9781405196949-5
D1693427

The Wiley Blackwell Encyclopedia of Gender and Sexuality Studies

Wiley Blackwell Encyclopedias in Social Science
Consulting Editor: George Ritzer

Published

The Wiley Blackwell Encyclopedia of Globalization
Edited by George Ritzer

The Wiley Blackwell Encyclopedia of Social and Political Movements
Edited by David A. Snow, Donatella della Porta, Bert Klandermans, and Doug McAdam

The Wiley Blackwell Encyclopedia of Health, Illness, Behavior, and Society
Edited by William C. Cockerham, Robert Dingwall, and Stella Quah

The Wiley Blackwell Encyclopedia of Consumption and Consumer Studies
Edited by Daniel Thomas Cook and J. Michael Ryan

The Wiley Blackwell Encyclopedia of Family Studies
Edited by Constance L. Shehan

The Wiley Blackwell Encyclopedia of Race, Ethnicity, and Nationalism
Edited by John Stone, Rutledge M. Dennis, Polly S. Rizova, Anthony D. Smith, and Xiaoshuo Hou

The Wiley Blackwell Encyclopedia of Gender and Sexuality Studies
Editor-in-Chief: Nancy A. Naples, Associate Editors: renée c. hoogland, Maithree Wickramasinghe, and Wai Ching Angela Wong

Forthcoming

The Wiley Blackwell Encyclopedia of Social Theory
Edited by Bryan S. Turner, Chang Kyung-Sup, Cynthia Epstein, Peter Kivisto, William Outhwaite, and J. Michael Ryan

The Wiley Blackwell Encyclopedia of Urban and Regional Studies
Edited by Anthony M. Orum, Marisol Garcia, Dennis Judd, Bryan Roberts, and Pow Choon-Piew

The Wiley Blackwell Encyclopedia of Environment and Society
Edited by Dorceta E. Taylor, Kozo Mayumi, Jun Bi, Paul Burton, and Tor A. Benjaminsen

Related titles

The Blackwell Encyclopedia of Sociology
Edited by George Ritzer

The Concise Encyclopedia of Sociology
Edited by George Ritzer and J. Michael Ryan

The Wiley Blackwell Encyclopedia of Gender and Sexuality Studies

Editor-in-Chief
Nancy A. Naples

Associate Editors
renée c. hoogland
Maithree Wickramasinghe
Wai Ching Angela Wong

Volume V
S–Y

WILEY Blackwell

This edition first published 2016
© 2016 John Wiley & Sons, Ltd.

Registered Office
John Wiley & Sons Ltd, The Atrium, Southern Gate, Chichester, West Sussex, PO19 8SQ, UK

Editorial Offices
350 Main Street, Malden, MA 02148-5020, USA
9600 Garsington Road, Oxford, OX4 2DQ, UK
The Atrium, Southern Gate, Chichester, West Sussex, PO19 8SQ, UK

For details of our global editorial offices, for customer services, and for information about how to apply for permission to reuse the copyright material in this book please see our website at www.wiley.com/wiley-blackwell.

The right of Nancy A. Naples to be identified as the author of the editorial material in this work has been asserted in accordance with the UK Copyright, Designs and Patents Act 1988.

All rights reserved. No part of this publication may be reproduced, stored in a retrieval system, or transmitted, in any form or by any means, electronic, mechanical, photocopying, recording or otherwise, except as permitted by the UK Copyright, Designs and Patents Act 1988, without the prior permission of the publisher.

Wiley also publishes its books in a variety of electronic formats. Some content that appears in print may not be available in electronic books.

Designations used by companies to distinguish their products are often claimed as trademarks. All brand names and product names used in this book are trade names, service marks, trademarks or registered trademarks of their respective owners. The publisher is not associated with any product or vendor mentioned in this book.

Limit of Liability/Disclaimer of Warranty: While the publisher and author have used their best efforts in preparing this book, they make no representations or warranties with respect to the accuracy or completeness of the contents of this book and specifically disclaim any implied warranties of merchantability or fitness for a particular purpose. It is sold on the understanding that the publisher is not engaged in rendering professional services and neither the publisher nor the author shall be liable for damages arising herefrom. If professional advice or other expert assistance is required, the services of a competent professional should be sought.

Library of Congress Cataloging-in-Publication data is available for this book.

ISBN 9781405196949 (hardback)

Cover image: Clockwise from top left: Artists of street theater group ASSA (Ankara Cinema and Art Atelier) during a demonstration on International Women's Day © Piero Castellano/Pacific Press/LightRocket via Getty Images; Banyana beat Mali, Women's Championship match, South Africa, 2010 © Gallo Images/Alamy; Young girl from Oaxaca © Jennifer Bickham Mendez; Demonstration over same-sex marriages, Taipei, Taiwan, 2015 © Sam Yeh/AFP/Getty Images

Set in 10/12pt Minion by SPi Global, Chennai, India
Printed and bound in Singapore by Markono Print Media Pte Ltd

1 2016

Contents

Volume I

Editors vii
Contributors ix
Lexicon xxxvii
Introduction and Acknowledgments xlix

Gender and Sexuality Studies A–D 1

Volume II

Gender and Sexuality Studies E–F 497

Volume III

Gender and Sexuality Studies G–I 931

Volume IV

Gender and Sexuality Studies J–R 1471

Volume V

Gender and Sexuality Studies S–Y 2051

Index of Names 2619
Index of Subjects 2633

Sadomasochism, Domination, and Submission

AMBER JAMILLA MUSSER
Washington University in St. Louis, USA

When used to refer to sexual practices, sadomasochism (S&M) is most commonly associated with BDSM (bondage, discipline, and sadomasochism). In this subculture partners often use erotic role playing and props to act out scenes that highlight power imbalances between the partners. This may or may not involve physical restraint, discipline, the ritualized infliction of pain, or humiliation. The manifestations of BDSM are diverse and may take on the form of emphasizing gendered or racialized power differentials. Until 2013, the American Psychological Association classified sadism and masochism as sexual disorders. In addition to rendering these desires pathological, this classification made practitioners of sadomasochism vulnerable to police surveillance, harassment, and legal prosecution under assault laws.

Sadomasochism entered the lexicon in 1890 in Richard von Krafft-Ebing's *Psychopathia Sexualis* as two separate entities – sadism and masochism. Both share a literary pedigree; sadism was named for the Marquis de Sade, who was famous for his violent erotic novels, while masochism was named for Leopold von Sacher Masoch and his novellas of submission, including *Venus in Furs* (1870). In Krafft-Ebing's view, sadism and masochism were linked because they were both the products of an overly active sexual instinct. Krafft-Ebing saw the sadist's desire to inflict pain as an intensification of masculine sexual aggression. Masochists, on the other hand, experienced a feminine desire to please their partner. Krafft-Ebing explained both as having arisen from normal feelings of love; they represented the pathological extremes of "active" (masculine) and "passive" (feminine) sexual roles.

In its guise as a psychological phenomenon, sadomasochism is used colloquially to describe different phenomena characterized by a combination of pleasure, pain, activity, and passivity. The problem of the self-defeating character, modeled after the protagonist in *Venus in Furs*, has been a popular literary trope; numerous books and articles purport to describe various characters as masochists. Werther, the suicidal, scorned lover in Goethe's *The Sorrows of Young Werther*, is described as masochistic because he seems to celebrate his suffering and eroticizes death. Similarly, Marcel Proust's lovesick protagonist in *Remembrance of Things Past*, Charles Swann, is labeled a masochist because of his unswerving devotion to Odette despite her affairs and abuse. The sadomasochistic label can also be applied to certain aesthetic formulations. In its most facile application, this refers to a cluster of paraphernalia associated with sadomasochistic sexual practices including whips, chains, high heels, and furs. In its more complex manifestation, it is used to describe representational strategies of delaying pleasure through suspense and repetition. As such Alfred Hitchcock's oeuvre and Henry James's novels have been described as adhering to this formal logic. These explorations of masochism, though disparate, understand sadomasochism as an analytic term that allows one to speak of power imbalances and understand them as born from a sense of inferiority and anxiety.

Within philosophy, sadomasochism rises to the fore because of its connection to questions of agency. Michel Foucault argues that the practice of S&M offered participants new and potentially subversive modes of embodying power and pleasure. Similarly Gilles Deleuze argues that masochism's valorization of passivity offered a new approach to thinking about the organization of society. In contrast, Jean-Paul Sartre argues that masochism is a failed attempt to deny one's agency.

The gendering of sadomasochism has produced controversy. Some psychoanalysts, including Marie Bonaparte, Karen Horney, and Hélène Deutsche, took masochism to be central to femininity, thereby naturalizing the connection between women and masochism. This close association proved to be problematic; the notion of woman as a willing victim in abusive situations delayed the legal rights for women in matters of rape, abuse, and domestic violence. The assumption that women unconsciously wanted to be abused was a contentious point of the American feminist movement in the 1970s. This schism contributed to the so-called sex wars of the 1980s, when some feminists argued that sadomasochism was harmful because it worked to perpetuate the ideology of violence against women while others argued that sadomasochism was a sexual practice that was not especially culpable for the prevailing conditions of patriarchy. Practitioners of sadomasochism argued that it was "safe, sane, and consensual." Proponents of sadomasochism such as Gayle Rubin argued that condemning it was a symptom of internalized repression, and others like Pat Califia argued that sadomasochism should be considered a subversive and liberatory practice. Here, activism to depathologize and decriminalize sadomasochism intersects with lesbian, gay, bisexual, and transgender (LGBT) activism and other calls for sexual freedom. There remain heated discussions about the ethics of sadomasochism. As the sexual practice of sadomasochism has become more mainstream, the conversations have shifted to tease out the erotics behind situations marked by power imbalances such as racism, neoliberalism, and sexism.

SEE ALSO: Sexualities; Taboo

FURTHER READING

Deleuze, Gilles. 1971. *Masochism: An Interpretation of Coldness and Cruelty*, trans. Jean McNeil. New York: George Braziller.
Farley, Anthony Paul. 1997. "The Black Body as Fetish Object." *Oregon Law Review*, 76(3): 457–535.
Foucault, Michel. 1997. "Sexual Choice, Sexual Act." In *Ethics: Subjectivity and Truth*, edited by Paul Rabinow, 141–157. New York: New Press.
France, Marie. 1984. "Sadomasochism and Feminism." *Feminist Review*, 16: 35–42.
Green, Richard. 2001. "(Serious) Sadomasochism: A Protected Right of Privacy?" *Archives of Sexual Behavior*, 30: 543–550.
Hart, Lynda. 1998. *Between the Body and the Flesh: Performing Sadomasochism*. New York: Columbia University Press.

Khan, Ummni. 2014. *Vicarious Kinks: S/M in the Socio-Legal Imaginary*. Toronto: University of Toronto Press.

Newmahr, Staci. 2010. "Rethinking Kink: Sadomasochism as Serious Leisure." *Qualitative Sociology*, 33(3): 313–331.

Rubin, Gayle. 1984. "Thinking Sex: Notes for a Radical Theory of the Politics of Sexuality." In *Pleasure and Danger: Exploring Female Sexuality*, edited by Carole Vance. Boston: Routledge and Kegan Paul.

Weinberg, Thomas S. 2006. "Sadomasochism and the Social Sciences: A Review of the Sociological and Social Psychological Literature." *Journal of Homosexuality*, 50(2–3): 17–40.

Weiss, Margot. 2011. *Techniques of Pleasure: BDSM and the Circuits of Sexuality*. Durham, NC: Duke University Press.

Same-Sex Families

JENNIFER POWER
La Trobe University, Australia

The term same-sex family generally refers to families parented by same-sex couples. This includes lesbian or gay male couples. However, the term is often used interchangeably with "same-sex attracted parents," so the definition may also include single parents who identify as lesbian, gay, or bisexual (LGB). Some definitions of "same-sex families" or "same-sex attracted parents" assume the inclusion of transgender parents. But, given not all transgender people identity as same-sex attracted, it is more appropriate to consider only those transgender parents who identify as LGB or non-heterosexual as being part of a same-sex family.

In recent decades, increasing numbers of LGB people have become parents. This has occurred in the context of broader social and cultural changes in the Western world, which have allowed for greater acceptance of non-traditional family forms – including single parent families, divorce, and re-marriage – along with the development of more flexible attitudes toward gender and sexuality.

It is estimated that up to six million children in the United States are being raised by an LGB parent or parents. The 2008/2010 General Social Survey in the United States indicated that 37 percent of LGB identifying adults are parents. Studies in several other western countries have also found a similar proportion of LGB adults are parents.

There are many ways in which LGB adults may become parents. Some people conceive or adopt children in a heterosexual relationship before they come out as LGB. But it is also common for same-sex couples or single people who identify as LGB to have children. There are a number of ways in which this might happen.

Lesbians or bisexual women may conceive children using donor sperm. Some women access anonymous donor sperm through a fertility clinic. Others conceive with sperm from a known donor, often a friend. In this case, conception may happen through a clinic (using artificial insemination or in vitro fertilization) or women may conceive at home using self-insemination techniques. Gay or bisexual men may conceive children through the help of a surrogate who carries the child.

Many LGB adults adopt or foster children. The 2011 American Community Survey estimated that same-sex couples in the United States are four times more likely than heterosexual couples to be raising adopted children and six times more likely to be raising foster children. However, not all countries allow same-sex couples to adopt. For example, in Australia current law allows same-sex couples to foster children (including permanent foster-care arrangements) but adoption by same-sex couples is not legal in many states and territories.

Some gay or bisexual men become parents by donating sperm to lesbian couples or single women. Donor arrangements vary. Some donors have little or nothing to do with the children conceived with their sperm and do not see themselves as fathers. Others may be involved in the children's lives as a close friend or father figure, while some are active fathers and play a large role in the day-to-day care of their children. Some lesbian couples or single women enter into co-parenting arrangements with a donor or a gay couple. This can mean that there are three or more adults raising children together. The children may spend time living with their parents across two households.

Step and blended families are common within LGB communities. This may include families where one or more adults are raising children from a previous heterosexual relationship or a previous same-sex relationship. For some LGB parents, step-parenthood is their first entry into parenting.

While laws regarding same-sex families vary across jurisdictions, the past few decades have seen many countries (or states and territories within countries) adopt laws that reflect greater recognition, and enable better protection, of families headed by LGB parents. For instance, some countries, including Australia, Denmark, The Netherlands, and some regions of Canada, allow the female partner of a birth mother to acquire the legal status of a parent without going through formal adoption processes. This includes the capacity for two women to be named as parents on a child's birth certificate.

Some individuals and groups within the broader community express concern that children being raised by LGB parents will be disadvantaged socially or emotionally. However, repeated studies have shown that this is not the case. Children raised by LGB families have at least equal social, emotional, educational, and developmental outcomes as their peers raised by heterosexual parents. Research has also shown that children raised by LGB parents are similar to other children in terms of their patterns of friendship and social networks.

Children with LGB parents, particularly as they move into their teenage years, may hold concerns about being teased or bullied due to negative social attitudes, stereotypes, and stigma surrounding homosexuality. There is mixed evidence regarding the extent to which these fears are grounded. Some studies have shown children with LGB parents are more likely than other children to experience bullying or harassment in a school environment, while other studies have shown little or no difference. Research has also shown that when bullying or discrimination does occur, children with LGB parents tend to be resilient and adopt positive coping strategies. What seems to be important is the general social climate regarding acceptance of homosexuality. In countries or regions where there is high visibility and acceptance of same-sex couples, children with LGB parents are less likely to experience teasing or bullying by their peers.

Attitudes toward parenting within the LGB community are diverse. Studies have shown that, today, younger LGB people are more inclined than LGB people of previous generations to assume they will become a parent at some point in their life. However, there are some people in the LGB community who consider having children to be kowtowing to heterosexual norms rather than embracing difference and diversity. Despite this, there are now many community groups and organizations within the LGB community – including children's playgroups and new-parent groups – that support parents and families.

SEE ALSO: Same-Sex Marriage; Sexualities

FURTHER READING

Berkowitz, D., and W. Marsiglio. 2007. "Gay Men: Negotiating Procreative, Father, and Family Identities." *Journal of Marriage and Family*, 69(2): 366–381.

Biblarz, T., and J. Stacey. 2010. "How Does the Gender of Parents Matter?" *Journal of Marriage and Family*, 72(1): 3–22.

Bos, H. M., N. K. Gartrell, F. Van Balen, H. Peyser, and T. G. Sandfort. 2008. "Children in Planned Lesbian Families: A Cross-Cultural Comparison between the United States and the Netherlands." *American Journal of Orthopsychiatry*, 78: 211–219.

Bos, H. M., and F. Van Balen. 2008. "Children in Planned Lesbian Families: Stigmatization, Psychological Adjustment and Protective Factors." *Culture, Health and Sexuality*, 10(3): 221–236.

Crouch, S., R. McNair, E. Waters, and J. Power. 2013. "What Makes a Same-Sex Parented Family?" *Medical Journal of Australia*, 199(2): 94–96.

Dempsey, D. 2013. "Same-Sex Parented Families in Australia," *Community Australia Paper No. 18*, Australian Institute of Family Studies Child Family, Melbourne.

Gates, G. 2013. *LGBT Parenting in the United States*. Los Angeles: The Williams Institute.

Grant, J. M., et al. 2011. *Injustice at Every Turn: A Report of the National Transgender Discrimination Survey*. Washington, DC: National Center for Transgender Equality and National Gay and Lesbian Task Force.

Mezey, N. 2008. *New Choices, New Families: How Lesbians Decide about Motherhood*. Baltimore: Johns Hopkins University Press.

Same-Sex Marriage

LARA AASEM AHMED and J. MICHAEL RYAN
The American University in Cairo, Egypt

Same-sex marriage is the matrimonial union of individuals who are of the same biological sex, with the term typically being used in reference to monogamous marriages involving only two partners. It is colloquially referred to as "gay marriage," the modifiers serving to distinguish it from "marriage," which is often used strictly in the context of heterosexual matrimony. Same-sex marriage is often studied at the macro level because of the structural political issues associated with it although there are also a range of studies analyzing the micro level including, for example, studies of the division of household labor and parenting duties among same-sex couples.

Same-sex marriage remains a controversial topic. In most countries, the current debate ranges around issues of acceptance and legalization. Opponents argue that same-sex marriage is a threat to the institution of family. This view holds that marriage, in the traditional sense, is a union between one man and one woman, the main purpose of which is the creation of offspring; because homosexual couples are incapable of biological reproduction, such unions are therefore seen as dysfunctional and unnatural. In popular culture, it tends to take on religious overtones. Orthodox readings of Judaism, Christianity, and Islam espouse the creationist story of Adam and Eve, as well as the tale of Sodom and Gomorrah, as proof of the sinfulness of homosexuality and thus the desecration of the sanctity of wedlock by same-sex marriage. In countries where legislative and judiciary institutions are intertwined with religious jurisprudence (as in much of the Middle East) or where conservative and religious groups have significant lobbying power (as in the United States), this attitude is often reflected in policy, with same-sex marriage being not only socially unacceptable but also illegal. The degree to which states are willing to go in order to maintain the status quo vis-à-vis sexuality and marriage is epitomized in the case of Iran – an Islamic nation which, in order to circumvent the issue of same-sex marriage, allows homosexual individuals to undergo sex reassignment surgery, after which they may marry members of (what the state views as) the now-opposite sex.

Not all religious belief systems are adamantly opposed to same-sex marriage. Some, such as Hinduism and Buddhism, are ambivalent on the topic. Revisionist readings of the Abrahamic religions, as well as many indigenous faiths, view same-sex marriage as a legitimate form of romantic and sexual union that is not incompatible with religion. Shared by many secularists as well, this stance has manifested itself in the public sphere in the LGBTQ+ and marriage equality movements taking place in many countries across the world, especially more secularized societies such as Canada, Western Europe, and some parts of Latin America. It has found its academic parallel in conflict theory, which analyzes attitudes toward same-sex marriage in terms of the power differentials between heterosexuals and sexual minorities, looking at how societal resources – including the image of the socially acceptable, traditional marriage – have been monopolized by the heterosexual nuclear family. (In a similar vein, recent economic analyses argue that legalizing same-sex marriage might boost consumption, as well as taxation and thus government revenue, prompting economic growth.) Also relevant are queer and feminist theories, which deconstruct the normalization of heterosexuality, a process in which heterosexuality is regarded as the default and other forms of sexual expression are marginalized as the deviant other. Queer and feminist scholars are often critical, condemning such heteronormative discourse for being homophobic.

Queer theory would go on to deconstruct the man–woman, male–female, and heterosexual–homosexual binaries inherent in the concept of same-sex marriage, arguing for the importance of acknowledging the arbitrary nature of the categorizations implicit in these divisions, especially with regards to the basis upon which sex is designated and reified as an innate biological attribute, with intersex individuals as an example.

Postcolonial theory also contributes to this deconstruction, regarding modern attitudes toward same-sex marriage as Western conventions that prohibit the organic expression of authentic cultural identity, be it in favor of or in opposition to the issue. In that sense, the marriage equality movement is often associated with the United States. However, homosexuality has been as geographically widespread and is as old as heterosexuality, with ritualized same-sex unions historically existing side by side with heterosexual ones, as in Mesopotamia, the Fujian province of China, and Egypt's Siwa Oasis, as well as among Native American tribes, where two-spirit unions still take place. Social constructionists would argue that historicizing same-sex marriage reveals how differences between formal and informal relationships are constructed, as well as how today's notion of what constitutes a traditional, ideal marriage is not ahistorical and universal, but relatively recent and context-dependent.

The fact that homosexuality, and in turn same-sex marriage, are not tolerated in many parts of the world places individuals who identify as homosexual in grave risk. It also prevents any given same-sex marriage from being internationally recognized; this may hinder partners from acquiring a divorce outside the jurisdiction within which they married. Even in places where same-sex partners can attain civil unions or domestic partnerships, they may still lack some of the legal protection accorded to married couples, such as joint taxation, hospital visitation rights, and inheritance. The fact that same-sex couples are often forced to resort to these alternatives to marriage, whereas heterosexual couples can choose freely between them, serves to further stigmatize same-sex unions, leading to increasing discrimination – as, for example, with regards to the right to adopt.

As of April 2015, same-sex marriage is legal nationwide in 18 countries: the

Netherlands, Belgium, Spain, Canada, South Africa, Norway, Sweden, Portugal, Iceland, Argentina, Denmark, France, Brazil, Uruguay, New Zealand, Britain, Luxembourg, and Finland. It is legal in some jurisdictions in the United States and Mexico, and is recognized but not performed in Israel. A legalization bill is currently pending in Slovenia.

SEE ALSO: Heterosexual Marriage Trends in the West; Lesbian and Gay Movements; Same-Sex Families

FURTHER READING

Bernstein, Mary, and Verta Taylor. 2013. *The Marrying Kind? Debating Same-Sex Marriage within the Lesbian and Gay Movement*. Minneapolis: University of Minnesota Press.

Sullivan, Andrew. 2004. *Same-Sex Marriage: Pro and Con*. New York: Vintage.

Same-Sex Sexuality in India

PRISCILLA ROSE SELVARAJ
Ohio University, USA

India has an established constitution that recognizes, protects, and celebrates diversity. In a country with the second largest population in the world, diversity exists across a broad spectrum spanning languages, castes, classes, religions, sexualities, and economic privileges. However, diversity in regards to sexual orientation has seldom been discussed in India, perhaps due to an unspoken rule of "don't ask, don't tell." A recent Indian Supreme Court ruling has drawn attention to same-sex sexuality in India. In this entry, current legal and social aspects of individuals with same-sex sexuality within the Indian context are discussed.

In historical India same-sex behaviors were accepted and celebrated. However, as time went on, and with the influence of British colonization, taboos around same-sex sexuality grew. In 2012, the Indian government estimated that there were about 2.5 million gay men in the country. The prevalence of same-sex sexuality in the Indian culture has been difficult to estimate for reasons such as associated stigma, social repression, unrepresentative sampling, and failure to capture the true essence of same-sex identity (Rao and Jacob 2012). There are divergent and changing perspectives in the understanding of same-sex sexuality ranging from a sin, to crime, to pathology, to normal variant of human sexuality, and back to a criminal act.

On December 11, 2013, India's Supreme Court overruled the 2009 judgment of the Delhi High Court by reinstating Section 377 of India's Penal Code, a law that bans and criminalizes consensual same-sex. Referred to as the "Sodomy Law," the law stipulates, "whoever voluntarily has carnal intercourse against the order of nature with any man, woman or animal shall be punished with imprisonment for life, or with imprisonment of either description for a term which may extend to ten years, and shall also be liable to fine." This archaic law, a legacy of the British colonial rule, is now being used to legitimize discrimination against same-sex couples, and to further criminalize and punish those engaging in consensual same-sex acts with imprisonment and fines.

India, by and large, remains a traditional sociocentric society rapidly moving to an egocentric society as a result of urbanization and industrialization under the overall impact of globalization. People supportive of Section 377 argue that "homosexuality," a term that is typically used in India, is a Western concept, imported into the country via colonization. Attitudes to same-sex sexuality are often negative, especially as heterosexual males in roles of fathers, brothers, and husbands in the patriarchal societies feel more threatened by variations in sexual behavior. Additionally, it is believed that the law's historic and moral underpinnings do not resonate with the historically held values in Indian society concerning sexual relations. Gay rights activists claim that the current law is not justified in contemporary Indian society as it rejects international human rights law on sexual orientation and gender identity. The verdict has emotionally disturbed members of the Lesbian, Gay, Bisexual (LGB) community and their families, especially those who had become open about their sexual orientation after the High Court judgment in 2009. These individuals are now at risk of prosecution under the reinstated criminal law of 2013. The concern of gay activists is the potential for this law to be abused by the police to force unwarranted arrests of individuals who identify as LGB and inflict undue harassment on workers, peer educators, and human rights activists who support this population.

In India, societal perceptions and attitudes toward same-sex sexuality have been ambivalent, and have a strong influence on whether individuals are "out" or "closeted." According to Verghese (2014), statistically, "homosexuality" forms a minority and gets skewed in the normal distribution, therefore, it has not been considered as a normal and acceptable behavior. The existence of prejudice and discrimination is evident among various religious and community leaders through the manifestation of their anti-gay attitudes. Their claim is from a philosophical and biological standpoint. According to them, sexual activity has two goals: (1) procreation to safeguard the continuation of the species; and (2) experience of pleasure to facilitate the sexual activity that strengthens the bond between husband and wife (Verghese 2014). In such a religious perspective, same-sex sexuality negates one of the goals of sexual activity, procreation, and contradicts God's institution of marriage between a man and a woman. There is even rhetoric equating same-sex behavior with pedophilia, which is viewed by many as a form of recruitment into same-sex sexuality. Additionally, an interesting fact is that large proportions of men who have sex with men (MSM) in India, unlike in the West, are married and have children (Rao and Jacob 2014). LGBT activists believe that criminalizing same-sex will spur more men to conceal their sexual orientation, leading more women into empty and isolating marriages. It also raises the question of whether there may be more bisexuals than gays in India, or whether the presence of married men who engage in gay sex is indicative of the stigma and a desire to hide their true sexual orientation.

A recent study on homosexuality found that discomfort with sexuality significantly correlates with levels of education, acceptance by friends and family, legal disadvantages, awareness, accessibility to non-heteronormative lifestyles, support systems, and trait affect (Maroky et al. 2014). These authors recommend that modifying external factors, reducing legal restrictions, and improving societal acceptance and support systems, could reduce "ego-dystonicity." Rao and Jacob (2012) report that much of the distress faced by people with same-sex orientation was due to the difficulties faced in living within the predominantly heterosexual world. The Naz Foundation, a non-governmental organization along with other advocacy groups continues to challenge the constitutional validity of Section 377 by claiming that it violates the rights to privacy, to dignity and health, to equality and non-discrimination, and to freedom of expression (Rao and Jacob 2014). These authors claim that the law prevents public health efforts of reducing the risk of transmission of HIV/AIDS by fostering the fear of prosecution and prevents people from discussing their sexuality honestly. It is an unfortunate reality that the MSM group remains at the epicenter of the AIDS pandemic which is increasing at an exponential rate in India. The laws, policies, and practices that lead to reduced access to healthcare services are limitations of the right to healthcare for these stigmatized sections of society. The World Health Organization (WHO) reports that decriminalizing and destigmatizing MSM, transgender, and other minority groups would greatly help in bringing down HIV infections among them. Additionally, the WHO recommends promoting condom use, wide-spread voluntary HIV testing, treating at-risk individuals with antiretroviral, voluntary male circumcision, and needle exchange programs for battling the disease. Therefore, discrimination of such at-risk and underrepresented population fuels the epidemic of HIV and further prevents effective healthcare interventions.

Between 2009 and 2013, the LGBT community in India has become increasingly visible – holding pride marches, opening gay businesses, and increasingly popularizing topics in movies and media with gay characters and themes (Potts 2013). Among the youth, the wide accessibility of the Internet seems to be yielding two possible consequences of the law reversal: (1) attitudes and behaviors may become more secretive, or (2) the coming out process and networking among LGBT community for support system may become easier and readily available. There is limited literature available in the field of psychotherapy and counseling in India that systematically investigates mental health status, issues, and psychological services rendered to this population. Developing professionals' competence and skills to deal with diversity, in addition to awareness of this complex phenomenon is pivotal. Further research into same-sex sexualities in India with regard to holistic (i.e., social, emotional, mental, physical, and psychological) behavior and psychosexual identity development is crucial.

SEE ALSO: Sexual Orientation and the Law; Sexualities

REFERENCES

Maroky, Ami Sebastian, et al. 2014 "'Ego-Dystonicity' in Homosexuality: An Indian Perspective." *International Journal of Social Psychiatry*, 61(4): 311–318. DOI: 0020764014543709.

Potts, Andrew. 2013. "India Supreme Court Recriminalizes Homosexuality." *Gay Star News*, December 11. Accessed September 28, 2014, at http://www.gaystarnews.com/article/india-supreme-court-finds-sodomy-law-constitutional-throws-issue-back-lawmakers111213#sthash.edNqjyjw.J21I15xU.dpuf.

Rao, Sathyanarayana T. S., and K. S. Jacob. 2012. "Homosexuality and India." *Indian Journal of Psychiatry*, 54(1): 1–3. DOI: 10.4103/0019-5545.94636.

Rao, Sathyanarayana T. S., and K. S. Jacob. 2014. "The Reversal on Gay Rights in India." *Indian Journal of Psychiatry*, 56(1): 1–2. DOI: 10.4103/0019-5545.124706.

Verghese, Abraham. 2014. "A Fresh Look at Homosexuality." *Indian Journal of Psychiatry*, 56(2): 209–210.

FURTHER READING

Badgett, Lee M. V. 2014. "The Economic Cost of Homophobia and the Exclusion of LGBT People: A Case Study of India." Preliminary results. Sogi, The World Bank.

Closson, Elizabeth F., et al. 2014. "The Other Side of the Bridge: Exploring the Sexual Relationships of Men Who Have Sex With Men and Their Female Partners in Mumbai, India." *Culture, Health & Sexuality*, 16(7): 780–791.

Das, Soumen. 2013. "Homosexuality in India Revisited: Some Recommendations and Research Directions." *Society Today*, 1: 9–16.

Drescher, Jack, and Vittorio Lingiardi. 2003. *The Mental Health Professions and Homosexuality: International Perspectives*. New York: Haworth Medical Press.

Scientific Motherhood

TAYLOR LIVINGSTON
University of North Carolina at Chapel Hill, USA

Scientific motherhood is the belief that mothers need to follow expert scientific or medical advice in order to rear healthy children (Apple 1995, 161). The belief became a guiding principle of motherhood in the United States during the late eighteenth century with the rise of germ theory, pediatricians, hospital births, and infant formula companies. One of the main outcomes of the popularity of this belief is the movement from breastfeeding to pediatrician-promoted bottle-feeding.

Scientific motherhood is a concept developed by scholar Rima Apple in 1995. Apple formulated this concept to explain the phenomenon of women seeking out scientific advice in matters of house-cleaning, childcare, and family nutrition. This marked a shift from receiving information on childrearing and other domestic duties from mothers, grandmothers, and other sources of knowledge to turning toward scientific "experts" like doctors, childcare educators, and public health officials – mainly white men – on how best to manage their households.

With the rise of the Industrial Revolution in the West, women's roles became more relegated to the private sphere and women became targets for consumerism. Women were expected to be the keepers of the home, and use modern, scientific information in taking care of their homes and families. Since family sizes were on the decline, young girls had fewer experiences to help prepare them for motherhood. Additionally, the way their mothers reared children was often incompatible with the new technologies of the day. All of these factors, along with the development of the germ theory of disease, led more middle-class white women to turn to experts in the field. These women did not directly go to pediatricians but received their information through magazine articles, advice columns, and books written by childcare authorities. One such text was *Treatise on Domestic Economy* authored by Catherine Beecher. This book, and others like it, instructed women to run their homes according to the modern way, such as having very clean houses and rearing children according to a doctor's advice. This advice was not just followed by middle-class white women; middle-class African American women also adhered to this advice and encouraged low-income African American women to do the same, in order to "lift the race."

Coinciding with the popularity of domestic advice books, doctors and pediatricians in particular began to gain more authority due to their work lowering the infant mortality rate. Most of the infant deaths were attributed to diarrheal diseases caused by contaminated milk consumed by young children. Milk was loaded from the dairy into an open vat in an unrefrigerated train car. Milk was exposed to flies, heat, and the open air. Pediatricians and public health officials in major cities undertook public health campaigns to educate mothers about the danger of unpasteurized milk. They set up "milk tents" throughout major cities that distributed pasteurized milk.

With more and more women seeking healthcare advice from trusted authorities and the rising status of doctors, government officials and public health workers undertook major campaigns throughout the United States to educate women about proper childcare and to encourage hospital births. These campaigns were organized and funded by the Children's Bureau in the 1910s. The Bureau dispatched nurses to go door to door to hand out their pamphlets on childrearing, even to rural and southern areas, although the campaigns in the South and in rural areas were largely unsuccessful because women did not have the money to follow the guidelines. New public health campaigns, such as the one initiated by the Children's Bureau, began to encourage formula feeding over breastfeeding. Doctors preferred formula feeding over breastfeeding because, unlike breast milk, the amount of formula babies consumed could be measured.

In addition to public health campaign pamphlets, childrearing books authored by pediatricians were marketed to mothers, beginning in 1894 with the publication of Dr. L. Emmett Holt's *Care and Feeding of Children*. Holt's book was extremely popular, being updated and republished until 1957. Another extremely popular childrearing text, which is still popular today, was Dr. Benjamin Spock's *The Pocket Book of Baby and Child Care* first published in 1946. Spock's publication differed from other scientific motherhood publications as it encouraged mothers to also "trust their instincts."

In addition to publications, scientific motherhood was also introduced via the classroom through the rise of domestic science courses in schools, which were often mandatory for girls. Domestic science curricula became increasingly popular in the 1920s and continued as required education for girls for many decades as part of home economics.

The effects of scientific motherhood can be seen in the decline of breastfeeding rates in the United States from 1890 to 1950 and the rise of yearly well-child checkups. Mothers are still encouraged today to follow pediatrician guidelines for healthy childrearing. Further, the ubiquity of childcare manuals shows that scientific motherhood is still a guiding principle for motherhood today.

SEE ALSO: Breastfeeding in Historical and Comparative Perspective; Cult of Domesticity; Household Livelihood Strategies; Midwifery; Private/Public Spheres

REFERENCES

Apple, Rima. 1995. "Constructing Motherhood: Scientific Motherhood in the Eighteenth and Nineteenth Centuries." *Social History of Medicine*, 8(2): 161–178. DOI: 10.1093/shm/8.2.161.

Spock, Benjamin. 1946. *The Pocket Book of Baby and Child Care*. New York: Pocket Books.

FURTHER READING

Apple, Rima. 2006. *Perfect Motherhood: Science and Childrearing in America*. New Brunswick: Rutgers University Press.

Litt, Jacquelyn S. 2000. *Medicalized Motherhood: Perspectives from the Lives of African American and Jewish Women*. New Brunswick: Rutgers University Press.

Wolf, Jacqueline H. 2001. *Don't Kill Your Baby: Public Health and the Decline of Breastfeeding in the Nineteenth and Twentieth Centuries*. Columbus: Ohio State University Press.

Scientific Sexism and Racism

SHARYN CLOUGH and JULIO OROZCO
Oregon State University, USA

The ideal of science is one of objectivity in the service of advancing knowledge. However, as feminist and anti-racist scholars have documented, the institutions and practices of science often serve instead to maintain a political status quo in the service of white, male, social elites (e.g., Haraway 1989; Harding 1993; Schiebinger 1993).

Sexism and racism in science overlap with each other and with other forms of social marginalization and oppression in complex ways. In the *Descent of Man*, Darwin argued that the pressure of natural selection responsible for the inferiority of white Victorian women compared to their male counterparts, was not in evidence in the "lower races." Among Africans, for example, he found little sex differentiation. According to Darwin, the inferiority of women to men was primarily a product of sexual selection among the "higher races." His sexism and racism were inextricably intertwined (Clough 2003).

Darwin's work is an exemplar of the tight links to be found between science and colonialism. While the Enlightenment period witnessed the possibility of equality across sexes and races – witness the appeals to equal rights during the French Revolution – the ideal of equality conflicted with lucrative colonialist projects. The Atlantic slave trade, for example, was predicated on the natural superiority of European elites. Science was one of many institutions called upon to rationalize the colonialist enterprise in the face of burgeoning egalitarian ideals. In *Nature's Body* (1993) Schiebinger discusses the strategic role played during this period by European anatomists, anthropologists, and naturalists. Appealing to the popular trope of the "great chain of being," which ranked in a strict hierarchy the natural order of plants, non-human animals, humans, and the divine, a more detailed version of the chain was articulated to show the ranks of the "different races of man," with economically privileged Europeans at the top. Schiebinger takes care to note that sexism complicated the straightforward hierarchy of the chain metaphor. In formulating hypotheses about racial hierarchies, differences between males were often highlighted. Females, however, were largely ignored because they were thought to be a subgroup of their respective "race." And when studies on sex differences were conducted, the samples were drawn almost exclusively from white European women; women of color were excluded almost entirely. Skull measurements were the most frequently used method of determining natural superiority. Facial angles were measured to compare the skulls of the great apes to the skulls of male humans of different "races." When women were compared across different "races" it was not the difference in skulls that was measured but the difference in secondary sex characteristics such as breast and pelvis size. These traits were not used to support a hierarchy within women, as much as they were used to identify particular women with their respective "races." The role of science in Western colonialist enterprises is further explored in Harding's *The Postcolonial Science and Technology Studies Reader* (2011). That the close relationship between science and racist/sexist colonialist projects is not unique to the West, is documented by Haraway's classic text *Primate Visions*, which examines the sexist threads of Japanese primatology within the context of Japanese colonialist identity (Haraway 1989).

Within the contemporary "postcolonial" period, people with marginalized social identities – people described as women, as black, as sexually transgressive, as poor – continue to be inequitably represented among science students, researchers, and grant recipients; they are discouraged from producing science about the world and about themselves; they are misrepresented as objects of scientific research in ways that further their marginalization; and in extreme but not unusual cases, their participation as subjects of scientific research leaves them maimed, poisoned, or dead.

The extreme cases of sexist/racist science, especially concerning the treatment of research subjects, are well known, though new examples continue to be brought to public attention (e.g., Skloot 2012). In the United States, well-documented examples of racist/sexist medical experimentation on Black men and women can be found from the colonial period to the present day (Washington 2007). In the early 1930s, the US Government sponsored experiments on black men from impoverished, rural communities of Tuskegee, Alabama. The experiments followed the course of untreated syphilis, without the informed consent of participants, long after treatment with antibiotics was known to be effective, and until as late as 1972 (Centers for Disease Control and Prevention). Indeed the experiments might have continued were it not for a whistleblower. Not only were these men refused adequate treatment (a refusal leading to a number of deaths), they were also kept from seeking treatment elsewhere, and their partners and children who contracted the disease from them were also victims. A similar set of studies sponsored by the US Government was conducted in the late 1940s involving the deliberate infection of marginalized populations (prisoners and sex workers) in Guatemala (U.S. Dept. of Health and Human Services). The horrific scientific research on prisoners in Nazi Germany presents other well-documented examples, and the sexist/racist elements of the motivations for the Nazi's research are clear. What is less known is the influence of British and American eugenics programs and anti-miscegenation laws on German colonialist policy in Africa prior to World War I, that in turn presaged the Nazi concept of "racial hygiene" in the 1930s (Haas 2008).

The moral condemnation provoked by these scientific studies stems in part from the fact that the problematic research involved failures to act on knowledge available at the time. Other cases, such as the extensive use of Agent Orange in Vietnam remind us that even acts of scientific ignorance can be morally culpable (McHugh 2015). Lab studies of risk assessment in the United States in the late 1950s and 1960s showed Agent Orange to have no adverse effects on humans. However, the conclusions about the safety for humans were reached using tests that were not done in the field, but in highly controlled lab settings, and they did not measure long-term effects. For these reasons alone, generalizations about human health beyond the lab setting were risky; the potential harm from ignorance was great. That the risks would be assumed primarily by Vietnamese women and children, half a world away, could not have failed to play a role in the decision to go ahead with widespread use of the chemical. A similar point can be made about a more recent case involving the use of depleted uranium munitions in the recent wars in Iraq and Afghanistan (Halfon 2008).

To be sure, the identification of sexist/racist features of science is more easily made in retrospect. There are no simple rules available to guide contemporary decisions about when a scientific research program should be abandoned because of racist/sexist features of the project, and when those who continue to pursue these kinds of projects deserve condemnation (see, for example, the lack of unanimity regarding the 1950 UNESCO statement condemning racist science). However, contemporary cases of scientific research that are empirically weak in ways that map on to available sexist/racist narratives, deserve critical attention.

Consider the work of Rushton, a Canadian social scientist. Working with Jensen he tried to establish biological explanations for "racial" differences in IQ scores, a racist chapter in American social science that has yet to close (Suzuki and Aronson 2005). Throughout a career spanning the late twentieth and early twenty-first centuries, Rushton argued that "Blacks" have naturally evolved capacities different from "Whites" and "Orientals." For example, he argued that people he identified as "Blacks" have evolved to be more promiscuous, that is, to be more interested in "gamete production" than are people he identified as "Whites" and "Orientals," and therefore that black people are less invested in parental care. The negative correlation between gamete production and parental investment can be found in a number of non-human species. That the pattern holds within humans is a doubtful claim that would need far more empirical support than he ever provided (Anderson 1991). However, even if he could show the correlation to be robust in humans, he failed to show that this pattern emerges from differential evolutionary strategies, let alone that these strategies are determined by "racial" categories. Reliable evidence shows that when there are differences in human parental caring, the underlying causal role is more likely played by local responses to social variables such as poverty and violence, rather than evolutionary pressures tied to membership in any given "racial" category (Zuckerman 2003). The empirical weaknesses in Rushton's work play into and reinforce sexist/racist narratives.

Unfortunately, his work is not an isolated phenomenon, but part of a reinvigoration of scientific defenses of racial and sexual difference – defenses that track new technological developments in genetics, computer software, medical imaging, and biomedicine. Despite the advances in technology, the underlying racist/sexist narrative has remained robust, if slightly more complex.

For example, in contrast to the eighteenth- and nineteenth-century practices of classifying individuals through racial phenotypic characteristics, contemporary geneticists have tried to classify individuals through statistical probabilities based on DNA samples that identify the geographic region of ancestral origin (Roberts 2011). Associated initially with the work of Rosenberg, computer software programs were designed to group individuals into clusters on the basis of similar genes. When applied to humans selected from different geographic regions, Rosenberg was able to identify a number of different possible clusters; one set of these corresponded to five major geographic regions sometimes associated with contemporary Western "racial" categories (Africa, Eurasia, East Asia, Oceania, and the Americas). Many commentators on Rosenberg's work were quick to proclaim that it supported the existence of those categories (e.g., Wade 2002). But others argued compellingly that the work did no such thing; the programs used are equally capable of detecting populations that do not correspond to ordinary "racial" categories, and the selection of individuals for inclusion is part of what determines the outcomes (e.g., Weiss and Fullerton 2005). It is worth noting that while the tiny amounts of genetic variation associated with a population can be used to uncover patterns of human migration and past gene flow, most genetic variation occurs *within* any population identified. This is a standard pattern routinely encountered when trying to identify differences across "races" (a pattern first highlighted by Lewontin 1972).

It is also a pattern that occurs when trying to identify differences across/between "sexes," such as "sex" differences in height and strength. Fausto-Sterling further complicates the science of "sex difference" in her essay "The Five Sexes: Why Male and Female Are Not Enough" (1993). Fausto-Sterling and a host of sound critical commentaries notwithstanding, searches for essential biological differences between humans labeled as either (and only) male and female continue in the form of neuroscience, aided by the new technology of functional magnetic resonance imaging (fMRI). That brains are malleable, rather than "hard-wired," and as likely to be changed by sexist/racist differences in the environment as to be the cause of those differences, is the latest corrective to be offered (e.g., Fine 2011).

As with the rise of racist/sexist science in the Enlightenment, economics is not a neutral force in the contemporary reinvigoration of scientific racism/sexism. Lucrative pharmacological and genetic therapies have been developed in response to differences in a variety of health outcomes that seem reliably to track differences in "race" and "sex." The development of BiDil, a medication marketed to treat heart failure in patients identified as African American men is a recent, problematic case (Pollock 2012). As with "sex" differences detected in brain structure and function, the question once again becomes one of causal order. What is clear is that oppressive social conditions contribute to any number of stress-mediated health conditions, from heart disease, to diabetes, to depression. When the oppressive social conditions are entrenched, the health conditions too become entrenched, reliably accompanying families and neighborhoods, across generations (Kaplan 2010). What is equally clear, however, is that, in most Western countries at least, to change the problematic social conditions requires a kind of political will not currently on offer. Biomedicine in contrast seems a quick fix. However, if the history of sexist/racist science is any guide, it will likely prove exorbitantly costly in terms of the further biological reification of inequitable social differences in the human community.

SEE ALSO: Feminist Studies of Science; Genetics and Racial Minorities in the United States

REFERENCES

Anderson, Judith. 1991. "Rushton's Racial Comparisons: An Ecological Critique of Theory and Method." *Canadian Psychology*, 32(1): 51–62. DOI: 10.1037/h0078956.

Centers for Disease Control and Prevention. *U.S. Public Health Service Syphilis Study at Tuskegee*. Accessed August 15, 2015, at: http://www.cdc.gov/tuskegee.

Clough, Sharyn. 2003. "Feminist Epistemology and Evolutionary Theory." In *Beyond Epistemology: A Pragmatist Prescription for Feminist Science Studies*. Lanham: Rowman & Littlefield.

Fausto-Sterling, Ann. 1993. "The Five Sexes: Why Male and Female Are Not Enough." *The Sciences* (March/April): 20–25.

Fine, Cordelia. 2011. *Delusions of Gender: How Our Minds, Society, and Neurosexism Create Difference*. New York: W.W. Norton & Co.

Haas, François. 2008. "German Science and Black Racism – Roots of the Nazi Holocaust." *The Federation of American Societies for Experimental Biology (FASEB) Journal*, 22: 332–337.

Halfon, Saul. 2008. "Depleted Uranium, Public Science, and the Politics of Closure." *Review of Policy Research*, 25(4): 295–311.

Haraway, Donna. 1989. *Primate Visions: Gender, Race, and Nature in the World of Modern Science*. New York/London: Routledge.

Harding, Sandra. 1993. *The "Racial" Economy of Science*. Bloomington: Indiana University Press.

Harding, Sandra. 2011. *The Postcolonial Science and Technology Studies Reader*. Durham, NC: Duke University Press.

Kaplan, Jonathan. 2010. "When Socially Determined Categories Make Biological Realities." *The Monist*, 93(2): 283–299.

Lewontin, Richard. 1972. "The Apportionment of Human Diversity." *Evolutionary Biology*, 6: 391–398.

McHugh, Nancy. 2015. *The Limits of Knowledge*. New York: SUNY Press.

Pollock, Anne. 2012. *Medicating Race: Heart Disease and Durable Preoccupations with Difference*. Durham, NC: Duke University Press.

Roberts, Dorothy. 2011. *Fatal Invention: How Science, Politics, and Big Business Re-Create Race in the Twenty-First Century*. New York: The New Press.

Schiebinger, Londa. 1993. "Theories of Gender and Race." In *Nature's Body*, 143–183. Boston: Beacon Press.

Skloot, Rebecca. 2010. *The Immortal Life of Henrietta Lacks*. New York: Broadway Books.

Suzuki, Lisa, and Joshua Aronson. 2005. "The Cultural Malleability of Intelligence and Its Impact on the Racial/Ethnic Hierarchy." *Psychology, Public Policy, and Law*, 11: 320–327.

U.S. Department of Health and Human Services. *Information on the 1946–1948 U.S. Public Health Service Sexually Transmitted Diseases (STD) Inoculation Study*. Accessed August 15, 2015, at: http://www.hhs.gov/1946inoculationstudy.

Wade, Nicholas. 2002. "Gene Study Identifies 5 Main Human Populations." *The New York Times*, December 20, 2002.

Washington, Harriet. 2007. *Medical Apartheid: The Dark History of Medical Experimentation on Black Americans from Colonial Times to the Present*. New York: Doubleday.

Weiss, Kenneth, and Stephanie Fullerton. 2005. "Racing Around, Getting Nowhere." *Evolutionary Anthropology: Issues, News, and Reviews*, 14(5): 165–169. DOI: 10.1002/evan.20079.

Zuckerman, Marvin. 2003. "Are There Racial and Ethnic Differences in Psychopathic Personality?" *Personality and Individual Differences*, 35(6): 1463–1469. DOI: 10.1016/S0191-8869(02)00362-8.

Sects and Cults

JAMES T. RICHARDSON
University of Nevada, USA

The terms sect and cult have a long history in sociology deriving from the work of German sociologist Ernst Troeltsch (1931). He defined sect as a spin-off group of a religion that sought to purify the beliefs and practices of the group which had supposedly strayed from the true path. Troeltsch then defined cult as something of a residual category focusing on more experiential and mystical religious experiences. Since this initial development, there has been much elaboration of both concepts, and the meanings have changed significantly, particularly for the term cult (for examples of this elaboration process see Yinger 1957; Nelson 1969; Wallis 1975; Campbell 1977; Richardson 1978, 1979, 1993a; Ellwood 1986).

A current working definition for sect is a religious group that is somewhat authoritarian in leadership style, voluntaristic in terms of membership, elitist in orientation (only they have the real truth), lay-led, and with definite boundaries of belief and behavior. A sect forms when members of another religious organization decide that the original group has abandoned the basic tenets that define the group. Those sharing this disenchantment then decide to withdraw and rebuild around the original tenets, thus "purifying" the beliefs and practices of the religion (Richardson 1979).

A working definition of a cult within the sociological tradition built on the work of Troeltsch is that "it is usually small in size, informal, lacking in a definite authority structure, somewhat spontaneous in development (although often possessing a somewhat charismatic leader or group of leaders), transitory, more mystical in orientation and individualistically oriented, and deriving inspiration and ideology from outside the predominant religious culture" (Richardson 1979, 159–160).

Both terms are somewhat "oppositional" in their character. Sects develop in opposition to an accepted religious group within a society, but even in their opposition they remain within the confines of the cultural values of the host society. Cults, however, develop on the fringes of a society's culture, in what Campbell (1977) refers to as the "cultic Milieu," and may espouse values and practices definitely at odds with those of the dominant culture (Richardson 1978). Richardson's treatment also generalizes the concept of cult considerably, as a cult can develop in opposition to any set of dominant values a society might have, be they religious, political, or any other type of value system. Indeed, a cult might even develop in opposition to subcultural values within a society.

Both sect and cult, and particularly the concept of cult, have become more negatively connoted in recent decades. This is a significant result of the "cult wars" that developed in America and spread to other countries in the 1960s and 1970s. The new religious movements (NRMs) that developed at that time in America and then spread to other nations caused great concern among parents and policymakers. These groups attracted young people from the middle and upper classes, and these recruits dropped out of their usual place in society to participate in movement groups. This development contributed to much concern about the new groups, which became designated as "cults" in a very popularized and negative manner (Beckford 1985; Richardson 1993a; Dawson 2006; Barker 2011). (In Europe, the term "sect" was the equivalent of "cult" in America, and it also became negatively connoted.) The mass media contributed greatly to the redefinition of NRMs as cults (or sects in Europe) which "brainwashed" supposedly unsuspecting youth. This new label was also functional for those who were concerned about young people withdrawing from society and joining the groups. To designate a group as a cult (instead of a "real religion"; see Dillon and Richardson 1994) meant that usual concerns about freedom of religion did not apply, thus allowing social control efforts by governmental agencies and self-help ones such as "deprogramming" thousands of participants in NRMs (Shupe and Bromley 1980; Richardson 2011).

Considerable attention has been paid by some scholars to the relationship between sects and cults, with some offering evidence that sometimes a cult-like group can change into a more sect-like group (Wallis 1975; Richardson 1979). This is not an automatic transformation, however, as many (perhaps most) cultic groups simply fade away. However, some cult groups do evolve into more sect-like forms, a process that requires certain conditions. Wallis (1975) describes the process based on his research on Scientology, which began as a more amorphous cultic phenomenon, but then achieved considerable structure and authority and became, Wallis claims, more sect-like. He posits three key elements that must be dealt with for a cult group to become a sect: (1) doctrinal precariousness; (2) authority; and (3) commitment of members.

Richardson (1979), using the Jesus Movement as his research focus, builds on Wallis's theories and elaborates a more detailed model of how the cult-like beginnings of a number of Jesus Movement groups changed over time into more sect-like organization forms. He posits four major factors that operate for a cultic group to move toward a more sect-like form: (1) group factors; (2) individual factors; (3) similarities or "bridges" between cultic and sect perspectives and lifestyles; and (4) external factors. In another paper, Richardson (1993b) discusses how a sect-like major Jesus Movement organization merged with an evolving, developing religious organization, Calvary Chapel, which was becoming a denomination through mergers, coalition formation, and other processes. This process of sects changing into denominations was pioneered nearly a century ago by Niebuhr (1929) and developed since by Martin (1962) and Black (1988), among others. Brasher (1992) has examined the process of denominationalization with research on Calvary Chapel, one of the fastest growing recent arrivals on the religious scene in America.

GENDER AND SEXUALITY IN CULTS AND SECTS

Research on gender roles and sexuality in sects and cults has revealed that such groups often develop alternative ways of dealing with gender and sexuality (Dawson 2006). The Shakers practiced total abstinence while other sect and cult-like groups go to the other extreme. The early years of a Jesus Movement group, the Children of God, practiced "sharing" and even used sex as a recruitment tool through "flirty fishing" (Richardson and

Davis 1983). However, most Jesus Movement groups practiced strict controls on sexuality and did not allow premarital or extramarital sex. The Unification Church ("Moonies") also exercised rigorous control over sexual activities of members, as did the Hare Krishna movement. However, all these groups practiced variations of traditional gender roles, and few NRMs allowed females prominent roles in the organization.

The fact that most NRMs practiced traditional gender roles has led to controversy about such groups. Jacobs (1989) has written about the exploitative nature of most new religions, and that many females leave such groups because of the sexism and even sexual exploitation in some. But Palmer (1994), in her research on several major NRMs, has countered with the view that many females use the newer religions to try out different lifestyles, including different sexual experiences. She also notes that females have occupied high leadership positions in some of these groups. Her more volitional approach meshes well with an overall more agency-oriented perspective which many scholars of NRMs have adopted (Dawson 2006). However, the debate on the role of females in sects, cults, and NRMs is ongoing.

SEE ALSO: Mysticism; Open and Affirming Religious Organizations; Religious Fundamentalism; Shaker Religion

REFERENCES

Barker, Eileen. 2011. "The Cult as a Social Problem." In *Religion and Social Problems*, edited by Titus Helm, 198–212. London: Routledge.

Beckford, James. 1985. *Cult Controversies: The Societal Response to New Religious Movements*. London: Tavistock.

Black, Alan. 1988. "A Marriage Model of Church Mergers." *Sociological Analysis*, 49: 281–292.

Brasher, Brenda. 1992. "Calvary Chapel: Understanding the Mega Church Phenomenon." Presented at annual meeting of the Society for the Scientific Study of Religion, Washington, D.C.

Campbell, Colin. 1977. "Clarifying the Cult." *British Journal of Sociology*, 28: 375–388.

Dawson, Lorne. 2006. *Comprehending Cults*. Oxford: Oxford University Press.

Dillon, Jane, and James T. Richardson. 1994. "The 'Cult' Concept: A Politics of Representation Analysis." *Syzygy: Journal of Alternative Religion and Culture*, 3: 185–197.

Ellwood, Robert. 1986. "The Several Meanings of Cult." *Thought: A Review of Culture and Idea*, 61: 212–224.

Jacobs, Janet. 1989. *Divine Disenchantment: Deconverting from New Religions*. Bloomington: Indiana University Press.

Martin, David. 1962. "The Denomination." *British Journal of Sociology*, 13: 1–14.

Nelson, Geoffrey. 1969. "The Spiritualist Movement and the Need for a Redefinition of Cult." *Journal for the Scientific Study of Religion*, 8: 152–160.

Niebuhr, Richard. 1929. *The Social Sources od Denominationalism*. New York: Holt, Rinehart, and Winston.

Palmer, Susan. 1994. *Moon Sisters, Krishna Mothers, Rejneesh Lovers: Women's Roles in New Religions*. New York: Syracuse University Press.

Richardson, James T. 1978. "An Oppositional and General Conceptualization of Cult." *Annual Review of Social Sciences of Religion*, 2: 29–52.

Richardson, James T. 1979. "From Cult to Sect: Creative Eclecticism in New Religious Movements." *Pacific Sociological Review*, 22: 139–166.

Richardson, James T. 1993a. "Definitions of Cult: From Sociological-Technical to Popular-Negative: *Review of Religious Research*, 34: 343–356.

Richardson, James T. 1993b. "Mergers, 'Marriages', Coalitions, and Denominationalization: The Growth of Calvary Chapel." *Syzygy: Journal of Alternative Religion and Culture*, 2: 205–223.

Richardson, James T. 2011. "Deprogramming: From Private Self-Help to Governmental Organized Repression." *Crime, Law, and Social Change*, 55: 321–336.

Richardson, James T., and Rex Davis. 1993. "Experiential Fundamentalism: Revisions of Orthodoxy in the Jesus Movement." *Journal of the American Academy of Religion*, 51: 397–425.

Shupe, Anson, and David Bromley. 1980. *The New Vigilantes: Anti-Cultists and the New Religions*. Beverly Hills: Sage.

Troeltsch, Ernst. 1931. *The Social Teachings of the Christian Churches*. New York: MacMillan.

Wallis, Roy. 1975. "Scientology: Therapeutic Cult to Religious Sect." *Social Research*, 41: 89–99.

Yinger, Milton. 1957. *Religion, Society, and the Individual*. New York: McGraw-Hill.

Self-Defense and Violence Against Women in the United States

DANIEL G. SAUNDERS
University of Michigan School of Social Work, USA

The legal concept of self-defense in the United States is based on English common law. The Model Penal Code, adopted by most states, says that "The use of force upon or toward another person is justifiable when the actor believes that such force is immediately necessary for the purpose of protecting himself against the use of unlawful force by such other person on the present occasion." The legal definitions have received a gender analysis when applied to both lethal and non-lethal situations. In most states there is no obligation to retreat from one's home in order to defend oneself, which applies in particular to women who are more likely to be victimized in the home than outside of it. Self-defense is also at the heart of the "gender symmetry" debate regarding intimate partner violence (IPV), which poses the question: are women the primary victims or are men and women equally victimized? In the 1970s the "subjective standard" – the belief that one is about to be harmed – was broadened for women, changing from the "reasonable man" to the "reasonable person" standard. In the case of abuse victims, the entire history of abuse can help explain a fearful state of mind at the time defensive force is used. A notion of the "special reasonableness of the battered woman" developed. The victim was seen as specially attuned to the nuances of her partner's behavior, allowing her to sense the gravest danger of all at the time she struck back and possibly killed her partner. Furthermore, courts ruled that women's vulnerability due to size and strength differences needed to be considered, as well as their vulnerability from women's history of gender discrimination.

Justifiable self-defense is often contrasted with "trauma" models that may form partial defenses or provide evidence of mitigating circumstances. However, trauma models, including the "battered women syndrome," are not defenses per se. "Battered women syndrome" is particularly imprecise and has changed definitions over time. Expert witnesses can testify with specialized knowledge, without the use of a "syndrome," to help explain survivors' sense of danger, emotional attachment, symptoms attributable to the abuse, and continued involvement in the abusive relationship. Nonetheless some fear that explanations of trauma feed stereotypes of women as weak (Keegan 2013), and, in particular, that "battered women syndrome" will pathologize survivors. Another term that raises concern is "violent resistance," which is used in some typologies of violent behavior. However, "violent resistance" includes two very different forms of violence: one is justifiable self-defense and the other is unjustifiable retribution.

Research shows that women kill their partners in self-defense to a much greater extent than men. These women are likely to feel hopelessly trapped, threatened with death, and suffering from the most severe forms of violence (Saunders and Browne 2000). Men, on the other hand, are often acting out of jealousy and a fear the relationship will end (e.g., Juodis et al. 2014). Women of color are likely to feel even more trapped and to mistrust majority institutions, for example, fearing their partners will be mistreated by the criminal justice system. Thus, they may be more likely to resort to force in response to assaults.

For non-lethal use of defensive violence, research shows it is also more common among women than men. In a systematic review of 23 studies, IPV survivors reported that self-defense was their primary motive (Bair-Merritt et al. 2010). However, the studies used varying definitions of self-defense and in some cases self-defense was not distinguished from retaliation. Less frequent, but still fairly common motives, were anger and attempts to gain attention. Such a systematic review has not been conducted on men's motives, but many studies show their predominant motives involve coercion, attempts to intimidate, punish unwanted behavior, or express anger (Swan et al. 2008). Such gender differences are most striking in help-seeking samples (Hamberger and Larsen 2015) as opposed to community samples (Graham-Kevan 2009). Specific measures of self-defense and other motives have been developed for use in research, but they can be used in clinical assessment as well.

Since 2005 more than twenty states passed "stand your ground" laws. The laws remove the duty to retreat when outside one's home. They often presume that imminent harm exists and they remove civil and criminal liability for those acting under the law. "Stand your ground" provisions do not benefit women attacked by men in public places. Prior to these statutes, women would not be expected to flee a man because she could not find "complete safety" in doing so (Franks 2014). However, if a survivor receives an order of protection against her partner or ex-partner, then the above presumptions hold if that person tries to enter the home (Dressler 2010). Research is emerging on the impact of "stand your ground" laws, with initial results showing they may actually increase violence (e.g., Cheng and Hoekstra 2013).

SEE ALSO: Violence Against Women in Global Perspective

REFERENCES

Bair-Merritt, M. H., et al. 2010. "Why Do Women Use Intimate Partner Violence? A Systematic Review of Women's Motivations." *Trauma, Violence, & Abuse*, 11(4): 178–189.

Cheng, C., and M. Hoekstra. 2013. "Does Strengthening Self-Defense Law Deter Crime or Escalate Violence? Evidence from Expansions to Castle Doctrine." *Journal of Human Resources*, 48(3): 821–854.

Dressler, J. 2010. "Feminist (or 'Feminist') Reform of Self-Defense Law: Some Critical Reflections." *Ohio State Public Law Working Paper*, 143.

Franks, M. A. 2014. "Real Men Advance, Real Women Retreat: Stand Your Ground, Battered Women's Syndrome, and Violence as Male Privilege." *University of Miami Law Review*, 68: 1099–1128.

Graham-Kevan, N. 2009. "The Psychology of Women's Partner Violence: Characteristics and Cautions." *Journal of Aggression, Maltreatment & Trauma*, 18(6): 587–603.

Hamberger, L. K., and S. Larsen. 2015. "Men's and Women's Experience of Intimate Partner Violence: A Review of Ten Years of Comparative Studies in Clinical Samples, Part I." *Journal of Family Violence*, 30(6): 699–717.

Juodis, M., A. Starzomski, S. Porter, and M. Woodworth. 2014. "A Comparison of Domestic and Non-Domestic Homicides: Further Evidence for Distinct Dynamics and Heterogeneity of Domestic Homicide Perpetrators." *Journal of Family Violence*, 29(3): 299–313.

Keegan, K. E. 2013. "The True Man & the Battered Woman: Prospects for Gender-Neutral Narratives in Self-Defense Doctrines." *Hastings Law Journal*, 65: 259–283.

Saunders, D. G., and A. Browne. 2000. "Intimate Partner Homicide." In *Case Studies in Family Violence*, edited by R. T. Ammerman and M. Hersen, 2nd ed. New York: Plenum.

Swan, S. C., L. J. Gambone, J. E. Caldwell, T. P. Sullivan, and D. L. Snow. 2008. "A Review of Research on Women's Use of Violence with Male Intimate Partners." *Violence and Victims*, 23(3): 301.

FURTHER READING

Coker, D. 2013. "The Story of Wanrow: The Reasonable Woman and the Law of Self-Defense." In *Criminal Law Stories*, edited by D. Coker and R. Weisberg. New York: Foundation Press/Thomson Reuters.

Self-Esteem

HEATHER KOHLER FLYNN
Sonoma State University, USA

Self-esteem is a commonly used term that is typically defined as thinking favorably of oneself. According to literature directed at a popular audience, if one has low self-esteem, "we can find a way to boost it!" Typing the phrase "self-esteem" into the search bar at Amazon.com turns up over one hundred thousand books – most of which are in the self-help genre – which shows just how ubiquitous self-esteem has become among pop psychologists and those whom they target. William James first introduced the concept in 1890, suggesting that self-esteem is the result of our successes (behavior) divided by our pretensions (values and goals). Indeed, self-esteem, an overall evaluation or appraisal of our own worth, isn't just for a popular audience.

The study of self-esteem has been of considerable importance in the social psychological research. The definition of self-esteem is generally conceptualized and measured as an internal, individual characteristic; however, this has been shown to be problematic when researching across cultures. Recent findings suggest that self-esteem is more of an implicit, collaborative task based on the dominant values of the culture, rather than an individual, personal undertaking.

MEASUREMENT

The most widely used and well-validated measurement of self-esteem is the 10-item Rosenberg Self-Esteem Scale developed by US sociologist Morris Rosenberg in 1965. It includes items such as "I feel I have a number of good qualities" and serves as an assessment of global self-esteem where an overall judgment of one's self-worth is not tied to any specific situation. In contrast, other domain-specific inventories measure one's value in a particular area, or subdomain, of self-esteem (i.e., academic, work, athletics, social, or appearance). More recent models account for cultural differences and focus less on individual values and more on the fulfillment of the dominant values of our culture. Such measurements include the self-concept enhancing tactician (SCENT) model, terror management theory (TMT), and values theory.

RESEARCH

The development of self-esteem is a lifelong process that is influenced by socialization beginning early in childhood. Findings using the Rosenberg Self-Esteem Scale with American respondents suggest that self-esteem is correlated with demographic factors including age, class, and race/ethnicity. Additional self-esteem measurements imply that cultural differences and gender also are influential predictors of self-esteem.

Socialization

Our socialization, the process by which society's values and norms are taught, influences our self-esteem. Parents transmit knowledge and values to their children and help to shape behavior and perceptions of self. Children also are actively constructing an understanding of their environment. The media constitutes an additional agent of socialization wherein, according to cultural studies scholars, children use the media to develop their identity and to test various identity representations. Debates include positive and negative contributions of the media to shaping constructions of the self and self-esteem. Feminist scholars argue idealized media images of women's bodies as a source of objectification are more detrimental than beneficial to self-esteem.

Age

Self-esteem increases from adolescence to middle adulthood, peaks around 50 years, and then decreases in old age. Generational studies of American children, parents, grandparents, and great-grandparents show that self-esteem influences depression, health, relationship satisfaction, and job satisfaction. These results remain across generations. Thus, regardless of age, positive self-esteem has significant benefits for people's experiences of love, work, and health, suggesting the advantages of high self-esteem.

Class

Increased self-esteem also is linked with socioeconomic status. Social class shapes socialization by influencing values and occupational aspirations within families. Depending on social class, parents may encourage a child's behavior toward conformity (often blue-collar occupations) or independence (often middle-class or white-collar jobs). Wealthier, more educated individuals do exhibit higher self-esteem, but this is a weak predictor explaining only 1 percent of the variance in self-esteem.

Race/ethnicity

Wade Nobles theorizes that self-concept is a social process that includes self-perceptions, internalized attitudes, and perceptions of one's racial or ethnic group. African Americans in the United States generally report higher self-esteem compared with white Americans, Asian Americans, Hispanics, and American Indians. Research indicates that African Americans take pride in and identify with their racial group and are less likely to value approval from others, hence preserving their self-esteem. Scholars extend these findings and show that African Americans score higher than white Americans on measures of self-esteem; however, white Americans score higher than all other racial and ethnic minority groups.

Cultural differences

Studies demonstrate that cultural differences are a stronger influence on self-esteem than are being of a certain class, race, or gender. Racial differences in self-esteem seem to extend beyond group identification and appear to be more about cultural differences. Cultures that place a greater emphasis on individualism (African American and Caucasian) exhibit higher self-esteem compared with those that value collectivism (many Asian cultures). This difference extends even wider when comparing Asians living in Asia with white Americans. These outcomes are consistent with the idea that cultural values about the self impact self-esteem, and these transformations happen over time and generations. Researchers contend this may be a consequence of how self-esteem is defined and measured. Cross-cultural researchers find systematic response bias in Likert-type scales, such as the Rosenberg Self-Esteem Scale. Japanese and Taiwanese cultures are more likely than Canadian and American cultures to use the midpoint on Likert scales; such biases also are found cross-nationally. In US response style studies, African Americans are more likely than white Americans to use extreme values while Asian Americans consistently rank themselves lower than other ethnic groups.

Importantly, debates have arisen regarding the applicability of the global self-esteem scale across cultures, perhaps accounting for disparate self-esteem results among different cultures. The SCENT model and TMT perspectives suggest individuals are motivated to embody internalized values from their culture. Those in individualist cultures may derive self-esteem from accomplishments that they personally achieve, whereas the self-esteem of people in more collectivist cultures is strongly tied to groups and to the communal contributions of that group. Statements such as "I feel that I'm a person of worth, at least on a level equal with others," have varied meanings depending on cultural norms. In some cultures, modesty may be a virtue, so one might disagree with the statement in order to appear humble. Consequently, the way society is organized – individualist versus collectivist – influences cultural perceptions of the self, identity, and presumably self-esteem.

Becker et al. (2014), however, suggest the focus on a bipolar concept – individualism–collectivism – provides a limited portrayal of cultural differences. Instead, these scholars employ a values theory perspective using longitudinal data from 5,000 members of 20 cultural groups, including Western and Eastern Europe, South America, Western and Eastern Asia, and sub-Saharan Africa. Results suggest that respondents base their self-esteem not on their own personal values, as has been widely assumed, but on the fulfillment of value priorities within their cultural environment based upon four key factors: controlling one's life, doing one's duty, benefiting others, and achieving social status. The importance of these values varies between cultures. For instance, Western Europeans were more likely to derive their self-esteem from the impression of controlling their lives, in contrast to those who are living in cultures that value conformity and tradition (areas of the Middle East, Africa, and Asia) who are comparatively more likely to base their self-esteem on the feeling of doing their duty.

Gender

Gendered self-esteem also is a frequently discussed research topic. Research using the Rosenberg Self-Esteem Scale shows that males consistently report higher self-esteem when compared with females, although the difference is quite small. Gender explains only about 1 percent of the variation in self-esteem. Contemporary explanations center on the measurement of self-esteem and compare it to cultural explanations: the scale has a masculine, individualistic bias. Boys in America are socialized to be independent while girls are socialized to be interdependent in a way that corresponds to the differences between North American (United States and Canada) and East Asian (Japan and Taiwan) cultures, accounting for the finding that females consistently report lower self-esteem than males. This may explain a gendered response bias induced methodologically. It is possible that girls may be more likely to use the midpoint, like East Asian cultures, and boys may be more likely to use the extreme points, similar to North American cultures. Further research is necessary to disentangle this presupposition. Indeed, investigations using the Collective Self-Esteem Scale and the Possible Selves Questionnaire instead of a global self-esteem measure indicate that girls, actually, do identify more strongly with a collective notion of self than do boys.

Nevertheless, contemporary research has shown global self-esteem gender differences are disappearing. Perhaps cultural shifts are occurring in America with Title IX and in other parts of the world, with the use of contemporary rhetoric such as "You Go Girl" having an effect on increasing girls' self-esteem. Future research will help to unravel these recent phenomena.

SEE ALSO: Identity Politics

REFERENCES

Becker, Maja, et al. 2014. "Cultural Bases for Self-Evaluation: Seeing Oneself Positively in Different Cultural Contexts." *Personality and Social Psychology Bulletin*, 40(5): 657–675.

James, William. 1890. *The Principles of Psychology*. Cambridge, MA: Harvard University Press.

Rosenberg, Morris. 1965. *Society and the Adolescent Self-Image*. Princeton: Princeton University Press.

FURTHER READING

Chen, Chuansheng, Shin-ying Lee, and Harold W. Stevenson. 1995. "Response Style and Cross-Cultural Comparisons of Rating Scales Among East Asian and North American Students." *Psychological Science*, 6(3): 170–175.

Orth, Ultrich, Richard W. Robins, and Keith F. Widaman. 2012. "Life-Span Development of Self-Esteem and Its Effects on Important Life Outcomes." *Journal of Personality and Social Psychology*, 102: 1271–1288.

Smith, Christine A. 1999. "I Enjoy Being a Girl: Collective Self-Esteem, Feminism, and Attitudes Toward Women." *Sex Roles*, 40(3): 281–293.

Self-Help Movements

HEATHER McKEE HURWITZ
University of California, Santa Barbara, USA

INTRODUCTION

Self-help movements create social change by inspiring personal transformation among participants. Participants provide reciprocal mutual aid to other participants in support groups, helping themselves and other members, thus the term "self-help." In the United States, recent estimates suggest 10 million Americans participate in support groups and more than 500 national self-help organizations coordinate and advocate for the support groups under their umbrella (Archibald 2007). There are thousands of healthcare and livelihood support groups nurturing community development on every continent. In developing countries self-help movements often focus on microfinance self-help groups, which are initiated by small community groups, non-governmental organizations (NGOs), or even large microcredit banks such as the Nobel Prize-winning Grameen Bank based in Bangladesh, with a membership of more than 7 million mostly female entrepreneurs.

Self-help movements pursue a variety of goals using diverse tactics. In support groups, volunteers share stories about their lives and provide medical or psychological assistance to the rest of the group. Support groups that are a part of national and international self-help organizations often share a similar goal or theme; for example, Self Help Africa organizes small savings and loans groups for women farmers to grow their businesses with the goal of alleviating hunger, poverty, and the effects of climate change. Support groups create a collective identity or sense of "we-ness," in part by mobilizing outside of dominant political, educational, medical, or economic institutions. Self-help movements aimed at transforming participants' health and families may provide group therapy for survivors of domestic violence, counsel participants addicted to sexual intercourse, comfort women transitioning to menopause, guide teen mothers, or advocate ways for transgender persons to access surgical treatments. Self-help movements for poverty reduction and education often focus on the participation of poor rural women in collectives such as seed libraries and grain banks, which collect and distribute surplus crops to improve village food security, or in La Leche League, which offers breastfeeding education and encouragement. When self-help movements shape public opinion, it is by both the sheer breadth and diversity of participation in support groups and self-help cultures and advocacy to transform the broader institutions that affect participants' lives.

Self-help movements have a long history of organizing groups to collectively transform both their participants and systems of authority that have failed to address their participants' problems. Since the 1600s, self-help and mutual aid groups have provided welfare for the poor and immigrant populations in England and the United States. The diversity and range of modern support groups emerged post-World War II and as part of the 1960s and 1970s global wave of social movements and countercultures. In the 1970s, social movement scholars tended to overlook self-help movements because they did not target collective action at the state. In the 1980s and 1990s, a variety of support groups blossomed. Self-help movements received broad visibility on daytime talk shows, through the publication of hundreds of self-help books aimed at solving almost every social psychological and relationship problem imaginable, and scholarship (Simonds 1992). The most recent mobilization inspired by self-help and mutual aid was the Occupy Wall Street movement. The movement emerged in the fall of 2011 by "occupying" or camping in hundreds of public squares and town centers around the world. In the encampments, volunteers protested economic inequality by sharing food, blankets, and tents, and by creating solidarity and mental health support systems with the homeless and victims of foreclosures and unemployment.

Although some self-help movements may be considered health movements, self-help has a controversial relationship with institutionalized healthcare. Hospitals may host groups and health professionals may attend or sponsor support group meetings. But many groups meet in community centers and eschew professional healthcare in favor of self-care. As a contentious and intentional act against healthcare authorities, support groups advocate alternative paths to health for conditions ranging from eating disorders to breast cancer. For example, in the 1980s, volunteer nurses and support groups motivated by the idea of mutual aid offered HIV-positive patients better information and care than hospitals, which feared contagion and stigmatization for serving AIDS patients. Still, critics of the booming self-help industry argue that self-help movements have strayed too far from the medical field and do more to promote pop psychology book sales than to promote well-being or the empowerment of women (Kaminer 1992).

Various ideological forces motivate self-help movements. Women's cultures of caretaking and valuing gender equality motivate groups dominated by women or groups in feminist communities. Support groups may also draw inspiration from anti-authoritarianism, participatory democracy, economic empowerment, and sustainable development ideologies that express the value of self-reliance. A variety of religious movements and New Age philosophies contribute to the development of self-help movements. Alcoholics Anonymous established a developmental process for recovery called a "12-step" program that draws on the idea of building a relationship with a "higher power." However, not all self-help groups use the "12-step" process. Many groups develop their own structures for recovery particular to each group's dynamics and ideologies.

GENDER AND SELF-HELP

While many groups are open to people of any gender, other groups are gender segregated. Groups may act on a shared sense of purpose around the cause of their group but also may act on the collective identity formed around their solidary identity, such as being mothers or being transgender. Gender-segregated groups include parenting groups for fathers, summer camps for transgender and gender-variant children, or groups for mothers with incarcerated children.

Like all social movements, self-help movements serve to reinforce, challenge, and/or reconfigure gendered inequalities. Although women work significantly more in the labor market than just a few decades ago, women tend to hold jobs that pay less and offer less security than men. Women turn to support groups to navigate the economic and emotional burdens associated with welfare, and to find ways to advance their careers in the face of workplace inequalities. For women who primarily work in the home, support groups have historically been spaces where they can create friendships with other women, relationships that have led to the formation of women's movements. Widely mobilized in India, Mexico, and many parts of the developing world, support groups termed Rotating Savings and Credit Associations (ROSCAs) or *tandas* encourage participants to pool their savings together and create small-scale cooperative craft or food businesses. Also, women participate in self-help movements to heal from date rape, stalking, anorexia, or other problems that stem from valuing male authority and male sexual enjoyment above the health and well-being of women. Because both self-help and women's cultures value expressions of femininity such as caretaking and exerting emotional labor, a majority of the participants in self-help are women and most self-help books are geared toward a female audience.

Self-help opposes hegemonic expressions of masculinity, such as hiding one's emotions or always being in control. Men who participate in self-help may object to typical hegemonic expectations for masculinity by joining support groups to reject the pressures of "manhood" and express their emotions and vulnerability. Men join self-help movements for many reasons including dissatisfaction with their romantic relationships, to build self-confidence, or to transform their families and sex lives. Self-help organizations also advocate for men who work in female-dominated or stigmatized industries, such as the American Assembly of Men in Nursing.

SEXUALITY AND SELF-HELP

The emergence and proliferation of self-help movements coincided with the post-World War II movement for sexual liberation. A variety of sex advice books, such as Alex Comfort's *The Joy of Sex*, encouraged readers to understand sexuality and talk more openly about it. However, the majority of early self-help books about sexuality were directed toward heterosexual audiences and maintained the marginalization of homosexuals.

Self-help movements have contributed resources to gay and lesbian movements and have frequently emerged out of lesbian, gay, bisexual, and transgender (LGBT) social movement communities. When sexual minorities have been ignored by mainstream culture or healthcare, support groups have legitimated the lives, identities, and health needs of gays, lesbians, and other sexual minorities. Drawing on both self-help movements and gay and lesbian movements, groups such as PFLAG (Parents, Families, and Friends of Lesbians and Gays) and gay and lesbian community centers improve the lives of sexual minorities by coordinating support groups, classes, and fundraisers that fight discrimination. Exemplary of the links between gay and lesbian movements and self-help movements is the tactic of "coming out," when activists reveal their sexual identity to friends and family. In addition to challenging societal prejudices, coming out is a personal realization and a process of working toward self-acceptance. A variety of movements have adopted coming-out strategies to develop emotional strength and pride using a "politics of visibility," such as survivors of sexual abuse who share their experiences to heal and to change how laws and medical institutions address child sexual abuse (Whittier 2009).

FEMINISM AND SELF-HELP

Many self-help movements emerged alongside feminist movements by drawing on feminist ideology and the belief in gender equality. Perhaps the best example of spillover between feminist and self-help movements is the idea of consciousness-raising (CR) circles, a tactic used widely by feminists in the 1970s. CR were support groups for women to share stories about their personal struggles with gender inequality in the home, workplace, classroom, and even the bedroom. By using the format of support groups and building collective identity and contention against the dual standards women faced in many institutions, CR expanded participants' self-confidence and stimulated political awareness about feminism (Rapping 1996).

Feminist self-help movements focus on improving women's lives by intentionally sharing personal stories and speaking out about women's unique biological and emotional experiences. Exemplary is the post-partum self-help movement, which revealed post-partum depression as a serious medical condition by using the strategies of support groups and appearing on daytime talk shows to educate families about the "baby blues," depression, and psychosis related to childbirth and early motherhood (Taylor 1996). In addition to support groups, self-help organizations Depression After Delivery and Postpartum Support International advocate changes to laws that criminalize infanticide and fail to acknowledge post-partum depression as a legitimate illness.

Self-help books have also been an important resource for women's and feminist movements. For example, Betty Friedan revealed her discontent as a modern housewife, sparking feminist action to change the alienation that women felt as devalued homemakers, in the self-help book *The Feminine Mystique* (1963). Likewise, the Boston Women's Health Book Collective recognized women's lack of information about their own bodies and the inadequacy of mainstream healthcare with respect to many health problems that affect women. They wrote *Our Bodies, Ourselves* (1970), a self-help book on women's health that continues to inspire the global women's health movement. Gloria Steinem's *Revolution from Within: A Book of Self-Esteem* (1992) is both a self-help book and feminist manifesto. In *Sisters of the Yam: Black Women and Self-Recovery* (1994), bell hooks argues for black women to oppose the negative psychological and emotional effects of racism and sexism with self-empowerment and support groups. And recently, drawing on feminist research and her life story, Sheryl Sandberg, chief operating officer of Facebook and author of *Lean In: Women, Work, and the Will to Lead* (2013), advises strategies to reduce workplace inequalities and improve women's leadership abilities. To reach a broad audience, a variety of feminists protest mainstream views about gender inequality using the format of self-help books and websites.

However, scholars debate whether self-help strengthens feminist movements or actually undermines feminism. Feminists question who benefits from microfinance and savings self-help groups. Although they have augmented transnational grassroots feminist networks in countries such as Morocco, international organizations and governments may profit more than the women who receive small business loans (Poster and Salime

2002). Self-help cultures may appear to "help" but actually manipulate women to think that they cannot be self-sufficient or that they are victims (Irvine 1999). Kaminer (1992) cautions that talk shows disempower women by portraying therapy as gossip, glamorize recovery, and offer anecdotes rather than scientific information. In addition, Tallen (1990) argues that 12-step programs view problems as personal failings and are therefore opposed to lesbian feminist analyses that view individuals' troubles as a result of larger systems of oppression such as sexism, ageism, and/or racism. Distinguishing whether self-help empowers women or serves as anti-feminist backlash is a postfeminist dilemma. Self-help movements may appear to help women improve their careers, mental health, or find romantic satisfaction, all of which may be considered feminist goals. At the same time, self-help may advocate for heteronormativity, consumerism, and individualism, ideologies that feminist values tend to critique. Like many new social movements, self-help movements have influenced the development, tactics, collective identities, and goals of other identity movements and movements focused on cultural and community change such as women's, feminist, and lesbian and gay movements.

SEE ALSO: Consciousness-Raising; Feminist Activism; Health, Healthcare, and Sexual Minorities; Medicine and Medicalization; Microcredit and Microlending; Occupy Movements; Self-Esteem; Women's Health Movement in the United States

REFERENCES

Archibald, Matthew E. 2007. *The Evolution of Self-Help: How a Health Movement Became an Institution*. New York: Palgrave Macmillan.
Irvine, Leslie. 1999. *Codependent Forevermore: The Invention of Self in a Twelve Step Group*. Chicago: University of Chicago Press.
Kaminer, Wendy. 1992. *I'm Dysfunctional, You're Dysfunctional: The Recovery Movement and Other Self-Help Fashions*. Reading, MA: Addison-Wesley.
Poster, Winifred, and Zakia Salime. 2002. "The Limits of Microcredit: Transnational Feminism and USAID Activities in the United States and Morocco." In *Women's Activism and Globalization: Linking Local Struggles and Transnational Politics*, edited by Nancy Naples and Manisha Desai, 185–215. New York: Routledge.
Rapping, Elayne. 1996. *The Culture of Recovery: Making Sense of the Self-Help Movement in Women's Lives*. Boston: Beacon Press.
Simonds, Wendy. 1992. *Women and Self-Help Culture: Reading Between the Lines*. New Brunswick: Rutgers University Press.
Tallen, Bette S. 1990. "Twelve Step Programs: A Lesbian Feminist Critique." *NWSA Journal*, 2: 390–407.
Taylor, Verta. 1996. *Rock-a-By Baby: Feminism, Self-Help, and Postpartum Depression*. New York: Routledge.
Whittier, Nancy. 2009. *The Politics of Child Sexual Abuse: Emotion, Social Movements, and the State*. Oxford: Oxford University Press.

FURTHER READING

Epstein, Steven. 2007. *Inclusion: The Politics of Difference in Medical Research*. Chicago: University of Chicago Press.

Senior Women and Sexuality in the United States

KATHERINE RAMOS
University of Houston, USA

JESSICA J. FULTON
Durham VA Medical Center, USA

Sexuality includes behaviors, beliefs, attitudes, values, orientation, and perceptions of intimacy and pleasure related to sex (Rheaume and Mitty 2008). International and US research on sexuality in elders remains scarce. Extant literature suggests men and women remain interested (albeit to a lesser degree) in sexual activity across the lifespan (Addis et al. 2006). Among US elders, 83.7 percent of men and 61.6 percent of women aged 57–64 and 38.5 percent of men and 16.7 percent of women aged 75–85 reported engaging in sexual activity in the past year (Lindau et al. 2007). Assumptions based on stereotypes and ageist attitudes may inadvertently suggest elders are not sexual or that sex is for the young. To improve understanding of sexuality and avoid faulty assumptions about sex among seniors (i.e., ages 65+), many factors should be considered. For instance, declining rates of sexual activity may be partially explained by physiological changes. Lindau et al. (2007) found that aging women report experiencing vaginal dryness (35.9–43.6 percent), inability to climax (34–38.2 percent), and pain during intercourse (11.8–18.6 percent). Women also experience declining estrogen levels, making sex less pleasurable (Rheaume and Mitty 2008). Moreover, illness and disability, including cardiovascular disease, diabetes, chronic pain, arthritis, stroke, and sexually transmitted diseases, hinder sexual interest and functioning among senior women (Rheaume and Mitty 2008).

Attitudes and social contexts also influence sexuality (Lindau et al. 2007). Today's older adult US women were forming attitudes about sexuality in the 1940s and 1950s, a context in which traditional morality drew a strong association between a woman's virginity and her worth and one where women were discouraged from expressing sexual desire (Allyn 2000). Early learning experiences may continue to influence aging women's sexuality. Indeed, only 4 percent of senior women report engaging in sex without a romantic partner (Lindau et al. 2007). This historical cultural context sheds light regarding why 35 percent of older adult women rate sex as "not important" (Lindau et al. 2007). Religious affiliations and cultural mores of what is acceptable further limit sexual expression (Rheaume and Mitty 2008). Moreover, older women's perceptions of ageist attitudes (e.g., elders should be asexual) and beliefs (e.g., sex in older age is repugnant) negatively impact comfort and willingness to discuss sexuality (Syme et al. 2015). Additionally, elders living in community living environments face insurmountable barriers to engaging in sexual activity. Nursing homes and assisted living facilities (ALFs) have limited to no accommodations (e.g., private rooms) to promote an active sex life (Rheaume and Mitty 2008). Furthermore, senior women outnumber their male counterparts so lack of available partners compounds limitations of sexual activity for heterosexual women.

Increased understanding of barriers to sex among senior women is important, as sexual activity impacts health and well-being (e.g., sexual satisfaction has been linked to lower body mass index and improved mental health; Addis et al. 2006). Recently, a longitudinal study with older English adults found sexual activity level was positively associated with sexual health and psychological well-being and negatively associated with sexual dysfunction among senior women (Lee et al. 2015). Given the positive benefits of healthy sexuality among elders, healthcare providers are increasingly recognizing the importance of addressing the unique needs and sociocultural context of elders (Syme et al. 2015). Providers may consider using the "five A's" (assess, advise, agree, assist, and arrange) and approach encounters with a collaborative, sex-positive stance. Assessment of current sexuality (e.g., behaviors, relationships, attitudes), sexual functioning (e.g., desire, excitement, arousal), well-being (e.g., sexual satisfaction), and history (e.g., sexual functioning history) can be followed by normalizing concerns. Providers can advise patients with basic sexuality education. Once providers and patients agree on identified treatment goals, providers can assist patients by identifying strategies to address specific concerns and arrange follow-up contact or refer for specialty services.

Issues related to sexuality and diverse older adult women must also be considered. Specifically, the increasing proportion of older adults is paralleled by an increasing representation of culturally, ethnically, and racially diverse older adult women. African American seniors will comprise at least 10 percent of the US population within the next 15 years and will have to navigate and overcome stigma and negative stereotypes related to their sexuality (Dickerson and Rousseau 2010; Laganá et al. 2013). Women within the lesbian, gay, bisexual, and transgender (LGBT) community face barriers to reception of their sexuality within healthcare systems, communities, and residences (e.g., heterosexist attitudes in ALFs; Syme et al. 2015).

Additional research, particularly international studies, is needed to better understand the nuanced aspects of sex and sexuality in older adulthood. Given that women outnumber men, addressing factors influencing women's sexual identity and needs in a forum that limits ageist perspectives and promotes understanding and psychological well-being is imperative. Finally, evidence-based program development on sexual health is needed to promote practical approaches to maintaining sexual health among seniors.

SEE ALSO: Aging, Ageism, and Gender; Menopause; Sex and Culture; Sexology and Psychological Sex Research

REFERENCES

Addis, L.B., et al. RRISK Study Group. 2006. "Sexual Actvitiy and Function in Middle-aged and Older Women." *Obstetrics and Gynecology*, 107: 755–764. DOI: 10.1097/01.AOG.0000202398.27428.e2.

Allyn, D. 2000. *Make Love, Not War: The Sexual Revolution, an Unfettered History*. New York: Routledge.

Dickerson, Bette, and Nicole Rousseau. 2010. "Black Senior Women and Sexuality." In *Black Sexualities*, edited by Juan Battle and Sandra L. Barnes, 423–442. New Brunswick: Rutgers University Press.

Laganá, Luciana, Theresa White, Daniel E. Bruzzone, and Cristine E. Bruzzone. 2013. "Exploring the Sexuality of African American Older Women." *British Journal of Medicine and Medical Research*, 4: 1129–1148. DOI: 10.9734/BJMMR/2014/5491.

Lee, D.M., et al. 2015. "Sexual Health and Well-being Among Older Men and Women in England: Findings from the English Longitudinal Study of Ageing." *Archives of Sexual Behavior*. DOI:10.1007/s10508-014-0465-1

Lindau, S.T., et al. 2007. "A Study of Sexuality and Health Among Older Adults in the United States." *New England Journal of Medicine*, 357: 762–774. DOI: 10.1056/NEJMoa067423.

Rheaume, C., and Mitty, E. 2008. "Sexuality and Intimacy in Older Adults." *Geriatric Nursing*, 29: 342–349. DOI: 10.1016/j.gerinurse.2008.08.004

Syme, M.L., C.C. Cordes, R.P. Cameron, and L.R. Mona. 2015. In *Handbook of Clinical Geropsychology*, edited by P. Lichtenberg and B. Mast, 395–412. Washington, DC: American Psychological Association.

Sex and Culture

JULIE A. WINTERICH
Guilford College, USA

What sex is, and who should and should not be having it, are beliefs and norms that vary across cultures and are shaped by dominant ideas about gender and sexuality. Sex is learned and socially controlled by various institutions including the medical, legal, and education systems. In the United States, sex researchers debate knowledge about gender, sexuality, and sex, and contest assumptions in research designs that focus on genital-based sex and frequency of sexual activity. Recent theorizing and research emphasize gender and sexual fluidity in identity and experiences.

What is a sex act in one time and place may be an act of power and status in another. For example, in ancient Athens adult male citizens could penetrate socially defined inferiors, whether they were male or female. Until the 1600s in Japan, boys were expected to desire both boys and girls until they ceremonially became a man at which point their role as a penetrated partner transitioned to that of a penetrator. Some scholars argue such relationships reflected shifts in status, and were educational as well as erotic. What Westerners now view as a person who is transgender or with a non-conforming gender identity was often valued within some native American groups as a person especially apt as a healer or shaman. A two-spirit person, or someone who possessed characteristics of both men and women, would live their life in the role of the "opposite" sex; more often they were men who lived as heterosexual women (Meem, Gibson, and Alexander 2010).

Historically, Western medical views of sexuality and sex reinforced cultural constructions of gender, heteronormativity, and normality. In the nineteenth century, homosexuality was first classified as a deviant sexual practice in the new field of sexology. The American Psychiatric Association published the original *Diagnostic and Statistical Manual of Mental Disorders* in 1952 and listed homosexuality as a disorder; that listing remained until 1973. In the nineteenth century, the medical establishment also arbitrated virginity statuses for young, white, middle-class women through pelvic exams to determine whether their hymens were intact. The cultural belief that an intact hymen reflected women's chastity persisted into the twentieth century even though gynecologists understood that the link between a hymen and virginity status was not definitive. Nonetheless, sometimes courts called for medical testimony in rape cases based on physicians' internal exams of victims (Brumberg 1998).

In the United States, federal and state laws throughout history have regulated the distribution of information about sex and controlled the sexual behavior of individuals by race and sexual identity. As part of a public purity campaign, the Comstock Law from 1873 to 1938 outlawed the dissemination of allegedly obscene materials including literature on sex, birth control, and sexually transmitted diseases. In the 1660s, Maryland was the first colony to prohibit interracial marriage, and by 1750, all southern colonies as well as Massachusetts and Pennsylvania defined such marriages as illegal. When the Supreme Court ruled in 1967 in *Loving v. Virginia* that anti-miscegenation laws were unconstitutional, 16 states had laws on the books banning interracial marriage.

Similarly, the legality of sodomy was determined at the state level until the Supreme Court ruled in 2003 in *Lawrence et al. v. Texas* that private sexual acts between two consenting adults were legally protected. Sodomy was not often defined by courts but was typically understood as any sexual act that was allegedly immoral or unnatural such as anal and oral sex, and bestiality. Courts did not regulate the sexual behavior of heterosexuals, however, and usually sodomy laws were used to punish gay men. Not until 1961 did Illinois become the first state to repeal its sodomy law. The Supreme Court ruling in 2003 overthrew the remaining sodomy laws in 13 states.

Same-sex legal unions were first recognized in the United States in 1997 when Hawaii provide some state benefits to same-sex couples, such as insurance and inheritance rights. Massachusetts was the first state to legally recognize same-sex marriage in 2003, affording gay couples the same rights as heterosexual couples. The Defense of Marriage Act, which defined marriage between a man and a woman with regard to federal rights, was struck down by the Supreme Court in 2013 in *United States v. Windsor* thereby guaranteeing federal benefits to couples in same-sex marriages. The Windsor ruling did not overturn states' prohibitions of same-sex marriage, but that ruling spawned a flurry of states acting either through their legislatures or courts to legalize same-sex marriages. As of June 2015, 37 states and the District of Columbia legalized same-sex marriage when the Supreme Court ruled by a vote of five to four that the Constitution guarantees same-sex couples the right to marry. Consequently, same-sex marriage is now legal in all 50 states.

Expectations of heterosexuality and gender dominate childhood and teen socialization through school curriculums, school practices, and sexual education. School curriculums contain heterosexual metaphors to illustrate course material. For example, heterosexual divorce is used to explain the constitutional division of federal and state power and, consequently, why states' laws vary on matters such as child custody and financial obligations. Biological descriptions of reproduction utilize gendered language that depicts sperm as dominating passive eggs rather than portraying mutually active unions. In addition, heterosexual rituals of dances including homecoming and prom presume that boys invite girls while dances in which girls do the asking are noted for their once-a-year occurrence. Homecoming and prom courts feature kings and queens thus valorizing heterosexual pairing as natural and inevitable. Non-heterosexual identities are largely invisible in school curriculums and rituals while the fag discourse in boys' language and interactions stigmatize and regulate boys' behavior (Pascoe 2007). One significant consequence is that gay, lesbian, bisexual, transgender, and queer (GLBTQ) students are at much greater risk for bullying and violence due to their non-conforming statuses. This violence polices dominant constructions of gender and sexuality in everyday life, and causes serious physical and mental health harm to GLBTQ students who attempt and commit suicide at greater rates than do heterosexual students.

Sex education in the United States varies by state from comprehensive to abstinence only. The overall focus in all sex education is a description of reproduction with an emphasis on avoiding pregnancy, sexually transmitted diseases, and HIV/AIDS. Mandated abstinence-only programs aim to control and regulate adolescent sexual behavior but have proven to be ineffective with regard to rates of sexually transmitted diseases and teen pregnancies when compared to rates in states with comprehensive education. Overall teen pregnancy rates in the United States are consistently dropping yet they continue to rank five to eight times higher than Western European countries.

Sex education curriculums impart desexualized instruction and do not provide knowledge on how to develop sexual agency, including how to identify sexual pleasure in the body, how to decide whether to act on it alone or with another person, and how to develop healthy, sexual relationships. This education also ignores information about non-heterosexual desires and behaviors with some research reporting that adolescent gay girls know they are attracted to girls but cannot visualize what they would do in a sexual relationship. They also fear retribution from letting others know about their same-sex desire (Tolman 2002).

Research on heterosexual adolescent sex consistently finds that girls' earliest sexual experiences are fraught with anxiety, pressure, coercion, and lack of pleasure. Girls and young women continue to contend with a sexual double standard in which they navigate a blurred line between sexually interested and promiscuous, resulting in rumors, gossip, and stigma. Findings conflict in scholarship on college hookup culture with some studies reporting that hookups are more detrimental to women than men while others find that hookups allow women to have casual and fun sex without competing demands on their time and schoolwork. Other scholars argue that gender inequity is the core problem, not the context of college sex, and that dismantling the sexual double standard would result in better sex for women in both relationships and hookups (Armstrong, Hamilton, and England 2010). Emerging research on queer women and college hookups finds that public kissing between women and threesomes may start as sexual behavior for heterosexual male pleasure but may turn into a chance for women to explore same-sex attraction and desire (Rupp et al. 2014). Some women report that college threesomes provide a socially accepted environment to experiment with same-sex sexual behavior, and an opportunity to approach women for future sex without men.

Some cultural beliefs about sex in the United States stem from methodological issues and controversies in sex survey research. For example, sex research in the twentieth century largely supported the dominant cultural assumption that problems in heterosexual couples' sex lives are primarily due to women's inadequate sex drives (Ericksen 1999). Quantitative research on sex, midlife, and aging similarly located the cause of couples' declining sex lives in women's menopausal bodies by narrowly focusing on rates of vaginal dryness, decreased libido, and sexual pleasure. In contrast, qualitative research with diverse menopausal heterosexual and lesbian women found that relationship quality and open communication about sex were more important social factors for couples' sex lives than the physiological change associated with menopause (Winterich 2003).

On the whole, scholars' assumptions about gender and sex influence their research designs, which questions they ask and do not ask, which may contribute to popular beliefs that frequency of sex defines a fulfilling sex life, and that men are more sexually active with more sexual partners compared to women. Research on heterosexual, gay, and lesbian couples found that men reported engaging in more frequent sex than women, and overall, lesbians reported the lowest rates of genital-based sex. Consequently the term "lesbian bed death" was coined in the 1990s, which became the source of jokes and debate in the gay, academic, and therapeutic communities. Subsequent research contends that underscoring frequent, genital-based sex overlooks the diversity of lesbians' intimate and erotic sex lives, and perpetuates the stereotype of lesbian sex as deviant.

Similarly, research that finds heterosexual men are more sexually active than heterosexual women may be the result of methodological limitations. Rarely do surveys include questions about consensual sex, so men may be reporting partners with whom sex was not consensual while women exclude such partners (Ericksen 1999). Indeed, a qualitative study informed by feminist methods with a diverse sample of women and men by sexual identity found that a greater percentage of women than men stated that virginity loss could not occur through rape (Carpenter 2005). Overall, emphasizing the number of partners bolsters the cultural view that sexual frequency and quantity are more important than consent, intimacy, and mutual sexual pleasure.

Recent theory and empirical work emphasizes the fluidity and complexity of gender, sexual identity, and sexual relationships. Queer theorists and activists argue that binary categories of gender and sexuality are social creations performed in daily interactions, and as such, can be challenged and destabilized. They resist gender and sexuality labels and they distinguish between biology and gender assignment based on biology. In addition, they challenge cultural expectations between gender expression and sexual desire, and emphasize the importance of recognizing the fluidity of gender presentation and sexual desire in daily life. For example, while critical legal scholars support the United Nation's protection of human rights based on gender identity and sexual orientation, some argue that those categories presume a pre-social and static identity and therefore risk overlooking discriminatory experiences for those with shifting and multiple gender presentations and sexual desires (Klesse 2014).

Scholarship on gender and sexual identity finds that many gay communities debate the meanings of identity and the complexity of experiences of sexism and homophobia. For example, queer identities can result in divisions within some lesbian communities concerning the meaning of the identity "woman." Some disagree whether those who transition from male-to-female can deeply understand the sexism biologically born females encounter in interactions and within institutions throughout their lives. Furthermore, people of color whose communities are hostile to gay identities and who face racism in some LGBTQ communities contend with multiple systems of oppression and thus debate the privileges and exclusions that different identities afford for different groups (Lorde 1999).

Some scholars argue that polyamory or consensual relationships with more than one person in any diverse combination of gender presentations and sexual desires has the potential to disrupt gender and sexuality binaries because this approach focuses on open and consensual relationships, not the preferred gender presentation or sexual desire of any one individual. Research conflicts on how individuals identify with some stating that polyamory describes their current status in relationships while others view it as a key aspect of their identities. Some research finds that polyamory can provide sexual freedom and the potential for gender equality. Other scholarship reports that those who engage in polyamorous practices tend to be privileged, white, and highly educated; consequently, such relationships do not address intersecting systems of oppression by gender, race, and able-bodiedness.

SEE ALSO: Gender Identities and Socialization; Heterosexism and Homophobia; Sex Difference Research and Cognitive Abilities; Sexualities

REFERENCES

Armstrong, Elizabeth A., Laura Hamilton, and Paula England. 2010. "Is Hooking Up Bad for Young Women?" *Contexts*, 9(3): 22–27.

Brumberg, Joan Jacobs. 1998. *The Body Project: An Intimate History of American Girls*. New York: Vintage Books.

Carpenter, Laura. 2005. *Virginity Loss: An Intimate Portrait of First Sexual Experiences*. New York: New York University Press.

Ericksen, Julia A., with Sally A. Steffen. 1999. *Kiss And Tell: Surveying Sex in the Twentieth Century*. Cambridge, MA: Harvard University Press.

Klesse, Christian. 2014. "Polyamory: Intimate Practice, Identity or Sexual Orientation?" *Sexualities*, 17 (1/2): 81–99. DOI: 10.1177/1363460713511096.

Lorde, Audre. 1999. "There is no Hierarchy of Oppressions." In *Dangerous Liasons: Blacks, Gays, and the Struggle for Equality*, edited by Eric Brandt. New York: New York Press.

Meem, Deborah T., Michelle A. Gibson, and Jonathan F. Alexander. 2010. *Finding Out: An Introduction to LGBT Studies*. Los Angeles: Sage.

Pascoe, C. J. 2007. *Dude, You're a Fag: Masculinity and Sexuality in High School*. Berkeley: University of California Press.

Rupp, Leila, Verta Taylor, Shiri Regev-Messalem, Alison Fogarty, and Paula England. 2014.

"Queer Women in the Hookup Scene: Beyond the Closet?" *Gender & Society*, 28(2): 212–235. DOI: 10.1177/0891243213510782.

Tolman, Deborah. 2002. *Dilemmas of Desire: Teenage Girls Talk about Desire.* Cambridge, MA: Harvard University Press.

Winterich, Julie. 2003. "Sex, Menopause, and Culture: Sexual Orientation and the Meaning of Menopause for Women's Sex Lives." *Gender & Society*, 17(4): 627–642. DOI: 10.1177/0891243203253962.

FURTHER READING

Bogle, Kathleen A. 2008. *Hooking Up: Sex, Dating, and Relationships on Campus.* New York: New York University Press.

Schwartz, Pepper, and Virginia Rutter. 2011. *The Gender of Sexuality*, 2nd ed. Walnut Creek, CA: Altamira Press.

Seidman, Steven, Nancy Fischer, and Chet Meeks. 2011. *Introducing the New Sexuality Studies*, 2nd ed. New York: Rowman & Littlefield.

Sex Difference Research and Cognitive Abilities

DAVID I. MILLER
Northwestern University, USA

Decades of research have investigated when and why females and males perform differently on cognitive tasks. This research has captured the attention of many people and has raised politically and emotionally charged questions. Overall, studies have not found evidence for a smarter sex. However, sex differences in some specific cognitive tasks are found, such as mental rotation (male advantage) or writing (female advantage). Importantly, these sex differences describe groups, *not individuals* (e.g., many women excel in mental rotation tasks, many men excel in writing tasks). Males and females also perform similarly on many other tasks, suggesting that focusing on differences may ignore the many ways in which the sexes are similar. Cognitive sex differences are sometimes substantial but often small in magnitude; both biological and environmental factors are necessary to explain these findings. Most research on cognitive sex differences has focused on three types of cognitive abilities: mathematical, spatial, and verbal. These abilities are multifaceted (e.g., some but not all spatial abilities show sex differences) and interrelated (e.g., some mathematical abilities require both spatial and verbal abilities).

EMPIRICAL EVIDENCE

Compared to males, females generally earn equal or higher grades in mathematics classes. In addition, average sex differences in mathematics test performance tend to be small. However, male advantages in mathematics test performance are sometimes found depending on factors such as age. For instance, small but notable male advantages in mathematics performance emerge in high school and college but are generally not found in earlier grades. Sex differences are also larger in highly selective samples, consistent with males being overrepresented in the higher-achieving "right tail" of the mathematics performance distribution (e.g., top 5 percent of test takers). These right-tail differences have been found in grades as early as kindergarten but vary substantially by children's ethnicity and socioeconomic status (Ceci, Williams, and Barnett 2009). These sex differences also vary substantially across nations. In a few nations, female advantages in average mathematics test performance are found and sex differences in the right tail of performance (e.g., top 5 percent) are not found (Halpern 2012). Male advantages among very highly performing students (higher than top 1 percent) are found globally but vary substantially in size across nations. In the United States, both average and right-tail differences have decreased during the 1970s to 1990s but have since remained constant; temporal changes in other nations are unclear. In sum, sex differences in average mathematics test performance tend to be small, although males outnumber females among high scorers in most nations.

Sex differences in spatial abilities strongly depend on the task considered. Males outperform females substantially in some spatial tasks such as mentally rotating 3-D objects but not consistently in other tasks such as mentally folding paper (Miller and Halpern 2014). Some spatial tasks such as remembering object locations moderately favor women. Many research studies have focused on mental rotation, perhaps because of the large sex differences found. One research synthesis found that sex differences in mental rotation emerged as early as middle school and increased during adolescence. Subsequent research with small to moderate sample sizes has found similar sex differences in second grade, preschool, and even infancy, although contradictory results are sometimes found. In one massive self-selected Internet sample, sex differences in mental rotation and spatial perception varied substantially across nations but favored males in all 53 nations analyzed. In sum, some spatial tasks such as mental rotation demonstrate remarkably robust and large male advantages. However, many other spatial tasks show no sex difference or, in one case, female advantage.

Research conducted before the 1990s suggested negligible sex differences in most verbal abilities. However, recent large international assessments of reading achievement reveal a different trend. In one recent analysis of the reading achievement of 1.5 million children, girls outperformed boys in all 75 nations in all four testing administrations (Miller and Halpern 2014). Sex differences in reading were moderately large in the majority of cases and three times as large as those in mathematics. Sex differences among low-performing students were also two times as large as among high-performing students; such findings are consistent with males being overrepresented in the "left tail" of the reading performance distribution and overrepresented among students with reading disabilities. These left-tail differences have been found in grades as early as kindergarten. Female advantages are even larger in writing achievement compared to reading achievement. Sex differences in reading and writing have not changed much in the United States during the 1970s to 1990s. However, according to some recent international research, female advantages in reading may have increased worldwide during the past decade. In sum, female advantages in reading and writing are moderate, global, and not decreasing.

BIOLOGICAL THEORIES

Some theoretical approaches have focused on biological factors such as hormones and brains to explain these complex patterns of cognitive sex differences. Although the term *biological* is often conflated with *innate* and *immutable*, these ideas are conceptually distinct. Environmental factors such as poor nutrition can cause biological differences (differentiating *biological* and *innate*) and biological traits such as hair color can be easily altered (differentiating *biological* and *immutable*). Hence, evidence for biological factors does not contradict the considerable evidence that cognitive sex differences are malleable and that all cognitive abilities can improve if nurtured and supported (Ceci, Williams, and Barnett 2009).

Early biological theories hypothesized that genes occurring on sex-linked chromosomes explain cognitive sex differences. Although sex-linked genes may partly explain the higher rates of mental retardation among males, genetic theories have failed to explain most other cognitive sex differences (Halpern 2012).

Some evidence exists that prenatal androgen exposure (e.g., exposure to testosterone in utero) may partly explain sex differences in mental rotation performance. Results have been inconsistent in studies using crude measures of prenatal androgens (e.g., the ratio of the index finger to ring finger) but have been more consistent in other studies. For instance, females with abnormally high prenatal androgen exposure (either because of having a genetic condition or a male fraternal twin) tend to have moderately superior mental rotation ability compared to control females (Miller and Halpern 2014). Hence, higher prenatal androgen exposure likely increases women's mental rotation performance, but the mechanisms of *how* remain unclear. Effects of prenatal androgens on any other cognitive abilities (spatial or non-spatial) also remain unclear.

Sex hormones encountered in adulthood may affect some cognitive abilities, but this evidence is mixed. For instance, in one well-controlled but small experimental study ($n = 26$), a single dose of testosterone improved women's mental rotation performance ($d \sim 0.4$). In some other small studies, circulating levels of testosterone predicted mental rotation performance both within and across adults. However, many other experimental and correlational studies (some with larger sample sizes) have failed to replicate these effects, sometimes even finding contradictory results (Ceci, Williams, and Barnett 2009). These inconsistencies have led some biologically oriented researchers, who believe in the cognitive effects of prenatal androgens, to conclude that the cognitive effects of postnatal hormones are either small or nonexistent.

Influential theories, with mixed empirical support, explain cognitive sex differences on the basis of brain lateralization (that is, the extent to which an individual's left or right brain hemisphere is more dominant for particular cognitive functions). According to these theories, prenatal androgens "organize" brain development resulting in men being more dominant in the right hemisphere and women being equally dominant in both. Based on other cognitive neuroscience research, right hemispheric dominance is thought to support spatial abilities and bilaterality is thought to support verbal abilities. Some evidence exists for these claims. For instance, during some spatial tasks, sex differences in brain lateralization have been found as early as 5 years of age. However, other evidence is inconsistent. For instance, during language tasks, sex differences in lateralization have not been found according to research syntheses (Miller and Halpern 2014).

Sex differences in the brain certainly exist (e.g., men have 10 percent larger brains). The bundle of fibers, called the corpus callosum, that connect the two hemispheres may be more bulbous in females, perhaps suggesting greater inter-hemispheric connectivity in females. However, many neuroscience researchers intensely debate this claim regarding the corpus callosum. Other researchers also point out that structural brain differences do not necessarily imply functional advantages (e.g., better verbal abilities) because women and men may use the same brain regions differently. Furthermore, such brain differences could reflect the accumulation of environmental experiences rather than the organizational effects of prenatal sex hormones. Differences in brain activation can even reflect the situational effects of making gender stereotypes salient (Halpern 2012). In sum, brain research has promise in helping to explain cognitive sex differences. However, the causal relationships between hormones, brains, and behavior are currently ambiguous.

Evolutionary theories propose that cognitive sex differences evolved in response to the demands of hunter-gatherer societies. For instance, men are thought to have better spatial ability because they had to track and hunt animals over long distances. Other scholars disagree, pointing out that women likely had to also navigate long distances to find edible crops that ripened in different locations throughout the year (Halpern 2012). These evolutionary theories are generally difficult to test empirically but offer interesting perspectives to consider.

ENVIRONMENTAL THEORIES

Environments contribute to cognitive sex differences, as evidenced by the substantial variability of cognitive sex differences across nations and across time. Researchers have proposed that specific environmental factors such as gender equity, sex-typed activities, and stereotypes explain this variability. Understanding these environmental causes offers promise to maximize the cognitive potential of both men and women.

Some sociocultural theories propose that national gender equity partly causes cognitive sex differences. Consistent with predictions, male advantages in mathematics are smaller and sometimes even reversed in nations with greater gender equity in education and in the workforce (e.g., percent women among students enrolled in school or among employed workers). However, these relationships are far less clear for sex differences in spatial and verbal abilities (Miller and Halpern 2014).

Other theories, for varied reasons, predict that economic prosperity should increase some cognitive sex differences. Consistent with predictions, sex differences in mathematical and spatial abilities tend to be larger in families with higher socioeconomic status and nations with more economic prosperity. These relationships are less clear for sex differences in verbal abilities.

Sex differences may increase with economic prosperity because the prevalence of sex-typed activities may also increase. For instance, some male-typical spatial activities (e.g., playing action video games) have been experimentally shown to increase spatial abilities. Males' more frequent engagement in these activities may therefore partly explain sex differences in some spatial abilities. Evidence for the effects of sex-typed activities on other cognitive abilities is less clear.

Much research has investigated whether the negative consequences of gender stereotypes may partly explain cognitive sex differences. For instance, women often perform worse if reminded of their gender before taking a mathematics test; this phenomenon is known as *stereotype threat*. Dozens of studies have replicated this basic effect. Other researchers have debated this evidence, arguing that these threat effects are small or not robust, according to a recent research synthesis. Stereotype threat researchers responded by arguing that the selection criteria of that research synthesis was biased and that a subsequent synthesis found threat effects that were both robust and meaningful (Miller and Halpern 2014). Research also suggests that gender stereotypes may partly explain male advantages in some spatial tasks (according to more than a dozen studies) and female advantages in some verbal tasks (according to a small handful of studies). Scholars continue to debate whether these stereotype threat effects exist in "real-world" settings such as when taking high-stakes standardized tests (e.g., the SAT).

Individuals tend to persist on tasks in which they expect and value success. Sex differences in these task expectancies and values might partly explain cognitive sex differences (Halpern 2012). For instance, females from across the world expect less academic success in mathematics than males, even when no sex differences in test performance are found. This lower confidence could cause women to avoid mathematics activities or underperform as the mathematics material becomes more challenging in high school and beyond. Extensive longitudinal evidence supports these claims, but these theories are generally difficult to test experimentally. Sex differences in other psychosocial constructs may also be important (e.g., women report higher math anxiety).

Some socialization theories propose that teachers and parents contribute to cognitive sex differences by influencing children's values and expectancies for success. For instance, teachers and parents may give boys more encouragement to pursue mathematics than girls because of biased perceptions of boys' abilities. Much evidence exists for some of these claims, but other evidence is inconsistent (Ceci, Williams, and Barnett 2009). For instance, in a recent nationally representative study, US elementary and middle school teachers rated girls' math achievement higher than boys' even when empirical data showed the opposite trend. Of course, teachers and parents may influence cognitive sex differences in many other ways than through differential treatment and biased perceptions. For instance, consistent with recent longitudinal and quasi-experimental evidence, female teachers' math anxiety could influence girls' math achievement by shaping girls' beliefs about which gender is good at math.

BIOLOGICAL AND ENVIRONMENTAL INTERACTIONS

Biopsychosocial theoretical frameworks describe biological and environmental factors as inseparable because they exert reciprocal effects on each other. Effects of biology can be mediated or moderated by environments and vice versa (Halpern 2012). For instance, higher prenatal androgen exposure could cause females to engage in male-typical activities (e.g., playing action video games) that are likely to enhance spatial cognition. In this way, effects of biology would be mediated by females' choices of activities and moderated by the availability of such activities. Recent research provides some direct evidence for this mediational pathway. Furthermore, environments cause biological changes. Effects of gender stereotypes on mental rotation performance are likely explained, in part, by changes in brain activation and perhaps circulating levels of testosterone. Hence, both prenatal androgens and gender stereotypes likely influence sex differences in mental rotation, and both factors interact with biology and environment. In other words, biology influences environments and environments influence biology in a continuous causal loop. Understanding how both biological and environmental factors interact is likely to identify strategies that can maximize both sexes' cognitive potential.

SEE ALSO: Educational Testing and Gender; Gender Difference Research; Psychology of Gender: History and Development of the Field

REFERENCES

Ceci, Stephen J., Wendy M. Williams, and Susan M. Barnett. 2009. "Women's Underrepresentation in Science: Sociocultural and Biological Considerations." *Psychological Bulletin*, 135: 218–261.

Halpern, Diane F. 2012. *Sex Differences in Cognitive Abilities*, 4th ed. New York: Psychology Press.

Miller, David I., and Diane F. Halpern. 2014. "The New Science of Cognitive Sex Differences." *Trends in Cognitive Sciences*, 18: 37–45.

Sex Discrimination

MADELINE HEILMAN and FRANCESCA MANZI
New York University, USA

Sex discrimination refers to any behavior or action that results in the unfavorable treatment of men or women because of their sex. Practices that constitute sex discrimination include, but are not limited to: restricted access to education, sexual harassment, unequal distribution of rights and duties, barriers to employment opportunities, and unequal payment. Because these practices tend to negatively affect one sex more than the other, and result in unfair conditions, they constitute sex discrimination.

Sex discrimination has been a particular problem for women, especially in employment settings. Although according to a recent United Nations report women comprise nearly 50 percent of the workforce in most developed nations, they remain dramatically underrepresented in jobs and roles that have been traditionally dominated by men. This is especially problematic given that these positions tend to hold the highest prestige and status, as well as monetary and social rewards. Women's full participation in the workplace is hindered by gender bias in evaluation, which in turn leads to discriminatory recruitment, selection, and promotion practices. It has been argued that gender stereotypes underlie the occurrence of gender bias and sex discrimination.

Gender stereotypes are generalizations about the characteristics of men and women. Research has demonstrated that while stereotypic conceptions of men tend to be predominantly agentic (e.g., dominant, forceful, independent), women are generally thought to be communal (e.g., caring, collaborative, understanding). Importantly, the content of gender stereotypes tends to be oppositional: women are seen as communal, but not agentic, while men are seen as agentic, but not communal. These beliefs are held by both men and women, and by those of different ages, education levels, geographic areas, and ethnic backgrounds.

Gender stereotypes are not inherently negative in their consequences; there are many instances in which the stereotyped attributes of men and women lead to positive evaluation. It is only in contexts in which stereotyped conceptions are inconsistent with what is desirable that they create problems. This is particularly relevant in work settings, in which many domains are gender-typed, or described in predominantly masculine or feminine terms. An occupation, job, or role can be characterized as being male-typed either because it has been historically dominated by men or because of culturally shared beliefs about its requirements for success. Male-typed occupational sectors (e.g., the military), professional fields within occupations (e.g., neurosurgery), organizational positions (e.g., chief executive officer), or academic fields (e.g., physics) are thought to require the attributes associated with men, not with women. Because of gender stereotypes, women tend to be perceived as deficient in the agentic attributes believed necessary for successful performance in male-typed jobs. This perceived incongruity or "lack of fit" between what women are thought to be like and what is thought to be necessary to succeed in male-typed positions is central to sex discrimination: it creates expectations of incompetence that have a profound effect on employment decisions.

Negative expectations about women's competence in male-typed fields are often activated without evaluators' awareness, making them particularly difficult to eliminate. They also have a tendency to perpetuate themselves by producing distortions in the way people process information, affecting what information is attended to, how it is interpreted, and whether it is remembered or forgotten. Because of these cognitive distortions, potentially disconfirming information can be ignored or dismissed, and incompetence expectations are reinforced and maintained in spite of information to the contrary. In fact, stereotype-based expectations about women's incompetence in male-typed fields and occupations have been shown to detrimentally affect women in recruiting, screening of application materials, selection decisions, compensation offers, and career advancement opportunities. They also have been shown to prevail unless there is disconfirming information that is overwhelming and unequivocal.

Certain aspects of evaluation processes can facilitate gender bias and therefore make sex discrimination more likely. In particular, aspects of the process that that heighten ambiguity provide opportunities for stereotype-based competence expectations to dominate in decision making. Ambiguity promotes reliance on inferences in making judgments, and inferences are strongly influenced by expectations. Some situations in which ambiguity is heightened are when the information about a candidate is incomplete, inconsistent, or irrelevant, when evaluation criteria are lacking or standards are not fixed, and when the source of responsibility for past performance is unclear.

Because men have not historically been targets of sex discrimination in work settings, less attention has been paid to male discrimination. However, there also can be perceptions that a job or role is female-typed. This can be a result of the overrepresentation of women in the field, or due to beliefs about what is required to do the job well. Female-typed occupations (e.g., kindergarten teacher), professional fields within occupations (e.g., pediatrics), organizational positions (e.g., human resources specialist), and academic fields (e.g., nutrition) all are thought to require communal attributes associated with women. However, the consequences of these beliefs for men seeking to advance in female-typed jobs are less conclusive than what has been found for women. It is possible that regardless of the gender-type of the field, work success is always seen as somewhat agentic and therefore never completely gender-inconsistent for men, rendering them less susceptible to sex discrimination than women.

Identifying the sources of gender bias can help evaluators and employers to prevent discrimination on the basis of sex. It is possible to curb the expectations of incompetence that give rise to sex discrimination by minimizing the activation of gender stereotypes or feminizing the conception of traditionally male jobs and roles. It also is possible to keep these expectations at bay by managing the evaluation process. For example, the effects of expectations have been shown to be mitigated when consistent and clear information about candidates is made available, when evaluation criteria are standardized, and when the source of performance is unambiguous. In addition, the reliance on stereotype-based expectations can be lessened if evaluators are held accountable for their decisions.

SEE ALSO: Gender Bias; Gender Stereotypes; Gender Wage Gap; Women in Non-Traditional Work Fields

FURTHER READING

Davison, Heather, and Michael Burke. 2000. "Sex Discrimination in Simulated Employment Contexts: A Meta-Analytic Investigation." *Journal of Vocational Behavior,* 56(2): 225–248. DOI: 10.1006/jvbe.1999.1711.

Eagly, Alice, and Linda Carli. 2007. *Through the Labyrinth.* Cambridge, MA: Harvard Business School.

Heilman, Madeline. 2012. "Gender Stereotypes and Workplace Bias." *Research in Organizational Behavior,* 32: 113–135. DOI: 10.1016/j.riob.2012.11.003.

Schein, Virginia. 2001. "A Global Look at Psychological Barriers to Women's Progress in Management." *Journal of Social Issues,* 57: 675–688. DOI: 10.1111/0022-4537.00235.

Sex Education in the United Kingdom and United States

LYNDA MEASOR
University of Brighton, UK

Sex education is a label with a wide range of uses and is defined in a number of different ways. Different disciplines and bodies of knowledge compete for space within it. Sex education has traditionally been framed in the context of physiological and biological knowledge and has focused on physical development, growth, and physiological change. It commands a strong knowledge based in the powerful and high-status scientific disciplines. In recent years sex education has become used as a shorthand term for the much broader subject of personal relationships, sexual health, and education about sexuality (Reiss 1990). The social science disciplines of sociology, psychology, and health promotion have become involved in this sexuality and relationships education. Reiss makes it clear that what is defined as sex education has changed significantly over time.

Sex education is offered to young people in a range of places and spaces and by a wide range of agencies. It is of course provided in some, although not all, family contexts (Farrell 1978; Allen 1987; Frankham 1993; Mueller, Gavin, and Kulkarni 2008). It has also been supplied by formal organizations: schools have been involved since 1943 in England.

An important issue that has influenced decisions on the provision of sex education is the sexual behavior of young people. We know that a high proportion (65 percent) of young people in Britain (defined as those under 19) are sexually active (Health Education Authority 1995). We also know that more and more young people are becoming sexually active at a younger age, often before the age of 16 (Wellings et al. 1994, 2001). Premarital sex has become the norm for young people in Western democratic countries (Wight 1990; Breakwell and Fife-Shaw 1992). What is controversial is the response that sex education should make to these patterns.

The provision of sex education by the state in schools has from its beginnings been controversial (Mort 1987; Moore and Rosenthal 1993; Irvine 2004). Questions about the age at which sex education should begin are common (Farrell 1978). Arguments consider whether sex education should deal only with the biological facts of sex and reproduction or whether it should include "sexuality in its broader sense" (Jackson 1982, 22). Feminist theorists have also drawn attention to the "silence on the subject of female desire and a missing discourse of female sexuality" (Fine 1988) within sex education.

Controversy centers on the impact that knowledge about sexuality and relationships has on attitudes to sexuality and, most significantly, on sexual behavior (Scott and Thomson 1992). The "restrictive" approach demands sex education should protect the innocence of children, the sanctity of marriage, and privilege heterosexuality (Santelli et al. 2005; Luker 2007; Kohler et al. 2008). The "liberal" model argues young people are empowered and kept safer through access to enhanced knowledge (Thorogood 2000, 425). Sexuality education, particularly in the United States, has become one battleground in the "culture wars," a phrase used since the 1960s to designate conflicting political and ideological values held by traditional–conservative and progressive–liberal groups (Irvine 2004; Kendall 2008).

One key question is whether offering sex education promotes or delays young people's sexual activity. Restrictive views argue their approaches delay its onset. Kirby's (2007) international studies make it quite clear, however, that effective sex education offering considerable information delays sexual interaction and renders it "safer." There are many countries in the world where no sex education is provided by a formal authority like school or college. In others a limited amount of information, mostly related to the processes of reproduction, is given. In some countries fuller programs that seek to work with issues of sexuality education have been developed (Häggström-Nordin 2002). Kirby's work (2007; Kirby et al. 1994) indicates that it is these programs that have most impact on early and unwanted pregnancy and sexually transmitted disease (STD) rates.

Many academic studies support the liberal views that we must respond to the fact that we live in a sexualized culture and produce sex education programs tailored to the realities of what adolescents are doing. Yvonne Roberts, for example, argued that we must provide information for young people to offer them maps through "the carnal jungle that passes for daily life" (*Guardian*, December 2, 1998). The international research evidence is absolutely clear. Providing full information about sexuality as well as reproduction delays the onset of sexual relationships and has positive effects on reducing the rate of teenage pregnancy and STDs (Kirby 2007).

One way of seeking to find a way through the controversies that rage amongst adults about how much sex education to provide and at what age to begin it is to ask children and young people what they feel about sex education they are given. Trudell comments that sex education "engages adults with distinct cultural, political and economic agendas in heated and acrimonious debates in which student voices are largely unheard" (Trudell 1993, 2).

Information on the users' views might enable us to move beyond the claims and counterclaims that are put forward in this debate (Measor, Tiffin, and Miller 2000). It is important to recognize that users' responses vary in different national contexts.

In the United Kingdom and the United States where the provision of full and open sex education is controversial, young people when asked are negative about the sex education they receive. They consider they are given "too little information too late in their lives" (Farrell 1978). They express bitter resentment toward sex education teachers who seem too embarrassed and insufficiently skilled to teach the material adequately. They also express strong opposition to government policies that seek to limit the topics and the material to which they can be exposed. Young people in school argue that they would appreciate the provision of explicit, relevant information given by skilled, confident medical people. Schemes that have worked with this model evaluate well in research (Mellanby et al. 1995). Young people also wish their parents would offer them more high-quality, less embarrassed sex education and are angry with parents who fail to do so (Frankham 1993). The primary source of information for many young people is their friends and many are acutely aware of the limitations of the accuracy of the information they access in this way.

In the United States in recent years sex education programs that have promoted abstinence-only approaches in young people have predominated in some states. In countries where a fuller sex education curriculum is provided, and crucially where education about sexuality rather than just sex and reproduction is offered, then young people when asked are much more positive about it (Oakley et al 1995).

We need also to recognize the increasing importance of the accessibility of pornography on the Internet. Many young people – especially young males – gain a considerable amount of their information about sex and sexuality from pornography, welcoming its explicit content, which shows them "exactly what to do" (Measor, Tiffin, and Miller 2000). There are inevitably serious concerns about the messages relating to the nature of sexuality and the place of love and affection within sexual relationships that young men gain from the pornography industry (Allen 2006). The development of access to Internet pornography raises the question once again and ever more urgently of the need for the provision of accurate, reliable, and comprehensive information in sex education schemes. It also raises the issue of the need to include within sex education programs space for discussion of the emotional aspects of the experience of sexuality as well as directions for what "happens."

SEE ALSO: Curriculum Transformation

REFERENCES

Allen, Isobel. 1987. *Education, Sex and Personal Relationships*. London: Policy Studies Institute.

Allen, Louisa. 2006. "Looking at the Real Thing: Young Men, Pornography and Sex Education." *Discourse Studies in the Cultural Politics of Education*, 27(1): 69–83.

Breakwell, G. M., and Chris Fife-Shaw. 1992. "Sexual Activities and Preferences in a UK Sample of 16–20 Year Olds." *Archives of Sexual Behaviour*, 21: 61–65.

Farrell, Christine. 1978. *My Mother Said … The Way Young People Learned about Sex and Birth Control*. London: Routledge and Kegan Paul.

Fine, Michelle. 1988. "Sexuality, Schooling and Adolescent Females: The Missing Discourse of Desire." *Harvard Educational Review*, 58(1): 29–51.

Frankham, Jo. 1993. *Parents and Teenagers: Understanding and Improving Communication about HIV and AIDS*. Horsham, UK: AVERT.

Häggström-Nordin, S. 2002. "Sex Behaviour amongst Adolescent Youth in Sweden." *Journal of Adolescent Health*, 30(4): 288–234.

Health Education Authority. 1995. *Sexual Health Interventions for Young People: A Methodological Review*. London: HEA.

Irvine, Janice M. 2004. *Talk about Sex: The Battles over Sex Education in the United States*. Berkeley: University of California Press.

Jackson, Stevi. 1982. *Childhood Sexuality*. Oxford: Blackwell.

Kendall, Nancy. 2008. "Sexuality Education in an Abstinence-Only Era: A Comparative Case Study of Two US States." *Sexuality Research and Social Policy*, 5(2): 23–44.

Kirby, D. B. 2007. "Sex and HIV Education Programs: Their Impact on Sexual Behaviours of Young People Throughout the World." *Journal of Adolescent Health*, 40: 206–217.

Kirby, D. B., et al. 1994. "School-Based Programs to Reduce Sexual Risk Behaviours: A Review of Effectiveness." *Public Health Reports*, 109: 339–360.

Kohler, Pamela K., et al. 2008. "Abstinence Only and Comprehensive Sex Education." *Journal of Adolescent Health*, 42(4): 344–351.

Luker, Kristin. 2007. *When Sex Goes to School: Warring Views on Sex and Sex Education*. New York: Norton.

Measor, L., C. Tiffin, and K. Miller. 2000. *Young People's Views on Sex Education*. London: Routledge.

Mellanby, Alex R., F. A. Phelps, N. J. Crichton, and J. H. Tripp. 1995. "School Sex Education: An Experimental Programme with Educational and Medical Benefit." *British Medical Journal*, 311(7002): 414–417.

Moore, Susan M., and Doreen A. Rosenthal. 1993. *Sexuality in Adolescence*. London: Routledge & Kegan Paul.

Mort, Frank. 1987. *Dangerous Sexualities: Medico-Moral Politics in England since 1830*. London: Routledge and Kegan Paul.

Mueller, Trisha E., Lorrie E. Gavin, and Aniket Kulkarni. 2008. "The Association Between Sex Education and Youth's Engagement in Sexual Intercourse." *Journal of Adolescent Health*, 1(42): 89–96.

Oakley, A., et al. 1995. "Sexual Health Interventions for Young People: A Methodological Review." *British Medical Journal*, 310(6973): 158.

Reiss, Michael Z. 1990. "What are the Aims of School Sex Education?" *Cambridge Journal of Education*, 23(2): 125–136.

Santelli, John, et al. 2005. "Abstinence and Abstinence-Only Education: A Review of US

Policies and Programs." *Journal of Adolescent Health*, 38: 72–81.
Scott, L., and R. Thomson. 1992. "School Sex Education: More a Patchwork than Pattern." *Health Education Journal*, 51(3): 132–135.
Thorogood, Nicki. 2000. "Sex Education as Disciplinary Technique: Policy and Practice in England and Wales." *Sexualities*, 3(4): 425–438.
Trudell, B. N. 1993. *Doing Sex Education*. London: Routledge.
Wellings, K., et al. 1994. *Sexual Behaviour in Britain: The National Survey of Sexual Attitudes and Lifestyle*. Harmondsworth, UK: Penguin.
Wellings, K., et al. 2001. "Sexual Behaviour in Britain: Early Heterosexual Experience." *The Lancet*, 358: 1843–1850.
Wight, Daniel. 1990. "The Impact of HIV/AIDS on Young People's Heterosexual Behaviour in Britain: A Literature Review." London: MRC Medical Sociology Unit.

Sex Reassignment Surgery

VARUNEE FAII SANGGANJANAVANICH
The University of Akron, USA

Sex reassignment surgery is a recognized medical intervention as an appropriate treatment for gender dysphoria, both male-to-female (MtF) and female-to-male (FtM) transsexuals. Sex reassignment surgery has also been referred to as sex change, gender reassignment surgery, and gender confirmation surgery. Sex reassignment surgery has been used not only to refer to actual surgical procedures altering one's primary (e.g., genital, reproductive organ) and secondary (e.g., breast, facial hair, voice) sex characteristics to match one's gender identity, but also to the overall gender transition process encompassing psychological, social, and legal aspects of one's life.

Harry Benjamin, a leading scholar of the Society for the Scientific Study of Sex, was credited as the "Father of Transsexualism" (Schaefer and Wheeler 1995, 73). Benjamin was different from medical professionals during his time. Instead of viewing cross-dressing behaviors and desires to become the opposite gender as forbidden and unlawful, Benjamin sought to better understand the condition where individuals feel trapped in their own bodies or have a sense of gender incongruence (i.e., one's gender identity does not match one's assigned sex at birth). Benjamin later defined transsexualism and its characteristics in his original work, *The Transsexual Phenomenon* (1966), and pioneered an affirmative treatment for individuals with gender dysphoria where he attended not only to the needs of individuals to alter their existing physical sex characteristics to match their gender identity, but also to many aspects of the gender transformation (e.g., hormone therapy, voice therapy, psychotherapy) (Schaefer and Wheeler 1995). Benjamin's marked contribution has influenced today's conceptualization of gender dysphoria treatment and has promoted a deeper understanding and greater acceptance of sex reassignment surgery.

In the context of sex reassignment surgery as actual surgical procedures, sex reassignment surgery includes reversible and irreversible interventions. Reversible interventions refer to temporary changes that facilitate one's gender transition (e.g., hormone suppressing) and do not cause a long-term effect or change in one's sex characteristics, whereas irreversible interventions refer to changes that are final (e.g., hysterectomy, phalloplasty, breast augmentation, vaginoplasty). Because sex reassignment surgery is a medical treatment for transsexual adults who experience gender dysphoria according to the *Diagnostic and Statistical Manual of Mental Disorders* (American Psychiatric Association 2013) or gender identity disorder according to the *International Statistical Classification of*

Diseases and Related Health Problems (World Health Organization 2010), individuals are required to meet the aforementioned diagnostic criteria in order to be eligible for the surgery. Particularly, in adolescents, sex reassignment surgery contains specific stages of physical interventions. Physical interventions can be categorized into three levels: fully reversible, partially reversible, and irreversible interventions. Fully reversible interventions refer to the utilization of gonadotropin-releasing hormone (GnRH) to suppress one's hormone production in order to delay puberty, whereas partially reversible interventions refer to hormone therapy to induce hormonal changes in one's body. Irreversible interventions are surgical procedures to alter one's assigned to desirable gender (Hembree et al. 2009). Although there are criteria for eligibility for each level of the interventions, treatment selection is individualized (World Professional Association for Transgender Health 2012).

When sex reassignment surgery is used to refer to the overall gender transition process, this term describes changes in psychological, social, and legal, in addition to hormonal and surgical, aspects of one's life (previously called Real Life Experience; RLE). Gender transition is a period where a person begins living full time as and adopts the gender role of a desired gender (i.e., *coming out* process). For instance, during gender transition, a biological male – living full time as a woman – is required to fully embrace the gender role of a woman and clearly express her gender identity in public. Although not required by the current *Standards of Care for the Health of Transsexual, Transgender, and Gender Nonconforming People* (WPATH 2012) – a document that outlines best practices concerning transgender care including specific requirements for sex reassignment surgery – living full time in a gender role that is congruent with one's gender identity is arguably necessary and has several benefits. Those benefits are to assist individuals in fully examining the consequences and implications of becoming a desired gender, developing clear and realistic expectations of further adopting this gender role, and making informed decisions regarding gender change (e.g., psychological impacts, social supports, employment opportunities, discriminations).

It is important, however, to note that an individual is required to complete 12 continuous months of living full time as a desired gender (including 12 continuous months of hormone therapy) prior to seeking genital surgery. This requirement is based on the idea that "the social aspects of changing one's gender role are usually challenging – often more so than the physical aspects" (WPATH 2012, 60–61). Living full time as a desired gender provides a unique opportunity for individuals to understand the consequences and implications of changing one's gender before pursuing irreversible surgery.

While many transsexual individuals seek sex reassignment surgery as a medical treatment to alleviate their gender discomfort or distress, some find that embracing the gender role, identity, and expression of a desired gender is sufficient and satisfying. Thus, after exploring all options and careful considerations, the decision to undergo sex reassignment surgery including treatment options and timing belongs to the individual.

SEE ALSO: Gender Dysphoria; Transsexuality

REFERENCES

American Psychiatric Association (APA). 2013. *Diagnostic and Statistical Manual of Mental Disorders*, 5th ed. (DSM-5). Washington, DC: American Psychiatric Association.

Benjamin, Harry. 1966. *The Transsexual Phenomenon*. New York: Julian Press.

Hembree, W. C., et al. 2009. "Endocrine Treatment of Transsexual Persons: An Endocrine Society Clinical Practice Guideline." *Journal of*

Clinical Endocrinology and Metabolism, 94(9): 3132–3154.

Schaefer, Leah C., and Connie C. Wheeler. 1995. "Harry Benjamin's First Ten Cases (1938–1953): A Clinical Historical Note." *Archives of Sexual Behavior*, 24: 73–93.

World Health Organization (WHO). 2010. *International Statistical Classification of Diseases and Related Health Problems*, 10th ed., text rev. (ICD-10). Geneva: World Health Organization.

World Professional Association for Transgender Health (WPATH). 2012. *Standards of Care for the Health of Transsexual, Transgender, and Gender Nonconforming People – Version 7*. Accessed July 27, 2015, at http://www.wpath.org/site_page.cfm?pk_association_webpage_menu=1351.

FURTHER READING

Bockting, Walter O., and Eli Coleman. 2007. "Developmental Stages of the Transgender Coming Out Process: Toward an Integrated Identity." In *Principles of Transgender Medicine and Surgery*, edited by Randi Ettner, Stan Monstrey, and A. Evan Eyler, 185–208. New York: Haworth Press.

De Cuypere, Griet, and Herman Vercruysse, Jr. 2009. "Eligibility and Readiness Criteria for Sex Reassignment Surgery: Recommendations for Revision of the WPATH Standards of Care." *International Journal of Transgenderism*, 11: 194–205. DOI: 10.1080/15532730903383781.

Dhejne, Cecilia, et al. 2011. "Longterm Follow-Up of Transsexual Persons Undergoing Sex Reassignment Surgery: Cohort Study in Sweden." *PloS ONE*, 6: 1–8. DOI: 10.1371/journal.pone.0016885.

Sex Segregation and Education in the United States

SUSAN W. WOOLLEY and THOMAS WILEY
Colgate University, USA

Sex segregation in education takes various forms across time periods, institutions, and practices. Institutional segregation has meant the formation of single-sex schools in addition to the structured separation of boys and girls within coeducational schools. Although the term "segregation" typically points to more formal, historically-embedded practices of legal and de facto separation between peoples, in this case it may also refer to the informal ways in which people are divided and socialized into binary gender roles and identities. This entry centers on both institutional and informal educational practices in the United States across public primary and secondary schools, religious schools, private preparatory and boarding schools, universities, and colleges.

PUBLIC SCHOOLS

American education during the colonial period focused primarily on schooling boys until the development of the dame school, the main function of which was to prepare boys for admission to town schools that were closed to girls. Dame schools often took root in the homes of older women in the community, offered instruction to both boys and girls in basic literacy, and helped to establish women as teachers in colonial America. Female students attended the informal dame schools and some continued in town schools, which, once they started admitting girls, arranged programming so that boys and girls attended at different times. Beyond the dame school and sex-segregated town schools, education for girls was single-sex and private, accessible only to the wealthy and only up through secondary education. During the American Revolution, schools gradually became more coeducational, but it was not until the rise of common schools in the 1830s that coeducation became the norm in the United States. Throughout the nineteenth century, one-room rural common schools were coeducational, whereas in cities throughout the Northeast and the South, single-sex public schools were more widespread. After the Civil War, the development of high schools rapidly accelerated, many of which were coeducational.

Prior to the arrival of colonial settlers, Native American tribes had long traditions of educating boys and girls in the skills and knowledge sets needed for their roles in gendered division of labor. Although not necessarily true of all groups, many indigenous peoples have educated boys and girls separately and differently in order to prepare them to be productive members of their communities. Such differential education was rooted in cultural practices relegated to domestic or public spheres, such as domestic arts like cooking, sewing, and housekeeping, tribal arts like weaving and pottery, and skills like hunting, fishing, and subsistence agriculture. The gendered division of labor and education in Native American tribes are not comparable to the gendered division of vocational education thrust upon Native children stolen from their families and placed in American Indian boarding schools in the late nineteenth and early twentieth centuries. In the American Indian boarding schools, differential education for boys and girls was aimed at producing manual laborers to fit into capitalist society as cooks, maids, seamstresses, blacksmiths, and farmers, for example.

During the first part of the twentieth century, reforms sought to differentiate education for boys and girls. With the rise of the comprehensive urban high school in the 1920s came progressive education reforms and the development of vocational education, which aimed to prepare students for gendered division of labor in life, work, and home. In public high schools, it became common to have sex-segregated vocational and physical education classes, different dress codes, and separate co-curricular activities with more emphasis placed on men's than women's sports. With the 1972 passage of Title IX – the federal law that prohibits discrimination on the basis of sex in schools that receive federal funding – access to higher education and also equal opportunity in athletics have been made more available to girls. For the most part, sex segregation in public schools had been limited to physical education, sex education, and athletics until the Bush administration changed Title IX regulations to expand single-sex public schools and sex segregation options within coeducational public schools in 2006.

RELIGIOUS SCHOOLS

Before the establishment of a public school system, much of the nation's early education reflected the Protestant demographics of the colonies. Protestant schools – especially Quaker schools – were generally coeducational. The Quaker belief that women could be called to serve in ministry has meant that girls and women have long been educated in Quaker communities. In Quaker schools, boys and girls have been educated together at both the elementary and secondary levels, yet Quaker higher education institutions were single-sex from the beginning, with the creation of several normal schools to prepare educated women to be teachers.

The first Catholic educational institutions to emerge in the New World were seminaries, which by 1640 were training an all-male priesthood for the missionary church. As the colonial period progressed, a more formalized college–seminary developed, which further split into three all-male institutions: seminaries exclusively for training priests, liberal arts colleges, and secondary schools. With most resources of the early American church supporting the education of men, charitable orders of European religious sisters created the first Catholic academies for girls, starting with a school founded by the Ursuline Sisters in New Orleans in 1727. The first parochial primary schools, which educated girls and boys together, also emerged during the colonial period. The American bishops' first Council of Baltimore in 1829 formally recommended the establishment of such schools supported by parish revenues. Meanwhile, Catholic secondary schools continued in a tradition of being single-sex. Boys' secondary schools focused at first on classical training and theology, whereas girls' schools had an emphasis on moral education as preparation for marriage and motherhood. Both schools, however, became more broadly academic over time. Pope Pius XI, in his 1929 encyclical *Christian Education of Youth*, denounced "the so-called method of 'coeducation'" as "false and harmful to Christian education," particularly during "the most delicate and decisive period" of adolescence. The reforms of the Second Vatican Council in the 1960s struck a new balance on gender roles, urging the full development of women's potential in the professions, while continuing to stress their role as mothers. The reforms of the council, along with financial concerns, led to an increasing number of coeducational Catholic schools, such that the majority of US Catholic schools today are coeducational.

Jewish religious schools were few and short-lived in the colonies, but they served both boys and girls – offering boys preparation for bar mitzvah while girls learned reading and needlework, embroidery, and music, but no formal instruction in Jewish studies. Private tutoring and also learning Hebrew reading and prayers in the family and synagogue provided the basis for some, but not all, girls' Jewish religious education throughout the nineteenth century. Following the Protestant Sunday school model, in 1838 Rebecca Gratz founded the Hebrew Sunday School Society of Philadelphia to teach basic Judaism to girls and boys. The Hebrew Sunday schools provided Jewish religious education to girls to counter the Protestant influence of their secular public education and gave American Jewish women opportunities to enter the teaching profession. Starting in the mid-nineteenth century, private Jewish day schools which were sex-segregated as boys-only or girls-only institutions and in other cases enrolled boys and girls in coeducational classes through the primary grades and then in sex-segregated upper-grade grammar classes, were first founded in New York City. In Orthodox communities, the separation of the sexes is stricter, maintaining separate classes and schools for boys or girls and fundamental differences in their studies.

Historically, the education of women in Muslim cultures has been of the utmost importance, producing female scholars and teachers competitive and respected with their male peers. Sex segregation in Muslim schools, however, has taken a number of forms, including the implementation of a gendered dress code, marking the difference between boys and girls through their school uniforms, in similar ways as the dress codes of preparatory, finishing, and some religious schools operate. Sex segregation in Muslim schools has also reflected the separation between men and women in mosques, with men placed at the front of the room for prayer or class and women at the back behind the men. Sex segregation in Muslim schools takes mundane forms in terms of how gendered bodies are to be dressed or positioned in the physical space of the classroom.

PRIVATE AND INDEPENDENT SCHOOLS

Private and boarding schools have long been the standard bearers for the sex-segregated school. The first private college preparatory schools in the United States tended to be founded on the model of the British public school, which in that country were specifically an exclusive, older, tuition-paying, and historically all-male private school. British public schools were first founded to educate the future gentlemen of Britain's aristocratic class and later to train a military and administrative elite for the Empire. A crucial component of the education process was isolating male students from their family and community, particularly its female members. Young men were then socialized by means of an all-male collective identity and a norming pedagogy oriented around the exercise of power and privilege. When all-male prep schools were founded in the United States, often to serve the emerging American business elite, their charters iterated their goal of preparing young men for positions of leadership similar to those of their British aristocratic counterparts. Military and reform schools also utilized gendered environments to shape students. These schools did not have the same expectations of privilege as the prep schools, so their application of masculine toughness and conformity is often at least perceived as "corrective" and in its own way prepares young men for their future place in society, whether in combat or the workforce. On the other hand, women's independent schools often radically broke down gender categories. The Troy Female Seminary, founded by Emma Willard in 1821, offered a liberal arts curriculum to young women and employed an all-female faculty.

HIGHER EDUCATION

The first colleges and universities founded in the United States were all-male and offered training in disciplines such as theology and rhetoric, which were seen as outside women's accepted sphere. Some of the first continuing education venues offered exclusively to women were in vocational or professional training in careers such as nursing or teaching. Small religious coeducational colleges, such as Oberlin College, which was founded in 1833, offered the first liberal arts educations for women, although classes were often separate and differentiated by gender. The first women's colleges, starting with Vassar College in 1861, were founded to improve the place of women in society and offer new opportunities to women similar to those of men. As the century moved forward, expansion in university education unexpectedly promoted opportunities for women. Schools such as Cornell College were obligated by law to educate women against the wishes of its administration because it was established in part on federal lands provided by the Morrill Land Grant Act of 1862. Changes such as these led to the rapid growth of women in universities and also the development of normal schools for teacher training primarily for women. Historically black institutions, on the other hand, have been coeducational since their inception, even hiring black women faculty. Originally, these institutions required specific courses of study for men and women, which combined industrial skills tailored to each gender with some liberal arts work. Industrial education, such as that promoted by the Tuskegee Institute, shaped vocational education for African American men and women towards careers in skilled and manual labor, yet their schools were also forced to compete with teacher training programs for federal resources. Following World War I, women at historically black institutions increasingly engaged in broader academic study and the academic profile of these schools also expanded.

The number of women attending college grew so rapidly towards the end of the nineteenth century and into the early twentieth century that a greater proportion of women compared with men attended university in

1920 than in 1970. The period saw cases of jealous patriarchal backlash against women, which included the University of Chicago's punitive sex segregation of classrooms starting in 1902 to marginalize female students, who that year won a majority of the school's academic honors. In the 1960s and 1970s, the tide turned back towards the inclusion of women as formerly all-male institutions increasingly accepted women. Women's colleges also declined steeply in number with the total number of schools falling from 268 in 1960 to fewer than 50 today.

INFORMAL SEX SEGREGATION

Although institutional sex segregation in schools has waned, there are still daily practices that segregate students into the category of boy and girl. In schools, boys and girls are frequently asked to line up in separate lines or to divide into separate groups. Pairing opposite-sex students together in "adopt an egg" or "adopt a bag of sugar" activities as a proxy for taking care of a baby in home-economics classes or in sex-education lessons may appear to integrate the two sexes, but instead highlight the heteronormative relations and assumptions of binary gender imposed on youth – bringing into stark relief anyone who does not fit the categories of heteronormative male or heteronormative female. The selection of prom king and queen could be said to do the same – segregating and surveying people into discrete opposite sexes before coupling them together. The built environment of schools reproduces the division of students into binary gender categories as locker rooms and bathrooms are designated as exclusively for either boys or girls. Transgender, genderqueer, and intersex students' struggles to incorporate gender-neutral bathrooms on school campuses highlight the everyday symbolic and sometimes physical violence done to those who do not fit rigid definitions of binary gender. In addition to such structures and practices that divide students by gender, students' segregation reflects the hidden curriculum of social relations. Perhaps lingering elements of formal and institutional sex-segregation structure choices reinforce children's decisions to play and socialize in groups predominantly divided, in some cases exclusively so, by sex. Peer groups and activities vary in their degrees of sex segregation, but research has demonstrated that the informal space of children's play and the playground tends to reflect patterns of sex segregation with ramifications for gender socialization and relations between the sexes across the lifespan.

SEE ALSO: Gender Equity in Education in the United States; Gender Identities and Socialization; Single-Sex Education and Coeducation

FURTHER READING

Bryk, Anthony S., Valerie Lee, and Peter B. Holland. 1993. *Catholic Schools and the Common Good*. Cambridge, MA: Harvard University Press.

Cookson, Peter W., and Caroline Hodges Persell. 1985. *Preparing for Power: America's Elite Boarding Schools*. New York: Basic Books.

Hansot, Elisabeth, and David Tyack. 1988. "Gender in American Public Schools: Thinking Institutionally." *Signs*, 13(4): 741–760.

LePore, Paul C., and John Robert Warren. 1997. "A Comparison of Single-Sex and Coeducational Catholic Secondary Schooling: Evidence from the National Educational Longitudinal Study of 1988." *American Educational Research Journal*, 34(3): 485–511.

Riordan, Cornelius. 1990. *Girls and Boys in School: Together or Separate?* New York: Teachers College Press.

Solomon, Barbara M. 1985. *In the Company of Educated Women: a History of Women and Higher Education in America*. New Haven: Yale University Press.

Thorne, Barrie. 1993. *Gender Play: Girls and Boys in School*. New Brunswick: Rutgers University Press.

Sex Selection

TEREZA HENDL
University of Sydney, Australia
BARBARA KATZ ROTHMAN
City University of New York, USA

Sex selection involves the determination of a future child's sex. It has most often been used to select against female offspring in many different countries around the world. Sex selection can be practiced at three stages: preconception (sperm selection prior to fertilization), prenatal (this involves preimplantation method of sex selection which combines prenatal genetic diagnosis (PGD) with in vitro fertilization (IVF) or post-implantation method of selective abortion), and postnatal (infanticide or neglect) (Sen 2003; De Wert and Dondorp 2010). Sex selection can be used to prevent the birth of a child with sex-linked hereditary diseases, or can be based solely on parental preference for a future child of a particular gender (this type of selection is often called gender selection).

The practice of sex selection for gender preference has had a severely negative social impact. Without technical intervention, the standard sex ratio at birth is 104–106 males born per 100 females (UNFPA 2012). However, in several societies around the world, sex ratios are significantly skewed in favor of males. In 1985, Mary Ann Warren reflected on the practice of infanticide against female offspring and came up with the concept of "gendercide," which signifies "the deliberate extermination of persons of a particular sex (or gender)" (Warren 1985, 22). She used a gender-neutral term to consider all victims of infanticide, yet acknowledged that the vast majority of the victims are female children. For this reason, the selective killing of newborn girls is often referred to as "gynocide" and "femicide" (Jones 2000).

In 1992, Amartya Sen estimated that there were 100 million women missing in Asia and North Africa, women who should have been born or grown up, but are missing because they were selectively aborted or killed by infanticide or neglect. Sen (1992, 2003) claims that these missing women are the result of a preference for male offspring in strongly patriarchal societies. Within such societies, various practices and beliefs lead to son preference; for example, it may be believed that only a son is capable of providing income for the family, while some traditions might nominate men only to perform a variety of socially and religiously important acts. Furthermore, daughters often require dowry and leave their parental home when married, and thus are seen as a resource for their husband's family and a burden for their own.

Currently, it is estimated that the number of missing women is around 126–134 million worldwide (UNDP 2010; Bongaarts and Guilmoto 2015), with approximately 117 million of these missing in Asia, particularly China and India (UNFPA 2012). Furthermore, recent data show that skewed sex ratios are also prevalent in regions such as Albania, Azerbaijan, Georgia, and Armenia (CoE 2011; UNFPA 2012).

The problem of skewed sex ratios leads to various forms of social crises. These include: discrimination against women; violations of women's bodily autonomy, reproductive and sexual rights; sexual violence; and forced marriages (Den Boer and Hudson 2004; UNDP 2010; UNFPA 2012). Some argue that women can benefit from being the rarer sex because they will be more valued (Sureau 1999). Others point out that such an argument fails to acknowledge that not allowing women to exist or grow up due to preference for male offspring is the most harmful act of discrimination against women (Hendl 2015). Furthermore, the lack of women in societies leads to reinforcement of women's oppression because existing women are perceived solely as prospective wives, sexual partners, and mothers (Rothman 1998; UNFPA 2012). Christian Mesquida and Neil Wiener (cited in Den Boer and Hudson 2004) also argue that large-scale gender selection against female offspring is a security threat, as the age composition of the male population is a crucial demographic factor influencing society's tendency to violent conflict. Den Boer and Hudson note that these imbalances can lead to a rise in sexual violence against women.

Owing to the severe social impact of sex selection based on strong gender preference, many affected countries, such as India, China, and South Korea, have introduced legislation banning prenatal gender selection, including bans on disclosure of chromosomal sex by medical staff (UNFPA 2012). Furthermore, preconception sex selection for social reasons is banned in many countries with standard sex ratios owing to its possible harmful impact (CoE 2011). At the same time, prenatal sex selection is legally available in countries such as the United States, and procreators engage in reproductive tourism for this purpose (Hendl 2015).

Liberal bioethicists such as John Robertson (1996) and Stephen Wilkinson (2010) argue that prenatal sex selection should be legally available, at least in Western countries, out of respect for reproductive choice. In their view, Western parents who want to undertake sex selection are doing so to have both sons and daughters, that is, for what they like to call "family balancing." They claim that family balancing avoids the harmful effects of sex selection motivated by a preference for male offspring, and will not lead to severely skewed ratios.

However, others argue that liberal arguments in favor of family balancing underestimate the negative impact of sexism, particularly gender stereotyping. Barbara Katz Rothman (1998) notes that undertaking embryonic selection based on a test for sex chromosomes means making stereotypical assumptions about the role of future children in the family and society. Parents do not select for sex but gender, and presume that girls and boys will give them different parental experiences (Rothman 2006). In this respect, gender selection is based on a biologically deterministic binary understanding of sex–gender roles and, as such, runs the risk of limiting future children's autonomy to develop diverse gender and sexual identities through the reinforcement of gender stereotyping (Rothman 2006; Hendl 2015).

So far there has been a lack of research into the impact of sex selection in societies without specific preference for male offspring. In particular, the claim that sex selection is ethically unproblematic in the West is based on an implicit assumption that there is a clear moral divide between the West and "the rest." Nevertheless, the worldwide penchant for essentialized understandings of gender calls for analysis that treats sex selection as a transnational issue.

SEE ALSO: Cisgender and Cissexual; Disability Rights Movement; Femicide; Gender Identity, Theories of; Genderqueer; Gender Stereotypes; Intersex Movement; Orientalism

REFERENCES

Bongaarts, John, and Christophe Z. Guilmoto. 2015. "How Many More Missing Women? Excess Female Mortality and Prenatal Sex Selection, 1970–2050." *Population and Development Review*, 41(2): 241–269.

CoE. 2011. Resolution 1829: Prenatal Sex Selection. Accessed February 10, 2015, at http://assembly.coe.int/Main.asp?link=/Documents/AdoptedText/ta11/ERES1829.htm.

De Wert, Guido, and Wybo Dondorp. 2010. "Preconception Sex Selection for On-Medical and Intermediate Reasons: Ethical Reflections." *Facts, Views and Vision in Obstetrics and Gynaecology*, 2(4): 80–90.

Den Boer, Andrea, and Valerie M. Hudson. 2004. "The Security Threat of Asia's Sex Ratios." *SAIS Review*, 24(2): 27–43.

Hendl, Tereza. 2015. *Ethical Aspects of Gender Selection for Non-medical Reasons*. PhD dissertation, Macquarie University.

Jones, Adam, ed. 2000. *Gendercide and Genocide*. Nashville: Vanderbilt University Press, pp. 1–38.

Robertson, John. 1996. *Children of Choice*. Princeton: Princeton University Press.

Rothman, Barbara Katz. 1998. *Genetic Maps and Human Imaginations: The Limits of Science in Understanding Who We Are*. New York: Norton.

Rothman, Barbara Katz. 2006. Choosing Your Child's Sex? John A. Robertson and Barbara Katz Rothman Debate. Accessed January 29, 2015, at http://www.legalaffairs.org/webexclusive/debateclub_sex-selection0306.msp.

Sen, Amartya. 1992. "Missing Women. Social Inequality Outweighs Women's Survival Advantage in Asia and North Africa." *BMJ*, 304(6827): 587–588.

Sen, Amartya. 2003. "Missing Women – Revisited." *BMJ*, 327(7427): 1297–1298.

Sureau, Claude. 1999. "Gender Selection: A Crime against Humanity or the Exercise of a Fundamental Right?" *Human Reproduction*, 14(4): 867–868.

UNDP. 2010. Human Development Report 2010: 20th Anniversary Edition. Accessed May 13, 2015, at http://hdr.undp.org/sites/default/files/reports/270/hdr_2010_en_complete_reprint.pdf.

UNFPA. 2012. Sex Imbalances at Birth. Accessed January 15, 2015, at http://www.unfpa.org/publications/sex-imbalances-birth.

Warren, Mary Anne. 1985. *Gendercide. The Implications of Gender Selection*. Totowa: Rowman & Allanheld.

Wilkinson, Stephen. 2010. *Choosing Tomorrow's Children*. Oxford: Oxford University Press.

Sex Tourism

MICHELLE TOLSON
Siem Reap Citizens for Health, Educational and Social Issues (SiRCHESI), Cambodia

Sex tourism at its most basic definition is travel for the purpose of engaging in sexual relations. Tourism researchers Stephen Clift and Simon Carter, in their edited volume *Tourism and Sex: Culture, Commerce and Coercion* (2000), note that pleasure and the possibility of sex are part of the overall marketing of tourism, whether the travel takes place in the Global North or South, and that it can be hard to separate "sex in tourism" from sex tourism. Scholars also contend that the setting of tourist locations and their marketing tend to intentionally promote hedonistic attitudes and titillation among tourists, and that the branding of locations as "exotic," desirable tourist destinations is inexorably linked to the racialized construction of local peoples as erotically "exotic" and sexually available. The study of sex tourism (with a focus on commercial sex) took on increased importance in the 1990s as a means of addressing sexual health and HIV prevention after the emergence of the disease in the 1970s and 1980s.

Destinations with an erotic tourism image, such as Las Vegas, Amsterdam, the Caribbean, Brazil, parts of the continent of Africa, and Southeast Asia, are places with thriving entertainment and hospitality industries in which sex tourism is embedded. Mark B. Padilla, Vincent Guilamo-Ramos, and Ramona Godbole (2012) call attention to the parallel growth of the multinational alcohol industry in nightclubs, bars, hotels, and resorts supporting tourism in developing countries that provide a jumping-off point for sex tourism, commercial or non-commercial. Most of the literature on sex tourism frames the issue within the context of commercial sex, with purchasers primarily being white, middle-aged, or older heterosexual males from the Global North traveling to the South to purchase sex, but research has also explored female heterosexual sex tourism, gay sex tourism, and the perspectives of local workers and migrant workers, including children working in sex tourism. While it is also common for heterosexual youth from Europe and North America on university holidays to abuse alcohol or recreational drugs and seek out casual sex, this remains a less discussed aspect of sex tourism by scholars.

Tourism in itself is described by researchers as a *liminal* state (stepping outside one's normal routine). The tourism environment sets the tone for travelers to access this liminal state of mind and encourages their taking greater risks while on holiday. This can include purchasing paid sex when an individual otherwise would not do so at home. Thomas G. Bauer and Bob McKercher, in their edited volume *Sex and Tourism: Journeys of Romance, Love, and Lust* (2003), describe tourism's role in enabling sex tourism as that of a facilitator of the provision of partners, encounters, and venue and a provider of setting and context.

Defining sex tourism in a commercial sex context in developing countries can be difficult and is open for debate in light of its placement within the informal economy. For instance, Nancy Wonders and Raymond Michalowski (2001), in their comparison of Amsterdam in the Netherlands and Havana, Cuba as two famous sex tourism destinations geared toward male tourists, found Amsterdam's legal sex tourism industry had clear lines of consumerism with straight cash transactions and government regulations, supplied by a diverse array of migrant sex workers from the Global South. The authors point out that tourism, as the largest industry in the world, holds a significant place in a global economy where developing countries face high rates of unemployment. They contend that emotional labor, a term coined by Arlie Russel Hochschild (1983) to describe how the status of the consumer is raised by service industry employees, is taken to a further extent in the sex industry. In this vein, they view women informally working Havana's sex tourism scene as using emotional labor in the form of a "soft sell," where prices are not named but gifts and money are expected for performing the role of "pseudo-girlfriend" for an evening, day, or several days.

Transactional sex has also been found to take place alongside formal tourism work positions such as bar tenders, tour guides, taxi drivers, and entertainment workers in the host city or country in the Global South who might engage in sexual relationships with tourists. While such relationships can have an economic aspect, they are not necessarily strict sex for cash. Rather, they may be based on providing companionship to the tourists during their stay for gifts (which can include cash), food, travel, and possible romance. Given that the Global North and South have a wide divide in income – with the Global South having fewer formal employment opportunities or low-paid formal work – researchers find local workers' relations with foreign tourists can provide a means for climbing out of poverty.

Researchers further note that women and men in the Global South who seek out foreign sex partners do not necessarily define themselves as commercial sex workers, but rather frame such relationships as a chance to improve their economic opportunities while working in touristic settings that oblige them to be emotionally warm, as required by transnational tourism industries. This group is characterized as mobile, having traveled from poorer rural areas, and even from neighboring countries, to urban areas with a tourism industry in search of opportunities.

Amalia Cabezas (2011) in particular discusses the exploitative nature of Western multinational tourism companies in the Caribbean that impose emotional labor on employees. While the practice is also seen in the hospitality sector in the Global North, Cabezas points to the monopoly these tourism corporations hold in the industry, setting the locals in the host country at a disadvantage for opportunities to earn a living wage. However, while Cabezas notes foreign corporations dictate that local staff interact with foreign guests in an emotionally warm and intimate manner, she observes they are able to leverage their affect in this oppressive structure into genuine opportunities to connect with wealthier foreigners, gain entry into international travel opportunities, and find greater financial benefits through their contacts, which can include sexual relationships. Her research found reciprocal arrangements played a large part in the apparent transactions. Cabezas contends that, within sex tourism literature, greater attention could be placed on the abusive labor practices of transnational tourism corporations rather than on foreigners' relationships with locals being inherently exploitative.

Research conducted by Padilla and colleagues (2012) in the Caribbean similarly pointed out that the parallel growth of multinational alcohol corporations in tourism locales played a large role in both tourism and the sex industry, impacting the local population with higher rates of HIV and sexual health risks due to decreased condom use from inebriation. Their work observed that both formal and informal tourism employees saw drinking as a requirement of their job to earn tourism venues more money through alcohol sales and increased customers. Transactional sex took place on the side of tourism work, with most research participants not identifying as sex workers (Padilla, Guilamo-Ramos, and Godbole 2012).

Male and female sex tourists do not tend to frame their relationships with locals as transactional, despite possible gifts or money transferred, because of their affective nature in contrast with straight cash for sex seen in prostitution in their home countries. Kempadoo (2001), in her studies in the Caribbean and Latin America, sees an overlap between sex tourism and "romance tourism" in both male and female sex tourists as they describe caring relationships with locals, with aspects of companionship, romance, and pleasure while still being transactional. However, she found local women selling sex often describe the relationships in business terms, finding economic empowerment in the arrangement, while local men selling sex did not describe their relationships with foreign women in economic terms, despite being paid, but rather found empowerment in leveraging their gender against the postcolonial framework. Their relationships with white women were seen to bring them status, which Kempadoo noted was supported by cultural norms that see Caribbean men as sexualized beings, a situation not afforded to local women, who are instead stigmatized as "whores." There is an additional "gray area" described for longer-term transactional relationships between mistresses or "girlfriends" and married foreign men, where the relationships are described as caring yet still transactional. This group is less likely to use condoms during sex.

However, Padilla (2007) argues that male sex workers in the Dominican Republic serving male tourists, many with local wives and girlfriends, are not benefiting from the region's gendered cultural norms but are marginalized. He suggests greater research is needed to include the perspectives of these men.

Researchers note studies on the sexual behaviors of gay and bisexual male tourists traveling internationally and domestically are also lacking in the literature compared to research on heterosexual tourists and are even more scant for lesbian tourists. Most studies on gay tourists focus on market research and tourism branding.

National histories and historical relations between nations have a profound impact on contemporary tourism practices. Thailand, for instance, was a rest and recreation (R&R) destination for military personnel during the Vietnam War in the 1960s and 1970s. When the conflict ended, military entertainment venues found a new market in the emerging modern international tourism sector made possible by advances in global travel (Clift and Carter 2000). Similarly, entertainment facilities that served the United Nations Transitional Authority in Cambodia (UNTAC) workers during the country's transition from conflict to open borders in 1991–1993 eventually became a thriving entertainment scene for both male locals and foreign tourists. This transition has, like the Caribbean, drawn the investment of a multinational alcohol industry that capitalizes on the companionship of local women to sell beer, while sex work occurs on the side. However, ethnographic researcher Heidi Hoefinger (2011) argues that Cambodian entertainment workers who sit with foreign customers and are known as "bar girls" use their agency within the "hedonistic" bar culture by crafting themselves as "professional girlfriends" to improve their economic situation. Within the liminal state of the bar, Hoefinger further contends, Cambodian entertainers craft a space to resist strict sexual and social norms while enjoying the consumption of alcohol.

Qualitative research undertaken by Heather Montgomery (2014) into the perspectives of children working in child sex tourism in Thailand shows that, like adult sex workers, this group faces limited economic opportunities and sees relationships with foreign clients as a preferable way to earn money compared to selling trinkets, small items, or other types of informal street-based work. Montgomery differentiates adolescent under-age sex workers (noting that the age of consent varies in each country) from pre-pubescent children working in the trade. For pre-pubescent children, she found familial duty tends to shape these children's placement in the industry, enabling them to support their families. Similar to adult sex workers, children with regular clients often framed these relationships in terms of affection for supporting their impoverished families through financial gifts. Montgomery's work sheds a light on the entrenched nature of this industry, highlighting how families' migration from rural to urban areas puts their children in unsafe situations with immense filial burdens. While her work was conducted two decades prior, she points out that due to greater legal protections now in place, the industry has largely relocated to countries with fewer social protections, like Cambodia. However, her work remains relevant, underscoring the risks faced by marginalized children who are forced to work the streets as beggars or informal sellers due to poverty and displacement. In such situations, the higher economic returns of sex work alleviate grinding poverty, and Montgomery suggests that greater attention be paid to these factors. It is also pertinent to note that the demographics of child sex tourists encompass domestic tourists who travel within the country specifically to procure sex and Asian men from other countries, exceeding that of white men (Thomas and Mathews 2006).

There is an emerging field of research discussing the role heterosexual women traveling from developed countries play in sex tourism, though this is often described as "romance tourism." Female sex tourists are usually seen to be middle-aged women from North American and European countries; however, female sex tourists are also young.

Researchers note fuller-figured women, who might have less romantic or sexual success in their home countries, find their body type appreciated more in Latin America, which does not idealize slimness. Female sex tourists, like their male counterparts, also tend to have relationships with some kind of gift, meal, or cash exchange. Their male partners usually work within the tourism and hospitality sector on a formal or informal basis and are sometimes described in the literature as "hustlers" who help tourists with their trip plans in exchange for financial support. Despite the exchanges of goods and services central to these relationships, they are often self-described by female tourists as non-commercial and based on affection. Indeed, Nancy Romero-Daza and Andrea Freidus (2008) researched an emerging trend of young American and European female sex tourists in their early to mid-20s traveling to Costa Rica to enjoy "sexual adventure," such as casual and group sex, in a nightclub setting with local men in which neither party described transactional exchanges.

Modern tourism has been described by researchers as a phenomenon of post-industrial societies with a division of time between formal work and non-work activities, and a clear line between who is a tourist and who is not. Laura Agustin (2007) questions assumptions on tourism as coming from a largely white male scholarly perspective, framing tourism as "'other' to work." Just as Cabezas urges researchers to look to the inequality inherent in multinational tourism corporations and Padilla sheds light on the exploitative nature of a multinational alcohol industry, Agustin points to inequality within tourism research itself. As a female researcher, she contends women consider tourism differently than men. She points out multiple aspects of travel that incorporate work and leisure, where workers would not fall under the banner of "tourist" such as those working in development work, budget travel combined with work, and even tourism work itself. These groups, she argues, also access the tourism industry for pleasure but are largely excluded by social science researchers. Agustin notes that migrant workers involved in tourism, whether domestic or international, are equally capable of seeking out pleasure and that, rather than their being cast as victims, their perspectives on liminal experiences deserve greater attention from researchers.

SEE ALSO: Sex Trafficking; Sex Work and Sex Workers' Unionization

REFERENCES

Agustin, Laura M. 2007. *Sex at the Margins: Migration, Labour Markets and the Rescue Industry*. London: Zed Books.

Bauer, Thomas G., and Bob McKercher, eds. 2003. *Sex and Tourism: Journeys of Romance, Love, and Lust*. New York: Haworth Hospitality Press.

Cabezas, Amalia. 2011. "Intimate Encounters: Affective Economies in Cuba and the Dominican Republic." *European Review of Latin American and Caribbean Studies*, 91: 3–14.

Clift, Stephen, and Simon Carter, eds. 2000. *Tourism and Sex: Culture, Commerce and Coercion*. Leicester: Pinter.

Hochschild, Arlie R. 1983. *The Managed Heart: Commercialization of Human Feeling*. Berkeley: University of California Press.

Hoefinger, Heidi. 2011. "Professional Girlfriends." *Cultural Studies*, 25(2): 244–266.

Kempadoo, K. 2001. "Freelancers, Temporary Wives and Beach Boys: Researching Sex Work in the Caribbean." *Feminist Review*, 67: 39–62.

Montgomery, Heather. 2014. "Child Prostitution as Filial Duty? The Morality of Child-Rearing in a Slum Community in Thailand." *Journal of Moral Education*, 43(2): 169–182.

Padilla, Mark B. 2007. *Caribbean Pleasure Industry: Tourism, Sexuality and AIDS in the Dominican Republic*. Chicago: University of Chicago Press.

Padilla, Mark B., Vincent Guilamo-Ramos, and Ramona Godbole. 2012. "A Syndemic Analysis of Alcohol Use and Sexual Risk Behavior

Among Tourism Employees in Sosúa, Dominican Republic." *Qualitative Health Research*, 22(1): 89–102.

Romero-Daza, Nancy, and Andrea Freidus. 2008. "Female Tourists, Casual Sex, and HIV Risk in Costa Rica." *Qualitative Sociology*, 31: 169–187.

Thomas, F., and L. Mathews. 2006. *Who are the Child Sex Tourists in Cambodia?* Melbourne: Child Wise.

Wonders, Nancy, and Raymond Michalowski. 2001. "Bodies, Borders, and Sex Tourism in a Globalized World: A Tale of Two Cities – Amsterdam and Havana." *Social Problems*, 48: 545–571.

FURTHER READING

International Labour Organization (ILO). 2010. "Developments and Challenges in the Hospitality and Tourism Sector." Issues paper for discussion at the Global Dialogue Forum, Geneva.

Montgomery, Heather. 2008. "Buying Innocence: Child-Sex Tourists in Thailand." *Third World Quarterly*, 29(5): 903–917.

Sex Toys

LOLA D. HOUSTON
University of Vermont, USA

Sex toys are generally material objects used in conjunction with a sexual act. They may be used as part of a solitary sexual experience, such as an aid to masturbation, or they may be used by two or more individuals. While the manufacture and distribution of sex toys have expanded greatly in the past 40 years, objects for use as sex toys have been in existence for much longer. While the usual sex toy is a physical object made of plastic, glass, or other material, some individuals may engage another individual to be their designated "sex toy" for a similar purpose, albeit in a somewhat different manner (it is obviously not possible, for example, to "insert" another whole body into the orifice of a second individual). In this way, the individual designated as the "sex toy" provides sexual services to one or more other individuals.

Historically, sex toys may have existed since very ancient times. A recent archaeological finding of an object that strongly resembles a phallus, made of a particular type of stone, suggests that early humans may have shaped particular materials into objects designed for the purpose of sexual gratification. Since it is not possible to determine with precision the intended use of such objects, this remains speculation. Various forms of sex toys have been alluded to in ancient texts such as the *Kama Sutra*, as well as being depicted on material art such as vases or sculpture. In these cases, the intended use of the object seems quite clear, as the context of the text or art is unambiguously expressed in a sexual manner.

More recently, sex toys, specifically dildos, have been subject to considerable study in regards to female sexuality. As the fields of Western psychiatry and medicine developed in the nineteenth and twentieth centuries, the practitioners of these fields began to consider situations in which a patient exhibited symptoms that were then seen as a disease. Early clinical evaluations of what was then termed "women's hysteria" were subject to careful study. Here, early clinicians believed that what they were seeing was an illness, something that required careful and detailed clinical study as well as some option for resolution – a treatment. During this same period, female sexuality, and the idea that women could have, much less enjoy, sexual pleasure, was still viewed with considerable suspicion and concern. One approach employed in the effort to "cure" so-called female hysteria was the use of the vibrator, a device that was made possible as electricity came into wider use. Maines (1999) details the emerging practice of vibrator use, as well as other approaches to clinical "cures" for female hysteria. The use of a mechanical device rather than the hands was seen in part as a kind of time-saving approach, a means to better clinical efficiency. While female sexual response and orgasm had long been noted and studied, it was not until the mid-eighteenth and early nineteenth centuries that the idea of hysteria took root in the West. By contrast, female sexuality in non-Western countries, and the idea of "female hysteria," was looked at very differently as being part of a larger social and, often, religious context.

Interestingly, it was the advent of train travel that, according to Maines (1999), elicited the discussion about vibration in conjunction with female sexuality, with many doctors advocating in favor of such vibration, and others opposing it. Since the object of the clinical practice around hysteria was to find the most efficient means to resolve the problem, and massage by hand having largely fallen out of favor because it was "tedious" to perform, the idea of a practical vibrational device that could reach into the smaller regions of the body was of significant interest. As a result, devices powered by hand, foot, and other mechanical means quickly appeared. It was not long afterward that the electromechanical vibrator made its debut.

These early devices were not seen as imparting pleasure, but rather as a means to cure the sick. In Western countries, it was only much later, in the mid-twentieth century, that the idea of a device instilling pleasure for its user became a reality – such devices, as noted above, seem to have been in use in many parts of the world for much longer. By this time, however, the dominant attitude toward not just female orgasm but sexual pleasure as a whole, at least in the West, had been strongly conditioned by the earlier debates in medicine and psychiatry. As a result, the devices one might obtain in the 1920s and beyond were, until only quite recently, marketed and sold as objects that provided "health benefits" and not as objects that could enhance sexual pleasure. Frequently, such devices were sold as "personal massagers" and not as sexual aids. It is important to note that while many Western attitudes toward female orgasm and sexual pleasure evolved around medical and clinical dictums, other parts of the world where sex toys had been in use (India and Africa, for example) had very different attitudes toward the same topics, placing them squarely in the context of social and religious norms and as a domain of male sexuality.

Today, sex toys are manufactured, sold, and distributed around the world with explicit and unambiguous intent: to facilitate a positive sexual experience for the user. While the availability of such devices is widespread, it remains illegal to sell or distribute sex toys in the state of Alabama in the United States, and ironically it is illegal to sell sex toys anywhere in the country of India. The growth of online markets in sex toys, as well as the ability to purchase them online, would appear to render such laws moot from the perspective of the customer.

There are no specific manufacturing guidelines, safety requirements or regulations governing the manufacture of sex toys, making it possible for anyone to make and sell a device that might have adverse health or safety consequences. Widespread public awareness of this problem first became apparent when the United States Food and Drug Administration reported that phthalates were possible human carcinogens. Phthalates have been used extensively in the manufacture of sex toys, specifically the class of toys called "insertables" (dildos and vibrators). Because of the perceived monetary value of the sex toy market, many manufacturers stopped using phthalates in their products following this revelation. The concern around what a sex toy is made of continues, however, with one report about the exposure to radioactive substances found in some toys serving as a highly visible example. The products not only are unregulated, but are invariably labeled "sold as a novelty only." This allows the maker to circumvent any problems that might arise in their use. Many of the newer sex toys have been manufactured with the explicit intention of being a sex toy designed to give sexual satisfaction, and manufacturers such as Lelo and JimmyJane have been forthright about what is used in the manufacture of the object.

The array of sex toy types is formidable. Dildos and vibrators are among the most popular. Masturbation aids also top the list. Strap-ons, cock rings, prostate massagers, as well as a wide array of BDSM (bondage, discipline, sadism and masochism) devices are easily located and purchased from online merchants in many countries. Additional browsing and buying options exist in the form of home-based parties, as well as a large number of "brick and mortar" store outlets in many major cities in the United States, Canada, and Europe.

SEE ALSO: Body Politics; Female Orgasm; Sexual Instinct and Sexual Desire; Sexualities; Strap-On Sex

REFERENCE

Maines, Rachel. 1999. *The Technology of Orgasm: "Hysteria," the Vibrator, and Women's Sexual Satisfaction*. Baltimore: Johns Hopkins University Press.

FURTHER READING

Iguchi, Jamie. 2010. "Satisfying Lawrence: The Fifth Circuit Strikes Ban on Sex Toy Sales." Accessed October 30, 2013, at http://www.lawreview.law.ucdavis.edu/issues/43/2/comments/43-2_Iguchi.pdf.
Joannides, Paul. 2009. *Guide to Getting It On: For Adults of All Ages*. Waldport, OR: Goofy Foot Press.
Taormino, Tristan. 2009. *The Big Book of Sex Toys: From Vibrators and Dildos to Swings and Slings – Playful and Kinky Bedside Accessories That Make Your Sex Life Amazing*. Beverly, MA: Quiver.
Vatsyayana. 1994. *The Complete Kama Sutra: The First Unabridged Modern Translation of the Classic Indian Text by Vatsyayana*, trans. Alain Daniélou. Rochester, VT: Park Street Press.

Sex Trafficking

MARY CRAWFORD
University of Connecticut, USA

Sex trafficking is the buying and selling of human beings for the purpose of sexual exploitation. Sex trafficking is widely held to be an egregious violation of human rights and a form of gender-linked violence that has affected millions of people, primarily girls and women. The tactics traffickers employ to compel individuals into sex work often include coercion, such as threats, abduction, and physical or sexual violence. Sex trafficking can also involve deception, particularly the promise of a marriage, educational opportunity, or paid employment which never materializes. Sex trafficking also encompasses situations where traffickers facilitate seemingly willing involvement in sex work by ensuring that sex work is the best or only choice for immediate survival, such as in the case of working off debts through sex work. Sex trafficking may or may not involve the organized movement of individuals from one country to another for the purpose of sex work.

Sex trafficking has only recently gained widespread attention, largely because of increased international concern with human rights violations, as well as increased interest in the ways the commercial sex industry contributes to the spread of HIV. However, sex trafficking is not a new phenomenon. Trafficking victims engage in a wide variety of activities in the commercial sex industry, including prostitution, work in strip clubs, work in pornographic films, and involuntary erotic servitude. Today, women are trafficked into Israel, the United States, and Canada to be employed in strip clubs. They are transported from Columbia and Nigeria to Europe and Japan to work as prostitutes. Children are sold into sexual slavery in Thailand, Sri Lanka, and the Philippines, and Nepali girls are taken from their villages into the red-light districts of Indian cities, where they are forced into prostitution. Human trafficking is the third biggest criminal activity worldwide, exceeded only by drug and weapons trafficking.

The critical factor that distinguishes sex trafficking from voluntary prostitution or sex work is lack of consent. According to the United Nations protocol on trafficking, a person under the age of 18 cannot consent to engage in sex work under any circumstances. Even in the absence of overt coercion, prostituting anyone under 18 constitutes trafficking (UN 2000). Going further, some anti-trafficking organizations take the position that all prostitution is abusive and exploitative and should be outlawed as a form of trafficking. Others differentiate between "forced" and "voluntary" prostitution. Meanwhile, organizations of commercial sex workers, and some feminist scholars, reject the term prostitution and use the term sex work, maintaining that it reflects women's choices to work in the sex industry. Some of the latter groups argue that the problem of trafficking has been exaggerated. These stances reflect long-standing (and ongoing) debates among feminist scholars and activists about women's sexual autonomy. Despite theoretical and political differences, all these factions agree in condemning violence against women.

Individuals who are trafficked are typically vulnerable to the tactics of traffickers for a variety of social and economic reasons, including poverty and a lack of social connections and protections. Homeless individuals, displaced individuals and refugees, adolescents and young adults running away from home, gender and sexual minorities, widows, job seekers, and addicts represent some of the populations most vulnerable to trafficking. In many contexts, women's subordinate status – particularly their lack of autonomy and educational and economic opportunities – means that women as a class are consistently vulnerable to trafficking. However, other factors such as ethnicity, social class, and age affect women's vulnerability, and a girl or woman is most vulnerable to being trafficked when she is impoverished, young, and belongs to a disadvantaged caste or ethnic group. The risk is higher in countries that have civil conflict and those that have high rates of migration. Another factor that increases the risk of being trafficked is a lack of governmental policy to facilitate prevention and to prosecute traffickers. However, the main factor underlying vulnerability to sex trafficking is gender inequality. Trafficking is most prevalent in cultures where women are subject to high levels of gender-based violence, denied equal opportunity for education and employment, and viewed as lesser human beings than are men.

Girls and women in these contexts who are most ambitious, agentic, and eager to work for a better life are, unfortunately, often those most vulnerable to trafficking. They are at risk because they hope and strive to escape from poverty and gender subordination. When a woman is trafficked, she may be sold by an acquaintance, or even a family member. Alternatively, she may have willingly consented to a romantic relationship or a marriage, to the chance to migrate for a better life, or even to commercial sex work under a set of promised conditions she believed livable. However, when she is trafficked, she is held against her will in conditions of sexual servitude. The most likely destination for a trafficked girl or woman is a brothel. There, she is forced to prostitute herself under the control of the brothel owner, often held captive by threats of physical and sexual violence and/or debt bondage.

There is no definitive measure of the prevalence of sex trafficking. Often, it is difficult to distinguish trafficking from consensual commercial sex work, sex tourism, the mail-order bride industry, the pornography industry, and the broader problem of trafficking for labor exploitation. As a criminal activity, it is underground and almost certainly under-reported. However, the United Nations has estimated that between 700,000 and 2,000,000 girls and women are trafficked each year. The most common mode of trafficking is deceptive and fraudulent job offers. A woman who is desperate for a way to support herself and her family is promised employment, and trusts the broker or employment contractor, who is actually a broker for the sex trade. The woman accompanies the trafficker in trust, only to find that she has been sold.

Sex trafficking occurs nearly everywhere around the globe, but not all women are equally at risk; instead, there are patterns of prevalence (Farr 2005). Source countries, from which girls and women are trafficked, tend to be poor and less developed (Cambodia, Vietnam) or industrialized countries where there is economic disruption and high unemployment (Ukraine and other states of the former Soviet Union). Destination countries tend to be relatively affluent and therefore desirable to migrant workers. Some nations or regions are hubs, or centers of trafficking where victims are bought, sold, and put in transit. These include countries that have large commercial sex industries (Thailand, the Philippines) and those that have powerful crime syndicates (Columbia, Nigeria, Albania). Often, women are trafficked by the same criminals and via the same routes as drugs and guns.

Overall, South Asian countries report the highest rates of trafficking, accounting for approximately one third of cases reported globally each year. Trafficking flourishes in this region because of its large and disadvantaged population, increasingly rapid urbanization and modernization, low level of development, and the occurrence of political insurgencies, such as those in Nepal, Pakistan, and Burma (Myanmar). Girls and women are trafficked within South Asian countries, for example from rural regions of Afghanistan to the capital, Kabul. They are trafficked across national borders; and they are trafficked out of the region, often to the Middle East (Crawford 2010).

Sex trafficking has grave consequences for trafficked girls and women and for the larger society. Many women who likely have been trafficked disappear and are never heard from again. When a girl loses contact after leaving a rural Nepali village, an isolated area of Vietnam, or a Columbian slum, her family and community may not have the resources to try to find her. Traffickers seize and hold passports and papers, and control the victims' access to others. No one knows how many trafficked women's lives have ended in degradation, abandonment, or sexual violence.

Girls and women who survive trafficking typically experience severe consequences to their physical health and well-being. There is little systematic research on this topic, but the few available studies show that 95 percent of trafficked women have experienced sexual violence. Nearly two thirds of survivors have 10 or more chronic health symptoms after exiting the trafficking situation, such as headaches, memory problems, dizziness, and back pain. Trafficked women's prolonged exposure to commercialized sexual activity heightens their vulnerability to sexually transmitted infections, including HIV/AIDS. Studies of HIV prevalence among trafficked women in South Asia show a pooled HIV/AIDS rate of 32 percent (Oram et al. 2012). With other risk factors held constant, the HIV risk is greater for girls who were trafficked at younger ages, likely due to increased biological susceptibility in immature females (Silverman et al. 2007). Even if a woman manages to escape the trafficking situation, her experience may seriously affect her health and shorten her life.

The psychological consequences of trafficking are severe. Across recent studies, survivors experience extremely high rates of anxiety (48–98 percent), depression (55–100 percent), and post-traumatic stress disorder (19–77 percent) (Oram et al. 2012). Case studies and accounts by counselors and therapists who offer support services to survivors report these same disorders along with a high incidence of somatic symptoms (e.g., chronic pain), dissociation, and withdrawal. Often, trafficked girls and women are stigmatized as immoral "fallen women" because they have worked as prostitutes. They also may be criminalized and prosecuted. Stigmatization and criminalization almost certainly exacerbate the post-trafficking adjustment problems of survivors; however, there has been virtually no systematic research on these factors.

The dominant scholarship on ending sex trafficking typically asserts that solving the global problem of sex trafficking requires at least three types of intervention, characterized as the "three Ps": prevention, protection, and prosecution. In efforts to prevent trafficking, governmental agencies and non-governmental organizations (NGOs) may conduct community education programs or public awareness campaigns in areas where trafficking is prevalent. They try to reach at-risk groups by means of street theater performances, informal education sessions, radio, video, posters, and meetings of community groups. Governments and NGOs may also increase border surveillance, designate a law enforcement division responsible for prevention, or otherwise try to stop sex trafficking before it happens or stop it in progress. NGOs in areas where trafficking is prevalent, such as South Asia, often offer women opportunities for income-generating activities, basic education, and vocational training, in efforts to reduce poverty and empower women. Some NGOs patrol border checkpoints, posting teams who are trained to recognize trafficking victims and intercept them before they leave the country. Finally, governmental and non-governmental agencies may conduct programs to educate police personnel in how to recognize trafficking and protect the human rights of its victims.

Keeping survivors safe from further victimization and providing the services they need is also considered a crucial component of addressing the consequences of sex trafficking. When a girl or woman leaves a trafficking situation, the exit itself may be traumatic and dangerous. She may manage to escape the brothel, or be caught up in a police raid and arrested as a prostitute, or she may be let go by the brothel owner if she becomes too ill to work, and thereby loses even the shelter and material support that she formerly had. Depending on the individual survivor's experience of sex work and exiting sex work, she may have a wide variety of needs, including a safe place to stay, medical care, psychological counseling, and legal support. She is likely to be depressed and suffering from post-traumatic stress disorder. She may be unable to trust anyone. All these issues need immediate attention as part of a comprehensive response to the harms wrought by sex trafficking.

Over the longer term, survivors also need education or employment training, follow-up care to ensure physical and psychological well-being, legal assistance in prosecuting their traffickers, and perhaps help in reconnecting with their families and communities.

Some women and girls cannot return to their homes and families because they are rejected for having been prostitutes. Anti-trafficking organizations may offer long-term residential and medical care for these women. For girls and women who are HIV-positive, some NGOs offer medical treatment and hospice care.

In less affluent countries with a high prevalence of sex trafficking, the central government may have few resources and may not view trafficking of women as a high-priority problem. Services for survivors, if they are available at all, are likely to be provided by charitable organizations. Although these NGOs often work heroically on behalf of trafficked girls and women, they may be unfamiliar with evidence-based practices, and often they lack the resources to systematically assess and treat survivors, as well as conduct longer-term follow-ups of their reintegration and adjustment.

When it comes to evaluating prevention and protection interventions, there has been very little systematic evaluation of whether the interventions produce the intended effects. NGOs may conduct community education programs, but it is uncertain whether these programs change attitudes and behavior. Charitable organizations may provide paraprofessional counseling for survivors, but it remains unknown whether such counseling reduces depressive symptoms. There is virtually no research that has rigorously evaluated whether an intervention has had an immediate or long-term impact on attitudes or behavior. This lack of research is an indicator that most societies do not yet regard sex trafficking as a serious social problem.

Many countries also lack anti-trafficking legislation and victim protection laws, while others do not enforce their existing laws, failing to prosecute traffickers. Each year, the United States Department of State publishes a Trafficking in Persons (TIP) report, which summarizes and evaluates governmental efforts to address human trafficking, including sex trafficking. The TIP report classifies countries into four categories. Tier One countries are those that meet the minimum standards for eliminating trafficking set out in the Trafficking and Violence Protection Act of 2000 and its updates: they have appropriate anti-trafficking legislation in place and are making vigorous efforts to enforce it. Compliance does not imply that a country has no trafficking. The Netherlands, for example, is a Tier One country in the 2014 TIP report, and also a trafficking hub, but one in which trafficking is prosecuted and victims are provided with protection and care. Other Tier One countries are the United States, the United Kingdom, and Canada.

Tier Two countries are those judged as failing to meet minimum standards, but making efforts to do so. Tier Two countries in 2014 include Croatia, India, and Nepal. A Tier Two Watch List, including such countries as Burma, China, and Sri Lanka, encompasses nations that have a high reported number of cases and/or an increase over the previous year, and do not meet minimum standards. Finally, Tier Three countries are those assessed as having a major human trafficking problem and which are doing little or nothing to either protect the victims or prosecute the perpetrators. Countries in this category include Thailand, Saudi Arabia, and Russia. In the 2014 TIP report, only 31 of 188 countries assessed achieved Tier One status, an indicator that sex trafficking is not yet being accorded a high priority among governments around the world (US Department of State 2014).

Trafficking is a complex area in which to conduct systematic research and to design and implement interventions. It is an illegal activity, hidden from public view. Access to trafficked women may be difficult, dangerous, or impossible. To date, social scientists have not yet developed adequate measures to assess the physical and psychological health of trafficking survivors, or conducted more than a few long-term studies of their post-trafficking adjustment. Designing and implementing research on sex trafficking is challenging. However, good research is an essential first step in preventing future trafficking and helping today's survivors. There are other essential steps toward ending trafficking. Governmental agencies and NGOs need to provide protection, resources, and assistance for survivors, so that they can return to society and lead productive lives. Finally, governments around the world need to enact and enforce anti-trafficking legislation and foster political and social equality for girls and women.

SEE ALSO: Gender-Based Violence; Human Rights, International Laws and Policies on; Human Trafficking, Feminist Perspectives on; Sexual Assault/Sexual Violence; Violence Against Women in Global Perspective

REFERENCES

Crawford, Mary. 2010. *Sex Trafficking in South Asia: Telling Maya's Story*. London: Routledge.

Farr, Kathryn. 2005. *Sex Trafficking: The Global Market in Women and Children*. New York: Worth.

Oram, Sian, Heidi Stöckl, Joanna Busza, Louise M. Howard, and Cathy Zimmerman. 2012. "Prevalence and Risk of Violence and the Physical, Mental, and Sexual Health Problems Associated with Human Trafficking: Systematic Review." *PLoS Medicine*, 9(5): e1001224. DOI: 10.1371/journal.pmed.1001224.

Silverman, J. G., et al. 2007. "HIV Prevalence and Predictors of Infection in Sex-Trafficked Nepalese Girls and Women." *Journal of the American Medical Association*, 298(5): 536–542.

United Nations (UN). 2000. "Protocol to Prevent, Suppress and Punish Trafficking in Persons, Especially Women and Children, Supplementing the United Nations Convention against Transnational Organized Crime." New York: United Nations.

US Department of State. 2014. *Trafficking in Persons Report 2014*. Washington, DC: US Department of State.

FURTHER READING

Crawford, Mary, and Michelle R. Kaufman. 2008. "Sex Trafficking in Nepal: Survivor Characteristics and Long Term Outcomes." *Violence Against Women*, 14: 905–916.

Kaufman, Michelle R., and Mary Crawford. 2011. "Sex Trafficking in Nepal: A Review of Intervention and Prevention Programs." *Violence Against Women*, 17: 651–665.

McCabe, Kimberly A., and Sabita Manian, eds. 2010. *Sex Trafficking: A Global Perspective*. New York: Lexington.

Sex Versus Gender Categorization

MAURA KELLY
Portland State University, USA

Scholars conceptualize gender as socially constructed, that is, categories of gender (and gender differences) are socially produced rather than naturally determined. As Simone de Beauvoir famously wrote: "One is not born, but rather becomes, a woman" (1973, 301). While the initial distinction between sex and gender suggested that gender follows from sex, that is, the social categories of gender are based on biological categories of sex, Anne Fausto-Sterling, Judith Butler, and others have contributed to a body of scholarship suggesting that sex is equally as socially constructed as gender. That is, average or typical differences in physical bodies are translated into a binary system of sex categorization that does not accurately reflect the actual diversity in bodies, agency to change the body, or the interaction between biological and social factors that play out on the body. As Butler argued, "perhaps this construct called 'sex' is as culturally constructed as gender; indeed, perhaps it was always already gender, with the consequence that the distinction between sex and gender turns out to be no distinction at all" (1999, 9–10).

The sex/gender distinction was first articulated by Robert Stoller in 1968 and was then adopted by feminists such as Ann Oakley and others (Brickell 2006). In this formulation, sex represents "biological" differences, while gender represents "social" differences. Sex (biological sex) is conceptualized as a classification of individuals as males and females based on biological criteria. These biological criteria include: chromosomes (XY, XX), hormones (e.g., androgen, testosterone, estrogen, progesterone), gonads (testes, ovaries), genitals (penis, vagina), and secondary sex characteristics. Although not all bodies align as typical male or typical female, sex is conceptualized as a binary (i.e., male, female) in most contemporary societies. Gender is a social identity ascribed to individuals on the basis of the gender assigned at birth (informed by an assessment of biological criteria), which dictates status, roles, and norms for behavior. Gender identities are also most commonly conceptualized as a binary (i.e., man, woman); however, some individuals take up identities that challenge this dichotomy and, in some cultures, a "third gender" is formally or informally recognized. The concept of gender is also used to describe performances of femininity, masculinity, and androgyny. Candace West and Don H. Zimmerman (1987) conceptualized gender as a routine accomplishment of everyday interaction. In articulating a theory of "doing gender," West and Zimmerman argued that gender is something that we *do*, not something that we *are*. A variation is Judith Butler's (1999) theory of gender as performative.

"Gender" rather than "sex" should be used to refer to gender identities as well as average or typical differences between men as a group and women as a group, as this indicates the socially constructed nature of differences. However, some scholars retain "sex" when discussing biological criteria or biological differences. To give some examples of the correct use of "gender," gender scholars are interested in examining gender socialization, occupational gender segregation, and same-gender attraction. However, some uses of "sex" have been retained where "gender" is more theoretically appropriate, for example the phrase "same-sex marriage." Notably, while gender scholars are concerned with differentiating the appropriate uses of the terms "sex" and "gender," this distinction has not been widely taken up in the broader culture. The terms "sex" and "gender" are often used interchangeably in public discourse and everyday speech. In the broader culture, gender identities are seen as following unproblematically from biological criteria and gender categories are assumed to be "natural" and asocial (i.e., not socially constructed). These sorts of essentialist assumptions often exaggerate differences between groups and minimize differences within groups.

Differentiating between "biological" and thus "unalterable" differences and "social" and potentially "changeable" differences has been useful in theorizing gender and gender inequality. Focusing on the ways in which society shapes the statuses, roles, and norms for behavior associated with gender allows for an understanding of how gender is shaped by society and how we might further projects of gender equality. For example, if boys' and girls' scores on math tests can be attributed largely to gender socialization rather than innate math ability, we are much more likely to be successful in promoting changes that will encourage more women to work in fields related to math and science. However, gender scholars have problematized the initial conceptualization of sex (biological) versus gender (social). Theoretical discussions of intersex and transgender bodies and identities have been used to examine the conceptual relationship between sex and gender, to theorize both sex and gender as socially constructed, and to challenge sex and gender as binary categories (Kessler 1998; Stryker and Whittle 2006). Intersex diagnoses include a variety of conditions in which bodies deviate from typical male or typical female alignment of biological characteristics. Scholars have noted that the analysis of social and medical responses to intersex bodies illustrates how systems of sex/gender/sexuality are regulated. That a child born with ambiguous genitals constitutes a "social emergency" demonstrates both the failure of genitals to be the definitive marker of sex (which is presumed to then dictate gender and sexuality) and the commitment to maintaining the appearance of the two-sex model (Kessler 1998). Transgender people have gender identities that do not align with the gender they were assigned at birth. Transgender people may choose to transition to their preferred sex, potentially using hormones or surgery (Stryker and Whittle 2006). Individuals with intersex and transgender identities, as well as non-binary gender identities such as genderqueer or gender non-conforming, pose challenges to sex and gender binaries and the presumed "naturalness" of the relationship between sex and gender. Scholars who understand both sex and gender as socially constructed have described this sort of diversity in bodies and the agency to change the body as well as noting that biological differences are not always clearly distinct from cultural differences. In other words, it is sometimes impossible to adjudicate between differences of "sex" (i.e., biological) and differences of "gender" (i.e., social) due to the complex and interrelated processes of physical development and socialization (Laqueur 1990; Fausto-Sterling 2000).

SEE ALSO: Gender as a Practice; Intersexuality; Transgender Politics

REFERENCES

Beauvoir, Simone de. 1973. *The Second Sex*. New York: Vintage Books.

Brickell, Chris. 2006. "The Sociological Construction of Gender and Sexuality." *Sociological Review*, 54(1): 87–113.

Butler, Judith. 1999. *Gender Trouble: Feminism and the Subversion of Identity*. New York: Routledge. First published 1990.

Fausto-Sterling, Anne. 2000. *Sexing the Body: Gender Politics and the Construction of Sexuality*. New York: Basic Books.

Kessler, Suzanne J. 1998. *Lessons from the Intersexed*. New Brunswick: Rutgers University Press.

Laqueur, Thomas W. 1990. *Making Sex: Body and Gender from the Greeks to Freud*. Cambridge, MA: Harvard University Press.

Stryker, Susan, and Stephen Whittle, eds. 2006. *The Transgender Studies Reader*. New York: Routledge.

West, Candace, and Don H. Zimmerman. 1987. "Doing Gender." *Gender & Society*, 1(2): 125–151.

Sex Work and Sex Workers' Unionization

GIULIA GAROFALO GEYMONAT
University of Lund, Sweden

Sex work is an umbrella term encompassing a broad variety of practices that involve the creation of a sexual experience for others in exchange for explicit remuneration, be it money or other material advantages such as presents, food, drugs, housing, and so on. The experience can involve contact between the sex worker and the client, whether through direct physical interaction, such as in prostitution or bondage and discipline, sadism and masochism (BDSM), or through the mediation of a technology such as a phone, webcam, or dance floor. In some sectors, for instance professional porn, workers' contact with each other might be more important than interaction with clients. However, most sex work involves aspects of emotional work and counseling with the client, and in some cases it may include massage, healing, and sex education. In the case of services supplied to seasonal workers, travelers, or tourists, people providing sex may also host clients in their home, and offer them washing, laundry, and cooking services. Some sex workers may be paid to accompany clients in social situations – to be literally an "escort" – for instance to a restaurant, social event, or sex party. In fact, the boundaries between commercial sex and other neighboring activities – entertainment, tourism, well-being, care, and even dating – are often blurred and in need of constant redefinition. This is increasingly visible in contemporary capitalist dynamics, as more jobs in the service industry explicitly tap on individuals' gendered, sexual, and racialized identities, and as intimate relationships become more openly negotiable, fragmented, and commercialized (Bernstein 2007; Boris and Parreñas 2010; Brents and Sanders 2010).

These processes may create social anxiety, and at the same time they contribute to exposing the deeply political content of the category of "sex work," or "prostitution." What is or is not "prostitution" or "sex work," who is or is not a "sex worker" (and their client), are not objective facts established once and for all, but are often contested and resisted (Pheterson 1996). For example, take the case of sex tourism. Many of those who are involved in these practices do not think about them as prostitution or as sex tourism (Truong 1990). Indeed, some of the local girls or boys are not "sex workers," but people who more or less frequently accompany tourists sexually as one of a series of activities in which they engage in order to access income. However, this perception and the words and the practices may change, becoming "sex tourism" whenever policymakers, non-governmental organizations (NGOs), churches, or health services decide to pay attention to these escorts by studying, classifying, taxing, controlling, and punishing them. Not too different is the process around the "birth of modern prostitution." According to Walkowitz (1980), before the nineteenth century there were no prostitutes in the modern Western sense of a class of clearly identifiable female workers. There certainly were young women from poor classes who, among other sources of income, such as factory work or marriage, earned money by providing sexual services, but it was only when state institutions started to repress them that the conditions were created for the separation and marginalization of these women's practices. Their social meaning changed and working class women were stigmatized as prostitutes, thereby excluded from other sources of income and from their community, and forced to look for protection from criminals in order to keep doing what had by all appearances become their job.

The variety of conditions and meanings in the sex industry has been widely documented by social and cultural studies in the last decade (Agustín 2007). Some people work independently and choose their clients, while others are controlled at several levels – by managers, traffickers, partners, and police – or are not able to refuse any client. Some people work safely and have two-hour sessions with their clients, while others put their lives at risk every time they go out in the streets, and struggle even to negotiate a condom. Most sex workers find themselves in between. However, all are subjected to the so-called stigma of prostitution. In the words of a conference of sex workers in Brussels:

> We recognize stigma as being the commonality that links all of us as sex workers, forming us into a community of interest – despite the enormous diversity in our realities at work in our lives. We have come together to confront and challenge this stigma and the injustices it leads to. (Sex Workers in Europe Manifesto 2005, 4)

Following this line of analysis, what appears ultimately to define "sex work" or "prostitution" is the very fact that it is labeled "sex work" or "prostitution": that is, the so-called "stigma of prostitution," a set of opinions, behaviors, and laws that isolate, discriminate, and punish anyone *explicitly* exchanging their sex labor for material advantages. It is not the sexual–economic exchange per se that is being stigmatized, as this takes place in many other situations, including with one's boss, professor, customer, husband or boyfriend, wife or girlfriend. According to materialist feminist Paola Tabet (2004), what distinguishes the transactions that are stigmatized as "prostitution" is that, compared with the other sexual–economic exchanges, they are explicit and transparent, and therefore women may more openly negotiate their deal with men. These elements may potentially expose a larger system of exploitation of women's reproductive labor, which instead remains largely informal, invisible, and unpaid – and so they are stigmatized and criminalized.

Interestingly, the history of the term "sex work" is itself connected to the struggle for women's emancipation: "sex work" was first introduced by Carol Leight (aka Scarlot Harlot), a feminist activist and prostitute with a Marxist background. This took place in California in the mid-1970s, and the importance of naming the labor of sex was understood as part of a larger political project of recognizing the social and economic value of services that had been traditionally expected from women as a natural expression of "love," or as part of an informal exchange of favors, in either case not implying entitlement to payment and proper labor rights.

Nowadays, while clients remain almost exclusively cisgendered men, and women constitute the large majority of workers, trans people and queer men have become more visible as providers across the world and have played an increasing role within the sex workers' movement. Since the 1990s, as the movement expanded and became more complex, it became clear that, across genders, young people, racialized minorities, migrants, queers, and working class people often represent a large proportion of the sex labor force, in addition to being more visible and targeted by the authorities. This is reflected in the analyses of an increasingly globalized sex workers' movement which, along with demanding rights for people engaging in sex work and their families, calls for public policies against poverty and for access to education and the labor market, in particular for runaway children, girls, queer youth, single mothers, and migrant or racialized minorities. In the eyes of the sex work movement, the right to engage in the selling of sex is indeed inseparable from the right *not* to engage in it, and to not be trapped in the sex industry – a very common experience for sex workers. This double claim is essential to grasping the activist idea that selling sex can be an act of resistance or even subversion, even when it is not an ideal choice. Indeed, activists argue that sex work may sometimes represent a relatively less exploitative activity than the actual alternatives women, queers, and racialized minorities might have in a supermarket, factory, office, bar, private home, or in their own families (DMSC 1997).

Furthermore, a growing body of personal accounts report how the practice of commercial sex may sometimes become a relatively safer space for both clients and workers to experience their non-normative pleasures, bodies, and identities – including trans, queer, and disabled bodies, as well as BDSM or forms of sacred and spiritual sex. Some queer theorists have gone as far as affirming that sex for money represents in itself a contestation of hegemonic construction of sexuality, in particular "the movement from anatomical sex to sexuality to identity and the maintenance of the public/private distinction through the isolation of sexuality and intimacy from productive work and commercial exchange" (Zatz 1997, 306). However, sex work rights activists are particularly aware that all these possibilities of resistance or even subversion are de facto largely prevented by the stigma that persists in legislation, institutions, and interactions, and which is internalized by sex workers themselves. The analogy with other struggles is made clear through activists' use of the term "whorephobia" (from French *putophobie*), which is seen as responsible for exposing sex workers to isolation, discrimination, blackmailing, criminalization, as well as a disproportionate level of exploitation, violence, and death.

People engaging in prostitution are currently criminalized in most countries in the world. For instance, they can be fined or arrested in Thailand, the United States (with the partial exception of Nevada), and Russia; in China they risk years in detention camps; and even the death penalty in the countries that follow Islamic shari'a law. *Prohibition* is prevalent in Africa and in the former socialist countries, and has recently reappeared in Europe under a new form, which criminalizes not the selling of sex, but buying it (the so-called Swedish model, devised in 1999). Even where prostitution is not directly criminalized as such, and prostitutes are considered as victims to be protected (the abolitionist model, invented in nineteenth century Britain), basic safety measures are often criminalized, such as working together, renting a flat, employing security, on the pretext of protecting sex workers from third parties. Sex workers also often risk losing custody of their children and are not considered credible by social services and in courts.

WHO, UNAIDS, UN Women, the ILO, and Amnesty International have repeatedly analyzed how the criminalization of sex work increases sex workers' vulnerability to violence, exploitation, and HIV, because it keeps sex workers away from public authorities, hospitals, NGOs, unions, as well as aggravating police corruption and the criminal control of the industry. Along similar lines, the medical journal *The Lancet* launched an important series "HIV and sex workers" in 2014. A few states, such as Germany, the Netherlands, and Australia, started taking this understanding seriously at the end of the 1990s, and have slowly introduced some labor rights and protections for some groups of sex workers, including the possibility for workers to work together legally, to employ security, and to have contracts, health insurance, and pensions. However, sex workers' unions report that even with these forms of rights-oriented legalization, vast parts of the industry are still underground, at least partly because the laws are designed to support the interests of large brothels and public institutions rather than those of workers. In particular, because of fears related to migration and trafficking, there is no possibility for migrants to obtain a visa to work in the sex industry – which means that in some cases the majority of the workforce has no possibility of working legally. Sex workers' organizations nowadays tend to support the full decriminalization of consensual adult sex work, a system developed in New Zealand since 2003.

While traditional political parties and funders have largely denied support to the sex workers' cause, in many contexts sex work activists have been part of grassroots movements inspired by labor, feminist, LGBTQ, anti-racist, and HIV-positive critiques, and have adopted these wider movements' strategies and tactics (Garofalo 2010). In France, in what is renowned as the first public action by sex workers, in 1975, a group of prostitutes occupied Saint Nizier church in Lyon in order to protest their harassment at the hands of police and institutions that supported criminal pimping organizations, and they threatened to out men who publicly spoke out against them while privately using their services. The 1980s saw the birth of a number of prostitutes' collectives in Latin America, the United States, Europe, Australia, Asia, and international conferences were organized in Amsterdam and Brussels in 1985 and 1986, and the World Whores' Charter was produced, in close alliance with feminists and lesbians (Pheterson 1989).

Sex workers have been crucial in international interventions against HIV/AIDS, and many organizations developed in the 1990s and 2000s around demands for access to condoms and treatment, extending their critique to the conditions that make sex workers vulnerable, including economic and social exclusion, exploitation, and judicial and police abuses, some of them in the name of the "anti-trafficking" cause. Exemplary cases are the work of the Durbar Mahila Samanwaya Committee (DMSC), created in Calcutta in 1992, which currently counts 65,000 members, and Empower in Thailand, started in 1984. In the 1990s, sex workers' groups in Australia and the United Kingdom developed sophisticated systems against violence, consisting of the centralized sharing of information on dangerous clients or aggressors posing as clients, "Ugly Mugs."

In 2000, the International Union of Sex Workers in London became affiliated to the country's third largest general union, the GMB. In Ecuador, brothel workers organized memorable strikes in 1988 and 2000, and AMMAR, the sex workers' union funded in Argentina in 2002, has organized numerous actions and campaigns with the support of one of the national confederation of unions, the CTA. The last decade has witnessed the explosion of an artistic activist scene, including film festivals (San Francisco, London, Hamburg), fashion shows (Daspu, Brazil), and music bands (Debby Doesn't Do it For Free, Australia). Following an increase in transnational activism, in particular through the work of the Network of Sex Work Projects (NSWP), the movement has recently established a common symbol, the red umbrella, and an International Day Against Violence Against Sex Workers, on December 17.

SEE ALSO: Feminisms, Marxist and socialist; Feminism, Materialist; Informal Economy; Prostitution/Sex Work; Sex Tourism; Sex Trafficking; Stigma

REFERENCES

Agustín, Laura, ed. 2007. "The Cultural Studies of Commercial Sex (Special Issue)." *Sexualities*, 10(4).

Bernstein, Elizabeth. 2007. *Temporarily Yours: Intimacy, Authenticity, and the Commerce of Sex.* Chicago: University of Chicago Press.

Boris, Eileen, and Rhacel Salazar Parreñas, eds. 2010. *Intimate Labors: Cultures, Technologies and the Politics of Care.* Stanford: Stanford University Press.

Brents, Barbara, and Teela Sanders. 2010. "Mainstreaming the Sex Industry: Economic Inclusion and Social Ambivalence." *Journal of Law and Society*, 37(1): 40–60.

Durbar Mahila Samanwaya Committee (DMSC). 1997. *Sonagashi Sex Workers' Manifesto, Calcutta.* Accessed August 5, 2015, at www.bayswan.org/manifest.html.

Garofalo, Giulia. 2010. "Sex Workers' Rights Activism in Europe: Orientations from Brussels." In *Sex Work Matters*, edited by Melissa Ditmore, Antonia Levy, and Alys Willman, 221–238. New York: Zed Books.

Pheterson, Gail, ed. 1989. *A Vindication of the Rights of Whores*. Seattle: Seal Press.

Pheterson, Gail. 1996. *The Prostitution Prism*. Amsterdam: Amsterdam University Press.

Sex Workers in Europe Manifesto. 2005. Brussels: ICRSE. Accessed August 5, 2015, at www.sexworkeurope.org/resources/sex-workers-europe-manifesto.

Tabet, Paola. 2004. *La Grande Arnaque: Sexualité des Femmes et Échange Économico-Sexuel*. Paris: L'Harmattan.

Truong, Thanh-Dam. 1990. *Sex, Money and Morality: Prostitution and Tourism in Southeast Asia*. London: Zed Books.

Walkowitz, Judith. 1980. *Prostitution and Victorian Society: Women, Class, and the State*. Cambridge: Cambridge University Press.

Zatz, Noah. 1997. "Sex Work/Sex Act: Law, Labor, and Desire in Constructions of Prostitution." *Signs*, 22(2): 277–308.

FURTHER READING

Ditmore, Melissa, ed. 2006. *The Encyclopedia of Prostitution and Sex Work, 2 vols*. Westport: Greenwood Press.

Kempadoo, Kamala, and Jo Doezema, eds. 1998. *Global Sex Workers: Rights, Resistance and Redefinition*. New York: Routledge.

Sex-Radical Feminists

NATALIE M. PELUSO
Concordia College, USA

The term "sex-radical feminists" refers to a subset of feminist scholars, activists, artists, and authors whose work explores the contours of female sexual expression, pleasure, and agency. Sex-radical feminism, also known as pro-sex feminism, is one of many strains of modern feminist thought. Sex-radical feminists are often defined in opposition to radical feminists, whose vigorous critiques of patriarchy, heterosexuality, pornography, and sex work set them apart both theoretically and politically. Some key themes present within sex-radical feminist scholarship, art, and literature include an emphasis on the importance of sexual revelry and pleasure, the reclaiming of "outlaw" or "bad girl" identities such as "slut," "whore," and "dyke," and the potential for female empowerment through sex.

Sex-radical feminism grew out of ideological rifts within the US feminist movement of the late 1970s and early 1980s. These philosophical divisions were primarily focused around issues of heterosexual and lesbian sex practices, bondage and discipline sadomasochism (BDSM), pornography, and commercialized sex. Framing power relations almost exclusively in terms of patriarchal domination, radical feminists asserted that sex and sexuality were social constructs designed to cater to the wants and needs of men. Sexuality and the reproductive arena, therefore, served as patriarchy's means of oppression of women. Radical feminists claimed that it would be impossible for women to know authentic sexual desire, pleasure, and liberation within a patriarchal society and culture. Following this reasoning, many radical feminist activists adopted staunchly anti-sex positions. Prominent members of the radical feminist community alleged that any kind of penetrative sex constituted institutionalized rape. Others contended that claims of "consensual" participation in the sex industry were antithetical and that such erotic labor was not freely chosen work but instead sexual slavery. Similarly, radical feminists argued that women who viewed or were involved in the production of pornography were either forced to engage in such activities against their will or were working in anti-feminist collusion with men. On more than one occasion (and with limited success), radical feminist activists such as Andrea Dworkin and Catharine MacKinnon joined political forces with right-wing religious and conservative institutions (including the Meese Commission) to frame pornography as coerced sex and, therefore, as a form of gender-based violence. Dworkin and MacKinnon also attempted to assert a causal link between the viewing of pornographic material and the committing of rape and other acts of violence against women. Simultaneously, intense debates raged within the United States women's movement as theoretical opposition grew to key radical feminist tenets and criticism mounted over radical feminism's seemingly bizarre choice of political bedfellows. One of the most famous clashes occurred at the Scholar and the Feminist IX: "Towards a Politics of Sexuality" conference at Barnard College on April 24, 1982 (commonly known as the "Barnard Conference on Sexuality"). Radical feminists outfitted with anti-pornography and anti-BDSM T-shirts, leaflets, and signage picketed the conference in protest. Years later these debates and conflicts within the women's movement would be collectively referred to as the "feminist sex wars."

The ideological distinctions that separated sex-radical feminists from radical feminists were numerous. Significantly, unlike radical feminism's overly deterministic theory of patriarchal oppression, sex-radicals believed that power relations were enacted on the institutional/macro-level as well as the interactional/micro-level. Due to the influence of social constructionist thought, sex-radicals accounted for historical and cultural context in their discussions of sexual expression, identity, and practice. For sex-radical feminists, social forces as well as interpersonal dynamics shaped the terrain of modern-day sexuality. This knowledge led Gayle Rubin (1984) to famously theorize the existence of a system of sexual hierarchy within the United States that oppressed erotic minorities including lesbians and gays, individuals who use or make pornography and sex toys, practitioners of BDSM and other forms of consensual "kink," non-monogamists, and sex workers. Acknowledging that these categories were subject to change over time, sex-radical feminists began working to combat what they saw as systematic erotic injustice. These intellectual insights had other discernable impacts on praxis, activism, and social policy. Not only did sex-radical feminists call attention to "whore stigma" (Queen 1997), but sex-radical feminist theory was directly informed by the personal narratives of current sex workers. Up until this point, most mainstream feminist interaction with erotic laborers involved former sex workers who saw themselves (or allowed themselves to be framed) as victims of sex trafficking and the sex trade more broadly. The sex-radical movement became a place where sex workers could mobilize and work to reform their industry without having to contend with factions of feminists bent on abolitionism. The very first international sex workers' rights conference was held in Amsterdam in 1985, aptly titled the World Whores' Congress. There, sex workers, their allies, and other feminists formed the International Committee for Prostitutes' Rights (ICPR) and created the World Charter for Prostitutes' Rights. This charter outlined and demanded the protection of sex workers' labor, health, and human rights. The initial and second World Whores' Congress (held in Brussels in 1986) prompted the rise of numerous sex worker organizations, publications, and conferences around the world.

Sex-radical feminists also asserted that women might delight in and gain political power from subverting normative constructions of gender and sexuality. The inclusion of symbolic interactionist theories allowed sex-radical feminists to frame individual social actors as agentic meaning-makers. Contrary to radical feminism's essentialist beliefs about the violence inherent in sex, sex-radicals believed that sexual acts and practices had no intrinsic meaning aside from that which the actor imparts. Therefore, it was entirely plausible that women could voluntarily (and perhaps even enthusiastically) engage in penetrative sex, BDSM, sex without commitment, erotic labor, sex with dildos and other sex toys, pornography, and public sex and derive feelings of power, pride, accomplishment, control, and pleasure from their experiences. By creating space within feminism for complex, diverse, and sometimes contradictory accounts of female sexuality, the sex-radical movement presented women with the reality of variation in sexual experience.

SEE ALSO: Empowerment; Feminism, Radical; Feminist Activism; Feminist Movements in Historical and Comparative Perspective; Feminist Sex Wars; Pornography, Feminist Legal and Political Debates on; Prostitution/Sex Work

REFERENCES

Queen, Carol. 1997. "Sex Radical Politics, Sex-Positive Feminist Thought, and Whore Stigma." In *Whores and Other Feminists*, edited by Jill Nagle, 125–135. New York: Routledge and Kegan Paul.

Rubin, Gayle. 1984. "Thinking Sex: Notes for a Radical Theory of the Politics of Sexuality." In *Pleasure and Danger: Exploring Female Sexuality*, edited by Carol Vance, 267–319. Boston, MA: Routledge and Kegan Paul.

FURTHER READING

Barton, Bernadette. 2002. "Dancing on the Möbius Strip: Challenging the Sex War Paradigm." *Gender & Society*, 16: 585–602. DOI: 10.1177/089124302236987.

Chapkis, Wendy. 1997. *Live Sex Acts: Women Performing Erotic Labor*. New York: Routledge and Kegan Paul.

Kempadoo, Kamala, and Jo Doezema, eds. 1998. *Global Sex Workers: Rights, Resistance, and Redefinition*. New York: Routledge and Kegan Paul.

Vance, Carol, ed. 1984. *Pleasure and Danger: Exploring Female Sexuality*. Boston, MA: Routledge and Kegan Paul.

Sex-Related Difference Research

STEPHANIE L. BUDGE and KATE E. SNYDER
University of Louisville, USA

Research on sex differences is highly contentious. One source of controversy stems from the interchangeable usage of "sex" and "gender," which confounds two distinct constructs. From a Western perspective, sex refers to a person's biological characteristics (e.g., chromosomes, hormones, reproductive organs, and secondary sex characteristics); conversely, gender refers to individuals' social, cultural, and psychological characteristics that pertain to stereotypes, norms, and traits that are considered masculine or feminine. Gender identity is an individual's sense of gender as it is privately experienced in one's behavior and self-awareness of being female, male, ambivalent, or at a defined point along a gender continuum; gender role is defined as the behaviors associated with a public expression of stereotyped masculinity, femininity, or ambivalence. However, the Western perspective of sex and gender provides a narrow, Eurocentric viewpoint of these constructs. From a majority world perspective, subcultures often construct sex and gender as fluid and non-binary aspects (Peletz 2006). A closer evaluation of these distinct constructs, as well as the theoretical approaches utilized in sex differences research, highlights new directions for research.

THEORETICAL APPROACHES

Broadly, essentialism (viewing sex differences as inherent to people) and social constructionism (conceptualizing sex differences as stemming primarily from environmental factors) represent polar ends of approaches to sex differences research. In essentialism, sex is conceptualized as dichotomous, such that men and women are believed to behave, think, and act in fundamentally unique ways. Basic biological characteristics (genotypes) are believed to directly contribute to observable differences (phenotypes) (Rudman and Glick 2008). Further, essentialism proposes that sex differences relate to unique characteristics assumed to be inherent to individuals, such that they are fixed, stable, and reside within the person. This view also assumes that characteristics for each sex are uniform; for example, if men do X behavior and women do Y behavior, women do not do X behavior.

Gender theorists have challenged the essentialist, dichotomous framing of sex and gender. Scholars contend that these dichotomous and essentialist viewpoints of gender often perpetuate Western, colonial thought that serves to exclude individuals based on sex and gender (Shohat 2002). Additionally, developmental variability in observed sex differences disputes the notion of inherent, stable differences (Hyde 2005). Social constructionism addresses these critiques by proposing that gender exists outside an individual. Here, gender is theorized to be socially constructed in order to give meaning in a cultural context. Social constructionism has also been criticized; for instance, this view overlooks biological contributions to an individual's construction of what sex and gender mean.

Criticisms of essentialism and social constructionism have led to the proposal of an interactionist approach (also called conjoint approach) in which biological and environmental factors interrelate, rather than compete. Biology sets the course for tendencies that are shaped by environment, and biological characteristics can also lead individuals to seek out reinforcing environments. Observed sex differences can be mutually formed through interactions between biology (genetic influences on physical characteristics), cognition (understanding and endorsement of gender constancy), and socialization (socializer's endorsement of gender roles, language, treatment by other individuals).

CONCEPTUALIZATION OF SEX DIFFERENCES RESEARCH

Apart from the essentialism and social constructionism debate, there are several conceptual issues with the operationalization of "sex" categories and with how research is conducted. Often, researchers of sex differences do not measure actual biological characteristics. Instead, participants are asked to indicate if they are male or female. In Western cultures, male/female are used as binary constructs to investigate statistical sex differences on a given variable; male/female categories are most often used as interaction variables, as control variables, or as independent variables.

This approach is problematic. First, although male and female are considered binary constructs in sex differences research, these constructs should be conceptualized as continuous variables. From a biological sex perspective, there are many variations of chromosomal makeups (e.g., XY, XX, XXY, X, XYY, etc.), hormone levels, phenotypes of secondary sex characteristics, and intersex conditions. From a gender perspective, gender is also a continuous construct. Many individuals identify as transgender (i.e., their sex assigned at birth is not congruent with their current gender identity) and/or gender non-conforming (e.g., individuals who perform their gender in a way that does not align with societal expectations of how men and women "should" represent their gender). This population may also identify with culturally specific, gender-diverse identities that include (but are not limited to) Bakla (Philippines),

Fa'afafine (Somoa), Hijra (India), Kathoey, Phet Tee Sam, or Sao Praphet Sorng (Thailand), Māhū/Māhūwahine (Hawai'i), Paksu mudang (Korea), Raerae (Tahiti), Khawaja Sara (Pakistan), Zapotec Muxe (Mexico), and Ashtime (Ethiopia). Among transgender individuals, many do not identify with a binary gender identity, but instead identify as both male and female (i.e., genderqueer or gender variant) or do not identify as male or female at all (e.g., agender). Further, many individuals do not conform to their cultural gender norms or social stereotypes of masculinity or femininity and maintain their sex assigned at birth. From a research perspective, treating groups of individuals as solely male or female does not account for the variance related to their current gender identity, expression, and/or socialization.

FOCUS ON VARIABILITY: WITHIN-GROUP VS. BETWEEN-GROUP

Researchers also tend to misinterpret observed sex differences. Because sex differences research stems from an essentialist view, in which differences are assumed to exist due to the very nature of sex and gender being a core determinant of an individual's identity (differences hypothesis), researchers often use this approach when interpreting their data. However, meta-analytic techniques used to synthesize sex differences research have instead provided support for the gender similarities hypothesis (Hyde 2005). In other words, within-group variability is much greater than between-group differences for studies that examine differences between men and women.

Relatedly, observed sex differences are often interpreted problematically. Researchers often conclude that an observed difference supports a *difference in kind* (males and females behave or think in entirely different ways). However, observing that males and females differ on a given characteristic and concluding that the sexes behave in fundamentally different ways, such that all males are similar to each other and dissimilar to all females (essentialist view), is an invalid extrapolation. It is more likely that the researchers are observing a *difference in degree* (there is an observed difference, but also a large overlap between sexes). Even when there is an observed difference on some characteristic, there may also be overlap; some males will score higher/lower than females on the characteristic and the same will be true of females. Thus, the appropriate conclusion must be made when interpreting sex differences findings.

Depending on the field (primarily medicine and psychology), sex differences research differs on methodology and focus. Medical researchers tend to focus primarily on sex differences based on the actual construct of sex, from brain differences to diabetes to autoimmune disorders. However, consumers of medical research should be skeptical of findings that indicate sex differences. For example, Kaiser et al. (2009) argue that most medical researchers do not use adequate statistical tests that are able to determine sex differences, should they exist. There continue to be unresolved issues in the medical field as to how to control for sex differences, specifically related to neuroscience research.

Similar criticisms apply to psychological research that focuses on biological sex differences. Psychological studies of sex differences most often study differences based on an individual's identification as male or female. For example, study participants are often provided with a forced choice option ("male or female") in the demographic form of the study and statistical tests are conducted using this gender variable. Thus, findings likely stem from gender roles and socialization. For example, researchers report that men score higher than women on spatial tests and that women scored higher than men on verbal fluency, extroversion, and agreeableness (Burton and Henninger 2013); these differences were attributed to the common neural substrate of verbal fluency and personality. These two studies are among thousands that argue for biological determinants of psychological differences between men and women. Aside from arguments about sex differences yielding zero to small effects (e.g., Hyde 2005), conclusions drawn from these psychological studies of gender differences are inaccurate, as actual biological factors are not being measured. Thus, it is inappropriate to draw biological conclusions from psychological data. In addition, all of the aforementioned studies in medical and psychological research interpret differences in kind rather than differences in degree.

Though much of the research related to sex differences can draw criticism, it is also important to note that research on developmentally related sex differences contributes to an understanding of how biological and environmental factors jointly influence observable sex differences. Self-selected sex segregation among young children is robust; preschool-aged children spend approximately half of their time with same-sex peers (Fabes, Hanish, and Martin 2003). This self-segregation derives from both a desire to be around same-sex peers, as well as a shared interest in similar (and perceived gender-appropriate) play (Martin et al. 2013). These "Petri dishes" of segregated sex groups exert a reinforcing influence on gendered behavior over time, explaining a portion of observed sex differences.

RECOMMENDATIONS

Based on the critiques of sex differences research outlined above, we offer four recommendations for research. First, researchers should consider sex and gender differences as separate questions, with both being influenced by socialization and biology. Thus, researchers need to represent findings that actually stem from the construct they are studying (rather than conflating sex and gender and biological etiology). Second, researchers should gather data related to participants' sex assigned at birth, current gender identity, and current gender expression, rather than just a single question assessing if someone is "male or female." This will allow researchers to make more valid conclusions about their samples and control for gender conformity and non-conformity, as well as appropriately identify individuals with culturally specific gender identities. After adjusting the conceptualization of sex and gender and measuring these constructs correctly, our third recommendation is for researchers to interpret their conclusions with a holistic perspective. In other words, researchers need to understand that null findings are just as important, if not more important, than differences. Further, differences in kind are distinct from differences in degree. Finally, we do not deny that there are differences that do stem from biology and also from socialization. Instead, we recommend that when researchers are investigating sex and/or gender differences, it is critical to delve into broader discussions of *why* the differences were found (interactionist perspective). Scholars recommend that the interactionist approach can be used to deconstruct Western notions of what sex and gender "should" be to provide collaborative, person-centered practice (CPCP; Khalili, Hall, and Deluca 2014). Researchers should embrace the shifting sands of change for sex and gender research to adequately address concepts of similarities and differences.

SEE ALSO: Biochemistry and Physiology; Cross-Cultural Gender Roles; Gender Bias in Research; Gender Difference Research; Gender,

Definitions of; Masculinity and Femininity, Theories of; Sex Versus Gender Categorization

REFERENCES

Burton, Leslie A., and Debra Henninger. 2013. "Sex Differences in Relationships between Verbal Fluency and Personality." *Current Psychology*, 32(2): 168–174.

Fabes, Richard A., Laura D. Hanish, and Carol Lynn Martin. 2003. "Children at Play: The Role of Peers in Understanding the Effects of Child Care." *Child Development*, 74(4): 1039–1043.

Hyde, Janet Shibley. 2005. "The Gender Similarities Hypothesis." *American Psychologist*, 60(6): 581.

Kaiser, Anelis, Sven Haller, Sigrid Schmitz, and Cordula Nitsch. 2009. "On Sex/Gender Related Similarities and Differences in fMRI Language Research." *Brain Research Reviews*, 61(2): 49–59.

Khalili, Hossein, Jodi Hall, and Sandra DeLuca. 2014. "Historical Analysis of Professionalism in Western Societies: Implications for Interprofessional Education and Collaborative Practice." *Journal of Interprofessional Care*, 28(2): 92–97.

Martin, Carol Lynn, et al. 2013. "The Role of Sex of Peers and Gender-Typed Activities in Young Children's Peer Affiliative Networks: A Longitudinal Analysis of Selection and Influence." *Child Development*, 84(3): 921–937.

Peletz, Michael G. 2006. "Transgenderism and Gender Pluralism in Southeast Asia since Early Modern Times." *Current Anthropology*, 47(2): 309–340.

Rudman, Laurie A., and Peter Glick. 2008. *The Social Psychology of Gender: How Power and Intimacy Shape Gender Relations*. New York: Guilford Press.

Shohat, Ella. 2002. "Area Studies, Gender Studies, and the Cartographies of Knowledge." *Social Text*, 20(3): 67–78.

FURTHER READING

Fausto-Sterling, Anne. 2012. *Sex/Gender: Biology in a Social World*. New York: Routledge and Kegan Paul.

DeLamater, John D., and Janet Shibley Hyde. 1998. "Essentialism vs. Social Constructionism in the Study of Human Sexuality." *Journal of Sex Research*, 35(1): 10–18.

Sexism

JULIA C. BECKER
Philipps-University Marburg, Germany

In comparison to how gender relations were considered 50 years ago, a shift away from considerable inequality to emerging gender equality can be observed – particularly in economically wealthier countries. However, gender discrimination is still prevalent around the world (see Glick et al. 2000; Swim et al. 2009) and reflected in women's underrepresentation in decision-making positions (e.g., in parliaments, in leadership positions), in the ongoing gender-specific division of labor, in violence against women, and in diverse forms of interpersonal everyday discrimination against women.

Sexism as a social psychological construct has been conceptualized from narrow definitions to broader and more refined assessments. Before the 1990s sexism was mainly characterized as an obvious and old-fashioned form of anti-female prejudice reflected in negative attitudes and beliefs about women. Today, sexism is defined as individuals' beliefs and behaviors or institutional practices that either reflect negative evaluations of individuals based upon their sex or promote unequal status between women and men (Swim and Hyers 2009). Although sexism can be directed at all genders, it is mostly a systematic discrimination of women. This broader definition of sexism includes more subtle and ostensibly positive beliefs about women. This entry focuses on three types of contemporary sexism, namely modern sexism, neosexism, and ambivalent sexism (see also Becker 2014).

Modern sexism (Swim et al. 1995) and neosexism (Tougas et al. 1995) measure hidden prejudice against women. Both concepts comprise denial of continued discrimination against women (e.g., "Discrimination against women is no longer a problem in the United States," Swim et al. 1995), negative reactions to complaints about inequality (e.g., "Women's requests in terms of equality between the sexes are simply exaggerated," Tougas et al. 1995), and resistance to efforts addressing sexism (e.g., "Over the past few years, women have gotten more from the government than they deserve," Tougas et al. 1995). Thus, both of these beliefs represent resistance to efforts made in the direction of addressing the problem of sexism and imply an inclination to maintaining current gender relations. In line with this, modern and neosexism are associated with a rejection of affirmative action programs, negative evaluations of feminists, and less endorsement of egalitarian values. Thus, modern and neosexist beliefs can be regarded as legitimizing ideologies that provide justification for existing social arrangements and status differences between women and men.

The third concept – ambivalent sexism (Glick and Fiske 1996) – explains how women can be loved and oppressed at the same time. Thus, ambivalent sexism theory takes into account that sexism is not necessarily only negative (as has been suggested in earlier research) but can also appear under the guise of chivalry.

Ambivalent sexism is comprised of hostile and benevolent sexism (Glick and Fiske 1996). Hostile sexism is the negative expression – grounded in the fear that women use their sexuality and feminist ideology to obtain control over men. Benevolent sexism is the subjectively positive expression – grounded in the beliefs that women should be protected and financially provided for by men (paternalism), that women are the "better" sex (women are characterized as morally superior to men), and that every man needs to have a woman whom he adores.

Although these benevolent beliefs appear in a positive light and many women feel flattered by being cherished, complimented, and protected, they have insidious downsides. Specifically, a characterization of women as wonderful and in need of protection goes along with the belief that women are weak, incompetent, and childlike. Thus, benevolent sexist ideology predisposes women for low-status roles. Moreover, research has indicted several negative consequences of benevolent sexism for the individual woman as well as women as a social category. For instance, women who are exposed to benevolent sexism decrease their cognitive performance and are less interested in engaging in collective action in order to change gender inequality (Becker and Wright 2011). Furthermore, women are more likely to accept discriminatory behavior from their intimate partners if the behavior was justified in a benevolent way.

Interestingly, research shows that benevolent and hostile sexism are positively correlated and that most women and men either accept or reject both forms of sexism, whereas the "pure benevolent sexists" (those who endorse benevolent but reject hostile sexism) as well as the "pure hostile sexists" (those who endorse hostile but reject benevolent sexism) are rare exceptions in society. Moreover, although men are more likely to endorse hostile sexist beliefs compared to women, women often show a stronger endorsement of benevolent sexist beliefs.

In sum, benevolent sexist beliefs reinforce patriarchy and work in concert with hostile sexism to stabilize gender inequality.

SEE ALSO: Affirmative Action; Gender Belief System/Gender Ideology; Gender Bias; Gender Stereotypes

REFERENCES

Becker, Julia C. 2014. "Sexism." In *Encyclopedia of Critical Psychology*, edited by Thomas Teo, 1727–1731. New York: Springer.

Becker, Julia C., and Stephen C. Wright. 2011. "Yet Another Dark Side of Chivalry: Benevolent

Sexism Undermines and Hostile Sexism Motivates Collective Action for Social Change." *Journal of Personality and Social Psychology*, 101: 62–77.

Glick, Peter, and Susan T. Fiske. 1996. "The Ambivalent Sexism Inventory: Differentiating Hostile and Benevolent Sexism." *Journal of Personality and Social Psychology*, 70: 491–512.

Glick, Peter, Susan T. Fiske, et al. 2000. "Beyond Prejudice as Simple Antipathy: Hostile and Benevolent Sexism across Cultures." *Journal of Personality and Social Psychology*, 79: 763–775.

Swim, Janet K., Kathryn J. Aikin, Wayne S. Hall, and Barbara A. Hunter. 1995. "Sexism and Racism: Old-Fashioned and Modern Prejudices." *Journal of Personality and Social Psychology*, 68: 199–214.

Swim, Janet K., Julia C. Becker, Elizabeth Lee, and Eden-Renée Pruitt. 2009. "Sexism Reloaded: Worldwide Evidence for its Endorsement, Expression, and Emergence in Multiple Contexts." In *Handbook of Diversity in Feminist Psychology*, edited by Hope Landrine and Nancy Felipe Russo, 137–172. Washington, DC: American Psychological Association.

Swim, Janet K., and Lauri L. Hyers. 2009. "Sexism." In *Handbook of Prejudice, Stereotyping, and Discrimination*, edited by Todd D. Nelson, 407–430. New York: Psychology Press.

Tougas, Francine, Rupert Brown, Ann M. Beaton, and Stéphane Joly. 1995. "Neosexism: Plus ça change, plus c'est pareil." *Personality and Social Psychology Bulletin*, 21: 842–849.

Sexism in Language

ANN WEATHERALL
Victoria University of Wellington, New Zealand

The topic of sexism in language emerged from feminist criticism of bias against women in language structures and in its use. Publications dating back to the late nineteenth century show women protesting against the negative and unequal treatment of women in language. The issues they raised included the ways women were addressed using diminutive forms, the practice of women and not men changing their name on marriage, and the trivialization of women's speech. However, it was with the women's movement, starting in the 1960s, that sustained criticism of male bias in language was undertaken. The area is a controversial one. There are disagreements over whether aspects of language identified by feminists are really sexist, what constitutes non-sexist language, and even whether the issue is one worth bothering about because language change will follow social change and not the reverse.

Robin Lakoff's *Language and Woman's Place* (1975), alongside other important feminist publications in fields including education, philosophy, and psychology, discussed the broad range of ways that language reflected the secondary social status of women. The features identified included the greater number of negative and demeaning terms for women than men; equivalent terms having more derogatory and sexualized connotations in the feminine form than the masculine one (e.g., bachelor versus spinster; slut versus stud; master versus mistress; she versus he is a professional), and in English the ways words are marked as feminine (e.g., the addition of -ess or -ette endings have diminutive connotations). Early work in the area also included observations about gender and interaction that were considered sexist. Examples included men interrupting women, the patronizing use of touch by men (e.g., bottom slaps), and street remarks that were directed at women (such as wolf whistles), which were considered both rude and objectifying. Another practice considered sexist was calling adult women "girls" and "ladies."

One of the single most controversial, well-researched, and ongoing issues in the area of sexism in language is the use of words marked as masculine to refer to people in general or to include women (e.g., manmade, postman). The matter at stake is whether this kind of male bias in language reflects women's secondary status in society or if it also plays a role in perpetuating it. Weatherall (2002) reviewed studies that provide convincing evidence that the use of masculine generic terms does have a negative impact. For example, women do not apply for jobs when they are advertised using masculine generic forms of titles and women's recall of written material using masculine generic terms is worse than when the same material is written using more neutral language.

Evidence that sexist language does indeed have a negative impact on women supports calls for non-sexist language policies. Feminist language planning has successfully resulted in some publishers, universities, and other professional organizations having guidelines and formal policies for gender. Gender-inclusive language (e.g., chairpersons, humans, people) is typically recommended. Wiley-Blackwell, the publisher of this Encyclopedia, rightfully instructs contributors to "avoid gendered language."

One aspect of sexism in language is the particular words that are used to refer to women and men. A more elusive aspect of language is the use of metaphors. Research has documented bias in the kinds of metaphors used to refer to women and men. For example, animal metaphors are used to refer to both women and men. However, the ones used to refer to women tend to be domesticated and compliant animals (e.g., women as chicks, cows, and mares), while metaphors for men use wild animals (e.g., tiger) and ones that communicate sexual virility (e.g., stud). Sexual metaphors tend to objectify women (e.g., honeypot, candy) or construe them passively in sexual acts (e.g., getting laid). In business settings, the common use of militaristic metaphors (e.g., going into battle) and sporting metaphors supports a masculine worldview that is not only possibly misogynistic, but also offputting for women who enter those workplaces.

How women are treated in the media is another facet of sexism in language. It has been repeatedly found that in newspapers and other written publications, powerful women (e.g., prime ministers, elite athletes, and chief executives of multinational companies) more often are reported on in terms of how they look and their family status than men in similar positions. A different but related issue is how their success is talked about. Studies of gender and sports commentary have found a bias where female sporting success tends to be described in terms of luck, but male success is explained in terms of their natural ability.

The issue of sexism in language remains a live one. Over time the number of languages being examined has increased and now includes French, Spanish, German, and Chinese. Ever-increasing arrays of linguistic contexts are documented for the use of language that negatively defines and stereotypes women. There are also studies of changes in language over time, indicating some changes for the better and some for the worse. The issue of linguistic bias has also become broader to include language use that derogates people on the basis of their sexuality – for example homophobic insults. The continuing relevance of issues of sexism and bias in language shows that the early feminist view that language issues are political issues remains valid today.

SEE ALSO: Androcentrism; Animality and Women; Discourse and Gender; Language and Gender; Non-Sexist Language Use

REFERENCES

Lakoff, Robin. 1975. *Language and Woman's Place*. New York: Harper and Row.
Weatherall, Ann. 2002. *Gender, Language and Discourse*. London: Routledge.

FURTHER READING

Bucholtz, Mary. 2004. *Language and Woman's Place: Text and Commentaries*. Oxford: Oxford University Press.

Gill, Rosalind. 2007. *Gender and the Media*. Cambridge: Polity.

Kramarae, Cheris, and Paula A. Treichler. 1985. *A Feminist Dictionary*. London: Pandora.

Mills, Sara, and Louise Mullany. 2011. *Language, Gender and Feminism*. London: Routledge.

Spender, Dale. 1980. *Manmade Language*. London: Routledge.

Thorne, Barrie, Cheris Kramarae, and Nancy Henley, eds. 1983. *Language, Gender and Society*. Rowley, MA: Newbury House.

Sexology and Psychological Sex Research

DAVID L. ROWL, DEVIN M. PINKSTON, and HOLLY M. REED
Valparaiso University, USA

THE SCOPE OF SEXOLOGY

The domain of sexology – translated quite literally as the "study of sex" – and sex research is broad and interdisciplinary. Academically, sexology spans the physical, biological, psychological/behavioral, and social sciences, as well as subdomains of these disciplines (e.g., biomedical sciences, sexual development, epidemiology and public health, and so on). Sexology generally assumes a *scientific* and *scholarly* approach to the understanding of human sexuality, and most commonly includes subject matter related to human sexual attitudes, interests, behaviors, development, problems, and aberrations, approached from any perspective along the biopsychosocial continuum. This approach, however, does not exclude analysis of other information and documents; for example, an anthropologist might attempt to understand cultural aspects of sexology in ethnic, national, or racial subgroups by examining various sources, including customs and laws, literature, art, religious tenets, and narrative histories. And this approach does not assume that human sexuality can be understood only by studying humans. Studies using non-human species may help inform processes in humans that would otherwise be unethical to investigate, for example, the potential for androgen binding in telencephalic regions of the human brain. Nevertheless, most research in sexology focuses on variables within the aforementioned topics, viewing them as outcomes, predictors, or covariates in studies that attempt to better understand sexual attitudes, behavior, function, or problems, as well as etiology and development, and causes and effects. Studies may be either qualitative or quantitative in nature, including narrative, observational, correlational, and experimental methodologies.

Sexology as a distinct discipline had its recent origins primarily in Western scientific thought, beginning in the latter half of the nineteenth century. Although not generally considered an appropriate topic for study – scientific or otherwise – during its earliest years, the study of human sexuality was led by bold researchers such as Richard von Kraft-Ebbing, Havelock Ellis, and Sigmund Freud. By the beginning of the twentieth century, however, sexology had become institutionalized, particularly in Germany, through the establishment of professional societies, journals, libraries, congresses, and courses of academic study. Post World War II, the focus of study shifted to other parts of Europe and expanded to the United States, most notably with the studies by Kinsey (1953) and, later, Masters and Johnson (1966). Today, the field of sexology encompasses topics of sexual and reproductive systems, sexual health and disease, sexual relationships and intimacy, sexual response and dysfunction, gender and gender identity, sexual orientation, sexual development, pregnancy and childbirth, and sexual paraphilia and legal issues. Moreover, sexology enjoys a position of respect in higher education in most nations – represented by academic departments, faculty appointments, majors and minors, undergraduate and graduate degrees, and a host of journals.

PSYCHOSEXUAL DEVELOPMENT

Sexual development, one of the earlier documented achievements of sexology, begins while the fetus is still in the womb and is initially directed by genetic influences and later by hormonal influences that differentiate both the bodies and brains of males and females at the time of birth. Early in life, infants and young children develop their capacity for attachment which may later affect their interest in and ability for establishing deep, secure relationships, including those involving sexual intimacy. Although overt sexuality is not prevalent until puberty, sexual development continues through latent processes. It is natural, for example, for toddlers to touch and fondle their sexual organs, behavior that is less about sexuality and more about exploring their body and finding pleasure. Young children are curious about those that are different from them, including the "opposite sex." Children play "doctor" or "house" as a way of discovering sex differences and similarities in each other. While sex play diminishes around 9 years old, the curiosity does not. Such play activities also serve as a social reference point, as young children learn to be like the people in their lives that mean most to them. Modeling from parents, along with parental and social reinforcement, often guide psychosexual processes during these stages of childhood and early adolescence.

For girls, puberty starts, on average, around 10–12 years old, whereas puberty for boys does not start until 12–14 years. Menarche, a girl's first menstrual period, is the culmination of many preceding endocrine and physiological changes, but is usually identified as the defining mark of puberty. The age of menarche in Western countries has decreased by several years over the past centuries, an effect generally attributed to better nutrition.

In both sexes, puberty is brought on by the activating effects of gonadal hormones, primarily estrogen in girls and androgens in boys, commencing as the result of hypothalamic brain stimulation of the pituitary gland. These steroid hormones from the gonads (ovaries in girls, testes in boys) are responsible both for accelerated body growth and eventually for closing bone epiphyses, thus terminating further elongation of the bones and preventing further growth. As girls go through puberty, fat begins to settle around the butt and hips, and breasts and pubic hair begin to grow. For boys, puberty is evidenced by muscle growth, body and facial hair, the growth of the testicles, scrotum, penis, and prostate gland, a process that is typically completed by about age 15 years.

Puberty changes how boys and girls view each other, and this developmental period typically marks the beginning of true sexual urges. Overt sexual activities begin in adolescence, as three out of four male teens have masturbated before 18 years old; by age 19, 60 percent of teens have engaged in vaginal intercourse. However, early-age partnered sexual experiences may be detrimental, as they can interfere with other important developmental tasks such as education. Early sexual activity onset is also correlated with higher incidence of depressive symptoms. Delayed sexual engagement, however, also has its downside, being associated with lower positive well-being. However, early and late sexual onset are correlated with numerous other factors, including social group membership, so precisely which factors are causal and which are merely correlative is not well understood.

In Western culture, 18–25 years old is typically the stage during which a person has more sexual partners than at any other time. By the time a person reaches full adulthood (26–39 years), 95 percent have participated in premarital sex and 66 percent have cohabitated. The first few years of marriage are typically the most sexually active years in a person's life, although late adulthood (40–59 years) does not instigate a sharp decline in sexual activities. Menopause signifies a woman's end to her periods, occurring naturally between the ages of 44 and 55. Men experience lower levels of testosterone beginning around the age of 55 – commonly referred to andropause although, unlike menopause, it has no distinct marker. Declining sexual hormones do not necessarily signal the end of sexual activity. On the contrary, 60 percent of adults over 70 years are still sexually active, despite ageist stereotypes. Past the age of 70, as men and women confront significant health issues, sexual activity typically declines substantially.

Cross-culturally, substantial variation occurs in patterns of psychosexual development. For example, adolescent brides may be considered the norm – meaning that the age of sexual activity onset may be younger in some populations or cultures; arranged marriages may alter expectations regarding courtship or romance, polygyny or other mating patterns may be permitted, extramarital liaisons may be prohibited and severely punished, and non-heterosexual behaviors during development may be more or less tolerated.

ISSUES CONFRONTED BY ADOLESCENTS AND YOUNG ADULTS

Adolescent sexual identity develops within the context of gender role stereotypes and sexual scripts received from individuals and institutions – particularly schools and religious organizations – within culture (Grose, Grabe, and Kohfeldt 2014). Reproductive and sexual health are often positioned within a broader social context of patriarchy, reflecting the social arrangement of males as the dominant group over the female group. These normative beliefs of traditional ideologies of masculinity (e.g., superiority) and femininity (e.g., passivity) are interconnected, and inform adolescents of the standards of male and female behavior. Moreover, women in more traditional relationships are more likely to experience forced sex by their partners and have less ability to negotiate safer sex, and they are more susceptible to unwanted pregnancies. Reciprocally, adolescent boys with more traditional beliefs of masculinity report more sexual partners, less consistent condom use, less belief that men too have responsibility to prevent pregnancy, and less intimacy in relationships. Some countries such as Norway have, for example, addressed issues of gender equity head on very successfully and instituted programs that reinforce healthy gender roles, thereby diminishing risk to girls and women; other countries retain systems of marginal equity or non-equity, placing girls and women in much more vulnerable positions.

Sex education also plays an essential role in adolescent sexual development. For example, STDs (sexually transmitted diseases) are more likely to affect sexually active adolescents and young adults than sexually mature individuals, who tend to have fewer sexual partners and engage in more stable, long-term relationships (Halpern 2010). Increasing knowledge about the consequences of sexual intercourse can provide a platform for lowering rates of STDs. STDs have been linked to certain behavioral characteristics: for example, adolescents that are defiant against authority are more likely to contract a STD.

Open communication channels with parental figures increase the chances of teens asking questions about sex before partaking and therefore decrease the risk of an STD. These open lines of communication encourage young adults to think about their actions before following through with their plans (Ryan et al. 2007). Future STD research needs to include same-sex couples and individuals with cognitive and emotional deficits, with the goal of improving sexual health in specific vulnerable populations.

Various events during child and adolescent development may lead to mental health and psychosocial issues later in life (Fergusson, Boden, and Hornwood 2008). Childhood sexual abuse, for example, is associated with increased rates of psychological disorders and adjustment problems, as well as more specific sexual complaints including sexual dysfunction, promiscuity, and, in the case of girls/women, vaginismus and dyspareunia. Females are typically at a higher risk of exposure to both sexual and physical abuse, and are more likely to report sexual problems as a result. With adequate and timely counseling and treatment, however, many of the negative consequences of abuse can be overcome.

SEXUAL HEALTH AND RELATIONSHIPS

In its early years, much of sexology focused on sexual disorders and sexual psychopathy, in some instances attempting to normalize what might have been considered abnormal (e.g., masturbation), in others attempting to catalog and enumerate specific behaviors (e.g., prostitution, homosexuality). In recent years, attention has included the study of healthy sexual relationships, including their psychological and physical benefits. For example, Sternberg sets forth critical elements of a healthy relationship, including passion, intimacy, and commitment (Sternberg and Barnes 1988). Others have demonstrated the power of sexual intimacy in maintaining a strong and lasting emotional bond, as well as in promoting good physical health and increased longevity. Sexual activity, for example, can assist in promoting and maintaining good relationships through shared intimate and rewarding experiences, heightened emotionality and passion, and a sense of exclusivity and trust. On the other hand, sex has its downsides when used as a means of control or power within the relationship, when done solely out of feelings of obligation, or when partners become frustrated because they are unable to communicate openly about their sexual needs. Sexual engagements outside of the primary relationship also have the potential to erode trust between the couple and compromise the relationship.

SEXUAL RESPONSE

Sexological research witnessed significant strides through the work of Kinsey, Masters and Johnson, and Kaplan. Their work provided descriptive and detailed analysis of sexual attitudes and sexual response. Sexual response itself is complex, requiring specific preconditions, incorporating a variety of behavioral responses, and including an array of psychosocial and interpersonal factors that relate to emotional, cognitive, and relationship dimensions. However, for purposes of simplification, it is usually divided into three phases: *desire*, *arousal*, and *orgasm* (Kinsey 1953; Masters and Johnson 1966; Kaplan 1979). More recent refinement distinguishes "unprompted" or "spontaneous" desire from arousability, the latter referring to sexual desire derived from a specific individual, object, or context. Further conceptualization has included separate pain–pleasure dimensions as well as attention to the feelings, motivations, and attitudes that surround sexual acts and relationships. While the various components of the sexual response cycle are essentially the same across the sexes, they may be manifested differently as the result of different genital structures. For example, in men genital arousal is manifested by penile erection; the analogous response in women is vaginal lubrication and clitoral erection. In addition, as is apparent later in this entry, sexual *dysfunctions* related to each component of the sexual response cycle are distributed differently across men and women, with men having greater problems with erection and ejaculating too quickly, and women having greater problems with sexual desire and reaching orgasm.

The above segmenting of the sexual response cycle into specific phases is helpful to health professionals because problems with each phase have their own etiology and causes and therefore may require their own specific treatment. Nevertheless, these categorizations have little meaning for most lay people who view their sexual experiences as holistic events that are either "satisfying or not satisfying." Furthermore, although an individual or couple may be dissatisfied with their sexual response and relationship, this does not necessarily signal a dysfunction – specific criteria are used for diagnosing a sexual dysfunction, and unless an individual meets those criteria, he or she may have a sexual problem or be "sexually dissatisfied," but not "sexually dysfunctional."

SEXUAL DYSFUNCTIONS

Any number of conditions or situations may interfere with normal sexual functioning and response, and understanding such problems constitutes an important area of sexological research. When sexual function is compromised, some men and women seek the help of an expert – typically a physician or counselor. Evaluation of the problem involves an analysis of the specific sexual problem, including severity, etiology, and factors associated with its maintenance. Such evaluations often include a medical and a psychosexual history that includes the individual's sexual partner (Rowland 2012). The first step in the process requires identifying a specific problem, typically associated with one of the phases of the sexual response cycle (desire, arousal, orgasm). For men, dysfunctions include low sexual desire, erectile and arousal difficulties, orgasmic difficulties (premature ejaculation, inhibited orgasms/ejaculation), or some combination of these. For women, the dysfunctions include low sexual desire, female sexual arousal disorder, female orgasmic disorder, sexual aversion disorder,

Table 1 Cataloguing of common sexual dysfunctions and related parameters

Disorder type	Name	Estimated prevalence	Physiological	Psychological	Relational	Age
Arousal disorders	Erectile dysfunction	5–50%	+++	++	+	+++
	Female arousal disorder	3–30%	+	++	++	++
Orgasmic disorders	Premature ejaculation	5–30%	++	+	+	+
	Anorgasmia (women)	20–30%	+	++	++	+
Low sexual desire	Hypoactive sexual desire disorder (men)	13–28%	+++	+	++	++
	Hypoactive sexual desire disorder (women)	26–43%	++	++	++	+

Key: Relevance to etiological influence: + mild, ++ moderate, +++ strong dyspareunia, and vaginismus, although these categorizations are likely to be modified in updated diagnostic manuals (Meana 2012) (Table 1). Furthermore, in non-Western countries, men's and women's sexual issues may be interpreted within the framework of other social values – for example, in India men may suffer Dhat syndrome, where sexual problems may be connected to concerns about the excessive loss of "valuable" semen; or in strongly patriarchal systems where women's sexuality (and therefore women's enjoyment of sex) is controlled through genital cutting.

Many sexual disorders can be diagnosed with the aid of validated self-administered tests that assess both somatic and psychological issues related to the problem. Whether issues are pathophysiological, psychological, or relationship based, a holistic strategy is often the best approach for both diagnosis and treatment. For any dysfunction, the level of distress, bother, or dissatisfaction regarding sexual response and function is usually important, both insofar as leading the individual to seek help and also for a clinical diagnosis of the problem. Identifying etiological factors sometimes serves as a marker for other health problems; for example, erectile dysfunction may be a marker for general cardiovascular disease. When a diagnostic process indicates co-morbidities, primary and secondary factors need to be clarified to determine which symptoms should be tackled first. By taking a holistic approach, the healthcare provider is better able to understand factors that may contribute to the sexual dysfunction and dissatisfaction and to devise, along with the patient, a more effective treatment plan.

TREATMENT OF SEXUAL PROBLEMS

To effectively treat sexual dysfunctions in men and women, healthcare providers can offer a variety of options, depending on the specific dysfunction. Possibilities include oral medications, biomedical treatments, bibliotherapy, individual sex therapy and counseling, and couples marital and/or sex therapy; all represent clinical "tools" that can be used to find the treatment most suitable for the patient and his/her partner (Rowland 2012). Over the past two decades, sexological research has made substantial gains regarding the treatment of male sexual dysfunction; however, the same cannot be said about women (Meana 2012). Many of their sexual problems go unnoticed because of lack of symptoms or because women are reluctant to seek treatment, having the impression that their problems are to be expected or are otherwise difficult or impossible to treat.

Education about sexual problems as well as open lines of communication between the couple constitutes a first important step in the resolution of sexual problems, dispelling myths and embarrassment that often accompany dysfunctional states. Erectile dysfunction and premature ejaculation most often lead men to seek help, and both conditions are readily treated using physiological/ pharmacological options, psychosexual counseling, or a combination of these therapies. Women are more likely to seek treatment for issues regarding lack of sexual desire and anorgasmia. For women, pharmacological options are limited (with only one FDA-approved treatment – flibanserin – for low sexual desire), but because relationship issues often play a pivotal role in their problems, psychosexual and couples counseling can have positive results. Of course, even within a supportive dyadic relationship, women may experience problems. A variety of treatment options can be implemented, including genital self-exploration, sensate focused procedures, stimulus control and behavioral activation, sexual fantasizing, directive masturbation, and lifestyle modification. With the help of the partner in a therapeutic context, women can often achieve (or regain) sexual satisfaction.

GENDER IDENTITY

The formation of gender identity is neither simple nor well understood, but prenatal (uterine) hormonal environment and sex of rearing have both been implicated. A fetus has the capacity to become male or female up until the seventh week of pregnancy, raising the question as to whether a person's identity is primarily nature driven or primarily nurture driven. Prenatal hormonal environment not only differentiates male and female bodies, but also produces "male" and "female" brains. To the extent that such differentiated brains affect childhood and adult functioning and behavior is not fully understood, but such brain differences may contribute to the establishment of specific cognitive abilities and preferences (sexual and non-sexual), behavioral tendencies, group identifications, and gender identity. Gender assignment and sex of rearing usually reinforce and reward identities already under development, often leading to the choices one makes regarding recreational, academic, occupational, and relationship activities (Egan and Perry 2001).

Thus, gender identity is a multidimensional construct encompassing individuals' membership within a gender category, their identification and compatibility with his or her gender group (e.g., self-perceptions of gender typicality and feelings of contentment with one's gender), pressures of gender conformity, and attitudes toward gender groups. Numerous investigations have explored gender identity in children and adults, comparing their self-perception of identity to masculine and feminine stereotypes. Children's and adults' adjustment appears optimal when individuals perceive themselves as having a mix of instrumental (masculine, task-oriented) and expressive (feminine, person-oriented) traits, although a bias toward instrumental traits and better adjustment is common in many Western countries.

For most individuals, biological sex, sex of rearing, and gender identity are all consistent with one another. Disorders in gender identity include biological, psychological, and cultural components. For example, incomplete differentiation as male or female may result in ambiguous genitalia and subsequent lack of confidence regarding gender identity. Gender identity disorder (GID) occurs when a child, adolescent, or adult displays an array of sex-typed behaviors that signal strong identification with the "opposite" sex, typically a condition leading to significant distress.

When disparity does occur among biological, psychological, and cultural components – originally thought to be a rarity but now appearing to be on the rise with the relaxation of strict sex/gender roles – various approaches may be taken. A typically Western "medical/disease" approach may attempt to "fix" the problem by making the "abnormal" once again "normal." In this scenario, adolescents and adults may opt for some or all steps (e.g., hormone therapy and/or gender reassignment) leading to transgender (transsexual) identification. However, the process of gender crossover typically occurs under the careful supervision of healthcare specialists and spans a period of several years that require trial, acclimation, and acceptance of incremental steps toward the "opposite" sex role. However, despite popular attention elicited by this condition in the media, research support and investigation have been limited in comparison with other disorders.

However, long before people sought Western-style medical solutions to help the "varied become less varied," cultures and societies found ways to recognize, accept, and incorporate variation in gender (Nanda 2008). Thus, many cultures have long recognized such diversity, as seen in the Hijras in India, the Travestis in Brazil, and the Kathoey in Thailand where such individuals are given an integrated (and sometimes special) role within society. Even in Western countries, binary gender categories are rapidly blurring, as issues of sexual orientation and transgender become increasingly discussed and vetted. On the other hand, through customs and laws, people of many countries continue to treat individuals expressing non-normative gender or sexual orientation behaviors with fear and disrespect. Indeed, in the worst scenarios, such variations may lead to imprisonment or capital punishment.

Sexual orientation

Typically categorized as heterosexual, homosexual, or bisexual, the origin of sexual orientation is unclear. Today, issues surrounding sexual orientation are not only scientific, but cultural, religious, and political as well. Attempts to identify specific genes or genetic markers have met with limited success. Identical twin studies suggest both genetic/biological and psychological/cultural contributions, as do studies that link specific prenatal hormonal environments to same- or opposite-sex orientation. Common thought currently suggests that no one single factor can account for homosexuality or bisexuality but that a combination of social, familial, environmental, endocrine, and genetic factors work together in as yet undefined ways. Indeed, so long as the understanding of factors leading to heterosexual orientation remains unknown, the origins of homosexuality and bisexuality are likely to remain elusive as well. To date, research seems to suggest that, whether biological or learned, individuals do not choose their orientation so much as come to realize it during their psychosexual development.

PARAPHILIA, CRIMINOLOGY, AND SEX LAWS

One of the most challenging areas of sexology relates to the understanding of paraphilia. Paraphilia refer to sexual arousal/behaviors that occur in inappropriate situations, or with inappropriate objects or people. The study of paraphilia raises questions about what is normal, what is psychopathological, what is a cultural variant, and what is healthy (Marshall, Marshall, and Serran 2006). Thus, the assumption is made that there exists a "natural," evolutionary grounded and cross-culturally invariant sexual development, which results in a normal sexual object choice with another adult human being. Normalcy of behavior is constituted by what society governs as permissible, and also by what is legal. Most types of paraphilia are not illegal, leaving a grey area when assessing when the behavior becomes unhealthy. However, one important criterion is whether or not the participating individuals do or can give consent. Paraphilia can be classified into different categories: those involving objects, people, or situations (Table 2).

Sexological research on paraphilia has focused on two issues: (1) whether various paraphilia have common etiologies and/or are likely to be more common among certain personality types; and (2) effective treatment strategies that enable those with paraphilia to replace unhealthy or injurious behaviors with

Table 2 Examples of paraphilia by classification

Objects	People	Situations
Fetishes	Rape	Exhibitionism
Bondage	Pedophilia	Voyeurism
Transvestitism	Bestiality	Sadism
	Necrophilia	Masochism

more socially acceptable sexual behaviors. Moderate progress has been made on both fronts, but scientifically this area of sexology is still in its infancy.

Some paraphilic behaviors are illegal, although wide variation occurs across nations and cultures, and laws are seldom enforced consistently (Sorrentino 2008). "Sex offenders" in the United States are sometimes demonized in the media and within law enforcement, perhaps even downplaying the potential value of rehabilitation – with proper counseling, recidivism rates following treatment tend to be lower for paraphilia than various other criminal activities (e.g., drug use) (Allison 2008). While most felony convictions engender infringements of an individual's rights and opportunities upon release, no other type of offense results in such pervasive post-release requirements than for sexual offenders. In the 1930s, the first generation of sex offender legislation originated in the form of sexual psychopath laws. The public criticized such laws, however, when the premature release of offenders resulted in sexual recidivism. In 1996, Megan's Law was signed, mandating all 50 states to develop requirements for convicted sex offenders to register with local law enforcement agencies and to notify the community.

As societal norms change, various laws regarding "normal" sexual behavior come and go. For example, sodomy laws were designed to prohibit sexual practices considered morally wrong. However, laws that criminalize sodomy have been criticized for suppressing the diversity of human sexuality by using criminal justice systems to confine activity to heterosexual vaginal intercourse. With the involvement of the gay rights movements, political persuasion, and the normalcy of sodomy practice by both heterosexual and homosexual communities, sodomy laws were eventually deemed unconstitutional.

CONCLUDING REMARK

This entry provides a brief overview of several topics and issues related to sexology and sex research. Many other topics fall into the realm of sexology and sex research, including the study of special populations (e.g., the disabled, the elderly, the diseased); contraception, pregnancy, and childbirth; pornography; sex trafficking; sexual addictions; and so on. In many cases, these topics can be subsumed under the broader topics mentioned above.

SEE ALSO: Adolescent Pregnancy; Gender Dysphoria; Gender Identification; Gender Identity, Theories of; Sex Reassignment Surgery; Intimacy and Sexual Relationships; Sexual Identity and Orientation; Sexually Transmitted Infections

REFERENCES

Allison, Gary D. 2008. "Sanctioning Sodomy: The Supreme Court Liberates Gay Sex and Limits State Power to Vindicate the Moral Sentiments of the People." *Tulsa Law Review*, 39: 65–105.

Egan, Susan K., and David G. Perry. 2001. "Gender Identity: A Multidimensional Analysis with Implications for Psychosocial Adjustment." *Developmental Psychology*, 37(4): 451. DOI: 10.1037/0012-1649.37.4.451.

Fergusson, David, Joseph Boden, and John Hornwood. 2008. "Exposure to Childhood Sexual and Physical Abuse and Adjustment in Early Adulthood." *Child Abuse and Neglect*, 32: 607–619. DOI: 10.1016/j.chiabu.2006.12.018.

Grose, Rose Grace, Shelly Grabe, and Danielle Kohfeldt. 2014. "Sexual Education, Gender Ideology, and Youth Sexual Empowerment." *Journal of Sex Research*, 51(7): 742–753. DOI: 10.1080/00224499.2013.809511.

Halpern, Carolyn T. 2010. "Reframing Research on Adolescent Sexuality: Healthy Sexual Development as Part of the Life Course." *Perspective on Sexual and Reproductive Health*, 42: 6–7. DOI: 10.1363/4200610.

Kaplan, Helen S. 1979. *Disorders of Sexual Desire*. New York: Taylor and Francis.

Kinsey, Alfred Charles. 1953. *Sexual Behavior in the Human Female*. Bloomington: Indiana University Press.

Marshall, W. L., L. E. Marshall, and G. A. Serran. 2006. "Strategies in the Treatment of Paraphilias: A Critical Review." *Annual Review of Sex Research*, 17: 162–182. DOI: 10.1080/10532528.2006.10559841.

Masters, William H., and Virginia E. Johnson. 1966. *Human Sexual Response*. Boston: Little, Brown.

Meana, Marta. 2012. *Sexual Dysfunction in Women*. Cambridge: Hogrefe Publishing.

Nanda, Serena. 2008. "Cross-cultural Issues." In *Handbook of Sexual and Gender Identity Disorders*, edited by David L. Rowland and Luca Incrocci, 457–485. Hoboken: John Wiley & Sons.

Rowland, David. 2012. *Sexual Dysfunction in Men*. Cambridge: Hogrefe Publishing.

Ryan, Suzanne, Kerry Franzetta, Jennifer Manlove, and Emily Holcombe. 2007. "Adolescents' Discussions about Contraception or STDs with Partners Before First Sex." *Perspective on Sexual and Reproductive Health*, 39: 149–157. DOI: 10.1363/3914907.

Sorrentino, Renee. 2008. "Legal and Privacy Issues Surrounding Sexual Disorders." In *Handbook of Sexual and Gender Identity Disorders*, edited by David L. Rowland and Luca Incrocci, 603–657. Hoboken: Wiley & Sons.

Sternberg, Robert, and Michael L. Barnes, eds. 1988. *The Psychology of Love*. New Haven: Yale University Press.

FURTHER READING

Laws, D. Richard, and William O'Donohue. 2008. *Sexual Deviance: Theory, Assessment, and Treatment*. New York: Guilford Press.

Lightfoot, Cynthia, Michael Cole, and Sheila Cole. 2008. *The Development of Children*. New York: Worth Publishers.

Reis, Elizabeth, ed. 2012. *American Sexual Histories*, 2nd ed. Hoboken: John Wiley & Sons.

Society for the Scientific Study of Sexuality. "What Sexual Scientists Know." Accessed April 17, 2014, at http://www.sexscience.org/resources/what_sexual_scientists_know/.

Weinberg, Thomas, and Staci Newmahr. 2014. *Selves, Symbols, and Sexualities: An Interactionist Anthology*. Thousand Oaks, CA: Sage.

Sexual Addiction

DENTON CALLANDER
University of New South Wales, Australia

Sexual addiction is a psychiatric condition that describes out of control or excessive behaviors, thoughts, or desires relating to sex. Historically, sexual addiction has been conceptualized in many ways and has had many names, such as nymphomania (for women) and satyrism (for men), but contemporary terminology tends to favor hypersexuality. The idea of sexual addiction, particularly when employed as a diagnostic label, is highly contested and many question whether it is appropriate to classify expressions of sexuality as "excessive." Debate also exists around whether it is best represented as an addiction, and some competing theories categorize excessive sexual behavior as a form of impulse control or obsessive-compulsive disorder. Although there have been many claims about the prevalence of sexual addiction in general populations, such claims are rarely substantiated with empirical evidence. Similarly, claims that sexual addiction is on the rise have not been supported by verifiable data.

Sexual addiction can be expressed through sex with other people but can also involve solo activities, such as masturbating, viewing pornography, or engaging in fantasy. Although no formal diagnostic criteria exist, there are many proposed ways of measuring, assessing, and characterizing sexual addiction. Common themes across such criteria include the use of sexual activity in response to anxiety and depression, interference of sexual activity in daily life, engaging in sexual activity with disregard for distress to self or others, and unsuccessful efforts to control sexual activity. Proposed diagnostic criteria commonly refer to context and individual circumstance as a way of understanding excess in terms of sex. What is an indicator of sexual addiction in one person may, for another, be a healthy and normalized part of their sexual life. Although there have been attempts to establish quantified markers of hypersexuality (see Kafka 2010), diagnosis remains largely under the miscellaneous psychological category of "sexual disorder not otherwise classified."

The lack of formal and empirically supported diagnostic criteria of sexual addiction may lead to over- or misdiagnosis. Sexual addiction may be particularly prone to clinical misdiagnosis because it is often conflated with other addictions, such as alcoholism, and with other mental conditions, such as obsessive-compulsive disorder. Improper self-diagnosis is also a risk, due partly to the large number of popular media accounts on sexual addiction, many of which have focused on the experiences of prominent "sex addicts" from the fields of sport, film, and politics. A number of readily available online diagnostic tools may also contribute to self-misdiagnosis.

Differing definitions of what constitutes normal and excessive in terms of sexual practice continue to plague efforts to diagnose and define sexual addiction. Although context and circumstance are commonly highlighted as key to appropriately diagnosing sexual addiction, many treatment programs and resources continue to define sexual expression in narrow and heteronormative terms. Portrayals of sexual addiction as a "disorder of intimacy" or a "relationship disorder" raise the issue of how society understands sex and the moral judgments that are applied to sex for pleasure, casual sex, and sex as a form of expression. By pathologizing aspects of sexual practice, the very idea that one can be addicted to sex may invite strong feelings of shame upon those who believe or are told to believe that their practices are harmful or abnormal. Such pathologization creates a therapeutic market and those who champion sexual addiction as a mental disorder often stand to benefit financially from its growing prominence.

Programs aimed at helping people overcome their addiction to sex started appearing in the mid-1970s. Such programs borrowed from the 12 steps of addiction recovery introduced by Alcoholics Anonymous, and modern treatment options continue to guide sex addicts through a similar recovery process that often incorporates aspects of religion. Public awareness of and interest in sexual addiction was awakened in the 1980s, largely through the writing of Patrick Carnes. Carnes's work continues to advocate for sexual behavior as susceptible to addiction and for 12-step approaches to recovery. Such approaches aim for "sexual sobriety," which has diverse meanings depending on the specific program and can range from no sexual activity whatsoever (including masturbation) to sexual activity only within the bounds of a monogamous relationship. Through processes such as admitting powerlessness over sex and apologizing to those harmed by sex, 12-step programs of recovery aim to improve how individuals understand self-worth, love, and sex. Neurochemical treatments that decrease libido have also been suggested to combat sexual addiction, but their effectiveness is not yet clear.

The Internet has been implicated as a key facilitator of sexual addiction because of the convenience with which it makes available countless sexual channels. For some, sexual addiction is based entirely around online sexual practices and a growing field of research and therapy has been developed to assist with the struggles of excessive online sexual activity. Sex addicts may use the Internet to view pornography, organize offline sexual encounters, or engage in sexual chatting. For some, however, such online behaviors may be a "virtual" way to engage normally with sex and sexuality. Other factors that have been linked to sexual addiction include a dysfunctional family life during childhood and a familial history of addiction (not necessarily sexual). It has also been suggested that those who experience sexual abuse in childhood may be more likely to become addicted to sex.

SEE ALSO: Cybersex; Heteronormativity and Homonormativity; Pornography, Feminist Legal and Political Debates on

REFERENCE

Kafka, Martin P. 2010. "Hypersexual Disorders: A Proposed Diagnosis for DSM-V." *Archives of Sexual Behavior*, 39: 377–400.

FURTHER READING

Carnes, Patrick. 2001. *Out of the Shadows: Understanding Sexual Addiction*. Center City, MS: Hazelden.
Ley, David. 2012. *The Myth of Sex Addiction*. Lanham: Rowman & Littlefield.
Reay, Barry, Nina Attwood, and Claire Gooder. 2013. "Inventing Sex: The Short History of Sex Addiction." *Sexuality and Culture*, 17: 1–19.

Sexual Assault/Sexual Violence

SARAH E. ULLMAN and MEGHNA BHAT
University of Illinois at Chicago, USA

Sexual violence is a serious, pervasive form of violence against women that affects women across all ages, social class, ethnicity, marital status, and national origin. The United Nations (UN) defines sexual violence as "being forced to have sexual intercourse without your consent, or because you feared of what your perpetrator or partner may do to you, or/and being sexually coerced to do something humiliating or degrading" (World Health Organization 2013, 6). Any person regardless of the relationship, in any setting, can perpetrate sexual violence. In addition, rape is defined as the physically forced or otherwise coerced penetration of the vulva or anus with a penis, other body part, or object. Sexual violence can include both physical or/and sexual violence perpetrated by a partner or a non-partner.

The high-profile gang rape cases of women in India in the mid 2010s and their victimization stirred public protests, public debates, and legal discussions among citizens, women's agencies, and human rights advocates. These cases of sexual violence highlighted the traumatic consequences of sexual violence on women and their families. Scholars assert that although sexual assault cases are universally underreported, reports of sexual violence in the news focus primarily on sexual assaults by strangers, not by intimate partners or spouses (*Japan Times* 2014). It should be remembered that women experience different forms of sexual violence in their daily lives in both public and private spaces.

According to the World Health Organization (2013), globally, 7 percent of women have been sexually assaulted by someone other than a partner, but there is less data on the health impact of non-partner sexual violence. Still, non-partner sexual violence is harmful, with women survivors of such violence over twice as likely as non-victims to have alcohol use disorders, and to experience depression or anxiety.

The sub-Saharan African countries (such as the Democratic Republic of Congo) are ranked the highest in rates of sexual violence followed by southern sub-Saharan Africa (Namibia, South Africa, Zimbabwe), North African and Middle Eastern countries (Turkey), and South Asian countries (India, Bangladesh) (Ghosh 2014). According to a report on world estimates of intimate partner and non-partner sexual violence by the World Health Organization (2013), approximately 35 percent of women across the globe reported experiencing either physical and/or sexual intimate partner violence or non-partner sexual violence.

Another form of sexual violence is street harassment – any action or comment between strangers in public places that is disrespectful, unwelcome, threatening, and/or harassing and that is motivated by gender. A 2010 study in New Delhi, India, found that 66 percent of women experienced sexual harassment at least two to five times annually in public spaces like the bus, train, and stores. Common examples of harassment included lewd verbal comments, leering at women and groping, touching, or leaning toward women (Jagori and UN Women 2010). Furthermore, a report by the UN General Assembly (2006) suggested that 40–50 percent of women in European Union nations experienced unwanted sexual, physical, and other forms of sexual harassment in their workplaces.

Some research on global sexual violence has examined perpetration. In a non-representative survey conducted in Phnom Penh, Cambodia, 47.4 percent out of 376 young men reported that they were willing to coerce their partner into having sexual intercourse on Valentine's Day. Another study in Cambodia indicated one in five men confessed to raping at least once in their life, and, most disturbingly, 50 percent of them had perpetrated sexual aggression at age 20 or younger (Hodal 2014). In a UN study of male perpetration of violence against women in Asia Pacific countries (Fulu et al. 2013), it was found that intimate partner rape was more common than non-partner rape, rape perpetration started early in life, most men were motivated by sexual entitlement, and had child abuse experiences. Men's rape of women was associated with having more sex partners, engaging in transactional sex, using physical violence against female partners, men's own victimization, and participation in violence outside the home.

Sexual violence is associated with serious and chronic debilitating physical and mental health consequences for the victims. Additionally, victims of sexual violence are also susceptible to mental illness, suicidal ideation, eating disorders, emotional stress, physical injuries, unintended pregnancies or abortions, and exposure to HIV infections (Japan Times 2014).

Unfortunately, most cases of sexual violence are not reported and, if they are investigated, most perpetrators never face any legal consequences; convictions are rare in such cases. According to the report by Fulu et al. (2013), 72–97 percent of men who perpetrated rape received no criminal sentence. In fact, those men who perpetrated intimate partner rape faced fewer legal consequences than men who perpetrated non-partner rape. These alarming findings suggest how the law trivializes marital rape, despite its high prevalence and serious consequences for women.

Violence against women emerged into the international limelight due to grassroots initiatives, violence prevention programs, and advocacy efforts by global feminist movements, women's agencies, and various stakeholders. It is very important to acknowledge and address the fact that violence against women is deeply rooted in gender inequality, patriarchy, and the historical context of the subordinate position of women in society (United Nations 2006). However, there is still a long way to go to achieve equality and social justice for women by implementing policies and laws protecting to protect them and their fundamental human right to be free of sexual violence.

SEE ALSO: Intimate Partner Abuse; Psychology of Gender: History and

Development of the Field; Rape Law; Violence Against Women in Global Perspective

REFERENCES

Fulu, Emma, et al. 2013. "Why Do Some Men Use Violence Against Women and How Can We Prevent It?" Quantitative Findings from the United Nations Multi-country Study on Men and Violence in Asia and the Pacific. Bangkok: UNDP, UNFPA, UN Women and UNV. Accessed August 14, 2015, at http://www.asia-pacific.undp.org/content/rbap/en/home/library/gender-equality/why-men-use-vaw-report.html.

Ghosh, Subir. 2014. "Non-Partner Sexual Violence in India among Lowest in World, Say Researchers." DNA India, February 13, 2014. Accessed February 25, 2014, at http://www.dnaindia.com/india/report-non-partner-sexual-violence-in-india-among-lowest-in-world-say-researchers-1961833.

Hodal, Kate. 2014. "Cambodian Valentine's Survey Raises Concerns over Rape and Sexual Violence." The Guardian, February 13, 2014. Accessed February 24, 2014, at http://www.theguardian.com/world/2014/feb/13/cambodia-valentine-survey-rape.

Jagori and UN Women. 2010. Safe Cities Free of Violence against Women and Girls Initiative: Report on the Baseline Survey. Accessed February 10, 2014, at http://jagori.org/wp-content/uploads/2011/03/Baseline-Survey_layout_for-Print_12_03_2011.pdf.

Japan Times. 2014. "Grim Global Stats on Sexual Assault." Accessed February 15, 2014, at http://www.japantimes.co.jp/opinion/2014/02/22/editorials/grim-global-stats-on-sexual-assault/#.Uw0vn2RDtOo.

World Health Organization. 2013. Global and Regional Estimates of Violence against Women: Prevalence and Health Effects of Intimate Partner Violence and Non-Partner Sexual Violence. Accessed February 21, 2014, at http://apps.who.int/iris/bitstream/10665/85239/1/9789241564625_eng.pdf.

United Nations. 2006. In-depth Study on All Forms of Violence against Women: Report of the Secretary-General. Accessed February 24, 2014, at http://www.un.org/ga/search/view_doc.asp?symbol=A/61/122/Add.1.

FURTHER READING

LaViolette, Alyce D., and Ola W. Barnett. 2014. It Could Happen to Anyone: Why Battered Women Stay. Thousand Oaks, CA: Sage.

Renzetti, Claire M., Jeffrey L. Edersen, and Raquel Kennedy Bergen, eds. 2011. Sourcebook on Violence against Women. New Delhi, India: Sage.

UN General Assembly. 2006. "In-depth Study on All Forms of Violence against Women: Report of the Secretary-General," A/61/122/Add.1, p. 42. New York. Accessed February 24, 2014, at http://www.unwomen.org/en/what-we-do/ending-violence-against-women/facts-and-figures#sthash.1v5Mh1N5.dpuf.

Sexual Citizenship in the Caribbean

RUTH NINA-ESTRELLA
University of Puerto Rico, Río Piedras Campus, Puerto Rico

Sexual citizenship (Evans 1993) refers to citizenship that enunciates, facilitates, defends, and promotes the access of citizens to the effective exercise of their rights, both sexual and reproductive, and to a political subjectivity that is not diminished by inequalities based on sex, gender, and reproductive capacity. Sexual citizenship as an ideal and an analytic lens allows greater understanding of the ways that democracies are predominantly heteronormative and structured according to rules and regulations that grant greater privileges to ideal sexual citizens who serve the interests of the state, typically heterosexual individuals in monogamous reproductive marital unions. Protections and privileges are thus systematically denied to other more vulnerable groups such as unmarried women, children and young people, and lesbian, gay, bisexual, and transgender (LGBT) populations.

Over a decade ago the notion of sexual citizenship began to provide a discursive foundation for addressing sexuality in relation to the state and civil society, filling a vacuum with reference to sexual rights, sexual health, and the need for greater social legitimacy and security of groups socially excluded on the basis of sexuality. It is through sexual citizenship that the following are recognized: (1) the diversity of sexualities and genders, whose expression changes dynamically at different times and in different contexts of each person's life; and (2) the rights of all citizens in general, with the effective support of laws, policies, and guarantees of non-discrimination. From this perspective sexuality becomes a political issue, and therefore a public affair, so it becomes necessary to begin to reflect on its democratization and exercise from the view of citizenship. The concept of sexual citizenship implies democracy, which refers to people having rights to live their sexuality and, at the same time, also be critical of existing sexuality-based oppressions. Central to the concept of sexual citizenship are the necessity of civic participation and the recognition and enforcement of rights. Rights that have more relevance to sexuality are: the right to physical integrity, health, non-discrimination, sexual diversity, freedom of sexual expression, and reproductive law (Richardson 1998).

Since the 1990s, sexual citizenship struggles have become more visible in Latin America and in the Caribbean region, as evidenced by varieties of social movements that have begun to address the issues of the rights violations of groups marginalized on the basis of gender and sexuality. Such movements have been integral to the process of reexamining meanings of sex, gender, and sexuality, both their configurations within modern nation-states and how they are implicated in constructions of citizenship.

Sexuality in the Caribbean follows heteronormativity, which determines not only heterosexual practices but also homosexual practices, while creating a moral hierarchy distinguishing between good and bad sexual citizens.

The discussion of sexual citizenship in the Caribbean focuses on access to rights, the laws that organize and shelter rights, and the struggles to acquire rights. In the Caribbean region, the struggle for the democratization of sexuality has evolved in the last decade mainly due to three factors: (1) the absence of legislation or public policies that protect the sexual rights of vulnerable groups; (2) responses to restrictive or oppressive cultural and social beliefs concerning appropriate sexual conduct and sexual practice, as this is a barrier to the advancement of sexual rights; and (3) short-term political opportunities that have emerged, in which sexual rights have been discussed and included in public policy and legal reform programs.

Some authors describe Caribbean sexualities as simultaneously hypervisible and obscured: sexuality is celebrated in popular culture and is considered an important ingredient in Caribbean social life, yet at the same time it is shrouded in double meaning, secrecy, and shame. Also, Caribbean sexualities are powerfully organized by patriarchal heteronormativity, even in cases such as bisexuality and same-sex relations. Important issues in the struggle for sexual citizenship in the Caribbean context include sexual and reproductive rights, HIV/AIDS prevention and education, and rights and protections for the LGBT community.

SEXUAL AND REPRODUCTIVE RIGHTS

Sexual and reproductive rights are recognized as an integral part of the public agenda. To that effect, most of the countries of the Caribbean have established standards and legislation to protect the right to sexual and reproductive health, responding primarily to international agreements since the 1990s.

There is, however, a huge gap between these standards and actual practices.

For example, family planning is almost universal in the region, which accounts for the decrease in birth rates with the exception of adolescent pregnancies. However, family planning is seen as a private matter, given the present laws and public policies that govern sexual behavior. Furthermore, the supply of birth control methods is not homogeneous in the region, Haiti being an example of a country where birth control methods are scarcely available. The rate of use of birth control methods is between 45 and 70 percent in countries where they are least used, Cuba and Puerto Rico being countries with the highest use, accounting for rates above 75 percent. Diverse factors are understood to have contributed to these rates, such as urbanization, increased education, media communication, and the modern acceptance of birth control. The lack of information regarding sources of birth control methods, poor support by the state, and cultural or religious values or norms are factors that can lead to a decision of not using birth control.

Questions over rights to abortion have generated intense debates, with contradictory positions between different people and social forces (feminists, religious groups, actors in the field of health, policy, and civil society) in all countries. Completely dichotomous groups have surfaced with some groups in favor of the decriminalization of its practice and others in favor of the ban. Among the countries of the region there are those where abortion is strictly forbidden (Haiti and Dominican Republic), others where it is authorized at the request of the woman (Barbados, Cuba, Guadeloupe, Martinique, St. Martin, and Puerto Rico), and finally, countries where abortion is authorized under certain conditions (Antigua, Dominica, Grenada, St. Kitts and Nevis, St. Lucia, Trinidad and Tobago, Barbados, Belize, and St. Vincent and the Grenadines).

Sexual violence against women affects a significant percentage of women and girls in the Caribbean. St. Vincent and the Grenadines show a higher than average rate of rape. At least 48 percent of adolescent girls report sexual initiation to be forced or somewhat forced in Caribbean countries. Violence to women is seen as a way in which Caribbean men seek to maintain patriarchal power, and sex becomes a primary means to exert control over and to inflict physical harm on women.

Sexual economic exchanges involve arrangements that have been described in three principal modalities: (1) prostitution or commercial sex work, (2) sex tourism, and (3) transactional sex, which involve a deliberate exchange of sex for some form of material goods and social status. Of these, the most prominent according to regional studies is sex tourism, particularly in the Dominican Republic and Jamaica. The stigmas, moral disapproval, and discrimination against persons who are engaged in sex work and other forms of sexual economic exchange are maintained in most Caribbean countries by legislation that criminalizes the commercialization of sex (i.e., prostitution) and by policies and international campaigns to combat the trafficking of persons.

HIV/AIDS PREVENTION AND SEXUAL EDUCATION

Recently, it was recognized that the inconsistency of public policies on sex education, the scarcity of resources, and the difficult implementation of projects affect the impact of educational programs. There are also diverse experiences regarding sex education and HIV/AIDS prevention programs in the region. However, a few common problems can be identified: the quality of education, its link with the preparation of teachers, and the implementation of these programs.

Sexual education is limited because it is oblivious to current debates on sexual rights, and the sociocultural context of sexuality is seen to be profoundly linked to gender relations. In terms of policies on sex education in the schools of the region, it is observed that most of the Caribbean countries do not have sex education policies, including Antigua and Barbuda, Bahamas, Barbados, Jamaica, St. Lucia, and Trinidad and Tobago. The exceptions are Dominican Republic, Cuba, and Puerto Rico, which recognize the rights of the adolescent population and the significance of receiving sex education. In these countries the programs focus more on family planning, on the labor rights of pregnant women, and the rules of family responsibility. However, public policy does not guarantee that the issues relevant to the prevention of HIV will be taught at schools.

In most of the countries of the region, sex education and educational programs for the prevention of HIV/AIDS are responsibilities of the state, with the exception of St. Lucia, where it is established that the family is primarily responsible for sex education. Sex education is addressed as part of the curriculum in other subjects, such as biology, rather than as a specific subject, and the teacher assumes the primary role of being the person responsible for transmitting most of the information. The issue of discrimination by sexual preference or orientation is not included in the school curricula.

On the other hand, among the countries that have granted rights in terms of sex education, Cuba is an example, establishing sex education as a state policy. Since 1996 Cuban schools have provided national sex education with a gender perspective and a program on prevention. In this way sex education was extended at all levels of the national education system (SNE) through the project "For a happy and responsible sex education," having an emphasis on high school and a gender perspective as its central axis.

The situation of Puerto Rico is worthy of mention as one of the contradictions arising in the region, being a territory of the United States. Law 149, the Organic Law of the Department of Education, recognizes the state's responsibility in the development and formation of students in their physical, mental, social, emotional, and moral aspects. The curricula are based on required information from research studies that identify the factors that lead to risky sexual behaviors. At the same time, programs are limited by conflicting positions that put morality and personal values ahead of the transmission of information based on scientific sex education. However, there is no regulation or policy requiring that all directors of the system maintain a uniform standard with regard to the implementation of the school curriculum.

In terms of educational programs on HIV/AIDS prevention, every country has some kind of legal framework to protect and promote human rights and combat discriminatory practices. Some anti-discrimination laws are based on national constitutions. Among the countries that contain protection laws related to HIV are Cuba, Bahamas, Dominican Republic, Puerto Rico, Dominica, St. Lucia, and Grenada. By contrast, areas where there are no rules or laws are St. Kitts and Nevis, Haiti, Antigua and Barbuda, Barbados, and St. Vincent and the Grenadines. HIV/AIDS programs have been developed on the premise that this group poses a particular health risk to the rest of the population. Social-cultural factors that influence sexual behavior are usually not taken into account. Religious groups are considered to be an obstacle to the development of adequate interventions for the LGBT community and for the development of public policy on HIV/AIDS.

LGBT COMMUNITY

Despite laws and agreements for the protection of human rights – which outlaw discrimination, intolerance, marginalization, and exclusion – LGBT persons in the Caribbean community are among the region's most vulnerable groups. In addition, there are no international agreements that may protect persons belonging to this community, which has led to these communities suffering exclusion and discrimination in a wide range of situations in their daily lives.

The reality is that most of the countries of the region lack a national plan for education, protection, and promotion of human rights. Also, religion exerts a strong influence, especially sectors of the fundamentalist right, which intervene in the laws or legislation that affect this population. It is also important to understand that there is widespread homophobia (Toro Alonso 2007) in the Caribbean. Its manifestations and variants are seen continuously in many contexts of everyday life, feeding prejudice, discrimination, and inequality.

In much of the Caribbean region there is an absence of public policies targeted to serve the LGBT community, which demonstrates how the state actively and passively helps legitimize discrimination and marginalization.

The prevailing situation in the Caribbean today is one of contrasts; there are differences between the English- and Spanish-speaking Caribbean. While countries like Cuba and Puerto Rico have experienced advances in favor of the rights of LGBT communities, in the English Caribbean there are laws that criminalize an individual's lesbian/gay status, and there is open demonstration of homophobia, as in the case of Jamaica. In this country gay, bisexual, and transgender people face a high degree of social rejection, violence, and legal sanctions. Sex between men is illegal and punished by up to 10 years in prison.

Antigua, Barbados, St. Vincent, Dominica, Grenada, Jamaica, St. Kitts and Nevis, St. Lucia, and Trinidad and Tobago prohibit relationships between people of the same sex, especially among men. Penalties imposed for this offense range from 10 to 50 years, depending on the laws of each country. In the cases of Grenada, St. Kitts and Nevis, Jamaica, and St. Lucia, only male homosexuality is punished, while these countries' current statutes allow, or simply are silent about, lesbianism. Since 1976, Trinidad and Tobago have prevented homosexual people from entering their territory. Due to the criminalization of homosexuality and the few historical links between some of these countries, activism and sexual rights movements remain scattered in this area. In countries with Spanish heritage, the situation varies from one nation to another; for example, in Cuba there is a proposed measure in parliament to recognize the unions of same-sex couples and their economic rights, as well as recognition of transgender as a legitimate expression of sexuality. Furthermore, some people have been able, with support from the state, to have sex change operations officially.

Since 2003 in Puerto Rico, criminalization of homosexuality has been removed by way of its new Civil Code, which has enabled greater visibility of the sector. To date, laws have been passed to prohibit discrimination based on sexual orientation in employment; domestic violence protection has been extended to include same-sex couples; and health insurance has been extended to unmarried couples living together, bringing refuge to a population that has previously lived without any legal protection.

In 2015, the Supreme Court of the United States legalized same-sex marriage. This historic decision makes same-sex marriage a constitutional right nationwide. Puerto

Rico is a territory of the United States and the island was forced to recognize gay marriage. The Department of the Family allows homosexuals to adopt children.

In contrast, although homosexuality is somewhat more acceptable socially in the Dominican Republic than other countries, manifestations of gay pride are systematically prohibited, although homosexual tourism is openly encouraged. Also, LGBT behavior is considered by many mental health professionals in the Dominican Republic as a mental disorder, exposing criteria and ideologies contrary to those established by the World Health Organization (WHO) and conducting practices directed at curing homosexuality by so-called repair therapies and even electric shocks. All this occurs with no competent state agency to regulate the situation. Religious groups of some power (e.g., Opus Dei and fundamentalist evangelicals) have created a hostile environment against the gay community, with an increase in violent acts.

In spite of advances in countries where state policies protect the sexual rights of citizens in the community, there is still a lack of recognition of sexual diversity. This highlights the urgency with which government and civil society must establish developmental and solidarity plans that can serve one of the most vulnerable sectors in our society.

SEE ALSO: Sexual Rights; Universal Human Rights

REFERENCES

Evans, David. 1993. *Sexual Citizenship: The Material Construction of Sexualities.* London: Routledge.

Richardson, Diane. 2000. "Constructing Sexual Citizenship: Theorizing Sexual Rights." *Critical Social Policy*, 20(1): 105–135.

Toro Alonso, José. 2007. *Por vía de la exclusión: homofobia y ciudadanía en Puerto Rico.* San Juan: Comisión de Derechos Civiles.

FURTHER READING

Caceres, Carlos, Timothy Frasca, Mario Pecheny, and Veriano Terto, eds. 2004. *Ciudadanía Sexual en América Latina: Abriendo el Debate.* Lima: Universidad Cayetano Heredia.

Flórez, Carmen, and Victoria Soto. 2008. "El estado de la salud sexual y reproductiva en America Latina y el Caribe." *Inter-American Development Bank*, 632: 1–60.

Kempadoo, Kamala. 2009. "Caribbean Sexuality: Mapping the Field." *Caribbean Review of Gender Studies*, 3: 1–24.

Lind, Amy, and Sofía Arguello. 2009. "Ciudadanía y Sexualidades en América Latina." *Iconos: Revista de Ciencias Sociales*, 35: 13–18.

Sexual Citizenship in East Asia

JOSEPH MAN KIT CHO
The Chinese University of Hong Kong, People's Republic of China

"Sexual citizenship" is a contested term. Its definition has not yet been settled despite the fact that a great deal of intellectual effort has been devoted to it (Evans 1993; Cooper 1995; Richardson 2000). However, the competing perspectives more or less recognize that sexuality constitutes one of the fundamental bases through which citizenship and its concomitant rights – be they legal, political, social, or economic – are granted or denied. Conceptualizing sexual citizenship as a "system of rights" (Richardson 2000), it provides a clearly delineated framework that classifies rights conducive to the realization of sexual citizenship into three types: conduct-based, identity-based, and relationship-based sexual rights. Each type is further divided into subcategories. Given that Richardson gives weight to legal rights at the expense of other rights and compartmentalizes sexual rights into separate entities, her framework is the most systematic in that it allows easier comparison of the ways, and to what extent, citizens are entitled to live as sexual subjects across East Asia. The following sections will compare some major countries and regions of East Asia according to Richardson's schema of sexual rights, examining in what ways and to what extent conduct-based, identity-based, and relationship-based sexual rights are granted, restricted, curtailed, and denied.

CONDUCT-BASED SEXUAL RIGHTS

The right to participate in sexual acts is fundamental to identity-based and relationship-based sexual rights. Although acquiring a sexual identity and forming a sexual relationship with others does not necessarily involve sexual acts, the legal and social recognition of them usually implies a sanction of sexual acts as one of the means through which sexual identities and sexual relationships are grounded. In that sense, the entitlement to conduct-based sexual rights is often a condition for identity-based and relationship-based sexual rights, circumscribing the legal boundary of how we can identify and express ourselves sexually and what relationships of a sexual nature can be socially recognized.

Age of consent

As is the case in many European countries and the United States, many countries and regions in East Asia also set a legal age of consent, an age at which one is presumed to be legally competent to express consent to sex. However, the variations are great in that some simply set a legal age while others adopt a more contextual approach that takes into consideration, for example, whether money or force is involved.

Section 236 of the Criminal Law of the People's Republic of China (PRC) stipulates that sexual intercourse with girls under the age of 14 is considered rape. It is unclear whether this applies to boys under the age of 14.

Article 177 of the Japanese Penal Code prescribes that sexual intercourse with girls under the age of 13 is considered to be rape. Of particular note is that the Japanese legal regime adopts a force-based determination of rape of girls over 13 instead of the consent-based determination that is in place in Europe and the United States (West 2011, 122–127). A person can only be found guilty of committing rape of girls over 13 when violence and intimidation that s/he imposes are "remarkably difficult" for the victim to resist. Lack of consent does not automatically render an act of sexual intercourse illegal. Hong Kong Special Administrative Region, whose sovereignty was handed over to the PRC by the British government in 1997, stands in sharp contrast to Japan in regulating sexual acts. With its colonial legacy, Hong Kong adopts the British common law system and sets the age of consent at 16 for heterosexual intercourse. Similar to the PRC's Criminal Law that outlawed male homosexual sex by categorizing it as a form of hooliganism, which was repealed in 1997 (Kam 2013, 24), Hong Kong subjected same-sex sexual acts to differential (and later ruled to be discriminatory) legal regulations by criminalizing sexual acts between consenting men in private, prior to 1991. A legal reform in 1991 decriminalized it by setting a higher age of consent for anal sex between consenting men at 21, five years higher than that applied to vaginal intercourse. Two landmark court cases in 2004 and 2005 overturned the regulations on constitutional grounds, equalizing the age of consent for vaginal and anal sex at 16. The rulings also serve as a strong impetus that enables LGBT people in Hong Kong to partially secure identity-based and relationship-based sexual rights through legal means.

Taiwan, the Republic of China, adopts a sophisticated legal framework for regulating sex. Although Article 227 of its Criminal Code prescribes that sexual intercourse with a male or female under the age of 14 is illegal, the age of consent is not universally applied but subject to change from context to context. For example, person A under the age of 16 who has sexual intercourse with another person B under 14 will not be subject to criminal trial unless B makes complaints. However, it is criminal for an individual over the age of 18 to have sex with another person under the age of 14 irrespective of the other person's intention. The law also applies different sets of charges to people aged between 14 and 16. For an individual over the age of 18, it is illegal only if s/he pays to have sex with another person aged between 14 and 16. Nevertheless, in practice, the law imposes tight legal regulations on sexual acts because it makes it illegal to spread, broadcast, or issue messages in whatever format that might seduce, suggest, or make innuendos about engaging a person to have sex for money. Scholars, activists, and lawyers have gathered quite a number of cases in which people were arrested and convicted simply because of the words they chose when discussing sex online. The struggle to repeal the Act is still underway.

Sex work

In the family of conduct-based rights, there are the right to pleasure and the right to sexual self-determination. The right to pleasure is traditionally concerned with the right to gain sexual gratification without fear of punishment. People who lay claims to such a right usually demand removal of legal restrictions on sexual matter. However, sex work as one of the most common ways to gain sexual gratification has still been subject to heavy legal regulations.

In addition to this negative understanding of right to pleasure that imposes an obligation on the state or government not to interfere with people's way of gratifying themselves sexually, there are groups in Japan and Taiwan that attend to the sexual needs of people with physical disabilities (Nakamura 2014). They train sex volunteers who mainly provide masturbation service to people whose mobility has been seriously impaired. The underlying philosophy is a positive conception of the right to sexual pleasure in that its fulfillment not only requires removal of existing legal restrictions but also proactive provision of resources. While the positive understanding of the right to sexual pleasure is being developed, legal restrictions curtailing the way people gain sexual gratification have not been lifted. For example, Article 80 of The Social Order Maintenance Act of the Republic of China, Taiwan prohibits sex work. Article 81 also prohibits procuring and soliciting for the purpose of sex work.

Sex work is also a criminal offense across the strait. In 1991, the Standing Committee of the National People's Congress of the PRC came to a legally binding decision on strict prohibition against prostitution and whoring. It outlaws selling sex, buying sex, organizing prostitution for benefits, operating brothels, procuring, and soliciting. Articles 66 and 67 of The Public Security Administration Punishment Law of the PRC further impose detainment and fines as penalties. In recent years, there have been an increasing number of high-profile large-scale crack-downs in, for example, Beijing (2010) and Dongguan (2014), raiding nightclubs, bars, saunas, saloons, and other premises where sex workers gather and work. Hundreds of brothels were closed, and thousands of sex workers were arrested (Kaufman 2011).

In Hong Kong, legal regulations on sex work are more or less in line with the British laws and practices that understand sex work to be a social nuisance to be controlled but not eradicated. In that sense, sex work itself is legal, although virtually every activity connected with it is illegal. Sex workers' disadvantaged social and legal position makes them highly vulnerable to exploitation, control, and abuse by gangs as well as the police. The Crimes Ordinance of Hong Kong makes it unlawful to control people for the purpose of prostitution, to live on earnings of the prostitution of others, to let premises for use as a vice establishment, and to solicit for an immoral purpose. One-woman brothels are a unique form of sex business in Hong Kong to get around the legal regulations that prohibit organized sex work. As its name suggests, there is only one sex worker working in a given premises. Although it makes sex work survivable by exploiting the legal loophole, such a setting also renders sex workers vulnerable to the risk of robbery, violence, and even murder.

Japan adopts a lenient approach to sex work. Technically speaking, sex work per se has been illegal since the enactment of the Anti-Prostitution Law (Baishun Bōshi Hō) in 1956 (Nakamura 2014, 205). However, as sex work is narrowly defined as penetrative sexual intercourse in which a penis penetrates a vagina, many other forms of sexual acts such as oral sex, anal sex, sadomasochism, among others, are offered by sex workers. Unless there are underage sex workers, the Japanese government seldom exercises the law against sex work and clients.

IDENTITY-BASED SEXUAL RIGHTS

Identity-based sexual rights consist of the right to self-definition, the right to self-expression, and the right to self-realization. Japan has never criminalized same-sex activity. In contrast, Hong Kong and mainland China only decriminalized homosexuality in 1991 and 1997 respectively. The Chinese Psychiatry Association formally declassified homosexuality from its list of mental disorders in 2001. It is clear that realizing the three strands of identity-based sexual rights requires more than decriminalization and depathologization.

Right to non-discrimination

To be able to identify, express, organize, and experience oneself through one's sexual orientation and/or gender identity without fear of adverse consequences – be they material, social, or legal – is crucial to the right to identity. It often demands states' recognition of gender and sexuality as a basis for personhood so that people can lead their lives openly as a certain gender irrespective of their sex assigned at birth and/or lead their lives as an openly lesbian, gay, bisexual, queer person. For this, discrimination can seriously hamper the right to identity not only because it inflicts material detriment, but because it impinges upon a person's human dignity.

Japan, Hong Kong, Macau, and the People's Republic of China lack comprehensive laws that prohibit discrimination on the grounds of sexual orientation and gender identity. Republic of China, Taiwan enacted the Gender Equity Education Act in 2013 and the Act of Gender Equality in Employment in 2014, which prohibit discrimination on the basis of sexual orientation in employment and education, giving partial protection to lesbian, gay, and bisexual persons. The Gender Equity Education Act, enacted in response to the tragic death of a student who had been bullied for being gender non-conforming in 2000, also makes it compulsory for schools to design and implement curriculums that foster sex equity education in senior forms.

In Hong Kong, the Court interpreted the Hong Kong Bill of Rights, a local ratification of the International Covenant on Civil and Political Rights, and the Basic Law to protect LGBT people from discrimination. However, as these legal documents only have binding power on government and statutory bodies, discrimination in the private sector is legal. The debate over legislating against discrimination on the grounds of sexual orientation, gender identity, and intersex status is still ongoing, with LGBT groups fighting for basic human rights protection while Christian rights groups defend their rights to religion and conscience.

Japan, Taiwan, mainland China, and Hong Kong have statutory laws and administrative guidelines on determination of post-operative sex that hampers people from leading their life in the preferred sex. Transgender people diagnosed as suffering from gender identity disorder or gender dysphoria are required to undergo complete sex reassignment surgery if they are to change their legal sex, which is usually the sex assigned at birth. In other words, sterilization (i.e., removal of uterus and ovaries and reconstruction of penis for female-to-male transsexuals; removal of penis and testes and reconstruction of vagina for male-for-female transsexuals) is a prerequisite for undergoing a sex change. For example, in 2009, the government of the PRC imposed a new regulation which requires people who seek sex reassignment surgery to be over 20 years old, and to be heterosexual and free from sexual disorders. In addition, they must be diagnosed as suffering from "transsexualism" and may not be married. The requirement of sterilization is highly controversial, as it neglects the fact that that many transgender people do not desire or are not physically suitable for sex reassignment surgery.

RELATIONSHIP-BASED SEXUAL RIGHTS

There are no countries or cities in East Asia that legally recognize same-sex marriage or same-sex partnership, but developments in Taiwan are rapid. It is expected that it might be the first place in East Asia to confer some form of legal recognition on same-sex relationships. There is also momentum, although small, in mainland China that asks for same-sex marriage. For example, Li Yinhe, an outspoken sociologist in Beijing, has been petitioning the Chinese People's Political Consultative Conference of the PRC to legalize same-sex marriage since 2004. Despite her insistence, her petition always draws a blank. Hong Kong and Macau do not recognize same-sex relationships.

Recognition of same-sex relationships

In 2007, the Hong Kong government expanded the scope of protection under the Domestic Violence Ordinance to nearly all family relations, including heterosexual cohabitants but deliberately excluding same-sex cohabitants on the grounds that their relationships were not recognized by law. After rounds of protests and discussions, the government conceded and devised a new legal construct of "cohabitation relationships" into the law to protect sexual minorities and accommodate the Christian right's insistence that sex-same cohabitants should not be recognized as a family.

Same-sex cohabitants in Macau faced the same fate of not being offered legal remedies in cases of domestic violence. In 2011, the Macau government consulted the public about the legislation of the Combating Domestic Violence Law. The clause that protects same-sex cohabitants was dropped in the consultation report in 2012 on the grounds that there is no social consensus as to whether same-sex cohabitants should be considered family members.

Regarding the prospect of having same-sex relationships legally recognized, Taiwan is expected to be the first region in East Asia to do so. The Taiwan Alliance to Promote Civil Partnership Rights in 2013 proposed a set of amendments to the existing laws by recognizing same-sex marriage, setting up a partnership scheme applicable to both heterosexual and same-sex partners in a monogamous relationship, and bringing in a registration system that allows for forming family among people living under the same roof by choice rather than by marriage or blood. The proposal attracted opposition from the Christian right. It was also criticized by queer scholars and activists for privileging monogamous relationships and family in terms of allocation of rights and resources. The proposal has been brought to the Legislative Yuan of Republic of China, a statutory body that enacts, amends, and repeals laws in Taiwan for debate.

Trans marriage

In contrast, the relationship-based sexual rights of transsexual people in Hong Kong are partially secured in a hard-won landmark case, *W v. Registrar of Marriage*. In 2009, a post-operative male-to-female trans woman Ms. W was prohibited by the Registrar of Marriage from marrying her biologically male fiancé on the basis that marriage, according to law, is "the voluntary union for life of one man and one woman to the exclusion of all others." Even with an identity card that labels her a female, Ms. W was considered a male for the purpose of marriage. In her final legal challenge, the Court of Final Appeal finally granted her the right to marriage as a member of her post-operative sex category and advised the administration to enact laws modeled on the UK's Gender Recognition Act within one year when the ruling was suspended. The amendment bill that requires sterilization was voted down.

People living in East Asia have not yet enjoyed full sexual citizenship. Gay, bisexual, lesbian, and transgender people have not been protected from discrimination by comprehensive legislation. Sex work is still subject to heavy legal regulations. However, the struggle for fuller sexual citizenship in mainland China, Taiwan, Hong Kong, and Japan is vibrant and has made some milestone achievements. Breakthroughs such as legal recognition of same-sex relations and legislation against discrimination on the grounds of sexual orientation and gender identity are expected to be seen in the coming decade.

SEE ALSO: Human Rights, International Laws and Policies on; Lesbian and Gay Movements; Prostitution/Sex Work; Queer Theory; Religious Fundamentalism; Same-Sex Marriage; Sexual Orientation and the Law; Sexual Rights; Transgender Movements in International Perspective

REFERENCES

Cooper, Davina. 1995. *Power in Struggle: Feminism, Sexuality and the State*. Buckingham, UK: Open University Press.

Evans, David T. 1993. *Sexual Citizenship: The Material Construction of Sexuality*. New York: Routledge.

Kam, Lucetta Yip Lo. 2013. *Shanghai Lalas: Female Tongzhi Communities and Politics in Urban China*. China: Hong Kong University Press.

Kaufman, Joan. 2011. "HIV, Sex Work, and Civil Society in China." *Journal of Infectious Diseases*, 204: 1218–1222.

Nakamura, Karen. 2014. "Barrier-Free Brothels: Sex Volunteers, Prostitutes, and People with Disabilities." In *Capturing Contemporary Japan*, edited by Satsuki Kawano, Glenda S. Roberts, and Susan Orpett Long, 202–220. Honolulu: University of Hawai'i Press.

Richardson, Diane. 2000. "Constructing Sexual Citizenship: Theorizing Sexual Rights." *Critical Social Policy*, 20: 105–135. DOI: 10.1177/026101830002000105.

West, Mark D. 2011. *Lovesick Japan: Sex, Marriage, Romance and Law*. Ithaca, NY: Cornell University Press.

FURTHER READING

Anti-Draconian Law Alliance. (In Chinese) Accessed March 15, 2015, at http://29.antilaw.info/.

GayJapanNews, Global Rights, International Gay and Lesbian Human Rights Commission (IGLHRC) and International Human Rights Clinic, Human Rights Program, Harvard Law School. 2008. "The Violations of the Rights of Lesbian, Gay, Bisexual and Transgender Persons in Japan: A Shadow Report."

Accessed August 26, 2015, at http://iglhrc.org/sites/default/files/159-1.pdf.

Immigration Department, The Government of the Hong Kong Special Administrative Region. "Identity Card." Accessed March 15, 2015, at http://www.immd.gov.hk/eng/faq/faq_hkic.html.

Rainbow of Macau. 2014. "Submission of Rainbow of Macau to United Nations Committee on Economic, Social and Cultural Rights 52nd Session: Shadow Report – Macau, China." Accessed August 26, 2015, at http://tbinternet.ohchr.org/Treaties/CESCR/Shared%20Documents/MAC/INT_CESCR_CSS_MAC_17092_E.pdf.

Sexual Coercion

LISA K. WALDNER
University of St. Thomas, USA

Social scientists define sexual coercion as occurring whenever someone is pressured or forced into unwanted sexual contact. As currently conceptualized, there are two dimensions, outcome and tactic (Waldner 2011). Outcomes range from kissing on the milder end of the continuum to sexual penetration or intercourse. Perpetration tactics also range from milder forms such as verbal or psychological pressure to more severe forms such as physical force (Christopher 1988). Sexual coercion is a broad concept that includes not only behaviors that constitute rape but also unwanted kissing or sexual touching. Because forced penetration can lead to higher social, mental, and physical costs (Basile 2005), this receives more attention from researchers (e.g., Shackelford and Goetz 2004). Most sexual coercion occurs between people who know each other (Basile 2005) and often are involved in an intimate relationship.

Coercion tactics are classified as verbal/psychological or physical, but there is also a range in severity within each of these types. Verbal strategies include pleading and making false promises, with lying and the use of blackmail considered more extreme. Verbal strategies may manipulate feelings such as saying things to make someone feel guilty or attacking someone's sexual or gender identity. Physical strategies such as the use or threat of force are considered more severe than persistent touching or groping. Even the use of drugs or alcohol as a coercion strategy can range from encouraging a partner to drink excessively to the intentional use of Rohypnol or other date-rape drugs.

Research on sexual coercion began in the 1950s with the discovery that female undergraduates experienced unwanted sexual activity with male partners (Kirkpatrick and Kanin 1957). Since then, researchers have expanded the definition to include more perpetration tactics, outcomes, and victims. Although most research considers only women victimized by men, in the 1980s researchers began asking both men and women about their victimization experiences (e.g., Struckman-Johnson 1988). Most research focuses exclusively on heterosexuals but there is a growing body of research on gays and lesbians that began in the late 1980s (e.g., Waterman, Dawson, and Bologna 1989). Sexual coercion research mostly relies on victims to estimate prevalence. When perpetration is measured, the samples are predominately male.

The prevalence of sexual coercion reported by researchers varies because of differences in how sexual coercion is defined and measured. Using a behavioral checklist that includes both a continuum of tactics and sexual outcomes will yield higher prevalence rates than using only a few items with a focus on the use of physical force resulting in penetration (Waldner-Haugrud 1999). Although there is not a standard measurement for sexual coercion, the Sexual Experiences Survey (SES) is one of the most commonly used instruments (Koss et al. 2007). One clear finding is that milder forms of coercion, in terms of both outcomes and tactics, exceed severe, with more instances of unwanted kissing and the use of verbal pressure than forced penetration and the use of physical force (Waldner-Haugrud and Magruder 1995).

Although both men and women report sexual coercion, women are more likely than men to report being physically forced into unwanted sex (Basile et al. 2007). Alcohol consumption increases victimization risk for women (Ullman, Karabatos, and Koss 1999). Coercive men have less empathy for women, more experiences with child abuse, a higher acceptance of relationship violence, and a greater level of distrust and anger towards women. This is also the case for men who only report using verbally coercive tactics (DeGrue and DiLillo 2004). There has been little research on female perpetrators beyond the child sexual abuse literature, so it is difficult to assess gender differences between men and women who coerce their intimate partners.

The shift to conceptualize same-sex intimate partners as victims has not come without methodological challenges. Representative samples of gays and lesbians are much more difficult to collect compared with heterosexuals, meaning that most of the research findings on same-sex victimization cannot be generalized. Further, because measurement tools were first developed to assess female experiences with male perpetrators, these items did not easily translate to a gay male or lesbian population. Phrases having a heterosexual connotation such as sexual intercourse have been replaced in newer versions of the SES and other victimization instruments (e.g., Koss et al. 2007).

Sexual coercion research tends to be more empirical than theoretical and, because researchers come from a variety of disciplines, the theoretical concepts are also varied. Criminological approaches that emphasize routine activities or lifestyles that increase victimization risk are reflected in research assessing the role of alcohol, number of sexual partners, exposure to delinquent peers, and age of first sexual experience. A feminist perspective that considers the importance of gender ideology in reinforcing male patriarchy is implicit in work that finds that attitudes towards women and adherence to traditional gender roles are important predictors of male-perpetrated sexual coercion. Minority stress theory emphasizing the role of internalized homophobia, stigma, prejudice, and heteronormativity is currently being applied to same-sex intimate partner violence and may also be useful in understanding sexual coercion (Kuyper and Vanwesenbeeck 2011).

SEE ALSO: Domestic Violence in the United States; Emotional Abuse of Women; Patriarchy; Rape and Re-Victimization, Treatment of; Rape Culture; Sexual Assault/Sexual Violence

REFERENCES

Basile, Kathleen C. 2005. "Sexual Violence in the Lives of Girls and Women." In *Handbook of Women, Stress, and Trauma*, edited by Kathleen A. Kendall-Tacket, 101–122. New York: Brunner-Routledge.

Basile, Kathleen C., Jieru Chen, Michele C. Black, and Linda E. Saltzman. 2007. "Prevalence and Characteristics of Sexual Violence Victimization Among U.S. Adults, 2001–2003." *Violence and Victims*, 22: 437–448.

Christopher, F. Scott. 1988 "An Initial Investigation into a Continuum of Premarital Sexual Pressure." *Journal of Sex Research*, 25: 255–266.

DeGrue, Sarah, and David DiLillo. 2004. "Understand Perpetrators of Nonphysical Sexual Coercion: Characteristics of Those Who Cross the Line." *Violence and Victims*, 19: 673–688.

Kirkpatrick, Clifford, and Eugene Kanin. 1957. "Male Sex Aggression on a University Campus." *American Sociological Review*, 22: 52–58.

Koss, Mary P., et al. 2007. "Revising the SES: A Collaborative Process to Improve Assessment of Sexual Aggression and Victimization." *Psychology of Women Quarterly*, 31: 357–370.

Kuyper, Lisette, and Ine Vanwesenbeeck. 2011. "Examining Sexual Heath Differences Between Lesbian, Gay, Bisexual, and Heterosexual Adults: The Role of Sociodemographics, Sexual Behavior Characteristics, and Minority Stress." *Journal of Sex Research*, 48: 263–274.

Shackelford, Todd K., and Aaron T. Goetz. 2004. "Men's Sexual Coercion in Intimate Relationships: Development and Initial Validation of the Sexual Coercion in Intimate Relationships Scale." *Violence and Victims*, 19: 541–556.

Struckman-Johnson, Cindy. 1988. "Forced Sex on Dates: It Happens to Men, Too." *Journal of Sex Research*, 24: 234–240.

Ullman, Sarah E., George Karabatos, and Mary P. Koss. 1999. "Alcohol and Sexual Assault in a National Sample of College Women." *Journal of Interpersonal Violence*, 14: 603–625.

Waldner, Lisa K. 2011. "Sexual Politics in Intimate Relationships." In *Introducing the New Sexuality Studies*, 2nd ed., edited by Steven Seidman, Nancy Fischer, and Chet Meeks, 49–56. London: Routledge.

Waldner-Haugrud, Lisa K. 1999. "Sexual Coercion in Lesbian and Gay Relationships: A Review and Critique. *Aggression and Violent Behavior*, 4: 139–149.

Waldner-Haugrud, Lisa K., and Brian Magruder. 1995. "Male and Female Sexual Victimization in Dating Relationships: Gender Differences in Coercion Techniques and Outcomes." *Violence and Victims*, 10: 203–215.

Waterman, Cynthia K., Lori J. Dawson, and Michael J. Bologna. 1989. "Sexual Coercion in Gay Males and Lesbian Relationships: Predictors and Implications for Support Services." *Journal of Sex Research*, 26: 118–124.

FURTHER READING

Black, Michelle C., et al. 2011. *The National Intimate Partner and Sexual Violence Survey (NISVS): 2010 Summary Report*. Atlanta: National Center for Injury Prevention and Control, Centers for Disease Control and Prevention.

Muehlenhard, Charlene L. 2011. "Examining Stereotypes About Token Resistance to Sex." *Psychology of Women Quarterly*, 35: 676–683.

Sexual Contract

CAROLE PATEMAN
University of California, Los Angeles, USA

References to the sexual contract conjure up the famous idea of a social or original contract, which originated in the work of political theorists in the seventeenth and eighteenth centuries. The phrase is often used in popular political discourse to refer to an explicit or implicit agreement between a democratic state and its citizens. "The sexual contract" came into currency in political theory in the early 1990s, after the publication of *The Sexual Contract* in 1988 (Pateman 1988), and has come to be used in two senses. The specific sense refers to the arguments of the book and to Anglo-American societies; the more general sense refers to forms of domination of women by men in any society or culture.

The Sexual Contract provides a reinterpretation from a feminist perspective of classic theories of an (hypothetical) original contract, together with an analysis of actual contracts, such as the marriage contract and employment contract, showing that these familiar contracts have been shaped in part by the ideas in the classic texts. The idea of an original agreement or contract was necessary for the classic theorists because of their premise of natural individual freedom and equality. The premise opened up the question of why self-governing individuals should submit to be governed in "civil society," that is, the modern state. The justification provided was that individuals freely gave their agreement by entering into an original contract. Feminist reinterpretation shows that, rather, the original contract is two-dimensional.

One dimension is the social contract that justified government of citizens by the state. The second dimension is the sexual contract that justified the government of women by men and thus the patriarchal structure of the modern state.

Three factors helped ensure that the sexual contract was ignored. First, political theorists failed to see that modern patriarchal government is not paternal, the traditional rule of fathers over sons (e.g., Filmer 1991); instead it is fraternal, the rule of (a fraternity of) men over women, maintained and reproduced through the mechanism of contract. Second, they did not pursue the political implications of the classic theorists' claim that women, by nature, lacked the characteristics and capacities of free and equal individuals and, therefore, cannot be self-governing. Mary Astell's question, posed in 1700 – why, if all men were born free, all women were born slaves? – was never mentioned (Astell 1996 [1700]). Third, political theorists accepted that the traditional marriage contract and the employment contract were unremarkable components of a free democratic society; that is, they did not analyze the place of the political fiction of property in the person (an idea that goes back to John Locke) in these two contracts (see Locke 1988 [1690]). The claim that it is pieces of property – capacities, talents, labor power, services – that are the subject of contract, not individuals themselves, allows relationships of subordination to be presented as free relations.

In the traditional marriage contract, when a single woman said "I do," she thereby became a wife, subordinate to her husband, who decided how the property in her person should be utilized. In Anglo-American jurisdictions, it was not until the early 1990s that the last remnant of the legal powers of husbands was finally eliminated. The employment contract can be seen as the exemplification of free labor if it is held that pieces of property are for sale, not, as in slavery, a person. But it is impossible for an individual to send a piece of the property in their person to a workplace. That is the fiction. The worker has to be there too if the property is to be "employed." But workers are instructed how to use their property by a boss; by entering the employment contract, the worker becomes a subordinate. The employment contract was also central to the patriarchal structure. In Anglo-American countries, the postwar welfare state was built around paid work and men's employment. Only the latter counted as the "contribution" required for benefits, and in the occupational structure men monopolized the skilled, supervisory, and better paid jobs. Women's unpaid work was, properly, performed in the household.

The heyday of the patriarchal structures analyzed in *The Sexual Contract* extended from the 1840s to the late 1970s. Since then, a great deal has changed, including the welfare state, the introduction of anti-discrimination laws, and social mores. Marriage law is now transformed (in various European countries and US states extending to same-sex couples). The economy is also transformed by neoliberal policies; the jobs that sustained the male "breadwinner" of the traditional marriage contract have been largely swept away, the employment contract is "flexible," and economic insecurity is widespread. The majority of wives, by choice and necessity, are in the labor force. A question currently being asked is whether, given such changes, the sexual contract is irrelevant. A definitive answer is difficult; many familiar elements of the sexual contract remain. Men occupy most of the authoritative positions in politics, the economy, higher education, the judiciary, and the military. Women earn less than men, and sexual harassment is still a feature of workplaces; they undertake most of the housework and childcare (including the women paid to do this work by the more affluent). The sex industry continues to grow and violence against women remains endemic.

That "the sexual contract" is used in its second, general sense to refer to the subordination of women in many different social and cultural settings is testament to the persistence and ubiquity of men's power. It is manifested in a variety of forms that extend, for example, from preference for boy babies, opposition to the education of girls, the legal powers of husbands, exclusion of women from inheritance of land, to obstacles that prevent women from earning a living. The subjection, ill-treatment, and neglect of women and girls are now well publicized, and bodies that range from a number of United Nations agencies to a multitude of women's organizations around the globe are now working against it. Nevertheless, men's government of women is one of the most deeply entrenched of all power structures, and the sexual contract is still vigorously defended.

SEE ALSO: Sexual Rights; Sexual Slavery

REFERENCES

Astell, Mary. 1996 [1700]. "Some Reflections upon Marriage." In *Mary Astell: Political Writings*, edited by Patricia Springborg, 15. Cambridge: Cambridge University Press.

Filmer, Sir Robert. 1991 [1680]. *Filmer: Patriarcha and Other Writings*, edited by Johann P. Sommerville. Cambridge: Cambridge University Press.

Pateman, Carole. 1988. *The Sexual Contract*. Cambridge: Polity Press and Stanford: Stanford University Press.

Locke, John. 1988 [1690]. *Two Treatises of Government*, edited by Peter Laslett. Cambridge: Cambridge University Press.

FURTHER READING

Coole, Diana. 1994. "Women, Gender and Contract: Feminist Interpretations." In *The Social Contract from Hobbes to Rawls*, edited by David Boucher and Paul Kelly, 193–212. London: Routledge.

Keating, Christine. 2011. *Decolonizing Democracy: Transforming the Social Contract in India*. University Park: Pennsylvania State University Press.

Mills, Charles. 1997. *The Racial Contract*. Ithaca: Cornell University Press.

Pateman, Carole. 2007. "On Critics and Contract." In *Contract and Domination*, edited by Carole Pateman and Charles Mills, 200–229. Cambridge: Polity Press.

Patil, V. 2013. "From Patriarchy to Intersectionality: A Transnational Feminist Assessment of How Far We Have Really Come." *Signs: Journal of Women in Culture and Society*, 38(4): 847–867.

Sexual Fetishism

LOLA D. HOUSTON
University of Vermont, USA

Sexual fetishism is most commonly understood as the specific sexual interest in an object, situation, or aspect or part of a person that results in a heightened sexual state in the individual so interested. This definition is not, however, without its problems.

The word fetish may have originated in Europe and describes an object imbued with some power. Commonly, such objects are human-made and are frequently thought to have some power over others. The term sexual fetishism was first used by Alfred Binet (1887) in the late nineteenth century, a period that saw an unquestionable spike in the investigation of different aspects of human sexuality, particularly in relation to pathologies. Richard von Krafft-Ebing (1887) expanded this in *Psychopathia Sexualis*. Concurrently, fetish was frequently the subject of ethnological research in different cultures, and often had little or no relation to sexuality. In this context the object is quite different, and, in addition to the idea of it being imbued with power, it may serve specific social functions as part of specific rituals. This dichotomy illuminates a number of the issues surrounding the difficulties in defining sexual fetishism. As a result, there are two distinctly different approaches to it: the clinical and the social.

From early studies of cultures and the human condition, fetishism has generally been associated with religion and religious practices. Late nineteenth-century interest in the nature of totems, for example, analyzed their role in what were then described as "primitive" societies. Totemism was often considered in the same context with particular taboos and linked to fetishes in part because of the use and inclusion of objects into this mix. Here, the notion of a sacred or special object was key, as was the idea that symbols – usually animals – found in nature were somehow special or held religious or other social significance. It was not until the mid-twentieth century that these ideas were seriously critiqued.

More recently, social science investigations into the sexual nature of different cultures began to connect fetishism with sexuality. Even as this work progressed, the more clinical aspect of the fetish, and more specifically the sexual fetish, began to enjoy greater currency in psychology and some of the social sciences. This parallel effort between two branches of the social sciences has led to a decided disconnect between the examination of actual practices that might be termed sexual fetishes, and the clinical application of psychology to individuals who might be deemed devious or abnormal due to their sometimes obsessive interest in a particular fetish object.

Over time, then, there has been a shift in how the concept of fetish is both interpreted and analyzed, and this shift has largely been from religious or social context to a behavioral or clinical context. A number of social scientists note that the fetishizing (whether sexual or not) of an object or, more particularly, some part or aspect of a person, effectively dehumanizes the person so venerated. The work of Herdt and Stoller (1990), for example, was done in the context of a sexual ritual, but they did not specifically suggest that this was a sexual fetish, nor was there any concern noted over the activities being "perverse" or "deviant." The difficulty, then, is that today, the entire idea behind fetish, once considered as part of a cultural whole, has now been more strongly pushed into a narrow definition that links "sexual" to it, and, more commonly, that a sexual fetish is a "problem" to be diagnosed and overcome rather than taken as part of how a culture or group or even an individual functions.

The clinical application of the term has most recently undergone a very slight change in how it is used in diagnostics. In *Different Loving*, a study of dominance and submission, Brame, Brame, and Jacobs (1993) suggest that sexual fetishism is a "translocation of desire." The use of the term "desire" can be seen to move the idea of "sexual fetish" from a problem into a simple facet of human sexual behavior, something to be celebrated, perhaps, but not necessarily pathologized.

Part of the challenge of current work, whether clinical or social, is to step back from the idea that all sexual fetishism is inherently wrong or "deviant." Recent research into the practice of sexual fetishism has begun to affect both the clinical and social perspectives. Ortmann and Sprott (2012), for example, suggest that those who practice fetishism are as healthy as those who do not. Others such as Taormino (2012) provide technical advice as well as stating that fetishism can provide an intimate experience. Still others, such as Carrellas (2007), incorporate both ritual and fetish as part of a larger practice. Currently, sexual fetishism may be understood simply as something humans do and enjoy.

SEE ALSO: Sexology and Psychological Sex Research; Sexualities; Taboo

REFERENCES

Binet, Alfred. 1887. "Du fétichisme dans l'amour." *Revue Philosophique*, 24: 143–167.

Brame, Gloria G., William D. Brame, and Jon Jacobs. 1993. *Different Loving: An Exploration of the World of Sexual Dominance and Submission*. New York: Villard Books.

Carrellas, Barbara. 2007. *Urban Tantra: Sacred Sex for the Twenty-First Century*. New York: Celestial Arts.

Herdt, Gilbert H., and Robert J. Stoller. 1990. *Intimate Communications: Erotics and the Study of Culture*. New York: Columbia University Press.

Krafft-Ebing, Richard von. 1887. *Psychopathia Sexualis: mit besonderer Berücksichtigung der conträren Sexualempfindung*. Stuttgart: Ferdinand Enke.

Ortmann, David, and Richard Sprott. 2012. *Sexual Outsiders: Understanding BDSM Sexualities and Communities*. New York: Rowman & Littlefield.

Taormino, Tristan. 2012. *The Ultimate Guide to Kink: BDSM, Role Play and the Erotic Edge*. Berkeley: Cleis Press.

FURTHER READING

Baudrillard, Jean. 1981. *For a Critique of the Political Economy of the Sign*. St. Louis, MO: Telos Press.

Seidman, Steven, Nancy Fischer, and Chet Meeks. 2011. *Introducing the New Sexuality Studies*. New York: Routledge.

Steele, Valerie. 1996. *Fetish: Fashion, Sex, and Power*. New York: Oxford University Press.

Sexual Freedom, Feminist Debates in the United States on

ABBEY WILLIS
University of Connecticut, Storrs, USA

Within feminist history in the United States, sexual freedom often refers to the movement headed by Victoria Woodhull (1838–1927) who advocated for sexual freedom (or free love), which, for her, meant the freedom for women to marry and divorce at will and without social stigma. A quote from one of Woodhull's (2005) famous speeches demonstrates that her meaning of sexual freedom meant much more than simply freedom to marry and divorce:

> Women are entirely unaware of their power. Like an elephant led by a string, they are subordinated by just those who are most interested in holding them in slavery ... Sexual freedom means the abolition of prostitution both in and out of marriage, means the emancipation of woman and her coming into control of her own body, means the end of her pecuniary dependence upon man ... means the abrogation of forced pregnancy, of anti-natal murder of undesired children and the birth of love children only.

Woodhull is clearly arguing for a more holistic form of sexual freedom which involves dismantling patriarchy and fostering bodily autonomy for women. However, scholars have written against Woodhull's support of eugenics (see, for example, Woodhull 2005). The Woodhull Sexual Freedom Alliance (n.d.) continues to advocate for sexual freedom as a fundamental human right but has distanced itself as an organization from Woodhull's earlier slide into eugenics, which was fairly common at the time. The Alliance advocates for "immigration equality, reproductive justice, prison reform, anti-discrimination legislation, comprehensive nonjudgmental sexuality education, and the right to define our own families." For the Alliance, sexual freedom encompasses a holistic and intersectional analysis of the oppressive and exploitative structures which curtail all people's experiences of sexual freedom, demonstrating that the ideas of what sexual freedom actually entails has vastly expanded since Woodhull's advocacy.

The sexual revolution in the United States in the 1960s and 1970s advocated for sexual freedom or "free love" which could be experienced outside of state-sanctioned heterosexual marriage. This was a time when changing social norms were the main goals of the overall movement. For the women's movement, the birth control pill played a large part in the ability for women to make more informed decisions with their bodies, as did the legalization of abortion (with restrictions). The gay rights movement was also advocating for sexual freedom, in large part by organizing to remove the pathologizing listing of homosexuality as a mental illness in the *Diagnostic and Statistical Manual of Mental Disorders* (DSM). These were not the only goals of the women's and gay rights movements, but were seen as the more mainstream strategic goals at the time.

Moving forward in feminist history, sexual freedom is often invoked in the dialogue surrounding the feminist sex wars in the 1980s between "sex positive" feminists and "anti-porn" feminists (Duggan 1995). More generally, this divide was between what can be understood as second-wave and third-wave feminists and their disagreements around topics such as pornography, prostitution, bondage, discipline, dominance and submission, and sadomasochism (BDSM) and other kink, media representation, as well as trans inclusion in lesbian and/or "women"-only spaces and communities (see, for example, Vance 1993). These sex wars divided the feminist movement as to which views could actually create sexual freedom, that being the goal of both poles. These debates have not been "resolved" per se, but rather reproduced in newer debates and dialogues around the same issues as well as additional feminist issues such as "slut shaming."

Within the same-sex marriage debates, sexual freedom is often used as shorthand for the legalization of same-sex marriage. However, this use of sexual freedom tends to limit the meaning to the legalization of marriage between two people of the same gender as the total goal rather than but one facet of a more holistic understanding of sexual freedom advocated by political radicals such as anarchist feminists which expands on what is meant by "freedom" and what that means for understanding what sexual freedom might require.

The idea of sexual freedom has been expanded by anarchist feminists to include a critique of "rights" and "justice" which are terms that often reify and rely on state power. The notion of sexual freedom, when used by anarchist feminists, describes a rejection of all institutionalized forms of inequality and oppression which hinder the ability to explore and create sexuality. Rather than "discovering" a "repressive sexuality," these theorists critique the forms of control that produce certain types of bodies, certain types of identities and orientations (or identities and orientations at all), and certain types of desires, as well as critiquing the normative equation that is used to "tie" bodies, identities, and desires together (for more on this see the introduction in Corber and Valocchi 2003). Sexual freedom in this sense is directly tied, though not completely determined by, political economy. Sexual freedom would necessitate a collective freedom rather than individual freedoms to pursue sexuality, including but not limited to freedom to define and form families and other types of kinship; explore and develop sexualities not contained and limited by sexual orientations and identity; fully control one's own reproduction (social and familial); one's own gender identity and expression; be involved sexually or romantically with as many people as desired, free from social and institutional stigma; access and safety vis-à-vis technology to enhance one's own desires and sexual health; move beyond the borders upheld between romantic, sexual, and other forms of intimacy; to not be sexual; have full control over one's body; and many others.

These sexual freedoms, because they are tied to a critique of political economy, have the ability to move beyond the question of, for example, whether sex work is liberating or demeaning to women. In the sex wars of the 1980s, this debate was often divorced from a critique of political economy which led some "third wavers" to find "liberation" in the labor–wage relationship (in this case, sex work). Although their critique was timely since some feminists refused to believe a woman would ever "choose" sex work on their own accord, the argument that some women do "choose" (sex-)work ends up erasing not only a critique of capitalism where very few own for a living while the vast majority rent themselves for their lifetimes, but erases even the existence of capitalism within these debates around sex work – as if it did not exist at all. Sexual freedom, then, seems to be most useful when coupled with a clear articulation of what "freedom" means, which will always vary across the political spectrum, and what types of creation and destruction of the structures we live under now would have to take place to not only secure "freedom" writ large, but sexual freedom, more acutely.

SEE ALSO: Feminism, Anarchist; Feminism, Radical; Feminist Sex Wars; Heteronormativity and Homonormativity; Intersectionality; Queer Theory; Sexual Identity and Orientation; Sexual Regulation and Social Control; Sexualities

REFERENCES

Corber, Robert J., and Stephen M. Valocchi, eds. 2003. *Queer Studies: An Interdisciplinary Reader*. Malden: Blackwell.

Duggan, Lisa. 1995. *Sex Wars: Sexual Dissent and Political Culture*. New York: Routledge.

Woodhull, Victoria. 2005. *Lady Eugenist: Feminist Eugenics in the Speeches and Writings of Victoria Woodhull*, introduction by Michael W. Perry. Seattle, WA: Inkling Books.

Vance, Carole S. 1993. *Pleasure and Danger: Exploring Female Sexuality*. Kitchener, Ontario: Pandora Press.

Woodhull Sexual Freedom Alliance. (n.d.) Accessed August 7, 2015, at http://www.woodhullalliance.org/.

FURTHER READING

Armand, Emile. 2004. "Anarchist Individualism and Amorous Comradeship." Accessed August 7, 2015, at http://theanarchistlibrary.org/library/emile-armand-anarchist-individualism-and-amorous-comradeship.

Armand, Emile. 2011. "On Sexual Liberty." Accessed August 7, 2015, at http://libertarian-labyrinth.blogspot.com/2011/09/emile-armand-on-sexual-liberty.html.

Brigati, A. J., ed. 2004. *The Voltairine de Cleyre Reader*. Oakland, CA: AK Press.

Daring, C. B., J. Rogue, Deric Shannon, and Abbey Volcano, eds. 2012. *Queering Anarchism: Addressing and Undressing Power and Desire*. Oakland, CA: AK Press.

de Cleyre, Voltairine. 1908. "They Who Marry Do Ill." Accessed August 7, 2015, at http://praxeology.net/VC-MDI.htm.

Goldman, Emma. 1910. *Anarchism and Other Essays*. New York: Mother Earth Publishing.

Goldman, Emma. 1914. "Marriage and Love." Accessed August 7, 2015, at https://www.marxists.org/reference/archive/goldman/works/1914/marriage-love.htm.

Moran, Jessica. 2004. "The Firebrand and the Forging of a New Anarchism: Anarchist Communism and Free Love." Accessed August 7, 2015, at http://theanarchistlibrary.org/library/jessica-moran-the-firebrand-and-the-forging-of-a-new-anarchism-anarchist-communism-and-free-lov.

Sexual Freedom Legal Defense and Education Fund. 2015. Accessed August 7, 2015, at www.sfldef.org/.

Vaneigem, Raoul. 2007. "The Book of Pleasures." Accessed August 7, 2015, at http://voidnetwork.blogspot.com/2007/11/book-of-pleasures-by-raoul-vaneigem_09.html.

Sexual Harassment Law

AUGUSTUS BONNER COCHRAN III
Agnes Scott College, USA

Sexual harassment "has a long past but a short history" (Fitzgerald 1996, 44). Vulnerable workers – slaves, indentured servants, immigrants, domestics, women in low-skill or predominantly male occupations – suffered harassment for centuries. Yet the term was only coined in 1975, identifying a problem that law could potentially address (Baker 2008, 31).

Methodological disparities make the prevalence of sexual harassment difficult to estimate. Different definitions, approaches, samples, time and cultural frames, and perceptions undermine generalizations. Cross-national statistics vary wildly, from 17 percent in Sweden to 80–90 percent in Spain, but a review of the literature concluded that roughly 50 percent of women employees in industrialized countries are affected. Estimates of incidence in the United States range from 28 to 90 percent; a survey of surveys found a median harassment rate of 44 percent. Men are sometimes targets, although probably 90 percent of victims are women and only 1 percent of victims are harassed by women (despite the notoriety of female predators in popular media). Even the lower estimates suggest the enormity of this social pathology (Cochran 2004, 29–41).

Sexual harassment involves gender harassment, unwanted sexual attention, and sexual coercion (Beiner 2005, 33). Explanations of sexual harassment include biological or psychological theories pointing to deviant individuals, social exchange theory analyzing the costs and benefits of relationships, sex-role spillover claiming that domestic female roles sexualize some jobs, and sex-ratio theories emphasizing that pioneering women likely will be harassed in traditionally male occupations. Other theories emphasize cultural norms and discourse, for example, in explaining the exaggerated incidence and persistence of sexual harassment in the military, while others stress the key role played by organizational factors and leadership. Crouch (2001) distinguishes a naturalistic approach that understands sexual harassment as natural behavior rooted in evolutionary sexual imperatives from a liberal approach viewing sexual harassment as individual deviance based in unequal power positions that could be prevented by sociolegal norms. The structural approach emphasizes asymmetrical power and cultural stereotypes, conceiving of sexual harassment as part of broader patriarchal dominance.

Sexual harassment's deleterious effects are legion: victims suffer psychological and health problems such as stress and physical ailments, family problems, and career consequences such as low morale, absenteeism, declining job performance, and transfers or job loss, with incidental costs such as legal or medical expenses. Sexual harassment entails enormous organizational and social costs. Absenteeism, turnover, reduced productivity, training, and formalization of work regulations may cost the US economy $1 billion annually, and litigation expenses can exceed $1 million, explaining the $50 million plus per year spent settling harassment claims (Kleiman, Kass, and Samson 2003–2004, 54).

Sexual harassment law is generally seen as a success story, an example of law reforming attitudes, conduct, and organizations. It also represents a paradigmatic instance of global diffusion; US law put sexual harassment on the international agenda, but other countries have adopted their own unique approaches (Saguy 2003; Zippel 2006). While American law prohibited sexual harassment as sex discrimination, other jurisdictions conceive the problem differently. Following the French approach, a number of countries (e.g., Brazil,

Peru) have criminalized sexual harassment as an abuse of hierarchical power or violence, with attendant advantages (targeting perpetrators, serious penalties) and disadvantages (neglecting hostile environments, reluctance to impose severe penalties) (Saguy 2003; Cochran 2012). Other countries have broadened protections, prohibiting harassment motivated by any reason rather than limiting the law's protection exclusively to harassment targeting victims based on sex. Jurisdictions banning harassment generally see this behavior (often called mobbing in English-speaking jurisdictions and Scandinavia or moral harassment elsewhere) as an affront to victims' dignity. Critics of the dignitary offense approach (which has some resonance with common law torts protections) criticize it for ignoring sexist social structures, while its defenders suggest that the US model is itself individualistic, especially in its reliance on litigation for relief (MacKinnon and Siegel 2004). Emphasizing moral harassment sometimes suggests more informal preventative and remedial solutions that may be more effective, for example, Germany (Zippel 2006). Some nations (e.g., Israel, Brazil) have tried to combine approaches to benefit from the strengths of diverse models. Most international norms target violence against women rather than sexual harassment per se, but the concept of violence is often sufficiently ample to encompass sex discrimination including sexual harassment (MacKinnon and Siegel 2004). Since the US approach has exerted both early and widespread influence, American sexual harassment law is emphasized here.

Sexual harassment law presents a classic example of lawmaking by judges in a common law system. When the women's movement first brought the problem to light in the late 1970s, no national law existed in the United States that explicitly prohibited sexual harassment. Some states had laws forbidding the practice (currently, 48 states do [Hemken 2011, 648]), and torts such as battery, false imprisonment, or intentional infliction of emotional distress can be used to recover damages from perpetrators if their harassment falls within the parameters of these traditional civil wrongs, but most claims would not be covered. Amidst feminist debates about strategies to combat sexual harassment, Catharine MacKinnon (1979) suggested that sexual harassment be considered a species of sex discrimination prohibited by Title VII of the 1964 Civil Rights Act making employment discrimination "because of sex" illegal.

Early cases were not encouraging as judges sometimes conceived of the harassment as strictly a personal "frolic" of supervisors rather than company practices for which employers were liable. Sometimes judges ruled that victims suffered discrimination because of their refusal to have sex rather than "because of sex," considering that term as a categorical meaning gender. Gradually courts found employers liable for their supervisors' abuse of company authority and began to concede that harassment targeted women because of their gender. Not until 1986 did the Supreme Court officially declare sexual harassment at work a type of sex discrimination prohibited under Title VII. In *Meritor Bank v. Vinson*, Justice Rehnquist's opinion for the Court also ruled that the test for harassment was not whether the victim voluntarily submitted but, rather, whether the conduct was unwelcome. The Court also recognized that conduct of a sexual nature that does not extort sexual favors on the basis of coercion but instead "has the purpose or effect of unreasonably interfering with an individual's work performance or creating an intimidating, hostile, or offensive working environment" constitutes illegal sexual harassment, effectively banning hostile work environments as well as quid pro quo sexual harassment. The Court also held that illegal harassment had to be "sufficiently severe or pervasive 'to alter the condition of [the victim's] employment and create an abusive working environment.'" The Court refused to rule inadmissible evidence of plaintiffs' dress and sexual fantasies. On the key issue of employer liability, the Justices divided, with Rehnquist somewhat mystically admonishing lower courts to "rely on agency principles," while Justice Marshall's concurrence argued that employers should be strictly liable for harassment committed by their supervisors.

Vinson left many questions unsettled. Critics challenged the logic of burdening the victim with proving unwelcomeness instead of presuming that harassment is unwelcome unless the accused perpetrator demonstrates that the conduct was in fact welcomed. Critics also question the relevance of evidence such as dress and sexual fantasies, especially unless directly linked to the harasser. Some charge that such aspects of the law reflect male judges' implicit bias toward gender hierarchies, in particular the traditional male privilege in initiating sexual relations. Judges have also been quite reluctant to "transform Title VII into a general civility code for the American workplace" (*Oncale v. Offshore Services* 1998) and often tolerate extremely obnoxious behavior and offensive work locales by finding them insufficiently severe or persuasive to constitute illegal sexual harassment. According to one judge, "The workplace that is actionable is one that is hellish" (Kleiman, Kass, and Samson 2003–2004, 59).

The vague "severe or pervasive" requirement generated controversy, with some critics contending that this standard should be judged from the perspective of a reasonable woman rather than the usual reasonable man (updated to the more inclusive reasonable person). These advocates argue that experience as well as some research shows that men have higher tolerance for sexual conduct in the workplace and that the perspective of women, less powerful and more vulnerable in the workplace, must set a more protective prohibition (*Ellison v. Brady* 1991). In *Harris v. Forklift Systems* (1993), the Supreme Court took a different tack, spelling out a two-pronged test: for conduct to be sufficiently severe or pervasive to constitute a hostile work environment, objectively, a reasonable person must consider it abusive, and subjectively, the victim must view it as abusive. The *Harris* Court also held that psychological injury, although relevant, was unnecessary to constitute an abusive environment, but suggested that courts consider "all the circumstances," including frequency and severity, whether harassment was physical or merely verbal, and whether it interfered with the victim's work performance. Many observers considered the issue of perspective conclusively settled, but in 1998 *Oncale* announced without elaboration that Title VII prohibits "conduct which a reasonable person in the plaintiff's position would find severely hostile or abusive," seemingly establishing a reasonable victim standard that is contextual rather than gender based.

Oncale also affirmatively answered whether same-sex harassment could be illegal. Oncale was harassed not out of sexual desire but apparently because his tormenters considered him insufficiently masculine. The opinion clarified that if victims are targeted "because of sex," the genders of those involved are irrelevant. The decision's reach is unclear, as harassment based on the way victims choose to perform their gender is not easily distinguishable from homophobic motivations, but sexual orientation is not an illegal basis of discrimination under Title VII.

Vinson left open the question of employer liability for harassment practiced by supervisors, an especially critical omission because non-employers are not liable under Title VII, which prohibits discriminatory employment practices, and employers are best positioned to remedy problems. Agency principles dictated that when supervisors practiced quid pro quo harassment, they misused authority delegated by their employers, who were generally held strictly liable for this abuse. When co-workers created a hostile environment, employers were deemed liable only if found negligent, that is, if they knew or should have known about the harassment and failed to remedy it. Left murky, however, was employers' liability for unfulfilled threats or hostile environments created by supervisors. Two 1998 Supreme Court cases presenting exactly these issues, *Burlington Industries v. Ellerth* and *Faragher v. City of Boca Raton*, instituted a new approach.

Jettisoning the traditional distinction between quid pro quo and hostile environment, the Court made tangible employment actions the touchstone for employer liability. It defined a tangible employment action as "a significant change in employment status, such as hiring, firing, failing to promote, reassignment with significantly different responsibilities, or a decision causing significant change in benefits" (*Faragher*), and ruled that employers were strictly liable for harassment involving such actions. For supervisors' harassment falling short of tangible employment actions, the employer is still liable but could raise an affirmative defense if it could prove by a preponderance of the evidence two necessary elements: first, "that the employer exercised reasonable care to prevent and correct promptly any sexual harassing behavior," and second, "that the plaintiff employee unreasonably failed to take advantage of any preventative or corrective opportunities provided by the employer or to avoid harm otherwise" (*Faragher*).

Beyond work, sexual harassment arises in diverse settings, ranging from street interactions to professional relationships involving housing, medicine, counseling, and religion. The problem appears particularly widespread and serious in education. As in employment, judicial interpretations of anti-discrimination laws rather than explicit statutory prohibitions on sexual harassment in education have made such practices illegal in education.

Title IX of the 1972 Education Amendments barred sex discrimination in education programs funded with federal money. From the late 1970s courts began to interpret the anti-discrimination statute as encompassing sexual harassment. Further cases established that beyond cutting funds for programs permitting discrimination, victims had an implied private right to sue and to recover money damages. In *Gebser v. Lago Vista Independent School District* (1998), the Supreme Court delineated a high hurdle for holding school districts liable for pecuniary damages: they would not be liable for harassment by employees unless "an official who at a minimum has authority to address the alleged discrimination and to institute corrective measures on the recipient's behalf has actual knowledge of discrimination in the recipient's programs and fails adequately to respond. We think, moreover, that the response must amount to deliberate indifference to discrimination." A year later the Court ruled that districts could be responsible for student harassment of fellow students, but raised the bar even higher for establishing liability. Beyond showing actual knowledge and deliberate indifference by an authoritative official, peer harassment must be so "severe, pervasive, and objectively offensive" that it "effectively deprives the victim of access to a federally funded educational opportunity" (*Davis v. Monroe County Board of Education*).

Sexual harassment law represents a triumph for common law approaches as judges extended anti-discrimination statutes to prohibit sexual harassment in employment and education. The impact of these changes goes well beyond formal legal arenas, as the "naming and blaming" educational effects of law have transformed culture, consciousness, everyday behavior, and business practices. One illustrative success is the Ellerth/Faragher rule, which not only tightens employer liability but also provides ample incentives for employers to engage in preemptive actions to prevent sexual harassment. The vast majority of American work organizations have instituted policies and procedures and train employees in order to sustain an affirmative defense if not avoid a sexual harassment lawsuit altogether.

Yet this success is not unalloyed. Even the attempt to internalize preemptive practices in organizations has been criticized as having perverse impacts: lower courts, accepting employers' effort to prevent sexual harassment as satisfying the first affirmative defense, too often turn the spotlight on victims' behavior and require them to prove that they reasonably tried to avail themselves of employers' procedures (Beiner 2005, 149–153). Many judges demonstrate little sympathy with employees and little understanding of the context in which harassment occurs and in which victims strive to cope with its consequences. Critics charge that various aspects of sexual harassment law, for example the unwelcomeness requirement, the severe or pervasive standard, the refusal to bar damaging but irrelevant evidence, and even the failure to avail defense, represent an unconscious predilection on the part of courts to protect male prerogatives in gender relations against feared unreasonable and even unscrupulous female claimants.

An even more serious limitation on the transformative impact of sexual harassment law is its reliance on a litigation model. In practice, suing to protect individual rights is beyond the reach of most victims who, lacking resources and support, usually conclude, not unreasonably, that the benefits of suing do not justify the steep costs. Isolated individuals often discover that legal rules are not supported by the collective power necessary to translate their rights into meaningful protection.

SEE ALSO: Sex Discrimination; Sexual Assault/Sexual Violence

REFERENCES

Baker, Carrie. 2008. *The Women's Movement Against Sexual Harassment*. Cambridge: Cambridge University Press.

Beiner, Theresa M. 2005. *Gender Myths v. Working Realities: Using Social Science to Reformulate Sexual Harassment Law*. New York: NYU Press.

Cochran, Augustus Bonner, III. 2004. *Sexual Harassment and the Law: The Mechelle Vinson Case*. Lawrence: University Press of Kansas.

Cochran, Augustus Bonner, III. 2012. "Legal Design and Reporting Harassment: Preliminary Considerations on the Comparative Efficacy of US and Brazilian Sexual Harassment Law." *Revista Direito Economica e Socioambiental*, 3(2): 401–446.

Crouch, Margaret. 2001. *Thinking about Sexual Harassment*. New York: Oxford University Press.

Fitzgerald, Louise. 1996. "Sexual Harassment: The Definition and Measurement of a Construct." In *Sexual Harassment on College Campuses*, edited by Michelle Paludi. Albany: SUNY Press.

Hemken, David. 2011. "State Regulation of Sexual Harassment." *Georgetown Journal of Gender and the Law*, 12(3): 647–666.

Kleiman, Lawrence S., Darrin Kass, and Yvetter Samson. 2003–2004. "Sexual Harassment and the Law: Court Standards for Assessing Hostile Environment Claims." *Journal of Individual Employment Rights*, 11(1): 53–73.

MacKinnon, Catharine A. 1979. *Sexual Harassment of Working Women*. New Haven: Yale University Press.

MacKinnon, Catharine A., and Reva B. Siegel, eds. 2004. *New Directions in Sexual Harassment Law*. New Haven: Yale University Press.

Saguy, Abigail. 2003. *What is Sexual Harassment?* Berkeley: University of California Press.

Zippel, Kathrin. 2006. *The Politics of Sexual Harassment*. Cambridge: Cambridge University Press.

FURTHER READING

Gregory, Raymond F. 2004. *Unwelcome and Unlawful: Sexual Harassment in the American Workplace*. Ithaca: Cornell University Press.

LeMoncheck, Linda, and James P. Sterba. 2001. *Sexual Harassment: Issues and Answers*. New York: Oxford University Press.

Sexual Identity and Orientation

LOLA D. HOUSTON
University of Vermont, USA

Sexual identity and sexual orientation are two different terms used to define, categorize, and understand specific facets of the sexuality of an individual. There is no clear consensus among clinicians or researchers about the precise definition of either term. Sexual orientation has been a subject of intense study for many decades, and while the predominant emphasis has been on the biological, the social aspect has recently gained wider attention.

Sexual orientation has most commonly been thought of as forming early in life and as defining the dominant sexual and romantic attractions of the individual and as being unchanging throughout the person's entire life. In this sense, it also describes the relationships that an individual has with others. It is often applied as a kind of umbrella term, subsuming multiple facets of individual sexuality including behavior, desire, and attraction as well as sexual identity. *Sexual identity*, on the other hand, is often understood as the means by which an individual may choose to self-identify as a sexual being to others, and thereby find affiliations with those others who might share similar interests.

While the prevailing view has been that sexual orientation develops early in life and remains more or less constant (American Psychological Association 2008), this idea has come under increasing scrutiny, with some recent research suggesting that sexual orientation can in fact change during an individual's lifetime and may be considerably more fluid than assumed (Savin-Williams 2006; Beckstead 2012). That these terms pose such a distinct challenge in definition also has a substantial impact on the many efforts to identify and understand the populations who inhere to the class of identities such as homosexual, bisexual, and transsexual (Gates and Newport 2012).

In the model where sexual orientation is seen as fixed, sexual identity becomes a variable component within individual sexuality, changing as the individual adopts or rejects other characteristics that may be felt as *part of* individual sexual orientation. Some clinicians and researchers view the degree of incongruence between sexual orientation and sexual identity as a key to individual self-resolution (Reiter 1989; Laumann et al. 1994).

Historically, two key arguments were at the heart of the debate over the nature of sexual orientation and sexual identity. *Essentialism* and *social constructionism* developed out of the interest in understanding homosexuality in the late 1970s. Essentialism argued that one's sexual orientation is innate, something that an individual is born with. For many researchers, this argument supposes that there is a biological or genetic factor that determines sexual orientation, and thus orientation is immutable and not a choice. Social constructionism, by contrast, argued that the various forces in a society – family, religion, politics, medicine, and so forth – were largely responsible for how an individual developed their sexual orientation, and thus sexual orientation was the result of these forces or was socially constructed.

Over the past several decades, considerable research has championed one side or the other as the correct and final arbiter of the question of sexual orientation. Part of the underlying rationale for the ongoing difference has to do with the place of homosexuality in society, and the political discourse and legal and medical considerations that often surround this question. Homosexuality, bisexuality, and transsexuality are often highly stigmatized, although the first of these has clearly been among the most visible and extensively vilified in many societies. Whether or not sexual orientation is innate or socially constructed, the individual who claims a particular sexual orientation may experience considerable social stigmatizing and shame. This may affect the choice of sexual identity, but does not result in the resolution of the difference between sexual orientation and sexual identity.

The difficulty in precisely defining sexual orientation and sexual identity can perhaps be better appreciated when one looks at the historical thread of efforts to understand these concepts. Earlier work on the nature of homosexuality (Laumann et al. 1994) was conducted in part as an attempt to comprehend the nature of homosexuality and to develop better protocols in the treatment of AIDS, which strongly stigmatized homosexuality. This research sought to better understand individual behavior, and thus attempted to define both sexual orientation and sexual identities, and yet these concepts were understood as being distinct. Much of this early work was based on the premise noted above: that orientation was innate, biological. But as the work in fields like epidemiology and psychology deepened, there were efforts to bridge the gap between biological and social factors. Many researchers felt that biological arguments for sexual orientation fell short, and noted that the experience of the population under study often seemed to shift the nature of sexual orientation away from this innate model (Daskalos 1998; Bem 2000; Hoffman 2012).

Similarly, considerable work was done to examine how different social categories, particularly youth, defined and then acted upon sexual interest. While sexual orientation figured in this work, some researchers began to focus on sexual behavior in order to address epidemiological concerns (Savin-Williams and Diamond 2000). More recent work further questions the largely biological or innate basis for sexual orientation (Kinnish, Strassberg, and Turner 2005) and suggests instead the possibility that different populations experience their sexual orientation differently, further reinforcing the claim that it is perhaps less fixed than first thought. Still others note that the definitions of sexual orientation emerged from work carried out by men, and that gender is a crucial part of understanding, and thus defining, sexual orientation, particularly when considering men and women (Peplau and Garnets 2000).

It is important to note that the majority of existing research on sexual identity and sexual orientation emerges from Western narratives and that perspectives from non-Western societies are at best thin, if present at all. The terms themselves – homosexual, bisexual, transsexual – rely largely on Western ideas about sexuality, gender, and identity and as such cannot be assumed to be "global" in any sense of the word. Kulick (1998, 2009) challenges assumptions about "male" and "female" via configurations of sexuality and gender in Brazil. Manalansan (2003, 2006) challenges notions of globalization, and his latter work introduces race and class identities into the notion of sexuality. These and other authors all present ideas about sexuality and sexual identity that speak to this problem, as well as examining the difficulty in separating ideas about sexuality and gender.

At the same time, the difficulty of defining these terms has also figured in the manner in which population estimates are made in sexual minorities such as homosexuals, bisexuals, and trans* (a shorthand term embodying both transsexual and transgender) individuals. Some have observed that the very nature of measuring such populations falls prey to respondents selecting an answer that is socially acceptable (Coffman, Coffman, and Ericson 2013). This in turn may render some of the data suspect, with the result not only that often, being "gay" is underreported, but also that it is socially acceptable to report anti-gay sentiments.

The absence of clarity in the question of sexual orientation and identity presents a particular dilemma when applied in the area of clinical or therapeutic work. For the clinician, much of how one understands a client may hinge upon a review of existing research and reported data. In the instance where a therapist does not self-identify as a member of one of the sexual minorities for whom he or she may be providing treatments, the inability to formulate an accurate understanding of sexual orientation and identity poses a challenge to providing balanced therapies (MacNish and Gold-Peifer 2011).

SEE ALSO: Bisexuality; Essentialism; Sexual Minorities; Sexual Orientation and the Law; Social Constructionist Theory

REFERENCES

American Psychological Association (APA). 2008. "Sexual Orientation and Homosexuality: Answers to Your Questions For a Better Understanding." Accessed August 1, 2015, at http://www.apa.org/topics/lgbt/orientation.aspx.

Beckstead, A. Lee. 2012. "Can We Change Sexual Orientation?" *Archives of Sexual Behavior*, 41(1): 121–134. DOI: 10.1007/s10508-012-9922-x.

Bem, Daryl J. 2000. "Exotic Becomes Erotic: Interpreting the Biological Correlates of Sexual Orientation." *Archives of Sexual Behavior*, 29(6): 531–548.

Coffman, Katherine B., Lucas C. Coffman, and Keith M. Marzilli Ericson. 2013. "The Size of the LGBT Population and the Magnitude of Anti-Gay Sentiment are Substantially Underestimated." *National Bureau of Economic Research Working Paper Series*. Number 19508. DOI: 10.3386/w19508.

Daskalos, Christopher T. 1998. "Changes in the Sexual Orientation of Six Heterosexual Male-to-Female Transsexuals." *Archives of Sexual Behavior*, 27(6): 605–614.

Gates, Gary J., and Frank Newport. 2012. "Special Report: 3.4% of U.S. Adults Identify as LGBT." Accessed August 1, 2015, at http://www.gallup.com/poll/158066/special-report-adults-identify-lgbt.aspx.

Hoffman, Heather. 2012. "Considering the Role of Conditioning in Sexual Orientation." *Archives of Sexual Behavior*, 41: 63–67. DOI: 10.1007/s10508-012-9915-9.

Kinnish, Kelly K., Donald S. Strassberg, and Charles W. Turner. 2005. "Sex Differences in the Flexibility of Sexual Orientation: A Multidimensional Retrospective Assessment." *Archives of Sexual Behavior*, 34(2): 173–183. DOI: 10.1007/s10508-005-1795-9.

Kulick, Don. 1998. *Travesti: Sex, Gender, and Culture among Brazilian Transgendered Prostitutes*. Chicago: University of Chicago Press.

Kulick, Don. 2009. "Soccer, Sex and Scandal in Brazil." *Anthropology Now*, 1(3): 32–42.

Laumann, E. O., J. H. Gagnon, R. T. Michael, and S. Michaels, 1994. *The Social Organization of Sexuality: Sexual Practices in the United States*. Chicago: University of Chicago Press.

MacNish, Melissa, and Marissa Gold-Peifer. 2011. "Families in Transition: Supporting Families of Transgender Youth." In *At the Edge: Exploring Gender and Sexuality in Couples and Families*, edited by A. I. Lev and J. Malpas, 34–42. AFTA Monograph Series, 7.

Manalansan, Martin F., IV. 2003. *Global Divas: Filipino Gay Men in the Diaspora*. Durham, NC: Duke University Press.

Manalansan, Martin F., IV. 2006. "Queer Intersections: Sexuality and Gender in Migration Studies." *International Migration Review*, 40(1): 224–249.

Peplau, Letitia Anne, and Linda D. Garnets. 2000. "A New Paradigm for Understanding Women's Sexuality and Sexual Orientation." *Journal of Social Issues*, 56(2): 329–350.

Reiter, Laura. 1989. "Sexual Orientation, Sexual Identity, and the Question of Choice." *Clinical Social Work Journal*, 17(2): 138–150.

Savin-Williams, Ritch C. 2006. "Who's Gay? Does It Matter?" *Current Directions in Psychological Science*, 15(1): 40–44.

Savin-Williams, Ritch C., and Lisa M. Diamond. 2000. "Sexual Identity Trajectories Among Sexual-Minority Youths: Gender Comparisons." *Archives of Sexual Behavior*, 29(6): 607–627.

Sexual Instinct and Sexual Desire

PAMELA C. REGAN
California State University, Los Angeles, USA

Sexual instinct or sexual desire (also called sexual interest, sexual attraction, libido, or lust) is the motivational component of sexuality, and it is generally experienced as an interest in sexual activities, a drive to seek out sexual objects or engage in sexual acts, or a wish, need, or craving for sexual contact (Regan and Berscheid 1999). Because desire is a subjective experience that cannot be readily observed, it is typically assessed via self-report. The Sexual Desire Inventory-2 (Spector, Carey, and Steinberg 1996) is a commonly used multi-item measure.

Sexual desire is considered distinct from other sexual responses, including sexual arousal (which involves physiological arousal, genital excitement, and the subjective awareness of physiological/genital arousal), sexual activity (overt sexual behaviors such as masturbation or intercourse), and sexual feelings and beliefs. However, because these responses frequently co-occur, they often are experienced relatively simultaneously (Kaplan 1979; Basson 2001).

Sexual desire varies along three dimensions. The first dimension is quantitative and concerns the magnitude of desire that is experienced. Both the intensity and frequency of desire can vary. A person may experience desire frequently one week, only to feel none the next; similarly, he or she may possess a powerful sexual urge at one point in time and a less intense need at another. People also differ in their chronic amount of desire, with some having a low level of sexual appetite and others habitually experiencing high levels. The second dimension is qualitative and concerns the specificity of the desired sexual goal and object. A person may wish to engage in a very specific sexual activity (e.g., intercourse) with a very specific other. Alternately, he or she may simply have an urge to engage in some form of sexual activity with an unspecified partner. The third dimension concerns the originating source of the sexual urge. Spontaneous sexual desire arises from an innate or internally generated cause, whereas responsive sexual desire is produced by an external event, cue, or situation.

Sexual desire is a complex phenomenon that is associated with a variety of factors (Regan and Berscheid 1999). These factors can be grouped into three broad categories: personal factors, or variables associated with the individual and the partner; relational factors, which emerge from the partners' interactions or result from the combination of their characteristics; and environmental factors located in the physical and social context surrounding the individual.

Research indicates that numerous personal variables are associated with sexual desire. For example, people with serious physical (e.g., cancer, diabetes, fibromyalgia) and mental (e.g., depression) illness typically report decreases in their overall level of sexual interest following the onset of their illness, and their desire levels usually are lower than those reported by healthy adults (see Regan and Berscheid 1999). Demographic variables also are associated with sexual desire. Sexual desire levels typically decrease with advancing age among both men and women, and men often report a higher frequency and level of spontaneous desire than do women (Regan and Atkins 2006).

Hormones represent another individual-level factor that is associated with sexual desire (for reviews see Regan 1999; Davis and Braunstein 2012). For example, testosterone levels are positively correlated with self-reported sexual desire in healthy adults; the higher the level of testosterone in a person's bloodstream, the more sexual desire he or she experiences. Similarly, the administration of testosterone (and other androgens) to men and women complaining of low sexual interest generally increases their desire levels. The hormonal fluctuations that occur during various female life events – such as menstruation, pregnancy, and perimenopause – also are associated with alterations in desire (Regan 1996). For example, many women experience reductions in sexual desire as they move through the trimesters of pregnancy (Stuckey 2008).

Relational factors play a particularly important role in sexual desire. Passionate love and sexual desire co-occur in romantic relationships, with higher levels of love predicting greater levels of desire (Regan 2000). Moreover, clinical research reveals that couples whose relationships are characterized by low levels of satisfaction, poor social support and conflict resolution strategies, interpersonal hostility, and maladaptive communication patterns, often report correspondingly low levels of desire (Stuart, Hammond, and Pett 1987). This does not imply, however, that partners in a healthy relationship will always feel a constant or high degree of desire; rather, sexual interest will wax and wane as each partner changes and as the relationship changes.

Although less investigated than other factors, physical and social environmental factors undoubtedly influence a person's ability, motivation, and opportunity to experience and express sexual desire. There is no scientific evidence for a naturally occurring aphrodisiac; however, low to moderate doses of some drugs (e.g., alcohol, stimulants) appear capable of increasing sexual interest (higher doses and chronic use decrease desire) (Regan and Berscheid 1999). Environmental stress negatively affects desire. People facing high levels of work- or school-related stress often report lacking sufficient time and energy to feel desire and act on their sexual urges (Murray and Milhausen 2012).

Social and cultural environmental forces, whose effects are often difficult to isolate and investigate, certainly affect how people experience desire. People learn the "rules" of desire – the situations in which, and individuals for whom, it is acceptable to feel desire, how desire should be communicated, and the meanings to attach to desire – from sociocultural norms about male and female sexuality; laws and religious doctrines that govern sexual behavior; media portrayals of sexuality; and the sexual attitudes and behaviors of peers, family members, and others (Tiefer 1995; Regan and Berscheid 1999). In Western societies, for example, it is commonly believed that male and female desire are different, that desire is an important part of romantic relationships, and that low levels of sexual desire are problematic. These beliefs inevitably shape the individual person's experiences with desire.

SEE ALSO: Sexualities; Socialization and sexuality

REFERENCES

Basson, Rosemary. 2001. "Human Sex-Response Cycles." *Journal of Sex and Marital Therapy*, 27: 33–43. DOI: 10.1080/009262301520235831.

Davis, Susan R., and Glenn D. Braunstein. 2012. "Efficacy and Safety of Testosterone in the Management of Hypoactive Sexual Desire Disorder in Postmenopausal Women." *Journal of Sexual Medicine*, 9: 1134–1148. DOI: 10.1111/j.1743-6109.2011.02634.x.

Kaplan, Helen Singer. 1979. *Disorders of Sexual Desire and Other New Concepts and Techniques in Sex Therapy*. New York: Simon and Schuster.

Murray, Sarah, and Robin Milhausen. 2012. "Factors Impacting Women's Sexual Desire: Examining Long-Term Relationships in Emerging Adulthood." *Canadian Journal of Human Sexuality*, 21: 101–115.

Regan, Pamela C. 1996. "Rhythms of Desire: The Association between Menstrual Cycle Phases and Female Sexual Desire." *Canadian Journal of Human Sexuality*, 5: 145–156.

Regan, Pamela C. 1999. "Hormonal Correlates and Causes of Sexual Desire: A Review." *Canadian Journal of Human Sexuality*, 8: 1–16.

Regan, Pamela C. 2000. "The Role of Sexual Desire and Sexual Activity in Dating Relationships." *Social Behavior and Personality*, 28: 51–60. DOI: 10.2224/sbp.2000.28.1.51.

Regan, Pamela C., and Leah Atkins. 2006. "Sex Differences and Similarities in Frequency and Intensity of Sexual Desire." *Social Behavior and Personality*, 34: 95–102. DOI: 10.2224/sbp.2006.34.1.95.

Regan, Pamela, and Ellen Berscheid. 1999. *Lust: What We Know About Human Sexual Desire*. Thousand Oaks, CA: Sage.

Spector, Illana P., Michael P. Carey, and Lynne Steinberg. 1996. "The Sexual Desire Inventory: Development, Factor Structure, and Evidence of Reliability." *Journal of Sex and Marital Therapy*, 22: 175–190. DOI: 10.1080/00926239608414655.

Stuart, Freida M., D. Corydon Hammond, and Marjorie A. Pett. 1987. "Inhibited Sexual Desire in Women." *Archives of Sexual Behavior*, 16: 91–106. DOI: 10.1007/BF01542064.

Stuckey, Bronwyn G. A. 2008. "Female Sexual Function and Dysfunction in the Reproductive Years: The Influence of Endogenous and Exogenous Sex Hormones." *Journal of Sexual Medicine*, 5: 2282–2290.

Tiefer, Leonore. 1995. *Sex is Not a Natural Act and Other Essays*. Boulder: Westview Press.

Sexual Minorities

ADELA C. LICONA and RYAN J. WATSON
University of Arizona, USA

In the United States, sexual minority/minorities refers to people who identify, or are identified, as distinct from a presumed dominant and thereby normativized population in terms of their sexual designations, desires, expressions, attractions, behaviors, performances, and/or pleasures. The concept can be traced to practices that medicalized, pathologized, psychologized, and bureaucratized homosexuality beginning in the late nineteenth century. The term can be traced to post-World War II United States when homosexuality was produced as an identity category and rights-based claims began to be expressed by those who were deemed or self-identified as members of a "sexual minority."

As a concept, "sexual minority" can be traced to the advent of sexology – the scientific study of human sexuality (see, for example, Richard von Krafft-Ebing's *Psychopathia Sexualis*, 1886). Early sexologists, who did not use the term, suggested and produced an identifiable category of human beings who expressed and/or experienced what was characterized as non-dominant and non-normative bodies and gender expressions as well as same-sex desires. Sexual minorities, as such, are conceptualized in early medicalizing literatures on human sexuality as inverts and emerge in psychologizing (and criminalizing) literatures as defective.

In the late 1940s and early 1950s, Alfred C. Kinsey, Wardell B. Pomeroy, and Clyde E. Martin claimed that while there was evidence of "homosexual activity" across their studied population, a stable percentage of the male and female population could actually be considered "homosexual." At this time, the medicalized concept of a "sexual minority" began to be statistically implied in that those represented as "homosexual" were always fewer in numbers than those represented as "heterosexual." As John D'Emilio noted, Kinsey's data "disputed the common assumption that all adults were permanently and exclusively either homosexual or heterosexual and revealed instead a fluidity that belied medical theories about fixed orientations" (1987, 35). However, it was the idea that a stable percentage of the population was homosexual that actually obscured gender and sexual fluidities (see, for example, Savin-Williams 2009, whose research consistently shows that individuals with same-sex behaviors and attractions identify as heterosexual, which potentially depresses an accurate answer to the question: "How many sexual minorities are there?" and thereby elucidates the complexity of categorizing, describing, surveying, and counting sexual minorities). While the statistics that Kinsey and colleagues reported have been reinterpreted, and/or dismissed, their ideas continue to, at least implicitly, inform some literatures on sexual minorities.

In *Sexual Politics, Sexual Communities*, John D'Emilio explicitly addressed "a sexual minority in the making" and a "gay emancipation movement," constituted by gays and lesbians (1987, 22).[1] He traced the concept to an emergent rights movement, noting that as early as 1915 "one observer of male homosexual life was already referring to it as a 'community distinctly organized'" (D'Emilio 1987, 12). However, he identified activist Harry Hay as the progenitor of the actual term sexual minority, which was also taken up in the late 1940s by other activists in the United States who argued for sexual rights based on either asserted sameness or asserted difference of those identified or self-identifying as a sexual minority. It became a term of self-identification deployed to intervene in the stigmatization of non-dominant sexualities, genders, and erotic behaviors. When the term began to be deployed as a label useful in arguing for rights, advocacy organizations most often used it to refer to homosexual males.[2] Later, lesbian-identified activists called attention to same-sex desire among women but the term was not often deployed. In acknowledging the "diverse subcultures" of the lesbian community, for example, Lillian Faderman's work suggests collective resistance to efforts to minoritize, homogenize, or otherwise erase "peripheries" in and across lesbian communities and lesbian communities of color through the use of such a term.

Today the term sexual minority circulates broadly in the United States, particularly in the social sciences and in law. In the social sciences, it is often used to study lesbian, gay, bisexual, and transgender (LGBT) populations to consider issues ranging from health disparities and stress, to risk and resiliency (particularly in youth), and to differential and unequal treatment in society based on a minoritized status. In law, sexual minority has been both narrowly and broadly defined and deployed to address those "rendered" minority by "legal or societal treatment" (Dunlap 1979, 1131; see also Valdes 1993 on "sexual minorityhood" and the emergence of queer legal theory).

Rebecca Young and Ilan Meyer (2005) have taken issue with presumably more neutral terms that have emerged to replace the term sexual minority, such as men who have sex with men (MSM) and women who have sex with women (WSW). They argue that such seemingly neutral terms can obscure the sociocultural dimensions of sexual relationships, reduce identity to behavior, and harbor unacknowledged racialized undertones. Contemporary critiques of the term sexual minority highlight how it, like other liberal identity categories, can imply static rather than dynamic identity and therefore potentially erase the complexities, fluidity, and flexibility of genders and sexualities and the possibilities of their varied expressions over time and across contexts. According to such critiques, by signaling a tacit knowing of who is included in the category of sexual minority, the term has the potential to discursively obscure how those belonging to either the sexual majority or sexual minority may slide in and out of majoritarian and/or minoritarian status. (For an elucidating insight into the broad concept of sexual minoritarians, see Muñoz 2002.) Its deployment can likewise also obscure intersecting social locations and abilities. Another important critique observes the location from which the term is deployed to highlight the different biopolitical implications of naming practices emanating from an authorized, "expert" space versus those emerging as self-determined. Some critics believe that discourses that minoritize a population can also function to stigmatize that population (see Blumenfeld 2012, which links minoritizing to scapegoating and stereotyping). Others question the sometimes uncritical use of the term sexual minority. (For a critique of sociological treatments of the sometimes reductive ways gender and sexuality are treated in sociology, see Lorber 1996.) Appeals to pleasure and to erotic justice have also emerged to promote a move away from rights-based claims and toward relatively broader justice-based movements (for examples, see Corrêa, Petchesky, and Parker 2008; Sexuality Policy Watch 2009).

SEE ALSO: Bisexuality; Gender Identity, Theories of; Heteronormativity and Homonormativity; Heterosexism and Homophobia; Lesbian and Gay Movements; Queer Theory; Sexualities; Trans Identities, Psychological Perspectives; Transgender Politics; Transsexuality

NOTES

[1] Swedish author and medical doctor Lars Ullerstam is often credited as having coined the term "sexual minorities." He expressed outrage at the "nauseating violations of a minority's rights" (Ullerstam 1966, 95), with specific concern about what he termed "erotic minorities."

[2] See, for example, Vicki L. Eaklor (2008), who notes that in 1924, Henry Gerber founded the Society for Human Rights as an advocacy and educational organization. Related homophile organizations emerged in the 1940s and 1950s and their members debated distinct strategies for best informing the social movement and activism for sexual rights. These include the Mattachine Foundation/Society; Bachelor's Forum; ONE; and the Daughters of Bilitis.

REFERENCES

Blumenfeld, Warren. 2012. "The 'Art' and Rhetoric of Stereotyping and Scapegoating LGBT People." Accessed August 10, 2015, at http://rhetoricraceandreligion.blogspot.com/2012/01/art-and-rhetoric-of-stereotyping-and.html.

Corrêa, Sonia, Rosalind Petchesky, and Richard Parker. 2008. *Sexuality, Health, and Human Rights*. New York: Routledge.

D'Emilio, John. 1987. *Sexual Politics, Sexual Communities: The Making of a Homosexual Minority*. Chicago: University of Chicago Press.

Dunlap, Mary C. 1979. "Constitutional Rights of Sexual Minorities: A Crisis of the Male/Female Dichotomy." *Hastings Law Journal*, 30: 1131–1149.

Eaklor, Vicki. 2008. *Queer America: A People's GLBT History of the United States*. Westport, CT: Greenwood Press.

Krafft-Ebing, Richard von. 1886. *Psychopathia Sexualis*. Stuttgart: Ferdinand Enke Verlag.

Lorber, Judith. 1996. "Beyond the Binaries: Depolarizing the Categories of Sex, Sexuality, and Gender." *Sociological Inquiry*, 66: 143–160. DOI: 10.1111/j.1475-682X.1996.tb00214.x.

Muñoz, José. 2002. "What is Performance Studies?" Interview by Diana Taylor. Accessed August 10, 2015, at http://hidvl.nyu.edu/video/003305734.html.

Savin-Williams, Rich C. 2009. "How Many Gays Are There? It Depends." In *Contemporary Perspectives on Lesbian, Gay, and Bisexual Identities*, edited by Deborah A. Hope, 5–41. New York: Springer.

Sexuality Policy Watch. 2009. "Position Paper on the Language of 'Sexual Minorities' and the Politics of Identity." Accessed August 10,

2015, at http://sxpolitics.org/working-paper-no-4-sexual-minorities-by-rosalind-petchesky/10855.

Ullerstam, Lars. 1966. *The Erotic Minorities*. New York: Grove Press.

Valdes, Francisco. 1993. "Coming Out and Stepping Up: Queer Legal Theory and Connectivity." *National Journal of Sexual Orientation Law*, 1: 1–34.

Young, Rebecca M., and Ilan H. Meyer. 2005. "The Trouble with 'MSM' and 'WSW': Erasure of the Sexual-Minority Person in Public Health Discourse." *Journal Information*, 95: 1144–1149. DOI: 10.2105/AJPH.2004.046714.

FURTHER READING

American Psychiatric Association (APA). 1987. *Diagnostic and Statistical Manual of Mental Disorders*, 3rd ed., revised (DSM-III-R). Washington, DC: American Psychiatric Association.

Canaday, Margot. 2009. *The Straight State: Sexuality and Citizenship in Twentieth-Century America*. Princeton: Princeton University Press.

Sexual Objectification

DAVID FREDERICK, GAGAN SANDHU, and KATHLEEN DOLL
Chapman University, USA

Sexual objectification consists of valuing the body, aspects of the body (e.g., breasts), or appearance separate from the individual (Bartky 1990). Sexual objectification has been framed as an issue affecting women, often directly targeting younger women. Pornography directly promotes objectification because the characters in this medium are valued primarily for their appearance and sexuality without regard to their desires, interests, or personality. Popular mass media and advertisements frequently reinforce the notion that women are valued for their sexuality and appearance rather than their thoughts and feelings. For example, advertisements focusing on specific body parts (e.g., chest) without showing the person's face are more likely to feature women than men (see Aubrey 2006).

Objectification theory proposes an explanation for how this exposure to sexual objectification can have negative effects on women's psychological well-being and body image (Fredrickson and Roberts 1997). This theory posits that experiencing sexual objectification leads women to begin self-objectifying. Self-objectification refers to the idea that women begin to view themselves as sexual objects and value themselves for their appearance and sexuality. Once a woman values herself for her sex appeal, this leads to a process known as appearance surveillance: habitually monitoring how one appears to others. This routine viewing of oneself from a third person's perspective has several consequences. One consequence is that routine monitoring leads women to detect or imagine flaws in their appearance. This surveillance can lead women to feel shame if they conclude that their appearance does not conform to the cultural ideals. Other consequences include feeling anxiety and the splitting of women's attention so that they cannot become fully immersed in other activities that require concentration or physical performance.

One common method for measuring constructs related to objectification theory is the Objectified Body Consciousness Scale. Participants respond to items on this measure using Likert scale responses to assess the extent to which women report experiencing three factors related to objectification: surveillance, shame, and appearance control beliefs (the extent to which women believe they can modify their appearance; McKinley and Hyde 1996). A second approach uses the Self-Objectification Questionnaire, which asks participants to rank how much they value aspects of their body related to appearance (e.g., sex appeal) versus physical competence (e.g., strength). Participants who rank appearance items higher are considered to be higher in self-objectification (Noll and Fredrickson 1998). The Interpersonal Sexual Objectification Scale assesses the extent to which people feel exposed to the sexually objectifying gaze and unwanted sexual advances (Kozee et al. 2007). These factors predict a host of negative psychological outcomes for women. Women who are higher in appearance surveillance are more likely than other women to report body dissatisfaction, disordered eating patterns, depression, experiences of sexual objectification and unwanted sexual advances, and greater discomfort during sex (Moradi and Huang 2008).

Wearing a swimsuit is one situation that may activate concerns regarding sexual objectification, self-objectification, and surveillance. In a study of over 50,000 adults, 31 percent of women and 16 percent of men reported that they avoided wearing a swimsuit in public (Peplau et al. 2009). Engaging in surveillance may exhaust cognitive resources and therefore impair cognitive functioning. In a series of experiments, women were asked to wear swimsuits or sweaters and then complete a math test. Women currently wearing a swimsuit, or who had recently tried on a bathing suit, performed more poorly on a math exam. Men wearing a bathing suit did not perform more poorly (although men who had been asked to try on Speedos did perform worse). In other experiments, women who are put into objectifying situations perform worse on tasks such as throwing a ball (see Moradi and Huang 2008). These experiments demonstrate that experiences related to objectification can impair performance.

The difference in body dissatisfaction between men and women is considered small to moderate in size and differences in preoccupation with weight and dieting are moderate to large. For example, heterosexual women and men differ in the percentage who consider themselves to be overall unattractive (21% vs. 11%), are dissatisfied with their weight (63% vs. 48%), attempt to hide at least one aspect of their body during sex (52% vs. 20%), state that their body image has a negative effect on their sex lives (30% vs. 20%), and have low overall evaluations of their appearance (38% vs. 24%; Peplau et al. 2009).

These results suggest there is a sizeable subgroup of men who experience intense body dissatisfaction (Pope, Phillips, and Olivardia 2000). Men with toned and muscular body types are idealized in mass media, whereas men who are overweight are more frequently the target of jokes or negative commentary. College men indicate that becoming more physically attractive to women is one of their main reasons for wanting to become more muscular. Measures of objectification also predict greater body dissatisfaction among men. Thus, although men's bodies are not sexually objectified to the extent that women's are, aspects of objectification theory apply to men's experiences (Frederick, Forbes, Grigorian, and Jarcho 2007; Frederick et al. 2007).

There are several limitations in research on the links between body concerns and objectification. Almost all of the research to date has been conducted on white college students in the United States, United Kingdom, and Australia. Objectification is prevalent in media across many cultures and thus the link between objectification and body concerns in different cultural contexts needs further consideration and examination. In the United States, there have been some attempts to examine whether aspects of objectification have different associations with body concerns among ethnic minority men and women (e.g., Frederick, Forbes, Grigorian, and Jarcho 2007) and gay and lesbian individuals (e.g., Kozee and Tylka 2006), but this research area is too new to make concrete conclusions. One further critique of objectification theory has been the widespread assumption that surveillance is inherently linked to body dissatisfaction when many participants with very high surveillance levels also report very high body satisfaction (Frederick, Forbes, Grigorian, and Jarcho 2007). One key future research direction will be to identify how being immersed in sexually objectifying environments, such as Hooters restaurants (where the waiting staff are primarily young and attractive women) and cheerleading teams, affects body concerns and perceived objectification.

SEE ALSO: Cosmetic Surgery in the United States; Eating Disorders and Disordered Eating; Feminist Theories of the Body; Psychology of Objectification; Self-Esteem; Skin Lightening/Bleaching

REFERENCES

Aubrey, Jennifer Stevens. 2006. "Effects of Sexually Objectifying Media on Self-Objectification and Body Surveillance in Undergraduates: Results of a 2-year Panel Study." *Journal of Communication*, 56: 366–386. DOI: 10.1111/j.1460-2466.2006.00024.

Bartky, Sandra Lee. 1990. *Femininity and Domination: Studies in the Phenomenology of Oppression*. New York: Routledge.

Frederick, David A., et al. 2007. "Desiring the Muscular Ideal: Men's Body Satisfaction in the United States, Ukraine, and Ghana." *Psychology of Men and Masculinity*, 8: 103–117. DOI: 10.1037/1524-9220.8.2.103.

Frederick, David A., Gordon B. Forbes, Kristina E. Grigorian, and Johanna M. Jarcho. 2007. "The UCLA Body Project I: Gender and Ethnic Differences in Self-Objectification and Body Satisfaction among 2,206 Undergraduates." *Sex Roles*, 57: 317–327. DOI: 10.1007/s11199-007-9251-z.

Fredrickson, Barbara L., and Tomi-Ann Roberts. 1997. "Objectification Theory: Toward Understanding Women's Lived Experiences and Mental Health Risks." *Psychology of Women Quarterly*, 21: 173–206. DOI: 10.1111/j.1471-6402.1997.tb00108.x.

Kozee, Holly B., and Tracy L. Tylka. 2006. "A Test of Objectification Theory with Lesbian Women." *Psychology of Women Quarterly*, 30: 348–357.

Kozee, Holly, Tracy T. Tylka, Casey L. Augustus-Horvath, and Angela Denchik. 2007. "Development and Psychometric Evaluation of the Interpersonal Sexual Objectification Scale." *Psychology Of Women Quarterly*, 31: 176–189. DOI: 10.1111/j.1471-6402.2007.00351.

McKinley, Nita Mary, and Janet Shibley Hyde. 1996. "The Objectified Body Consciousness Scale: Development and Validation." *Psychology of Women Quarterly*, 20: 181–215. DOI: 10.1111/j.1471-6402.1996.tb00467.

Moradi, Bonnie, and Yu-Ping Huang. 2008. "Objectification Theory and Psychology of Women: A Decade of Advances and Future Directions." *Psychology of Women Quarterly*, 32: 377–398. DOI: 10.1111/j.1471-6402.2008.00452.x.

Noll, Stephanie M., and Barbara L. Fredrickson. 1998. "A Mediational Model Linking Self-Objectification, Body Shame, and Disordered Eating." *Psychology of Women Quarterly*, 22: 623–636. DOI: 10.1111/j.1471-6402.1998.tb00181.

Peplau, Letitia Anne, et al. 2009. "Body Image Satisfaction in Heterosexual, Gay, and Lesbian Adults." *Archives of Sexual Behavior*, 38: 713–725. DOI: 10.1007/s10508-008-9378-1.

Pope, Harrison G., Katharine A. Phillips, and Roberto Olivardia. 2000. *The Adonis Complex: The Secret Crisis of Male Body Obsession*. Sydney: The Free Press.

Sexual Orientation and the Law

MACARENA SÁEZ
American University Washington College of Law, USA

This entry on sexual orientation and the law (SO&L) analyzes the legal treatment of the categories sexual orientation and gender identity and the impact of legal practices, doctrines and customs in the lives of individuals and groups who define themselves or are defined by societies, communities, or other individuals as non-heterosexuals. The entry analyzes the experiences and interactions with legal systems of lesbian, gay, bisexual, transgender, intersex, and all other individuals who do not conform to the sex and gender binaries man–woman, male–female. They are usually grouped under the acronym LGBTI or LGBTIQ, to include the more inclusive and self-identification idea of queer. Until the 1960s, individuals who did not conform to heterosexuality were invisible to legal systems and acquired legal relevance mainly in criminal law through the criminalization of sexual behaviors and in family law or civil law through processes that stripped them of legal capacity by being declared mentally incapacitated. The new international world order created after World War II as a response for the horrors of the Holocaust also ignored the harms suffered by thousands of victims abused and killed because of their sexual orientation. International conventions and treaties, therefore, ignored LGBTIs and their rights, replicating the lack of protection suffered by these individuals at national level.

SO&L draws on different disciplines, such as psychology, philosophy, psychiatry, religion, critical legal studies, feminist legal theory, and queer theory, to provide a framework to the legal treatment of LGBTIs. Legal regulations that negatively affect LGBTIs are often based on medical, religious, and philosophical understandings of the role of sexuality. SO&L covers, among others, criminal sanctions to homosexuality and sexual conducts between individuals of the same sex and the right to privacy; criminal sanctions to non-conforming gender stereotypes such as "cross-dressing," and umbrella statutes used to control sexuality such as vagrancy laws; discrimination in public or private employments, including the military, and in educational institutions; the right to freedom of speech and association; discrimination and the right to freedom of religion; the right to family and to the formation of different forms of family; the right to integrity and life, including the concept of hate crimes and crimes of passion as criminal law concepts; and the right to health.

The regulation of sexuality is a feature of every country in the world. Legal regulations of sexuality include the criminalization of individual sexual behaviors, and also conducts that require interaction among different individuals. Examples of the first group are masturbation, cross-dressing, and pornography, and also the status of being a homosexual. Regulated sexual interactions have included at times all sexual relations outside marriage, with criminal sanctions for some sexual interactions such as adultery, especially in the case of a married woman having sex with a man who is not her husband. It has also included some sexual practices within marriage considered "unnatural." Anal sex and bestiality have been typically considered among the latter. These conducts were part of the influential British Buggery Act of 1533 brought to the British colonies by their settlers. Although the main objective of SO&L is to unveil and understand the treatment of non-conforming sexualities by legal institutions and systems, the analysis of the regulation of sexuality in general, including between individuals of different sex, is an important part of SO&L. It is not possible to understand the legal constrains and struggles of LGBTI people outside the role of sexual control in general. SO&L, therefore, covers the legal regulation of sexuality, including how different concepts of sex and sexuality are legally construed.

The twenty-first century is marked by the widest range of legal treatment towards LGBTIs ever seen in history, from countries with the death penalty for sexual acts between individuals of the same sex, to countries where same-sex couples can marry, and raise children, and countries where discrimination on the basis of sexual orientation and gender identity is illegal. SO&L not only documents and analyzes this broad spectrum of treatment but has in part contributed to the liberalization and acceptance of LGBTIs by raising the level of discussion and challenging prohibitions and exclusions throughout the world, starting with criminalization of sexual conduct and status.

The treatment of LGBTIs has not been a progressive history toward liberalization and inclusion. There is evidence of cultures and historical periods where same-sex encounters were accepted or completely ignored. By the end of the nineteenth century, however, and through the first half of the twentieth century, most countries of the world had strict legal rules against homosexual conduct. Criminalization of same-sex relations has been one of the greatest obstacles toward inclusion of LGBTI people in society. It is very hard to argue for equality when an important part of the lives of individuals, as the capacity to engage emotionally and sexually with another, is treated as criminal conduct. SO&L, therefore, has a special focus on anti-sodomy statutes and their application by courts. Criminalization of sexual activity is strongest in countries where legal systems are controlled totally or partially by religious beliefs. Muslim countries, for example, tend to criminalize more sexual conducts outside marriage than secular countries. By 2014, at least 10 countries, all of them officially Muslim or with a majority of the population practicing Islam, applied the death penalty either by statute or through interpretation of shari'a law for the crime of sodomy. It is important to note, however, that not all Muslim countries have a ban on homosexual conducts and the rise of the Judeo-Christian tradition in Europe, especially when transmitted through British colonialism, has been responsible for much of the contemporary legal repression against LGBTIs (Wilets 2011, 642). Many countries that today criminalize sodomy are former British colonies that inherited the Buggery Act of 1533 from the British Empire. Although criminalization in former British colonies is a legal transplant, several leaders from postcolonial African nations have argued that homosexuality is "un-African," adding a questionable cultural element to discrimination against LGBTIs. At the same time, the most vocal countries against LGBTI rights are those former British colonies where the presence of Christian churches is very strong, as is the case in Uganda, Nigeria, and the British Caribbean region. Religion, therefore, may not be the only variable that explains the criminalization of sexual behavior, but certainly it hinders the liberalization of anti-sodomy statutes. There are other factors specific to different traditions and cultures that contribute to the ban on homosexuality in countries of every continent. As some countries move toward the inclusion of LGBTIs, others react with stricter anti-sodomy and anti LGBTI statutes using the argument that homosexuality is a Western imposition. In the Americas, the only countries that criminalize sexual activity among individuals of the same sex are in the British Caribbean region. At least 13 of the 15 countries of the region use never-repealed buggery laws from colonial times that allow the prosecution of individuals for consented sex between two individuals of the same sex.

The influence of buggery laws from the British Empire in today's criminalization of LGBTIs has been contrary to the view of LGBTI rights in the United Kingdom since 1967 when these laws were repealed. Decriminalization was the result of the Report of the Committee on Homosexual Offences and Prostitution, known as the Wolfenden Report, issued in 1957. The report recommended that "homosexual behavior between consenting adults in private be no longer a criminal offence" (Committee on Homosexual Offences and Prostitution 1957, 25). The Report did not advocate for "homosexual acts" but it considered that the role of the law was to preserve public order and decency rather than to intervene in the private life of citizens. The 1967 Sexual Offenses Act decriminalized homosexual acts among consenting adults using a narrow concept of privacy. Thus, hotel rooms and even private homes where third parties could be present were excluded. The Report generated enriching debates on the relationship between law and morality. In part influenced by the Report, advocates of decriminalization of anti-sodomy statutes used the privacy argument in other countries such as the United States and Canada to push for legal reforms.

The English colonists brought to the United States the crime of sodomy, which until the nineteenth century was considered in many states a capital crime. In 1986, the Supreme Court of the United States upheld a Georgia statute that criminalized oral and anal sex between adults of the same sex. The plaintiffs had argued that the sodomy statute violated the constitutional right to privacy. The decision stated that under the United States Constitution there was no fundamental right to homosexual consented sodomy. According to the Court, a statute based on the sentiment of the majority that homosexual sodomy was immoral was not unacceptable rationale. On the contrary, it stated that the law "is constantly based on notions of morality, and if all laws representing essentially moral choices are to be invalidated under the Due Process Clause, the courts will be very busy indeed" (*Bowers v. Hardwick* 1986, 196). Less than 20 years after, the same court overturned this decision in *Lawrence v. Texas*, the landmark US case that declared sodomy laws unconstitutional in the United States. The decision stated that in *Bowers v. Hardwick* the court had "misapprehended the claim of liberty" presented to it and it stated that the petitioners were entitled to respect for their private lives. "The State cannot demean their existence or control their destiny by making their private sexual conduct a crime" (*Lawrence v. Texas* 2003, 567, 578).

Most of the discussion on criminalization of sodomy relates to whether the right to privacy includes the right to engage in sexual intercourse with a person of the same sex. The Wolfenden Report and the scholarly work that followed it in Europe and the Americas focused on the existence of a sphere of action where the government should not intervene. *Lawrence v. Texas* advanced arguments of privacy that could not be translated into claims about sexual conduct that took place in public spaces. It could not reach the treatment of LGBTIs in other areas different than sexual conducts in the confines of private homes or similar spaces. Once sexual conduct among individuals of the same sex is legal within private boundaries, in addition to the question of the extension of the concept of privacy (i.e., does it cover hotel rooms, private spaces that are visible from the outside, etc.), the issue that becomes more visible is whether there are legitimate grounds to treat individuals differently on the basis of their sexual orientation. Once anti-sodomy statues are repealed, countries can start a dialogue on non-discrimination in other areas such as pensions, labor, health, and family law. It is, therefore, no surprise that countries where LGBTIs enjoy more freedom are the ones where sodomy statutes were repealed early on. Denmark, the first country to regulate civil unions in 1989, had decriminalized consensual sodomy in the 1930s. Norway repealed its sodomy statutes in the 1970s and was the second country in enacting a registered partnership regime in 1993.

In addition to control of sexuality through criminal law, throughout history, and in many parts of the world today, many statutes have been enacted that explicitly discriminate against individuals on the basis of their sexual orientation and gender identity. Many more do not explicitly discriminate against LGBTIs but effectively do so. Examples of explicit discrimination are statutes or constitutional provisions that ban same-sex marriage or ban LGBTIs from specific jobs such as the military. Examples of covert discrimination are vagrancy and cross-dressing laws, and laws that prohibit conducts against moral and good customs. These broad statutes are discriminatory when used by police to harass and persecute sexual minorities. Although most regulations that create a difference in treatment based on a person's sexual orientation or gender identity are aimed at excluding LGBTIs from services and spaces available to heterosexuals, some differentiations may effectively exclude heterosexuals from enjoying specific benefits. This exceptional situation happens in countries where marriage is not available to same-sex couples and a registered partnership system is implemented only for same-sex couples. Although marriage usually brings more tangible benefits than partnerships, the two-track system prevents heterosexual couples from choosing an association model different than marriage. This is the situation in Germany, where the Constitutional Court rejected a regime of registered partnerships open to same-sex and different-sex couples because it would undermine the constitutional institution of marriage.

One of the main obstacles faced by LGBTIs has been discrimination in the workplace. SO&L analyzes whether employers have a right to not hire, treat differently, or terminate a person's job because of their sexual orientation. Discussions on the treatment of non-heterosexuals in the workplace show the complexity of providing a legal definition of homosexuality and sexual orientation. An employer may refuse to hire or decide to terminate a person's employment based on his or her perception of the employee's sexuality. This perceived non-heteronormativity may be based on gender stereotypes. Individuals who do not conform to traditional gender roles expected by their peers may suffer discrimination. What conduct triggers discrimination is complex because "homosexuality" as a legal category can mean different things. For example, barring homosexuals from the military may require active sexual conduct with individuals of the same sex or it may only require that the sexual orientation of a person be known to others. The United States had a history of prohibitions of homosexuality in the military which was confirmed in 1993 through a federal statute that prohibited people who demonstrated a propensity or intent to engage in homosexual acts from serving in the armed forces. In 1994, an executive directive prohibited harassing or forcing individuals to disclose their sexual orientation but reinforced the prohibition of serving in the military with regard to individuals who recognized their sexual orientation. The so-called "don't ask, don't tell" policy was in place until 2011, when President Barak Obama certified its repeal. Many law suits were brought to US courts before the "don't ask, don't tell" policy was repealed. Many of those cases show the problem of trying to separate conduct from orientation. Although a considerable number of countries still prohibit LGBTIs from serving in the military, others, including countries outside Europe and the Americas, such as Taiwan, South Africa, New Zealand, and the Philippines, allow gay and lesbians to serve.

Discrimination in the workplace is even more complex in the case of private employers. In Europe and in the United States there are several cases where employees sued their employers or former employers, arguing that they were fired or denied promotion because of their gender non-conformity. Even in countries where discrimination on the basis of sexual orientation and gender identity is illegal in the workplace, there is still discrimination of LGBTI people in the job market (van Balen et al. 2010, 18). This discrimination affects even more profoundly trans individuals who have little access to education and less job opportunities.

An area where LGBTIs have experienced an important change is family law. SO&L analyzes the different normative family models and their evolution in the last three decades. This is an area where legal systems have experienced one of the most rapid and profound structural transformations. The heteronormative family has ruled family law systems around the world for centuries. The heterosexual marriage has been treated as the ideal institution for family formation with many countries setting constitutional protections for marriage and the family. The family is as much a private association between individuals as a public institution that fulfils an important role in society. Families care for dependent individuals, support each other, and to a certain extent guarantee the survival of societies, especially in countries where governments provide little to no welfare support. Until the late 1980s, the only families legally recognized were formed by men and women (either one or several women and one man, with a few isolated examples of one woman and several men). In the 1980s, several countries started to challenge the heteronormative family. The first move came from Denmark in 1989 with the first registered partnership regime aimed at recognizing the relationship between individuals of the same sex. Many countries followed and created frameworks that allowed same-sex couples to be legally recognized and enjoy some "marriage-like" benefits, mostly related to the administration and distribution of property. Even though the first regimes did not create legal family relations, these statutes contributed to a change in the family law landscape. In less than 15 years, marriage was opened to same-sex couples. In 2001, The Netherlands was the first country to give same-sex couples access to marriage. Between 2001 and 2015, 19 countries have amended their marriage statutes to include same-sex couples in all or part of their territory. In some countries, marriage was the result of court decisions that deemed the lack of same-sex marriage unconstitutional. This is the case in Brazil, the United States, and some of the states of Mexico. In other countries, such as Argentina, Belgium, Denmark, France, Iceland, The Netherlands, New Zealand, Norway, Portugal, Spain, Sweden, Uruguay, England and Wales, Luxembourg, and some states of the United States and Mexico, the legislature has amended marriage statutes to include same-sex couples. In some of these cases the political processes have later been confirmed by courts. This is the case in Canada, Federal District of Mexico, Spain, Portugal, France, and the United States. In a few cases, such as South Africa, recognition has been triggered by courts mandating that legislatures seek a solution for same-sex couples, or rejecting political processes against same-sex marriage. Colombia also followed this model, although the legislature failed to comply with the Constitutional Court's mandate and in 2013 rejected a Bill opening marriage to same-sex couples. It is important to note that marriage does not guarantee equal treatment. In Belgium in 2003 and Portugal in 2010, marriage was allowed but adoption was barred for same-sex married couples. Marriage and same-sex marriage, therefore, may be different institutions if the latter cannot access the same methods of family formation as heterosexual married couples. Belgium amended its statute in 2005, eliminating differences between marriages. In

Portugal, an amendment allowed the adoption of the spouse's biological child by her or his spouse of the same sex (second-parent adoption), but by July 2015 joint adoption by same-sex couples was still barred.

The same-sex marriage debate, as it was referred to in the late 1990s and early 2000s, and the marriage equality debate as it is known today, is the most visible struggle of the LGBTI movement for the recognition of family rights. LGBTI activists in different countries have used different strategies and arguments to gain access to legal marriage. One early difference was between countries that moved toward the recognition of heterosexual unmarried couples as family units and countries that only recognized unmarried same-sex couples and established legal frameworks exclusive for them in areas such as property distribution, pension system, and inheritance rights. In the former case, same-sex couples were able to become visible by highlighting their similarities with unmarried heterosexual couples. In the latter case, same-sex couples highlighted the unfairness of not being able to access marriage because it was viewed as an exclusively heterosexual institution. The difference is important because countries that have granted rights to unmarried heterosexual and same-sex couples have created frameworks where individuals who do not marry for reasons not related to their sexual orientation or gender identity but rather to their social and economic vulnerability may be able to have their families legally recognized. Mexico, for example, already recognized some rights for unmarried couples when the Supreme Court had to review the constitutionality of the Federal District's same-sex marriage statute passed by the Legislature. The Supreme Court had no difficulty in concluding that same-sex marriage was not unconstitutional and that the Mexican legal system recognized families as socially constructed. It was not the role of the law to create families but to recognize already existing ones.

In the United States, the legal struggle for marriage equality started to gain ground in the 1990s after the Supreme Court of Hawai'i ruled that the denial of marriage to same-sex couples was discriminatory. In response to this decision, the legislature amended the Hawai'i constitution defining marriage as a union between a man and a woman. More than 30 states had at some point amended their constitutions to define marriage as a union of a man and a woman. In 2003, Massachusetts became the first state to recognize marriage equality when its Supreme Court declared the exclusion of same-sex couples from the institution of marriage unconstitutional. Several states followed. The federal government also played its part by passing in 1996 a statute that defined marriage for federal purposes as a union between a man and a woman. Section 3 of the Defense of Marriage Act (DOMA) impeded same-sex couples legally married in the United States or abroad to be treated as married by the federal government. Several cases were brought to courts challenging the statute. A major game changer came in 2013 when the US Supreme Court decided *Windsor v. United States* declaring section 3 of DOMA unconstitutional. *Windsor v. United States* was not a case on marriage equality but the Court used arguments on the right to privacy and dignity that could easily translate to decisions on marriage equality. Within 2 years following the *Windsor v. United States* decision, more than 40 decisions favoring same-sex marriage were issued and only two decisions favoring marriage equality. In June 2015, the US Supreme Court decided *Obergefell v. Hodges*. This decision recognized that marriage was a fundamental right applicable to different and same-sex couples, making same-sex marriage legal throughout the country. In Canada, same-sex marriage became legal in 2005, and in Latin America, by 2015 it was legal in Uruguay, Argentina, Brazil, and parts of Mexico. Colombia's Constitutional Court has paved the way to marriage equality but by 2015 it was still unclear whether same-sex couples could legally marry. Several countries, however, have registered partnerships or equivalent regimes for unmarried couples. In Africa, only South Africa recognizes marriage equality. In Asia and the Middle East, no country allows same-sex couples to marry, although Israel allows same-sex couples legally married abroad to have their marriages registered and same-sex unmarried couples have access to the majority of benefits as unmarried heterosexual couples. In New Zealand, marriage equality has been available since 2013. Europe is the region with more countries with marriage equality and other models of legal recognition for unmarried couples.

THE ROLE OF PRIVACY, EQUALITY, AND DIGNITY

In the legal struggle for recognition of LGBTI rights, three legal arguments repeat with slight differences. The right to privacy helped to decriminalize sexual conduct between individuals of the same sex. Privacy, however, does not require the acceptance of LGBTIs as equals to heterosexuals. There can still be – and there is still is for the most part – a legal system where sexuality is based on heterosexuality as the normative ideal and non-heterosexual sexuality is at most tolerated provided that it takes place in private. While heterosexual couples can hold hands and kiss in public, same-sex couples cannot do that if only privacy reaches their right to engage in sexual intimacy with persons of their same sex. SO&L is in part responsible for advancing arguments on equality and conceptualizing legal definitions of discrimination on the basis of sexual orientation and gender identity. From discussions on the right to be let alone, countries in the Western world have moved to discussions on equality of treatment in areas such as housing, health, pension systems, and finally, family law. Some countries have interpreted privacy in a broader sense, as related to the right to autonomy or the free development of one's personality. That interpretation surpasses privacy. Under the gaze of autonomy, individuals should be granted the right to work in the area of their like, to choose their partner and family without government intervention, and live according to their own life plan.

The other argument often provided in courts and legislatures is the right to equality. The use of the right to equality requires proving that LGBTIs are similarly situated to heterosexual individuals and, therefore, should have equal access to institutions. Equality has been used by litigators in both local and international litigation. Additionally, the use of dignity to support LGBTI rights has gained ground through marriage equality litigation and has spread to claims in other areas such as health and parenting. Countries as diverse as South Africa, Mexico, Brazil, the United States, and Portugal have referred to the dignity of all human beings regardless of their sexual orientation and gender identity to support marriage equality. The use of dignity may prove to be a turning point for the protection of trans people, whose rights are still far behind those of gay and lesbian individuals even in countries that have embraced LGBTI rights.

THE FUTURE OF SO&L

SO&L analyzes the shift from criminalization to full recognition and the strategies that allowed the change of treatment of LGBTI individuals. Thus, although there are many countries where sexual orientation and gender identity have not yet emerged as legal categories, there are others where the struggle for equality has moved to family law, health regulations, and the right to identity. In the last two decades of the twentieth century, the focus of SO&L was criminalization of sexual conduct and status, in addition to discussions on what constituted for legal purposes homosexuality and other sexual categories created by mainstream institutions and disciplines. SO&L in the twenty-first century has added new discussions on equality and inclusion of LGBTIs. Concepts used by SO&L, but construed by the heterosexual society to *name* the non-heterosexual such as homosexuality, hermaphroditism, and cross-dresser, have been replaced by concepts advanced by the LGBTI community such as gay, lesbian, bisexual, trans, and intersex. To the concept of sexual orientation – encompassing gay, lesbian, and bisexual – the concept of gender identity has been added, providing a specific space to analyze the distinct marginalization and discrimination of trans individuals. Concepts have become more complex and diverse. The queer theory movement has invited the use of "queer" to refer to all non-conforming sexualities. The acronyms LGBT, LGBTI, and LGBTQ, however, have transcended the boundaries of the United States, where they originated, and are now used in other countries and languages. The diversity of concepts shows also a diversity of opinions and theories behind the regulation of non-heterosexuals. The topics of discussions have diversified and they now include more thorough discussions on trans people and their rights, including the right to define one's identity instead of having it established at the moment of birth. These new legal models include the option of not including information on sex in birth certificates or including a third box for unspecified sex. More countries are passing statutes on gender identity that recognize the right of each individual not to be discriminated against on the basis of their actual or perceived gender identity. In many cases, these statutes aim at eliminating medical requirements or procedures in order for a person to legally change their sex or gender. In 2012, Argentina passed a gender identity statute that has been considered by LGBTI activists as a model to follow. This statute allows an individual to seek a change of sex in their legal identification record, pictures, and any legal document without the need to show psychiatric or medical evaluations. Among other situations, statutes such as this allow individuals to show passports with the name and physical appearance that correspond to their sense of identity rather than showing a picture and identity that do not correspond to their actual appearance/identity. Issues of access to health for trans people have also emerged. These include access to hormone treatment, surgical procedures, and medicines.

Discussions on family law are no longer focused on marriage and civil unions. Instead, a complex discussion on parenting and the creation of families through assisted reproductive technologies has emerged. Many countries, including some where marriage for same-sex couples is not available, are discussing the right of same-sex couples to be eligible to become adopting parents jointly. Another current discussion is the legal relationship of a person and the biological children of their same-sex partner. This discussion goes from applying the paternity presumption historically granted to the husband of the birth mother to the creation of second-parent adoption procedures for same-sex couples. Courts in different countries have seen an emergence of cases of child support or custody battles between couples of the same sex. Judges in these cases must decide if a person who has no biological ties to a child, but has actively participated in the decision of having that child and has treated the child as their own since birth, can have the same rights that legal systems easily grant to biological parents. New topics also include whether children could have more than two parents registered at birth.

The contrast between countries that harshly criminalize the sexual conduct and status of LGBTIs and countries where legislation prohibits discrimination on the grounds of sexual orientation and gender identity has triggered an increasing number of asylum-seeking claims in European countries and in the United States. The claims of persecution for sexual orientation and gender identity and the risk to life if returning to home countries seem to be ever more recurrent.

SO&L IN LAW SCHOOLS

As Rubenstein (1997) pointed out, before the 1990s there were no materials on sexual orientation and the lives of gays and lesbians were for the most part invisible to law students and professors. SO&L, and also other disciplines that have made sexual orientation and gender identity visible categories, have emerged thanks to the efforts of LGBTIs themselves. One of the first prominent legal arguments against the criminalization of sodomy in the United Kingdom, however, was written around 1785 by Jeremy Bentham, and the Wolfenden Report came in 1957. Throughout the twentieth century, there were also isolated law suits against anti-sodomy statutes and on same-sex marriage. The study of sexual orientation as a legal category in law schools, however, did not emerge until the last decade of the twentieth century. Despite the fact that discrimination and violence against LGBTIs requires the support of legal systems, law schools stayed mostly out of the lives of LGBTIs until recently. This may be explained by the fact that during a long period, law was viewed by gay rights activists as a tool for social control of sexual minorities rather than as a tool of protection and liberation. The contemporary gay rights movement, many authors claim, has its origin in the riots of the gay bar Stonewall in New York City in 1969. For those activists, the law had not been anything but an instrument of repression. The first scholars in making SO&L a legal discipline were US law professors who gathered the few secondary sources on the legal treatment of gays and lesbians available at the time and enriched them with their own discussions and available case law. The focus of SO&L courses, as had been the case before with feminist legal theory classes, was the study of law from the perspective of those who had traditionally *suffered* the law rather than of those who had benefitted from it due to their sexual orientation. The first materials on SO&L were limited to the life experiences of gay, lesbian, and bisexual individuals. As the LGBTI movement gained ground in more countries, classes and materials on SO&L became broader and the life experience of trans individuals was also included. The emergence of SO&L in law schools throughout the United States, Canada, and some European countries is reflected in the rising scholarly literature on the topic. An advanced search in the largest network of library contents and services of the world, Worldcat, shows five books with the terms "sexual orientation" and "law" as subject matter between 1900 and 1950, 45 between 1951 and 1980, 1009 between 1981 and 2000, and 4915 between 2001 and 2015.

SEXUAL ORIENTATION AND INTERNATIONAL LAW

Although international law ignored the problems suffered by sexual minorities, since the early 1980s it has contributed to the visibility of LGBTIs and to the construction of legal categories that have helped to protect them in different countries. Often national courts cite international and comparative law to support their decisions advancing LGBTI rights. The European Court of Human Rights (ECourtHR) was the first international organ, in 1981, to decide a case on sexual orientation. In *Dudgeon v. United Kingdom*, the ECourtHR decided that the buggery statute in Northern Ireland constituted an unjustified interference with Mr. Dudgeon's right to respect for his private life protected by the Convention for the Protection of Human Rights and Fundamental Freedoms (ECHR). In 1994, the United Nations Human Rights Committee (HRC) decided a similar case in *Toonen v. Australia*. Both systems were faced with similar cases later on and reinforced their case law in similar terms. In addition to criminal statutes, these international organs have reviewed cases on exclusion of gays in the military, pension systems, labor law, and family law. Even though by 2015 the ECourtHR had still refused to declare marriage equality, in 2010 it decided *Schalk and Kopf v. Austria*, rejecting marriage equality but accepting that same-sex couples were protected by the right to family.

The first decision on sexual orientation by the Inter-American Court of Human Rights (ICourtHR) came much later, in 2012, when the ICourtHR decided *Atala and daughters v. Chile*. This case referred to a woman who lost custody of her three children for living with her lesbian partner. The Court decided against Chile, stating that discrimination on the basis of sexual orientation and gender identity was prohibited by the American Convention on Human Rights and that it was a violation of the rights to family and privacy to base a custody decision on the sexual orientation of the mother per se. It also stated that the Convention did not protect only one model of the family. The *Atala and daughters v. Chile* decision has been cited by the Mexican Supreme Court to support its decisions in favor of marriage equality. It has also been cited by the European Court of Human Rights. The African system of Human Rights has not yet decided a case on sexual orientation. In addition to court and treaty body decisions, international law has contributed to the protection of LGBTI rights by referring to the discrimination and violence suffered by LGBTIs as human rights violations.

SEE ALSO: Gender Stereotypes; Queer Theory; Same-Sex Families; Sexual Minorities

REFERENCES

Balen, Barbara van, Ursula Barry, Ronald Holzhacker, Elisabeth Villagomez, and Katrin Wladash. 2010. *Synthesis Report 2010. Part I – The Situation of LGBT Groups in the Labour Market in European Member States*. Network of Socio-Economic Experts in The Non-Discrimination Field, VT-2008-007. Accessed January 20, 2015, at http://ec.europa.eu/justice/discrimination/files/sen_synthesisreport2010 parti_en.pdf.

Bowers v. Hardwick, 478 U.S. 186, 196, 106 S. Ct. 2841, 2846-47, 92 L. Ed. 2d 140 (1986).

Committee on Homosexual Offences and Prostitution. 1957. *Report of the Committee on Homosexual Offences and Prostitution*. London: HMSO. Accessed January 20, 2015, at http://www.humandignitytrust.org/uploaded/Library/Other_Reports_and_Analysis/Wolfenden_Report_1957.pdf.

Lawrence v. Texas, 539 U.S. 558, 123 S. Ct. 2472, 156 L. Ed. 2d 508 (2003).

Rubenstein, William B. 1997. *Sexual Orientation and the Law*. St. Paul, MN: West Publishing.

Wilets, James D. 2011. "From Divergence to Convergence? A Comparative and International Law Analysis of LGBTI Rights in the Context of Race and Post-Colonialism." *Duke Journal of Comparative and International Law*, 21(3): 631–686.

FURTHER READING

Eskridge, William N. 2002. *Gaylaw: Challenging the Apartheid of the Closet*, Boston: Harvard University Press.

Greenberg, David F. 1990. *The Construction of Homosexuality*, Chicago: University of Chicago Press.

Habib, Samar. 2010. *Homosexuality and Islam*, vols. I and II. Santa Barbara: Praeger

Haggerty, George, ed. 2000. *Encyclopedia of Gay Histories and Cultures*. New York: Garland Publishing.

International Commission of Jurists. 2015. Sexual Orientation and Gender Identity Casebook Database. Accessed February 3, 2015, at http://www.icj.org/sogi-casebook-introduction/.

Sexual Regulation and Social Control

DEBORAH BROCK
York University, Canada

There may be no other area of human activity as highly regulated as sexual expression, including erotic practices involving bodies, textual practices such as producing images and writing about sex, communicating about sex through public channels such as the mail or on the Internet, or transporting sexually explicit material across borders. The criminal codes of Western nations include a taxonomy of prohibitions addressing what can and cannot be done sexually, by whom, and with whom, and also regulations for the production and dissemination of sexually explicit materials. Well-known legal statutes are provisions regulating sexual assault, sexual offences against children, prostitution, pornography, and sex in public places, among a plethora of less well-known provisions. Historical sociolegal research suggests that sex-related legislation was and is created to uphold certain gender, age, race, and class relations of a particular time, and changes to this legislation can signal significant social and cultural shifts.

Sexuality is now conceptualized as a locus of both pleasure and danger (Vance 1984). It is personal, political, and inextricable from power. Studies of sexuality in the social sciences share a common understanding that sexualities are enmeshed in a complex nexus of power that intersects with gender, racialization, class, age relations, citizenship, and so on. Claiming certain "truths" about sexuality is, for example, closely tied to constructing gender by attributing appropriate forms of conduct to women and men, to racialization through the sexualization of non-whites, and so on. Sexuality is a matter of social, ethical, religious, medical, and political concern, a frequent target of regulatory practices by the state, of professional organizations and institutions, and of pedagogical initiatives. It is a preoccupation of numerous social movements invested in its liberation or its suppression. As such, while sexuality is a distinct area of research in its own right, the regulation of sexuality can best be understood in conjunction with other facets of identity and experience.

Studies explicitly addressing sexual regulation as a distinct area of research are of relatively recent origin, with a notable moment being the publication of Jeffrey Weeks' *Sex, Politics, and Society* in 1981 (Weeks 1981). This research was motivated by the critique of law and juridical authority being posed by movements for social and sexual liberation as they sought greater recognition by, and sometimes freedom from, social control and state regulation. A key scholarly moment for *how* this research was to be undertaken was the publication of Michel Foucault's (1926–1984) *History of Sexuality*, Volume 1, in English in 1978 (Foucault 1978) and the subsequent flourishing of sexuality research, both historical and contemporary. By the late twentieth century, sexuality in Western societies was no longer governed by a shared moral, religious, or political framework, bringing its mode of regulation into question. It had become a contested terrain, according to Jeffrey Weeks (Weeks 1989).

Most significantly, the women's movement, the lesbian and gay liberation movement, and queer politics have sought greater sexual freedoms through law reform. Some sex-related issues have been the target for more regulation (including rape, sexual abuse, and other gender-based violence) and for other issues less (most notably the decriminalization of homosexuality and abortion), while still others (including pornography and prostitution) remained highly contested within and between these social movements. These social movements have been instrumental in shifting public opinion and culture, providing the conditions of possibility for significant legal judgments on the regulation of homosexuality, abortion and birth control, prostitution, pornography, and so on.

We might assume from the character of sex-related legislation that sexual regulation is largely negative and prohibitive in character. Indeed, the history of sexual regulation in the West originated with a conservative perspective on sexuality, through which sexuality is primarily regarded as a negative disruptive force that needs to be repressed and regulated lest people fall into moral turpitude.

At the far end of this spectrum, some religious conservatives regard reproduction as the primary purpose of sexuality, occurring between differently sexed (female and male) married partners, in the heterosexual, monogamous family. Many religious conservatives call for a "return" to a largely mythical traditional family and the sexual values associated with it.

Western states continually negotiate between conservative demands and a liberal legal perspective, in which sex between consenting adults, which does not cause harm, is essentially a private matter. The liberal view of sexuality is that what goes on between consenting adults in private is not the law's business, and toleration can be exercised toward some forms of public sexual expression.

Research foci on state regulation, political ideologies, and the role of social movements continue to make significant contributions to studies of sexual regulation. This research has been both challenged and enriched by the publication in English of Michel Foucault's three-volume exploration of *The History of Sexuality* (Foucault 1978, 1985, 1986).

First, the disciplines of criminology and sociolegal studies have taken up a critique of sex-related legislation that analyzes it primarily within the context of its social and historical construction and effects. This research takes the position that sexuality is constituted by how it is regulated, including the norms that govern it, the social practices and relationships through which it is understood, and the discourses that give it meaning. However, the making of law must simultaneously refer to social conditions to judge that which is constituted (Craig 2012).

This mutually constitutive process can be attributed, above all, to practices of *normalization*, something that Foucault considered to be among the most effective means of regulation in contemporary Western societies. The juridical system of law has not become less important (on the contrary, the legal realm is ever-expanding), but rather law itself has become normalized, and the judicial system is increasingly becoming integral to medical, administrative, and other apparatuses that are also characterized by regulatory functions (Foucault 1978).

Law is now interdependent with an array of disciplines, such as medicine, the psy-disciplines, and criminology; these comprise the governmental technologies that together organize social life. Nikolas Rose and Mariana Valverde furthered Foucault's *governmentality* approach in their exploration of the "legal complex" (legal mechanisms, arenas, functionaries, reasoning, etc.) by challenging the typical approach; that is, how law regulates sexuality (Rose and Valverde 1998). Instead, they ask how sexual "problems" such as homosexuality come to be understood as targets for government, and suggest further investigation of the legal complex in strategies of regulation (Rose and Valverde 1998).

The second interrelated direction for studies in sexual regulation focuses on the exercise of what Foucault referred to as *biopower*. Biopower takes two main forms: disciplining the body through shaping our very sense of ourselves, and through intervention into the life of the population as a whole (for example, the statistical measurement of births, deaths, and illnesses) through the development of knowledges and techniques to administer populations for the "management of life" in a calculated way (Foucault 1978, 140). These two forms of biopower intersect in sexuality, which is saturated with flows of power (Foucault 1978). Sustaining the normal life, and life itself, emerged as the key objective in the exercise of biopower, displacing the focus on punishment and death. Biopower was a constituent element in emerging disciplines in the social sciences and medicine, and became a focus of the expanding apparatus of the state.

Many sexuality scholars employ a governmentality approach and explore biopolitical power because they are such effective constructivist tools for understanding the making of beliefs, feelings, identities, and actions in a socially and historically contextualized way. Some governmentality research suggests that the most common form of sexual regulation in the West today is not law but *self-governance*. We can find this in the impetus to be healthy, responsible, self-managing, skilled, open-minded, empowered, self-actualizing, sexually fulfilled, ethical, and so on.

Governmentality research on sexual regulation now surpasses the scope of deviancy studies, which was the dominant sociological approach to the study of sexuality from the 1950s until the 1970s. Deviancy theorists' focus on sexual transgressors, including the pervert, the prostitute, the criminal sexual psychopath, the pornographer, and the pedophile, played a part in the definition and regulation of difference. As a discipline, sociology (often inadvertently) contributed to the identification, naming, and judging of behaviors, identities, ideas, and appearances, and so on as violations of social norms, rules or laws. For example, the naming of people as homosexual, pervert, delinquent, slut, sex addict, nymphomaniac, frigid woman, swinger, exhibitionist, and so on are part of both the mutual constitution of the person and the sexual meaning being ascribed to the person, as well as suggestive of how that person, and those actions, should be treated. For their part, the psy- and medical professions rely on *The Diagnostic and Statistical Manual* (American Psychiatric Association 2013), which now surpasses law in its detailed taxonomy of "abnormal" sex. Foucault's research on the history of psy- professions and institutions was instrumental in bringing attention to their construction as much more than a means of diagnosis and treatment, but as a regulatory apparatus (e.g., Foucault 2003b).

Foucault's influence on studies of sexual regulation, however, takes us beyond the constitution of the abnormal (Foucault 2003a) to think about the significant regulatory power of positive identities and prescriptions. For example, heterosexual women are now increasingly responsibilized to engage in practices of self-examination and self-improvement in order to produce better sex. These practices have become a new form of regulation, casting women into a position of greater uncertainty and self-critique (Attwood 2006). The process through which we have come to regard sexuality as central to our sense of self, and as crucial to our health and happiness, is yet another dimension of sexual regulation.

We can also use the example of a relatively new phenomenon known as *homonormativity*. Lisa Duggan suggested that "the new homonormativity" is embodied in the white middle class gay, who is family oriented, consumption motivated, and a patriotic citizen, and thus deserving of social recognition and legal rights (Duggan 2002). The homosexual, in other words, has accomplished some limited legitimacy through assimilation in all matters but the sex of one's partner. This entails the adoption of *heteronormative* values and beliefs such as marriage, child-rearing, economic interdependence, and home ownership. Homonormativity, then, is not simply a matter of gaining increasing freedom *from* regulation. We can also conceptualize homonormativity *as* a new mode of governance: few other pressures are so pervasive as the impetus to be "normal" – to embrace domesticity and familialism, neoliberal capitalism, patriotism, and nationalism.

How does this alter our understanding of sexual regulation? First, in keeping with the directions established by Foucault, we need to reconceptualize power as relational, as everywhere, and coming from everywhere. Second, we need to reconceptualize sexual regulation as something that occurs well beyond the realm of the state and its legal apparatus. Law and the state are indeed produced *through* power, they are not simply the sources of power. Governmentality extends well beyond the state, meaning that the state is a component (albeit a central and crucial one) of a network of *governmentalities* (Foucault 2004). Third, while domination can indeed be produced through power, power is more than this, and has a productive and creative character. For example, we find power in the production of new identities, discourses, and desires. Fourth, it is not possible to free ourselves from power. Desire itself suggests that power is already present (Foucault 1978). For Foucault, pleasure and power are joined in sexuality; pleasure proliferates through power. One does not wrest oneself from power in the interests of sexual freedom or pleasure. Finally, Foucault's concept of biopower provides insights into the organization of power and knowledge about sexuality, suggesting that sexual regulation ultimately targets people's capacities and energies, and the potential of human bodies.

SEE ALSO: Governance and Gender; Heteronormativity and Homonormativity; Normalization; Sexualities

REFERENCES

American Psychiatric Association. 2013. *The Diagnostic and Statistical Manual*, 5th ed. Washington, DC: American Psychiatric Association.

Attwood, Fiona. 2006. "Sexed Up: Theorizing the Sexualization of Culture" *Sexualities*, 9(1): 77–94.

Craig, Elaine. 2012. *Troubling Sex: Toward a Legal Theory of Sexual Integrity*. Vancouver: University of British Columbia Press.

Duggan, Lisa. 2002. "The New Homonormativity: The Sexual Politics of Neoliberalism." In *Materializing Democracy: Toward a Revitalized Cultural Politics*, edited by Russ Castronovo and Dana D. Nelson, 175–194. Durham, NC: Duke University Press.

Foucault, Michel. 1978. *The History of Sexuality: An Introduction*, vol. 1. New York: Vintage Books.

Foucault, Michel. 1985. *The Use of Pleasure*. New York: Vintage Books.

Foucault, Michel. 1986. *The Care of the Self*. New York: Vintage Books.

Foucault, Michel. 2003a. *Abnormal: Lectures at the College de France, 1974–1975*. New York: Picador.

Foucault, Michel. 2003b. *Psychiatric Power*. New York: Palgrave Macmillan.

Foucault, Michel. 2004. *The Birth of Biopolitics: Lectures at the College de France, 1978–1979*. New York: Picador.

Rose, Nikolas, and Mariana Valverde. 1998. "Governed by Law?" *Social and Legal Studies* 7(4): 541–551.

Vance, Carole S., ed. 1984. *Pleasure and Danger: Exploring Female Sexuality*. London: Routledge and Kegan Paul.

Weeks, Jeffrey. 1981. *Sex, Politics, and Society: The Regulation of Sexuality Since 1800*. London: Longman.

Weeks, Jeffrey. 1989. *Sexuality*. London: Routledge.

Sexual Rights

ALISON PLUMB
Independent Scholar

Sexual rights have been defined as an evolving set of entitlements related to sexuality that contribute to the freedom, equality, and dignity of all people. Sexual rights are human rights related to sexuality that address a wide range of issues and often intersect with several other rights. Examples of sexual rights issues include, but are not limited to, sexuality education, reproductive rights, maternal morbidity and mortality, and sex work. More broadly, sexual rights are one field that falls under sexual and reproductive health and rights (SRHR). Three other related but separate fields in SRHR are sexual health, reproductive health, and reproductive rights. In the broad concept of SRHR, these four fields are treated as separate, but are inherently intertwined. Beyond this broad definition, what constitutes sexual rights is contested and means different things to different groups. Wilson acknowledges how varied the concept of sexual rights is, and the many things it may encompass: "Sexual rights refer variously to sexual orientation, gender identity, intimate relations, erotic practices, health, reproduction, bodily integrity, autonomy, and the potential for pleasure" (Wilson 2002, 251).

On the international stage, demands are increasingly being made by a variety of political groups, which are articulated in the language of sexual rights and citizenship. However, sexual politics is a relatively marginalized theme in the Western democracies, and beyond there it remains even more marginal. Sexual rights are denied to women and gay and lesbian groups in most Muslim-majority and African countries. To a large extent, they are also neglected in Asian and Latin American nations. Only a few states outside the European Union have been actively involved in extending civil rights to gay men and lesbians. Among them are South Africa, Brazil, Mexico, Canada, Australia, and the United States. Other countries that had no anti-homosexual criminal laws, such as Japan and Thailand, have been slow to offer safeguards to sexual communities in civil law. The concept of sexual citizenship draws our attention to all kinds of social exclusions that the various sexual communities experience. These exclusions inhibit these communities' political, social, cultural, and economic participation. The various constraints point to the necessity of more inclusive and diverse institutions. However, simply allowing sexual minorities into these organizations on an individual basis does not challenge the heterosexist assumptions that govern most societies. Sexual citizenship refers to the transformation of public life into a domain that is no longer dominated by male heterosexuals, but that is based in gender and sexual diversity. The goal is a society in which diverse people can take responsibility for their own sexual lives. Three key political groups that may benefit from a redefinition of sexual citizenship and rights-based discourses are: women, disabled people, and gay, lesbian, and bisexual people.

One political group that has seen some international recognition of sexual rights is women. The 1994 International Conference on Population and Development (ICPD) in Cairo was a milestone in the history of women's rights. ICPD delegates reached a consensus that the equality and empowerment of women is a global priority. It approached this not only from the perspective of universal human rights, but also as an essential step toward eradicating poverty and stabilizing population growth. A woman's ability to access reproductive health and rights is a cornerstone of her empowerment. It is also the key to sustainable development. A total of 179 governments signed up to the ICPD Programme of Action, which set out, among other goals, to provide universal access to family planning and sexual and reproductive health services and reproductive rights. Following this, the Platform for Action from the 1995 Beijing Conference on Women established that human rights include the right of women to have control over, and make decisions concerning, their own sexuality, including their own sexual and reproductive health freely and without coercion, violence, or discrimination. This paragraph has been interpreted by some countries, such as Sweden, as the applicable definition of women's sexual rights. Four years later, in 1999 at the 14th World Congress of Sexology in Hong Kong, the World Association for Sexual Health (WAS) adopted its Declaration of Sexual Rights. The Declaration included 11 sexual rights, including the right to: sexual freedom; sexual autonomy, sexual integrity, and safety of the sexual body; sexual privacy; sexual equity; sexual pleasure; emotional sexual expression; sexually associate freely; make free and responsible reproductive choices; sexual information based upon scientific inquiry; comprehensive sexuality education; and the right to sexual health care.

One of the most important fronts in the struggle for women's human rights is around sexual and reproductive autonomy, and the coercive and often violent ways in which that autonomy is suppressed. Some ways in which women's sexual and reproductive autonomy are suppressed include: women and girls may be forcibly sterilized because they have HIV, were born with intersex conditions, or are a member of a repressed ethnic group; they may be subjected to virginity testing. In other cases, coercion takes the form of a lack of access to basic health care and contraception. The core goals of women's advocacy groups, such as the Global Fund for Women, are that all women and girls are free to make their own reproductive and sexual choices and that sexual and reproductive health services and information are readily available.

One important group that has played a role in the advancement of women's sexual rights is the Global Fund for Women. The Global Fund for Women was founded during the mid-1980s in Palo Alto California by three women: Anne Firth Murray, founding president, Frances Kissling, and Laura Lederer. The three women were convinced that women's human rights and dignity were essential to the advancement of global agendas for social, economic, and political change. Frustrated by the lack of interest of traditional philanthropic organizations in funding women's groups and human rights, they forged a new path, founding an organization that would fund women-led organizations directly. On this basis, the Global Fund for Women envisions: "a just, equitable and sustainable world in which women and girls have resources, voice, choice and opportunities to realize their human rights." The group has played a key role in the advancement of the rights of women and girls worldwide by increasing the resources for and investing in women-led organizations and women's collective leadership for change. In relation to sexual rights, the Global Fund for Women supports campaigns, service delivery, advocacy, and education to influence attitudes and achieve policy change that secures women's and girls' full access to sexual and reproductive health and rights. In 1989, Global Fund for Women awarded its first grant to advance the rights of sexual minorities; during this time very few funders supported the issue. The group's support of LGBTQI activism in the Global South has made them one of the most significant funders of this global movement today. The group has provided nearly US$3.5 million in support to 260 groups working to advance the rights of LGBTQI individuals, in 61 countries, of which at least ten criminalize homosexuality.

It has been recognized that women's ability to exercise their reproductive rights is integrally related to their empowerment. This is the process by which unequal power relations are transformed and women gain greater equality with men. At the government level, women's empowerment implies the extension of all fundamental social, economic, and political rights to women. Alternatively, on the individual level, empowerment implies women gaining the power to express and defend their rights and gain greater self-esteem and control over their own lives and personal and social relationships. Empowerment of women was a central policy goal of both the International Conference on Population and Development in Cairo in 1994 and the Fourth World Conference on Women in Beijing in 1995. Women's empowerment has also been underlined in agreements of other important international, regional, and national conferences during the past two decades, including in the fifth-year review of ICPD implementation (ICPD+5) in 1999 and at the World Food Summit in 1996 and Habitat II in 1996.

Mirroring the rise of the recognition of women's sexual rights, over the past three decades a proliferation of disability rights advocacy organizations has led the campaign to grant sexual rights for disabled people. A large part of the work of these groups has been to gain recognition that disabled people have sexual needs and desires and to overcome the stigma attached to disabled sex. In many societies there is a widespread view that disabled people do not have sex, and disabled people have been the focus of sexual stigma. Research on attitudes and perceptions toward disability and sexuality suggests that individuals with disabilities are commonly viewed as asexual due to a predominant heteronormative idea of sex and what is considered natural. Lack of information and education on sexuality and disability is felt to be a major contributing factor toward the stigma attached to disability and sexuality (Esmail et al. 2010).

Campaigners for the rights of disabled people argue that denying a sex life is to deny disabled people their full human rights. Those campaigning for the rights of disabled people argue that disability does not alter the right of an individual to express his or her sexuality. These rights include the right to marry, parent, and care for children; to make choices about these areas; and to have access to accurate information that will enable them to make good choices and take appropriate actions. Over the past thirty years, paralleling the rise of these organizations, there has been a proliferation of literature on disability and sexuality. A key moment in the field was the founding of the journal *Sexuality and Disability* in 1978, which is a forum for the study of the psychological and medical aspects of sexuality in relation to rehabilitation.

It is only recently – in the past decade or so – that projects aiming to aid disabled people's sexual expression have officially been set up. One way that has begun to be officially recognized as a means for disabled people to access sexual pleasure is through the use of sex workers. Advocacy groups, such as Touching Base in Sydney, Australia, have formed to assist people with disabilities and sex workers to connect with each other. The group focuses on addressing issues of access, discrimination, human rights, legal issues, and the attitudinal barriers that these two marginalized communities can face.

In Sweden, Denmark, the Netherlands, and Germany, sexual assistants for people with disabilities have legal status. In some of these Western European countries, people with a disability can use public funds to allow them to access sex assistants once a month. However, this group is still at risk from legislation that seeks to criminalize the clients of sex workers. On February 26, 2014, the European Union voted to support criminalization of clients of sex workers, as recommended in a committee report from MEP Mary Honeyball. Although this does not legally bind EU countries, it will have an impact on future legislation in Europe and elsewhere. However, there have been calls in other countries to follow the Netherlands and other countries that have developed official programs to allow disabled people means to express their sexuality.

The third group of people campaigning for sexual rights are gay, lesbian, and bisexual people. The main principles guiding the rights approach on sexual orientation relate to equality and non-discrimination. Human rights advocates, lawyers, and other activists seek to ensure social justice and guarantee the dignity of lesbians, gays, and bisexuals. Lesbians, gays, and bisexuals do not claim any "special" or "additional rights," just the observance of the same rights as those of heterosexual persons. Historically, lesbian, gay, bisexual, and transgender (LGBT) persons have been denied – either by law or practices – basic civil, political, social, and economic rights. Violations to these rights have been documented in all parts of the world. For example, arbitrary arrests occur in a number of countries with individuals suspected of having a homo/bisexual identity. In addition, the freedom of movement is denied to bi-national couples by not recognizing their same-sex partnerships. Binding treaties can be used to force governments to respect the treaty provisions that are relevant for the human rights of LGBT individuals. Alternatively, non-binding instruments, such as declarations and resolutions, can be used in relevant situations to embarrass governments by public exposure.

The following international and regional treaties determine standards for the protection of lesbian, gay, bisexual, and transgender persons: the Convention on the Elimination of All Forms of Discrimination against Women (CEDAW) (1979) can be relevant in cases of discrimination against lesbian, bisexual, or transgender women; Article 2 of the Convention on the Rights of the Child (1989) prohibits discrimination and requires governments to ensure protection against discrimination. This treaty can be relevant in addressing sexual orientation discrimination of lesbian, gay, or bisexual children and/or parents; since April 1993 the United Nations High Commissioner for Refugees (UNHCR) has recognized in several Advisory Opinions that gays and lesbians qualify as members of a "particular social group" for the purposes of the 1951 Convention and the 1967 Protocol Relating to the Status of Refugees. Several European Union laws offer protection from discrimination based on sexual orientation, and additional requirements refer to the human rights situation in accession countries. In addition, the founding treaties on the EU have been amended in the Treaty of Amsterdam to enable EU to fight sexual orientation discrimination.

SEE ALSO: Disability Rights Movement; Sex Work and Sex Workers' Unionization; Sexualities; Stigma

REFERENCES

Esmail, S., K. Darry, A. Walter, and H. Knupp. 2010. "Attitudes and Perceptions towards

Disability and Sexuality." *Disability & Rehabilitation*, 32(14): 1148–1155.

Wilson, A. 2002. "The Transnational Geography of Sexual Rights." In *Truth Claims: Representation and Human Rights*, edited by M. P. Bradley and P. Petro, 251–265. New Brunswick: Rutgers University Press.

FURTHER READING

Bell, D., and J. Binnie. 2000. *The Sexual Citizen: Queer Politics and Beyond*. Cambridge: Polity.

YAI/National Institute for People with Disabilities. 2004. *Relationships and Sexuality Policy*. New York: YAI.

Sexual Scripts

NAAMA NAGAR
University of Wisconsin – Madison, USA

Sexual scripts are organized cognitive schema, which people employ in order to understand their own actions and desires sexually, to consider certain bodily activities as pleasurable, to interpret certain social situations as potentially sexual, and to recognize appropriate behavior for each situation. In other words, scripts are widely shared ideas about sexuality through which people learn what sex is, what is sexual, what is sexy, how to experience pleasure, and how to conduct oneself sexually. Social script theory argues that the "private world" of desire does not originate merely in the self, but evolves at the interaction between sociocultural ideas and ongoing processes of self-creation and meaning making. No bodily act or social conduct has sexual meaning without the prior existence of sexual scripts. In directing people's self-definition, orientations, beliefs, and behaviors, scripts may have a beneficial impact of reducing anxiety through providing guidance, but they also convey confining norms, which confer social inequality and limit individual expression.

DEVELOPMENT

Sexuality was not always understood in terms of learned behavior. The concept of scripts reflects the central place that sexuality holds in "the project of the self" in the twentieth century (Kimmel 2007). The metaphor of sexual scripts was first expressed in the 1970s, as part of a paradigm shift in the sciences, from naturalism in biology and functionalism in sociology, to constructionism. Prior to that period, sexuality was understood as a behavior driven by biological urges and was seen as "natural." Gagnon and Simon (1973) were the first to describe sexuality in terms of social rules, and to assert that sexual encounters were learned interactions that follow predictable sequences.

Sexual script theory (SST) leaves room for human agency, which actively engages with the culture within which it is embedded (Simon and Gagnon 2003). According to the theory, scripts consist of three distinct levels: cultural scenarios at the macro societal level, interpersonal scripts at the interactional middle level, and intra-psychic scripts at the micro level of oneself (Simon and Gagnon 1986). At the macro level, cultural scenarios prescribe the How, When, With Whom, Where, and Why of expected sexual conduct. These cultural arrangements are neither universal nor uniform but particular to a given society. Despite similarities in repertoires of bodily activities usually associated with sexuality, there is no similarity in the meanings attributed to them. At the middle level, people learn the scripts by picking up cues and directions unintentionally and intuitively from their environment, and apply them in specific social contexts in ways that facilitate sexual exchange. The interpersonal scripts serve to mediate individuals' relation to the norms and regulate their social interactions. At the intrapsychic level, cultural meanings are internalized, allowing individuals to manage their experiences and construct sexual "selves:" desires, beliefs, fantasies, and values.

GENDER AND SEXUAL SCRIPTS

Sexual scripts are embedded in social, political, and economic structures and are organized through class, ethnicity, age, and other social factors, primarily gender meanings and conduct (Mahay et al. 2000).

Sexual scripts and concepts of gender construct each other. In many cultures, *heteronormativity* – the idea that heterosexual relations are the only normal and desired form of sexual relations – constitutes the basis for kinship relations, and oppresses sexual minorities. Heteronormativity requires, by definition, two, and only two, mutually exclusive sexes (males and females) and two, and only two, mutually exclusive gender identities (men and women), thus grounding the idea of a gender binary. Men and women are expected to follow separate, overlapping and complementary scripts. Western heteronormative scripts convey a *double standard*: men are supposed to be responsible for sexual activity, to be knowledgeable about sex, to conduct themselves as assertive and often aggressive predators, and to initiate the first moves, whereas women are posited as seductive stimulus, and at the same time gatekeepers. Women should employ strategies of avoiding sex and prefer sex in committed, exclusive, and emotionally intimate relationships, or face negative sanctions. They should conduct themselves within a passive and compliant air, and must appear pleased and responsive at men's advances (Wiederman 2005).

In modern times, lesbian, gay, bisexual, transsexual, and queer (LGBTQ) relations have been considered deviant, and are still largely marginalized. Gay male identities and relations tend to be regarded as highly sexualized, and lesbian relations are regarded as less sexual, because men's sexuality is considered automatically driven, whereas women's sexuality is thought to be passive.

Variations in concepts of gender and sex influence sexual scripts. For example, among the Gerai of Borneo, men and women are believed to have the same sexual organs, and male genitalia are considered more vulnerable than women's because they are outside the body. Neither is men's sexuality considered active or aggressive, nor women's passive or vulnerable. Intercourse is conceptualized as mutual and reciprocal, and the idea of coercing someone into sex is almost unthinkable (Helliwell 2000).

Disputes over sexuality, morality, and religious and political rule politicize women's status. In Indonesia, for example, control over women's bodies has radically fluctuated over the centuries with medieval Islamization of the indigenous society, later European colonization, independent nation building, and contemporary influence of global Islamist movements and discourse (Wee 2012).

CHANGES IN CONTEMPORARY SEXUAL SCRIPTS

Sexual scripts change over time as a result of economic, technological, and political changes, and through the power of grassroots movements, whether feminist, LGBTQ, or health-related, religious movements. In Western cultures, the "sexual revolution" and the invention of oral contraceptives, for instance, loosened the link between sexual relations and marriage, and gave women more sexual control and freedom. In recent decades sexual scripts have become more globalized, owing greatly to the proliferation of global media, including porn (Kimmel 2007). At the same time, contemporary scripts remain multiple and contradictory, not uniform. In the United States, for example, two central contradictory trends are noticeable. On the one hand, growing liberalism, for example increased acceptance of LGBTQ relations, most notably seen in the recent institutionalization of same-sex marriage. At the same time, there is also growing conservatism. For example, while the lingering power differences between men and women still characterize heterosexual scripts, the gendered double standard is gradually being replaced, as both men and women who behave in overtly sexual ways face negative sanctions in some subcultures (Sakaluk et al. 2014).The sexual scripts that suggest men act as aggressors and women as gatekeepers are also diminishing; however, they are not replaced by gender-balanced scripts.

CONCLUSION

Sexual script theory aligns with queer theories in that both consider sexualities to be relative, and contingent upon social contexts, with room for actors to exercise their agency, even if constrained. Sexual script theory contributed to a revolutionary transformation in the understanding of sexualities as neither fixed nor unitary but rather varied, changing, self-conscious and reflective, and advanced liberating politics of sexuality and sexual rights (Plummer 1996).

SEE ALSO: Heteronormativity and Homonormativity

REFERENCES

England, Paula. 2011. *Understanding Hookup Culture: What's Really Happening on College Campuses.* DVD. Northampton, MA: Media Education Foundation.

Gagnon, John H., and William Simon. 1973. *Sexual Conduct: The Social Sources of Human Sexuality.* Chicago: Aldine.

Helliwell, Christine. 2000. "It's Only a Penis: Rape, Feminism, and Difference." *Signs: Journal of Women in Culture and Society*, 25(3): 789–816.

Kimmel, Michael. 2007. "Introduction: John Gagnon and the Sexual Self." In *The Sexual Self: The Social Construction of Sexual Scripts*, edited by Michael Kimmel, vii–xvi. Nashville: Vanderbilt University Press.

Mahay, Jenna, Edward O. Laumann, and Stuart Michaels. 2000. "Race, Gender and Class in Sexual Scripts." In *Sex, Love, and Health in America: Private Choices and Public Policies*, edited by Edward O. Laumann and Robert T. Michael, 197–238. Chicago: University of Chicago Press.

Plummer, Ken. 1996. "Foreword." In *Postmodern Sexualities*, edited by William Simon, ix–xvi. London: Routledge.

Rutter, Virginia, and Pepper Schwartz. 2011. *The Gender of Sexuality: Exploring Sexual Possibilities*, 2nd ed. Lanham: Rowman & Littlefield.

Sakaluk, John K., Lea M. Todd, Robin Milhausen, and Nathan J. Lachowsky. 2014. "Dominant Heterosexual Sexual Scripts in Emerging Adulthood: Conceptualization and Measurement." *Journal of Sex Research*, 51(5): 516–531.

Simon, William, and John H. Gagnon. 1986 "Sexual Scripts: Permanence and Change." *Archives of Sexual Behavior*, 15(2): 97–120.

Simon, William, and John H. Gagnon. 2003. "Sexual Scripts: Origins, Influences and Changes." *Qualitative Sociology*, 26(4): 491–497.

Wee, Vivienne. 2012. "The Politicization of Women's Bodies in Indonesia: Sexual Scripts as Charters for Action." in *Sexuality in Muslim Contexts: Restrictions and Resistance*, edited by Anissa Hélie and Homa Hoodfar, 17–51. London: Zed Books.

Wiederman, Michael. 2005. "The Gendered Nature of Sexual Scripts." *The Family Journal*, 13(4): 496–502.

Sexual Slavery

WENDY CHAPKIS
University of Southern Maine, USA

Sexual slavery is sexualized abuse of a continuing nature enacted in the context of a severe deprivation of physical liberty. Victims are predominantly women and girls, perpetrators men. Sex slavery can take both individual and organized forms. Individual acts of sexual enslavement include such high profile cases as the 2013 conviction of Ariel Castro for kidnapping, rape, and imprisonment of three young women for 8–11 years in a home in the US state of Ohio, and the 2008 prosecution of Josef Fritzl in Austria found guilty of physically and sexually assaulting his daughter during 24 years of captivity in a secret area of the family basement. The extensive media attention given to these cases reflects the fact that the crimes were not only horrific but committed in violation of both law and social norms. Far more common, though less sensational, are individual acts of sexual slavery that may correspond with, rather than directly violate, social conventions such as rape within marriage, domestic violence and abuse, and rape within prisons.

Some forms of sexual slavery are enabled, or even authorized, by the state. Until the abolition of the trade in, and possession of, African slaves in British territories (in 1833) and the United States (in 1863), the sexual abuse of enslaved women was both commonplace and considered to be a right of ownership. Rape, and other forms of sexual violence, has also been a common feature of war. In the contemporary period, examples include the 2014 kidnapping and "forced marriage" of 200 girls by Boko Haram fighters in Nigeria; the detention of large numbers of women in "rape camps" in the early 1990s by Bosnia Serb forces in the former Yugoslavia; and the coercive recruitment into, and sexual abuse within, state-organized brothels servicing Japanese military personnel in the "comfort station" system during World War II. Not until 1997, with the Rome Statute of the International Court (Articles 7 and 8), was a specific category of sex-related war crimes defined as "crimes against humanity" including "rape, sexual slavery, enforced prostitution and forced pregnancy."

Organized sexual slavery can also have a commercial dimension; prostitution and sexual slavery are thought by some to be synonymous. In the late nineteenth century, following the abolition of African slavery in the British territories and the United States, new abolitionist campaigns targeted "traffic in women" or so-called "White Slavery." Despite relatively few documented cases of forced prostitution, campaigners succeeded in creating a moral panic focused on the supposed threat to white women and girls posed by immigrants and newly freed African slaves. In 1910, in the United States, the White Slave Traffic Act, also known as the Mann Act, was passed prohibiting unmarried women from crossing state lines "for the purpose of prostitution or debauchery." White Slavery was also the focus of a series of international agreements drafted in the early twentieth century (1904, 1910, 1921, and 1933) culminating in the 1949 United Nations Convention for the Suppression of the Traffic in Persons and the Exploitation of the Prostitution of Others. Significantly, none of these agreements, domestic or international, made a distinction between sexual slavery and consensual prostitution. The 1949 convention, for example, prohibits "enticing, procuring, or leading away of a person for the purpose of prostitution … even with the consent of the person."

In the late twentieth century, second-wave feminist anti-prostitution activists in the United States – most prominently, Kathleen Barry and the Coalition Against Trafficking in Women (CATW) – drew renewed attention to the issue of prostitution as a form of sexual slavery (Barry 1979). Simultaneously, however, other feminist activists began challenging the conflation of prostitution and sexual slavery and arguing for worker rights within the sex trade. The tension between these two perspectives helped to shape the Feminist Sex Wars of the 1970s and 1980s.

Debates have continued among feminist scholars and activists over whether prostitution is inevitably a form of sexual slavery. But, by the early 1990s, the abolitionist perspective no longer found direct expression in international agreements. Instead, through the work of such groups as the Network of Sex Work Projects (NWSP) and the Global Alliance Against Trafficking in Women (GAATW), most UN instruments now distinguish between "forced" and "voluntary" prostitution.

Scholar and sex worker rights activist Jo Doezema (1998, 2010) has argued that, while the distinction between forced and voluntary prostitution has been useful, it is also inadequate: international agreements all focus exclusively on the abuse of those coerced or deceived into entering prostitution without concern about violations of the human rights of sex workers' who were not "forced." The use of the distinction "forced" and "voluntary" has also been criticized for the ways it is differentially applied to women from different parts of the world: women in the Global North are often depicted as capable of choosing sex work while those from the Global South are frequently reduced to sex slaves unable to choose (Doezema 1998; Kempadoo, Sanghera, and Pattanaik 2007).

Estimates vary widely on the magnitude of the problem of contemporary "sex slavery." This is due in part to the methodological challenge of measuring a stigmatized, underground, criminal activity. But it also reflects differing conceptions of who counts as a slave and what constitutes slavery-like conditions. For example, according to the US Centers for Disease Control, there are over 10 million incidents of intimate partner violence and over two million intimate partner rapes each year; these acts, however, are rarely defined as sexual slavery (CDC 2014). A more common measure of contemporary slavery involves coerced labor, both sexual and otherwise. The US State Department estimates between 14,500 and 17,500 people may be trafficked in the United States annually into agricultural work, sweatshop labor, domestic labor, and sexual slavery (Clawson et al. 2009). But, since the passage of the Trafficking Victims Protection Act of 2000 (reauthorized in 2005, 2008, and 2013), there have only been a few hundred confirmed cases each year nationwide (Brenna 2014). International estimates vary widely as well. The International Labour Organization (ILO) has estimated a total of 21 million people globally may be victims of forced labor with 22 percent of them (4.5 million) victims of forced sexual exploitation (ILO 2012). The UN Office on Drugs and Crime, in contrast, estimates roughly 2.4 million people may be victims of human trafficking with 53 percent of identified victims experiencing sexual slavery; UNODC observes, however, "there is no methodologically sound available estimate" of the total number of victims (UNODC 2014).

One of the most critical debates surrounding sexual slavery in the early twenty-first century focuses on the strategic responses to the problem. Those who view the problem of sexual slavery largely as a problem of trafficking women into prostitution tend to favor criminal justice responses coupled with rescue and rehabilitation efforts for victims. Those who see prostitution as a possible site of abuse, but not inevitably abusive, argue instead for strategies that emphasize worker empowerment, including immigration and prostitution law reform. Feminist activists on all sides, however, share a common commitment to structural changes within and between nations designed to reduce inequality and enhance self-determination for all persons.

SEE ALSO: Child Prostitution; Comfort Women; Feminist Sex Wars; Human Rights,

International Laws and Policies on; Prostitution/Sex Work; Sex Trafficking; Sexual Coercion; War, International Violence, and Gender

REFERENCES

Barry, Kathleen. 1979. *Female Sexual Slavery*. New York: Avon Books.

Brenna, Denise. 2014. "Life Beyond Trafficking." *Contexts*, Winter: 20–21.

Centers for Disease Control (CDC). 2014. National Intimate Partner and Sexual Violence Survey. Accessed November 20, 2014, at http://www.cdc.gov/violenceprevention/nisvs/.

Clawson, Heather, Nicole Dutch, Amy Solomon, and Lisa Goldblatt Grace. 2009. Human Trafficking Into and Within the United States: A Review of the Literature. Accessed September 10, 2015, at http://lastradainternational.org/lsidocs/index.pdf.

Doezema, Jo. 1998. "Forced to Choose." In *Global Sex Workers*, edited by Kamala Kempadoo and Jo Doezema, 34–50. New York: Routledge.

Doezema, Jo. 2010. *Sex Slaves and Discourse Master*. New York: Zed Books.

International Labour Organization (ILO). 2012. 21 Million People are Now Victims of Forced Labour. Accessed September 10, 2015, at http://www.ilo.org/global/about-the-ilo/newsroom/news/WCMS_181961/lang–en/index.htm.

Kempadoo, Kamala, Jyoti Sanghera, and Bandana Pattanaik, eds. 2007. *Trafficking and Prostitution Reconsidered*. Boulder: Paradigm Publishers.

UNODC. 2014. Global Report on Trafficking in Persons. Accessed November 20, 2014, at http://www.unodc.org/documents/data-and-analysis/glotip/GLOTIP_2014_full_report.pdf.

FURTHER READING

Bernstein, Elizabeth. 2010. "Militarized Humanitarianism Meets Carceral Feminism." *Signs*, 36(1): 45–71.

Brownmiller, Susan. 1975. *Against Our Will*. New York: Fawcett Columbine.

Chacon, Jennifer. 2006. "Misery and Myopia." *Fordham Law Review*, 74: 2977–3040.

Coalition Against Trafficking in Women. n.d. Accessed September 10, 2015, at http://www.catwinternational.org/.

Donovan, Brian. 2006. *White Slave Crusades*. Urbana-Champagne: University of Illinois.

Global Alliance Against Trafficking in Women. n.d. Accessed September 10, 2015, at http://gaatw.org/

Kara, Siddarth. 2008. *Sex Trafficking and the Business of the Modern Slave Trade*. New York: Columbia University Press.

Yoshiaki, Yoshimi. 2002. *Comfort Women*. New York: Columbia University Press.

Sexual Subjectivity

MURIEL DIMEN
New York University, USA

Sexual subjectivity refers to how people think about themselves as sexual beings. It includes their experiences of sex and erotism, as well as their conception and assessment of their own erotic and sexual desires, acts, and fantasies. It encompasses their sexual pleasures and displeasures; their appetites, revulsions and apathies; and the way they speak of or otherwise represent their sexual experience(s) and their sexual dreams. By implication, it comprises as well the unfelt or unregistered forces of unconscious and cultural life that inform sexual experience. It is also undergirded by whether and how sexuality is set up as a system of power that structures individual lives (see Dimen and Goldner 2011).

Sexuality, like gender, is differently salient for different people, which means that the importance of sexual subjectivity varies. For some, sexuality is a means of self-expression, where you come into your own. For others, it is a site of creativity, where a great deal of play takes place. For many, it is a serious matter, its significance linked to the begetting of children and reproduction of family or the religious or ethnic group or the species itself. For some, sexuality is the aim of life, for others, it is a "good, not a great," as a patient of mine put it. For some people, it holds very little, if any interest at all. And for others it is unwelcome, even noxious.

It is possible to think of sexual subjectivity as emerging within a single person, and trace that process from birth through adulthood to old age. Yet what sex is for each person depends on the culture each person belongs to and the meanings bestowed on sexuality within that culture. Each person, in other words, develops in a cultural context in which sexuality is given meaning and form in various ways. Each individual comes to be in a social unit – family, community, institution – that is made and marked by the particular ways sexuality is understood and handled and evaluated. Each child is born to adults with already formed sexual feelings and gender identities, their ideas and values about sex congruent or at odds with the cultural ethos of embedding them. So the subjective acquisition or creation of sexual desire is never black and white, it is always already colored by culture.

In the immediate experience of sex, the earliest relationships of life are central if not definitive. The primary connection between infants and caretakers, the emotions arising therein, the processes of development, including attachment, separation-individuation and recognition, and the passions of love and hate – these early object-relations infuse sexuality to the degree that they are affected by other concurrent processes. Gender identity, its construction and negotiation, in itself can eroticize primary object ties insofar as the duality of feminine and masculine is implicated in heterosexuality as a structure of erotic life. Sexual subjectivity is also emergent in such erotic feelings as swirl among infants and caretakers, between caretakers and their partners and others. The family or household or institution in which children come of age creates a medium in which the emergence of desire takes on color and form.

Sexual desire links to many other dimensions of life. Sexuality may be a way to achieve independence, or to attach to others or identify with them. It may function as a means to protect oneself from, or relieve, unwelcome feelings like depression or anxiety. It can be a way to work through trauma or it can itself be a site of trauma. Sex may feel empowering or disempowering; it may be a route to power; or it may be a place where one works through difficulties around power.

It is possible to consider sexual subjectivity as produced at the intersection of four axes: phenomenology, fantasy, power, and the enigmatic. Phenomenology refers to the way sexuality presents itself in conscious life. More formally, one might say that sexual phenomenology means the structure of various types of sexual experience ranging from perception, thought, memory, imagination, emotion, desire, and volition to bodily awareness, embodied action, and social activity, including linguistic activity. It denotes individuals' registry of their desires, their preferences for sexual pleasure, their intentions, the sorts of people and bodies and acts that excite and draw them. One can speak of sexual self-states, by which is meant states of mind in their orientation toward sexual desire and its expression. Key to sexual self-states is how one relates to others: as objects of desire, or participants in sexual practices, or objects to be avoided.

Also central to sexual subjectivity is one's sexual narrative. Everyone has a story about how they came to be sexual (Person 1980). Such an account includes memories of one's first conscious feelings of desire; of those whom one desired; of sexual acts; and of the sexual narrative's place in one's personal life story. Key to a sexual narrative is one's sexual orientation or what psychoanalysts have called "object choice," that is, which sex one prefers to have sex with, or the sexual preference by which one identifies oneself. Traditionally, only heterosexuality was deemed healthy and normal. Currently, homosexuality has joined that rank, as has bisexuality, in some quarters. More variations in desire, identification, and practice are on the near and far horizons, including transsexualities and polyamories.

The influence of fantasy in sexuality is immense. Sometimes sexual fantasy is conscious, always it is unconscious. Conscious sexual daydreams may guide one's sexual acts, but they also have the capacity to reveal, to oneself and to others, wishes that one did not quite know one had. What is most important in such conscious fantasies is how sexuality unfurls, that is, the drama of desire they depict and trace.

Unconscious sexual fantasy, which can be inferred from dreams and marginal thoughts and slips of the tongue, is another matter, for it shows up outside ordinary awareness, is not at all under immediate control. Perhaps unconscious sexual fantasy is the most unsettling of all because, in telling what it will without our say-so, it can unveil desires that one consciously deems repugnant and that one fears others will repudiate. It is very hard to receive the news of unconscious sexual wishes in a matter-of-fact way.

The relation between power and sexuality, and the place of power in sexual subjectivity, is complicated, subtle, and controversial (Butler 1990). Sexuality develops from the beginning of life largely outside conscious awareness, choice, and intent, and as such has a sway over individual experience that is unsettling. Desire is the psychic engine that runs us. One does not control when a longing will strike. Rather, desire can be said to have its way with us. Indeed, one source of sexual anxiety is in fact the loss of power one faces in the strength of desire. It is no surprise, then, that sexual subjectivity may entail conscious play with power itself between the parties to a sexual encounter. Such sexual play can show up as bondage and domination; formalized exchanges of power that sometimes take shape as sadomasochistic practices; and role-playing that entails costumes and scripts. And any of these may borrow on the others.

Quite a profound link between power and sex that manifests in sexual subjectivity is found in feelings about and experiences of the hierarchies of gender and age as they influence sexuality. Central to these is patriarchy: a system of power in which masculinity carries more weight than femininity, in which social customs and law skew toward men at the expense of women, in which female sexuality remains more hedged by moral judgment and social stricture than male sexuality, and in which men at the apices of various power structures dominate. This system of gendered power tends to find its way into cycles of desire, into fantasies of desirability, into preferences for sexual acts and positions, into patterns of eroticization.

Finally, something there is about sexual desire that does not want to be known, an enigma that is inextricably entangled with trauma. People come to desire through a circuit of desire present before their birth. The mother's (or caretaker's) mind is already touched and formed by sexuality, and it is the mother's bodymind that is the infant's first world. However, infants have no capacity to comprehend sexuality as such. Rather, the caretaker's desire is transmitted in an osmotic way such that the infant receives, among messages it can understand – "food is coming right now" or "you will soon dry" – one that it cannot comprehend, nor does the transmitter know s/he is sending it. The message of the caretaker's desire is enigmatic to the baby and the caretaker, and takes up residence in the infant's psyche as an "alien internal entity," a disturbing demand that lives forever at the heart of sexuality (Laplanche 1976).

Call it ordinary sexual trauma. On this foundation are layered other sorts of sexual experience that come with intense emotions: the excitements and disturbances of gender identity and difference, of incestuous wishes and the prohibition on acting on them, and of the first experiences of sexual activity itself. If sexual experience turns traumatic – as in incest or rape – then the entire negotiation of pleasure and danger that constitutes sexual subjectivity becomes all the more complicated.

SEE ALSO: Gender Identity, Theories of; Intimacy and Sexual Relationships; Sexual Coercion; Sexual Instinct and Sexual Desire; Sexual Scripts; Sexual Slavery; Socialization and Sexuality

REFERENCES

Butler, Judith. 1990. *Gender Trouble*. New York: Routledge.
Dimen, Muriel, and Virginia Goldner. 2011 "Gender and Sexuality." In *American Psychiatric Association Publishing Textbook of Psychoanalysis*, 2nd ed., edited by Glen O. Gabbard, Bonnie E. Litowitz, and Paul Williams, 133–152. Washington, DC: American Psychiatric Association Publishing Inc.
Laplanche, Jean. 1976. *Life and Death in Psychoanalysis*. Baltimore: Johns Hopkins University Press.
Person, E. 1980. "Sexuality as the Mainstay of Identity." *Signs*, 5: 605–630.

Sexual Terrorism

DAVID ROSEN
Independent Scholar

Sexual terrorism is a form of violence – or the threat of violence – employed officially or informally in wars and civil conflicts. It is also referred to as gender-based terrorism and most often targeted at women and young girls. The International Criminal Court (ICC) recognizes such acts of terrorism as war crimes. Legal scholars (Phelps 2006) use a narrow definition of sexual terrorism. It is a practice executed in the name of a state, an oppositional entity, or their surrogates as part of a political, racial, religious, or ethnic armed conflict. It is waged against combatants, prisoners, and/or noncombatants. It involves a wide range of practices including individual rape, gang rape, forced impregnation, and sexual mutilation. For these scholars, sexual terrorism is distinguished from interpersonal or domestic sexual violence, which can involve the same acts of terror, but neither the state nor another political entity is involved.

Other scholars use a broader interpretation based on the work of the psychiatrist Frederick Hacker (1977), for whom terrorism is a tactic. Carole Sheffield defines such terrorism as "a system by which males frighten and, by frightening, control and dominate females." She argues, "women's lives are bounded by both the reality of pervasive sexual danger and the fear that reality engenders" (Sheffield 1995).

Both definitions assume the use of nonconsensual sexual practices to foster "fright" so as to enforce tyranny. Sexual terrorism serves two purposes: to physically harm and to emotionally scar those subjected to such abuse. Historically, females have been the principal targets of sexual terrorism, but an increasing number of males and children are now victims of such attacks.

Sexual terrorism is a worldwide phenomenon with historic roots reaching back to Greek mythology and the Bible (Laqueur 2007). It finds its most barbaric expression during war, especially under conditions of modern "total war." In the United States, William Tecumseh Sherman, the celebrated Civil War general, pioneered the concept of total war during the Second Seminole War of 1840–1842. "We are not only fighting hostile armies, but a hostile people, and must make old and young, rich and poor, feel the hard hand of war," he declared. He urged his fellow soldier, "make the war so terrible ... [and] make them [noncombatants] so sick of war that generations would pass away before they would again appeal to it." Sherman implemented this policy in his infamous 1864 Civil War "march to the sea" campaign.

The concept of total war was the cornerstone of twentieth-century military strategy and is the basis for sexual terrorism. During World War II, the Japanese inflicted sexual terrorism on an estimated 200,000 Chinese, Korean, Filipino, and other colonized women in rape camps, euphemistically called "comfort stations." Susan Brownmiller, in *Against Our Will* (1975), exposed the wide-scale use of rape by the US military during the Vietnam War. In these and subsequent military conflicts, the targeted civilian casualties of total war came to be known as "collateral damage."

In the wake of the genocidal wars taking place throughout the world over the last quarter-century, sexual terrorism has become an increasingly common feature of military conflict. It was first systematically used as part of the military strategy of "ethnic cleansing" in the 1992 Bosnian conflict (Ray 1997). It was a feature in the 1994 Rwandan ethnic war (Green 2002) and the 1994–1996 Democratic Republic of Congo (Pratt and Werchick 2004).

During the 1990s and 2000s, still other incidents of gender-based terrorism were reported in countries across the globe. They apparently took place in Afghanistan and Iraq, in Chechnya and Columbia, and in Sri Lanka, Burma, and East Timor. In Zimbabwe, President Robert Mugabe has been accused of using sexual terror to maintain near-dictatorial power (AIDS-Free World 2009). Most recently, episodes of sexual terrorism – known as "rape jihad" – are reported being committed by Islamic fundamentalists in West Africa, most notably in Somalia, Mali, and in northern Nigeria (Salifu 2013).

In the United States, sexual terrorism acquired a different meaning following the attacks of September 11, 2001. The US government adopted "enhanced interrogation techniques" designed to get information from alleged enemy combatants. At Abu Ghraib, Guantánamo, and black-site prisons, captives were subject to not only waterboarding, but a host of other acts of sexual dehumanization, if not terrorism.

These activities included: forcing naked male detainees to wear women's underwear; forcing groups of male detainees to masturbate while being photographed and videotaped; placing a dog chain or strap around a naked detainee's neck and having a female soldier pose for a picture; and sodomizing a detainee with a chemical light or a broomstick (Taguba 2004).

SEE ALSO: Comfort Women; Genocide; Sex Trafficking; Sexual Slavery

REFERENCES

AIDS-Free World. 2009. *Electing to Rape: Sexual Terror in Mugabe's Zimbabwe*. Accessed June 10, 2015, at http://www.aidsfreeworld.org/Publications-Multimedia/Reports/Electing-to-Rape.aspx.

Brownmiller, Susan. 1975. *Against Our Will: Men, Women and Rape*. New York: Simon and Schuster.

Green, Llezlie L. 2002. "Gender Hate Propaganda and Sexual Violence in the Rwandan Genocide: An Argument for Intersectionality in International Law." *Columbia Human Rights Law Review*, 33: 733–776.

Hacker, Frederick J. 1977. *Crusaders, Criminals, Crazies: Terror and Terrorism in Our Time*. New York: Bantam Books.

Laqueur, Walter. 2007. "Terrorism: A Brief History." In *Countering the Terrorist Mentality*, US Department of State, Bureau of International Information Programs, 33: 21 (May).

Phelps, Andrea R. 2006. "Gender-Based War Crimes: Incidence and Effectiveness of International Criminal Persecution." *William & Mary Journal of Women and the Law*, 12: 499–520.

Pratt, Marion, and Leah Werchick. 2004. Sexual Terrorism: Rape as a Weapon of War in Eastern Democratic Republic of Congo. USAID/DCHA Assessment Report.

Ray, Amy E. 1997. "The Shame of it: Gender-Based Terrorism in the Former Yugoslavia and the Failure of International Human Rights Law to Comprehend the Injuries." *American University Law Review*, 46(3): 793–840.

Salifu, Uyo. 2013. "*Sexual Terrorism in Africa: A Case of Two Crimes in One.*" Institute for Security Studies. Accessed June 10, 2015, at http://www.issafrica.org/iss-today/sexual-terrorism-in-africa-a-case-of-two-crimes-in-one.

Sheffield, Carole J. 1995. "Sexual Terrorism." In *Women: A Feminist Perspective*, edited by Jo Freeman, 5th ed., 409–424. Palo Alto: Mayfield Publishing.

Taguba, Antonio M. 2004. "AR 15-6 Investigation of the 800th Military Police Brigade." Taguba Report.

Sexual Violence and the Military

HEATHER D. CYR
Southern Connecticut State University, USA

In 2012, approximately 26,000 US soldiers were sexually harassed and/or assaulted at the hands of peers and superiors, though only a fraction of victims came forward to report the incident/s (Project Vote Smart 2013). Verbal and physical retaliation by peers and superiors is a common reason victims of sexual violence often remain silent. Another reason soldiers do not come forward to report sexual harassment and assault is the threat of being involuntarily discharged from the military. For these same reasons many women and men within the armed forces who have experienced sexual violence do not seek medical help.

For many, the aftermath of sexual violence is as devastating as the actual assault. Those who have met with sexual violence in the military, commonly referred to as MST (military sexual trauma), generally experience stress, depression, substance abuse, suicidality, and post-traumatic stress disorder (PTSD). Untreated PTSD combined with MST has led to an increase in homelessness for US veterans.

Despite the physical and emotional damage caused by MST those who perpetuate sexual violence within the armed forces and those who allow it to happen are rarely brought to justice. In many cases those accused of sexual violence receive little more than a verbal warning. The history of military sex scandals in the United States illustrates both the prevalence of sexual violence within the armed forces and the lack of consistency in disciplining those who are accused of sexual harassment and assault.

The Tailhook scandal of 1991 was the first time in American history that the incidence of sexual harassment and assault within the armed forces became public knowledge. Shortly after the 1991 Tailhook convention, which took place at the Las Vegas Hilton, servicewomen, servicemen, and female civilians came forward to report incidents of sexual harassment and assault that they experienced at the hands of US Navy pilots. The investigation of the 1991 Tailhook convention was due, in large part, to Lt. Paula Coughlin of the United States Navy.

Lt. Coughlin was attacked while walking through a hotel hallway aptly referred to as the gauntlet. The young lieutenant reported the incident to her superior on several occasions and on each occasion the incident was dismissed as harmless frivolity. She then took the matter up the chain of command until her accusations of sexual assault were taken seriously. Lt. Coughlin's charges against the men who attacked her, combined with the accusations of the other victims, led to an investigation of approximately 175 officers.

At the end of the Tailhook hearings less than a handful of male officers met with disciplinary action and Lt. Coughlin, due to continuous harassment by peers, resigned from the Navy.

Since the Tailhook scandal there have been many more publicized cases of sexual violence within each of the four branches of the United States military. In 1996 at Aberdeen Proving Ground, drill sergeants were accused of raping female enlistees, then passing the names of the enlistees on to other male sergeants who raped them as well. One of the men accused of participating in the scandal admitted not only to having sex with female recruits, but also to covering for the other drill sergeants who participated in the sexual coercion and rape of female enlistees. The outcome of the trial, in which nearly a dozen men were accused of rape and coercion, led to a 25-year imprisonment term for one of the male participants while the other male attackers met with lesser prison terms or administrative punishment.

In 2003 more than 20 women from the Air Force Academy in Colorado Springs claimed that reports of sexual harassment and assault were ignored by academy officials. Furthermore, those who reported sexual harassment and assault were retaliated against by peers and superiors. As a result of the military's apathetic treatment of sexual violence, lawsuits filed on behalf of sexual harassment and sexual assault victims began to hold military officials accountable for harms done to US soldiers.

In 2011 a lawsuit was filed on behalf of 25 servicewomen and 3 servicemen who were raped in the military then harassed and/or involuntarily discharged from military service for reporting the attacks. The case of *Kori Cioca et al. v. Donald Rumsfeld et al.* was a direct result of the continued lack of reaction to sexual harassment and assault within the armed forces. Kori Cioca, one of the soldiers filing the complaint, was sexually harassed by a superior. Although she reported him several times, no formal charges were brought against her superior and no protection was afforded Cioca, who was eventually beaten and raped by the man she reported. The other women and men who appeared in court with Cioca testified to similar treatment. After they were raped, they received no help from superiors. Furthermore, when the incidents were reported, the complainants were harassed by peers and superiors. In December of 2011 the court found in favor of *Donald Rumsfeld et al.*, stating: "rape is an occupational hazard of military service" (Dick 2012).

A similar lawsuit was filed against Defense Secretary Leon Panetta and several former defense secretaries on behalf of women and men who were harassed and/or raped while serving in the US Navy and Marine Corps. The complainants filed the case against the Defense Department for failure to confront the problem of sexual harassment and rape within the US military. One of the complainants asserted that after she reported the men who raped her, she was harassed by peers and told by superiors to forget the incident and move on. The other women and men involved in the lawsuit experienced similar treatment. At the end of the trial the presiding judge held that the plaintiff's constitutional rights were not violated and that the defendants did not have the obligation to protect the soldiers from harm (*Ariana Klay, et al., Plaintiffs, v. Leon Panetta, Secretary of Defense, et al., Defendants*).

Currently veterans and civilians are working together to end sexual violence in the United States armed forces. Online organizations such as the Service Women's Action Network (SWAN) and Protect Our Defenders strive to educate civilians on the issue of sexual trauma and offer aid to survivors. In 2012 the documentary *The Invisible War* was released in hopes of bringing attention to the seriousness of sexual violence within the US armed forces. The creators of the film interviewed men and women veterans who were sexually traumatized by peers and superiors while serving in the United States military. Others interviewed for the film were military personnel and civilians who have worked tirelessly to bring attention to the prevalence of sexual trauma. US Congresswoman Jackie Speier, a longtime advocate of sexual trauma survivors, was also interviewed for the film. In 2013, Congresswoman Speier (D-CA) alongside Congressman Patrick Meehan (R-PA) introduced a bill known as the STOP Act, which would allow victims of military sexual violence to seek help outside of the usual chain of command. The bill, which calls for an amendment to military article 32, has been co-signed by a number of Democratic and Republican Congressional leaders whose aim is to aid survivors of sexual violence in the military, though it has not been passed at time of this writing.

SEE ALSO: Militarism and Gender-Based Violence; Militarism and Sex Industries; Post-Traumatic Stress Disorder

REFERENCES

Dick, Kirby, dir. 2012. *The Invisible War*. Produced by Amy Ziering and Doug Blush. USA: Docuramafilms.

Project Vote Smart. 2013. "Hirono, Colleagues Introduce Bipartisan Bill to Protect Military Sexual Assault Victims During 32 Proceedings." Accessed August 10, 2015, at http://votesmart.org/public-statement/824368/hirono-colleagues-introduce-bipartisan-bill-to-protect-military-sexual-assault-victims-during-32-proceedings.

FURTHER READING

D'Amico, Francine, and Laurie Lee Weinstein. 1999. *Gender Camouflage: Women and the U.S. Military*. New York: NYU Press.

Dean, Donna M. 1997. *Warriors without Weapons: The Victimization of Military Women*. Pasadena, MD: Minerva Center.

Dutra, Lissa, et al. 2011. "Women at War: Implications for Mental Health." *Journal of Trauma and Dissociation*, 37: 25–37.

Hunter, Mic. 2007. *Honor Betrayed: Sexual Abuse in America's Military*. Fort Lee, NJ: Barricade Books.

Nelson, T. S. 2002. *For Love of Country: Confronting Rape and Sexual Harassment in the U.S. Military*. New York: Haworth Maltreatment and Trauma Press.

Service Women's Action Network (SWAN). 2015. "Serving Military Women and Veterans." Accessed August 10, 2015, at http://servicewomen.org/.

Zurbriggen, Eileen L. 2010. "Rape, War, and the Socialization of Masculinity: Why Our Refusal to Give Up War Ensures That Rape Cannot Be Eradicated." *Psychology of Women Quarterly*, 34: 538–549.

Sexualities

M. MORGAN HOLMES
Wilfrid Laurier University, Canada

The use of the term "sexualities" is best understood as a corrective response to the commonly held notion that human beings have one shared, universal sexuality determined primarily by reproductive biology, largely unchanging over time, and common to all cultures, even if there are some variations on the generally reproductively oriented theme. It is, for example, still common to encounter titles in medicine, psychology, and reproductive biology that speak to "human sexuality."

From the highly popular and deeply influential medico-sexological work of William Masters and Virginia Johnson (1982), to the mid-1990s anthropological work of Edgar Gregerson (1994), or the more contemporary psychology/evolutionary biology-based work of Simon LeVay (LeVay and Baldwin 2009), titles with a focus on "human sexuality" abound. Ironically, many of these singularly focused titles that give a false impression of unity and simply paper over the very diversity of practices, feelings, and identifications of the cultures and regions written about within their pages. Even Jeffrey Weeks's important text, *Sexuality*, first published in 1986, and again in an updated edition in 2003, presents a historicized, rather than biologized, account of diverse practices and politics under a homogenized, single-word title. And Gregerson, for instance, writes about a literal world of diverse cultural practices that contemporary readers can recognize as being sexual, but nonetheless titles the book monolithically as *The World of Human Sexuality*. In other words, in spite of claims to a scientific neutrality, "sexuality," as a singular term, does not operate as an accurate description of human behaviors, feelings, and identifications. Instead, its singularity functions as a normative ideal: a generally reproductive and heterosexual act, and carried out – at least in the contemporary, dominant, Western location of its provenance – between adults. Moreover, in the face of a world of complex geographically, historically, and culturally specific practices, the gathering together of all these under the heading of "sexuality" has allowed the acts to be easily categorized as either "common to all humans" or "odd deviation."

In contrast, scholars who have chosen to adopt the plural "sexualities" both as their object of study and as a description of their interests have decided to draw deliberate attention to the multiplicity of contexts, histories, practices, and politics of sexualities around the world, across time, and between/across groups. As the favored term or mode for conceptualizing one's area of interest, "sexualities" focus from the outset on a critical mandate to recognize how sexual identities and relationships are made to bear meaning for and within a range of contexts from the institutions of family to religion, education, government, and medicine, and are formed through personal practices that are shaped by local cultures and historically specific contexts. For example, Hunt and Curtis (2006) on the discursive production of appropriate uses of oral sex:

> There is a common assumption that pervades everyday life that such practices as "sexual intercourse" and "oral sex" are natural and unchanging and that "we" all know what these terms mean. One reason we should all be grateful to President Clinton [during his impeachment trial] is that he drew attention to the fact that there was no self-evident consensus about what "having sex" means. What gets subsumed under the umbrella of "oral sex" often involves a dispersed set of practices and meanings. (2006, 70)

The work of sexualities scholarship is predominantly interdisciplinary and often informed by feminist, poststructuralist, and queer theories/politics, and either implicitly or explicitly traces how certain categories of sexual experience and behavior – namely those practices that are disciplined and moderated, heterosexual, pair-bonded, and reproductively oriented – come to be considered "sacred," "healthy," or "normal" while others – those that reject the centrality of children and the family unit, defy propriety, embrace relative states of "excess," and resist easy classification as heterosexual – are regarded as "deviant," and, thus, socially undesirable. At the forefront of work in this critical vein, Gayle Rubin's 1984 essay, "Thinking Sex," draws attention to the ways that various practices, starting with masturbation and moving outward – away from what she refers to as the "charmed circle" of monogamy, reproductively oriented sex within marriage – "organized" sexual desires and practices into sacred, approved categories and into ejected ones which, if discovered, could result in a variety of punishments (including clitorectomy, binding of hands, incarceration in mental hospitals or prisons, etc.).

In addition, the scholarship on sexualities draws heavily from the work of the twentieth-century French theorist, Michel Foucault. Foucault's main focus on the combined importance of context and the relationships between power and the production of knowledge has been used to challenge two key precepts: first, the notion that our sexual world has only recently been marked by the arrival of discrete categories of sexual experience and identifications; and second, the notion that our political sensibilities always progress toward greater liberalization of our treatment of sexual minority groups. Foucault argues these points in the three-volume series *The History of Sexuality*, which, in spite of its singular form in the title, demonstrates that *sexualities* have proliferated and changed across time and place. Foucault's observations have been important in developing an understanding of how Euro-American encounters with medicine have become, over the last two centuries, increasingly the source of our thinking about how to live our sexual lives, and most particularly how to think of ourselves in terms of having a particular, unchanging *sexual identity*. In addition, Foucault's history demonstrates the illogic of insisting that the same-sex activity of the classical period can be read as evidence that people have always understood themselves to be "gay" or "homosexual," and shows how sexual practices, recognized as plural within Hellenic culture, were managed through a *diet* or *regimentation* based on an "economy of humors" – or bodily energies, flows, and substances – and thus allowed for all kinds of desires, so long as none dominated to the point that it would drain one's energies and threaten one's health.

Writing as a rough contemporary of Foucault, and taking a similar view, Vern L. Bullough, historian at California State University Northridge, wrote in the 1970s on the manner in which the medical model of thinking about sex had produced a particular view of "homosexuality" as a diagnosis (Bullough 1974). Bullough's work demonstrates that the historical production of sexual types, whether heterosexual or homosexual, served prevailing medical interests in the eighteenth and nineteenth centuries to identify what was considered to be "normal" human behavior, and to cure those diseases brought about by immoderate or unbalanced sexual appetites. Bullough explains that in this context, "homosexuality" was largely understood as "a symptom of hereditary weakness, and along with those individuals suffering from nymphomania, satyriasis, or engaging in bestiality, rape, or profanation of corpses ought to be regarded as a pathological condition and delivered to the asylum rather than imprisoned [as criminals]" (1974, 107). That the apparent commonsense perception of same-sex desire and activity belonged to a disease cluster that rendered homosexual behavior in the same register as it rendered the act of rape will likely seem absurd if not incomprehensible to contemporary readers demonstrates not only that our ideas about sexuality are culturally and historically changeable, but also that they are grounded in a specific sociopolitical and cultural context.

These examples also show us why scholars have turned to the use of the term "sexualities": to mark the different meanings and uses for categories that are at least nominally "the same." In other words, the study of sexualities allows us to understand and to mark the different connotations of "heterosexual" and "homosexual" over the last 250 years, to understand that the same-sex activity well known in the records left by the classical Greeks does not have the same social meaning as the identifications of gay, lesbian, and bisexual persons and acts now.

At the forefront of the social science and humanities disciplines that have adopted a critical, pluralist approach to the study of human sexualities are anthropology, sociology, and gender studies. Of key importance in the fields are the journal *Sexualities* established by Ken Plummer in 1998; the 2011 edited collection *Sexualities in Anthropology* edited by Andrew and Harriet Lyons; and Steven Seidman's 1991 monograph, *Romantic Longings: Love in America, 1830–1980*. Each of these examples has contributed to the ability of scholars to recognize the ways that different forms of sexual activities, desires, communities, and so forth have been constituted as identifiable and discrete sexualities.

The practical utility of thinking in the corrective terms of "sexualities" rather than "sexuality" is not limited to the world of academic research. Precisely because it is a corrective term with an indexical relationship to the plural and fluid character of sexual identifications and affiliations, "sexualities" has had great importance for social and political movements and for community-based activism. In other words, because it is not limited by the guiding principles of sexologists and biologists to determine the singularly normative standard that governs human behavior and identifies its deviations, "sexualities" has been hailed by those who wish to speak about divergences and interconnections in human sexual behavior without positing a normative standard against which personal proclivities and community practices ought to be measured.

Outside academia, "sexualities" first appeared in the American poet and essayist Audre Lorde's talk, "I am Your Sister: Black Women Organizing Across Sexualities," delivered in 1985 at Medgar Evers College, in which Lorde challenges black women's rights groups not to continue to allow homophobia and heterosexism to act as barriers to black women's civil rights work (1988, 57). For Lorde, "sexualities" operates as an expedient way to gesture toward the different lives that women lead, and works as a tacit acknowledgment that some, like her, are lesbians, while the center of power in black women's organizations belonged to family-oriented, straight women. In her essay, Lorde challenged the assertions that black lesbians (like her) did not have families, and were not part of the larger black family or black sisterhood, and she lists the many ways in which, over more than three decades, she and her friends had worked as unacknowledged black lesbians, and so demands in the essay that she and her friends start to be recognized, and to become visible. She calls for an alliance across these different sexualities, rather than for a reassertion that the only "family" that counts is the family that serves men first and disavows the contributions of lesbians to the black civil rights and black feminist movements.

Lorde's example, then, shows us that "sexualities" in its first popular usage could refer to the popular awareness in grassroots organizations that, contrary to powerful earlier social, cultural, and medical assertions, while people do not all share the same sexual experiences, orientations, or perceptions, they may still share overlapping goals. Additionally, it is important to note that in Lorde's deployment of the term, she still assumes that heterosexuality is one thing, and that lesbianism is another, each its own discrete and distinct category of desire. More recent work on sexualities has highlighted the ways in which a single person may experience over the course of a lifetime a variety of experiences best described in the plural. Taking a sociological perspective, Kimmel (2015), for example, observes that:

> the sexual world is dramatically different from the world of our parents' or grandparents' generations. … there have been so many changes in

the technologies of sex – from pills that prevent pregnancies to those that promise to increase sexual functioning … sex is now something that we expect to be doing throughout our lives … (xiv)

Finally, the use of the term "sexualities" is found in research and activist work on the human rights entitlements of trans-identified persons, and also for those who have experienced the particular form of biomedicalization that Lena Eckert (2010) refers to as "intersexualization." As a framework that neutrally describes the diversity in sexual identifications, configurations, and behaviors, "sexualities" provides a critical and intellectual framework that is capable of bringing trans and intersex studies within the purview of academic and community-based scholarship where the sexological tradition of sexuality studies had treated these two groups as medical and/or psychological examples of pathology. It is within the arena of sexualities that critical intersex studies (Morland 2009; Reis 2009; Eckert 2010; Holmes 2010) has been able to develop, and through which various activist groups (e.g., Organization Internationale Intersexe) have been able to make human rights claims to bodies such as the United Nations. Similarly, it is under the umbrella of "sexualities" that critical trans studies (Namaste 2000; Noble 2004; Stryker 2006) have been able to develop in fields that span the humanities and social sciences. The development of these research areas, and of activist alliances across sexualities in the manner suggested by Lorde, are certainly heralded in some of the more radical work published on sexuality, but could only come fully into positions of intellectual, political, and academic legitimacy by virtue of the legitimacy granted to human plurality by the term "sexualities."

SEE ALSO: Bisexuality; Feminism, Poststructural; Heterosexism and Homophobia; Intersexuality; Queer Theory; Sexuality and Human Rights; Trans Identities, Psychological Perspectives

REFERENCES

Bullough, Vern. 1974. "Homosexuality and the Medical Model." *Journal of Homosexuality*, 1: 99–116.

Eckert, Lena. 2010. "*Intervening in Intersexualization: The Clinic and the Colony*." Doctoral dissertation, University of Utrecht.

Foucault, Michel. 1985. The History of Sexuality, Vol. 2: *The Use of Pleasure*, trans. Robert Hurley. New York: Vintage Books.

Gregerson, Edgar. 1994. *The World of Human Sexuality*. New York: Irvington Publishers.

Holmes, M. Morgan. 2010. *Critical Intersex*. Farnham, UK: Ashgate Press.

Hunt, Allan, and Bruce Curtis. 2006. "A Geneology of the Genital Kiss: Oral Sex in the Twentieth Century". *The Canadian Journal of Human Sexuality*, 15(2): 69–84.

Kimmel, Michael, and The Stony Brook Sexualities Research Group. 2015. *Sexualities: Identities, Behaviors, and Society*. New York: Oxford University Press.

LeVay, Simon, and Janice Baldwin. 2009. *Human Sexuality*, 3rd ed. Sunderland, MA: Sinauer Associates.

Lorde, Audre. 2009. "I am Your Sister: Black Women Organizing Across Sexualities." In *I am Your Sister: Collected and Unpublished Writings of Audre Lorde*, edited by Rudolph Byrd, Johnnetta Cole, and Beverly Guy-Sheftall. New York: Oxford University Press.

Lyons, Andrew, and Harriet Lyons, eds. 2011. *Sexualities in Anthropology: A Reader*. Malden, MA: Wiley-Blackwell.

Masters, William H., and Virginia E. Johnson. 1982. *Human Sexuality*. Boston, MA: Little, Brown.

Morland, Iain. 2009. "Between Critique and Reform: Ways of Reading the Intersex Controversy." In *Critical Intersex*, edited by Morgan Holmes, 191–213. Farnham, UK: Ashgate.

Namaste, Viviane. 2000. *Invisible Lives: The Erasure of Transsexual and Transgendered People*. Chicago: University of Chicago Press.

Noble, Jean. 2004. *Masculinities Without Men?* Vancouver: University of British Columbia Press.

Reis, Elizabeth. 2009. *Bodies in Doubt: An American History of Intersex*. Baltimore, MD: Johns Hopkins University Press.

Rubin, Gayle. 1984. "Thinking Sex: Notes for a Radical Theory of the Politics of Sexuality." In *Pleasure and Danger*, edited by Carol Vance. New York: Routledge and Kegan Paul.

Seidman, Steven. 1991. *Romantic Longings: Love in America, 1830–1980*. New York: Routledge and Kegan Paul.

Stryker, Susan. 2006. *The Transgender Studies Reader*. New York: Routledge and Kegan Paul.

Weeks, Jeffrey. 1986. *Sexuality*. Harlow, UK: Ellis Horwood and Tavistock Publications.

Sexuality and Human Rights

SHWETA MAJUMDAR ADUR
California State University, Fullerton, USA

In 2011, a study commissioned by the United Nations Human Rights Council (UNHRC) found that more than 76 countries around the world have "sodomy laws" criminalizing consensual, adult, same-sex sexual relations and in at least five there are provisions for the death penalty (A/HRC/19/41 2011). The World Health Organization (WHO) estimates that approximately 800 women die from pregnancy and childbirth-related causes every day (WHO 2014). Approximately 133 million girls and women worldwide have experienced female genital mutilation or cutting (UN Women 2014). Countries may criminalize marital rape. Trafficking victimizes millions worldwide. Women and girls represent 98 percent of the estimated 4.5 million forced into sexual exploitation (UN Women 2014).

Sexuality and human rights represent a contemporary, albeit contested, development in the field of post–World War II international human rights. Though discrimination and violence on the basis of gender and sexual identity existed long before and continued long after the adoption of the Universal Declaration of Human Rights (UDHR) in 1948, activists and scholars have recently begun the task of linking the two. The UDHR is one of the most influential documents of global governance. Based on the premise that "all human beings are born free and equal in dignity and rights," it outlines a list of rights that are deemed universal, inalienable, and indivisible. Broadly, the rights pertain to matters of security, slavery, torture, protection of the law, freedom of speech and movement, religion, and rights to social security, work and health, education, culture, and citizenship.

For the first three decades (1945–1975) of the existence of United Nations (UN) there were a few cursory references to sex discrimination in official UN documents. A handful of women who were signatories of the UN Charter struggled for women's recognition in the UN Charter's contents and for women's inclusion in political positions within the UN. Their tenacious activism was also responsible for the formation of the Commission on the Status of Women, an entity dedicated to the global promotion of gender equality, but, overall, during this period, conversations concerning gender and sexuality were largely unheard.

The UN Decade for women (1975–1985) was a major turning point. The decade included landmark women's conferences sponsored by the UN in Mexico City (1975), Copenhagen (1980), and Nairobi (1985), wherein gender began to be seen as an important variable for discrimination. Yet, here too women's issues were discussed more prominently in the context of *discrimination* in the socioeconomic sphere. In 1979, the UN General Assembly approved the Convention on the Elimination of All Forms of Discrimination against Women (CEDAW), which became the starting point for discussing women's human rights.

By the 1990s, gender-based violence against women had emerged on the international agenda but as an issue of women's rights and crime prevention (Coomaraswamy 1999). In 1993, at the World Conference of Human Rights in Vienna, the Declaration on the Elimination of Violence against Women (DEDAW) was adopted. It defined violence against women as: "any act of gender-based violence that results in, or is likely to result in, physical, sexual or psychological harm or suffering to women, including threats of such acts, coercion or arbitrary deprivation of liberty, whether occurring in public or in private life."

In 1994, the UN appointed the Special Rapporteur on Violence Against Women whose mandate included the collection and analysis of comprehensive data regarding gendered violence at international, national, and regional levels. In the same year, the International Conference on Population and Development (ICPD) linked reproductive health and gender equality in a human rights-based framework. Amongst other provisions, the goals included access to reproductive and sexual health services including family planning. Female genital cutting was also explicitly acknowledged as a human rights violation.

The Fourth World Conference on Women (Beijing Platform) in 1995 was a major breakthrough as it consolidated the idea of women's rights as human rights. It identified 12 areas of concern and urged national governments to develop strategies to implement the Platform locally. In 2000, the UN Security Council Resolution 1325 on Women, Peace and Security required parties in conflict to recognize women's rights and supported women's participation in peace talks and post conflict reconstruction. The UN Entity for Gender Equality and the Empowerment of Women (UN Women) was created in 2010 by merging four distinct branches of the UN system. Michelle Bachelet, the former president of Chile, was the inaugural executive director until 2013 followed by Phumzile Mlambo-Ngcuka.

Until recently, sexuality and sexual rights were narrowly defined to address heterosexual concerns of sexual violence experienced by women and children, contraception, maternal health, in conversations surrounding "safe sex," and in relation to HIV/AIDS and sexually transmitted diseases. It is only in the last decade or so that sexual rights has come to include all of these and also gender identity and sexual orientation.

In 2006, Yogyakarta Principles extended the International Human Rights Law to include gender identity and sexual orientation and outlined obligations of states to protect individuals from discrimination and violence regardless of gender identity and sexual orientation. In 2011, the UN issued the first report on human rights of lesbian, gay, bisexual, and transgender (LGBT) people (A/HRC/19/41 2011). This documents human rights violations experienced by LGBT persons and argues that violence against lesbian, gay, bisexual, transgender, and questioning (LGBTQ) people tends to be more vicious than other bias-motivated crimes. It calls for the annulment of repressive laws that criminalize on the basis of gender identity and consensual adult same-sex sexuality and, finally, petitions for protection against homophobic and transphobic behaviors.

Scholars argue that international human rights instruments have created a master frame of reference, which is sufficiently broad in interpretive scope, inclusivity, and flexibility (Keck and Sikkink 1998). Merry (2006) argues that the framing of local events into the global language of violence and human rights facilitates a script easily understood across borders. Conversely, intermediaries translate international documents into terms relevant to particular localized political struggles.

Injured individuals view themselves as experiencing a human rights violation – which is meant to be inalienable. It has facilitated coalitions across different cultural and socioeconomic contexts (Moghadam 2000). A *boomerang pattern* of influence exists when domestic groups in a repressive state bypass their government and directly seek out international allies to bring external pressure on their states (Keck and Sikkink 1998). Using a human rights framework also delinks rights and protection from "citizenship" status. Most modern states structure rights as entitlements to "citizen" status, thus in effect marginalizing vast numbers of people who may not fall within this category (e.g., undocumented migrants, migrant women with dependant visa status, trafficked persons, and refugees). Human rights instruments promise protection regardless of "citizen" status and hold states responsible for upholding the dignity and humanity of all individuals within their borders. It also challenges violence that is tolerated, perpetrated, and justified in the name of tradition, culture, abetted in the shadow of religion, culture, and tolerated in the name of cultural relativism (Ertürk 2007).

Despite its advantages, scholars have also pointed to some of the challenges which include reification of cultures and the dangers of "decontextualized" readings (Merry 2006; Tripp 2006); problems of implementation, weak political will, and recalcitrant states (Ertürk 2007); difficulties even in defining the content of the discourse (Ertürk and Purkayastha 2012), and the consolidation of inequalities between the Global North and the Global South (Naples 2002).

SEE ALSO: Female Genital Cutting; Gender-Based Violence; Reproductive Justice and Reproductive Rights in the United States; Sexualities; Sodomy Law in Comparative Perspective; Transphobia; UN Decade For Women; Universal Human Rights; Yogyakarta Principles

REFERENCES

A/HRC/19/41. 2011. "Discriminatory Laws and Practices and Acts of Violence against Individuals Based on Their Sexual Orientation and Gender Identity." New York: United Nations Human Rights Council. Accessed August 4, 2015, at http://www2.ohchr.org/english/bodies/hrcouncil/docs/19session/a.hrc.19.41_english.pdf.

Coomaraswamy, Radhika. 1999. "Reinventing International Law: Women's Rights as Human Rights in the International Community." In *Debating Human Rights: Critical Essays for United States and Asia*, edited by Peter Van Ness, 167–183. New York: Routledge.

Ertürk, Yakin. 2007. "Intersections between Culture And Violence Against Women: Report of The Special Rapporteur On Violence Against Women – Its Causes And Consequences." Accessed August 4, 2015, at http://www.refworld.org/pdfid/461e2c602.pdf.

Ertürk, Yakin, and Bandana Purkayastha. 2012. "Linking Research, Policy and Action: A Look at the Work of the Special Rapporteur on Violence against Women." *Current Sociology*, 60(2): 142–160. DOI: 10.1177/0011392111429216.

Keck, Margaret E., and Kathryn Sikkink. 1998. *Activists Beyond Borders: Advocacy Networks in International Politics*. Ithaca: Cornell University Press.

Merry, Sally E. 2006. *Human Rights and Gender Violence: Translating International Law into Local Justice*. Chicago: University of Chicago Press.

Moghadam, Valentine. 2000. "Transnational Feminist Network: Collective Action in the Era of Globalization." *International Sociology*, 15(1): 57–85. DOI: 10.1177/02685809000015001004.

Naples, Nancy A. 2002. "The Challenges and Possibilities of Transnational Feminist Praxis." In *Women's Activism and Globalization: Linking Local Struggles and Transnational Politics*, edited by Nancy. A. Naples and Manisha Desai, 263–277. New York: Routledge.

Tripp, Aili M. 2006."Challenges in Transnational Feminist Mobilization." In *Global Feminism: Transnational Women's Activism, Organizing and Human Rights*, edited by Myra Marx Ferree and Ali Mari Tripp, 296–312. New York: New York University Press.

UN Women. 2014. "Facts and Figures: Ending Violence against Women" Accessed August 4, 2015, at http://www.unwomen.org/en/what-we-do/ending-violence-against-women/facts-and-figures.

World Health Organization (WHO). 2014. "Maternal Mortality". Accessed August 4, 2015, at http://www.who.int/mediacentre/factsheets/fs348/en/.

FURTHER READING

Armaline, William T., Davita Silfen Glasberg, and Bandana Purkayastha. 2011. *Human Rights in our Own Backyard: Injustice and Resistance in the United States*. Philadelphia: University of Pennsylvania Press.

Collins, Dana, Sylvanna Falcón, Sharmila Lodhia, and Molly Talcott, eds. 2011. *New Directions in Feminism and Human Rights*. London: Routledge.

Cook, Rebecca J., ed. 1994. *Human Rights of Women: National and International Perspectives*. Philadelphia: University of Pennsylvania Press.

Corrêa, Sonia, Rosalind Petchesky, and Richard Parker. 2008. *Sexuality Health and Human Rights*. New York: Routledge.

Desai, Manisha.1999. "From Vienna to Beijing: Women's Human Rights Activism and Human Rights Community." In *Debating Human Rights: Critical Essays for United States and Asia*, edited by Peter Van Ness, 183–196. New York: Routledge.

Donnelly, Jack. 2003. *Universal Human Rights in Theory and Practice*. Ithaca: Cornell University Press.

Ferree, Myra M., and Aili Mari Tripp. 2006. *Global Feminism: Transnational Women's Activism, Organizing, and Human Rights*. New York: New York University Press.

Merry, Sally E. 2001. "Rights, Religion, and Community: Approaches to Violence against Women in the Context of Globalization." *Law and Society Review*, 35(1): 39–88.

Molyneux, Maxine, and Shahra Razavi. 2002. *Gender Justice, Development and Rights*. Oxford: Oxford University Press.

Morgaine, Karen. 2007. "Domestic Violence and Human Rights: Local Challenges to a Universal Framework." *Journal of Sociology and Social Welfare*, 34(1): 109–129.

Sexualizing the State

JYOTI PURI
Simmons College, USA

Seeing the state as a crucial source of governance in contemporary life, "sexualizing the state" is an approach that analyzes sexuality's impact on the state towards a more critical appraisal of it. Despite the many claims about the diminished role of states due to privatization, reduction in social services, and other such neoliberal policies, states still continue to have a decisive influence in just about every aspect of our lives – life and death, bodies, relationships, mobility, behaviors and practices, rights, work, health, and, not least, gender and sexuality. For the most part, though, the state is seen as an institutional, territorial, and sovereign form of power that impacts our sexual lives through policies and discourses, while sexuality is understood primarily as an attribute of individuals or social collectives (women, children, gay men) and a social problem. Thus, it appears commonsensical that states would regulate sexuality, which is also what makes them obvious sites of activism and redress – for example, legalizing gay marriage, introducing laws and policies against sex trafficking, making stricter the laws curbing and punishing sexual violence. What receives less attention, however, is the extent to which sexuality is not simply an object of state regulation but a domain upon which the state relies, that is, inasmuch as states impact sexuality, they are impacted by it. Extending this view, sexualizing the state investigates the ways that regulating sexuality affirms the state and state-based governance as essential and indispensable aspects of social life.

Grappling with this approach entails revisiting ideas of sexualization as well as statehood. As a verb, "sexualizing" has long been in circulation, but endowed with more precise meaning by Michel Foucault. Laying the groundwork for it in the first volume of the *History of Sexuality* (Foucault 1978) and then speaking to it more directly in a seminal interview, "Truth and Power" (Foucault 1980), he undoes commonplace views of sexuality as a form of identity (heterosexual), a quality (to be sexual), or a condition (doing sex work). Making the path-breaking argument that sexuality aids in the dispersal of power, he addresses the ways that the anxieties, concerns, and pleasures related to sexuality actually assist power's reach into both intimate and institutional spheres. Stressing the productive rather than the repressive aspects of how power functions, Foucault usefully draws attention to the stimulating effects of sexuality. Exemplifying his point through burgeoning concerns about children's sexuality since the eighteenth century in the West, he notes that preoccupations with ensuring that children are not sexual actually resulted in " ... a sexualizing of the infantile body, a sexualizing of the bodily relationship between parent and child, a sexualizing of the familial domain" (Foucault 1978, 120). Sexualizing a person, a relationship, an institution, or a social structure, therefore, becomes a means of critically understanding and analyzing how sexuality aids in the proliferation of power.

To sexualize the state, in particular, also means upending popular perceptions of states as freestanding material realities. Consider here how we talk about "the state" as somehow distinct from society and how we often render "it" a monolith, or, in the inimitable words of Philip Corrigan (1994), we "thingify" it. However, as Corrigan and Derek Sayer (1985) effectively argue, states are culturally produced, which is to say, states are not natural, self-generating entities but are actively fashioned through a myriad of practices, policies, and discourses. If they appear to be enduring material realities, it is partly due to their illusory aspects, an insight first offered by Philip Abrams (1988). Abrams noted that states are systems – as nexuses of practices and institutional structures – but states are also fundamentally ideas, which make them seem real, self-evident. In other words, in the United States, for example, there is a "thereness" to the state, it appears obvious, somehow unified despite the many and varied agencies and institutions at the federal and regional levels, symbolized by buildings, flags, rituals, speeches, and much more. The US state, following the insights of political anthropologists such as James Ferguson and Akhil Gupta (2002) and Timothy Mitchell (1999), also appears to be not only distinct from society, but also as somehow existing "above" and "encompassing" it. Instead, seeing the state in the United States and elsewhere as varying across time and space helps demystify it and undermine its seemingly immense power.

Bringing the state into the fold of culture and history also helps recast it as an intense rather than principal site of governance, a view deriving from Foucault's reflections on matters of state, sovereignty, and governance. Using the concept of governmentality, by which he means the ensemble of techniques, practices, and strategies aimed at governing populations, Foucault (1991) clears the ground for a capacious understanding of governance that is not overly focused on the territorial and sovereign state. Rather, taking a decentered approach that allows for multiple sites (media, corporations, self-help literature, for example) through which people and things are governed, he argues " ... the state is no more than a composite reality and a mythicized abstraction, whose importance is more limited than many of us think" (p. 244). Foucault's cautions dovetail with additional concerns that nineteenth century political dualisms of state/civil society, public/private, power/resistance are no longer adequate to understanding the nature of governance, which is why Nikolas Rose (1999) has theorized governance away from the state towards gated residential communities, for example. Although such contributions are undoubtedly important, especially since sites of governance are expanding (think here of the ways in which the Internet or even Facebook allows for greater scrutiny of our lives), states are hardly becoming obsolete to our analyses of power and politics. Undeniable is the fact that "the state" continues to endure in our language and imaginations as well as in systems of surveillance, regulations, and power. The state may not be the sole source of power, as Foucault (1978) cautions, but its institutions, structures, discourses, and practices fully impact our lives.

While these approaches to sexuality and the state help provide the necessary scaffolding, feminist and sexuality studies scholarship give substance to what it means to sexualize the state. First, sexualizing the state draws on a structural, or non-identity-based, understanding of sexuality, following preeminent queer theorist Eve K. Sedgwick. Indeed, as Sedgwick (1985) showed in her early work on relationships between men, sexuality does not only obtain at the level of individuals, but also at the level of institutions and structures in ways that are analogous to how we understand the differences between gender and gendering. Cynthia Enloe's contributions in *Bananas, Beaches, Bases: Making Feminist Sense of International Politics* (Enloe 1990) powerfully illustrate what it means to see international politics from a gendered lens, for she points not only to international politics' impact on women in their capacities as diplomatic wives, domestic workers, and service providers around military bases, but also usefully underscores the gendered aspects of tourism, colonialism, nationalism, and the state. With the proviso that gender and sexuality are interrelated but not the same, it becomes possible to take a comparable view of the sexualized aspects of states.

Second, what is also necessary is to see the state as not rational but characteristically subjective. Understanding the state in this way does not imply, as do some social scientists and international relations experts, that the state is an actor – motivated by biases and idiosyncrasies much like a person. Rather, this approach examines the state as a messy, complex assemblage of structures, discourses, and practices that are characterized by inconsistencies, irrationalities, and affect, what Thomas Blom Hansen and Finn Stepputat (2001) summarized as disaggregating and denaturalizing the state. Jacqueline Rose (1996) effectively juxtaposes the psychic and the political to highlight the similarities between the public connotations of "the state" with the psychological emotional dimensions of being "in a state," so to speak. Unsettling the state as inherently rational, she argues:

> Look a little more closely at the word 'state' in its political significance as polity, commonweal, commonwealth. Place it alongside that other meaning of 'state' (and of 'fantasy') as loss of authority, and it appears that the private and public attributes of the concept 'state' are not opposites but shadows – outer and inner faces precisely – of each other. (Rose 1996, 8)

Sidestepping a psychoanalytical view of the state, M. Jacqui Alexander (1991, 1997) also foregrounds the subjective characteristics of the state but by highlighting its preoccupations with sexuality. In a set of interventions, one predating Rose and another coming soon after, Alexander comes to grips with legislation prohibiting homosexuality in Trinidad and Tobago and the Bahamas and, in so doing, gestures to the ways that regulating sexuality helps constitute the state:

> A great deal of analytic work has been done by feminists in different parts of the world on

demystifying the state's will to represent itself as disinterested, neutered, and otherwise benign. We now understand how sex and gender lie, for the state, at the juncture of the disciplining of the body and the control of the population and are, therefore, constitutive of those very practices. ... Much less work has been done, however, on elaborating the processes of heterosexualization at work within the state apparatus and charting the ways in which they are constitutively paradoxical: that is, *how heterosexuality is at once necessary to the state's ability to constitute and imagine itself, while simultaneously marking a site of its own instability*. (Alexander 1997, 65; present author's emphasis)

Almost simultaneously, two other scholars honed the argument that state and sexuality are co-constituted, thereby shifting the needle towards looking at their mutual impact. Making explicit the point that the British state does not only impact sexuality and the struggles around it, but that it is itself influenced by sexual identities, ideologies, and culture, Davina Cooper (1993) broke new ground. Although Cooper's article is infrequently cited, especially compared with the wide attention received by Alexander and Rose, she appears to be the first scholar to use the idea of sexualizing the state. She presciently notes, "... to change state practice, it may be necessary to focus on transforming those processes and relations that shape and influence state form. In the context of sexuality, this means, amongst other things, considering the ways in which the state is sexualized" (Cooper 1993, 266). In so doing, Cooper gestures toward the tight connections between the state, governance practices, and sexuality in ways that echo in Lisa Duggan's article, "Queering the State" (Duggan 1994). Writing in response to the state- and national-level political influence of the Christian rightwing in the United States, Duggan suggests that scholars and activists should divest the state of its efforts to promote heteronormativity. Pointing to the ways that state policies and discourses reinforce heterosexuality, she argues compellingly that just as the state cannot support a particular religion, it ought not to uphold a particular sexuality.

Another scholar, Elizabeth Povinelli (1998), makes further headway into this analytical approach by raising questions of state and sexuality in the Australian context. From the angle of ethnographic work among Aboriginal communities in Australia, she shows that even as the state grants land rights to these communities, it is attentive to issues of sexuality in ways that preserve the Australian state's sovereignty and the sway of non-Aboriginal groups. Begoña Aretxaga (2005) is a further noteworthy scholar who effectively weaves together the psychic, the political, and the sexual in her analysis of state power. Writing about the practice of strip-searching political prisoners in 1992 in the high-security prison of Maghaberry in Northern Ireland, Aretxaga notes that state power and desire co-mingle to unleash violence and hurt on Irish women's bodies that cannot be justified as rational or necessary. Stressing the irrational, excessive dimensions of the state, Aretxaga observes, "The embodied being of what counts as the state is not a neutral body, but is instead a thoroughly sexualized one, whose sexual operations are invested with political power" (p. 265). Thus, she analyzes the mass strip-search of Irish women political prisoners as a replication of heterosexual rape in order to draw attention to the convergence of state fantasy and techniques of subjugation. Notably, Margot Canaday (2011) has shifted attention to the historical context of the United States to analyze the growth of the bureaucratic state and its interest in homosexuality through the idea of the "straight state." Emphasizing state formation and preoccupations with homosexuality, Canaday calls attention to the expanding reach of the state, and specifically the roles of the Bureau of Immigration, the military, and federal agencies, that not only institutionalized policies regulating homosexuality but also rendered people so identified unequal citizens.

More recently, questions of state fantasy and desire have been more thoroughly pursued by Jyoti Puri in light of the struggle to decriminalize homosexuality in India. The mobilization against the anti-sodomy law, Section 377 of the Indian Penal Code, was set into motion by a public interest litigation filed in Delhi High Court in 2001 asking that consensual private same-sex adult sexual activity be excluded from the statute's purview. Based on fieldwork among state institutions and agencies named in the writ petition, such as the Government of India and Delhi Police, among other respondents, Puri sexualizes the state in order to uncover how sexuality variously impacts these institutions, agencies and their practices. Analyzing the government's first legal response to the writ and police discourses on the anti-sodomy law's enforcement in an earlier article, "Sexualizing the State: Sodomy, Civil Liberties, and the Indian Penal Code," she reveals sexuality's constitutive effects on state institutions and practices (Puri 2012).

Expanding this approach and analysis into the concept of the sexual state in the book *Governance and the Struggle Over the Antisodomy Law in India*, Puri (in press) crystallizes what sexualizing the state would entail and why that is necessary. It means undoing the oppositions between sexuality (subject-oriented, irrational, messy) and state (structural, rational, monolithic), identifying the subjective and, more precisely, sexual foundations of states, and underscoring the relevance of multiple modes of state-based governance that are practiced in ordinary and seemingly insignificant ways. By following the mobilization to decriminalize homosexuality through its various twists and turns over more than a decade and juxtaposing it with other struggles against state regulation in the Indian context, *Sexual States* uncovers how governing sexuality helps power and reaffirm the state as a normal and, even, natural feature of contemporary life. Highlighting the stakes of sexualizing the state, it reveals that state institutions, discourses, and practices continue to lean on the domain of sexuality to reinforce the imperatives of state governance. Most importantly, the book shows that this reliance on sexuality is particularly salient at this moment when states are losing some of their other functions under the pressures of privatization and deregulation associated with neoliberal policies.

Feminist and sexuality studies scholars in a variety of disciplines, including sociology, anthropology, and political science, continue to complicate how we think of and critically assess the state and state governance, and the contributions noted here have usefully helped further such endeavors by defining the meaning and significance of sexualizing the state.

SEE ALSO: Sexualities

REFERENCES

Abrams, Philip. 1988. "Notes on the Difficulty of Studying the State (1977)." *Journal of Historical Sociology*, 1(1): 58–89.

Alexander, M. Jacqui. 1991. "Redrafting Morality: the Postcolonial State and the Sexual Offences Bill of Trinidad and Tobago." In *Third World Women and the Politics of Feminism*, edited by Chandra Talpade Mohanty, Ann Russo, and Lourdes Torres, 133–152. Bloomington: Indiana University Press.

Alexander, M. Jacqui. 1997. "Erotic Autonomy as a Politics of Decolonization: an Anatomy of Feminist and State Practice in the Bahamas Tourist Economy." In *Feminist Genealogies, Colonial Legacies, Democratic Futures*, edited by M. Jacqui Alexander and Chandra Talpade Mohanty, 63–100. New York: Routledge.

Aretxaga, Begoña. 2005. *States of Terror: Begoña Aretxaga's Essays*, edited by Joseba Zulaika. Reno: Center for Basque Studies.

Canaday, Margot. 2011. *The Straight State: Sexuality and Citizenship in Twentieth Century America*. Princeton: Princeton University Press.
Cooper, Davina. 1993. "An Engaged State: Sexuality, Governance, and the Potential for Change." *Journal of Law and Society*, 20(3): 257–275.
Corrigan, Philip. 1994. "State Formation." In *Everyday Forms of State Formation: Revolution and Negotiation of Rule in Modern Mexico*, edited by Gilbert M. Joseph and Daniel Nugent. Durham, NC: Duke University Press.
Corrigan, Philip, and Derek Sayer. 1985. *The Great Arch: English State Formation as Cultural Revolution*. Oxford: Blackwell.
Duggan, Lisa. 1994. "Queering the State," *Social Text*, 39: 1–14.
Enloe, Cynthia. 1990. *Bananas, Beaches, Bases: Making Sense of International Politics*. Berkeley: University of California Press.
Ferguson, James, and Akhil Gupta. 2002. "Spatializing States: Toward an Ethnography of Neoliberal Governmentality," *American Ethnologist*, 29(4): 981–1002.
Foucault, Michel. 1978. *History of Sexuality, Volume 1: An Introduction*, trans. Robert Hurley. New York: Vintage Books.
Foucault, Michel. 1980. "Truth and Power." *Power/Knowledge: Selected Interviews and Other Writings 1972–1977*, edited by Colin Gordon; trans. Colin Gordon, Leo Marshall, John Mepham, and Kate Soper, 109–133. New York: Pantheon Books.
Foucault, Michel. 1991. "Governmentality." In *The Foucault Effect: Studies in Governmentality*, edited by Graham Burchell, Colin Gordon, and Peter Miller, 87–104. Chicago: University of Chicago Press.
Hansen, Thomas Blom, and Stepputat, Finn. 2001. "Introduction." In *States of Imagination: Ethnographic Explorations of the Postcolonial State*, edited by Thomas Blom Hansen and Finn Stepputat, 1–40. Durham, NC: Duke University Press.
Mitchell, Timothy. 1999. "Society, Economy, and the State Effect." in *State/Culture: State-Formation After the Cultural Turn*, edited by George Steinmetz, 76–97. Ithaca: Cornell University Press.
Povinelli, Elizabeth A. 1998. "The State of Shame: Australian Multiculturalism and the Crisis of Indigenous Citizenship." *Critical Inquiry*, 24(2): 576–610.
Puri, Jyoti. 2012. "Sexualizing the State: Sodomy, Civil Liberties, and the Indian Penal Code." In *Contesting Nation: Gendered Violence in South Asia. Notes on the Post Colonial Present*, edited by Angana Chatterji and Lubna Chowdhury. New Delhi: Zubaan Books.
Puri, Jyoti. In press. *Governance and the Struggle Over the Antisodomy Law in India*, Durham, NC: Duke University Press.
Rose, Jacqueline. 1996. *States of Fantasy*. Oxford: Clarendon Press.
Rose, Nikolas. 1999. *Powers of Freedom: Reframing Political Thought*. Cambridge: Cambridge University Press.
Sedgwick, Eve K. 1985. *Between Men: English Literature and Male Homosocial Desire*. New York: Columbia University Press.

Sexually Transmitted Infections

MARTIN HOLT
University of New South Wales, Australia

Sexually transmitted infections (STIs) are bacteria and viruses passed from person to person during sex. Stigma remains a major barrier to prevention and treatment; people delay seeking healthcare, and those diagnosed with an STI are often reticent to tell partners. The most common and infectious STIs can be transmitted through vaginal intercourse, anal sex, oral sex, and kissing. Many STIs are asymptomatic. Ease of transmission, a frequent lack of symptoms, and enduring stigma suggest why STIs are so prevalent; it is estimated that worldwide there are 500 million new cases each year of infections like chlamydia, gonorrhoea, and syphilis (World Health Organization 2014). Among viral STIs, human papillomavirus is the most common and is a significant cause of cervical cancer among women. Although human immunodeficiency virus (HIV) is less common, 2.3 million people are infected with HIV annually and the majority of these infections are due to sexual transmission (UNAIDS 2013).

Reflecting inequities in access to healthcare and power differentials in the ability to negotiate sex or use preventive measures like condoms, the global burden of STIs disproportionately affects poor people, women, children, and marginalized populations (particularly indigenous people, sex workers, gay and bisexual men, and transgender people). In many countries, women are particularly vulnerable to STIs and HIV because they lack the power and economic independence to refuse sex or insist upon safe sex. Women's lower social status in traditional, patriarchal societies means that they are often blamed for the spread of STIs, even when male cultural norms (such as promiscuity and sexual conquest) are responsible for increasing vulnerability in both men and women. Gender-based violence can be a particular barrier to women seeking HIV testing or disclosing that they are HIV-positive, for fear that they will be abandoned or driven out of their homes.

Current responses to STIs have been influenced by the social history of venereal disease, moral panics about population health, and the emergence of medical disciplines like sexology (Foucault 1978; Weeks 1985). In Europe in the fifteenth and sixteenth centuries, syphilis (known at the time as the "great pox") was more prevalent than leprosy and plague (Quétel 1990). The infection's rapid spread and virulent symptoms (initially sores and pustules, then physical deformation, madness, and death in its later stages) caused great fear. It was recognized that the pox was driven by sexual activity, even if the exact cause was not understood. This led to pox-sufferers being excluded and condemned for what was judged to be their moral weakness and degeneracy. Moral outrage in response to STIs has been an enduring phenomenon. Prophylactic measures for syphilis initially involved shunning and excluding those deemed to be spreading the disease (particularly the promiscuous, the poor, and prostitutes). Early, partially effective but potentially toxic treatments included mercury. Abstinence was viewed as the most acceptable way to avoid infection. In the early twentieth century the male condom was recognized as a way to significantly reduce infection rates.

In the West, fear of syphilis reached its apogee between World Wars I and II, with both physicians and moral campaigners aligned in their concern about the threat of syphilis to public health and moral hygiene. Anti-venereal disease campaigns focused on scaring people to abstain from sex outside marriage. During this period the infamous Tuskegee syphilis experiment was conducted in the United States (Brandt 1978). Six hundred poor African American men were enrolled under the guise of receiving free healthcare. Most of the men had syphilis but were not told about the infection; the study was designed to observe the natural history of the disease. During the 40 years the study was conducted, numerous men died, and many wives and children were infected. The study was only stopped in the early 1970s after whistleblowers went to the press; the public was shocked to learn that no participant had been treated for syphilis, even after effective antibiotics became available. The outcry forced the development of formal ethical guidelines for medical studies.

The development of antibiotics, particularly penicillin in the 1940s, revolutionized the treatment of syphilis and other bacterial infections. In some countries, large-scale campaigns encouraged people to be tested and treated, virtually eliminating infections like syphilis. However, the latter part of the twentieth century saw the resurgence of many STI epidemics, driven in part by the greater popularity of sex outside marriage, urbanization, and an increased tolerance of homosexuality in some countries. In China, for example, syphilis was nearly eliminated in the 1960s. The development of a market-based economy since the 1980s has, however, created the conditions for a sharp increase in syphilis (Tucker, Chen, and Peeling 2010). A significant proportion of the population has moved to urban areas and there has been an increase in the demand for commercial sex work. As well as female sex workers, men who have sex with men are disproportionately affected by syphilis in China. Yet the response to syphilis continues to be hampered by formal and informal condemnation of prostitution and homosexuality, with police fines, public shaming, and detention reducing the chances of people coming forward for testing and treatment. Confronting the fear and stigma associated with syphilis and other STIs remains a major barrier to reducing the global burden of these diseases.

SEE ALSO: AIDS-Related Stigma; Gender-Based Violence; Health Disparities; Purity Versus Pollution; Sexology and Psychological Sex Research

REFERENCES

Brandt, Allan M. 1978. "Racism and Research: The Case of the Tuskegee Syphilis Study." *Hastings Center Report* 8(6): 21–29. DOI: 10.2307/3561468.

Foucault, Michel. 1978. *The History of Sexuality*, vol. 1. Harmondsworth, UK: Peregrine.

Quétel, Claude. 1990. *History of Syphilis*. Cambridge: Polity.

Tucker, Joseph D., Xiang-Sheng Chen, and Rosanna W. Peeling. 2010. "Syphilis and Social Upheaval in China." *New England Journal of Medicine*, 362(18): 1658–1661. DOI: 10.1056/NEJMp0911149.

UNAIDS. 2013. *Global Report: UNAIDS Report on the Global AIDS Epidemic 2012*. Geneva: UNAIDS.

Weeks, Jeffrey. 1985. *Sexuality and its Discontents: Meanings, Myths and Modern Sexualities*. London: Routledge.

World Health Organization (WHO). 2014. *Report on Global Sexually Transmitted Infection Surveillance 2013*. Geneva: World Health Organization.

Sexuopharmaceuticals

TIINA VARES
University of Canterbury, New Zealand

The development of the medical field of sexuopharmacology is a relatively recent one (although there is a long history of various substances being used for sexual enhancement). Sexuopharmaceuticals refer to medications (pills or creams) that are designed to improve or maintain sexual function, the first and best known being Viagra (sildenafil citrate). In the 1990s, the pharmaceutical company Pfizer began testing sildenafil citrate for the treatment of cardiovascular problems when it found that it had an unanticipated side effect for men: it created and sustained erections. Viagra went through clinical trials and received approval by the United States Food and Drug Administration (FDA) in 1998 (crucial to the international release of any new drug) as the first oral treatment for men with erectile dysfunction or male erectile disorder.

Erectile dysfunction (ED) is defined as the persistent inability to achieve or maintain penile erection sufficient for satisfactory sexual performance. However, it was not very long ago that the medical establishment considered that erectile difficulties (more commonly referred to as impotence) were primarily psychological in origin, with treatment falling to psychologists. Any physical interventions consisted of mechanical devices such as vacuum pumps and penile implants. Today, however, following the advent of pharmacological preparations, it is claimed that at least 90% of all male sexual dysfunctions have an organic or medical cause. Viagra was followed by similar pills such as Levitra (Vardenafil) produced by Bayer and GlaxoSmithKline, Cialis (Tadalafil) by Eli Lilly, and, more recently, Stendra (Avanafil) manufactured by Vivus. Like Viagra, these work by relaxing the smooth muscle of the arteries to the penis, thus enabling blood flow. Worldwide sales of Viagra are estimated at nearly US$2.3 billion.

Given the blockbuster status of Viagra for the treatment of male erectile dysfunction, it is not surprising that pharmaceutical companies turned their efforts to finding a similar drug that might work for women (the so-called "pink" Viagra). However, there first needed to be clearer identification and classification of women's sexual problems. In 1999, a group of 19 international sexuality researchers and clinicians, 18 of whom had links to pharmaceutical companies (Moynihan 2003), met as The Consensus Committee on FSD (female sexual dysfunction). The aim was to make changes in the categorization of women's sexual difficulties that would shift these from the arena of mental health (DSM IV – the American Psychiatric Association's *Diagnostic and Statistical Manual of Mental Disorders*) to biomedicine. The nomenclature was expanded and a clause added to each category regarding "personal distress." Although this meant that the focus on women's sexual problems would be biomedical, it also acknowledged that, for women, a sexual disorder is determined according to personal experience and distress (Potts 2007).

Although many pills and creams for FSD have been trialed, none (to date) have been approved by the FDA. Lybrido (a combination of testosterone and a Viagra-like drug) is currently undergoing clinical trials. Femprox, a topical genital cream for women with FSAD (female sexual arousal disorder), is also undergoing clinical trials. Some existing hormonal drugs are also being investigated as possible treatments for FSD, for example, Tibolone (a synthetic steroid used for postmenopausal osteoporosis). Anecdotal reports suggest that Viagra is used by some women (although this is "off-label" use, that is, used for indicators other than those approved by the FDA). A book by Jennifer and Laura Berman (co-directors of the University of California at Los Angeles Female Sexual Medicine Center) describes how they often prescribe Viagra for women patients and suggests that it might have benefits for women with sexual problems (Fishman 2004, 203). There is also a variety of creams such as Lyriana, Provestra, Climestra, and Mycreme (among many others) that occupy a space somewhere between "novelty sex products and medically sanctioned treatments" (Treacher 2004, 3).

The development of sexuopharmaceuticals can be located in a broader context of medicalization in which aspects of life previously outside the jurisdiction of medicine come to be framed as medical problems. The medicalization of sexuality, for example, not only privileges scientific and medical solutions to sexual concerns but also constructs them as more effective. However, some social scientists argue that the recent merging and expansion of science, medicine, and technology signals a new era of "biomedicalization" (Clarke et al. 2003). Biomedicalization takes account of the intensification of medicalization, the increasing commercialization of medicine and medical products, and changes in healthcare systems that put increasing emphasis on individuals being responsible for their own health (Clarke et al. 2003). The development and marketing of Viagra (and other ED medications), for example, have come to resemble those of other commodified products in a competitive marketplace (Fishman 2004, 188–189). Although this is most evident in the Unites States and New Zealand, which allow direct-to-consumer advertising (DTCA), the expansion of the Internet indicates that information and marketing about sexual disorders and products extend well beyond pharmaceutical company advertising.

Biomedicalization is premised on a medical model of sexuality that subscribes to a mechanistic view of the body in which sexual response is broken down into a series of consecutive stages as part of a supposedly universal "human sexual response cycle." This cycle is considered to be a biological given and to operate in individuals without taking into account sociohistoric factors. Deviation from the normal sexual response cycle thus constitutes a sexual dysfunction. Within a context of biomedicalization, ED and FSD manifest through disorders of arousal, orgasm, desire, and pain (with the latter two constituting FSD only). These are now considered abnormal medical conditions that require medical intervention in order to make the man or woman sexually functional or normal again. Furthermore, in medical constructions of ED, there is little attention to factors outside the body. This differs from medical constructions of FSD in which "personal distress" is part of each FSD category.

Social scientists, among others (including some within the medical establishment), have been critical of the deterministic view of health and illness espoused by medicine. Critiques have focused on the way in which Western medicine is based on a distinction between the normal and the pathological. This framework for the definition of disease or dysfunction depicts difference as pathological. It is assumed that constancy represents normalcy, whereas fluctuations are rendered abnormal or indicative of "disease processes" (Birke 1999). This is apparent in the uncritical application of the human sexual response model in which healthy and normal sexual experience is restricted to an individual's correct physiological progression through the various stages of the cycle (Potts et al. 2004).

Feminist and gender scholars have also critiqued the reductionist and androcentric constructions of normative sexuality. Paula Nicolson (1993) identified three prevalent discourses operating in medical constructions of "normal" sex: a reproductive model of sexuality (which privileges biological and procreative aspects of sex), a coital imperative (the notion that penile-vaginal sex is the most natural and usual form of sexual activity), and an orgasmic imperative (the idea that orgasm – particularly male orgasm – is the goal towards which all sexual activity is directed, and the measure of successful sex). Medical constructions of normal sexuality are thus informed by the framing of sex as a natural act involving heterosexual coitus and ending in (male) orgasm/ejaculation, while sexual dysfunctions or disorders are constructed in opposition to these.

Following the release of Viagra (1998), a number of critical studies were produced by gender, aging, sexualities and media scholars. Informed by social constructionist frameworks, gender theorizing, and critiques of the biomedicalization of sexuality, these studies considered media representation and marketing of Viagra (Mamo and Fishman 2001; Loe 2004), responses of readers and viewers to these representations (Vares et al. 2003), the sociocultural implications of men's use of Viagra (Potts et al. 2004, 2006), and the sociocultural implications of partners' experiences of Viagra use (Potts et al. 2003).

Popular cultural representations and DTCA of Viagra have both drawn on and reproduced normative assumptions of male sexuality, heteronormativity, and appropriate sexuality (Mamo and Fishman 2001; Loe 2004). Given that sexuality is integral to the construction of masculinity, an erection is seen as important to both having "real" sex and being a "real" man. Viagra can thus be seen as a pill to restore erections and "repair masculinity" (Loe 2004). Media representations of Viagra have included couples in mid–later life and focus on the value of penetration for men but also for their female partners, the assumption being that penetrative sex is what she wants and needs for a happy sexual relationship. They therefore construct a heterosexual relationship without an erection and without penile–vaginal penetration as necessarily problematic and undesirable. The possibility that such a relationship, without such sex, but possibly with other forms of sex, might be desirable or even preferable to a relationship in which penile–vaginal penetration does take place, is absent.

Such images of "sexy oldies" (Gott 2005) can be located in a broader cultural scientific shift to successful aging in which lifelong sexual function is a primary component (Katz 2000). Rather than images of old age as a period of sexual decline, sexual activity in later life is now framed as essential for a happy and healthy old age. It is possible to read Viagra advertisements as both reinforcing and disrupting normative aging scripts. On the one hand, images of older people engaged in sexual activity are refreshing as they challenge the idea that older people are asexual. The images of caring and happy older couples can be read as privileging intimacy, relationships, relational sex, attending to the needs of one's female partner, and sexually desiring women expecting to be satisfied (although coitally). On the other hand, they also set up an imperative that sex is a necessary part of aging – that to be healthy and happy you need to be sexually active.

It has only been fairly recently that the marketing for Viagra shifted from a focus on older couples to younger men and potentially gay men, for example, a man in an advertisement walking along a beach worrying about a relationship could be hetero- or homosexual. ED is no longer constructed as a "serious medical condition" but rather something that increasing numbers of (ever younger) men could have. In the past decade, the numbers of younger men (including teenagers) using Viagra has increased. Researchers have also indicated the growth in gay men's recreational use of Viagra (Crosby and Di Clemente 2004). A prominent Pfizer-sponsored urologist, Irwin Goldstein, has recommended that men use Viagra as a prophylactic against erectile difficulties (that is, taking a small dose of Viagra on a daily basis to "prevent impotence") (Moynihan and Cassels 2005, 31). The emphasis for masculine sexuality (whether heterosexual, gay, or bisexual) is therefore on performance and improving one's performance. While heteronormativity is challenged, penis-centered understandings of masculinity are reproduced.

Studies on men's and their partners' experiences of Viagra use both complicate and challenge biomedical understandings of a universal body and its accompanying categorization as either normal or pathological. Potts et al. (2003, 2004, 2006), for example, suggest that Viagra produces different effects and experiences – bodily, emotional, and relational – for different individuals, and impacts in a variety of ways on relationships. Whereas some see erectile difficulties as part of a disorder of the male body and welcome the restoration or the erections and penile–vaginal penetration, others resisted the idea that erectile difficulties were abnormal or dysfunctional. For example, some participants with erectile changes experimented with non-penetrative (and non-erection) sex and accepted or even celebrated such changes rather than seeing them as conditions that require fixing.

With respect to FSD, the focus has been less on the sexuopharmaceuticals in the production pipeline and more on the construction of the disorder that informs the search for the "female Viagra." The escalating biomedicalization of women's sexuality prompted Leonore Tiefer (2001) to think about a "new view" of women's sexual problem. Tiefer, together with a grassroots group of feminist social scientists, sex educators, therapists, sex researchers, physicians, and activists, developed *The Campaign for a New View of Women's Sexual Problems*. In contrast to the medical model, the new view emphasizes sexual diversity, social context, education, empowerment, and attention to the ways in which sexual norms are constructed.

Future research directions could include: recreational use of sexuopharmaceuticals for men and women (and their partners), including a range of ages, sexualities, and national contexts; the (currently debated) relationship between Viagra use and STD risks in gay men; the demedicalization (where medical aspects are challenged and reduced) of sexuality through Internet technologies and the increasing difficulty of distinguishing between dysfunction and enhancement; continuing shifts in pharmaceutical marketing; the production of new sexuopharmaceuticals (particularly the expected development of an FDA-approved treatment for FDS); and more qualitative and interdisciplinary research into the subjective and interpersonal aspects of sexuopharmaceutical use.

SEE ALSO: Asexuality; Masculinities; Sexualities

REFERENCES

Birke, Linda. 1999. *Feminism and the Biological Body*. New Brunswick: Rutgers University Press.

Clarke, Adele, Janet Shim, Laura Mamo, Jennifer Fosken, and Jennifer Fishman. 2003. "Biomedicalization: Technoscientific Transformation of Health and Illness and U.S. Biomedicine." *American Sociological Review*, 68: 161–194.

Crosby, Richard, and Ralph Di Clemente. 2004. "Use of Recreational Viagra among Men having Sex with Men." *Sexually Transmitted Infections*, 80: 466–468. DOI: 10.1136/sti.2004.010496.

Fishman, Jennifer. 2004. "The Commodification of Female Sexual Dysfunction." *Social Studies of Science*, 34: 187–218. DOI: 10.1177/0306312704043028.

Gott, Merryn. 2005. *Sexual Health and Ageing*. Maidenhead, UK: Open University Press.

Katz, Stephen. 2000. "Busy Bodies: Activity, Aging and the Management of Everyday Life." *Journal of Aging Studies*, 14: 137–138.

Loe, Meika. 2004. *The Rise of Viagra*. New York: New York University Press.

Mamo, Laura, and Jennifer Fishman. 2001. "Potency in All the Right Places: Viagra as a Technology of the Gendered Body." *Body and Society*, 7: 13–35. DOI: 10.1177/1357034X01007004002.

Moynihan, Ray. 2003. "The Making of a Disease: Female Sexual Dysfunction." *British Medical Journal*, 326: 45–47.

Moynihan, Ray, and Alan Cassels. 2005. *Selling Sickness: How Drug Companies are Turning Us into Patients*. Sydney: Allen and Unwin.

Nicolson, Paula. 1993. "Public Values and Private Beliefs: Why Do Women Refer Themselves for Sex Therapy?" In *Psychological Perspectives on Sexual Problems: New Directions in Theory and Practice*, edited by Jane M. Ussher and Christine D. Baker, 56–78. London: Routledge.

Potts, Annie. 2007. "The 'Female Sexual Dysfunction' Debate: Different 'Problems', New Drugs, More Pressures?" In *Contesting Illness: Processes and Practices*, edited by Pamela Moss and Katherine Teghtsoonian, 259–280. Toronto: Toronto University Press.

Potts, Annie, Nicola Gavey, Victoria Grace, and Tiina Vares. 2003. "The Downside of Viagra: Women's Experiences and Concerns." *Sociology of Health and Illness*, 25: 697–719. DOI: 10.1046/j.1467-9566.2003.00366.x.

Potts, Annie, Victoria Grace, Nicola Gavey, and Tiina Vares. 2004. "'Viagra Stories': Challenging Erectile Dysfunction." *Social Science and Medicine*, 59: 489–499. DOI: 10.1016/j.socscimed.2003.06.001.

Potts, Annie, Victoria Grace, Tiina Vares, and Nicola Gavey. 2006. "'Sex for Life'? Men's Counter-stories on 'Erectile Dysfunction', Male Sexuality and Ageing." *Sociology of Health and Illness*, 28: 323–324. DOI: 10.1111/j.1467-9566.2006.00494.x.

Tiefer, Leonore. 2001. "A New View of Women's Sexual Problems: Why New? Why Now?" *Journal of Sex Research*, 38: 89–96. DOI: 10.1080/00224490109552075.

Treacher, Geraldine. 2004. "Sex, Drugs and Women: Exploring the Construction of Technologies and Sexualities in the Development and Use of Sexuopharmaceuticals for Women," Unpublished Master's Thesis, University of Canterbury, Christchurch, New Zealand.

Vares, Tiina, Annie Potts, Nicola Gavey, and Victoria Grace. 2003. "Hard Sell, Soft Sell: Men Read Viagra Ads." *Media International Australia*, (108): 101–114.

Shaker Religion

R. CASEY DAVIS
Independent Scholar

The Shakers are a religious group that rose to prominence during the Second Great Awakening in the United States of America during the middle of the nineteenth century. Shakers' theology is unique to not only the time and place, but to the approach in understanding divine revelations. One of the founders, Ann Lee, known later as "Mother Ann," challenged the long-held conventions of religion, primarily promoting the equality of the genders in religious worship and practice. The last time a woman had been a religious leader in American history prior to Ann Lee was when Anne Hutchinson led the Quakers in the Massachusetts Bay Colony in the 1600s.

Like Hutchinson, Lee was branded an outcast for her understanding of Christianity. Lee led the early Shaker movement, which was deemed heretical by mainstream Protestant churches in the United States. Primarily, the equality of the sexes as well as their communal approach to property and living shocked many of the other Protestant denominations (Lindley 1996).

The Shakers got their name from the fact that, during church service, members would literally shake. Shakers believed this to be evidence of the Holy Spirit moving the person. Their worship services included dancing and charismatic speaking. Originally, the Shakers referred to themselves as the United Believers in Christ's Second Appearing.

The Shakers as a distinct, organized group originated under the leadership of Jane Wardley in 1747. Wardley was an engaging and charismatic speaker. In her preaching, Wardley admonished her followers to prepare for the imminent return of Jesus Christ. Shakers believed that this return would soon befall the Earth and its inhabitants. As such, Shakers were part of the millennial movement that was sweeping through the United States at the time.

When Ann Lee joined the small community in 1756, she added to Wardley's theology. In preparation for the imminent Second Coming of Christ, Lee preached sexual purity in the form of complete abstinence. While both males and females shared an equality unknown within the Christian Church up to this time, Lee's understanding of sexual intercourse framed the daily lives of the Shakers.

Lee received her vernacular title of "Mother" from the early Shakers as a result of her stirring sermons. She survived the death of all four of her children prior to becoming a leader within the ranks of the Shakers. Lee proclaimed that she was the mother of a new creation. She believed that this new creation would only come through the following of a simple, but strict rule of life.

According to Lee's understanding of the story of Adam and Eve, humanity's expulsion from the Garden of Eden and fall from Grace was tied to sexual intercourse. As such, male and female Shakers lived in sex-segregated dormitories. Males and females were separated during the work day as well. This was not necessarily due to gender-specific roles;

rather, it was to keep the temptation of sexual intercourse in check.

The craftsmanship and ingenuity of the Shakers quickly made their products highly valued and much sought after. The attention to detail and simplicity of their products are the trademarks of Shaker arts and crafts. Like the monastics in the early Christian Church, the Shakers were self-supporting through their labors.

Mirroring their simple life, Shaker work changed little through the years. Farming, husbandry, carpentry, and other traditional labors filled the workday. One of the more popular pieces of Shaker work is the ladder-back chair.

Like their crafts, Shaker clothing was handmade and also reflected the precept of simplicity. In fact, this was perhaps the primary difference between the men and women living in the Shaker colonies. Clothing was meant to provide function primarily, and tame temptation as well. Shaker women, in contrast to their contemporaries, regularly wore pants (Lindley 1996).

After the passing of Mother Lee, Lucy Wright took over leadership of the Shakers in the early 1790s. It was under Mother Wright that the Shakers began to expand westward in the United States. Mother Wright maintained the Shaker beliefs and traditions established by Lee, and Wardley before her. Primary of these foundational beliefs was the need for celibacy and the equality among all members. As Mother Lee had preached, it was sexual intercourse that was to blame for the fall from Grace that Adam and Eve had experienced. This led to expulsion from the Garden of Eden by God.

Along with the practice of celibacy, Wardley, Lee, and Wright added the practice of confession. Mother Lee was the first Shaker leader to directly address the act of confession. Lee's simple approach to this defining act was quickly adopted by the Shakers. According to Lee, individuals needed to confess their sins to God regularly.

From the foundation of these two acts, the Shakers continued to shock the established Protestant churches in the United States. Celibacy and confession were matched with gender and racial equality. Work was seen as a blessing by God and as a means of abating temptation and sin.

Only recently have historical and theological analyses of the Shakers opened more of an objective and positive perspective on this shrinking religious community (Lindley 1996). Prior to the last few decades of the twentieth century, most historians and theologians interpreted the Shakers as fringe Christians with a radical theology. The rise of liberation theology as well as other more socially engaged understandings of Christianity opened the way to this new point of view on Shakers.

This new vantage point provided by these innovative analyses of Shakers has resulted in the community, their practices, as well as their theology being introduced into the mainstream of theological and historical debate. Connections between the Shakers and the environmental movements beginning in the 1970s in the United States, as well as around the world, have been suggested.

Many of the remaining Shaker communities are now state and federal historical sites. In fact, some of the last Shakers were still living and using Shaker communities as they became part of historic trusts. The remaining Shakers moved to the last surviving community in Maine.

Even though the Shakers operated orphanages, their numbers dwindled during the nineteenth century. This was in direct relation to their practice of celibacy. The only surviving Shaker colony is located in Sabbathday Lake, Maine. The last practicing Shakers continue to live out their lives in ritual simplicity, continuing to wait for the Second Coming of Christ.

SEE ALSO: Pacifism, Quakers, and Gender

REFERENCES

Lindley, Susan Hill. 1996. *You Have Stept out of Your Place: A History of Women and Religion in America*. Louisville, KY: Westminster John Knox Press.

FURTHER READING

Brewer, Priscilla J. 1986. *Shaker Communities, Shaker Lives*. Labanon, NH: University Press of New England.
Foster, Lawrence. 1991. *Women, Family, and Utopia: Communal Experiments of the Shakers, the Oneida Community, and the Mormons*. Syracuse, NY: Syracuse University Press.
Stein, Stephen J. *The Shaker Experience in America: A History of the United Society of Believers*. New Haven, CT: Yale University Press.

Shakti Shanti

METTI AMIRTHAM
Holy Cross Social Centre, India

Shanti in Sanskrit means "peace," "tranquility," "bliss," and so on. But from its Hindu and Buddhist origins, T. S. Eliot once translated the Sanskrit word to mean, "The Peace which passeth understanding." Rather than passive or inactive, Shanti is said to represent more of a moving, fluid, or "living" peace that can be realized in an ever-present state of being – right here, right now – and actively engaged through personal practice. In other words, the subtle nuance of Eliot's translation conveys the idea of a peace that can be continually discovered, experienced, reaped – not as an outcome, but as a never-ending practice and experience.

As a result, one begins to understand life, everyday actions, simple thoughts, and even daily words as "streams" of peace through which understanding passes from self and from beyond to every facet of the world that surrounds. This is what Panikkar would call cosmotheandric experience. "All the forces of the universe … are intertwined," to the extent that "individualistic souls do not exist: we are all interconnected, and I can reach salvation only by somehow incorporating the entire universe in the enterprise" (Panikkar 1993).

In order to experience Shanti deep within, one needs to be in touch with Shakti, which links together and energizes all things. According to the Indian tradition, Shakti (in Sanskrit *shak* – "to be able" or "power" or "empowerment") is ultimately the primordial cosmic energy that represents the dynamic forces that are thought to move through the entire universe. Shakti is, accordingly, the all-pervading and intangible energy principle that propels the cosmos and its endless human dimensions with the life-throbs of activity, culture, and with peace and harmony.

Shakti in Hinduism is energy/power identified as female. She is responsible for creation. She is "*Prakriti*," Nature. The energy of god is feminine and almost every god is static, even dead, without his Shakti. But Shakti is complete in herself because her existence does not depend on extraneous force. The male gods are incomplete without a consort, even powerless. When the energies of male gods prove inadequate, they have to turn to the females for protection. Shakti is the feminine counterpart to male deities, representing their "power" or "energy" embodied in the female form, such as Kali or Lakshmi. Her adherents worship Shakti as the force that maintains the universe and makes all life possible. Thus, the worship of Shakti or the feminine aspect of Divinity is an integral element of the religious fabric of the entire Indian subcontinent.

In Hindu philosophy and theology Shakti is understood to be the active dimension of the godhead, the divine power that underlies the godhead's ability to create the world and to display itself. Within the totality of the godhead, Shakti is the complementary pole of the divine tendency toward quiescence and stillness. Therefore, attainment of peace demands that we live in harmony with the universe, with universal Shakti. One of the spiritual paths within Hinduism called *Tantra* also speaks of Shakti as the only energy in the whole of the universe and to experience that energy is the human task. According to its belief, the Shakti form of goddesses comes to the aid of human beings and gods in periods of cosmic darkness by killing the demons that threaten the cosmic order and by bringing harmony and peace. In Tantrism the female manifestation called Shakti has been viewed as a significant agent in the cosmogony and the material cause of creation.

According to Indian tradition, women share in the Shakti of Devi, the Great Goddess of Hinduism, and are thought to embody both creative and destructive power. However, such embodiment does not, in and of itself, result in the ability to exercise power and authority in socially and culturally meaningful ways. Although some feminists criticize this dichotomy between theory and reality, still others argue that the idea of Shakti can be used to empower Indian women to resist patriarchy and to affirm their sexuality. For Indian women to become powerful, it is necessary for them to remake their *akti* (adherence) through culturally prescribed actions and transform the Shakti given by nature into moral power and authority, "a cultural artifact." When women are awakened to that primeval creative principle underlying the cosmos and realize the presence of the Divine Mother/Shakti in themselves and in the creation, they shall experience Shanti or integrative peace within.

However, this experience is attained only through awakening of the Shakti through yoga. Yoga is about living in the ever divine state of awareness of self as Shakti. Self is the essence of our very existence. There are many branches of yoga leading to the ultimate goal of self-realization. The integration of different yoga practices controls the body, nerves, and mind through physical discipline, breath or *prana*, and mental concentration and awakens the hidden energy dormant in human beings to produce an extremely profound mystical experience of bliss, happiness, and peace. This experience brings the total being into harmony and rhythm with the whole universe (cosmotheandric communion).

Through inner peace, genuine world peace can be achieved. In this the importance of individual responsibility is quite clear; an atmosphere of peace must first be created within oneself, then gradually expanded to include families, human communities, and ultimately the whole planet.

SEE ALSO: Hinduism; Sexualities

REFERENCE

Panikkar, Raymond. 1993. *The Cosmotheandric Experience: Emerging Religious Consciousness*. New York: Orbis Books.

FURTHER READING

Eliot, T. S. 1922. *The Waste Land*. New York: Horace Liveright.

Harish, Ranjana, and V. Bharathi Harishankar. 2003. *Shakti: Multidisciplinary Perspectives on Women's Empowerment in India*. New Delhi: Rawat.

Kinsley, David. 1986. *Hindu Goddesses: Vision of the Divine Feminine in the Hindu Religious Traditions*. Berkeley: University of California Press.

Kinsley, David. 1998. *Tantric Vision of Divine Feminine: The Ten Mahavidyas*. Delhi: Motilal Banarsidass.

Mehi, Maharishi. 1998. *Philosophy of Liberation: A Manual of Sant Mat Mysticism*. Chandrapur: Santmat Satsang Samiti.

Woodroffe, Sir John. 1959. *Shakti and Shakta*. Madras: Ganesh.

Shaman Priestesses

DAWN M. RUTECKI
Indiana University, USA

Shamanism was conceptualized in the late nineteenth century to broadly encompass diverse religious practices from across the world to describe spiritual beliefs and rites related to hunting, healing, divination, and conducting offerings to spirits. First used to describe male and female spiritual practitioners in Central Siberia, shaman originates from the Tungus word *šaman*, incorporating *ša*, meaning "to know," to denote a particular kind of knowledgeable religious practitioner (Eliade 1964). Shaman priestesses distinguish female shamans who transgress the boundaries of the natural and supernatural worlds usually on a varying part-time basis, from other priestesses who are full-time spiritual leaders and contrary to the malevolence often associated with witches.

Mircea Eliade's extensive *Shamanism: Archaic Techniques of Ecstasy* (1964) cemented the fluidity and vagueness of the term *shaman* in research and discussion by arguing its origins to be in the Upper Paleolithic, approximately 30,000 years ago, and marking it as the most primitive foundation of religion. Subsequently, it designates religious specialists from distinct spiritual practices throughout the world. In addition to a Siberia ritual specialist, shaman is used to describe, among many others, a Korean *masin* and *mudang*, Nepalese *jhākri*, Mapuche (Chilean) *machi*, sangoma of southern Africa, and an Okinawan (Ryūkyūan Islands) *yuta*. Within this far-reaching use of the term, shamans and shaman priestesses are identified by their direct contact with the spirit world through traces and other altered states of consciousness (ASC), who use their connection to and control of spirits aided by ritual paraphernalia to act on behalf of the community. Due to the ambiguity of the term, shaman continues to be inaccurately used to describe many traditional healers, mediums, and other religious specialists involved in spiritual possession or trances, such as many Native American and First Nation healers who separate themselves from the world (Kehoe 2000).

Despite historically contingent, cultural differences between shaman priestesses of diverse communities, the general progression between stages from selection to fully initiated shaman display similarities. First, a spirit or group of spirits select a shaman. While this may happen at any age in most communities, usually the dreams, trances, or possessions identified with a shaman's calling result from some kind of distress, sickness, or trauma. As a result, shamans are often associated with the idea of being "healed madwomen" or a similar conceptualization (Harvey 1979, 6). After commencing their training, many shamans recognize previous dreams, fits, and other experiences as earlier attempts by the spirits to call them. Some argue that these beliefs support theoretical positions maintaining that shamans are psychopathic or were mentally ill, but are healed through therapeutic initiation rites (Walsh 1997). However, research demonstrates that ASC experienced by shamans are within a normal range of behavioral variance, not psychosis – largely distinguished by awareness and subsequent mental stability surrounding shamanistic ASC and absent in, for example, schizophrenic patients (Krippner 2002).

After a shaman has accepted her call, she undergoes an extensive apprentice period with an older shaman. While all shamanistic trainings involve extended time lengths and high intensity, specifics regarding exact length of time, order of rites learnt, specific progress markers toward initiation, and other facets vary by spiritual community. Often fasting, sexual abstinence, and dancing are part of apprenticeship, while use of herbs, medicines, and hallucinogens varies widely (Sered 1994). Some shaman priestesses interact with the supernatural world through ecstatic flight, where the soul leaves the body to journey in the spirit realm and return with information. Other shamans act as mediums, where the body is possessed by a spirit. Both types of interaction with the spirit world involve exceptional levels of control and danger. Each part of training helps the shaman priestess learn the requisite skills to make contact with the spirt world, build connections with a spirit guide, and control the ASC needed to perform her tasks.

Upon completion of her apprenticeship, she becomes a fully recognized shaman through an initiation rite that usually includes some kind of rebirth. A shaman priestess's ability to call upon spirits successfully and move between worlds relies both on her ability to control this movement and her ability to transform. The importance of shamanistic transformation and transgression may require dressing as (becoming) an animal or other being, cross-dressing, or occupying a gender-ambiguous space. This results in further misapplication of the term shaman to transgender and third-gender individuals in a variety of cultures. Transgressing the natural and supernatural worlds is dangerous, exhausting, and requires significant spiritual power; as a result, while a shaman priestess occupies a special, socially recognized position, she and her family are often viewed with some suspicion, if not as social outcasts.

Suspicion of shamans and shaman priestesses extends beyond local communities. Shamans are often seen as the main obstacle to progress, and mocked, demonized, stripped of their paraphernalia and regalia, and sometimes exiled or executed by governments. In some cases, such as in Siberia, shaman priestess escaped the persecution experienced by male shamans and were able to keep working for their communities (Kehoe 2000). Shamans in most societies that document a long, cohesive history of shamanism experienced government persecution, even if shamanism or neo-shamanism is currently celebrated in that society.

SEE ALSO: Cross-Dressing; Gender Transgression; Indigenous Knowledges and Gender; Traditional Healing; Witches

REFERENCES

Eliade, Mircea. 1964. *Shamanism: Archaic Techniques of Ecstasy*. Princeton: Princeton University Press.

Harvey, Youngsook Kim. 1979. *Six Korean Women: The Socialization of Shamans*. St. Paul: West Publishing.

Kehoe, Alice B. 2000. *Shamans and Religion: An Anthropological Exploration in Critical Thinking*. Long Grove: Waveland Press.

Krippner, Stanley. 2002. "Conflicting Perspectives on Shamans and Shamanism: Points and Counterpoints." *American Psychologist*, 57(11): 962–977. DOI: 10.1037/0003-066X.57.11.962.

Sered, Susan S. 1994. *Priestess, Mother, Sacred Sister: Religions Dominated by Women*. New York: Oxford University Press.

Walsh, Roger. 1997. "The Psychological Health of Shamans: A Reevaluation." *Journal of the American Academy of Religion*, 65(1): 101–124.

Shari'a

HAMID MAVANI
Claremont Graduate University, USA

Muslims view the shari'a (divine law), which initially referred to a well-trodden path or road that leads to a water supply to quench one's thirst, as a comprehensive and all-encompassing divine law that addresses both the religious and mundane aspects of their lives at the individual and societal levels. The Qur'an and the hadith (statements and practices attributed to the Prophet) constitute the foundational sources from which the law is derived. The latter also serves as the source for the majority of rulings, for only about 10 percent of the Qur'an deals with legal questions. Later on, the consensus of the religious scholars or the Muslim community (*ijma'*), along with analogical reasoning (*qiyas*) in Sunni Islam and reason (*'aql*) in Shi'i Islam, were added to the sources of divine law as part of Islamic legal theory. Subsidiary sources, such as public welfare (*maslaha*) and convention or customary practice (*'urf*), were also added so that the derived law would be harmonious with the objectives of divine law: the preservation of one's life, property, mind, religion, and offspring. The different level of emphasis placed on these sources as reflected in the jurists' approaches and methodologies is evident in the four Sunni legal schools (Hanafi, Shafi'i, Maliki, and Hanbali) and in the majority Shi'i legal school (Ja'fari).

Islamic law developed gradually from its rudimentary form of proto-judges, who possessed extensive discretionary powers and were assigned administrative responsibilities and authority. In its mature form during the tenth century, the law acquired a robust methodology, a developed judiciary, and a crystallization of various schools of thought from the personal schools. The substantive or positive law that emerged from these developments divided the subject matter into two major components: acts of worship (*'ibadat*), which are considered to be constant and unchanging, and interpersonal relations (*mu'amalat*), which can be viewed as bound by time and context. The former constitutes about one third of the legal corpus and covers such acts as ritual purity and ablution, prayers (*salat*), fasting during the month of Ramadan (*sawm*), pilgrimage to Makkah (*hajj*), and giving alms (*zakat*). The second category would generally include, among other things, marriage, divorce, oaths, child custody, religious endowments, inheritance, last will and testament, contracts, blood money, criminal penalties, and war and peace (jihad).

It is in the domain of personal status laws that codification figures prominently. Women are subject to serious disabilities under the existing laws, which are based on a patriarchal system and do not take into account the new context or circumstances. For instance, women are required to obey their husbands and be sexually available so long as this would not lead to a violation of any divine law; the husband remains the absolute guardian of the children and after his death the right would be transferred in his lineage. This, of course, has implications on parenting and custody of children in the event of a divorce. The husband has an unconditional right of divorce, which he can exercise without any just cause, whereas the wife has to petition for divorce through the court and needs to provide evidence to substantiate her case. The Qur'anic verse on polygamy is interpreted as a license to engage in it, provided that the husband can be equitable, instead of being viewed as a restrictive clause whose intent was to evolve toward the norm of monogamy. This is akin to slavery, which was tolerated during Muhammad's time with the aim of eradicating it, even though there is no explicit text that prohibits slavery. On many occasions conjugal violence is substantiated by invoking Qur'an 4:34 as the basis, even though stringent conditions and steps have been set forth in the books of law before the husband can forcibly demand wifely obedience. Present-day Islamic law does not recognize shared matrimonial resources and thus the wife would not be entitled to any share of assets accumulated during the term of marriage, nor could she demand alimony upon divorce.

The divine law occupies a central place in a Muslim's life and identity formation at the psychological level, even though institutionally it no longer plays a pivotal role. European colonialism during the eighteenth and nineteenth centuries had a great impact on the Muslim legal system; in fact, it replaced all aspects of this system except for family law, intestate succession, and pious endowments. After achieving independence, many Muslims viewed the shari'a as an obstacle to progress and modernization and, as a result, little effort was made to restore it to its former position. Recently, calls to restore the shari'a as the law of the land through a process of Islamization have become more frequent in some Muslim majority countries. This call has resulted in a surge of Islamism and attempts to codify the law. However, it is unlikely that this undertaking will attain much success, as was the case in Iran, if it continues to limit the scope of *ijtihad* (a jurist's exertion to deduce new legal rulings from the sources) and ignores the changing context and circumstances while trying to apply the shari'a's norms and principles.

The impetus for Islamization, as was evident in some Arab countries after the Arab Spring, has focused primarily on instituting criminal punishments and on minority rights and women's rights, in order, it is claimed, to protect the public space and the family from any kind of immorality or corruption resulting in moralization of public space. This is partly because the small portion of the Qur'an that deals with legal questions provides no more than general principles from which historically conditioned and context-bound rulings can be derived. Acknowledging this fact would open up a space for secularity, one in which the public could negotiate those rules and regulations that impinge upon their lives as citizens of a modern nation-state. Such an approach would also allow an indigenous form of liberal democracy based on a civil society model to emerge. The end result of this process would be a mechanism that could address and resolve the inequities faced by Muslim women in regards to autonomy, testifying in court, marriage, divorce, child custody, inheritance, and other issues. Moreover, it would reduce the tension between Islamic law and Western legal codes that has prompted many states in America to enact legislation or introduce such measures that would prohibit judges from considering shari'a in the adjudication of cases.

SEE ALSO: Feminism, Islamic; Islam and Gender; Islam and Homosexuality

FURTHER READING

Abou El Fadl, Khaled. 2001. *Speaking in God's Name: Islamic Law, Authority and Women*. Oxford: Oneworld Publications.

Berger, Maurits S., ed. 2013. *Applying Sharia in the West: Facts, Fears and the Future of Islamic Rules on Family Relations in the West*. Leiden: Leiden University Press.

Duderija, Adis. 2011. *Constructing a Religiously Ideal "Believer" and "Woman" in Islam: Neo-Traditional Salafi and Progressive Muslims' Methods of Interpretation*. New York: Palgrave Macmillan.

Hallaq, Wael B. 1997. *A History of Islamic Legal Theories: An Introduction to Sunni Usul al-Fiqh*. Cambridge: Cambridge University Press.

Kamali, Mohammad Hashim. 2003. *Principles of Islamic Jurisprudence*. Cambridge: The Islamic Texts Society.

Mir-Hosseini, Ziba, Kari Vogt, Lena Larsen, and Christian Moe, eds. 2012. *Gender and Equality in Muslim Family Law: Justice and Ethics in the Islamic Legal Process*. London: I. B. Tauris.

Tucker, Judith E. 2008. *Women, Family, and Gender in Islamic Law*. Cambridge: Cambridge University Press.

Vogel, Frank E. 2000. *Islamic Law and Legal System: Studies of Saudi Arabia*. Leiden: Brill.

Shinto

NORIKO KAWAHASHI
Nagoya Institute of Technology, Japan

Shinto is an ethnic religion, and it is considered a particular, traditional, and indigenous religion that is unique to Japan. Shinto means "the way of the gods," and its beliefs and rituals are practiced at some 80,000 shrines that exist in Japan today. However, the content of Shinto, and its definition, are now being subjected to scholarly scrutiny (Havens 2006).

A distinctive feature of Shinto in general is that it includes elements of nature worship, in which mountains, trees, fields, and so on are worshipped as sacred; animism, in which plants and animals are perceived to have spirit; and shamanism, in which the spirits of gods possess human beings. With regard to shamanism, Shinto mythology such as the *Records of Ancient Matters* (Kojiki) and the *Chronicles of Japan* (Nihongi) record the activities of women who possessed special shamanistic abilities. The key point here is that the highest supreme deity in the Shinto pantheon is the sun goddess named Amaterasu Omikami. Moreover, Japanese mythology positions this goddess as the ancestral deity to the imperial house, and she is enshrined even today as the supreme deity in the Inner Shrine of the Grand Shrines of Ise. In other words, the deity that has been represented as symbolizing the unity of the Japanese state is not a male deity but a female deity.

Hinduism and esoteric Buddhism (Mikkyo) present instances of gender-based symbols, such as goddesses, that affirm the gender of women. It does not follow, however, that women are perceived as capable and wise in the cultures concerned. In other words, the fact that the highest deity is a goddess does not guarantee a positive attitude toward actual women. This is clear also from the fact that even those Shinto-related new religions that have roots in Shinto and that were founded by women have undergone such change that their religious institutions today are run by men. Even more noteworthy, however, is the fact that Shinto is a religion that exhibits a strong non-tolerance and even aversion to blood, and that places emphasis on blood pollution. This is apparent in the *Code of the Engi Era* (Engishiki). Compiled in the tenth century, this text objects to childbirth, menses, and other matters relating to women's reproductive function as impurities that pollute the sacred nature of the state rituals centered on the imperial household that were being formed into established practices at that time (Yusa 1994). Despite the necessity of childbirth for the imperial succession, blood was made into a ritual impurity. Even today there are localities where women are not allowed to take part in carrying portable shrines (*mikoshi*) and other practices of local Shinto festivals. In the sport of sumo, which has close connections with Shinto, women are prohibited from setting foot in the wrestling ring. Consequently, no woman governor or cabinet minister has yet made the customary awards presentations to winning sumo wrestlers in the ring. When a woman was governor, the award would be presented by a male vice governor representing her.

This kind of exclusion of women (*nyonin kinsei*) exists in Japanese religious tradition in general, not just in Shinto. It is, however, particularly conspicuous in Shinto (Kawahashi 2006). The above examples show how women's reproductive capability, which is not itself reasonably to be considered polluting, nevertheless comes to be construed as polluting and unclean when it is linked with religious ideology. Moreover, as a result of women's exclusion because they offend against the sacred, religious authority or orthodoxy becomes even more rigid and unbending.

Even though women make up more than 10 percent of priests in the Shinto religious community today, almost all of these women are priests of small shrines. The important positions in the religious community are occupied by men. The Shinto community is opposed to having a woman succeed to the position of emperor. It is also against allowing married couples to have separate surnames, a practice it stigmatizes as undesirable individualism and Westernization. The lobbying group known as the Shinto Association of Spiritual Leadership continues to issue political messages with a right-leaning slant. One of this group's important objectives is the revision of Japan's postwar "peace" constitution (Havens 2006).

About this lack of enthusiasm in the Shinto community for achieving gender equality, Bocking has cogently remarked: "Some observers have suggested that Shrine Shinto will continue to decline until it can offer women real opportunities to achieve leadership within the priesthood and in other important roles currently occupied only by men" (2005, 8369).

SEE ALSO: Buddhism; Hinduism; Purity Versus Pollution; Shaman Priestesses

REFERENCES

Bocking, Brian. 2005. "Shinto." In *Encyclopedia of Religion*, vol. 12, edited by Lindsay Jones. Detroit: Macmillan Reference USA.

Havens, Norman. 2006. "Shinto." In *Nanzan Guide to Japanese Religions*, edited by Paul L. Swanson and Clark Chilson. Honolulu: University of Hawaii Press.

Kawahashi, Noriko. 2006. "Gender Issues in Japanese Religions." In *Nanzan Guide to Japanese Religions*, edited by Paul L. Swanson and Clark Chilson. Honolulu: University of Hawaii Press.

Yusa, Michiko. 1994. "Women in Shinto: Images Remembered." In *Religion and Women*, edited by Arvind Sharma. Albany: SUNY Press.

Single-Parent Households

JENNIFER E. LANSFORD
Duke University, USA

Estimates from census and demographic surveys suggest that about 18% of children worldwide live with single parents (OECD 2013). Single-parent households can result from divorce, death of a parent, parents living apart, and from parents who were never married. The origins of single parenthood and percent of single-parent households at a population level differ widely across countries and socioeconomic groups within countries. To illustrate, in the United States, more than 40% of children are born to single women, and about 50% of children will experience their parents' divorce. In contrast, divorce is illegal in the Philippines, so single parenthood in this context originates from factors other than divorce. In Zambia, more than 20% of children experience the death of one or both parents, making death a common route to single parenthood. Children in Asia and the Middle East are less likely to live with single parents than children in other world regions. Thus, the demography of and reasons for single parenthood differ across countries.

Single-parent households are predominantly female headed, particularly in the case of unmarried women becoming mothers. However, after divorce, mothers are also much more likely than fathers to have custody of their children. Likewise, after the death of a parent, children are more likely to continue living with the other parent rather than extended family or other caregivers if it is the father rather than mother who died. Female-headed and female-supported households are increasingly common in many nations. A wide range of societal-level factors such as increasing proportions of women in the work force and social norms regarding the perceived acceptability of non-marital childbearing has been argued to have affected these demographic changes in the prevalence of female-headed and female-supported households.

Single parenthood is strongly linked to socioeconomic status. Mothers with only a high school education are much more likely to be unmarried than mothers with a college education. In addition, single parenthood is predictive of future poverty. Becoming a single parent at an early age by giving birth to a child outside of marriage predicts lower educational attainment (e.g., teenagers often drop out of school if they become pregnant) and, thereby, lower income potential. Becoming a single parent through divorce or death of a spouse also predicts a reduction in income, particularly for women. In any comparisons of single-parent and two-parent families, it is crucial to control for socioeconomic status to avoid confounding the effect of having fewer economic resources with the effect of being in a single-parent family.

Researchers have investigated whether being in a single-parent household is related to parents' and children's adjustment. The largest body of relevant research examines whether children who live in single-parent households because their parents divorced show worse adjustment than children whose parents have not divorced. Reviews of this research generally conclude that divorce has some negative effects on children's adjustment but that these effects may be small in magnitude and not universal (Lansford 2009). Hetherington and Kelly (2002) concluded that 25% of individuals whose parents divorce have serious long-term social, emotional, or psychological problems in adulthood in comparison with 10% of individuals whose parents have stayed together; still, this means that 75% of individuals whose parents divorce do not have serious long-term impairment during adulthood. Even studies that do find long-term effects of divorce generally report that the effect sizes are small. For example, Allison and Furstenberg (1989) concluded that although divorce was related to behavior problems, psychological distress, and low academic achievement, the effect sizes for divorce were smaller than those found for gender differences. Taken together, these findings indicate that children whose parents have divorced have higher levels of externalizing behaviors and internalizing problems, lower academic achievement, and more problems in social relationships than do children whose parents have not divorced. However, even though children whose parents divorce have worse adjustment on average than do children whose parents do not divorce, most children whose parents divorce do not have long-term negative outcomes.

Experiencing the death of a parent is among the most stressful events a child can face, and children in single-parent families resulting from the death of a parent are at increased risk for negative outcomes such as depression and anxiety. However, these children typically show better adjustment outcomes than children in other types of single-parent families (Amato 2005). Children of never-married single mothers are typically at risk of more adjustment problems than children in other types of single-parent families, in large part because never-married mothers have lower levels of education and higher levels of poverty than divorced or widowed mothers.

Most researchers no longer simply compare the adjustment of individuals in single- versus two-parent families. Instead, several scholars have argued that processes occurring in all types of families are more important than family structure in relation to the well-being of children. Taking family process variables into account attenuates the association between family structure and children's adjustment. For example, being a single parent can increase parents' stress and anxiety, making it more difficult for parents to monitor and supervise children effectively, to discipline consistently, and to provide warmth and affection, all of which can negatively affect children's adjustment (more so than single parenthood per se).

Not all single-parent families follow the same patterns. Thus, patterns of adjustment that may be typical of many single-parent families may not be exhibited by a given family. Furthermore, what initially appear to be effects of single parenthood are likely to be a complex combination of parent, child, and contextual factors that precede and follow single parenthood in conjunction with single parenthood itself.

SEE ALSO: Families of Choice; Same-Sex Families

REFERENCES

Allison, Paul D., and Frank F. Furstenberg, Jr. 1989. "How Marital Dissolution Affects Children: Variations by Age and Sex." *Developmental Psychology*, 25: 540–549.

Amato, Paul R. 2005. "The Impact of Family Formation Change on the Cognitive, Social, and Emotional Well-Being of the Next Generation." *The Future of Children*, 15: 75–96.

Hetherington, E. Mavis, and John Kelly. 2002. *For Better or Worse*. New York: Norton.

Lansford, Jennifer E. 2009. "Parental Divorce and Children's Adjustment." *Perspectives on Psychological Science*, 4: 140–152.

OECD (Organization for Economic Cooperation and Development). 2013. "OECD Family Database." Accessed February 18, 2014, at: www.oecd.org/social/family/database.

Single-Sex Education and Coeducation

URSULA KESSELS
Freie Universität Berlin, Germany

Coeducation means that both genders are taught together in the same schools and in the same classes, whereas single-sex education means that boys and girls attend boys-only or girls-only schools and/or classes. Nations vary in their ratio of single-sex and coeducational educational settings, both currently and historically. Wiseman (2008) analyzed the 46 nations participating in TIMSS 2003 and found that 19 percent of eighth-graders were enrolled in single-sex schools. Ten nations had no single-sex schools at all, 17 nations had very few (below 4 percent of schools), and in Saudi Arabia, Jordan, and Iran schools were (almost) exclusively single-sex.

Before the twentieth century, single-sex education beyond the elementary level was common in most European countries and the United States. In single-sex education at that time, not only were boys and girls separated at school, but they studied different curricula, with the education offered to female students being less academic and also less well funded. These highly gendered curricula were intended to track males and females into different roles in society, which assigned women to subordinate tasks and careers. In the wake of the women's rights movement and promotion of gender equality, coeducation became more universal and is now the status quo in most countries of the world. A fierce debate on single-sex schooling has broken out recently, most notably in the United States. Starting in 1972, sex segregation was equated with sex discrimination and prohibited in public schools by federal law, but in 2006 Congress voted to ease restrictions on single-sex schooling. Of course, these amendments were not intended once again to provide females with a different or inferior education. Instead, coeducational schools were perceived as not always offering optimal and equal opportunities to both sexes. Proponents particularly hoped that single-sex settings would overcome the underrepresentation of females in mathematics and sciences, as several researchers have stated that both boys and girls are less likely to pursue sex-atypical subjects in mixed schools than in single-sex schools (Sullivan, Joshi, and Leonard 2010).

Research on single-sex education versus coeducation addresses different empirical and theoretical questions that are influenced by normative questions. Empirical research is designed to test whether (female and/or male) students in coeducational and single-sex settings differ on important outcome variables and whether any such differences are causally related to students' being taught in single-sex or coeducational settings. Theoretical questions inquire as to why and how a single-sex setting should yield different outcomes than a coeducational setting. The overarching normative questions inquire which important educational outcome variables should be studied and whether some values that a society intends to convey to their youth may be inherently in contradiction with single-sex (or coeducational) settings.

Results of empirical studies on the effects of single-sex schools are inconsistent and often suffer from methodological problems, mainly linked to selection bias. Because single-sex schools tend to be highly selective with respect to both students and teachers, it is difficult or nearly impossible to rule out factors other than group composition that might account for differences in achievement or interest between students from single-sex versus coeducational schools. One possible way to resolve that problem is by controlling for many potentially confounding background variables. Using large data sets, these studies usually result in smaller or no differences between school types (when compared with uncorrected apparent differences). Which confounding variables should be controlled for in order to allow for causal interpretations of differences between school types has been the subject of intensive debates. Another way to resolve the selectivity problem is through experimental design, using randomization of students to single-sex or coeducational classes within coeducational schools. Here a positive effect of single-sex classes on girls' physics-related self-concept has been found and the underlying psychological mechanism which made single-sex physics lessons beneficial for girls clarified (Kessels and Hannover 2008), contributing not only to the empirical body of research, but also to its theoretical foundation.

Because findings have been inconsistent and even contradictory, both supporters and opponents of the recent implementation of many single-sex education programs in the United States currently claim that research comparing coeducational and single-sex settings supports their own position. The discussion on the pros and cons of single-sex education often seems based less on science than on ideology. Because the rationale for defending single-sex education or coeducation can vary so fundamentally, support of or opposition to single-sex education is not diagnostic of any coherent ideology. Very different argumentation can lead to advocating an outwardly similar educational setting. Whereas some researchers who see advantages in single-sex settings base their theoretical argumentation and empirical research on the relevance of (culturally defined and socially transmitted) gender stereotypes (e.g., Kessels and Hannover 2008), others, in contrast, express essentialist views on profound differences between the sexes that require separation in order to adapt education to the special needs of each. Whereas some authors argue that one possible way to foster *gender equity* might be to offer single-sex settings, others who promote single-sex settings seem to emphasize the value of existing *gender differences*. Some researchers (e.g., Halpern et al. 2011) even see single-sex educational settings as inherently threatening to gender equity and comparable to racial segregation.

SEE ALSO: Gender Equity in Education in the United States; Sex Segregation and Education in the United States; Women in Science

REFERENCES

Halpern, Diane F., et al. 2011. "The Pseudo-science of Single-Sex Schooling." *Science*, 333: 1706–1707. DOI: 10.1126/science.120503.

Kessels, Ursula, and Bettina Hannover. 2008. "When Being a Girl Matters less: Accessibility of Gender-Related Self-Knowledge in Single-Sex and Coeducational Classes and Its Impact on Students' Physics-Related Self-Concept of Ability." *British Journal of Educational Psychology*, 78: 273–289. DOI: 10.1348/000709907X215938.

Sullivan, Alice, Heather Joshi, and Diana Leonard. 2010. "Single-Sex Schooling and Academic Attainment at School and Through the Lifecourse." *American Educational Research Journal*, 47: 6–36. DOI: 10.3102/0002831209350106.

Wiseman, A. W. 2008. "A Culture of (In) Equality?: a Cross-National Study of Gender Parity and Gender Segregation in National School Systems." *Research in Comparative and International Education*, 3: 179–201. DOI: 10.2304/rcie.2008.3.2.179.

Sisterhood

SONJA VIVIENNE
University of Queensland, Australia

Sisterhood is a multivalent term. Literally, it connotes the relationship between sisters. More broadly it has come to signify a feeling of closeness or affinity among a group of women or all women. The group may be affiliated around common interests, political or spiritual beliefs, race, class, sexuality or employment. While some groups affirm a clearly articulated identity, other groups may be more fluid or resistant to categorization. Iterations that are affirmed by social policy, political activity, and/or media representation gain fortitude and have a constitutive influence on individuals and groups who are seeking to define identity.

In a historical context, the term sisterhood emerged hand in hand with first-wave feminism, post-World War I, as predominantly white, Western, privileged women sought to unify *all* women against officially mandated inequities, and in battle for suffrage. Precedents for female unification against opposition were arguably established in the mid-nineteenth century in the form of sororities (from the Latin *soror* meaning sister), when previously all-male universities started to admit women. However, some argue that these were merely female equivalents of the male fraternities of the time, principally Latin literary societies.

Second-wave feminism, flourishing throughout the 1960s and 1970s, brought together numerous sisterhoods (e.g., women of color, lesbian women, women on campus, women for peace) in pursuit of social and political change on numerous fronts. *Sisterhood is Powerful* (1970) is a renowned anthology, edited by Robin Morgan, which canvases many of the central tenets of the women's liberation movement during this period. However, critiques from minority women emphasized the many distinctions between racism and sexism and challenged the primacy of the latter, resulting in the publication of the deliberately eclectic *Sisterhood is Global* anthology in 1984. In 2003, the anthology was again revisited, with *Sisterhood is Forever* addressing divergent generations, ethnicities, sexualities, and beliefs.

Despite many differences of agenda, feminism across the decades is, arguably, unified by the maxim "the personal is political." However, divisions between opposing groups of women (exemplified during "the sex wars," fraught with hostility over definitions of pornography and sexual liberation) problematize a politics of unity. Proponents of third-wave feminism draw attention to the very different forms of oppression borne by women in different cultural and social contexts. Interwoven with poststructuralist thinking, much current feminist theory emphasizes the power of institutions and social structures in defining "woman" and encourages critique of fixed or essentialist categories of any kind. Greater awareness of transgender, transsexual, and intersex identity also contributes to ruptures in biological gender categories.

"Sisterhood" and "feminism" may appear interchangeable in some contexts, but the two terms also have distinct connotations. While feminism is widely held to address the common concerns of women, sisterhood may be utilized to affirm affinity based not solely in gender. For example, numerous religious orders refer to a community of women living together with common beliefs as "sisters" or in some cases "nuns." Sisters in Islam (SIS) emerged in 1990 in Malaysia as a collective of lawyers, activists, scholars, and journalists who seek to challenge misogynist social and legal principles commonly justified by specific interpretations of the Qur'an.

Beneath any equivalence drawn between sisterhood and feminism lurk many different understandings of gendered identity performed in social context. The notion of performativity, emerging originally in linguistics and refined by Butler (1990) and other queer theorists, posits gender as a social construction that emerges through repeated gendered performance, something one *does* rather than an essential or biological state. As such, any unification of a gendered category like sisterhood must be realized through mutual recognition of social affinity rather than prescribed anatomy.

Scholars working with notions of the public sphere have systematically deconstructed the social conditions of affinity and collective expression of identity. Berlant (1997) presents the idea of an "intimate public" as a kind of assumed audience of people with common life experiences and beliefs. Meanwhile Warner (2005) argues for a "counter-public" unified by perceived differences to dominant paradigms (e.g., heteronormativity). These analyses draw attention to the complex nuances of affinity beyond binary oppositions.

The ubiquitous role technology now plays in mediating social relations has revealed the phenomenon of social convergence in which formally discrete audiences are potentially witness to discordant or inconsistent performances of identity across face-to-face and online spaces. The fact that digital articulations of identity are persistent and searchable amplifies the potential for schisms in unified categorizations of both individual and collective representations. Further, algorithms (Gillespie 2014) that shape how search engines recognize and categorize what is "trending" or "most discussed" are of great pertinence to notions of affinity.

While early iterations of feminism sought unification as empowerment, more recent theoretical developments (e.g., queer theory) problematize stable categorizations. Analysis of how individuals and groups orient themselves and are oriented by social structures, both real and perceived, deconstructs oversimplified notions of collectivity with which terms like sisterhood are inscribed. While sisterhood still has some significance in symbolizing unity, modern utilization may equally be ironic. Further developments in the study of gender, feminism, and affinity seem likely to continue the deconstruction and complication of finite parameters of identity, focusing instead on the pervasive context that undergirds any social category.

SEE ALSO: Essentialism; Feminism, Poststructural; Feminisms, First, Second, and Third Wave; Identity Politics; Queer Theory

REFERENCES

Berlant, Lauren Gail. 1997. *The Queen of America Goes to Washington City: Essays on Sex and Citizenship*. Durham, NC: Duke University Press.

Butler, Judith. 1990. *Gender Trouble: Feminism and the Subversion of Identity*. New York: Routledge.

Gillespie, Tarleton. 2014. "The Relevance of Algorithms." In *Media Technologies: Essays on Communication, Materiality, and Society*, edited by Tarleton Gillespie, Pablo J. Boczkowski, and Kirsten A. Foot. Cambridge, MA: MIT Press.

Morgan, Robin. 1970. *Sisterhood is Powerful: An Anthology of Writings from the Women's Liberation Movement*. New York: Random House.

Morgan, Robin. 1984. *Sisterhood is Global: The International Women's Movement Anthology*. Garden City, NY: Anchor Press/Doubleday.

Morgan, Robin. 2003. *Sisterhood is Forever: The Women's Anthology for a New Millennium*. New York: Washington Square Press.

Warner, Michael. 2005. *Publics and Counterpublics*. New York: Zone Books.

Skin Lightening/Bleaching

SUSAN LEVINE, CRYSTAL POWELL, LESTER M. DAVIDS, and MEAGAN JACOBS
University of Cape Town, South Africa

Skin bleaching, also known as skin lightening, has long been a practice among black and dark skinned populations around the world. Despite the variety of well-known iatrogenic effects, the use of skin bleaching products ("Xessel" as they are referred to by the Senegalese) among women around the world continues to increase. Skin bleaching involves the use of various cosmetic products such as cream, soap, and lotions. Other products include the use of gel, toothpaste, bleach, washing powder, and battery acid. It is believed that the most common reasons for using skin-lightening products is the notion of colorism, meaning the preference for lighter skin and a social hierarchy based on skin tone. Other reasons for continued use of skin-lightening cosmetics include combating uneven skin tone, reducing the signs of aging, and treating other dermatological problems including "acne, melasma, and post inflammatory hyperpigmentation" (Dlova, Hendricks, and Martincgh 2012, 51). This entry looks at the practices of and motivations behind the use of skin-lightening products in different areas of the world, with a focus on South Africa.

As Francis Nyamnjoh and Divine Fuh observe, "beauty is as much a work of nature as it is the outcome of working on nature" (2014, 52). Hamed et al. (2010) suggest that 62.3 percent of women regard lighter skin as beautiful and associate dark skin with evil, disease, and dirt. Lightness and darkness have moral connotations: lightness can be associated with innocence, purity, virginity, spirituality, and vulnerability, whereas darkness can refer to threat, aggression, and danger. The connotations have serious health implications. The majority of skin lighteners are combinations of compounds which include the "toxic 4" – hydroquinone (HQ), mercury, corticosteroids, and retinoids (different isoforms of vitamin A). Biologically, they combine to inhibit the enzyme tyrosinase, which is specific to the epidermal cell, the melanocyte. Inhibiting tyrosinase reduces the formation of the pigment melanin and consequently leads to skin lightening. This process is effective over the short term but chronic use of skin lighteners lead to an accumulation of these toxic compounds causing irreversible damage to the upper and underlying skin layers. Moreover, the skin, ironically, hyperpigments (goes very dark), resulting in a dismal cosmetic outcome.

Elysia Pan explains how East Asian women, for example, protect themselves from the sun, variously using umbrellas "with UV300 protection" to wearing gloves in summertime (Pan 2013). According to Yaba Blay, a leading scholar in African cultural aesthetics, the history of skin lightening can be traced to the Elizabethans (Blay 2009, 2011) but, in its current manifestations, is practiced disproportionately within communities "of color" (Blay 2011, 5). As Blay argues for the African context, "skin bleaching represents one attempt to approximate the White ideal and consequently gain access to both the humanity and social status historically reserved for Whites" (Blay 2011, 5).

The predominantly female use (although use by men is increasing) of these products can be attributed to complex processes of white supremacy, global aesthetic regimes that associate lightness with success and attractiveness, and the pervasive effects of capitalist and cultural domination. In addition to the powerful force of colonial discourse, there is an overriding influence of colorism driven by popular media.

A SOUTH AFRICAN HISTORY OF SKIN LIGHTENERS

The use of skin lighteners in South Africa dates to the 1950s with the Coloured Labour Preference Act, which reserved certain jobs for people classified colored under the race classification act. This historical legacy may in part explain why some black people lightened their skin to remove the color stigma (Bellow and Alster 2004). Popular magazines further fueled the notion that fair skin set the standard for beauty. Dark skin was considered a marker of dirt and lower social status, leading to a "pigmentocratic society" (Westerhof 1997). The hierarchy of women in terms of skin lightness, known as pigmentocracy, employs a historically established notion of beauty. Individuals approximate the appearance of others with the hope of being "like them" (Jablonski 2012). Paradoxically, the custom of skin-lightening creams increased after South Africa's liberation in 1994. Lighter skin continues to inform a beauty ethic, despite black empowerment initiatives that seek to rupture colonial and Western domination.

MEDIA'S PSYCHOSOCIAL IMPACT

The impact of black celebrities including Beyonce and Nicky Minaj who endorse skin lightening cannot be overstated (Glenn 2008). Billboard advertising together with print and social media rely on lighter skinned individuals to sell their products. Hamed et al. (2010) suggest that television advertisements possibly contribute most to influencing skin-lightening practices, with slogans such as "lighter and lovelier." The unspoken message is that black women are unhappy, ignored by men, and less likely to succeed (Olumide et al. 2008).

SEE ALSO: Cosmetic Surgery in the United States; Embodiment and the Phenomenological Tradition; Footbinding

REFERENCES

Bellow, S. G., and T. S. Alster. 2004. "Treatment of Ochronosis with a Q Switched Alexandrite (755) Laser." *Dermatologic Surgery*, 30: 555–558.

Blay, Yaba A. 2009. "Struck by Lightening: The Transdiasporan Phenomenon of Skin Bleaching." *JENdA: A Journal of Culture and African Women Studies,* special issue, 14: 1–10.

Blay, Yaba A. 2011. "Skin Bleaching and the Global White Supremacy: By Way of Introduction." *Journal of Pan African Studies,* 4(4): 4–46.

Dlova, Ncoza C., Nicole E. Hendricks, and Bice S. Martincgh. 2012. "Skin-lightening Creams Used in Durban, South Africa." *International Journal of Dermatology,* special issue, 51(suppl. 1): 51–53.

Glenn, E. N. 2008. "Yearning for Lightness: Transnational Circuits in the Marketing and Consumption of Skin Lighteners." *Gender & Society*, 22(3): 281–302.

Hamed, S. H., R. Tayyem, N. Nimer, and H. S. Alkhatib. 2010. "Skin Lightening Practice among Women Living in Jordan: Prevalence, Determinants, and User's Awareness." *International Journal of Dermatology*, 49(4): 414–420.

Jablonski, N. G. 2012. *Living Color: The Biological and Social Meaning of Skin Color*. Berkeley: University of California Press.

Nyamnjoh, F., and D. Fuh. 2014. "Africans Consuming Hair, Africans Consumed by Hair." *Africa Insight*, 44(1): 52–68.

Olumide, Y. O., et al. 2008. "Complications of Chronic Use of Skin Lightening Cosmetics." *International Journal of Dermatology*, 47: 344–353.

Pan, Elysia. 2013. "Beautiful White: An illumination of African Skin-Whitening Culture." Unpublished Thesis. Durham, NC: Duke University.

Westerhof W. 1997. "A Few More Grains of Melanin." *International Journal of Dermatology*, 36: 573–574.

FURTHER READING

Coard, S. I., A. M. Breland, and P. Raskin. 2001. "Perceptions of and Preferences for Skin Color, Black Racial Identity and Self-Esteem among African Americans." *Journal of Applied Social Psychology*, 31: 2256–2274.

Lewis, K. M., N. Robkin, K. Gaska, and L. Njoki. 2011. "Investigating Motivations for Women's Skin Bleaching in Tanzania." *Psychology of Women Quarterly*, 35(1): 29–37. DOI: 10.1177/03616848310392356.

Mahe, A., F. Ly, G. Aymard, and J. M. Dangou. 2003. "Skin Diseases Associated with the Cosmetic Use of Bleaching Products in Women from Dakar, Senegal." *British Journal of Dermatology*, 148(3): 493–500.

Thomas, L. M. 2009. "Skin Lighteners in South Africa: Transnational Entanglements and Technologies of the Self." In *Shades of Difference Why Skin Color Matters*, edited by E. N. Glenn, 188–211. Stanford: Stanford University Press.

Social Constructionist Theory

KEITH KLOSTERMANN and DAVID FORSTADT
Medaille College, USA

Social constructionism can be referred to as any social influence on an individual experience (DeLamater and Hyde 1998). According to social constructionism, almost all aspects of human behavior and experience are developed by culture, contrasting the biological essentialist view that describes human behavior as being "biologically essential or natural to the human condition" (Giles 2006).

DeLamater and Hyde explain Berger and Luckmann's (1966) paradigm of social constructionism in five parts. First, our experience of the world is ordered, and we perceive the world through a collection of specific events and interactions with specific people that shape our reality. Second, language provides a foundation to make sense of the world and helps us categorize and classify events and persons. Third, the reality of daily life is shared through interpersonal experiences, and is a product of social interaction. Fourth, shared experiences of reality become institutionalized by society and are habituated to produce predictability in interactions and roles. Fifth, knowledge may be institutionalized by society or subgroups of people, which can either unify individuals or cause conflict. There appears to be passive and radical approaches in how theorists define social constructionism, with little agreement around the exact nature of the theory (Vance 1991; Richters 2001; Giles 2006). This may be attributed to the way in which social constructionism has evolved as a theoretical model throughout history.

Beginning in the Middle Ages, the expression of sexuality had been defined solely by religion, and "the sins of the flesh" (Foucault

1978; Weeks 1985, 1991; Parker 2009). By the twentieth century, alternatives to religious perspectives and moral focuses of sexuality began to emerge, shifting to more scientific, empirical descriptions (Parker 2009), which defined sexuality as a "natural force that exists in opposition to civilization, culture or society" (Robinson 1976; Weeks 1985, 1991; Parker 2009). In the 1960s, previous scientific paradigms were not able to fully describe the facets of sexuality, causing social theorists as well as feminist and gay and lesbian activists to aide in the redirection of the sexual paradigm (Parker and Gagnon 1995; Parker 2009). As a result, in the 1970s and 1980s, perspectives of sexuality as a social, cultural, and historical construction were developed (Plummer 1984; Parker 2009). These stated that the development of sexuality was "not the result of irreversible human behavior, but was the product of a social, cultural and historical processes" (Parker 2009). This new perspective of sexuality focused on the interpersonal experiences that defined sexual meaning and the integration of this meaning on the collective whole of society (Parker 2009). As a result, understanding individual behavior became less important than understanding the context of human sexual interactions (Parker 2009).

A new emphasis arose, which focused on assessing the cultural categories and systems of classification that defined sexual experience in various social and cultural contexts (Parker 1991; Parker 2009). DeLamater and Hyde quote Gagnon to describe the influence of sexuality experience in social and cultural contexts stating: "sexuality is not a universal phenomenon, which is the same in all historical times and cultural spaces" (Gagnon 1990 cited in DeLamater and Hyde 1998). They further state that sexuality is created by culture through defining certain behaviors and relationships as sexual, which are taught to the members of society (DeLamater and Hyde 1998).

Social constructionist theory explains that our mating preferences are determined by socialization and through learning the meaning of our subcultures. Mate selection is influenced by culturally specific attributes such as physical attractiveness, education, age, and virginity (Hatfield and Rapson 1996; DeLamater and Hyde 1998). As a result, sexual desire is created and defined because culture and history have determined it to be expressed in a specific way (Giles 2006). Even though the desire for an attractive mate is universal, there is no universal standard for what is deemed attractive (DeLamater and Hyde 1998). This is attributed to the fact that sexuality is grounded in biological drives for sexual interaction, but it does not determine what "object" a person engages in sexual behavior with (Berger and Luckmann 1966; DeLamater and Hyde 1998).

Further, human sexuality is not an inner drive or a biological quality, which is consistent across time; it is a cultural construct derived from the language and structure set by an institution in society (Foucault 1978; DeLamater and Hyde 1998). "Sexuality is not definable as a fixed object of analysis. It encompasses all those acts, desires, identities, and relationships understood as in some sense erotic – but the erotic itself is a fluid concept" (Giles 2006). Parker indicates that categories such as homosexuality, prostitution, masculinity, and femininity may be variable in different social and cultural settings and may not fit into the categories designed by Western science (2009). Because of this, social constructionists expect significant variations across cultures in the behaviors associated with homosexuality and heterosexuality (DeLamater and Hyde 1998). As a result, the social construct of how we define not only sexuality, but gender and gender identity has now been questioned

(Parker 2009). "What it is to be male or female, masculine or feminine, in different social and cultural contexts may vary greatly and gender identity is clearly not reducible to any underlying biological dichotomy" (Parker 2009).

All people, despite their biological gender, experience a process of sexual socialization where definitions of masculinity and femininity are shaped by culture, and through this process, individuals learn the "sexual desires, feelings, roles and practices" of their societal structure (Parker 2009). Social constructionists describe gender by the interactions between people, by language, and the dialogue of a culture, not by biological trait (DeLamater and Hyde 1998).

SEE ALSO: Biological Determinism; Essentialism; Nature–Nurture Debate; Social Role Theory of Sex Differences; Structuralism, Feminist Approaches to

REFERENCES

Berger, Peter, and Thomas Luckmann. 1966. *The Social Construction of Reality: A Treatise in the Sociology of Knowledge*. Harmondsworth, UK: Penguin.

DeLamater, John D., and Janet S. Hyde. 1998. "Essentialism vs. Social Constructionism in the Study of Human Sexuality." *Journal of Sex Research*, 35(1): 10–18. DOI: 10.1080/00224499809551913.

Foucault, Michel. 1978. *The History of Sexuality: An Introduction*. New York: Random House.

Giles, James. 2006. "Social Constructionism and Sexual Desire." *Journal for the Theory of Social Behaviour*, 36(3): 225–238. DOI: 10.1111/j.1468-5914.2006.00305.x.

Hatfield, Elaine, and Richard L. Rapson. 1996. *Love and Sex: Cross-Cultural Perspectives*. Boston, MA: Allyn and Bacon.

Parker, Richard G. 1991. *Bodies, Pleasures, and Passions: Sexual Culture in Contemporary Brazil*. Boston, MA: Beacon Press.

Parker, Richard G. 2009. "Sexuality, Culture and Society: Shifting Paradigms in Sexuality Research." *Culture, Health & Sexuality*, 11(3): 251–266. DOI: 10.1080/13691050701606941.

Parker, Richard G., and John H. Gagnon, eds. 1995. *Sexuality: Approaches to Sex Research in a Postmodern World*. London: Routledge.

Plummer, Ken. 1984. "Sexual Diversity: A Sociological Perspective." In *The Psychology of Sexual Diversity*, edited by Kevin Howells, 219–253. Oxford: Basil Blackwell.

Richters, Julie. 2001. "The Social Construction of Sexual Practice: Setting Sexual Culture and the Body in Casual Sex Between Men." Dissertation. University of Sydney, Public Health and Community Medicine.

Robinson, Paul A. 1976. *The Modernization of Sex: Havelock Ellis, Alfred Kinsey, William Masters, and Virginia Johnson*. Ithaca: Cornell University Press.

Vance, Carole S. 1991. "Anthropology Rediscovers Sexuality: A Theoretical Comment." *Social Science and Medicine*, 33(8): 875–884.

Weeks, Jeffrey. 1985. *Sexuality and its Discontents*. London: Routledge.

Weeks, Jeffrey. 1991. *Against Nature: Essays on History, Sexuality, and Identity*. London: Rivers Oram Press.

FURTHER READING

Fausto-Sterling, Anne. 2012. *Sex/Gender: Biology in a Social World*. New York: Routledge.

Social Identity

JOHANNA E. FOSTER
Monmouth University, USA

Generally speaking, "social identity" refers to the cultural meanings that individuals give to their own, and to others', social locations, or status positions, within a social structure. For instance, one might define oneself as a "woman," a "college student," or an "activist" in a social system, and also recognize oneself as sharing these social positions with others. This recognition that one defines oneself as someone who inhabits or enacts status positions in ways that share similar values, beliefs, attitudes, or practices as others in similar status positions constitutes one's "social identity."

The concept of social identity is closely related to classic sociological notions of the self, which contemporary sociologists define as a relatively stable set of socially constructed ideas one holds about one's own existence (Johnson 2008). As articulated most famously by George Herbert Mead (1962), human beings acquire a mind and self only through social interaction with significant others who, through language transmission and face-to-face interaction across a series of distinct phases of cognitive development, socialize individuals to internalize the cultural and structural relationships of the larger social system, including the meanings of the social positions they inhabit within their social groups.

Also in the classic tradition, W. E. B. Du Bois (1989), in his analysis of the relationship between US racial apartheid and black identity during reconstruction, set forth some of the most central principles of the nature and formation of social identity. His work studied the impact of structures of racial stratification on the development of a double-consciousness, or a sense of seeing oneself through the lens of the oppressive status position of whites and the subordinate position of one's own social location as a black American. In a similar way, Charles Horton Cooley (2013), in his notion of "the looking glass self," theorized that human beings develop a sense of themselves as distinct individuals only by interpreting the perceptions that others hold of themselves, and the subsequent construction of a self-concept in relation to these interpretations. More contemporary notions of the self and of identity as the meanings one assigns to one's self were further articulated by Erving Goffman (1982) who argued that one's sense of who one is in relation to others must be socially produced and maintained in ongoing interaction rituals that set forth and protect the sacredness, or validity, of the self in everyday life, and that these rituals of social identity form the basis of social order.

Since the late twentieth century, feminist scholars in the social sciences and the humanities, as well as critical theorists informed by postmodernism, queer theory, and postcolonialism, have further emphasized that the meanings individuals assign to social identities, and particularly the social identities of sex, gender, sexuality, race, and nation, are not based on universal, stable, or fixed social categories, but are variable and contextual, and imbued with multiple meanings.

Moreover, theorists in these contemporary intellectual spaces suggest that one's sense of self is a dynamic process that is not inevitably tied to essential attributes or properties of individuals as given by biology or psychology, but embedded in intersecting social practices, social institutions, and intersecting systems of social inequality that are inseparable from other systems of inequality that become routinized (see also Kessler and McKenna 1978; Mohanty 1984; Connell 1987; Spivak 1987; West and Zimmerman 1987; Fuss 1989; Butler 1990; Collins 1990; West and Fenstermaker 1995). In other words, what constitutes both the boundaries between and also the very meanings assigned to gender and sexual identity categories in any social context are always in relation to race, class, age, ability, and geopolitical location. Even more consequential for feminist and critical scholars, individuals' sense of their own gender and sexual identities are always tied to the larger and shifting sociohistorical systems of classification and cultural definitions in which people live, and also to the systems of distribution that rely on identity categories to justify unequal allocations of valuable social resources, such as income, wealth, political power, access to employment, education, healthcare, and leisure time, among other social goods.

The voluminous body of scholarship on gender and sexuality identity includes Michel Foucault's (1978) foundational work on the emergence of "homosexual" as an identity category, and Lacquer's (1990) work on the invention of binary sex categories, all constructed in various political and economic forces of modernity; Fausto-Sterling's (1993) widely popularized research on "the five sexes"; Kessler's (1998) investigation of social construction of intersex identity; Garber's (1992) study of third sex and third gender categories around the world; Kennedy and Davis's (1993) groundbreaking work on the butch/femme identities of white and black working class lesbians in the 1930s and 1940s; and Bornstein's (1994) trailblazing work on transgender identities, to name but a few of the scores of examinations of the meanings of gender and sexual identities; the very lines we draw socially between gender and sexual identity categories, and the lived experiences people share "performing" these identities.

Of central importance to contemporary scholars of gender and sexuality, contextual meanings and expressions of gender and sexual identities are constitutive of one's experiences of gender and sexual privilege and oppression such that, for instance, some groups of women will experience sexism and heterosexism differently from others based on their experience of "multiple jeopardy" (King 1988), given their location in what Patricia Hill Collins (1990) famously called the "matrix of domination." So, too, for men's ability to exercise male privilege, or, say, for transwomen to navigate employment, public space, or medical care free of harassment and violence. For example, Byrd's (2004) work on misogyny in hip–hop culture shows the compounding impact for black women who are sexualized in ways that serve to dehumanize black women and also black men in relation to racist and sexist constructions of white women's supposedly virginal sexual identities. Similarly, Atkin and Rich's (1988) work examines the construction of the "Jewish American princess" identity to show how young, college-educated Jewish women are demonized in different ways from both Jewish men and non-Jewish women in ways that suggest they bear the brunt of the Anglo elite's resistance to the massive structural mobility of working class racial and ethnic "others" into the American higher education system in the mid-twentieth century.

Finally, increasingly, feminist and critical scholars have studied the social and political implications of "liminal," "boundary crossing," or "transgressive" gender and sexual identities as expressed in, among others, the explicit challenges to fixed notions of sex, gender, and sexual identities made by intersex, bisexual, transgender, and queer activists, including Devor's (1989) work on transgender identities and "gender blending"; Lorber's (1999) work on the paradoxes of "crossing borders and erasing boundaries"; Preves' (2004) work on the impact of intersex activism; and Enke's (2013) edited volume on transfeminist practices.

SEE ALSO: Butch/Femme; Status of Women Reports; Social Role Theory of Sex Differences

REFERENCES

Atkin, Ruth, and Adrienne Rich. 2006. "'J.-A.-P.'-Slapping: The Politics of Scapegoating." In *Reconstructing Gender: A Multicultural Anthology*, edited by Estelle Disch, 67–70. Boston: University of Massachusetts Press. First published 1988.

Bornstein, Kate. 1994. *Gender Outlaw: On Men, Women, and the Rest of Us*. New York: Routledge.

Butler, Judith. 1990. *Gender Trouble*. New York: Routledge.

Byrd, Ayana. 2004. "Claiming Jezebel: Black Female Subjectivity and Sexual Expression in Hip-Hop." In *The Fire this Time: Young Activists and the New Feminism*, edited by

Vivien Labaton and Dawn Lundry Martin. New York: Anchor Books/Random House.
Collins, Patricia Hill. 1990. *Black Feminist Thought: Knowledge, Consciousness and the Politics of Empowerment*. New York: Routledge.
Connell, Raewyn W. 1987. *Gender and Power: Society, the Person, and Sexual Politics*. Palo Alto: Stanford University Press.
Cooley, Charles H. 2013. "The Social Self." In *Human Nature and the Social Order*. New York City: The Classics. First published 1902.
Devor, Holly (Aaron). 1989. *Gender Blending: Confronting the Limits of Duality*. Bloomington: Indiana University Press.
Du Bois, W. E. B. 1989. *The Souls of Black Folk*. New York: Penguin Books. First published 1903.
Enke, Anne. 2013. *Transfeminist Perspectives In and Beyond Transgender and Gender Studies*. Philadelphia: Temple University Press.
Fausto-Sterling, Anne. 1993. The Five Sexes: Why Male and Female is Not Enough. *The Sciences*, March–April, 20–25.
Foucault, Michel. 1978. *The History of Sexuality*, vol. 1. New York: Pantheon.
Fuss, Diana. 1989. *Essentially Speaking: Feminism, Nature and Difference*. New York: Routledge.
Garber, Marjorie. 1992. *Vested Interests: Cross-Dressing and Cultural Anxiety*. New York: Routledge.
Goffman, Erving. 1982. *Interaction Ritual: Essays on Face-to-Face Behavior*. New York: Pantheon Press.
Johnson, Allan. 2008. *The Forest and the Trees: Sociology as Life, Practice, and Promise*. Philadelphia: Temple University Press.
Kennedy, Elizabeth Lapovsky, and Madeline D. Davis. 1993. *Boots of Leather, Slippers of Gold: The History of a Lesbian Community*. New York: Routledge.
Kessler, Suzanne, J. 1998. *Lessons From the Intersexed*. New Brunswick: Rutgers University Press.
Kessler, Suzanne, and Wendy McKenna. 1978. *Gender: An Ethnomethodological Approach*. Chicago: University of Chicago Press.
King, Deborah. 1988. "Multiple Jeopardy, Multiple Consciousness: The Context of Black Feminist Ideology." *Signs: The Journal of Women in Culture and Society*, 14: 265–295.
Lacquer, Thomas. 1990. *Making Sex: The Body and Gender from the Greeks to Freud*. Cambridge, MA: Harvard University Press.
Lorber, Judith. 1999. "Crossing Borders and Erasing Boundaries: The Paradoxes of Identity Politics." *Sociological Focus*, 32: 355–369.
Mead, George Herbert. 1962. *Works of George Herbert Mead: Mind, Self, and Society from the Standpoint of a Social Behaviorist*, vol. 1, edited by Charles W. Morris. Chicago: University of Chicago Press. First published 1934.
Mohanty, Chandra Talpade. 1984. "Under Western Eyes: Feminist Scholarship and Colonial Discourses." *Boundary 2*, 12(3): 333–358.
Preves, Sharon. 2004. Out of the O.R. and Into the Streets: Exploring the Impact of Intersex Activism. *Research in Political Sociology*, 13: 179–223.
Spivak, Gayatri Chakravorty. 1987. *In Other Worlds: Essays in Cultural Politics*. New York: Metheun.
West, Candace, and Sarah Fenstermaker. 1995. "Doing Difference". *Gender & Society*, 9(1): 8–37.
West, Candace, and Don H. Zimmerman. 1987. "Doing Gender". *Gender & Society*, 1(2): 125–151.

Social Role Theory of Sex Differences

ALICE H. EAGLY
Northwestern University, USA

WENDY WOOD
University of Southern California, USA

Social role theory is a social psychological theory that pertains to sex differences and similarities in social behavior. Its key principle is that differences and similarities arise primarily from the distribution of men and women into social roles within their society. Through socialization and the formation of gender roles, the behaviors of men and women generally support and sustain the division of labor. In industrialized economies, for example, social roles are organized so that women are more likely than men to be homemakers and primary caretakers of children and to hold caretaking jobs in the paid economy. In contrast, men are more likely than women to be primary family providers and to assume full-time roles in the paid economy, often ones that involve physical strength, assertiveness, or leadership skills.

The division of social roles between women and men is flexible, but nevertheless constrained by the inherent attributes of women and men and by each society's socioeconomic development and ecology. Specifically, sex-typed roles arise from an interaction between (1) the sex differences represented by each sex's physical attributes and related behaviors, especially women's childbearing and nursing of infants and men's greater size, speed, and upper-body strength, and (2) the variable factors represented by the social, economic, technological, and ecological forces present in a society. Because of these physical differences, certain activities are more efficiently performed by either men or women. For example, highly strength-intensive activities are more efficiently performed by men. In short, human biology and the environment together produce a division of labor that differs across societies. The division of labor may also reflect inherited temperamental sex differences – specifically, the greater surgency, including greater motor activity, that is more typical of young boys and the greater effortful control, or self-regulatory skill, that is typical of young girls (Else-Quest et al. 2006). Through proximal mediators, this division of labor yields the psychologies of women and men that people observe in their own society (Wood and Eagly 2012).

The division of labor underlies each society's gender roles, which are consensually shared expectations about men and women. As also argued by theorists of expectation states theory (e.g., Ridgeway 2011), these expectations emerge from everyday observations of what women and men do. To the extent that people observe the sexes engaging in different types of activities, they infer differing psychological traits that match these activities. For example, if women commonly are observed performing nurturing activities in caretaking roles (e.g., as mothers, nurses, and teachers of young children), people assume that women tend to be nurturing and caring. The tendency to infer dispositions that correspond to observed behavior is a basic social cognitive principle known as *correspondent inference* or *correspondence bias*. By this process, observation of the social roles of women and men yields beliefs about the attributes typical of each sex. Yet, rather than viewing these attributes as merely reflecting the pressures of social roles, social perceivers generally essentialize them by regarding them as deeply embedded in the biology or social experience of women and men.

Consistent with the correspondent inference of traits from each sex's typical behaviors, research has repeatedly established that people have differing beliefs, or gender stereotypes, about men and women. These stereotypes are *descriptive* of the actual characteristics of the sexes and also *prescriptive* of what women and men are expected to do. In most societies, much of the content of gender roles pertains to the broad trait dimensions of communion and agency, with more minor themes involving physical characteristics, cognitive abilities, and other qualities (Williams and Best 1990). Communal traits consist of qualities such as friendly, unselfish, concerned with others, and expressive – traits ascribed more to women than men. Agentic traits consist of qualities such as mastery, assertiveness, independence, and instrumental competence – traits ascribed more to men than women.

Gender role expectations, as they are shared within cultures, influence the behavior of both sexes to conform to these beliefs. In childhood, socialization acts to impart these expectations to children and to encourage related behaviors through the mediation of parents and other socializing agents. As children mature and in adult life, gender roles influence behavior by working through a trio of biosocial mechanisms to influence behavior in role-appropriate directions. These proximal mechanisms implicate others' stereotypic expectations and one's own gender identity, plus biological processes involving hormonal fluctuations. These three types of influences work together to yield both differences and similarities in male and female behavior.

One mechanism involves behavioral confirmation to gender roles, as people respond to others' expectations. Specifically, people learn that behavior inconsistent with gender roles often elicits negative sanctions, including dislike and social exclusion. Consistent with theories that emphasize the performative aspects of gender (e.g., West and Zimmerman 1987), behavior consistent with gender roles fits expectations and thus receives more positive reactions. These negative and positive responses from others make it easier to follow gender roles than to disregard them.

A second mechanism involves the personal adoption of gender norms as standards for judging one's own behavior. People self-regulate their behavior to gender norms to the extent that they have incorporated gender roles into their self-concepts. Both men and women may evaluate themselves favorably to the extent that they conform to personal gender standards and unfavorably to the extent that they deviate from them.

A third mechanism involves hormonal changes, especially in testosterone and oxytocin, that act to facilitate culturally masculine and feminine behaviors (Van Anders, Goldey, and Kuo 2011). Hormones and related neural structures were shaped in part through ancient selection pressures associated with the basic perceptual, sensory, and motivational processes that humans share with other animals. Yet, humans activate these biological processes to support the sociocultural constraints that guide their behavior. For example, engaging in competitive behavior activates testosterone in both sexes. To facilitate such reactions, subcortical structures interact with more recently evolved, general-purpose, higher brain functions associated with the neocortex. Biology thus works with psychology to facilitate role performances, yet the main limitation of social role theory is that its proponents have not yet elaborated these biosocial interactions.

Social role theory allows for non-traditional as well as traditional behaviors. For example, to encourage non-traditional behaviors, some parents avoid conveying gender-stereotypical norms to their children, and some social environments convey atypical gender norms. Also, with changes in the occupational structure involving, for example, new service and managerial roles demanding complex social skills, many women have entered these occupational roles. By emphasizing the multiple processes that underlie sex-differentiated behavior, social role theory allows for variability in behavior within each sex as well as change over time and across societies in the typical behaviors of women and men.

Social role theory is particularly well known in psychology as a theory of gender, and its influence has extended to European psychologists (e.g., Fischer and Evers 2011). As a theory of psychological sex differences and similarities, its main competition is evolutionary psychology (e.g., Buss and Schmitt 2011). In the evolutionary tradition, theorists have maintained that most psychological sex differences derive from evolved attributes that were genetically coded early in the history of the human species. These traits are then elicited by cues in the current environment. In contrast, social role theory takes the interactionist position that nature and nurture work together in producing the behaviors of women and men, which are in part socially constructed to take account of the current sociocultural environment.

SEE ALSO: Division of Labor, Domestic; Gender Belief System/Gender Ideology; Gender Stereotypes

REFERENCES

Buss, David Michael, and David P. Schmitt. 2011. "Evolutionary Psychology and Feminism." *Sex Roles*, 64: 768–787. DOI: 10.1007/s11199-011-9987-3.

Else-Quest, Nicole M., Janet Shibley Hyde, H. Hill Goldsmith, and Carol A. Van Hulle. 2006. "Gender Differences in Temperament: A Meta-Analysis." *Psychological Bulletin*, 132: 33–72. DOI: 10.1037/0033-2909.132.1.33.

Fischer, Agneta H., and Catherine Evers. 2011. "The Social Costs and Benefits of Anger as a Function of Gender and Relationship Context." *Sex Roles*, 65: 23–24. DOI: 10.1007/s11199-011-9956-x.

Ridgeway, Cecilia L. 2011. *Framed by Gender: How Gender Inequality Persists in the Modern World*. New York: Oxford University Press.

Van Anders, Sari M., Katherine L. Goldey, and Patty X. Kuo. 2011. "The Steroid/Peptide Theory of Social Bonds: Integrating Testosterone and Peptide Responses for Classifying Social Behavioral Contexts." *Psychoneuroendocrinology*, 36: 1265–1275. DOI: 10.1016/j.psyneuen.2011.06.001.

West, Candace, and Don H. Zimmerman. 1987. "Doing Gender." *Gender & Society*, 1: 125–151. DOI: 10.1177/0891243287001002002.

Williams, John E., and Deborah L. Best. 1990. *Measuring Sex Stereotypes: A Multination Study*. Newbury Park: Sage.

Wood, Wendy, and Alice H. Eagly. 2012. "Biosocial Construction of Sex Differences and Similarities in Behavior." In *Advances in Experimental Social Psychology*, vol. 46, edited by James M. Olson and Mark P. Zanna, 55–123. London: Elsevier.

FURTHER READING

Bussey, Kay. 2013. "Gender Development." In *The Sage Handbook of Gender and Psychology*, edited by Michelle K. Ryan and Nyla R. Branscombe, 31–99. Los Angeles: Sage.

Wood, Wendy, and Alice H. Eagly. 2010. "Gender." In *Handbook of Social Psychology*, vol. 1, 5th ed., edited by Susan Fiske, Daniel Gilbert, and Gardner Lindzey, 629–667. Hoboken: John Wiley & Sons.

Socialization and Sexuality

DIEDERIK F. JANSSEN
Independent Researcher, The Netherlands

The notion of sexual socialization or enculturation refers to the lifelong process of attunement to social and cultural norms, value systems, conceptual fixtures, and legal frameworks governing the broad area of human intimacy. Encompassing attitudinal alignment with and negotiation of truth claims, the issue poses questions of social regulation, ideology, and discourse formation that extend beyond the derivation of sexual wisdom from family, school, peer, and media environments. Questions readily appeal to specifically sociological, and more broadly social scientific, models of sexuality as an integral – often cardinal – dimension of personhood, particularly of childrearing. Such models are testament to the notable burdening of sexuality (a historical, specifically modern, rubric) with developmental and pedagogical discourses. Nevertheless, research in the context of sexuality has championed a broad shift from notions of social adjustment, regulation, and knowledge acquisition to conceptions of social production, literacy, and meaning-making. An enduring and inevitable leitmotif in sexuality studies is the salience of family sexual culture – read: the primacy and promotion of the modern nuclear family as a cradle of socio-sexual individuality – as it is rivaled worldwide by multiplying, encroaching, and interlocking spheres of value negotiation: social and global media, consumer and entertainment industries, peer networks, school curricula, and social movements.

HISTORIES

Much variation exists worldwide in figurations of sexuality as a teachable or schoolable subject. In Daoist and Tantric texts, ingredients for an arguable *ars erotica* (a cult of the erotic) included an advisory literature spelling out intimacies' spiritual objectives and technicalities. Until recently, comparable Western apologies for the cultivation of "erotic capital" have had to wrestle free from Western sexuality's Judeo-Christian imprint. In the circum-Atlantic West since the mid-nineteenth century, pedagogical circumscriptions of sexual intimacy became marked by a gradual, but still far from complete, divorce between knowing God's intentions for Man to knowing parameters of personal health and hygiene. Exegetic, confessional, legal, and folkloric templates for the tutoring of chastity and decency gradually cross-faded with increasingly empirical formulations of "moral" and "sexual development." In Europe from the late seventeenth century onward, popular vernacular manuals providing advice on courtship and marital love had become widely available in all main languages. Anti-masturbation tracts were circulated widely as of the early eighteenth century. Today's familiarity with this dual advisory–cautionary outlining of approved and pathologized forms of intimacy, respectively, is integral to sexuality's rise as a modern, Western European concept (Foucault 1978) and in particular its entanglement with notions of child development (Egan and Hawkes 2010), its concomitant adoption in institutional education contexts (Sauerteig and Davidson 2009), and the many modes of friction and contestation this adoption triggers when facing ideological structures and regulatory frameworks that make up civil society (Irvine 2004; Kendall 2013). Emerging alongside a growing sense of cultural distinction and difference from the nineteenth century onward, these modes of confrontation importantly animate the formation of the European family as well as the European bourgeois self (Stoler 1995).

To a large degree sexuality's late nineteenth-century scientification and medicalization intimately coordinated with legal, scriptural, and pastoral frameworks and vocabularies for regulating and protecting family life. Worldwide and on many fronts, faith-based and medical intuitions about sexuality's "development" remain remarkably consonant, at least notably conversant. *Socialization* against this background came importantly to mean the disclosure and decryption of the unmentioned (because complex and delicate, if not trauma-induced) and unseen (because private, if not molecular and genetic) mysteries of the desiring body. Revelations of divine purpose and courtesies were traded for instructions about apparent functions and mechanisms. Programs that formalized and circumscribed sexuality in this tentative new way knew various telling headings, including *sexual enlightenment, social hygiene, sex instruction, sex training,* and *family-life* or *parenthood education.*

Anthropologists saw that in preindustrial and tribal contexts, the facts of life had been securely tied to core taboos upholding often kinship-, age-, gender- and class-structured social systems. Incest/exogamy rules in clan, moiety, extended family, and tribe contexts are cases in point. Matrimonial lore was disclosed, often with remarkable frankness, at the ritualized occasion of initiations or weddings. Into the 1960s even in advanced postindustrial settings, sexual socialization was mostly preoccupied with chaste courtship leading to fruitful and lifelong marriage. In the United States and beyond, as recently as the early 1990s "virginity pledges," "chastity clubs," and "purity balls" evidence a re-ritualization of sexual pedagogy around evangelical themes of fatherly authority and the primacy of heterosexual marriage. Problems including the seduction of the innocent and wrongful seduction of the nubile, teen and premarital pregnancy, minors' "exposure" to explicit materials (Heins 2007), and the sexualization or vulgarization of youth culture and courtship are among the historically recurrent and globally attested focal points at which older generations urge for, or simply enforce, moderation and delay in the younger. Across the West the militancy and emotional ardor of such moderations reveal the part entanglement of, part clash between traditionalist, progressive (e.g., feminist), biomedical, and most recently neoliberalism-inspired approaches to sex as a multiplex liability and danger to personal "integrity." Irvine (2004) chronicles how in the United States sex education served as a bridge issue between the Old Right (early twentieth century) and the New Christian Right (late twentieth century) such that opposition to and restrictions on school-based sex education (with "abstinence-only" replacing "comprehensive" curricula) became and remained a major vehicle for political mobilization.

Around the world, debates on sexual socialization remain experienced as touching upon the kernel value structure at once of society, nation, and personhood. Within the post-World War II international context of human rights and child rights, sexuality and its education are progressively refocused from concerns for "intact" families and "holy" matrimonies to entitlements of the purportedly free-standing person. Around such structures as the World Health Organization (WHO) and the United Nations Children's Fund (UNICEF), for instance, this has meant a focus on minors' protection, education, health, and self-determination. The extent to which these concerns are or, given their universal scope, really aim to be "culture-sensitive," as is claimed, is debated. The United States, Holy See, and Islamic conservative block have often monopolized policy and funding directions for global reproductive health education frameworks, down to the very terms used in policy statements.

THEORIES

With the exclusion of psychodynamically oriented and evolution-minded authors, few canonical socialization theorists of the twentieth century stand out as theorists of the socialization of sexuality. Congruently, contemporary handbooks on childhood social development may barely mention sexuality (e.g., Smith and Hart 2011). Yet sex education and socialization fascinated many early twentieth-century theorists, including Sigmund Freud, Émile Durkheim, Bronisław Malinowski, Margaret Mead, and Wilhelm Reich. Of importance to the theoretical outlining of the subject across the modern West have been: mental hygiene and sex education movements since the late nineteenth century, which blended moral precepts (virtue, chastity) with increasingly scientific-sounding probes into what came to be called moral and sexual development (resonating with a broad interest in precocities, retardations, and developmental stages); Freud's theory of psychosexual development and G. Stanley Hall's child study movement, culminating in the latter's conceptualization of "the adolescent," both around 1905; cross-cultural sex research since the late 1940s; clinical research on gender dysphoria since the late 1950s; feminist, interactionist, and social constructionist elaborations of gender "role" and identity development since the

1960s; anti-authoritarian, Marxist, Lacanian, Foucauldian critical historical (1970s) and later queer theoretical (1990s) reflections on sex, pedagogy, and the family; sex pedagogy's preventative, forensic, diagnostic, and therapeutic turns to child sexual abuse and exploitation since the early 1980s (a paradigm summed up in Bromberg and O'Donohue 2013); and finally the concurrent mainstreaming of the meta-theory of evolutionary psychology, centralizing the theme of reproductive, or "mating," strategies in developmental psychology.

Approaches to sexual socialization in anglophone literature and culture, in short, have fanned out considerably over a century's time. Mentioned perspectives vary substantially in their emphasis on evolved, neurological, or environmental factors in sexual learning. Adaptationist perspectives, for instance, single out confirmations of or predictions by evolutionary theory on the balancing of human "mating efforts" and "parenting efforts" and their implications for adolescent "mating intelligence" acquisition and parental mentoring. Recent research suggests family relationships and family composition independently affect even girls' pubertal timing. Social psychologists may rather search for models of adolescent peer network interactions capable of predicting sexually transmitted disease (STD) transmission, coital onset, or subjective measures of well-being. Cross-cultural studies, lastly, have tied cultural tendencies to inculcate modesty or chastity in the young to sociopolitical variables, including the social and economic value of children and the exchange of goods accompanying arranged marriages.

CONTEMPORARY ISSUES

The subject of young sexualities has often seemed more outrage- and law- than theory- or even fact-driven. Since the late 1970s divergent themes have appealed to pedagogical intervention and monopolized empirical literature. Among these are the mise-en-scène of the lesbian, gay, bisexual, or transgender (LGBT) adolescent; the internationalization of sexual and reproductive health (SRH) education; the epochal thematization of child sexual abuse; and the social ecologies of Internet and new (mobile and social) media. Corresponding topics of outstanding interest in the Anglo-American context since the 1990s have been shifting frames for the global mainstreaming of sexual diversity as a leitmotif both for curriculum design and pedagogical theory; for understanding trends in media content (including pornography) and dimensions of media literacy (media as "identity toolkit"); lastly, for conceptualizing peer influence.

A focal point for many concerns, late 2000s inquiries into the "sexualization of childhood" across Anglo-American nations have been seen dividing public, political, and policy rhetoric of endangered and stolen childhoods on the one hand, and critical perspectives on issues of children's agency, autonomy, and rights, on the other (Egan 2013). Two lines of criticism stand out. First, sexualization debates are seen as out of touch with the empirical lives and critical opinions of children, erratically overestimating and caricaturing the latter's lack of resolve in situations of "premature exposure." Second, public debates are considered to expound a regulatory and universalist construction of childhood that effectively precludes acquisition of necessary skills and controls to prevent unwanted situations.

Anglo-centric research suggests that adolescents' use of sexual content in media is linked to their sexual cognitions, affect, and behavior (Peter 2013). However, effect sizes are small, inferences of causal direction delicate, and research methods ethically problematic and thus limited. Moreover, cross-cultural, long-term, and positive angles often remain underrepresented (Tolman and McClelland 2011; Peter 2013). Adolescents appear active and critical users, increasingly also producers, whose relation to sexual content is cyclical and importantly peer-mediated (Shafer, Bobkowski, and Brown 2013). Ethnographic attention in recent decades has centralized the production of meaning and negotiation of identities within children's and youth's sexual and gender cultures (Renold 2005). Sexting (Internet-based sharing of risqué "selfies" or erotic imagery in general) among under-18s, unsurprisingly, has been a paradigm case study (Klettke, Hallford, and Mellor 2014). Qualitative researchers suggest that sexting's contemporary legal containment lags behind shifts in how even preteenagers, in new and significant ways, participate fully and resiliently in their own enculturation.

Nevertheless, parents still have a broad range of effects on measures of adolescent sexuality (de Graaf et al. 2011). Review suggests that across Western societies, scores across three dimensions of parenting effort (parental support, "age-appropriate" levels of control, and knowledge of children's whereabouts) relate to children's delay of first sexual intercourse, safer sexual practices, and higher sexual competence. Today's multitude of studies notwithstanding, researchers express a need for more dynamic, dialectical studies of parenting and children's sexual development. Studies focusing on enculturation of youth in multi-ethnic environments, moreover, have reported outcome differences along the degree to which youths take their cue from heritage culture, from mainstream culture, or from an amalgamation of the two.

Research further reports evidence on the role of social cognitive development, gender conceptions, and social experiences of both gender- and sexual orientation-based discrimination (Horn and Sinno 2013). Issues of gender and sexual diversity have been duly centralized in recent decades. An emergent (late 2000s) trend from Russia and the Balkans to Asia and Africa, same-sex intimacies have been significantly problematized by discourses and even specific laws against any form of LGBT-themed "propaganda" directed to minors. In sub-Saharan Africa and Asia, this often resonates with the invariably politicized moves from "traditional" to "modern" and from colonial back to purportedly indigenous ways of socializing sex.

SEE ALSO: Adolescent Pregnancy; Gender Identities and Socialization; Sex Education in the United Kingdom and United States

REFERENCES

Bromberg, Daniel S., and William T. O'Donohue, eds. 2013. *Handbook of Child and Adolescent Sexuality: Developmental and Forensic Psychology*. Oxford: Academic Press.

de Graaf, Hanneke, Ine Vanwesenbeeck, Liesbeth Woertman, and Wim Meeus. 2011. "Parenting and Adolescents' Sexual Development in Western Societies: A Literature Review." *European Psychologist*, 16: 21–31.

Egan, R. Danielle. 2013. *Becoming Sexual: A Critical Appraisal of the Sexualization of Girls*. Cambridge: Polity.

Egan, R. Danielle, and Gail Hawkes. 2010. *Theorizing the Sexual Child in Modernity*. Basingstoke: Palgrave Macmillan.

Foucault, Michel. 1978. *The History of Sexuality*, vol. 1. New York: Pantheon Books. First published 1976.

Heins, Marjorie. 2007. *Not in Front of the Children: "Indecency," Censorship, and the Innocence of Youth*. New Brunswick: Rutgers University Press.

Horn, Stacey S., and Stefanie M. Sinno. 2013. "Gender, Sexual Orientation, and Discrimination Based on Gender and Sexual Orientation." In *Handbook of Moral Development*, 2nd ed., edited by Melanie Killen and Judith G. Smetana. New York: Psychology Press.

Irvine, Janice M. 2004. *Talk About Sex: The Battles over Sex Education in the United States*. Berkeley: University of California Press.

Kendall, Nancy. 2013. *The Sex Education Debates*. Chicago: University of Chicago Press.

Klettke, Bianca, David J. Hallford, and David J. Mellor. 2014. "Sexting Prevalence and Correlates: A Systematic Literature Review." *Clinical Psychology Review*, 34: 44–53.

Peter, Jochen. 2013. "Media and Sexual Development." In *The Routledge Handbook of Children, Adolescents and Media*, edited by Dafna Lemish. London: Routledge.

Renold, Emma. 2005. *Girls, Boys, and Junior Sexualities*. London: RoutledgeFalmer.

Sauerteig, Lutz, and Roger Davidson, eds. 2009. *Shaping Sexual Knowledge: A Cultural History of Sex Education in 20th Century Europe*. London: Routledge.

Shafer, Autumn, Piotr Bobkowski, and Jane Brown. 2013. "Sexual Media Practice: How Adolescents Select, Engage With, and Are Affected by Sexual Media." In *Oxford Handbook of Media Psychology*, edited by Karen E. Dill. New York: Oxford University Press.

Smith, Peter K., and Craig H. Hart, eds. 2011. *The Wiley-Blackwell Handbook of Childhood Social Development*, 2nd ed. Oxford: Wiley-Blackwell.

Stoler, Ann Laura. 1995. *Race and the Education of Desire: Foucault's History of Sexuality and the Colonial Order of Things*. Durham, NC: Duke University Press.

Tolman, Deborah L., and Sara I. McClelland. 2011. "Normative Sexuality Development in Adolescence: A Decade in Review, 2000–2009." *Journal of Research on Adolescence*, 21: 242–255.

FURTHER READING

Adams, Vincanne, and Stacy Leigh Pigg, eds. 2005. *Sex in Development: Science, Sexuality, and Morality in Global Perspective*. Durham, NC: Duke University Press.

Francoeur, Robert T., Raymond J. Noonan, and Beldina Opiyo-Omolo, eds. 2004. *The Continuum Complete International Encyclopedia of Sexuality*. New York: Continuum. Accessed August 17, 2015, at http://www.kinseyinstitute.org/ccies.

Savin-Williams, Ritch C. 2005. *The New Gay Teenager*. Cambridge, MA: Harvard University Press.

Schalet, Amy T. 2011. *Not Under My Roof: Parents, Teens, and the Culture of Sex*. Chicago: University of Chicago Press.

Sodomy Law in Comparative Perspective

VICTOR ASAL
University at Albany, State University of New York, USA

UDI SOMMER
Tel Aviv University, Israel

Although there have been significant changes in legal views towards sodomy recently, the dominant legal prescription towards sodomy has been criminalization cross-nationally for a majority of countries globally for the last 200 years (Asal, Sommer, and Harwood 2013). Sodomy is usually defined as anal sex (and for some, oral sex or sex with animals) and could be something practiced by both same-sex and heterosexual couples. Despite this broad definition, sodomy laws most often focus specifically on sex by same-sex couples or are targeted for enforcement against same-sex couples. An example of a law that frames the criminalization of sodomy specifically at same-sex relations (and in this case only male same-sex relations) is that of Zimbabwe, which states that:

> Any male person who, with the consent of another male person, knowingly performs with that other person anal sexual intercourse, or any act involving physical contact other than anal sexual intercourse … shall be guilty of sodomy and liable to … imprisonment for a period not exceeding one year or both. (ILGA 2013, 62)

Such laws are often understood to be used to target sexual minorities and the political discourse about the law is focused on the criminalization of homosexuality. Given the dominant use of criminalization and enforcement of sodomy laws to target sexual minorities we focus on this interpretation of sodomy laws and their repeal.

Over the last 40 years there has been a sea change in the treatment of lesbian, gay, bisexual, and transgender (LGBT) individuals and communities around the world. (An excellent resource for data on anti-sodomy laws and the treatment of homosexuals in general can be found in Itaborahy and Zhu's report (ILGA 2013) "State-Sponsored Homophobia. A World Survey of Laws: Criminalisation, Protection and Recognition of Same-sex Love" from which much of the data cited in this review was drawn.) In 1975, 60 countries (or approximately 38% of the countries in the world) did not outlaw sodomy with punishments ranging from imprisonment and beating to death. By 2008 that number had greatly expanded with 103 countries (or nearly 54% of countries worldwide) where sodomy was legal while many countries have moved farther down the road of treating sexual minorities as equal citizens with 59 countries prohibiting employment discrimination based on sexual orientation and 12 countries legalizing same-sex couple marriages. Despite the significant changes in how the LGBT community is being treated legally there are still large swathes of the world where being gay can get you killed – not just by people in the street acting out their biases, which also happens – but by state executioners sanctioned by the legal power of the state. Seven countries still have the death penalty for sodomy (ILGA 2013) and in at least one country in Africa – Uganda – there is an ongoing effort to make "aggravated homosexuality" punishable by death (Cheney 2012, 78). The threat of the death penalty is not an empty one, as such executions can take place (ILGA 2013).

An example of a country where members of the LGBT community are killed by the state is Saudi Arabia where, despite news restrictions and censorship, research by human rights organizations suggests that this kind of treatment of homosexuals is not rare. Amnesty International reported that, "in April 2000 it was reported that a Saudi court had sentenced nine young men to prison sentences and up to 2,600 lashes each for 'deviant sexual behavior'. Six men were executed in July 2000 on charges partly relating to their sexual orientation and Amnesty International feared that these six may in fact have been among the nine men sentenced to the flogging and prison sentences" (Amnesty International UK 2002). While few countries punish sodomy with the death penalty many still arrest people and punish them with prison sentences for same sex relations. For example, Roger Jean-Claude Mbede of Cameroon died in prison in 2014 where he had been sentenced to three years of jail time for homosexual acts (Nzouankeu 2014).

Before we focus on the regional distribution of anti-sodomy laws and possible factors that led to such laws, it is important to note that just because a country may lack laws specifically criminalizing sodomy does not mean that homosexuals are not socially discriminated against or that they are not being oppressed by the government. A good example of this is in Russia, where the city of St. Petersburg passed a law banning homosexual and lesbian propaganda which would harm morality. Though not a law against sodomy per se, it is a law that can be used to prosecute gay activists or members of the LGBT community in general and as one Russian gay rights activist put it, it is a law that " … will create a negative atmosphere in society around gays and lesbians as well as our organizations" (Schwitzr 2012).

The prevalence of laws criminalizing same-sex relations is shrinking. Yet, a good number of countries in Asia, the Indian subcontinent, most of the Middle East, the Caribbean and large sections of Africa still have such laws on their books and those laws are enforced – often with many years of imprisonment or death as a punishment. The Americas (outside of the Caribbean) have only a few instances of anti-sodomy laws.

Western Europe, Eastern Europe, and Russia strikingly lack laws against sodomy – though as noted above there are significant cases of government targeting of homosexuals in this area – not just in Russia but also in other countries of Eastern Europe (ILGA 2013).

The criminalization of sodomy goes back thousands of years. While some ancient polytheistic civilizations were more or less accepting of homosexual relations, monotheistic religions tended to be hostile – and to legally proscribe same-sex relations when they had the political power to do so. The very word "sodomy" comes from the evil behavior of the townspeople of Sodom who proved their depravity and evil by demanding that Lot let them rape his (male) guests. While there are ongoing arguments about whether the sin of the Sodomites was homosexuality, rape, or xenophobia, it is very clear that the God of the Bible is against same-sex intercourse given what Leviticus says about it. Leviticus tells the Israelites that "If a man practices homosexuality, having sex with another man as with a woman, both men have committed a detestable act. They must both be put to death, for they are guilty of a capital offense" (Leviticus 20:13). The monotheistic Children of Judaism, Christianity, and Islam have also historically had very negative attitudes towards same-sex relations (Helminiak 2008). It is important to note that these broad characterizations should come with some serious caveats. In particular periods and particular centuries there were clearly times when homosexuality was tolerated more in certain places in Christian and Islamic civilizations. Nonetheless the legal codes of these civilizations were generally negative and proscribed same-sex relations. Given the continuing power of religion – specifically in certain regions – it should not be too much of a surprise that countries that are monotheistic religious states which discriminate against other religions are more likely to also make same-sex relations illegal. Interestingly the relationship between anti-sodomy laws and the Common Law at its source can be traced back to the same strong negative religious attitudes about homosexuality – but the relationship is almost 500 years old.

Many of the countries of the world have a legal system that is based in part or in whole on the British Common Law system and there is strong quantitative evidence that having a common law system makes a country much more likely to have anti-sodomy laws (Asal et al. 2013; Sommer et al. 2013). The reason for this also ties back to religious attitudes but unlike the impact of current religious states the religious attitudes that shaped the anti-sodomy laws related to the Common Law are views that were held by state leaders almost 500 years ago. In the sixteenth century, during the break with Roman Catholicism, King Henry VIII and Thomas Cromwell his chief minister instituted a host of new laws that replaced religious law. One of those was the Buggery Act of 1533 which outlawed sodomy by punishment of death. The British then went out and conquered two-thirds of the world bringing their law with them. For example, using statutes such as the Indian Penal Code, after taking over India the British colonial administration made sodomy a crime (Bhaskaran 2004, 85–86). On the other hand the Civil Law code created by Napoleon and spread around the world to French and Spanish colonies did not have a prohibition against sodomy as part of its mandate for its colonies because " … buoyed by Enlightenment ideals of individuality, rationality, privacy and secularism, the French National Assembly abolished the country's old sodomy prohibition on the ground that 'liberty consists in the freedom to do everything which injured no one else' (Declaration of the Rights of Man 1789)" (Frank, Boutcher, and Camp 2009, 136). Thus a decision made a little less than 500 years ago has played a large part in major differences in the legality of sodomy worldwide.

The fight for decriminalization in modern times has taken various forms in different countries, and in some cases even within the same country in different jurisdictions. Some movements for the repeal of sodomy laws fought their way through the court system, in some cases winning a nod from the nation's highest court. Such cases include South Africa and the United States; in its ruling in *Lawrence v. Texas* (539 U.S. 558) the Supreme Court of the United States struck down the sodomy laws of Texas (and several other states) effectively making such laws unconstitutional in the entire country. Conversely, certain movements for change in the direction of decriminalization pursued a legislative strategy. Indeed, in certain countries – such as Canada (1969 Criminal Law Amendment Act) – repeal of sodomy provisions happened in their legislative branches. Strong religious constituencies seem to decrease the likelihood that legislatures would be the venue for repeal of sodomy laws. Interestingly, it is the legal system that largely determines where decriminalization takes place; whereas legislative repeal constitutes 97% of the cases of decriminalization in Civil Law countries, in Common Law countries 6 in every 10 repeals were judicial (Sommer et al. 2013).

SEE ALSO: Civil Rights Law and Gender in the United States; Colonialism and Gender; Colonialism and Sexuality; Gender and the Death Penalty in Comparative Perspective; Human Rights and Gender

REFERENCES

Amnesty International UK. 2002. "Saudi Arabia: 'Sexual Orientation' Executions Condemned." Accessed February 22, 2014, at: http://www.amnesty.org.uk/press-releases/saudi-arabia-sexual-orientation-executions-condemned.

Asal, Victor, Udi Sommer, and Paul G. Harwood. 2013. "Original Sin: A Cross-National Study of the Legality of Homosexual Acts." *Comparative Political Studies*, 46: 3. DOI: 10.1177/0010414012453693.

Bhaskaran, Suparna. 2004. *Made in India: Decolonizations, Queer Sexualities, Trans/National Projects*. New York: Palgrave Macmillan.

Cheney, Kristen. 2012. "Locating Neocolonialism, 'Tradition,' and Human Rights in Uganda's 'Gay Death Penalty.'" *African Studies Review*, 55: 2. DOI: 10.1353/arw.2012.0031.

Frank, David J., Steven A. Boutcher, and Bayliss Camp. 2009. "The Reform of Sodomy Laws from a World Society Perspective." In *Queer Mobilizations: LGBT Activists Confront the Law*, edited by Scott Barclay, Mary Bernstein, and Anna-Maria Marshall, 123–141. New York: New York University Press.

Helminiak, Daniel A. 2008. "Homosexuality in World Religions: A Case Study in the Psychology of Spirituality." *Journal of Individual Psychology*, 64: 2.

ILGA (International Lesbian, Gay, Bisexual, Trans and Intersex Association). 2013. "State-Sponsored Homophobia: A World Survey of Laws: Criminalisation, Protection and Recognition of Same-sex Love." Accessed January 11, 2014, at: http://old.ilga.org/Statehomophobia/ILGA_State_Sponsored_Homophobia_2013.pdf.

Nzouankeu Anne Mireille. 2014. "Gay 'Prisoner of Conscience' Jailed for Sending Text Message Dies in Cameroon." *Associated Press*. Accessed February 22, 2014, at: http://globalnews.ca/news/1076899/gay-prisoner-of-conscience-jailed-for-sending-text-message-dies-in-cameroon/.

Sommer, Udi, Victor Asal, Katie Zuber, and Jonathan Parent. 2013. "Institutional Paths to Policy Change: Judicial Versus Nonjudicial Repeal of Sodomy Laws." *Law and Society Review*, 47: 2. DOI: 10.1111/lasr.12017.

Schwitzr, Michael. 2012. "Russian City Passes Law Banning Gay 'Propaganda'." *International Herald Tribune*, March 1.

FURTHER READING

Frank, David John, and Elizabeth H. McEneaney. 1999. "The Individualization of Society and the Liberalization of State Policies on Same-Sex Sexual Relations, 1984–1995." *Social Forces*, 77: 3. DOI: 10.2307/3005966.

Frank, David John, and Nolan Edward Phillips. 2013. "Sex Laws and Sexuality Rights in Comparative and Global Perspectives." *Annual Review of Law and Social Science*, 9: 249–267. DOI: 10.1146/annurev-lawsocsci-102612-134007.

United States Commission on International Religious Freedom. 2013. "*Annual Report of the United States Commission on International Religious Freedom.*" Accessed August 20, 2014, at: http://www.uscirf.gov/sites/default/files/resources/2013%20USCIRF%20Annual%20Report%20%282%29.pdf.

Status of Women Reports

SUSAN HARRIS RIMMER
Australian National University, Canberra, Australia

The idea of "status of women" reports originated in the Commission on the Status of Women (hereafter referred to as "CSW"), a functional commission of the United Nations Economic and Social Council (ECOSOC). The Commission was established by ECOSOC resolution 11(II) of 21 June 1946 with the aim to *inter alia* prepare recommendations and reports to the Council on promoting women's rights in political, economic, civil, social, and educational fields. Every year, representatives of Member States gather at United Nations Headquarters in New York to "evaluate progress on gender equality, identify challenges, set global standards and formulate concrete policies to promote gender equality and women's empowerment worldwide."

At the same time, the body of international law setting out women's rights has progressed, and increasingly requires reporting by states on their progress towards certain standards. The Convention for the Elimination of All Forms of Discrimination Against Women (CEDAW) was adopted by the UN General Assembly in 1979 and now has 186 state parties (but with many states making serious reservations to certain provisions). At least every four years, the States parties are expected to submit a national report to the Committee, indicating the measures they have adopted to give effect to the provisions of the Convention. During its annual session, the Committee members discuss these reports with the Government representatives and explore with them areas for further action by the specific country.

Apart from the hard law of treaties there is also increasing "soft law" in the area of women's rights at the United Nations which has led to the production of "status of women" reports at the global and national level. For example, the Beijing Conference for Women in 1995 adopted a Platform for Action, which has been reviewed every five years with country-by-country surveys and updates.

The Security Council has issued a series of resolutions on women, peace, and security (WPS). A cluster of UN Security Council Resolutions (UNSCR) comprise the WPS agenda. Those resolutions are UNSCR 1325 (2000), UNSCR 1820 (2008), UNSCR 1888 (2009), UNSCR 1889 (2009) and UNSCR 1960 (2010), and UNSCR 2106 (2013). In essence, the WPS agenda states that women and girls experience conflict differently from men and boys. Women have an essential role in conflict prevention, peace building, and post-conflict reconstruction, and States are required to ensure women are represented in all decision-making. The resolutions have led to annual reporting by the Secretary-General. One of the key obligations on states is to formulate National Action Plans measuring annual compliance with the resolutions.

Another extension of the concept of status of women reports came with the publication of the first Human Development Index by the United Nations Development Programme in 1990, created by Mahbub ul Haq and Amartya Sen. The first Human Development

Report introduced a new way of measuring development by combining indicators of life expectancy, educational attainment, and income into a composite human development index. The Gender Inequality Index (GII) is a new index for measurement of gender disparity that was introduced in the 2010 Human Development Report. It measures proxies such as the maternal mortality rate, number of seats women hold in government bodies, and the labor force participation rate.

In 2000, leaders at UN Headquarters adopted the United Nations Millennium Declaration, committing their nations to a new global partnership to reduce extreme poverty and setting out a series of time-bound targets – with a deadline of 2015 – that have become known as the Millennium Development Goals (MDGs). The MDGs include two specific goals focused on women, MDG 3 and MDG 5.

MDG 3 seeks to promote gender equality and empower women by achieving the following target: eliminate gender disparity in primary and secondary education, preferably by 2005, and in all levels of education no later than 2015. The indicators are:

1. Ratios of girls to boys in primary, secondary, and tertiary education
2. Share of women in wage employment in the non-agricultural sector
3. Proportion of seats held by women in national parliament

MDG 5 aims to improve maternal health. The targets are to reduce by three-quarters the maternal mortality ratio, and achieve universal access to reproductive health with six indicators.

In the *Millennium Development Goals Report 2013*, the UN Secretary-General outlines both global progress but also progress of country groupings against these goals.

As a matter of national public policy, states may present their own status of women updates through reports or campaigns. For example, the Australian Government created the Workplace Gender Equality Agency which is tasked with compiling reports from employers under the *Workplace Gender Equality Act 2012* against a range of indicators.

Non-governmental organizations also produce status of women reports, the most well known being *The Global Gender Gap Report*, introduced by the World Economic Forum in 2006.

These status of women reports are sometimes criticized for drawing too much attention to women's lives in one sphere (formal employment) and not others (such as unpaid care work), and focusing only on quantitative indicators.

SEE ALSO: Governance and Gender

REFERENCES

United Nations, Commission on the Status of Women website. Accessed August 24, 2015, at: http://www.unwomen.org/en/csw.

ECOSOC resolution 11(II) of 21 June 1946. Accessed August 24, 2015, at: http://www.un.org/womenwatch/daw/csw/pdf/CSW_founding_resolution_1946.pdf.

United Nations Development Programme (UNDP). 2010. *2010 Human Development Report: The Real Wealth of Nations: Pathways to Human Development*. Accessed August 24, 2015, at: http://hdr.undp.org/sites/default/files/reports/270/hdr_2010_en_complete_reprint.pdf.

United Nations. 2013. *Millennium Development Goals Report 2013*. Accessed August 24, 2015, at: http://www.un.org/millenniumgoals/pdf/report-2013/mdg-report-2013-english.pdf.

FURTHER READING

Human Rights Resource Centre. 2012. *Violence, Exploitation, and Abuse and Discrimination in Migration Affecting Women and Children in ASEAN: A Baseline Study*. Jakarta, Indonesia: HRRC.

Partners for Prevention, for UNDP, UNFPA, UN Women and UNV. 2013. *The UN Multi-country*

Study on Men and Violence in Asia and the Pacific.
The World Economic Forum. 2013. *The Global Gender Gap Report 2013.* Davos: WEF.

Sterilization

VÉRONIQUE MOTTIER

University of Cambridge, UK and University of Lausanne, Switzerland

Sterilization refers to medical interventions that prevent men and women from reproducing. The term covers a variety of both surgical and non-surgical procedures. For men, these include vasectomy (cutting the tubes between the prostate and the testicles) and castration (removal of the testicles), and for women, tubal litigation (cutting and tying of the Fallopian tubes), ovariotomy (excision of the ovaries), hysterectomy (removal of the uterus), and techniques such as chemical sterilization or the Essure procedure (where inserts are placed into the Fallopian tubes), which do not require surgery.

Practices such as castration have existed since the beginning of human societies, often carrying religious or symbolic meanings (such as the ritualistic humiliation of defeated enemies). Late nineteenth-century doctors believed that hysterectomy could cure "female diseases" such as hysteria, and that male sterilization had a moderating effect on "perverse" sexual desires. As a surgical technique used primarily for contraceptive purposes, sterilization became more widespread in the course of the twentieth century, and closely intertwined with wider social and political aims.

In the 1920s and 1930s, organizations that promoted sterilization sprang up in many Western countries, while sterilization practices justified by arguments against overpopulation and poverty rose sharply in Puerto Rico from the late 1930s and in Japan in the aftermath of World War II. Worldwide, it remained a deeply contested practice well into the second half of the twentieth century, however, owing to fierce opposition from the Catholic Church in particular.

In the first half of the twentieth century, sterilization practices often became intertwined with the rise of eugenic movements. Eugenicists saw the hereditary transmission of "inferior" mental and physical characteristics as the source of a process of national degeneration, and called upon the state to encourage "fitter" citizens to have more children, while discouraging "unfit" citizens from reproducing. Many (though not all) eugenicists promoted the coerced sterilization of "inferior" citizens to prevent them from reproducing. National and international Leagues promoting eugenic sterilization were founded worldwide, for example, in Hong Kong and Australia in 1936 and Mexico (International Latin Federation of Eugenics Societies) in 1935. The first eugenic sterilization law was adopted by Indiana in 1907, with 33 American states following suit. Switzerland, Sweden, Finland, Denmark, Norway, Iceland, Estonia and Nazi Germany all introduced sterilization laws that allowed for the coerced sterilization of citizens declared "unfit," according to eugenic criteria such as mental and physical disabilities, between the late 1920s and early 1930s, followed by Japan in 1940. Although eugenic sterilization programs fizzled out in most contexts by the late 1950s, coerced sterilization programs continued to occur especially in non-Western contexts, as part of birth control campaigns. For example, during the so-called State of Emergency in India (1975–1977), in Peru under Fujimoro (1996–2000), in East Timor under Indonesian rule (1975–1999), and in post-Mao China, thousands of men and women were allegedly sterilized without informed consent, or explicitly against their will.

Such programs have attracted increasing political controversy in recent decades, and this is reflected in the critical scholarship that has emerged since the 1990s. Three major lines of critique can be identified. First, post-World War II sterilization campaigns that were often organized and funded by international agencies but implemented in post-independence contexts such as Bangladesh, Sri Lanka, Pakistan, and many African states in the 1960s and 1970s have been accused of only portraying "overpopulation" (itself a contested term) in non-Western, but not Western, countries, as "a problem." Financial incentives to undergo sterilization and inadequate information provision have been additionally criticized for blurring the notion of consent, thereby ignoring the basic human right to reproductive autonomy.

Second, feminist theorists and critical historians of eugenics have explored the gendered nature of coerced sterilization practices, pointing out that such programs often targeted women. This was especially pronounced in countries such as the United States, Sweden, and Switzerland, where the great majority (over 90%) of victims of coerced sterilization were women, although eugenic ideas present both men and women as equally liable to be "unfit" for reproduction. The notion of coercion in this context has been questioned by some, however, on the grounds that eugenic sterilization could offer women an effective means of birth control at a time when access to contraception or abortion was highly restricted, and other methods were unreliable. Such arguments often refer to a study by Johanna Schoen (2005) on eugenic sterilizations in North Carolina between 1929 and 1975, even though her research shows that only a very small minority of women who were sterilized on eugenic grounds consented to this intervention.

Third, critical race scholars such as Dorothy Roberts (1997) have argued that the role of gender and social class in sterilization practices needs to be further unpacked, also taking into account race factors. In the United States, for example, Puerto Rican, American Indian and African American women have been disproportionately targeted by government programs that saw sterilization as a means to curtail welfare costs until well into the 1970s.

Against this backdrop, recent scholarship generally approaches the analysis of sterilization practices through the critical lens of the "reproductive rights" of women and men, referring to the freedom to determine if, when, and how often to have children.

SEE ALSO: Birth Control, History and Politics of; Eugenics, Historical and Ethical Aspects of; Family Planning; Reproductive Health; Reproductive Justice and Reproductive Rights in the United States; Women's Health Movement in the United States

REFERENCES

Roberts, Dorothy E. 1997. *Killing the Black Body. Race, Reproduction and the Meaning of Liberty*. New York: Vintage Books.

Schoen, Johanna. 2005. *Choice & Coercion. Birth control, Sterilization and Abortion in Public Health and Welfare*. Chapel Hill: University of North Carolina Press.

FURTHER READING

Bashford, Alison, and Philippa Levine, eds. 2010. *The Oxford Handbook of the History of Eugenics*. Oxford: Oxford University Press.

Dowbiggin, Ian. 2008. *The Sterilization Movement and Global Fertility in the Twentieth Century*. Oxford: Oxford University Press.

Hansen, Randall, and Desmond King. 2013. *Sterilised by the State. Eugenics, Race, and the Population Scare in Twentieth Century North America*. Cambridge: Cambridge University Press.

Mottier, Véronique. 2013. "Reproductive Rights." In *The Oxford Handbook of Gender and Politics*, edited by Georgina Waylen, Karen Celis, Laurel Weldon, and Johanna Kantola, 214–235. Oxford: Oxford University Press.

Steroids

KATHRYN HENNE
Australian National University, Canberra

Anabolic-androgenic steroids, more commonly referred to as anabolic steroids or simply as steroids, are drugs that are synthetic derivatives of testosterone, the principal male sex hormone. Like testosterone, anabolic steroids have anabolic and androgenic effects. In other words, they promote muscle growth (anabolic) and the development of male sexual characteristics (androgenic) in men and women. Anabolic steroids, as synthetic androgens, are designed to maximize anabolic effects while attempting to limit androgenic effects. In popular culture, steroid use is often associated with hypermasculinization, in terms of both physique and behavior. It has emerged as responsible for the growth of seemingly unnatural masculine bodies, which are characterized as larger, more muscular, and more aggressive.

Although anabolic steroids are more commonly used for their anabolic properties, they were originally developed in the 1930s to treat male hypogonadism, a condition in which the testes do not produce enough testosterone to support normal growth or sexual function. These traits are often characterized as side effects. Among women, such changes can include a deepened voice, enlarged clitoris, acne, and abnormal body hair growth (hirsutism), which can be accompanied by an irregular menstruation and a heightened libido. The excess testosterone in men can yield distinctly different side effects, such as testicular atrophy, a reduction in sperm count, and gynecomastia, which is the development of breast-like tissues on the chest.

Recent global epidemiological studies characterize non-medical anabolic steroid use as a serious public health problem (Sagoe et al. 2014, 383), finding that 3.3 percent of the world's population (6.4 percent of men, 1.6 percent of women) has used them. Quantitative research supports claims that non-medical steroid use has increased, but there are limited numbers of in-depth inductive studies on users. To date, studies have identified attributes of steroid users in high-income Western countries, but have offered little insight into the social networks and conditions that facilitate steroid use (Sagoe, Andreassen, and Pallesen 2014, 11–12). Evidence suggests that most users are men who begin taking steroids before the age of 30, with the average user in the United States being a college-educated, white-collar worker with an above-average income (Griffiths 2014). Many users do, however, exhibit psychological conditions or disorders and lack social support (Sagoe, Andreassen, and Pallesen 2014). "Disordered" masculinity and muscle dysmorphia are common explanations for steroid use (Keane 2005). Pharmaceutical companies market a number of synthetic testosterone hormone drugs and therapies as rejuvenation treatments, which buttresses perceptions of steroids' masculine enhancement potential (Hoberman 2006). Although providing important gendered insights, most studies focus primarily on a particular kind of steroids user, one who is cisgender male, of European descent, and pursuing bodily enhancement.

Research challenges public discourses that often connect steroid use and violence. The connection reflects a broader cultural belief that hypermasculinity is deviant in ways that cause aggression and, in turn, crime. For example, concerns around "roid rage" – hyperaggression attributed to steroid users – have served to justify stronger penalties for steroids possession; however, studies to date show that steroid use does not necessarily result in acts of aggression or violence toward others (Griffiths 2014). In addition, in-depth research on the trafficking of steroids reveals that not only do recreational users take calculated measures to obtain illegal substances, but also that the growth of black markets reflects a broader medicalization of Western societies in which citizens seek out medical interventions for individual enhancement (Kraska, Bussard, and Brent 2010). Thus, to frame steroid use as simply gendered deviance misses the broader social milieu influencing users, their consumption, and their modes of accessing steroids.

In addition to findings about recreational use, there is a well-documented history of steroid use among elite athletes in the twentieth century. In the mid-1950s, accusations surfaced that weightlifters on the United States and Soviet national teams were systematically using anabolic steroids. By the late 1960s steroid use in elite sports had become more widespread. An unofficial poll of Olympic athletes from a variety of sports and countries found that two thirds of respondents had used steroids during the lead-up to the 1972 Olympic Games. Amidst these findings and concerns that steroid use provided athletes with an unfair competitive advantage, pressure mounted to develop a test that could detect the metabolites of anabolic steroids, which researchers successfully developed in 1973. Since then, an elaborate, transnational regime has replaced simple drug testing in order to detect a range of drugs used by athletes (Henne 2015).

Scholarship on doping in sport draws attention to the gendered dimensions of the politics surrounding anabolic steroids and their regulation in sport. During the Cold War, Western media accounts portrayed female Soviet bloc athletes as men masquerading as women, as "not fully" women, or as drug users. In contrast, US athletes emerged as more feminine, presumably drug-free and "fully" female. Accordingly, these depictions portrayed female Soviet bloc athletes' bodies as reflective of communism's unethical pursuit of winning at all costs, which required women to go against their feminine "nature" (Beamish and Ritchie 2005; Henne 2015). As the history of doping in sport yields a number of instances where female masculinity emerges as grounds for suspicion, feminist and queer critiques suggest that anti-doping regulation reveals the tacit assumption that the absence of normative femininity is not only undesirable to the heteronormative gaze of authorities, but also emerges as seemingly unreal or unlike "true" women (Lock 2003). Thus, female masculinity emerges as suspicious because it appears to transgress the presumed boundaries of womanness, a category assumed to be naturally feminine and not capable of achieving the same level of physical ability as men.

In sum, empirical evidence suggests that the majority of anabolic steroid users do not identify as elite athletes, which has prompted additional scholarly efforts to document and identify patterns of illicit anabolic steroid use by bodybuilders and other (usually male) gym-active persons. Despite the critical attention paid to athlete and recreational users, few analyses examine steroid use beyond physical cultural settings. Allegations of steroid use among police officers and in the military are notable but underinvestigated. Although using steroids can assist sex reassignment treatment and in treating muscle and weight loss among HIV/AIDS patients, some cancers, and osteoporosis, there remains limited research on medical patients and the values that they attribute to such drugs. In sum, while studies of steroid use and regulation have yielded important gendered insights, their emphasis on recreational users and athletes provides a narrow picture of what could be broader or differential gendered patterns of use.

SEE ALSO: Athletics and Gender; Drug and Alcohol Abuse; Hypermasculinity; Masculinities

REFERENCES

Beamish, Rob, and Ian Ritchie. 2005. "The Spectre of Steroids: Nazi Propaganda, Cold War Anxiety and Patriarchal Paternalism." *International Journal of the History of Sport*, 22(5): 777–795.

Griffiths, Scott. 2014. "Scapegoating Steroids Won't Make a Safer Night Out." *The Conversation*, September 2. Accessed August 15, 2015, at http://theconversation.com/scapegoating-steroids-wont-make-for-a-safer-night-out-31062.

Henne, Kathryn. 2015. *Testing for Athlete Citizenship: Regulating Doping and Sex in Sport*. New Brunswick: Rutgers University Press.

Hoberman, John. 2006. *Testosterone Dreams: Rejuvenation, Aphrodisia, Doping*. Berkeley: University of California Press.

Keane, Helen. 2005. "Diagnosing the Male Steroid User: Drug Use, Body Image and Disordered Masculinity." *Health*, 9: 189–208.

Kraska, Peter, Charles R. Bussard, and John J. Brent. 2010. "Trafficking in Bodily Perfection: Examining the Late-Modern Steroid Marketplace and Its Criminalization." *Justice Quarterly*, 27(2): 159–185.

Lock, Rebecca Ann. 2003. "The Doping Ban: Compulsory Heterosexuality and Lesbophobia." *International Review for the Sociology of Sport*, 38(4): 397–411.

Sagoe, Dominic, Cecile S. Andreassen, and Ståle Pallesen. 2014. "The Aetiology and Trajectory of Anabolic-Androgenic Steroid Use Initiation: A Systematic Review and Synthesis of Qualitative Research." *Substance Abuse Treatment, Prevention and Policy*, 9(27). DOI: 10.1186/1747-597X-9-27.

Sagoe, Dominic, Helge Molde, Cecile S. Andreassen, Torbjørn Thorsheim, and Ståle Pallesen. 2014. "The Global Epidemiology of Anabolic-Androgenic Steroid Use." *Annuals of Epidemiology*, 24: 383–398.

Stigma

EMILY R. CABANISS SAM
Houston State University, USA

Following the publication of Erving Goffman's (1963) book *Stigma: Notes on the Management of Spoiled Identity*, research on the creation, sources, experiences, and consequences of stigma have proliferated in the social sciences. Offering a concise and widely cited definition, Goffman (1963, 3) proposed that a stigma is "an attribute that is deeply discrediting." To be stigmatized is to be "reduced … from a whole and usual person to a tainted, discounted one." In developing what remains the most comprehensive and influential introduction to the topic, Goffman drew on his earlier, year-long ethnographic research in a mental hospital. In that case study, he observed that patients, once labeled mentally ill, found it nearly impossible to shed this devalued status. Every attempt they made to redeem themselves and claim a "normal" identity was interpreted by institutional authorities as further evidence of their mental illness. The disparaging label acted as a lens through which all of their behaviors were seen and understood in this setting, by this audience.

If the same behaviors could be interpreted differently by different audiences or under different circumstances, Goffman concluded, stigma must not inhere in individuals. Rather, it must be a situational condition that arises when an individual or group deviates in important ways from normative expectations for that situation and/or for that audience. Stigma, he argued, is better understood as a relationship between an "attribute and stereotype" (Goffman 1963, 4), a failure to live up to deeply rooted cultural assumptions about how someone with a particular social status should behave in a particular situation. Stigma is thus context-dependent and relational. "An attribute that stigmatizes one type of possessor," Goffman argued, "can confirm the usualness of another, and therefore is neither creditable nor discreditable as a thing in itself" (1963, 3). Thus, one might find oneself stigmatized in one situation, but perceived as entirely normal in another. Likewise, under particular circumstances, anyone may find their claims to a valued identity discredited and, thus, become vulnerable to stigmatization.

In recent years, social psychologists have emphasized the ways in which stigma and stigmatization are implicated in the reproduction of inequality. Link, Phelan, and Hatzenbuehler (2014, 52) contend that "Stigmatization is entirely contingent on access to social, economic, and political power that allows the identification of differentness, the construction of stereotypes, the separation of labeled persons into distinct categories, and the full execution of disapproval, rejection, exclusion, and discrimination." Some people, in other words, have more power than others to impose stigma, or to brand individuals and entire categories of people as unworthy of recognition as "whole and usual" persons. "For stigmatization to occur," Link and Phelan (2001, 363) assert, "power must be exercised."

In patriarchal societies, men as a group have more social, economic, and political power than women as a group. To justify and perpetuate this unequal social arrangement, men (and some women) have generally tried to tie women's subordination to cultural stereotypes that cast them as manifestly different from and inferior to men. During the 2008 US presidential campaign, for instance, Hillary Clinton was routinely denounced by politicians and members of the media as too emotional for the job, as riding her husband's political coat-tails, and as dangerously ill-equipped (as a woman) to lead the country especially in times of war. At campaign events, she even faced protesters with signs reading "Iron my shirt!" As a woman attempting to be taken seriously in what has historically been a male-dominated public arena, she was violating normative expectations and was thus vulnerable to stigmatization. Because of racism, people of color also face uniquely pejorative stereotypes that threaten their ability to claim identities as social equals to their white counterparts. As a result, they often feel pressure to shift their gender performances in order to counter or distance themselves from racial and ethnic stigma.

As a social process, stigmatization occurs at both the macro- and micro-levels of society. At the macro-level, powerful actors in government, corporate, media, religious, and educational institutions establish laws, policies, and conventions that normalize some behaviors and attributes and marginalize others. In heteronormative societies, for instance, heterosexuality is treated as the standard and expected form of sexuality, and rights and privileges flow to those who are perceived as heterosexual. Non-conformity to heterosexist expectations, on the other hand, can result in the denial of basic civil rights, including those related to employment, housing and public accommodations, parental rights, rights to inheritance, and so on. In the extreme, stigma that is perpetuated by institutional actors can be deadly. In the 1980s, when HIV/AIDS was ravaging many gay communities, prevention efforts were stymied by perceptions – reinforced by outspoken political and religious elites – that it was a "homosexual" disease. When the stigma of disease was linked with a stigmatized group, people died (Gamson 1989).

At the micro-level, individuals and groups create and reinforce normative expectations and police violations as they interact with each other in different social contexts. In a "heteronormative gender system," gender, sex, and sexuality are linked and seen as determined by one's biological makeup (Schilt and Westbrook 2009, 449). Those with male bodies are expected to present themselves as men and desire relationships with women, and vice versa. Hegemonic constructions of masculinity and femininity include expectations of heterosexuality. Those who fail or refuse to conform to these normative expectations risk being stigmatized as not "real" women or men. However, situational norms shape responses to deviance, including the imposition of stigma. In their research on transwomen and transmen in the workplace, Schilt and Westbrook (2009) found that organizational leaders had a central role in setting expectations for how openly transitioning transgender employees would be received by their "gender-normal" colleagues. When bosses were supportive of their transgender employees, gender-normal employees tended to accept and normalize their colleagues' transitions. In workplaces where organizational leaders were less supportive, transwomen and transmen encountered more resistance from their colleagues and their gender-nonconformity was more stigmatized.

Stigma and stigmatization are implicated in every aspect of the reproduction of gender and sexual inequalities, from labeling and stereotyping gender and sexual nonconformists as immoral, threatening, or otherwise less than fully human, to justifying their political, economic, and social subordination. Yet, as scholars beginning with Goffman have shown, stigma is not inevitable. It is created and imposed by individuals and groups with situational power. Thus, at the interactional level, it can be resisted by other individuals and groups who find creative ways of leveraging new sources of situational power. At the institutional level, it can be challenged by reducing the power of particular groups to stigmatize others.

SEE ALSO: Gender as a Practice; Heteronormativity and Homonormativity; Normalization

REFERENCES

Gamson, Josh. 1989. "Silence, Death, and the Invisible Enemy: AIDS Activism and Social Movement 'Newness'." *Social Problems*, 36(4): 351–367.

Goffman, Erving. 1963. *Stigma: Notes on the Management of Spoiled Identity*. New York: Simon & Schuster.

Link, Bruce G., and Jo C. Phelan. 2001. "Conceptualizing Stigma." *Annual Review of Sociology*, 27: 363–385.

Link, Bruce G., Jo C. Phelan, and Mark L. Hatzenbuehler. 2014. "Stigma and Social Inequality." In *Handbook of the Social Psychology of Inequality*, edited by Jane D. McLeod, Edward J. Lawler, and Michael Schwalbe, 49–64. Dordrecht: Springer.

Schilt, Kristen, and Laurel Westbrook. 2009. "Doing Gender, Doing Heteronormativity: 'Gender Normals,' Transgender People, and the Social Maintenance of Heterosexuality." *Gender & Society*, 23(4): 440–464.

FURTHER READING

Goffman, Erving. 1961. *Asylums: Essays on the Social Situation of Mental Patients and Other Inmates*. Garden City: Doubleday.

Herek, Gregory M. 2007. "Thinking about AIDS and Stigma: A Psychologist's Perspective." *Journal of Law, Medicine, and Ethics*, 30(4): 285–303.

Major, Brenda, and Laurie T. O'Brien. 2005. "The Social Psychology of Stigma." *Annual Review of Psychology*, 56: 393–421.

Stone Butch

KAI KOHLSDORF
University of Washington, USA

Stone butch is an identity term that was popularized in the 1940s and 1950s in a largely US white, working-class, lesbian context. While there are several characteristics of those who identify as a stone butch, the primary defining characteristic is their presumed or identified sexual untouchability. To be untouchable means to gain sexual pleasure through the satisfaction of one's partner, from giving pleasure to them, and to be uninterested in having one's own genitalia stimulated. Stone butches most often identify as female but do not identify as women. Stone butch brings together two disparate concepts that operate individually with their own definitions, "stone" and "butch." Stone butches most often partner with femmes, who sometimes may identify as "stone femmes" to reference their attraction to stone butches. "Stone femme" may alternatively refer to someone who identifies with the designator "stone" referencing their own sexual untouchability or identity as a sexual top. Stone butch gender presentation is very masculine or very butch and this characteristic is as important as sexual untouchability. Other significant characteristics of stone butches include identifying as the aggressive partner, taking on traditional masculinity codes in both clothing and mannerisms, and identifying with stoicism. Stone butches are often described as a link between the supposed butch/FTM border wars, but this is too simple an analysis. Some stone butches identify as trans men and some trans men identify as stone; the categories are far from distinct. Identities are complex and the ways in which these terms circulate are not exclusive, nor do they exist on a linear continuum.

A prevalent stereotypical assumption regarding stone butches holds that previous sexual abuse caused their disinterest in stimulation of their own genitalia. At the heart of this stereotype is that a stone butch's sexuality is abject, negative, and embodies a kind of gender dysphoria that causes a rejection of their own sexual pleasure. This is a reductive reading that denies sexual agency to the stone butch to enact a sexuality they choose, and also disregards their sexual pleasure gained from giving pleasure to their partners. Halberstam (1998) critically engages the concept of the abject as written onto stone butch bodies in *Female Masculinity* while also arguing for alternative constructions of a sexual self. Halberstam's work enables us to question how it is that a stone butch's sexuality has largely been described in terms of what they do not do, as opposed to what they do. The presumption that a stone butch has something wrong with their sexuality is an indication of general judgment and resistance to gender variance and queer sexuality.

Assumptions operate also within lesbian and queer communities. In a study of stone butches in the 1940s and 1950s butch/femme community in Buffalo, NY, Kennedy and Davis describe that in the 1950s there was significant pressure for all butches to identify as stone (Kennedy and Davis 1993, 203–214). This expectation coded the stone butch as the only "real" butch, a stereotype that butches then felt compelled to enact, regardless of their interest or identification with the role. The ensuing popularity of the identity in the 1950s could explain the shift in the term's expectation of untouchability, as Kennedy and Davis report many butches articulated they were untouchable but had a varying degree of openness with their bodies being touched by their partners. Regardless of the degree to which a stone butch's body was or was not touchable, untouchability is the most defining trait of the identity and is often conflated with that of being the sexual aggressor, or sexual top. These are not the same thing, but both traits are expected in the stone butch identity. Sexual tops or aggressors are not always untouchable, and those who are untouchable are not always sexual tops or aggressors. As with all identity categorization, the realities of those who identify with being stone butch vary along each of these characteristics and traits. Importantly, there is overlap with those who identify as "studs," who follow the same characteristics of sexuality and gender as described above. Studs are usually African American or black identified and reject the utilization of butch or stone butch as identities given their largely white historical framing and origination.

Additionally, stone butches experienced significant ostracism within feminist and lesbian communities in the 1960s and 1970s for supposedly taking on the role of the oppressor. Other tensions exist from femmes and partners who resent the lack of reciprocal sex and desire to touch their stone butch partner's bodies, and contribute to rhetoric around their partner's sexuality as being negative, as sad, as operating in response to trauma, or as something they should work through instead of embrace (Kate 2012). Leslie Feinberg's novel *Stone Butch Blues* traces some of these stereotypes and is a well-known text that thinks through the supposed tragedy of the stone butch body (Feinberg 1993).

More recently, stone has extended beyond the borders of butch to be applied to other identities. For instance, stone may operate as a descriptor for femme, trans, male, or other identities and may operate with a variety of meanings that may or may not include the primary defining characteristic defined above, that of sexual untouchability. Some of the other things that may be meant when using the designator "stone" include having emotional armor, being a sexual top, identifying at the end of the spectrum of masculinity and/or butchness, and a bodily experience of violation with certain kinds of touch (West 2014).

SEE ALSO: Butch/Femme; Gender as a Practice; Gender Identification; Gender Identity, Theories of; Gender Performance; Masculinities; Sexual Identity and Orientation; Trans Identities, Psychological Perspectives

REFERENCES

Feinberg, Leslie. 1993. *Stone Butch Blues: A Novel*. Ithaca: Firebrand Books.

Halberstam, Judith. 1998. *Female Masculinity*. Durham, NC: Duke University Press.

Kate. 2012. "Butch Please: Sticks and Stones." *Autostraddle*, December 14, 2012. Accessed March 4, 2015, at http://www.autostraddle.com/butch-please-sticks-and-stones-151966/.

Kennedy, Elizabeth Lapovsky, and Madeline D. Davis. 1993. *Boots of Leather, Slippers of Gold: The History of a Lesbian Community*. New York: Routledge.

West, Xan. 2014. "What is Stone?" *Kink Praxis*, March 9, 2014. Accessed March 12, 2015, at https://xanwest.wordpress.com/2014/03/09/what-is-stone/.

Strap-On Sex

LOLA D. HOUSTON
University of Vermont, USA

Strap-on sex denotes a specific form of sexual practice that involves one participant wearing a device that is used to penetrate the other participant in either the vagina or the anus (sometimes the mouth). The device consists of a strap-on harness and a dildo that is attached to the harness. The harness part may be attached to the waist area or worn as a band or other configuration on other body parts such as a leg or arm or foot.

No definitive historical evidence of strap-on sex as a practice exists. Most evidence is derived from artwork (e.g., vase paintings) and a few texts, both ancient and modern. The dildo has a more robust historical portfolio, with evidence from objects, artwork, and written descriptions.

Ample evidence for dildos exists from ancient times. Numerous representations dating back 2,500 years appear in Greek, Roman, and Chinese sources. Ancient texts mention them, including the *Kama Sutra*, the poetry of Sappho, and Aristophanes' play *Lysistrata*. Unambiguous archaeological evidence from prehistory, especially the Paleolithic, is much harder to decipher. Some objects seem compelling, yet there is not any way to clearly establish use. A recent, widely publicized discovery of a siltstone object that strongly resembles a phallus was suggested to be a sex aid or dildo. While the nature of the carved object, replete with frenulum of prepuce of the penis, strongly alludes to its intended use, it is impossible to determine with any certainty that this is the case.

There is a reference to dildos in the diaries of Anne Lister, whose diary of 1823 gives a detailed account of her erotic interest. The word phallus is used, but it is not clear that this refers to a dildo per se. Clark (1996, 44) suggests that Lister was not specifically noting a dildo, but rather notes the passage as suggestive of one.

Historical evidence for the strap-on is even more scant, possibly because use of the strap-on harness without the dildo makes little sense as a sex toy. Some depictions exist on Greek vase paintings, and there is apparently a quite specific mention in the *Kama Sutra* (Vatsyayana 1994, 510). Michael Haberlandt (1899, 669) documents the use of single and double dildos with a "tie strap" as a kind of strap-on in an ethnological report about Zanzibar.

While reliable historical evidence is clearly lacking, it would be shortsighted to presume that these objects are not part of human history and prehistory. Sexual activity is unabashedly part of the historical account of all human activity, whether or not it has been suppressed, lost, or simply overlooked. The abundance of suggestive evidence seems to support the idea that use of the strap-on and the dildo has been extant for thousands, if not multiple thousands of years.

The use of the strap-on and dildo today is more readily documented, but again, historical data are also limited. Kennedy and Davis (1993, 227) note that in the 1950s, for example, sexual exploration generally did not include sex toy use, despite the concurrent stereotyping of lesbians as being unable to function without a toy. Currently, the sheer variety of devices available, as well as the broad distribution of information about both the dildo and the strap-on harness, suggests an extremely large audience for this particular sex toy combination. This interest extends to a wide range of sexual subcultures, including gay, lesbian, and transgender populations, as well as those that practice bondage and discipline.

There is a staggering variety of strap-on equipment that is readily available to those who seek it or are able to seek it out, something accomplished using any type of Internet access provided the site(s) or access are not blocked. Educational resources exist for both the novice and advanced user in the form of online forums and merchants, again subject to the obvious limitations of the controls imposed on such access. There is considerable scope for hands-on educational opportunities, both at stores selling the products and at major national events focusing on sexuality and sexual practices of all types.

Much of the history of the dildo and the strap-on is obscured by the taboo nature of this kind of sexual activity, and the way that sex toy use is often seen or classified as a "deviant" or "perverse" practice. The pathologizing of sexuality is well documented (see Foucault 1988, 1994, for example), and sex toys have certainly been, at various points in time, part of this pattern of medicalizing sexual practices. Sex toys in general have been included in the definition of *paraphilia*, and it is only recently that such a label has been partially destigmatized in the *Diagnostic and Statistical Manual of Mental Disorders* (DSM), the authoritative clinical manual used in psychology and psychiatry to evaluate and treat persons seeking help resolving personal difficulties. For this reason alone, perspectives on the use of sex toys can present a challenge, and much of the narrative data must be viewed with caution. It is not always obvious if one is dealing with a clinical perspective that holds a particular sexual practice as "deviant" or simply as a variation on a normal, healthy sexuality.

SEE ALSO: Sex Toys; Sexualities; Taboo

REFERENCES

Clark, Anna. 1996. "Anne Lister's Construction of Lesbian Identity." *Journal of the History of Sexuality*, 7(1): 23–50.
Foucault, Michel. 1988. *The History of Sexuality*. New York: Vintage Books.
Foucault, Michel. 1994. *The Birth of the Clinic: An Archaeology of Medical Perception*. New York: Vintage Books.
Haberlandt, Michael. 1899. "Conträre Sexual-Erscheinungen bei der Neger-Bevölkerung Zanzibars." *Zeitschrift für Ethnologie*, 31: 668–670.
Kennedy, Elizabeth Lapovsky, and Madeline D. Davis. 1993. *Boots of Leather, Slippers of Gold: The History of a Lesbian Community*. New York: Routledge.
Vatsyayana. 1994. *The Complete Kama Sutra: The First Unabridged Modern Translation of the Classic Indian Text by Vatsyayana*, trans. Alain Daniélou. Rochester, VT: Park Street Press.

FURTHER READING

Lister, Anne, and Helena Whitbread. 1992. *I Know My Own Heart: The Diaries of Anne Lister, 1791–1840*. New York: NYU Press.
Taormino, Tristan. 2009. *The Big Book of Sex Toys: From Vibrators and Dildos to Swings and Slings – Playful and Kinky Bedside Accessories That Make Your Sex Life Amazing*. Beverly, MA: Quiver.
Taormino, Tristan. 2012. *The Ultimate Guide to Kink: BDSM, Role Play and the Erotic Edge*. Berkeley, CA: Cleis Press.

Strategic Essentialism

ELISABETH EIDE
Oslo and Akershus University College, Norway

In postcolonial and feminist studies "strategic essentialism" has long been a disputed concept in connection with both feminism and minority representation. The same holds for essentialism; or as Fuss (1990) claims, we need to speak about "essentialisms." At some occasions, Gayatri Spivak, who is said to have introduced the phrase (Spivak 1988, 1996), has been regarded as being representative of "Third World Women," as if this was an easily apprehensible category, or as if billions of women share an essence of sorts. This way of grouping together people from vast areas with a diversity of experiences, still often occurs in public sphere representations. Modern history, not least with its patriarchal and colonialist discourses, is full of related examples.

Essentialism is the assumption that groups, categories, or classes of objects have one or several defining features exclusive to all members of that category (Ashcroft, Griffiths, and Tiffin 1998). Essentialist studies of race or gender have promoted binaries of superiority or inferiority, of the colonial subject or women as inferior, and such discourses were vital for the perseverance of patriarchal and colonial hegemony. This hegemony practiced oppression by assigning the role of *subaltern* to its subjects, whose identity became their difference. Essentialism simplifies and reduces human identity, which is more justly seen as multifaceted (see, for example, Maalouf 2000). Assuming a certain "nature" of one group of human beings, be it through ethnification, culturalization, or sexism, is strongly related to essentialism.

Categorization of women in general – as Simone de Beauvoir has also eloquently documented – as the "second sex" entails granting more diversity to the "first sex" while at least to a degree depriving the members of the "other" sex of their individualities and abilities to transcend their assigned places in society, and she recommends radical strategies for overcoming this otherness. On the other hand, throughout history, women's organizations have at times emphasized a female essence, such as, for example, nurturing and caring abilities while demanding parental leave or specific work protection, in their struggle for human rights and representation. Thus, a struggle for equal rights and to escape the "other" position, may at times conflict with demands for special rights for women in need. In addition, minorities within the "women" category (lesbians, transsexuals, ethnic and religious minorities) may feel estranged by majority discourses and priorities.

Gayatri Spivak discusses the experiences of the Subaltern Studies Group, whose aim it is to rewrite the history of India with a perspective from below (subaltern), deconstructing the imperial version. She reads their work as "a strategic use of positivist essentialism in a scrupulously visible political interest" (Spivak 1996, 214). She compares the application of strategic essentialism to deconstruction, arguing that although she uses deconstruction, it does not make her a deconstructivist. A reasonable interpretation is that strategic here can be read as *pragmatic*, since Spivak sees this essentialism as having little to do with theory, it rather defines a certain political practice: "I think we have to choose again strategically, not universal discourse, but essentialist discourse … In fact I must say I am an essentialist from time to time" (Grosz 1984). An illustrative example is that we may imagine fighting for more visibility for women artists in concrete cultural-political situations, but simultaneously be fiercely opposed to notions such as "women literature," "girl bands," and so on. These examples clearly demonstrate the dilemmas inherent in promoting certain group rights, although often justified and necessary.

Spivak, while stating that she is at times an essentialist, warns against the application of the concept, as other theorists also do, since strategic essentialism may encourage the survival of frozen identities and deepen differences. In the same interview with Grosz, Spivak urges the "need to take a stand against the discourses of essentialism … but strategically we cannot. Even as we talk about *feminist* practice, or privileging practice over theory, we are universalizing – not only generalizing but universalizing." She recommends being "vigilant about our own practice and use it as much as we can rather than make the totally counterproductive gesture of repudiating it" (Grosz 1984).

Strategic essentialism may thus be seen as a political strategy whereby differences (within a group) are temporarily downplayed and unity assumed for the sake of achieving political goals. In political practice, its usage in opposing and fighting against gender oppression is recommended, be it for judicial or social rights; but so is opposing and fighting against *theories* and *discourses* that imprison groups within unifying categories, which are by necessity narrowing. Strategic essentialism may help bringing down oppressive structures and diminish suffering, but should not be allowed to affect world views and encourage reductive views against the human dignity. Thus "the ideal that we may have to 'take the risk of essence' in order to have any political purchase remains an important theme in feminist theory and politics" (Phillips 2010). On the other hand strategic essentialism is theoretically unviable.

Essentialism may be used to subjugate or liberate, but strategic essentialism ought to be seen as a temporary political strategy and not as a universalizing theory or as a universal way of conducting political struggle.

SEE ALSO: Essentialism; Feminism, Postcolonial; Gender Analysis

REFERENCES

Ashcroft, Bill, Gareth Griffiths, and Helen Tiffin. 1998. *Key Concepts in Post-Colonial Studies*. London: Routledge.
Fuss, Diana. 1990. *Essentially Speaking: Feminism, Nature & Difference*. London: Routledge.
Grosz, Elizabeth. 1984. "Criticism, Feminism and The Institution" [interview with Gayatri Spivak]. *Thesis Eleven*, 10(11): 184.
Maalouf, Amin. 2000. *On Identity*. London: Harvill Press.
Phillips, Anne. 2010. "What's Wrong with Essentialism?" *Distinktion: Scandinavian Journal of Social Theory*, 11(1): 47–60.
Spivak, Gayatri. 1988. "Can the Subaltern Speak?" In *Marxism and the Interpretation of Culture*, edited by Larry Grossberg and Cary Nelson, 66–111. Houndmills: Macmillan.
Spivak, Gayatri. 1996. "Subaltern Studies: Deconstructing Historiography?" In *The Spivak Reader*, edited by Donna Landry and Gerald MacLean, 203–237. London: Routledge.

Stratified Reproduction

KAREN M. McCORMACK
Wheaton College, USA

Stratified reproduction is a concept that refers to the various policies, practices, and beliefs that create a system wherein conception, childbearing, nurturing, and raising children are encouraged and supported for some and discouraged and made far more difficult for others across the globe. By allocating resources unequally, such as access to high-quality healthcare and education, the reproductive practices of the privileged are supported and celebrated, while these same practices are made difficult and even dangerous or impossible for others. The term draws our attention to the consequences of political, economic, and social arrangements on the bodies of parents and children.

Shellee Colen (1995) first coined the term stratified reproduction in her study of West Indian childcare workers and their employers in New York. She argued that "physical and social reproductive tasks are accomplished differentially according to inequalities that are based on hierarchies of class, race, ethnicity, gender, place in a global economy, and migration status" (1995, 78). Colen demonstrated reproductive labor is experienced and valued differentially depending on access to resources and particular contexts.

Stratified reproduction is held in place by public policies – such as unpaid maternity leave, which makes it very difficult for working-class or poor parents to take time from work to be with their new children – to eugenics policies that actively discourage or prohibit reproduction among ethnic minorities, immigrants, or the poor. Policies also can be used to encourage reproduction to increase the population, build the nation, and maintain ethnic, national, or religious dominance. Struggles over issues as varied as abortion, access to contraception, assisted reproductive technologies (ART), and family leave highlight the disparities in the treatment of parents and often revolve around questions of whether reproduction within and of a particular group is desirable.

The concept of stratified reproduction can highlight inequalities within nations but is most often employed transnationally, to examine global practices. Analyses of ART demonstrate both within-nation and transnational stratification, as medical technology enables resource-rich adults – primarily those in industrialized countries – to bear their own biological children. Yet the enormous expense and relatively low rates of success highlight the vastly unequal value placed on children. According to the American Society of Reproductive Medicine, the average cost of one cycle of in vitro fertilization is $12,400. Yet young children continue to die in the developing world from infectious diseases that could be treated at little expense. Stratified reproduction highlights the differential value placed on human life, where some children are allowed to die while others are born only with Herculean medical interventions.

The movement of women and children (through adoption) within and across national borders highlights the politics of reproduction. Along with the importation of care workers and children, women's bodies in the developing world are also commodified to produce surrogate children for affluent parents. Rudrappa (2012) describes India as an emerging key site for surrogacy. Pande (2010) examines how rural Indian women are recruited and "manufactured" into perfect worker-mothers through enclosure in hostels and strict discipline in order to provide children for wealthier families.

Stratified reproduction is both transnational and intersectional, highlighting the complex interplay of race, class, gender, and sexuality. Hochschild's (2000) analysis of global care chains demonstrates how care of children and the elderly is often performed by immigrant women working as nannies, home health workers, and maids in industrialized countries in the West, while the children of these workers are often left at home and cared for by relatives. Hondagneu-Sotelo (2001) points to the vulnerability of immigrant care workers in California due to gender, economic vulnerability, and immigration status. The caregiving that women do for the children of those with resources, often white, wealthy children in the West, is valued – and paid – while the same care and nurturing for their own children or elderly parents is made impossible by economic conditions.

Stratified reproduction provides ideological justification for inequality and neoliberal policies. Roberts demonstrates how policies that control population and technologies that allow for genetic selection – allowing doctors and parents to select only healthy eggs or embryos – "reinforce biological explanations for social problems" (2009, 785). These technologies and policies privatize risk and responsibility, shifting responsibility for well-being away from the government and onto individuals to bear and raise healthy children. And while more resources flow to those families that are highly valued, when children in low-resource families run into trouble, the practices of their parents are often blamed. The political, economic, and social contexts that produce opportunity and unequal life chances become invisible, as stratified reproduction makes unequal outcomes appear natural and provides an ideological framework in which they are expected and make sense.

SEE ALSO: Assisted Reproduction; Global Care Chain; Intersectionality

REFERENCES

Colen, Shellee. 1995. "'Like a Mother to Them': Stratified Reproduction and West Indian Childcare Workers and Employers in New York." In *Conceiving the New World Order: The Global Politics of Reproduction*, edited by Faye Ginsburg and Rayna Rapp, 78–102. Berkeley: University of California Press.

Hochschild, Arlie. 2000. "Global Care Chains and Emotional Surplus Value." In *On The Edge: Living with Global Capitalism,* edited by Tony Giddens and Will Hutton, 130–146. London: Sage.

Hondagneu-Sotelo, Pierrette. 2001. *Domestica: Immigrant Women Cleaning and Caring in the Shadows of Affluence.* Berkeley: University of California Press.

Pande, Amrita. 2010. "Commercial Surrogacy in India: Manufacturing a Perfect Worker-Mother." *Signs*, 35(4): 969–992.

Roberts, Dorothy E. 2009. "Race, Gender, and Genetic Technologies: A New Reproductive Dystopia?" *Signs*, 34(4): 783–804.

Rudrappa, Sharmila. 2012. "India's Reproductive Assembly Line." *Contexts*, 11(2): 22–27.

Strong Objectivity

HEIDI GRASSWICK
Middlebury College, USA

Strong objectivity operationalizes the central tenet of feminist standpoint theory that all knowing is socially situated. It does so by insisting that researchers consider the effects of social situation on their research in order to be maximally objective. Strong objectivity marks a key development in Sandra Harding's specific version of standpoint theory in its attempt to reconcile the tension between standpoint's two claims: all knowing is socially situated, and some social situations (those of the socially underprivileged) are better suited to revealing the world's structure (or some parts of it) than others. Harding argues that in order to maximize objectivity, and thus achieve strong objectivity, researchers must "ground research in women's lives" (1991, 142). Her more general articulation of this idea is that researchers must "start thought from marginalized lives" (1993, 50), and her work over the years has examined many different axes of marginalization and their effects on knowledge production. Strong objectivity demands that researchers look outside of themselves and consider the variety of ways in which adopting the perspectives of marginalized lives and experiences can contribute to knowledge, especially knowledge of social relations.

Strong objectivity serves as both a critique of standard versions of value-free objectivity, and a demonstration of how standpoint theory can make use of the language and framework of objectivity rather than being viewed as rejecting any claims or goals of objective knowledge and thus falling outside of important discussions of how to achieve objective scientific research. Harding argues that standard models of value-free objectivity are really quite weak. Although they purport to keep values and interests out of the knowledge generated through their standards of objective research, the models are operationalized in such a way as to only be capable of eliminating those values and interests that differ across researchers (Harding 1991, 142). The end result is not value-free knowledge at all, but rather knowledge that represents the values and interests shared by those who manage to participate in the (relatively privileged) research communities. Absent from the research, however, are the values and interests of the marginalized, who typically are underrepresented in research communities. By way of contrast, strong objectivity requires broad consideration of the socially situated background assumptions and cultural agendas that shape knowledge. Harding points to a similarity between her strong objectivity and the "strong programme" in the sociology of knowledge in their common demand that we examine the social causes of our well-formed beliefs and not just those of our badly formed beliefs (Harding 1991, 149). Harding argues that in order to be maximally objective, researchers need to engage in a kind of strong reflexivity, through which they become critically aware of how their own situation shapes their research. They must counter this influence by coming to "value the Other's perspective and to pass over in thought into the social condition that creates it" (Harding 1991, 151). Starting one's research in this way allows for a more critical (and objective) view of the background assumptions and cultural agendas that shape research.

Strong objectivity offers an important contribution to standpoint theory in its attempt to clarify the tight link posited between knowledge and social identity or experience. Standpoint theory has been accused of positing unbridgeable chasms between knowers (Nelson 1990; Walby 2001), such that only the socially underprivileged, through their experiences of oppression, have the possibility of accessing a deep understanding of social relations. Harding's strong objectivity suggests that, indeed, researchers from privileged social positions can develop deep understandings of social relations, but only if they engage in strong reflexivity and begin their research by thinking through the positions of the marginalized, placing the experiences of the marginalized at the center of research. It loosens the link between certain social experiences and knowledge, while maintaining the standpoint insistence that attention to the social experiences of the marginalized is particularly important to developing robust knowledge of social relations.

The concept of strong objectivity also offers a significant contribution to debates in philosophy of science insofar as it attempts to break down the classic distinction between the context of justification, wherein the research methods are applied, and the context of discovery, wherein decisions are made concerning what kind of research questions will be taken up or funded. Harding understands her concept as strengthening objectivity in part because it encompasses questions regarding the role of values and interests in directing research. Value-free models of objectivity are weak in that they are only applied to the realm of scientific methods and their results, leaving the role of values in the context of discovery open and outside mechanisms of scrutiny. Strong objectivity, however, includes a critical assessment of the values and interests that direct the research, and by demanding that the research must start from the lives of the marginalized, helps work toward scientific research that better serves the interests of the marginalized. But strong objectivity is not only valuable in generating knowledge of importance for the marginalized; research that employs strong objectivity will help explain the relationship between the marginalized lives and "the rest of social relations," revealing the mechanisms of institutions of dominance and how they affect all social positions (Harding 1998, 158).

Strong objectivity also clarifies the value of standpoint theory as a research methodology, not just an epistemology. Harding notes that regardless of its controversial status within epistemological debates, standpoint theory has been extremely useful to feminist researchers, offering a transdisciplinary and general logic of inquiry that can be harnessed within particular fields of study to develop feminist research (Harding 2009). The concept of strong objectivity, with its call for starting research from the lives of the marginalized, is the key element of standpoint theory that most clearly articulates such methodological guidance that many feminist researchers have embraced.

SEE ALSO: Feminist Epistemology; Feminist Methodology; Feminist Objectivity; Feminist Standpoint Theory; Reflexivity

REFERENCES

Harding, Sandra. 1991. *Whose Science? Whose Knowledge? Thinking from Women's Lives*. Ithaca: Cornell University Press.

Harding, Sandra. 1993. "Rethinking Standpoint Epistemology: What is Strong Objectivity?" In *Feminist Epistemologies*, edited by Linda Alcoff and Elizabeth Potter, 49–82. New York: Routledge.

Harding, Sandra. 1998. *Is Science Multicultural? Postcolonialisms, Feminisms, and Epistemologies*. Bloomington: Indiana University Press.

Harding, Sandra. 2009. "Standpoint Theories: Productively Controversial." *Hypatia*, 24(4): 192–200.

Nelson, Lynn Hankinson. 1990. *Who Knows: From Quine to a Feminist Empiricism*. Philadelphia: Temple University Press.

Walby, Sylvia. 2001. "Against Epistemological Chasms: The Science Question in Feminism Revisited." *Signs*, 26(2): 485–509.

FURTHER READING

Roy, Deboleena. 2008. "Asking Different Questions: Feminist Practices for the Natural Sciences." *Hypatia*, 23(4): 134–157.

Wylie, Alison. 2003. "Why Standpoint Matters." In *Science and Other Cultures*, edited by Robert Figueroa and Sandra Harding, 26–48. New York: Routledge.

Structural Adjustment

GÜNSELI BERIK
University of Utah, USA

Structural adjustment refers to the process of restructuring national economies using a standard package of policies that emphasizes the market as the main mechanism for the allocation of economic resources. Feminist researchers have examined the gender-differentiated effects of structural adjustment programs (SAPs) from the 1980s onwards when these programs were implemented in heavily indebted developing countries as a condition for loans from the International Monetary Fund (IMF) and the World Bank. Feminist researchers argue that SAPs are a key area of concern for feminists as they constrain the possibilities for securing livelihoods and well-being.

SAPs encompass an initial macroeconomic stabilization component (currency devaluation in order to reduce the balance of payments deficit and an austerity program to curb the domestic debt). Stabilization policies are followed by long-term adjustment of the economy so as to prevent the recurrence of macroeconomic imbalances. The basic policies for adjustment are the following: (1) removal of government regulation of prices and subsidies; (2) privatization of public services and industrial enterprises so as to ensure their operation according to market criteria of profitability and to eliminate budget support for state-owned companies; (3) reduction of restrictions on trade and orientation of domestic production towards export markets; (4) removal of restrictions on foreign direct investment and financial flows; and (5) maintenance of balanced government budgets.

SAPs have been a key contributor to contemporary economic globalization. Variants of the SAP model were implemented in the United States, United Kingdom, and Canada starting in the early 1980s under the label of supply-side economics, in the Eastern European economies after 1989 in order to ensure their transition to a capitalist economy, and as the required remedy in each of the financial crises of the 1990s and the new millennium, including the financial crisis of 2008. The SAP has become the model for standard macroeconomic policies and is now referred to as market reforms, structural reforms, austerity packages, or neoliberal policies. While the SAP was replaced by the Poverty Reduction Strategy Papers (PRSPs) in 1999 (and other loan programs in 2010), the same loan conditionalities have continued (Elson and Warnecke 2011).

Despite methodological and data constraints in sorting out the direct and indirect gender impacts of SAPs, the consensus is that the economic adjustment envisioned by SAPs is likely to have disproportionate adverse impacts on women, particularly among low-income groups. Feminist research identified these channels of impact and documented them (Benería and Feldman 1992; Sparr 1994; Elson 1995; Elson and Çağatay 2000): the contractionary nature of the fiscal and monetary policies causes job losses (or stagnant job growth). Given the pattern of gender job segregation in many economies, often men lost jobs in declining domestic industries. Privatization of public services or introduction of user fees contributes to pressures for additional family members to generate income to pay for these more expensive or new budget items. Not only do women enter the labor force but also their unpaid hours of work increase as they seek to substitute home-prepared goods and services for formerly market-sourced ones to provision basic needs of the family. These adjustments at the household level often result in daughters' education being cut short as they help mothers with daily chores of provisioning. And if there are any safety nets that survive the budget cuts, they stipulate that women access them as dependents, which may leave some groups of women without social support.

SAPs accelerated women's entry into the labor force, supporting the trend referred to as global feminization of labor (Standing 1999): export orientation, along with pressures on women to generate additional income, contributed to the rise in women's share of labor-intensive export employment. However, under conditions of deregulation of investment, companies have tapped into pools of low-wage labor in different parts of the world, creating downward pressure on wages and working conditions in export jobs. Similarly, increased international mobility of financial capital has constrained governments' ability to generate full employment and has ensured the continuity of the contractionary macroeconomic policy approach that keeps inflation low and protects asset values of the wealthy or financial companies. Moreover, the costs of financial crises (job losses, foreclosure of homes and businesses, decline in social services) that result from deregulated capital flows are borne by low-income groups.

Feminist research on SAPs has been instrumental in the development of gender-aware macroeconomics (Elson 1995; Çağatay 2003). This research showed that (1) the adverse gender impacts of SAPs are due to the gender bias of macroeconomic models that guide SAPs (for example, an implicit assumption is that women in low-income families will become providers of last resort and produce the efficiency of markets that SAPs seek); and (2) not only do macroeconomic policies affect gender inequalities, as in the case of SAPs, but also gender inequalities affect economic growth. This research has led to design of strategies for a broadly shared development where gender equality is compatible with economic growth (Seguino and Grown 2006; Elson and Warnecke 2011).

SEE ALSO: Economic Globalization and Gender; Feminist Economics; Gender Inequality and Gender Stratification

REFERENCES

Benería, Lourdes, and Shelley Feldman, eds. 1992. *Unequal Burden: Economic Crises, Persistent Poverty and Women's Work*. Boulder: Westview Press.

Çağatay, Nilüfer. 2003. "Engendering Macro-Economics." In *Macro-Economics: Making Gender Matter*, edited by Martha Gutiérrez, 22–41. New York: Zed Books.

Elson, Diane, ed. 1995. *Male Bias the Development Process*, 2nd ed. Manchester: Manchester University Press.

Elson, Diane, and Nilüfer Çağatay. 2000. "The Social Content of Macroeconomic Policies." *World Development*, 28: 1354–1361.

Elson, Diane, and Tonia Warnecke. 2011. "IMF Policies and Gender Orders: the Case of Poverty Reduction and Growth Facility." In *Questioning Financial Governance from a Feminist Perspective*, edited by Brigitte Young, Isabella Bakker, and Diane Elson, 110–131. Abingdon: Routledge.

Seguino, Stephanie, and Caren Grown. 2006. "Gender Equity and Globalization: Macroeconomic Policy for Developing Countries." *Journal of International Development*, 18: 1081–1104.

Sparr, Pamela, ed. 1994. *Mortgaging Women's Lives: Feminist Critiques of Structural Adjustment*. London: Zed Books.

Standing, Guy. 1999. "Global Feminization through Flexible Labor: a Theme Revisited." *World Development*, 27: 583–586.

Structuralism, Feminist Approaches to

SAM WARNER
Salford University, UK

Structuralism is traced from its semiotic linguistic origins through social anthropology, psychoanalysis, and feminist deconstructions of naturalized gender hierarchies. Ideological and genealogical critiques pave the way for an overview of poststructuralism's decentering of gender as the starting point for politics and life. This theoretical move is located within the transition from second- to third-wave feminism and is explored through reference to sex/gender identity, desire, abuse, and intersections with race. Current reinvestments in feminism are considered.

INTRODUCTION TO STRUCTURALISM

Structuralism can be traced back to the semiotic (from the Greek *semeîon* meaning "sign") linguistic approach of Saussure (1857–1913). Saussure argued that language can be understood as a system of signs, in which words – and images – are composed of two parts: the signifier, the word – or image; and the signified, the concept or meaning attached to the word or image. Because there is no absolute relationship between signifier and signified, signs are understood to derive their meaning from their relationship with other signs: that which they are not. Central to the project of structuralism then is identifying the binary oppositions that are implicated, not just in language, but in any social activity. The ways in which these binary oppositions are made manifest are thought to indicate the deep structures that underlie dominant understandings and beliefs about human culture. For example, in social anthropology, Lévi-Strauss (1908–2009) demonstrated that in traditional societies, women are exchanged as gifts in marriage between men (from father to husband), and it is women-as-gifts that bind men to one another (Lévi-Strauss 1968). From this, he argued that kinship rules, rather than blood affiliations, shape human relationships, and that kinship rules are based on the binary opposition of man/woman and underlying structures of gender differentiation.

According to Lacan (1901–1981) the unconscious mind is structured in a similar way to social culture, because it is also language-based. Indeed, according to Lacan (2006) it is the unconscious which functions as the repository of the rules and rituals of culture and society. Individual subjectivity is thought to be achieved when individuals map themselves against idealized representations of masculinity and femininity, for example, which operate in the unconscious as the symbolic order. For Lacan, subjectivity is always gendered and is defined in reference to the presence/absence of the Phallus. Culture and the unconscious mind, therefore, work together to cement gender hierarchy and division; whereby within this phallocentric universe women can only ever be constituted as that which is lacking, excluded, or wrong.

FEMINIST APPROACHES

Feminist theorists in France sought to challenge the naturalization of gender division and hierarchy implicated in Lacanian theory. Irigaray (1985) argued that women should resist their figuration within the phallocratic autocracy by developing their own language and system of representation that more authentically expresses their own ideas and multiple desires. Irigaray thus posited a feminized form of biological determinism. Like Irigaray, Cixous (2014) also advocated that women should take the female body as the starting point for subjectivity, because the female body provides a means to resist the law of the father and women's specification in a masculinized discourse. This is because women do not have to be defined in reference to the phallus, which Cixous argues is inevitable when subjectivity is reduced to the binary opposition of man/woman. Like Derrida (2001), Cixous believed that all dualisms are hierarchical. According to Kristeva (1986) this is because femininity, being excluded, can only ever negatively define subjectivity, which is always already encoded as masculine. Kristeva goes further than Irigary and Cixous to challenge the idea that gender difference is foundational. According to Kristeva there is no essence to femininity, rather there is only positionality. Kristeva therefore resists the notion, as posited by Cixous, that there is an authentic, body-based *l'ecriture feminine* that can act as a revolutionary force to resist masculinized language structures. Indeed, Kristeva does not see language as having any stable meaning. Subjectivity is therefore also destabilized. For Kristeva, gender differences only exist on entry into the symbolic order, and hence femininity and sexuality are linguistically driven, rather than biologically determined: even if they feel natural and inevitable.

Althusser (1971) also sought to challenge the assumption of a natural social order. He argued that dominant beliefs about gender perpetuate because people fail to recognize that their felt sense of self is achieved via psychosocial processes of identification. Althusser argues that people learn to recognize themselves as "subjects" (whether immanent or lacking) through establishing an imaginary relationship with their social network and the ideological knowledges therein that hail or interpellate them. Dominant power interests that structure ideological knowledge, and which organize the unconscious, therefore, are reinforced through ensuring that people come to overlook how their identities are always under construction. Foucault (1926–1984) developed a genealogical approach within structuralism in order to track how these regimes of truth, which serve to regulate gendered bodies, are socially constructed through language. Foucault (1978) reinvests subjectivity, by arguing that the subject is not an object set in opposition to society. Rather power/knowledge systems both regulate bodies and reinforce gender hierarchies, and invest and generate them too.

FEMINIST CRITIQUES AND POSTSTRUCTURALISM

The recognition that language does not simply reflect the social world, but rather constructs it gave rise to a variety of feminist critiques of structural determinism, and paved the way for feminist poststructuralist approaches. This led some (*pace* Derrida) to reject the search for unity and to search for contradiction and tension within social texts. This deconstructive turn signaled the "death of the author" as meaning began to be understood not simply as being derived from that which is written/said but in reference to how it is interpreted too.

For example, Rubin (1975) reinterpreted Lévi-Strauss's analysis of gendered kinship systems, refuting the idea of naturalized gender archetypes. Rather the subordination of women is understood to be an effect of culture rather than an invariant biological given on which culture rests. Rubin, therefore, argues that gender difference is a pernicious construct because sex/gender systems in patriarchal societies iterate and naturalize inequality through, for example, the exchange of women in marriage. Female subjugation is perpetuated through engaging in these gendered social activities and through a process of internalization via the unconscious mind. Rubin's work, and that of the above feminist and constructionist structural theorists, paved the way for an increasingly deconstructive account of sexuality and gender, in which marginality took center stage and naturalized, universalized, or normalized concepts of identity were critiqued. Such approaches share with the Lacanian feminists a skepticism about phallocentric language and social structures, while also going further to reject all metanarratives of gender and sexuality. Such approaches directly challenge the modernist assumption of an objective world, and with this the implication of any singular understanding of gender and sexuality, or the automatic right of any one group (of women, men, etc.) to define the truth about sex and gender.

Feminist appropriation of poststructuralism coincided with significant upheaval within Westernized feminism. It marked the transition from the second wave to the third wave of feminism. The first wave of feminism occurred in the late nineteenth and early twentieth centuries and focused on women's suffrage within urbanized environments. The second wave began in the 1960s, crescendoed in the 1970s, and gradually dissipated through the 1980s. Again, it was located in Westernized economies that were witnessing the emergence of a number of social liberation movements (the women's movement, gay pride, and black power) that first demanded equality, then recognized the need for autonomy, and finally as the third wave took shape called for deconstruction. The third phase in which feminist critiques of structuralism primarily emerged and can be situated arose out of a concern with differences between women and in response to criticisms that feminism and "the women's movement" excluded more women than it contained. Women's identity was increasingly coming under critical scrutiny.

Butler (1990) argued that the fiction of a stable gendered identity is achieved through performative reiteration of society's norms and values. However, the mimetic effects of performativity are concealed by theories that locate biological sex as a story of the origins of identity. This is because biology obscures the social production of subjectivity and the normalizing effects of constructing gender in this way. Hence, from this perspective the assumption of gender as foundational to both normative and critical political practices is problematized. Even feminist theories which essentialize (gender) differences ultimately reproduce that which they seek to transform. Therefore, for Butler, identity must always remain open as a site of political contestation, so that normative versions of sex, gender, and desire can be resisted and subverted.

Alongside Butler, theorists such as De Lauretis (1991) drew on the notion of performative resistance to challenge heteronormative discourses by focusing on non-heteronormative sexual identities and practices. This approach became known as queer theory and its aim was to unsettle the naturalized and expected relationships between sex/gender identity and sexual practices/desire. There is recognition that social institutions deploy power to position both dominant and deviant sexualities in fixed identity categories that reify each other. Queer theory thus provides a critical and sustained engagement with explicating how sex/gender identity and desire is always under construction and how cultural constraint operates via dominant social institutions that signify and shape how sex/gender identity can be apprehended and understood. From this perspective, because identity is thought to be performative rather than essential, parodic identities, such as butch/femme, drag, and cross-dressing, are understood to subvert heteronormativity precisely because they demonstrate the contingent and imitative structure of sex and gender (Butler 1990). Queer theory therefore represents a challenge to the heteronormative phallocentric order because it embraces multiplicity and thereby again disinvests gender as the starting point for politics and life.

Many feminists took issue with the decentering of gender. There was concern that such approaches appeared to deny the reality of women's experiences, which seemed to imply that if there was no shared identity there could be no collective action (e.g., Benhabib 1990). And an emphasis on gender-as-performance (*pace* Butler) seemed to trivialize and underestimate the constraining effects of socially constructed femininity. Finally, too much emphasis seemed to have been placed on the politics of pleasure, rather than the iniquities of abuse and cultural erasure. Yet some poststructuralist feminists have focused their attention on sexual abuse (e.g., Warner 2009). Such feminists argued that child sexual abuse was not denied by acknowledging its social construction through language. Rather, understanding language use was seen as central to exposing the deployment of privilege and (gendered) power within sexually abusive relationships.

At the same time that queer theory reimagined sex/gender identity, and various theorists reconsidered sexual violence, a sustained attempt was also being made to rethink race, culture, and colonialism. This was heralded by critical concern with the politics of representation. For example, Mohanty (1984) argued that when Westernized feminists wrote about third world women they often discursively recolonized them by reducing their material and historical heterogeneities to an amorphous unifying Other. Spivak (1993) developed this critique further to explicate how subjugated persons, such as third world women, not only have their experiences appropriated but are concomitantly often denied the right to speak about themselves. As the silenced Other, the subaltern's experiences can only ever reflect and reveal the vested interests of the Westernized speaking subjects who seek to represent her.

Crenshaw (1993), among others, attempted to address the problem of representational marginalization by developing a critical theory of race that emphasized the intersectionality of different identity formations. Crenshaw recognized that race and gender do not function independently of each other, but culturally interact to produce complex intersectional subjects. As such, she demonstrated how processes of subordination and privilege create and maintain social hierarchies and structure individual subjectivity. Intersectional theory illuminates the too frequent erasure of the multiply marginalized (e.g., black women) in single issues groups (e.g., women's groups or black and minority ethnic/BME groups). Intersectional theorists not only argue for the need to recognize the interactive effects of multiple stratification, but also note that where there is multiple oppression there is also greater insight and knowledge. This is because persons so positioned are ideally placed to identify positive and negative aspects of partial membership of multiple groups. Thus, BME women are primed to recognize racism in women's organizing and sexism within BME groupings. In its commitment to valorizing subjugated standpoints, intersectionality theory has been critiqued for reinstating materialism. Yet the valorization of marginalization does not necessitate a return to materialism.

Haraway (1991) articulates a poststructuralist version of standpoint theory. According to Haraway, knowledge is not located in stable subjects (female or BME, for example), but in positions of subjugation. For Haraway subjugation affords clarity of perspective because subjugated subjects are able to access subjugated knowledges, as well as dominant ideologies that are available to all. Those in privileged positions have little need to process, and therefore limited access to, subjugated perspectives which would otherwise enrich understanding. Haraway rejects being nowhere (as in modernism) and everywhere (as in relativism) in favor of speaking from somewhere – however mobile this polyvocal standpoint is. This type of poststructuralist theory avoids the relativist trap of mistaking epistemological equivalence for structural and political equality: not all marginalized voices have the same value.

CURRENT CONCERNS IN THEORY, RESEARCH, AND PRACTICE

Feminist contestations of (post) structuralism have sustained concern with illuminating, articulating, and problematizing marginality in theory, research, and practice. For some this has continued the focus on the micro-politics of self-defined individual acts of performative resistance. This has instigated an anti-academic character to some third-wave feminist theorizing that can be characterized as a do-it-yourself approach, supported by ready access to and use of the Internet (Wlodarczyk 2010). For some younger Westernized feminists, the structural impact of widespread feminism has always provided the backdrop to their lives and therefore is hardly noticed (Baumgardner and Richards 2000). Yet there is also evidence of a resurgent commitment to addressing macro-structural inequalities that shape abuse and oppression. While feminism can still be collectivized, it is more about where one speaks from, rather than who one is. This is about epistemological, rather than ontological integrity.

Recent activisms reflect a poststructuralist concern with subverting signs and resisting heteronormative specification. This is typified by the North American Riot Grrrl movement in the 1990s and more recently in the slut walks of the early 2010s. Riot Grrrl punk musicians used their writings politically to challenge gender-based violence, advocate for women's emancipation, while recognizing diverse routes toward this. As with previous generations it can be argued that the rebellious ethic of the Riot Grrrl movement was neutered as radical opposition gave way to mainstream commodification. Like the Reclaim the Night marches of the 1970s and 1980s that asserted that women out at night are not asking to be raped, SlutWalks protest "rape culture" which suggests that what women wear and how women look can be used, at least partially, to explain why rape happens. Although there have been numerous criticisms of the name, focus, and potentially exclusionary politics of SlutWalks, it has been one of the most successful global feminist activisms of recent years.

Feminism, in research and activism, is currently enjoying a renaissance. The dissolution of belief in an interior and stable gendered identity and a more mobile reading of semiotics did give rise to an individually focused post-feminist age. Yet there has been a return to a concern with collectivized action centered on feminist identity (however mobile that is). Wlodarczyk argues that paradoxically the rejection of feminism, engendered in the deconstructive turn which typified the 1990s, opened up a space in which femininity could be rediscovered. And it is this embodied engagement with gender that has heralded the more recent return to feminism and the semiotics of representation, of finding voice and claiming social space, and an ongoing concern with analyzing inequality, oppression, and marginalization.

SEE ALSO: Critical Race Theory; Feminism, Poststructural; Feminisms, First, Second, and Third Wave; Queer Theory

REFERENCES

Althusser, L. 1971. *Lenin and Philosophy and Other Essays*, London: New Left Books.

Baumgardner, J., and A. Richards. 2000. *Manifesta: Young Women, Feminism, and the Future*, New York: Farrar, Strauss and Giroux.

Benhabib, S. 1990. "Epistemologies of Postmodernism: A Rejoinder to Jean-Francois Lyotard." In *Feminism/Postmodernism*, edited by L. Nicholson. London: Routledge.

Butler, J. 1990. *Gender Trouble: Feminism and the Subversion of Identity*. London: Routledge.

Cixous, H. 2014. "The Laugh of the Medusa Source," trans. K. Cohen and P. Cohen. *Signs*, 1(4): 875–893.

Crenshaw, K. 1993. "Mapping the Margins: Intersectionality, Identity Politics and Violence against Women of Color." *Stanford Law Review*, 43(6): 1241–1299.

De Lauretis, T. 1991. "Queer Theory: Lesbian and Gay Sexualities." *Differences*, 3(2): iii–xviii.

Derrida, J. 2001. *Writing and Difference*. London: Routledge.

Foucault, M. 1978. *The History of Sexuality. Volume 1: The Will to Knowledge*. Harmondsworth, UK: Penguin.

Haraway, D. 1991. *Simions, Cyborgs and Women: The Reinvention of Nature*. New York: Routledge.

Irigaray, L. 1985. *The Sex Which Is Not One*, trans. C. Burke and C. Porter. New York: Cornell University Press. First published 1977. Accessed September 10, 2015, at http://caringlabor.files.wordpress.com/2010/11/irigaray-this-sex-which-is-not-one.pdf.

Kristeva, J. 1986. *The Kristeva Reader*, edited by Toril Moi. New York: Columbia University Press. Accessed September 10, 2015, at https://archive.org/stream/TheKristevaReader/The%20Kristeva%20Reader#page/n1/.

Lacan, J. 2006. *Ecrits: The First Complete Edition in English*, London: Norton.

Lévi-Strauss, C. 1968. *Structural Anthropology*. London: Allen Lane.

Mohanty, C. T. 1984. "Under Western Eyes: Feminist Scholarship and Colonial Discourses." *Boundary*, 2(12/13): 333–358.

Rubin, G. 1975. "The Traffic in Women: Notes on the 'Political Economy' of Sex." In *The Second Wave: A Reader in Feminist Theory*, edited by L. Nicholson, 27–62. London: Routledge.

Spivak, G. C. 1993. "Can the Subaltern Speak?" In *Discourse and Post-Colonial Theory*, edited by P. Williams and L. Chrisman, 66–111. London: Harvester Wheatsheaf.

Warner, S. 2009. *Understanding the Effects of Child Sexual Abuse: Feminist Revolutions in Theory, Research and Practice*. London: Routledge.

Wlodarczyk, J. 2010. *Ungrateful Daughters: Third Wave Feminist Writing*. Newcastle upon Tyne: Cambridge Scholar's Writing.

Subaltern

MIEKE VERLOO
Radboud University, The Netherlands

Subaltern as a concept is best understood as related to issues of domination and power, democracy and citizenship, resistance and transformation. According to Gayatri Chakravorty Spivak, *subalternity* is a position without identity, a position "*where social lines of mobility, being elsewhere, do not permit the formation of a recognizable basis of action*" (Spivak 2005, 476). Originally used as just meaning lower status, the term was used more metaphorically and politically by Antonio Gramsci (1971) to describe and analyze the political and historical dynamics of subordinated social classes, using examples of groups such as slaves, peasants, religious groups, women, different races, and the proletariat as subaltern social groups. For Gramsci, the ultimate goal was to transform the subordination of subaltern social groups, through writing and analyzing the histories of different subaltern groups and contributing to the development of historical understandings of potential strategies for such transformation. During his time in prison, he developed the outline of such understandings, always starting from historical analysis, stressing explicitly the crucial necessity of broad alliances of subaltern groups, the need for developing new conceptions of cultural values, social relations, and state that transcend the hegemonic legitimizations of existing domination in order for a postsubaltern state to be possible.

Subsequently, the notion of the subaltern has been adapted in a game-changing intervention in the writing of South Asian history by a group of historians producing the Subaltern Studies series (Guha 1982–1985). The work of this group is at the base of the later and current adoption of the concept of subaltern or subalternity in postcolonial studies. Criticizing not only mainstream historiography about former South Asian colonies, but also Marxist inspired history writing that saw only a development of class consciousness in these contexts for silencing the non-elite people actually living there, they set out to create an intellectual and political space for the experiences of subaltern people. In recovering history on behalf of the dominated masses, they intended to recuperate the agency of subaltern people, studying the ways they practiced living with and resisting the dominations that they were entangled in. While their purpose was to create presences instead and out of the previously existing silences and absences, intervening in knowledge creation as well as in political practice, they in their turn have been criticized. The criticism especially targeted what is still one of the most crucial frictions in any scholarly endeavor about social and political domination and the possibilities of resistance and transformation: how to combine acknowledging the subordinating effects of hegemonic power on subjectivities and actions with the conceptualization of subaltern groups as autonomous agents that can change the course of history and disallow social relations in which one group dominates others.

Gayatri Chakravorty Spivak (1988), in her seminal work "*Can the subaltern speak?*", addressed exactly this problem, exposing how the Subaltern Studies group too readily assumes autonomy for subaltern groups and essentializes them. According to Spivak, there is no unproblematically constituted subaltern identity that can be derived simply from the position of a group in a stratification scheme. In fact, such identity or subjectivity is already constructed by the imperialist project, and in this context of colonial production, the subaltern cannot speak, and "the subaltern as female is even more deeply deeper in the shadow" (p. 287). Spivak argues for the strategic use of essentialism, but with a permanent awareness of the dangerousness of this. In her own analysis of the practice of sati (widow sacrifice) reform by the British colonial rulers, she navigates carefully, in an ongoing process of critiquing colonial discourse, to make visible where, when, and how this practice did and did not involve agency for Indian widows. Criticizing first world philosophers such as Michel Foucault and Gilles Deleuze, Spivak exposes their false claim that they can be the "absent nonrepresenter who lets the oppressed speak for themselves" (p. 292), when they are unwilling to acknowledge and question their own subjectivity and privilege as constructed by the imperialist project.

Spivak's comprehensive analysis of the subaltern combined with her meta-analysis of the role of first and third world intellectuals in studying the subaltern has been taken up across a wide range of disciplines: history, philosophy, and literature, but also social and political sciences. In line with her critique of first world scholarship and theory, her work, and the concept of the subaltern or of subalternity is highly present across disciplines studying geopolitics (Roy 2011), social movements in the context of globalization (Escobar 2001), and in area studies focusing on South Asia or the Global South, making the concept of the subaltern a core concept in postcolonial studies (Ashcroft, Griffiths, and Tiffin 2013). Her work is also prominently part of feminist theory in her theorizing of the subaltern as female (Hennessy 1993). Based on Spivak's theoretization, one can problematize, as she does, many well intended Western interventions by international civil society or by counter-globalist resistances as "philanthropy without democracy" or as "feudality without feudalism," because of the failure of these interventions to end subalternity and to learn from and give a voice to subaltern groups. One of the most interesting theoretical cross-overs is done by Nancy Fraser, who elaborated on the conditions for subaltern counter-publics to be able to find spaces where they can "invent and circulate counter discourses which in turn permit them to formulate oppositional interpretations of their identities, interests and needs" (Fraser 1990, 67). Fraser's work puts the concept of the subaltern firmly with debates on democracy and citizenship, hoping for a way that, as Spivak would say "unrecognizable resistance becomes recognizable" (Spivak 2005, 478).

SEE ALSO: Essentialism; Feminism, Postcolonial; Identity Politics; Indigenous Knowledges and Gender; NGOs and Grassroots Organizing; Postcolonialism, Theoretical and Critical Perspectives on; Strategic Essentialism; Suttee (Sati); White Supremacy and Gender

REFERENCES

Ashcroft, Bill, Gareth Griffiths, and Helen Tiffin. 2013. *Postcolonial Studies: The Key Concepts*. New York: Routledge.

Escobar, Arturo. 2001. "Culture Sits in Places: Reflections on Globalism and Subaltern Strategies of Localization." *Political Geography*, 20: 139–174.

Fraser, Nancy. 1990. "Rethinking the Public Sphere: A Contribution to the Critique of Actually Existing Democracy." *Social Text*, 25/26: 56–80.

Gramsci, Antonio. 1971. *Selections from the Prison Notebooks of Antonio Gramsci*, trans. and edited by Q. Hoare and G. Nowell-Smith. New York: International Publishers.

Guha, Ranajit, ed. 1982–1985. "Subaltern Studies." In *Writings on South Asian History and Society*, vol. I, viii, 241; vol. II, x, 358; vol. III, x, 327; vol. IV, vi, 383. Delhi: Oxford University Press.

Hennessy, Rosemary, ed. 1993. *Materialist Feminism and the Politics of Discourse (RLE Feminist Theory)*. New York: Routledge.

Roy, Ananya. 2011. "Slumdog Cities: Rethinking Subaltern Urbanism." *International Journal of Urban and Regional Research*, 35: 223–238.

Spivak, Gayatri C. 1988. Can the Subaltern Speak? In *Marxism and the Interpretation of Culture*, edited by Cary Nelson and Larry Grossberg, 271–313, Chicago: University of Illinois Press.

Spivak, Gayatri C. 2005. "Scattered Speculations on the Subaltern and the Popular." *Postcolonial Studies*, 8: 475–486.

FURTHER READING

Green, Marcus. 2002. "Gramsci Cannot Speak: Presentations and Interpretations of Gramsci's Concept of the Subaltern." *Rethinking Marxism*, 14: 1–24.

O'Hanlon, Rosalind. 1988. "Recovering the Subject Subaltern Studies and Histories of Resistance in Colonial South Asia." *Modern Asian Studies*, 22: 189–224.

Spivak, Gayatri Chakravorty. 1999. *A Critique of Postcolonial Reason: Toward a History of the Vanishing Present*. Cambridge, MA: Harvard University Press.

Suffrage

BEATRICE HALSAA
University of Oslo, Norway

"Woman has the right to mount the scaffold, so she should have the right equally to mount the rostrum," insisted the French revolutionary Olympe de Gouge in her *Declaration of the Rights of Woman and of the Citizen* (1791). At that time, "citizens" referred to men only, and "coverture" (DuBois 1998) gave husbands exclusive power over their wives. de Gouge's early plea for women's suffrage was brushed aside, however, and she was beheaded in 1793 (Offen 2000, 52–59), but her words have survived.

Claims for women's citizenship, including the right to vote, re-emerged in Europe during the revolutionary mid-eighteenth century, when feminism as a social movement was formed. Gradually, suffrage evolved as a core feminist demand, and before the turn of the century, mobilized women, and some men, in a number of states worldwide. The timing, strategies and outcome of the struggles depended on the particular sociopolitical context, but periods of general political mobilization have been beneficial: women have obtained political skills, resources, networks and alliances through participation in other movements. Thus, broad support for women's suffrage coincided with struggles such as the anti-slavery movement in the mid-eighteenth century, the working-class movement since the late eighteenth century, and the national liberation movements of former colonies since World War II.

In no state have women been enfranchised before men. Women's right to vote has generally been more limited than men's, whether this was restricted to property holders, to members of a racial, ethnic or religious group, to level of education, and so forth.

Universal suffrage has been adopted in fits and starts. In Australia, New Zealand, Finland, and Norway, it occurred before World War I; in Oman, Kuwait, and Saudi Arabia, it happened during the last 10 years; and in-between, only 15 more states by 1920; another 24 by 1945; 32 more up to 1955, 47 new states by 1965, and a further 15 states since.

Scale and political system matter: suffrage was often granted at local or state level, before the national or federal level (some Swedish women could vote in local elections from the 1860s). Universal suffrage has generally been delayed in states with bicameral systems, such as the United States, Britain, and France, owing to more conservative voices in the upper house.

Woman's suffrage has always been a transnational movement (DuBois 1998). For example, the British women's Chartist campaign for universal suffrage in 1838 inspired women in the US anti-slavery campaign who inscribed it in the "Declaration of Sentiments" at Seneca Falls in 1848. This declaration was embraced by French suffragists who were in turn acknowledged by the American feminists (Dubois 1991), and so on. John Stuart Mill's seminal book *The Subjection of Women* (1869) was quickly translated into Japanese and other languages, and boosted suffragist movements (Rossi 1974). The militant suffragettes in England attracted worldwide attention at the beginning of the twentieth century; for example, in China in 1912, women stormed the parliamentary chambers and smashed the windows, consciously imitating British suffragettes (Edwards 2000).

Suffrage has been transformative because the demand contradicted claims of women's fragile and subservient nature, and set a radical new standard for women as citizens. But the vote was also an agonizing, contentious issue. Suffragists have had to maneuver within a complex set of ideas of women as equal and/or different from men, and to negotiate opposing loyalties to class, race, and political party.

The tactical choice between demands for suffrage on the same, limited terms as men, or universal suffrage, caused painful organizational splits. The principal motives were mixed with class interests whether the vote was restricted by income/marriage, race, age and/or education. Where property and taxation were crucial requirements, and married women were denied access to property, class and marriage were fundamentally intertwined. In Britain, this was the major issue in a lengthy struggle, during which suffrage was gradually extended in relation to marriage, income, and education between 1869 and 1928.

Women's suffrage was a class issue, but it was not merely a bourgeois claim (DuBois 1998). Although leading socialist women argued fiercely against collaboration with bourgeois feminists, they supported women's universal suffrage from the 1890s, and also established autonomous women's organizations. They wanted to stop non-socialist women from becoming too influential among working-class women; and they were afraid that limited suffrage would benefit the interests of middle-class women only. Many individual socialist women, however, supported limited suffrage, which was often the only feasible strategy.

Race was another major issue in the early suffrage movements (Hannam et al. 2000; Sulkunen et al. 2009). The US Civil War had made the Black vote possible, but not certain, and abolitionist leaders thought that mixing Black and women's suffrage would "doom Negro suffrage to failure" (Banks 1981, 134). Thus, the alliance between suffragism and the anti-slavery campaign came to a halt. When the Fourteenth Amendment (1868) enfranchised black Americans, it caused a split between those women and men who were in favor, and those who opposed it because women would then be the only disenfranchised group. In Australia, "white" women were enfranchised in 1894, indigenous women only in 1949; and in South Africa, white women had the vote in 1930, but black women did not until 1994.

Since the French Revolution, women's vote has been justified by references to universal human rights. With the growth of the suffrage movement, however, mixed references to women's difference from men, their role as mother, and their perceived moral superiority were also embraced. Equality and difference could be opposing ideas, but more often they existed simultaneously as expressions of the different interests and identities involved. The suffragists had to negotiate their claims in relation to their specific time and place, opportunities and constraints.

The demand for suffrage was met with stubborn resistance, and for many years, the protagonists were far outnumbered by the adversaries. The basic counter-arguments were echoed around the world: women's vote would undermine men's privileges; it would ruin the patriarchal family; citizenship was fundamentally contrary to women's place; women were too different from men to vote; women were not equipped with sufficient reason or were simply too silly. Women's vote was also opposed for economic reasons; for example, in Britain and the United States where brewers and the liquor interests engaged in fierce anti-suffrage campaigns (Banks 1981). Generally, liberals against suffrage thought that women's vote would move the political center to the right; conservatives were worried about a liberal or socialist turn.

Suffrage was not necessarily the outcome of prolonged, militant mobilization, however. Contrary to Britain, where militant suffragettes and less radical suffragists fought for decades, peaceful campaigns were successful elsewhere, such as in New Zealand (1893), Australia (1902), Norway (1913), and Sweden (1921). In some states, suffrage was granted without much struggle, as in Turkey where the president promoted suffrage in 1934 as part of the democratization process (Abadan-Unat 1994).

In order for suffrage to be a real right, women must have freedom of speech and of organization during free elections. The right to vote is a political right, and as such it is not won once and for all. In times of war and revolutions, the right to vote does not exist, for example, Spanish women lost their citizenship during the Franco dictatorship 1936–1976, and Afghan women lost the right to vote during the Taliban regime 1996–2001.

SEE ALSO: Anti-Racist and Civil Rights Movements; Class, Caste, and Gender; Democracy and Democratization; Empowerment; Feminisms, Postmodern; Gender Equality; Gender, Politics, and the State: Overview; History of Women's Rights in International and Comparative Perspective; Human Rights and Gender; Politics of Representation; Women's Political Representation

REFERENCES

Abadan-Unat, Nermin, and Oya Tokgöz. 1994. "Turkish Women as Agents of Social Change in a Pluralist Democracy." In *Women and Politics Worldwide*, edited by B. J. Nelson and N. J. Chodorow. New Haven/London: Yale University Press.

Banks, Olive. 1981. *Faces of Feminism. A Study of Feminism as a Social Movement*. Oxford: Martin Robertson.

DuBois, Ellen C. 1998. *Woman Suffrage and Women's Rights*. New York: New York University Press.

Edwards, Louise. 2000. "Women's Suffrage in China: Challenging Scholarly Conventions." *Pacific Historical Review*, 69(4): 6617–6638.

Hannam, June, Katherine Holden, and Mitzi Auchterlonie, eds. 2000. International Encyclopedia of Women's Suffrage. Santa Barbara: e-book.

Offen, Karen. 2000. *European Feminisms 1700–1950. A Political History*. Stanford: Stanford University Press.

Rossi, Alice S., ed. 1974. *The Feminist Papers*. New York: Bantam Books.

Sulkunen, Irma, Seija-Lenna Nevala-Nurmi, and Pirjo Markkola, eds. 2009. *Suffrage, Gender and Citizenship. International Perspectives on Parliamentary Reforms*. Cambridge: Cambridge Scholars.

Surrogacy

AMRITA PANDE
University of Cape Town, South Africa

Surrogacy is a term commonly used for the practice of assisted reproduction in which a woman gestates and gives birth to a child for others to raise. There are two types of surrogacy: the first, called traditional surrogacy, involves the surrogate being artificially inseminated with the intended father's sperm. The second, termed gestational surrogacy, is done through in vitro fertilization (IVF), in which the egg of the intended mother or of a donor is fertilized in a petri dish with the sperm of the intended father or of a donor and the embryo is transferred to the surrogate's uterus. If the surrogate receives monetary payment beyond the reimbursement of medical and other reasonable expenses, the arrangement is labeled commercial surrogacy; otherwise, it is referred to as altruistic surrogacy. The appropriateness of the term "surrogacy" itself has been debated by feminists who have argued that this terminology of "surrogate" or substitute and replacement mother suggests that the woman who is gestating and giving birth is somehow less important than the social and/or the genetic mother.

The practice of using another woman to bear a child is not new. Historically women in socially subservient positions, for instance slaves and domestic workers, have served as surrogates. With development in artificial insemination, conception could be delinked from sexual intercourse, making it possible for a man to impregnate a woman without any physical contact. The next step in assisted reproduction – the development of IVF – meant that the genetic mother (the woman who provided the eggs) could be separated from the gestational (surrogate) mother. The separation of the two roles had several effects: it reduced the connections between the surrogate and the baby and was expected to decrease the likelihood of custody battles. It increased the supply of surrogates since women were more willing to become surrogates if the child they were carrying was not genetically related to them. It also expanded the pool of surrogates, particularly to women across national borders, since the intended parents were less interested in the surrogates' characteristics like race, physical appearance, educational background, and so on (Spar 2006).

Surrogacy, especially commercial surrogacy, has been generating feminist, ethical, legal, and social debates for over three decades. Advocates of surrogacy, often following the liberal feminist approach, emphasize a woman's right to use her body as she chooses, and see surrogacy as an avenue of empowerment as well as an opportunity for economically marginalized women to better their situation. Others have highlighted the potential of surrogacy for redefining families and making parenthood feasible for gay couples. But for many other scholars commercial surrogacy is inherently unethical as it allows for the extension of the market into the private and intimate sphere of reproduction. It defies laws of nature, family, and religion, and is perceived to be a commercialization of motherhood, the act of giving birth, and of children. Other critics focus on the potential exploitation of women, especially women from disadvantaged races and class, within surrogacy. The recent ethnographic turn in the literature around surrogacy has served to dispel some of the moral certainty about the need to reject surrogacy practices in the earlier writings and shifted attention to surrogacy as a lived practice, negotiated in complex and varied ways by women in different contexts. The fraught nature of surrogacy becomes more evident when surrogacy involves clients from countries in the Global North hiring economically disadvantaged women in the Global South to bear children for them. There is a burgeoning literature on the rising incidence of such cross-border surrogacy cases. While feminists focus on its potential to stratify reproduction by race, class, and nation, others have debated on its legal dimensions, especially the ambiguous citizenship of children born out of cross-border surrogacy arrangements.

The policy responses of countries reflect the anxieties regarding the future developments in surrogacy. Most countries continue to treat commercial surrogacy with caution. Some countries, like China, France, Germany, Italy, Saudi Arabia, Switzerland, and Turkey, ban surrogacy in all its forms. Some allow altruistic surrogacy, for instance Australia (Victoria), Brazil, Canada, Denmark, Hungary, Mexico, South Africa, and the United Kingdom (Markens 2007). Even the United States, which usually takes a laissez-faire approach to fertility treatments, is more cautious in the context of commercial surrogacy arrangements – surrogacy is not regulated by the federal government but through a combination of legislative actions and court decisions. With the rise in cross-border surrogacy, countries have started recognizing the need to incorporate new complexities in their policies around surrogacy. Some countries, for instance Turkey and Malaysia, prohibit their citizens from crossing borders to obtain surrogacy procedures. Some like France, the United Kingdom, Germany, Spain, and Japan, attempt to discourage their citizens from pursuing surrogacy abroad by withholding legal recognition to such cases (Storrow 2010). There are other countries, Iceland, Norway, and Sweden, for instance, which are currently debating a shift toward a less restrictive approach and allowing altruistic surrogacy at home to discourage their citizens from resorting to cross-border surrogacy.

SEE ALSO: Assisted Reproduction; Fertility Rates; Stratified Reproduction; Wet Nursing

REFERENCES

Markens, Susan. 2007. *Surrogate Motherhood and the Politics of Reproduction.* Berkeley: University of California Press.

Spar, Debora L. 2006. *The Baby Business: How Money, Science, and Politics Drive the Commerce of Conception.* Cambridge, MA: Harvard Business School Publishing.

Storrow, R. F. 2010. "The Pluralism Problem in Cross-Border Reproductive Care." *Human Reproduction*, 25(12): 2939–2943.

FURTHER READING

Gürtin, Z. B., and Inhorn, M. C., eds. 2011. Special Issue Symposium: Cross-Border Reproductive Care – Ethical, Legal, and Socio-Cultural Perspectives. *Reproductive BioMedicine Online*, 23(5).

Hochschild, Arlie. R. 2012. *The Outsourced Self: Intimate Life in Market Times.* New York: Metropolitan Books.

Pande, Amrita. 2014. *Wombs in Labor: Transnational Commercial Surrogacy in India.* New York: Columbia University Press.

Ragoné, Helena. 1994. *Surrogate Motherhood: Conception in the Heart.* Boulder: Westview Press.

Raymond, J. G. 1993. *Women as Wombs: Reproductive Technologies and the Battle over Women's Freedom.* San Francisco: Harper.

Rothman, Barbara K. 2000. *Recreating Motherhood.* New Brunswick: Rutgers University Press.

Thompson, Charis M. 2005. *Making Parents: The Ontological Choreography of Reproductive Technologies.* Cambridge, MA: MIT Press.

Twine, France W. 2011. *Outsourcing the Womb: Race, Class, and Gestational Surrogacy in a Global Market.* New York: Routledge.

Sustainable Livelihoods

WENDY HARCOURT
International Institute of Social Studies, Erasmus University, The Netherlands

Sustainable livelihoods (SL), unlike sustainable development, is a community and people-centered approach to environment and resource management. SL views environmental concerns from a human perspective with a focus on the lives and resources of largely poor rural and marginal urban dwellers. Even though SL acknowledges rural women's importance in sustaining community lives and environments, it has not closely engaged with the debates around gender and sexuality. Running parallel to the SL approach have been feminist political ecology (FPE) and queer ecology (QE).

The SL approach first emerged in the 1970s, evolved during the 1980s, and has been in wide use since the 1990s as both a framework of analysis and an advocacy strategy by researchers, United Nations (UN) agencies, and non-governmental organizations (NGOs) (Krishna 2012). Countering mainstream sustainable development focus on economic growth, the SL view promoted economic and environmental management through participation, equity, and the sustainability of community groups. In this period SL approaches focused on local knowledges in order to understand and support community coping strategies in the face of "the violence of development" (Kothari and Harcourt 2004).

Women's environmental struggles such as the tree-hugging Chipko tree movement in the Himalayan forests of northwest India (Shiva 1988) or the tree-planting Green Belt movement in Kenya (Maathai 2006) are examples often given of women's knowledge and action to sustain livelihoods. But though women were seen as part of SL narratives, gender relations were not examined, nor were sexuality issues seen as part of the power dynamics determining sustainable livelihoods.

One problem of the SL approach was that issues of power and conflict were not taken into account. The gap in SL approaches has been addressed in recent years by focusing on gender decision-making in family and communities, as well as looking directly at power and conflict around SL. This has involved looking at collective political action as a way to bring in women's gendered experience of sexual, cultural, political, and economic subordination. Analyzing collective political action encompasses an understanding of how gender power relations inform the struggle of men and women to sustain ecologically viable livelihoods and community well-being (Argawal 2010). The discussion of rural women's gender power struggles in different settings illustrates how environmental rights and justice are deeply enmeshed in and determined by gender relations, allowing a bridge to be built between SL, FPE, and QE.

The FPE and QE link SL to gender roles and body politics. They examine: the intersection between the environment and the struggle for a healthy and well body; the right to produce, prepare, and consume healthy and culturally appropriate food; the right to reproductive choice and desire; and the gender relations that determine who is caring for the household, the community, and landscape. FPE and QE expand the understanding of SL strategies at both local and global levels to include power struggles around body politics, health, and cultural survival alongside family and community economic needs.

FPE and QE take up an implicit interest in the well-being of the body, community, and culture in environmental struggles not only in the Global South, but as a global phenomenon that encompasses the impact of all peoples' actions on environmental change. They speak of "the interconnectedness of all life and the relevance of power relations including gender relations in decision making about the environment" (Rocheleau, Thomas-Slayter, and Wangari 1996).

FPE and QE approaches look at women's economic and environmental struggles around livelihoods and how they are grounded in embodied realities culturally situated within their own sexual practices, understandings of desire, bodies, and nature (GESEC 2011).

This discussion is deeply informed by Donna Haraway's work on "naturecultures" (Haraway 2003). Haraway states that "nature and culture are tightly knotted in bodies, ecologies, technologies and times" (Haraway 2011). In her work on queer ecology Catriona Mortimer-Sandilands takes Haraway's concept of naturecultures further in her construction of a "queer ecological" sensibility that questions the link between power, sexuality, and gender in humanity's relations with nature (Mortimer-Sandilands 2005).

Mortimer-Sandilands explores how heteronormativity (the way in which gender and sexuality are hierarchically organized in societal structures) informs the understanding of nature. She proposes to queer nature as a way to reinstate diverse experiences of embodiment, including the gendered diversities and sexual expressions of poor rural and urban dwellers.

Bringing in gender and sexuality to SL approaches allows for an honoring of local knowledge(s). It recognizes community struggles to ensure healthy bodies and caring communities in the face of the "violence" of modern development. It brings the SL approach closer to a more balanced and healthy living within the finite resources of humanity's and the Earth's shared commons.

SEE ALSO: Gender and Development; Heteronormativity and Homonormativity; Queer Theory

REFERENCES

Argawal, Bina. 2010. *Gender and Green Governance*. Oxford: Oxford University Press.

GESEC (Gender and Environment Series Editorial Committee). 2011. "Feminist Political Ecology." In *The Women, Gender and Development Reader*, edited by Nalini Visvanathan, Lynn Duggan, Nan Wiegersma, and Laurie Nisonoff. London: Zed Books.

Haraway, Donna. 2003. *The Companion Species Manifesto: Dogs, People, and Significant Otherness*. Chicago: Prickly Paradigm Press.

Haraway, Donna. 2011. "Speculative Fabulations for Technoculture's Generations: Taking Care

of Unexpected Country." *Australian Humanities Review*, 50: 100–107.
Kothari, Smitu, and Wendy Harcourt. 2004. "The Violence of Development." *Development*, 47(1): 1–6.
Krishna, Sumi. 2012. "Sustainable Livelihoods." In *Women Reclaiming Sustainable Livelihoods: Spaces Lost, Spaces Gained*, edited by Wendy Harcourt. London: Palgrave Macmillan.
Maathai, Wangari. 2006. *Unbowed: A Memoir*. New York: Knopf.
Mortimer-Sandilands, Catriona. 2005. "Unnatural Passions: Notes Toward a Queer Ecology." *Invisible Culture*, 10. Accessed June 8, 2015, at https://www.rochester.edu/in_visible_culture/Issue_9/sandilands.html.
Rocheleau, Dianne, Barbara Thomas-Slayter, and Esther Wangari, eds. 1996. *Feminist Political Ecology: Global Issues and Local Experiences*. New York: Routledge.
Shiva, Vandana. 1988. *Staying Alive: Women, Ecology and Development*. London: Zed Books.

Suttee (Sati)

ANDREA MAJOR
University of Leeds, UK

Few practices are as controversial as the Hindu rite of sati/suttee (widow immolation). Literally translated, sati means "virtuous woman" and it is used to denote the Hindu widow who burns on her husband's funeral pyre. In the nineteenth century, the British applied the anglicized form "suttee" to the process of immolation, with the result that sati/suttee is often used to describe both the practice and the practitioner. Although this application of the word to the custom suggests that sati is something that one performs, those who revere sati understand it as something a woman becomes, as *sat* (goodness) accumulated through a lifetime of devotion to her husband finds its ultimate expression in immolation. For some orthodox Hindus, sati is a miraculous and divinely inspired act worthy of veneration; historic and mythic satis are worshipped both in the community at local sati *stals* (shrines), and at major temples such as the Rani Sati temple in Jhunjhunu, which is one of wealthiest in India. For others, however, sati is an act of socially and culturally sanctioned violence, while the ideology behind it is indicative of the subjugation of women inherent in some strands of Hindu tradition. Thus, as the virulent debate that surrounded the immolation of Roop Kanwar in 1987 demonstrates, opinion on sati is polarized between those who believe in the potential for "authentic" (voluntary and/or miraculous) sati, and those who see all sati as murder.

The oldest known historical instance of sati occurred in 316 BCE, when Greek observers recorded the immolation of the wife of Hindu General Keteus during Alexander's invasion of India, although archaeological and literary evidence suggests that the rite long predates this. Although the *Vedas* (4000–1000 BCE) do not refer to sati as an act to be practiced, there is a verse in the *Rg Veda* that has been (mis)quoted by exponents of the rite to prove its Vedic origin. The long tradition of validating it in religious laws began in earnest in the medieval period, however, and the famous passages extolling its virtue (e.g., "she who follows her husband into death dwells in heaven for as many years as there are hairs on a human body, viz., $3\frac{1}{2}$ crores of years" – *Angirasa*, c.700 CE), date from around 600 CE onwards. Although the origins of sati are obscure, growing support for it within Hindu legal and religious texts in this period may have been a response to contemporaneous calls for improved inheritance rights for women in Bengal, high levels of widowhood among some caste groups, and an emerging *kshatriya* warrior tradition in Rajasthan that used sati to emphasize elite social and ritual status. While explorations of the textual origins of sati have emphasized its scriptural and social sanction, it is important to note that there was also a strong tradition of opposition to the rite, from Banabhatta and Medhatithi to Raja Rammohan Roy and Gandhi.

In modern times, sati has become a site of political and cultural conflict for groups within India, and beyond. In the colonial period, sati became a key trope in Western accounts of India that emphasized the rite as a "barbaric oriental custom" and used its presence, and eventual prohibition by the British in 1829, to justify colonial rule. Indeed, Lata Mani has argued that British preoccupation with sati in the early nineteenth century was less about burning women than it was about defining the parameters of colonial control and extending it into the social, cultural, and religious world of the colonized – an interpretation that emphasizes the political nature of the sati debate, and challenges traditional image of Bentinck's regulation on sati as one of the crowning glories of the so-called "civilizing mission" (Mani 1998). The British prohibition of sati did not eradicate the custom, or its veneration, however, and isolated cases of sati continued to occur, both before and after Independence.

The most high-profile case of sati of the late twentieth century was that of Roop Kanwar in 1987. Although only one of a series of immolations in postcolonial India, Kanwar's sati provoked a particularly intense debate between those who presented the sati as part of a glorified version of Hindu (and specifically Rajput) tradition and culture, and those who opposed the act as murder and saw its veneration as another indicator of Indian women's oppression. Doubts surrounding the nature of Kanwar's complicity in the sati raised fundamental questions about a widow's right over her own life and about the nature of religious and societal structures that might make her wish to end it, while the glorification of event by some groups raised questions about the role of "religious tradition" in a modern, secular state, in the context of emergent Hindu nationalism. Debates about sati in both colonial and postcolonial period India thus go far beyond the tragic deaths of individual women, raising fundamental questions about the politicized nature of tradition, identity, and belief.

SEE ALSO: Hinduism; Colonialism and Gender

REFERENCE

Mani, Lata. 1998. *Contentious Traditions: the Debate on Sati in Colonial India, 1780-1833*. Berkeley: University of California Press.

FURTHER READING

Bose, Mandakranta. 2000. "Sati: The Event and the Ideology." In *Faces of the Feminine in Ancient, Medieval and Modern India*, edited by Mandakranta Bose, 21–32. New York: Oxford University Press.

Fisch, Joerg. 2006. *Burning Women: a Global History of Widow Sacrifice from Ancient Times to the Present*. New York: Seagull.

Hardgrove, Anne. 1999. "Sati Worship and Marwari Public Identity in India." *Journal of Asian Studies*, 58(3): 723–752.

Loomba, Ania. 1993. "Dead Women Tell No Tales: Issues of Female Subjectivity, Subaltern Agency and Tradition in Colonial and Post-Colonial Writings on Widow Immolation in India." *History Workshop Journal*, 36(1): 209–227.

Major, Andrea. 2006. *Pious Flames: European Encounters with Sati, 1500–1830*. New Delhi: Oxford University Press.

Major, Andrea. 2007. *Sati: an Historical Anthology*. New Delhi: Oxford University Press.

Major, Andrea. 2011. *Sovereignty and Social Reform: the British Campaign Against Sati in the Princely States, 1830–1860*. Abingdon, UK: Routledge.

Narasimhan, Sakuntala. 1998. *Sati, a Study of Widow Burning in India*. New Delhi: Viking Penguin Books.

Oldenburg, Veena Talwar. 1994. "The Roop Kanwar Case: Feminist Responses." In *Sati: the Blessing and the Curse*, edited by John Stratton

Hawley, 101–130. New York: Oxford University Press.

Vaid, Sudesh, and Kumkum Sangari. 1991. "Institutions, Beliefs, Ideologies: Widow Immolation in Contemporary Rajastan." *Economic and Political Weekly*, 26(17): WS2–WS18.

Weinberger-Thomas, Catherine. 1999. *Ashes of Immortality*. Chicago: University of Chicago Press.

Yang, Anand A. 1989. "Whose Sati? Widow Burning in Early 19th Century India." *Journal of Women's History*, 1(2): 8–33.

Taboo

KEITH ALLAN
Monash University, Australia

The word *taboo* derives from the Tongan *tabu* which came to notice toward the end of the eighteenth century. Taboos are proscriptions of behavior arising out of social constraints on the individual's behavior where it is perceived to be a potential cause of discomfort, harm, or injury. People are at metaphysical risk when dealing with sacred persons, objects, and places; they are at physical risk from powerful earthly persons, dangerous creatures, disease, and contaminated food. A person's soul or bodily effluvia (sweat, feces, menstrual fluid, etc.) may put them at metaphysical, moral, or physical risk and may contaminate others; a social act may breach constraints on politic and/or polite behavior. Infractions of taboos can lead to illness or death as well as to the lesser penalties of corporal punishment, incarceration, social ostracism, or mere disapproval. Even an unintended contravention of taboo risks condemnation and censure; generally, people avoid tabooed behavior unless they intend to violate a taboo.

Religious ideology is a fecund source for taboo with dire consequences for transgressors. According to the Bible, God told Moses "You shall not permit a sorceress to live" (Exodus 22:18); implementing scripture, hundreds of heretics and witches were burned in Europe when Christianity had unfettered political power. Under some Islamic regimes the shari'a is interpreted to rule that a woman who commits adultery can be stoned to death.

Killing people is taboo in most societies. Nevertheless, human sacrifice has been practiced to propitiate gods or natural forces that it was thought would otherwise harm the community. Killing enemies is normally approved and judicial execution of traitors and murderers is common. Some Islamists believe that blowing themselves up along with a few infidels leads to Paradise. The Bible sanctions execution for murder in Exodus 21:12 and the wartime murder of males and abduction of females in Numbers 25 and 31 – still common practice in today's world.

There are taboos in which notions of uncleanliness are the motivating factor. Many communities forbid contact with a corpse such that no one who has touched the cadaver is permitted to handle food. More pervasive is that very many communities forbid physical contact with a menstruating woman, believing it pollutes males. Across the world, many places of worship forbid menstruating women because they would defile holy sites.

Genital mutilation, often referred to as "circumcision," is practiced on both males and females. It is usually perpetrated by

The Wiley Blackwell Encyclopedia of Gender and Sexuality Studies, First Edition. Edited by Nancy A. Naples.
© 2016 John Wiley & Sons, Ltd. Published 2016 by John Wiley & Sons, Ltd.

adults on children under religious auspices. The excuse, when any is offered, is that it benefits the physiological and moral health of the victim and, thence, the community. In the West, female genital mutilation (FGM) is generally tabooed and often illegal but, until very recently, male genital mutilation has not been seen in the same light – partly because it has long been practiced in the West and partly because removal of the foreskin does not adversely affect male sexual abilities. The situation is very different for FGM, of which there are three types: clitoridectomy (Type I), the added excision of the labia minora (Type II), full infibulation (Type III), which removes part of the labia majora too, leaving nothing of the normal anatomy of the genitalia except for a wall of flesh from the pubis to the anus, with the exception of a pencil-size opening at the inferior portion of the vulva to allow urine and menstrual blood to pass through (World Health Organization 2008). With Type III, the adult woman will often suffer reverse infibulation to allow for sexual intercourse, sometimes effected by the husband using a knife on their wedding night. During childbirth, the enlargement is too small to allow vaginal delivery and so the infibulation must be opened completely by enlarging the vagina with deep episiotomies. Afterwards, the mother will often insist that what is left of her vulva be closed again so that her husband does not reject her nor her friends and family ostracize her.

FGM is described by UNICEF as "one of the worst violations of the Convention on the Rights of the Child" (www.unicef.org/pon96/womfgm.htm) because it is usually performed on girls between the ages of 4 and 8, but up to menarche. FGM is inflicted on about 2 million girls a year, mostly by people with no medical training who perform the cutting without anesthetic, sterilization, or the use of proper medical instruments. The result is often scarring and/or obstructed flow of urine and menstrual blood, which leads to urinary- and reproductive-tract infections and infertility. Infibulated women have a 70 percent increase in postpartum hemorrhage compared to women without FGM.

One motive for FGM is to decrease the risk of female promiscuity, since it reduces and may remove the woman's sexual pleasure – though this is sometimes hotly disputed (Lightfoot-Klein 1989). Infibulation supposedly provides a proof of virginity, which is a necessary condition for marriage in many FGM communities such that men cannot marry uncircumcised women; hence FGM creates an economic advantage by permitting parents to demand a high bridal price. So, the push for a universal prohibition on FGM is unlikely to succeed any time soon.

There is an assumption that both accidental breach and defiance of taboo will be followed by some kind of trouble to the offender, such as lack of success in hunting, fishing, or other business, and the sickness or the death of the offender or one of their relatives. In many communities, a person who meets with an accident or fails to achieve some goal will infer, as will others, that s/he has in some manner committed a breach of taboo. However, those who violate a taboo can often purify themselves or be purified by confessing their sin and submitting to a ritual. For instance, Catholic Christians confess their sins to a priest and are given absolution on behalf of God.

There is no such thing as an absolute taboo – one that holds for all worlds, times, and contexts. *Taboo* refers to a proscription of behavior for a specifiable community of one or more persons at a specifiable time in specifiable contexts. Some taboos are enshrined in legal enforcement such that breaking the law violates a taboo; but social attitudes mutate and laws get repealed or revised as what was once taboo is reevaluated. And, to the contrary, once acceptable behaviors are made illegal as institutionalized taboos. In principle, any kind of behavior can be tabooed. For behavior to be proscribed it must be perceived as in some way harmful to an individual or their community; but the degree of harm can fall anywhere on a scale from a breach of etiquette to downright fatality.

SEE ALSO: Animality and Women; Clitoridectomy, Female Genital Cutting Practices, and Law; Double Standard; Gender Identities and Socialization; Human Rights, International Laws and Policies on; Purity Versus Pollution; Reproductive Health; Sex and Culture

REFERENCES

Lightfoot-Klein, Hanny. 1989. *Prisoners of Ritual: An Odyssey into Female Genital Circumcision in Africa*. Binghamton: Harrington Park Press.

World Health Organization. 2008. Eliminating Female Genital Mutilation: An Interagency Statement – OHCHR, UNAIDS, UNDP, UNECA, UNESCO, UNFPA, UNHCR, UNICEF, UNIFEM, WHO. Geneva: World Health Organization. Accessed July 29, 2015, at http://whqlibdoc.who.int/publications/2008/9789241596442_eng.pdf?ua=1.

FURTHER READING

Allan, Keith, and Kate Burridge. 2006. *Forbidden Words: Taboo and the Censoring of Language*. Cambridge: Cambridge University Press.

Mead, Margaret. 1937. "Tabu." In *Encyclopaedia of Social Sciences*, edited by Edwin Seligman and Alvin Johnson, vol. 7, 502–505. London: Macmillan.

Radcliffe-Brown, Alfred R. 1939. *Taboo*. Cambridge: Cambridge University Press.

Tattooing and Piercing

FRANCES E. MASCIA-LEES
Rutgers University, New Brunswick, USA

Tattooing and piercing are practices of body modification with deep historical roots and wide geographic distribution. Traditionally, they were the scholarly purview of anthropologists and archaeologists focused on their role in non-Western and prehistoric societies and psychologists concerned with them as forms of self-mutilation in Western societies. Today, they are researched by a range of scholars, including sociologists interested in subcultural identity and feminist scholars in body politics.

The oldest tattoo, a permanent mark made by inserting pigment under the skin, and the oldest piercing, an opening made through a body puncture into which jewelry is inserted, belong to Ötzi, the European "Iceman" (3300 BCE). Evidence of tattooing exists for almost every region of the world, suggesting it developed independently in various locations. Piercing of various body parts is widely documented in the archaeological record: for example, there is evidence for ear piercing from Ancient Egypt, nipple piercing from Ancient Rome, genital piercing from Ancient India, tongue piercing from Aztec society, and lip piercing from Africa.

Body modifications have had various functions throughout history and across societies. Anthropologists have documented their central role in initiation ceremonies in many cultures, where tattooing and piercing are symbolic ritual actions that transform young girls or boys into adults. They have also researched their use as body adornments and markers of status, rank, and group affiliation. Historians have revealed multiple uses of tattoos in the past, including among early Celtic Christians who wore them to symbolize religious commitment and Ancient Romans who used them to mark the foreheads of slaves. Tattoos have served as amulets for protection for sailors, marks of bravery for men of the Kalinga in the Philippines, and badges of courage for contemporary women who place them over mastectomy scars.

Differences in meanings of tattooing and piercing are embedded in fundamental differences in ideas about, and experiences of, the body and its relationship to self and society. They cannot be understood without knowledge of the particular cultural context in which they are practiced. Much current scholarship on tattooing and piercing focuses on the renaissance of these practices in European and US society in the last decades of the twentieth century when they moved out of subcultural groups into the mainstream after a long history of fluctuating meanings.

Although tattooing in Europe is old, it experienced a significant resurgence in the eighteenth century when Captain James Cook returned to England from the Pacific Islands where tattooing was widely practiced. It became associated with "primitiveness," and its co-optation was deeply embedded in European colonialism and notions of "otherness." Soon tattoos became signs of adventure and travel as well; in the nineteenth century, they briefly signaled the wealth and leisure of British aristocrats. At the turn of the twentieth century, working-class men in Europe and the United States donned tattoos as symbols of masculinity. Not long after, tattoos emerged as a predominantly US male practice, connected with patriotism and servicemen's devotion to, and love of, their country and the women they left behind. Although several women became famous for their tattoos during the 1920s, few were "inked" outside of the carnival circuit, where they were displayed as "freaks." During this entire period in Europe and the United States, piercing of any body part was uncommon for both men and women; even ear piercing remained largely socially unacceptable for women until the 1960s.

The popularity of tattoos declined in the United States after World War II as they lost patriotic appeal and became associated with bikers and criminals whose body modifications expressed challenges to mainstream values and traditional designs. By the 1970s, tattoos and piercings were increasingly worn by disaffected US middle-class youth searching for symbols of rebellion against society. Precisely because tattooing and piercing have long been associated with non-Western "others" and "outcast" groups, they provided a resource for middle-class individuals to protest parental or larger societal constraints. British punk subcultural style was particularly influential during this time; its rebellious use of razor blades and safety pins in the ears, nose, or mouth was largely responsible for introducing piercing into mainstream US society (Wojcik 1995). The contemporary rage for piercing, especially nipples and genitals, also grew out of the West Coast S&M subculture of the period where it was simultaneously a transgressive act and means to enhance sexual1 pleasure.

The transformation in meanings of body modification during the 1970s to 1990s in the United States was influenced by the anti-war, feminist, and gay rights movements as well as "new class social movements" focused on personal transformation, self-actualization, and spiritual growth (DeMello 2000). A primary motivation for getting tattooed or pierced is to create one's own identity and express individuality. Many US women get tattoos and piercings to protest constraining cultural inscriptions of femininity, using their body as a canvas for self-expression, exerting control over its meaning (Mascia-Lees and Sharpe 1992). The ability of body modifications to also challenge hegemonic meanings of masculinity helps explain their association with the gay rights movement and queer culture. The process of being tattooed or pierced is often significant in people's desire to modify their bodies; it can test their physical endurance and provide them with experiences of personal growth or spiritual transcendence.

By the twenty-first century, tattooing and piercing were deeply enmeshed in consumer culture, part of global fashion, and the subject of numerous scholarly and popular books, museum exhibitions, and documentary films. Today, in the United States, members of all economic classes and age groups have tattoos, as do both sexes, although slightly more US women have them than men (Mifflin 2013). Women's earlobes remain the most frequently pierced body part, followed by the navel.

SEE ALSO: Archaeology and Genealogy; Body Politics; Cross-Cultural Gender Roles; Gender Identification; Initiation Rites; Masculinities

REFERENCES

DeMello, Margo. 2000. *Bodies of Inscription: A Cultural History of the Modern Tattoo Community*. Durham, NC: Duke University Press.

Mascia-Lees, Frances E., and Patricia Sharpe, eds. 1992. *Tattoo, Torture, Mutilation, and Adornment: The Denaturalization of the Body in Culture and Text*. New York: SUNY Press.

Mifflin, Margot. 2013. *Bodies of Subversion: A Secret History of Women and Tattoo*. Brooklyn: Powerhouse Books.

Wojcik, Daniel. 1995. *Punk and Neo-Tribal Body Art*. Jackson: University Press of Mississippi.

FURTHER READING

Atkinson, Michael. 2003. *Tattooed: The Sociogenesis of a Body Art*. Toronto: University of Toronto Press.

Caplan, Jane, ed. 2000. *Written on the Body: The Tattoo in European and American History*. Princeton: Princeton University Press.

Pitts, Victoria. 2003. *In the Flesh: The Cultural Politics of Body Modification*. New York: Palgrave Macmillan.

Romanienko, Lisiunia A. 2011. *Body Piercing and Identity Construction: A Comparative Perspective*. New York: Palgrave Macmillan.

Sanders, Clinton, and D. Angus Vail. 2008. *Customizing the Body: The Art and Culture of Tattooing*. Philadelphia: Pennsylvania University Press.

Vale, Vivian, and Andrea Juno, eds. 1989. *Modern Primitives*. San Francisco: Re/Search Publications.

Tearoom Trade

CHRIS ASHFORD
Northumbria University, UK

The publication of Laud Humphreys' *Tearoom Trade* in 1970 established itself as the first – and to date only – detailed study of sex in public toilets. The ethnographic study originally formed Humphreys's PhD thesis and sought to document men's anonymous sexual encounters in public restrooms, or "tearooms" as they are colloquially known in the United States, "bogs" in New Zealand, or "cottages" in the United Kingdom.

Humphreys performed the role of "watchqueen," ostensibly keeping a lookout for the men in a public convenience, to ensure that they were not surprised by the appearance of an unwitting member of the public or law enforcement agencies. For 2 years, commencing in the spring of 1966, Humphreys surveyed a number of restrooms in St. Louis, Missouri. He observed the men arriving, often via motor vehicles, and recorded their license plate details, along with descriptions of the men and details of their arrival.

It was to be these data, combined with public records, which were to prove one of the most controversial aspects of the study. Humphreys used the combined data to obtain the addresses of the men he had observed and then visited their homes, posing as a survey interviewer. He arrived with a deliberately changed appearance and motor vehicle, and completed 50 interviews through this technique. It is an approach that has ensured Humphreys's work continues to be highlighted as a troubling example of research methods on research ethics courses today.

Humphreys chronicled the "rules and roles" that were experienced in the tearoom, the men who inhabited the sexualized space, and the patterns of action that took place. He sought in *Tearoom Trade* to detail the strategies and ritual, which he suggested could be distilled down to the often-spotted toilet graffiti slogan of "show hard – get sucked."

He divided "players" into two subcategories: the insertee and the insertor. The insertee would be the fellator, the person who has a penis inserted into them (orally or anally). The insertor is the person who does the said inserting. Lookouts (the "watchqueens") can be waiters, masturbators, or voyeurs. Straights were those who did not participate in the "action," although Humphreys suggested that these individuals would melt into one of the other categories.

Teenagers (or "chicken") were divided into straights (as described), enlisters (who watch and learn), toughs (youths who harass other tearoom participants), and hustlers (enlisters who are seeking payment to act as insertors but can become toughs if payment is refused). Finally, Humphreys categorized agents of social control as being vice squad members, park policemen, or other park employees.

Humphreys described a series of stages of behavior that tearoom participants would engage in to pursue a successful sexual encounter and to "hide" that behavior from unwanted attention.

These ritualistic gestures would begin with "approaching," which signifies the initial moves one might make into the tearoom, for example parking a car, or watching from a distance others entering the tearoom. This is followed by "positioning" which is where one positions oneself within the tearoom, or what Humphreys described as "the interaction membrane." This was then followed by "signaling" in which a potential participant would indicate their desire by a form of "casual masturbation," and – especially if a hopeful insertor – step or lean back from the urinal in order to flash his penis to the man stood adjacent at a urinal. "Contracting" describes the next stage in which consent is essentially provided to an encounter. "The payoff," which comprises of the sexual act, follows an optional fifth stage of "foreplay." This is followed by the final stage of "clearing the field" in which the men remove themselves from the scene and might involve the cleaning of their penis or the washing of hands.

The men who frequented tearooms were categorized through a taxonomy that divided men into four types. Type I (trade) who are or have been married and typically undertake the insertor role; type II (ambisexuals) who are typically unmarried and may switch between the role of inserter and insertee; type III (the gay) is unmarried and openly participates in the gay community; and finally type IV (the closet queen) who is unmarried and does not reveal his homosexual identity.

Humphreys developed the concept of "the breastplate of righteousness" in order to describe the ways in which these men would seek to "hide" their behavior from wider society and to present themselves as "respectable members of society." This would typically take the form of marriage (conceptualized in an exclusively heterosexual context) and holding – or at least appear to hold – right wing social and political views.

Tearoom Trade continues to be cited as a key work relating to methodologies and research ethics, but has also influenced a number of more recent academic examinations of public sex (see, for example, Ashford 2006, 2012; Dalton 2012).

SEE ALSO: Sexualities; Sexual Orientation and the Law

REFERENCES

Ashford, Chris. 2006. "The Only Gay in the Village: Sexuality and the Net." *Information and Communications Technology Law*, 15(3): 275–289.
Ashford, Chris. 2012. "Heterosexuality, Public Places and Policing." In *Policing Sex*, edited by Paul Johnson and Derek Dalton, 41–53. London: Routledge.

Dalton, Derek. 2012. "Policing 'Beats' in Australia." In *Policing Sex*, edited by Paul Johnson and Derek Dalton, 67–81. London: Routledge.

Humphreys, L. 1970. *Tearoom Trade: Impersonal Sex in Public Places*. New York: Aldine Transaction.

FURTHER READING

Delph, Edward W. 1978. *The Silent Community: Public Homosexual Encounters*. Beverly Hills: Sage.

Galliher, John F., Wayne H. Brekhus, and David P. Keys. 2004. *Laud Humphreys: Prophet of Homosexuality and Sociology*. Madison: University of Wisconsin Press.

Johnson, Paul, and Derek Dalton, eds. *Policing Sex*. London: Routledge.

Leap, William L., ed. 1999. *Public Sex/Gay Space*. New York: Columbia University Press.

Pry, Paul. 1937. *For Your Convenience*. London: George Routledge & Sons.

Reynolds, Bryan. 2010. "Rest Stop: Erotics at Harvard." In *Toilet: Public Restrooms and the Politics of Sharing*, edited by Harvey Molotch and Laura Norén, 43–46. New York: NYU Press.

Technosexuality

SHAOWEN BARDZELL and JEFFREY BARDZELL
Indiana University, USA

Technosexuality is an emergent research area in human sexuality and technology studies that explores the interplay between technology and sexuality. Human sexuality comprises both subjectively experienced and also socially mediated experiences and practices, including tactual experiences, body habits, socially prescribed norms and taboos, and interpersonal relationships. The academic study of technosexuality considers "the ways in which technology has produced or configured sexuality, how technology become sexualized and how sexuality has in turn configured technology in society" (López and Cleminson 2004). More specifically, this study entails the examination of these private and social aspects of sexual life in connection with information and communication technology.

In popular culture, the term "technosexuality" has been appropriated to characterize individuals who are sexually attracted to technologies, either as a sexual fetish or more broadly as an attraction towards technology-mediated sexual experiences (see, for example, the entries on Technosexuality in Urban Dictionary, Wikipedia, and Wiktionary). Common to both academic and popular understandings is a view of sexuality that is somewhat plastic, that is, not fixed but rather capable of change; and an understanding of technology as partly constitutive of, rather than external to, human experience, desire, and self-expression.

Technosexual practice can involve any of the following technologies: webcamming, instant messaging ("sexting"), mobile phone applications (e.g., bedpost.com, OvuView, Glow), social networking (e.g., FeltLife), massively multiplayer role-playing games (e.g., Sociolotron), virtual worlds (e.g., Red Light Center/Utherverse, sex-themed communities in Second Life), sex-oriented blogging (e.g., Fleshbot), Internet pornography, erotic uses of Twitter (see, e.g., the #HitachiMagic hashtag), online dating (e.g., eHarmony.com, Adam4Adam.com), and Google Maps API-enabled sexual interactions (e.g., ijustmadelove.com), among others.

The rise of social media in particular has been accompanied by a rise in technologies devoted to various forms of sexual interaction. New forms of technological sexual interactions thus call into question how we think about our bodies online, especially the "lived, subjective experience of corporeality" (Blackman 2008), focusing on the body not as it "is" in-itself but rather the body as it is understood, experienced, and enacted or performed. Practices such as virtual tattoos and virtual branding in virtual worlds, or practices of anonymous exhibitionism (i.e., sharing one's sexual exploits behind the wall of anonymity), and anonymous voyeurism are mediated by online communities of practice, who establish their significances and limits in ways that often reflect but also depart from their physical world analogues. An important way they depart from physical world analogues is in the plasticity of gender – online gender changes are often only a checkbox away. Additionally, it is possible and often easy to perform gender in exaggerated ways (e.g., designing and performing with hypermasculine avatars), though doing so raises issues of authenticity – both to the self and in social interactions (Marshall 2003).

A related phenomenon, cybersex, colloquially known as "cybering," "cybersex," "camming" or "c2c," refers to two (or more) users derive sexual pleasure using chat and/or videoconferencing tools. In commercial webcamming, for example, users express their sexual fantasies and desires via text chat and direct sex workers' on-camera performances. Such live sex shows, a new form of online sex work enabled by the easily assessable Internet and inexpensive gadgets, raises issues concerning the sexual body online and transformations in the meaning and experience of sex as labor.

Another significant development in technosexuality is digitally enabled designer sex toys. Companies such as Lelo, Jimmyjane, and Je Joue have helped inaugurate a new area of sex toys, one that is aligned with sex-positive feminist activism, using high quality body-safe materials in designs holistically targeted at sexual health and overall well-being while providing physical pleasure (Bardzell and Bardzell 2011). Other examples in this genre include customizable teledildonic devices that combine tangible interactions, DIY, and open-source software to enable sexual pleasures (e.g., slashdong, thethrillhammer).

Because of the impacts and intellectual implications of these quickly emerging practices, it is not surprising that several research disciplines have contributed studies of technosexuality. Humanists from gender studies and cultural studies have viewed the history of technologies invented for sexual use. These histories have shown that such technologies have not only reflected diverse technological configurations, but also social ones. For example, at different times sex-related technologies have been viewed as medical devices, as novelty items distributed by the porn industry, and as mediators of emerging forms of sexual self-representation and erotic practice. Each of these also reflects different cultural understandings of sexuality itself (e.g., the early medical notion that orgasms needed to be induced in women by doctors to relieve symptoms of hysteria – which led to the invention of electric vibrators – is nowhere to be found in sex toy design today).

In human computer interaction (HCI), a discipline that involves the study of digital interaction design, scholars have investigated the ways that humans interact with computers, and more broadly technology, or with each other through technology, in a context that is considered sexual by any or all of the participants. In this research, notions of sexual pleasure, sexual health, sexual identity, self-expression, cultural mores, and technology and design are all seen as interdependent. That is, not only do technologies reify the contemporary sexual attitudes, but they also bring into focus new practices, and with them new desires, which did not exist before. These emergent desires in turn become objects of inquiry for scholars as well as material for the imagination of new designs and technologies.

The study of technosexuality can be productive in understanding the changing dynamics between the user, sexuality, and technology and prompt questions such as what the characteristics of technology-mediated sexuality are, and how technologists and designers can build both practical and theoretical understandings of this important locus of embodied interaction. In all this, researchers are better able to understand the surge of technology-mediated sexual interactions. These technology-mediated sexual forms tend to be both abstract and anonymous, touching upon issues such as distance and immediacy in sexual interaction, anonymity and self-disclosure, and physical and mental/emotional aspects of human sexuality.

SEE ALSO: Body Politics; Cybersex; Sex Toys; Sex Work and Sex Workers' Unionization

REFERENCES

Bardzell, Jeffrey, and Shaowen Bardzell. 2011. "'Pleasure is Your Birthright': Digitally Enabled Designer Sex Toys as a Case of Third-Wave HCI." *Proceedings of the SIGCHI Conference on Human Factors in Computing Systems, 2011*, 257–266. New York: ACM Press.

Blackman, L. 2008. *The Body: The Key Concepts*. Oxford: Berg.

López, Ángel J. Gordo, and Richard Cleminson. 2004. *Techno-Sexual Landscapes: Changing Relations Between Technology and Sexuality*. London: Free Association Books.

Marshall, J. 2003. "The Sexual Life of Cyber-Savants." *Australian Journal of Anthropology*, 14(2): 229–248.

FURTHER READING

Ben-Ze'ev, Aaron. 2004. *Love Online: Emotions on the Internet*. Cambridge: Cambridge University Press.

Boellstorff, Tom. 2008. "Intimacy." In *Coming of Age in Second Life: An Anthropologist Explores the Virtually Human*. Princeton: Princeton University Press.

Döring, Nicola M. 2009. "The Internet's Impact on Sexuality: A Critical Review of 15 Years of Research." *Computers in Human Behavior*, 25: 1089–1101.

Kannabiran, Gopinaath, Jeffrey Bardzell, and Shaowen Bardzell. 2011. "How HCI Talks About Sexuality: Discursive Strategies, Blind Spots, and Opportunities for Future Research." *Proceedings of the SIGCHI Conference on Human Factors in Computing Systems, 2011*. ACM: New York.

Third Genders

CHRISTINA RICHARDS
Nottinghamshire NHS Trust Gender Clinic, UK

Third gender[1] people, more often called pangender, bigender, genderqueer, or queer, are those people who do not identify as male or female and so fall outwith the gender binary (the notion that men and women are fundamentally different in kind). Note that we are only considering gender here (one's felt sense of oneself) rather than biological sex. Although approximately 1.728 percent of the population (Blackless et al. 2000) cannot be defined as wholly male or female in terms of their biological sex (and may consequently be termed as being intersex or having a diversity or disorder of sex development – DSD), most, but not all, intersex/DSD people nonetheless identify as wholly male or wholly female and not as third gender (Harper 2007).

Third gender people may have a single identity outside of the gender binary, or have a more fluid sense of gender that shifts with time. Third gender people are differentiated from *neutrois* people – people without genders; *cisgender* people – people who are happy to remain the gender they were assigned at birth; and *transsexual* people – people who transition gender to an unequivocally male role or an unequivocally female role. In the past this differentiation has not been the case, with some authors suggesting that cisgender gay, lesbian, and bisexual people, as well as transsexual people, might constitute a third gender category as men would necessarily be attracted to women and women attracted to men, with no crossing between these categories (e.g., Hirschfeld 1952). However, this is not so as, in general, gay, bisexual, lesbian, and transsexual people will be unequivocally male or female (Richards and Barker 2013).

Third gender people have been found across time and culture from America to Polynesia (Herdt 1996), and from the Bronze Age to the present day. In each case the exact expression will vary somewhat, just as cisgender expression varies across time and geographical/cultural regions. For example, people who opt for an "X" category on their Australian or New Zealand passport for indeterminate/unspecified/intersex (rather than "M" for male or "F" for female) have a different expression of gender available than do people in countries where such legal facilities are not available.

Similarly, people who identify as *hijra* in South Asia are undertaking activism toward legal recognition of this third gender position. Hijra may identify as men (transsexual), women, or as third gender. Traditionally hijra are people who are birth-assigned male who are devotees of the Bahuchara Mata and may officiate at some Hindu ceremonies. Hijra may gain their spiritual power through removal of their genitals and through living as women, often in all-hijra communities. However, as with many such third gender identities, there are people who identify as hijra outside of this strict definition, and some people who historically might have so identified may now use the term *khwaaja sira* instead of hijra and/or identifying as transsexual.

Another group of people who may be considered to be third gender are the *two-spirit* people who are indigenous to North America. Two-spirit people may generally be birth-assigned males who take on aspects and roles of femininity or birth-assigned females who take on aspects and roles of masculinity, but they need not take on all aspects or roles of the "other" sex. Similar to the hijra, two-spirit people may traditionally have a spiritual and healing role as a medicine[2] person or as a nurse, although this will by no means always be the case, with two-spirit people holding a variety of roles within society.

There are various terms used by First Nation peoples for two-spirit people such as *wiŋkte* by the Lakota, *hwame* by the Mohave, *nádleehé* by the Navajo, and *ilhamana* by the Zuni as well as several others. These terms are not exactly analogous and indeed ilhamana defies direct translation into English – a point that is worth bearing in mind for readers based in a two-sex/two-gender cultural system. Two-spirit itself is not a term that is universally accepted as it suggests a spiritual/cultural system that does not accord with all First Nation understandings and is only used here as a loose umbrella term. Indeed, it is worth noting that such is the diversity of the peoples discussed in this entry, there will be many people who identify as something outwith the terms used here.

Similar to the hijra and the two-spirit people, the Samoan *fa'afāfine* (literally, the way of a woman) may be considered to be third gender, although again in a different way and within a specific cultural context that inflects basic understandings about the world. For example, Herdt (1996) suggests that, while gender liminality in Polynesia is generally accepted, it is not afforded the status of a third gender within cultural praxis. The fa'afāfine are usually birth-assigned males who foreground traditionally feminine behaviors at certain times and are often especially engaged with their community. Within Polynesia there are also other "third gender" groups such as the *māhū* from Hawaii and Tahiti, who are birth-assigned males who have feminine gender identities and roles and are attracted to men, and the *fakaletī* of

Tonga, who are birth-assigned males who identify as women.

Many of the terms above have been adapted by vernacular slang into terms of abuse. This is perhaps because many cultures that had previously embraced gender diversity have grown less tolerant with the move to evangelize native peoples during the historic wars of conquest; and more recently with the spread of other, less diverse, understandings through cultural colonialism. This marginalization of third gender people has led some to seek legal recognition, as with the hijra above, and others to adopt a (medical) discourse of "transsexualism" from postindustrial nations, instead of the traditional understandings touched on above. For those people who are marginalized there can be increasing isolation as communities no longer have a place that once existed for third gender people, which in turn can lead to minority stress, homelessness, and work within underground economies. However, the rise of the identities of trans*, transgender, and genderqueer within some areas, while supplanting traditional understandings, can offer community or a sense of identity to third gender people who would otherwise be marginalized.

As part of this non-traditional (medical) discourse, some workers have argued that third genders are pathological. Indeed, the two main psychiatric taxonomies, the *International Classification of Diseases*, 10th edition (ICD-10) and the *Diagnostic and Statistical Manual of Mental Disorders*, 5th edition (DSM-5), contain diagnoses that might pertain to these gender forms. One of the key criteria for a diagnosis of gender dysphoria is "A strong conviction that one has the typical feelings and reactions of the other gender (or some alternative gender different from one's assigned gender)" (American Psychiatric Association 2013, 452). That these diagnoses exist is somewhat paradoxical as rates of psychopathology for people who transgress gender boundaries are no higher than in the general population (Hoshiai et al. 2010). Indeed it has been suggested that psychological androgyny is healthier than maintaining a strictly uni-gendered identity (Bem 1974). The primary reason for retention of these diagnoses in the DSM-5, especially gender dysphoria, was simply to maintain access to physical healthcare such as surgeries and hormones that allow some third gender people to have a body which more closely matches their gender. For this reason the APA altered the name of the diagnosis from gender identity *disorder* in the DSM-4 to gender dysphoria in the DSM-5. Not all third gender people wish to have such physiological interventions, however. For those who do, the development or removal of breasts and hair are probably the most commonly requested interventions (Barrett 2007). Cessation of menses, either though medication or surgery, is also quite common and some people also request the surgical creation of a penis or vagina, although this is rarer. Whether third gender people access physiological interventions depends on the choice of the individual, the availability of interventions, and cultural factors. Consequently, while some people may access such interventions, others may not have them available, or may find them in conflict with traditional understandings.

Lastly, variation of gender expression outside of the two-gender model is not limited to *homo sapiens*. Roughgarden (2004) enumerates many animals across a diversity of species that have a variety of gender forms, from the hummingbird to the sunfish, suggesting that biology, as well as culture, may have a role in the etiology of third genders. Indeed a neurological basis for people who transition from their gender of birth has been found (cf. Kruijver 2004), which suggests that third gender people too may have a neurological base for non-binary feelings and behaviors.

Third gender people, then, are fairly ubiquitous across time and geography/culture; may or may not wish to have physical interventions to alter their bodies as identity and opportunity allow; and are perhaps best understood as another illustration of the diversity of natural expression.

SEE ALSO: Cross-Dressing; Drag; Gender Dysphoria; Gender Variance; Genderqueer; Hijra/Hejira; Kathoey; Kothi; Ladyboys; Tomboys and Sissies; Two-Spirit

NOTES

[1] For taxonomological reasons this entry is titled "third gender." However, the term is less often used than some other terms listed above. Nonetheless, for clarity, third gender will be used throughout.
[2] In the First Nation sense of the word.

REFERENCES

American Psychiatric Association (APA). 2013. *Diagnostic and Statistical Manual of Mental Disorders*, 5th ed. (DSM-5). Washington, DC: American Psychiatric Association.
Barrett, James, ed. 2007. *Transsexual and Other Disorders of Gender Identity*. Oxford: Radcliffe.
Bem, Sandra. 1974. "The Measurement of Psychological Androgyny." *Journal of Consulting and Clinical Psychology*, 42(2): 155–162. DOI: 10.1037/h0036215.
Blackless, Melanie, et al. 2000. "How Sexually Dimorphic Are We? Review and Synthesis." *American Journal of Human Biology*, 12: 151–166. DOI: 10.1002/(SICI)1520-6300(200003/04).
Harper, Catherine. 2007. *Intersex*. Oxford: Berg.
Herdt, Gilbert. 1996. *Third Sex, Third Gender: Beyond Sexual Dimorphism in Culture and History*. New York: Zone Books.
Hirschfeld, Magnus. 1952. *Sexual Anomalies and Perversions*. London: Encyclopaedic Press.
Hoshiai, Masahiko, et al. 2010. "Psychiatric Comorbidity among Patients with Gender Identity Disorder." *Psychiatry and Clinical Neurosciences*, 64: 514–519. DOI: 10.1111/j.1440-1819.2010.02118.x.
Kruijver, Frank P. M. 2004. *Sex in the Brain*. Amsterdam: Netherlands Institute of Brain Research.
Richards, Christina, and Meg Barker. 2013. *Sexuality and Gender for Mental Health Professionals: A Practical Guide*. London: Sage.
Roughgarden, Joan. 2004. *Evolution's Rainbow*. Berkeley: University of California Press.

Third World Women

WENDY HARCOURT
International Institute of Social Studies, Erasmus University, The Netherlands

Feminist and postcolonial scholar Gayatri Chakravorty Spivak (Landry and MacLean 1996) identifies the moment when the term "third world" was first used at the 1955 Bandung Conference, which sowed the seeds of non-aligned movements and Afro-Asian economic and cultural cooperation to resist the old imperial powers. The term was coined to describe a huge economic, political, and geographical imaginary – all the countries in the non-Western and non-Eastern part of the then emerging new world order.

In the last decades the term has been the subject of intense debate in relation to who defines and who speaks for or about the third world in international relations and international development studies. These debates have been reflected also in women and gender studies as well as feminist activism around the term (and imaginary) of "third world women."

Third world women in the early work of international development and women's studies emerged as a stereotype where US and European scholars such as Ester Boserup, Perdita Huston, and Irene Tinker depicted the majority of the world's women as poor, vulnerable, home-bound, and repressed by centuries of patriarchal regimes in the third world (Mohanty 2011, 85). This dominant imaginary of the 1970s and 1980s has since been challenged with the opening up of women's studies to gender studies, and the questioning of development and modernity and postcolonialism (Graves 2012).

Feminist scholar Chandra Talpade Mohanty (2011) was one of the first to problematize the term third world women. In her famous 1991 text "Under Western Eyes" she criticizes "the production of Third World woman as a singular monolithic subject" by scholars who "take as their referent feminist interests as they have been articulated in the USA and western Europe." She sees third world feminism as resisting and working against this "western feminist discourse" (2011, 83). She refutes the idea of third world women as an already constituted group regardless of class and ethnic or racial location formed through an uncritical understanding of patriarchy, gender power relations, and sexual difference. Such uncritical analysis, she argues, has led to a "homogeneous notion of the oppression" of third world women, producing the imaginary of "an average third world woman [as] ignorant, poor, uneducated, tradition-bound, domestic, family-oriented, victimized" (2011, 84). She decries the notion of third world women as "politically immature women who need to be versed and schooled in the ethos of western feminism" (2011, 85). Mohanty is particularly damning of the "women in development" literature with its failure to acknowledge third world women's agency and its implicit racism and neocolonialism of projects of Western women "saving" other women. She points to the example of Afghan women under the Taliban as part of this discursive cultural (and economic) colonization.

The emerging discourse on sexuality and third world women during the 2000s continues this critical attack on the imaginary of third world women. Note that in this period the term "third world" shifted to "Global South." Put simply, the reason for this shift is that the term Global South removes the implicit hierarchy of first, second, and third worlds and better reflects post-Cold War geopolitical arrangements where essentially the "second world" ceased to exist. The discussions on sexuality and women in the Global South in the last decade have comprised several strands.

The first strand in the tradition of Spivak and Mohanty examines the dichotomies between the Global North and South in relation to debates around sexuality, identity politics, and anti-colonial and postcolonial critiques of globalization. The multidisciplinary, highly creative, and visual critiques aim to undo stereotyped gendered sexual behaviors. As Anne McClintock states, "sex is the other of civilization and the global south continues to be the porno tropics for the European imagination" (quoted in Harcourt 2009, 113). This set of writing exposes the racialized and sexualized meanings of bodies and desire that inform gender and development discourse that focuses on third world women.

The work of international relations feminist scholar Cynthia Enloe (2007) is an important example of such scholarship that unpacks race, class, sexuality, and gender in colonial, imperial, and postcolonial discourse. Another key collection on development and sexual rights (Lind 2010) challenges global hegemonies on sexual rights by proposing that gender transgression is a key strategy practiced by women around the world, including in the development projects of the Global South. The collection looks at "how emergent sexual subjectivities have provided important challenges to heterosexist biases and gender normativity in post/neocolonial state planning traditions and technologies" (Lind 2010, 1).

Other recent work in this tradition has elaborated on sexual diversity in the Global South. The collection by Saskia Wieringa and Horacio Sivori (2013) explicitly addresses what a Global South perspective means to sexuality and sexual politics, looking at how sexuality has been articulated in contexts that are located on the margins of a Eurocentric postcolonial discourse. The case studies historically examine precolonial realities of sexuality as well as the role of the sexual in contemporary societies, including China and the Middle East. The studies by scholars based in the Global South reveal multiple sexual relations, identities, and subjectivities. The book contributes to the growing body of transnational sexuality studies that moves out of hegemonic Western concerns with third world women by carefully tracing in a historical, material, cultural, and political analysis biopolitics and heteronormativity, sexual science and political control, and the emergence of sexual rights and sexual citizenship (Wieringa and Sivori 2013, 14–16).

Another important collection on sexuality in Muslim contexts (Hélie and Hoodfar 2012) brings together scholars from the Middle East, North Africa, and Islamic countries in South Asia to explore the emerging trends that expressly affect women's sexuality. The collection challenges the assumed denigration of all Muslim women as sexually oppressed, as Anissa Hélie argues in her introduction: "bodily rights, sexual conduct and gender expressions are regulated in all societies" (2012, 1). The book counters the "widespread tendency to posit gender equality and emancipation within the sexual realm as products of 'Western'-inspired reforms" and instead presents a series of studies that recognize the way women in Muslim societies have "designed empowerment strategies within their own societies that draw on exisiting traditions" (2012, 1–2).

The second strand is around gender-based violence, trafficking, and sex work, which for decades built the imaginary of poor third world women, girls, and young boys as victims, oppressed and exploited by men and patriarchal structures. While there is undoubtedly violence and exploitation of women, the recent writings on sex work in the Global South, for example, challenge the construction of women as purely victims, examining how selling sex, for example, is perceived as a valid livelihood choice where children, women, and transgender people have agency. Studies in Asia by Tahmina and Moral (2004), Misra and Chandiramani (2005), Menon (2007), and Banerji (2008) and in Africa by Tamale (2011) and Currier (2012) build on the realities of sexual experience in different locations in the Global South, including sex workers. The literature presents counter-imaginaries of exploited victims, showing how women in many different contexts have politically confronted religious fundamentalism, police brutalities, and heteronormativity in marriage and other legal institutions determining women's economic and social lives.

A further strand aims to break the silence around sexual pleasure as an entry point for change in women's lives globally. Andrea Cornwall and her colleagues in the UK-based Pathways of Empowerment Programme (Jolly, Cornwall, and Hawkins 2013; Institute of Development Studies 2014) have produced a series of studies working with activist scholars in the Global South that focus on how the pursuit of sexual pleasures is pivotal to social and cultural arrangements and behaviors. These studies show how, for example, the mobilizing of resources to respond to HIV and AIDS has provided a space for once marginalized identity groups identifying as coalitions of lesbian, gay, bisexual, transsexual, transgender, queer, and intersex (LGBTQI) to speak about their lifestyles and sexual choices.

This academic work is closely linked to the feminist call for sexual rights and erotic justice. One such global advocacy network is Sexual Policy Watch, a global forum of feminists and sexual rights advocates and academics including Rosalind Petchesky and Sonia Correa, who are tracking the discourse on demography, sexual and reproductive health, trafficking, and AIDS as well as the struggles of LGBTQI movements and communities. The report *SexPolitics* (Parker, Petchesky, and Sember 2012) presents a comparative study of the politics of sexuality, sexual health, and sexual rights, illustrating how sexuality has become both a point of political controversy and a domain for social change that has helped move international gender and sexuality studies beyond the troubling term of "third world women."

SEE ALSO: Gender and Development; Postcolonialism, Theoretical and Critical Perspectives on

REFERENCES

Banerji, Rita. 2008. *Sex and Power: Defining History, Shaping Societies*. New Delhi: Penguin Books India.

Currier, Ashley. 2012. *Out in Africa: LGBT Organising in Namibia and South Africa*. Minneapolis: University of Minnesota Press.

Enloe, Cynthia. 2007. "Feminist Readings on Abu Ghraib: Introduction." *International Feminist Journal of Politics*, 9(1): 35–37.

Graves, Nicola. 2012. "Third World and Third World Women." *Postcolonial Studes @ Emory*. Accessed August 16, 2015, at https://scholarblogs.emory.edu/postcolonialstudies/2014/06/21/third-world-and-third-world-women/.

Harcourt, Wendy. 2009. *Body Politics in Development: Critical Debates on Gender and Development*. London: Zed Books.

Hélie, Anissa. 2012. "Policing Gender, Sexuality and Muslimness." In *Sexuality in Muslim Contexts: Restrictions and Resistance*, edited by Anissa Hélie and Homa Hoodfar. London: Zed Books.

Hélie, Anissa, and Homa Hoodfar, eds. 2012. *Sexuality in Muslim Contexts: Restrictions and Resistance*. London: Zed Books.

Institute of Development Studies (IDS). 2014. "Overview of Pathways of Empowerment Programme." Accessed January 10, 2014, at http://www.ids.ac.uk/project/pathways-of-women-s-empowerment-research-programme-consortium.

Jolly, Susie, Andrea Cornwall, and Kate Hawkins. 2013. *Women, Sexuality and the Political Power of Pleasure*. London: Zed Books.

Landry, Donna, and Gerald MacLean, eds. 1996. *The Spivak Reader: Selected Works of Gayatri Chakravorty Spivak*. London: Routledge.

Lind, Amy, ed. 2010. *Development, Sexual Rights and Global Governance*. Abingdon: Routledge.

Menon, Nivedita, ed. 2007. *Sexualities*. New Delhi: Kahli for Women.

Misra, Geetanjali, and Radhika Chandiramani, eds. 2005. *Sexuality, Gender and Rights: Exploring Theory and Practice in South and Southeast Asia*. New Delhi: Sage.

Mohanty, Chandra Talpade. 2011. "Under Western Eyes: Feminist Scholarship and Colonial Discourses." In *The Women, Gender and Development Reader*, 2nd ed., edited by Nalini Visvanathan, Lynn Duggan, Nan Wiegersma, and Laurie Nisonoff. London: Zed Books.

Parker, Richard, Rosalind Petchesky, and Robert Sember, eds. 2012. SexPolitics: Reports from the Frontlines. Accessed August 16, 2015, at http://www.sxpolitics.org/frontlines/book/pdf/sexpolitics.pdf.

Tahmina, Qurratul Ain, and Shishir Moral. 2004. *Sex-Workers in Bangladesh: Livelihood at What Price?* Dhaka: Society for Environment and Human Development.

Tamale, Sylvia, ed. 2011. *African Sexualities: A Reader*. Oxford: Pambazuka Press.

Wieringa, Saskia, and Horacio Sivori, eds. 2013. *The Sexual History of the Global South*. London: Zed Books.

Tokenism

YOLANDA FLORES NIEMANN
University of North Texas, USA

Tokenism research formally began with Rosabeth Moss Kanter's (1977) landmark work, *Men and Women of the Corporation*. Examining corporate power, interaction dynamics, and workplace experiences, she identified overarching group types: numerical dominants, who represent the majority; and tokens, who are rare among their demographic groups within the context. Kanter stipulated that tokenism occurs, in part, when the tokens account for 15 percent or less of the workforce. In the corporate world of Kanter's research, men were typically dominants and women were tokens. Tokenism research has evolved to examine the perception, treatment, behaviors, and experiences of persons from visible racial/ethnic groups in predominantly white workplaces and on women who work in male-dominated environments (Niemann and Dovidio 1998; Niemann 2003, 2011; King et al. 2009; Gutierrez y Muhs et al. 2012). The interrelated phenomena associated with tokenism, which are exacerbated by intersections of race/ethnicity and gender, include isolation, loneliness, visibility, distinctiveness, representativeness, role encapsulation, stereotyping, stereotype threat, and attributional ambiguity.

Tokenized contexts fuel heightened visibility and feelings of chronic distinctiveness, especially for persons of color (Pollak and Niemann 1998). They afford exaggeration of differences between tokens and dominants, leading observers to assimilate tokens to their preconceived notions about their group and to question their goodness of fit for a given environment, role, and/or occupation (Hewstone et al. 2006). As such, tokens may be evaluated under different, and more stringent, criteria from their dominant colleagues (Jones, Dovidio, and Vietze 2014). They also attract disproportional attention and causality.

Tokens are perceived as homogeneous. Their actions, decisions, values, and mannerisms are interpreted in a stereotype-consistent manner (Sekaquaptewa and Thompson 2003). Stereotypic expectations may lead to the encapsulation and entrapment of tokens in particular roles, such as specialists in ethnic or gender matters and symbols of workplace diversity. They may trigger in the token feelings of inadequacy, stigma, inequity in the workplace, and stereotype threat, which refers to the fear of proving true the stereotypes about one's group (Steele 1997). Stress is added when tokens' imperfections and mistakes are perceived as reflective of their group, while their successes are deemed exceptions to the group stereotype.

Tokenism can damage tokens' interactions with colleagues, thus intensifying feelings of cultural isolation, loneliness, alienation, and distrust. They also lead to persistent attributional ambiguity, which refers to not knowing the intentions of the feedback or actions toward or against them (e.g., feedback may be grounded in support and helpfulness), and/or in racist or sexist biases. Without trusted feedback tokens's career progress may be slowed or stopped. In addition, simultaneously managing their distinctiveness (e.g., through self-monitoring and impression management strategies), as well as their job, can strain tokens's cognitive resources, physical and psychological health, and job performance.

While Kanter focused primarily on numerical proportions between men and women in the workplace as the foundation of different group-based experiences, current research identifies numerical status as a critical but insufficient identifier of tokenism (Yoder 1994). Antecedents, moderators, and added impacts of tokenism that have been the focus of recent research include: subordinated gender status within the context; placement of the minority group on the social hierarchy; organizational structure; perception of gender and race appropriateness for the occupation; solo status, job satisfaction; interactive effects of other visibly stigmatized status (e.g., weight; institutional climate; performance context; and formal role in the institution; Viallon and Martinot 2009;

Stickman, Hassell, and Archbold 2010; Torchia, Calabro, and Huse 2011).

SEE ALSO: Intersectionality; Sexism; Stigma

REFERENCES

Gutierrez y Muhs, G., Yolanda F. Niemann, C. Gonzales, and A. Harris, 2012. *Presumed Incompetent: The Intersections of Race and Class for Women in Academia*, 446–500. Boulder: Utah State University Press/University Press of Colorado.

Hewstone, M., et al. 2006. "Tokens in the Tower: Perceptual Processes and Interaction Dynamics in Academic Settings with 'Skewed', 'Tilted,' and 'Balanced' Sex Ratios." *Group Processes and Intergroup Relations*, 9(4): 509–532.

Jones, James M., John F. Dovidio, and Deborah L. Vietze. 2014. *The Psychology of Diversity: Beyond Prejudice and Racism*. Chichester: John Wiley & Sons.

Kanter, Rosabeth Moss. 1977. *Men and Women of the Corporation*. New York: Basic Books.

King, E.B., M.R. Hebl, J.M. George, and S.F. Matusik. 2009. "Understanding Tokenism: Antecedents and Consequences of a Psychological Climate of Gender Inequity." *Journal of Management*, 36(2): 482–510.

Niemann, Yolanda F. 2003. "The Psychology of Tokenism: Psychosocial Reality of Faculty of Color." In *The Handbook of Racial and Ethnic Minority Psychology*, edited by G. Bernal, J.E. Trimble, A.K. Burlew, and F.T. Leong, 100–188. Thousand Oaks: Sage.

Niemann, Yolanda F. 2011. "Diffusing the Impact of Tokenism on Faculty of Color." In *To Improve the Academy*, edited by Judith E. Miller and James E. Groccia, 216–229. San Francisco: Jossey-Bass.

Niemann, Yolanda F., and J.F. Dovidio. 1998. "Relationship of Solo Status, Academic Rank, and Perceived Distinctiveness to Job Satisfaction of Racial/Ethnic Minorities." *Journal of Applied Psychology*, 83(1): 55–71.

Pollak, K., and Yolanda F. Niemann. 1998. "Black and White Tokens in Academia: A Difference of Chronic vs. Acute Distinctiveness." *Journal of Applied Social Psychology*, 11: 954–972.

Sekaquaptewa, D., and M. Thompson. 2003. "Solo Status, Stereotype Threat, and Performance Expectancies: Their Effects on Women's Performance." *Journal of Experimental Social Psychology*, 39(1); 68–74.

Steele, C.M. 1997. "A Threat in the Air: How Stereotypes Shape Intellectual Identity and Performance." *American Psychologist*, 52(6): 613–629.

Stichman, A.J., K.D. Hassell, and C.A. Archbold. 2010. Strength In Numbers? A Test of Kanter's Theory of Tokenism. *Journal of Criminal Justice*, 38(4): 633–639.

Torchia, M., A. Calabro, and M. Huse. 2011. "Women Directors on Corporate Boards: From Tokenism to Critical Mass." *Journal of Business Ethics*, 102(2): 299–317.

Viallon, M.L., and D. Martinot. 2009. "The Effects of Solo Status on Women's and Men's Success: The Moderating Role Of The Performance Context." *European Journal of Psychology of Education*, 24(2): 191–205.

Yoder, J.D. 1994. "Looking Beyond Numbers: The Effects of Gender Status, Job Prestige, and Occupational Gender-Typing on Tokenism Processes." *Social Psychology Quarterly*, 150–159.

Tomboys and Sissies

ROBERT B. HEASLEY
Indiana University of Pennsylvania, USA
BETSY CRANE
Widener University, USA

The words tomboys and sissies are colloquial expressions used to describe children who do not confirm to gender expectations. The girl who is seen as a tomboy, and the boy labeled a sissy, both display qualities that call into question the idea that biological males and biological females are by nature "opposites." Such qualities include behaviors, appearance, or other social characteristics that have been culturally assigned to the "opposing" sex. As Reeser (2010) argues, the transgression in either direction "destabilizes imagined binary oppositions between male masculinity and female femininity" (p. 133).

The term sissy "emerged out of the boy culture of the nineteenth century" as "not only an epithet hurled by schoolyard bullies but a clinical term suggestive of psychological pathology and sexual inversion" (Grant 2004, 829). Sexual inversion was a term used in late 1800s and early 1900s to refer to homosexuality (Ellis 1927). It was during this period when gender non-conformity for both males and females (though there was greater obsession about boys) became associated with homosexuality, the prevention of which was viewed as critical (Kimmel 2012).

The use of "tomboy" has older roots, appearing in the English language in the sixteenth century and used initially to refer to loud or boisterous males. The name Thomas during this period was an archetypical male name, used to indicate maleness, hence the word tomcat. The *Online Etymology Dictionary* reports that in the 1550s, the word tomboy meant a "rude, boisterous boy," from *Tom* + *boy*. The use of the term to describe a girl who acts like a spirited boy is first recorded in the 1590s. It also could mean "strumpet, bold or immodest woman" (Harper, n.d.).

The use of both "tomboy" and "sissy" to refer to those who are gender non-conforming requires an appreciation of Connell's (1995) ideas about hegemonic masculinity and emphasized femininity. Connell's framework acknowledges the ways in which gender is a power-based social construction, one associated with dominance (male) and submissiveness (female). This binary sees male-ness and female-ness as both absolute and biologically based constructs that serve as the justification for opposing sets of expectations in gender expression. The binary also suggests that the absence of sex-appropriate qualities – being biologically male, but having feminine qualities – is to be "not male." To be "not male" creates the child as "other" which comes to be labeled "sissy."

It is important to differentiate between children who have some qualities generally associated with the other sex, and may be seen as tomboys or sissies, from children who are transgender. That some children, starting as young as 3 or 4, strongly state that they see themselves as the other sex, has only recently been acknowledged. Such children have a persistent and consistent desire to dress and present as the other sex, and thus can be understood as having a transgender identity. With tomboys and sissies we do not necessarily see children who want to *be* the other sex; rather, these are children who act in ways that belies the narrow constraints of what a boy or girl is supposed to look like and act like. The children themselves are most often fine with their sex (Gottschalk 2003). The response they are likely to receive from others is the source of their problems and that response has more to do with the meaning we give to masculinity and femininity.

Historically both males and females are valued to the extent to which they conform to being appropriately masculine and feminine, an expectation that leads to society reinforcing qualities from birth that are perceived as gender appropriate. Placing emphasis on gender conformity can, however, result in discouraging, or even punishing children for exhibiting qualities that do not conform. The socialization process also establishes the within-gender hierarchy wherein children learn to value other children who most readily conform to the gender binary. Thus, the sissy and the tomboy are likely to be exposed to ridicule, bullying, and social isolation by peers. There is even a hierarchy between these terms, in that a boy being called a sissy is often a much more damaging epithet than a girl being called a tomboy. This may be related to the overall valuing of the male versus the female, in that it is considered worse for a boy to act like a girl than vice versa.

Tomboys and sissies disrupt both the essentialist perception of gender and threaten the hierarchy established by a history of patriarchy that positions a particular type of masculinity as legitimizing male dominance over females. "Sissy" males are not seen as exercising that dominance or having the qualities associated with dominance over females (or other males). While females with masculine qualities associated with being "tomboys" may be valued for their physical or athletic prowess, they may not be seen by males as sufficiently feminine (and thus submissive) to be desirable spouses (Crane, Towne, and Crane-Seeber 2013). However, the gender non-conforming child is likely to lack encouragement to be non-conforming even when parents and others may indicate their acceptance. Such difference is accentuated in that these children are unlikely to have other immediate family members or even peers, who outwardly exhibit non-conforming gender presentation (Ehrensaft 2011).

At a core level the terms sissy and tomboys are linked to societal fears and rejection of homosexuality. Gender conformity is associated with heterosexuality. To "be a man" or to be seen as a "real women" assumes a heterosexual identity and orientation. Boys identified as having feminine qualities are likely be bullied and called "fag" while girls who similarly seen as tomboys, particularly due to both physical appearance (for instance, dressing primarily in male clothing and having short hair and no makeup in high school) are likely to be ridiculed for also being lesbian. The tomboy doesn't, after all, devote a great deal of attention to appeasing males to attract their attention. In his research on lesbian and gay youth, LaSala (2010) found that many parents displayed as much or even more concern that their son or daughter conform to gender norms then whether they identified as homosexual. As LaSala notes, the mother of a gay, feminine-acting male told her son, "I don't care if you are homosexual or not. I just like men who look like men and act like men" (LaSala 2011, para. 8).

When society holds a punitive attitude about gender non-conforming girls and boys, "reducing" them to "tomboys" and "sissies," it denies the beneficial characteristics of such children that may be desirable as they become adults, for example, women who can hold their own in male–female relationships, males who can be part of a nurturing, empathic community. Yet because of the close association of gender performance and sexuality, the stigma of non-conforming children as possibly homosexual is substantial. Gender non-conforming children queer the gender binary (Heasley 2005), which may be positive, contributing to a broader set of behaviors that might be allowed in males and females.

SEE ALSO: Gender Bias; Gender Inequality and Gender Stratification; Gender Oppression; Gender Performance; Gender Stereotypes; Heterosexism and Homophobia; Language and Gender

REFERENCES

Connell, R. 1995. *Masculinities*. Berkeley: University of California Press.

Crane, B., A. Towne, and J. Crane-Seeber. 2013. "The Four Boxes of Gendered Sexuality: A Framework And Lesson Plan for Teaching about the History and Effects of Gendered Sexuality." *American Journal of Sexuality Education*, 8(4): 274–305. DOI: 10.1080/15546128.2013.854008.

Ellis, H. 1927. *Studies in the Psychology of Sex Volume II: Sexual Inversion*, 3rd ed. Accessed July 19, 2015, at http://www.gutenberg.org/ebooks/13611?msg=welcome_stranger.

Ehrensaft, D. 2011. "Boys Will Be Girls, Girls Will Be Boys: Children Affect Parents as Parents Affect Children in Gender Nonconformity." *Psychoanalytic Psychology*, 28(4): 528–548.

Gottschalk, L. 2003. "Same-Sex Sexuality and Childhood Gender Non-Conformity: A Spurious Connection." *Journal of Gender Studies*, 12(1): 35–50. DOI: 10.1080/0958923032000067808.

Grant, J. 2004. "A 'real boy' and Not a Sissy: Gender, Childhood, and Masculinity, 1890–1940." *Journal of Social History*, 37(4): 829.

Harper, D. n.d. Tomboy. Accessed July 19, 2015, at http://www.etymonline.com/index.php?allowed_in_frame=0&search=tomboy&searchmode=none.

Heasley, R. B. 2005. "Queer Masculinities of Straight Men: A Typology." *Men and Masculinities*, 7(3): 310–320.

Kimmel, M. 2012. *Manhood in America*. New York: Oxford University Press.

LaSala, M. C. 2010. *Coming Out, Coming Home: Helping Families Adjust to a Gay or Lesbian Child*. New York: Columbia University Press.

LaSala, M. C. 2011. Problem with Sissy Boys? Get Over It! Pathologizing Cross-Gender Behavior Is Culturally Bound [Blog post], June 13. Accessed July 19, 2015, at http://www.psychologytoday.com/blog/gay-and-lesbian-well-being/201106/problem-sissy-boys-get-over-it.

Reeser, T. W. 2010. *Masculinities in Theory*. Malden: Wiley Blackwell.

Traditional and Indigenous Knowledge

KIM ANDERSON
Wilfrid Laurier University, Canada

Traditional and indigenous knowledge regarding gender and sexuality is distinct among the many tribes and nations located worldwide, but there are some common characteristics related to land-based ways of knowing. In general, the term "indigenous" refers to peoples who have an ancestral connection to a particular geographical territory as well as ongoing links to those lands in terms of worldview and cultural practices. Indigenous peoples are distinct from the dominant cultural groups of the nation-states that have colonized them. "Traditional" refers to the beliefs and practices that come from precolonial cultures, but which may continue to be exercised, if only by degrees. This entry is based on literature that has been produced in English, and is primarily from knowledge about indigenous peoples in North America.

The land-based lifestyles of indigenous people in the past, and to some extent the present, underpinned gendered domains, including the economic, social, spiritual, and political. These distinctions were so intrinsic to indigenous cultures that some had societies and even languages that were particular to gender. Among North American indigenous peoples, it has often been said that men's responsibilities were to "protect and provide" by bringing in resources through hunting and ensuring community security through warfare, while women were known to "create and nurture" through birth and early childrearing, harvesting or cultivating plants for medicine and food, and governing the internal relations of the family and community. The work required to sustain land-based communities was thus typically assigned according to sex and the respective physical abilities of women and men.

Balance and respect between genders was considered integral to the survival and well-being of the people as indigenous economies were built on the gendered labor of women and men. Neither was valued over the other as it was understood that both were necessary and that the work of women and men was interdependent. Men might bring in large game through hunting, for example, but they needed the women to process and manage these resources to ensure the community was fed, housed, and clothed. Within these roles, however, there was flexibility according to capacity and need; women also hunted and men tended to internal affairs, some more than others. The ultimate goal was to create and support life, which was done through the collective and typically by females and males respectively (Anderson 2000).

Traditional governance systems, though varying across indigenous societies, reflected this ethic of balance through gender. In some societies, such as the Haudenosaunee situated in the northeastern United States and Canada, only men could be chiefs. Yet these men were selected and, when necessary, dismissed by older women who were clan mothers. Women held political authority in other tribal groups through women's councils and societies and as matriarchs of their extended families. They held spiritual authorities as ceremonial leaders, medicine women, traditional doctors, and herbalists. Many societies were also matrilocal, with communities built on the kinship of women. Men would move in to these environments with the expectation that they would contribute as protectors and providers.

A closer look at traditional indigenous practices reveals that, beyond these categories of women and men, there were multiple expressions and dimensions of gender. These expressions involve variables of sex, gender, sexuality, and spirituality, which intersected in non-binary ways. Historians, ethnographers, and indigenous theorists have documented the presence of more than two genders in indigenous societies, sometimes four, sometimes six, running along a continuum of masculine and feminine, and including categories such as womanly men and manly women, or not-men and not-women (Brown 1997; Roscoe 1998). Traditionally, it was gender and not sex that influenced participation in the community; thus, a womanly man might engage in domestic labor typically done by females; a manly woman might engage in warfare. Sexual practices could occur between or across genders, removing sexuality from the binaries associated with gay/straight. A female who took on a male gender role and engaged in sexual practice with another female, for example, would not be considered homosexual as the term has been defined in Western culture, as this would constitute a relationship across genders. As Sabine Lang has commented, "a same sex relationship in many Native American cultures is not necessarily at the same time a same gender relationship" (Jacob, Thomas, and Lang 1997, 104).

Spirituality figures prominently in traditional indigenous articulations of gender as there are notions of masculine and feminine "spirit," which correspond to entities in creation. The feminine has been associated with the land (Mother Earth) and moon (Grandmother Moon) whereas the masculine is associated with sky (Father Sky) and sun (Grandfather Sun). These associations and the qualities of the masculine and feminine are said to bring about and then maintain a necessary balance within creation. Indigenous creation stories reflect these gendered notions of spirit and honor the birthing capacity of the earth mother and her ongoing ability to nurture.

Traditionally, there was an understanding that individuals had the ability to carry masculine and feminine spirit to varying degrees, which allowed for a flexibility of gendered identities independent of sex. As Lester B. Brown has noted, "Gender has always been viewed as a spiritual calling and not determined by a person's anatomy" (1997, 5). The term "two-spirited," coined in 1990 at the third Native American/First Nations gay and lesbian conference in Winnipeg, Canada, reflects this understanding. Two-spirit refers to indigenous peoples who carry a combined masculine and feminine spirit. In the past, this would have allowed them to transgress domains typically defined by sex, and without judgment. This is evident through European narratives of contact depicting indigenous males who dressed as females, did their work, and engaged in same-sex relations.

Gender variance among indigenous peoples, shame-free sexuality, and the empowered position of indigenous women shocked, frightened, and disgusted the Europeans who first encountered them. Missionaries and colonists responded by forcing heteronormative and patriarchal sexual and social practices and systems on indigenous peoples, subverting them to the moral and legal authority of settler societies. The introduction of heteropatriarchy and gendered violence was thus not just a cultural response, it was critical to colonization. The strength of indigenous societies, built on a balance of gendered roles and masculine/feminine spirit within the collective, was ripped apart when extended kin networks came under attack through the introduction of nuclear family systems in which men were the ultimate authority. Governance, spiritual, and social systems where women previously held authority were replaced by Euro-Western institutions that privileged males over females. Same-sex or same-gender sexual practices were reconstructed as deviant and punishable. All of this had the effect of dismantling indigenous societies and gaining access to indigenous lands.

As part of the decolonization movement, contemporary indigenous peoples and their allies are investigating these disruptions to traditional and indigenous knowledges and practices of gender and sexuality. In addition to seeking out traditional knowledge located within their own oral histories, indigenous peoples are able to draw on ethnographic, historical, sociological, literary, and theoretical works. Early twentieth-century ethnographic literature concerning gender was largely drawn from male informants and paid scant attention to women's lives or the presence of two-spirited peoples, but can be used as primary sources. Second-wave feminism and the development of social history influenced the emergence of historical, sociological, autobiographical, and literary accounts of indigenous women's lives from the 1980s forward (Woodsum 1995). These works reclaimed an empowered place for indigenous women by affirming their political, economic, social, and spiritual authorities in traditional societies. From the early 1990s on, anthropological works recording the presence of "berdache" or two-spirited individuals in indigenous societies across the Americas began to emerge. This material documented the widespread and distinct practices of gender variance in indigenous societies of the Americas (Williams 1992; Jacob, Thomas, and Lang 1997; Roscoe 1998).

In recent years, theoretical work on gender and sexuality in indigenous communities has become more prominent. In the past, indigenous scholars and activists have been slow to engage with feminist theory, as feminism was viewed as a colonial space that carried risks of imposing Western, white, and middle-class definitions and priorities on indigenous women. The centrality of motherhood as a place of empowerment and what might be perceived as essentialized feminine identities in many indigenous cultures was a particular fault line between traditional indigenous knowledge and Western feminism. In the last 10 years, however, an emerging field of "indigenous feminism" has been exploring the intersection between feminist theories and practices and indigenous and traditional knowledge around gender (Green 2007; Suzack et al. 2010). Indigenous feminists have emphasized connections to the land, environmental protection, indigenous sovereignty, and women's responsibilities related to lifegiving, family, and community organizing, while calling attention to the impact of patriarchy on indigenous women's lives.

There has been relatively little gender-based analysis about indigenous men and/or work on indigenous masculinities. Most of the work has been led by indigenous scholars of Oceania (Tengan 2007; Jolly 2008; Hokowhitu 2012). Indigenous masculinities work is congruent with indigenous feminist work as it examines the impact of Euro-Western heteropatriarchy on indigenous communities. It also examines the colonial practice of imposing hegemonic masculinities, and what this has meant in terms of indigenous men's identities. More work is needed to explore traditional and indigenous knowledge about men and masculinities, and to document the identities and gendered experiences of indigenous men in historical and contemporary contexts.

Recent indigenous queer theory has drawn together traditional and indigenous knowledge about gender and sexuality, gender-based analysis of colonization, indigenous feminism, and indigenous masculinities studies to challenge heteropatriarchy in indigenous and settler communities, and to envision an alternative (Driskill et al. 2011). This work offers promising direction for scholars and activists with an interest in understanding non-Western systems of gender and sexuality and then finding ways to apply this knowledge to social justice. It is in keeping with the decolonization efforts of many indigenous peoples who wish to challenge hegemonic and heteropatriarchal notions of gender, and who envision a healthier future by looking to the past as expressed in traditional and indigenous knowledge, theories, and practices.

SEE ALSO: Berdache; Colonialism and Gender; Colonialism and Sexuality; Gender, Politics, and the State: Indigenous Women; Gender, Politics, and the State, and the Māori; Indigenous Knowledges and Gender; LGBT Activism in Native North America; Two-Spirit

REFERENCES

Anderson, Kim. 2000. *A Recognition of Being: Reconstructive Native Womanhood*. Toronto: Sumach/Canadian Scholars' Press.

Brown, Lester B., ed. 1997. *Two-Spirit People: American Indian Lesbian Women and Gay Men*. New York: Harrington Park Press.

Driskill, Quo-Li, Chris Finley, Brian Joseph Gilley, and Scott Lauria Morgensen. 2011. *Queer Indigenous Studies: Critical Interventions in Theory, Politics, and Literature*. Tucson: University of Arizona Press.

Green, Joyce, ed. 2007. *Making Space for Indigenous Feminism*. Black Point: Fernwood Publishing.

Hokowhitu, Brendan. 2012. "Producing Elite Indigenous Masculinities." *Settler Colonial Studies, Special Issue: Gender, Sexuality, and Settler Colonialism*, 2(2): 23–48.

Jacob, Sue Ellen, Wesley Thomas, and Sabine Lang, eds. 1997. *Two Spirit People: Native American Gender Identity, Sexuality and Spirituality*. Champaign: University of Illinois Press.

Jolly, Margaret, ed. 2008. The Contemporary Pacific, *Special Issue: Re-membering Oceanic Masculinities*, 20(1).

Roscoe, Will. 1998. *Changing Ones: Third and Fourth Genders in Native North America*. New York: St. Martin's Press.

Suzack, Cheryl, Shari Huhndorf, Jeanne Perreault, and Jean Barman, eds. 2010. *Indigenous Women and Feminism: Politics, Activism, Culture*. Vancouver: University of British Columbia Press.

Tengan, Ty P. Kāwika. 2007. *Native Men Remade: Gender and Nation in Contemporary Hawai'i*. Durham, NC: Duke University Press.

Williams, Walter L. 1992. *The Spirit and the Flesh: Sexual Diversity in American Indian Culture*. Boston: Beacon Press.

Woodsum, Jo Ann. 1995. "Gender and Sexuality in Native American Societies: A Bibliography." *American Indian Quarterly*, 19(4): 527–554.

FURTHER READING

McKegney, Sam, ed. 2014. *Masculindians: Conversations about Indigenous Manhood*. Winnipeg: University of Manitoba Press.

Slater, Sandra, and Fay A. Yarbrough. 2011. *Gender and Sexuality in Indigenous North America: 1400–1850*. Columbia: University of South Carolina Press.

Traditional Healing

ROY MOODLEY
University of Toronto, Canada

In response to globalization and migration, and as a result of liberal and humanistic ideas that inform current health and social care practices, traditional healing practices are now becoming part of the alternative and complementary ways in which people seek solutions to psychological and physical problems (Moodley 2011, 2013). Research, teaching, and the use of traditional and cultural healing practices have been on the increase in the West, with a particular focus on mental health issues (see Vontress 1991; Moodley and West 2005). Indeed many middle-class North Americans make use of alternative and complementary healing practices, which include meditation, spiritual healing, network chiropractics, craniosacral therapy, Shiatsu, Reiki, therapeutic touch and energy healing, naturopathy, occult, New Age therapies, Christian Science, acupuncture, Ayurveda, herbalism, yogic meditation, and many others for their mental and physical well-being (Heber et al. 1989). In researching South Asian women's use of traditional healing practices in Canada, Hilton et al. (2001) found that they use a wide variety of traditional healers and healing practices, such as homeopathy, naturopathy, babajis (wise men), pundits and granthis (holy men), and jyotshis (fortune tellers or astrologers). This engagement and interest in traditional healing has, in part, been fueled by the Asian, African, and South American immigrant communities in the West, since traditional and cultural healing has been a primary means of addressing problems among these ethnic minority communities (Constantine et al. 2004). Dein and Sembhi (2001) argue that this happens due to the limitations of Western healthcare practices, while the argument is made that traditional healers have profound knowledge and understanding of their particular community's historical, religious, and cultural beliefs, as well as the current economic despair, political conflict, and changing values they experience (Crawford and Lipsedge 2004). The use of cultural symbols, rituals, and artifacts consistent with the spiritual and religious belief systems of the patient provides them with an opportunity to interpret illness in a culturally specific context and to predict and prescribe various kinds of treatments for particular conditions in an individualized way (Moodley 2013).

In North America ethnic minority cultural and traditional healing practices appear to be complementing existing Aboriginal practices such as storytelling and healing circles, sweat lodge ceremonies, medicine wheel, the Pimaatisiwin circle, and so on (McCormick 1997; Poonwassie and Charter 2005; McCabe 2007). Indeed, many psychologists, amongst them a growing number of counseling psychologists of Aboriginal descent, are now integrating Aboriginal traditional healing practices into their mainstream counseling and clinical psychology work (Oulanova and Moodley 2010).

In the United States and Canada, traditional healing has been changing in relation to the sociopolitical and economic conditions that prevailed. For example, in the Caribbean and South and North America, traditional healing evolved as a response to the inhumane conditions of slavery and colonization, and practices such as Voodoo and black magic have been a direct response to slavery and racism (Chireau 2003). Over time other forms of healing practices evolved to accommodate racial discrimination and cultural marginalization. Mekada Graham (2005) points to Maat, an Afrocentric healing method that empowers individuals and groups to resist the racial discrimination and cultural marginalization in the inner cities of Britain and North America. In these instances, the healers may not be Voodoo priests but Afrocentric mentors; indeed there could be others who are not Afrocentric that engage intensely and deeply with anti-oppressive and anti-racist empowerment practices, such as teachers, priests, and counselors. In this way, it seems that these contemporary anti-racist healers are the carriers of cultural and religious ideas, keeping indigenous healing traditions alive by acting as guardians of the old world's social and cultural history against the onslaught of colonial Christianity, oppression, marginalization, racism, and capitalism (Moodley 2013).

However, as older and newer forms of healing intersect, converge, collide, and/or compete with each other, the traditional healing practices themselves have transformed, changing not only the definition of traditional healing but also the ways in which we represent and present health, illness, and wellness (Moodley 2013).

SEE ALSO: Alternative Medicine and Therapies; Complementary and Alternative Medicine; Medicine and Medicalization

REFERENCES

Chireau, Yvonne, P. 2003. *Black Magic: Religion and the African American Conjuring Tradition.* Berkeley: University of California Press.

Constantine, Madonna G., et al. 2004. "Exploring Indigenous Mental Health Practices: The Roles of Healers and Helpers in Promoting Well-Being in People of Color." *Counseling and Values* 48: 110–125.

Crawford, Tanya A., and Maurice Lipsedge. 2004. "Seeking Help for Psychological Distress: The Interface of Zulu Traditional Healing and Western Biomedicine." *Mental Health, Religion & Culture*, 7(2): 131–148.

Dein, Simon, and Sati Sembhi. 2001. "The Use of Traditional Healing in South Asian Psychiatric Patients in the U.K.: Interactions between Professional and Folk Psychiatries." *Transcultural Psychiatry*, 38(2): 243–257.

Graham, Mekada. 2005. "Maat: An African-Centered Paradigm for Psychological and Spiritual Healing." In *Integrating Traditional Healing Practices into Counseling and Psychotherapy*, edited by Roy Moodley and William West. Thousand Oaks: Sage.

Heber, Alexandra Sharon, et al. 1989. "Dissociation in Alternative Healers and Traditional Therapists: A Comparative Study." *American Journal of Psychotherapy*, 43: 562–574.

Hilton, B. Ann, et al. 2001. "The Desi Ways: Traditional Health Practices of South Asian Women in Canada." *Heath Care for Women International*, 22: 553–567.

McCabe, Glen. 2007. "The Healing Path: A Culture and Community Derived Indigenous Therapy Model." *Psychotherapy: Theory, Research, Practice, Training*, 44(2): 148–160.

McCormick, Rod. 1997. "Healing through Interdependence: The Role of Connecting in First Nation Healing Practices." *Canadian Journal of Counselling*, 31: 172–184.

Moodley, Roy. 2011. "The Toronto Traditional Healers Project: An Introduction." *International Journal of Health Promotion and Education*, 49(3): 74–78.

Moodley, Roy. 2013. "Spirit Based Healing in the Black Diaspora." *Therapy Today*, 24(6): 17–20.

Moodley, Roy, and William West, eds. 2005. *Integrating Traditional Healing Practices into Counseling and Psychotherapy*. Thousand Oaks: Sage.

Oulanova, Olga, and Roy Moodley. 2010. "Navigating Two Worlds: Experiences of Canadian Mental Health Professionals who Integrate Aboriginal Traditional Healing Practices." *Canadian Journal of Counselling and Psychotherapy/Revue canadienne de counseling et de psychothérapie*, 44(4): 346–362.

Poonwassie, Ann, and Ann Charter. 2005. "Aboriginal Worldview of Healing: Inclusion, Blending, and Bridging." In *Integrating Traditional Healing Practices into Counseling and Psychotherapy*, edited by Roy Moodley and William West. Thousand Oaks: Sage.

Vontress, Clemmont E. 1991. "Traditional Healing in Africa: Implications for Cross-Cultural Counseling." *Journal of Counseling and Development*, 70: 242–249.

Trans Identities, Psychological Perspectives

VARUNEE FAII SANGGANJANAVANICH
The University of Akron, USA

Transgender people are recognized and have their place in many cultures and societies across the world (e.g., hijras or third gender in the Indian subcontinent, two-spirits in indigenous groups in North America). "Transgender" refers to individuals who experience incongruence between their assigned and expressed gender, and therefore their gender identity differs from a binary view of gender – female or male. Trans identities refer to a transgender identity umbrella overarching a variety of gender non-conforming people within the transgender community. In general, trans identities represent transgender, transsexual, crossdresser, drag queen, intersex, androgyny, genderqueer, genderless, and bigender people. People from the mainstream culture sometimes use the aforementioned terms interchangeably to refer to the transgender community. It is important, however, to note that while transgender is a broader term used to refer to gender non-conforming people, diversity within the transgender community exists.

Although transgender and transsexual are used interchangeably, these two terms are different. "Transgender" is a broader term that refers to people who adopt gender identities that differ from the one assigned at birth. Transsexual, however, is a specific term derived from a recognized medical condition coined by Harry Benjamin (1966). Transsexual refers to individuals, male-to-female (MtF) and female-to-male (FtM), who may experience gender discomfort and distress and seek to align their bodies or appearance with a gender other than the one assigned at birth. This condition has been categorized by health professionals as *gender dysphoria* according to the *Diagnostic and Statistical Manual of Mental Disorders* (APA 2013) and *gender identity disorder* in the *International Statistical Classification of Diseases and Related Health Problems* (World Health Organization 2010).

Unlike transgender, transsexual individuals not only adopt gender roles and expressions, but also choose to live full-time as a member of the desired gender and usually seek *sex reassignment surgery* (also known as sex change, gender reassignment surgery, or gender confirmation surgery) – a standard medical intervention believed to alleviate gender discomfort by altering primary and secondary sex characteristics to match with gender identity, including hormone therapy and surgical procedures (World Professional Association for Transgender Health 2012). Through the use of cosmetic and reconstructive surgeries (e.g., breast augmentation for MtF, mastectomy for FtM), individuals can achieve a sense of gender congruence through their new physical appearance. However, not all transsexual people decide to pursue sex reassignment surgery due to various reasons (e.g., financial constraints, physical health). Additionally, in many cases sex reassignment surgery is often used to describe *gender transition* – a process where one undertakes an identity transformation from the assigned gender at birth. Gender transition involves psychological, biological, social, and legal aspects of one's life. Thus, gender transition has implications for important aspects of the individual including legal, education, career, and mental health.

"Cross-dresser" is a term used to refer to individuals who prefer to wear clothing of the opposite gender (e.g., a woman wearing men's clothing), which, in many cultures, is considered a violation of social norms. In fact, it is inaccurate to refer to cross-dressers as transvestites and vice versa. Cross-dressers, sometimes called drags (i.e., drag queen and king), enjoy wearing clothing of the opposite gender for certain purposes (e.g., entertainment, personal pleasure). Transvestic disorder (APA 2013) or transvestic fetishism (WHO 2010) is considered a form of paraphilic disorder – atypical sexual interest and stimulation (e.g., urge, fantasy) exclusively through unusual objects (e.g., clothing), situations (e.g., public), or individuals (e.g., corpse) – that causes significant distress or impairment in one's social and occupational functioning. There are criticisms surrounding whether cross-dressing behaviors should be considered a mental disorder because those behaviors simply reflect diversity of sexual expression, not illness.

Genderqueer, genderless, and bigender are newer terms that are used to describe a gender identity of individuals who do not conform to the traditional gender binary – a belief that only two genders, female and male, exist – and reject being identified with either gender. These individuals are opposed to the idea of having to identify with either female or male gender identity. Rather, they promote gender neutrality (e.g., using gender-neutral language) and create a self-identified gender identity that, too often, may not fit with conventional ways of gender identity conceptualization.

Researchers have attempted to estimate the number of transgender individuals; however, there are various factors that may contribute to an inaccurate estimation. First, it is difficult to estimate the size of the transgender community because the number of transgender people, under the transgender umbrella, is usually diversified through self-constructed meanings. Second, trans identities are self-identified and sometimes underreported. Many transgender people do not want to publicly identify as transgender due to guilt and shame of being labeled as transgender and fear of discrimination and stigmatization.

The World Professional Association of Transgender Health (WPATH 2010) issued a statement to address the issue of over-pathologization and stigmatization toward transgender people. WPATH emphasized that "the expression of gender characteristics, including identities, that are not stereotypically associated with one's assigned sex at birth is a common and culturally diverse human phenomenon which should not be judged as inherently pathological or negative" (2010, 1). People with trans identities have historically been marginalized in many social structures including family unit, healthcare, housing, education, and employment (Grant et al. 2010). These individuals are involuntarily stigmatized through the negative perceptions and sociopolitical implications of being transgender (e.g., mentally ill). Institutionalized oppression, marginalization, exclusion, and discrimination seem to be ongoing issues that the transgender population around the world encounters (e.g., lack of social and legal protection and support when compared to their non-transgender counterparts). These issues may lead transgender people to experience an increased risk to their mental and physical well-being such as anxiety, depression, substance abuse behaviors, self-injury behaviors, and suicidal ideation (Bockting, Knudson, and Goldberg 2006).

Despite the struggles, transgender communities remain present in many societies around the globe, such as hijras on the Indian subcontinent and kathoey in Thailand. In recent years, transgender people across cultures are more represented in various industries, including education, politics, media, and sports (Chonwilai 2012). The visibility of transgender people in these industries increases public awareness of their potential and a degree of acceptance of trans identities, although there are still problems in practice (Sharma 2012). Some subgroups of trans identities (e.g., transsexualism and transvestism) are currently considered mental disorders by medical classifications. Many critiques advocate that trans lived experience and gender diversity should be viewed neither as deviant nor as abnormal behaviors. Rather, gender and sexual diversity is a freedom that one can choose to embrace as a part of one's lifestyle. Trans identities are reflections of diverse human sexuality.

SEE ALSO: Androgyny; Bisexuality; Cross-Dressing; Drag; Gender Dysphoria; Genderqueer; *Hijra/Hejira*; Intersexuality; Kathoey; Sex Reassignment Surgery; Third Genders; Trans Theorizing; Transgender Health and Healthcare; Transgender Movements in International Perspective; Transgender Movements in the United States; Transgender Politics; Two-Spirit

REFERENCES

American Psychiatric Association (APA). 2013. *Diagnostic and Statistical Manual of Mental Disorders*, 5th ed. (DSM-5). Washington, DC: American Psychiatric Association.

Benjamin, Harry. 1966. *The Transsexual Phenomenon*. New York: Julian Press.

Bockting, Walter, Gail Knudson, and Joshua M. Goldberg. 2006. *Counselling and Mental Health Care of Transgender Adults and Loved Ones.* Vancouver: Vancouver Coastal Health Transgender Health Program.

Chonwilai, Sulaiporn. 2012. "Kathoey: Male-to-Female Transgenders or Transsexuals." In *Thai Sex Talk: The Language of Sex and Sexuality in Thailand*, edited by Pimpawun Boonmongkon and Peter A. Jackson, 100–117. Chiang Mai, Thailand: Mekong Press.

Grant, Jamie M., et al. 2010. "National Transgender Discrimination Survey: Report on Health and Health Care." National Center for Transgender Equality and National Gay and Lesbian Task Force. Accessed August 17, 2015, at http://transequality.org/PDFs/NTDSReportonHealth_final.pdf.

Sharma, Preeti. 2012. "Historical Background and Legal Status of Third Gender in Indian Society." *International Journal of Research in Economics and Social Sciences*, 2: 64–71.

World Health Organization (WHO). 2010. *International Statistical Classification of Diseases and Related Health Problems*, 10th ed., text rev. (ICD-10). Geneva: WHO.

World Professional Association for Transgender Health (WPATH). 2010. "Statement Urging the De-psychopathologisation of Gender Variance." Accessed August 17, 2015, at http://www.wpath.org/uploaded_files/140/files/de-psychopathologisation%205-26-10%20on%20letterhead.pdf.

World Professional Association for Transgender Health (WPATH). 2012. "Standards of Care (SOC) for the Health of Transsexual, Transgender, and Gender Nonconforming People." Accessed August 17, 2015 at http://www.wpath.org/site_page.cfm?pk_association_webpage_menu=1351.

FURTHER READING

American Psychological Association Task Force on Gender Identity and Gender Variance. 2009. Report of the American Psychological Association Task Force on Gender Identity and Gender Variance. Washington, DC: American Psychological Association.

Bockting, Walter O., and Eli Coleman. 2007. "Developmental Stages of the Transgender Coming

Out Process: Toward an Integrated Identity." In *Principles of Transgender Medicine and Surgery*, edited by Randi Ettner, Stan Monstrey, and A. Evan Eyler, 185–208. New York: Haworth Press.

Coleman, E., et al. 2012. "Standards of Care for the Health of Transsexual, Transgender, and Gender Nonconforming People, 7th Version." *International Journal of Transgenderism*, 13: 165–232.

Trans Theorizing

ANDRZEJ KLIMCZUK
Warsaw School of Economics, Poland

MAŁGORZATA BIEŃKOWSKA
University of Białystok, Poland

"Trans" is an umbrella term encompassing all of the gender practices and identities that fall outside of the binary gender system. Trans theorizing is the formation of a system of ideas used to explain the nature of gender and gender identity in understanding the lived experiences of trans people. In the beginning, trans theories were mainly medical concepts developed in the 1950s and 1960s and psychiatric theories in the 1970s. Later, the medical approach was criticized by scholars and others including trans people who challenged the way in which it pathologized trans and gender nonconforming people. These criticisms opened the way for constructionist theories, which led to the development of the performative perspective and queer theory in the 1990s. Physical embodiment in gender identity is integrated with socially constructed aspects of selfhood in contemporary trans theories. Incorporating this approach with the lived experiences of trans people, contemporary trans theorizing reconciles feminist and queer theoretical scholarship with activism and advocacy for trans people and to larger issues of group identity and social oppression (Nagoshi and Brzuzy 2010).

MEDICAL AND PSYCHIATRIC THEORIES

The concept of "transsexualism" was popularized in the 1950s by Harry Benjamin, an endocrinologist (Stryker 2006). In the 1960s, the scientific approach to this issue was dominated by a medical perspective. It affected the way in which trans people were described and analyzed in the social sciences. Medical discourse mentions "being trapped in the wrong body" and the necessity of sex reassignment surgery to change one's body to match one's gender identity. Benjamin created the classification of "transsexualism" and determined standards of medical care for transsexual people. Doctors considered it to be a medical disorder that can be treated by surgical procedures to allow trans people to embody their "authentic" sex rather than the physical sex in which they were born. The emphasis on authenticity meant that trans people were forced to attempt to "pass" as the "opposite" sex (and to be heterosexual) in order to be considered authentically transsexual and to be eligible for medical intervention. In the 1970s, this focus on authenticity was intensified by psychiatrists who insisted that surgical procedures were an appropriate method to adjust to the "real sex" with which a transsexual person identified (Hines 2010).

The American Psychiatric Assocation (APA) adopted that term "transsexual" in the *Diagnostic and Statistical Manual (DMS-III)* in 1980. The term was replaced in 1987 in the *DSM-IV* by "gender identity disorder" (GID) to assist in diagnosis of individuals whose assigned gender at birth diverged from their self identity and who experienced distress as a result. In 2013, the APA removed GID and replaced it with "gender dysphoria" in the *DSM-5* to reflect new understanding of the diverse ways the people experience and perform gender outside social expectations.

PERFORMATIVITY AND CONSTRUCTIONIST THEORIES OF TRANSSEXUALITY

When trans people began telling their own stories rather than being spoken about by the medical community, the limitations of medical and psychiatric trans theories became clear. During the 1960s, the first autobiographies of transsexual people began to be published. In 1974 Jan Morris wrote *Conundrum*, in which she described her own path toward sex reassignment surgery. Since then, many transsexual people published autobiographies and memoirs describing their experiences of the transition process. They became a main source from which to analyze transsexual people from perspectives other than medical and psychiatric theories.

In the late 1960s sociologists began to explore the social construction and performative aspects of gender (Hirn 2002). In 1967, sociologist Harold Garfinkel – who developed the perspective of ethnomethodology – detailed the proactive ways in which Agnes, a transgender person, convinced a team of doctors to support her request for gender transition. In *Changing Sex: Transsexualism, Technology, and the Idea of Gender* (1995) Bernice L. Hausman furthered the constructionist perspective by analyzing the social assumptions of medical discourse on trans people (see also Prosser 1998). Social construction theories demonstrate how the lived experiences of trans people can expose the day-to-day construction of gender in nuanced ways that reveal how gender is socially constructed by all of us in our daily lives (Kessler and McKenna 2000).

Judith Butler (1990) is credited as having developed the theory of gender performativity in which gender is understood as what someone *does*, rather than what someone *is*. This idea of gender as performative was the springboard for queer trans theories in that she argues against the distinction between sex and gender and for the power of discourse to construct what we take as natural or normal. In her now classic book *Gender Trouble* (1990), Butler explains that "Gender is the repeated stylization of the body, a set of repeated acts within a highly rigid regulatory frame that congeal over time to produce the appearance of substance, of a natural sort of being" (p. 45). Butler addresses some of the criticism that her book garnered including lack of attention to transgender and intersexuality in the introduction to the 1999 edition of the book (Salih 2002). She also takes on other questions that her *Gender Trouble* evokes in *Bodies That Matter* (1993). Here she discusses the regulatory production of race and explores how "race" is "lived in the modality of sexuality" and how gender is "lived in the modality of race" (p. 117) to offer a more intersectional understanding of performativity.

TOWARD QUEER THEORY

In the 1990s, the concept of transgender was introduced as a replacement for the term "transsexual" in order to diminish the primacy of medical discourse. Transgender is the less clinical umbrella term under which transsexual, genderqueer, and other trans identities are covered. Purely medical perceptions of transgender were further undermined by queer theory that developed at the time and deconstructed the idea of biological sex being entirely natural. For example, *Queer Theory/Sociology* (1996), edited by Steven Seidman, reflected on the changes in scientific discourse concerning sexuality, sex, sexual orientation, and demonstrates how gender is historically and socially constructed. Seidman and other authors in the volume challenged the knowledge concerning sexual minorities from earlier "naive modernist assumptions."

Queer trans theory contests rigid boundaries and the presumed stable or fixed nature of gender. It views gender and sexuality as always implicated in relations of power that are woven throughout everyday life, discourse, and culture. In this way it is itself a shifting intellectual and activist project.

SEE ALSO: Essentialism; Genderqueer; Social Identity; Social Role Theory of Sex Differences; Transsexuality; Transvestitism; Queer Theory

REFERENCES

Bornstein, Kate. 1994. *Gender Outlaw*. New York: Routledge.
Butler, Judith. 1990; (Anniversary edition 1999). *Gender Trouble: Feminism and the Subversion of Identity*. New York: Routledge.
Butler, Judith. 1993. *Bodies That Matter: On the Discursive Limits of 'Sex'*. New York: Routledge.
Ekins, Richard, and Dave King. 1999. "Towards a Sociology of Transgendered Bodies." *The Sociological Review*, 47(3): 580–602.
Garfinkel, Harold. 1967. *Studies in Ethnomethodology*. Englewood Cliffs NJ: Prentice Hall.
Hausman, Bernice L. 1995. *Changing Sex: Transsexualism, Technology, and the Idea of Gender*. Durham, NC: Duke University Press.
Hines, Sally. 2010. "Introduction." In *Transgender Identities: Towards a Social Analysis of Gender Diversity*, edited by Sally Hines and Tam Sanger, 1–22. New York: Routledge.
Kessler, Suzanne J., and Wendy McKenna. 2000. "Gender Construction in Everyday Life: Transsexualism (Abridged)." *Feminism & Psychology*, 10(1): 11–29.
Nagoshi, Julie L. and Stephan/ie Brzuzy. 2010. "Transgender Theory: Embodying Research and Practice." *Affilia*, 25(4): 431-443.
Prosser, Jay. 1998. *Second Skin: The Body Narratives of Transsexuality*. New York: Columbia University Press.
Salih, Sara. 2002. *Judith Butler*. New York: Routledge.
Seidman, Steven, ed. 1996. *Queer Theory/Sociology*. Cambridge, MA: Blackwell.
Stryker, Susan. 2006. "(De)Subjugated Knowledges: An Introduction to Transgender Studies." In *The Transgender Studies Reader*, edited by Susan Stryker and Stephen Whittle, 1–17. London: Routledge.

FURTHER READING

Bieńkowska, Małgorzata. 2012. *Transseksualizm w Polsce: Wymiar indywidualny i społeczny przekraczania binarnego systemu płci* [Transsexualism in Poland: Individual and Social Dimension Crossing Binary Gender System]. Białystok, Poland: Wydawnictwo Uniwersytetu w Białymstoku.
Hausman, Bernice L. 2001. "Recent Transgender Theory." *Feminist Studies*, 27(2): 465–491.
Hines, Sally. 2007. *TransForming Gender: Transgender Practices of Identity, Intimacy and Care*. Bristol: Policy Press.
Hird, Myra J. 2002. "For a Sociology of Transsexualism." *Sociology*, 36(3): 577–595.

Transgender Health and Healthcare

RACHEL R. BOGAN
The City University of New York, USA

Transgender health and healthcare refer to the diagnosis, treatment, and prevention of health issues for transgender or gender-nonconforming people. The study of transgender health examines how transgender people interact with medical and mental health practitioners, institutions, laws, and insurance practices while seeking gender-confirming healthcare. Scholarship reflects the transgender community's diverse and individualized needs as not all transgender people desire hormones or surgery and many of their healthcare needs are similar to those of the general population. However, transgender people are less likely to have their healthcare needs addressed, owing to factors such as discrimination, absence of practitioner competency, and insurance exclusions.

Like the general population, transgender people desire access to safe, non-discriminatory, culturally sensitive, and affordable healthcare. When the necessary care is provided, the population's mental health improves and suicide rates drop. However, transgender people frequently experience discrimination when receiving care, including being refused treatment, harassed, or misgendered. Low-income and transgender people of color (when compared with other sexual minorities) describe higher rates of discrimination when accessing knowledgeable and inclusive care. Discrimination and stigma experienced inside and outside healthcare settings can lead to negative health outcomes. For transgender people, fear of discrimination (transphobia) can be just as harmful to their health as active discrimination.

In order to stay healthy, transgender people require access to a range of medical, surgical, and psychological services. Their acute and preventive care needs are often similar to those of the cisgender community (a term used to describe people who do not identify as transgender or gender non-conforming). These services include screenings and treatment for sexually transmitted infections, HIV/AIDS, cancer, substance use, mental health issues, and gender-specific care such as mammograms, PAP smears, and prostate examinations. Rates of HIV infection for the transgender community are four times higher than the national average and are even higher for trans women of color, trans people who engage in commercial sex work, and homeless trans people. Transgender people seek out mental healthcare for help with a variety of issues: transition care, depression, anxiety, discrimination, and management of identity issues.

Although their healthcare needs are similar to those of the cisgender population, transgender people also have specific health needs (physical and psychological) related to their transgender identity – such as support surrounding gender transition. Transgender people desire individualized gender-confirming healthcare, such as feminizing or masculinizing hormones, psychotherapy, and genital surgery – care connected to how they express their gender identity. Yet, when transgender healthcare becomes synonymous with gender transition care, it may produce a narrative that all transgender people desire to undergo genital surgery – an account that is not accurate.

The availability of transgender-friendly healthcare correlates with the health of the transgender community. When a lack of gender-confirming healthcare exists, transgender people may suffer negative health consequences. Lack of competent services may force them to seek services outside the mainstream healthcare system, potentially compromising their health. For example, people who cannot legally access hormones may seek out "street hormones" that can be unsafe or unclean and seriously harm them, putting them at risk for contracting HIV or blood-borne pathogens. Like other groups experiencing discrimination, transgender people have higher rates of HIV infection, drug and alcohol use, smoking, and suicide attempts.

One key aspect of transgender healthcare is gender transition care. People seek this type of care when they believe their gender identity differs from their sex assigned at birth.

Gender transition treatment is heterogeneous and includes various mental health, surgical, and medical procedures. One transition option is gender-confirming surgery, also known as sex reassignment surgery (SRS) or gender reassignment surgery (GRS). Gender-confirming patients want to align their primary and secondary sex characteristics with their gender identity. Surgical transition procedures to change primary or secondary sex characteristics include breast or chest surgery, genital reconstruction, and hysterectomies. Although not the first American to undergo SRS, Christine Jorgensen's 1950's European SRS was sensationalized by the US press – making her the first widely known person in the United States to undergo gender-confirming surgery.

Although some transgender people medically or surgically change their bodily sex or gender presentation, others do not. Not all desire or can afford surgery (often surgeries) and care must be individualized due to the multiplicity of goals. The most common transition treatment is hormone therapy that feminizes or masculinizes bodies. However, transition care is more than hormones and surgery and can include: psychotherapy, hair removal, changes in hairstyle or clothing, breast binding or padding, genital tucking, penile prostheses, and name or gender changes on documents.

For the past century, Western medicine has been involved in the treatment of trans bodies – most frequently in "sex change" surgeries. Lili Elbe, a Danish artist, was one of the first known people to transition medically from male to female. In the twentieth century, European medical practitioners were among the first to publicize and conduct surgeries to change people's "sex" before the availability of synthetic hormones and modern plastic-surgery techniques. German physician and sexologist Magnus Hirschfeld headed the first institute for the study of sexuality (Institut für Sexualwissenschaft) from 1919 until the Nazis destroyed the institute and its libraries in 1933. Among the institute's many services, it offered the first modern "sex-change" surgeries (in the 1930s) to patients they named "transvestites." A colleague of Hirschfeld, German-born American endocrinologist and sex researcher Harry Benjamin, became well known for introducing transsexuality to the American medical field and developing medical procedures for transsexuals. Benjamin advocated for transsexuals to receive (sex) hormones and for medical professionals to offer transsexual patients surgery.

In addition to transition care, diagnoses also contribute to the medicalization of trans bodies. Medical and mental health practitioners may diagnose transgender patients using the *Diagnostics and Statistical Manual of Mental Disorders* (*DSM*) classification of gender dysphoria (before the DSM-5, the classification was gender identity disorder). Gender dysphoria refers to the discomfort between a person's assigned gender and their experienced gender. Treatment for gender dysphoria includes hormone therapy, surgery, psychotherapy, name or gender changes on documents, hair removal, breast binding or padding, and genital tucking.

Not all transgender people experience gender dysphoria, and if they do, they may only experience it at a certain point in their lives. A diagnosis of gender dysphoria often allows transgender people access to medical or surgical transition care. However, the use of a diagnosis to receive healthcare is controversial, as transgender activists argue that no diagnosis should be needed to access care.

In the 1970s, the Chair of Johns Hopkins University School of Medicine's Gender Identity Clinic, Paul McHugh, spoke out against SRS, arguing for the use of psychotherapy instead of hormones and surgery to treat gender dysphoria. McHugh coordinated a study, led by psychiatrist Jon Meyer and co-investigator Donna Reter, examining the effects of SRS on transgender women's daily lives. Although Meyer and Reter assessed approximately 60 subjects pre- and post-treatment (in their jobs, education, and martial status) and found that transgender women had the same or better outcomes, the pair did not find a statistically significant difference between patients who had undergone transition surgery and those who had not. Despite the study's flaws, its results attracted significant attention as they were published in a well-known psychological journal. McHugh used these results to reinforce his viewpoint that gender-confirming surgery was not beneficial *and* to validate the institute's closure.

When the Johns Hopkins Gender Identity clinic closed, it triggered other academic clinics to close (except for the University of Minnesota). Treatment moved out of the academic medical sphere and into private heath practices. During the same timeframe, insurance plans that covered transgender treatment began to remove this coverage. Although a majority of current insurance policies expressly exclude coverage for transgender care – despite doctors deeming this care medically necessary – regulations are shifting in favor of coverage of transgender care. A number of private insurance carriers currently cover transgender-related healthcare under the rubric of "transgender services," "medical and surgical treatment of gender identity disorder," and "gender reassignment surgery." Nine states (California, Colorado, Connecticut, Illinois, Massachusetts, New York, Oregon, Vermont, and Washington) and the District of Colombia mandate that most private insurance plans cover medically necessary healthcare for transgender patients.

The transgender community is less likely than the general population to be insured (although they are not the only population to be uninsured). This lack of insurance is related to various factors: the trans community's lower employment rates and the fact that many people access insurance via their employer, and the difficulty of getting one's name or gender on documents in order to apply for public insurance. Lack of coverage can lead to high expenses, lack of needed care, or accessing non-legal care that can be harmful. In fact, these desired services are often the same ones that cisgender people receive, such as mastectomies and augmentation mammoplasty that practitioners use for treatment and reconstruction after breast cancer.

Medicaid, a federal health insurance program for low-income residents, leaves the regulation of the coverage of gender-confirming healthcare up to each state. Many states exclude transgender care in one of two ways: with specific regulations or by using a case-by-case basis to evaluate need. There are some states, such as New York, that now require Medicaid to cover (most) transgender care.

A rich history of spaces where transgender people seek medical and surgical care exists. In 1965, the Johns Hopkins Gender Identity Clinic became the first US academic institution to perform SRS. The clinic also served as teaching space, educating doctors and researchers about transition surgery, until it closed in 1979. However, Johns Hopkins was not the only hospital to treat transsexual people in the 1960s and 1970s. In 1968, Stanford University opened the first "sex change" clinic on the West Coast and the Center for Sexual Health at the University of Minnesota's Program in Sexuality has provided transgender care since 1973.

Transgender people need to work with transgender-friendly practitioners who provide competent care and are educated about transgender health issues. Practitioners must consider the race, class, age, sexuality, disability, and geographic location of the transgender population when providing services. Medical providers who are aware of their patients' transgender identity are more likely to provide sensitive and trans-positive care. Beyond providing competent care, primary care providers can advocate for their transgender clients, especially with other specialists, making sure they receive the care they need. In addition, it is important that practitioners, medical forms, and interpersonal communication do not use gendered language to make assumptions about a transgender person's identity or body. The use of appropriate language affects levels of care as it can increase comfort levels and trust – and misuse of gendered language can contribute to lack of quality of care.

The World Professional Association for Transgender Health's (WPATH) Standards of Care (SOC) – a set of non-binding clinical guidelines outlining treatment requirements for people who desire to transition to the opposite sex – influence how practitioners treat transgender patients. (Until 2007, WPATH was known as the Harry Benjamin International Gender Dysphoria Association.) Before the SOC, no consensus about the medicalization of transgender bodies existed; similar guidelines exist worldwide, with the SOC being the best known. First published in 1979, the SOC provide clinical guidelines for health practitioners on how to help transsexual, transgender, and gender-non-conforming people receive the best possible healthcare. The most updated SOC (2011) relax the guidelines that detail how transgender patients can access care, view conversion therapy unethical, and depathologize gender non-conformity. For example, the standards no longer require patients to undergo psychotherapy before receiving hormones or surgery.

SEE ALSO: Health Disparities; Health, Healthcare, and Sexual Minorities; Medicine and Medicalization; Trans Identities, Psychological Perspectives; Transgender Politics; Transsexuality

FURTHER READING

Coleman, Eli, et al. 2011. "Standards of Care for the Health of Transsexual, Transgender, and Gender-nonconforming People, Version 7." *International Journal of Transgenderism*, 13: 165–232. DOI: 10.1080/15532739.2011.700873.

Gorton, Nick, and Hilary Maia Grubb. 2014. "General, Sexual, and Reproductive Health." In *Trans Bodies, Trans Selves: A Resource For the Transgender Community*, edited by Laura Erickson-Schroth, 215–240. Oxford: Oxford University Press.

Lombardi, Emilia. 2010. "Transgender Health: A Review and Guidance for Future Research – Proceedings from the Summer Institute at the Center for Research on Health and Sexual Orientation, University of Pittsburgh." *International Journal of Transgenderism*, 12: 211–229. DOI: 10.1080/15532739.2010.544232.

Spade, Dean, Gabriel Arkles, Phil Duran, Pooja Gehi, and Huy Nguyen. 2010. "Medicaid Policy and Gender-confirming Healthcare for Trans People: An Interview with Advocates." *Seattle Journal for Social Justice*, 8: 497–514.

Stroumsa, Daphna. 2014. "The State of Transgender Health Care: Policy, Law, and Medical Frameworks." *American Journal of Public Health*, 104: e31–e38.

Stryker, Susan. 2008. *Transgender History*. Berkeley: Seal Press.

Transgender Movements in International Perspective

DANIELA JAUK
University of Graz, Austria

Gender non-conforming people have worked together in political movements and organizations seeking social justice for people with diverse gender identity expressions since the 1800s. It was not until the 1990s, however, that a vibrant and increasingly globalized trans*gender movement bolted forward into the public eye and onto the political stage. Transgender, linguistically shortened and conceptually expanded to trans*, is an umbrella term for a wide array of individuals, including individuals whose gender identities do not match their sex assignment at birth and individuals who do not conform to the binary gender order. Trans* folk may or may not permanently or temporarily change their gender presentation, with or without surgical or chemical help. The term trans*gender has been used since the early 1990s, primarily through the influence of Leslie Feinberg's 1992 pamphlet *Transgender Liberation: A Movement Whose Time Has Come* (Feinberg 1992). It originated as a catchall term meant to resist pathologizing terminology and bring people of non-conforming gender identities together in one imagined community. The asterisk in trans*gender is recently becoming widely used by trans*activists and scholars to create a more inclusive trans*gender category (although it is also sometimes contested). Yet trans*gender is not in itself an identity term. In contrast to other forms of identity politics, the trans*gender movement is unique because it builds communities around gender identities, while simultaneously working to deconstruct and denaturalize oppressive gender identity categories. In the international context, the trans*gender label is not universally embraced because it does not account for mutable and fluid gender constructs across cultures. Latin American activists, for instance, speak of "travesti" identities, whereas indigenous activists of "hijras" or "metis." Some Asian and Oceanic cultures embrace forms of a "third gender." Nevertheless, trans*gender movements create political categories for individuals who face discrimination and violence because they do not conform to culturally enforced gender norms worldwide.

Trans*gender movements address numerous issues for gender non-conforming populations across the globe. Trans* people face massive discrimination and marginalization in all social institutions, including the family, labor market, housing, health, education, and religion. Trans* folk deal with great levels of hate and violence across societies, which leads some authors to suggest that a trans*gender genocide is taking place worldwide. The majority of countries in the world make it difficult or do not allow trans* people to amend identity documents (such as birth certificates, passports and national ID cards) to reflect their gender identities. Without proper identity documentation, trans* people are denied citizenship rights. Trans* people have less access to healthcare than the general population, due to discrimination and harassment by providers, inability to pay, lack of insurance, and a host of other socioeconomic barriers. It is difficult for trans* people to navigate gender-segregated services, including public restrooms, homeless shelters, drug-therapy facilities and prisons. Trans* people in prison face challenges not only related to gender segregation and violence, but also due to lack of access to proper clinical care and medication – especially in relation to transition-related medical care. Trans* rights activists are confronted with torture, prison, and death in many parts of the world.

Trans*gender social activism made gains in the 1960s when transgender issues resonated with larger cultural shifts such as the rise of feminism, the anti-war movement, the civil rights movement, and sexual liberation. The movement's momentum increased over the last three decades, spurred by, inter alia, the new political concept of queerness, the AIDS epidemic, and the development of the Internet as an outlet for trans*gender networking "that has not yet reached its crest," according to Susan Stryker in her classic work *Transgender History* (Stryker 2008). One of the first recorded trans* riots in US history took place 1966 around the Compton Cafeteria in the Tenderloin district of San Francisco. Trans* people were also heavily involved in the New York City Stonewall Riots of 1969, which marked the onset of the contemporary lesbian gay bisexual transgender (LGBT) movement. Trans* activists of the Stonewall era, such as Sylvia Rivera, distanced themselves later from the usurpation of trans* issues by the LGBT umbrella. More recent trans* movement literatures also criticize the LGBT movement's homonormative and neoliberal factions. Since the early 1990s, trans*gender movements have moved beyond the narrow scopes of sexuality and gender identity politics. Trans*gender movements seek new forms of collaboration and networking including trans* leaders of color (e.g., The Sylvia Rivera Law Project and the Trans People of Color Coalition). Trans*gender individuals also deal with a very specific set of problems that do not necessarily pertain to other LGBT groups, including problems with state-issued IDs, questions of citizenship, immigration, and undocumented work.

Many accounts of the trans* movement are US-centric due to the accessibility of literature and the location of trans* research communities. Yet trans* movement networks also exist in the Global South, such as the Asia Pacific Transgender Network, the Latin American and Caribbean Transgender Network, and the Africa Transgender Network. Efforts are being made to facilitate better information exchange and funding for global trans*gender movements. GATE (Global Action for Trans*Equality) conducted a survey of 340 trans* or intersex groups and found that trans* and intersex movements are young, diverse, and growing rapidly worldwide. Trans* and intersex groups exist in every region of the world, with sub-regional patterns. For example, there are many more groups in Eastern Africa than in Southern or Western Africa, and Western Europe has more organizations than Eastern Europe. Most trans* and intersex groups work locally, with a few global and regional groups. The groups surveyed in the study work primarily within their home countries, with the greatest number working at the local level (38%), national level (34%), and provincial/state level (20%). Not surprisingly, GATE finds that trans* and intersex groups are generally severely underfunded, yet there are stark differences in the budget sizes of groups led by trans* or intersex people and groups that are not. Discrimination is perpetuated on this level, as trans*-led groups have only one-third to one-fifth of the median annual budget and receive significantly less external funding than groups without trans* leadership.

Trans*gender activists bring transgender discrimination to the forefront of the political debate in their countries, and also push for the acknowledgement of trans* issues in the context of international human rights. In 2011, the United Nations (UN) Human Rights Council passed the first-ever UN resolution on the human rights of lesbian, gay, bisexual and transgender persons (United Nations Human Rights Council 2011). The Yogyakarta Principles of 2006 state that LGBTQIA populations *are in fact protected under current human rights law*; accordingly, member states are expected to protect people from transphobic and homophobic violence and to prohibit discrimination. Numerous cities and states throughout the United States and Europe have introduced anti-discrimination ordinances. In the United States since 2009, gender identity has been covered by federal hate crime law under the Matthew Shepard Act. The controversial Employment Non-Discrimination Act (ENDA), which would prohibit employment discrimination on the basis of sexual orientation and gender identity, is yet to be introduced in the 114th Congress. More than 30 countries in Europe have legal provisions to recognize a trans* person's gender identity, yet trans* people's existence is *de facto* made illegal in 16 countries, and more than 20 countries in Europe require by law that trans people undergo sterilization before their gender identities can be recognized. Acknowledging existing human rights law is one way to counter transphobia. Some countries, including Brazil, Ecuador, Germany, Malta, The Netherlands, and Uruguay, have used the Yogyakarta Principles to guide policy responses to incidents of violence and discrimination. Other initiatives, such as teacher-training programs, the establishment of "safe spaces" for LGBT youths in schools, the installation of gender-neutral bathrooms, and more general awareness-raising campaigns, increasingly include the perspectives of trans* activists.

Trans*gender activists point out that despite the gains made, trans* people – particularly trans* people of color, sex workers, and those who are incarcerated – remain vulnerable to social and medico-legal regulation and violence. Yet trans* gender movements fight injustice by remembering history, creating common denominators, and establishing movement platforms for the future. For example, the Transgender Day of Remembrance (TDOR) is an international day of commemoration for the victims of transphobic killings. The event is held in November. In the past, the TDOR took place in more than 180 cities in more than 20 countries in North America, Europe, Asia, Africa, and Oceania. The TDOR 2014 update reveals a total of 226 cases of reported killings. In total, the preliminary results show 1612 reports of murdered trans* people in 62 countries since January 2008. The TDOR is simultaneously critical and political in its content, yet creates community and identity across borders.

After decades of political activism, trans* individuals increasingly are recognized as subjects and experts on trans* people and trans* movements. They have created their own safe spaces, such as the "Southern Comfort" conference first held in Atlanta, GA, in 1991. The conference remains a hub for the US trans*gender movement. Extensive archival material on the trans*gender movement is located in The Transgender Archives at the University of Victoria in Victoria, British Columbia, Canada. Trans*gender movements inspire new forms of trans*gender knowledge production, art, literature, and culture. Conferences, journals, and academic programs in trans*gender studies witness that "transgender issues are now clearly at the cutting edge of the social justice agenda" and that "the growing acceptability of transgender representation in mass media … suggests that sometime in the future – the near future – transgender people will finally be accepted as full, equal members of society" (Stryker 2008, 153).

SEE ALSO: Human Rights, International Laws and Policies on; Identity Politics; Trans Identities, Psychological Perspectives; Trans Theorizing; Transgender Politics; Transphobia

REFERENCES

Feinberg, Leslie. 1992. *Transgender Liberation: A Movement Whose Time Has Come.* New York: World View Forum.

Stryker, Susan. 2008. *Transgender History.* Berkeley: Seal Press.

United Nations Human Rights Council. 2011. *Discriminatory Laws and Practices and Acts of Violence Against Individuals Based on Their Sexual Orientation and Gender Identity.* A/HRC/19/41. Geneva: Office of the United Nations High Commissioner for Human Rights. Accessed April 9, 2015, at http://www2.ohchr.org/english/bodies/hrcouncil/docs/19session/a.hrc.19.41_english.pdf.

FURTHER READING

Broad, Kendal L. 2002. "GLB + T?: Gender/Sexuality Movements and Transgender Collective Identity (De)Constructions." *International Journal of Sexuality and Gender Studies*, 7(4): 241–264. DOI 10.1023/A:1020371328314.

Davidson, Megan. 2007. "Seeking Refuge Under the Umbrella: Inclusion, Exclusion, and Organizing Within the Category Transgender." *Sexuality Research & Social Policy: Journal of NSRC*, 4(4): 60–80. DOI: 10.1525/srsp.2007.4.4.60.

Devor, Aaron H. 2014. *The Transgender Archives: Foundations for the Future*. Victoria: University of Victoria Libraries. Accessed April 9, 2015, at http://www.uvic.ca/library/about/ul/publications/Devor_Foundations_for_the_Future.pdf.

Eisfeld, Justus, Sarah Gunther, and Davey Shlasko. 2013. *The State of Trans* and Intersex Organizing: A Case for Increased Support for Growing But Under-funded Movements for Human Rights*. New York: Global Action for Trans* Equality and American Jewish World Service. Accessed April 9, 2015, at http://transactivists.org/resources/documents/funding-report/.

Kidd, Jeremy D., and Tarynn M. Witten. 2008. "Transgender and Trans Sexual Identities: The Next Strange Fruit – Hate Crimes, Violence and Genocide Against the Global Trans-Communities." *Journal of Hate Studies*, 6(1): 31–63.

Silverman, Victor, and Susan Stryker, Directors. 2005. *Screaming Queens: The Riot at Compton's Cafeteria* (documentary film). Accessed September 12, 2015, at http://www.imdb.com/title/tt0464189/.

Transgender Europe. 2015. Trans Murder Monitoring Project. Accessed April 8, 2015, at http://tgeu.org/tmm/.

Transgender Movements in the United States

SIMONE KOLYSH
CUNY Graduate Center, New York, USA

To speak of transgender movements in the United States requires careful consideration of definitions, histories, and activism. There is, after all, tremendous variation of identities under the umbrella of "transgender." The term gained popularity in the 1990s within a white, middle-class context but may now be used by other individuals and communities. In addition, any account of transgender histories should include how European colonizers engaged with gender difference within indigenous, immigrant, and enslaved communities. Finally, transgender activism is inextricably linked to other social movements for racial, gender, economic, and sexual equality. The fact remains that people, be they indigenous, part of immigrant or diasporic communities, or able to trace several generations of family history in the United States, have lived experiences that do not fit the white Western gender binary.

Though the term "transgender" is not applicable or accessible to all who differ in terms of gender, Susan Stryker's definition of "transgender" as a "movement across a socially imposed boundary away from an unchosen starting place" may help in locating gender non-conforming people at different historical points (Stryker 2008, 1). When applied to the formation of the United States, the unchosen starting place of the white Western gender binary was imposed on indigenous communities, many of which had alternative constructions of gender which appeared alien to European colonizers. Historical records indicate that Europeans, upon discovering what they considered to be cross-dressing men and women engaged in "masculine activities," slaughtered indigenous people for being guilty of sodomy. In response, two-spirit and native queer people's movements continue to reject Western heteropatriarchy and pursue decolonization (Morgensen 2011).

The European concept of the "sodomitical body" was tied to gender difference perceived in other groups affected by colonialism and enslavement. Sodomy laws were also used to prevent immigration and successful integration of groups considered to be a homosexual threat. Specifically, the legacy of slavery in the United States is that sexual and gender characteristics within black bodies have been classified as abnormal, in direct contrast to a white, heterosexual, and gender-conforming subject. Deeply racist and purportedly scientific accounts of nineteenth-century sexologists like Havelock Ellis marked both black and homosexual people as physiologically and psychologically different, mapping a racial hierarchy onto a sexual hierarchy. The historical construction of homosexuality as a pathology reinforced the link between people of color, gender difference, and sexual difference. As a result, many early scientific accounts conflate "transgenderism" with homosexuality or intersexuality.

The link between gender and sexual deviance was reinforced at the intersection of the legal system and the public sphere. In the nineteenth century, jurisdictions passed laws against cross-dressing in public and other sumptuary legislation that reinforced gender and sexual norms. At the time, social movements around race, gender, and sexuality contributed to the policing of gender and sexuality in public. There was an assumption that gender non-conforming individuals were likely to engage in unacceptable sexual practices (Mogul, Ritchie, and Whitlock 2011). Despite these barriers, transgender people wishing to inhabit a gender identity different from the one they were assigned at birth did so through changes to clothing and behavior. It is important to note the distinction between sex and gender. Sex, a construct applying to the body and physical markers that congeal "female," "male," and "intersex" as categories, and gender, a construct applying to the social and behavioral markers that congeal "woman," "man," and "transgender" as categories are not synonymous. Those wishing to make extensive changes to their sex as part of their gender transition had few options.

In was not until the beginning of the twentieth century that autobiographical accounts of male-to-female and, to a lesser extent, female-to-male transsexual people emerged. These stories helped shape the idea that transsexual people are born in the "wrong body" and need medical intervention in the form of hormones and sex reassignment, sometimes called gender confirmation, surgery. Endocrinologist Harry Benjamin acknowledged a variety of transgender experiences, mostly for people on the male-to-female spectrum. The Harry Benjamin International Gender Dysphoria Association solidified the relationship between gender dysphoria and medical transition by outlining steps to manage "gender disorders" and secured clinical behavioral scientists as gatekeepers of any legal sex changes. Those who did not want to alter their bodies were not considered "true" transsexuals.

The popular mass media did its part by focusing on stories of transsexual people who were white, middle-class Americans who would, upon completion of their medical transition, be like other heterosexual people. Following 1950s accounts of "successful" transsexual people like Christine Jorgensen, transgender people interested in medical intervention told similar stories, describing a fixed set of symptoms that "proved" their "disorder." As a result, some doctors blamed transsexual people for being deceptive, when these individuals were simply navigating a rigid medical understanding of transsexuality. After all, not everyone within the medical community wanted to help transsexual people; John Money, an endocrinologist supporting the "fixing" of intersex infants, and Richard Green, a psychiatrist committed to eliminating "effeminacy" in young boys, were part of a group that wanted to prevent or "cure" transsexuality.

By the early 1980s, the director of the Johns Hopkins Gender Identity Clinic wanted to discredit trans women as "caricatures of women." Dr. John McHugh's methodologically flawed research study of trans women was very influential. He said there were no significant benefits to surgery. This led to the closure of all clinics offering care to transsexual people and elimination of any insurance coverage for transgender care. At the same time, "gender identity disorder" (GID) was introduced into the *Diagnostic and Statistical Manual of Mental Disorders* (DSM) produced by the American Psychiatric Association. In 2013, it was changed to "gender dysphoria" but many activists argue being transgender is not a disorder and that it should be removed from the DSM. Some transgender people labeled with disabilities or working within disability movements consider it ableist to fight for removal of gender dysphoria without also critiquing the way in which the field of psychiatry categorizes difference and creates "disorders" out of normal human experiences. Instead, transgender people should have access to medical care when it comes to gender-related body alteration without being labeled pathological and the fields of medical and psychiatry should lose their gatekeeper status.

Because sex and gender are not synonymous, medical transition and transsexual identity is not part of every trans person's journey. Autobiographies and texts published in the latter half of the twentieth century offered a corrective to the traditional narrative. Activist Kate Bornstein spoke of not being a man or a woman, neither male nor female (Bornstein 1994). Leslie Feinberg's novel *Stone Butch Blues* had a protagonist who took hormones in order to be a man in a homophobic and racist society as a result of not being accepted as a person of butch identity (Feinberg 1993). Narratives that do not link one's transgender identity to medical transition also allow for a critique of the white Western gender binary and cisgender privilege, a term used to refer to individuals whose gender identity matches their sex assigned at birth, or rooting gender dissonance within the individual. For example, the conversation around "passing" exposes the cissexual assumption that those who do not "pass" have failed to achieve transgender status (Serano 2007).

The relationship between sex and gender may be complicated by sexuality. When mid-twentieth century physicians acknowledged the difference between gender and sexuality, and between transsexual people and "sexual deviants," there were nevertheless overlaps. For one, many transgender people did not identify as heterosexual and worked with communities of cross-dressers, drag performers, and people labeled as "transvestites." Certain transvestite individuals distanced themselves from transsexual individuals but others were encouraged when transsexual people went through medical transition. As for gay and lesbian groups, there was a similar bifurcated response. Some members of homophile organizations like the Mattachine Society maintained that gay people are not like transsexual people, insisting on a gender normative presentation as part of their assimilationist strategy. Some gay and lesbian people, in solidarity with transsexual people, formed common social networks and communities.

In response to police surveillance and harassment of street sex workers, many of whom were transgender women, the 1966 Compton's Cafeteria riot in San Francisco led to the formation of several transsexual advocacy groups such as the California Advancement for Transsexuals and the National Transsexual Counseling Unit. The Street Transvestite Action Revolutionaries, co-founded by the legendary transgender activist Sylvia Rivera, and the Labyrinth

Foundation formed in Los Angeles and New York City. Today, organizations like TransJustice, FIERCE!, the Sylvia Rivera Law Project, and the Transgender, Gender Variant, and Intersex Justice Project follow in their steps and engage in broad-based, intersectional activism.

In 1969, after yet another "routine" police raid of the Stonewall Inn, a crowd comprised of drag queens, gay people, and transgender women, also targeted for being poor and of color, began to throw objects at the police. The number of protesters rose over the next several nights and clashes with the police reached a peak. This moment of resistance has been largely credited with sparking the gay and lesbian rights movements in the United States. Almost immediately, the efforts of transgender women of color leading these rebellions were co-opted by the Gay Liberation Front and the more conservative Gay Activists Alliance, to advance a white, middle class, gay men's agenda. As a result, feminist lesbian and queer women formed their own organizations, which continue to struggle with racial diversity and including trans women and other trans people.

For example, gender critical feminism, an offshoot of radical feminism sometimes called trans exclusionary radical feminism, espouses an essentialist philosophy that transgender people, especially transsexual women, are just tools of sexist male doctors and of patriarchy. To these "feminists," many of whom are lesbian and queer women, transsexual women are "still men" who are trying to infiltrate spaces of "real women," which are defined as women sexed female at birth. Trans women have therefore been excluded from women's social and political organizations like Daughters of Bilitis and events like the Michigan Womyn's Music Festival. Only four years after the Stonewall riots, a group of lesbian feminists prevented Sylvia Rivera from speaking at the 1973 Stonewall commemoration.

Throughout the 1970s and the 1980s, gay and lesbian activists continued to prioritize their concerns over transgender people's concerns even though many transgender people fought for sexual liberation. For example, part of the struggle for gay and lesbian rights focused on the removal of homosexuality from the DSM. One of the strategies employed to achieve this goal was to make a clear distinction between homosexuality and transgender experiences. Homosexuality was removed as a disorder in 1980, the same year GID made its debut. Another example is that when the AIDS epidemic occurred, much of the energy and resources went to addressing gay men's issues at the expense of women's and transgender people's issues. In reality, many transgender people were hit hard by the epidemic due to reliance on sex work for survival, having to share needles for hormone injections, and general lack of healthcare. The tension between gay, lesbian, and feminist communities and transgender communities set the stage for a reinvigorated transgender movement.

In the early 1990s, the term "transgender" began to circulate as an umbrella term for many different expressions of gender difference as a lived experience. Leslie Feinberg's (1999) pamphlet, *Transgender Liberation: A Movement Whose Time Has Come*, and Sandy Stone's (1992) article "The 'Empire' Strikes Back: A Post-Transsexual Manifesto" helped the term gain political and academic dimensions. The "T" for "transgender" became a part of the lesbian, gay, bisexual, transgender, and queer (LGBTQ) acronym and trans studies, as a field, overlapped with women's and LGBTQ studies. When it comes to labels, it appears that a transgender identity is distinct from sexuality, which belies a particularly white, middle-class context. For example, some communities of color use the term "gay" to describe a lived experience that others might define as transgender (Valentine 2007). Many other groups – immigrant or indigenous – do not find the term "transgender" adequate in describing their gender identity. Instead, they use terms like "two-spirit," "third-gender," or specific terms from their native language.

When transgender movements are made to appear uniform through whitewashing or single-issue narratives, much oppression facing transgender people is overlooked. For example, even though all transgender people sometimes experience transphobia or poverty, trans people of color often face additional burden of structural racism. Racism, when combined with transmisogyny, results in black trans women being killed at an extraordinary rate, an issue that requires immediate attention. Another pressing concern is police harassment and brutality. Upon transition, some trans men learn that being a man of color, regardless of sexuality, means having to face racial profiling and an increased risk of becoming part of the prison industrial complex.

Economic barriers are another factor. For many trans women, "walking while trans" is a phrase coined to address the frequency with which they experience verbal and physical abuse by police officers who make assumptions about their being involved in sex work. One of the reasons so many trans women are involved in sex work is lack of educational and job opportunities because of unchecked harassment and discrimination faced by transgender people. Given the disproportionate criminalization of trans people, many face significant abuses within prisons where they are not placed according to their gender nor have their gender-related medical needs addressed. Transgender people also have a harder time finding and maintaining stable housing, childcare, or legal services. When it comes to legal protection, immigrant and undocumented people have a harder time because they do not have legal documents matching their gender identification. Therefore, the future of transgender movements in the United States lies with addressing a range of issues within transgender communities that connect to racial, gender, economic, and sexual equality.

SEE ALSO: *Diagnostic and Statistical Manual of Mental Disorders* (DSM), Feminist Critiques of; Gender Identities and Socialization; Transgender Politics

REFERENCES

Bornstein, Kate. 1994. *Gender Outlaw: On Men, Women and the Rest of Us*. New York: Routledge.

Feinberg, Leslie. 1993. *Stone Butch Blues: A Novel*. New York: Alyson Books.

Feinberg, Leslie. 1999. *Trans Liberation: Beyond Pink and Blue*. Boston: Beacon Press.

Mogul, Joey L., Andrea J. Ritchie, and Kay Whitlock. 2011. *Queer (In)Justice: The Criminalization of LGBT People in the United States*. Boston: Beacon Press.

Morgensen, Scott L. 2011. *Spaces Between Us: Queer Settler Colonialism and Indigenous Decolonization*. Minneapolis: University of Minnesota Press.

Serano, Julia. 2007. *Whipping Girl: A Transsexual Woman on Sexism and the Scapegoating of Femininity*. Berkeley: Seal Press.

Stone, Sandy. 1992. "The 'Empire' Strikes Back: A Posttranssexual Manifesto." *Camera Obscura*, 10(2): 150–176.

Stryker, Susan. 2008. *Transgender History*. Berkeley: Seal Press.

Valentine, David. 2007. *Imagining Transgender: An Ethnography of a Concept*. Durham, NC: Duke University Press.

FURTHER READING

Erickson-Schroth, Laura. 2014. *Trans Bodies, Trans Selves: A Resource for the Transgender Community*. Oxford: Oxford University Press.

Myerowitz, Joanne. 2002. *How Sex Changed: A History of Transsexuality in the United States*. Cambridge, MA: Harvard University Press.

Transgender Politics

DAN IRVING
Carleton University, Canada

Derived from the Latin root *trans*, meaning to move across, transgender is defined in terms of horizontal movement across the sex/gender binary structuring Western and non-Western societies. While sex and gender are categories that can function independently, they operate as relationally within particular ruling relations such as heteronormativity. According to heteronormative logics, or a system of governance based on normalizing particular embodiments, gender performances, and sexual desires, one is born either male or female, and receives masculine or feminine socialization to become a man or a woman whose desire is for the opposite sex. Such dominant discourses render the diversity of sex and gender invisible. For instance, the erasure of sex and gender pluralism first occurs through assigning sex at birth and, in the case of some intersex individuals, surgical interventions to construct female or male embodiment (Fausto-Sterling 2000). In various political milieus, transgender acts as an umbrella term that encapsulates non-normatively sexed bodies and gender non-conforming identities that disrupt the governing logic of sex/gender dualisms.

Transgender politics takes multiple forms and addresses numerous issues. In spite of such plurality, there is a central divide that creates two broad branches of transgender politics. The first approach operates within wider liberal democratic frameworks espousing recognition of single identities within a larger society (Gan 2012, 292), hence trans politics is framed as a single-issue movement. The second approach to transgender politics is geared toward social justice and self-determination of all people (Gan 2012, 300). Street-active individuals who are impoverished, under-housed, or homeless and working within criminalized economic sectors often play central roles in social justice approaches to trans politics. This particular manifestation of transgender politics is typically a grassroots initiative and functions as a multi-issue movement. Both approaches to transgender politics often occur simultaneously and need not be understood as diametrically opposed. Single-issue or trans rights approaches can function as a means to an end that is defined in ways that understand transgender subjectivities as mediated by class and race in the midst of specific local, national, and global contexts. As will be demonstrated below, however, transgender politics are fraught with significant tensions.

HISTORICAL EMERGENCE OF TRANSGENDER IDENTITIES AND POLITICS

Transsexuality (i.e., an identification opposite to one's birth-assigned sex and the desire to embody one's gender identity often through medicalized processes) is a significant identity under the transgender umbrella. Transsexual activism emerged in the United States during the early 1950s in response to the pathologizing of transsexual individuals by medical and psychiatric professionals. For transsexual activists, their individual right to self-determine their sexed and gendered embodiment was key. Transsexual activists fought against their objectification by medical and psychological practitioners and the gate-keeping role that these professionals played. Advancing and protecting their individual agency, these advocates focused their efforts on gaining access to medicalized transition procedures such as hormone replacement therapy and sexual reassignment surgeries. Such efforts gained some momentum from the media-sensationalized accounts of Christine Jorgenson's transition in 1952. Jorgenson, a former GI in the US military, turned "blond bombshell," who made her living as an entertainer and educator, points to the ways that single-issue politics – achieving rights to gender self-determination – obscures socioeconomic and cultural inequalities amongst transsexual demographics. Not only was the means to pay for medical transition taken for granted in arguments for gender self-determination, but also many debates concerning medical transition further marginalized dis/abled transsexual people. For example, a key issue involved delinking sex and/or gender alterity from mental illness, given that one's ability to transition depended on meeting particular diagnostic criteria as laid out in the DSM (e.g., gender dysphoria) and the Harry Benjamin Standards of Care (e.g., being diagnosed as a primary transsexual). Such arguments further removed the chance of surgery from those who needed the diagnosis to have the procedure covered under insurance, and degraded those with mental illness.

For many transsexual people, battling for access to surgery was not a high priority and framing transgender politics in terms of rights to trans-specific healthcare did not speak to their everyday experiences. For many trans people, their gender (mainly trans women), race, and class location rendered them hyper-visible and vulnerable to unemployment, under-housing and physical, sexual, and spiritual violence. Their approach to politics was intersectional and focused mainly on multiple issues that would improve their immediate life chances.

Often involved with or taking inspiration from more militant liberationist groups, some trans women of color, drag queens, and two-spirit persons who often worked as prostitutes rebelled against state authority, structural violence, and micro-aggressions that endangered their daily existence. The central role that the aforementioned played in the Compton Cafeteria Riot in San Francisco in 1966 (Silverman and Stryker 2005) and the Stonewall riots in New York in 1969 (Gan 2013) illustrate such resistance. The primary role that transsexual, transgender, and two-spirit prostitutes played in developing a vibrant and diverse community in Vancouver's West Side and their leadership in protesting its gentrification and the expulsion of the poor, disabled, and racialized minorities to the downtown East Side is a lesser known example (Hamilton 2014).

Given the plethora of non-normative gender expressions existing in society, other trans subjectivities also emerged through advocacy. Transgender first appeared during the 1960s out of "organic, grassroots process[es] that emerged from many sources, in many conversations, happening in many different locations" (Williams 2014, 223). Transgender political actors worked to garner awareness of their specific gender identity and experiences while some also sought to differentiate themselves from other trans people to gain respectability within mainstream society. Virginia Prince popularized the term transgenderist in an attempt to garner widespread acceptance for individuals who cross the gender binary to live full-time as women. Indicative of the tensions in transgender politics along the lines of achieving legibility versus protecting life chances for a multiplicity of marginalized subjects, Prince distinguished transgenderists by distancing them from transsexuals and transvestites; the former group Prince argued to be mentally ill for desiring to alter their body surgically and the latter was debased because they donned women's clothes for sexual arousal (Salah 2014).

Although various efforts continued through the 1970s and 1980s, it was not until the early 1990s that trans politics gathered momentum in the United States and

Canada. Trans activists and allies struggled on multiple community, institutional, organizational, governmental, and artistic fronts. The ascendency of neoliberalism as the dominant policy paradigm and governing rationality within society buttressed transgender politics focusing on sociolegal status and achieving transgender human rights. Employment and housing discrimination, refusal of service, and other issues were fought individually through the courts. Transgender activists also struggled for inclusivity within and representation by established lesbian and gay rights lobby groups and labor organizations. The most marginalized segments of transgender demographics who were castigated as being unrespectable by middle-class professional trans people organized their own programs to feed and house street-active trans-identified people, and also to educate trans sex workers about HIV/AIDS, to gain access to Violence Against Women Shelters and to provide a sense of community and support for each other through hosting community radio shows, operating trans telephone lines from their homes, and writing 'zines and newsletters.

Sandy Stone's article "The Empire Strikes Back: A Posttranssexual Manifesto" (Stone 2006/1991) pioneered the emergence of trans studies as an interdisciplinary field of critical academic inquiry. Illustrative of the interrelationship between academic analysis of power relations and resistance that define transgender studies, Stone engaged with the radical feminist logic that had resulted in her being fired from her position at Olivia Records, a women-only collective, when it was "discovered" that she was a transsexual. Stone responded to Janice Raymond's arguments in her book *The Transsexual Empire: The Making of the She-Male* that male-to-female transsexuals are not authentic women (Raymond 1994/1979). Raymond asserts that trans women unreflectively accept hyper-feminine gender expressions which indicates their complicity with patriarchal male fantasy. Furthermore, transsexual women's penetration of the women's movement is for destructive purposes. She demonstrated the ways that gender identity clinics (GICs) functioned as governing technologies to ensure the production of normatively feminine and thereby depoliticized subjects. Nevertheless, trans subjects do not have to disappear as prescribed by practitioners working within GICs; Stone calls for visible gender alterity which, consistent with feminist politics, destabilizes dominant narratives of sex and gender.

Stone's response laid the foundation for pillars of analysis that helped define transgender studies: she argued that embodied gendered subjectivities were *produced relationally* through interactions with the state and within institutions and other organizations that legitimize governing social, political, and cultural relations. Susan Stryker, Paisley Currah, and Lisa Jean Moore reassert the importance of trans resisting containment to horizontal movement. They assert "trans-" as a flexible and open-ended approach that enables broader understandings of the ways that gendered embodiment interfaces with biopolitical and biomaterial regimes of social regulation (Stryker et al. 2008). In so doing, trans studies research can contribute to ongoing resistance efforts within and beyond the academy.

TRANSGENDER POLITICS AND IMAGINED COMMUNITY: RACE, COLONIALISM, AND IMPERIALISM

Approaches to transgender politics are not necessarily progressive. Colonialist and nationalist experiences of sex/gender that privilege whiteness tend to define intelligible trans identities and set the agenda for trans politics within the Global North and South. Intellectual critiques of transgender politics remind us of uneven development and inequities between nations. Viviane Namaste's work serves as an example of the insidious ways that transgender politics reproduces Anglo-chauvinism and intrinsic components of Canadian nationalism Namaste 2011). Namaste points out that transgender is an English term – there is no French word for gender. In fact, most of the identities under the transgender umbrella are English words that reflect anglophone experiences. Namaste demonstrates how transgender political activity can unwittingly reproduce nationalism and perpetuate the exclusion of those believed to not belong to the nation as "imagined community" (Anderson 1996). She called the conference organizers of "Sexin' Change: Reclaiming Our Genders and Bodies" to account, listing trans identities such as "femme" in their invitations. In English LGBTQ activist contexts, femme denotes reconstructed femininities rooted in queer desires, whereas in French it translates to "woman." Additionally, recent campaigns to enshrine gender identity in the *Canadian Human Rights Code* and Hate Crimes legislation ignore the fact that activists within Quebec won formal legal protection for gender non-conforming individuals on the grounds of civil status 20 years ago (Namaste 2011).

Tensions between rights-based and social justice approaches to transgender politics have opened spaces for scholastic and political debate concerning transnational relations. Campaigns for trans rights and recognition are critiqued for their complacency with colonialism and imperialism. In the US and Canadian contexts, single-issue movements to protection from discrimination based on gender identity ignore the interconnectivity between the sex/gender binary system and settler-colonialism. In the early 1990s, indigenous people whose territories are within the United States and Canada coined the term "two-spirit" at a conference held in Winnipeg. Two-spirit is a keyword that functions as part of a de-colonial project to reclaim the various forms of indigenous sexual and gender expressions that were subject to physical and cultural genocidal attacks during colonization. Not only does two-spirit challenge the rigid categorical separation between gender and sexuality that is definitive of transgender identities, two-spirit activism also interconnects gender self-determination with issues of national sovereignty and redistributive justice that includes equitable access to the land (Muñoz 2012).

Arguments for recognition of trans identities from the broader public appeals to the state for formal rights protection and arguments made with various institutions (e.g., healthcare, education, social assistance) take for granted the ways that whiteness, nationalism, and citizenship as a broader social category produce a particular sense of belonging that many racialized im/migrants cannot access. Singular approaches to transgender often employ discourses of "home" and rely on affective states of belonging to frame their arguments for the granting of individual agency over one's embodied gender expressions and the necessity of state protection against discrimination. Such discourses erase the experiences of racialized trans im/migrants and foreclose upon the possibilities of "trans-" epistemologies and activism that can adequately address multiple vectors of oppression (Bhanji 2013).

Social justice and gender activists based in non-Western locations are wary of the "transnational expansion of 'transgender' as a rubric of identity and activism" (Dutta and Roy 2014, 320) and seek to interrupt the unidirectional linguistic politics within trans/national borders (Dutta and Roy 2014, 322). The imposition of "transgender" raises significant issues concerning the politics of naming identities and framing particular issues as being pertinent to transgender activism and movements. Transgender-based terminology and politics produce hierarchical and divisive categories such as the "cosmopolitan citizen subject" versus "traditional" or "local" non-conforming sexual and gender-based identities. Such divisions can also cultivate a politics of respectability where more affluent trans-identified individuals residing within urban areas are framed as deserving of rights contrary to Other identities that signify gender and sexual alterity, as well as engagement in criminalized activities such as sex work. Privileging Western-imposed meanings and political frameworks diverts attention away from the already existing grassroots activism taking place within many locations in the Global South.

SEE ALSO: Human Rights and Gender; Trans Identities, Psychological Perspectives; Trans Theorizing; Transgender Movements in International Perspective; Transphobia; Transsexuality; Two-Spirit

REFERENCES

Anderson, Benedict. 1996. *Imagined Communities: Reflection on the Origin and Spread of Nationalism.* London: Verso.

Bhanji, Nael. 2013. "Trans/scriptions: Homing Desires, (Trans)sexual Citizenship and Racialized Bodies." In *The Transgender Studies Reader 2*, edited by Susan Stryker and Aren Z. Aizura, 512–526. New York: Routledge.

Dutta, Aniruddha, and Raina Roy. 2014. "Decolonizing Transgender in India: Some Reflections." *Transgender Studies Quarterly*, 1(3): 320–337.

Fausto-Sterling, Anne. 2000. *Sexing the Body: Gender Politics and the Construction of Sexuality.* New York: Basic Books.

Gan, Jessi. 2013. "'Still at the Back of the Bus': Sylvia Rivera's Struggle." In *The Transgender Studies Reader 2*, edited by Susan Stryker and Aren Z. Aizura, 291–301. New York: Routledge.

Hamilton, Jamie Lee. 2014. "The Golden Age of Prostitution: One Woman's Account of an Outdoor Brothel in Vancouver, 1975–1984." In *Trans Activism in Canada: A Reader*, edited by Dan Irving and Rupert Raj, 27–32. Toronto: Canadian Scholars' Press.

Muñoz, Vic. 2012. "Gender/Sovereignty." In *Transfeminist Perspectives In and Beyond Transgender and Gender Studies*, edited by Anne Enke, 23–33. Philadelphia: Temple University Press.

Namaste, Viviane. 2011. *Sex Change, Social Change: Reflections on Identity, Institutions, and Imperialism*, 2nd ed. Toronto: Women's Press.

Raymond, Janice G. 1994. *The Transsexual Empire: The Making of the She-Male.* New York: Teachers' College Press. First published 1979.

Salah, Trish. 2014. "Gender Struggles: Reflections on Trans Liberation, Trade Unionism, and the Limits of Solidarity." In *Trans Activism in Canada: A Reader*, edited by Dan Irving and Rupert Raj, 149–168. Toronto: Canadian Scholars' Press.

Silverman, Victor, and Susan Stryker, Directors. 2005. *Screaming Queens: The Riot at Compton's Cafeteria* [documentary film]. Accessed September 12, 2015, at http://www.imdb.com/title/tt0464189/.

Stone, Sandy. 2006. "The Empire Strikes Back: A Posttranssexual Manifesto." In *The Transgender Studies Reader*, edited by Susan Stryker and Stephen Whittle, 221–235. New York: Routledge. First published 1991.

Stryker, Susan, Paisley Currah, and Lisa Jean Moore. 2008. "Introduction: Trans-, Trans or Transgender?" *WSQ: Women's Studies Quarterly*, 36(3–4): 11–22.

Williams, Cristan. 2014. Transgender. *Transgender Studies Quarterly*, 1(1–2): 232–234.

FURTHER READING

Cotton, Trystan T., ed. 2012. *Transgender Migrations: The Bodies, Borders, and Politics of Transition.* New York: Routledge.

Currah, Paisley, Richard M. Juang, and Shannon Price Minter, eds. 2006. *Transgender Rights.* Minneapolis: University of Minnesota Press.

Driskell, Qwo-Li, Chris Finley, Brian Joseph Gilley, and Scott Lauria Morgenson, eds. 2011. *Queer Indigenous Studies: Critical Interventions in Theory, Politics, and Literature.* Tucson: University of Arizona Press.

Spade, Dean. 2011. *Normal Life: Administrative Violence, Critical Trans Politics, and the Limits of the Law.* Boston: South End Press.

Stryker, Susan. 2008. *Transgender History*. Berkeley: Seal Press.

Valentine, David. 2007. *Imaging Transgender: An Ethnography of a Category*. Durham, NC: Duke University Press.

Transnational Labor Movements

SUZANNE FRANZWAY
University of South Australia, Australia

Transnational labor movements uniting workers across borders have been the goal as much as the instrument for workers' organizations since the early period of labor movement history. It is assumed that workers everywhere share fundamental interests in improving or challenging their conditions of employment – workers of the world unite. However, union solidarity on any level is always hard won in the face of multiple conflicting interests and needs. Gender is a central, if not always visible, element in this story.

Labor movements are made up of trade unions, political parties, and, increasingly, of non-governmental organizations (NGOs) and networks oriented toward the economic and political interests of workers. Trade unions are formally structured to represent their members on the local and national levels. They connect their members at international levels through the union's formal membership in international labor bodies and, less formally, through strategic partnerships and alliances with transnational social movements, NGOs, and intergovernmental agencies.

The history of working women, since industrialization, is not a simple one of gradually increasing participation in the workforce, but rather, women are sometimes centrally involved, while at others they are explicitly excluded from whole sectors of industries and occupations. Generally, women are more likely to occupy the lowest paid, lowest valued sectors of the workforce with the worst conditions, relative to men in any place and at any level. The reasons for these conditions also impact on their struggles for recognition and representation within labor movements.

RESEARCH

Our knowledge of these complexities depends very much on the creative and persistent efforts of feminist social and historical researchers. Labor movement researchers generally have been as reticent as those in any other field to integrate women or gender and sexuality into their theoretical frameworks or empirical investigations (Cobble 2004; Ledwith 2012). Such research limitations lead to distortions in our understandings of gender and transnational labor movements (see, for example, Flanders 1968). Karl Marx and Frederick Engels both paid some attention to working women but one of the more comprehensive of the earliest researchers to examine women's roles in labor movements is Barbara Drake with her classic account of women and trade unionism first published in 1920 (Drake 1984). Drake was following her aunt, Beatrice Webb who with Sidney Webb set up the Labour Research Department in London in 1912. The Webbs, like researchers in the United States, Germany, and other industrialized countries were advocates of sociological research as a tool of social change. This work revealed dangerous working conditions and served to encourage activists to establish organizations such as the Women's Trade Union League in the United States. It was built from an uneasy alliance of feminists, unionists, and social reformers and was also an example of the internationalism of early twentieth-century feminism (Kirkby 1991). Some research was conducted in the following years but it took the renewal of the women's movement in the late 1960s before a more systematic challenge to women's absence from labor history and social theory began to develop (Rowbotham 1973; Boston 1980).

It must be clear, however, that the research had lagged behind the participation of women in labor across the previous century. It is equally important to recognize that gender was integral to labor whether or not women themselves were directly involved. Thus, feminist researchers have moved from rediscovering the women who were hidden from history to developing sophisticated theories of gender. Gender is now understood in terms of gender relations, sexual politics, and sexualities and is integral to the history, meanings, and issues of labor movements. Feminists assume that women and non-heterosexual people in general share common interests at local and international levels in overcoming the oppressiveness of heterosexual male power. However, differences of race, class, cultural, sexual, and national diversity complicate the task (Rupp 1997). The site of transnational labor movements epitomizes the case (Ledwith and Hansen 2013). The challenge is at least twofold: one, to find space in labor organizations in order to engage with gendered workplace issues, which in turn depends on confronting the prevailing sexual politics of both labor and the workplace; and two, to find resources as well as union practices that work across organizational, cultural, and national boundaries (Briskin and McDermott 1993; Kirton 2006; Baron and Boris 2007).

Transnational feminist activism in trade unions changes across time, scale, and space from large international institutions like the International Labour Organization (ILO) to local campaigns (Franzway and Fonow 2011). Conflicts over the political and strategic importance of class versus gender interests have been almost perennial extending back to the earliest women's and labor movements of the nineteenth century (Rowbotham 1973; Tax 1980). In order to work together effectively, both movements face complex challenges posed by class, race, and sexual politics.

HISTORY

Unions in transnational labor networks have often faced tensions between states and between nationalism and internationalism (Bendt 2003). Socialism promoted the advantages of building international movements in order to confront the growth of industry beyond national borders. Early feminists and socialists called for international labor organization to unite workers without regard to sex, politics, religion, or national boundaries. They argued for egalitarian principles to include women, but the argument was lost by the mid-1840s when class struggles became the central concern of trade unions while gender relations and women's position were constructed as "other" (Alexander 1976). Women's labor activism became largely invisible over the following decades at the international levels. Men did most of the writing, debating, and traveling while women did the cleaning, cooking, and fundraising that made it possible for men to participate.

Transnational union cooperation was built through trade secretariats, with 33 established by World War I. Mostly based in male-dominated industries, they aimed to create worker solidarity. However, the 1914–1918 war between nation-states broke these early attempts at transnational organizing. A burst of internationalism followed the war leading to the creation of influential formal bodies, such as the ILO, and international trades unions, including the International Confederation of Free Trade Unions (ICFTU). The first attempt by women trade unionists was in 1919 at the International Congress of Working Women where women from 19 countries established the International Federation of Working Women (IFWW). It was short-lived and merged in 1924 with the ICFTU (Cobble 2004). Union solidarity was challenged by the 1930s worldwide depression, and World War II followed rapidly by the Cold War divided international labor movements as well as feminist and other social movements for decades.

TRANSNATIONAL LABOR BODIES

Three of the most significant transnational labor bodies for those concerned with gender and sexuality issues are the International Labour Organization (ILO), the Global Union Federations (GUFs), and the International Trade Union Confederation (ITUC).

The ILO was established in 1919 to reconcile the interests of governments, employers, and labor unions. From its inception, women have had to actively seek representation and attention to their specific issues at every level. Persistent efforts by feminist activists inside the United Nations, established in 1949, slowly created a women's policy machinery, which has been important to the recognition of gender issues at the ILO. These include the Convention on the Elimination of Discrimination against Women (CEDAW) adopted by the UN in 1979, as well as the 1995 Beijing Platform for Action and its follow-up, and the Millennium Development Goals. The ILO's mandate to promote gender equality is enshrined in its constitution and gender mainstreaming has become ILO policy. The four key ILO gender equality conventions are the Equal Remuneration Convention (No. 100), Discrimination (Employment and Occupation) Convention (No. 111), Workers with Family Responsibilities Convention (No. 156), and Maternity Protection Convention (No. 183).

Equity became a key component of the ILO Declaration on Fundamental Principles and Rights at Work, adopted in 1998 and is one of four core labor rights spelled out in the declaration. They are: (1) freedom of association and the effective recognition of the right to collective bargaining; (2) the elimination of all forms of forced or compulsory labor; (3) the effective abolition of child labor; and (4) the elimination of discrimination in respect of employment and occupations. Whether they have ratified the declaration or not, each member state of the ILO has the obligation to respect, to promote, and to realize, in good faith, these core labor rights. The Action Plan for Gender Equality 2010–2015 operationalizes policy on gender equality (ILO 2007).

Global Union Federations are transnational labor bodies that are organized regionally and by sector, representing millions of workers across the world. Each has an active women's committee and sponsors gender-specific events and activities. Campaigns may be coordinated across the GUFs such as the ITUC's Organizing Women Workers campaign. Other campaigns may be sector specific, such as the Public Service International's (PSI) Water, Women, Workers campaign, or focused on the social rights of women and the prevention of violence against women. The campaign "Unions for Women, Women for Unions" targets specific groups of women workers including those working in the informal economy, young women, migrant women, women from ethnic minorities, and women employed in the export processing zones.

In 2006, the ICFTU merged with the World Federation of Labor (WFL) to form the ITUC. At the time, the ICFTU was the largest international labor federation with a worldwide membership of 158 million workers from 150 different countries. Sharan Burrow, an Australian labor feminist is the president of the ITUC. The ITUC has an equality department that coordinates anti-discrimination activities and campaigns. It produces and disseminates policy reports, training manuals, fact sheets, newsletters and brochures, and coordinates with the ILO and the GUFs various transnational campaigns for women's rights including campaigns to end violence against women and girls, for maternity protection, and for pay equity. The ITUC Action Programme for Achieving Gender Equality in Trade Unions actively encourages the adoption of similar programs at regional and local levels.

The damaging effects of the globalization of capital on the conditions of women workers has led to renewed efforts to forge transnational alliances between women's organizations, particularly feminist NGOs, and union women. Union feminists connect to other feminist NGOs at the UN through the affiliation of their unions and peak labor bodies with the GUFs, the ITUC, and the ILO (Moghadam 2005). The Women Working Worldwide organization emerged in the UK in the early 1980s in support of networks of women workers' organizations in the export processing zones (EPZs) in Asia (Hale and Wills 2007). It links women workers in different countries who work for the same multinationals, as well as fighting for women's rights in the informal sector in Asia and Central America. Union women joined with other women's groups at the 1995 UN Beijing women's conference to campaign for women workers' rights, with a strong focus on vulnerable workers in EPZs. The Women's International Coalition for Economic Justice (WICEJ), founded in 2000, is a transnational network of 45 women's economic and human rights organizations that focuses on the link between gender, race, and macro-economic policy.

CAMPAIGNS

Both labor movements and women's movements organize campaigns to achieve their goals. Campaigns are a series of collective actions, are not spontaneous, and require focus on specific goals. They also need material and discursive resources, as well as the capacity to frame issues. Campaigns are key sites for alliances between women's movements and labor movements. They can focus on local issues, such as legislative change, or international goals such as the eradication of human trafficking (Bendt 2003).

A campaign that spread through international feminist networks as a challenge to the sexual politics of the labor movement was based on the Working Women's Charter. Campaigns for the charter and its demands from the late 1960s until the early 1990s generated enormous popular support. A network of WWC groups organized with labor movements in the United Kingdom, Australia, New Zealand, and elsewhere in spite of the suspicions of some labor leaders (Coote and Campbell 1982). The contentious demand for free, safe, and legal abortion delayed its adoption by union peak bodies. The issues surrounding women's work were so numerous and diverse that it was difficult to agree on what the best strategy was. The addition of multiple demands led to it becoming an unwieldy document. Union feminists did not occupy enough leadership positions to ensure that the charter was implemented in their own organizations or women's workplaces. The charter did raise awareness about what women want in their work and in their unions.

In 1951, the ILO adopted Convention 100 for equal pay for equal work by men and women for work of equal value. It has since been ratified by most of its members, an important advance that recognizes the discriminatory impact of the sexual division of labor. Over time, the goals have shifted from "pay equity" between women's and men's work even when their jobs were not equal or even similar to redressing the undervaluation of jobs typically performed by women and remunerating them according to their value. National and international women's movements took up pay equity and began pushing labor movements to recognize the unequal effects of the sexual division of labor on women workers. The Working Women's Charter campaigns argued that "equal pay for equal work" is not enough. The campaigns often led to complex industrial and legal arguments, so that in 2007, the ILO was still reporting that the notion of "equal pay for work of equal value" is perhaps one of the least understood concepts in the anti-discrimination field (ILO 2007).

Transnational labor movements have historically been dominated by masculine heterosexuality and so the representation and organization of LGBTI workers has been a major challenge. These workers experience high rates of discrimination and prejudice (Colgan and Ledwith 2002). At national levels, trade unions can provide vital support and legal protection for LGBTI workers. Much depends on queer activist unionists themselves as to whether labor movements will respond to the needs and interests of LGBTI workers. Transnational alliances and organizing have been utilized with moderate success. The international "Out at Work!" conferences first held in 1998 grew out of global/local networks of gay, lesbian, and transgender workers. Two of the GUFs, the Public Services International (PSI), and Education International (EI) argue for the social and economic rights of LGBTI workers within the network of global union federations. Mutual support across labor movements is both possible and necessary, but much needs to be done to create political opportunities, forums, and spaces for lesbian and gay workers in and around the trade union movement (Franzway 2014).

The so-called traditional industrial worker has long been under challenge: from capital and employers looking for cheaper labor, and from the great diversity of alternative workers (women, immigrants, non-white groups, and so on) seeking to make their living however they can. Labor movements attempt to respond in ways that support already hard-won conditions while trying to meet new demands from rapidly changing conditions. For example, the ILO campaign for "decent work" has been expanded by the ITUC and the GUFs into the Global Campaign for Decent Work, Decent Life for Women. Likewise, the global growth of the informal economy including small-scale producers, service providers, paid domestic workers, home workers, sweatshop workers, and self-employed is deeply gendered and outside the traditional reach of trade unions (Vosko 2007). Yet, transnational organizations like Women in Informal Employment: Globalizing and Organizing (WIEGO) have developed alliances with transnational labor bodies to push for changes that recognize and advocate for such workers.

TRANSNATIONAL SITE

The World Social Forum has been an important site for transnational labor movements since its first meeting in 2001 in Brazil in which international labor bodies played a central role. By contrast, and in spite of its proclaimed respect for diversity and the strength of feminist global justice movements and transnational NGOs, feminist activists have had to be always alert to ensure that women's issues are integral to the forum's agendas (Eschle 2005). Two feminist networks, the World March of Women (WMW) and the Mercosur Feminist Articulation (AFM), organized two of the forum's five axes or themes: (1) principles and values, human rights, diversity, and equality; and (2) political power, civil society, and democracy.

The erosion of women's economic security and citizenship by neoliberal globalization is a central concern but the feminist organizations rarely engage with issues of workers' rights, in particular the issues faced by women workers in the Global South. Here too, sexual politics privileges men's political activism at transnational levels.

In summary, transnational labor movements can be vehicles through which women workers are mobilized to struggle for economic justice for themselves and their communities. Unions have the resources to bring women together to build new forms of transnational labor solidarity. It must be a solidarity that recognizes women's differences and encourages the productive use of these differences to expand ideas about democracy and human rights. Without the material resources, networks, and discourses of transnational labor movements and their unions, women workers everywhere have little opportunity to fight for their interests and conditions.

SEE ALSO: Gender Equality; NGOs and Grassroots Organizing; United States' Women's Movements in Historical Perspective

REFERENCES

Alexander, Sally. 1976. "Women's Work in Nineteenth Century London." In *The Rights and Wrongs of Women*, edited by Juliet Mitchell and Ann Oakley. London: Penguin.

Baron, Ava, and Eileen Boris. 2007. "'The Body' as a Useful Category for Working-Class History." *Labor: Studies in Working-Class History of the Americas* 4(2): 23–43.

Bendt, H. 2003. *Worldwide Solidarity: The Activities of Global Unions in the Era of Globalization*, trans. A. Brinkmann. Bonn: Friedrich-Ebert-Siftung.

Boston, S. 1980. *Women Workers and the Trade Union Movement*. London: Davis Paynter.

Briskin, Linda, and Patricia McDermott, eds. 1993. *Women Challenging Unions: Feminism, Democracy and Militancy*. Toronto: Toronto University Press.

Cobble, Dorothy Sue. 2004. *The Other Women's Movement: Workplace Justice and Social Rights in Modern America*. Princeton: Princeton University Press.

Colgan, Fiona, and Sue Ledwith, eds. 2002. *Gender, Diversity and Trade Unions: International Perspectives*. London: Routledge.

Coote, A., and B. Campbell. 1982. *Sweet Freedom*. London: Picador.

Drake, Barbara. 1984. *Women in Trade Unions*. London: Virago.

Eschle, Catherine. 2005. "'Skeleton Women': Feminism and the Antiglobalization Movement." *Signs*, 30(3): 1742–1769.

Flanders, Allan. 1968. *Trade Unions*, 7th ed. London: Hutchinson.

Franzway, Suzanne. 2014. "Sexual Politics and Queer Activism in the Australian Trade Union Movement." In *Sexual Orientation at Work: Contemporary Issues and Perspectives*, edited by Fiona Colgan and Nick Rumens. London: Routledge.

Franzway, Suzanne, and Mary Margaret Fonow. 2011. *Making Feminist Politics: Transnational Alliances between Women and Labor*. Urbana: University of Illinois Press.

Hale, Angela, and Jane Wills. 2007. "Women Working Worldwide: Transnational Networks, Corporate Social Responsibility and Action Research." *Global Networks*, 7(4): 453–476.

ILO (International Labour Organization). 2007. *Equality at Work: Tackling the Challenges*. Global Report under the Follow-up to the ILO Declaration on Fundamental Principles and Rights at Work. Report of the Director-General. Geneva: ILO.

Kirkby, Diane. 1991. Alice Henry: The Power of Pen and Voice. *The Life of an Australian-American Reformer*. Melbourne: Cambridge University Press.

Kirton, Gill. 2006. *The Making of Women Trade Unionists*. Aldershot: Ashgate.

Ledwith, Sue. 2012. "Outside, Inside: Gender Work in Industrial Relations." *Equality, Diversity and Inclusion*, 31(4): 340–358.

Ledwith, Sue, and Lize Lotte Hansen, eds. 2013. *Gendering and Diversifying Trade Union Leadership*. Abingdon: Routledge.

Moghadam, Valentine. 2005. *Globalizing Women: Transnational Feminist Networks*. Baltimore: Johns Hopkins University Press.

Rowbotham, Sheila. 1973. *Hidden from History: 300 Years of Women's Oppression and the Fight against It*. London: Pluto Press.

Rupp, Leila, J. 1997. *Worlds of Women: The Making of an International Women's Movement*. Princeton: Princeton University Press.

Tax, Meredith. 1980. *The Rising of the Women: Feminist Solidarity and Class Conflict 1880–1917*. London: Monthly Review Press.

Vosko, Leah F. 2007. "Representing Informal Workers: Emerging Global Strategies and Their Lessons for North American Unions." In *The Sex of Class: Women Transforming American Labor*, edited by Dorothy Sue Cobble. Ithaca: Cornell University Press.

Transphobia

Y. GAVRIEL ANSARA
University of Surrey, UK

ERICA J. FRIEDMAN
The Graduate Center, City University of New York, USA

The term transphobia was first used in English to describe hostile responses to people perceived as "trans," a term typically used to describe people whose own designations of their gender are independent from their assigned gender or from the administrative sex category listed on their original birth certificate. "Trans" has also been used to describe people whose characteristics and behavior differ from expected gender norms in a particular context. The prefix "trans-" is Latin for "across from." The suffix "-phobia" is derived from the Greek word *phobos*, which means fear. In psychiatry, "-phobia" is used to describe intense fear that is considered unfounded or treated as pathological.

The transphobia framework is an adaptation of the "homophobia" concept, which explored negative responses to and hostility toward people perceived as having same-gender attractions or relationships. Similar to homophobia, transphobia was originally framed as an irrational, intrapsychic response of fear and disgust to people who do not conform to the gender norms and expectations of their society (Hill 2002). Research shows that transphobia can lead to violence and to discriminatory treatment for reasons unique to a person's perceived gender.

Historically, researchers searched for negative stimuli to explain the existence of "trans people" and explored ways to reduce "cross-gender" behavior and identity. In the last decade, researchers have used the transphobia concept to shift professional discourse from a focus on why "trans people" exist, a line of inquiry sometimes described as "the transsexual problem," to a focus on why discriminatory responses toward people of trans and/or non-binary experience exist. This shift has allowed researchers to challenge negative views of "trans people" and to expose hostile and explicit forms of the discriminatory behavior they experience. Thus, the term transphobia has been used as an anti-oppressive linguistic device to redefine "the transsexual problem." Transphobia is used in popular culture and by many trans activists as an imprecise label for all mistreatment of people perceived as "trans." Findings from transphobia research have informed the development of interventions to reduce discrimination and resolve hostile treatment.

Hill and Willoughby (2005) were the first to develop and validate a scale to measure transphobia. Their Transphobia Scale includes items that incorporate emotional responses (e.g., fear and disgust) and physical responses (e.g., harassment and discrimination). Although some researchers have identified limitations such as the lack of discriminant validity with measures of homophobia (see Nagoshi et al. 2008), the scale is widely used and accepted as a reliable measurement of "anti-trans prejudice."

Nagoshi et al. (2008) incorporated broader concepts of social prejudice when designing their Transphobia Scale. Nagoshi et al.'s final version of the scale had items all loading on one factor, indicating good inter-item reliability. The scale correlated with a measure of homophobia, but differences were found between homophobia and transphobia when comparing the scales to people's responses on measures of adherence to social norms about gender roles. Women's adherence to traditional gender roles was a stronger predictor of transphobia than homophobia. In contrast, men's adherence to traditional gender roles equally predicted transphobia and homophobia. According to Nagoshi et al., this finding indicates that transphobia is a response to gender-related challenges to the self in women and a challenge to aspects of both gender and sexuality in men.

Transphobic behavior can involve verbal abuse, physical assault, and murder. Research in various cultures, including Hong Kong, the United Kingdom, and the United States, has evaluated the impact of transphobia. Being targeted for transphobia has been linked to physical and emotional trauma (Mizock and Lewis 2008) and higher rates of attempted suicide (Clements-Nolle, Marx, and Katz 2006). Transphobia has also been linked to decreased use of barriers for sexually transmitted infection (STI) and HIV prevention (Sugano, Nemoto, and Operario 2006). Whittle, Turner, and Al-Alami (2007) identified several additional life situations impacted by transphobia: significant financial problems due to either unfair employment termination or resignation as a result of hostile workplace conditions; difficulties in obtaining official identity documents; and negative experiences at home and in family contexts, schools, public and community spaces, and public accommodations such as goods, services, and housing.

Individual difference factors that have been highly correlated with transphobia and anti-trans prejudice include: limited contact with "trans people" (King, Winter, and Webster 2009), identifying as a man (Hill and Willoughby 2005; Nagoshi et al. 2008; King, Winter, and Webster 2009; Willoughby et al. 2010), low self-esteem (Willoughby et al. 2010), religious fundamentalism (Nagoshi et al. 2008; Willoughby et al. 2010), authoritarian beliefs (Willoughby et al. 2010), ego-defensiveness (Willoughby et al. 2010), and moral dogmatism (Willoughby et al. 2010).

Transphobia is still a relatively understudied area (Nagoshi et al. 2008). Some researchers have called for more research on transphobia (Whittle et al. 2007). However, other researchers have suggested that conceptual limitations to transphobia indicate a need for a new approach (Ansara and Hegarty 2013).

Some critics of the transphobia framework have raised concerns that research using this concept may undermine equality by reifying a new gender essentialism that merely shifts from a previous "woman/man" binary to a "transgender/cisgender" binary (Ansara and Hegarty 2013). The transphobia framework inaccurately assumes people can be neatly categorized as either "transgender people" or "cisgender people." The focus in transphobia research on people perceived as trans excludes those whose identities, histories, and experiences do not neatly conform to a cis–trans binary (e.g., people who have a non-binary experience of gender, people who experience themselves as not having any gender, and people who live part of the time as a gender that is typically classified as "cis" and part of the time as a gender that is typically classified as "trans"). Some authors (e.g., Ansara 2012;

Ansara and Hegarty 2012; Blumer, Ansara, and Watson 2013) have described the concept of "trans," and thus transphobia, as ethnocentric for not acknowledging culturally specific genders (e.g., Kathoey, Kinnar, Bissu). The emphasis on the category "trans people" in transphobia research also frames professional discourse in a way that excludes discriminatory approaches to intersex people and to people with disability labels.

Transphobia does not address benevolent and unintentional forms of differential treatment. As the field of research on racism has shifted away from studying explicit bias toward a focus on implicit bias and the field of sexuality research has moved from studying homophobia to heterosexism, so too have some researchers begun to shift away from the transphobia framework toward research on cisgenderism.

SEE ALSO: Cisgenderism; Gender-Based Violence; Gender Inequality and Gender Stratification; Gender Oppression; Heterosexism and Homophobia; Strategic Essentialism; Trans Identities, Psychological Perspectives

REFERENCES

Ansara, Y. Gavriel. 2012. "Cisgenderism in Medical Settings: How Collaborative Partnerships Can Challenge Structural Violence." In *Out of the Ordinary: LGBT Lives*, edited by I. Rivers and R. Ward, 102–122. Cambridge: Cambridge Scholars Publishing.

Ansara, Y. Gavriel, and Peter Hegarty. 2012. "Cisgenderism in Psychology: Pathologizing and Misgendering Children from 1999 to 2008." *Psychology & Sexuality*, 3: 137–160. DOI: 10.1080/19419899.2011.576696.

Ansara, Y. Gavriel, and Peter Hegarty. 2013. "Misgendering in English Language Contexts: Applying Non-Cisgenderist Methods to Feminist Research." *International Journal of Multiple Research Approaches*, 7: 160–177.

Blumer, Markie L. C., Y. Gavriel Ansara, and Courtney M. Watson. 2013. "Cisgenderism in Family Therapy: How Everyday Clinical Practices Can Delegitimize People's Gender Self-Designations." *Journal of Family Psychotherapy, Special Section: Essays in Family Therapy*, 24(4): 267–285.

Clements-Nolle, Kristen, Rani Marx, and Mtichell Katz. 2006. "Attempted Suicide Among Transgender Persons: The Influence of Gender-Based Discrimination and Victimization." *Journal of Homosexuality*, 51: 53–69. DOI: 10.1300/J082v51n03_04.

Hill, Darryl B. 2002. "Genderism, Transphobia, and Gender Bashing: A Framework for Interpreting Anti-Transgender Violence." In *Understanding and Dealing with Violence: A Multicultural Approach*, edited by Barbara C. Wallace and Robert T. Carter, 113–136. Thousand Oaks: Sage.

Hill, Darryl B., and Brian L. B. Willoughby. 2005. "The Development and Validation of the Genderism and Transphobia Scale." *Sex Roles*, 53: 531–544. DOI: 10.1007/s11199-005-7140-x.

King, Mark E., Sam Winter, and Beverley Webster. 2009. "Contact Reduces Transprejudice: A Study on Attitudes towards Transgenderism and Transgender Civil Rights in Hong Kong." *International Journal of Sexual Health*, 21: 17–34. DOI: 10.1080/19317610802434609.

Mizock, Lauren, and Thomas K. Lewis. 2008. "Trauma in Transgender Populations: Risk, Resilience, and Clinical Care." *Journal of Emotional Abuse*, 8(3): 335–354. DOI: 10.1080/10926790802262523.

Nagoshi, Julie L., et al. 2008. "Gender Differences in Correlates of Homophobia and Transphobia." *Sex Roles*, 59: 521–532. DOI: 10.1007/s11199-008-9458-7.

Sugano, Eiko, Tooru Nemoto, and Don Operario. 2006. "The Impact of Exposure to Transphobia on HIV Risk Behavior in a Sample of Transgendered Women of Color in San Francisco." *AIDS and Behavior*, 10: 217–225. DOI: 10.1007/s10461-005-9040-z.

Whittle, Stephen, Lewis Turner, and Maryam Al-Alami. 2007. "*Engendered Penalties: Transgender and Transsexual People's Experiences of Inequality and Discrimination*." London: BM Network.

Willoughby, Brian L. B., et al. 2010. "Who Hates Gender Outlaws? A Multisite and Multinational Evaluation of the Genderism and

Transphobia Scale." *International Journal of Transgenderism*, 12: 254–271. DOI: 10.1080/15532739.2010.550821.

FURTHER READING

Lombardi, Emilia L., Riki A. Wilchins, Dana Priesing, and Diana Malouf. 2001. "Gender Violence: Transgender Experiences with Violence and Discrimination." *Journal of Homosexuality*, 42: 89–101.

Transsexuality

LAL ZIMMAN
University of California, Santa Barbara, USA

Transsexuality was first introduced to a broad public audience by Harry Benjamin in his 1966 book, *The Transsexual Phenomenon*. Drawing on the insights of German sexologists from the late nineteenth century like Karl Heinrich Ulrichs, Benjamin identified transsexuality as a condition driven by gender dysphoria, or a feeling of discomfort, distress, or sadness over one's assigned gender role. In a metaphor that has retained its potency for over a century, Ulrichs described the experience that Benjamin labeled as transsexuality as that of being "a female soul enclosed within a male body." According to Benjamin's typology of gender non-normativity, which includes multiple categories of individuals who do not adhere to expectations for their assigned sex and who may experience gender dysphoria, transsexuals experience a deep and enduring identification with the gender role "opposite" to their assigned sex. Key in Benjamin's account of transsexuality is a separation between homosexuality (same-sex desire), transvestism (cross-dressing in the absence of self-identification with the other sex), and transsexuality (identification with the other sex extending beyond self-presentation). Benjamin's volume lays out diagnostic criteria for the "true transsexual," etiological theories for transsexual development, and recommendations for treatment in the form of hormone therapy and surgery. These ideas have remained influential in the intervening decades even as many of the particulars of his account have fallen out of popularity (such as the distinction "true" and "pseudo" forms of transsexuality) and sex-changing medical practices have extended beyond the particular Western subjectivities centered by Benjamin and his colleagues.

The rise of transsexuality as a concept, then, occurred in tandem with the development of medical techniques, procedures, and practices that allow transsexuals to bring their bodies in line with sociocultural expectations for members of the gender with which they self-identify. The connection between transsexuality and medicine established by Benjamin and furthered by transsexuals' demand for medically administered body-changing technologies created a lasting impression that transsexuality is first and foremost a medical condition. For some transsexuals, this association provides legitimacy in the face of intense social stigma, while others consider transsexuality to be characterized by pathologizing discourses about gender variance. In trans activism, this schism is currently reflected in the sometimes contentious debate about whether to end the psycho-medical diagnosis of transsexuality. The replacement of gender identity disorder with gender dysphoria in the 2013 revisions of the *Diagnostic and Statistical Manual of Mental Disorders* (American Psychiatric Association 2013) constitutes an attempt to answer this critique by shifting the locus of pathologization away from transsexuals' identities and toward the experience of gender dysphoria.

The medical and pathological associations attached to transsexuality were intensified by the coinage and ascent of the word *transgender*, which offered an alternate framework of trans identification for those who might otherwise be classified as (pseudo) transsexuals. First introduced in the late 1960s by Virginia Prince, an American activist for self-identified heterosexual male cross-dressers, *transgender* originally referred to those who make a social transition from one gender role to another without pursuing a change in physiological sex. In the 1990s, the word came to serve as an umbrella label for English speakers that included transsexuals, transgenderists (a now outdated term that has been replaced by the phrase *transgender people*), and others who do not fit easily into culturally dominant classifications of gender and/or sex. More than an umbrella label, though, transgender represented a shift away from the compulsory gender normativity that characterized diagnoses of transsexuality. The diagnostic criteria identified by Benjamin and enacted by several generations of medical practitioners who followed relied on their own contemporary – and heavily racialized, classed, and otherwise culture-bound – models of gender normativity. The "true" male-to-female transsexual not only self-identified as a woman, but also preferred normatively feminine occupations and pastimes, wished to attain a physical appearance considered feminine and attractive by hegemonic cultural standards, and was exclusively attracted to men. Some doctors notoriously even used their own degree of sexual attraction to a patient as one measure of whether she would have a "successful" transition. Without displaying these attributes, a patient would likely be denied services by the gender identity clinics that were a primary source of institutionally sanctioned sex-changing interventions for much of the twentieth century. This gatekeeping process ensured that medical establishments treating transsexuals did not produce women or men who would fundamentally disrupt the gender order; transsexuals should blend into society rather than challenge it. It is in this context that transsexuality came to stand for not only body modification over non-modification, but also gender normativity over gender subversion and assimilation into the new gender role over its denaturalization. Today, many who could be classified as transsexual based on their diagnosis and/or pursuit of body-changing medical technology nevertheless make use of *transgender* or simply *trans* as their preferred identity label.

Despite the cultural shift toward transgender, both as a terminological choice and as a distinctive subjectivity, research on transsexuality remains a significant force in the framing of academic work on trans issues. As might be expected based on the intellectual history detailed above, one line of inquiry in this body of work consists of medical research on the physiological processes of transsexual transition. However, a more recent humanistic and social scientific literature aims to recuperate transsexuality by virtue of its connection to sexed embodiment. Indeed, the theorization of the gendered body has become one of the primary projects of transgender studies as an interdisciplinary field. In this work, strictly medico-scientific notions about embodiment are discarded in favor of psychosocial, poststructuralist, and culturally contingent understandings of the body. Ultimately, however, scholars of transgender studies have expressed skepticism of purely discursive theories of sex associated with queer theory, and instead aim to blend poststructuralist and materialist approaches to embodiment that allow for a recognition of the importance trans people themselves place on corporeality as well as the ways trans bodies are a site of regulation and surveillance in transphobic cultural and institutional contexts.

SEE ALSO: Embodiment and the Phenomenological Tradition; Intersexuality;

Queer Theory; Sex Reassignment Surgery; Transgender Movements in International Perspective; Transgender Movements in the United States; Transgender Politics

REFERENCES

American Psychiatric Association. 2013. *Diagnostic and Statistical Manual of Mental Health Disorders*, 5th ed. Washington, DC: American Psychiatric Association.

Benjamin, Harry. 1966. *The Transsexual Phenomenon*. Ann Arbor: Julian Press.

FURTHER READING

Meyerowitz, Joanne. 2002. *How Sex Changed: A History of Transsexuality in the United States*. Cambridge, MA: Harvard University Press.

Prosser, Jay. 1998. *Second Skins: The Body Narratives of Transsexuality*. New York: Columbia University Press.

Salamon, Gayle. 2010. *Assuming a Body: Transgender and Rhetorics of Materiality*. New York: Columbia University Press.

Transvestitism

JOANNA McINTYRE
University of Queensland, Australia

Transvestitism, or transvestism, refers to certain modes of, and behaviors associated with, cross-dressing; that is, temporarily wearing clothing and adornments designated to the opposite sex/gender. Transvestitism tends to manifest either as an expression of cross-sex/gender identification (distinct from sexual orientation), or for the purposes of sexual gratification. Those who practice transvestitism are known as transvestites. Transvestitism has appeared in human societies for centuries, but the term arose first in medical discourse in the early twentieth century. Since then, "transvestitism" has been applied to differing transgender phenomena, and remains a variable term.

Transvestitism entails the transvestite temporarily wearing attire and/or adornments that belie their anatomically assigned gender, and typically involves the transvestite also taking on behavioral aspects of that corresponding gender. Broadly the term encompasses a wide range of cross-dressing; however, transvestitism can be distinguished from the flamboyant cross-dressing of drag, which is parodic and purposefully excessive in nature, and it is also distinct from the permanent psychological and/or corporeal sex/gender-crossing of transsexualism. Transvestitism is often used to refer to cross-dressing that is unrelated to gender identity or sexuality, such as ceremonial cross-dressing performed as part of cultural or religious rituals, and cross-dressing used for the purposes of a temporary cross-sex disguise. The latter often arises as a comic ploy in fictional narratives, but there are also historical accounts of female-to-male transvestites masquerading as males for safety while travelling or to gain access to male-only domains. Nevertheless, transvestitism usually manifests as an expression of queer gender identity, or as a result of a sexual fixation with garments of the opposite sex/gender.

Pioneering German sexologist Magnus Hirschfeld coined the term "transvestite" in reference to what is now understood as range of transgender subjectivities. Although terminology has evolved considerably, in Hirschfeld's work and that of those who followed him, as well as in contemporary psychiatric discourse and academic theory, a distinction is delineated between forms of transvestitism associated with gender identity and transvestic fetishism, which is characterized by sexual arousal. In its most common current usage, transvestitism denotes cross-dressing that functions as an outward expression of an identification with the opposite sex/gender. Such transvestitism comprises a diverse range of participants, and is independent of sexual orientation, as transvestites can identify as homosexual, bisexual, or heterosexual. In some cases, habitual transvestitism of this nature is a stage in an individual's progression to transsexualism, for others it remains a significant ritual within their lives. At its most extreme, transvestitism manifests as transvestic *passing*. Passing transvestites cross-dress and behave in such a way that they pass, or at least intend to pass, as members of the opposite sex, bearing no deliberately visible traces of cross-gendering (though some may still be apparent). Transvestic passing is achieved through the production of an appearance that represents realistically the desired gender and often involves the adoption of a name, vocal qualities, mannerisms and/or demeanor stereotypically appropriate to that gender. The resulting effect is usually a dramatic alteration of the transvestite's appearance. In these circumstances the transvestite assumes, for the duration of their passing, a cross-gender identity: for a male transvestite the cross-gender identity of a "woman," for a female transvestite the identity of a "man."

Cross-sex/gender-identified transvestitism has caused debate across and within academic disciplines concerned with gender. Anti-essentialist queer studies scholars tend to valorize the figure of the transvestite and expound its transgressive possibilities. From this point of view, transvestitism (along with drag) can work to reveal the constructedness of gender, demonstrating that any*body* can enact either masculinity or femininity, or a coupling of both. On the other hand, in relation to male-to-female transvestites, some feminist scholars take the stance that such gender-crossing is a destructive appropriation of femininity that works to oppress women. Such a position situates these queer models of gender in opposition to the goals and motivations of feminism.

As noted above, a distinction exists between transvestitism that is associated with cross-sex/gender identification and transvestic fetishism, wherein the transvestite's cross-sex/gender garments function as fetish objects. A mode of transvestitism typically associated with heterosexual males, transvestic fetishism indulges erotic desire and sexual urges connected with particular items of clothing. The types of articles of clothing that are fetishized vary, as does the methods of fetishistic engagement with them. For example, a man may wear women's lingerie underneath conventional clothing so as have his fetish object close to him, or a complete feminine outfit may be worn in a manner aesthetically akin to passing transvestites. The sexual behaviors associated with transvestic fetishism are often autoerotic and sometimes autogynephilic. The *Diagnostic and Statistical Manual of Mental Disorders*, fifth edition (DSM-5 2013) defines transvestic fetishism as a diagnosable paraphilic disorder only if this behavior causes significant distress or impairment.

Transvestic fetishism is often explained in terms of psychoanalysis. From a psychoanalytic standpoint, transvestic fetishism is a symptom of a not properly completed oedipal journey. These fetish objects stand in for the displaced maternal phallus; that is, the imagined phallus of the mother that represents infantile pre-separation completeness, which is "lost" upon the (male) child's realization that she is without a phallus and subsequent belief that she has been castrated. Such fetishism indicates a denial of the mother's "castration," as the maternal phallus is substituted with the fetishized object. However, because a need for substitution is consequently recognized, at the same time the mother's castration is also acknowledged. According to psychoanalysis, fetishism is therefore understood as a balance between the symbolic (social, patriarchal, language-related) stipulation that the mother be renounced and the preservation of maternal attachment. It is believed that this balance allows the fetishist to remain a signifying subject while maintaining pre-symbolic libidinal drives.

SEE ALSO: Drag; Psychological Theory, Research, Methodology, and Feminist Critiques; Queer Theory; Transgender Movements in International Perspective; Transsexuality

REFERENCE

American Psychiatric Association. 2013. *Diagnostic and Statistical Manual of Mental Disorders*, 5th ed. (DSM-5). Arlington: American Psychiatric Publishing.

FURTHER READING

Butler, Judith. 1999. *Gender Trouble: Feminism and the Subversion of Identity*. New York: Routledge.
Garber, Marjorie. 1993. *Vested Interests: Cross-dressing and Cultural Anxiety*. New York: Harper Perennial.
Hirschfeld, Magnus. 2006. "Selections from The Transvestites: The Erotic Drive to Cross-Dress." In *The Transgender Studies Reader*, edited by Susan Stryker and Stephen Whittle, 28–39. New York: Routledge.
Lewins, Frank. 1995. *Transsexualism in Society: A Sociology of Male-Female Transsexuals*. Melbourne: MacMillan Education Australia.
Modleski, Tania. 1991. *Feminism Without Women: Culture and Criticism in a "Postfeminist" Age*. New York: Routledge.
Newton, Esther. 1979. *Mother Camp: Female Impersonators in America*. Chicago: University of Chicago Press.
Stryker, Susan. 2008. *Transgender History*. Berkeley: Seal Press.
Stryker, Susan, and Stephen Whittle, eds. 2006. *The Transgender Studies Reader*. New York: Routledge.

Two-Spirit

MICHAEL ANHORN
Independent scholar

Over 150 of the indigenous cultures of North America had words, traditions, and/or ceremonies for more than two gender identities. In 1990, at the third annual intertribal Native American/First Nations gay and lesbian conference in Winnipeg, the term "two-spirit" became the preferred English term to refer generally to the various Native American/First Nations' gender identities that are outside of the gender concepts of man and woman as defined in the contemporary hegemonic culture of North America. The term comes from the Ojibwa words *niizh manitoag* (two-spirits). In most understandings of the term, two-spirit refers to having both male and female spirits within one person (though for some nations this understanding is problematic). Across North America, two-spirit has now mostly replaced the colonial term of "berdache," which was originally coined by the French and meant "kept boy."

Prior to European contact, most nations had their own understanding and terminology for concepts which in English are now grouped together under the term two-spirit. The Dine'é (Navaho) used the term *nádleehé*, the Zuni used *lhamana*, the Lakota *winkte* (sometimes spelled *wintke*, both a contraction of the word *Winyanktehca*) and the Squamish *g!a:uk*. The traditional understanding and roles of two-spirit people varied greatly from nation to nation, sometimes even between nations within the same language group. The traditional concepts on which the contemporary concept of two-spirit is based were a complex intersection between the contemporary concepts of gender and sexual orientation. In some nations, the traditional role of a two-spirit person saw them dress and do the work of the other sex. In others, the person may dress the same as others of the same sex, but might have had sexual relations with others of the same sex. In some nations two-spirit people were expected to be celibate, in others it was considered a great honor and very good luck to have sex with a two-spirit person before battle or hunting. In many nations, two-spirit people held the rights for ceremonies and rituals that could only be performed by a two-spirit person. In yet others, two-spirit people were the only ones trusted to raise children whose parents had died. Although most nations view two-spirit people with honor and respect, there were some that viewed them with disdain and would chastise and ridicule them or even banish them from the community.

Since the 1980s, many Aboriginal and First Nations people (two-spirit and non-two-spirit identified) have been working to reclaim, and where necessary recreate, the traditions of two-spirit people both on reserve and in urban settings. This re-emergence of two-spirit people and their participation in spiritual ceremonies, in both their home communities and urban Aboriginal communities, has led to a wide range of experiences from acceptance and welcoming, to rejection and discrimination. Groups such as the Greater Vancouver Native Cultural Society, Gay American Indians, and Dancing to Eagle Spirit Society have provided camaraderie, activism and experiential exploration of cultural and spiritual traditions for two-spirit people in urban settings. On reserve, individuals have been working to reclaim their nation's specific two-spirit traditions, stories and ceremonies (often while working to overcome the stigma and hatred ingrained in their people by colonization).

SEE ALSO: Berdache; Colonialism and Gender; Colonialism and Sexuality; Cross-Cultural Gender Roles; Indigenous Knowledges and Gender; LGBT Activism in Native North America; Traditional Healing

FURTHER READING

Brown, Lester B. ed. 1997. *Two Spirit People: American Indian Lesbian Women and Gay Men*. New York: Harrington Park Press.

Conner, Randy P., David H. Sparks, and Mariya Sparks. 1997. *Cassell's Encyclopaedia of Queer Myth, Symbol, and Spirit: Gay, Lesbian, Bisexual, and Transgender Lore*. New York: Cassell.

Driskill, Qwo-Li, Daniel H. Justice, Deborah Miranda, and Lisa Tatonetti. eds. 2011. *Sovereign Erotics: A Collection of Two-Spirit Literature*. Tucson: University of Arizona Press.

Gilley, Brian J. 2006. *Becoming Two-Spirit: Gay Identity and Social Acceptance in Indian Country*. Lincoln: University of Nebraska Press.

Jacobs, Sue-Ellen, Wesley Thomas, and Sabine Lang. 1997. *Two-Spirit People: Native American Gender Identity, Sexuality and Spirituality*. Chicago: University of Illinois Press.

Laframboise, Sandra, and Michael Anhorn. 2008. "The Way of the Two Spirited People: Native American Concepts of Gender and Sexual Orientation." Accessed August 19, 2015, at http://www.dancingtoeaglespiritsociety.org/twospirit.php.

Lang, Sabine. 1998. *Men as Women, Women as Men: Changing Gender in Native American Cultures*. Austin: University of Texas Press.

Roscoe, Will. 1998. *Changing Ones: Third and Fourth Genders in Native North America*. New York: St. Martin's Press.

Roscoe, Will., ed. 1988. *Living the Spirit: A Gay American Indian Anthology*. New York: St. Martin's Press.

Roscoe, Will. 1991. *The Zuni Man-Woman*. Albuquerque: University of New Mexico.

Young, Jean C. 1997. *Alternative Genders in the Coast Salish World: Paradox and Pattern*. Unpublished Master's Thesis, University of British Columbia, Vancouver, BC.

U

UN Decade for Women

STEPHANIE CHABAN
University of Ulster, UK

Regarded as a significant institutional forum for the international women's movement to meet and further develop their agendas, the United Nations Decade for Women (the Decade) took place from 1975–1985 and began with the International Women's Year (1975). A succession of world conferences followed: the World Conference of the International Women's Year in Mexico City (1975), the World Conference of the United Nations Decade for Women: Equality, Development and Peace in Copenhagen (1980) and the World Conference to Review and Appraise the Achievements of the United Decade for Women: Equality, Development and Peace in Nairobi (1985). The Conferences centrally placed women's issues in the international arena and provided a forum for women's voices and opportunities for women to share their oppression, network, and strategize globally. Significant documents were produced that eventually challenged and changed the discourse surrounding equality, development, peace, and the discrimination of women. The text of the Convention on the Elimination of All Forms of Discrimination against Women (CEDAW, 1979) was introduced during this timeframe. The trio of conferences led the way for the important transformations of the 1990s, most significantly at the Fourth World Conference on Women in Beijing (1995) and enumerated within the Beijing Declaration and the Platform for Action.

In 1975, dedicated by the United Nations as International Women's Year (IWY), the Commission on the Status of Women (CSW) called for a global world conference on women. The conference was held to commemorate the 25th anniversary of the CSW in 1972.

The Mexico City Conference aimed to address discrimination against women at a global level; it was the first such conference of its kind set up to address women's issues at the international level. A parallel forum ran, entitled the International Women's Year Tribune. The conference document, the World Plan of Action, outlined the three main themes advocated for by the delegates: equality, development, and peace. The Plan of Action provided minimum goals to be addressed within a five-year span: improve the status of women in education, employment, political participation, health, housing, and family planning. Despite the agreed-upon goals, tensions arose between delegates, recreating Cold War divisions. Additionally, the Plan of Action was critiqued for not addressing the causal explanations for women's subordination. The language used in the document tended to identify women in the family context while continuing to utilize patriarchal discourse. States were tasked with creating a national strategy for improving the situation of women.

After the conference in Mexico City, 127 Member States committed to creating national women's machineries, women's ministries, and Women in Development programs. As a result of the Conference, the United Nations Development Fund for Women (UNIFEM) and the International Research and Training Institute for the Advancement of Women (INSTRAW) (now both part of UN Women) were created.

The Second World Conference on Women was held in Copenhagen in 1980. Building on the document produced at the Mexico City Conference, the Copenhagen Conference chose to address more deeply the issues of access to education, employment, and health. During this time CEDAW was officially launched. Tensions over politicized issues surfaced during the conference, with calls from the United States to focus only on "women's issues." The most controversial issue to arise was the inclusion of Zionism as a form of racism in the text of the Programme of Action. Similar to the Mexico City Plan of Action, the Copenhagen Programme of Action contained issues representing the different political blocs associated with the Cold War.

Overall, the Programme of Action called for national measures to address women and property, inheritance, child custody and nationality. The call to collect sex-disaggregated data was also a unique component of the document. Compared to the Mexico City Plan of Action, the Copenhagen Programme of Action placed women at the center of the development agenda, discussed women outside of the family context, and equated peace with the elimination of discrimination against women.

The Nairobi Conference in 1985 was, at the time, considered the largest gathering of women in history; an estimated 1400 official delegates from 157 countries attended, in addition to 15,000 NGO representatives. Formally titled the World Conference to review and appraise the achievements of the United Nations Decade for Women: Equality, Development and Peace, the Conference was comprised of official government delegate meetings and unofficial gatherings of individuals and organizations at the Non-Governmental Organization Forum (Forum '85).

A 350-point plan of action was proposed as the Nairobi Forward-looking Strategies (FLS) for the advancement of women to the year 2000 and was unanimously adopted by 157 governments in attendance. While Cold War tensions continued to play out during the conference, the greatest obstacle occurred when the United States lobbied for and obtained voting by consensus on all conference documents. Thus, there was an effort to have the term "Zionism" as a form of racism removed from the text of the FLS. In the end, an agreement was reached that substituted the phrase "all forms of racial discrimination" for Zionism, thus securing consensus on the document. The text of the FLS went further than previous conference documents in that it critiqued domestic and international causes related to the discrimination of women.

A significant outcome of the United Nations Decade for Women, as mentioned above, was the creation of the UN Development Fund for Women (UNIFEM, which eventually grew to UN Women) at the international level. Women's transnational networks, especially those situated in the Global South, such as Development Alternatives with Women for a New Era (DAWN), the International Women's Rights Action Watch (IWRAW), and the Association for Women in Development (AWID) also emerged providing an institutional foundation for an international women's movement.

SEE ALSO: Feminist Movements in Historical and Comparative Perspective; Feminist Organizations, Definition of; Women in Development; Women's Movements: Early International Movements; Women's Movements: Modern International Movements

FURTHER READING

Bunch, Charlotte. 2012. "Opening Doors for Feminism: UN World Conferences on Women." *Journal of Women's History*, 24(4): 213–221.

Reilly, Niamh. 2009. *Women's Human Rights*. Cambridge: Polity Press.

Tinker, Irene, and Jane Jaquette. 1987. "UN Decade for Women: Its Impact and Legacy." *World Development*, 15(3): 419–427.

Zinsser, Judith P. 2002. "From Mexico to Copenhagen to Nairobi: The United Nations Decade for Women, 1975–1985." *Journal of World History*, 13(1): 139–168.

United States' Women's Movements in Historical Perspective

NICHOLAS PEDRIANA
University of Wisconsin–Whitewater, USA

INTRODUCTION

Although collective efforts to improve the status and opportunities of women in the United States go back to the republic's founding, many movement historians refer to and compare specific "waves" of women's mobilization. There is near consensus that the "first" wave roughly spanned the period from 1840 to 1920, that women's suffrage was the overarching objective, and that the movement fragmented and ceased to be a major political force for several decades after passage of the 19th Amendment. Many movement scholars further agree that a "second" wave emerged in the mid- to late 1960s and culminated sometime in the 1980s; and that, the franchise notwithstanding, it was during this wave that women achieved many of their greatest accomplishments with respect to individual rights and formal legal equality. Reproductive freedoms and equal employment and educational opportunities are considered among the second wave's most important and longstanding achievements. There is less agreement among scholars and historians as to whether the women's movement is currently in the midst of a distinct "third" wave or whether women's mobilization in the last 20 years is simply a continuation of the second wave.

Space limitations preclude a highly detailed and nuanced treatment of each; rather, the major events, debates, organizations, objectives, and outcomes of each successive period are highlighted and summarized. Each wave is also placed into a broader structural and cultural context that enables and constrains the possibilities for collective action. Finally, the third wave is treated as a distinct phase of the US women's movement with the acknowledgment that not all will agree with this characterization, and that some would situate the last two decades of women's mobilization as a current phase of second-wave activism (for a detailed treatment of this issue, see Reger 2005).

THE FIRST WAVE (1840–1920)

The rise of industrial capitalism transformed work and family relationships in ways that marginalized women's economic "value," significantly lowered fertility rates, and fostered gender norms, roles, and stereotypes that restricted women to the "nonproductive" private sphere of home and family. "It was in this context that a new role of domesticity was created and promoted as a distinctly feminized complement to the masculinized role of economic provider" (Buechler 1990, 13), and contributed in part to a distinct feminine identity and new possibilities for collective action.

The seeds of independent women's activism were planted within other established movements, including the abolitionist, temperance, progressive, and other religious/charitable causes (DuBois 1978). While many of these movements themselves had patriarchal tendencies, they nonetheless provided women's advocates with the experience, associational networks, and organizational skills necessary for an (eventual) independent women's movement. The Seneca Falls conference in 1848 – widely seen as the event that formally launched the US women's rights/suffrage movement – took place within this historical context.

The first national women's suffrage organizations emerged in the later decades of the nineteenth century. Elizabeth Cady Stanton and Susan B. Anthony formed the National Women's Suffrage Association (NWSA) in 1869. Soon after, Lucy Stone and Henry Blackwell formed the American Women's Suffrage Association (AWSA). Although the two organizations began as rival groups, neither had much political success advancing the suffrage cause between 1870 and 1890, at which point they merged to form the National American Women Suffrage Association (NAWSA).

If, however, the political environment at the end of the nineteenth century was temporarily unfavorable to the suffrage cause, rapid structural changes in economy and society created new social identities and political cleavages that were entangled with women's rights and claims to the franchise. The ongoing expansion of American capitalism and productive technologies, immigration, urbanization, and expanded education for females diversified the class and occupational structure and prompted calls for social reform in ways that contributed to women's growing relevance and strength as a political constituency in their own right (Cott 1987).

All these changes coincided with the spread of new social problems – real and perceived – associated with urbanization, poverty, and immigration (e.g., overcrowding, child-labor, strained social services, hygiene, alcoholism, etc.) and enticed many middle- and upper-class women into the progressive movement and its calls for civilizing social reforms. Women's distinct experiences and viewpoints intermingled with the broader progressive cause and yielded new political alliances that further revealed women's relevance in public life that, while nowhere near equal to men, could no longer be ignored (Flexner 1959; DuBois 1978). Such was the context in which the nascent suffrage movement brought together disparate and rival elements of women's activism into a unified call for the right to vote.

To be sure, there were intra-movement rivalries and conflicts over philosophy and tactics during this period. In 1913, a group of NAWSA members led by Alice Paul and Lucy Burns, split from the NAWSA to form the Congressional Union (CU) (renamed the National Women's Party (NWP) in 1917). The NWP was hierarchical and brought many state-level suffrage organizations under the authority of its wider national umbrella; it tolerated little internal dissent and was uncompromisingly committed to a national amendment for female suffrage (as opposed to winning the vote on a state-by-state basis). The NAWSA, led by Carrie Chapman Catt, soon followed suit and stepped up its own national strategy, although it retained its greater tolerance of diverse perspectives and tactics within the organization and eschewed the NWP's comparative militancy.

By the start of World War I, the movement had gained the upper hand politically. A combination of nationally coordinated state and local activity, congressional lobbying, pressure politics, and even a series of direct action protest marches eventually brought an ambivalent President Wilson and cautious Congress to support a constitutional amendment, culminating with ratification of the 19th Amendment in 1920. Once the vote was won, most historians concur that the suffrage movement's broad coalition fragmented and activists kept a comparatively low profile for the next several decades (see Rupp and Taylor 1987).

If first-wave women's activism achieved formal political equality for women via the franchise, it arguably did so without fundamentally challenging widespread gender norms and stereotypes surrounding assumed female characteristics and the primacy of women's domestic roles. Some early activists – Susan B. Anthony and Elizabeth Cady Stanton among them – did raise broader challenges to a patriarchal culture that devalued women inside and outside the home and thus restricted women's opportunities and life chances beyond mother, wife, and homemaker. Yet historical evidence suggests that the first-wave movement to a significant extent embraced gender difference and in fact persistently argued that the right to vote would benefit society by enabling women to *better fulfill* their sex-specific natures and obligations. As summarized by activist Jane Frohock, "[I]t is woman's womanhood, her instinctive femininity, her highest morality that society now needs to counter-act the excess of masculinity that is everywhere to be found in our unjust and unequal laws" (quoted in Cott 1987, 19). The second wave of the women's movement would begin to challenge these gender assumptions and taken-for-granted sex differences, calling for women's full and equal participation in social, economic, and political life well beyond the right to cast a ballot.

THE SECOND WAVE (1960–1980s)

Several interrelated structural and demographic changes contributed to a renewed wave of activism in the mid- to late 1960s. They included a steady decline in birthrates; more young single women delaying marriage; strong growth in percentage of women attaining bachelors, graduate, and professional degrees; significant increases in labor force participation; and ongoing occupational diversity among women (Freeman 1975, 28–31). As noted by movement historian Sara Evans (2003, 18):

> the terrain on which [women] lived their lives was changing at a remarkable pace, pulling their experiences increasingly out of line with the words and concepts available to describe them. The pressure that built up in this disjuncture explains much of the explosive force of the [second-wave] women's movement

Renowned feminist Betty Friedan articulated this "disjuncture" in her seminal 1963 book *The Feminist Mystique* and is often credited with sparking a renewed women's consciousness that jumpstarted second-wave activism. Many women were also influenced by the black civil rights movement and subsequently used its struggle for equal treatment and equal opportunity as a model to frame and challenge their own oppression throughout the late 1960s and 1970s.

In the early 1960s, many progressive women's advocates were institutionally located within the US Department of Labor's Women's Bureau and/or the President's Committee on the Status of Women (PCSW), created by President Kennedy in 1960. Women leaders from large, private organizations such as the UAW, AFL-CIO, YWCA, and American Association of University Women (AAUW) were also key institutional players promoting women's issues and women's rights. While most advocates generally promoted an expansion of women's rights – particularly in the areas of employment and education – few initially called for an aggressive equal rights agenda and/or direct challenges to culturally embedded gender norms and stereotypes. That would change when Congress unexpectedly added "sex" to Title VII of the 1964 Civil Rights Act, the law banning employment discrimination on account of race, religion, and national origin.

Title VII's sex provision was initially greeted with ambivalence and condescension by the Equal Employment Opportunity Commission (EEOC), the press, and many employers. Nearly all women's movement historians agree that failure to take the sex provision seriously helped spark the formation of the National Organization for Women (NOW) and the "second wave" of the women's movement. Employment discrimination against women – in all its forms – illuminated the connection between traditional gender norms and the structural obstacles to women's opportunities outside the home. NOW and its allies immediately set to work pressuring the EEOC and filed numerous lawsuits in the federal courts to enforce Title VII. For the next decade and a half, the EEOC and the federal judiciary consistently struck down longstanding practices that openly discriminated against working women, including sex-specific help-wanted advertisements; "protective" laws such as hours, travel, and weightlifting restrictions for female employees, exclusion of women from traditionally "male" jobs (and vice versa), discrimination on the basis of pregnancy or pregnancy related conditions, discrimination against women workers with children (but not males with children); and so forth. At the root of most of these legal/administrative decisions was a crucial principle: that employers could no longer justify gender discrimination on the basis of traditional cultural norms regarding women's inherent natures or traditional roles in society (Freeman 1975; Harrison 1988).

Thus, a universal "equality" frame that challenged accepted assumptions about women's interests and capabilities became one dominant theme for second-wave activists within and beyond the workplace (see Pedriana 2006). Indeed, it was during this period that second-wave activists and their allies lobbied aggressively for an equal rights amendment to the US Constitution. And although the ERA effort eventually failed, significant cultural, legal, and political changes favoring greater women's equality throughout social life continued apace. Major legislative achievements included enactment of Title IX in 1972, which banned gender discrimination in educational institutions (and today is most associated with women's equal access to sports and athletic programs) and the 1978 Pregnancy Discrimination Act, prohibiting employment discrimination on the basis of pregnancy.

A second major strand of second-wave activism emphasized women's "liberation," particularly with respect to the sexual oppression of women (inside and outside the home) and reproductive rights (Evans 2003). Liberation activism saw control of women's bodies and regulation of female sexual behavior as cornerstones of patriarchal oppression in ways that not only limited women's life chances and opportunities, but also tolerated – indeed often legitimated – violence against women. Accordingly, second-wave activists pushed for laws protecting women's access to contraception and the right to abortion, both of which were codified as fundamental constitutional rights by the Supreme Court, respectively, in *Griswold v. Connecticut* (1965) and *Roe v. Wade* (1973). They also sought to significantly reform and strengthen America's archaic laws governing violence against women, especially spousal abuse and rape laws.

The "equality" and "liberation" categories of second-wave activism are heuristic devices and ought not be seen as distinct, self-contained approaches to women's rights; rather, the strands overlapped in ways that painted a larger, systemic picture of women's disadvantage and oppression throughout society and whose amelioration called for a wide range of cultural, political, and legal changes that continued throughout the 1990s into the present day with varying degrees of success. Whether one views these ongoing efforts as seamless continuations of the second wave, or whether one draws attention to substantive differences and rivalries within the current US women's movement will likely influence whether it makes sense to speak of a distinct "third wave" of the women's movement. The final section summarizes some of the highlights of the past 20 years of women's activism and suggests that both characterizations may be accurate.

THE "THIRD" WAVE (1990s–PRESENT)

For those who do promote the "third wave" label, most date its beginning to the early 1990s, partly as a critical response of a new generation of feminists to perceived biases and rigidity of their second-wave predecessors. One central criticism is the claim that second-wave feminism rested largely on a white, middle class model of women's rights and identities. A growing chorus of activists and scholars pointed out that such a model marginalized the experiences of women facing multiple forms of oppression, especially poor women, women of color, and/or those of different sexual orientations (Walker 1995; Evans 2003; Reger 2005). Many third-wave activists also perceived rigidity in second-wave definitions and assumptions of what it meant to be a feminist. Third wavers instead emphasized the fluid nature of gender identity and a belief that "feminism" can mean different things to different individuals, depending on one's background, experiences, and personal identity (Baumgardner and Richards 2010). Such ideas have led to new internal debates and conflicts among and between third- and second-wave feminists about questions involving women's ongoing victimhood versus women's progress and substantive gains; the existence of racism and/or heteronormative biases within feminism; whether sexual assertiveness – symbolized by Madonna and a new generation of female performers – is empowering and liberating or simply reinforces the stereotype of women as sex objects; whether feminism can accommodate women who choose family over career; the extent to which women today are responsible for their own opportunities and success (or lack thereof) in the workplace; whether and with what consequences women are now surpassing men; and so forth. Hanna Rosin's book *The End of Men* (2012); Facebook COO Sheryl Sandberg's writings about professional women aggressively "leaning in" to advance their careers (Sandberg 2013); and recent articles in academia and the popular press about whether women really can "have it all," women's general reluctance to negotiate for better salaries and benefits, and related questions are examples of current third-wave issues and debates.

That said, third-wave (to the extent that the term applies) activists have continued to tackle many of the same entangled issues of the prior wave including violence against women and sexual harassment; limitations on reproductive freedoms; difficulties in balancing work–family obligations and the lack of family friendly workplace policies; institutional glass ceilings; the pay gap and comparable worth; and persistent gender stereotypes that continue to assume the primacy of women's domestic roles (Reger

2005; Baumgardner and Richards 2010). In this sense, the third wave could plausibly be classified as a continuation of the second wave conceived on a longer time horizon.

Some examples of third-wave policy/legal successes include enactment of the 1993 Family and Medical Leave Act (FMLA), the 1994 Violence against Women Act (VAWA), and the 2009 Lily Ledbetter Fair Pay Act, along with the Supreme Court's 1996 ruling that the Virginia Military Institute (VMI) may not exclude qualified women. Conservative backlash, however, has persistently challenged and in some cases rolled back women's gains, particularly with recent laws/court rulings curtailing women's access to abortion and contraception. These issues are likely to remain front and center among third-wave activists, further connecting them to their second-wave predecessors even as feminist identities, discourse, and cultural representations are themselves in transition and moving in multiple new directions.

SEE ALSO: Feminisms, First, Second, and Third Wave; Feminist Movements in Historical and Comparative Perspective; Gender, Definitions of; Women's and Feminist Activism in the United States and Canada

REFERENCES

Baumgardner, Jennifer, and Amy Richards. 2010. *Manifesta: Young Women, Feminism, and the Future*, 10th anniversary ed. Farrar, Straus and Giroux.

Buechler, Steven. 1990. *Women's Movements in the United States: Women's Suffrage, Equal Rights and Beyond*. New Brunswick: Rutgers University Press.

Cott, Nancy F. 1987. *The Grounding of Modern Feminism*. New Haven: Yale University Press.

DuBois, Ellen. 1978. *Feminism and Suffrage*. Ithaca: Cornell University Press.

Evans, Sara M. 2003. *Tidal Wave: How Women Changed America at Century's End*. New York: Free Press.

Flexner, Eleanor. 1959. *Century of Struggle: The Women's Rights Movement in the United States*. Cambridge, MA: Harvard University Press.

Freeman, Jo. 1975. *The Politics of Women's Liberation: A Case Study of an Emerging Social Movement and Its Relation to the Policy Process*. New York: David McKay.

Griswold v. Connecticut, 381 US 479, decided June 7, 1965.

Harrison, Cynthia. 1988. *On Account of Sex: The Politics of Women's Issues 1945–68*. Berkeley: University of California Press.

Pedriana, Nicholas. 2006. "From Equal to Protective Treatment: Legal Framing Processes and Transformation of the Women's Movement in the 1970s." *American Journal of Sociology*, 111: 1718–1761.

Reger, Jo. 2005. *Different Wavelengths: Studies of the Contemporary Women's Movement*. New York: Routledge.

Roe v. Wade, 410 US 113, decided January 22, 1973.

Rosin, Hanna. 2012. *The End of Men: And the Rise of Women*. New York: Riverhead Publishing.

Rupp, Leila, and Verta Taylor. 1987. *Survival in the Doldrums: The American Women's Rights Movement, 1945 to the 1960s*. New York: Oxford University Press.

Sandberg, Sheryl. 2013. *Lean in: Women, Work, and the Will to Lead*. New York: Knopf.

Walker, Rebecca. 1995. *To Be Real: Telling the Truth and Changing the Face of Feminism*. New York: Anchor Books.

FURTHER READING

Baker, Paula. 1984. "The Domestication of Politics: Women and American Political Society, 1780–1920." *The American Historical Review*, 89: 620–647.

Duerst-Lahti, Georgia. 1989. "The Government's Role in Building the Women's Movement." *Political Science Quarterly*, 104: 249–268.

Kay, Katty, and Claire Shipman. 2014. "The Confidence Gap." *The Atlantic*, May.

Ouellette, Laurie. 2009. "Building the Third Wave: Reflections of a Young Feminist, 1992." In The American Women's Movement 1945–2000: A Brief History with Documents, edited by Nancy MacLean, 160–165. New York: St. Martin's Press.

Slaughter, Anne-Marie. 2012. "Why Women Still Can't Have it All." *The Atlantic*, July–August.

Universal Human Rights

FRANCINE J. D'AMICO
Syracuse University, USA

Universal human rights principles came to the international stage in the mid-1800s as citizens petitioned governments to sign multilateral treaties abolishing the slave trade (1890), trafficking in women and children (1904), and the opium trade (1912). Advocates argued these rights to freedom and security of person applied to all people everywhere, as human beings, in contrast to national rights, which applied only to citizens in a particular country, or humanitarian protections, which applied only to soldiers in armed conflict. Today, over one hundred human rights treaties prohibit specific acts, such as genocide, torture, and discrimination, and aim to protect categories of persons, such as refugees, migrant workers, and persons with disabilities who experience particular or targeted forms of rights violations (United Nations 2015). Recent human rights campaigns focus on gender-based violence and discrimination against sexual minorities (Yogyakarta Principles 2006) and confirm that women's rights and sexual orientation and gender identity rights are fundamental human rights. Domestic courts and international tribunals enforce these treaties, and non-governmental organizations (NGOs) police state compliance. Critics claim international human rights law is Eurocentric, neocolonialist, masculinist, and heteronormative, challenging the concept of "universality" of rights. Supporters contend states are obligated to promote and protect these rights regardless of their political, economic, and cultural systems and that new treaties and more progressive juridical interpretations extend the promise of rights protections to groups previously excluded or ignored by mainstream human rights advocacy organizations and enforcement mechanisms.

From the Treaty of Westphalia (1648) on, countries were the only entities with rights under international law. People in a particular country were subjects of their sovereign, and their rights were national rights only – conferred by that government and applied only within that territory. States could do whatever they wanted to people in their territory, and international law applied only to how states behaved toward other states. During World War I, the concept of the nation-people – a group with a shared identity grounded in the principle of self-determination – began a gradual shift from this state-centric view to a more people-centric perspective, beginning with the League of Nations Covenant (1919). The League promoted disarmament, conflict resolution, decolonization, and "fair and humane conditions of labour for men, women, and children" (Article 23a).

This principle of self-determination, coupled with the world's reaction to the Holocaust during World War II, made human rights central to the new United Nations (UN) organization. UN supporters believed respect for human rights would prevent war. The UN Charter (1945) begins: "We the peoples of the United Nations" and commits member states "to reaffirm faith in fundamental human rights." The UN General Assembly adopted the non-binding Universal Declaration of Human Rights on December 10, 1948. The declaration holds that people ought to have their rights respected everywhere, by everyone, and passed with 48 votes in favor, none opposed, and 8 abstentions (United Nations 2015). The United Nations observes International Human Rights Day annually on December 10.

The norms articulated in the Universal Declaration of Human Rights (UDHR) were codified in two treaties, the International

Covenant on Economic, Social, and Cultural Rights (ICESCR) and the International Covenant on Civil and Political Rights (ICCPR), concluded in 1966 and entered into force in 1976 (United Nations 2015). These treaties are legally binding on all states whose representatives have signed and ratified or acceded to the agreements. Taken together, these three documents – the UDHR, the ICESCR, and the ICCPR – comprise the International Bill of Human Rights. These documents commit state governments to respect and to protect the rights of all people within their territory. In 1970, the International Court of Justice held that all UN member states and the international community as a whole must respect human rights and punish violations. Additional multilateral treaties ban such practices as apartheid, race and gender discrimination, and child labor, marriage, and military service (United Nations 2015). Regional and bilateral human rights treaties have also proliferated. However, under international law, only states that have signed and ratified treaties or have otherwise explicitly agreed to be bound by the rules codified in the treaties have a legal obligation to obey these rules.

Enforcement presents challenges. The UN Human Rights Council, the UN High Commission for Human Rights, and numerous NGOs, such as Amnesty International and Human Rights Watch, promote respect for human rights. Treaty bodies, such as the Human Rights Committee, attempt to hold states accountable for their promises through reporting and review processes. Human rights violations are adjudicated in domestic courts, in regional human rights courts, such as the Inter-American Court of Human Rights and the European Court of Human Rights, in ad hoc tribunals, such as the International Criminal Tribunal for Rwanda and the Special Court for Sierra Leone, and, since 2002, by the International Criminal Court, which tries individuals for war crimes, crimes against humanity, genocide, and aggression.

A central question concerns the "universality" of human rights. During the Cold War, Western capitalist democracies emphasized civil and political rights, like free expression, while communist regimes emphasized economic rights, like the right to unionize. Contemporary critics argue the emphasis on individual rights reflects a Eurocentric conceptualization of an atomistic individual divorced from other citizens and the environment, whereas alternative views emphasize communal or collective rights. For example, in the Eurocentric view of individual rights, the land belongs to the people – a person can purchase land, build on it, and sell it – whereas in many indigenous communities, the people belong to the land, which cannot be owned by any one person or group of people, or can only be held in common. Islamic and Asian perspectives on international law reflect this precedence of communal or collective rights over individual rights, and some critics view the concept of universality as neocolonialism (Mandami 2000). Advocates of the universality of human rights reject these arguments as cultural relativism.

Feminist legal scholars have also critiqued the "universality" of the rights articulated in the International Bill of Human Rights and other treaties as masculinist in that they are read as applying in the "public" rather than the "private" sphere, as in cases of sexual assault or domestic violence, and are enforced in confrontational rather than cooperative ways and venues that value masculine over feminine behaviors (MacKinnon 2007). Other legal scholars critique human rights law as heteronormative in that these laws fail to extend rights explicitly to people based on perceived sexual orientation and gender identity, such as the right to marry the person of one's choice or to be employed in any profession for which one is qualified, and fail to prevent or punish violations targeting sexual minorities, such as physical assault or "gay bashing" or being jailed or put to death for loving someone of the same sex (Wilde et al. 2007).

To date, no human rights treaty is "universal" even on paper, as no treaty has been signed and ratified or acceded to by every country in the world. The Convention on the Rights of the Child (CRC) of 1989 is most nearly universal in terms of states promising to abide by legal obligations arising from the treaty, with 194 states parties. Only two countries – Somalia and the United State of America – have signed but not ratified this treaty (United Nations 2015). The Convention on the Elimination of All Forms of Discrimination against Women (CEDAW) of 1979 has 188 states parties. Palau and the United States have signed but not ratified this treaty, and non-signatories include Iran, Somalia, Sudan, and the Holy See (United Nations 2015). Many states parties have registered reservations to these and other human rights treaties, claiming exemptions from certain rules for social, cultural, political, or historical reasons. Additionally, legislatures and courts in different countries have interpreted and applied the treaty obligations differently (MacKinnon 2007), leaving "universality" of human rights a promise as yet unfulfilled.

SEE ALSO: Convention on the Elimination of All Forms of Discrimination against Women; Disability Rights Movement; Employment Discrimination; Eurocentrism; Fetal Rights; Human Rights and Gender; Human Rights, International Laws and Policies on; Sex Discrimination; Sexual Rights; Sexuality and Human Rights; Yogyakarta Principles

REFERENCES

League of Nations. 1919. "The Covenant of the League of Nations." Accessed June 25, 2015, at http://avalon.law.yale.edu/20th_century/leagcov.asp.

MacKinnon, Catharine. 2007. *Are Women Human? And Other International Dialogues*. Cambridge, MA: Harvard University Press.

Mandami, Mahmood, ed. 2000. *Beyond Rights Talk and Culture Talk: Comparative Essays on the Politics of Rights and Culture*. New York: St. Martin's Press.

United Nations (UN). 1948. "Universal Declaration of Human Rights." Accessed June 25, 2015, at http://www.ohchr.org/EN/UDHR/Pages/Introduction.aspx.

United Nations (UN). 2015. *Treaty Collection*. Chapter IV: Human Rights. Accessed June 25, 2015, at https://treaties.un.org/pages/Treaties.aspx?id=4&subid=A&lang=en.

Wilde, Ralph, Dianne Otto, Doris E. Buss, Amr Shalakany, and Aeyal Gross. 2007. "Queering International Law." *American Society of International Law Proceedings*, 101: 119–132.

Yogyakarta Principles. 2006. Accessed June 25, 2015, at http://www.yogyakartaprinciples.org/.

FURTHER READING

Viljoen, Frans. 2009. "International Human Rights Law: A Short History." *UN Chronicle*. Accessed June 15, 2015, at http://www.unchronicle.un.org/article/international-human-rights-law-short-history/.

Victim Blaming

MICHELLE CASARELLA ESPINOZA
Alliant International University, USA

Victim blaming is the process of observers finding instances within victims' behavior to hold them at least partially responsible for their fate (Schwartz and Leggett 1999). Essentially, it is the practice of blaming victims to varying degrees based on personal and contextual variables. It is an ideological process, resulting from beliefs and ways of viewing the world that is based on distorted perceptions of reality. Such distortions may be subtle and are generally made on an unconscious level, and therefore not necessarily intentional. Additionally, there is certainly a purpose served in the process of victim blaming. The principle function of this self-serving attribution is that it allows people to distance themselves from any possibility of meeting a similar fate (Ryan 1971). It is important to consider that personal motivations to endorse rape myths are not necessarily intentional or conscious. A personal violation as intense as sexual assault contradicts cultural values stipulating the need for personal safety and justice (Brinson 1992). The mere existence of a rape victim threatens this delicate façade. By being faced with a threat to the system, people become motivated to preserve the world in which they live.

Victim blaming is disproportionally related to victims of rape and sexual assault (Ryan 2011). Traits such as rape myth acceptance and hostile masculinity are positively correlated with tendencies to blame rape victims (Viki, Abrams, and Masser 2004). Victim blaming is also associated with victim behaviors such as prior willingness to have consensual romantic contact with a victimizer, wearing revealing clothing, or accompanying one's date to his home (Pollard 1992; Bell, Kuriloff, and Lottes 1994; Maurer and Robinson 2008). Rape myths deny and trivialize sexual violence against women by transferring the blame for the rape from the perpetrator to the victim (Burt 1980). They serve ego-defensive and self-protective functions for the individual, resulting in biases in the attribution process. Attitudes toward sexual assault are socially influenced in complex and intricate ways. Gender, ethnicity, and stereotypes dominate how we perceive sexual activity. Continual denial of the presence of the rape culture that exists within the United States and the world, and of the violence against women in general will only perpetuate such injustices.

It has been postulated that blaming victims of rape occurs as a result of biased processes, a consequence of self-serving motives and irrational tendencies of the attributor which result in "anomalies in the judgment process" (Krahé 1991, 280). Research has illustrated the tendency to believe accepted misconceptions or "myths" about rape, defined as "attitudes and beliefs that are generally false but are widely and persistently held, and that serve to deny and justify male sexual aggression against women" (Lonsway and Fitzgerald 1994, 134). Rape myths include positive endorsements of general statements such as "women lie about rape" or "real rape victims have signs of injury to prove it." Social psychological research has examined rape myth acceptance by focusing on individual rape myths and examining the effect of the myth on attributions of blame ascribed to the victim. Examples include the influence of rape myths and the effect of the victim's physical attractiveness, previous sexual activity, degree of victim intoxication, and what the victim was wearing at the time of the attack.

The notion of victim blaming is a complex, mystifying, and concerning issue; however, it is indeed not a novel one. It has deep-seated roots ingrained in prejudices such as racism and sexism and is greatly influenced by perceptions resulting from various theories of attribution. Many of these theories, to some degree, serve to personally motivate humans to subscribe to certain beliefs when evaluating the circumstances of a victim's role in their own sexual assault. One theory is referred to as the just-world belief (Lerner and Montada 1998). Humans need to believe the world they live in includes a society that is not only fair and just, but also organized and free of chaos. Just-world beliefs are particularly evident when the events that occurred cannot be changed, such as in the incidence of a rape. By drawing the conclusion that the victim in some way deserved their fate, the belief in a just world is restored: good things happen to good people; bad things happen to bad people (Van den Bos and Maas 2009). Additionally, this emerges when people have a lack of experience or knowledge on a specific topic, such as sexual assault, and essentially rely on this because they are fearful of the unknown (Stahl, Eek, and Kazemi 2010).

Another theory is the defense attribution model (Walster 1966). This theory states that when there is a high degree of similarity between the victim and the person observing, they are more likely to attribute responsibility to someone or something other than the victim. In contrast, if the victim is unlike the observer, then the possibility of blaming the victim increases. The personal motivation component of this theory comes from an inner need to protect one's self-esteem. Furthermore, this is also a way to avoid any potential self-blame in the future if the person ever found themselves in the victim's circumstances. The need for control model states many people desire controllable, and therefore predictable, environments. Observers feel more in control of their own environments when they are able to attribute parts of the victim's personality or their actions as the cause for the attack. This allows them to maintain the mentality that they remain in control over their own lives. Otherwise, many people would be forced to confront the reality that they really have limited control over their own lives (Gray, Palileo, and Johnson 1993).

The final theory that attempts to explain the underlying need to blame victims is referred to as system justification. It proposes that humans are motivated to defend the status quo. Inherently, people hold on to favorable perspectives about themselves as well as society, even if in reality it is disadvantageous to certain groups of people (Jost, Mahzarin, and Nosek 2004). In part, this theory describes the practice of ignoring the reality that injustices such as sexism and violence against women are still rampant in modern society. It is much more comforting to believe that our society is not gender biased and equality exists for both sexes (Stahl, Eek, and Kazemi 2010).

SEE ALSO: Rape Culture; Victimization

REFERENCES

Bell, S. T., P. J. Kuriloff, and I. Lottes. 1994. "Understanding Attributions of Blame in Stranger Rape and Date Rape Situations: An Examination of Gender, Race, Identification, and Students Social Perceptions of Rape Victims." *Journal of Applied Social Psychology*, 24(19): 1719–1734.

Brinson, S. L. 1992. "TV Rape: Television's Communication of Cultural Attitudes toward Rape." *Women's Studies in Communication*, 12(2): 23–36.

Burt, M. R. 1980. "Cultural Myths and Supports for Rape." *Journal of Personality and Social Psychology*, 38(2): 217–230.

Gray, N. B., G. J. Palileo, and G. D. Johnson. 1993. "Explaining Rape Victim Blame: A Test of Attribution Theory." *Sociological Spectrum*, 13(4): 377–392.

Jost, J. T., R. B. Mahzarin, and B. A. Nosek. 2004. "A Decade of System Justification Theory: Accumulated Evidence of Conscious and Unconscious Bolstering of the Status Quo." *International Society of Political Psychology*, 25(6): 881–919.

Krahé, B. 1991. "Social Psychological Issues in the Study of Rape." *European Review of Social Psychology*, special issue, 2(1): 279–309.

Lerner, M. J., and L. Montada. 1998. "An Overview: Advances in Belief in a Just World Theory and Methods." In *Responses to Victimizations and Belief in a Just World*, edited by Leo Montada and M. J. Lerner. New York: Plenum Press.

Lonsway, K. A., and L. F. Fitzgerald. 1994. "Rape Myths in Review." *Psychology of Women Quarterly*, 18(2): 133–164. DOI: 10.1111/j.1471-6402.1994.tb00448.x.

Maurer, T. W., and D. W. Robinson. 2008. "Effects of Attire, Alcohol, and Gender Perceptions of Date Rape." *Sex Roles*, 58: 423–434. DOI: 10.1007/s11199-007-9343-9.

Pollard, P. 1992. "Judgments about Victims and Attackers in Depicted Rapes: A Review." *British Journal of Social Psychology*, 31: 307–326.

Ryan, K. M. 2011. "The Relationship between Rape Myths and Sexual Scripts: The Social Construction of Rape." *Sex Roles*, 65: 774–782. DOI: 10.1007/s11199-011-0033-2.

Ryan, W. 1971. *Blaming the Victim*, 1st ed. New York: Pantheon Books.

Schwartz, M. D., and M. S. Leggett. 1999. "Bad Dates or Emotional Trauma? The Aftermath of Campus Sexual Assault." *Violence Against Women*, 2: 134–147.

Stahl, T., D. Eek, and A. Kazemi. 2010. "Rape Victim as System Justification: The Role of Gender and Activation of Complementary Stereotypes." *Social Justice Research*, 23(4): 239–258.

Van den Bos, K., and M. Maas. 2009. "On the Psychology of Belief in a Just World: Exploring Experiential and Rationalistic Paths to Victim Blaming." *Society for Personality and Social Psychology*, 4(2): 203–210. DOI: 10.1177/0146167209344628.

Viki, G. T., D. Abrams, and B. Masser, B. 2004. "Evaluating Stranger and Acquaintance Rape: The Role of Benevolent Sexism in Perpetrator Blame and Recommend Sentence Length." *Law and Human Behavior*, 28(3): 295–303.

Walster, E. 1966. "Assignment for Responsibility for an Accident." *Journal of Personality and Social Psychology*, 3(1): 73–79.

Victimization

VICTORIA M. NAGY
La Trobe University, Australia

Victimization is defined as the process of becoming a victim of a crime, and the field of study associated with it is called victimology (Doerner 2011). Victimization can take various forms. Generally there are crimes which are victimless (for example, theft or fraud), or those which are against a person or persons (for example, assault, sexual violence, or, in its most extreme, murder). A power imbalance between the victim and the perpetrator of the crime is what typically exemplifies the relationship between the person being victimized and the offender, and can be a significant factor in the abuser's decision-making process to victimize, as it is often illustrated in domestic abuse cases as well as child maltreatment and abuse.

Various forms of victimization have been identified. These include not only the traditionally accepted view of victimization – a more powerful abuser victimizing a less powerful individual – but can also include peer victimization, secondary victimization, and revictimization (Olweus 1995; Doerner 2011, 38; Patterson 2011). Peer victimization is used to describe child-on-child/youth-on-youth violent activity where there might not be a power imbalance; secondary victimization is when the victim (adult or child) is further victimized in relation to the initial offense, for example, being treated without care by investigative officers or medical staff after having reported being the victim of a crime; revictimization is when an individual becomes a victim of a crime that is not (necessarily) linked with the first offense, for example, being the victim of any crime once heightens the chance that the individual will become the victim of another crime in the future (Finkelhor et al. 2011). Reasons for why revictimization occurs centers around victim vulnerability (which may be used by opportunistic abusers, or abusers in domestic abuse scenarios), such as depression, negative feelings about oneself, isolation, and even not recognizing the initial victimization as an offense (for example, marital rape may not be recognized by the victim who may assume this is the accepted form for marital relations) (DAIP 1984).

The concept of the "ideal victim" was first described by Nils Christie in 1986. Christie defined the ideal victim as "a person or category of individuals who – when hit by a crime – most readily is given the complete and legitimate status of being a victim" (Christie 1986, 18); and this ideal victim is characterized by being (1) weak, (2) carrying out a respectable project, (3) not blameworthy, and is victimized by a big and bad offender who is unknown to the victim (Van Wijk 2013). Individuals who do not fit this image of the ideal victim risk being blamed for their victimization. This is common in cases of sexual violence where the victim's prior behavior, clothing, or demeanor are questioned and used as the explanation for why the perpetrator committed the offense and often to exonerate the actions of the perpetrator. The other dynamics of sexual assault and violence – that the majority of victims are assaulted by someone who is known to them (partner, friend, an acquaintance or family member) and that two thirds of victims know their attacker – also complicates how the offense is viewed by the victim's friends, family, and the broader community including police and the criminal justice system (RAINN 2014a). In these scenarios the victim may be informed by verbal or physical cues that they are to blame for their victimization and that they are undeserving victims (i.e., victims who do not deserve protection and justice from the criminal justice system and society).

In both developed and developing countries women are more likely to be victims of child sexual abuse, sexual assault, and domestic/intimate partner and family violence than men. In the United States, it is estimated that 1 in 6 women have been the victims of attempted or completed rape (approximately 17.7 million women) in comparison to approximately 1 in 33 men (approximately 3.2 million men) (RAINN 2014b). The World Health Organization calculates that over 35 percent of women around the world have been victims of sexual violence (World Health Organization 2013, 2). Approximately 22–40 percent of women have experienced intimate partner violence during their lives (European Institute for Crime Prevention and Control, affiliated with the United Nations 2013).

While men can be victims of sexual violence, it is a highly gendered crime that affects more women than men.

Feminist scholars have repositioned debate around heterosexual male-on-female sexual assault as a crime about male power and violence, not sexual desire. The majority of rape reported to authorities, and rape reported in victimization surveys is male-on-female sexual assault. This is the most common form of sexual assault although male-on-male, female-on-female, or female-on-male rape also occur, however rape myths (such as the myth that men cannot be victims or that women cannot rape people) and social stigmas prevent victims from coming forward even more so than in cases of male-on-female rape. While historically sexual violence was explained as either resulting from male desire and biology, or due to women's appearance (for instance, the clothing worn by victims), today there is a greater understanding about the causes of violence against women. Feminist scholars argue that societal as well as individual factors are at play in sexual assault perpetration, and gender inequality, cultural and religious beliefs, and legislation which treats sexual violence and violence against women and children leniently are all considered contributors, on a societal level, to the victimization of women (Donat and D'Emilio 1992; Heberle and Grace 2010).

Around the world, the majority of violent crimes are committed by men against men – men are more likely to be victims of murder, violent assaults, street crimes, and gang related offenses than women (Bricknell, Boxall, and Andrevski 2014). Individuals who are not heterosexual, that is, homosexual, queer, trans-, or gender non-conforming are significantly more likely to be the victim of sexual or physical abuse than heterosexuals (Fileborn 2012). Heterosexism (the privileging of heterosexual relationships in religion, communities, society, and law) can be an underlying cause of intolerance and stigmatization of non-heterosexuals, which can then manifest itself in abuse and violence against those who identify as lesbian, gay, bisexual, transgender, intersex, or queer (LGBTIQ). Rates of victimization are not conclusive from official records as individuals may not report their victimization (if they believe that authorities will not help them or will further victimize them), official statistics often do not delineate along sexuality lines (heterosexuality is considered the norm), and because LGBTIQ individuals may conceal their gender identity as a precaution to (further) victimization (Fileborn 2012).

Victimization rates are drawn from not only official records (i.e., crimes recorded by police) but also self-reporting victimization surveys. Because victims of physical or sexual crime often do not report their experiences to the authorities owing to feelings of shame, embarrassment, fear of retaliation, or because they do not identify as a victim, victimization surveys offer a way of discovering the dark figure (or unknown number) of crime. Victimization surveys tend to reveal that there are a much higher number of victims of crime than what are reported to the police.

SEE ALSO: Gender Stereotypes; Gender Violence

REFERENCES

Bricknell, Samantha, Hayley Boxall, and Hannah Andrevski. 2014. "Male Victims of Non-Domestic and Non-Sexual Violence: Service Needs and Experiences in Court." AIC Reports: Research and Public Policy Series 126. Canberra: Australian Institute of Criminology. Accessed November 11, 2014, at http://www.aic.gov.au/media_library/publications/rpp/126/rpp126.pdf.

Christie, Nils. 1986. "The Ideal Victim." In *From Crime Policy to Victim Policy*, edited by E. A. Fattah, 17–30. Basingstoke: Macmillan.

Doerner, William G., and Steven P. Lab. 2011. *Victimology*, 6th ed. Burlington: Elsevier.

Domestic Abuse Intervention Programs (DAIP). 1984. Power and Control Wheel. Accessed November 20, 2014, at http://www.theduluthmodel.org/pdf/PowerandControl.pdf.

Donat, Patricia L. N., and John D'Emilio. 1992. "A Feminist Redefinition of Rape and Sexual Assault: Historical Foundations and Change." *Journal of Social Issues*, 48(1): 9–22.

European Institute for Crime Prevention and Control, Affiliated with the United Nations (HEUNI). 2013. International Violence against Women Survey, IVAWS. Accessed July 10, 2014, at http://www.heuni.fi/en/index/researchareas/violenceagainstwomen/internationalviolenceagainstwomensurveyivaws.html.

Fileborn, Bianca. 2012. "Sexual Violence and Gay, Lesbian, Bisexual, Trans, Intersex and Queer Communities: ACSSA Resource Sheet." Melbourne: Australian Institute of Family Studies. Accessed November 20, 2014, at http://www.aifs.gov.au/acssa/pubs/sheets/rs3/.

Finkelhor, David, Heather Turner, Anne Shattuck, and Sherry Hamby. 2011. *The Role of General Victimization Vulnerability in Childhood Sexual Re-Victimization*. Durham, NH: Crimes Against Children Research Center.

Heberle, Renee J., and Victoria Grace. 2010. *Theorizing Sexual Violence*. London: Routledge.

Olweus, Dan. 1995. "Bullying or Peer Abuse at School: Facts and Intervention." *Current Directions in Psychological Science*, 4: 196–200.

Patterson, Debra. 2011. "The Linkage between Secondary Victimization by Law Enforcement and Rape Case Outcomes." *Journal of Interpersonal Violence*, 26(2): 328–347.

RAINN. 2014a. The Offenders: The Rapist Isn't a Masked Stranger. Accessed July 1, 2014, at https://www.rainn.org/get-information/statistics/sexual-assault-offenders.

RAINN. 2014b. Who Are the Victims? Accessed July 1, 2014, at https://www.rainn.org/get-information/statistics/sexual-assault-victims.

Van Wijk, Jan. 2013. "Who Is the 'Little Old Lady' of International Crimes? Nils Christie's Concept of the Ideal Victim Reinterpreted." *International Journal of Victimology*, 19(2): 159–179.

World Health Organization. 2013. Global and Regional Estimates of Violence against Women. Accessed July 1, 2014, at http://apps.who.int/iris/bitstream/10665/85239/1/9789241564625_eng.pdf.

FURTHER READING

Bourke, Joanna. 2007. *Rape: A History from 1860 to the Present*. London: Virago.

Cain, Maureen, and Adrian Howe, eds. 2008. *Women, Crime, and Social Harm: Towards a Criminology for the Global Age*. Oxford: Hart Publishing.

Gerdes, Louise I. 2008. *Sexual Violence (Opposing Viewpoints)*. Farmington Hills: Greenhaven Press.

A Vindication of the Rights of Woman

BARBARA ELLEN LOGAN
University of Wyoming, USA

A Vindication of the Rights of Woman with Strictures on Political and Moral Subjects by Mary Wollstonecraft (1759–1797) is a treatise written between the storming of the Bastille (July 14, 1789) and before the "Terror" (September 5, 1793–July 27, 1794) in response to trends in social-contract theory. Although developments in the French Revolution sparked some of the texts that *Vindication* is in conversation with, the larger context includes Anglo-Liberal and Franco-Republican theories of citizenship, the nation state, public versus private education, property rights, religious freedom, morality, rationality, and class and sexual difference.

Wollstonecraft's *Thoughts on the Education of Daughters: With Reflections on Female Conduct in the More Important Duties of Life* (1787) and *A Vindication of the Rights of Men, in a Letter to the Right Honorable Edmund Burke* (1790) contain the seeds of *Vindication*'s argument for educating the citizen and nation in morality through rationality, while *An Historical and Moral View of the Origin and Progress of the French Revolution* (1794) explains Wollstonecraft's position on the French revolution after the "Terror" and execution of Louis XVI (January 21, 1793) and Marie Antoinette (October 16, 1793).

Edmund Burke's (1729–1797) *Reflections on the Revolution in France* (1790) was a conservative attack on the French Revolution in particular and revolutionary movements in general; although Burke had originally been a supporter of the American Revolution, his politics changed as he became older and wealthier. He characterized the revolutionaries as "the swinish multitude" and regretted the loss of medieval ideals such as chivalry, which had allowed the "pleasing illusions" that made the execution of power "gentle" and obedience to authority "light." This Romantic nostalgia for a kinder, gentler hierarchy was likewise espoused by Jean-Jacques Rousseau (1712–1778), whose *magnum opus* on education, *Emile* (1762), observes that woman's natural role is to be subjugated to man and that her "particular strength lies in her charms."

In contrast, Wollstonecraft's *Vindication* argues from a position that denies patriarchy and the hierarchal relations that it supports via its polite veneer, and against Romanticism's appeal to the "passions," "sentiment," and traditional gender roles. Rousseau, Burke, and the authors of "conduct for ladies" manuals such as James Fordyce (*The Character and* Conduct *of the Female Sex*, 1776) and John Gregory (*A Father's Legacy to his Daughters*, 1761) argued for a model in which the protection of "privileges" for the disempowered – women, children, the elderly, the disabled, the poor, and African slaves – was regarded as sufficient to replace rights. The conservative argument therein is that the wealthy and powerful have traditionally protected the poor and powerless in return for the right – and responsibility – to rule unquestioned. Wollstonecraft rejected the conservative "privileges versus rights" model, in small part because of her personal experience with the failure of this ideal (her father had destroyed the family finances and brutalized his wife and children) and in large part because of the rational, Enlightenment argument that while privileges and protection may be withdrawn or rescinded, rights (according to the arguments of her day) were inalienable.

While some feminist scholars, such as Carol Poston (1995), Mary Poovey (1982), and Cora Kaplan (2002), have expressed trepidation about Wollstonecraft's language addressing sexuality and femininity in the *Vindication*, Wollstonecraft's concern about girls in boarding schools undressing in front of one another, or of picking up "bad habits" from servants, simply reiterate key discussions of the era concerning female sensitivity and sensibility. The larger, and more trenchant, argument regarding the female sex and sexuality in *Vindication* is that the language of Romanticism about women's "natural" propensity to sentiment and passion is false, dangerous, and must be rejected. As with the "privileges versus rights" argument, women's "feelings" are explained by conservatives as proof of women's inferiority, even as it is argued that they are a form of manipulation: Women's tears are supposed to prevent rape; her "charms" are explained as a kind of covert power that is capable of diverting, subverting, or defeating men's overt power. Accordingly, Rousseau argued that man's sexual drive is such that it can never be quenched, and that alone is sufficient to make men into women's (secret) slaves. Burke argued that tradition alone keeps woman from being classified as an "animal," and an "inferior" animal at that, because of her susceptibility to "the passions." Wollstonecraft's counterpoint is that the body politic includes female bodies and that those female bodies are not "naturally" any different from male bodies. She argues that education, by which she means nurture, not simply school subjects, is what differentiates the rational, moral, citizen from the sly and corrupt parasite. Consequently,

Wollstonecraft uses terms reified as feminine (soft, gentle, sentimental, spoiled, smooth, weak, enervated, submissive, capricious, wily, passionate, artificial) to describe institutions that she regards as illegitimate: The wealthy, Church authorities, military officers, aristocrats, and traditional training for marriage for girls are labeled as "feminine" and "emasculated" to stress that qualities praised or accepted as characteristic in women are suspiciously despicable when applied to men or powerful classes. For Wollstonecraft, "liberty is the mother of virtue." Although she confessed that "my blood runs cold" at the violent excesses of the French revolution, her essay argues that even anarchy is preferable to enslavement.

SEE ALSO: Discourse and Gender; Feminism, Eighteenth-Century Britain; Gender Identity, Theories of; Gender Inequality in Education; Gender, Politics, and the State in Western Europe; Governance and Gender; Social Identity; Women's Movements: Early International Movements

REFERENCES

Kaplan, Cora. 2002. In *The Cambridge Companion to Mary Wollstonecraft*, edited by Claudia L. Johnson, 246–270. Cambridge: Cambridge University Press.

Poovey, Mary. 1982. "Mary Wollstonecraft: the Gender of Genres in Late Eighteenth-Century England." *Novel: a Forum on Fiction*, 15(2) (Winter), 111–126; http://www.jstor.org/stable/1345219.

Poston, Carol. 1995. "Mary Wollstonecraft and the 'Body Politic'." In *Feminist Interpretations of Mary Wollstonecraft (Re-Reading the Canon)*, edited by Maria J. Falco, 85–104. University Park: Penn State University Press.

FURTHER READING

PRIMARY SOURCES:

Todd, Janet. 2003. *The Collected Letters of Mary Wollstonecraft*. London: Allen Lane/Penguin.

Wollstonecraft, Mary. 2013. *A Vindication of the Rights of Woman with Strictures on Political and Moral Subjects: an Authoritative Text, Backgrounds and Contexts Criticism*. London: Joseph Johnson. 3rd ed., edited by Deidre Shauna Lynch. New York: Norton. First published 1792.

SECONDARY SOURCES:

Falco, Maria J., ed. 1996. *Feminist Interpretations of Mary Wollstonecraft*. University Park: Penn State Press.

Johnson, Claudia L., ed. *The Cambridge Companion to Mary Wollstonecraft*. Cambridge: Cambridge University Press.

Jump, Harriet Devine. 1994. *Mary Wollstonecraft: Writer*. New York: Harvester Wheatsheaf.

Sapiro, Virginia. 1992. *A Vindication of Political Virtue: the Political Theory of Mary Wollstonecraft*. Chicago: University of Chicago Press.

Violence Against Women in Global Perspective

ANGELA LEWELLYN JONES
Elon University, USA

Violence against women continues to be one of the world's most disturbing social problems. Despite this truth, we continue to struggle with how to define this activity – in broad or narrow terms, in strictly scientific measurable terms or in politically and culturally specific terms (DeKeseredy and Schwartz 2011). Violence worldwide must be understood through a cultural lens, but cautiously without stereotyping or overgeneralizing. Globally, women and girls face violence from the moment of their inception and throughout their lives. Half a million female fetuses are aborted annually in India and many more young girls are "missing" in India, China, Taiwan, South Korea, Pakistan, Vietnam, and some parts of sub-Saharan Africa where the preference for male children is still practiced.

Sexual and physical violence of young girls is widespread globally. Many report that their first sexual encounter was not consensual (24 percent in rural Peru, 28 percent in Tanzania, 30 percent in rural Bangladesh, and 40 percent in South Africa), and research in Western countries has shown a strong linkage between this early exposure to sexual violence and later problems of both a physical and psychological nature, including teen pregnancy, substance abuse, and homelessness. Prior to marriage, young girls around the world are forced to find their way in a world where the sexual double standard is alive and well, which creates an environment that is conducive to rape, sexual assault, and ultimately "honor" killings and assaults.

Marriage brings additional threats of its own. Where forced marriages are the norm, young girls are often compelled into marriages with much older male partners (e.g., 60 percent in Afghanistan, 56 percent in Mozambique, 51 percent in Nepal, and 75 percent in Niger). Later, within marriages, women face the threat of ongoing violence. In industrialized nations where nuclear family structure is the norm, such as the United States, this violence often remains hidden within the household making it more challenging for the woman to escape. Later in life, widowed females face additional threats in nations where their worth to society is tied to their husbands' value. When their husbands die, widows are often seen as a drain on the family's resources and are encouraged to commit suicide or may be murdered (e.g., in Ghana, Nigeria, India, and other parts of Africa).

Lastly, lesbian women face the constant threat of homophobic violence as well as the reality of potential violence in lesbian partnerships, thus violence against women is not only international in scope but is also unrelenting, in that all women are impacted by the ever-present threat (Fontes and McCloskey 2011).

International data on violence against women are drawn from police and court records as well as population-based surveys (e.g., the Centers for Disease Control and Prevention, International Reproductive Health Surveys; Demographic and Health Surveys; World Health Organization (WHO) studies on women's health and domestic violence against women). The diversity of the data sources creates challenges when comparing data to assess the extent of this social problem (Jaquier, Johnson, and Fisher 2011). However, focusing specifically on rates of physical violence in intimate partner relationships and/or non-partner encounters as well as sexual violence in intimate partner relationships and/or non-partner encounters, the numbers reveal a picture of when and where women are most at risk of violence.

PREVALENCE

The global frequency of physical and/or sexual intimate partner violence among all ever-partnered women reporting is 30 percent. Looking regionally, this type of violence is most common in African, the Eastern Mediterranean, and Southeast Asian regions (with an average of 37 percent), followed by the Americas (30 percent). The Western Pacific and European regions reported 25 percent of ever-partnered women experiencing intimate partner violence. The global frequency of non-partner sexual violence is 7.2 percent, and regional differences reflect the highest prevalence in Africa and the Americas. Regional differences are challenging to explain because of wide variation in the reporting of violence, particularly for sexual violence which continues to be highly stigmatized across the world, and in many cases women fear for their lives when reporting. Conflict-affected countries are very likely to have a much higher rate of sexual violence against women; however, collection of these data are significantly hampered by the dangers in place. When combining the data on occurrence of intimate partner violence and non-partner violence, 35.6 percent of women around the world have ever experienced either non-partner sexual violence or intimate partner violence (physical and/or sexual). Regionally, Africa (45.6 percent) and Southeast Asia (40.2 percent) have the highest prevalence, followed by the Eastern Mediterranean (36.4 percent) and the Americas (36.1 percent) (WHO 2013).

Examining the variety of data sources available on violence against women across countries around the world reveals a more detailed picture. The data are collected from police reports, court statistics, health records, and population-based surveys, so comparisons are challenging at best. Despite these shortcomings, the preponderance of violence against women around the world is made clear. Women are exposed to physical violence (e.g., pushing, grabbing, pulling hair, slapping, kicking, biting or hitting, strangulation, burning, and threats with weapons) throughout their lives. The proportion of women reporting exposure to physical violence in their lifetimes ranges from 11 percent in Kiribati and 12 percent in China, Hong Kong SAR, to 52 percent in the United States, 64 percent in the Democratic Republic of the Congo, and 68 percent in Slovakia (UN Women 2011). When narrowing the focus to intimate partners, available data reveal that the proportion of women reporting exposure to physical violence in their lifetimes ranges from 6 percent in China, Hong Kong SAR, and Morocco, to 22 percent in the United States, 57 percent in the Democratic Republic of the Congo, and 48 percent in Bangladesh (UN Women 2011).

Data further indicate that women are at risk of both moderate and severe physical violence from intimate partners throughout their lives, and the likelihood of one or the other varies by country. The greatest likelihood of severe physical violence is in Peru (province) and Ethiopia (province), while the greatest likelihood of moderate physical violence is in Peru (city) and Bangladesh (province) (latest available data 2000–2008; United Nations 2012). Age-specific data reveal that young women, particularly those between the ages of 15 and 24, are at greater risk of exposure to intimate partner physical violence than older women. For example, more than one third of women in the younger age group are exposed to violence in Ethiopia (province) and Peru (province), while closer to 15 percent of their counterparts 40 years of age and older face the same threat.

Examining the international distribution of sexual violence, defined broadly as unwanted touching, forced intercourse, and rape, reveals that sexual and physical violence most commonly occur in the same contexts (Fontes and McCloskey 2011). The most recent data (2000–2008) show that women report the greatest exposure to sexual violence in Uganda (39 percent) and the Czech Republic (35 percent) and the least exposure in Côte d'Ivoire (0.3 percent) and Turkey (3 percent). In the United States, the rate of exposure is 17.6 percent. However, of the 86 nations providing data on the prevalence of violence against women, 52 had no data sources for sexual violence (irrespective of the perpetrator) in women's lifetimes. When focusing specifically on sexual violence by intimate partners, for which many more data are available (70 out of 86 nations), the least likelihood of exposure to sexual violence is reported in Georgia (1.5 percent) and Cambodia (2.7 percent), while the greatest is in Ethiopia (province) (58.6 percent) and Solomon Islands (54.7 percent); for the

United States, the rate of exposure to sexual violence by an intimate partner is 7.7 percent (United Nations 2012).

International data on the prevalence of femicide (i.e., the intentional murder of women and girls) suggest that women live with the constant threat of death, as well as violence more generally. Studies by the WHO and the London School of Hygiene and Tropical Medicine suggest that more than 35 percent of all murders of women globally are reported to be committed by an intimate partner, while this is true for only 5 percent of all murders of men. Pregnant women are at increased risk of intimate partner femicide. A UK study found that the female partner is often not the only victim in these situations, as children, innocent bystanders, other relatives, attorneys, and new partners are often victims of the violence too (WHO 2012). Additional data reveal that approximately 5,000 women and girls are killed in the name of "honor" each year globally, with most occurring in the Middle East and South Asia, as well as in migrant communities in Australia, Europe, and North America. Similarly, dowry-related femicide is common in India, where the National Crime Records Bureau reported an estimate of 7,600 dowry-related deaths in 2006, while other sources have reported more than double that amount. Dowry-related murders and maiming, many of which involve burnings, are very common in the region. Burns are the seventh most common cause of death for women aged 15–44 globally, which is partly a result of the greater amount of time they spend cooking worldwide; however, data from the WHO's Southeast Asia region indicate that burns are the third most common cause of death for women aged 15–44, as a result of the dowry-related femicide practices in the region (WHO 2012).

The single encouraging indicator in the data on violence against women is a decrease in the prevalence of female genital cutting (FGC) among young women compared with older generations in several countries. When examining countries where FGC is traditionally practiced, they all show a decrease in the practice since the late 1990s and early 2000s, except for Burkina Faso and Yemen. When comparing age groups in Kenya, 43 percent of women between 30 and 49 years have experienced FGC, while only 26 percent of 15- to 29-year-olds have experienced FGC. Similar patterns were found in Benin, Central African Republic, Ghana, and Nigeria. There were no differences between younger and older women in Egypt, Guinea, Mali, and Mauritania, and in Niger more young women were undergoing the procedure than older ones (the overall prevalence in Niger is only around 5 percent of women aged 15–49; United Nations 2012).

The data are a reminder that women continue to confront the real effects of long-standing unequal power relations between women and men around the world. Violence against women is manifested in physical, sexual, economic, and psychological abuses, by intimate partners, acquaintances, and strangers. Some of the violence is a product of historically accepted cultural practices (e.g., acid burnings and dowry deaths, "honor" killings, female genital cutting), while other forms of violence are expressions of power and control in conflict ridden areas of the world (e.g., sexual assaults in the context of war). Every woman around the world lives with the persistent fear of violence simply because of her gender and her perceived sexual availability to men, who possess gender privilege. For many women who live with the reality of violence in their own homes, this is a particularly acute threat because those from whom one would expect to receive love and support are more likely to bring severe injury and hatred to the relationship. The everyday violence that women face worldwide is largely routine and fails to draw our attention (Fontes and McCloskey 2011).

REMEDIES, LAWS, AND ACTIVISM

Finding a solution to the problem of violence against women is extremely challenging in a world where male privilege is still prevalent, and cultural traditions that reinforce male privilege and female disadvantage are deeply rooted. Women and men have to take a stand against this type of violence, and that is challenging while many parts of the world are still very accepting of violent traditions. The World's Women 2010 report contains data that examine women's attitudes toward wife-beating. Women were asked whether a husband was justified in hitting or beating his wife if she (1) burnt the food, (2) argued with him, (3) refused to have sex with him, (4) went out without telling him, or (5) neglected the children. The greatest proportion of women believed that husbands would be justified in their abuse if women neglected the children (41 percent). If they went out without telling him, 36 percent believed the husband would be justified in hitting or beating his wife. Lesser proportions accepted the idea of beating for arguing with the husband (29 percent), refusing to have sex with the husband (25 percent), and burning the food (21 percent).

Despite these attitudes, there are multiple national treaties and charters to address the problem of violence against women globally, including the Universal Declaration of Human Rights, the International Covenant on Civil and Political Rights, the Convention on the Elimination of All Forms of Discrimination against Women, and the Declaration on the Elimination of Violence against Women. Rwanda and Yugoslavia both declared rape in the context of war as a violation of international law and human rights norms in their war crimes tribunals in 1998 and 2001, respectively (Goodmark 2011), but there is still much work to be done in the international arena to address the rampant violence against women.

The UN Secretary-General tackled the problem of violence against women by starting the UNiTE Campaign to End Violence against Women. The objective of the campaign is to raise public awareness, increase political conviction to address the problem internationally, and encourage more resources to be invested in the cause. One of the primary goals of the campaign is to improve data collection around the issue, thereby improving the ability to understand the problem and its international scope (United Nations 2012). Organizations such as Amnesty International have shone a bright light on the preservation of human rights for decades. They prominently post the Declaration on the Elimination of Violence against Women on their webpage, stating that violence against women refers to "any act of gender-based violence that results in, or is likely to result in, physical, sexual or psychological harm or suffering to women, including threats of such acts, coercion or arbitrary deprivation of liberty, whether occurring in public or in private life" (Article 1). The declaration further avows that states have an obligation to "exercise due diligence to prevent, investigate and, in accordance with national legislation, punish acts of violence against women, whether those acts are perpetrated by the State or by private persons" (Amnesty International 2015a, Article 4-c). Currently, Amnesty International is encouraging support of the bipartisan International Violence Against Women Act (H.R. 1340 and S. 713), also known as IVAWA, which makes "ending violence against women and girls a top diplomatic, development, and foreign assistance priority by ensuring the United States government has a strategy to efficiently and effectively coordinate existing cross-governmental efforts to prevent and respond to gender-based violence globally" (Amnesty International 2015b).

In February 2015, the United Kingdom launched the femicide census at a special conference to increase awareness of how often women are killed by intimate male partners in the United Kingdom. There are comparable initiatives worldwide where groups are taking on the need to educate others about the rampant reality of violence against women and work to change the distribution of resources to address the problem. The Rwanda Men's Resource Center holds training sessions, where positive messages about masculinity and femininity are taught and necessary changes to cultural norms to promote equality are addressed. In Cairo, Egypt, a Safe City Programme began in 2011 to prevent and respond to sexual violence in urban spaces. Jackson Katz (2015), the founder of the Mentoring Violence Prevention program, has spread his message of the critical role men play in stopping violence against women around the United States by visiting various sports organizations and schools. His message has spread to the University of Cape Town in South Africa, encouraging men and boys to be proactive in the prevention of gender-based violence. The reach of Mentoring Violence Prevention has extended to Stockholm, Sweden, Australia, the Dominican Republic, and Scotland (www.mvpnational.org). These efforts are encouraging, as they suggest that there are movements afoot around the world to address the problem of violence against women.

SEE ALSO: Battered Women; Domestic Violence in the United States; Dowry Deaths; Femicide; Intimate Partner Abuse; Militarism and Gender-Based Violence; Rape Culture; Sexual Assault/Sexual Violence

REFERENCES

Amnesty International. 2015a. "The International Violence Against Women Act (IVAWA)." *Amnesty International: Issue Brief*, No. 4. Accessed August 19, 2015, at http://www.amnestyusa.org/our-work/issues/women-s-rights/violence-against-women/international-violence-against-women-act.

Amnesty International. 2015b. "Women's Rights." Accessed August 19, 2015, at http://www.amnestyusa.org/our-work/issues/women-s-rights/.

DeKeseredy, Walter S., and Martin D. Schwartz. 2011. "Theoretical and Definitional Issues in Violence Against Women." In *Sourcebook on Violence Against Women*, 2nd ed., edited by Claire M. Renzetti, Jeffrey L. Edleson, and Raquel Kennedy Bergen, 3–22. Thousand Oaks: Sage.

Fontes, Lisa Aronson, and Kathy A. McCloskey. 2011. "Cultural Issues in Violence Against Women." In *Sourcebook on Violence Against Women*, 2nd ed., edited by Claire M. Renzetti, Jeffrey L. Edleson, and Raquel Kennedy Bergen, 151–169. Thousand Oaks: Sage.

Goodmark, Leigh. 2011. "State, National, and International Legal Initiatives to Address Violence Against Women." In *Sourcebook on Violence Against Women*, 2nd ed., edited by Claire M. Renzetti, Jeffrey L. Edleson, and Raquel Kennedy Bergen, 191–208. Thousand Oaks: Sage.

Jaquier, Veronique, Holly Johnson, and Bonnie S. Fisher. 2011. "Research Methods, Measures, and Ethics." In *Sourcebook on Violence Against Women*, 2nd ed., edited by Claire M. Renzetti, Jeffrey L. Edleson, and Raquel Kennedy Bergen, 23–48. Thousand Oaks: Sage.

Katz, Jackson. "Mentors in Violence Prevention." Accessed August 19, 2015, at http://www.mvpnational.org/.

United Nations. 2012. "The World's Women 2010: Trends and Statistics 2010." Accessed August 19, 2015, at http://unstats.un.org/unsd/demographic/products/Worldswomen/wwVaw2010.htm.

United Nations Entity for Gender Equality and the Empowerment of Women. 2011. "Violence Against Women Prevalence Data: Surveys by Country." Accessed August 19, 2015, at http://

www.endvawnow.org/uploads/browser/files/vaw_prevalence_matrix_15april_2011.pdf.

World Health Organization. 2012. *Understanding and Addressing Violence against Women: Femicide.* Geneva: WHO.

World Health Organization, Department of Reproductive Health and Research. 2013. *Global and Regional Estimates of Violence Against Women: Prevalence and Health Effects of Intimate Partner Violence and Non-Partner Sexual Violence.* Geneva: WHO.

Violence Against Women, Movements Against

MARTHA E. THOMPSON
Northeastern Illinois University, USA

Historically, violence against women has been an accepted practice across the globe. Violence against women activism emerged as part of women's rights, women's liberation, and womanist movements of the late 1960s and early 1970s. Although these were not the first protests, violence against women was central to the massive late twentieth century feminist agenda to create gender equality and end women's oppression.

Feminist activism has influenced international, national, state, and local governmental and non-governmental bodies to reframe violence against women as a social issue and to search for solutions to what is now viewed as a major social problem throughout history and across the globe. Collective actions to end violence against women reflect three broad themes: accountability, victim support, and empowerment. Because of the enormity of the undertaking, groups typically emphasize one theme or another with different meanings across groups, but these three interrelated themes are found to some extent in all social movements against violence against women.

Accountability refers to holding perpetrators responsible for their actions, providing victims with meaningful redress, and promoting community responsibility. Beliefs that violence against women continues because the public tolerates perpetrators' behavior and underestimates victims' trauma underlie accountability.

Victim support refers to the need for immediate and long-term support and services for victims of violence, their families, and their communities because of the possible traumatic ramifications of violence and the importance of interrupting cycles of violence. Underlying the need for victim support are assumptions that violence and acceptance of violence flow across relationships and generations and healing from violence is delayed, or even impossible, if victims are isolated, are shamed, and do not receive trauma-sensitive health, economic, legal, emotional, and social support.

Empowerment refers to the belief that women and girls are capable and powerful, have agency, can effectively develop and use knowledge and skills to stop violence, and can participate in identifying and creating respectful and peaceful relationships, communities, and societies. To reduce vulnerability to violence necessitates enhancing women's and girls' educational and economic opportunities and life choices.

In addition to these three broad themes, feminist organizing to stop violence against women varies in terms of scope. International and national governing bodies have accepted a socioecological model of prevention, also useful for understanding variations in levels of activism: individual, relationship, community, and societal. A group may advocate primarily at one level, but influence multiple levels. For instance, INCITE! addresses interpersonal and state violence, with a focus on ways women of color experience multiple oppressions. The group holds communities and police accountable for violence against women of color and trans people; medical institutions accountable for sterilization abuse of poor women, women with disabilities, and women of color; and the US government accountable for the War on Terror which has resulted in increased violence against women. INCITE! is a national organization consisting of grassroots chapters and affiliates through which individuals engage in critical dialogue and develop their knowledge and skills to build healthy relationships and improve their communities.

Women Against Violence Against Women (WAVAW) also illustrates the interconnectedness of accountability, victim support, and empowerment, and influence on individuals, relationships, communities, and society. WAVAW provides services to women who have experienced sexualized violence, such as a toll-free rape crisis line, hospital accompaniment, services for aboriginal women and youth, for families of missing and murdered aboriginal women, counseling, and support groups. In addition to these individual and relationship services, WAVAW also provides community education for youth, offers a campus anti-violence initiative, partners with other community groups, engages men and boys as allies, and organizes campaigns to challenge social values and practices that contribute to violence against women.

The third example of feminist advocacy that highlights interrelated themes with multi-level influence are national and international Empowerment Self-Defense (ESD) coalitions (e.g., IMPACT International, National Women's Martial Arts Federation Self-Defense Group, and Empowerment Self-Defense Advocacy) dedicated to women and girls learning self-advocacy and self-protection. Individual women and girls increase their self-defense knowledge and skills through ESD, providing themselves with tools to build healthy relationships based on consent and directly challenge the ideas that violence is inevitable and that aggressors are invincible. Cornerstones of ESD programs are building community and social consciousness across age, class, disability/ability, race, and sexual orientation while also heightening awareness of women's and girls' survival, resiliency, and resistance. ESD programs hold perpetrators, not victims, responsible for violence; promote trauma sensitive learning environments; and offer compassionate support to victims of violence.

These examples illustrate ways different groups uniquely integrate different themes and levels in their advocacy work. Addressing thematic expressions of accountability, victim support, and empowerment at different levels of advocacy reveals similarities and differences in how groups prioritize and mobilize and is a way to communicate the complexities of and variations in feminist activism against violence against women and to increase understanding of interconnections and divisions.

Collective actions directed toward individuals highlight individuals' attitudes, beliefs, behavior, choices, responsibilities, and opportunities. Activism for individual accountability highlights processes for increasing perpetrators' accountability with collective actions promoting increased perpetrator accountability through criminal justice (e.g., sentencing, incarceration, and education) and rehabilitation to modify thoughts and behaviors that lead to violence against women. Other collective actions go beyond the criminal justice system and focus on supporting perpetrators to recognize the harm they have done, accept accountability for their actions, and change their behavior.

Victim support activism focuses on women and girls with particular attention to those who are at risk of or have experienced violence. Collective actions highlight the need for a variety of services (e.g., counseling and therapy, support groups, medical care, legal assistance, housing, and employment) for individuals to deal with trauma and with their alteration in life circumstances. Individual empowerment activism highlights women's and girls' freedom and safety, encompassing a variety of goals, such as women and girls expanding their educational, economic, political, and social opportunities; developing their self-confidence, self-efficacy and self-reliance; and living their lives to their fullest potential. Empowerment activism includes women and girls creating forums to speak out; developing knowledge, skills, and resources for self-protection; educational advancement; and economic independence.

Collective actions also emphasize relationships between victims and perpetrators, victims and their personal support networks, and victims and interpersonal relationships within the social environments within which violence occurs, health and social service providers, and police and others within the criminal justice system. The focus here is on altering violent dynamics in relationships and increasing the quality of support offered to women and girls from a continuum of relationships, from their most intimate to professional.

Accountability activism addresses ways to improve the responses of those who witness or suspect crimes of violence and to hold people accountable. All those who deal with an alleged perpetrator within the criminal justice system must follow the required laws of their state or nation and collective actions often focus on improving the criminal justice process and minimizing missteps in following the law while also increasing sensitivity to the causes and consequences of violence. Efforts include training mandatory reporters; engaging members of the legal profession; and improving policing, prosecuting, sentencing, and monitoring of perpetrators. Using a transformative justice model, other collective actions for accountability focus on supporting people who harm to transform their relationships by developing an understanding of the social conditions and systems of oppression within which they engaged in violence.

Activism for victim support addresses how others can increase and improve their responses to women and girls who witness violence, are threatened, attacked, or are coping in the aftermath. Others can speak out and step in to interrupt or minimize violence and offer support to victims. Post-violence, the reaction of others to victims and perpetrators affects the healing process. Compassionate support enables victims of violence to move forward from violence when ready whereas expressions of disbelief, blame, belittling, or ignoring the effects of violence increase the possibility of post-traumatic stress and other negative consequences. Activism for victim support includes awareness campaigns, bystander intervention training, and training for professional service providers.

Empowerment activism prioritizes women's and girls' choices and power in their relationships and having skills and tools to assess the quality of relationships; to communicate, problem-solve, resolve conflict assertively and effectively; and to have awareness, verbal, and physical skills to create and maintain safe relationships and prevent, interrupt, and minimize dangerous ones. Empowerment activism aims for women and girls to have access to programs that build, restore, and enhance the quality of relationship, such as empowerment self-defense, affirmative consent, and transformative justice.

Collective efforts for stopping violence in community highlight safe social and physical environments. Accountability activism challenges values and practices of social institutions (e.g., family, police, schools and universities, religion, workplaces) that promote violence and work to create social institutions that inhibit violence. Activism promotes shared community values, public awareness of violent offenders in the community, and acts of violence against women; sufficient funding to collect and process evidence; specialized and coordinated community responses to violence, such as special police units; and educational opportunities to increase understanding of gender-based violence and its intersections with other forms of oppression.

Private and public spaces for victims of violence to find safety, healing, information, medical care, legal assistance, housing, and empowerment exemplify community advocacy for victim support. Collective actions for victim support have resulted in shelters, hotlines, emergency services, crisis centers, and networks for victims of violence and their families. Advocacy for victim support includes demands for improved inter-institutional coordination and communication among professionals working with victims (e.g., courts, medical, housing, employment).

Empowerment community actions promote ways that women and girls can envision and participate in developing safe and liberating social and physical environments, including schools, universities, workplaces, and public spaces. These efforts, which can involve male allies, focus on challenging values, norms, traditions, practices, procedures, and spaces that contribute to violence against women and girls and creating social and physical environments that promote women's and girls' safety and freedom. Empowerment activism creates spaces where women and girls develop solidarity and a collective consciousness about their life experiences; have opportunities for full participation and leadership regardless of gender, age disability/ability, race, sexual orientation, or social class; and have experiences where they are valued as people and not sexually objectified or rendered invisible. Collective actions include leadership opportunities for women and girls; school curricula highlighting women's contributions to history, politics, and social life; forums for sharing life experiences and stories of survival, resiliency, and resistance.

Efforts to stop societal violence pinpoint social and cultural values, institutions, and practices that promote inequalities and support violence and push for ways to decrease social inequalities and inhibit violence. Societal efforts go beyond the specific and local school, job site, or public arena and address values and practices characteristic of large social institutions (e.g., higher education, religious institutions, the workplace, media) and commonalities across institutions.

Collective actions for societal accountability represent a commitment to ending violence against women and creating shared societal understandings of violence and accountability through legislation, policymaking, and awareness campaigns. Across the globe, activists have advocated for legislation prohibiting and punishing violence against women and today most countries have passed anti-violence against women legislation, although consistent enforcement remains a goal of social movement mobilization. Legislation, policies, and procedures may be comprehensive (e.g., Violence Against Women Act, National Action Plans), specific (e.g., redefining prostitution laws), or limited, such as data gathering (e.g., National Crime Victimization Survey), orders of protection (e.g., Civil No Contact Order), or registering offenders (e.g., National Sexual Offender Registry). Societal accountability efforts also expose ways that social institutions tolerate, perpetuate, and benefit from violence.

Societal victim support challenges the isolation and silencing of victims through campaigns to expose the extent of violence and to raise awareness of its consequences. In addition to national campaigns, advocacy for victim support includes increasing trauma-sensitive education, medical care, and social services. Societal empowerment activism focuses on enhancing women's and girls' opportunities to envision and participate in societies where human potential is fully realized and in creating inclusive, democratic, and socially just solutions to societal problems. Advocacy includes building coalitions across issues and social location (e.g., age, class, disability/ability, race, sexual orientation) to raise awareness of women's and girls' potential and social contributions; to create inclusive forums, networks, and resource sharing; and to expand women and girls' participation in political, economic, and educational decision-making. Empowerment activism includes women and girls creating and participating in vigils, marches, speak outs, protests, learning environments, and coalition building to resist social values and practices that contribute to violence and to fight for values and practices that enhance safety and increase choices.

The global level is not part of the socioecological model, but it is a logical extension and vitally important to collective efforts to end violence against women. There are common issues across societies (e.g., the gender gap in political participation, the wage gap, rigid gender expectations), but violence against women also crosses national borders and reflects global inequalities, whereby policies or actions in one country produce violence against women and girls elsewhere. Advocating for accountability globally includes working for international cooperation and shared understandings of violence, its consequences, and ways to stop it. Global mobilization has put violence against women on the international agenda, resulting in international agreements (e.g., Convention on the Elimination of All Forms of Discrimination against Women, UN Declaration on the Elimination of Violence against Women). These international agreements make it more possible for countries to develop consistent legislation, policies, and enforcement procedures. Global action is also essential to stopping trafficking of women and girls by holding customers, procurers, and traffickers responsible for their actions. Global networks, international conferences, and virtual resources provide the opportunity to share knowledge and resources to enhance victim support and victim services for people who have been trafficked within and across borders as well as for activists to share information and strategies. Globally, empowerment advocates share resources and critical dialogue through virtual and conferencing networks to expand women's and girls' opportunities worldwide, to interrupt human supply chains, and develop more comprehensive and critical understandings of gender inequalities and violence against women.

Activism against violence against women has had many successes, such as influencing international and national governments and civil organizations to frame violence against women as a social issue and to develop models, strategies, and approaches to stopping violence. Independent feminist advocacy is the most important factor accounting for national and transnational change in addressing violence against women. Communities across the globe have established extensive services for women and girls who have experienced violence and prioritized attention to violence against women in training social service, medical, police, and legal professionals. Anti-violence movements have also successfully expanded women's legal protections, educational and economic development, and political participation and decision-making. Feminist activism continues to challenge entrenched values and practices that condone violence against women and continues to deepen understanding of connections among different types of violence against women, state violence, and global inequalities. Critical analysis of intersections of gender and other forms of oppression and creating cultural values and practices supporting communication, problem-solving, and conflict resolution without violence remain central to social movements against violence against women.

SEE ALSO: Violence Against Women in Global Perspective

FURTHER READING

Greenberg, Max A., and Michael A. Messner. 2014. "Before Prevention: The Trajectory and Tensions of Feminist Antiviolence." In *Gendered Perspectives on Conflict and Violence: Part B (Advances in Gender Research, Volume 18B)*, edited by Marcia Texler Segal and Vasilikie Demos, 225–249. Binghamton: Emerald Group.

Hutn, Mala, and S. Laurel Weldon. 2012. "The Civic Origins of Progressive Policy Change: Combating Violence Against Women in Global Perspective, 1975–2005." *American Political Science Review*, 106(3): 548–569.

INCITE! Women of Color Against Violence. 2006. *The Color of Violence: The Incite! Anthology*. Boston: South End Press.

Martin, Patricia Yancey, and Schmitt, F.E. 2007. "The History of the Anti-rape and Rape Crisis Center Movements." In *Encyclopedia of Interpersonal Violence*, edited by C.M. Renezetti and J. Edleson. Thousand Oaks: Sage.

McCaughey, Martha, and Jill Cermele. 2014. *Special Issue of Violence Against Women: Self-Defense Against Sexual Assault*, 20: 247–251.

Virginity

HANNE BLANK
Emory University, USA

Virginity may be nominally defined as the sexual status of an individual (particularly a female) who has never experienced sexual activity with another person. The precise parameters of virginity in any specific social or historical context, however, are inevitably both more specific and entirely culturally constructed.

Historically, virginity has been defined in the terms of three primary interpretive structures: the religio-moral, legal, and biomedical. These interpretive structures rarely exist independently, and are typically combined and even conflated to form internally self-consistent models and ideologies of virginity that answer to the social and political needs of given times and places.

Moral and behavioral definitions of virginity have historically been difficult to separate from religious ones. Particularly in cultures influenced by Abrahamic religions, modesty, chastity, humility, and submissiveness in women are among the traditional markers of female virtue and also of virginity.

Specific virginity dogmas and doctrines, however, have varied widely, with the best developed and documented examples existing within the Catholic Church. Catholicism historically posited virginity as the ideal form of human existence, teaching that only virgins received the full rewards of Heaven. Luther repudiated this teaching during the Reformation; in turn, the Council of Trent declared the Protestant dismissal of the virgin ideal heretical. Despite doctrinal battles, both Catholicism and Protestantism have continued to uphold virginity as both a moral and spiritual value to the present day.

Legally, the loss of virginity has been an expected coterminant of marital status. Lack of sexual consummation of a marriage has historically been considered grounds for annulment, whereas sexual intercourse, whether in the context of a ceremonialized marriage or not, has sometimes been considered to constitute legal marriage, as when rape victims have at times been legally compelled to marry their rapists. The strength of this relationship between virginity loss and marriage is reflected in the linguistic use of words meaning "virgin" to indicate unmarried young women, for example English "maiden" and German *Jungfrau*.

The prior virginity of women has also been considered materially relevant in the prosecution of rape cases in that punishments for rapists have often been lighter (or nonexistent) if judges and juries could be convinced that the woman was no longer a virgin at the time of the rape.

There exists no significant documentation of biomedical concern for the diagnosis of male virginity. Diagnosis of virginity has, biomedically speaking, related exclusively to the bodies of women and girls. As such it has been materially complicated by changes in the understanding of female genital anatomy and physiology.

An ongoing debate concerning the existence of physical telltales of virginity has been documented since the second century CE, when Greek physician Soranus detailed his failed attempts to locate a rumored obstacle to penetration within the vaginas of virgin women. The works of eleventh-century Persian physician Ibn Sina (Avicenna) reveal that speculations about some sort of intra-vaginal structure (variously described as a "web" or "veil" of tissue) that would be damaged and bleed upon first vaginal penetration were common in Arab medicine as well.

However common these rumors and speculations may have been, however, they were by no means universally accepted. The hypothetical structure did not receive a name until 1461, when Michele Savonarola used the term "hymen" (Greek "membrane") to identify a "subtle membrane" that he claimed covered the cervix, but this name was rapidly taken up, and was standardized in Thomas Elyot's 1538 *Dictionary* where it is defined as "a skinne in the secrete place of a maiden, which whanne she is defloured is broken."

The naming and description of the hymen, therefore, considerably predates any actual anatomical confirmation of its existence.

In 1544, Andreas Vesalius became the first anatomist to confirm the existence of the hymen in dissection. Vesalius did not ever illustrate the structure, however, and published only a very vague verbal description of his dissections in an otherwise unrelated text, the 1546 *Letter on the China Root*. The lack of visual referent did nothing to deter a new generation of physicians (and quacks), including Severin Pineau, from expanding on the "true" nature and appearance of the hymen and its relation to virginity. No anatomically accurate drawing of the hymen was published until the 1668 *Anatomy* of Danish anatomist Thomas Bartholin.

The relationship between the hymen and virginity – if there is one – has yet to be reliably determined. Twentieth-century anatomists have revealed hymens to be vastly more variable than had been previously thought, with dramatic naturally occurring variation in size, tissue thickness and resilience, vascularization, and morphology. It has also been shown that the physical attributes of the hymen can change spontaneously over the lifespan due to hormonal and other factors. Since the 1980s, research into the utility of hymen examination as a means of evaluating claims of sexual assault and child sexual abuse has yielded no reliable diagnostic. It is now generally accepted in the West that the hymen cannot be used to diagnose prior vaginal penetration. Relatedly, as there are no other known tests that can reliably determine virginity, despite a long history of virginity testing, it is safe to say that virginity cannot in fact be diagnosed.

Increasingly, in the first world late twentieth- and early twenty-first centuries, virginity is viewed as a matter of personal experience and discernment. Challenging earlier notions that non-consensual and/or non-sexual experiences could constitute the end of virginity, women (and some men) have begun to decide for themselves what virginity means to them and which personal experiences they believe constitute its boundaries. The ability to negotiate virginity in this way is a strong indicator of the degree to which religious, legal, and medical concepts of virginity have lost their power in a culture strongly influenced by egalitarianism, feminism, and secular individualism.

SEE ALSO: Adolescent Pregnancy; Buddhism; Celibacy; Chastity; Christianity, Gender and Sexuality; Hinduism; Islam and Gender; Judaism and Sexuality

FURTHER READING

Carpenter, Laura M. 2001. "The Ambiguity of 'Having Sex': The Subjective Experience of Virginity Loss in the United States." *Journal of Sex Research*, 38(2): 127–139.

Castelli, Elizabeth. 1986. "Virginity and Its Meaning for Women's Sexuality in Early Christianity." *Journal of Feminist Studies in Religion*, 2(1): 61–88.

González-López, Gloria. 2004. "Fathering Latina Sexualities: Mexican Men and the Virginity of their Daughters." *Journal of Marriage and Family*, 66(5): 1118–1130.

Schlegel, Alice. 1991. "Status, Property, and the Value on Virginity." *American Ethnologist*, 18(4): 719–734.

Zhou, Xiao. 1989. "Virginity and Premarital Sex in Contemporary China." *Feminist Studies*, 15(2): 279–288.

Visual Culture

JUDITH LAKÄMPER
Wayne State University, USA

The term visual culture has been used to describe both the nature of contemporary culture as predominantly visual and an emerging academic interdisciplinary field with the goal of studying this culture. Academic, legal, medical, religious, and most other discourses rely increasingly on visual images embedded in medial forms ranging from photography, motion pictures, and advertising to visual data presentation and, more recently, digital images. Images are relevant to our experience of the world because they allow us to reflect on and express our position in the world, and they carry both informational and entertainment value. A number of readers and handbooks published at the turn of the millennium have contributed to an increasing institutionalization of the field (see, e.g., Mirzoeff 1999; Sturken and Cartwright 2001). Visual culture studies analyzes how images and the visual contribute to and reflect on our perception of the world, both synchronically and diachronically. Other terms that have been used to describe philosophical interest in the visual are picture theory, image studies, and visual studies.

As an academic field of interest, visual studies rejects the primacy of the spoken and written word as it has dominated science and scholarship since the Enlightenment. Instead, it emphasizes how the visual contributes to how we make sense of ourselves and the world as well as the need to approach images differently than linguistic representation. Proposing a "pictorial turn," W. J. T. Mitchell (1994) claims that the book and the written word are no longer the most dominant cultural forms, and that contemporary Western culture is instead pervaded by and oriented toward the image. Whether one evaluates this change as positive or negative, Mitchell argues that images contribute to our lives and identities in ways that are different from texts, and thus need to be approached from a different critical angle. With this argument, Mitchell contributed significantly to the emergence of the new scholarly field of visual culture studies.

As an interdisciplinary field, visual culture employs different approaches to exploring the nature of the visual. The most important approaches include art history, semiotics, phenomenology, and psychoanalysis. Traditionally, art historians tend to evaluate images based on formal qualities and their monetary value on the art market, and this continues to be an important approach within the visual culture framework. The other disciplines, whose interventions into the study of visual culture are more recent, analyze the ways in which we experience and make sense of the multitude of images we encounter daily. The field is thus also closely related to the more institutionalized academic discipline of cultural studies, as visual culture can be seen as one of its subfields.

Visual culture studies employs these multiple approaches synchronically in analyzing the significance of images and the visual in contemporary culture. In addition, it produces diachronic analyses of the relevance of the visual in the past. Before literacy came to be widespread in Western cultures, images were central to disseminating both general information and religious messages. Within religious discourses, the centrality of images was highly contested, and frequently led to violent conflicts between different religious groups. Iconoclasm was one of the central driving forces behind the Protestant Reformation, and the dispute over images has thus facilitated one of the most consequential conflicts in Western history. In early modern times, when institutionalized religion began losing its impact on the everyday, perspective and portrait painting became central art forms that aimed specifically at an implied spectator. This change in artistic technique correlated with the emergence of a humanistic worldview distancing itself from religious beliefs and instead focusing on the nature of human agency and individuality. The implication of oneself as (intended) spectator evoked in the viewer a sense of identity. In this sense, these early art forms illustrate that the visual has a long history of structuring our relation with the world.

At the same time, the relationship between the painted object and the spectator/owner provides insight into the conventionalized gender relationships that surround visual culture and its embeddedness in larger cultural phenomena. John Berger (1972) demonstrates how the relationship between the mostly male owners of the images and the mostly nude female objects depicted in the paintings codified women as passive objects to be looked at and possessed. Berger's analysis not only emphasized the relevance of images as a separate field of study, but it also offered an important precursor to approaches that focus on gender relations and relations of power as central to practices of looking. Berger thus laid the groundwork for the feminist psychoanalytical approaches that have provided pivotal analyses of visual culture.

The invention of photography in the early nineteenth century coincided with the rise of positivist science and was thus both enabled by and promoted a desire to depict reality more accurately than was possible through painting. Photography was considered a more reliable because mechanical device to gather visual evidence for scientific theories. Indeed, as Roland Barthes emphasizes, analog photography has an indexical relationship to reality; it comes into existence only through chemical processes occurring between the camera and an object which must coexist both spatially and temporally for a distinct amount of time. Photography thus is evidence that "the thing has been there" (Barthes 1980, 76). However, despite this sense of objectivity, critics were quick to emphasize the subjective dimensions involved in creating photographs as well. First, one needs to note that it is the photographer who selects and frames some objects and deliberately excludes others. Thus, the photograph always offers merely an extract from reality, and one that is deliberately chosen by the photographer. Second, every image contains an array of cultural content that is activated by the viewer. Photographs never merely denote their content; viewers bring knowledge about this content to their encounter with the photograph, and incorporate this knowledge into the process of making sense of what the image represents.

The advent of photography also heralds a change in the evaluation of images. Walter Benjamin (1969) discusses how the reproducibility of images changes what is valued about them. Whereas paintings were considered valuable due to their uniqueness and authenticity, what Benjamin called their "aura," photographs and films fulfill very different functions culturally. Writing in the historical context of the emerging Third Reich, Benjamin was interested in the relationship between the mass media and politics. The ability to quickly reproduce and disseminate images allowed for important information to spread much faster, but it also provided the premise for the successful propaganda tactics employed by the Nazis. Due to this dynamic, the prevalence of images in/and the mass media has been both welcomed for its democratic potential to educate and inform the masses, and criticized for the detrimental effects of using imagery and technology in the perpetuation and dissemination of fascist ideologies.

Benjamin's critique of the mass media forms the basis for the Frankfurt School scholars and their critique of consumer culture. Adorno and Horkheimer (2002) hold that the mass media fulfill quasi-religious functions for a mass audience in what they call the "culture industry." The products of mass media are seen as commodities to be consumed by passive audiences, who, by way of consuming such products, are lured into contentment despite economic and other hardships that are caused by the cultural apparatuses of capitalism. The images used in advertising play a significant role in creating desire for these products that claim to solve whatever ailments the audience might experience. This critique relies significantly on the assumption that audiences fail to distinguish between the real conditions of their existence and the representations of these conditions in the media. Mass media are thus seen to take a significant part in creating false consciousness among the masses and in recreating the conditions that are necessary to uphold capitalist structures.

Adorno and Horkheimer's distinction between representation and the real collapses even further in postmodern theoretical discourse. Guy Debord (1983) suggests that in the society of the spectacle, the visual is no longer merely a representation of the real, but replaces real human interaction. It is the consumption of images as commodities that structures human experience. Jean Baudrillard (1994) takes this argument a step further by claiming that representation exists without an original that is represented. Representation thus is so central to how we make sense of our lives that our own connections with reality become void.

These negative views of visual culture are opposed by other scholars who emphasize the democratizing potential of the mass media. Marshall McLuhan (1962) emphasized how mass media transmit information globally, thereby spreading information and ideas in democratic fashion around the world. One instance of this was certainly the news coverage of wars that began in World War II and culminated in the detailed coverage of the Vietnam War. Discussions surrounding the Arab Spring and the Occupy movement continue to reflect on the democratizing potential of imagery in media, specifically as they are used to mobilize the masses in global popular movements.

Images have been central to psychoanalytical thought as it developed from Freud's notion of the unconscious to Lacan's discussion of the gaze and beyond. In these accounts, images figure pivotally in the subject's imagination of individual identity. Lacan (1981) conceptualizes the self as inherently split and decentered, an aspect which it constantly – and unsuccessfully – tries to overcome via identification with images that are made available by image technologies. Psychoanalytic film theory illustrates how in watching film, the self is temporarily lost in the process of identification with the world on screen.

Psychoanalysis has functioned as a central tool for feminist approaches to analyzing visual culture. Laura Mulvey (1975) emphasizes how male and female spectators are interpellated differently by the imagery presented on screen. Mulvey argues that film tends to address an assumedly male spectator, and female characters are presented as passive spectacles, according to male fantasies. Thus, Mulvey claims, spectators do not so much identify with the entire world on screen as with the active male protagonist and his experience of the fictional world. The female spectator internalizes the male gaze of desire and attempts to fashion herself in accordance with the ideal imagery presented on screen. In that sense, spectators are also always already socialized as either male or female, approaching a filmic viewing experience from a gendered subject position. Mulvey's account draws attention to the ways in which images do not merely represent, but also create ideas about masculinity and femininity.

In the context of poststructuralist Foucauldian thought, the internalized gaze becomes a central concept to understand the relationship between images, knowledge, and the power relations that structure practices of looking. In mass media culture, where consumers are constantly confronted with a variety of images, the implied (male) gaze induces mechanisms of self-regulation in accordance with dominant ideologies as perpetuated in these images. Foucault (1975) uses the structure of the panopticon, a circularly constructed jail in which all cells can potentially be observed from a central watchtower without the inmates' ability to see whether or not they are momentarily being observed, as an analogy for the surveillance society. It is the potential of being observed that forces citizens into compliant behavior. Learning and internalizing the male gaze through representations in film, TV, and advertising teaches subjects, specifically women, to regard themselves through the camera lens. The desire to conform to the images seen via this gaze positions women in a constant struggle to reproduce the image content.

Mulvey's ideas have been criticized by other scholars, specifically because her conceptualization of spectatorship constructs women as passive viewers who fall victim to ideological construction rather than considering, for instance, deconstructive or resistant viewing practices. Nonetheless, Mulvey's arguments have provided a pivotal basis for a psychoanalytical feminist branch of visual culture studies. The application of her ideas has expanded from the initial focus on cinema to including other fields of visual culture, such as TV and Internet imagery.

In the digital age, the images lose their indexical function as they no longer depend on the actual presence of an object to be represented in the image. Images thus increasingly challenge established habits of reading images for truth content, in regards to both digital and analog image production. In addition, the digital age entails a dispersal of formerly large mass audiences – even though these audiences were never as homogeneous as their critics insinuate. A variety of cable networks, Internet streaming websites, and other Internet portals have created a complex market for images, which can no longer be assumed to target merely one mass audience. At the same time, image content can quickly and easily be distributed globally, creating a market that is not only more diverse than twentieth-century mass media's audiences, but also less predictable.

Recently, scholars have utilized the turn to affect that has occurred across all disciplines, but most forcefully in the humanities, to inform approaches to the interdisciplinary field of visual culture studies. These approaches emphasize the primacy of material experiences in processes of knowledge construction. From this perspective, visual culture engenders encounters that precede linguistic representation, which require the scholar to account for the immediacy and materiality of such an encounter. Ultimately, visual culture thus invites a perspective that breaches the Cartesian mind–body dualism and emphasizes the significance of material ways of knowing.

SEE ALSO: Feminism and Postmodernism; Feminisms, Postmodern; Gaze; Images of Gender and Sexuality in Advertising; Media and Gender Socialization; Representation; Visual Culture and Gender

REFERENCES

Adorno, Theodor W., and Max Horkheimer. 2002. "The Culture Industry: Enlightenment as Mass Deception." In *Dialectic of Enlightenment: Philosophical Fragments*, edited by Gunzelin Schmid Noerr and translated by Edmund Jephcott. Stanford: Stanford University Press.

Barthes, Roland. 1980. *Camera Lucida: Reflections on Photography*, trans. Richard Howard. New York: Hill and Wang.

Baudrillard, Jean. 1994. *Simulacra and Simulation*, trans. Sheila Faria Glaser. Ann Arbor: University of Michigan Press.

Benjamin, Walter. 1969. "The Work of Art in the Age of Mechanical Reproduction." In *Illuminations: Essays and Reflections*, edited by Hannah Arendt and translated by Harry Zohn. New York: Schocken.

Berger, John. 1972. *Ways of Seeing*. London: Penguin.

Debord, Guy. 1983. *Society of the Spectacle*. Detroit: Black & Red.

Foucault, Michel. 1975. *Discipline and Punish: The Birth of the Prison*, trans. Alan Sheridan. New York: Random House.

Lacan, Jacques. 1981. *The Seminar of Jacques Lacan Book XI: The Four Fundamental Concepts of Psychoanalysis*, edited by Jacques-Alain Miller and translated by Alan Sheridan. New York: Norton.

McLuhan, Marshall. 1962. *The Gutenberg Galaxy: The Making of Typographic Man*. Toronto: University of Toronto Press.

Mirzoeff, Nicholas. 1999. *An Introduction to Visual Culture*. New York: Routledge.

Mitchell, W. J. T. 1994. *Picture Theory*. Chicago: University of Chicago Press.

Mulvey, Laura. 1975. "Visual Pleasure and Narrative Cinema." *Screen*, 16(3): 6–18.

Sturken, Marita, and Lisa Cartwright. 2001. *Practices of Looking: An Introduction to Visual Culture*. Oxford: Oxford University Press.

Visual Culture and Gender

ERIN BROWN BELL
Wayne State University, USA

Visual culture is a broad term that is inclusive of cultural and artistic productions that privilege vision over the other senses. Human beings have demonstrated an enthusiasm for visual representations for thousands of years (consider the cave paintings at Lascaux or the hieroglyphs in the Egyptian pyramids), and as such, visual culture is pervasive and holds an esteemed status within many societies. Though visual culture is present in numerous aspects of contemporary culture, feminist and gender theorists are especially interested in how visual culture represents, constructs, and perpetuates gender roles and stereotypes.

The composition of visual culture has adapted over time (and continues to metamorphose) due to changes in both the medium of the visual productions and the modes of their presentation and transmission. Though its parameters continue to expand, visual culture today is a broad term that includes (but is not limited to) numerous types of fine arts such as painting, theater, photography, architecture, and sculpture. Visual culture also includes mainstream cultural objects such as television programs, films, advertisements, magazines, fashion, Internet clips, social networking profiles, comic strips, graphic novels, video games, graffiti, and any other media that are imbued with a visual component.

Privileging vision over the other senses is often described as ocularcentrism, and understanding the scope and breadth of ocularcentrism within the world is important in exploring why feminists and other theorists consider certain visual representations of gender problematic. Put simply, it is commonplace in the Western world to assume that "seeing is believing," yet human eyesight is not at all infallible. Indeed, the shortcomings of relying upon vision in order to gain knowledge are numerous, but perhaps the most obvious failure is that many people simply have poor or limited vision; hence the range of their sight as well as their ability to focus can be flawed. A mere blinking of the eyes can limit the content of one's field of vision as well. Though many consider an "eyewitness account" to be reliable, for example, a group of eyewitnesses may all see an event in very different ways and offer varying descriptions of the same occurrence.

Despite the limitations of human vision, it is not often treated as such; the flawed eyewitness report mentioned above is often considered as concrete evidence. There is also a tendency to assume the veracity of televised or print images at *all* times, even though there have been many instances when the media has produced inaccurate or incorrect reportage of events. If, then, the media and other avenues of visual culture present problematic images of gender, and if, as stated above, many viewers believe in the fidelity of such representations, it is arguable that visual culture is complicit with the circulation of sexist images and partially responsible for the instruction of viewers to behave in ways deemed sexist or misogynistic. That is, because a viewer *sees* a sexist character on a television program, the viewer might *believe* such behavior to be appropriate and then engage in it in their own life. The idea that visual culture "instructs" viewers on modes of behavior is one critique of ocularcentrism.

Another point of contention between visual culture and feminist and gender studies has to do with the creation and editing of visual images. Certainly human vision is not always reliable, but mediated representations (like a photograph in a fashion magazine or the digital portrait of a celebrity on a website), as stated earlier, cannot always be considered accurate either. Though these mediated images are typically considered to be "true to life," a photographic, filmic, or digital representation is just that – a representation of an object and not its actuality. Photographic images can be, and often are, manipulated in a multitude of ways. Photographs printed from film can be altered in the darkroom through the addition of ink, the double-exposure process, or even through cropping a photograph in such a way as to change its content. The advent of digital technology has introduced even more techniques to alter and enhance images. This process is often referred to in slang terms as "photoshopping a picture" (designated as such after the Adobe image editing software of the same name). While some experts in the field of graphic design claim these types of alterations are benign, other critics question the ethics of such manipulations. A renowned photographic magazine met with dissent when it was revealed that its designers altered an image of the Egyptian pyramids, making them appear closer together in order to fit the image on the magazine's cover. In the 1990s, a leading American news publication was criticized for altering a police photograph of former American football player Orenthal James "O.J." Simpson. The photograph placed on the cover of the publication was altered to make Simpson's skin appear much darker than in the original photograph, causing critics to claim that the digital changes made to the image belied overt racism in the publication.

These examples of photographic manipulation have been the object of much scrutiny and certainly warrant scholarly examination, but instances of the alteration of photographs of the bodies of models and celebrities are especially prevalent in visual culture and are relevant to this particular discussion. Print publications for both men and women can arguably create unrealistic standards for viewers to emulate through the production and presentation of digitally altered images. Fashion and fitness magazines, for example, distort images of women and men by using digital software to edit and enhance the images in numerous ways. Photo editors use computer programs to edit the images of models. Through a variety of digital tools, editors are able to shrink models' waistlines, increase their bust sizes, lengthen their legs, and slim the hips. Likewise, editors may erase or airbrush wrinkles and other skin permutations, lighten skin tone, whiten teeth, and edit out unruly hair and other physical details in the photographs of models through the use of this software. In certain instances, the images that result from these procedures are clearly distorted. In other cases, overzealous photo editors and page designers have accidentally erased entire limbs and digits from the model's form, producing a bizarre, mutated image that is obviously unrealistic. More subtle forms of editing, however, are often used as well. These muted manipulations are more difficult for viewers to detect, making these particular images appear realistic, perhaps even offering an image that might seem obtainable to the average viewer. Because the digital enhancements are understated and not often recognized, readers do not realize that these images are only obtainable with the help of a digital airbrush.

Though print and online magazines and websites produce images in a manner that creates unrealistic body image norms for society, these formats are not the only form of visual culture complicit with perpetuating unrealistic gender stereotypes. Filmic images, whether televised or presented in a theater, often not only manipulate the images of women's and men's corporeality through editing, but alter and distort gender images through plot devices as well. Feminist film theorists such as Laura Mulvey and Teresa de Lauretis trouble the relationship between media and gender. In her book *Technologies of Gender*, de Lauretis writes that "the representation of gender is its construction" (1987, 3), which underscores the practices explained earlier. Mulvey (1989) explicates the manner in which women are rendered objects through the camera's eye, arguing that the viewer of such media, whether male or female, then becomes complicit with a masculine mode of viewership. Still other critics and theorists have noted how women are often the objects of violence in film and television. Victimized, tortured, and beaten, images of brutalized women are common in popular culture.

While graphic violence against women is commonplace on both the large and small screen, television programs also arguably create female and male characters that are one-dimensional and saturated in common gender stereotypes. Situational comedies from the 1950s on often present images of a "perfect" family in which the father figure is completely responsible for the financial well-being of the family and the mother is the portrait of domestic productivity – minding her children, cleaning the home, and performing a number of other domestic duties. Though these images are not digitally altered, they, like the photoshopped magazine cover, also portray unrealistic and possibly unobtainable portraits of gender. And though the cultural tide seems to be turning by becoming more inclusive of a multiplicity of sexualities in programs and movies, for many years these visual artifacts disseminated images that not only suggested compulsory heterosexuality and marriage, but even insisted upon it.

Though it might seem as though advances in visual technology are accountable for the perpetuation and circulation of unrealistic and problematic representations of gender, visual artifacts that objectify the female form are numerous and have been in existence for generations. In his book titled *Ways of Seeing* (1990), English art critic and novelist John Berger illustrates the manner in which women have been objectified by the male master painters in countless artistic depictions. Referring to European oil paintings as well as advertisements contemporaneous to the time of publication as evidence, Berger explains that women have systematically been placed on display as the objects of spectatorship by men in such visual artifacts for centuries. In fact, "in one category of European oil painting women were the principal, ever-recurring subject," writes Berger. "That category is nude" (1990, 47). In most of these European oil paintings the woman appears to be aware that she is being watched (Berger 1990, 49). Berger's assertion is that there is not a rupture between the sexist images of European oil paintings and sexist publicity images but a continuity; that popular sexist advertising images that feature women are just one more artifact in a long line of such evidence. Teresa de Lauretis also highlights the ongoing relationship between gender and representation in her *Technologies of Gender*, stating that "the construction of gender goes on as busily today as it did in earlier times, say the Victorian era" (1987, 3); she cites the media as a site for such construction.

While many painters and other artists have objectified women or represented gender stereotypes in their work, many others have sought to subvert such imagery. Modern, postmodern, and contemporary artists have challenged sexist representations of gender in their productions and frequently contested expected gender norms. Cindy Sherman, an American photographer and model, shot a series of self-portraits that parody commonly circulated cinematographic images of women. American photographer Sherrie Levine is well known for photographs in which she re-photographs the work of male masters in their current settings and locations, and American collage artist Barbara Kruger's work often combines captions with iconic images of men and women that question common gender stereotypes and their practice within the realm of artistic production. Male artists such as Robert Mapplethorpe have also contested stereotypical gender roles in their work. Mapplethorpe's photographs of male nudes destabilize the female eroticized object image and focus in on a homoerotic subject.

Enthusiasm for visual culture persists, and as such the study of visual culture continues to be an area of scholarship in which numerous theorists are engaged. A number of cultural critics from the Frankfurt School, a group of Marxist intellectuals in Germany in the 1920s that included Theodor Adorno and Walter Benjamin, wrote extensively on visual culture. Benjamin's essay titled "The Work of Art in the Age of Mechanical Reproduction" is frequently cited in visual culture studies and continues to be a touchstone for scholars interested in critiquing the place of technological reproductions (such as photographs and film) in our aesthetic experiences in society (Benjamin 1969). Benjamin's prescience rings especially true in the era of new media.

Likewise, the image is especially critical to the work of French psychoanalyst and psychiatrist Jacques Lacan, who interprets and analyzes "the gaze" in a key number of his works. Lacan's studies constitute a break from the earlier Freudian psychoanalytical models, and in turn Lacan's methodology and interest in the visual influenced a number of critical theories and theorists, especially as pertaining to gender, poststructuralism, and other areas of scholarship.

Contemporary studies of visual culture continue to surge, offering a plethora of commentaries, positive, negative, and ambivalent, regarding visual culture and the image. Both Roland Barthes in his book *Camera Lucida: Reflections on Photography* (2010) and Susan Sontag in her book *On Photography* (2005) illustrate the shortcomings of the photographic image. While Barthes laments the fact that photographs of his deceased mother never quite capture her true essence, Sontag traces a variety of behaviors that are interconnected with photography, ranging from voyeurism to tourism and scopophilia. By immersing ourselves in images, Sontag seems to suggest, we might miss out on actual events, activities, and spaces for intervention.

Today, W. J. T. Mitchell is among one of the most notable scholars engaged with visual culture. Mitchell, who has written extensively about what he describes as the "pictorial turn" in Western culture, challenges readings of images as simply passive vessels. In his *What Do Pictures Want? The Lives and Loves of Images* (2005), Mitchell asserts that "art historians may 'know' that the pictures they study are only material objects that have been marked with colors and shapes, but they frequently talk and act as if the pictures had feeling, will, consciousness, agency and desire. Everyone knows that a photograph of their mother is not alive, but they will still be reluctant to deface or destroy it" (2005, 31). According to Mitchell, it is not only high art that "speaks," for "every advertising executive knows that some images, to use the trade jargon, 'have legs' – that is, they seem to have a surprising capacity to generate new direction and surprising twists in an ad campaign" (2005, 31). While Mitchell continues to think of images in new and surprising ways, the manner in which gender is represented in visual culture continues to adjust and adapt as well.

SEE ALSO: Chick Flicks; Feminist Art Practice; Feminist Film Theory; Feminist Magazines; Gaze; Images of Gender and Sexuality in Advertising; Media and Gender Socialization

REFERENCES

Barthes, Roland. 2010. *Camera Lucida: Reflections on Photography*, trans. Richard Howard. New York: Hill and Wang.

Benjamin, Walter. 1969. "The Work of Art in the Age of Mechanical Reproduction." In *Illuminations: Essays and Reflections*, edited by Hannah Ahrendt, translated by Harry Zohn. New York: Schocken.

Berger, John. 1990. *Ways of Seeing*. London: Penguin.

De Lauretis, Teresa. 1987. *Technologies of Gender: Essays on Film, Theory, Fiction*. Bloomington: Indiana University Press.

Mitchell, W. J. T. 2005. *What Do Pictures Want? The Lives and Loves of Images*. Chicago: University of Chicago Press.

Mulvey, Laura. 1989. *Visual and Other Pleasures*. Bloomington: Indiana University Press.

Sontag, Susan. 2005. *On Photography*. New York: Rosetta Books.

FURTHER READING

Nancy, Jean-Luc. 2005. *The Ground of the Image*, trans. Jeff Fort. New York: Fordham University Press.

Volunteerism and Charitable Giving

CHRISTOPHER J. EINOLF
DePaul University, Chicago, USA

PAMALA WIEPKING
Erasmus University Rotterdam, The Netherlands

Gender differences in overall levels of volunteerism and charitable giving are small but vary across countries. While women are more motivated to help others, men have more of the resources of income and education that facilitate giving and volunteering. Structural inequalities tend to depress women's volunteerism and giving, which in turn may contribute to the perpetuation of gender inequality.

Volunteerism is the voluntary donation of time and charitable giving is the voluntary donation of money to organizations that benefit others or create public goods and services. Women score higher on most measures of prosocial motivations, behave more generously in most economics experiments, and are more likely to help friends and family members. However, women currently volunteer only slightly more than men in the United States (Einolf 2011) and volunteer less than men in Europe (Wiepking and Einolf 2012). In Europe (Wiepking and Einolf 2012) and the United States (Einolf 2011), women are about equally as likely as men to give money to charity.

Men and women tend to give time and money to different types of organizations. In both the United States and Europe, men are more likely to support organizations they might be directly involved with, such as organizations involved in sports, outdoor recreation, culture, hobbies, unions, professional associations, consumer groups, and political associations. Women are more likely to give time and money to organizations supporting more distant beneficiaries, such as humanitarian, human rights, and human services organizations (Themudo 2009; Wiepking and Einolf 2012). Gender differences in donations of time and money to religious charities and congregations vary by country (Wiepking and Einolf in press). In the United States, men concentrate their volunteering and giving among a few types of organizations rather than spreading them out among many types of organizations (Andreoni, Brown, and Rischall 2003). In Europe, however, women are more likely than men to concentrate their donations of time and money to a small number of types of organizations (Wiepking and Einolf 2012).

Turning to the causes of volunteerism and giving, women tend to score higher on psychological measures of prosocial motivations known to stimulate volunteering and giving behavior. Women score higher on agreeableness, moral obligation, prosocial role identity, and intrinsic religiosity (Einolf 2011), benevolence, universalism, and belief in the importance of volunteering (Wiepking and Einolf 2012), and empathic concern and the principle of care (Mesch et al. 2011). The only motive predictive of volunteerism and giving that is stronger for men is political interest (Wiepking and Einolf 2012).

However, women's higher motivations to volunteer and give are canceled out by their lower levels of resources. Men typically make more money and feel more financially secure, which allows them to give to charity. In most countries, men still have more education, which provides them with the skills needed for volunteering and facilitates better understanding of beneficiaries' needs in the case of charitable giving (Einolf 2011; Wiepking and Einolf 2012).

Men's and women's levels of social capital, or the norms, networks, and trust that facilitate cooperation, vary according to the type of social capital measured (O'Neill and Gidengil 2006). Participation in social networks makes it more likely that people will be asked to volunteer and give, while trust and external norms of helpfulness and reciprocity make it more likely that they will say yes. Men tend to have higher levels of trust and more integration into social networks related to employment and recreation, while women tend to participate more in networks related to relatives, children, and religion. Overall, social capital differences have no net effect favoring either male or female volunteerism and giving (Einolf 2011; Wiepking and Einolf 2012).

Not only inequalities in individual characteristics, but also inequalities in social context affect volunteering and giving. In countries where women's incomes, education, workforce participation, and political participation are more nearly equal to men, their levels of volunteering and giving are more equal to men. In gender-unequal countries, even wealthy and highly educated women are less likely to give and volunteer due to structural gender inequalities (Themudo 2009; Wiepking and Einolf 2012).

Gender inequalities in volunteering and giving may serve to reinforce gender inequalities in other aspects of society. Volunteering brings health benefits, helps volunteers learn job-related skills, and encourages greater political participation (Musick and Wilson 2008), and charitable giving provides donors with influence over the policies of non-profits. Structural inequalities in income, education, employment, and access to high-status social networks tend to deprive women of the opportunity to volunteer and give, and their lower levels of volunteerism and giving tend to further deprive them of the opportunities for career advancement, political voice, and influence on non-profits. Few studies exist on the mutually reinforcing relationships between structural inequality and volunteerism and giving, making this an important area for future research on gender.

SEE ALSO: Democracy and Democratization; Division of Labor, Gender; Ethic of Care; Ethics, Moral Development, and Gender; Gender Inequality and Gender Stratification

REFERENCES

Andreoni, James, Eleanor Brown, and Isaac Rischall. 2003. "Charitable Giving by Married Couples: Who Decides and Why Does It Matter?" *Journal of Human Resources*, 38: 111–133.

Einolf, Christopher J. 2011. "Gender Differences in the Correlates of Volunteering and Charitable Giving." *Nonprofit and Voluntary Sector Quarterly*, 40: 1092–1112.

Mesch, Debra J., Melissa S. Brown, Zachary I. Moore, and Amir D. Hayat. 2011. "Gender Differences in Charitable Giving." *International Journal of Nonprofit and Voluntary Sector Marketing*, 16: 342–355.

Musick, Marc A., and John Wilson. 2008. *Volunteers: A Social Profile*. Indianapolis: Indiana University Press.

O'Neill, Brenda, and Elisabeth Gidengil, eds. 2006. *Gender and Social Capital*. New York: Routledge.

Themudo, Nuno S. 2009. "Gender and the Nonprofit Sector." *Nonprofit and Voluntary Sector Quarterly*, 38: 663–683.

Wiepking, Pamala, and Christopher J. Einolf. 2012. "Gender Differences in Charitable Giving in Europe." Presented at the Annual Meeting of the Association for Research in Nonprofit Organizations and Voluntary Action (ARNOVA), November 15, Indianapolis, Indiana.

War, International Violence, and Gender

STEPHANIE CHABAN
University of Ulster, UK

War is inherently gendered, as is the violence that stems from such conflict. The experiences of men and women during conflict vary; therefore the experiences of men and women during war cannot be generalized, including their experiences of violence. Men are often viewed as warriors, protectors, or diplomats, whereas women are usually perceived to be victims, nurturers, or peacemakers. Specifically, while women may be survivors of sexual assault and suicide bombings, or deemed as innocent bystanders or collateral damage, or viewed as mothers, daughters, sisters, or wives of soldiers, their lives during violence conflict are more complex and nuanced. While sexual and gender-based violence (SGBV) are the most reported forms of violence inflicted on women during war, violence can occur in different forms; in some instances, such violence can be rendered invisible. Gendered stereotypes, poverty, displacement, and institutional reform can have a negative impact on women during conflict. The roles of men and women in peacemaking and peacebuilding are also perceived from different vantage points – women are often seen as making peace at the local or grassroots level whereas men work at the international level and make peace between states. However, not all these assumptions about the roles of men and women in war are true. These are the gendered aspects of war and international violence.

MILITARIZED MASCULINITIES AND FEMININITIES

Gender is defined as the socially constructed roles, behaviors, activities, and attributes that a given society considers appropriate for its men and women, young and old. It is not a synonym for "women," nor is it a synonym for "women and men." Gender gives rise to masculinities and femininities that can be defined as ways in which the gender order is maintained by practice and through performance (see Connell 2005). War and violence produce and reproduce different types of masculinities and femininities that mutually reinforce one another. Feminist researchers who look at war and its ensuing violence have identified the privileging of militarized masculinities as a means of legitimizing and encouraging war and violence (Elshtain 1995; Enloe 2000). Militarization is the "step-by-step process by which a person or a thing gradually comes to be controlled by the military or comes to depend for its well-being on militaristic ideas" (Enloe 2000, 3). Militarized masculinities are about violence; they are about upholding state violence and a violent form of security.

In direct contrast, the types of femininities that war benefits from include portrayals of women as mothers or nurturers, or what Elshtain (1995) refers to as the "Beautiful Soul." This theory supports the traditional roles of conflict where men are involved with fighting while women tend to hearth and home and theoretically and literally reproduce the nation; they are rewarded for creating more fighters and supporting the war effort. In turn, these fighters (traditionally males) will go to war to protect the women left behind. The "Beautiful Soul" imagines a woman who is inherently associated with pacifism and maternalism and is in need of protection.

War and violence are more complicated than these gendered stereotypes. When looking at the lives of men and women impacted by war and international violence, it is necessary to look at the myriad situational factors, both local and international, that affect their experiences and their abilities within the conflict.

INTERNATIONAL LAW AND WOMEN, PEACE, AND SECURITY

In 2000, the United Nations (UN) took on the issue of women, peace, and security and issued the innovative United Nations Security Council Resolution 1325. UNSCR 1325 is known as the "Women, Peace and Security" Resolution. This resolution stresses the important role of women in the prevention and resolution of conflicts, peace negotiations, peacebuilding, peacekeeping, humanitarian response, and post-conflict reconstruction. The Resolution also stresses the importance of women's equal participation and full involvement in all efforts related to the maintenance and promotion of peace and security.

Subsequent resolutions include UNSCR 1820 which demands that steps be taken to protect civilians, including women and girls, from all forms of sexual violence; UNSCR 1888 which reaffirms the need to address sexual violence during and after conflict; UNSCR 1889 which encourages member states in post-conflict situations to design concrete strategies for gender-responsive law enforcement and access to justice; UNSCR 1960 which creates institutional tools to combat impunity, and outlines specific steps needed for both the prevention of and protection from sexual violence in conflict; UNSCR 2106 which emphasizes the important role women can play concerning armed conflict and sexual violence and calls for women's greater role in disarmament, demobilization, and reintegration (DDR), security sector reform (SSR), and justice reform; and UNSCR 2122 which calls for the promotion of gender equality and the empowerment of women in conflict and post-conflict situations, for women's full participation in DDR, SSR, judicial reform, and post-conflict reconstruction, for an increase in women's participation in the maintenance of peace and security and post-conflict peacebuilding, and which requests funding to enable women's leadership development regarding the implementation of UNSCR 1325.

Within international humanitarian law (IHL), women have been afforded special protection due to women being viewed primarily as victims, noncombatants, and mothers or expectant mothers. Much focus is on women's vulnerability to sexual violence, rape, and sexual exploitation. In detail, the Geneva Conventions (1949) outline the following in regard to the status of women:

- Article 12(4), Geneva Convention I: "Women shall be treated with all consideration due to their sex."
- Article 12(4), Geneva Convention II: "Women shall be treated with all consideration due to their sex."
- Article 14(2), Geneva Convention III: "Women shall be treated with all the regard due to their sex."
- Article 27(2), Geneva Convention IV: "Women shall be especially protected against any attack on their honour, in particular against rape, enforced prostitution, or any form of indecent assault."
- Article 76(1) of the Additional Protocol I (1977): "Women shall be the object of special respect."

The Rome Statute (2002), the treaty that established the International Criminal Court (ICC), has defined crimes against women, primarily sexual assault, as crimes against humanity, war crimes, and genocide. Prior to the Rome Statute, ad hoc tribunals were established, most notably the International Criminal Tribunal for the former Yugoslavia (ICTY, 1993), the International Criminal Tribunal for Rwanda (ICTR, 1994), and the Special Court for Sierra Leone (SCSL, 2002). Each tribunal stands out for the ways in which it uniquely responds to sexual violence and violence against women and girls. These efforts are significant in that previous tribunals that tried war crimes, like Nuremberg and the Tokyo Tribunal, did not fully address rape and other forms of sexual violence as war crimes.

Significant cases heard at the ICTY include *Prosecutor v. Duško Tadić* (1997) where Tadić, as a former member of a paramilitary force, was convicted for participation in widespread and systematic beatings, torture, and sexual assaults against non-Serbs. Tadić was found guilty of crimes against humanity, including sexual violence. In the *Čelebići Case* (1998), the outcome confirmed that rape and sexual violence are acts of torture. Finally, the *Prosecutor v. Anto Furundzija* (1998) judgment expanded the definition of rape and expanded the definition of torture to include rape. The most significant case heard at the ICTR involved *Prosecutor v. Jean Paul Akayesu* (1998). The judgment of this trial recognized for the first time that acts of sexual violence can be prosecuted as elements of a genocidal campaign. Finally, the SCSL recognized forced marriage as a crime against humanity.

Other types of tribunals and hybrid courts have surfaced in the wake of conflict where gendered violence is discussed and acknowledged, such as Truth Commission (South Africa) or Gacaca Courts (Rwanda). These forums are generally for public healing and reconciliation rather than for prosecution.

THE GENDERED IMPACT OF CONFLICT

Socioeconomic impact

Poverty increases for men and women alike during conflict, though oftentimes women endure a very specific type of socioeconomic impact. The poverty faced by women in any society is often invisible (as is the case in times of peace); it becomes even greater in the midst of social upheaval. Women's impoverishment takes on many forms as a carry-over from peacetime, brought on by displacement, by the death, detention, or migration of male breadwinners, exacerbated by a lack of access to resources, or instigated by sexist practices. Female-headed households increase, causing women to bear full economic responsibility for the immediate and extended household. Women and girls are most likely the ones to take up care work; it is their job to attend to the elderly, the sick, and the young, further adding to other duties. In general, women are less likely to own property or land; this has long-term impacts during conflict and displacement. Issues such as food insecurity, degradation to the environment, and the fact that many women already work in the informal sector further amplifies their situation. The informal economy endangers women overall, but during conflict women may turn to other forms of work to make ends meet, such as sex work, where they may be left vulnerable to further violence or disease.

Displacement

Displacement is an inevitable consequence of contemporary wars given that most are intrastate rather than interstate. The length of displacement varies though it is estimated that the average length is nearly 17 years. This results not only in refugees but also internally displaced persons (IDPs). Accurate data on who makes up the displaced is hotly contended as generalizations claim that women and children make up more than three quarters of those on the move. Women are typically regarded as "vulnerable" in emergencies as physical displacement can severely impact a community's social and economic structures, thus greatly affecting gender relations. Displacement can also provide a setting where gender norms are transformed, both positively and negatively.

Women and girls may encounter violence during flight or where they receive asylum; they maybe be harassed or assaulted by armed forces, police, or militias, border officials, males from the locale where they seek asylum, male family members, or other male refugees. They maybe taken advantage of by peacekeepers, humanitarian workers, or others tasked with their protection. The government of asylum may actively or passively tolerate actions or policies that allow violence against displaced females to occur. As refugees, there should be a framework that women and girls can turn to in order to address their needs, yet this is not always the case. As IDPs, their vulnerability, along with others, may increase due to a breakdown in the state.

In many instances, "refugee camps can be conflict zones" (Giles and Hyndman 2004, 193). Within a refugee camp or IDP settlement, displaced females are at risk for increased domestic and sexual violence. Abuse can occur due to poor camp set-up or may occur outside the camp – for instance, when women and girls use latrines or bathe, or when displaced women and girls go in search of firewood or to market, as was the case in Darfur. Girls may be vulnerable in that, in an effort to preserve their honor or secure their future, their families marry them off at an early age to a financially secure individual or an older suitor. This has occurred with refugees based in Jordan, Lebanon, and other host countries, who fled the conflict in Syria begun in 2011. To address these issues, there have been efforts by United Nations and humanitarian organizations to include women in the design and construction of refugee camps, as well as in decisions about the distribution of humanitarian assistance.

In urban settings, displaced females may not have access to any services and may remain barricaded in the residence for fear of exploitation, detention, or abuse. Syrian refugee populations in Jordan and Lebanon have faced discrimination and increasing poverty. Women and girls often do not leave their homes for fear of harassment. These populations tend to become invisible and do not access the services often made available to those in refugee camps.

Returning home, when possible, does not always guarantee security or rights. Community upheaval can result in increased family violence. Disrupted communities also mean that the common protective factors, such as the extended family, may no longer be intact.

Despite these significant issues, war can impact gender relations in positive ways. While many may be in a vulnerable position due to a loss of males, some are able to assume roles that would not normally be available to them in time of perceived peace. An example of women's empowerment during displacement occurred in the Western Sahara. Sahrawi refugee camps in western Algeria were comprised predominantly of women during the fighting years (1975–1991) when the men were away, which has resulted in their control of much of the camp's infrastructure.

Political, legal, and judicial breakdown

Legal institutions commonly break down during war; in some cases they were never properly developed. Other institutions associated with rule of law are also impacted, like the government, the judiciary, and the police. There is a focus on security of the state rather than human security. When this occurs, laws are often modified or suspended, resulting in a loss of rights for all. In these instances women may face obstacles in having their rights respected and their voices heard. Liberation and emancipation movements reveal the ways in which the concerns of women are often sidelined or ignored. Legal reform, where women's rights are respected and implemented, is often argued to be a post-conflict endeavor and women are told to wait out the conflict and then to ask for "their" rights. This was seen after the Algerian War (1954–1962): once independence was achieved, promises made concerning women's rights were put on the back burner and women continued to struggle for their rights.

Laws are commonly introduced that either reinstitute oppressive practices or create new ones. Occasionally, repressive laws are drafted or reinstituted in the vein of "protecting" women. In Iraq, the previously liberal and secular Iraqi Law of Personal Status (1959) was transformed after the US occupation, expanding the power of religious courts to rule in all disputes related to the family and limiting the rights of women. Legislation relating to domestic violence may not be as empowering as is publicized. In Afghanistan, the Elimination of Violence Against Women Law (2009) appeared to be quite progressive on the surface but has been ignored by the criminal justice system. Additionally, attempted amendments to the criminal code have contradicted its efforts.

Efforts at mainstreaming gender into other processes, like constitutional revision and developing quotas for political or security sector institutions, vary from community to community. In the aftermath of the Rwandan genocide (1994), Rwandan women achieved near parity in the parliament, a first in the world. Other contexts have seen quotas written into legislation to ensure women's participation.

Sexual and gender-based violence, health, and reproductive health

Many researchers acknowledge that the violence women experience throughout war is directly linked to a "continuum of violence" (Cockburn 2004) that women and girls experience, even during times of peace. The "continuum of violence" asserts that such violence is not necessarily a product of war; rather, it is violence directed at women because they are women. Conflict exacerbates this violence.

During conflict, it is well documented that rates of sexual and physical violence against women tend to increase, but men and young boys also encounter gender-specific forms of violence. Sexual and gender-based violence (SGBV) appears in many forms. The United Nations defines SGBV as "violence that is directed against a person on the basis of gender or sex. It includes acts that inflict physical, mental or sexual harm or suffering, threats of such acts, coercion and other deprivations of liberty ... While women, men, boys and girls can be victims of gender-based violence, women and girls are the main victims." There can be many different types of perpetrator during a conflict, including intimate partners, community members, opposing forces, security forces, and humanitarian actors. Oftentimes, women and girls are the targets, their bodies and wombs used as a means to "dilute" their ethnic or religious communities or to serve as means for sending messages between male fighters.

One of the most well known forms of SGBV is rape as a weapon of war. History has been mute on the subject, though such violence did occur with great frequency. During World War II and the Holocaust, Jewish and non-Jewish women alike endured sexual violence. In the aftermath of World War II, revelations of "comfort women" – women enslaved by the Japanese army for sexual purposes – came to light. Such violence persists in conflicts as varied as those occurring in Darfur, the Former Yugoslav Republics (FYR), the Democratic Republic of Congo, and Timor Leste, among others. The conflict in the FYR during the 1990s is when sexual violence became an international human rights and humanitarian concern. Other conflicts have been characterized by campaigns of mass rape such as in East Timor (1999).

Trafficking and exploitation have all become significant forms of gendered violence during conflict. During the Balkan War, trafficking of women became so commonplace that even peacekeeping forces were participating. The increase in trafficking can be tracked to the increase in criminal networks, the increase in the trade of arms and drugs, and the increasing poverty of those impacted by conflict.

Researchers such as Meintjes, Pillay, and Turshen (2001) argue that there is no such thing as a post-conflict aftermath for women since violence continues to persist. While violations may occur at the hands of opposing forces, local menfolk are just as likely to be perpetrators. Males may mirror the violence inflicted upon them in the conflict zone, importing it into the domestic sphere, or they may feel compelled to reproduce violence against women deemed as acceptable in the conflict zone. The increase in small arms and light weapons (SALW) is also connected to increases of gender-based violence not only during conflict, but also in the post-conflict setting. It is claimed that the increase of domestic violence hotline calls in the aftermath of the conflict in Bosnia-Herzegovina was due to the influx of SALWs and the loss of an "enemy." Links have also been drawn between paramilitary violence and domestic violence during the Troubles in Northern Ireland (1969–1998).

Proximity to peacekeeping forces and military bases can result in increases of violence against women and girls. Peacekeepers have been charged with assault and trafficking in locales as diverse as Angola, Bosnia, Cambodia, the Democratic Republic of Congo, Mozambique, and Somalia. Peacekeeping forces and other humanitarian staff were implicated in rape and sexual abuse in the Balkans in the 1990s. US soldiers have committed rape and other forms of sexual violence in the communities that host their bases, including Okinawa, the Philippines, and South Korea. US service members have also been held to account for the murders and attempted murders of women in Okinawa. Women and human rights groups have frequently protested their presence.

Access to health and reproductive health services is greatly impaired during conflict. There may be a lack of services due to a drain on healthcare professions, increasing segregation of the sexes, or a dismantled infrastructure. International sanctions may also make it difficult for those most in need to access services.

Access to hygienic products for menstruation or to sanitary facilities compounds health problems. Women who are pregnant or post-partum have specific nutritional needs and may be more prone to treatable ailments like anemia (Palestine and Somalia) or scurvy (Afghanistan). Surrounding violence impacts pregnancy. In the Palestinian West Bank, checkpoints created situations where women would choose to go to the hospital early in order to obtain a cesarean section rather than risk having a checkpoint birth. During Operation Cast Lead (2008–2009) in the Gaza Strip, a number of women miscarried or had premature births due to the bombardments.

COMBATANTS, SOLDIERS, AND TERRORISM

The participation of men in armed combat is often seen as a given and, in some cases, expected. It is assumed that men primarily serve as soldiers, fighters, and combatants. Men make war and women make peace. However, women's roles are more varied and women's participation in active fighting does exist (both by choice and by coercion), though this varies from society to society. Recent conflicts have also seen documentation proving that women torture and abuse the opposing forces, as has been evidenced in conflicts in Iraq and Rwanda. Women serve as fighters and also carry out acts of terrorism.

Women's formal participation in modern conflict takes the form of military service. There is a long history of women serving as nurses and in other supporting roles in armies during World War I and World War II. After World War II women's military service became more structured and routinized in certain parts of the world and a significant number of armies in the West have allowed women to fill active combat roles. Israel is the only military in the world where women are conscripted (since 1948), though in practice about one third of women actually serve and those who do most commonly serve in noncombat roles.

Concerns over women's participation in the military center on their vulnerability to sexual violence by opposing forces. Recent evidence has shown in the United States that women are more likely to be sexually assaulted by their military colleagues than die in combat. Women's presence in combat also does not necessarily lessen the likelihood of male soldiers committing crimes against the local population. This is evidenced by the high-profile participation of Specialist Lynndie England during the torture and prisoner abuse scandal at Abu Ghraib Prison (2003–2004).

Women's informal participation in modern conflict occurs when they are participants of militias, rebel groups, and suicide missions. Occasionally this participation is coerced. In conflicts such as those in the Democratic Republic of Congo, Uganda, and Sierra Leone, child soldiering has been a frequent occurrence; some of these children are girls. In certain instances, as with the Lord's Resistance Army (LRA) in Uganda, girls are recruited not only as child soldiers but as bush wives or sex slaves.

The fighters the Liberation Tigers of Tamil Eelam (LTTE) in Sri Lanka had women's wings entitled Malathi and Sothiya Brigades. Thenmozhi Rajaratnam was a female suicide bomber aligned with the LTTE who assassinated Rajiv Gandhi in 1991. In Chechnya, there are the Black Widows who are best known for their participation in a hostage crisis that took place in a Moscow theater in 2002. In the early days of the Second Intifada (2000), a handful of Palestinian women based in the West Bank and the Gaza Strip became suicide bombers.

As fighters, women have served in Turkish Kurdistan, in the Kurdistan Workers' Party (PKK). The PKK has stood out as a rebel force that embraces the participation of women in its fighting forces as part of its Marxist-Leninist doctrine. In many instances, women's participation in the PKK has been viewed as empowering and as contributing to a more egalitarian Kurdish society. During the Eritrean War for Independence (1961–1991) with Ethiopia, nearly a quarter of soldiers within the Popular Front for the Liberation of Eritrea (EPLF) were women. Similarly, while there are female fighters in the Marxist-Leninist Revolutionary Armed Forces of Colombia (FARC), it has been documented that young female recruits have been sexually assaulted by older male members of the FARC as a form of indoctrination.

ORGANIZING FOR PEACE, PEACEMAKING, AND PEACEBUILDING

Equating women with peace has both pros and cons in the international realm, as women may be perceived as inherent peacebuilders and less likely to participate in any type of conflict. Furthermore, conflating their identities with motherhood and civilians is also seen as limiting. Yet, there is significant documentation that women do organize for peace both at the informal, local level and at the formal, international level.

While not all women can be considered peacemakers, many women have organized across borders, ethnic lines, and religious lines to end conflict and build peace within their communities. One of the earliest peace organizations to bring women together was the Women's International League for Peace and Freedom (WILPF). WILPF was born out of the International Women's Congress against World War I in 1915; its first president was Jane Addams. Women have been prominent in other peace and anti-military movements. The Greenham Common Women's Peace Camp formed in 1981 (until 2000) in protest at the British government allowing cruise missiles to be housed at an RAF airbase in the area. The Peace Camp is significant in that a conscious decision was made that only women would be involved in the ongoing protests, utilizing the concept of women as mothers and nurturers. Other activists and women's organizations have adopted this approach in their work in conflict zones as diverse as Israel/Palestine, Russia, Northern Ireland, and the United States. Among the most well known of maternal activists is the Las Madres de la Plaza de Mayo. The Madres began in Buenos Aires, Argentina when mothers of the "disappeared" from the Dirty War of the military dictatorship (1976–1983) took to the main plaza for weekly protests for information on the disappeared. The Madres gained currency in the local and international communities due to their utilization of motherhood as a protest strategy and their unwavering public defiance of the local regime. Women in Black (WiB) serves as a network of women concerned about war and militarism. WiB vigils are characterized by public gatherings of women standing silently, dressed in black, carrying placards in protest against a conflict or militarized intervention. Founded in 2001 in response to the Israel/Palestine conflict, WiB has been exported to other regions of the world as a way for women to use non-violent protest to raise awareness of militarism. Women have initiated cross-border cooperation and discussions in a number of divided communities such as Israel and Palestine, Cyprus, Northern Ireland, and North and South Korea.

Women have also served as United Nations peacekeepers in the wake of revelations that male peacekeepers were complicit in human trafficking, forced prostitution, and other forms of sexual violence. While women have served as UN peacekeepers in many contexts, the most prominent has been the number of female peacekeepers in post-conflict Liberia.

In 2011, the Nobel Committee awarded the Peace Prize to Ellen Johnson Sirleaf and Leymeh Gbowee, both of Liberia, and Tawakkol Karman of Yemen "for their nonviolent struggle for the safety of women and for women's rights to full participation in peace-building work." Only a few women had previously been acknowledged in such a formal manner for their peacebuilding efforts.

SEE ALSO: Comfort Women; Gender Mainstreaming; Gender-Based Violence; Greenham Common; Militarism and Gender-Based Violence; Military Masculinity; Pacifism, Peace Activism, and Gender; Refugee Women and Violence Against Women; Refugees and Refugee Camps; Sexual Violence and the Military

REFERENCES

Cockburn, Cynthia. 2004. "The Continuum of Violence: A Gender Perspective on War and Peace." In *Sites of Violence: Gender and Conflict Zones*, edited by Wenona Giles and Jennifer Hyndman, 24–44. Berkeley: University of California Press.

Connell, R. W. 2005. *Masculinities*, 2nd ed. Berkeley: University of California Press.

Elshtain, Jean Bethke. 1995. *Women and War*. Chicago: University of Chicago Press.

Enloe, Cynthia. 2000. *Maneuvers: The International Politics of Militarizing Women's Lives*. Berkeley: University of California Press.

Giles, Wenona, and Jennifer Hyndman, eds. 2004. *Sites of Violence: Gender and Conflict Zones*. Berkeley: University of California Press.

Meintjes, Sheila, Anu Pillay, and Meredeth Turshen, eds. 2001. *The Aftermath: Women in Post-Conflict Transformation*. London: Zed Books.

FURTHER READING

Bouta, Tsjeard, Georg Frerks, and Ian Bannon, eds. 2005. *Gender, Conflict, and Development*. Washington, DC: The World Bank.

Coomaraswamy, Radhika. 2001. "Violence against Women Perpetrated and/or Condoned by the State During Times of Armed Conflict (1997–2000)." E/CN.4/2001/73. Accessed August 19, 2015, at http://www.unhchr.ch/Huridocda/Huridoca.nsf/0/8a64f06cc48404acc1256a22002c08ea/$FILE/G0110444.pdf.

Farr, Vanessa, Henri Myrttinen, and Albrecht Schnabel, eds. 2009. *Sexed Pistols: The Gendered Impacts of Small Arms and Light Weapons*. Tokyo: United Nations University Press.

Goldstein, Joshua S. 2001. *War and Gender: How Gender Shapes the War System and Vice Versa*. Cambridge: Cambridge University Press.

Lorentzen, Lois Ann, and Jennifer Turpin, eds. 1998. *The Women & War Reader*. New York: NYU Press.

Moser, Caroline O. N., and Fiona Clark, eds. 2001. *Victims, Perpetrators or Actors?* London: Zed Books.

Rehn, Elisabeth, and Ellen Johnson Sirleaf. 2002. *Women, War and Peace: The Independent Experts' Assessment on the Impact of Armed Conflict on Women and Women's Role in Peacebuilding*. New York: United Nations Development Fund for Women (UNIFEM).

Sjoberg, Laura, and Caron E. Gentry. 2008. *Mothers, Monsters, Whores: Women's Violence in Global Politics*. London: Zed Books.

Turshen, Meredeth, and Clotilde Twagiramariya, eds. 1998. *What Women Do in Wartime: Gender and Conflict in Africa*. London: Zed Books.

Wet Nursing

ANNA DODSON SAIKIN
Rice University, USA

Wet nursing, or the practice in which a woman breastfeeds an infant who she has not birthed and/or is not the mother of, has served as an alternative to a mother's breast milk throughout much of modern history. The practice of wet nursing was safeguarded by legal contracts in ancient Mesopotamia, and non-medical sources demonstrate the widespread use of wet nurses in Ancient Egypt, Greece, and Rome, typically by the wealthier classes. Islamic physicians followed the Qur'an by recommending that babies should be breastfed for two years, but did not outlaw the use of wet nurses. Wealthier mothers typically used lower class wet nurses, but the vast majority of women breastfed their own babies.

Women could find work as wet nurses depending on their husband's occupation. Certain professions such as laborers, tailors, brick-makers, and blacksmiths were more visible, and thus their wives were more frequently put in the path of mothers who could afford to employ them. Wet nursing provided an extra source of income for pre-industrial families, though the amount that women were paid varied depending on whether the wet nurse was hired by a private individual or by the parish to suckle foundlings. In early periods, the wet nurse typically came to the infant's home so that the mother could supervise. By the medieval period, the practice evolved so that infants were sent away from their home to the country.

Beginning in the sixteenth and seventeenth centuries, European physicians began to discourage women from using wet nurses. If a woman chose to employ a wet nurse, strict codes of conduct were recommended which were thought to guard against infant mortality. For example, doctors and midwives counseled that a wet nurse should abstain from sexual intercourse during her employment as sexual activity was thought to decrease the quality and amount of her breast milk. Similarly, wet nurses were scrutinized for the onset of menses, as menstruation was thought to cause milk to spoil. Other conditions that precluded work as a wet nurse included pregnancy, venereal disease, and physical traits such as red hair and freckles.

Even taking these factors into account, many worried that the quality of wet nurses was not always consistent. If the wet nurse had taken too many infants, the babies may have been dry nursed or undernourished. In eighteenth-century France, twice as many infants who were wet nursed died than those who had been breastfed by their mothers. Accounts that wet nurses tried to swap infants who had died in their care generated anxiety that wet nurses would try to collect money for deceased infants. Generally, these fears proved to be exaggerated, as wet nurses were used as scapegoats for other issues associated with infant mortality during this time. Wet nurses were blamed for several infant diseases including "the pox," which was said to result from venereal disease, rickets, thrush, consumption, and gastrointestinal conditions.

Though the practice of wet nursing increased during the early part of the eighteenth century, medical and philosophical writers during this time were strongly in favor of maternal breastfeeding. In France, Jean-Jacques Rousseau's recommendation that women breastfeed their children extended his philosophy that favored a natural, simplistic life. Rousseau's educational treatise *Émile*, published in French in 1762 and translated into English the same year, sparked a transnational obsession with motherhood. In England, Mary Wollstonecraft's *A Vindication of the Rights of Woman* (1792) argued that women's involvement in the public sphere stems from their role as mothers to future citizens. An increased attention to motherhood, and in particular breastfeeding, became a way for women to enter the emerging public sphere. Breastfeeding thus became a political choice in the eighteenth century, and subsequently wet nursing began to decline in Western countries.

European medical advice had a profound effect on American families, where wet nursing grew out of favor by the late eighteenth century. Yet the need for an alternative source of breast milk meant that the practice continued to a lesser degree in the nineteenth century. In the southern United States, wet nursing became linked to the plantation system, yet the availability of African American slave wet nurses did not necessarily mean that wealthy white women used slaves as wet nurses at a greater rate than poorer white women. Concerns regarding cross-racial wet nursing limited the use of slaves, though African American women continued to have a significant role in childcare on plantations. By the mid-nineteenth century, ethical concerns over the fate of the children born by wet nurses coupled with concerns over the safe use of the breast milk of wet nurses caused the practice to go into sharp decline.

The development of infant formula after World War II effectively eliminated the need for wet nurses in Western countries. Mothers who cannot produce milk but prefer to use it instead of formula can purchase milk from a milk bank. Milk banks, or places where women can buy human milk, were established as early as the 1920s, and allow women to buy nourishment for their infants without the ethical concerns raised by wet nursing. Yet the use of infant formula or milk banks is not so widespread in some parts of the world. In China, for example, where the quality of formula has been called into doubt by recent instances of contaminated or poisoned formula, the use of wet nurses has seen a resurgence, signaling that the practice still has value in certain parts of the world.

SEE ALSO: Breastfeeding in Historical and Comparative Perspective; Division of Labor, Gender; Midwifery

FURTHER READING

Fildes, Valerie A. 1986. *Breasts, Bottles, and Babies: A History of Infant Feeding*. Edinburgh: Edinburgh University Press.

Golden, Janet. 1996. *A Social History of Wet Nursing in America: From Breast to Bottle* Cambridge: Cambridge University Press.

Stuart-Macadam, Patricia, and Katherine A. Dettwyler, eds. 1995. *Breastfeeding: Biocultural Perspectives*. New York: Aldine de Gruyter.

Sussman, George D. 1982. *Selling Mother's Milk: The Wet-Nursing Business in France, 1715–1914*. Urbana: University of Illinois Press.

White Supremacy and Gender

ABBY L. FERBER
University of Colorado, Colorado Springs, USA

Gender and race are intertwined systems of inequality which shape the lives of everyone, including people who benefit from them. Over the past 25 years, research on whiteness and white supremacy that focuses on gender has grown, as has research on gender which takes into consideration whiteness. This work has developed in three strands of scholarship and critique: intersectional feminist theory; privilege studies; and whiteness studies.

INTERSECTIONALITY

Intersectional theories argue that race and gender, as well as other salient social identities, are intertwined and inseparable and cannot be fully comprehended on their own. Though the term is new, intersectional theory has a long history. Early African American theorists like Sojourner Truth, Frederick Douglass, Ida B. Wells, and Anna Julia Cooper critiqued the ways race divided the suffrage movement, and sex limited black women's participation in the abolitionist movement. Mid-century women of color again fought for full inclusion within the civil rights, Chicano, and women's movements. Intersectional scholarship grew out of the activism and scholarship of women of color arguing that their lives are simultaneously shaped by their race and their gender. For example, the battle for abortion rights became a central focus of the women's movement, reflecting white middle-class women's needs. Throughout US history, many women of color and disabled women have been sterilized without their consent. Once the intersections of race and gender were explored, a shift to focusing on the broader claim of reproductive rights and justice occurred. Over the past few decades, explicitly intersectional feminist analysis has accelerated.

WHITE PRIVILEGE

Privilege refers to the systemic favoring, valuing, validating, and including of certain social identities over others. Whiteness is a privileged status. To be white is to have greater access to rewards and valued resources simply because of group membership. Whites are seen as the average, normal, universal human. W. E. B. Du Bois and other African American scholars and activists have been writing about white privilege throughout US history. However, it was the work of Peggy McIntosh that spurred a focus on white privilege among white scholars across disciplines, especially sociology, psychology, and women's studies. McIntosh's classic article "White Privilege and Male Privilege" in 1988 was one of the first attempts by a white person to document the unearned advantages and conferred dominance whites experience on a daily basis. McIntosh's analysis of white privilege grew out of her understanding of the role of male privilege as an obstacle to women's equity.

Works by literary theorists, legal scholars, anthropologists, historians, and sociologists have contributed to the burgeoning field of whiteness studies, which examines the construction of white identity and the maintenance of white supremacy throughout Western European and US history (Morrison 1992; Brodkin 1998; Jacobson 1998).

Scholars have examined the construction of the United States as a white republic, and many feminist scholars have examined the role of gender in the construction of whiteness. Citizenship has been examined as both racialized and gendered. Schloesser (2002), for example, examines the ways that race was constructed through ideologies of white femininity during the founding period in the United States. As classifications of race were invented, the borders between races were maintained by policing sexuality and reproduction. The history of slavery and Jim Crow segregation depended upon firm knowledge of who was white and black for their support. As race mixing increased in the early Americas, punishments for interracial sexuality were instituted. In 1662, Virginia passed the first laws discouraging miscegenation and defining mulattoes born to slave mothers as slaves. Slave owners could reproduce slave labor by raping and impregnating their female slaves. The one-drop rule gained increased acceptance in the eighteenth century, regulating sexuality and births, so that any child born to a black woman would automatically be black. The regulation of women's sexuality was key to constructing white racial identity.

After the Civil War, the myth of the black male rapist was invented and became an excuse for lynching black men. The institution of lynching and the continued rape of black women contributed to maintaining the economic and political domination of African Americans. The pioneering works of Ida Wells Barnett, Mary Church Terrell, Anna Julia Cooper, and other black women at the time argued that the mechanisms of lynching and rape bolstered both racial and gender hierarchies maintaining white male dominance (Guy Sheftall 1995). Black men were denied access to patriarchal power and black women were defined as outside the construction of "womanhood." More recently, research on white men has found that they still harbor strong fears of interracial marriage and want to maintain their white lineage.

Gender has also been explored as playing a role in the incorporation of European ethnic immigrants into the category of whiteness. As immigrants arrived from new nations in Eastern and Southern Europe they occupied a middle position between whites and blacks. Feminist scholars have examined the specifically gendered identities these immigrants embraced in order to assimilate into the ideal of "whiteness." For example, specific images of the assimilated Jewish woman were constructed as the ideal to which immigrant Jews should aspire (Prell 1999).

Much of the contemporary work in whiteness studies does not include issues of gender beyond a side note. However, intersectional feminist scholarship has taken seriously the task of exploring whiteness and gender in a wide range of contexts, ranging from research in social work and development studies on the history of white women in charity work, and the desire to "help" the less fortunate; depictions of white femininity in the media and the law; the impact of race on white men and women's work histories; the experience of white mothers mothering children of color and examining their own whiteness; white women teaching children of color; white lesbian privilege in coming out and starting families, and many more. In sum, any issue that had previously been studied through a feminist lens is now subject to examination through a racialized feminist lens, where whiteness is taken as a subject to study in addition to the racial identities of minority women.

WHITE SUPREMACIST MOVEMENT

White racial purity has been the operating assumption underlying the construction of racial categories throughout US history, and also in the context of Western imperialism and colonialism around the globe. The white supremacist movement organized in the name of protecting white purity and maintaining white supremacy (they also do not see Jews as white). The Ku Klux Klan, historically the most influential white supremacist organization in the United States, was founded in 1865. The Klan grew in size and respect in the 1920s; membership increased from 5,000 in 1920 to between 4 and 5 million in 1925. It was not until the 1990s that scholars began studying the role of women and gender in the movement, beginning with Kathleen Blee's work on the Klan of the time, which engaged approximately 500,000 women as members of the women's auxiliary, Women of the Ku Klux Klan (2008).

Other scholars have since examined why the organized white racist movement has traditionally attracted and represented the position and interests of men, documenting both micro-level psychological and macro-level sociological reasons revolving centrally around issues of masculinity. Research on women in the movement has also found that they join for gendered reasons that reflect ideologies of women's place in society as well as their own gendered concerns. Blee has explored the various factors precipitating the increased recruitment of women into certain white supremacist organizations. The homegrown nature of the movement is due, in large part, to the reproductive and socialization labor of women. Women in the movement are responsible for the bearing and rearing of children, fulfilling their duty to reproduce the white race, and also educating and socializing their children to the racist beliefs, thereby reproducing the movement.

Many scholars have documented conflicting views within the movement regarding women's place. The greater participation of women in the contemporary movement has brought many of these issues to the fore. Nevertheless, the issue of gendered tactics is central to the roles played by both men and women in the movement, and the movement is being forced to respond to changing notions of appropriate gendered tactics for women as broader social constructs of womanhood have changed. Some research argues that women are now the glue that holds the movement together, forming and strengthening the social ties among members and forging a sense of collective identity. Women also make the movement more accessible and less threatening to the mainstream. They contribute to the seeming ordinariness of life in the movement. While women rarely fill leadership positions, they carry out a variety of informal activities nevertheless essential to the success of this social movement.

The movement voices both racialized and gendered goals throughout its literature and language. For example, in order to secure the existence of the white race, there is a strong emphasis upon the responsibility of white women to bear pure white children. The politics of reproduction is central to the movement and the goal of preserving the white race. The movement's tactics, behaviors, displays, and activities all take gendered forms as well. For example, while there is variation among the specific organizations, the men of the movement tend to adopt highly masculinized and warrior-like wardrobes, tattoos, boots, and so on. For women involved in the movement, the gendered tactics vary. For example, in some of organizations, women are encouraged to adopt an overly traditional, feminine role, serving refreshments at meetings and taking care of the men. Within other groups, however, this feminine image is questioned, and women seek to participate in the tactics defined as "masculine." Gendered tactics such as these are connected to the construction of gendered identities by the movement. Movement members select and perform specific, gendered identities. Finally, gendered attributions come into play. Outsiders to the movement attribute certain gendered attributes to movement members. For example, members of organized racist movements are often overly simplified by outsiders, and women are often dismissed as simply meek, submissive followers in the movement. Blee's life histories of 34 women in the movement dispel this myth. The movement itself also constructs gendered attributes *for others*. A number of scholars have examined the racialized, gendered identities and attributes constructed for people of color and Jews. The gendered white identities constructed by the movement for themselves are in direct opposition to the identities they construct for African Americans, Jews, and other non-whites.

There is much room for growth in research on the intersections of race and gender in the white supremacist movement, as well as in the field of whiteness studies more generally. At this point, the majority of the work on gender and whiteness is carried out by feminist and critical race scholars. There is a great deal of research that continues to examine whiteness in historical, legal, sociological, and psychological terms, without including any examination of gender. Intersectional theory and research has demonstrated the intertwined nature of social identities. Bringing gender more centrally into the study of the white supremacist movement and whiteness studies would advance our knowledge and scholarship, providing more complex and nuanced knowledge. In addition, work on gender and whiteness can further grow by adding in an examination of other systems of oppression and privilege where relevant, including class, disability, religion, and more.

SEE ALSO: Black Feminist Thought; Critical Race Theory; Rape Culture; Reproductive Justice and Reproductive Rights in the United States; Right-Wing Women's Movements; United States' Women's Movements in Historical Perspective

REFERENCES

Blee, Kathleen M. 2008. *Women of the Klan: Racism and Gender in the 1920s.* Berkeley: University of California Press.
Brodkin, Karen. 1998. *How Jews Became White Folks and What That Says About Race in America.* New Brunswick: Rutgers University Press.
Guy Sheftall, Beverly. 1995. *Words of Fire: An Anthology of African-American Feminist Thought.* New York: Norton.
Jacobson, Matthew Frye. 1998. *Whiteness of a Different Color: European Immigrants and the Alchemy of Race.* Cambridge, MA: Harvard University Press.
Morrison, Toni. 1992. *Playing in the Dark: Whiteness and the Literary Imagination.* New York: Vintage Books.
Prell, Riv-Ellen. 1999. *Fighting to Become American: Jews, Gender, and the Anxiety of Assimilation.* Boston: Beacon Press.
Schloesser, Pauline. 2002. *The Fair Sex: White Women and Racial Patriarchy in the Early American Republic.* New York: NYU Press.

FURTHER READING

Blee, Kathleen M. 2003. *Inside Organized Racism: Women in the Hate Movement.* Berkeley: University of California Press.
Collins, Patricia Hill. 2008. *Black Feminist Thought: Knowledge, Consciousness, and the Politics of Empowerment.* New York: Routledge.
Davis, Angela Y. 1983. *Women, Race, & Class.* New York: Vintage Books.
Ferber, Abby L. 1998. *White Man Falling: Race, Gender, and White Supremacy.* Lanham: Rowman & Littlefield.
Ferber, Abby L., ed. 2004. *Home-Grown Hate: Gender and the White Supremacist Movement.* New York: Routledge.
McIntosh, Peggy, with Michael Kimmel, eds. 2003, 2010, 2013. *Privilege: A Reader,* 1st ed. 2003; 2nd ed. 2010; 3rd ed. 2013. Boulder: Westview Press.
Roediger, David R. 2007. *The Wages of Whiteness: Race and the Making of the American Working Class.* New York: Verso.

Wicca

RENE A. JONES and KEITH KLOSTERMANN
Medaille College, USA

Wicca is an often misunderstood religious practice. Its roots stem from earth-based religions. In the 1940s, Gerald Gardner's book, *High Magic's Aid,* launched the religion into the public's eye. Wicca influenced the feminist and sexual revolution and continues to be one of the fastest growing religions in North America.

Wicca is a branch of the larger belief system of Paganism and is a nature-based religion. Pagans believed goddesses and gods were nature spirits; Sun, Fire, Rain, Thunder, etc. The supreme Goddess was in charge of human fertility. The God was usually horned to show his connection with animals and dealt with the fertility of animals. The connection with nature guided their beliefs and celebrations.

Those that practice Wicca are called Wiccans or witches. Their main purpose is to create balance within the self and the environment. One of the symbols that encompasses this concept is the pentagram (i.e., a five-pointed star). The five points represent the elements: air, earth, fire and water with the top point corresponding to "spirit." The pentagram, with a circle around it, can symbolize a cross-legged human with his/her hands out, surrounded by universal wisdom. Wicca is often confused with Satanism and its symbol, the upside-down pentagram. Wicca does not acknowledge a heaven or hell thus does not believe in Satan or a devil so therefore does not worship either creation.

Witches practice magick. Note: It is spelled with a "k" to differentiate itself from the illusionary magic conducted by performers. When working magick, there is a respect of all life and the primary premise is to harm none. The Threefold Law guides Wiccans by stating that whatever energy, thought, or wish a person puts into the universe, the universe will send back multiplied by three. Therefore witches do not use magic to harm or manipulate others. Free will is a fundamental aspect of the religion. Magick cannot be performed on behalf of anyone, without that person's permission.

Wicca honors the male and female energies and does not promote one sex as being greater than the other. This approach honors both the female/feminine and male/masculine and places emphasis on the female and the Goddess. The human body is considered beautiful and is honored. In addition, sexuality is viewed as pleasurable, positive, and healthy when consensual. Wiccans can practice monotheistic, duotheistic, polytheistic, henotheistic, or atheistic religion (no belief in a deity or deities). Many witches practice on their own, although there are covens (group of witches) that one may join. The ceremonies are guided by the cycles of nature and honor the environment.

Today, there are eight Wiccan Sabbats that are acknowledged and spaced about 45 days apart during the year. Four of these are minor Sabbats: the two equinoxes of March 21 and September 21 when the daytime and nighttime are each 12 hours long and the two solstices of December 21 (the longest night of the year), and June 21 (the shortest night of the year). The major Sabbats occur roughly midway between the minor Sabbats, typically at the end of the month. Different Wiccan traditions assign various names and dates to these festivals. Perhaps the most common names are Celtic: Samhain – October 31; Imbolc – February 2; Beltane – April 30; and Lammas – August 1.

In 1949, Gerald Gardner wrote *High Magic's Aid* under the pseudonym Scire (Hugh 2006). Gardner claimed he was initiated into a witch cult called the New Forest Coven, led by Dorothy Clutterbuck or "Old Dorothy." He said the work was fictional because the coven did not want their rituals revealed. Critics state that Gardner's work was based on the works of Aleister Crowley and Margaret Murray. Other criticisms concluded that Gardner was not actually a part of the coven and that the coven did not exist.

Despite the criticism, Wicca grew because of its beliefs of equality of the sexes and harmony with nature. It also reflected new attitudes towards sexuality. Gardner believed the human body contained its own inherent power, which could be awakened and channeled using various techniques or rituals (Hugh 2006). Gardner was a nudist and believed that magic should be practiced in this state, so as to not block the energy and the power of the magic. Many of the rituals in *Gardner's Book of Shadows* are done in the nude. Today most Wiccans practice clothed. There are those that practice sexual magic, but again most do not.

The rise of Wicca merged with radical feminism and the sexual revolution of the 1960s and 1970s (Hugh 2006). Both represent a rejection of political oppression and recognition of the inherent goodness of sexual pleasure for both males and females. They celebrated the female body and sexuality as something unique and different from male sexuality. The movements rejected patriarchal culture and affirmed female power. Although there was a preaching of female empowerment, the roles of women in Wicca were still traditional. They remained maidens, mothers, and crones or embodiments of Earth, nature, and fertility as opposed to adding hunters and warriors. Today, there seems to a shift in Wicca providing non-traditional roles and there are a variety of homosexual pagan movements like the Radical Faeries.

Wicca in the United States is a growing religion that continues to fight to be recognized by the government and other citizens. According to Kosmin and Keysar (2009) who were the primary investigators conducting the *American Religious Identification Survey (ARIS)* in 2008, there were 342,000 households practicing Wicca and 340,000 households who identified as Pagan. However, because many Wiccans keep their practice private, accurate numbers are difficult to acquire. Although the numbers are growing, the acknowledgment of Wicca as a legitimate religion by the United States is still a battle. Recent victorious court cases include prisons allowing incense for Wiccan rituals and the US military permitting deceased Wiccan veterans to have the pentagram on their grave stones.

SEE ALSO: Witches

REFERENCES

Kosmin, Barry, and Ariela Keysar. 2009. *American Religious Identification Survey 2008*. Hartford: Trinity College.

Urban, Hugh. 2006. *Magia Sexualis: Sex Magic, and Liberation in Western Esotercism*. Berkeley: University of California Press.

FURTHER READING

Curott, Phyllis. 2001. *Witch Crafting: A Spiritual Guide to Making Magic*. New York: Broadway Books.

Gibbons, Jenny. 2014. "Recent Developments in the Study of The Great European Witch Hunt." Accessed August 16, 2015, at http://web.archive.org/web/20051029023619/http://www.cog.org/witch_hunt.html.

Religious Tolerance. 2014. "Wicca: a Neopagan, Earth-Centered Religion." Accessed January 10, 2014, at http://www.religioustolerance.org/witchcra.htm.

Witches

DANIELLE DUMAINE and MARY-MARGARET MAHONEY
University of Connecticut, USA

The question of why women as a group were particularly vulnerable to accusations of witchcraft has served as a long-standing source of fascination. Between 1580 and 1650, scholars estimate that 100,000–200,000 men and women were brought to trial under accusations of witchcraft in Europe. Approximately 80 percent of those tried were women. Of the 342 accused witches in New England, 78 percent were women. That the history of witchcraft in the West is necessarily a history of gender and sexuality is undeniable. However, this history of witchcraft from the early modern period to the present is also bound up in histories of society, power, capitalism, and religious authority. Scholars have focused on discrete moments of crisis driven by the perceived threat of witches and, more recently, the heightened popularity of the popular practice of witchcraft.

The majority of women accused and executed for witchcraft date to the early modern period. Witch-hunting occurred throughout Europe, but was concentrated in Germany, France, and Britain. Scholars have focused their attention on the cultural and societal shifts that made witch-hunting possible in this period. Prior to the second half of the sixteenth century, witches, or "cunning folk" as they were more commonly referred to, coexisted with secular authorities and Christianity as a non-threating part of community life. Around the time of the Reformation, what had been a common belief in magic and sorcery was transformed into a site of conflict and suspicion. Whereas before individuals had been accused of witchcraft as a way of explaining common misfortune, witches were now seen as part of what historian John

Demos (2008) termed "a general plot to destroy God."

The *Malleus Maleficarum*, a guide to identifying witches authored by German Catholic clergyman Heinrich Kramer in 1486, is a source of particular interest in this history. While its use by witch-hunters has been debated, it is frequently referenced as an example of the potential misogyny inherent in the ways that women's bodies and sexuality figure in witch-hunting. When the figure of the witch became more threatening, they were no longer depicted as symbols of healing and magic, but instead as women who held midnight sabbats and engaged in sexual relationships with the devil.

Perhaps the most well known historical example of witch-hunts in the United States is the Salem witch trials of 1692. Over the course of several months, over 200 people were accused of witchcraft. Of the 20 who were convicted and executed, 13 were women. Some scholars have disregarded gender as a possible motivation for accusations, citing instead anxieties over the transition from an agrarian to capitalist economy, disputes between families, or reassertions of power by secular and religious authorities. Historian Mary Beth Norton (2002) argued that latent trauma from conflicts with local American Indians incited the witch trials. The most significant feminist intervention came from Carol Karlsen (1987), who argued that accusations of witchcraft were a means by which accusers could curtail the power of land-holding widows and the very poor. This built on a shared understanding by most scholars that women were targeted as witches because they were independent widows, marginal figures, or otherwise displayed non-normative behavior.

The practice of witchcraft and witch-hunting continues to the present although practices have diversified with increasing immigration and the import of newly developed neopagan beliefs. Witchcraft remained a marker of otherness, but took on the symbolism of racial, ethnic, religious, and class difference. In some cases the "witch-hunt" operated as a metaphor to describe the perceived domestic threat of communism that defined the Cold War. Arthur Miller's (1953) *The Crucible* explicitly connected contemporary attempts to demonize whole groups based on non-normative behaviors and beliefs to the literal witch-hunts of early America. Neopagan witchcraft emerged in post-World War II Britain as part of a rejection of modernity, socialism, and Christianity.

The "father" of modern witchcraft, also referred to as Wicca, is Gerald Gardner. Gardner claimed a spiritual ancestry to pre-Renaissance witches. His texts and practices traveled to the United States where they were adopted and reworked by radical feminists in the 1960s and 1970s. The feminist groups WITCH and Reclaiming are prominent examples of this practice. The New York based group Women's International Terrorist Conspiracy from Hell (WITCH) used the iconography of witches to protest capitalism and normative visions of femininity through guerrilla theater actions. The Reclaiming community of San Francisco, meanwhile, was defined by what sociologist Jone Salomonsen (2002) has described as "an attempt to construct new cultural visions and new religious agency and identity by means of nature oriented goddess worship and magical ritual performance."

The second half of the twentieth century also saw an increase in women as witches in mainstream popular culture. The 1960s sitcom *Bewitched* has been examined by scholars as representative of contemporary debates about women's power and domesticity (Herzog and Rollins 2012). The sitcom, which starred Elizabeth Montgomery as a witch trying to negotiate her magical powers while living as a "normal" housewife in a suburb, has been studied for what it can tell us about witches and witchcraft as a metaphor for cultural debates about communism, feminism, civil rights, anti-Semitism, and homosexuality. The show has been derided for depicting home as a site that stifles women's power while more recent scholarship has questioned whether it actually presents domestic life as a queer space that can showcase women's agency.

Sociologists have attributed the rise in the popularity of witchcraft among young women in the 1990s to positive depictions of witches in mainstream popular culture. Some examples of these depictions include *Sabrina the Teenaged Witch*, *Hocus Pocus*, *Charmed*, and *Buffy the Vampire Slayer*. While in the 1970s, sociologists observed that witchcraft provided a means for community building, in the 1990s, witchcraft served as a technology of selfhood and self-actualization, representative of a larger trend towards individualism (Berger and Ezzy 2009). The more recent popularity of the Harry Potter series of books and movies has fostered public discussion about witchcraft in popular culture. The series, which follows the training of a young boy in witchcraft to serve the public good, has complicated traditional gendering of witchcraft as something that is practiced by women and/or consumed and marketed towards them.

In the West, the figure of the witch has always solicited fascination and fear. Scholarship on witches will continually have to contend with the ways it shapes and is shaped by the culturally specific demands placed on the category of witch, both as a historical figure and on witchcraft as an ongoing spiritual practice.

SEE ALSO: Christianity, Gender and Sexuality; Feminist Theories of the Body; Mysticism; Wicca

REFERENCES

Berger, Helen A., and Douglas Ezzy. 2009. "Mass Media and Religious Identity: A Case Study of Young Witches." *Journal for the Scientific Study of Religion*, 48(3): 501–514.

Demos, John. 2008. *The Enemy Within: 2000 Years of Witch-hunting in the Western World*. New York: Viking.

Herzog, Amy, and Joe Rollins. 2012. "Editors' Note: Strange Magic." *Women's Studies Quarterly*, 40(3): 9–12.

Karlsen, Carol F. 1987. *The Devil in the Shape of a Woman: Witchcraft in Colonial New England*. New York: Norton.

Norton, Mary Beth. 2002. *In the Devil's Snare: The Salem Witchcraft Crisis of 1692*. New York: Random House.

Salmonsen, Jone. 2002. *Enchanted Feminism: The Reclaiming Witches of San Francisco*. New York: Routledge.

FURTHER READING

Boyer, Paul, and Stephen Nissenbaum. 1974. *Salem Possessed: The Social Origins of Witchcraft*. Cambridge, MA: Harvard University Press.

Briggs, Robin. 1996. *Witches and Neighbors: The Social and Cultural Context of European Witchcraft*. New York: Viking.

Women Suicide Bombers (LTTE, Sri Lanka)

V.G. JULIE RAJAN
Rutgers University, New Jersey, USA

Women suicide bombers have been active in various insurgencies and terrorist groups since the 1980s. In rebel movements arising in Lebanon, Turkey, Chechnya, Sri Lanka, Jordan, Iraq, Uzbekistan, Pakistan, Palestine/Israel, Kashmir, and Afghanistan, many women willingly strap bombs to themselves in order to fight for their cause – most often nationalist struggles – killing themselves in order to kill their enemies. This entry focuses on the case of the Liberation Tigers of Tamil Eelam (LTTE), a group in Sri Lanka that fought for 40 years to liberate themselves from the racist postcolonial policies of the Sri Lankan majority.

Women suicide bombers deployed by the LTTE are notorious for executing missions killing high-level targets and mass numbers of people. The ethnic Tamil, predominantly Hindu (90 percent) LTTE used these bombers, known as Black Tigresses, in its decades-long struggle (which killed upwards of 65,000 and displaced over 700,000) against the Sri Lankan government (Swamy 1994; Hopgood 2005; Whaley Eager 2008; Roberts 2010). The LTTE aimed to establish a separate Tamil nation (Tamil Eelam) within Sri Lanka that would secure the Tamil minority (16 percent of Sri Lanka) community against nearly a century of socioeconomic, militant violence by Sri Lanka's majority (74 percent) Buddhist, ethnic Singhalese. Tamils occupy lands primarily in the north (Jaffna and Vavuniya) and east (Trincomalee and Batticaloa) (Bloom 2005; Hopgood 2005). Established in 1976 by Velupillai Prabhakaran, the LTTE claimed affiliations with over 14 front organizations globally, and by 2000 boasted cadres numbering from 10,000 to 14,000 (Pape 2005).

While some LTTE did train for suicide missions with Hezbollah, the LTTE perfected the suicide vest and belt emulated in most suicide missions globally today (Neary 2009). Since its first mission in July 1987, the rebel group pursued the most consistent, lengthy suicide campaign globally in the postcolonial era. Executing anywhere from 76 to 200 attacks during the 1990s, the LTTE targeted politicians such as Sri Lankan president Ranasinghe Premadasa in 1993; national infrastructures, such as oil depots and financial centers; and Sri Lanka's military, wiping out half of its air force planes (Hopgood 2005; Pape 2005; Miller 2007).

The LTTE is known for its active recruitment of numerous Tamil women; approximately 4,000 of the 14,000-strong LTTE in the 1990s (Pape 2005). Although in some cases women were abducted and forced to join the LTTE, numerous women have joined the LTTE of their own accord for various reasons: to secure Tamil Eelam; for protection against sexual violence in the conflict; to escape poverty; fighting for women's rights; and fighting against violence against Tamil women in the war (Jordan and Denov 2007). LTTE women cadres engaged in direct combat through a separate women's wing, *Viduthali Pulikal Munani* (Women's Front of Liberation Tigers). They were housed separately; planned and ran their own operations; and underwent six months of training to acquire expertise in combat, explosives, and strategy (Whaley Eager 2008). Women also participated in the LTTE's naval squad, the Sea Tigers. The prevalence of LTTE women cadres engaging in direct combat is evidenced in Sri Lankan government estimates of LTTE deaths: of the 17,648 total deaths recorded through 2002, 3,766 were of women (Gonzalez-Perez 2009).

The LTTE is most notorious for its deployment of numerous women to affect suicide missions, which the LTTE references as martyrdom operations. Like men, LTTE women applied to become suicide attackers and, if accepted, underwent year-long trainings in preparation for their missions. Black Tigresses executed from 29 to 40 percent (thwarted and successful) of the LTTE's total suicide missions (Whaley Eager 2008; Speckhard 2009) and some of its most notable missions including 25-year-old Dhanu's (Thenmozhi Rajaratnam) assassination of then Indian prime minister Rajiv Gandhi in 1991, killing 17; and on February 9, 2009, a Black Tigress targeting Brigadier Shavendra Silva, the commander of Sri Lanka Army's 58 Division, blew herself up at an internally displaced person rescue center in Mullaitivu, killing 30 and injuring 64. The success of LTTE women-initiated bombings, experts suggest, has proven a role model for women suicide bombers in other movements globally, notably in Palestine.

SEE ALSO: Nationalism and Gender; Third World Women; War, International Violence, and Gender

REFERENCES

Bloom, Mia. 2005. *Dying to Kill: The Allure of Suicide Terror*. New York: Columbia.

Gonzalez-Perez, Margaret. 2009. *Women and Terrorism: Female Activity in Domestic and International Terror Groups*. New York: Routledge.

Hopgood, Stephen. 2005. "Tamil Tigers, 1987–2002." In *Making Sense of Suicide Missions*, edited by Diego Gambetta. New York: Oxford University Press.

Jordan, Kim, and Myriam Denov. 2007. "Birds of Freedom? Perspectives on Female Emancipation and Sri Lanka's Liberation Tigers of Tamil Eelam." *Journal of International Women's Studies*, 9(1): 42–62.

Miller, Debra A. 2007. *Suicide Bombers*. New York: Lucent.

Neary, Lynn. 2009. Interview with Robert Pape. "Tamil Tigers: Suicide Bombing Innovators." Accessed August 21, 2015, at http://www.npr.org/templates/story/story.php?storyId=104391493.

Pape, Robert A. 2005. *Dying to Win: The Strategic Logic of Suicide Terrorism*. New York: Random House.

Roberts, Michael. 2010. "Killing Rajiv Gandhi: Dhanu's Sacrificial Metamorphosis in Death." *South Asian History and Culture*, 1(1): 25–41.

Speckhard, Anne. 2009. "Female Suicide Bombers in Iraq." *Democracy and Security*, 5(1): 19–50.

Swamy, M.R. Narayan. 1994. *Tigers of Lanka: From Boys to Guerillas*. Colombo: Vijatha Yapa.

Whaley Eager, Paige. 2008. *From Freedom Fighters to Terrorists*. Aldershot: Ashgate.

FURTHER READING

Rajan, V.G. Julie. 2011. *Women Suicide Bombers: Narratives of Violence*. London: Routledge.

Skaine, Rosemary. 2006. *Female Suicide Bombers*. Jefferson: McFarland.

Woman-Centeredness

GLORIA GIARRATANO
Louisiana State University Health Sciences Center
New Orleans, USA

Woman-centeredness is an ideological statement for societal or institutional transformation to liberate women and put women at the center. The movement to transform institutions in order to express and embody women-centeredness has its roots in radical feminism. Theoretical tenets of radical feminism are based on the belief that patriarchal power structures oppress women and are so embedded in societal institutions that even legal, economic, or political means alone can correct them. Only when these patriarchal structures become transformed or recreated within to reverse the oppression of women and instill the practice of feminist values can women-centeredness be achieved.

Both feminist values and deliberate actions are key to the praxis of woman-centeredness. Only by promoting the empowerment and education of women and by disrupting the power structures from within can the transformation of institutions occur and the philosophy of women-centeredness be practiced. Then the services, products, or relationships within the societal institution can change to support and focus on the best interests of women. In optimal circumstances, women's best interests are defined from a post-modern perspective which acknowledges that women of different cultural, ethnic, or social circumstance require alternative options which become available to them in a women-centered, liberated environment.

Women-centeredness is a term found in varied fields such as education, art, religion, business, and healthcare to describe changes required to recreate environments so that women are at the center. Using the concept of women-centeredness, discourse focuses on how to transform institutions so that women's perspectives and needs are at the forefront, which will give women power and authority to make decisions that affect them.

Healthcare discourse using woman-centeredness ideology is the most explicit in describing how to liberate women. Woman-centeredness ideology in healthcare is described and disseminated as frameworks, models, or approaches to deliver care guided by this philosophy. Led primarily by birth anthropologists and feminist caregivers, including midwives, nurses, women's health and childbirth advocates, and childbirth organizations, woman-centeredness models of healthcare go beyond reproductive issues. It includes liberating and changing women's healthcare for young girls, for immigrant women experiencing violence, for cardiac rehabilitation, and for breast care.

The focus on changing the healthcare environment using woman-centeredness ideology was a response to the oppression women experienced in traditional healthcare institutions. Modern medicine emerged in the twentieth century as primarily a paternalist structure that medicalized the female body and its normal reproductive ability. In Western countries, reproductive health experiences of women were highly controlled, especially with regard to contraception and childbirth. In response to these constrictions, the Women's Health Movement worked to transform the traditional institutions of women's healthcare delivery into a women-centered philosophy of healthcare. Feminist Women's Health Centers (FWHCs) emerged in the United States in the 1970s (Ruzek 1978). According to Thomas and Zimmerman (2007, 360) the FWHCs were designed as woman-centered places where "women cared for other women, women were the subject of care, and women were partners and active participants in their healthcare."

Likewise, nurses, childbirth advocates, childbirth organizations, and midwifery maternity care providers in the United Kingdom, Australia and the United States worked to transform the modern culture of childbirth to reflect woman-centeredness in the twentieth century. Because midwife means "with woman," and centers on supporting a woman's power and authority to give birth in the way she chooses, the literature sometimes interprets the midwifery model of childbirth and woman-centeredness in childbirth to mean the same (Rothman 1991; Carolan and Hodnett 2007).

Feminist values that convey woman-centeredness in healthcare may differ with the specific healthcare providers and organizations, but each shares commonalities. In woman-centered healthcare environments, the caregivers acknowledge and respect the personal context of healthcare needs in a woman's life. Childbirth, contraceptive, or abortion services, for example, are not medical procedures or sporadic events, but major life experiences that carry with them personal meanings for women. These woman-centered healthcare providers respect and support the decisions that women make about their healthcare. Caregivers practicing woman-centeredness maintain equal partnerships and meaningful relationships with women where shared decision-making with the woman and her family is the norm. To establish this relationship, the woman has full access to appropriate educational and medical information related to her care which would ensure that she understands the implications for decisions that she may have to make. Since women are made aware of all their options and have full access to choices, they can exert control over their experiences. The institution where the caregiver practices (hospital, clinic) makes effort to offer the preferred services or may refer women to institutions that can provide these services. Finally, women make their own decisions by consulting with whom they choose (intimate partners, family members, healthcare professionals, religious leaders) but without coercion by other people. The goal is to provide education and a supportive environment that empowers women to make the best decisions for themselves (Center for Health and Gender Equality 2010; Australian College of Midwives 2011).

One controversial issue debated among childbirth providers using woman-centeredness philosophy concerns the role of modern medical technology in natural childbirth. On the one hand, childbirth advocates describe woman-centered care to mean that women are to be supported in such a way that pain medication or continuous electronic monitoring should not be used or be warranted. However, other childbirth providers not only recognize the supportive environment for natural childbirth as primary, but also see the use of technology as an issue that women should be knowledgeable about before childbirth, which includes knowing how certain technology and pain medication might impede natural childbirth. In the end, however, women make their own personal decisions in a woman-centered care environment. More recently, physicians developed techniques referred to as woman-centered cesarean birth for those situations where a surgical birth is indicated for medical reasons. These surgical techniques are aimed at a gentle, slow birth of the baby and provide the mother an opportunity to view and hold the baby in the surgical suite (Camann and Barbieri 2013).

Co-optation of woman-centeredness is also documented and identified as a concern among healthcare activists seeking to change institutions. Stratigaki (2004, 1–2) defines co-optation as occurring when "the [feminist] goals of … proposals are undermined by shifting the meanings of the original concepts to fit into the prevailing political and economic priorities … resulting in the loss of their potential for changing gender relations." Co-optation of woman-centered healthcare was a response to the early feminist women's movement as patriarchal institutions recognized the potential economic gain in promoting women's health as a commodity. The 1990s saw a proliferation of women's health centers, programs, pavilions, and birthing centers. These "women's centers" were marketed as special places where care is responsive to women's preferences and their special needs. However, many of these institutions focus on superficial, cultural meanings of femininity to include cosmetic touches, such as rooms painted with soft tones, fluffy robes, on-call masseuse, and special meals. Birthing balls and water tubs are placed in birth units to simulate natural childbirth practices, while technological devices such as fetal monitors are hidden in armoires until the woman is admitted to the room. The preferred use of technology and medical procedures during birth remain the norm and the woman has less decision-making power and fewer choices about the labor experience. Nurses and midwives who practice in co-opted birth environments describe how the desire to use woman-centeredness to guide care is often thwarted by institutional systems not centered on women, but on the medical system. This practice includes, for example, the routine use of induction or forceps to speed the time of birth (Davis-Floyd and Sargent 1997; Giarratano 2003). These types of healthcare centers may appear to address women's needs but are actually developed for economic gain by hospitals that entice women as consumers rather than liberating women and eliminating oppression.

SEE ALSO: Feminism, Radical; Patriarchy; Reproductive Health; Women's Centers;

Womanism

KIMBERLY P. JOHNSON
Tennessee State University, USA

Womanism is a liberation movement that originated as a result of feminism's racial divide and the gender divide of the civil rights movement. The moment black women were called to the aid of white feminists to put black males "in their place," black men and black women entered into a crisis relationship with each other. As long as black men are unable to break the strongholds of a white patriarchal society, they will continue to see feminism and feminist movements as a threat to their upward mobility. Likewise, the more women are expected to stay silent in exchange for the advancement of the black male, women's liberation will never be achieved. Although men sympathized with the cause of women's rights activists, they were not willing to risk their own political advancement for the right to vote. As a result, black women were placed between supporting either "women's suffrage" or "manhood suffrage." To align themselves with the women's suffrage movement would partner them with white feminists who were already openly racist against black men. Yet, if they aligned themselves with manhood suffragists, civil rights activists, this would cause them to endorse a patriarchal social order that would inevitably continue to silence women.

Alice Walker questioned the paradigms of oppression and she credits the civil rights movement as the influence that caused her to redefine her own existence from feminist to womanist, which then propelled the ideological practices of womanism into action. The civil rights movement gave Walker a reason to look beyond herself and her gender, and it encouraged her to get involved not only in the life of her community, but also in the world at large. Walker was already a feminist

---

Women's Health Movement in the United States

REFERENCES

Australian College of Midwives. 2011. *AMC Philosophy for Midwifery*. Accessed May 8, 2014, at http://www.midwives.org.au/scripts/cgiip.exe/WService=MIDW/ccms.r?pageid=10019.

Camann, William, and Robert L. Barbieri. 2013. "Mother-, Baby-, and Family-Centered Cesarean Delivery: It Is Possible." *OBG Management*, 25(3): 10–15.

Carolan, Mary, and Ellen Hodnett. 2007. "'With Woman' Philosophy: Examining the Evidence, Answering the Questions." *Nursing Inquiry*, 14(2): 140–152.

Center for Health and Gender Equality. 2010. *A Woman-Centered Approach to the U.S. Global Health Initiative*. Washington, DC: Center for Health and Gender Equity.

Davis-Floyd, Robbie E., and Carolyn F. Sargent, eds. 1997. *Childbirth and Authoritative Knowledge: Cross-Cultural Perspectives*. Los Angeles: University of California Press.

Giarratano, Gloria. 2003. "Woman-Centered Maternity Nursing Education and Practice." *The Journal of Perinatal Education*, 12(1): 18–28.

Rothman, Barbara K. 1991. *In Labor: Women and Power in the Birthplace*. New York: Norton.

Ruzek, Sheryl B. 1978. *The Women's Health Movement*. New York: Praeger.

Stratigaki, Maria. 2004. "The Cooptation of Gender Concepts in EU Policies: the Case of 'Reconciliation of Work and Family'." *Social Politics*, 11(1): 30–56.

Thomas, Jan E., and Mary K. Zimmerman. 2007. "Feminism and Profit in American Hospitals: the Corporate Construction of Women's Health Centers." *Gender and Society*, 21: 359–383.

FURTHER READING

Holmes, Helen B., Betty B. Hoskins, and Michael Gross, eds. 1980. *Birth Control and Controlling Birth: Woman-Centered Perspectives*. Clifton: Humana Press.

Shields, Sara G., and Lucy M. Candib. 2010. *Woman-Centered Care in Pregnancy and Childbirth*. Oxford: Radcliffe Publishing.

before the civil rights movement. She knew about standing in solidarity with her fellow African American sisters, but she had not yet stood in or fought for the solidarity of the American people as a whole. According to Walker, to fight is to exist and existence means knowing the difference between what you are and what you were, being capable of looking after yourself both intellectually and financially, knowing when you are being wronged and by whom, being able to protect yourself and the ones you love, being part of the world community, being alert to which part of the community you have joined, and knowing how to change to a different part if that part does not suit you (Walker 1983). Walker's fight for liberation included the freedom for her to define her own existence and the freedom of choice to not be forced into supporting one movement over the other.

Alice Walker's activism is what set womanism into motion. The 1979 publication of a short story, "Coming Apart," represents the first time that Walker gave utterance to the term *womanist*. Then, in 1983, she supplied the meaning of her newly defined womanist existence through the publication of her book, *In Search of Our Mothers' Gardens: Womanist Prose*. Her definition is as follows (Walker 1983):

1. From womanish. (Opp. of "girlish," i.e., frivolous, irresponsible, not serious.) A black feminist or feminist of color. From the black folk expression of mothers to female children, "You acting womanish," i.e., like a woman. Usually referring to outrageous, audacious, courageous or *willful* behavior. Wanting to know more and in greater depth than is considered "good" for one. Interested in grown-up doings. Acting grown up. Being grown up. Interchangeable with another black fold expression: "You trying to be grown." Responsible. In charge. *Serious*.
2. *Also*: A woman who loves other women, sexually and/or nonsexually. Appreciates and prefers women's culture, women's emotional flexibility (values tears as natural counter-balance of laughter), and women's strength. Sometimes loves individual men, sexually and/or nonsexually. Committed to survival and wholeness of entire people, male and female. Not a separatist, except periodically, for health. Traditionally universalist, as in "Mama, why are we brown, pink, and yellow, and our cousins are white, beige, and black?" Ans.: "Well, you know the colored race is just like a flower garden, with every color flower represented." Traditionally capable, as in: "Mama, I'm walking to Canada and I'm taking you and a bunch of other slaves with me." Reply: "It wouldn't be the first time."
3. Loves music. Loves dance. Loves the moon. *Loves* the Spirit. Loves love and food and roundness. Loves struggle. *Loves* the Folk. Loves herself. *Regardless*.
4. Womanist is to feminist as purple is to lavender.

Walker's definition claims that a womanist is committed to the survival and wholeness of all people regardless of race, class, gender, or sexuality. Womanists love life, love being responsible, and most importantly love themselves.

BROADER PERSPECTIVES ON WOMANISM

Womanist theology came out of the dissatisfaction with feminist theology, which neglected to look at issues of race and class, and black liberation theology (and black preaching), which neglected to consider the issue of gender (Flake 2007). African American women needed a theology that would address and confront all of the sins that oppressed them and the black community. In 1985, womanist theology emerged as a methodological perspective of religious scholars. Katie Geneva Cannon, Jacquelyn Grant, and Delores Williams are acknowledged as the founders of womanist theology within the American Academy of Religion

(Floyd-Thomas 2006). These three women discovered that economic exploitation, discrimination, racism, sexism, and segregation require African American women to construct their own set of values and virtues that will allow them to conduct themselves with moral integrity in the midst of suffering. As a result, they began to follow in the footsteps of Walker by not letting society define who they are; and so, they redefined themselves within their own theological understanding of Christianity.

In 1985, Chikwenye Okonjo Ogunyemi also questioned the ability of feminism, more specifically white feminism, to represent fully African and Afro-American women, which led her to coin the term *African womanism*. This perspective is situated in the African experience and it applies to the traditional African religions in addition to the African-derived religions in the global African diaspora. The main focus of African womanism is to combat racism. This type of womanism understands black sexism as a microcosmic replica of Euro-American racism – a racist hegemonic power structure exercised over African and Afro-American women by Western culture (Ogunyemi 2006).

Two years later, in 1987, Clenora Hudson-Weems (2006) coined the term *Africana womanism*. This perspective is situated within the Africana culture and it examines womanism through the lenses of African studies, black nationalism, and pan-Africanism. Africana womanism recognizes racism and classism, on both national and global levels, as their most prominent obstacles in their collective struggle toward survival. This type of womanism requires African women and men to work together within Africana communities to fight collectively for the survival and wholeness of all Africana people.

Ultimately, the practices and ideologies of womanism work toward dismantling the hegemonic power structures that continue to oppress those who are marginalized. Womanism broadens the goal of the Women's Liberation Movement and even reaches beyond the African American female to give voice to all who are silenced (male and female – within the United States, Africa, and the global African diaspora) and to liberate all who are oppressed. This liberation movement promotes freedom from economic, political, social, and religious oppression worldwide. Womanist activism is expressed through womanist literature, womanist theology, womanist preaching, womanist discourse, womanist epistemology, and womanist ethics.

SEE ALSO: Womanist; Womanist Theology

REFERENCES

Flake, Elaine. 2007. *God in Her Midst: Preaching Healing to Wounded Women*. Valley Forge: Judson Press.

Floyd-Thomas, Stacey M., ed. 2006. *Deeper Shades of Purple: Womanism in Religion and Society*. New York: NYU Press.

Hudson-Weems, Clenora. 2006. "Africana Womanism (1993)." In *The Womanist Reader*, ed. Layli Phillips, 47. New York: Routledge.

Ogunyemi, Chikwenye Okonjo. 2006. "Chikwenye Okonjo Ogunyemi's African Womanism." In *The Womanist Reader*, ed. Layli Phillips, 22–26. New York: Routledge.

FURTHER READING

Cannon, Katie. 1995. *Katie's Canon: Womanism and the Soul of the Black Community*. New York: Continuum.

Houston, Marsha, and Olga Idriss Davis, eds. 2002. *Centering Ourselves: African American Feminist and Womanist Studies of Discourse*. Cresskill: Hampton Press.

Mitchem, Stephanie Y. 2005. *Introducing Womanist Theology*. Maryknoll: New York.

Phillips, Layli, ed. 2006. *The Womanist Reader*. New York: Routledge.

Spelman, Elizabeth V. 1998. *Inessential Woman: Problems of Exclusion in Feminist Thought*. Boston: Beacon Press.

Thomas, Linda. 1998. "Womanist Theology, Epistemology, and a New Anthropological Paradigm." *CrossCurrents*, 48: 488–499.

Townes, Emilie M. 1996. "Ethics as an Art of Doing the Work Our Souls Must Have." In *The Arts of Ministry: Feminist–Womanist Approaches*, edited by Christie Cozad Neuger, 143–161. Louisville: Westminster John Knox Press.

Walker, Alice. 1983. *In Search of Our Mothers' Gardens: Womanist Prose*. Orlando: Harcourt.

Womanist

KHADIJAH O. MILLER
Norfolk State University, USA

In 1983, Alice Walker's *In Search of Our Mothers' Gardens* defined "womanist" as:

> From *womanish*. (Opp. of "girlish," i.e., frivolous, irresponsible, not serious.) A black feminist or feminist of color. From the black folk expression of mothers to female children, "You acting womanish," i.e., like a woman. Usually referring to outrageous, audacious, courageous or willful behavior. Wanting to know more and in greater depth than is considered "good" for one. Interested in grown-up doings. Acting grown up. Being grown up. Interchangeable with another black folk expression: "You trying to be grown." Responsible. In charge. *Serious*. (Walker 1983, xi)

Womanism or a womanist comes from womanish (Tsuruta 2012, 4). Womanist stems from an African American or black American cultural context and resonates in their history. It is a term that alludes to self-agency and empowerment of black women (and girls) who are boisterous, brave, sassy, bold, and bodacious. Womanist is a self-defining term that has been considered and actualized among black women for centuries; credit is given to Walker for re-presenting this idea of being "womanish" among African Americans. Tsutura clarifies that womanist comes from womanish, rooted in the black community idea of having gumption. "The concept of "gumption" means common sense, courage, and intuitive, points toward the importance of self-determination in defining womanism and maintaining the cultural integrity of it and its root ideal, womanish" (2012, 5).

A womanist is one who speaks, acts, and responds according to her lived experiences as a black woman. A womanist places black women at the center of inquiry; she does not negate others nor does she purport that her situation is universal; rather, creates a safe space of inquiry, dialogue, research, expression, analysis, and syntheses in an authentic black woman-centered process. A womanist is devoted to the wholeness and survival of her people. She is community-centered and survival-focused. JoAnne Banks-Wallace surmises,

> Walker's definition provides a space to (1) recognize the uniqueness of African American women's experiences, (2) articulate the similarities and differences between these experiences and those of other women of color, and (3) address explicitly the important bond between African American women and men (Banks-Wallace 2006, 316).

Womanists do not assert that there is a composite black woman or composite/universal experience of black women or women of color. Womanists accommodate diversity in thought, expression, and experience. Womanists identify as African-centered womanists, Africana womanists, and Afrocentric womanists (see Ogunyemi 1985; Kolawole 1997; Hudson-Weems 2004). Naming is important; it serves as identification and placement of space, location, validity, and purpose. Afrocentric, Africana, and African-centered womanists seek to explicitly link their experiences, foci, and analysis on their culturally distinct, self-determined and self-standing intellectual, social, political, cultural, and historical elements. It is framed within African culture for its intellectual and practical initiatives. For some, Walker's definition is a fine starting place to assert and self-define black women's experiences throughout the world, with many adding, refining, and executing particularities. However, Ogunyemi attests to the specific and unique experiences of African women and separates her use of womanism distinctly from Walker. All definitions speak to the complexities of African, Africana, black, African American, and women of color.

Womanists are self-confident and independent of comparisons to others. Womanists are not defined by whom they are not, but rather defined by who they are and to what they belong – the black community. Although in Walker's definition, womanists are defined as black feminists, they are not. There are black feminists who are not womanists (bell hooks, Angela Davis, Beverly Guy-Sheftall, Audre Lorde, Barbara Smith) as there are womanists who are not black feminists. The terms are not the same and have different meanings, connotations, and implications.

The term "womanist" is often used among academicians, but it is also used in political, social, and community circles. Womanist academicians offer a methodological position that is conversational in approach – often writing in first person and/or first person plural. Womanists create space – literal and figurative, questioning, challenging, engaging, and reinforcing their own knowledge construction. Major thinkers include Ogunyemi (1985), Cannon (1995), Phillips (1995), Kolawole (1997), Hudson-Weems (2004), Banks-Wallace (2006), and Tsuruta (2012).

A womanist is concerned with the wholeness of women – her connection to her community and humanity as a whole. Hudson-Weems states that a womanist's "sense of wholeness is necessarily compatible with her cultural consciousness and authentic existence" (Hudson-Weems 2004, 69). A womanist is responsible, serious, and in charge of her life. A womanist sees herself and her sisters – black women – as active agents in their lives and the lives of their community.

SEE ALSO: Critical Race Theory; Feminism, Black; Postfeminism

REFERENCES

Banks-Wallace, JoAnne. 2006. "Womanist Ways of Knowing: Theoretical Considerations for Research and African American Women." In *The Womanist Reader*, edited by Layli Phillips, 316–326. New York: Routledge.

Cannon, Katie. 1995. *Katie's Canon: Womanism and the Soul of the Black Community*. New York: Continuum.

Hudson-Weems, Clenora. 2004. *Africana Womanism: Reclaiming Ourselves*. New York: Bedford Publishers.

Kolawole, Mary E. Modupe. 1997. *Womanism and African Consciousness*. Trenton: Africa World Press.

Ogunyemi, Chikwenye Okonjo. 1985. "Womanism: The Dynamics of the Contemporary Black Female Novel in English." *Signs: Journal of Women in Culture and Society*, 11(1): 63–80.

Phillips, Layli and Barbara McCaskill. 1995. "Who's Schooling Who? Black Women and the Bringing of the Everyday into Academe, or Why We Started 'The Womanist'." *Signs*, 20(4): 1007–1018.

Tsuruta, Dorothy Randall. 2012. "The Womanish Roots of Womanism: A Culturally-Derived and African-Centered Ideal (Concept)." *The Western Journal of Black Studies*, 36(1): 3–10.

Walker, Alice. 1983. *In Search of Our Mothers' Gardens: Womanist Prose*. San Diego: Harcourt Brace Jovanovich.

FURTHER READING

Arndt, Susan. "African Gender Trouble and African Womanism: An Interview with Chikwenye Oguynyemi and Wanjira Muthoni." *Signs*, 25(3): 709–726.

Karenga, Maulana, and Tsuruta, Dorothy Randall. 2012. "African-Centered Womanism: Recovery, Reconstruction and Renewal." *The Western Journal of Black Studies*, 36(1): 1–2.

Womanist Theology

KHADIJAH O. MILLER
Norfolk State University, USA

Womanist theology is a God-centered conceptual framework and practice. It is grounded in the religious and spiritual scholarship and experiences of women of color – African American/black, African, Caribbean, Latina. In its infancy womanist theology craved a space outside of black liberation theology (Cone 1998) and feminist theology, with particular religious focus on black Christian women's experiences. However, as it has developed over the last 25 years, womanist theology is a responsive resolve to include the silent, forgotten, unsung voices of women of color and faith; with a deconstructionist, reconstructionist, and revivalist intent to empower women, and assert their place in God's world and word.

Womanist theology was developed out of Alice Walker's 1983 definition of womanist, meaning one who is "acting womanish … wanting to know more and in greater depth than is good for one – outrageous, audacious, courageous and willful behavior." A womanist is also "responsible, in charge, serious" (Walker 1993, xi-xii). Womanist theology provides a rational inquiry to provide an authentic assessment, reflection, review, analysis, and framework for intellectual, religious scholarship that focuses on African American women, and in later development, women of color, and her relationship with God.

Not feminist theology or black liberation theology, Womanist theology builds upon the unique dimensions of liberation, life experiences, and spaces of inquiry for African American women. Womanist theology includes a methodology that has multi-dialogical, liturgical, and didactic intents. Womanist theology revisits the social construction of black womanhood in relation to her role in the African American community, a community of faith, and in the world in general. Using women's voices in history, literature, folklore, storytelling, song, poetry, narratives, and other sources, womanist theology provides humanity to the full experiences of African American women.

First-wave womanist theologian scholar, Katie G. Cannon refers to womanist theology as "the methodological framework that the vast majority of African American women have been using … [since 1985] to challenge inherited traditions of androcentric patriarchy, and as a method of engaging in revolutionary acts of resistance as members of the American Academy of Religion and the Society of Biblical Literature" (1998, 96). Womanist theology affords a name for African American religious scholars to critically identify "the particularities of God's presence in our everyday realities, because such clarity enhances our ability to tap the sacred foundation of our common humanity" (1998, 96).

Womanist theology is fluid and lucid. The first wave of womanist theologians includes Cannon, Jacqueline Grant, and Renita J. Weems. Their seminal texts, *Black Womanist Ethics* (Cannon 1988), *White Women's Christ and Black Women's Jesus: Feminist Christology and Womanist Response* (Grant 1989), and *Just a Sister Away: A Womanist Vision of Women's Relationships in the Bible* (Weems 1988) carved space for a discussion that continues to develop today. Delores Williams, another founding womanist theologian, wrote *Sisters in the Wilderness: The Challenge of Womanist God Talk* in 1993, which established that womanist theology is woman talk about God. It creates a space for another voice and interpretation of God, God's word and God's truth as it relates to black women. Womanist theology doesn't purport to have one singular black woman's truth – but instead creates a space for her multiple truths including class, gender/sex, sexuality, ability, age, race, and ethnicity.

Other first-wave womanist theologians include Emilie Townes, Cheryl Townsend Gilkes, Delores Williams, Kelly Brown Douglas, Shawn Copeland, Clarice Martin, Francis Wood, Karen Baker-Fletcher, Jamie Phelp, Marcia Riggs, and Cheryl Kirk-Duggan. Contemporary or third-wave womanist theologians include A. Elaine Brown Crawford, Monica Coleman, LaReine-Marie Mosely, and Darnise Martin. Womanist theologians are in seminary, university and divinity schools as well as practicing preachers. Womanist theologians include ordained and lay women in all facets of extraordinary life.

Womanist theology purports to unearth the quiet, often overlooked aspects of women's lives – struggles, survival, plights, and highlights. Combining both sacred and secular sources and applications to uncover, challenge, create and define, womanist theology defines African American women in their vast complexities. Womanist theology uses Black women as "agents of culture and community" (Gilkes 2001, 5) to provide a broad-based humanist perspective that "signals the unity of the sacred and the secular in African American reality" (Williams 1993, 160).

In simple terms, womanist theology centralizes African American women's languages and showcases their lens of the world in a conscientious and conscious manner allowing voice, community, and identity. Womanist theology gives priority to African American women as "positive affirmation of gifts from God" (Thomas 1998, 2). Overlapping with black liberation theology, feminist, and black feminist theories, womanist theology carves a unique space giving authority to the diversity of black women theologians. Womanist theology is faith-conscious, culturally based on African American traditions, and woman-centered lending voice and actions for African American women. Womanist theology challenges hegemonic structures in theology and feminism, providing a hermeneutical perspective. Among its goals is to seek understanding and enlightenment of others, confront oppression in all its many forms, and seek justice, human agency, harmony, and balance – carving a space for all in God's world and word.

SEE ALSO: Critical Race Theory; Feminism, Black

REFERENCES

Cannon, Katie. 1998. *Black Womanist Ethics*. Atlanta: Scholars Press.

Cone, James H., and Gayraud S. Wilmore, eds. 1993. *Black Theology: A Documentary History*, vol. 1, 1966–1979, 2nd ed., revised; vol. 2, 1980–1992. Maryknoll: Orbis Books.

Gilkes, Cheryl. 2001. *If it Wasn't for the Women … Black Women's Experience and Womanist Culture in Church and the Community*. Maryknoll: Orbis Books.

Thomas, Linda. 1998. "Womanist Theology, Epistemology, and a New Anthropological Paradigm." *Cross Currents*, 48(4): 488–499.

Walker, Alice. 1983. *In Search of Our Mothers' Gardens: Womanist Prose*, xi–xii. San Diego: Harcourt Brace Jovanovich.

Weems, Renita. 1993. "Womanist Reflections on Biblical Hermeneutics." In *Black Theology: A Documentary History*, 2nd ed., vol. 2, 1980–1992, edited by James H. Cone and Gayraud S. Wilmore, 216–224. Maryknoll: Orbis Books.

Williams, Delores. 1993. *Sisters in the Wilderness*. Maryknoll: Orbis Books.

FURTHER READING

Baker-Fletcher, Karen. 1998. *Sisters of Dust, Sisters of Spirit: Womanist Wordings on God and Creation*. Minneapolis: Fortress.

Townes, Emilie. 1993. *Womanist Justice, Womanist Hope*. Atlanta: Scholars Press.

Women in Combat

LISA DeLANCE
University of California, Riverside, USA

Women in combat refers to the direct participation of women, those individuals whose sexual identity is female, regardless of gender identity, in military combat operations. Combat means any organized military action undertaken by soldiers against an opposing group, including guerrilla fighting and political rebellion. Cultural constructions of gender, popularized gender ideology, population demographics, political salience, and national threat all influence the decision to either allow or deny women the opportunity to serve as combatants in a national military unit.

In a study of women's military roles, Mady Weschsler Segal (1995) notes several trends regarding women in combat positions and hypothesizes that in situations where the threat to national security is significant, women will be active combatants until the threat subsides, at which point they will return to their pre-threat gendered roles. In societies where national security is not threatened, but cultural values encourage equal treatment, women are likely to pursue combat-related vocational positions in the military. In societies where national security is not significantly threatened and cultural values are not egalitarian, women will not participate extensively, if at all, in combat. Additionally, women tend to take active and sometimes prominent positions in revolutionary fighting. Women combatants were featured prominently among Viet Cong soldiers during the Vietnam conflict of the 1960s and 1970s. In the mid-nineteenth century, women actively participated in the Taiping Rebellion of southern China as administrators of the Taiping Heavenly Kingdom and as military officers. During the Nicaraguan Revolution, women were active participants in the Sandinista National Liberation Front. During World War II, women were active insurgents and resistance fighters against Nazi Germany. Women also played a crucial role as freedom fighters in the Zimbabwean struggle for independence from colonial rule. In cases of revolution or rebellion, gender ideology is suspended as women and men both fight for their cause; however, once the revolutions are complete and combat is no longer necessary, traditional gender ideology is often reinvigorated and women often become excluded from political and military communities that they helped to found.

Historically, women have served in direct combat positions in many different cultures and over many different time periods. In Roman Britain, Queen Boudica (Boadicea) not only fought but led Celtic soldiers into battle against Roman forces. Similarly, female members of the Germanic tribes participated in combat operations against invading Roman forces during the first century CE. In Shang-dynasty China, Fu Hao served as a military general and high priestess, as well as one of the wives of King Wu Ding. In the 1400s, Joan of Arc led French troops to several important victories during the Hundred Years' War before being burned at the stake as a heretic. Between 1600 and 1900, approximately 4,000 Dahomean women, dubbed "Amazons" by European observers, served as combatants during wars with invading French forces. In some instances, women who were prohibited from participating in active combat disguised their sexual identity in order to fight. In the sixteenth century, Brita Olofsdotter disguised her identity and fought for the Swedish military in Lavonia. During the American Revolution, Deborah Sampson served as a male in the Continental Army, taking on the identity "Robert Shurtliff." During the United States Civil War, Loretta Janeta Velazquez disguised her gender and took on the identity of "Confederate Lieutenant Harry T. Buford," fighting in several notable battles. Greek mythology highlights Epipole of Carystus, a woman who disguised her identity and fought with the Greeks in the Trojan War. In China during the Middle Ages, the Ballad of Mulan celebrated a female who assumed the identity of a male and fought in combat on behalf of her family.

The participation of women in combat became an issue on a global scale starting with World War I in the early twentieth century. Intense and large-scale fighting in Eastern Europe required women to fight in battles, both as soldiers and as civilian combatants. Although not officially sanctioned, many Russian women volunteered for duty on the front lines during this engagement, and Russian soldier Maria Bochkareva formed the first all-female combat battalion of World War I.

During World War II, United States women served in a variety of units with many different positions. In 1942, women from the Women's Auxiliary Combat Corps were trained in the use of anti-aircraft guns. Despite the fact that the women from these units performed well above the standard of achievement and despite the fact that they were recommended by training officers for combat duty, they were not assigned to official combat roles and were placed in administrative positions at the behest of lawmakers who decried any deviation from the gendered norms of the time. In Great Britain, women were trained as anti-aircraft gunnery operators during World War II. While not allowed to actually fire the anti-aircraft gun, they served alongside male counterparts and were granted official military status in 1941. In Germany, Nazi ideology prohibited the training of women in the use of weapons, although several women participated in piecemeal combat operations in times of urgent necessity. Although a women's infantry unit was finally authorized in the final months of the war, the unit never materialized and the few German women who participated in combat operations were considered anomalies. In 1939, the Soviet Union authorized women to serve not only in traditional roles such as nursing and training, but also as tank drivers, anti-aircraft operators, combat pilots, and snipers. During World War II, Lyudmila Pavlichenko served as a sniper for the Soviet Army and became one of the most decorated snipers on either side of the war. After World War II, female soldiers returned to their standard positions as administrative assistants and nurses.

During the last half of the twentieth century, social movements fighting for the rights of women to equal opportunity in the workplace have reinvigorated a discussion of training female soldiers for combat. While women have been gaining immense ground in equal opportunity struggles, the discussion of women in combat remains a contentious issue. Contemporary debates regarding the suitability for women in combat operations focus on issues that question the combat effectiveness of mixed gendered military units and tend to use both biologically and psychologically based arguments. Limitations-style arguments stress that women are by nature physically and mentally unsuited to perform in combat. Effects-style arguments stress that men would not be able to control their own physical and mental drives around women in a combat situation.

Proponents of the *biological limitations* argument stress the biological structure of the female body limits its effectiveness in combat operations. Furthermore, these arguments tend to stress the role of women as progenitors of society and demand that they be kept out of harm's way in order to safely reproduce. The biological processes used to argue this point include pregnancy and personal hygiene needs and emotions related to menses; however, the determination as to what exactly these needs are is as much a cultural issue as a biological one. Proponents of these types of arguments claim that natural biological processes are incompatible with the unsanitary conditions that combat soldiers are required to live in; however, there are many ways to deal with feminine hygiene that are compatible with unsanitary conditions. These arguments further state that women naturally lack the requisite upper body strength to be able to carry and use combat equipment; however, critics point out that when combat equipment is designed to be compatible with female physiology, women will be able to carry and use combat equipment with little issue.

Proponents of the *psychological limitations* argument stress the psychological nature of combat will irrevocably damage the female psyche. These arguments tend to stress the sensitivity of women as nurturers and their inability to perform under intense and often deadly conditions due to their emotional temperament. This argument tends to be used in conjunction with studies that demonstrate a higher rate of reported stress and anxiety on behalf of women rather than their male colleagues, although these studies generally project an arguable bias in data collection. The psychological limitations argument obfuscates cultural components of stress and anxiety, and attempts to implicitly demonstrate that females are naturally ill-equipped to manage intense stress and make emotional decisions under stress. Critics argue that there is nothing in the psychological makeup of women that makes them necessarily more mentally fragile than men and note that the very definition of mental fragility is culturally constructed.

Proponents of the *biological effects* argument stress that female combatants are a sexual distraction for their male comrades, which will result in decreased combat effectiveness of the overall unit as male soldiers will inevitably be physically and uncontrollably attracted to their female comrades and will form romantic attachments to them. At issue in this argument is males' ability to control their biological sexual drives for women; however, this argument makes the assumption that all male combat soldiers have a biological attraction to women, something that has yet to be proven. This argument also fails to take into account that it is possible that there are combat soldiers who form intimate relationships with their male comrades. Although these relationships are generally not made public, no evidence has been presented that they damage the combat effectiveness of the military unit. A second element of this argument discusses the phenomenon of combat rape, in which female soldiers in combat zones are sexually assaulted by their male comrades. Proponents of biological effects arguments claim that such sexual assault damages unit integrity and the most effective way to curb this is to not allow women to be in combat zones in the first place. Critics of these arguments state that the responsibility for male physical control should be placed on males themselves rather than on females.

Proponents of *psychological effects* arguments stress that the combat effectiveness of male soldiers will decrease as they become distracted by their drive to protect their female comrades and psychologically devastated when or if they are unable to protect them. An extension of this argument claims that men are genetically programmed to protect and care for women, something that will interfere with the performance of their duties and endanger lives. This argument was used successfully in 1948 by the Israeli Defense Force (IDF) when it claimed that male soldiers developed a protective instinct for their female comrades and experienced severe psychological damage at seeing female combatants killed in action. After this incident, women were prohibited from combat in Israel, a decision that stood until 2001 when the IDF allowed women to serve in combat on a trial basis. This incident framed further arguments against women in combat by multiple countries for a large portion of the later twentieth century. Critics of psychological effects arguments claim that there is no evidence to support the contention that men have a psychological drive to protect women, and that any such behaviors are culturally construed.

Currently, the majority of countries in the world prohibit women from serving in combat-related positions; however, in many countries, women are allowed, even encouraged, to pursue other military-related vocations that do not directly involve combat. Countries that currently allow women to pursue combat-related military positions are Australia, Canada, New Zealand, Norway, Sweden, and, most recently, the United States; however, the logistics of implementation are still being debated. Few countries prohibit any female involvement in military operations.

Feminist scholars (e.g., Enloe 2004) who are researching the phenomenon of women in combat generally note the impact of militarism on gender ideologies. The act of combat is a small subset of the larger phenomenon of militarism, and it has been suggested that militarism itself creates a model for the masculinization of both male and female subjects. Yet for females in the military, the choice to embody masculinization comes at the cost of being assumed to be homosexual, while the choice to embody femininity comes at the cost of being assumed to be weak, physically and mentally.

Due to significant technological developments in the practice of warfare, many argue that the "front line" has effectively disappeared, as battles are waged from a distance using technology such as drone machines and fighter planes. In many cases, official warfare is conducted from controlled rooms utilizing computerized systems that value hand–eye coordination as much as physical prowess. In recent years, actual combatants have used guerrilla-style tactics, as seen in the wars in both Iraq and Afghanistan; close combat fighting generally includes ambushes, suicide bombings, and other attacks on military personnel who are not primarily considered combatants. As a result, female soldiers in non-combat vocations frequently encounter and participate in close-quarter combat alongside their male comrades. Women who have experienced this type of combat have frequently been given accolades for intelligence and bravery under fire by their male comrades. In addition to technological changes in the way that war is conducted, social attitudes favoring comprehensively equal treatment for both women and men are becoming more salient in discussions of combat readiness and compulsory military service. Although many countries allow for males to be drafted into military service, most do not permit the same for females. Some countries allow women to be conscripted into medical or administrative vocations but not into combat roles; however, that is changing as the debate to allow women to serve in combat roles intensifies. As dialogues concerning the militarization of women evolve to critically examine the nuances of gender ideology, it is likely that more combat positions will be opened to and fulfilled by women globally.

SEE ALSO: Amazons, Dahomey; Gender Role Ideology; Militarism and Gender-Based Violence; War, International Violence, and Gender

REFERENCES

Enloe, Cynthia. 2004. "'Gender' Is Not Enough: The Need for a Feminist Consciousness." *International Affairs (Royal Institute of International Affairs 1944–)*, 80(1): 95–97.

Segal, Mady Weschsler. 1995. "Women's Military Roles Cross-Nationally: Past, Present, and Future." *Gender & Society*, 9(6): 757–775.

FURTHER READING

Campbell, D'Ann. 1993. "Women in Combat: The World War II Experience in the United States, Great Britain, Germany and the Soviet Union." *Journal of Military History*, 57(2): 301–323.

Carreiras, Helena. 2006. *Gender and the Military: Women in the Armed Forces of Western Democracies*. New York: Routledge.

Enloe, Cynthia. 2000. *Maneuvers: The International Politics of Militarizing Women's Lives*. Berkeley: University of California Press.

Fenner, Lorry, and Marie deYoung. 2001. *Women in Combat: Civic Duty or Military Liability?* Washington, DC: Georgetown University Press.

Firestone, Juanita M. 1984. "Sexist Ideology and the Evaluation Criteria Used to Assess Women's Integration into the Army." *Population Research and Policy Review*, 3(1): 77–95.

Gailey, Christine Ward. 1991. "The Case for Women Warriors." *Boston Sunday Herald*, August 18: 25.

Partlow, Frank A., Jr. 1984. "Womanpower for a Superpower: The National Security Implications of Women in the United States Army." *World Affairs*, 146(4): 290–317.

Thompson, Mark. 2013. "American Amazons: Hiding in Plain-Jane Sight." *Time US*, January 28.

Women as Cultural Markers/Bearers

BRONWYN WINTER
The University of Sydney, Australia

Women have been mobilized as cultural markers/bearers most particularly in relation to nationalist discourse, including in the (re-)invention of tradition (Hobsbawm and Ranger 1992). Within subnational identity politics, women have similarly taken on symbolic roles, both within and outside (post)colonial frameworks. Feminist scholarship has looked at the use of women as markers and bearers of culture in relation to three main areas: nationalism and in particular the extreme right, such as Nazism, with its notorious Kinder–Küche–Kirche (children, kitchen, and church) ideology, although the party never used the actual slogan in so many words (Koonz 1987); anti-colonial/anti-imperialist national movements; and (ethno-)religious identity, this last having been treated most copiously, albeit not exclusively in relation to Islam, notably since the Islamic revival which began in roughly the 1970s. The scholarship examines both the deployment of women as symbols through their appearance and behavior, and women's own ambiguous relationships to these cultural roles, whether as participants (willing or not), defenders, and advocates, educators through maternal transmission of values to daughters and sons, or alternatively as resistants who attempt to create new cultural values.

WOMEN, CULTURE, AND NATION 1: INCARNATING THE NATION

Female symbols have come to represent the nation and its values for both the right and the left. One can see a proliferation of such symbols in post-revolutionary Republican contexts such as Marianne in France (Winter 2009), the Statue of Liberty, offered as a gift from France to the United States in 1886, or the (also French-inspired) Efígie de la República in Portugal (short-lived) and particularly Brazil (enduring). There are also a number of "Mother of the Nation" symbols throughout Eastern Europe and extending into Scandinavia, sometimes associated with regional mythology. All of these female symbols have been laden with incarnating both ideal national values (justice, liberty, national cohesion) and ideal-type women: mother, protector, prioritizing duty and nation.

Other female symbols of national/cultural identity have emerged as sometimes semi-mythologized "founding mother" figures, often through their association through marriage or blood relationship to male figures. Thus, Neang Neak, wife of Preah Thong, is considered the pre-Angkorian "mother" of Khmer nation and culture in Cambodia, and Fatima Jinnah, sister of Muhammad Ali Jinnah and founding member of the Muslim League, is considered the "mother" of Pakistan. Other legendary but perhaps rarer figures have symbolized national resistance to invaders, such as Boudicca, Queen of the Iceni, who in the first century led a rebellion against Roman invasion of what is now Britain, or Al-Kahina, the Berber queen who led resistance in what is now Algeria to the Arab Islamic expansion in North Africa in the seventh century. Significantly, Boudicca disappeared from medieval histories of Britain, and was not rehabilitated until the nineteenth century, when she was romanticized through a symbolic and literary association with Queen Victoria. As for Al-Kahina, she featured in a number of legends, often being attributed with supernatural powers, and has been celebrated by North African-born feminist writers such as the late Assia Djebar (1995) and the lawyer and activist Gisèle Halimi (2006). Indeed, some warrior women have been "rehabilitated" by second-wave feminists, not because they embodied the nation and its values, but because they embodied female strength and resistance. Joan of Arc, a fifteenth-century Catholic mystic who cross-dressed in order to fight for Catholic France in the Hundred Years War, is one of the most celebrated examples of such feminist reclaiming, although she is also a rather unfortunate choice because her primary values were God, King, and Country, and she is furthermore claimed as a symbol by the extreme-right French party the National Front. The "unearthing" of women warriors and legendary figures has nonetheless inspired second-wave feminists in search of evidence of pre-patriarchal traditions or women's resistance to masculinist prescriptions (e.g., Davis-Kimball and Behan 2003; Miles and Cross 2011; Mayor 2014). Thus, Joan of Arc figures in feminist iconography because of her defiance of norms dictated to her sex at that time, and has even been celebrated in performance as a lesbian–feminist hero (Gage 2008).

Beyond these ideal-type fictional and legendary symbols, flesh-and-blood "ordinary" women have fairly consistently been used as markers of culture and national cohesion, most conspicuously during times of crisis or perceived crisis. Thus, during the two world wars of the twentieth century, Western countries mobilized women as "keepers of the homefires," performing feminized tasks associated with the war effort, especially during World War I, and – particularly during World War II – as participants in the national war effort through their paid labor. The well-known US image of Rosie the Riveter has been part of this nationalist cultural campaign, although research suggests that national policies towards women and labor during World War II were not as unified or progressive as the Rosie the Riveter image may suggest, and enforced gendered behavior along class and race lines, as well as maintaining prescriptions of dutiful wife behavior alongside the imagery of working women (Honey 1984; Knaff 2012). Post-World War II, women's magazines and popular culture ensured that the induction of women into an ostensibly democratizing mass culture and increasing participation in public life remained firmly rooted to women's idealized role within heterosexuality and family, the bedrocks of national culture (Winter 2013). Accompanying these cultural prescriptions were prescriptions about clothing and appearance, as the new consumerism fashioned the middle-class, high-heeled, properly undergarmented, bejeweled and made-up woman as its most significant icon.

WOMEN, CULTURE, AND NATION 2: ANTI-COLONIAL AND ETHNO-RELIGIOUS EXPRESSIONS

The iconography of the appropriately dressed and appropriately behaving woman as representative of culture and nation has similarly been played out in anti-colonial contexts. Control of women's appearance and behavior has been the stake in the conflict between the "penetrating" colonizer and the "emasculated" and "raped" colonized nation – metaphors commonly used in colonial and anti-colonial imagery (Enloe 1990; hooks 1990). Both colonizers and colonized thus engaged in prescriptions concerning the appropriate national/cultural behavior of women, and a number of feminist scholars have pointed out that Western feminists often reproduced colonial attitudes in their critiques of "traditional" gendered cultural practices (Narayan 1997). Feminist scholarship has also shown, however, and across a variety of contexts, that post-colonial or anti-imperialist cultural identity politics have nonetheless rested heavily on the shoulders of women, who are expected to dress and behave in culturally appropriate ways, even when these cultural "traditions" are often invented or imported from elsewhere and then reified as "indigenous" to the cultures/nations in question (Moghadam 1993, 1994; Narayan 1997; Yuval-Davis 1997). Among the aspects of women's appearance and gendered cultural practices that have been fetishized by men, none has been more copiously discussed than the Islamic headscarf. Debates over veiling have led to the production of vast amounts of both mainstream and scholarly literature that has argued the point about the whys and wherefores of veiling and its relationship to national or Islamic culture, to personal expressions of faith or identity politics, to cultures of racism or fundamentalism, and indeed to female resistance and feminism (e.g., Moghadam 1993; Moghissi 1999; Mahmood 2005; Winter 2008; Ahmed 2011). The debate over the headscarf and veil has been one of the most heated and polarized in women's studies forums, and shows little sign of abating, given the geopolitical framework in which it has been waged since at least the 1980s, with an added edge since 9/11. The fact that this item of clothing has also been so important to both Muslim and Western *men*, and so fiercely politicized, is in itself indicative of the significance attached to women's appearance as a marker of cultural/ethnic/national belonging.

Beyond the hijab debates, however, feminist practitioners and scholars have also engaged more with religion and spirituality, both mainstream and alternative, as forms of resistance to male cultural and religious supremacy. Either they have challenged religious traditions from within – such as Wadud's "gender jihad" (Wadud 2006; Trible and Lipsett 2014) – or sought affirmations of an alternative spiritual culture that is woman-centered and feminist in its expression (Christ and Plaskow 1979; Christ 1998). These various feminist challenges from both within and outside male-dominated religions are indicative of the continued importance of religion in culture and politics, including for those who identify as cultural resistants. The question of the imbrication of religious traditions within gendered cultural practices, and indeed political and social life, even in supposedly secular countries, has been a fraught one for feminist scholars. Regardless of their personal views on religion and/or spirituality, they have had to grapple with the fact that religious beliefs, norms, and customs regulate a great deal of women's lives and are indeed deeply internalized by women themselves. Moreover, religious values are also often imbricated with questions of race and class, both within and across nations. Battles over cultural/religious identities and meanings reveal the difficulties encountered by feminists in attempting to envision and to theorize alternative cultural practices when the dominant ones are all around us and indeed within us, especially when women's culturally appropriate behavior is so minutely scrutinized and policed.

WOMEN AS AGENTS OF CULTURAL TRANSMISSION

Women themselves also participate in such cultural policing of other women, and nowhere more so than through the delegated authority they hold as mothers. Already in the 1970s feminists were writing of the transmission of woman-hating cultures and gendered role prescriptions from mother to daughter [one of the most famous early works on the subject being that of Belotti (1973)] The extension of parental transmission of gendered cultural values and practices to other contexts, such as the education system, has also been discussed (e.g., Thorne 1993). Another area of feminist scholarship on the role of mothers in cultural transmission has focused on son preference and concomitant devaluing of daughters, as well as on the status women derive from being mothers of sons (e.g., Lacoste-Dujardin 1985). Son preference has had particularly disastrous demographic consequences in China (Attané 2013).

Given the importance attached to women as markers and bearers of culture, the concurrent lack of attention paid to girl children may appear somewhat paradoxical at first glance. Yet there is no real contradiction. First, the scholarship shows that girl children are paid attention, but they are paid attention in specifically gendered ways, learning early to perform the cultural roles expected of them. Second, the status women derive from son preference is consistent with the expectation that women's primary function, including cultural function, is to serve the needs of men. Moreover, that status is contingent on having sons and is only a temporary delegated authority. Third, the symbolic function of women as cultural markers, bearers, and transmitters is not to be cultural actors as such but rather to represent masculinist conceptualizations of culture and women's place within it.

SEE ALSO: Gender as a Practice; Nationalism and Gender; Popular Culture and Gender

REFERENCES

Ahmed, Leila. 2011. *A Quiet Revolution: The Veil's Resurgence, from the Middle East to America.* New Haven: Yale University Press.

Attané, Isabelle. 2013. *The Demographic Masculinization of China: Hoping for a Son.* Paris: INED/Springer.

Belotti, Elena Gianini. 1973. *Dalla parte delle bambine.* Milan: Feltrinelli.

Christ, Carol. 1998. *Rebirth of the Goddess: Finding Meaning in Feminist Spirituality.* New York: Routledge.

Christ, Carol, and Judith Plaskow. 1979. *Womanspirit Rising, a Feminist Reader in Religion.* New York: Harper and Row.

Davis-Kimball, Jeannine, and Mona Behan. 2003. *Warrior Women: An Archaeologist's Search for History's Hidden Heroines.* New York: Warner Books.

Djebar, Assia. 1995. *Vaste est la prison.* Paris: Albin Michel.

Enloe, Cynthia. 1990. *Bananas, Beaches and Bases: Making Feminist Sense of International Politics.* Berkeley: University of California Press.

Gage, Carolyn. 2008. *The Second Coming of Joan of Arc and Selected Plays.* Parker: Outskirts Press.

Halimi, Gisèle. 2006. *La Kahina.* Paris: Plon.

Hobsbawm, Eric, and Terence Ranger, eds. 1992. *The Invention of Tradition.* Cambridge: Cambridge University Press.

Honey, Maureen. 1984. *Creating Rosie the Riveter: Class, Gender and Propaganda During World*

War II. Amherst: University of Massachussetts Press.
hooks, bell. 1990. *Yearning: Race, Gender, and Cultural Politics*. Boston: South End Press.
Knaff, Donna B. 2012. *Beyond Rosie the Riveter: Women of World War II in American Popular Graphic Art*. Lawrence: University Press of Kansas.
Koonz, Claudia. 1987. *Mothers in the Fatherland: Women, the Family, and Nazi Politics*. London: St Martin's Press.
Lacoste-Dujardin, Camille. 1985. *Des Mères contre les femmes. Maternité et patriarcat au Maghreb*. Paris: La Découverte.
Mayor, Adrienne. 2014. *The Amazons: Lives and Legends of Warrior Women Across the Ancient World*. Princeton: Princeton University Press.
Miles, Rosalind, and Robin Cross. 2011. *Warrior Women: 3000 years of Courage and Heroism*. New York: Metro Books.
Mahmood, Saba. 2005. *Politics of Piety: The Islamic Revival and the Feminist Subject*. Princeton: Princeton University Press.
Moghadam, Valentine M. 1993. *Modernizing Women: Gender and Social Change in the Middle East*. Boulder: Lynne Rienner Publishers.
Moghadam, Valentine M., ed. 1994. *Identity Politics and Women: Cultural Reassertions and Feminisms in International Perspective*. Boulder: Westview Press.
Moghissi, Haideh. 1999. *Feminism and Islamic Fundamentalism: The Limits of Postmodern Analysis*. London: Zed Books.
Narayan, Uma. 1997. *Dislocating Cultures: Identities, Traditions and Third World Feminism*. New York: Routledge.
Thorne, Barrie. 1993. *Gender Play: Girls and Boys in School*. New Brunswick: Rutgers University Press.
Trible, Phyllis, and B. Diane Lipsett. 2014. *Faith and Feminism: Ecumenical Essays*. Louisville: Westminster John Knox Press.
Wadud, Amina. 2006. *Inside the Gender Jihad: Women's Reform in Islam*. London: Oneworld Books.
Winter, Bronwyn. 2008. *Hijab and the Republic: Uncovering the French Headscarf Debate*. Syracuse: Syracuse University Press.
Winter, Bronwyn. 2009. "Marianne Goes Multicultural: Ni putes ni soumises and the Republicanisation of Ethnic Minority Women in France." *French History and Civilization: Papers from the George Rudé Seminar*, vol. 2. www.h-france.net/rude/rudepapers.html.
Winter, Bronwyn. 2013. "Politicising the Personal: Questioning the Public/Private Divide." In *A Cultural History of Women in the Modern Age*, edited by Liz Conor (vol. 6 of *A Cultural History of Women*, edited by Linda Kalof), 97–118. London: Bloomsbury.
Yuval-Davis, Nira. 1997. *Gender and Nation*. London: Sage.

Women in Development

JENNA BASILIERE
Indiana University, USA

Women in development (WID) is a term used to describe a number of different development policies deployed by governments, donor agencies, and non-governmental organizations (NGOs) in the developing world in the 1970s and 1980s. The WID approach to development represents one of many attempts to incorporate issues of gender inequality into existing development policies. WID policies focus primarily on issues of gender equity and women's productive contributions to local economies. These approaches to development draw heavily on the principles of second-wave feminism in the West, and resist "trickle-down" approaches to economic growth. Rather, WID policies emphasize participatory approaches to economic development.

Prior to 1970, development policies either took women for granted or were interested in the welfare of women as mothers, primarily in the contexts of family health and lowering of fertility rates in overpopulated countries. The gender-neutral assumptions of welfare politics were first challenged by the Danish economist Ester Boserup (1970), who made groundbreaking claims that development had a differential impact on men and women;

that women did not necessarily benefit when male heads-of-household gained increases in income and social status; and that women's economic contributions to local economies were invisible to policymakers.

The women in development (WID) approach was introduced into public discourse through the 1975 United Nations World Conference of the International Women's Year at Mexico City and the United Nations Decade for Women (1976–1985). These public events illustrated the global interest in development issues concerning women in the 1970s and 1980s. The key strands of WID are identified by Caroline Moser (1993) as welfare, equity, anti-poverty, efficiency, and empowerment. These strands shared the goal of elevating women out of poverty through a change in their relationship to capital and production. In particular, the empowerment strain sought to make women agents of change in their own economic future, and transform their relationship to the mode of production in their community. This approach was more collective than other WID strands, and sought to elevate women as a community rather than as individuals.

The WID framework focused primarily on ways to incorporate women into the already existing development framework, assuming that the same economic relief strategies that worked for men could be unilaterally applied to women with only minor changes to allow for gendered differences in need.

Different strands of the WID model were used to advocate for gender equality in a number of ways. The first was through a substantive rejection of women's classification primarily as mothers. Under the anti-poverty strand of WID, women's subordination was seen as economic. This assumption brought with it an understanding that power and status were intrinsically linked to economic contributions. Thus, improving women's position would also decrease the gendered disparities between men and women. Proponents of this WID model took steps such as highlighting the agricultural contributions of women in rural communities and lobbying to have women's labor more accurately included in gross national products (GNPs).

Second, strategies such as the efficiency strand of WID policies countered the perceived gender bias in existing development projects through the creation of women-only development initiatives. These initiatives sought to counter assumptions about labor production within familial structures, and provided women opportunities to generate revenue outside of their households. Practices such as hands-on job training and the advance of small loans (microcredit) available only to women provided the opportunity for women to combat their own social position by changing their relationship to poverty. The efficiency approach argues that development work is more effective when relations between men and women are accounted for, and rests on the premise that women have something unique and valuable to contribute to development projects.

Finally, WID policies interested in empowerment provided women in developing countries with a voice to articulate their identities. Women's organizations and other self-identified feminist groups began using the language of WID to make justice claims in their home contexts. Even though WID policies never explicitly addressed issues of social justice, they provided a language for those interested in doing justice work to make legitimized claims to women-centered organizing.

While the WID approach arguably brought about a number of positive changes in international development communities, there were several critiques of this model. First, there was concern that the exclusive focus on economic inequality overlooked other systemic social inequalities. Second, many claimed that the WID approach treated women as a homogeneous category, and in doing so overlooked issues of race, ethnicity, class, religion, marital status, or age. Finally, the exclusive focus on women in the WID approach arguably forecloses opportunities for men to act as allies or potential beneficiaries of WID development policies.

In response to these critiques, there was a push toward a more nuanced approach to gendered issues of development that focused on the construction of gender roles, and the sociological necessity of investigating gender roles independently before attempting to address gendered issues of development. The series of approaches that arose out of this critique are now colloquially referred to as gender and development (GAD) policies. While GAD has emerged as a significant discursive shift in our understanding of the relationship between gender and development, its implementation has been less universal. In the absence of a universal language to talk about gender relations and their relationship to inequality, many development agencies still return to WID policies to drive their daily interventions.

SEE ALSO: Economic Globalization and Gender; Feminism, Materialist; Feminisms, Marxist and Socialist; Gender and Development; Microcredit and Microlending; Poverty in Global Perspective

REFERENCES

Boserup, Ester. 1970. *Women's Role in Economic Development*. London: Allen and Unwin.
Moser, Caroline. 1993. *Gender Planning and Development: Theory, Practice and Training*. New York: Routledge.

FURTHER READING

Rai, Shirin M. 2008. *The Gender Politics of Development*. New York: Zed Books.
Rathgeber, Eva M. 1990. "WID, WAD, GAD: Trends in Research and Practice." *Journal of Developing Areas*, 24(1): 489–502.

Razavi, Shahra. 1997. "Fitting Gender into Development Institutions." *World Development*, 25(7): 1111–1125.
Razavi, Shahra, and Carol Miller. 1995. "From WID to GAD: Conceptual Shifts in the Women and Development Discourse." *United Nations Research Institute for Social Development*, Occasional Paper 1.

Women in Non-Traditional Work Fields

VIVIAN PRICE
California State University, Dominguez Hills, USA

Women try to raise their standard of living by entering non-traditional occupations, jobs from which they have long been excluded or marginalized for reasons of culture, discrimination, contract, or law. They have been attracted to these jobs in part because male-dominated employment generally pays better than female-dominated jobs. Aside from pay, there have always been women who sought ways to follow their own interests, or reshape the profile of jobs in society and further equal opportunities. The US Department of Labor Women's Bureau begins its definition of non-traditional occupations in quantitative terms, as ones "in which women comprise 25 percent or less of total employment." This definition encompasses a spectrum of jobs from manual labor to the highest managerial positions. The bureaucratic wording hides a harsh reality: like women who work in construction, transportation, mining, and other manual or protective and security services work, many women in management, science, engineering, architecture, even law and medicine, find themselves a small minority in their workplace. Many are concentrated in the lowest status jobs in their field and are often treated as tokens or anomalies.

This categorization also masks tremendous challenges. Some women in non-traditional jobs find ways to adapt, survive, and even thrive; some suffer from injury, stress, humiliation, isolation, lack of training, sexual harassment, or assault. Some will not have any privacy or running water, while others will have a key to the bathroom. This entry focuses on the non-traditional as found in manual "blue-collar" jobs. This entry is written from personal experience, both as a white journey-level union electrician living in the United States, and as a researcher, scholar, organizer, and filmmaker of the issues facing women in non-traditional jobs internationally.

The literature on non-traditional jobs straddles many disciplines. Theories about the participation of women in male-dominated jobs consider the role of the economy and the organization of labor and technology, international development discourse and practices, gender stereotyping, intersectionality and critical race theory, psychology of masculinity, the development of anti-discrimination policies through social movements, organized labor and issues around training and education, occupational safety and health, and, finally, the meaning of empowerment. A core question concerns why women's involvement in many non-traditional fields remains so low and what conditions would lower racial and gender barriers in the workplace.

The gendered and racialized division of labor relates directly to how employment is organized and regulated on national and local levels, and to the position of each country in the world system of power relations. Feminist scholars Amott and Matthaei (1991) explain the structure of segmented employment, in which work in the secondary sector is temporary, lower paid, lower status than the more stable, higher paid primary sector (further subdivided into upper and lower in each category). These two sectors make up what is considered the formal economy, and are – at least nominally – under state regulation and enforcement. In contrast, a looser set of rules regulates the underground or informal sector. In the Global South, the formal sector is generally a small percentage of workers, while it is much broader in the Global North (though even there a vast underground economy exists which relies on migrant labor). These distinctions are important for understanding the valences of meanings of non-traditional work in the Global North and South. Comparing the concept "non-traditional" internationally and historically raises important paradoxes about the social construction of work.

What does the term "non-traditional" job mean in the Global South? In a labor-intensive country, with a large informal economy, it may be traditional for more than 25 percent of women to work in male-dominated jobs. As in the pre-industrial history of Britain, when children and women worked alongside men in coal mines, labor-intensive economies often rely on the physical labor of whole families. In poor communities all over the world, women and children work at hard physical labor. Status (manifested in the intersectionality of gender, nationality, race, age, caste, place of origin, sexual orientation, disability, political ideology, relationship to owner, etc.), is a key element employers use to control and discipline workers and organize employment. Accepting all status differentiation as normal, together with resultant forms of inequality, is critical to macro-level social control, and shapes mass psychology and ideology.

Gendering and racializing jobs saves employers money in the short term. In some instances, like headloading, the carrying of cement and bricks in construction sites, both genders do the same job, but women and children are paid less or only the men are on the payroll. Women are often referred to as "helpers" in construction and mining, doing heavy manual work but barred from working in the skilled trades or in the mines, sometimes by religious rationale, or even superstition. The discourse of gender stereotyping is used both by employers to justify paying women less, and by male workers to defend their entitlement to higher paying skilled jobs in the Global South and North.

In East and South Asia and sub-Saharan Africa, a large portion of the population work in family-based agriculture. During the fallow season, they find work in construction and mining. In India, Pakistan, Afghanistan, Nepal, China, Thailand, Myanmar, Vietnam, Japan, Singapore, and Korea, women have worked seasonally on building sites and related construction, like road work, for many years (Figure 1). The historical record shows that in India women carried headloads in the sixteenth century, as captured in the miniatures printed in the *Akbarnama*.

Lahiri-Dutt and McIntyre's (2006) edited collection on women miners provide historical and contemporary insights about that industry. The first European mining textbook, Agricola's *De Re Metallica,* published in 1556, contains illustrations of women breaking lumps of ore with a hammer, sieving the crushed mass to separate mineral from dirt. An image of Japanese women doing similar work was published in the *Kudo Zuroku* (on the smelting of copper) in 1801. Yet even today Namibian women can still be seen doing similar work sifting pulverized tin ore. One third of the approximately 13 million artisanal miners in 55 countries are women. In Asia, generally less than 10 percent of artisanal miners are women; in Latin America, they are up to one fifth; and in Africa up to half of miners are women. Women primarily transport ore and water, pound rocks, sieve,

Figure 1 Kausar and Fatima, two sisters from the Rajput Odh community, work on a construction site outside of Lahore, Pakistan, 2005. Reproduced with permission from Sobia Aslam.

sort, and purify the metals, and these jobs are considered secondary to men's collection of the ore, which is paid more. In Burkina Faso, between 45,000 and 85,000 women work in gold mining alone, which is very dangerous work.

The demand for low-paid workers in labor-intensive economies in the South and labor shortages in the North are the primary factors influencing the employment of women in male-dominated jobs. During World Wars I and II women in the United States worked on railroads, in defense plants and shipyards, as skilled workers, but their employment often ended with peace. Ironically, after many legal battles keeping women out, the rise in the prison and military industrial complex requires more workers and offers non-traditional jobs for women, and particularly for women of color. Integration into these fields is a global trend. According to a Center for Strategic and International Studies publication (2012), many law enforcement agencies in Latin America started admitting women into their ranks in the 1970s, and there is now an average of 5.5 percent of women police in Latin America, while Uruguay has the highest proportion of female police at 26 percent. The International Women's Police Association website shows affiliate groups in the Emirates, Kenya, Trinidad and Tobago, and many other countries.

International bodies have had an impact on women's entry into non-traditional fields. The United Nations declared 1976–1985 the Decade for Women: Equality, Development, and Peace. This resulted in a series of international conferences on women and the development of significant gender policies to be put before legislatures around the world. For example, the Convention Concerning the Elimination of all Forms of Discrimination Against Women (1979) inspired national laws, like the Equal Employment Opportunity Act passed in Japan in 1986 that led to openings for women in male-dominated jobs such as plumbing, and truck-driving. The International Maritime Organization encouraged academies worldwide to increase recruitment of women students.

When it suits them, states can reverse the dominant narratives about gender and race. They can launch successful ideological campaigns and control government funding to legitimize and implement gender and racial equality of employment, even free childcare. The United States famously called for Rosies to join assembly lines and shipyards during World War II. Marxist-based countries like the former Soviet Union, the Eastern bloc, and later China and Cuba used state power to break down the barriers to male-dominated work. In the USSR, women became construction workers and machine operators in heavy industry and industrial agriculture, as well as entering the professions of medicine and engineering, where women's participation went beyond 25 percent. Thousands of Soviet women served in the navy in the 1940s, and many rose high in the ranks of officers. In China in the 1950s, the Great Leap Forward policy enlisted women into tending the backyard steel furnaces and driving heavy machinery in agriculture. With the fall of the Soviet Union, the rise of international migration has provided additional exploitable labor. State support for gender inclusion is dissipating in the privatized economies of postsocialist countries.

The power of the state to undermine gender and racial stereotyping is a key area of study. Clarke et al. (2004) examined the legacy of Eastern European efforts to integrate women into male-dominated professions and blue collar work, contrasting them with what they see as the limited pressure from the social partners (government, labor, and employers) of Northern European countries. Clarke et al. argue that in Germany and Scandinavia where work is more stable and unionized, with education and formal requirements needed for entry into skilled jobs, states have more power to influence hiring and apply the goals for women's inclusion adopted by the European Union (e.g., Maastricht procedures). Therefore, they surmise that the low percentage of women in non-traditional jobs is a result of the lack of political will. Similar studies find patterns of low inclusion of ethnic minorities and immigrants in skilled work in Europe.

Likewise, Eisenberg (1999) argues for the importance of political will in the United States and suggests that there needs to be a critical mass of women in non-traditional jobs for women to be able to have staying power. She documents the dismantling of the procedures that began in 1978, when pressure from women's organizations, workers, the movement against sexual harassment, and the positive results in cities like Seattle and Madison resulted in federal regulations that set goals and timetables to hire women in non-traditional fields.

In the United States, the movement to open up work for women in non-traditional jobs marked a convergence of a mainly middle-class white women's movement with the multi-class black freedom movement that was challenging occupational racial apartheid, along with other ethnic groups and the emerging lesbian movement in the 1960s and 1970s. Powerful social movements compelled the government to desegregate the workplace, chiefly through Title VII of the Civil Rights Act, along with an executive order calling for affirmative action, and a structure of monitoring and enforcing agencies.

On the basis of these laws and other orders, people were able to sue employers and unions for racial and gender discrimination. The National Association of Colored People and the National Organization for Women jointly challenged discrimination in many industries, and consent decrees followed in the telephone, steel, auto and shipping industries in the mid-1970s. Critical to the successful verdicts were refutations of the employers' argument that the absence of women or blacks in skilled jobs or management was due to their lack of interest, beating back a more subtle form of gender and racial stereotyping.

Changing legal tests had other consequences. Vicki Schultz (1990) contends that African American men were successful in early race discrimination litigation because the courts interpreted statistical evidence of their absence in these positions relative to their proportion in the population as discrimination, with the understanding that people do not apply for jobs for which the effort is futile. However, the futility doctrine, as it is known, was soon supplanted with the requirement for proof of discrimination by a more conservative judiciary, proof that is much more difficult to establish, and legal actions against racial or gender discrimination became less effective. The courts were less likely to accept the futility doctrine for women and the conservative stance that women intrinsically preferred female-dominated jobs regained its foothold, alleviating employer responsibility.

A conservative movement, rising in reaction to the civil rights movement and subsequent desegregation of jobs and schools, together with the rise of neoliberalism, succeeded in dismantling much of the state apparatus for achieving equality. Meanwhile, both liberal and conservatives invested a great deal in the idea that job training by itself can eliminate barriers to good jobs. The World Bank and other international investment agencies have recommended that training for women in non-traditional fields could lead to financial independence and women's empowerment, and suggested that programs be instituted in places where they extend loans. Adubra (2005) evaluated such a program in Togo, and found that while some women were able to practice their trade after training, many women had difficulty finding work, or setting up their own shops. In contrast, she theorized that women's empowerment would be furthered by programs that prepared women for sustainable employment, including non-traditional training, but which were based on understanding underlying needs of local conditions. The work of the Self Employed Women's Association in India (SEWA) offers other case studies of the strengths and weaknesses of short-term training programs in masonry and other non-traditional fields. How to encourage more equal opportunity for women has to be rooted in understanding the contexts of local communities.

Of course, training does not automatically result in jobs elsewhere in the world. Scholars of both European and US labor argue that participating in a union apprenticeship results in higher rates of employment for women and ethnic and racial minorities. But studies have also documented the problems outsiders have getting and keeping employment even in unionized sectors.

Organized labor has been ambivalent about women and non-whites entering fields that are male-dominated. Labor unions in the United States and Europe grew powerful as working class movements, and in the skilled trades and related areas, largely as white working class male bastions. Most unions in the United States have been forced to accept some openness to men of color and women, in some ways similar to German unions accepting workers from Turkey, or French the Algerians and Senegalese (Figure 2). Women and men of color have been able, in some situations, to influence union leadership to become more progressive, and have created safer environments in the workplace.

Recent scholarship explores the reasons why men resist accepting women as equals. Moccio (2006) argues that unlike the class solidarity of industrial workers, the craft union brotherhood embraces the concept of fraternalism, which is based on the idea that workers should bond with their employers along gender lines to achieve success. She contends that the structure of the joint industry and union board that oversees training, hiring, and so on, provides a "nexus that privileges white male workers, unionists, and employers, to the exclusion of women" (Moccio 2006, 18). Paap (2006) takes this a step further. She theorizes that unethical contractors benefit from encouraging male workers' identification with an "animalistic" masculinity, in which workers put up with dirty toilets, excessive physical risks, unsafe working conditions, and treat women and people of color as inferior "affirmative action hires." Paap argues that women and men, whatever their race, gender, national status, or sexual orientation, thrive on jobsites where contractors have zero tolerance for racial and sexual harassment, and safe working conditions. Ibáñez and Narocki (2011) refer to Paap's ideas in their analysis of the "low road" model that characterizes the unsafe conditions and strong competition among small contractors in the mostly non-unionized construction industry in Spain. Ibáñez and Narocki argue that the lack of worker power to negotiate better conditions is related to men's acceptance of a masculine work culture that helps them tolerate safety risks and contingent work while practicing the social exclusion of women and non-white men.

The intersectionality of class consciousness with constructions of masculinity and racial identity emerge from critical race theory, such as the work of Kimberlé Crenshaw. These analyses suggest that by organizing around issues of respect across race and

Figure 2 Denise Johnson, union ironworker, on the construction site of the Mandalay Bay Casino in Las Vegas, 1998. Reproduced with permission from Susanne Davis.

gender lines, unions could improve working conditions and strengthen membership.

Understanding the psychology of identity and consciousness contributes to the broader analysis of how economics and politics affect gender and racial stereotyping and the organization of work. As international corporate power interacts with government to shape employment policies, these studies can provide alternative strategies to men and women inside and outside of unions, in the Global North and Global South, seeking to build strategies for change.

SEE ALSO: Gender Stereotypes; Occupational Segregation; Sexual Harassment Law

REFERENCES

Adubra, Ayélé L. 2005. *Non-Traditional Occupations, Empowerment, and Women: A Case of Togolese Women.* London: Routledge.

Amott, Teresa, and Mattaei, Julie. 1991. *Race, Gender, and Work: A Multicultural Economic History of Women in the United States*. Montreal: Black Rose Books.

Clarke, Linda, Elsebet F. Pedersen, Elisabeth Michielsens, Barbara Susman, and C. Wall. 2004. *Women in Construction*, 8–22. Brussels: CLR/Reed Business Information.

Eisenberg, Susan. 1999. *We'll Call You If We Need You: Experiences of Women Working Construction*. Ithaca: Cornell University Press.

Ibáñez, M., and C. Narocki. 2011. "Occupational Risk and Masculinity: The Case of the Construction Industry in Spain." *Journal of Workplace Rights*, 16(2): 195–217.

Lahiri-Dutt, Kuntala, and Martha Macintyre, eds. 2006. *Women Miners in Developing Countries: Pit Women and Others*. Aldershot: Ashgate Publishing.

Moccio, Fran. 2010. *Live Wire: Women and Brotherhood in the Electrical Industry*. Philadelphia: Temple University Press.

Paap, Kris. 2006. *Working Construction: Why White Working-Class Men Put Themselves – and the Labor Movement – in Harm's Way*. Ithaca: Cornell University Press.

Schultz, Vicki. 1990. "Telling Stories about Women and Work: Judicial Interpretations of Sex Segregation in the Workplace in Title VII Cases Raising the Lack of Interest Argument." *Harvard Law Review*, 103: 1749.

FURTHER READING

Baker, Carrie N. 2008. *The Women's Movement Against Sexual Harassment*. Cambridge: Cambridge University Press.

Belcher, P. 2003. *Women Seafarers: Global Employment Policies and Practices*. Geneva: International Labour Office.

Byrne, J., L. Clarke, and M. Van Der Meer. 2005. "Gender and Ethnic Minority Exclusion From Skilled Occupations in Construction: A Western European Comparison." *Construction Management and Economics*, 23(10): 1025–1034.

Chin, C.B. 2008. *Cruising in the Global Economy: Profits, Pleasure and Work at Sea*. Aldershot: Ashgate Publishing.

Honey, Maureen. 1984. *Creating Rosie the Riveter: Class, Gender, and Propaganda During World War II*. Amherst: University of Massachusetts Press.

Kalpagam, U. 1994. *Labour and Gender: Survival in Urban India, New Delhi*. Thousand Oaks: Sage.

Ramakrishnan, Geetha, 1996. "A Struggle Within A Struggle: The Unionization of Women in the Informal Sector in Tamil Nadu." In *Speaking Out, Women's Economic Empowerment in South Asia*, edited by Marilyn Carr, Martha Chen, and Renana Jhabvala, 167–182. London: IT Publications.

Reskin, Barbara F., and Patricia A. Roos, eds. 2009. *Job Queues, Gender Queues: Explaining Women's Inroads into Male Occupations*. Philadelphia: Temple University Press.

Women as Producers of Culture

DUSTIN KIDD
Temple University, USA

Women comprise many of the greatest authors, artists, and creators of culture in all forms. However, women have often had limited or no access to the institutional structures that control the production and distribution of culture. Historically, women who have found success in producing cultural objects – such as books, paintings, plays, and films – have often had to present their ideas in coded form in order to appease the male power figures within these institutions. Cultural objects produced by women have often been devalued compared with similar objects produced by men. Women are much less likely to be recognized for their cultural contributions than men. As of 2014, women have received only 11.7% of the Nobel Prizes in Literature. Only one woman has ever received an Academy Award for best director. Women have received only 10 awards in the 29 years of the prestigious Ruth Lilly Poetry Prize.

Producers of popular culture sit at one of the four points on what sociologist Wendy Griswold (1994) calls the "cultural diamond."

In addition to production, the other points are the cultural object, the audience, and the social world in which culture is situated. Gender disparities are rampant in the social world, but the disparities found within culture are not merely a reflection of the larger society. Cultural systems have their own histories and logic that powerfully shape how gender works within those systems. For instance, in the arts, the trope of the male genius who is born with creative skills has resulted in a devaluation of women artists who have sought to bring greater attention to issues of training and institutional access. For this reason, the production point on the cultural diamond needs particular attention within the analysis of gender and culture.

In many realms of cultural production, women's participation is not improving. Martha Lauzen's annual report "Boxed In: Employment of Behind-the-Scenes and On-Screen Women in 2013–14 Prime-time Television" (Lauzen 2014) found that only 27% of behind-the-scenes professionals in television are women. That number has shown no significant increase over recent years – 28% in 2012–2013; 27% in 2009–2010 – and only a slight increase from the 21% of television professionals who were women in 1997–1998.

The numbers are worse in the film industry. According to the report "The Celluloid Ceiling," also by Martha Lauzen (2015), women comprised just 17% of off-screen professionals in film in 2014. That shows no particular change over previous years: 16% in 2013, 17% in 2005, 19% in 2001, and 17% in 1998. So there is no indication of recent improvement.

The careers of those women who do work in the film and television industries tell an important story as they do not fare well compared with male professionals. A 1996 study by sociologists Denise Bielby and William Bielby found that women writers in the film industry suffer from a "cumulative disadvantage" (Bielby and Bielby 1996). They begin their careers with a gap between their incomes and those of men and that gap widens over the course of their careers. As a result, men benefit financially far more than women from accumulating experience. Sociologists Anne E. Lincoln and Michael Patrick Allen have found that women suffer more than men from the detrimental impact of age on acting careers. In addition, they found that although the gender gap in the number of film roles is lessening; the presence of women as prominent cast members still lags behind men in significant ways (Lincoln and Allen 2004).

The absence of women in film and television is not necessarily the result of an absence of women preparing for careers in these fields. According to the Annual Survey of Journalism and Mass Communication Enrollments (Becker et al. 2013), two-thirds of students in those fields are women, and that proportion has been consistent since at least 1988. The numbers are lower for film-specific programs. According to 2011–2012 data from the National Center for Education Statistics (2015), women comprise only 37.8% of bachelor-level students in film studies, only 30.8% in cinematography, and only 43.0% in film and video production. Women may be the minority in these programs, but women still make up a larger proportion of the undergraduate programs than they do in the film and television industries.

Women do not fare well in literature either. Although studies indicate that women read more than men, and purchase more books than men, men publish far more books than women. An annual study by the literary organization VIDA finds that men are published more than women in most literary journals, and their works are reviewed more than works by women (King 2014).

Women represent only about one-third of professionals in the music industry. The communications scholar Kristin Lieb has argued that female musicians are treated as brands, rather than artists, that are carefully controlled and packaged and all too quickly abandoned (Lieb 2013). In music reviews, women's careers are discussed on different terms from those of men. Sociologists Vaughn Schmutz and Alison Faupel conducted a qualitative analysis of the reviews presented alongside a *Rolling Stone* list of the top 500 albums of all time (Schmutz and Faupel 2010). Whereas the male artists who made the list were discussed in terms that focused on their creative genius, the female artists were discussed in terms of their relationships and their access to social networks that helped them to succeed – primarily networks composed of men.

In the growing field of digital culture and social media, women have very little industry influence. Currently, for instance, Sheryl Sandberg is the only woman on the five-person management team at Facebook and she is one of just two women on the board of directors. Twitter has one woman on its 10-person management team and one woman on its board. Google has three women on its 20-person management team and three women on its board. New media follow old patterns when it comes to leadership and hiring.

Gender is one of several fault lines that create what is known as the digital divide. Since the early days of the worldwide web, studies have consistently shown that women lag behind men in terms of experience with the Internet and related technologies, frequency of use, and familiarity with digital literacy (Jones et al. 2009). Eszter Hargittai and Gina Walejko shift the focus from a digital divide to a participation divide, asking whether men and women create and share information online at different rates (Hargittai and Walejko 2008). They find that men and women actually have similar levels of digital creation – 62.3 percent of men and 60.0 percent of women claim to have made content in the form of music, artistic photography, poetry/fiction, or film/video. However, men are more likely than women to publish their work online in a way that allows them to find an audience for their creations. Also, men and women create different kinds of culture using digital technology. Men are more likely to create music, film, and video whereas women are more likely to create photography, poetry, and fiction.

The trend of studying gender demographics in cultural production owes much to the social activism of a group called the Guerrilla Girls. The Guerrilla Girls began as an anonymous feminist collective of artists who used social action and visual culture to address gender disparities in the arts. They formed in New York City in 1985. They are known for appearing in public wearing guerrilla masks to protect their identities and they take the names of dead female artists. The visual works for which they are best known are images on posters and billboards that combine powerful imagery with striking statistics. For instance, one iconic image showed a reclining female nude wearing a guerrilla mask with the headline "Do women have to be naked to get into the Met. Museum?" Copy below the headline offered powerful data: "Less than 5% of the artists in the Modern Arts sections are women, but 85% of the nudes are female." The Guerrilla Girls call themselves "the conscience of the art world" and their work serves as a reminder that for all its alleged progressivism, the art world is persistently sexist, racist, classist, and homophobic (Kidd 2010).

Audiences for cultural objects determine what those objects mean through sets of ideas that are often referred to as interpretive strategies. Interpretive strategies are "ways of seeing" – to use John Berger's phrase (Berger 1972) – that help audiences make sense of objects, determine what the message is, and decide how to use that message as social actors. Interpretive processes intersect with processes of gender. The development of feminist aesthetics has provided new lenses for interpreting culture produced by women. Those feminist lenses have been important tools for renegotiating some cultural works by women into literary and artistic canons. This process of cultural valorization is documented by the work of Sarah M. Corse and Saundra Davis Westervelt, who show that Kate Chopin's novel *The Awakening* moved from a position of critical disdain to acceptance into the Western canon due to the increasing embrace of feminist aesthetics (Corse and Westervelt 2002).

Adding an intersectional lens to the analysis of women as producers of culture reveals that those women who do succeed in developing professional careers in the culture industries – from the arts to the mass media and digital technology – are overwhelmingly white, heterosexual, non-disabled, and more likely to come from middle- and upper-class backgrounds (Kidd 2014).

Sociologist Patricia Hill Collins has discussed the ways in which black women have had especially limited access to the institutional structures that are used to create, legitimate, and share knowledge (Collins 1990). Creating new systems for producing and distributing knowledge and culture is both a tool for liberating oppressed groups and an opportunity for expanding the kinds of knowledge that are available to all. Expanding the opportunities for women to be producers of culture and expanding the ways in which social institutions recognize how women have long been producers of culture promote social equality and generate innovation in the creation of knowledge.

SEE ALSO: Feminist Art Practice; Images of Gender and Sexuality in Advertising; Popular Culture and Gender; Representation; Visual Culture and Gender

REFERENCES

Becker, Lee B., Tudor Vlad, and Holly Anne Simpson. 2013. Annual Survey of Journalism and Mass Communication Enrollments. Accessed March 22, 2015, at http://www.grady.uga.edu/annualsurveys/Enrollment_Survey/Enrollment_2013/2013EnrollCombined.pdf.

Berger, John. 1972. *Ways of Seeing*. London: Penguin.

Bielby, Denise D., and William T. Bielby. 1996. "Women and Men in Film: Gender Inequality Among Writers in a Culture Industry." *Gender and Society*, 10: 248–270.

Collins, Patricia Hill. 1990. *Black Feminist Thought: Knowledge, Consciousness, and the Politics of Empowerment*. New York: Routledge.

Corse, Sarah M., and Saundra Davis Westervelt. 2002. "Gender and Literary Valorization: The Awakening of a Canonical Novel." *Sociological Perspectives*, 45: 139–161.

Griswold, Wendy. 1994. *Cultures and Societies in a Changing World*. Thousand Oaks: Sage.

Hargittai, Eszter, and Gina Walejko. 2008. "The Participation Divide: Content Creation and Sharing in the Digital Age." *Information, Communication, and Society*, 11: 239–256.

Jones, Steve, Camille Johnson-Yale, Sarah Millermaier, and Francisco Seoane Perez. 2009. "U.S. College Students' Internet Use: Race, Gender and Digital Divides." *Journal of Computer-Mediated Communication*, 14: 244–264.

Kidd, Dustin. 2010. *Legislating Creativity: The Intersections of Art and Politics*. New York: Routledge.

Kidd, Dustin. 2014. *Pop Culture Freaks: Identity, Mass Media, and Society*. Boulder: Westview Press.

King, Amy. 2014. The VIDA Count 2013 – Lie by Omission: The Rallying Few, The Rallying Masses. Accessed March 22, 2015, at http://www.vidaweb.org/the-count-2013/#count-2013.

Lauzen, Martha M. 2014. Boxed In: Employment of Behind-the-Scenes and On-Screen Women in 2013–14 Prime-time Television. Accessed March 22, 2015, at http://womenintvfilm.sdsu.edu/files/2013-14_Boxed_In_Report.pdf.

Lauzen, Martha M. 2015. The Celluloid Ceiling: Behind-the-Scenes Employment of Women on the Top 250 Films of 2014. Accessed March 22, 2015, at http://womenintvfilm.sdsu.edu/files/2014_Celluloid_Ceiling_Report.pdf.

Lieb, Kristin J. 2013. *Gender, Branding, and the Modern Music Industry*. New York: Routledge.

Lincoln, Anne E., and Michael Patrick Allen. 2004. "Double Jeopardy in Hollywood: Age and Gender in the Careers of Film Actors, 1926–1999." *Sociological Forum*, 19: 611–631.

National Center for Education Statistics. 2015. Digest of Education Statistics. Bachelor's, Master's, and Doctor's Degrees Conferred by Postsecondary Institutions, by Sex of Student and Discipline Division: 2011–12. Accessed March 22, 2015, at http://nces.ed.gov/programs/digest/d13/tables/dt13_318.30.asp.

Schmutz, Vaughn, and Alison Faupel. 2010. "Gender and Cultural Consecration in Popular Music." *Social Forces*, 89: 685–708.

FURTHER READING

Alexander, Victoria D. 2003. *Sociology of the Arts: Exploring Fine and Popular Forms*. Malden: Blackwell.

Becker, Howard. 1982. *Art Worlds*. Berkeley: University of California Press.

Blau, Judith R. 1989. *The Shape of Culture: A Study of Contemporary Cultural Patterns in the United States*. Cambridge: Cambridge University Press.

Dubin, Steven C. 1992. *Arresting Images: Impolitic Art and Uncivil Actions*. London: Routledge.

Freeland, Cynthia. 2001. *But Is It Art?* Oxford: Oxford University Press.

Halle, David. 1993. *Inside Culture: Art and Class in the American Home*. Chicago: University of Chicago Press.

Levine, Lawrence. 1988. *Highbrow/Lowbrow: The Emergence of Cultural Hierarchy in America*. Cambridge, MA: Harvard University Press.

Press, Andrea L. 1991. *Women Watching Television: Gender, Class, and Generation in the American Television Experience*. Philadelphia: University of Pennsylvania Press.

Radway, Janice. 1984. *Reading the Romance: Women, Patriarchy, and Popular Literature*. Chapel Hill: University of North Carolina Press.

Wolff, Janet. 1981. *The Social Production of Art*. London: Macmillan.

Women in Science

JACOB CLARK BLICKENSTAFF
Pacific Science Center, USA

Women have made many notable contributions to science discovery and today make up a significant percentage of practicing scientists worldwide. At the same time in many cultures, the stereotypical image of "scientist" remains a white man, usually with unkempt hair and holding a test tube. When asked to name important woman scientists, very few students can go beyond Marie Curie (who is still the only person to win the Nobel Prize in two different academic disciplines). Female scientists are paid less than their male counterparts, receive less grant support, and are less likely to be selected for postdoctoral fellowships. The twentieth-century perception of science as a "male subject" has resulted in women avoiding academic preparation in the sciences even though girls in elementary school express just as much interest in science as boys (Baker and Leary 1995). The sciences are not seen as uniformly masculine, though. The physical sciences (physics, chemistry, and geology, for example) are generally seen as the most "male," while the life sciences (biology, environmental science, and medicine) are perceived as more "female." The participation of women in these fields tracks with those perceptions, with the representation of women in physics among the lowest, and in biology among the highest.

Formal and informal educators, professional societies, and federal funders have all worked for some time to ameliorate the underrepresentation of women in many science disciplines. This work has brought about some change in the numbers of women who receive undergraduate preparation in the sciences, but participation in postgraduate work and the science workforce remains unbalanced.

CURRENT PERCENT REPRESENTATION OF WOMEN IN THE SCIENCES

Internationally there is even more variation in the representation of women in science, not least because the representation of women in the workforce overall is widely variable. Members of the former Soviet Union tend to have greater female participation in the physical sciences than other parts of the world, while African and Asian nations tend to have fewer women in the sciences. Those countries with the lowest participation rates of women in science tend to have the greatest social and cultural pressures impacting girls' access to education.

According to the US Census Bureau's (2011) American Community Survey (ACS), 48 percent of the workforce in the Unites States is female, so professions with less than 48 percent women show underrepresentation, and in those with more than 48 percent women are overrepresented. The ACS data reveals that women are at approximate parity in the biological sciences with 47 percent of the workforce female. On the other hand only 16 percent of atmospheric and space scientists are women, and just 20 percent of astronomers and physicists. In the social sciences, women are overrepresented in psychology (70 percent) and sociology (61 percent), but underrepresented in economics (33 percent).

EFFORTS TO ENCOURAGE GIRLS AND RETAIN WOMEN IN SCIENCE

Many initiatives have been put in place over the last 40 years to keep girls interested in science beyond elementary school. While some focus on specific sciences (those efforts put in place by the professional societies, for example) many see bringing young women into STEM generally as their goal. In the United States, for example, The National Girls Collaborative Project (www.ngcproject.org/) is a good example of a STEM-wide effort to encourage and retain girls. Most of the projects shared through the collaborative are after school, weekend, or summer enrichment experiences intended to give young women positive experiences with science. The strongest emphasis is often in the middle school grades, when young girls tend to lose interest in science. There is less attention on the transition from high school and into college.

As young women complete college and consider graduate study in the sciences, there are some programs to facilitate that shift. The American Physical Society supports the Conferences for Undergraduate Women in Physics (CUWIP, www.aps.org/programs/women/workshops/cuwip.cfm) program, which has grown dramatically since the first CUWIP event at the University of Southern California in 2006.

The undergraduate conferences grew out of an international program also in physics, the International Conference on Women in Physics. As one of the sciences with the greatest underrepresentation of women, physics and the physics societies have paid particular attention to addressing the issue. Beginning in 2000, the International Union of Pure and Applied Physicists has held international conferences for women in physics every four years. Attendance has grown dramatically, and the event gives women scientists an opportunity to meet and form international collaborations.

In 1999 the MIT faculty newsletter published the results of an internal study of the status of women faculty in science. The report found that female and male faculty had unequal access to resources and very different experiences, particularly after tenure was granted. In response to the MIT report and other calls for action the National Science Foundation (NSF) has worked since 2001 to support the careers of women in science in the United States through the ADVANCE Program (www.nsf.gov/crssprgm/advance/). This program focuses on ensuring that women faculty consider academia as a viable and attractive career option through supporting career development for new faculty, institutional transformation, and mentor/mentee relationships between female scientists.

BACKLASH AGAINST WOMEN IN SCIENCE

Even as substantial efforts have been made to attract and retain women in science, some men have argued that the current representation of women in the sciences is appropriate, and due to real masculine superiority in the subject. One of the more notorious incidents occurred in 2005 when Lawrence Summers, then president of Harvard, hypothesized that the underrepresentation of women in science was due to women being unable to put in long hours in the laboratory, or to the greater variability in mathematical aptitude present in males. (The aptitude argument says that since there is more variability in male math scores, there will be more males at the top – and bottom – of the ability scale. Those very able math students might then become the best scientists.) Summers's comments were widely criticized by researchers who study sex differences, though he also had supporters who argued his comments were taken out of context.

Political and social power affects the kind of questions that scientists ask and how scientists interpret the answers they obtain. If only one group asks the questions and interprets the results, then the field of scientific inquiry will be narrowed, and important scientific work will not be done. Questions and observations are two fundamental elements of science practice, and they are clearly affected by gender roles.

BIAS IN SCIENCE PRACTICE

Scientific ideas have been used in the past to support claims that we now see as biased. In the nineteenth century, white male scientists thought that blacks and women had inferior mental capacity, either because of head size or facial structure. Women have been excluded from medical research trials because doctors thought the menstrual cycle would invalidate their results. Virtually all scientists working today would dismiss such work as flawed. Many might then argue that scientists have learned how to be more objective, so science is no longer biased toward the masculine. A very different position is taken by a number of feminist critics of science including Sue V. Rosser, Sandra Harding, Donna Haraway, and Helen Longino. These scholars suggest that aspects of scientific structure, epistemology, and methodology reflect masculine ideals and take the male perspective and experience as standard.

Modern scientific tradition is based upon using the senses and objective rationality to interrogate nature, which is seen by some feminist scholars as overly masculine and therefore closed (or unattractive) to women. There are three alternative perspectives described by Kerr (2001) and Harding (1991):

Feminist Standpoint Theory – Sandra Harding argues that science should be done from the perspective of women, because their position outside the dominant social order endows women with a more objective view of the world than men have. The perspective of those in power is clouded by that power, while the powerless have a clearer view. Harding argues that knowledge claims should be judged upon the social context of their production.

Situated Knowledge – While agreeing with the idea that people have different points of view from which they see the world,

Donna Haraway believes that everyone takes on different standpoints at different times, and people can temporarily take on the standpoint of others. Haraway conceptualizes varied research perspectives as different ways of seeing and argues that every view has both blind spots and focal points.

Feminist Empiricism – Instead of evaluating knowledge claims on their social context, Helen Longino argues for "contextual empiricism," testing truth claims against available evidence, but also recommending that scientists use their political beliefs to guide their theoretical positions. Instead of trying to avoid political bias, scientists should acknowledge the biases they have and work with it from their political position.

Many women respond to these feminist critics of science by pointing out that the above arguments overemphasize the commonality of women's experience, and fail to account for the experiences of women of color in the sciences. Many women who have become successful scientists are quite vehement in their opposition to the feminist critiques of science described above.

Some science disciplines are perceived as more masculine than others; biology and other life sciences are at one end of the spectrum, while physics and engineering are at the other end. Esther Saraga and Dorothy Griffiths (1981) point out the sciences most strongly identified as masculine are those that are closely tied to improving economic production and developing weapons, two tasks that male-dominated society has decided are valuable. Biology has been less clearly tied to economic development (except in agricultural science, another male province) and weapons than physics or engineering.

RESEARCH QUESTIONS

When men are the only people doing scientific research, the kinds of questions scientists ask can be very different from the questions asked by women. As Sue V. Rosser (1994) points out, medical research is particularly subject to androcentric errors: diseases that affect both men and women were initially only studied in male patients, and those studies of women's health that were conducted focused only on reproduction. The early signs of heart attack are different in men and women, but this was only realized when doctors studied female victims more carefully.

OBSERVATIONS

When scientists observe animal behavior, they cannot help but project human social roles on animal groups. Primate science is perhaps the most obvious area where the perspective of male and female scientists can be quite different, and Londa Schiebinger's (1999) work clearly delineates the differences. In observing a group with one male and several females, the male scientist might call the group a "harem," implying that the females are there as involuntary breeding partners for the male. A female primatologist might call the same group a "single male troop," which does not carry the same implications as "harem."

SEE ALSO: Feminist Studies of Science; Gender Bias in Research; Sexism

REFERENCES

Baker, D., and R. Leary. 1995. "Letting Girls Speak Out About Science." *Journal of Research in Science Teaching*, 32(1): 3–27.

Harding, S. 1991. *Whose Science? Whose Knowledge? Thinking from Women's Lives*. Milton Keynes: Open University Press.

Kerr, E. A. 2001. "Toward a Feminist Natural Science: Linking Theory and Practice." In *The Gender and Science Reader*, edited by

M. Lederman and I. Bartsch, 386–406. New York: Routledge.

Rosser, S. V. 1994. "Gender Bias in Clinical Research: The Difference It Makes." In *Reframing Women's Health: Multidisciplinary Research and Practice*, 253–265. New York: Sage.

Saraga E., and D. Griffiths. 1981. "Biological Inevitabilities or Political Choices? The Future for Girls in Science." In *The Missing Half: Girls and Science Education*, edited by A. Kelly, 85–97. Manchester: Manchester University Press.

Schiebinger, L. 1999. *Has Feminism Changed Science?* Cambridge, MA: Harvard University Press.

US Census Bureau. 2011. American Community Survey. Accessed August 1, 2014, at http://www.census.gov/acs/www/.

FURTHER READING

Blickenstaff, J. Clark. 2005. "Women and Science Careers: Leaky Pipeline or Gender Filter?" *Gender and Education*, 17(4): 369–386.

Haaken, J. 1996. "Field Dependence Research: A Historical Analysis of a Psychological Construct." In *Gender and Scientific Authority*, edited by B. Laslett, S. G. Kohlstedt, H. Longino, and E. Hammonds, 282–301. Chicago: University of Chicago Press.

Hill, Catherine, Christianne Corbett, Andresse St. Rose, and American Association of University Women. 2010. *Why so Few? Women in Science Technology Engineering and Mathematics*. Washington, DC: AAUW

Hyde, J. S. 1996. "Meta-Analysis and the Psychology of Gender Differences." In *Gender and Scientific Authority*, edited by B. Laslett, S. G. Kohlstedt, H. Longino, and E. Hammonds, 302–322. Chicago: University of Chicago Press.

MIT Faculty Newsletter. 1999. A Study on the Status of Women Faculty in Science at MIT. Accessed July 17, 2015, at http://web.mit.edu/fnl/women/women.html.

Pierson, E. 2014. "In Science, It Matters That Women Come Last." *Gender Gap*, August 5. Accessed July 17, 2015, at http://fivethirtyeight.com/features/in-science-it-matters-that-women-come-last/.

Rosser, S. V. 1990. *Female-Friendly Science: Applying Women's Studies Methods and Theories to Attract Students*. New York: Pergamon.

Women Travelers

BRUCE PRIDEAUX
Central Queensland University, Australia
PETRA GLOVER
University of West London, UK

Women travelers comprise about half of all travelers. As with their male counterparts, they travel for a variety of reasons, including business, to visit friends and relatives, for recreation, and for leisure. Depending on their cultural origins, women may travel with companions, families, or alone. Previous research (Laroche et al. 2000) has shown that gender can influence purchasing decisions and the selection of holiday destinations (Jönsson and Devonish 2008). Surprisingly, the tourism literature has paid relatively little attention to this important group of travelers, particularly those who choose to travel alone. Solo independent women travelers are defined as women who choose to travel independently without a packaged tour and without a companion (McNamara and Prideaux 2010). They are regarded as a growing and influential market segment. Initially viewed as part of the backpacker market, solo independent women travelers may now be grouped into a distinct market segment. Nevertheless, given the size of this group of travelers as well as the broad definition based on gender and travel party, it is unsurprising that they are not a homogeneous group. Although it is often posited that these travelers are particularly safety conscious and conservative in their choice of activities and destinations, they have also been characterized as bold, confident, and gutsy adventurers. Some researchers (Jackson and Henderson 1995; Wilson and Little 2008) argue that solo independent women travelers face greater constraints than their male counterparts in their choice of tourist activities and destinations. Common barriers to independent solo travel include a fear of violence and concerns for personal safety and well-being, in particular being subjected to sexual harassment and violence. Such concerns have been associated with destinations ranging from natural to urban environments. In natural environments, locations such as national parks and forests, remoteness, and isolation contribute to a sense of fear, whereas in urban environments places such as cinemas and pubs as well as public transport are considered frightening, especially at night. Broadly speaking, outdoor activities and public places have been identified as spaces of fear where large numbers of women feel vulnerable and threatened and hence hesitate or decline to visit. To mitigate these concerns, women may choose to undertake leisure activities close to home and may decide not to engage in independent travel.

Concerns for personal safety may not necessarily be felt by solo independent women travelers themselves but may be expressed by others, including partners, family members, friends, and work colleagues. These concerns often extend to disapproval and lack of support and demonstrate a widespread perception that it is socially unacceptable for women to travel alone and independently (Wilson and Little 2008). Contrary to these concerns, crime statistics in many countries including Australia and the United Kingdom reveal that women are more likely to experience sexual assault in their own home. The perceived risk of traveling independently may be higher than the actual risk.

Women who decide to undertake solo independent travel often feel self-empowered and report a sense of pride and achievement, potentially because they have overcome their perceptions of fear. Their motivation is often founded on an aspiration to extend themselves and stems from a desire to meet new people, to challenge themselves, to move outside their comfort zone, and to develop their autonomy. The challenge may lie simply in the pursuit of solo independent travel but it may also be expressed through the chosen destination or the activities they participate in. In a study into activities undertaken by solo women travelers McNamara and Prideaux (2010) found that they participate in risk-taking activities, confidently take part in night-time social activities, and travel well beyond their home or accommodation base. In addition, research into women travelers' engagement in adventure tourism has demonstrated that their participation extends the self-challenge of solo independent travel and is also pursued to impress others, thus enhancing their self-confidence and self-importance (Myers 2010). For others, traveling independently has a deeper and more reflective purpose. Characterized as "meaningful travel" (Wilson and Harris 2006), it is undertaken to help define or shape women's identity, contemplate and assess their interpersonal relationships, and reevaluate their perceptions and attitudes toward life and community. There is also a more pragmatic group of women who appear to travel independently simply due to lack of a traveling companion.

Following the push–pull concept of destination choice, which states that travelers' motivations (push factors) must be aligned with destination attributes (pull factors) (Dann 1981), destinations hosting solo independent women travelers must ensure that the destination environment aligns with these travelers' expectations and demands. Given the dominant constraints among women travelers, the safety of the destination or activity is a vital decision-making factor. This does not necessarily mean that solo independent women travelers only choose destinations and activities that have a strong reputation for safety. Rather, they assess the potential risks of a destination or activity more carefully than other travelers and may put in place additional contingency measures. Similar to other groups of travelers, risk aversion among these women is varied, resulting in diverse choices for destinations and tourist activities.

SEE ALSO: Self-Esteem

REFERENCES

Dann, Graham M. S. 1981. "Tourist Motivation: An Appraisal." *Annals of Tourism Research*, 8(2): 187–219.

Jackson, Edgar L., and Karla A. Henderson. 1995. "Gender-Based Analysis of Leisure Constraints." *Leisure Sciences*, 17(1): 31–51.

Jönsson, Cristina, and Dwayne Devonish. 2008. "Does Nationality, Gender, and Age Affect Travel Motivation? A Case of Visitors to the Caribbean Island of Barbados." *Journal of Travel and Tourism Marketing*, 25(3–4): 398–408.

Laroche, Michel, Gad Saad, Mark Cleveland, and Elizabeth Browne. 2000. "Gender Differences in Information Search Strategies for a Christmas Gift." *Journal of Consumer Marketing*, 17(6): 500–522.

McNamara, Karen Elizabeth, and Bruce Prideaux. 2010. "A Typology of Solo Independent Women Travellers." *International Journal of Tourism Research*, 12(3): 253–264.

Myers, Linda. 2010. "Women Travellers' Adventure Tourism Experiences in New Zealand." *Annals of Leisure Research*, 13(1/2): 116–142.

Wilson, Erica, and Candice Harris. 2006. "Meaningful Travel: Women, Independent Travel and the Search for Self and Meaning." *Tourism*, 54(2): 161–172.

Wilson, Erica, and Donna E. Little. 2008. "The Solo Female Travel Experience: Exploring the 'Geography of Women's Fear'." *Current Issues in Tourism*, 11(2): 167–186. DOI: 10.2167/cit342.0.

Women-Church

MARY E. HUNT
Women's Alliance for Theology, Ethics and Ritual (WATER), USA

Women-church is a movement of feminist base communities that seeks to create a church and society that reflect a "discipleship of equals." Theologian Elisabeth Schüssler Fiorenza (1993) coined that term and the name "ekklesia of women," which she and liturgist Diann L. Neu translated as "women church." Women-church is the locus of both ecclesial and political actions shaped by and for women and others who are marginalized in kyriarchal structures. "Kyriarchy," another term developed by Schüssler Fiorenza, is the interlocking forms of oppression, including racism, sexism, heterosexism, colonialism, and so forth, that result in discrimination for many and privilege for a few.

Women-church is not a church for women only, as Rosemary Radford Ruether (1985) explains in her eponymous book. It is a way to live out the Christian tradition with specific attention to equality, participation, and empowerment of all members, especially women, who have heretofore been marginalized.

The movement began in the 1970s in the United States when the non-ordination of Roman Catholic women scandalized many people into action, as Diann L. Neu and Mary E. Hunt (1993) chronicled in a sourcebook on the movement. Rather than simply trying to bring about women's ordination, which the Vatican opposed, Catholic feminists created communities in which leadership and ministry are shared without hierarchical clerical structures. Ruether claims that these reflect the early Christian community house-churches and operate effectively in many settings.

US women-church groups are linked through the Women-Church Convergence (www.women-churchconvergence.org), which is "a coalition of autonomous Catholic-rooted organizations/groups raising a feminist voice and committed to an ekklesia of women which is participative, egalitarian and self-governing." Groups meet in

Switzerland, Germany, and Chile, among other countries. For instance, in Korea, a Presbyterian community with a woman pastor called itself "women church," while in Iceland a Lutheran woman priest started *Kvenna Kirkjan* (women church). No one has a copyright on the name. The range of uses signals the dynamic, if sometimes diffuse, nature of the movement.

The US women-church movement is characterized by local communities that meet usually for a meal and worship. While the roots of women-church are in the Catholic tradition, members of local groups include women from many religious backgrounds and practices. For example, some Protestant women ministers belong to such groups; their ordination does not confer any special status on them as members of women-church groups.

The Women-Church Convergence is made up of member organizations, as Kathleen Kautzer details (2012). The Women's Ordination Conference, Dignity USA, the Sinsinawa Dominican Women's Network, and the Women's Alliance for Theology, Ethics, and Ritual (WATER) among others are all members of the Convergence. They work in coalition on a wide range of social and ecclesial issues, always prioritizing the perspectives of those who are left aside.

Three large gatherings sponsored by the Convergence show the development of the movement. In 1983, Catholic feminist groups organized "From Generation to Generation: Woman-Church Speaks" in Chicago, Illinois. Several thousand participants explored social justice themes, including ecclesial injustice, and spoke in one voice as church. Taking on moral and spiritual agency as women-church was new and exciting for women, albeit unwelcome by the kyriarchal church.

It meant that women were not begging for ordination in a church that did not want their time and talents. Instead, women were going about the works of mercy, as well as their theo-political work as church, without asking permission or making apologies. This offensive rather than defensive approach was eventually understood as a power-changing model, leading to subsequent kyriarchal critiques of feminism. Since women celebrate Eucharist without ordained, male, celibate clergy, the movement challenges the sacramental power at the heart of the kyriarchal church.

A second meeting in 1987 in Cincinnati, Ohio focused on "Women-Church: Claiming Our Power." Three thousand women discussed sexual, spiritual, political, and economic power, encountering the wide diversities of class and ethnicity that enhance the movement, but make cooperative work challenging. Thus the name changed from "woman" to "women" church to signal the many and varied ways women experience kyriarchal oppression.

In that era, the movement was successful in shifting the default conversation from ordaining women to being church. Rather than responding to the Vatican's intransigence, women-church people let the needs of the world and not the failings of the church set their agenda. This led to cooperation with other groups, both religious and non-religious, on issues of reproductive justice, LGBT equality, and the like, creating new voices that call themselves "Catholic" despite efforts by bishops to claim that only the Roman Catholic hierarchy speaks for the Catholic community.

A third gathering was held in Albuquerque, New Mexico, in 1993 entitled "Women-Church: Weavers of Change." This reflected the movement's strong commitment to social justice. Economic disparities, racial differences, and discrimination against persons with physical disabilities came to the surface. While the assembly could not solve these problems, members showed their willingness to work on hard issues as part of their faith commitment.

Women-Church Convergence functions as the organizing umbrella for the movement. Educational programs, theological discussions, and liturgical/ritual innovations are developed and shared by member groups. At times Convergence groups take corporate stances on justice issues, amplifying their individual voices. The members work together to create opportunities for people to experience church as equal partners, something that Catholic women simply do not find in their parishes.

By 2007, when the Women-Church Convergence celebrated its 25th anniversary, the Catholic feminist flavor was much in evidence in the conference title: "Celebrating Catholic Feminist Ministries: A Women-Church Forum." By then, women were being ordained through Roman Catholic Women Priests and other organizations. But it is the focus on feminist ministries, not on ordination, that distinguishes women-church religiously and strategically. Such work is not under the control of or even in direct opposition to the kyriarchal church. It is instead determined by the best insights of the women themselves. Interestingly, two Roman Catholic Women Priests (RCWP) groups, the original as well as the newer Association of Roman Catholic Women Priests, belong to the Convergence, proving there is room in women-church for a wide range of approaches to transforming religious kyriarchy.

Women-church remains a relatively small, but vital part of religious movements for inclusion and equality. It occupies an important rhetorical and strategic space in feminist struggles in religion.

SEE ALSO: Feminist Christology; Feminist Theology; Open and Affirming Religious Organizations; Woman-Centeredness

REFERENCES

Kautzer, Kathleen. 2012. *The Underground Church: Nonviolent Resistance to the Vatican Empire*, ch. 4, esp. 121–123. Leiden: Koninklijke Brill NV.

Neu, Diann L., and Mary E. Hunt. 1993. *Women-Church Sourcebook*. Silver Spring: WATERworks Press.

Ruether, Rosemary Radford. 1985. *Women-Church: Theology and Practice of Feminist Liturgical Communities*. San Francisco: Harper & Row.

Schüssler Fiorenza, Elisabeth. 1993. *Discipleship of Equals: A Critical Feminist Ekklēsia-logy of Liberation*. New York: Crossroad.

FURTHER READING

Hunt, Mary E. 2000. "Woman-Church." In *Routledge International Encyclopedia of Women*, edited by Cheris Kramare and Dale Spender, 2129–2130. New York: Routledge.

Hunt, Mary E. 2006. "Women-Church." In *Encyclopedia of Women and Religion in North America, Part XIII: Contemporary Women's Issues in Religion*, edited by Rosemary Skinner Keller, Rosemary Radford Ruether and Marie Cantlon, 1243–1249. Bloomington: Indiana University Press.

Hunt, Mary E. 2009. "Women-Church: Feminist Concept, Religious Commitment, Women's Movement." *Journal of Feminist Studies in Religion*, 25(1): 85–98.

Women's and Feminist Activism in Aboriginal Australia and Torres Strait Islands

PAT DUDGEON and ABIGAIL BRAY
University of Western Australia, Australia

Aboriginal and Torres Strait Islander women in the country the British invaders named Australia have always been engaged as warriors and activists in defending their land

and people. The population of Aboriginal and Torres Strait Islander people of Australia as of June 30, 2011 was 669,900 people, or 3 percent of Australia's total population (Australian Bureau of Statistics 2011). Indigenous Australia is made up of two distinct cultural groups: the majority, mainland Aboriginal people and a minority, Torres Strait Islander people. This entry uses the term Aboriginal to refer to both groups.

Of the many issues, land rights and environmental survival and protection, the forced removal of children by government agencies, education, health, and labor issues have been central. Given over two centuries of white patriarchal oppression of Aboriginal women, the early history of resistance and activism has yet to be fully reclaimed. Although Aboriginal women had equal relationships with men within cultures that long preceded the invasion of the British in 1788, white colonial patriarchy was not able to comprehend such equality. Moreover, the erasure of Aboriginal agency which accompanied the official verdict that Australia was uninhabited by humans intensified the invisibilization of Aboriginal women. Although male Aboriginal resistance leaders are mentioned in the emerging history of the frontier wars against white invaders, the women who fought with warriors such as Yagan, Musquito, Pemulwuy, Jandamarra, and Windradyne are not recorded (Reynolds 2006). While there are numerous accounts of settlers murdering Aboriginal women during combat, the names of women warriors and resistance fighters is studiously ignored in colonial records (Dudgeon 2008).

In Tasmania, the resistance leader Walyer taught her people to shoot white men after many years of being raped and exploited by sealers and witnessing the death of her family and people. Several years after her death, in 1837 other women who had escaped capture by sealers formed together to resist the power of a local colonial tyrant, Robinson. Ten years later, "the survivors addressed a petition protesting against hardships imposed by one of the white superintendents, Henry Jeanneret. It was the first written document of black protest in Australian history" (Marxist Interventions 2015). It is logical to assume that women fought during the most notorious recorded massacres such as Pinjarra (1834) and Forrest River (1926) in Western Australia, and Mount Isa (1884) in Queensland where the Kalkadoon warriors resisted.

Aboriginal women resistance fighters and activists have been central to the collective efforts to reclaim land and rights. In 2014, Arrernte Elder Rosalie Kunoth-Monks, one of the most important grassroots activist leaders in Australia and central to the indigenous self-determination movement, was prominent in the nationwide call for the 2014 Alice Springs Freedom Summit. The summit brought together leaders from across the country to reignite the civil rights movement. Between the warrior Walyer's death in 1831, and her women warrior survivors historically unique petition in 1847, to Kunoth-Monks' call for a national summit in 2014, Aboriginal women too numerous to mention here have empowered resistance against oppression.

Among the activists combating the mental health crisis that has emerged within indigenous communities during over 200 years of systemic racist oppression, Lorna Hudson is an elder working to heal young people through a connection to the land. Hudson is part of a movement to combat an epidemic of youth suicide among Aboriginal peoples. Pat Dudgeon, Australia's first Aboriginal psychologist, is also at the forefront of movements to restore emotional and social well-being and prevent suicide.

Jane Duren was an early activist in the first national indigenous political body, the Australian Aboriginal Progressive Association (AAPA), which was headed by Charles Maynard in 1924. The AAPA focused on recovering stolen land and improving life for Aboriginal people, and also combating the New South Wales Aborigines Protection Board, which forcibly removed children from their mothers. Although it was not until 1993 that the Native Title Act was passed by the Australian government, Duren's impact on focusing the AAPA on protesting the loss of land should not be underestimated. Duren sent a strong letter to King George V on June 14, 1926 protesting against the injustices inflicted on her people which included, among other abuses of human rights, the exclusion of Aboriginal children from school (Maynard 2007). Pearl Gibbs was a central figure in this era of Aboriginal activism and was part of the Aborigines Progressive Association (APA) and in 1938 established the Day of Mourning on Australia Day to protest against the national white celebration of invasion.

There is some evidence that Aboriginal women were involved in strikes, protests, letter writing, and other forms of activism in the nineteenth century. A central tactic of colonial oppression was the systematic breaking of Aboriginal girls, women, and mothers, and many women were silenced. The role of women activists in the important strikes of the twentieth century has not yet been recovered, partly due to a tendency within the white male dominated Left to ignore gender relations and partly because of the invisibilization of Aboriginal women by white colonial patriarchy. Aboriginal men and women walked off their reserve in Cummeroogunga in 1939 in protest. The first important act of worker resistance in Australia occurred when Aboriginal people conducted a lengthy strike in the Pilbara in 1946–1949. Marxist labor historians recognize the Pindan Pilbara strike as the most significant of Australian history; however, the women involved have not been discussed in the records apart from a fleeting mention of Mumaring, or Daisy Bindi, who was involved in worker resistance at the Ethel Creek Station.

The role of Aboriginal women activists in the 1963 Yirrkala Arnhem Land bark petition to the House of Representatives against the appropriation of land by a mining company is also yet to be highlighted by historians. However, it is logical to assume that mothers, aunties, and sisters, along with women Elders, would have been a vital (and natural) part of the community force. Indeed, it is important to point out that although various leaders have emerged from within Aboriginal resistance cultures, the collective nature of community means that such figureheads carry the voices of community, which in a culture that has achieved gender equality, means the voices of women, and not just men. In other words, it is a mistake to assume that the interests of women are not carried by male resistance leaders within the Aboriginal movement, and that while white history might have ideological problems with the inclusion of indigenous women as powerful actors, it is likely they were instrumental in defending their land and children during the frontier wars and defending their peoples' rights during strikes, as well as part of protests against colonization such as the 1972 Canberra Tent Embassy. The battles that erupted between police, government, and Aboriginal people over the removal of the Tent Embassy by the McMahon government ignited a strong protest in 1972, with many women playing key roles. It has been acknowledged that community-controlled organizations which had emerged from the civil rights movement and practiced self-determination were often led by women and focused on caring for women and children.

Of the many women activists who protested and agitated for social justice, Alice Nannup held flash protests against the racist oppression of her people in Geraldton, Western Australia (Nannup 1992). In 1947,

Helena Clarke established the Coolbaroo League which led to the establishment of the *Westralian Aborigine* newspaper in 1954. The focus was on self-determination and social justice. In South Australia in the 1960s, the Council for Aboriginal Women spoke out on a range of issues impacting on indigenous people and was instrumental in the formation of the Aboriginal Legal Rights Movement and the Aboriginal Land Rights Support Group. During the 1970s, larger groups of women activists were able to build on the gains of their foremothers. Key figures in national debates within the movement were Jackie Huggins and Pat O'Shane. Aboriginal women activists spoke to white middle-class Australian feminists who, they argued, demanded that Aboriginal women conform to their own unexamined ideas of what they should be and do, while also entrenching prejudice about Aboriginal men as deviant oppressors which were both toxic legacies of colonial oppression.

Denis Walker, the son of internationally acclaimed writer and activist Oodgeroo Noonuccal or Kath Walker, was central to the formation of the militant Black Power movement in the 1970s. Kath Walker mobilized for Aboriginal suffrage (Australian Women's Register 2013). Shirley Smith (Mum Shirl) a Wiradjuri woman, was also involved in the Black Power movement along with militant activists such as Gary Foley. Smith spoke out against the high rates of Aboriginal incarceration, an issue which continues to be an issue in 2015. She supported the poor, single mothers and their children, alcoholics, and those damaged by racism. She was active in mobilizing changes in housing, land rights, and in the black ghetto of Redfern she helped establish the Aboriginal Medical Service and the Redfern Aboriginal Legal Service in 1971 (Goodall 1996).

Aboriginal and Torres Strait Islander women activists have been at the forefront of the Stolen Generations movement for justice, from Duren in the 1930s onwards. Mollie Dyer, the daughter of Margaret Tucker, created the aboriginal child placement principle which recognized that removed Aboriginal children should be placed with Aboriginal families, and not white families. This policy was rolled out by many welfare departments in the 1980s (Haebich 2000). Barbara Cummings (1990), a victim of forced removal as a child, documented the forced removal of children in the Northern Territory in her authoritative book *Take This Child: From Kahlin Compound to Retta Dixon Children's Home*, organized the 1996 Going Home Conference in Darwin after the 1995 start of the National Inquiry into the Separation of Aboriginal and Torres Strait Islander Children from their Families, and with other women created the Karu Aboriginal Support Agency and the Aboriginal and Islander Child Care Agency in Darwin. In 2014, the New South Wales Gunnedah grandmothers formed to challenge the continuing removal of children from their mothers by various state governments. A key figure in this movement is grandmother Hazel Collins. As Collins pointed out, the new euphemism for forced removal by the Department of Child Protection is "out of home care."

Significant indigenous women leaders are emerging within the Australian parliamentary system. In 2001, Carol Martin won the seat of Kimberley for the Australian Labour Party and so became the first Aboriginal woman to be elected to the Australian parliament. Martin has long been active in supporting young women's health and encouraging indigenous women into entering public life. Olympic and Commonwealth gold medal winner and senator Nova Peris became the first Aboriginal woman elected to federal parliament in 2013, representing the Northern Territory as a member of the Australian Labour Party. Peris has a lengthy history of activism promoting health for children and adolescents. She blocked the conservative Abbott government's attempt to repeal Section 18C of the Racial Discrimination Act on the grounds that it would enable racist abuse (Summers 2013). In 2014, Peris was subjected to a racially motivated media smear campaign and Peris and her children have also been subjected to numerous racist threats.

Aboriginal women have also been at the forefront of activism to protect their land from mining. In 1998, Jacqui Katona mobilized one of Australia's largest blockades against the Northern Territory's Jabiluka uranium mine. Pitjantjatjara and Aranda women also led the Pine Gap Women's Peace protest in 1983. Pine Gap is a high security military base near Alice Springs in central Australia. However, contemporary Australian feminist hagiographies continue to ignore the agency of Aboriginal women activists. For example, in her history of the Pine Gap protests, Alison Bartlett merely writes that "the presence of Aboriginal women reminds the white women of the violent settler history of the land, and for some white protestors, their encounters with indigenous women are profound" (Bartlett 2013, 192). Nameless, but providing the conscientizing service of reminding white women of colonization, "some" white women manage to have "profound encounters" with these nameless Aboriginal women, some of whom are probably Elders. The process of the forgetting of Aboriginal women activists continues in early twenty-first century Australia.

Given the multiple layers of oppression that Aboriginal women experience, the very act of living is a form of resistance in itself. The process of activism is always already a collective becoming, energized by a multitude of people who do not always receive public recognition. There are numerous women who have not been recognized, by the white public sphere, in the ongoing work of liberation.

SEE ALSO: Anti-Racist and Civil Rights Movements; Gender, Politics, and the State: Indigenous Women; Indigenous Knowledges and Gender; White Supremacy and Gender

REFERENCES

Australian Bureau of Statistics. 2011. "The Health and Welfare of Australia's Aboriginal and Torres Strait Islander Peoples, October 2010." Accessed August 6, 2015, at http://www.abs.gov.au/AUSSTATS/abs@.nsf/lookup/4704.0Chapter935Oct+2010.

Australian Women's Register. 2013. "Oodgeroo Noonuccal (1920–1993)." Accessed August 6, 2015, at http:www.womenaustralia.info.biogs/IMP0082b.htm.

Bartlett, Alison. 2013. "Feminist protest and cultural production at the Pine Gap Women's Peace Camp, Australia 1983." *Women: A Cultural Review,* 24: 179–195.

Cummings, Barabara. 1990. *Take This Child: From Kahlin Compound to Retta Dixon Children's Home.* Canberra: Aboriginal Studies Press.

Dudgeon, Pat. 2008. *Mothers of Sin: Indigenous Women's Perceptions of their Identity and Gender.* Doctoral thesis, Murdoch University, Perth, Western Australia.

Goodall, Heather. 1996. *Invasion to Embassy: Land in Aboriginal Politics in New South Wales, 1770–1872.* Sydney: Allen & Unwin.

Haebich, Anna. 2000. *Broken Circles: Fragmenting Indigenous Families 1800–2000.* Fremantle Press: Fremantle.

Marxist Interventions. 2015. "'Difficult to Get Into a Black-Fellow's Head': Black Resistance in Colonial Australia." Accessed August 6, 2015, at http://www.anu.edu.au/polsci/marx/interventions/kooris.htm.

Maynard, John. 2007. *Fight for Liberty and Freedom: The Origins of Australian Aboriginal Activism.* Canberra: Aboriginal Studies Press.

Nannup, Alice. 1992. *When the Pelican Laughed.* Fremantle: Fremantle Art Centre Press.

Reynolds, Henry. 2006. *The Other Side of the Frontier: Aboriginal Resistance to the European Invasion of Australia.* Sydney: University of New South Wales Press.

Summers, Anne. 2013. "A Stellar Debut." Accessed August 26, 2015, at http://www.annesummers.com.au/wp-content/uploads/2014/10/asr10_stellardebut.pdf.

FURTHER READING

Bell, Diane. 1990. *Daughters of the Dreaming*. Sydney: McPhee Gribble/Allen & Unwin.

Bringing Them Home: Report of the National Inquiry into the Separation of Aboriginal and Torres Strait Islander Children from their Families. 1997. Human Rights and Equal Opportunity Commission. Commonwealth of Australia: Sydney.

Convict Creations. 2015. "Walyer, the Tasmanian Amazon." Accessed August 6, 2015, at http://www.convictcreations.com/history/walyer.html.

Elder, Bruce. 1988. *Blood on the Wattle: Massacres and Maltreatment of Australian Aborigines Since 1788*. Frenches Forest, NSW: Child & Associates.

Reynolds, Henry. 1995. *Fate of a Free People*. Sydney: Penguin.

Smith, Shirley. 1992. *MumShirl: An Autobiography*. Port Melbourne: Mammoth.

Walker, Kath. 1964. *We Are Going*. Brisbane: Jacaranda.

Women's and Feminist Activism in Australia and New Zealand

SANDRA GREY

Victoria University of Wellington, New Zealand

FIRST WAVE – WOMEN'S ENFRANCHISEMENT

The first wave of women's activism in Australia and NZ came in the mid-nineteenth century. Aimed at gaining for women the political and civil rights afforded to men, it was founded on fundamental claims of women as human beings and rejected practices that made women the property of men.

This first wave achieved one major gain – women's enfranchisement – which was hard fought for in both nations and set them as world leaders with regard to women's political rights: NZ was the first nation in the world where women won the right to vote (1893) and Australia was the first nation where women won both the right to vote and to stand for parliament (1902).

Feminist accounts of the first wave (Grimshaw 1987; Oldfield 1992) retell the herstories of the courageous women who fought social conventions and political elite to win the vote – women such as Kate Sheppard (NZ), Mary Ann Müller (NZ), Vida Goldstein (Australia), and Mary Lee (Australia). Feminist historians have also worked to ensure that the writings of early activists are preserved and recognized for their significance to political and social thought.

The herstories of the first wave of the women's movements in both Australia and NZ note the importance of the Women's Christian Temperance Union (alongside groups such as the Australian Womanhood Suffrage League) in advancing the political rights of women. It was thought if women could vote they would "banish the demon drink" from the two British colonies.

While political rights were central to the first wave, attention was also given to other formal rights. The NZ National Council of Women, for example, sought legal equality for women in areas such as marriage and employment. And in both countries activists sought major social and cultural changes through organizations such as the Rational Dress Movement.

SECOND WAVE – WOMEN'S LIBERATION

The next period of intense women's activism came nearly three generations later with the rise of the women's liberation movement in Australia and NZ (Kedgley and Varnham 1993; Henderson 2006). This activism must be set against the backdrop of these nations as male-wage earner welfare states which established clear boundaries between the public and private spheres and cast women as "housewives" and mothers.

This view was challenged when women moved out of the home and "onto the factory floors" during World War II. What follows, post-World War II, is a level of discontent from women forced back into the private sphere when the "men came home."

The rise of feminist collectives in both nations was also a reaction to male-dominated post-material social movements of the 1960s. Throughout the peace, anti-war and environmental movements, women found themselves charged with traditional "women's roles" such as making sandwiches and writing up minutes, while men dominated decision-making positions. Australian and NZ left-wing women found these roles constricting and sought to establish their own space for debate and action.

The women's liberation movements of Australia and NZ flourished under the social democratic consensus of the 1960s and 1970s, winning state funding for services such as women's health centers; refuges for victims of domestic violence; and rape crisis counselling services. Activists also won major law changes on equal pay; gender-based discrimination; domestic violence, rape, and sexual harassment; and access to contraception and abortion.

However, these gains were not won easily. The rise of the women's liberation movement in both Australia and NZ sparked counter-movements. Frequently the resistance to feminist ideals came from church-led organizations, with perhaps the bitterest disputes centered on access to "the right to choose" (Smyth 2000). For example, concerted campaigns opposing abortion in NZ raged during the 1980s, with scare campaigns outside hospitals and the fire-bombing of an abortion clinic.

Both in terms of their claims and forms of organizing, feminists challenged the patriarchal world and the oppression of women that resulted. Much of the early organizing was done through small consciousness-raising groups that were leaderless and non-hierarchical. This style of organizing was taken by feminists into the public sector, and while women's policy units survive in both the NZ and Australian public sectors today, the feminist models of operating were often short-lived in a political sphere structured around male-dominated hierarchies.

THIRD WAVE – POSTFEMINISM

By the 1990s, in both Australia and NZ, there is significant academic writing and populist rhetoric about the "death of feminism" (Sawer 2010). For some, this "death" in fact signaled the third wave of the women's movement (Maddison 2008) – a move to postfeminism and an era in which feminist activists accept the contradictions, pluralism, and hybrid nature of women's struggles as a given.

Third-wave activists engage in a broad range of activities, particularly those centered on the body, sexual health and reproduction, and cultural production. Younger feminists note that postfeminism signals a change in the nature of the movement and the modes of organizing; one example being the flourishing cyber activism they engage in – a type of activist tactic which is often eschewed by older feminists as too individualist, consumer-culture oriented, and which has little real-world impact.

Feminist activists in Australia and NZ have also continued in the early twenty-first century to take action over, and make gains on, a range of public sphere issues, particularly in areas focused on women's labor force participation such as better access to paid parental leave and childcare.

A MOVEMENT BEYOND BORDERS

All three waves of women's movement activism in Australia and NZ sit within transnational feminist movements. The herstories of the first wave retell how the tactics and messages of the suffrage movement were shared between English-speaking democracies through letters and by activists travelling beyond their home territories.

The second-wave women's movement organizations in Australia and NZ connected to the transnational realm by importing a wide range of feminist texts from authors such as Betty Friedan and Simone de Beauvoir, and through setting up "feminist" libraries and bookshops. Groups also brought international feminists to the nations for speaking tours (Dann 1984).

For third-wave feminists the task of working across borders is aided by information communications technology. One example was the spread of the SlutWalk concept in 2011 which began in Toronto following a police officer's comments that "women should avoid dressing like sluts in order not to be victimized," and was quickly picked up in both Australia and NZ.

A POLITICAL AND CULTURAL MOVEMENT

A crucial feature of feminist activism in Australia and NZ has been the focus on both political and cultural change. While much of the literature looks at movement interactions with the state, feminists have long recognized the importance of cultural production and reproduction in empowering women.

There is a strong history of women's movement publishing: first, in suffrage pamphlets; then, in women's liberation magazines; and finally, through third-wave zines and blogs. The earliest women's movement magazine in Australia was *The Dawn*, published first in 1888. NZ's longest running feminist magazine was *Broadsheet*, published from 1972 to 1997. Publishing was a way of transmitting women's experiences and voices without moderation; a way of sharing movement tactics and information about services for women; and a challenge to mainstream media constructions of women.

Activists were also involved in the production of films, theater, and music. Perhaps the best-known musical contribution is Australian singer Helen Reddy's "I Am Woman," which became an anthem for the women's liberation movement.

Women in Australia and NZ knew the importance of knowledge production, and were actively involved in research and writing centered on gendered experiences. Both nations have spawned international feminist authors with two of the most well known internationally being Australian Germaine Greer (1970) and New Zealander Marilyn Waring (1988). And from the late 1970s women's studies departments were established in most universities in Australia and NZ. By the 1990s many of these were mainstreamed into other departments or shut down due to the pressures of operating within neoliberal tertiary education markets. The difficulty of maintaining feminist structures in hostile political and cultural climates is a theme seen across both nations.

THE TENSION OF REVOLUTION OR REFORM

Women's movement activists in Australia and NZ have long debated whether insider or outsider tactics would bring an end to women's oppression. However, in both nations feminists often directed activism toward the state. While the state's role in creating the division between the public and private spheres was rightly questioned by feminists in Australia and NZ, the interventionist states also provided shape to activism. For example, feminists sought legislation on maternity leave and childcare provision; laws around domestic violence; and changes to tax and labor laws that privileged "working" men.

To advance their project for formal equality, liberal feminists in Australia and NZ sought to change the very nature of the state itself. They agitated for and won the establishment of feminist bureaucratic structures inside the state and the "femocrat" was born (Curtin and Teghtsoonian 2010).

Liberal feminists in Australia and NZ also fought to get women into elected political office, forming groups to advance women's political interests such as the Women's Electoral Lobby (Preddy 2003; Sawer 2008).

Feminists in the second wave also set their sights on changing other male-dominated domains such as churches and trade unions (unions in both nations had protected the labor market as the preserve of men). Accordingly, feminists took a range of actions within the trade union movement to raise the profile of women and "women's issues" inside trade unions, setting up women's structures, for example.

A reliance on the state and the ability to bring change from within formal political institutions was challenged from the start by those who feared co-optation of the activists. What is evident in both nations is the triumph of liberal feminism and a focus on formal equality. This dominance in the nations' women's movements silenced the more revolutionary liberations (Maddison and Sawer 2013). In hindsight, the reliance on an active social democratic state being kept honest by feminists outside the institutional structures was problematic (Grey and Sawer 2008).

DEATH OR RENEWAL?

From the 1990s the women's liberation movement in both nations was under strain and women's groups had to fight to hold onto what they had won in earlier decades. In Australia, for example, the early twenty-first century has seen women's organizations defunded due to a rise in rhetoric that Australia is "postfeminist."

Scholars and activists alike have argued that the political and cultural opportunities of the two nations enabled the rise of new social movements, but also led to the ebb in more "contentious" and "radical" activism towards the end of the twentieth century. The rise of neoconservatism in Australia and NZ, as well as neoliberal marketization approaches in state and society, impacted negatively on the ability of feminist activists to continue their agitation against patriarchal oppression. Feminists from the 1990s found it much more difficult to pursue equality for women through the state. And the neoliberals were able to co-opt the autonomy and freedom-language of the women's liberation movement, albeit using it in a different way than feminists of the second wave.

It was not just external forces which impacted on radical feminist and women's liberationist activity: endogenous factors impacted on the unity and strength of the movement. Internal tensions in the women's liberation movement were seen as renting the movement apart. In NZ, the movement is seen to have splintered during the infamous "Black Olive Affair" at Piha, where challenges to the dominance of liberal feminism from both Māori activists (mana wahine) and lesbian-feminists arose. In Australia, a major change occurred in the 1980s when the women's movement divided along two tracks – those who go into personal politics, and those who enter the public realm (Maddison 2008). Throughout the second wave, Aboriginal and Torres Strait Islander women found they had to challenge the white feminism that dominated the Australian women's movement (Moreton-Robinson 2000).

However, the proclamations of the death of the women's movements of Australia and NZ have been challenged by activists and scholars alike. Feminist scholars have noted that the women's liberation movement may have either gone into abeyance due to hostile social and political environments (McLeay, Leslie, and McMillan 2009), or morphed into something new because of changing modes of organizing.

The scholarly challenge is reflected in intergenerational debates between feminists, in which older feminists in Australia and NZ have challenged younger women to take up the baton and younger women have responded saying "we are, but in different ways." Cast in the framework of being a mother–daughter debate in which the "daughter" is seeking to assert her independence and uniqueness, this postfeminist phase is most certainly a reaction to the second-wave women's liberation ideology and practices.

Whatever the truth, persistent gender-based inequalities in Australia and NZ mean that feminism as a political philosophy is likely to be used as a base for ongoing agitation to seek the further empowerment of women.

SEE ALSO: Empowerment; Feminisms, First, Second, and Third Wave; Gender Equality; Postfeminism; Women's Movements: Modern International Movements

REFERENCES

Curtin, Jennifer, and Katherine Teghtsoonian. 2010. "Analyzing Institutional Persistence: The Case of the Ministry of Women's Affairs in Aotearoa/NZ." *Politics and Gender*, 6(4): 545–572. DOI: 10.1017/S1743923X1000036X.

Dann, Christine. 1985. *Up from Under: Women and Liberation in New Zealand, 1970–1985*. Wellington, NZ: Allen & Unwin.

Henderson, Margaret. 2006. *Marking Feminist Times: Remembering the Longest Revolution in Australia*. Bern: Peter Lang.

Grey, Sandra, and Marian Sawer, eds. 2008. *Women's Movements: Flourishing or in Abeyance?* London: Routledge.

Grimshaw, Patricia. 1987. *Women's Suffrage in NZ*. Auckland: Auckland University Press.

Kedgley, Sue, and Mary Varnham, eds. 1993. *Heading Nowhere in a Navy Blue Suit and other Tales from the Feminist Revolution*. Wellington, NZ: Daphne Brasell.

Maddison, Sarah. 2008. *Collective Identity and Australian Feminist Activism: Conceptualising a Third Wave*. Germany: VDM Verlag.

Maddison, Sarah, and Marian Sawer, eds. 2013. *The Women's Movement in Protest, Institutions and the Internet: Australia in Transnational Perspective*. London: Routledge.

McLeay, Elizabeth, John Leslie, and Kate McMillan, eds. 2009. *Rethinking Women and Politics: NZ and Comparative Perspectives*. Wellington, NZ: VUW Press.

Moreton-Robinson, Aileen. 2000. *Talkin' Up to the White Woman: Indigenous Women and White Feminism*. St Lucia, Australia: University of Queensland Press.

Oldfield, A. 1992. *Woman's Suffrage in Australia: A Gift or a Struggle?* Melbourne: Cambridge University Press.

Preddy, Elizabeth. 2003. *The WEL herstory: the Women's Electoral Lobby in NZ 1975–2002*. Wellington, NZ: WEL NZ (with Fraser Books).

Sawer, Marian. 2008. *Making Women Count: A History of the Women's Electoral Lobby in Australia*. Sydney: UNSW Press.

Sawer, Marian. 2010. "Premature Obituaries: How Can We Tell if the Women's Movement is Over?" *Politics and Gender*, 6(4): 602–609. DOI: 10.1017/S1743923X10000383.

Smyth, Helen. 2000. *Rocking the Cradle: Contraception, Sex, and Politics in NZ*. Wellington, NZ: Steele Roberts.

FURTHER READING

Greer, Germaine. 1971. *The Female Eunuch*. New York: McGraw-Hill.

Waring, Marilyn. 1988. *Counting For Nothing: What Men Value & What Women Are Worth*. East Melbourne: Allen & Unwin/Port Nicholson Press.

Women's and Feminist Activism in the Caribbean

PATRICIA MOHAMMED
University of the West Indies, Trinidad

In 1917 Amy Ashwood Garvey accompanied her husband Marcus Garvey to New York. She was a colored woman now, and no longer possessed the "browning" class status that she would have enjoyed at the time in Jamaica. The segregation she encountered outside of the West Indies shaped a consciousness of race and gender that generated her pioneering support for Pan-Africanism and a community feminism that she introduced into activism in the region (Vassell 1993). In Puerto Rico, Luisa Capetillo (1880–1922) is revered as an extraordinary socialist labor organizer and writer who militantly struggled for equal rights for women and for human emancipation. In the 1980s when Drupatie Ramgoonai, a housewife from Trinidad, defied taboos to publically perform the chutney songs that were once restricted to Indo-Caribbean female ritual spaces, the message was an affirmation of women's cultural contributions and of the increasing visibility of an Indo-feminist presence in an Afro-European dominated space (Puri 2004). In 2011 a group of young female and male university students, calling themselves "Support for Change" and networking primarily though not exclusively through Facebook, picketed the entrance to the Trinidad and Tobago parliament where the cabinet was debating the draft National Gender Policy. These examples illustrate the breadth and changing nature of the varied contestations in women's and feminist activism in the Caribbean from the twentieth into the twenty-first century.

The historical past renders up variations by societies and among women and various groups who by their actions and words have challenged diverse forms of gender discrimination (de Haan 2013). A narrow definition that sees feminist actions derived primarily from a consciousness of female subordination denies those whose actions were impelled by political, class, ethnic, or national identity concerns as underscored by gender. Such an inelastic definition also fails to contemplate fully the distinctive nature and evolution of feminist activism in the Caribbean, a region framed first by its decimation of indigenous populations and settlement, through different European colonial systems of migrating labor, including African slavery and Asian indentures (Lewis 2004). This legacy of varied languages and vastly differing cultural practices and gender belief systems makes the construction of any master narrative of feminism in the Caribbean, including one that denies male solidarity, impossible to construct. Universalizing frameworks that are conventionally framed in terms of waves or phases of a women's movement also do not fit the internal struggles within nations of the Caribbean. To avoid the pitfalls of definitions that exclude, I view feminism in the region as overlapping and emerging consortia that provide cyclical strength and possibilities for sustained growth of a feminist and gender consciousness. I separate feminist and women's activism into three distinct yet overlapping categories and illustrate with specific national examples. The categories are self-defined feminist and non-governmental women's organizations; the state machinery and gender; and tertiary-level teaching and research in gender studies, with greater attention paid to the first of these three categories, and all spanning the time period of the twentieth century to the present.

SELF-DEFINED FEMINISTS AND NON-GOVERNMENTAL WOMEN'S ORGANIZATIONS

There are distinctive variations in the traditions of women's activism that emerged in different Caribbean territories. For example, Cuba was a forerunner in naming activities or groups as feminist. *Aspiraciones* (1918) is an early feminist journal published by the Partido Feminista Aspiraciones, and *La Mujer Moderna* (1926) was the journal for the Club Femenino de Cuba, the oldest Cuban feminist organization. Jamaica also boasts a very early tradition of self-acclaimed feminists. Among these was Una Marson, born in 1905, the daughter of a Baptist parson. She was the first woman editor and publisher recorded in that society, and rose to international fame as a journalist, social activist, and BBC broadcaster. Power and resource imbalances as a result of race and class differences were as present then as they are today in women's activism. Mary Morris-Knibb, who ran a private preparatory school, had to form alliances with other black and colored Jamaican women like Una Marson and Amy Bailey in order to highlight poor laboring conditions suffered by black women in Jamaica in the 1930s.

Social work and community care was another foundational space for women's activism throughout the region. Audrey Jeffers in Trinidad was responsible for the formation of the Coterie of Social Workers in the 1920s, thus initiating the spread of similar activity in neighboring territories. There were parallel developments in Haiti. Calling themselves the Ligue Feminine d'action sociale (1934), women in Haiti consolidated around interclass cooperation. They founded the Association des Femmes Haitiennes pour l'Organisation du Travail in 1935, a foundation for homemakers in 1937, and an organization working on behalf of children's rights in 1939. These were viewed largely as acceptable pastimes for middle- and upper-class women of Jamaica, Guyana, Barbados, and other Caribbean countries. From such experience in civic activity, however, some women were able to move into political office. In 1940, Audrey Jeffers became the first woman in Trinidad nominated to the Legislative Council (Reddock 1994).

Alongside these were the less forthright but equally committed women who worked in church and charity organizations such as the Anglican Mother's Union and the umbrella organization of the Young Women's Christian Association. Gema Ramkeesoon observed that from such beginnings, she also became involved in the founding of the Caribbean Women's Association. There was "a drift away from the purely social welfare organizations. We entered the field of labour relations as in 1952 the government set up a three member panel to adjudicate over the Minimum Wages Council" (Ramkeesoon 1999). Ramkeesoon would become the deputy chair of this council while Lenora Pujadas Mc-Shine was an independent member. Nesha Haniff of Guyana recorded the victories of individual women in this society involved in unions, political unrest, and in struggles in their homes and villages, many unproclaimed feminists (Haniff 1988). The period of the 1950s saw an increase in women sliding unobtrusively into the political milieu, as evidenced in the testimony of Nesta Patrick, the first recipient of the Caribbean Community Secretariat Triennium award for women, conferred for her service to several social work organizations and, among others, her pioneering role in the League of Women Voters in Trinidad.

By the 1960s we see a confirmed presence of women as political activists. Christina Ramjattan, who had escaped death in the scourge of racial violence that erupted in Guyana between warring groups, emerged as a leading female activist, and in 1965 was made a senator in the People's Progressive Party, the first female in Guyana to hold that post. The Hermanas Mirabal (Mirabal sisters) in the Dominican Republic were not so fortunate. The four women dared to oppose the political dictatorship of Rafael Trujillo and were assassinated in 1960. Their iconic status in the women's movement in this society and in the wider region draws attention to the revolutionary militancy that is also part of the earliest feminist traditions, a potency that recurs in the example of the young Beverley Jones's tragic involvement in the Black Power movement of Trinidad and Tobago (Pasley 2001). She was gunned down in action in September 1973, as was Jacqueline Creft in the socialist revolution of Grenada in the 1983.

The radical messages that were being transmitted in these early schools of feminist thought and action would not reveal themselves fully until the next generation of activists – the second wavers who were labeled licentious women's libbers. The period of the 1970s and 1980s ushered in a new and more strident brand of feminism that was taken up throughout the region, influenced by a parallel global internationalism of feminism. By the late 1970s and early 1980s in Jamaica the Committee of Women for Progress, the women's arm of the leftist Workers Party of Jamaica, was formed. Similarly, the Concerned Women for Progress in Trinidad was the women's face of the People's Popular Movement, a socialist party rooted in the trade union movement. The Antiguan-Caribbean Liberation Movement led by Tim Hector bolstered the efforts of Arah Hector in a women's movement that between the late 1970s and 1990s had threaded its way across the Anglophone Caribbean, forging sisterhood links to the Hispanophone, Francophone, and Dutch Antillean islands.

The debates generated by these groups were not restricted to labor or social welfare issues. From the 1990s the National Coordinating Committee for the Advocacy of Women's Rights (CONAP) in Haiti brought together five feminist organizations to negotiate directly with the Haitian parliament to modify texts of existing laws unfavorable to women (Lebon and Maier 2010).

Anti-abortion platforms, crisis centers for rape survivors, and shelters for women and children from violent domestic situations sprang up across the region. In Trinidad, under the support of the Caribbean Conference of Churches, the first Rape Crisis Centre, under my coordination, was opened in the compound of the Catholic Centre in Port of Spain 1985. In 1986, the Business and Professional Women's Club of Barbados established a "Crisis Centre" offering a confidential hotline service, counseling, and support services to victims of abuse. Many such centers and resources were supported in part by church and professional women's associations. By this time also, the network of funding for non-governmental organizations who engaged in institutional protections on issues such as gender-based violence was available from international agencies, and supplemented by government subsidies. Many if not most of these institutional initiatives continue to form the backdrop to gender interventions in the region today, by the millennium becoming more and more mainstreamed and legitimated. The discourse of feminism had expanded and the areas of sexual and reproductive rights, including gay and lesbian rights, and the advance in technologies that allowed greater global communication flows stimulated new activisms. The once seemingly radical groups such as the Ligue Feminine d'action sociale of the 1930s and the Caribbean Women's Association of the 1950s have transformed into an unapologetic feminist activism today, although many women still do not avow the term "feminist." In organizations such as Red Thread in Guyana, Code Red for Justice in Barbados, and Support for Change in Trinidad, there have emerged groups of women and men who continue the radical strain of feminist activism that is vital to its continuity.

THE STATE MACHINERY AND GENDER

Despite nearly a century of women's activism, gender issues remained marginal to the compelling ones of self-governance and national identity formation in Caribbean states. Freedom from colonial clutches was privileged as the primary battle. Men led the independence movements. The few women visible were the supporting act. Leaders such as Eric Williams in Trinidad and Tobago and Norman Manley in Jamaica became the first prime ministers of these nations at independence. In the first 50 years of independence and postcolonial rule, only one woman, Dame Eugenia Charles in the Commonwealth of Dominica, rose to the national leadership.

Women's autonomous activism in the Caribbean cannot, however, be fully distanced from the state machinery initiatives. Women comprised half the voters from the time adult suffrage fully included the female sex. The governmental platform of gender surfaces more visibly from the 1980s, accelerated by United Nations programmatic support. The International Decade for Women (1975–1985), the Convention against the Elimination of Violence against Women (CEDAW 1979), which required governments' ratification, the sponsoring of World Conferences of Women between 1985 and 2000, sent a clear mandate to governments that gender equality must be placed on their agendas if they wanted to benefit from global links and development loans (Antrobus 2004).

From the 1980s, the global women's movement and the gender and development discourse proved to be a steady pressure group. Caribbean states were either encouraged or forced to establish women's desks or women's bureaus to address gender inequality and discrimination. These bureaus/desks were the result of tireless work by feminist activists who lobbied for governments to be accountable to women. The women's bureaus/desks were typically overworked, understaffed, institutionalized to fail, vulnerable to co-optation, and of marginal importance due to their focus on women's issues, the latter which were and are still viewed as intrusive into the realpolitik of nations. These limbs of state were informed by current progressive global developments by gender theory that argued for the mainstreaming of gender into all facets of government policy and ministries. In order to comply with the UN conventions they had ratified and with the growing demands of more enlightened populations of women and men who demanded gender equity and equality as the right of the modern citizen, several governments in the Caribbean committed to formulating national gender policies for equity and equality. Among these Belize, Guyana, Cayman Islands, Jamaica, Dominica, and the British Virgin Islands are currently implementing policies that include addressing discriminatory laws against gender equality. This new institutionalized level is, however, toothless without their constituency of non-governmental and women's organizations, and without the backing of the new space where gender specialists and opinion leaders are being shaped, in the tertiary-level departments for gender studies.

TERTIARY LEVEL AND GENDER STUDIES

It would be impossible in the Caribbean to separate women's and feminist activism from the growth of tertiary-level education and research in gender. The creation of this interdisciplinary area of studies at tertiary level was highly political. Many of the early pioneers in woman and gender studies had spent their formative years in activism. Two examples are illustrative of the distinctive ways in which feminist activism and gender studies in the Caribbean has operated as an integrated space. In the late 1960s, the ruling party in Jamaica, in order to assist with relief programs for unemployed women, recruited Grenadian-born Peggy Antrobus. A popular theater group called SISTREN, comprised of working- and middle-class Jamaican women, supported her. This total immersion in the field provided the rich experiential data from which Antrobus would later build the first Women and Development Unit of the University of the West Indies, as an extra-mural department. In Barbados, Joycelin Massiah, director of the Institute for Social and Economic Research, spearheaded a region-wide research project entitled Women in the Caribbean which drew in older disciplinary trained scholars and new budding ones who would make gender studies their main preoccupation. Among these young scholars were young university-educated women from the Caribbean. Inspired by the female authors of the global women's movement, among them were Rhoda Reddock, Patricia Mohammed, and Eudine Barriteau. They had begun graduate dissertations on women in labor, migration, and economy in the Caribbean and were founding members of the early feminist organizations, the Concerned Women for Progress and Women Working for Social Progress, the former being the first second-wave feminist group in Trinidad.

The need for culturally apposite theoretical and policy frameworks became increasingly crucial under conditions of globalization. While the earlier problems of women's invisibility and abuse had not disappeared, the 1980s and 1990s were characterized by the emergence of many feminist groups who developed their activism around a greater variety of issues in which there was a paucity of raw data to support programmatic changes. The rolling out of gender studies departments committed to research, teaching, and outreach filled this gap. Among the institutions that emerged in the last two decades of the twentieth century, with the cooperation of Dutch expertise and funding, was the Institute for Gender and Development Studies. Units were located at the University of the West Indies in Trinidad, Barbados, and Jamaica, and in the latter the first Professor of Women Studies, Elsa Leo-Rhynie, was appointed by 1992. In Puerto Rico, programs in the United States spurred on the growth of women studies. Centers were created within universities such as the Centro de Estudios, Recursos y Servicios a la Mujer (CERES), and Proyecto de Estudios de la Mujer (Pro Mujer) at the University of Puerto Rico (Crespo 2002). Tertiary-level education is the think tank for the women's movement, grappling with the increasing complexity of issues related to gender inequality and undertaking to train a more informed and articulate voice for the region's present and future feminist activists.

SEE ALSO: Anglophone Caribbean Feminism; Feminism, Indo-Caribbean

REFERENCES

Antrobus, Peggy. 2004. *The Global Women's Movement: Issues and Strategies for the New Century*. London: Zed Books.

Crespo, Elizabeth. 2002. "Feminist Activism and Women's Studies in Puerto Rico." Accessed June 21, 2014, at http://pages.towson.edu/ncctrw/working%20papers/puertoricoWMST.html 2002.

de Haan, Francisca. 2013. *Women's Activism: Global Perspectives from the 1890s to the Present*. London: Routledge.

Haniff, Nesha. 1988. *Blaze a Fire: Significant Contributions of Caribbean Women*. Caribbean Women Series. Toronto: Sister Vision.

Lebon, Nathalie, and Elizabeth Maier. 2010. *Women's Activism in Latin America and the Caribbean: Engendering Social Justice, Democratizing Citizenship.* New Brunswick, NJ: Rutgers University Press.

Lewis, Gordon K. 2004. *The Growth of the Modern West Indies.* Jamaica: Ian Randle Publishers.

Pasley, Victoria. 2001. "The Black Power Movement in Trinidad: An Exploration of Gender and Cultural Changes and the Development of a Feminist Consciousness." *Journal of International Women's Studies,* 3(1): 24–40.

Puri, Shalini. 2004. *The Caribbean Postcolonial: Social Equality, Post/Nationalism and Cultural Hybridity.* Basingstoke: Palgrave Macmillan.

Ramkeesoon, Gema. 1999. "Early Women's Organizations in Trinidad." In *Gender in Caribbean Development,* 2nd ed., edited by Patricia Mohammed and Cathy Shepherd. Kingston: University of the West Indies Press.

Reddock, Rhoda. 1994. *Women, Labour and Politics in Trinidad & Tobago: A History.* London: Zed Books.

Vassell, Linette, ed. 1993. *Voices of Women in Jamaica, 1898–1939.* Kingston: Department of History, University of the West Indies.

FURTHER READING

Bailey, Barbara Evelyn, and Elsa Leo-Rhynie. 2004. *Gender in the 21st Century: Caribbean Perspectives, Visions and Possibilities.* Kingston: Ian Randle Publishers.

GaleCengage Learning. Archives Unbound: "Feminism in Cuba 1898–1958." Accessed June 21, 2014, at http://gdc.gale.com/archivesunbound/archives-unbound-feminism-in-cuba-18981958/.

Horizons Guyana. 2013. "First Woman in Guyana's Politics Christina Ramjattan." Accessed June 20, 2014, at http://www.horizonsguyana.com/first-woman-in-guyanas-politics/.

Mohammed, Patricia. 2003. "Like Sugar in Coffee: Third Wave Feminism in the Caribbean." *Social and Economic Studies,* 52: 5–30.

Reddock, Rhoda. 1998. "Women's Organizations and Movements in the Commonwealth Caribbean: The Response to Global Economic Crisis in the 1980s." *Feminist Review,* 59: 57–73.

Women's and Feminist Activism in East Asia

JULIA C. BULLOCK
Emory University, USA

Because "East Asia" is a diverse and populous region that cannot be discussed thoroughly in the space allotted, this entry will focus primarily on the Chinese, Japanese, and (South) Korean cultures, with some attention to the transnational frameworks of feminist activity that have developed therein. The reader is encouraged to view the following as a concise summary of the role of women's and feminist organizations in select East Asian nations, and to consult the sources listed below for further detail.

From the beginning of the modern period, Chinese feminist activity was intimately connected with nationalist movements to resist imperialism, first by Western nations and later by the Japanese. For example, the Women's Suffrage Alliance was formed in 1912, soon after the fall of the Qing dynasty, by women revolutionaries who had fought against the Manchu regime. In addition to suffrage, these early feminist activists struggled for women's rights to education and freedom of marriage, and for the abolition of oppressive cultural practices such as footbinding. As the rise of the May Fourth Movement (1919) fostered broader societal support for women's rights, United Women's Associations were created in various urban centers. These activists managed to secure guarantees of gender equality in some provincial constitutions in the early 1920s, and were later active in the successful campaign to include women's right to suffrage in the Constitution of the Republic of China (promulgated 1947). However, this government was forced to relocate to Taiwan when the civil war concluded with the communist victory in 1949, and democratic elections were not held until 1987.

With the transition to democratic rule, the number of Taiwanese women's organizations and the issues they addressed expanded rapidly to include explicitly feminist groups like the Feminist Studies Association (academic), the Warm Life Association (divorced women), the Taipei Association for the Promotion of Women's Rights and Pink Collar Solidarity (working women), and the Taipei Women's Rescue Foundation (domestic violence), as well as more traditionalist organizations like the Homemakers Union (environmental protection) and the Compassionate Relief and Merit Society (Buddhist charity). Additionally, the Awakenings Foundation (*Funü xinzhi*) has been particularly active in protesting sexism in Taiwanese society, in spite of suppression by the authoritarian government. Formed in 1982 to support women's liberation activist Hsiu-lien Annette Lu, who was imprisoned for her feminist activities, the Awakenings Foundation has launched high-profile campaigns against sexual harassment, sex tourism, and other forms of gender discrimination.

Women were granted suffrage by the People's Republic of China in 1949, and the government established the All-China Women's Federation (ACWF) in the same year. While this organization is dedicated to protection of women and promotion of their interests, it is also structurally and ideologically subordinate to the Communist Party. While the Party has given verbal and legal support to gender equality – for example, by passing a Marriage Law (1950) that gave women the legal standing to make autonomous decisions about marriage and divorce – patriarchal traditions have remained strong in Chinese society and institutions. The ACWF has therefore been active in protesting employment discrimination, advocacy of women's rights within the family, and increasing women's representation in the political power structure by recommending talented women for official positions within the Party, in addition to promotion of government-sponsored initiatives such as family planning. While the ACWF disbanded during the Cultural Revolution (1966–1976), its activities resumed afterward. In the wake of the market reforms of 1978 that removed many of the quotas and incentives intended to promote gender equality in the political structure and the workplace, the ACWF has proven a powerful advocate for women who have faced pervasive discrimination in spite of legal guarantees of equality. It effectively campaigned for passage of the Law on Protecting Women's Rights and Interests (1992), which provides broad legal protections for women in the areas of employment, education, and family relations.

Japanese women were vocal participants in the People's Rights Movement (*Jiyū Minken Undō*) of the early Meiji era (1868–1912). However, the passage of the Law on Political Associations and Assembly (1890) and the Public Peace Police Law (1900) curtailed their rights to political participation, thus hampering the development of women's political organizations during this period, with the exception of nationalistic groups like the Patriotic Women's Society (*Aikoku Fujinkai*, founded 1901). However, the transition to the Taisho era (1912–1926), a time of relative political liberalization, saw a proliferation of feminist activity. Groups emerging during this time included the Bluestocking (*Seitō*) Society (1911–1916), a literary group that published increasingly politicized essays on the role of women both inside and outside the home, and the socialist-feminist Red Wave Society (*Sekirankai*, 1921). The New Women's Association (*Shin Fujin Kyōkai*, 1919) successfully lobbied the government to legalize women's political organizations (but not suffrage) with the repeal of Article

Five of the Public Peace Police Law (1922). This enabled the founding of more explicitly political organizations like the Women's Suffrage League (*Fusen Kakutoku Dōmei*, 1924). As Japan slid toward total war as a result of the 1931 Manchurian Incident, women rallied to the nationalist cause, and organizations like the Greater Japan National Women's Defense Association (*Dai Nihon Kokubō Fujinkai*) were formed to provide moral support for troops fighting abroad. In 1942, all women's voluntary associations were subsumed underneath the Greater Japan Women's Association (*Dai Nihon Fujinkai*), which mobilized women to support the war effort through their labor on the homefront.

After Japan's defeat in World War II, its women were finally granted suffrage under an Allied Occupation that sought to restructure Japan legally and culturally as a democratic nation, leading to the election of 39 women to the Diet in 1946. New political organizations like Ichikawa Fusae's Women's Committee on Postwar Policies (*Sengo Taisaku Fujin Iinkai*), which successfully pushed for the inclusion of women's suffrage in the new election law of 1945, sprang up to capitalize on this turn to democracy. Other organizations, like the Housewives Association (*Shufuren*, 1948) and the Mothers' Conferences (*Hahaoya Taikai*, beginning 1955), leveraged women's status as guardian of the home and hearth to lobby for consumer protection, the peace movement, and other reforms to improve the material conditions of family life. In the 1970s, women who rejected the sexism of their New Left comrades during the 1960s formed a diverse spectrum of small-scale activist collectives under the rubric of "women's liberation" (*ūman ribu*), which sought to problematize both the sexual exploitation of women in Japanese society and the ease with which it conflated womanhood with motherhood. Japanese women's organizations that formed after the International Women's Year of 1975 were, generally speaking, less politically radical and more institutionally powerful, as a result of the growth of women's studies as an academic discipline and the increasing representation of women in governmental bureaucracies and advisory councils dedicated to improving the status of women in society.

Women's organizations in Korea first developed as a consequence of the modernization process that followed the signing of the Kanghwa Treaty with Japan, which forcibly opened the country in 1876. The first such organization was the Praise and Encouragement Association (*Ch'anyanghoe*), formed in 1898, a social reform society dedicated to promoting women's education. Women also joined and formed patriotic societies, sometimes in cooperation with men, that developed as a response to the increasing threat of Japanese colonialism on the peninsula. After Korea was annexed by Japan in 1910, women's organizations like the Friends of the Rose of Sharon (*Kŭnuhoe*) and the Korean Patriotic Women's Society (*T'aehan Aeguk Puinhoe*) sprang up to protest the various types of discrimination experienced by Korean women in the context of both Japanese imperialism and the sexism of their own countrymen.

Japanese rule ended in 1945 with its defeat in World War II, and the Korean War (1950–1953) subsequently split the peninsula into South and North Korea. Since then feminism in North Korea has been subordinated to communist ideology, and femininity has been subsumed beneath maternalist rhetoric. In South Korea, the education level, employment rate, and standard of living of women have risen with industrialization and the global integration of the South Korean economy. However, the persistence of traditional Confucian views of women's place in society has made it necessary for Korean women to struggle for gender equality in the family and the workplace. Lee T'aeyong, the first female lawyer in South Korea, founded the Korea Legal Aid Center for Family Relations in 1956 to advocate for more legal rights for women. She successfully lobbied for creation of a family court to address problems of divorce and domestic violence. The Council of Korean Women's Organizations (CKWO), an umbrella group of centrist women's organizations formed in 1959, was likewise active in advocating for greater rights for women in the workplace and the family.

In 1973, 61 Korean women's organizations united to form the All Women's Federation to Revise the Family Law. Their efforts ultimately resulted in the passage of laws granting women equal rights of inheritance, marriage, divorce, and child custody (effective 1991). The Korean Women's Association United (KWAU), founded in 1987, has advocated for the rights of women workers and housewives, and challenged the state to address urban poverty and the needs of rural women. In the early 1990s, the Korean League of Women Voters, the Korean National Council of Women, and Korean Women's Association United collaborated in a campaign to revise election laws to facilitate election of more female representatives, to rectify women's historic underrepresentation in elected office. This joint effort resulted in the successful passage of a bill in 2000 requiring that 30 percent of candidates running for proportional representation seats in the National Assembly be women.

While East Asian women's organizations are unarguably grounded in the local and sociohistorically specific contexts of their origin, they have also taken inspiration from transnational movements of ideas and activist tactics. From the beginning of the modern period, Christian reformers were active across East Asia in promoting education for women, and works by Western feminist thinkers like Ellen Key and Margaret Sanger contributed to the development of Japanese feminist theory. In China and Japan, during the early decades of the twentieth century, local branches of the international Women's Christian Temperance Union were active in the struggle for women's suffrage, and in Korea, the Young Women's Christian Association (YWCA) has been a vocal advocate for women, particularly concerning themselves with women's employment issues, since 1922. Additionally, participation in socialist organizations gave some Asian women the political experience necessary to organize on their own behalf, spawning many more explicitly feminist groups. More recently, the international women's liberation movement of the 1970s nurtured similar developments in Japan and Taiwan, as women from these countries were exposed to new ideas as a result of travel to the United States and other Western countries, or received and translated information from abroad that bolstered their own feminist activity.

In response to the United Nations (UN) designation of 1975 as the International Year of the Woman, 41 Japanese women's organizations formed an International Women's Year Liaison Group to lobby their government for more effective policies to ensure sexual equality. This group successfully pressured the government to sign the 1979 UN Convention on the Elimination of All Forms of Discrimination against Women, committing it to a process of extensive legal revision designed to redress various types of sexual discrimination. As a result, new laws were passed to foster equality in education (by making home economics compulsory for both sexes, not just girls, beginning 1994); employment (with the passage of the 1985 Equal Employment Opportunity Law); and legal status (by changing the Nationality Law in 1985 to give equal status to men and women married to foreign nationals). Participation in the 1975 conference also encouraged inter-Asian cooperation among women's organizations. For example, the Asian Women's Association was founded in 1977 as a means of linking feminist activity in Japan, South Korea, the Philippines, Thailand, and other Asian nations to protest the exploitation of women and the environment as a result of increasing globalization and the legacies of Japanese colonialism.

In the wake of the 1995 UN Fourth World Conference on Women, held in Beijing, there has been a proliferation of non-governmental Chinese women's organizations that provide women with legal aid and counseling, protect migrant women and HIV/AIDS patients, advocate for environmental protection and lesbian, gay, bisexual, transgender, and queer (LGBTQ) populations, and sponsor initiatives to combat poverty and domestic violence. The 1995 conference also spurred the Chinese government to implement three major National Programs for Women's Development to raise women's political participation, education and employment rates, and other determinants of women's social status. This increasing openness to information from abroad has encouraged the participation of Chinese women in international organizations and conferences, and spurred the development of gender studies research and activism. In Japan, the commitments made by the government as a result of participation in the Fourth World Conference likewise have put more pressure on the government to increase the number of women members on national advisory councils and committees. This has resulted in a strengthening of the provisions of existing laws that protect women, such as the 1997 revisions to the Equal Employment Opportunity Law, as well as the passage of new laws to promote gender equality (1999) and to address social problems like domestic violence (2001).

SEE ALSO: Convention on the Elimination of All Forms of Discrimination against Women (CEDAW); Employment Discrimination; Footbinding; Gender, Politics, and the State in East Asia; International Women's Day; Nationalism and Gender; Sexism; Sexual Harassment Law; Suffrage; UN Decade for Women; Women's Movements: Modern International Movements

FURTHER READING

Edwards, Louise. 2010. "Women's Suffrage in China: Challenging Scholarly Conventions." In *Globalizing Feminisms, 1789–1945*, edited by Karen Offen, 275–285. London: Routledge.

Gelb, J., and M. L. Palley. 1994. *Women of Japan and Korea: Continuity and Change*. Philadelphia: Temple University Press.

Gelb, J., and M. L. Palley. 2009. *Women and Politics around the World*. Santa Barbara: ABC-CLIO.

Jones, Nicola A. 2006. *Gender and the Political Opportunities of Democratization in South Korea*. New York: Palgrave Macmillan.

Lee, K. C. 1995. "Confucian Ethics, Judges, and Women: Divorce Under the Revised Korean Family Law." *Pacific Rim Law and Policy Journal*, 4(2): 479–503.

Mackie, Vera. 2003. *Feminism in Modern Japan: Citizenship, Embodiment and Sexuality*. Cambridge: Cambridge University Press.

Molony, Barbara. 2004. "Frameworks of Gender: Feminism and Nationalism in Twentieth-Century Asia." In *A Companion to Gender History*, edited by T. A. Meade and M. E. Wiesner-Hanks, 513–539. Oxford: Blackwell.

Women's and Feminist Activism in Eastern Africa

ALIZA LUFT
University of Wisconsin–Madison, USA

In the last five decades, Eastern Africa has experienced the fastest and highest rate of change in women's political representation worldwide. In the 1960s, less than 1 percent of all legislators were women, yet by January

1, 2015, Rwanda, Tanzania, Uganda, and Burundi were among the top 35 countries globally in terms of women's representation in national legislatures (Inter-Parliamentary Union 2015). Additionally, in 2010, Kenya adopted a new constitution that created a special post to represent women's issues in the National Assembly. The result was 47 women representatives in each county after the 2013 elections – a total of 19.7 percent in Kenya compared to 63.8 percent in Rwanda, 36 percent in Tanzania, 35 percent in Uganda, and 30.5 percent in Burundi (representation of women in parliament, all in the lower or single house). Rwanda notably became the first country in the world to have more women than men in its parliament in 2008, which is a status it currently maintains.

In most cases, these changes in women's representation in parliament are attributable to the introduction of gender quotas in sub-Saharan African politics. However, women's movements have supported the construction and subsequent implementation of such policies.

This entry is an overview of women's movements in Eastern Africa from precolonial times to the present. A word of caution: in this entry it is impossible to do justice to the specifics of the women's movements in each Eastern African state. The ways in which different factors have combined to shape women's movements in Rwanda, Burundi, Uganda, Tanzania, and Kenya are distinct and tied to local histories and knowledge.

Women in Eastern Africa were politically active prior to colonialism and often held positions of political authority. According to some accounts, precolonial women leaders were as common as male rulers, and women had central roles in religious rituals and belief ceremonies (Saidi 2010). Women were also involved in local organizations that addressed women's issues, such as the *ndundu* (council) in the Kenyan Mitero village. The *ndundu* was comprised of Kikuyu women, organized by age, and while its central function was cooperative cultivation, it also provided women with a base by which to address their juridical, social, and agricultural concerns (Stamp 1986). Additionally, there is evidence that prior to colonialism, matrilineal societies existed among the Mbugwe of north-central Tanzania and the Mijikenda in coastal Kenya (Saidi 2010, 14). Here, many of the central elements of the societal order were organized and administered by women, in particular mothers and their spheres of activity (Saidi 2010, 18).

Colonialism brought profound changes to Eastern African women's political status and their ability to organize. The loss of land experienced by most Africans especially affected women in Eastern Africa as it also meant an intensification of their economic reliance on men. Furthermore, colonialism pulled women away from their traditional roles in land cultivation and food production by forcing them into waged labor where they were often subject to acts of physical and sexual abuse. Victorian ideals of gender also were introduced in Eastern Africa as a result of colonialism, excluding women from politics and positions in the administration, relegating them to the domestic sphere, and seeking to control women's sexuality and reproductive rights (Geiger, Musisi, and Allman 2002).

In several cases, women responded with force. In the area that today is southern Uganda and Rwanda, Muhusa, a woman described as having had an "extraordinary character," led armed protests and raids against German colonial authorities (Sheldon 2005, xxxviii). In Burundi and Tanzania, women mobilized to protest rising taxes during colonialism. As movements formed to overthrow the colonial system, women became active here as well. Bibi Titi Mohammed had a major role in the Tanzanian Nationalist Movement by organizing a women's section of the Tanganyika African National Union (TANU; Geiger 1987). This women's section of TANU participated in the battle to secure independence. Women elsewhere in Eastern Africa likewise were active in their own independence movements, and many fought to guarantee social, political, and economic women's rights in the new systems that followed independence.

Unfortunately, nearly all women's movements that emerged in the struggle to end Eastern African colonialism were co-opted upon independence by the new nationalist political parties. These new, and frequently massive, organizations used women to campaign for their own objectives and prevented other organizations from forming. A classic example is the national woman's organization *Umoja wa Wanawake wa Tanzania* (United Women of Tanzania; UWT) which first began as an affiliate of TANU. Although Tanganyikan women formed the backbone of the Tanzanian nationalist movement and were vital to its success, toward the end of colonialism male TANU leaders enlisted the help of the UWT to fundraise for male leader's salaries and trips abroad. Once Tanzania achieved independence, only a few women maintained their political roles in the new system, and those who had held a variety of party positions prior to independence now took jobs as sweepers, cleaners, and in clothing factories (Geiger 1987, 25). The independent government determined that some women were only suitable for domestic positions, with educated women in particular called upon to teach their "less fortunate" sisters lessons in sewing, nursing, and cookery (Geiger 1987, 25).

Elsewhere, such as in Kenya, the state-run women's organization *Machdeleo Ya Wanawake*, which had the largest membership of any in the country after colonialism, confined women to domestic and childcare, handicrafts, agriculture, literacy, and sports.

The absorption and co-optation of women's movements often by authoritarian ruling parties in Eastern Africa made it dangerous for women to campaign for issues at odds with the ruling party (Tripp 2003b; Fallon 2008; Tripp et al. 2009). As a result, women who were active across Eastern Africa in fighting for anti-colonial independence movements were often pushed aside once new governments came to power and were unable to campaign for women-specific issues. Unless they were willing to mobilize for the interests of the new regime, women in Eastern Africa could not be socially and politically active without incurring high costs.

Paradoxically, then, it was a combination of the 1970s global economic crisis along with a shift in international attention towards women's rights that allowed women's movements in Eastern Africa to re-emerge. The global economic crisis forced women to mobilize in order to improve their economic situations, often combining resources in order to make goods that could be sold. Additionally, the year 1975 was declared International Women's Year by the United Nations (UN) and included the adoption of a World Plan of Action focused on securing equal access for women across a variety of institutional fields (education, employment, health, housing, family, nutrition, and political participation). In turn, many of the movements that women in Eastern Africa formed at this time drew on legacies of precolonial women's organizations already discussed, as well as organizations that existed during colonial times to mobilize for independence. However, they rose to prominence especially as a result of the new UN priorities.

Women's organizations were still limited at this time in what they could achieve as a result of their ties to the political party in power and the extent to which they depended on government funding. In many of the mass party-affiliated organizations, women's leadership roles had first to be approved by the ruling party that dictated the organization's agenda and, as a result, infrequently challenged the status quo. Women's organizations' activities were also often monitored to ensure compliance with government initiatives. Consequently, many of them were organized around religion, domestic concerns, and "development," narrowly defined to mean only income-generating enterprises such as handicrafts and farming to the neglect of women's rights. Issues of concern to women that were not approved by the state-run women's organizations were too dangerous to push for under authoritarianism.

Beginning in the late 1980s and early 1990s, state-affiliated women's organizations declined in significance and new independent associations burst onto the scene. This was largely a result of three factors. First, the global push for democracy also resulted in a shift among donors towards funding non-governmental organizations (NGOs) as opposed to states. These changes in global politics and priorities provided women with non-state-based forms of funding, which led to new opportunities and the possibility of functioning independently from the state. As independent mobilization became possible, so did independent women's movements.

Second, the continuing global emphasis on women's rights sustained and even increased the focus of international donors on improving the status of women worldwide. International women's movements motivated by the UN Conference on Women in Nairobi in 1985 and another UN Conference on Women in Beijing 10 years later encouraged women's organizations in Eastern Africa to push their governments to improve women's status and implement gender-based reforms (Snyder 2006). Many of these topics had been considered taboo in the past. However, the women's rights agendas that were promoted by international organizations allowed new women's networks to form, the proliferation of new norms concerning women's rights, and the diffusion of new strategies by which to achieve them. Conferences that focused on women's education, women's reproductive rights, violence against women, and other women-specific concerns profoundly affected women's movements in Eastern Africa. Coupled with access to resources separate from the state, women could now create organizations and mobilize to address a host of issues, which they did: land rights; violence against women including domestic violence, genital cutting, and rape; women's political representation and constitutional reforms to secure it; among others. Women in Eastern Africa mobilized around political agendas that had once been unthinkable (Tripp et al. 2009).

Third and finally, the end of numerous civil wars, and even genocide in the case of Rwanda, provided the social and political ruptures necessary for reconstruction. Women seized the opportunities provided by such upheavals, often insisting they have a role in rewriting state constitutions and restructuring the political order to include legislative changes for gender equality. Often, war itself would alter traditional gender roles and provide women with new opportunities. In many cases, women in Eastern Africa demanded their inclusion in peace talks at the war's end. With the exception of Tanzania, all countries with the highest rate of women's legislative representation in Eastern Africa (Rwanda, Burundi, Uganda) emerged out of violent conflicts that took place in the 1980s and 1990s. Unique to women's movements, the autonomy obtained in recent decades by women's organizations has allowed women to select their own leaders and forge alliances across patronage networks, including cleavages defined by ethnicity, race, religion, urban–rural, and general divides (Tripp 2003a, 253).

The impact of the recent remarkable rise of women in formal Eastern African politics remains to be seen. Each country is currently under authoritarian or semi-authoritarian rule, but unlike the past where states co-opted some women's organizations and dismantled others, so far it seems as if women MPs have been working to advocate on behalf of women's interests without eliminating local women's organizations. In Rwanda, for example, the Forum of Rwandan Women Parliamentarians has worked closely with women's organizations and government ministries to enact an inheritance law that allows women to own property in their own names, to inherit property, to enter into legal contest, and to seek paid employment. Similarly, women MPs in Rwanda have initiated pro-child legislation and anti-gender-based violence legislation, even passing a Gender Based Violence Bill in 2008 and creating an anti-violence movement in Rwanda in the process. In Uganda, women members of the constitutional assembly have also fought to secure provisions for women such as a Domestic Violence Bill, an Anti-Female Genital Mutilation Bill, and a Marriage and Divorce Bill in 2009. In Tanzania, women's increasing legislative representation has resulted not only in an attempt to advocate for laws that represent women's interests (including access to university education, maternity leave, land reform, and prevention of, as well as punishment for, gender-based violence), but also the establishment of a women's caucus to provide parliamentary skills training. This has led to a more interactive parliamentary system between women and men in Tanzania, as well as a rise in women MPs' contribution to parliamentary debates and articulation of women's interests. These are but a few examples of how, at the formal institutional level, women's movements in Eastern Africa have contributed to significant progress for women's rights.

However, at the same time, increased pressure by women's movements to transform the laws and culture of their respective countries has resulted in some cases in a backlash. For example, despite Uganda's gains noted here, men in parliament have recently introduced several bills that set women back. In particular, the Anti-Pornography Bill, signed in 2013 and which was quickly renamed the Mini-skirt Bill, restricts women from wearing clothing such as mini-skirts and cleavage-bearing tops deemed to excite public sexual cravings. Similarly, in 2004, the Kenyan government passed a bill allowing polygamy allowing men to marry as many women as they wished. While the bill originally provided women with the right to veto their husband's choice, male members of parliament introduced a wording that dropped this clause. In both cases, numerous women's movements have mobilized to protest these laws. Nonetheless, examples such as these call into question Eastern African governments' genuine commitment to advance the rights of women beyond their formal legal representation. There are also concerns that electoral gender quotas are being used by authoritarian regimes in Eastern Africa such as Rwanda and Uganda to quiet international dissent and calls for democracy.

SEE ALSO: Colonialism and Gender; NGOs and Grassroots Organizing; Postcolonialism, Theoretical and Critical Perspectives on; Representation; Third World Women; Women's Political Representation

REFERENCES

Fallon, Kathleen. 2008. *Democracy and the Rise of Women's Movements in Sub-Saharan Africa*. Baltimore: Johns Hopkins University Press.

Geiger, Susan. 1987. "Women in Nationalist Struggle: TANU Activists in Dar es Salaam." *International Journal of African Historical Studies*, 20(1): 1–26.

Geiger, Susan, Nakanyike Musisi, and Jean Marie Allman, eds. 2002. *Women in African Colonial Histories*. Bloomington: Indiana University Press.

Inter-Parliamentary Union. 2015. "Women in National Parliaments." Accessed August 18, 2015, at http://www.ipu.org/wmn-e/world.htm.

Saidi, Christine. 2010. *Women's Authority and Society in Early East-Central Africa*. New York: University of Rochester Press.

Sheldon, Kathleen. 2005. *Historical Dictionary of Women in Sub-Saharan Africa*. Metuchen: Scarecrow Press.

Snyder, Margaret. 2006. "Unlikely Godmother: The UN and the Global Women's Movement." In *Global Feminism: Transnational Women's Activism, Organizing and Women's Rights*, edited by Myra Marx Ferree and Aili Marie Tripp, 24–50. New York: New York University Press.

Stamp, Patricia. 1986. "Kikuyu Women's Self-Help Groups." In *Women and Class in Africa*, edited by Claire C. Robertson and Iris Berger, 27–46. New York: Africana Publishing.

Tripp, Aili Mari. 2003a. "Women in Movement: Transformations in African Political Landscapes." *International Feminist Journal of Politics*, 5(2): 233–255.

Tripp, Aili Mari, ed. 2003b. *Greenwood Encyclopedia of Women's Issues Worldwide: Sub-Saharan Africa*. Westport: Greenwood Press.

Tripp, Aili Mari, Isabel Casimiro, Joy Kwesiga, and Alice Mungwa. 2009. *African Women's Movements: Changing Political Landscapes*. Cambridge: Cambridge University Press.

FURTHER READING

Bauer, Gretchen, and Hannah E. Britton, eds. 2006. *Women in African Parliaments*. Boulder: Lynne Rienner.

Bauer, Gretchen, and Faith Okpotor. 2013. "'Her Excellency': An Exploratory Overview of Women Cabinet Ministers in Africa." *Africa Today*, 60(1): 76–97.

Berger, Iris. 2012. "Decolonizing Women's Activism: Africa in the Transformation of International Women's Movements." In *Women and Social Movements, International*, edited by Tom Dublin and Katherine Kish Sklar. Alexandria: Alexander Street Press.

Berger, Iris. 2014. "African Women's Movements in the Twentieth Century." *African Studies Review*, 57(3): 1–19.

Berger, Iris, and Francis White. 1999. *Women in Sub-Saharan Africa: Restoring Women to History*. Bloomington: Indiana University Press.

Burnet, Jennie. 2008. "Gender Balance and the Meanings of Women in Governance in Post-Genocide Rwanda." *African Affairs*, 107(428): 361–86.

Tamale, Sylvia. 1999. *When Hens Begin to Crow: Gender and Parliamentary Politics in Uganda*. Kampala: Fountain Publishers.

Tripp, Aili Mari. 2001. "Women and Democracy: The New Political Activism in Africa." *Journal of Democracy*, 12(3): 141–155.

Yoon, Mi Yung. 2001. "Democratization and Women's Legislative Representation in Sub-Saharan Africa." *Democratization*, 8(2): 169–190.

Women's and Feminist Activism in Eastern and Central Europe

SONNET D. GABBARD and JILL M. BYSTYDZIENSKI
Ohio State University, USA

Women's organizations in Eastern and Central Europe (ECE) are as vast and diverse as the region itself. To summarize in a grand narrative the swath of land that includes countries as different as Albania, Bulgaria, the Czech Republic, Estonia, Hungary, Poland, Romania, Serbia, and Ukraine[1] fails to capture the historical, economic, geographic, religious, and cultural contexts and complexities that make up the region. However, with the fall of the Iron Curtain and the simultaneous development of the European Union (EU), a number of trends regarding the role of women's and feminist organizations in ECE can be discerned.

To clarify, women's organizations include all those groups and associations that are established by and for women, whether they have progressive or regressive goals. Feminist organizations are dedicated to achieving gender equality and eradicating sexism and discrimination against women. In the ECE countries, feminist organizations, progressive women's groups that do not identify as feminist, and conservative women's organizations have proliferated in recent years. In some cases, organizations have been openly feminist, even including the term in their names (e.g., "Feminist Foundation" in Poland; "AnA – The Romanian Society for Feminist Analyses" in Romania), although they are more likely to identify simply as *women's* organizations. The organizations are very diverse and include associations, federations, clubs, foundations, charitable and religious groups, sections of political parties and trade unions, and women's and gender studies centers. Many have obtained nongovernmental organization (NGO) status and have oriented their activities to foreign donor agencies. Most women's organizations tend to be small (such as SOS Corpo in Serbia), although some function at the national level as umbrella structures that include many groups (e.g., Federation of Polish Women's Clubs; the Kosovo Women's Network in Kosovo; Budi Aktiva Budi Emancipiran or Babe [Be Active, Be Emancipated], in Croatia), and some are international (e.g., La Strada, a foundation against trafficking in women, has chapters in Poland, Ukraine, the Czech Republic, Italy, and France as well as other countries).

The development of women's and feminist organizations in Eastern and Central Europe does not follow the patterns of Western women's movements. Instead, much of their development has happened in relation to the decades of socialism and the rapid economic, social, political, and ideological shifts that the region underwent during the late 1980s and 1990s and is still experiencing. In order to fully comprehend the breadth of work of women's organizations, it is important to understand the historic role of socialism in the region and its impact on women and their rights.

Under socialism, ECE women were expected to work outside the home while maintaining their domestic responsibilities of childrearing and housekeeping. Women were working in public, but sexism in terms of gender inequality continued, despite the state's commitment (if in name only) to equality. State propaganda showed women as capable and powerful workers, and yet images glorifying domestic violence, rape, and hypersexuality were common media tropes, especially in comedic cinema. In several countries (e.g., Poland), women were excluded from a number of occupations and from high-level managerial and political positions. Under communist party rule in many ECE states, reproductive healthcare, including birth control and abortion, were legal, but access was not always assured. Many women were still forced to go underground to obtain abortion services, and certain types of contraception were not available. On paper, at least, under socialism ECE women seemed to have many more rights than their Western contemporaries.

During this time, there were formal communist party-sponsored women's groups, and those who worked outside of these organizations were often isolated and pushed behind closed doors or underground. In some areas, women's groups not affiliated with communist parties existed, but their sway was extremely limited.

The fall of the Berlin Wall in 1989 not only signified the beginning of the end of the Cold War, it also sparked a wave of political revolutions in ECE. From Solidarity in Poland, to the Velvet Revolution in the Czech Republic, to the more violent Romanian Revolution, to the Orange Revolution in Ukraine, powerful and entrenched socialist states began the rapid process of political liberalization and economic privatization. The effects of these shifts left women's organizations in a unique place. In countries such as Poland, Romania, Bulgaria, and Ukraine, women's groups were caught between battling the communist legacy of espoused gender equality with the increasing need for women's political representation, reproductive healthcare, and with states' retreat from social welfare and direct provision of social services. Thus, activists and professionals in the women's organizations were forced to walk a fine line – distancing themselves from the legacies of the socialist era while many were still working toward what might be characterized as feminist goals. This inevitably led to cultural backlash and tensions. Many resisted supporting women's rights efforts, seeing them as yet another hangover of socialism. As a result, most women's rights advocates and activists shifted away from identifying themselves as feminists and instead reached out to a broader audience, including conservative women's groups and constituents.

In addition to breaking from their socialist associations, women's organizations, and especially those with feminist goals, were also confronted with a rise in populism and nationalism that held "family values" with conservative politics and religious affiliations at their core. While the notion of family values is not anti-women per se, it created political, economic, and social barriers for women's rights advocates. To criticize governmental policies and rulings meant to criticize the nation. Thus, women's organizations were stuck between the past and the present. This was, and still is, particularly striking in regards to women's access to reproductive healthcare and family planning, equal employment opportunities, sexism in the media, and violence against women. Directly following the fall of socialism, women's rights advocates faced political resistance regarding reproductive healthcare access, international funding, and political recognition for women's NGOs. These trends have continued, although certain gains have been made. Some of these gains can be attributed to the joining of the EU by many of the ECE states.

For the post-socialist transitional states, participating in the EU represents transitioning from socialism to joining the global stage. EU accession not only provides international recognition and clout, it also opens up borders, creates more economic trade opportunities, and provides political support and allies. With EU accession, however, come certain mandates and political expectations. These demands are particularly evident in the Balkans, Poland, Latvia, Romania, and Bulgaria. In order to join the EU, candidate countries must comply and implement various social, political, and economic policies. Anti-discrimination laws, gender mainstreaming policies, designing and implementing anti-human trafficking safeguards, anti-corruption laws and prosecutions, and defending human rights are examples of EU policy demands that have directly affected women's organizations in ECE.

Romania's and Bulgaria's accessions provide examples of the complicated relationship ECE feminists have with EU membership. Following the fall of socialism in these states, some international feminists (mostly Western feminists and women's groups) approached women's organizations about joining the EU. They espoused the benefits of EU membership, particularly in regard to equality in the workplace and universal women's struggles. This approach did not resonate with activists in Romania and Bulgaria where women had been working outside the home for decades. Women's progress, for many in Bulgaria and Romania, meant that they did not *have* to work outside the home and could choose what they wanted to do. Many scholars have pointed to the troubling dynamics between Western and Eastern European feminists and women's rights advocates at this time. Some scholars have gone so far as to call the Western feminists' political approach and agenda setting as colonialist (Weiner 2009). In the case of Bulgaria and Romania, the EU delegates pressured politicians to pass gender equality legislation. Even though the employment-based gender equality law being mandated did not necessarily pertain to these two countries, their parliaments quickly passed the bills in order to comply with EU demands. In the end, local women's organizations in Bulgaria and Romania were not consulted, and were expected to support moot legislation that did very little to promote women's rights. The approach to promote Western-specific politico-ideologies in order to join the EU has been used in a number of other ECE states. One such approach, gender mainstreaming, has had mixed results and is increasingly undergoing scrutiny from feminist scholars and women's organizations.

The EU has made a major push to promote gender mainstreaming through quotas, policy, funding, and as a standard for inclusion. Gender mainstreaming programs (GMPs) are designed to create meaningful change that promotes gender equality in realms beyond those typically associated with women (such as the family and reproductive health). Since 1997, the EU has invested significant amounts of money and people power in GMPs in member and applicant states. Feminist scholars, practitioners, and activists alike have voiced concerns about the inefficacy of GMPs due to the weight and reliance they put on structural and institutional frameworks and policy implementations. Funding models have privileged professionalized NGOs and governmental programs at the expense of smaller, less professionalized organizations and groups. Additionally, feminist scholars question GMPs' ability to profoundly challenge the social, political, economic, and cultural forces that maintain and perpetuate gender inequality.

While most of the EU policies are designed to protect and promote women's rights, one glaring omission and inconsistency regarding accession involves women's reproductive health and rights. For many EU member countries, providing access to birth control, safe and timely abortions, and other forms of family planning and reproductive health services is required. In the case of Poland, however, the EU waived reproductive health requirements, citing Poland's avowed Catholicism (and thus religious freedom) as the reason for the waiver. In 2006, Poland, a new member state of the EU, banned abortions. Rather than require that Poland repeal its law, the EU issued a waiver and left the law intact. Women's rights advocates and organizations in Poland and abroad had worked to defeat the law, citing that it was a gross violation of women's rights and would lead to an increase in illegal abortions, abortion tourism (where women travel outside of the country to obtain an abortion), and unwanted pregnancies. Even though activists faced defeat, this event helped bolster women's rights groups and transnational relations and organizing between feminist and women's movements, strengthening new networks working for women's rights. This rise in transnational discourse and dialogue is not unique to Poland, or to the EU waiver phenomenon, but is indicative of international involvement and intervention and local and regional feminist/women's organizations' response and activism.

An example of regional feminist outcry and activism bringing gross human rights violations to the international stage comes from the Balkans, and the ethnically charged wars that led to the disintegration of Yugoslavia in the 1990s. Women's organizations played a major role during these wars, which led to the fall of Yugoslavia and involved Serbs, Croats, and Bosnians participating in ethnic cleansing, the displacement of thousands of people, as well as systematic rape and torture. During the wars, women's groups such as Women in Black organized anti-war demonstrations in the capital, Belgrade, as well as other major cities in the former Yugoslavia. Women's organizations and advocates also played an integral part in transitioning to peace in the region. Following the bloodshed, women's organizations provided direct services, aiding survivors of sexual and domestic violence. Additionally, they helped those who were displaced during the war to return to their homes and villages, developing economic aid services, which administered micro-loans, worker training programs, and other forms of employment opportunities. They also hosted support groups and hotlines for war survivors, and developed public programs designed to engage public memory and begin the healing process. Many of these programs are still in existence in Bosnia and Herzegovina, Montenegro, Kosovo, Serbia, and Croatia. Additionally, regional feminist organizations acted as a unifier during the divisive time among ethnic Croat, Serb, and Bosnian feminists. Twenty years later, these networks remain intact and regional organizing, cooperation, and communication continue.

Much of the funding for the women's groups' direct services in postwar Balkans comes from international aid organizations, and many of the women's organizations that emerged as a response to the horrors of war have transitioned into direct social service providers. As a result, many of the major actors in the women's organizations in the Balkans have shifted from being a tight-knit group of grassroots organizers and activists to professionalized NGO and civil society actors. However, feminist activists in the former Yugoslavia have not abandoned their critical view of the government and politicians, and many groups continue to agitate the state, engage in anti-war and anti-nationalism actions, and continue to promote peace transformation efforts through community reconciliation and collective memory projects. At the same time, smaller women's foundations are beginning to develop as the push for professionalized women's organizations is promoted. One such example is the Rekonstrukcija Ženski fond in Serbia, which was founded in 2009 and is the first locally developed and run women's foundation in Serbia.

Since the beginning of the global economic recession in 2008, the status of the EU and member states is becoming increasingly questionable. With major austerity measures occurring in Greece and other parts of Southern Europe, social unrest is on the rise. Despite the EU economy being in flux, and member states' autonomy and power in question, gender mainstreaming programs, development efforts, and privatization of social services continue in ECE states. Women's organizations, groups, and networks continue to play a major role in strengthening civil society and providing social services. As the region continues to transform, it is clear that women's organizations, too, will continue to change.

NOTE

[1] Which specific countries constitute East Central Europe is a contested matter among scholars of the region. Most, however, include the Balkans and nations of the former Yugoslavia, as well as the now independent eastern states of the former USSR, such as Ukraine. In this entry we do not include Russia due to its particularly complex history and role in the region.

SEE ALSO: Feminist Activism; Feminist Organizations, Definition of; Gender and History of Revolutions in Eastern and Central Europe; Gender Mainstreaming; Gender, Politics, and the State in Central and Eastern Europe

REFERENCES

Weiner, Elaine. 2009. "Dirigism and Déjà vu Logic." *European Journal of Women's Studies*, 16(3): 211–228.

FURTHER READING

Bystydzienski, Jill M. 2001. "The Feminist Movement in Poland: Why So Slow?" *Women's Studies International Forum*, 25(5): 501–511.

Bystydzienski, Jill M. 2005. "Negotiating the New Market: Women, Families, Women's Organizations and the Economic Transition in Poland." *Journal of Family and Economic Issues*, 26(2): 239–265.

Mršević, Zorica. 2001. "The Opposite of War Is Not Peace – It Is Creativity." In *Frontline Feminisms: Women, War, and Resistance*, edited by Marguerite R. Waller and Jennifer Rycenga, 42–57. New York: Garland.

Orenstein, Mitchell A., Stephen R. Bloom, and Nicole Lindstrom. 2008. *Transnational Actors in Central and East European Transitions*. Pittsburgh: University of Pittsburgh Press.

Squires, Judith. 2007. *The New Politics of Gender Equality*. Basingstoke: Palgrave Macmillan.

Stratigaki, Maria. 2005. "Gender Mainstreaming vs. Positive Action: An Ongoing Conflict in EU Gender Equality Policy." *European Journal of Women's Studies*, 12(2): 165–186.

Women's and Feminist Activism in Latin America

NATHALIE LEBON
Gettysburg College, USA

Latin America boasts one of the most diverse and vibrant women's/feminist movements in the world today. Autonomous women's/feminist organizations, and women's formalized groups embedded in labor, social, and racial liberation movements, and political, cultural, religious, or social organizations and institutions, have played a vital role over the past 100 years in improving equity in gender and sexual power relations. They have also contributed in important ways to deepening democracy by bringing in new political subjects, nationally and internationally.

Obvious contributions include a host of political and civil rights for women, including, in the mid-twentieth century, the right to vote, as well as changing social norms and gender socialization for greater empowerment for women in the public and private spheres. The culture change work is key yet difficult to attribute to specific actors. Numerous public discussions, consciousness-raising groups, workshops, efforts at non-sexist and non-racist education and media campaigns have helped produce a new consciousness among women concerning their role and opportunities in society. According to the OECD, Latin America and the Caribbean is the developing region that has made the most progress in recent years in the formal recognition of women's rights (CIM-MESECVI 2012). Many women's/feminist organizations now focus on monitoring the implementation of those rights, especially in the area of gender-based (and race-based) violence. In addition, important thrusts of women's/feminist organizations today include securing full reproductive and sexual rights, improved political participation, and better redistribution of societal resources to combat poverty and improve working conditions.

Analysts have also documented women's/feminist organizations' contributions to a much broader range of political and social processes. These include: (1) the toppling of ruthless dictatorships in the 1970s and 1980s, by participating in armed struggle, organizing human rights campaigns – the most famous of which is that of the Argentine Mothers of the Plaza de Mayo – and participating in other movements for the return to formal democracy; (2) the improvement of living conditions through pressing the state to invest in the marginalized urban settlements established by internal migrants on the edges of large megapolises; (3) the transformation towards greater gender and racial/ethnic equity of rural and urban labor unions and movements, as well as political parties, especially since the 1980s; (4) the similar transformation of the global social justice/alter-globalization movement, since 2000; (5) the transformation of movements for ethnic, racial, and sexual equity, towards greater gender equity; (6) the overall deepening of democracy of national (political) cultures along racial, class, and sexual/gender identity lines; (7) experimentation with horizontal organizational dynamics for more participatory decision-making; and (8) greater space and attention to the negotiation of difference among social groups.

Each South and Central Latin American nation presents a specific political-economic reality and historical trajectory of feminist/women's activism. Hence, timing and contributions vary: self-identified feminist organizations appeared earlier in the larger, more industrialized countries of the Southern Cone than in the smaller Central American countries, for example.

Women's/feminist organizations include those who self-identify as feminist and whose explicit goal is to eliminate the power imbalance in social relations between men and women, and the devaluation of the feminine, as well as those who do not, but who work to contribute to women's well-being as women, especially in their gendered roles as mothers, wives, and workers. Relatively permanent forms of organization include consciousness-raising groups, autonomous collectives, caucuses or commissions in racial, ethnic, popular and labor movements, as well as more institutionalized gender and sexuality research and studies programs, lobbying groups, and non-governmental organizations. However, more fluid and/or temporary forms of organization have also promoted much transformation. These include national and Latin American women's/feminist specialized thematic networks (women's rights, violence, or sexual and reproductive health) and sectorial networks (of Afro-Latina feminists, lesbian feminists, indigenous women, etc.), the socialist–feminist coalition of the World March of Women against Poverty and Violence against Women, especially vibrant in the Americas, and the *Encuentros Feministas Latinoamericanos y del Caribe*, the large-scale, week-long, gatherings where feminists from all corners of the continent have met about every three years since 1981 for a plethora of workshops, political discussions, creative activities, and transnational networking.

The first half of the twentieth century witnessed the first wave of feminist organizations which contributed to women's right to vote, achieved as early as 1929 in Ecuador and 1932 in Brazil, but much later in Mexico (1947), Nicaragua and Peru (1955), and Paraguay (1961). As related by Pinto (2003), the Brazilian case exemplifies the variety of ways in which women organized to secure the right to vote. Despite the lack of formal women's organizations, the political know-how gained by women involved in the struggle for the abolition of slavery deserves a mention here. As early as 1910, some Brazilian feminists organized the Women's Republican Party despite their lack of political rights. The largest and least controversial organization in the struggle for suffrage, the Brazilian Federation for Women's Progress, founded in 1922, brought together upper-class women. Journals of the feminist press worked to spread ideas and information, while women workers close to the Anarchist Movement, such as the Union of Seamstresses, Hat-makers, and Related Categories, presented the most radical critique of women's oppression and a clear understanding of the structural role of gender in labor relations. Today, women's limited participation in politics remains a target for feminist organizations. Women account for 25 percent of national parliamentarians on average in the Americas, with substantial national discrepancies, (compared to 18.9 percent in the United States Congress). Nevertheless, quota initiatives and gender equity campaigns, instigated by feminist organizations since the 1990s, may explain the region's second place in the world regional ranking, after Nordic Countries (Inter-Parliamentary Union 2013).

Women's/feminist organizations were less visible after the conquest of the right to vote up until the 1970s, but organized middle- and upper-class women kept working at broadening women's access to and presence in the public sphere, notably in higher education, while organized working-class women continued improving labor conditions and protesting against the high cost of living.

The second wave of highly visible women's/feminist organizations arose in the 1960s and 1970s amidst the authoritarian military dictatorships that then cloaked the region. Women's human rights organizations, such as the Mothers of the Plaza de Mayo in Argentina, were among the first to dare to protest openly. Similar women's organizations sprang up in Chile and El Salvador, among others, to protest against the regime for the disappearance of their loved ones. They organized peaceful weekly marches, as in Argentina, and/or acts of civil disobedience, such as chaining themselves to the gates of the presidential palace, as in Chile. In the following decades, these organizations contributed to the campaigns that brought former military leaders to justice.

Urban and rural popular movements, which constituted a majority of women – including Afro-descendants and indigenous women, were among the first spaces where awareness of people's citizenship rights, including women's rights, could flourish. In neighborhood associations, mothers' clubs, communal kitchens, and other community-based organizations, these women fought against the lack of infrastructure and difficult living conditions faced by their neighborhoods. They became the foot soldiers of the opposition movement and over time came to swell the demonstrations in favor of ousting military leaders.

In countries where open civil war broke out, women did not generally constitute separate combat units but contributed to the logistics effort, most often in gendered roles, as cooks and nurses, but also at times in actual combat. Feminist organizations of former guerrillas publicly protested and thus raised awareness, in El Salvador in the 1990s for example, about the complete erasure of women's contribution to both the armed struggle and the peace process that followed, and of women's needs and gender equity issues in the reconstruction effort.

With the return to democratic rule in the 1980s in the Southern Cone, and in the 1990s in Central America, women's/feminist organizations were able to impact, in some national settings more than in others, their nation's new constitution, public policy, and state institutions, often working in collaboration with women/feminist elected representatives. Civil, penal, and family codes started to be reformed to formally recognize women rights. Innovative mechanisms, such as Brazil's women's police stations, charged with dealing with domestic violence, or Maternal Mortality Committees, investigating the causes of maternal deaths, among others, were instituted. Reproductive and sexual rights have remained elusive though, in particular abortion rights on the one hand, in the face of strong Catholic and Evangelical resistance, and the elimination of sterilization abuses on the other – especially for marginalized women of color. Nevertheless, feminist organizations, working with progressive governments, obtained the legalization of abortion in the first 12 weeks of gestation in Mexico City (2007), and in Uruguay (2012), only the third country with such a law, besides Cuba (1965) and Guyana (1995). The Mexico City law also requires the provision of free services by public healthcare services. Despite these gains, the rise of religious and economic fundamentalisms in the New Millennium has generally put feminist organizations on the defensive, as illustrated by the total ban on abortion passed in Nicaragua in 2007, resulting in criminalization and jail time even for women victims of spontaneous miscarriages but suspected of induced abortion.

Women's/feminist effective work to render public the many manifestations of violence against women (i.e., domestic violence, sexual assault, rape) motivated and provided support to the Inter-American Commission of Women, an organ of the Organization of American States which is largely constituted of female representatives, to seek the establishment of the first international agreement addressing violence against women. The Inter-American Convention on the Prevention, Punishment and Eradication of Violence against Women, known as Belém do Pará Convention, took effect in 1995, facilitating the adoption of national legislation, and a policy and strategic framework for implementation. However, in too many countries, enforcement of various provisions has remained thwarted (CIM-MESECVI 2012). Women's/feminist organizations have used the Convention to file violation claims against States before the Inter-American Commission on Human Rights to bring about justice and policy change. In addition, feminist networks have promoted the dissemination across borders of successful experiences in addressing these deficits.

For example, in 1992, CLADEM, the Latin American and Caribbean Committee for the Defense of Women's Rights, provided activists with a forum to share experiences about feminist popular legal education programs, already in place in Argentina and Chile, that train women from marginalized neighborhoods to become resource persons, known as *Promotoras Legales Populares*, on women's rights and the justice system, and to monitor policy implementation. Indeed many women's/feminist organizations are now focusing on monitoring and ensuring the implementation of hard-won rights, including through working with municipal and local authorities.

Women's/feminist organizations have been full participants in the deepening of citizenship for women (and men) of color and marginalized ethnicities, which have been excluded from political, economic, and social power since European colonization of the region. Since the mid-1980s, autonomous Afro-descendant feminist/women's organizations have been empowering their participants and beneficiaries, building networks to strengthen their voice as a political actor at the local, national, and transnational levels, publicly denouncing the racialized nature of the gender discrimination they faced in everyday life or in the public sphere, and working to build public institutions designed to combat racial inequality without neglecting gender differences. Women are also the majority of participants in a wide range of Afro-Latin religious and cultural organizations, as well as many neighborhood associations in their quest for land rights, better housing and infrastructure. Similarly, albeit more recently, in the Andes and in Central America, areas with a majority of indigenous people, indigenous women have built their collective voice often from within indigenous rights movements. Unsurprisingly, these women's caucuses have also pushed for gender equity within Afro-descendant and/or indigenous rights movements.

Besides working-class women's massive participation in the urban popular movements of the 1970s and 1980s to improve housing, infrastructure, and other aspects of living conditions in their neighborhoods, women workers, including women rural workers, have been organizing within trade unions with greater vigor since the 1970s. Today, women's commissions are present in most large rural and urban trade unions and have brought about, with varying degrees of success, the notion that women too are workers. When trade unions were no longer able to fulfill their role in the face of multinationals' strategies of production across multiple nation-states, women workers' transnational networks have been innovating with new forms of organization to share information across borders to defend wages and working conditions.

Lesbian organizations have contributed to the strength of the feminist movement and of the LGBT movement in the region since the 1970s, leading, in recent years, to the recognition of sexual rights, such as the legalization of gay marriage in a few countries, and cities. They have also called attention to heterosexism in the women's movement and sexism in the LGBT movement. More research is needed around women's/feminist organizations' role in the rising visibility of disability and children's rights.

At the global governance level, Latin American feminist organizations have been called upon as consultants since the 1990s United Nations conference cycle (Rio 1992, Vienna 1993, Cairo 1994, Beijing 1995, and Durban 2001) for their expert knowledge on gender/race relations to help draft official reports and accompany official delegations. They shore up relatively progressive government positions, such as those of Costa Rica or Brazil, to influence international documents, such as the Beijing Platform of Action, which was later used by activists at the national level to call their own governments to task by reminding them of their international commitments.

Latin American feminist theoretical visions and their experience in building transnational solidarity networks during this UN conference cycle, and during the Latin American and Caribbean *Encuentros*, became an important source of inspiration for the global justice movement, in particular the World Social Forum, born in the region and which has been thriving since 2001.

Finally, feminist organizations, especially more radical and early consciousness-raising organizations, highlighted the importance of horizontalism, of building organizations that promote the participation of all in decision-making and the non-specialization of roles. As feminist organizations have become more enmeshed with mainstream institutions in the neoliberal 1990s and 2000s, faced with time and financial constraints, they met increasing challenges to work in this way. Nevertheless, concerns with "methodology" have always been present. Over time, feminist organizations have also become pioneers in recognizing the need to deal with difference of race, ethnicity, class, and/or sexual identity, and so on, among women, and to grapple with the challenges presented by consensus decision-making in the presence of informal power differences.

SEE ALSO: Women's and Feminist Activism in the Caribbean

REFERENCES

CIM-MESEVIC (Follow-up Mechanism to the Belém do Pará Convention). 2012. Second Hemispheric Report on the implementation of the Belém do Pará Convention. OAS Official Records Series; OEA/Ser.L/II.6.10: Washington.

Inter-Parliamentary Union. 2013. Women in National Parliaments, Situation as of December 1, 2013. Regional Averages. Accessed February, 26, 2014, at http://www.ipu.org/wmn-e/world.htm.

Pinto, Céli Regina Jardim. 2003. *Uma História do Feminismo no Brasil*. São Paulo: Fundação Perseu Abramo.

FURTHER READING

Alvarez, Sonia. 1990. *Engendering Democracy in Brazil: Women's Movements in Transition Politics*. Princeton: Princeton University Press.

Di Marco, Graciela. 2011. *El Pueblo Feminista: Movimientos Sociales y Lucha de las Mujeres en torno a la Cuidadanía*. Buenos Aires: Biblos.

Maier, Elizabeth, and Nathalie Lebon, eds. 2010. *Women's Activism in Latin America and the Caribbean: Engendering Social Justice, Democratizing Citizenship*. New Brunswick: Rutgers University Press.

Mogrovejo, Norma. 2000. *Un amor que se atrevió a decir su nombre: La lucha de las lesbianas y su relación con los movimientos homosexual y feminista en América Latina*. Plaza y Valdés.

Perry, Keisha-Kahn. 2013. *Black Women against the Land Grab: The Fight for Racial Justice in Brazil*. Minneapolis: Minnesota Press.

Safa, Helen. 1990. "Women's Social Movements in Latin America." *Gender & Society*, 4(3): 354–369.

Women's and Feminist Activism Among Māori

MICHÈLE D. DOMINY
Bard College, USA

Māori women's activism came to prominence with rural women's involvement in voluntary associations in the mid-twentieth century, in the form of the Māori protest movement, Māori feminism, radical separatism, and Māori sovereignty in the 1970s and 1980s, and in the realization of the Māori Renaissance as a transformative cultural, social, and political movement by the turn of the twenty-first century. The shared foundation of activist and radical Māori feminisms rests on interpretations of precolonial Māori social structures and cultural beliefs – the tribal structure of the *iwi* (descent group), the Māori language (*te reo Māori*), and customary practices (*ngā tikanga*), in addition to the messages conveyed in the stories of prominent Māori women's lives. These structures and beliefs have been reintroduced through the restoration of Māori cultural practices in society, in language renewal, in literature, media, and the arts, and in legislative revision of Crown policy in the Māori cultural Renaissance.

Precolonial Māori women's status and role (*mana wahine*) is understood to rest on the principle that women are *te whare tangata* – the house of humanity – and honored for their life-giving capacities and the derivation of their *mana* (strength or dignity) from the *atua* or gods. Māori goddesses embody natural features that inextricably link life and the land (Higgins and Meredith 2013). Scholars have interpreted these aspects of Māori practice and belief as responsible for the high rank and positions of authority held by some Māori women in precolonial and colonial Māori society. Some had formal roles on the *marae*, some signed The Treaty of Waitangi with the British Crown in 1840, and others were queens, most notably Te Ārikinui Dame Te Atairangikaahu. Positive interpretations of Māori women's status have provided the basis for contemporary activism for many women (Mikaere 1994; Higgins and Meredith 2013). For others, the past presents activists and scholars with considerably more ambiguity in their understandings of its source for women's power and its implications for precolonial gender roles and postcolonial feminism.

Māori women's activism intensified in rapidly urbanizing postwar Aotearoa/New Zealand as rural Māori women migrated to cities and began to extend their spheres of influence nationally through organizing national voluntary associations to address social welfare needs. Initially this was a sociological response to the disruptive effects of the structural separation of Māori women from traditional social forms of *whānau* (the kin group), *hapū* (extended kin group including several *whānau*), and *iwi* (a people, a descent group of several *hapū*). It was a response to their separation from the land as a site of location and identity (*tūrangawaewae*), from land resources, and from rural Māori cultural and spiritual values best understood as Māori custom and law (*tikanga Māori*). It also was a response by Māori women leaders to the effects of colonialism and white settlement that led to changing perceptions of precolonial *mana wahine* (Māori women's dignity or authority). Māori legal scholar Annie Mikaere (1994) attributed this shifting status to the effects of English common law on women under colonization and suggested that colonization is responsible for the declining influence and authority of Māori women. Women's activism had evolved by the 1970s into national movements for the restitution of rights to land and fisheries through turbulent protest, for language revitalization, Māori sovereignty and self-definition in the 1980s, and in the 1990s through the work of the Waitangi Tribunal established in 1975 by the Treaty of Waitangi Act.

Māori women leaders initially honed their networking, organizational, and political skills in partnership with Pākehā women through their involvement with rural women's committees, organizations such as the Women's Institutes founded in 1921, and the Women's Health League, founded in Rotorua in 1937 by rural women and district nurses (Rei 1994). Māori women's commitments were to social welfare issues – housing, education, health, and employment – and with urbanization they also drew upon the resources of their tribal base, turning to the *marae* (meeting place) and to traditional leaders and tribal committees as models for leadership. Essential to their activism in the late 1950s was the revitalization of Māori language and culture in the schools through immersion programs, especially through the Māori language preschool movement (*kōhanga reo*) introduced in the early 1980s. Women's participation as agents of cultural transformation was based on *tikanga Māori* (culture broadly conceived) and its foundational tribal principles (*kaupapa*) and genealogical lines of descent (*whakapapa*).

These skills led to prominent expressions of autonomous Māori women's leadership, and Māori women's activism was best represented by the national efforts of individual women. Amiria Stirling's *Amiria: The Life Story of a Maori Woman* (co-authored with anthropologist Anne Salmond) (Stirling and Salmond 1976) and historian Michael King's biography *Whina: A Biography of Whina Cooper* (King 1983) portray the strength of both tribal identity and personal individuality through the life histories of singular women leaders or *kuia* (an elderly woman or female Māori leader). Notably, Dame Whina Cooper served as the first dominion president of the Maori Women's Welfare League (MWWL) or Te Ropu Wahine Māori Toko it te Ora from 1951 to 1957, with Dame Miraka (Mira) Szazy as secretary and later president. The League's founding and rapid expansion with 300 branches throughout the country marked the influence of Māori women as they expanded their domestic roles into the public sphere, promoted economic development, and realized their political agency through direct negotiation with the state. These strategies were later dismissed by radical activists as assimilationist and potentially destructive of Māoriness (Rei 1994, 202; Higgins and Meredith 2013). Even so the work of the MWWL continues into the twenty-first century.

Influenced by international indigenous movements of the late 1960s, historian Ranginui Walker organized a conference at the University of Auckland, and from this emerged the modern Māori protest movement in the form of Ngā Tamatoa (The Warriors). By rejecting the presumed assimilationist agenda of the New Zealand nation state and by extension the strategies of the MWWL, Ngā Tamatoa called for the celebration of Māori ways of seeing and doing through the expression of Māoritanga in the Māori Renaissance. By extension, it also called for the return of Māori lands and fisheries to the *iwi* and marked a forceful beginning to Māori land rights movement. In 1975 Whina Cooper, aged 79, led the Māori Land March on Parliament from Te Haupua in the far north to Wellington to promote the political position that Māori identity is inextricably linked to the people's connection to land and heritage. The land march (*hīkoi*) was a powerful form of activism led by women, but it also signaled an emerging fragmentation in the community between those, like Cooper, who were committed to appealing to Parliament through established structures, and those who rejected the elders' trust in Pākehā structures and sought more radical and less integrationist strategies.

A newer generation of Māori women radical activists, who had been influenced by international third world independence movements, Marxism, women's liberation, and separatist feminism, emerged from within the turbulent Māori protest movements of the late 1970s and early 1980s and defined and established Māori sovereignty (Dominy 1990; Locke 2012). One such protest was the 1977 Orākai Māori occupation of Bastion Point in Auckland, which demanded restitution of these lands to the Ngati Whatua by the Crown. Led by Joe Hawke, treasurer of Whina Cooper's group, the occupation marked the emergence of a radical feminist consciousness that signaled a new form of activism that broke with the women of the League and initially with Māori men. Civil disobedience advocate Eva Rickard led protesters in their occupation of the Raglan golf course, which had been taken from its tribal owners during World War II for use as a military airstrip. The protestors also challenged traditional Māori leadership as similarly patriarchal, and others addressed tribal variations in women's speaking rights on the *marae* and pointed to ambiguous and conflicting Māori expressions of *mana wahine* (Locke 2012; Higgins and Meredith 2013).

The fourth national United Women's Convention in Hamilton in 1979 was a definitive moment in the expression of Māori activism and feminist protest. Self-ascribed black women activists joined white lesbian separatists in an alliance against a "white women's convention" that they characterized as heterosexist and patriarchal in its structure. Taking the podium at the closing session, Ripeka Evans voiced a shared ideology with white lesbian separatists in rejecting hierarchy, individualism, materialism, spiritual detachment, and racism as inextricably and metonymically linked (Dominy 1990, 244). Throughout the convention, their strategies of symbolic inversion included graffiti, loud chanting, and disruptive behavior as ways of rejecting what they believed to be New Zealand white middle-class values. In self-ascribing as black, these women signaled a politicized identity that included the allied and separate interests of other colonized peoples and also white separatists. Initially this response was possible because of the analytic equation of patriarchy with a nation state that was conceptualized as racist.

The Black Women's Movement, fostered by activist spokeswomen Donna Awatere and Ripeka Evans, linked the power relations of race, gender, and class as a tripartite form of oppression at the National Black Women's Hui (meeting) in 1980 (Locke 2012, 254). The fusion of the analytic categories of race, gender, and class rejected the primacy of gender oppression voiced at the United Women's Convention and was the foundation of a movement that called for the overthrow of the New Zealand state as racist, and the restitution of traditional land, fisheries, and sovereignty to Māori people. By 1981, these activists, led by women as part of an expanding anti-apartheid movement in opposition to the 1981 South African Springbok rugby tour of Aotearoa/New Zealand, clashed with police. The following year, Donna Awatere wrote a four-part series of articles for the New Zealand feminist publication *Broadsheet*, later collected with a new conclusion, "Exodus," in her influential manifesto, *Maori Sovereignty* (Awatere 1984). The essay collection served as a touchstone for activism and feminist scholarship on Māori sovereignty as a politicized and self-conscious formulation of cultural identity and its relationship to Māori feminisms as distinct from Western feminisms (Dominy 1990; Yeatman 1994).

From 1984 through the 1990s, this generation rapidly turned its attention to the matter of Māori land alienation and the restitution of lands to the *iwi*. Awatere's concept of sovereignty promoted Māori political and economic self-determination and a dissociation from European cultural values, the capitalist state, and white feminists whom she saw as inevitably the beneficiaries of land settlement and land alienation. The Fourth Labour Government implemented the Treaty of Waitangi Amendment Act in 1985 and in the following years the work of presenting Māori claims for land restitution came from varied Māori constituencies including from the "flaxroots," from a new Māori elite of "corporate warriors," and from "tribal executives." In 1993, a group of Māori women joined the settlement process and alleged systematic discrimination since the signing of the Treaty through the failure of the New Zealand state to affirm and protect *mana wahine* (Poata-Smith 1996; Higgins and Meredith 2013).

Scholarship on Māori feminism was generated most intensively between 1979 and 1995, primarily by New Zealand-based feminist scholars, and served as a form of intellectual activism intrinsic to the movement. From the 1990s until the present, Māori women's activism has continued to set itself apart from Western feminisms with the emergence of indigenous scholarship and new decolonized methodologies. Linda Tuhiwai Smith has been especially influential in illustrating that "new ways of theorizing by indigenous scholars are grounded in a real sense of, and sensitivity towards, what it means to be an indigenous person" (Smith 1999, 38). *Mana wahine* has become a theoretical framework within the academy that not only gives voice to Māori women's historical, embodied, spatial, and spiritual experiences but also has applied consequences for transitional justice. Within the new context provided by the Waitangi Tribunal hearings of the *iwi*'s land claims against the Crown, these voices seek land restitution through the Treaty of Waitangi, promote an authentic decolonized Māori identity for women and men, work to preserve the Māori language, and promote cultural nationalism (Mikaere 1994; Smith 1999; McNicholas 2004). In this way, these postcolonial revisionings by Māori women are multiple and situated forms of "perspectival dialogism" as they "express a negotiated compromise between different perspectives" (Yeatman 1994, 87). The most influential scholarship argues that Māori feminisms are multiple, and that they share an underlying theory through which Māori women "can and must design new tools – Māori feminist theories, to ensure that we have control over making sense of our world and our future" (Irwin 1992, 5).

SEE ALSO: Feminist Activism

REFERENCES

Awatere, Donna. 1984. *Maori Sovereignty*. Auckland: Broadsheet Magazine.

Dominy, Michele D. 1990. "Maori Sovereignty: A Feminist Invention of Tradition." In *Cultural Identity and Ethnicity in the Pacific*, edited by Jocelyn Linnekin and Lin Poyer, 237–257. Hawaii: University of Hawaii Press.

Higgins, Rawinia, and Paul Meredith. 2013. "Te mana o te wāhine – Māori women." In *Te Ara – The Encyclopedia of New Zealand*. Accessed June 17, 2015, at http://www.TeAra.govt.nz/en/te-mana-o-te-wahine-maori-women/.

Irwin, Kathie. 1992. "Towards Theories of Māori Feminisms." In *Feminist Voices: Women's Studies Texts for Aotearoa/New Zealand*, edited by Rosemary Du Plessis, 1–21. Auckland: Oxford University Press.

Locke, Cybele. 2012. "Māori Sovereignty, Black Feminism, and the New Zealand Trade Union Movement." In *Indigenous Women and Work: From Labor to Activism*, edited by Carol Williams, 254–267. Urbana: University of Illinois Press.

King, Michael. 1983. *Whina. A Biography of Whina Cooper*. Auckland: Hodder and Stoughton.

McNicholas, Patty. 2004 "Maori Feminism: A Contribution to Accounting Research and Practice." Paper presented at the Fourth Asia Pacific Interdisciplinary Research in Accounting Conference, Singapore.

Mikaere, Annie. 1994. "Māori Women: Caught in the Contradictions of a Colonised Reality." *Waikato Law Review*, 2: 125–149.

Poata-Smith, Evan S. Te Ahu (1996) "He Pokeke Uenuku I Tu Ai: The Evolution of Contemporary Māori Protest." In *Nga Patai: Racism and Ethnic Relations in Aotearoa/New Zealand*, edited by Paul Spoonley, Cluny Macpherson, and David Pearson, 97–116. Palmerston North: Dunmore Press.

Rei, Tania. 1994. "Te Tiriti O Waitangi, Māori Women, and the State." In *Feminist Thought in Aotearoa/New Zealand: Differences and Connections*, edited by Rosemary Du Plessis and Lynne Alice, 198–207. Auckland: Oxford University Press.

Smith, Linda Tuhiwai. 1999. *Decolonizing Methodologies: Research and Indigenous Peoples*. Dunedin: University of Otago Press.

Stirling, Amiria Manutahi, and Anne Salmond. 1976. *Amiria: The Life Story of a Maori Woman*. Auckland: A.H. and A.W. Reed.

Yeatman, Anna. 1994. *Postmodern Revisionings of the Political*. New York: Routledge.

FURTHER READING

Okeroa, Erina. 2012. "*Unfurling Routes of Self-Determination in Aotearoa New Zealand: The Black Women's Movement 1978–1982*." Master's thesis, Victoria University of Wellington, New Zealand.

Simmonds, Naomi. 2011. "Mana Wahine: Decolonising Politics." *Women's Studies Journal*, 25: 11–25.

Yarwood, Lisa. 2013. "Women, Transitional Justice and Indigenous Conflict: The Role of Women in Addressing New Zealand's Colonial Past." In *Women and Transitional Justice: The Experience of Women as Participants*, edited by Lisa Yarwood, 8–33. New York: Routledge.

Women's and Feminist Activism in the Middle East

MOHA ENNAJI
University of Fès, Morocco

Middle East feminists endeavor to promote women's empowerment through education, awareness, and knowledge of new legal rights. They also propagate information about family law and the labor code through their non-government organizations (NGOs) and community-based groups. Women's activism has contributed considerably to democracy in the region, particularly in North African countries such as Tunisia, Morocco, and Algeria. because of its greater involvement in social and political affairs and the proliferation of women's associations, and to their access to the media. Women's activism is essential to modernization and democracy, as it has significantly contributed to the advance of civil society and democratic culture. One cannot imagine the success of democracy in this region of the world without the full emancipation of women.

This entry deals with women's activism within a broader sociopolitical approach. The emergence of women's NGOs is a response to the crisis of the nation-state model of governance. Such grassroots movements are treated as a way to ensure democracy and sustainable development. They create social dynamism through the mobilization and participation of the masses. They also decentralize governance in a more globalized world. Their modes of action raise new challenges for government development policies and open up new ways of thinking about the issues of sustainability.

To understand the significance of women's activism in the Middle East, it is essential to underscore the role of feminist NGOs, taking into account women's own interpretations, needs, and views of gender and development in order to fit local realities and satisfy these needs and demands. Women's NGOs have a major role in the struggle against gender inequalities and highlight their agency to consolidate democracy and social justice and to challenge traditional thinking and practices of governance.

Women's issues have recently become an important political topic in the region attracting the attention of decision-makers, activists, researchers, and politicians. Both women and men have been involved in the birth of modern feminism in the Middle East. Together, they resisted the forces of patriarchy, which deprived them of their civic rights. The men who were involved were mostly highly educated, with legal training and exposure to European thought, and the women belonged to a generation where educated daughters had illiterate mothers. This was accompanied by a wave of enlightenment and awakening in the realms of philosophy and political thought. One of the Egyptian male pioneers of women's rights is Gamal Eddine Al-fghany, who had a crucial political role in spreading progressive ideas on the emancipation of women. His work was continued by his disciples, Abdallah Nadeem and Muhammad Abdu. Historically, the most well-known feminist leader in the region is Huda Shaarawi in Egypt. In 1923 she became the first president of the Egyptian Feminist Union.

Across the region, women have a crucial role in socioeconomic development despite the fact that there are large inequalities between men and women in access to resources. In the labor market, which is marked by labor and gender division between men and women, women have growing responsibilities in ensuring the survival and well-being of the family, and in doing their share of farming and of production, small trade, and services.

State feminism, which may be defined as the government's official policy that seeks to achieve the emancipation of women, started to develop in the Middle East since the independence in the late 1950s and the early 1960s. State feminism is considered a historical strategy that has been adopted in different parts of North Africa to improve women's conditions and to contribute to their well-being. Thus, the provision of education, health, and work for women helped to improve the image of the state. In Egypt, state feminism started to develop during Nasser's regime (1960s and 1970s), and promised the equality of men and women and better quality of life. However, in the long term, its main beneficiaries have been the aristocracy and the upper class (Ennaji 2008).

In the 1980s, with the application of economic reforms (the structural readjustment plan), the economic and social retreat of the state began, which weakened the prospects for a better future for working class and middle class women. Thus, although state feminism succeeded in giving women access to education, health, and employment, it did not really challenge the negative social attitudes toward women who are still regarded as dependent on men.

It is important to note that Middle East men's feminist views are different from women's: the latter aim at improving their lives, whereas men's feminist views have more abstract goals in the sense that their attitude is part of their search for the causes of the "backwardness" of their country and their action to prove that it cannot progress without educating and training women. However, for both Middle East men and women feminism in one way or another needs to be concerned with the revitalization and empowerment of women (Sadiqi 2003).

Secular feminism in the region adopts Western feminist views while maintaining national and cultural identity. Its proponents think that although feminism can be easily rejected in the name of religious and ideological conservatism, it cannot be easily rejected in the name of cultural authenticity.

The Islamic revivalist movements, which have been flourishing throughout the Middle East since the mid-1980s, have ignited debate over the role of women in contemporary society. The social agendas of these revivalists propagate Islamic practices, although there has always been lack of consensus on the content of those practices. Islamic modernists preach the improvement of women's lives within the precepts of Islam.

Present-day feminists, on the other hand, emphasize the Islamic character of their feminist activities. Some consider that character is the only guarantee to women's liberation. They also think that the state regulates the public life of Moroccans, but religion regulates family life, as Islam has been used to shore up family-based patriarchal controls and prerogatives.

By contrast, the radicals adhere to the view that Islam is incompatible with feminism. Their doctrines are often rooted in leftist political movements, which do not see any compatibility between the concepts of Islam and feminism. For these radical feminists, women's liberation requires a thorough de-Islamization of all aspects of life. In fact, a number of radical scholars attribute the problems of contemporary Arab women to Islam.

While not rejecting the text, reconciliatory feminists adhere to the view that Islam as culture is compatible with feminism in a compromised view of the pro-Islamists and the radicals. The Moroccan writers Fatima Mernissi and Leila Abouzeid are good cases in point.

For some Egyptian feminists, such as Nawal Saadawi (1997, 246), Islam is not the only culturally legitimate framework of reference. She argues that present-day feminists from the Arab Islamic world need to reread their history to understand their culture.

A natural follow-up of feminist journalistic and academic writings is the expanding development of feminist activism through women's NGOs. These associations attest to the dynamism of civil society. Most associations, which struggle for secular feminism and civil rights, are mainly led by upper and middle class women.

One of the major challenges is the choice between modernity and tradition. In a country like Morocco, which has opted for multilingualism, liberal economy, and political pluralism within a constitutional monarchy, the choice cannot be insensitive either to Islam or to the country's image at the Islamic, Arab, African, and international levels. The internal context is also important, as it is challenged by the struggle for economic and social development and the place of women in this development.

In Morocco, for instance, women's organizations have a decisive role in the democratization and modernization of society. From the 1970s, women's NGOs have severely criticized the ways in which policymakers overlooked women's demands for emancipation and gender equity.

At the sociopolitical level, after the political reforms of the 1990s (re-amendment of the constitution and law on elections), which led to more democratization, a large number of women's associations emerged; this had great national and regional impact: for example, *l'Union Féminine Marocaine* and *l'Organisation Démocratique des Femmes*. These NGOs often have links and form networks. However, despite the dynamism of their organizations, women are still disfavored at the judiciary level in legal matters (e.g., in polygamy and inheritance). Nevertheless, the conservative forces regard women's role to be limited to home, reproduction, and childrearing.

Women's NGOs promote women's emancipation, participation, and social mobilization. They encourage women's empowerment and participation in decision-making and in public affairs. They have enabled women to assess their own situation critically and shape a transformation of society (Sadiqi and Ennaji 2006).

Women's NGOs take part in diverse activities, and have so far accumulated a great deal of experience in local development; their experience should be known, studied, and analyzed profoundly to show that Morocco's women are dynamic and problem-solvers (Mernissi 1989). Unlike in many Arab countries, Moroccan women's NGOs are allowed by the government to receive financial aid from foreign organizations and donors. The challenge facing these NGOs is to devise autonomous strategies and to establish themselves as independent forces in their partnership with the state and with political parties.

Over the past two decades, many Moroccan women's advocacy organizations have emerged to combat violence against women, illiteracy and poverty among women, gender-based legal and cultural discrimination, and under-representation of women in policy-making. They have made important steps forward: the ratification of CEDAW (Convention for the Elimination of All Forms of Discrimination against Women) by Morocco on June 21, 1993; it is no longer required for the husband to authorize the wife to practice a trade activity (1995); or for the signature of a work contract (1996); the revision of the work code and of the penal code (2003); and the reform of the nationality code which now allows a Moroccan woman to transmit her citizenship to her children. Yet, the most remarkable achievement is the reform of the family code (in October 2004). The latter code came after more than 20 years of struggle by feminists and women's NGOs.

The principal changes brought out by this code are, briefly: (1) the family is considered to be the responsibility of both the husband and the wife, while the previous personal status law treated the husband as the only tribunal in marriage and divorce; (2) couples must appear before a judge before contracting marriage and when filing for divorce; (3) both boys and girls can marry at the age of 18, as under the previous code girls could get married at 16; (4) the elimination of tutorship for women as women now can marry without the authorization or agreement of their father; (5) divorce is regulated by new laws, which are enforced by the Ministry of Justice, represented by a judge in the family court; (6) in case of divorce, the property and financial resources accumulated by the household during marriage are shared by the two spouses, under the previous family code the wife had no right to claim a portion of the property and money of the husband; and (7) women now have the right of custody over their children, even if they remarry, as previously the mother lost custody of her children when she remarried.

However, the new family code has its own limitations and imperfections despite its advantages and its positive impact on women and families. For example, although polygamy is significantly controlled, it is legally accepted, and inequality concerning inheritance is still maintained, whereby a woman inherits only half the share of a man. When there are no males among the inheritors, the females inherit only part of the legacy and the rest goes to the family of the deceased male.

Over the last decade, Moroccan women's NGOs have intensified their efforts to improve women's living conditions. Thus, many associations fight gender-based violence and assist battered women by giving them shelter and legal advice. A network of associations has been created, organizing numerous activities and campaigns to raise awareness about gender equality, the promotion of women's rights, tolerance, and citizenship. They have been successful in using the media, especially television, to make their voices heard and to contribute to the debate on equality between the sexes. In 1998, the first national campaign against violence against women was organized. This campaign mobilized many government administrations and ministries, as well as civil society. As an outcome of this campaign, the Ministry of Family has adopted a national strategy to combat violence against women, and recently the government has initiated a phone line for women victims of violence who want to seek help or make a complaint about domestic violence.

However, there are still limitations and barriers in the path of women's emancipation and legal rights in the Middle East. Most countries have not agreed to all the articles of CEDAW, and have not ratified international agreements about women's rights. Similarly, the principle of the quota is not officially recognized in the constitution, which implies that the representation of women depends on the political agendas of individual leaders. There is also weak commitment by many governments in the region to protect women from violence, especially domestic violence, and concerning their legal rights in police investigations, sanctions, and as victims of violence.

Furthermore, cultural hurdles and patriarchal traditions, illiteracy, and lack of information prevent women from invoking their rights or reporting crimes against them, such as rape, child abuse, sexual exploitation, and domestic violence. Concerning such cases, lawyers do not often make legal arguments based on international human rights treaties.

Thus, women's organizations and civil society in general have a major role in alerting women, families, and social actors to the importance of integrating women in economic, social, and cultural development. Further steps in favor of protecting women's rights are necessary to ensure their strong contribution to sustainable development. Likewise, education and training are important for women to enable them to meet the new challenges, and to help them safeguard their rights and interests. The development of society cannot be achieved without the integration of women in the processes of growth and democratization.

SEE ALSO: Gender and History of Revolutions in Northern Africa; Gender, Politics, and the State in Northern Africa; LGBT Activism in the Middle East; NGOs and Grassroots Organizing; Sexual Citizenship in East Asia

REFERENCES

Ennaji, Moha. 2008. "Steps to the Integration of Moroccan Women in Development." *British Journal of Middle Eastern Studies*, 35(33): 339–348.
Mernissi, Fatema. 1989. *Doing Daily Battle*. New Jersey: Rutgers University Press.
Saadawi, Nawal. 1997. *The Nawal Saadawi Reader*. New York: Zed Books.
Sadiqi, Fatima. 2003. *Women, Gender, and Language in Morocco*. Leiden: Brill Academic.
Sadiqi, Fatima, and Moha Ennaji. 2006. "The Feminization of Public Space: Women's Activism, the Family Law, and Social Change in Morocco." *Journal of Middle East Women's Studies*, 2(2): 86–114.

FURTHER READING

Ennaji, Moha. 2006. "Social Policy in Morocco: History, Politics and Social Development." In *Social Policy in the Middle East*, edited by Massoud Karshenas and Valentine Moghadam, 109–134. London: Palgrave.
Ennaji, Moha, and Fatima Sadiqi, eds. 2011. *Gender and Violence in the Middle East*. London: Routledge.
Frazer, Francis. 1989. *Feminist Talk and Talking about Feminism*. Oxford: Oxford University Press.
Moghadam, V. 1997. *Women, Work, and Economic Reform in the Middle East and North Africa*. Boulder: Lynne Rienner.
Sadiqi, Fatima, and Moha Ennaji, eds. 2010. *Women in the Middle East and North Africa*. London: Routledge.
Zoglin, Katie. 2009. "Morocco's Family Code: Improving Equality for Women." *Human Rights Quarterly*, 31: 964–984.

Women's and Feminist Activism in the Native United States and Canada

EMILY J. MACGILLIVRAY
University of Michigan, USA

Native American women have long engaged in activism – movements large and small to effect social change. Much of that activism has been directed toward fighting colonialism, the violent process through which Native people were dispossessed of their land after contact with Europeans. Indigenous women scholars have frequently interpreted this activism within the framework of Native feminist thought, which recognizes that gender has been a key signifier and instrument of colonial power throughout centuries of contact between Native and non-Native peoples (Huhndorf 2009, 108).

Native feminist scholar Kim Anderson (2010) links Native feminism to a profound reverence for all forms of life – a foundational principle in indigenous societies. As a result, Anderson defines Native feminism as seeking social justice for all forms of life by organizing around multiple axes, such as gender, sexuality, race, and class (Anderson 2010). Under this framework, social justice and gender are inextricably linked, and neither the terms "Native" nor "feminism" take precedence in "Native feminism." If Native feminism is to take seriously its responsibility in seeking social justice for all peoples, both terms must be considered mutually reinforcing and equally important.

This approach takes into account national histories and cultural practices of Native women throughout key periods in North American history. In the late eighteenth century, Native women faced challenges such as increasing violence due to the American Revolutionary War and increased settlement by non-Native peoples. Despite these challenges, Native American women advocated for political and economic self-sufficiency for themselves and their communities. In the northeast, women like Molly Brant (Mohawk) drew on their influence to advocate for their Native communities and families. Brant worked as a trader and interpreter during the Revolutionary War, and used her access to the British military's supplies to ensure her family and friends remained well fed, given that they lacked Brant's economic and political privilege (Feister and Pulis 1996). In the south, Cherokee women, such as Nancy Ward, resisted land cessations in Cherokee politics and treaties with the United States (Miles 2009). Ward attended treaty meetings and, along with other Cherokee women, frequently spoke out against larger cessions of Cherokee territory and the removal of those who lived on the land in question (Miles 2009). However, despite Cherokee women's activism, on May 28, 1830, President Andrew Jackson signed the Indian Removal Act into law. Removal would be a national policy, freeing lands east of the Mississippi for agricultural development and settlement.

In the late nineteenth century, both the United States and Canada legislated acts to overhaul Native families, governance, and property. In 1887, the United States Congress passed the General Allotment (also known as the Dawes Severalty Act) of 1887, dissolving communal Native property laws. The Allotment Act ushered in an era of dwindling land bases for Native peoples, and ensured that land ownership on reservations would be consolidated into privately held property owned disproportionately by men (Huhndorf and Suzack 2010). In 1867, Canada assigned parliament exclusive jurisdiction over "Indians and Lands reserved for Indians" under the Indian Act, and in 1876 a highly gendered amendment to the Act defined "Indian status" by patrilineal descent (Lawrence 2004).

If a status woman married a man without status, she lost status in the band of her birth, while status men could marry non-status women and extend status to them and their children. The Indian Act contributed to the corrosion and devaluation of women's participation within Native governance, economics, and cultural life. However, despite the radical reorganization of Native familial relations and conceptions of property by the General Allotment Act and the Indian Act, Native women like Alice Jemison, Laura Cornelius Kellogg, Sarah Winnemucca, and Zitkala-Sa organized in resistance to these policies and promoted Native languages, Native-controlled education, land claims, and treaty rights in the early twentieth century (Mihesuah 2003).

In the early 1960s, women in the Pacific northwest, like Janet McCloud (Tulalip) and Ramona Bennet (Puyallup), participated in protests over fishing rights (Jaimes and Halsey 1992, 311). The government attempted to remove non-treaty Indians from their fishing grounds on the Nisqually River in Washington, despite their right to harvest salmon. The fishing rights activism in the 1960s set in motion the activist movements that would follow, such as the American Indian Movement (AIM) and Women of All Red Nations (WARN) (Jaimes and Halsey 1992, 311). AIM formed in 1968 to address the issues faced by Native Americans in urban areas, such as poverty, discrimination, and incarceration. The movement gained notoriety when participants occupied Alcatraz Island near San Francisco, the Bureau of Indian Affairs building in Washington D.C., and the community of Wounded Knee on Pine Ridge Reservation in South Dakota. Dynamic female Native women activists emerged from AIM, such as Stella Leach, LaNada Means, and Anna Mae Aquash (Smith and Warrior 1996, 70; Mihesuah 2003). Leach and Means occupied leadership roles in Alcatraz, and became outspoken critics of federal Indian policies (Smith and Warrior 1996). Aquash became involved with AIM during protests on the East Coast, and later participated in Wounded Knee (Mihesuah 2003). On February 25, 1976, she was found shot dead in the northeast corner of Pine Ridge Reservation. Her influence within Native communities extends beyond her death with the ANNA Foundation – an international non-profit organization started in 1999 to preserve Native languages, cultures, and traditions.

In 1974, WARN organized as an extension of AIM to explicitly address issues relevant to women, such as exposing the widespread practice of the forced sterilization of Native women (Huhndorf and Suzack 2010). Native women pressured Congress to investigate, and the resulting government report brought public attention to the issue in 1976 (Smith 2005, 82). WARN also published a study about the dangers to women of radiation poisoning found at the Pine Ridge Reservation (Huhndorf and Suzack 2010). Some of the women associated with WARN, such as Winona LaDuke (Anishinaabe), founded the Indigenous Women's Network (IWN) in 1985 – a global movement aimed at achieving sustainable change for Native communities by supporting women's leadership (Huhndorf and Suzack 2010). The IWN also presents the annual Annie Mae Awards to honor the lifetime achievement of Native activist women (Mihesuah 2003). LaDuke has exposed a variety of environmental issues that affect women, like the disposal and storage of nuclear waste on Indian Reservations, uranium mining on Native lands in northern Canada, and the increasing prevalence of dioxin and other heavy metals in breast milk, particularly in communities near the Great Lakes and Hudson's Bay.

The Native Women's Association of Canada (NWAC) formed in 1974 in response to the gender inequalities in the Indian Act (Huhndorf and Suzack 2010). In 1981, the United Nations determined the Indian Act denied Native women cultural rights because they were barred from living in their communities. In response, Canada passed Bill C-31 in 1985 containing three fundamental principles: the removal of gender-based discrimination in the Indian Act; the restoration of status and membership rights to eligible individuals; and the recognition of band control over membership (Lawrence 2004). While approximately 127,000 individuals have since regained status, more than 106,000 were denied reinstatement (Lawrence 2004). Furthermore, many of the women who regained status will be unable to pass it down other than to the first generation of their children, so Native families' experience of gender discrimination is deferred to a future generation. Bill C-31 failed to alter the Indian Act's discriminatory provisions. Native women throughout Canada have protested their reinstatement of status on the grounds that it constitutes a lesser category of Indian registration.

In the 1970s and 1980s, Native women in both countries such as Paula Gunn Allen, Jeanette Armstrong, Louise Erdrich, Joy Harjo, Leslie Marmon Silko, Maria Campbell, Beatrice Culleton-Mosionier, and Lee Maracle began to publish to widespread acclaim in various genres (Jaimes and Halsey 1992; Huhndorf and Suzack 2010). Published in 1986, Paula Gunn Allen's *The Sacred Hoop: Recovering the Feminine in American Indian Traditions* is an early attempt to expose the patriarchal aspects of colonization and to retrieve what Allen terms "gynocratic" indigenous traditions as the foundations for feminist practice in the present (Huhndorf and Suzack 2010). Allen defines woman-centered social systems as including free and easy sexuality and wide latitude in personal style, meaning that a diversity of people, including gay men and lesbians, are accepted and honored (Allen 1992). While Allen's statements may be true for some Native groups, other Native women have pointed out that there is too little research on the sexuality of the hundred of indigenous groups within North American to make such sweeping assertions (Mihesuah 2003, 43).

From the 1970s to the present, Native women in the United States and Canada have experienced high rates of domestic and sexual abuse perpetrated by non-Native and Native men (Jaimes and Halsey 1992; Mihesuah 2003, 56). In the 1980s, rape became the number one crime on certain reservations (Jaimes and Halsey 1992). Poverty, the breakup of multigenerational families, fewer ties to the land with increased immigration to the cities, substance abuse, and mental health issues, all contribute to violence within Native communities (Jaimes and Halsey 1992; Mihesuah 2003, 57). In Canada, over 500 Native women went missing or were murdered with little attention from the police or dominant society between 1990 and 2005 and, due to the complex jurisdictional issues in the United States, perpetrators of sexual violence can usually commit crimes against Native women with few legal consequences (Smith 2005, 30).

In the twenty-first century, Amnesty International produced two reports on the violence that Native women face in Canada and the United States illustrating how Native women are frequently targeted for acts of sexual violence and denied access to justice on the basis of their gender and Native identity (Amnesty International 2004, 2007). The reports feature the voices of Native women as a way of validating and reclaiming the worth and voices of those murdered, assaulted, and missing, and Amnesty's international reputation as a pioneering human rights non-governmental organization lent credibility to the extensive amount of literature, narratives, and analyses produced by Native women in both countries since the 1960s (Million 2013, 33).

Native women also addressed sexual violence through grassroots organizing and cultural productions. In the early 1990s, Native and non-Native women's organizations within the low-income Downtown Eastside neighborhood of Vancouver, British Columbia, declared February 14 a day of remembrance to honor women who were murdered or disappeared. They organized the Women's Memorial March, which has become an annual event, transforming Valentine's Day into a protest against racism, poverty, and sexual and gender violence against women, and a celebration of resistance, solidarity, and survival (Culhane 2009). Rebecca Belmore (Anishinaabe) produced the play *Vigil* in 2002, and Marie Clements (Métis) produced and published the play *The Unnatural and Accidental Women* in 2005. The plays reconstruct the lives and voices of the murdered and missing women of the Downtown Eastside – creating space for the voices of women who experienced systemic racism, misogyny, and violence and whose deaths were described by the coroner as "unnatural and accidental." In the United States, Louise Erdrich (Ojibwe) published *Love Medicine* in 1984, which due to its popularity, the novel about multi-generational families on the Turtle Mountain Indian Reservation of North Dakota, was reissued in 1993 and 2009. *Love Medicine* opens with the death of an Ojibwe woman, and exposes the historical connections between colonialism and present-day violence on reservations, including domestic and sexual abuse. Erdrich's 2012 award-winning novel *The Round House* focuses on the sexual assault of a Native American woman and exposes the struggle for Native women and their families to attain justice within the present-day US legal system.

In the twenty-first century, the Idle No More movement – an ongoing grassroots effort founded in November 2012 by Native women in Canada that has attracted global participants – exemplifies Native women's activism surrounding environmental issues and gender violence. Idle No More makes the voices and concerns of Native women central to its platform and protests, such as organizing around the proposed (and passed in 2013) Bill C-45, which included amendments to the Indian Act, the defunding of Native reservations, and the changes to the Navigable Waters Act (Morris 2014). The movement exemplifies coalitional, Native feminist activism by asking the government to reverse course and respect the sovereignty and treaty rights of Native peoples.

Native feminist activism provides a flexible rubric through which to understand the political and social organizing of indigenous women. Native women, who have faced a variety of related but distinct issues throughout North America, are connected through a common colonial history. As gender continues to structure the contemporary effects of colonialism on Native communities, Native women remain engaged in activism on multiple fronts.

SEE ALSO: Colonialism and Gender; Colonialism and Sexuality; Domestic Violence in the United States; Environment and Gender; Gender, Politics, and the State: Indigenous Women; Sexual Assault/Sexual Violence

REFERENCES

Allen, Paula Gunn. 1992. *The Sacred Hoop: Recovering the Feminine in American Indian Traditions*. Boston: Beacon Press.

Amnesty International, Canada. 2004. *Stolen Sisters: A Human Rights Response to Discrimination and Violence against Indigenous Women in Canada*. Ottawa: Amnesty International Canada.

Amnesty International. 2007. *Maze of Injustice: The Failure to Protect Indigenous Women from Sexual Violence in the USA*. New York: Amnesty International USA.

Anderson, Kim. 2010. "Affirmations of an Indigenous Feminist." In *Indigenous Women and Feminism: Politics, Activism, Culture*, edited by Cheryl Suzack, Shari M. Huhndorf, Jeanne Perreault, and Jean Barman, 81–91. Vancouver: University of British Columbia Press.

Culhane, Dara. 2009. "Their Spirits Live within Us: Aboriginal Women in Downtown Eastside Vancouver Emerging into Visibility." In *Keeping the Campfires Going: Native Women's Activism in Urban Communities*, edited by Susanne Applegate Krouse and Heather A. Howard, 76–92. Lincoln: University of Nebraska Press.

Feister, Lois M., and Bonnie Pulis. 1996. "Molly Brant: Her Domestic and Political Roles." In *Northeastern Indian Lives 1632–1816*, edited by Robert S. Grumet, 295–320. Amherst: University of Massachusetts Press.

Huhndorf, Shari M. 2009. *Mapping the Americas: The Transnational Politics of Contemporary Native Culture*. Ithaca: Cornell University Press.

Huhundorf, Shari M., and Cheryl Suzack. 2010. "Indigenous Feminism: Theorizing the Issues." In *Indigenous Women and Feminism: Politics, Activism, Culture*, edited by Cheryl Suzack, Shari M. Huhndorf, Jeanne Perreault, and Jean Barman, 1–20. Vancouver: University of British Columbia Press.

Jaimes, M. Anette, and Theresa Halsey. 1992. "American Indian Women: At the Center of Indigenous Resistance in North America." In *The State of Native America: Genocide, Colonization, Resistance*, edited by M. Annette Jaimes, 311–344. Boston: South End Press.

Lawrence, Brenda. 2004. *"Real" Indians and Others: Mixed-Blood Urban Native Peoples and Indigenous Nationhood*. Vancouver: University of British Columbia Press.

Mihesuah, Devon. 2003. *Indigenous American Women: Decolonization, Empowerment, Activism*. Lincoln: University of Nebraska Press.

Miles, Tiya. 2009. "'Circular Reasoning': Recentering Cherokee Women in the Antiremoval Campaigns." *American Quarterly*, 61: 221–243. DOI: 10.1353/aq.0.0078.

Million, Dian. 2013. *Therapuetic Nations: Healing in an Age of Indigenous Human Rights*. Tucson: University of Arizona Press.

Morris, Amanda. 2014. "Twenty-First-Century Debt Collectors: Idle No More Combats a Five-Hundred-Year-Old Debt." *WSQ: Women's Studies Quarterly*, 42: 244–256. DOI: 10.1353/wsq.2014.0025.

Smith, Andrea. 2005. *Conquest: Sexual Violence and American Indian Genocide*. Cambridge: South End Press.

Smith, Paul Chaat and Robert Allen Warrior. 1996. *Like a Hurricane: The Indian Movement from Alcatraz to Wounded Knee*. New York: The New Press.

FURTHER READING

Suzack, Cheryl, and Shari M. Huhndorf, Jeanne Perreault, Jean Barman, eds. 2010. *Indigenous Women and Feminism: Politics, Activism, Culture*. Vancouver: University of British Columbia Press.

Women's and Feminist Activism in Northern Africa

VALENTINE M. MOGHADAM
Northeastern University, USA

The history of feminist activism in North Africa – or the Maghreb – dates back to the 1970s, when women-and-development study groups were formed. In the 1980s, academics and activists mobilized to warn about the growing Islamist influence, and in the latter part of the 1980s they became part of feminist sociologist Fatima Mernissi's Maghreb-wide anti-fundamentalist network. In the early 1990s feminists from Algeria, Morocco, and Tunisia formed the Collectif 95 Maghreb-Egalité to push for egalitarian family laws and full citizenship for women. Since then, a number of key legal reforms and policy initiatives for women's rights have been achieved. In addition, women played prominent roles in the Arab Spring protests of 2011, which led to the collapse of governments in Egypt and Tunisia, constitutional changes in Morocco, and promises of reform in Algeria.

Algeria, Morocco, and Tunisia form a geocultural subregion in that they are contiguous in territory; share an experience of French colonialism; retain some francophone identity as well as French-influenced institutions such as the education system, the judiciary, and trade unions; and are home to some of the most prominent women's rights groups in the Middle East and North Africa (MENA) region. A common pattern is attention to labor and social rights issues as well as to the enhancement of women's civil and political rights. Maghrebian women are major contributors to, and participants in, civil society and democracy movements; they see a democratic polity as both a desirable alternative to authoritarianism and a pathway to their own equality and rights. Noteworthy is that until 2011, the only MENA countries with women political party leaders were Algeria and Tunisia; Louisa Hanoune and Maya Jribi led left-wing parties; Khalida Toumi (Messaoudi) co-led the ruling party. Because of these shared characteristics, this essay focuses on the three countries. And although non-feminist forms of women's activism, such as the activities of women associated with Islamist movements and parties, exist in the Maghreb, this paper focuses on *feminist* activism.

The immediate postcolonial period saw women involved almost exclusively in either official women's organizations or charitable associations, but new organizations formed in the 1980s and 1990s, including Morocco's Association Démocratique des Femmes du Maroc (ADFM), Algeria's SOS Femmes en Détresse, Tunisia's Association Tunisienne des Femmes Démocrates (known as Femmes Démocrates), and women-led professional associations. In the absence of significant female participation in the labor force or in government, critically minded educated women could establish their authority, take part in decision-making, engage with various publics, develop their civic skills, and exercise political rights in their own organizations. Another form of women's participation in civil society has involved literary efforts, including the production of books, magazines, and films. These developments reflect sociodemographic changes in the female population, including greater educational attainment, the rising age at first marriage, smaller family size, and women's presence in an array of professional fields and occupations. Travel abroad, access to satellite TV, and knowledge of information technology facilitates international connections and fosters civic and feminist activism. Participation in media, including a feminist press, and in cultural production enables women to access the public sphere and thus national debates and dialogues.

At the same time, the Maghreb participates in the world economy and world society, which makes it vulnerable to the vagaries of global capitalism and the recipient of global discourses. Thus, when states began implementing structural adjustment policies from the late 1970s into the 1990s, not only unions but also the burgeoning feminist groups began to raise objections. While the unions protested on the streets, the feminist groups wrote critiques in their domestic publications as well as in documents prepared for the UN's Third World Conference on Women, held in Nairobi in 1985, and the Fourth World Conference, held in Beijing in 1995. The Collectif was able to draw on the emerging global women's rights agenda, notably the UN's Convention on the Elimination of All Forms of Discrimination against Women (CEDAW), as well as funding from German foundations, to advance its case for an egalitarian family code and to launch campaigns to improve their legal status and social positions and to ensure that their governments implement international agreements. The group also relied on the support of other transnational feminist networks, such as Women Living under Muslim Laws (WLUML) and the Women's Learning Partnership for Rights, Development, and Peace (WLP). The WLP's translation service produced an English-language version of an important Collectif study of family law across the Maghreb.

The contemporary discourses of women's participation, human rights, civil society, modernity, citizenship, and democratization reflect the changing sociopolitical dynamics of women's activism. Advocacy becomes more pointed, with a focus on the need to reform discriminatory family laws and bring them in line with constitutional guarantees of equality and with CEDAW; to criminalize domestic violence and prohibit sexual harassment; to grant women equal nationality rights so that their children may acquire citizenship through the mother and not just the father; and to create mechanisms to facilitate women's access to employment and political decision-making. The demands and strategies are indicative of the political maturity of the women's rights movement.

TUNISIA

Tunisian scholar-activists have underscored the importance to women's rights of the 1956 Code du Statut Personnel (Tunisia's family law), introduced by President Bourguiba. Still, progressive women were aware of discrimination and oppression. The *Women's Condition Study Club* celebrated International Women's Day on March 8, 1980 and subsequently a group of women intellectuals formed the Taher Haddad Club – named after a famous liberal thinker – which became a center for the discussion of social problems and women's rights. Themes included low-income and rural women's precarious conditions, the plight of divorced mothers without family support or resources, girls forced to leave school, household violence, and media images of women. A bilingual (Arabic and French) feminist magazine called *Nissa* (Woman) appeared in 1985; feature articles over the first year of publication included discussions of the problem of illegitimate children, the personal status laws of Tunisia and Egypt (both under attack that year), the Israeli bombing raid of the PLO headquarters in a suburb of Tunis, the pros and cons of sex-segregated activities, the risks of childbirth, and feminism. The magazine folded in 1987 mainly because of disagreements among its staff members, who then went on to join some of the associations mentioned earlier.

Political opportunities specific to Tunisia, even in an authoritarian context, enabled the women's rights movement to grow. The Tunisian government signed CEDAW in July 1980, though it would be another five years until ratification. In 1982, Tunis was host to UNESCO's Expert Meeting on Multidisciplinary Research on Women in the Arab World. Two autonomous feminist organizations appeared in 1989: the Association of Tunisian Women for Research and Development (known by its French acronym AFTURD) and the Femmes Démocrates, which would come to have close ties to the Women's Commission of the General Union of Tunisian Workers (UGTT). Other women's organizations – notably the National Union of Tunisian Women and the Association of Tunisian Mothers – were more closely linked to the state. Khedija Arfaoui has argued that government policies and programs enabled the emergence of women's organizations and other NGOs in that period. Still, as law professor Alya Cherif-Chammari noted in a 1992 book, women remained unequal in inheritance and the law prohibited the marriage of a Muslim woman to a non-Muslim man while allowing a Muslim man to marry a Christian or Jewish woman. Women activists also were concerned about the economic crisis and the rise of *intégrisme* in Tunisia and elsewhere in North Africa.

As a result of women's activities – and possibly, too, because of their stated opposition to Islamic fundamentalism – the Tunisian state under President Ben Ali introduced wide-ranging amendments to the family law in 1993. The mother's consent was now required in addition to the father's for the marriage of a minor; a wife's duty of obedience to her husband was replaced by her right to be treated with care and concern; she gained the right to participate in the management of the family's affairs, such as children's education, travel, and financial matters; the couple could choose joint or separate financial holdings, to be stipulated in the marriage contract. If a child is born out of wedlock and the father is known, the child carries the father's name, has the right to the father's support until reaching adulthood, and inherits the same portion as a daughter. In 1998, a law criminalizing crimes of honor was adopted; what is more, the punishment for domestic violence was made double that of an ordinary offense.

At the 2004 Arab League Summit held in Tunis, as described by Lilia Labidi, the host nation called on the member states to "consider the promotion of the rights of Arab women as a fundamental axis of the process of development and modernization of Arab societies." Thus were the Femmes Démocrates able to secure the passage in 2004 of the country's first legislation combating sexual harassment; the association also established the first *centre d'écoute*. This counseling center and hotline was followed by one in Algeria hosted by the country's main trade union.

With the launch of the Arab Spring in Tunisia in January 2011 and the collapse of the Ben Ali government, feminist groups mobilized to ensure a democratic transition *with* women. Fearing that the "Dignity revolution" in which they had taken part would come to favor Ennahda – the Islamic party that had been banned since the early 1990s – and recalling Ennahda's regressive stance on women's issues in the past, Tunisian feminists staged a protest on the eve of leader Ghannouchi's return from exile in January 2011. When the constituent assembly, which was dominated by Ennahda, sought to replace the term *equality* with words akin to *complementarity* or *partnership*, women's rights activists and their male supporters in the secular and left-wing parties took to the streets and to the domestic and international media in protest. The constituent assembly retained the term *equality*. The new Tunisian constitution was finalized and adopted in January 2014.

MOROCCO

Long subject to a highly patriarchal family law, the Mudawana, Moroccan women saw its replacement in 2004 with a more egalitarian set of laws and norms for marital life and family affairs – the result of a 12-year feminist campaign led by feminist groups such as l'Union de l'Action Feminine and the ADFM, as the latter noted:

> The new law embodies the principle of shared family responsibilities between the spouses. It was the product of extensive public discussion of challenges women faced under the previous law, as well as analysis of the implications of human rights standards and religious texts. To help ensure effective implementation of the new rights that have been guaranteed, the legislative changes were accompanied by the creation of dedicated Family Courts, and the Ministry of Justice is enhancing the provision of support services and training for judges and court officials.

Introduction of the new family code was part of a broader wave of important reforms within the country, including changes to the electoral code (in 2002), which introduced a "national list" that reserved 30 parliamentary seats for women, to the labor code (in 2004) to introduce the concept of sexual harassment in the workplace, and to the nationality code (in 2007) to give women and men equal rights to transmit nationality to their children as required by CEDAW's Article 9. In February 2004, a coalition to ensure the implementation of Morocco's new labor law was launched by the Centre des Droits des Gens, the Ligue Démocratique pour les Droits des Femmes, and the Association Marocaine des Droits des Femmes, and in November of that year it was joined by the Union Marocaine du Travail, the Confédération Démocratique du Travail, and the Association Marocaine des Droits Humains. The campaign also issued a report entitled *Protection des Droits des Femmes*, which, among other things, pointed out that Morocco had yet to sign and ratify ILO Convention 183 on maternity protection, designed to protect the rights of working mothers. More recently, Moroccan feminist groups formed a coalition with physicians' groups and human rights organizations, called the Springtime of Dignity, to urge the government to revise the penal code to criminalize all forms of violence against women and "preserve the dignity of women, their physical and psychology integrity, and their autonomy."

Following the Arab Spring, ADFM hosted a regional seminar in Rabat in May 2011 on Women and Democratic Transitions in the MENA region, which was attended by representatives from civil society, women's rights organizations, UN Women and other international organizations and the diplomatic corps from Morocco, Tunisia, Egypt, Syria, and Lebanon. The Moroccan Minister of Women's Affairs at the time, Nouzha

Skalli, announced that after years of advocacy by women's rights organizations, the Moroccan government would officially ratify CEDAW's Optional Protocol. Minister Skalli, a socialist well known for her commitment to women's equality and rights, discussed the challenges and prospects for equality in the constitutional reform process in Morocco and noted that women made up 5 of the 18 members of the Consultative Commission for the Constitutional Reform Coalition. Morocco's constitutional amendments were approved in a referendum in July 2011.

ALGERIA

The Algerian women's movement has endured – but stood against – patriarchal laws and norms and Islamist terrorism, and it helped to build the Collectif. It has shown a most audacious opposition to both Islamism (and state autocracy) in a manner that cost a number of women activists their lives during the wave of Islamist terror in the 1990s. Algerian feminists saw their movement as simultaneously democratic and feminist, fighting for modernity and individual rights while also holding on to the socialist legacy of equality of citizens. They were critical of past practice subsuming the woman question under national liberation and the building of Algerian-style socialism. The ideological and cultural divide between Islamist and non-Islamist women activists was enormous; feminists distinguished "women of the modernist trend" from the women of the Islamist movement. According to one such activist-theorist, Doria Cherifati-Merabtine, the modernist women's movement, comprised mainly of older university women from the first post-independence generation of intellectuals, "have learned at their expense that no change is possible if the outlook on woman and her place within society does not evolve." These modernist women are committed to both "an egalitarian social project" and recognition of the rights of the "Woman-Individual."

In previous work, I have examined three waves of Algerian women's collective action since the 1980s: against the conservative family code in the immediate post-Boumediènne period, against the Islamist movement and the terrorism of the 1990s, and for gender justice in the new century. Algerian feminist groups have worked with each other, with human rights groups and the country's main trade union, and with the Collectif to achieve policy and legal reforms, including some amendments to the family law in 2005, and a law against sexual harassment. Still, feminist groups gathered in March 2010 to call for the total repeal of the family law and its replacement with a new, egalitarian code. In this they were supported by Louisa Hanoune, leader of the Workers' Party. (Her party won 20 seats – out of 462 – in the 2012 parliamentary elections.)

In 2002, in recognition of the feminist movement and its valiant stance in the face of Islamist terrorism, Algerian president Bouteflika appointed five well-known women's rights advocates to his cabinet. Although the government fell after one year, the remarkable 25 percent female composition of the cabinet was unprecedented and has yet to be replicated elsewhere in the region. In May 2012, as a result of the adoption of a gender quota for the new parliamentary elections, women came to comprise 31 percent of parliamentary seats – the highest in the region. (Elsewhere in North Africa, women's parliamentary share in 2013 was 27 percent in Tunisia, 17 percent in Morocco, and a mere 2 percent in Egypt.) As of late 2013, the Interparliamentary Union's ranking of women in national parliaments placed Algeria at 26 out of 142 countries examined. The cabinet was less impressive: just three women – including the well-known feminist Khalida Toumi,

Minister of Culture – out of a total of 39 ministers.

Turning to feminist studies in the Maghreb, Fatima Mernissi's first book, *Behind the Veil: Male-Female Dynamics in Modern Muslim Society* – which appeared in 1976 as the product of her doctoral dissertation in sociology at Brandeis University in the United States – influenced a generation of scholars and set the stage for the fields of North African women's studies, Middle East women's studies, and the study of women and Islam. Mernissi's sociological insights and bold analyses laid bare some of the key contradictions in women's status and gender relations in Muslim societies generally and in Morocco in particular: the application of shari'a-based family law privileged men, subordinated women, and prevented companionate marriage. The second edition of her book appeared in 1987 in revised form with a new Introduction that now examined Islamic fundamentalist movements and found them to be the products of the contradictions of modernization, including changes in gender relations and women's roles. As she memorably noted in the Preface: "If fundamentalists are calling for a return of the veil, it must be because women have been taking off the veil."

Founded in 1987 by Leila Chaouni, the publishing house *Le Fennec* promoted writing by and on women. As Loubna Skalli notes, Le Fennec's multidisciplinary and multilingual research strengthened regional research networks of Moroccan, Tunisian, and Algerian activists, media professionals, and academics; published texts in both Arabic and French to cater to needs of larger circles of writers and readers; and encouraged men and women researchers/activists to work, write and publish together. In Algeria, women academics such as Cherifa Bouatta, the novelist and essayist Assia Djebar, and the filmmaker Horria Saihi have sought to uncover women's roles in the 1950s liberation movement and the building of the new state and society, and have boldly criticized fundamentalist thinking and Islamist terrorism. Saihi's documentary *Algérie des Femmes* recounts the horror of kidnapping, torture, and rape inflicted on women during the years of Islamist terrorism. The combination of women's literary production, advocacy efforts, mobilizing structures, access to various media, use of new information and communication technologies, and engagement with various publics has been called by Valentine Moghadam and Fatima Sadiqi "a gradual feminization of the public sphere" in North Africa.

SEE ALSO: Women's Political Representation; Women's Writing

FURTHER READING

ADFM 2009. "Report on the Application of CEDAW in the Arab World," May 2009. Accessed August 16, 2015, at http://cedaw.files.wordpress.com/2009/07/adfm-report-on-the-application-of-cedaw-in-the-arab-world.pdf.

Arfaoui, Khedifa. 2005. "Origins of the Women's Movement in Tunisia." Paper prepared for the Sixth Mediterranean Research Meeting, Montecatini, Italy (16–20 March), workshop on Women's Activism and the Public Sphere.

Chékir, Hafidha, and Khedija Arfaoui. 2011. "Tunisia: Women's Economic Citizenship and Trade Union Participation." In *Making Globalization Work for Women*, edited by Valentine M. Moghadam, Suzanne Franzway, and Mary Margaret Fonow, 71–92. Albany: SUNY Press.

Chérif Chamari, Alya. 1992. *La Femme et la Loi en Tunisie*. Rabat: Le Fennec.

Cherifati-Merabtine, Doria. 1994. "Algeria at a Crossroads: National Liberation, Islamization, and Women." In *Gender and National Identity: Women and Politics in Muslim Societies*, edited by Valentine M. Moghadam. London: Zed Books.

Collectif 95 Maghreb-Egalité. 2003. *Dalil pour l'égalité dans la famille au Maghreb*. Rabat: Association Démocratique des Femmes du Maroc. [Available in English as *Guide to Equality in the Family in the Maghreb*, published in 2005 by the Women's Learning Partnership's Translation Series, Bethesda, MD.]

Labidi, Lilia. 2007. "The Nature of Transnational Alliances in Women's Associations in the Maghreb: The Case of AFTURD and AFTD in Tunisia." *Journal of Middle East Women's Studies*, 3(1): 6–34.

Mernissi, Fatima. 1987. *Behind the Veil: Male-Female Dynamics in Modern Muslim Society*, Revised ed. Bloomington: Indiana University Press.

Moghadam, Valentine M. 2013. *Modernizing Women: Gender and Social Change in the Middle East*, 3rd ed. Boulder, CO: Lynne Rienner Publishers.

Moghadam, Valentine M., and Fatima Sadiqi. 2006. "Introduction and Overview: Women and the Public Sphere in the Middle East and North Africa." *Journal of Middle East Women's Studies*, 2(2): 1–7.

Skalli, Loubna. 2006. "Communicating Gender in the Public Sphere: Women and Information Technologies in the MENA Region." *Journal of Middle East Women's Studies*, 2(2): 35–59.

Tchaicha, Jane. D. 2005. "Technology in the Service of Maghribi Women." *The Journal of North African Studies*, 10(2): 155–171.

Women's and Feminist Activism in Russia, Ukraine, and Eurasia

KATALIN FÁBIÁN
Lafayette College, USA

ALEX HRYCAK
Reed College, USA

JANET ELISE JOHNSON
Brooklyn College, City University of New York, USA

Women in Russia, Ukraine, and Eurasia have expressed their interests and demands through numerous forms of activism shaped by varied experiences of colonialism and national liberation struggles, Soviet totalitarianism and Communist Party-led emancipation, and post-Soviet democratization, authoritarianism, economic instability, and warfare.

Many cases in the region teach us that small pockets of women's activism can have great effect. Mass women's mobilization has also been central to attaining universal suffrage and addressing social needs, especially before the formation and after the collapse of the Soviet Union. A minority of women's activists identify as feminist because feminism has often encountered suspicion and rejection. Emerging women's movements tended either to pursue proto-feminist aims while rejecting the feminist label or to take up conservative, traditional gender-conforming goals that allowed cooperation with and co-optation by the state.

Before 1917, most of this region was conquered and deeply influenced by the Russian Empire, which imposed restrictions on organizing, especially for non-Russians. Activism in the Russian Empire ranged from clandestine operations to innocuous women's circles, informal networks within larger organizations that expressed interests through women's writing, organizing charities, and participating in trade unions and federated professional organizations. Women activists in the Russian Empire fought against girls' exclusion from education and agitated for universal suffrage and the protection of women workers from exploitation. Women's rights were understood through the lens of the "woman question," with a focus on how to balance women's role as mothers with professional calls and obligations. Small-scale actions, such as individual petitions, allowed upper-class women to enter secondary schools, university preparatory classes, and, in 1872, professional training in teaching and medicine. A few female activists committed terrorist acts, such as the assassination attempt on the governor general of St Petersburg for his abuse of prisoners, and participated in the assassination of Tsar Alexander II in 1881. Women joined Marxist groups to resolve their extremely few personal options and the economic–political impoverishment of the masses.

In Habsburg-ruled Western Ukraine, women organized more freely. A notable leader was the socialist feminist Natalia Kobrynska, who is considered to be the founder of the Ukrainian women's movement. In addition to campaigning for suffrage and women's rights to university education, activists founded numerous mass membership organizations for the empowerment of working women, demanding subsidized cafeterias, representing the interests of domestic servants, and establishing a federated women's cooperative and nursery schools.

Russian feminists were more radical than many counterparts in connecting women's liberation with freedom and equality for all. Women protesting about bread shortages led to the February 1917 revolution and then mass demonstrations persuaded the provisional government to be the first major international power to grant women's suffrage. Feminists and socialist women's movements parted ways, with socialists and later communists accusing feminists of focusing on upper-class concerns.

Under Soviet rule, the leadership banned preexisting women's organizations but passed laws granting women equality and established a system of women's sections within the Communist Party – headed first by feminist Inessa Armand and then by Aleksandra Kollontai. These sections trained local women activists, recruited local women into the Party, and directed community relief work among orphans, wounded soldiers, and the homeless. In the 1920s, women Party members held women's conferences of delegates from local women's groups. In the 1930s, women's sections merged with local Communist Party organizations and some of the early Soviet laws intended to grant women equality were repealed: abortion was banned, sex outside marriage condemned as bourgeois, and motherhood awards encouraged large families. In the late 1950s (and again in the 1980s), when fertility rates and economic productivity began to slow considerably, the Party formed Women's Councils. By the late 1970s, along with other feminist samizdat publications, a small group of women in Leningrad started the *Women's Almanac* that critiqued the Soviet claim of women's emancipation. Such views were so unwelcome that the regime exiled the *Almanac*'s founder, Tatiana Mamonova.

While some scholars viewed the Soviet state-sponsored economic and political gains afforded to women as a form of "state feminism," these were top-down, often symbolic measures that did not challenge patriarchal relations in the home and gender inequalities in employment and public life. In the Central Asian Soviet republics, Muslim women were forcibly unveiled, not in response to women's activism, but as part of the colonizing project. The political and economic reforms of the 1980s allowed more open debate on, among other problems, women's double burden of work and family. Women became active in a variety of protest organizations, bringing attention to the issue of violence in the military through committees of Soldiers' Mothers and to the environment (including in response to the Chernobyl nuclear accident), while also joining the emergent movements demanding independence throughout the USSR.

Russia, Ukraine, and other post-Soviet states became independent in 1991. Feminist groups, scholarship, literature, and various kinds of women's organizations emerged to challenge public and government attitudes promoting a narrowly traditional cult of domesticity and motherhood, and offering alternatives that empower women. Given the dramatic economic and political losses they experienced with the collapse, women's activism generally called for new approaches to welfare and political representation (such as quotas). Some of these groups remained small in scale and gained little public attention and political support. Others who couched their demands in ways that resonated with immediate public or state interests often managed to develop followings outside their immediate membership. In Russia and Ukraine, activists created women's parties (e.g., Women of Russia, the only such party to experience a brief electoral success) and women's organizations that allied with parties. In Ukraine, leadership of women's organizations is one of the primary channels to national or local legislatures. Among the few women activists to achieve positions of political prominence is Ruslana Lyzhychko, who has been a central figure in public campaigns to prevent sex trafficking, served in the parliament, and has been an active leader in Ukraine's democracy and human rights movements. Similarly in Russia, Elena Ershova, head of the Consortium of Women's Nongovernmental Associations, served in the Public Chamber, and Ekaterina Lakhova (from Women of Russia) acted as head of the Presidential Commission on the affairs of women and children and as a Duma Deputy.

Soldiers' Mothers groups continued building on activism during the 1980s. The Union of the Committees of Soldiers' Mothers of Russia used a maternalist–nationalist discourse to bring attention to hazing in the military and object to the country's wars in Chechnya in the 1990s. Various groups of Soldiers' Mothers in Ukraine also continued to fight violence and abuse of conscripts and lobbied successfully for reforms in military conscription. New gender studies centers also became important in shaping policy and scholarship, in particular the Saint Petersburg Center for Gender Issues, the Moscow Center for Gender Studies, the Kyiv Gender Studies Institute, and the Kharkiv Center for Gender Studies.

Participation in the 1995 United Nations Conference on Women in Beijing and support from Western women's programs and donors helped spur women's activists to raise new women's rights issues, most notably violence against women. This problem has been a central focus of global women's rights advocacy and it also appeared to worsen amidst economic downturn and political turmoil. Lobbying by women's advocates led to the passage in 2001 of Ukraine's Law on the Prevention of Family Violence, the first legislation in Central and Eastern Europe and the former Soviet Union that defines domestic violence as a specific offense, introduces temporary restraining orders, and mandates state support for nationwide networks of crisis centers, shelters and other services to assist victims of abuse. Activists also secured laws in Kyrgyzstan (2003) and Georgia (2006), but with less weight. In Russia, a small but effective women's crisis center movement changed public opinion about domestic violence and nudged the government to establish its own support centers for women, albeit with a less feminist orientation and no national legislation. Crisis hotlines and at least some shelters serving victims of domestic violence appeared nearly everywhere in the region. In Central Asia, the few women's NGOs and shelters are faced with multiple, interlocking problems when re-emerging traditional gender segregation decreases women's access to education and opportunities to work outside the home leading to increased frequency of child marriage, bride kidnapping, and psychological and physical violence against girls and especially widowed and older women.

Anti-trafficking emerged as part of the movement to combat violence against women. One of the prominent women's rights

NGOs has been La Strada Ukraine, whose president (Kateryna Levchenko) served as a member of parliament during 2006–2007 and as an advisor to the government on the prevention of human trafficking. Lobbying led in 1999 to the definition of human trafficking as a crime and to the creation of a series of state agencies and comprehensive programs to coordinate trafficking prevention in Ukraine. The UN Protocol against Trafficking was ratified by Tajikistan in 2002, Armenia, Azerbaijan, Belarus, and Kyrgyzstan in 2003, Russia and Ukraine in 2004, Moldova and Turkmenistan in 2005, Georgia in 2006, and Kazakhstan and Uzbekistan in 2008.

Ukrainian women's organizations have built on extensive historical legacies and international networks. The Union of Ukrainian Women, founded in 1921, continues to coordinate transnational support for women's participation in the United Nations and other international events. Of the more than 1500 women's organizations founded since 1991, many are self-help community groups focused on assisting disadvantaged families and children. Several dozen non-feminist women's associations have raised concerns about the status of women and mobilized support for gender equality policies and laws. The most politically significant groups that organized conferences assessing the status of women, produced election campaigns to increase women's representation in legislatures, and lobbied the Ukrainian parliament to strengthen women's legal rights included nationwide women's federations such as the Women's Community, The Union of Women of Ukraine (the successor to official Soviet Women's Councils), the Olena Teliha International Women's Society, and the League of Women Voters 50/50.

The direction of the cross-border encounters has been a contentious theme among activists and observers. Critics charge that feminism has been imported mainly through Western European and North American aid projects and academic exchanges and assisted by international bodies, such as the UN CEDAW and the Council of Europe. International funders tend to favor short-term support for a cycle of issues and approaches that are externally determined, hence these themes may lack relevance and are difficult to adapt to local women's concerns.

Because of the legacy of Russian and Soviet imperialism, connections between women activists from different countries have also been contentious. For example, the US–NIS Women's Consortium founded in 1993 aimed to forge ties among women's organizations in the United States, Russia, Ukraine, and other post-Soviet countries. However, all that remains are separate Russian and Ukrainian versions of this organization, both of which still serve as hubs for inter-organizational cooperation on projects to empower women politically.

The shift in international funding from the region and increasing authoritarianism in Russia and Central Asia have limited space for activism, leading most women's organizations to embrace a "maternalist" style of activism that focuses on improving the welfare of children or families, rather than the status of women. Nascent gender equality machineries developed in the 1990s in some countries were dismantled and gender equality dropped from the state agenda. Laws in Russia, such as a 2012 requirement that organizations engaged in political activity register as "foreign agents," have established new mechanisms for the state's arbitrary control over women's organizations. In Ukraine, whose 2004 Orange Revolution had opened more opportunities for social movements, women's activism and gender equality mechanisms faced similar restrictions after 2010. The Ukrainian president's impeachment in 2014 and the ensuing conflict with Russia have further distracted the attention both of these states, their populations, and the international community from addresing gender inequality.

Even with these extensive pressures, there have been new feminist voices in public life and academia. The Russian Pussy Riot, Ukrainian FEMEN, and the Feminist Initiative have drawn extensive domestic and worldwide attention for challenging authoritarian practices. FEMEN is known for its controversial bare-breasted protests against sex trafficking and neoliberalism. Members of the punk band Pussy Riot attracted worldwide attention when three of its members were sentenced to prison for a performance that critiqued the close ties between church and state. Dozens of groups continue to critique ongoing patriarchal structures, articulate new feminisms, and expose the role of economic violence in perpetuating gender inequality.

Social media are also helping new feminisms emerge through collective blogs such as Russia's *feministki* or *womenation, Za Feminizm* (http://www.zafeminizm.ru/) and the Moscow Feminist Group (https://www.facebook.com/ravnopravka?fref=ts/), and Ukraine's feminism-ua. These and other informal virtual discussion groups have created a new forum for issues of gender equality in addition to engaging in new causes that were rarely discussed earlier, such as LGBTQ politics, intersectionality, restrictions on abortion, legalization of prostitution, in and out migration, polygamy, body image, and the media's representation of women and girls.

It is undeniable that women's and feminist organizing have contributed substantially to the paths of political, economic, and cultural developments in the territory that the Russian Empire and the Soviet ruled until 1992. The deep historical scars of past dictatorial systems continue to produce erratic political and economic developments, profoundly mediating the emergence and influence of women's groups and feminist activism.

SEE ALSO: Democracy and Democratization; Feminist Activism; Human Trafficking, Feminist Perspectives on

FURTHER READING

Bohachevsky-Chomiak, Martha. 1988. *Feminists Despite Themselves: Women in Ukrainian Community Life, 1884–1939*. Edmonton: University of Alberta.

Fábián, Katalin, ed. 2010. *Domestic Violence in Postcommunist Europe and Eurasia: Local Activism, National Policies, and Global Forces*. Bloomington: Indiana University Press.

Hrycak, Alexandra. 2002. "From Mothers, Rights to Equal Rights: Post-Soviet Grassroots Women's Associations." In *Women's Community Activism and Globalization: Linking the Local and Global for Social Change*, edited by Nancy Naples and Manisha K. Desai, 64–82. New York: Routledge.

Gessen, Masha. 2014. *Words Will Break Cement: the Passion of Pussy Riot*. New York: Riverhead Trade.

Johnson, Janet Elise. 2009. *Gender Violence in Russia: the Politics of Feminist Intervention*. Bloomington: Indiana University Press.

Kay, Rebecca. 2000. *Russian Women and Their Organizations*. New York: St Martin's Press.

McDermid, Jane, and Anna Hillyar. 1999. *Midwives of Revolution: Female Bolsheviks and Women Workers in 1917*. Athens, OH: Ohio University Press.

Matland, Richard, and Kathleen Montgomery, eds. 2003. *Women's Access to Political Power in Post-Communist Europe*. New York: Oxford University Press.

Noonan, Norma Corigliano, and Carol Nechemias, eds. 2001. *Encyclopedia of Russian Women's Movements*. Westport: Praeger.

Phillips, Sarah. 2008. *Women's Social Activism in the New Ukraine: Development and the Politics of Differentiation*. Bloomington: Indiana University Press.

Rueschemeyer, Marilyn, and Sharon Wolchik, eds. 2009. *Women in Power in Post-Communist Parliament*. Washington, DC: Woodrow Wilson

Center Press and Bloomington: Indiana University Press.
Ruthchild, Rochelle Goldberg. 2010. *Equality and Revolution: Women's Rights in the Russian Empire, 1905–1917*. Pittsburgh: University of Pittsburgh Press.
Sperling, Valerie. 1999. *Organizing Women in Contemporary Russia: Engendering Transition*. Cambridge: Cambridge University Press.
Sperling, Valerie. 2015. *Sex, Politics, and Putin: Political Legitimacy in Russia*. New York: Oxford University Press.
Sundstrom, Lisa McIntosh. 2010. "Russian Women's Activism: Two Steps Forward, One Step Back." In *Women's Movements in the Global Era*, edited by Amrita Basu, 229–254. Boulder: Westview Press.

Women's and Feminist Activism in Southeast Asia

SHARON A. BONG
Monash University, Malaysia

Women's/feminist activism in Southeast Asia (SEA) offers a reimagining of the global vision and practice of women's human rights. It does so by drawing from both rights-based and faith-based frameworks in mobilizing gender equality and gender equity for women and men and, by extension, gender and sexual minorities.

The conflation of women's activism and feminist activism faithfully reflects the historical privileging of a woman-centered activism and one that is sustained by campaigns against violence against women (VAW) or gender-based violence (GBV) within women's non-governmental organizations (NGOs) in Southeast Asia. In this sense, women's/feminist activism is tied to the genesis of most women's NGOs in this region, and this focus remains the current emphasis given the transnational exacerbation of VAW or GBV. Global trends of VAW and GBV include but are not limited to trafficking in human persons and the gendered impact of changing configurations of marriage (e.g., mail-order brides), migration, ethnic and religious conflict, state-sponsored victimization (e.g., trauma inflicted on women during the Khmer Rouge regime, sexual slavery of Muslim Rohingya women in Myanmar), and so on. Yet, in another sense, the conflation of women's activism and feminist activism less faithfully reflects the ethos of some women's NGOs. This is because some women's NGOs maintain reservations in identifying as feminist, as articulated in their organizational vision and mission statements even though the nature of advocacy or services that they offer are aimed at the elimination of gender inequality and inequity. Eschewing a feminist identity is politically strategic given that Southeast Asian states often position human rights and women's human rights as western values that are antithetical to Asian values (e.g., a rhetoric propagated by the then prime ministers of Malaysia and Singapore in the 1980s that privileges the common good over and above individual well-being).

In view of this tension, the term women's/feminist activism henceforth refers to both women's NGOs that identify as "feminist" and those who do so albeit to a lesser extent. Women's/feminist activism in Southeast Asia coheres with a feminist postcolonial framework within an intellectual social context. The essential understanding of feminism, when operationalized, would be the advancement of women's human rights in realizing gender equality and gender equity. These two concepts are differentiated. Gender equality is often appreciated as sameness between genders; women having the equal right to vote as men, for instance. Whereas gender equity takes into account the ways in which women are differently and disproportionately affected by GBV, which, in turn, calls for woman-centered or women-specific policies and agendas and in some cases, affirmative action.

Equality as such – between men and women and even among women from the north and south, first worlds and developing worlds – is not always synonymous with sameness. These differences that matter are made more apparent when states attempt to mainstream women's human rights in national developmental projects: from women in development (which foregrounds the ways women are differently and disproportionately affected by poverty, for instance) to the more integrative gender and development approaches (which uses a gendered lens, to view the gendered dimensions of structural poverty).

Feminist postcolonial approach privileges not only gender but also ethnicity, class, cultures, and religions as analytical categories in making sense of gender inequalities and gender inequities in Asia. As such, there is not just one definition of feminism; it is not a monolithic body of knowledge and practices. The emergence of feminist postcolonial theory offers a counter-discourse that challenges the unexamined assumptions of white, western, and middle-class feminists. Its ethos seeks to de-colonize (hence the prefix "post" in postcolonial) by opening up feminisms that have greater resonance with the lived realities of Southeast Asia, in particular its poverty and the plurality of its political, social, and cultural contexts.

Whereas first-wave feminisms (e.g., liberal, radical, or lesbian feminism) positioned women as an oppressed class under the rubric of "sisterhood is global," feminist-postcolonial theorists, as third-wave feminists, posit that not all women are oppressed or oppressed in the same way. Identity politics that are integral to setting apart Asian women's/feminist activism particularly within the arena of global women's human rights, calls for a degree of essentialism: that the "Asian woman" is marginalized and triply marginalized on account of her sex, her poverty, her lower status as an ethnic, cultural, religious, and sexual minority.

However, in drawing the parameters of, making sense of and practicing Asian women's feminisms, it is important to avoid the pitfall of homogenization; flattening out differences among Asian women under the tyranny of sameness, as not all Asian women are oppressed or oppressed in the same way. And assigning the fixed attribute of victimhood to "Asian women," however politically strategic in mobilizing resources (e.g., foreign funding, political will of governments, consciousness-raising of the public), also risks the pitfall of reductionism where women are not just disempowered but also empowered as activists and feminist activists. As negotiations in claiming and reevaluating a politics of identity of women's/feminist activism in Southeast Asia remain a continuing challenge, the prefix "post" in postcolonial does not suggest that the work is done. But it does point to the coming-of-age of women's/feminist activisms in this Asian region.

SEA's women's/feminist activism engages with the rhetoric and practice of women's human rights. Framed within a feminist postcolonial perspective, SEA's women's/feminist activism takes into account these ideological and pragmatic contestations and pluralities on the ground. It does so to more effectively bring global women's human rights conventions home, that is, to realize global women's human rights at a local level. In terms of global women's human rights conventions, the singular women's treaty is the 1979 UN Convention on the Elimination of All Forms of Discrimination against Women that all Southeast Asian countries are states parties to in having ratified it, albeit with reservations. In doing so, governments are held accountable by incrementally realizing gender equality and equity for women – in overcoming these reservations – through a faithful documentation of achievements and obstacles in periodic government reports to the CEDAW Committee. The complementary Shadow Report provided by women's/feminist NGOs is often positioned as a counter-narrative to the government report on the country-specific position and treatment of women and the girl-child. The Shadow Report inadvertently also showcases good practices of women's/feminist activisms in working together with states in overcoming reservations in operationalizing the goals of CEDAW.

Some of these good practices involving women's/feminist activisms in Southeast Asia include, among many others: the Vietnam Women's Union, founded in 1930, which was initially immersed in mobilizing women in nationalist struggles, for example, anti-feudalism and anti-imperialism movements led by the Communist Party to struggle for the "power of the people," subsequently, resistance against American aggressors and is currently mandated to protect women's legitimate rights and strive for gender equality with achievements such as the new Law on Gender Equality signed in 2006 (Chiricosta 2010, 139); GABRIELA Philippines, established in 1984, is a nationwide alliance of over 200 women's NGOs at the forefront of not only women's rights but also the "Filipino women's struggle for freedom and democracy"; the Foundation For Women in Thailand formed in 1984, "implements activities by applying human rights principles" aimed at "respecting, protecting, and promoting the rights of individual women and girl child," launched a community-based education project (Kamla) to combat child prostitution in 1988 as well as campaigned for safe migration and community participation in protecting workers against trafficking; the Joint Action Group Against Violence Against Women formed in 1985, now the Joint Action Group for Gender Equality (JAG) of Malaysia, a coalition of women's NGOs, had spearheaded multiple campaigns and legal reform efforts, leading to milestones as the 1994 Domestic Violence Act and the inclusion of "gender" under Article 8(2) of the Federal Constitution in 2001; AWARE Singapore, founded in 1985, whose vision is to realize "true gender equality," seeks to provide a "feminist perspective in the national dialogue"; Fokupers of Timor-Leste, established in 1997, works on the "empowerment of women from a women's human rights perspective," investigates women's human rights violations and provides support, including counseling, to women political prisoners, wives of political prisoners, war widows, and survivors of violence against women; Komnas Perempuan of Indonesia (formerly, the National Commission on Violence Against Women) was formed in 1998 and their mission is, among others, to "strengthen efforts to prevent and deal with all forms of violence against women and to promote survivors' rights to truth, justice, multidimensional rehabilitation that includes economic, social, political and cultural rights based on rights of self-integrity"; Chab Dai Cambodia, founded in 2005, is a coalition of over 50 member organizations working to address sexual abuse and trafficking whose initiative, the Cambodia Leaning Community, is set up to hone in collaboration and encourage best practices among anti-trafficking NGOs, from grassroots to large organizations on "raising the standard of care for survivors and those at risk of being exploited," sharing resources and building capacity; and the Gender Equality Network of Myanmar is an inclusive network of over a hundred civil society organizations, national and international NGOs, UN agencies, and technical resource persons, with the mandate to "support the development and implementation of enabling systems, structures, and practices for the advancement of women, gender equality, and the realization of women's rights in Myanmar."

A further example of good practice in bringing CEDAW home is evidenced by many women's/feminist NGOs that operate within rights-based and faith-based frameworks. The rationale for this lies in the diversity of cultures and religions in Southeast Asia that have an impact on the rhetoric and practice of women's human rights. This hyphenated strategy – in localizing a global vision and potentially globalizing a local practice – offers a unique positioning of women's human rights as not merely secularist (in dismissing or undervaluing cultural and religious considerations). It offers a standpoint and praxis, a *critical relativism* (Bong 2006) that, in embracing both the universalism of women's human rights and the particularities of cultures and religions, more effectively realizes gender equality. Critical relativism considers the lived realities of women and men whose lives, in particular their sexual and reproductive health and rights, remain greatly influenced by cultures and religions. The Philippines is overwhelmingly Catholic as is Timor-Leste; Indonesia is home to the largest Muslim population globally; Brunei Darrusalam is now an Islamic State with shari'a law recently imposed; Malaysia is often mistaken as one given its state-sponsored Islamization; and Buddhism is the dominant spirituality of Cambodia, Lao PDR, Myanmar, Singapore, Thailand, and Vietnam.

The following selected initiatives embody the intersection of politicizing spirituality and spiritualizing politics within women's/feminist activism in Southeast Asia.

To politicize spirituality is to direct one's faith towards political and social change and to spiritualize politics is to direct the state's policies and programs towards social justice (which includes gender equality) and inclusiveness. Women's/feminist activism that operates from rights-based and faith-based frameworks, politicizes spirituality and, in doing so, potentially, spiritualizes politics. In terms of Muslim women's/feminist activism in Southeast Asia to politicize spirituality is what Rinaldo terms as "pious critical agency" and "pious activating agency" (2013, 19): where the former engages with "the interpretation of texts" whilst the latter deploys religious texts to make claims for political and social change. To illustrate, the Sisters in Islam's (Malaysia) long-term objective, among others, is "to promote a framework of women's rights in Islam which takes into consideration women's experiences and realities," which it articulates and implements through its press statements, publications (often banned), and gender-sensitization training amid personal threats including death threats. SIS has vocally and visibly championed women's rights on issues as diverse as Muslim family law (e.g., polygamy, child marriage, divorce), *hudud* (Islamic law), and greater civil and political liberties that have periodically come under threat (e.g., sedition law) that allows the government to suppress the freedom of expression as well as the moral policing of gender and sexual minorities, for example, *mak nyahs* or male-to-female trans persons.

In terms of Catholic women's/feminist activism in Southeast Asia, Talitha Kum Southeast Asia (meaning little girl, arise, in Aramaic), is part of the International Network of Consecrated Religious (i.e., Catholic sisters) aimed at exchanging information and referrals for integration, sharing modules for the schools, communities, congregations and networking for advocacy, lobbying, and mobilization to "counteract human trafficking." Its representatives in Southeast Asia are based in Indonesia, Malaysia, Thailand, and Timor-Leste. Its vision "to renew the values of the church to respect and uphold the dignity of women and men created in the image and likeness of God" coalesces with a fundamental human liberty which runs counter to slavery in any form. The involvement of "feminist nuns" in women's/feminist NGOs on prostitution (Roces 2009) and reclaiming faith as a feminist practice by nuns of the Missionary Benedictine congregation in their negotiation of their gendered, religious, and national identities (Claussen 2001) are well documented.

In terms of Buddhist women's/feminist activism in Southeast Asia, Venerable Dhammananda Bhikkhuni, formerly Chatsumarn Kabilsingh, a well-known academic, is the first Thai woman to receive *bhikkhuni* ordination (monkhood) in the Theravada tradition. Along with three other *bhikkhuni*s, she founded Sakyadhita International Network of Buddhist Women, which has been integral in canvassing for the restoration of the *bhikkhuni* order globally (Falk 2010). The *bhikkhuni* movement explicitly challenges the official standpoint that deems the *bhikkhuni* order as extinct and their continued rejection by the Thai *sangha* (monks). By according legitimacy to *bhikkhuni*s, Sakyadhita realizes gender equality within the Buddhist world order.

Future directions of women's/feminist activism on SRHR concerns lies in complementary sexuality rights activism that is well supported by the Yogyakarta Principles drafted in 2006 on comprehensive human rights standards on sexual orientation and gender identity (Wieringa 2013).

SEE ALSO: Feminism in Southeast Asia; Gender Equality; LGBT Activism in Southeast Asia; Women's and Feminist Organizations in South Asia

REFERENCES

Bong, Sharon A. 2006. *The Tension between Women's Rights and Religions: The Case of Malaysia*. Lewiston: Edwin Mellen Press.

Chiricosta, Alessandra. 2010. "Following the Trail of the Fairy-Bird: The Search for a Uniquely Vietnamese Feminist Movement." In *Women's Movements in Asia: Feminisms and Transnational Activism*, edited by Mina Roces and Louise Edwards, 124–143. London: Routledge.

Claussen, Heather L. 2001. *Unconventional Sisterhood: Feminist Catholic Nuns in the Philippines*. Ann Arbor: The University of Michigan Press.

Falk, Monica Lindberg. 2010. "Feminism, Buddhism and Transnational Women's Movements in Thailand." In *Women's Movements in Asia: Feminisms and Transnational Activism*, edited by Mina Roces and Louise Edwards, 110–123. London: Routledge.

Rinaldo, Rachel. 2013. *Mobilizing Piety: Islam and Feminism in Indonesia*. Oxford: Oxford University Press.

Roces, Mina. 2009. "Prostitution, Women's Movements and the Victim Narrative in the Philippines." *Women's Studies International Forum*, 32(4): 270–280.

Wieringa, Saskia E. 2013. "Marriage Equality in Indonesia? Unruly Bodies, Subversive Partners and Legal Implications." *The Equal Rights Review*, 10: 97–110.

FURTHER READING

Blackburn, Susan, and Helen Ting, eds. 2013. *Women in Southeast Asian Nationalist Movements: A Biographical Approach*. Singapore: NUS Press.

Ford, Michele, ed. 2013. *Social Activism in Southeast Asia*. London: Routledge.

Ng, Cecilia, Maznah Mohamad, and tan beng hui. 2006. *Feminism and the Women's Movement in Malaysia: An Unsung (R)evolution*. London: Routledge.

Norani Othman, ed. 2013. *Muslim Women and the Challenge of Islamic Extremism*, 2nd ed. Petaling Jaya: SIS Forum (Malaysia).

Women's and Feminist Activism in Southern Africa

MARY HAMES
University of the Western Cape, South Africa

During the liberation struggles in the respective colonized countries women tended to establish separate women's caucuses within the male-dominated organizations. The African National Congress (ANC) had the ANC Women's League, in Angola the Organization of Angolan Women (OMA) was affiliated to the People's Movement for the Liberation of Angola (MPLA), in Mozambique the Organização da Mulher Moçambicana (OMM) was the women's structure within the ruling Frelimo (Front for the Liberation of Mozambique), the SWAPO Women's Council is found in Namibia as a substructure of the South West Africa People's Organization (SWAPO), and in Zimbabwe the ZANU PF Women's League is associated with the Zimbabwe African National Union – Patriotic Front (ZANU-PF). With independence these women's structures were incorporated into the newly formed democratic governments. Women's organizations have now started to collapse their interests with those of the ruling political party. Post-independence brought a focus on conventional political expedience and a demand for representation in political parties and government.

The histories and struggles of Southern African women's and feminist organizations are situated in divergent cultural, socioeconomic, geographical, and political backgrounds. The common denominator is that Southern African countries have been colonized, albeit by different colonial powers. The activism in these organizations has therefore centered on the oppressiveness of both patriarchy and colonization. The organizations under discussion are geographically located within the formal Southern African Development Community (SADC). The member states in the SADC include Angola, Botswana, Lesotho, Malawi, Mauritius, Mozambique, Namibia, South Africa, Swaziland, United Republic of Tanzania, Zambia, and Zimbabwe. With the signature of the SADC to regional and international agreements such as the Beijing Platform of Action, attempts have been made to find strategies to attain gender equality.

Colonization subjected women in Southern Africa to a dualistic legal system. The one was the formal codification of the rule of law of the colonial master and the second was the formalization of customary practices. This system allowed the colonial authorities to use the customary practices to their advantage and reinterpret them as bureaucratic governmental policy. African women in particular were affected by the dual legal system as subjects of both the colonial laws and the customary law, which was enforced by the specially created courts. The hybrid system made allowances for the existence of traditional authorities and the formalization of cultural practices such as polygamy, arranged marriages, and the payment of bridewealth (*lobola*) amongst others. Under both customary and Western/metropolitan law women could not own property, draw up contracts, own land or inherit, and women remained perpetual minors when they married. In both the traditional and the Western system, therefore, African women in particular were regarded as third-class citizens in their own countries. Their struggles against oppression have thus been multiple and rooted in a long history of organizing against oppression.

The postcolonial states became signatories of various international and regional treaties, agreements, conventions, and protocols.

One of the conventions signed by the SADC countries was the United Nations (UN) Convention on the Elimination of All Forms of Discrimination against Women (CEDAW). The constitutions of the postcolonial states were couched in the liberal human rights language that included commitments to the equality and empowerment of women. The government invariably became the custodian of women's rights and empowerment. Initially the feminists in government were seen as allies of the broader women's movement. They advocated for women and gender-inclusive legislation and various women's departments, women's desks, women's focal points, and women's ministries were introduced. For instance, in South Africa the members of the ANC Women's League (ANCWL) were part of the Women's National Coalition (WNC), which lobbied for the inclusion of women as a category in the Constitution's equality clause and the writing of a Women's Charter. The mobilization for the WNC went beyond race, class, culture, language, political affiliation, and religion.

After independence many countries established national gender machinery (NGM) for women to promote equality, but as Mama (2000, 15) noted, they have done very little to alleviate the plight of the ordinary woman. A few examples of NGMs are the Department of Women's Affairs (DWA) in Namibia; the Department of Women's Affairs in the Ministry of National Affairs, Employment Creation and Cooperatives in Zimbabwe; the Ministry of Community Development, Gender and Children (MCDGC), formerly known as the Ministry of Community Development, Women Affairs and Children (MCDWAC), in Tanzania; and in Swaziland, the Women's Desk, which is located in the Ministry of Home Affairs. South Africa has perhaps the most advanced national gender machinery in the region, but since its inception concerns have been raised whether the Commission on Gender Equality (CGE) would be able to effectively represent women's voices within state policy discussions and simultaneously mobilize women in civil society. The initial belief was that the national gender machineries would open up the opportunity for mechanisms to be developed to ensure the enforcement of international instruments (Gouws 2005). However, lessons learned from Mozambique and Zimbabwe showed that as soon as women are incorporated into the state, women's initiatives become demobilized and depoliticized (Meintjes 1996).

State feminism (government structures charged with promoting women's rights) and its accompanying "femocrat phenomenon" became a reality in Southern Africa. Mozambique in particular was a forerunner in institutionalizing feminism shortly after liberation, but the OMM was soon perceived as a threat to the privileges that men have always been entitled to. Feminists in Southern Africa addressed issues such as polygamy, bridewealth (*lobola*), and other oppressive cultural practices; they were concerned about access to education, healthcare, childcare, and representation in decision-making processes. They were acutely aware that these specific women's concerns were negated during the liberation struggles. The universal human rights framework became the tool for women and feminists to ensure that feminist jurisprudence is implemented in the region. Women's rights were mainly seen through the lens of legal equality.

Women's specific concerns were framed in a rights-based language and organizations became issue driven. The rights-based approach assisted with the building of global and transnational partnerships and solidarity with women's organizations sharing similar concerns. The postcolonial period is marked by two discernible trends; one is state-driven feminism and the affiliation between women's wings and ruling parties, and the other is the dynamic issue-driven activism of women's organizations, especially with regard to violence against women.

State-driven feminism and the universality of the rights-based approach in gender mainstreaming ignore the cultural relativism of women in different settings (Ndashe 2005). CEDAW raises concerns about the persistence of harmful practices such as polygamy and bride-price and argues that such customs and practices are perpetuating discrimination against women and children. Article 16 of CEDAW prohibits polygamy, but polygamy is widely practiced and lives alongside the most progressive laws in South Africa. Contradictions in law exist, such as the fact that the South African Constitution makes provision for both an advanced NGM and ensconcing the rights of traditional authorities. There are no mechanisms within the international and regional instruments that compel countries to abide with the protocols. This makes the instruments weak and frustrating for women's and progressive feminist organizations. State feminism in effect watered down feminist activism.

Critical women's and feminist organizations have long realized that the existence of a benevolent state is a myth and that they had to find ways to raise awareness with regard to their particular concerns. Some of the remedies that organizations have turned to have been alternative reports to the United Nations. After the disappointment of the first South African CEDAW report, the Masimanyane Women's Support Centre compiled a shadow report in protest against the one submitted by government (Pillay 2010). Other countries, like Botswana, started to submit shadow reports when they realized the paralysis of the state with regard to the implementation of gender mainstreaming and the fact that male privilege and patriarchy remained largely intact. There was also the realization that the NGMs were usually located at a low level on the government hierarchy or in many instances disappeared. There has also been non-compliance with some of the signatory countries' obligations of regular reporting to CEDAW. South Africa, for instance, failed to report in 2001, 2005, and 2009. The implication is that women's organizations became watchdogs of the NGMs and the respective governments in their commitments to ensure gender mainstreaming.

Gender mainstreaming is also part of the nation-building exercise. Formal or legal equality did not translate into equality for all women. Neither did the international and regional instruments offer solutions to the country-specific challenges to gender equity. Some countries ratified these international instruments with reservation and that often increased the tension between universal rights and cultural relativism. The notion of the universal human rights approach did not necessarily relate in real terms to the particular cultural roles that women occupy in the local communities. The challenge was to domesticate the international conventions and still maintain the power to advocate for social justice and human rights.

Southern African feminists have politicized personal experiences and formally built organizations and networks around these women-specific concerns. Violence against women in all its manifestations remains an important concern for women. For example, Rape Crisis is the oldest feminist organization of its kind in South Africa and continues to offer free and confidential support to rape and sexual assault survivors over the age of 16. The Musasa Project in Zimbabwe addresses rape and domestic violence against women. In Botswana, the Young Women's Christian Association (YWCA) and Women

Against Rape (WAR) started shelters and safe houses. The organization People Opposing Women's Abuse (POWA) and the lesbian organization Forum for the Empowerment of Women (FEW) have been powerful lobby groups against violence against women in South Africa.

Women's organizations and other civil society bodies incessantly advocate and lobby institutions to become transformative. The Women of Farms Project together with the New Women's Movement mobilized with other organizations and made submissions to the South African parliament, resulting in the promulgation of the Domestic Violence Act (1998). There are campaigns with other social movements pertaining to a living wage, fair trade, housing, and land. The lesbian and gay movement in South Africa had to consistently lobby and organize to persuade government to repeal, amend, or promulgate inclusive laws. Paradoxically, the international, regional, and country-specific instruments further opened the way for women to start or intensify existing work in women's legal centers or organizations in testing the women's equality promises of these progressive legal instruments and laws. The Women and Law in Southern Africa Research and Education Trust (WLSA) is active in seven countries, namely Botswana, Lesotho, Malawi, Mozambique, Swaziland, Zambia, and Zimbabwe, and deals with issues such as inheritance, gender-based violence, and sexual and reproductive rights. WLSA does action-oriented research on the legal status of women in these countries and uses the data to influence policy and law reform.

Many postcolonial activist organizations have been situational or issue driven. For example, women in South Africa have organized and protested against carrying passbooks, and in both South Africa and Botswana women have campaigned for the right to produce traditional beer. Other examples of specific concerns are when women affected by wars in distinctive ways organized around disarmament, peace, refugees, rape, and sexual crimes that were committed during the periods of war. Where codified cultural practices were particularly oppressive and harmful, feminists have campaigned and advocated for their eradication.

While the quest for gender mainstreaming allowed gender legislation to flourish in the region, laws often lacked particular feminist nuances in their language and their interpretation. South Africa remains the only country that embraced the feminist principle of women's bodily integrity and reproductive choice, and one of the first women-sensitive pieces of legislation that was passed post-1994 was the Choice on the Termination of Pregnancy Act, 1996. Women can now make the choice to terminate their pregnancy within the first 12 weeks of gestation without the consent of their partner. Another progressive stance of this piece of legislation was that a girl child from the age of 12 could have a termination of pregnancy without the consent of her parents. There is a range of suitable abortion clinics available. The rest of the governments in the SADC region consider the termination of pregnancy as a criminal act.

Countries in the region are well aware of the fact that the law could be a powerful enabler for gender equity. Emang Basadi Women's Association in Botswana challenged the proposed Amendment of the Citizenry Act because they perceived it as discriminatory against women. The Women's Legal Centre (WLC) in South Africa is a feminist organization that works in five strategic areas, namely violence against women, fair access to resources in relationships, access to land/housing, access to fair labor practices, and access to healthcare, in particular reproductive healthcare. It provides free legal advice and assistance to women. The Tshawaranang Legal Advocacy Centre (TLAC), also in South Africa, promotes and defends the rights of women to be free from violence and for women to have access to appropriate and adequate services.

Feminists belong to a wide range of social movements that advocate for women's rights, from accessing and owning land to healthcare, housing, and education opportunities. The Treatment Action Campaign (TAC) is regarded as one of the most influential social movements in South Africa. It originated to ensure that government provide affordable antiretroviral drugs (ARVs) to HIV- and AIDS-positive people, especially pregnant women. Although TAC is not an exclusive women's organization and does not regard itself as feminist, the fact remains that the majority of its members are women. It has been noted that TAC missed a golden opportunity to advance feminist jurisprudence in forwarding its prevention of mother-to-child transmission (PMTCT) campaign as a right to healthcare instead of women's right to sexual and reproductive health.

In 2006 over 100 feminist activists met in Accra, Ghana and adopted the "Charter of Feminist Principles," in which they acknowledge their multiple and varied identities as feminists and their "shared commitment to a transformatory agenda for African societies and African women in particular."

SEE ALSO: AIDS-Related Stigma; Battered Women; Convention on the Elimination of All Forms of Discrimination against Women (CEDAW); Customary Laws; Feminism in South Africa; Feminist Activism; Feminist Jurisprudence; Feminist Organizations, Definition of; Gender Equality; Gender Mainstreaming; LGBT Activism in Southern Africa; Polygamy, Polygyny, and Polyandry; Reproductive Health; Violence Against Women, Movements Against

REFERENCES

Gouws, Amanda. 2005. "Assessing the National Gender Machinery in South Africa: Gains and Weaknesses." In *Gender Instruments in Africa: Critical Perspectives, Future Strategies*, edited by Christi van der Westhuizen, 112–127. Midrand: Institute for Global Dialogue.

Mama, Amina. 2000. *National Machinery for Women in Africa: Towards an Analysis*. Accra: Third World Network – Africa.

Meintjes, Sheila. 1996. "The Women's Struggle for Equality during South Africa's Transition to Democracy." *Transformation*, 30: 47–64.

Ndashe, Sibongile. 2005. "Using International Human Rights to Re-Envision Gender in Customary Law." In *Gender Instruments in Africa: Critical Perspectives, Future Strategies*, edited by Christi van der Westhuizen, 77–95. Midrand: Institute for Global Dialogue.

Pillay, Anu. 2010. "Women's Activism and Transformation: Arising from the Cusp." *Feminist Africa*, 14: 63–78.

FURTHER READING

Da Silva, Terezinha, and Ximena Andrade. 2000. *Beyond Inequalities: Women in Mozambique*. Maputo and Harare: Centre for African Studies, University of Eduardo Mondlane and SARDC-WIDSAA.

Dos Santos, Naiole Cohen. 2000. *Beyond Inequalities: Women in Angola*. Luanda and Harare: ADRA/DW/SARDC.

Essof, Shereen. 2013. *SheMurenga: The Zimbabwean Women's Movement 1995–2000*. Harare: Weaver Press.

Geisler, Gisela. 2004. *Women and the Remaking of Politics in Southern Africa*. Uppsala: Nordiska Afrikainstitutet.

Hames, Mary. 2006. "Rights and Realities: Limits to Women's Rights and Citizenship after 10 Years of Democracy in South Africa." *Third World Quarterly*, 27(7): 1313–1327.

Hassim, Shireen. 2006. *Women's Organizations and Democracy: Contesting Authority*. Madison: University of Wisconsin Press.

Walker, Cherryl. 1982. *Women and Resistance in South Africa*. Cape Town: David Philip.

Women's and Feminist Activism in the United States and Canada

CHRISTA CRAVEN
College of Wooster, USA

There has been much debate over where to begin a history of women's/feminist activism in North America. The United States-based feminist organization INCITE! Women of Color Against Violence makes this point powerfully in their slogan "Feminist since 1492," arguing against a Eurocentric, Global North-focused, single history of women's/feminist activism. Following suit, this entry considers key moments for feminist activism and women's rights movements in the United States and Canada over the past 150 years, recognizing both the limits of space and the dearth of written histories for much of the organizing by historically marginalized groups. Even in recent history, it would be impossible to cover the many struggles, alliances, victories, and defeats that feminists have experienced, often alongside activists for civil rights, socialist reforms, indigenous rights, disability rights, LGBTQ rights, environmental justice, natural childbirth, and so on (many of which are covered elsewhere in this encyclopedia). Thus, although limited in scope, this entry provides an overview of US and Canadian efforts toward – and intersections between – women's suffrage, anti-racism and civil rights organizing, reproductive rights/justice activism, anti-violence campaigns, indigenous activism, and LGBTQ rights organizing.

Feminist historians and sociologists have argued for several decades for a need to redefine politics and political activism to understand women's participation in social change efforts. In short, they suggest that scholars depart from analyses that focus solely on electoral and legislative arenas, where men's influence has long predominated, to include the important activist work that women do in their local communities. Sociologist Nancy Naples (1998) has emphasized the importance of "activist mothering," through which women extend their nurturing of their families towards their communities. This "community caretaking," Naples argues, is often overlooked by scholars of politics and political activism because it falls outside legislative and electoral politics. Moreover, many female activists – especially indigenous, aboriginal, and women of color, who have perceived feminism as largely a white, middle-class movement – have rejected the label "feminist," but developed ideas and participated in actions that echo feminist efforts. Research on working-class women's activism and women of color's activism that community reform efforts and grassroots organizing often goes unreported. The brief history presented here begins with the groundswell of well-documented collective organizing by women in the United States and Canada during the nineteenth century.

SUFFRAGE AND WOMEN'S HEALTH CAMPAIGNS

By the late 1800s, women in both countries had begun to organize around several issues, including women's suffrage, better access to education, the improvement of access to medical services, and anti-lynching campaigns in the southern United States. Many organized through religious groups, such as the Women's Christian Temperance Union, which was formed in Ohio and Ontario in the 1870s, with the intent of creating a sober world where women could contribute to social reforms, such as suffrage. Moreover, in contrast to the modern association of feminists with pro-choice politics, many nineteenth-century feminists were strong supporters of the womanly duty to bear children. Indeed, the well-known proponent of women's rights in the United States Elizabeth Cady Stanton described abortion as "the degradation of women," although she argued that voluntary motherhood – through access to birth control and the legal ability to say no to her husband's sexual demands – was key to women's salvation. Many feared that the availability of birth control and abortion services would encourage male promiscuity, contribute to the loss of women's control over their bodies and morality to men, and diminish husbands' commitment to their families (Ehrenreich and English 1978).

Some feminists, however, became ardent proponents of birth control during the early 1900s and the first birth control clinics were opened in the United States by Margaret Sanger in 1916 and in Canada by the 1930s. Sanger, who founded the American Birth Control League (which later became known as Planned Parenthood), advocated for women's control over their fertility as a means of social mobility. Initially, some US clinics reserved services for white women, and pressure from African American women for birth control expanded access dramatically. Despite this interracial interest, Sanger and other white organizers ultimately alienated many supporters when they built alliances with the population control establishment, which promoted eugenic goals of selective breeding under the framework of public health. Eugenics proponents became a primary source of funding for fertility control clinics in the United States, which led to controversial alliances between feminists struggling to assure access to birth control for a broad range of women and eugenicists who hoped that these technologies would limit births among poor and non-white women. As a result, many African American women began to organize instead through their own community networks, both for access to fertility control and against the compulsory sterilization of many African American women (Nelson 2003). The support of fertility control was not unanimous, however, and some African American and aboriginal women in Canada continued to resist birth control into the 1900s, arguing that it was an attempt at genocide, a policy designed to reduce the size of their populations. Thus, although there is some evidence of multiracial feminist activism during the early to mid-twentieth century, white women and women of color often worked in separate organizations towards suffrage, community reform, anti-sterilization efforts, and access to birth control and abortion.

With the increasing public scrutiny of childbirth practices at the turn of the twentieth century, the improvement of maternal and child healthcare became a primary political concern for many women. Many suffragists hoped to affect healthcare change through governmental reform. In fact, historians have suggested that the movements for women's health and feminism became nearly indistinguishable at this point, and reproductive healthcare remained central to feminist organizing throughout the twentieth century.

LEGISLATIVE STRUGGLES AND LOCAL ACTION

After suffrage was achieved federally for women in Canada in 1919 and in the United States in 1920, Canadian women achieved additional governmental reform in 1929 when the "Famous Five," a group of five female activists, successfully petitioned the Supreme Court of Canada to clarify that women would be legally considered "persons" and could therefore be appointed to political office. In contrast, although US feminists made initial legislative gains, politicians – many of whom were initially fearful of women's power at the polls – quickly realized that women were not voting as a cohesive bloc. Therefore, many state and federal initiatives shifted funding away from concerns that the women's movement had emphasized. For instance, the Sheppard–Towner Maternal and Infancy Protection Act, which was the first explicit federal social welfare legislation in the United States (passed in 1921 just following suffrage), was repealed in 1929.

National feminist activist campaigns quieted during the mid-1900s, although local struggles continued to demand access to education and reproductive services at a community level (Silliman et al. 2004). It also became increasingly evident that universal equality for women had not been achieved through suffrage alone. Women's rights – to equal pay, educational equity, and reproductive rights – had not been fully achieved, and remained stratified significantly by race and class. In addition, Canada relied heavily on immigration to supply a work force during the twentieth century, and the resultant social and institutional racism that developed among many native-born Canadians heightened inequities faced by many women of color and immigrants. The increase in female immigrants to the United States during the twentieth century, coupled with contentious debates over illegal immigration, have further complicated legal and political recognition for women born outside the country.

Notably, during the 1960s and 1970s, the history of social democratic political traditions in Canada strengthened the legitimacy of movements toward equality. For instance, a Royal Commission was established in the late 1960s to examine the status of women and found substantial inequities in pay and job advancement opportunities. The Commission made broad recommendations to the Canadian federal government, including the prohibition of discrimination based on gender and marital status, expansion of education and job training programs for women, enhancement of maternity leave, and access to birth control and day care. Ultimately, the results of the Commission's work created significant government funding for women's rights groups. In 1972, the National Action Committee (NAC) created a coalition of women's groups to advocate more effectively for the Commission's recommendations, and eventually became the largest feminist organization in Canada with 700 affiliated groups. The goals of the NAC also extended to combat poverty, racism, LGBTQ discrimination, and violence against women.

COALITIONS AND SCHISMS

In the United States, women's organizing became central in the Civil Rights Movement during the 1950s and 1960s, which significantly influenced the emergence of the so-called "second wave" of the feminist movement in the early 1960s. Feminist efforts and Civil Rights organizing made significant gains, such as the Civil Rights Act of 1964 and toward reproductive rights (see below). Yet it is important to note the frictions that also occurred: many black women experienced alienation both within male-led civil rights organizations and in primarily white feminist groups, leading many to create their own organizations, such as the National Welfare Rights Organization, to make demands that emerged from their unique experiences of gender, race, and class oppression. Frictions during this time were also evident in Canada as Aboriginal women's organizations struggling for self-determination and land rights in the face of colonization allied to form a Native women's movement and a francophone women's movement in Quebec focused on issues related to sovereignty. Thus, in both Canada and the United States, women's organizations have often served the needs of individual constituencies and engaged in national coalitions around shared concerns. In Canada, and to a lesser extent the United States, the "second wave" of feminism was greatly influenced by socialist feminism, following Marxist analyses of class and critique of capitalism and placing class struggle at the center of struggles for equality. Left-wing activists in Canada, for instance, initially distinguished themselves from liberal equality-seeking feminists by avoiding the term "feminist" altogether, in favor of advocating women's liberation.

Another schism in the "second wave" centered on the emergence of lesbian feminism, which emphasized efforts against heteronormativity, the assumption that society should be structured around heterosexual relationships. Although many lesbians were active in feminist organizing in both the United States and Canada, they were excluded from prominent organizations such as the National Organization for Women (NOW), founded in 1966. Then-president of NOW Betty Friedan courted the ire of prominent lesbian feminists – such as Charlotte Bunch, Adrienne Rich, Audre Lorde, and Marilyn Frye – after firing several lesbian staff members, including Rita Mae Brown, and allegedly referring to the growing lesbian visibility within feminist organizing as the "lavender menace." Lesbian feminism intensified during the 1970s as a part of mainstream feminist organizing, and also within the Gay Liberation movement, which encouraged "coming out" as a form of public activism, in addition to community events such as pride marches, which remain popular throughout North America and many other areas of the world.

REPRODUCTIVE RIGHTS, REPRODUCTIVE JUSTICE

Women's activism for reproductive rights also intensified in both Canada and the United States during the 1960s and into the early 1970s. In the United States, the right to obtain legal access to birth control and abortion was achieved through a series of legal decisions that culminated in the 1973 US Supreme Court decision in *Roe v. Wade* to legalize abortion. In Canada, the Planned Parenthood Federation of Canada was successful in generating support for government-funded birth control across Canada in the early 1970s, but funding waned toward the end of the decade. Abortion became legally available in 1988, but access to abortion clinics has been uneven across the provinces, as it has by state in the United States. Historian Rickie Solinger (2005) has argued that these successes inaugurated the "era of choice" in the 1970s that did not take into account the constraints that have historically and currently restricted the reproductive decisions of poor women and women of color. The uneven effects of laws legalizing abortion and contraception continue to be felt as recent laws have further restricted the ability of clinics and healthcare facilities to provide abortion and frequently require parental notification. Feminist efforts toward reproductive rights as "consumer rights" have continued to intensify to the present day (Craven 2010) and the promotion of "choice" – although widely criticized by many feminists, and recently dropped by some mainstream organizations, such as Planned Parenthood in 2013 – has remained a central rallying cry for many contemporary feminist organizers.

Although the primary focus for mainstream feminists in the 1960s and 1970s centered on access to abortion and contraception, some feminists also allied themselves with the Natural Childbirth Movement (NCM). In both the United States and Canada, this created a unique alliance between feminists and religiously and politically conservative women who also rallied around efforts to support midwives and homebirth. Although some historians have argued that feminists have generally supported women's "right to choose" during pregnancy *and* childbirth, explicit feminist support of homebirth and midwives was spotty even into the late twentieth century, and some historians have called the NCM anti-feminist since it allied with pronatalist interests. It was only in 1999 that NOW issued a resolution to expand "reproductive freedom" to include the support of women's choice to seek midwives as their birthcare providers in hospitals and birthcenters and for homebirths. Efforts to legalize midwifery in both Canada and the United States have been largely successful in increasing access to midwives, particularly for middle-class white women, but have been critiqued for reproducing racial inequality by excluding midwives who practiced historically in indigenous and African American communities, and also those who have immigrated from the Global South (Nestel 2006).

Since the 1960s, many women of color have centered their efforts toward reproductive rights on sterilization abuse and uneven access to pre- and postnatal healthcare and childcare. The term "reproductive justice" emerged in the United States during the 1980s among organizations promoting the rights of indigenous women and women of color, linking feminist reproductive rights struggles with social justice aims. As Asian Communities for Reproductive Justice (recently renamed Forward Together) wrote in their Vision Statement: "Reproductive Justice is the complete physical, mental, spiritual, political, economic, and social well-being of women and girls, and will be achieved when women and girls have the economic, social, and political power and resources to make healthy decisions about our bodies, sexuality, and reproduction for ourselves, our families, and our communities in all areas of our lives." The SisterSong Women of Color Reproductive Health and Sexual Rights Conference popularized the term in 2003 and groups such as NOW and Planned Parenthood have begun to adopt the language of reproductive justice in recent advocacy efforts. Several international organizations, including the United Nations, have also promoted reproductive justice, such as the emphases on access to family planning services in the Convention on the Elimination of All Forms of Discrimination against Women and the Convention against Torture and Other Cruel, Inhuman, or Degrading Treatment.

CONTINUED DEBATES AND TRANSNATIONAL ALLIANCES

The "sex wars" that developed among feminists in the 1980s – heated debates over pornography, prostitution, BDSM, and transgender rights/identities – continue to create tensions in feminist organizing (Duggan 1995). In Canada, for instance, the Supreme Court used language by feminists Andrea Dworkin and Catherine MacKinnon in a 1992 revision of obscenity laws that restricted pornography. "Sex-positive" feminists staunchly opposed these efforts, encouraging sexual freedom and arguing that anti-pornography laws unfairly targeted LGBTQ materials. The emergence of queer theory in the 1990s reignited controversies over the prominence of sexuality within feminist organizing efforts. With an emphasis on embracing gender fluidity, queer activists criticized essentialist understandings of gender, while radical feminists have maintained small, but vocal, opposition to trans liberation politics and denied intersections between feminist and queer activism. Mainstream LGBTQ efforts, however, such as the promotion of same-sex marriage and the expansion of adoption laws, have become widely supported by many women's rights organizations, despite earlier feminist critiques of marriage as a patriarchal institution that served primarily to limit women's autonomy. Recent efforts to promote transgender inclusion, such as appeals to Planned Parenthood and NARAL in 2013 to remove reference to gender (i.e., "women's health" and "women's reproductive choice") in the names of their health clinics and reproductive justice campaigns, have continued to meet with resistance among some feminist organizers.

Efforts to combat violence against women – including domestic violence, rape, and sexual harassment – that were central to feminist organizing in the 1970s when rape crisis centers were first established, have taken new forms in twenty-first-century North American feminist organizing. The highly publicized Slutwalk protest marches, for instance, emerged in response to a Toronto police officer's admonishment that women should "avoid dressing like sluts in order not to be victimized." The first rally and protest march occurred in Toronto in 2011 and subsequent marches have been organized throughout Asia, Europe, Latin America, and North America. Prominent feminist pundits and bloggers have accused the movement of trivializing women's experience and excluding women of color, reigniting concerns about racialized divisions in mainstream feminist organizing.

Increasingly, US and Canadian feminists have engaged with transnational efforts to promote women's rights and social justice, particularly reproductive rights and anti-violence campaigns. Wealthy Western donors have actively supported particular feminist initiatives throughout the world (perhaps most notably, and controversially, efforts to end female genital surgery), but scholars note that the support of North American-based international agencies and nongovernmental organizations can reproduce inequalities between Northern "experts" and donors and recipients of aid (Naples and Desai 2002). Following the rise of neoliberalism in the 1980s, with the promotion of open markets and structural adjustment, feminist responses have been notoriously different for women in the Global North and the Global South, leading to what sociologist Manisha Desai has called "scattered resistance." Although some have suggested that feminist organizing has lessened in North America in recent years, transnational and multiracial feminist alliances have continued to form within the United States and Canada around issues such as the feminization of exploitative labor conditions, aboriginal and indigenous women's rights, access to reproductive healthcare, cuts to welfare provisions, and anti-violence campaigns focused on women and LGBTQ people.

SEE ALSO: Activist Mothering; Feminisms, First, Second, and Third Wave; Feminist Activism; Feminist Movements in Historical and Comparative Perspective; Pro-Choice Movement in the United States; Reproductive Justice and Reproductive Rights in the United States

REFERENCES

Craven, Christa. 2010. *Pushing for Midwives: Homebirth Mothers and the Reproductive Rights Movement*. Philadelphia: Temple University Press.

Duggan, Lisa. 1995. *Sex Wars: Sexual Dissent and Political Culture*. New York: Routledge.

Ehrenreich, Barbara, and Deirdre English. 1978. *For Her Own Good: 150 Years of the Experts' Advice to Women*. Garden City: Anchor Books.

Naples, Nancy A. 1998. *Grassroots Warriors: Activist Mothering, Community Work, and the War on Poverty*. New York: Routledge.

Naples, Nancy A., and Manisha Desai. 2002. *Women's Activism and Globalization: Linking Local Struggles and Transnational Politics*. New York: Routledge.

Nelson, Jennifer. 2003. *Women of Color and the Reproductive Rights Movement*. New York: New York University Press.

Nestel, Sheryl. 2006. *Obstructed Labour: Race and Gender in the Re-emergence of Midwifery*. Vancouver: UBC Press.

Silliman, Jael Miriam, Marlene Gerber Fried, Loretta Ross, and Elena R. Gutiérrez, eds. 2004.

Undivided Rights: Women of Color Organize for Reproductive Justice. Cambridge, MA: South End Press.

Solinger, Rickie. 2005. *Pregnancy and Power: A Short History of Reproductive Politics in America*. New York: New York University Press.

FURTHER READING

Green, Joyce, ed. 2007. *Making Space for Indigenous Feminism*. Black Point: Fernwood Books.

Luxton, Meg, and Kate Bezanson, eds. 2006. *Social Reproduction: Feminist Political Economy Challenges Neo-Liberalism*. Montreal: McGill-Queen's University Press.

Wine, Jeri Dawn, and Janice Lynn Ristock, eds. 1991. *Women and Social Change: Feminist Activism in Canada*. Toronto: James Lorimer.

Women's and Feminist Activism in West Africa

PEACE A. MEDIE
University of Ghana, Ghana

Women's organizations in West African states have been pivotal to the advancement of women's rights and have contributed to development in the region. Although their leaders and members are women, these organizations are characterized by key differences in structure, focus areas, and efficacy. They range from loosely coordinated grassroots groups that lack written mission statements to highly professionalized non-governmental organizations (NGOs) with multi-year action plans. While some organizations have limited their activism to problems that they consider to be women's interests, others have adopted broader agendas, thus mobilizing to influence political, social, and economic issues that affect all of society at the subnational, national, and international levels. Similarly, while the majority of these groups have self-identified as women's organizations, a few have embraced the "feminist" label and have placed the campaign for gender equality at the forefront of their efforts. However, even when they have not prioritized equality between men and women, some women's organizations have challenged the patriarchal status quo and improved women's status. To accomplish this, they have adopted a variety of strategies that have evolved over time in response to national and international political, economic, and technological transformations. These strategies have enabled women's organizations to challenge dominant and often discriminatory political and socioeconomic beliefs, practices, and structures, and sometimes to effect changes in them.

The presence and activism of women's organizations in West Africa predate colonialism. Women organized in formal and informal groups to protest decisions and practices that threatened their livelihoods. They formed market networks to protect their trading interests and, in the process, gained relative autonomy from men in the domestic sphere (Tamale 2000). They frequently stood up to authority in the colonial period. Not only did women's organizations challenge colonial laws and institutions that discriminated against women, but they also played key roles in the fight against colonialism and the struggle for independence. While under British rule in 1951, Sierra Leonean women demonstrated against the proposed steep increase in food prices and market dues brought about by Lebanese traders' monopolization of wholesale food distribution (Steady 2005). Their protests won them the right to purchase food directly from the government and paved the way for the formation of the Sierra Leonean women's movement. In southeastern Nigeria, the anticipated taxation of women by British colonial authorities, combined with a litany of other grievances including corruption among members of the Native Court, led Igbo women to launch the

Women's War in 1929 (Mba 1982). The uprising lasted for about a month and involved demonstrations, the burning of Native Court buildings, and violent clashes between the women and colonial forces. The war, which resulted in the deaths of over 50 women, led the British authorities to assure the women that they would not be taxed, although many of the exploitative and oppressive governing practices persisted.

Women's organizations also sought to address women's concerns in the domestic sphere. They did not limit their activities to issues that were specific to women, however, but also opposed colonial policies that were inimical to men and mounted strong resistance to colonial rule. Ghanaian women fed activists at countrywide rallies and mobilized citizens to join the struggle for independence (Ampofo 2008). Kwame Nkrumah, the country's first president, in his autobiography lauded the contributions of women to Ghana's independence. These and other challenges to colonial authority across the region bolstered the anti-colonial struggle and paved the way for independence.

Women's political activism did not end with colonialism. However, their expectations of inclusion in governance were largely unmet. This is partly because post-independence governments had inherited political structures that consolidated male domination and female subordination and partly because of a lack of sufficiently strong and independent women's organizations (Tamale 2000). Women were, therefore, poorly represented in the governments of most newly independent West African states. Nonetheless, women's groups continued to advocate for women's socioeconomic rights, with attention paid to issues such as land tenure, education, and employment. However, their autonomy was compromised in several countries, including Ghana and Nigeria, with the entrenchment of one-party systems in the 1980s. Women's organizations were co-opted and turned into cheerleaders and extensions of the ruling parties, a move that prevented them from holding their governments accountable. This phenomenon was evidenced in Ghana where the ruling Provisional National Defense Council (PNDC) created the 31st December Women's Movement in 1982 and used it to mobilize women in support of the party (Fallon 2003, 2008).

The second wave of democratization and the introduction of multiparty systems in the 1990s weakened states' control of civil society organizations and opened up the political space to the participation of autonomous women's organizations in most countries. Women's organizations have begun to campaign for the passage and amendment of laws in favor of a range of issues. They have launched several campaigns including ones for the introduction of gender quota laws to increase the representation of women in parliament, for the criminalization of female genital mutilation and other forms of gender-based violence, and to make basic education compulsory for girls. These calls for legal change have been accompanied by the implementation of programs to educate women on their rights and to give them the skills and tools to empower themselves socially and economically. In Niger, women's organizations mobilized to ensure the implementation of the country's 2000 gender quota law. Among other things, they supported female candidates and pressured political parties to respect the law. Their efforts have contributed to the mainstreaming of women in Nigerian politics (Kang 2013).

Whether working independently or as part of national women's movements, organizations have employed a variety of advocacy tools including demonstrations, strikes, awareness-raising campaigns, lobbying, and negotiations to attain their goals. While activism in the precolonial, colonial, and immediate post-independent stages of West African history was aimed at the mostly male leadership of local institutions, the past two decades have seen women organize transnationally with the goal of placing their concerns on the agenda of international organizations such as the United Nations (UN), the African Union (AU), and the Economic Community of West African States (ECOWAS), and of harnessing the influence of these agencies to pressure their respective governments to pass and enforce women-friendly laws. Their efforts have been facilitated by changing international norms that emphasize respect for women's rights (Tripp et al. 2009). This appeal to powerful international actors has not only provided women's organizations with political clout but has also enabled them to acquire financial as well as technical assistance.

Women organizing across national borders have also pushed for the resolution of West African conflicts. The Mano River Women Union Peace Network (MARWOPNET) formed in 2000 by peace activists from Guinea, Liberia, and Sierra Leone pressured the ECOWAS to find solutions to the violence and other forms of human insecurity that threatened people in the conflict-ridden Mano River countries. They have combined this transnational activism with in-country activism. In Liberia, women's groups began to call for peace at the outbreak of the country's civil war in 1989 and were later joined by other women's organizations that were formed during the war. Women fought to have their voices heard at the many peace conferences that were held during the 14-year war. A coalition of Muslim and Christian women, the Women in Peacebuilding Network (WIPNET), demanded an end to the violence. At the 2003 peace talks in Accra, which produced the Comprehensive Peace Agreement (CPA), they protested the warring factions' unwillingness to accept the terms of the peace negotiations (African Women and Peace Support Group 2004). Their activism has not ended with the signing of peace agreements. Women's organizations have participated in the disarmament, demobilization, and reintegration of ex-combatants and have fought to be included in the reconstruction of their countries. Sierra Leonean women were at the forefront of the passing of gender-based violence laws in the aftermath of the country's civil wars. In Liberia, a favorable political opportunity structure combined with the political and financial support of international organizations, such as the UN, have enabled women's organizations to have an influence on police response to rape (Medie 2013).

Despite their contributions to social development and peacebuilding, women's organizations confront several challenges that limit their impact. Women's organizations face resistance in some countries. Religious norms and extremism limit women's organizing and the issues they can include on their agendas in places such as northern Nigeria. Furthermore, many organizations across the region are hampered by a lack of funding. Not only has this hindered their ability to organize and implement programs, but it has also resulted in an overdependence on international organizations for funding. Consequently, the agenda of some organizations has been dictated by donor interests and has led to, among other things, the neglect of issues that are not on donors' agendas. Competition for resources and poor coordination have led to the duplication of programs in some areas, a practice that not only wastes financial and human resources but also takes them away from other areas that deserve attention. Another problem is the NGO-ization of women's organizing. This phenomenon is characterized by dependence on donors as well as by the lack of a mass base and of accountability, the preference for a technocratic approach instead of one that could be construed as political, and the prioritization of a "short-term project-based approach" over "long range broad agendas" (Tsikata 2009, 186). This has rendered women's organizations less capable of challenging the actors, beliefs, and practices that perpetuate all forms of discrimination against women.

The research on women's organizations in West Africa is expanding to address the outcomes of women organizing. Feminist organizations such as the Association of African Women for Research and Development (AAWORD) are producing work that explores feminism and women's organizations in Africa. Scholars have also begun to examine more systematically the impact that women's organizations have on the advancement of women's rights and to establish the conditions under which organizations are influential (Kang 2013; Medie 2013). These studies are providing new insight into the significance of women's organizations, using comparative case studies and large-*n* analyses. Their findings educate not only on the roles of women's organizations but also on how the contributions of these groups can be enhanced in West Africa.

SEE ALSO: Colonialism and Gender; Community and Grassroots Activism; Gender, Politics, and the State: Overview

REFERENCES

African Women and Peace Support Group. 2004. *Liberian Women Fighting for the Right to be Seen, Heard and Counted*. Trenton: Africa World Press.

Ampofo, Akosua A. 2008. "Collective Activism: The Domestic Violence Bill becoming Law in Ghana." *African and Asian Studies Review*, 7: 395–421. DOI: 10.1163/156921008X359597.

Fallon, Kathleen M. 2003. "Transforming Women's Citizenship Rights within an Emerging Democratic State: The Case of Ghana." *Gender & Society*, 17: 525–543. DOI: 10.1177/0891243203253657.

Fallon, Kathleen M. 2008. *Democracy and the Rise of Women's Movements in Sub-Saharan Africa*. Baltimore: Johns Hopkins University Press.

Kang, Alice. 2013. "The Effect of Gender Quota Laws on the Election of Women: Lessons from Niger." *Women Studies International Forum*, 1–8. DOI: 10.1016/j.wsif.2013.03.005.

Mba, Nina E. 1982. *Nigerian Women Mobilized: Women's Political Activity in Southern Nigeria, 1900–1965*. Berkeley: Institute of International Studies, University of California.

Medie, Peace A. 2013. "Fighting Gender-Based Violence: The Women's Movement and the Enforcement of Rape Law in Liberia." *African Affairs*, 112: 377–397. DOI: 10.1093/afraf/adt040.

Steady, Filomena C. 2005. *Women and Collective Action in Africa: Development, Democratization and Empowerment*. Gordonsville: Palgrave Macmillan.

Tamale, Sylvia. 2000. "'Point of Order, Mr. Speaker': African Women Claiming Their Space in Parliament." *Gender and Development*, 8: 8–15. DOI: 10.1080/741923783.

Tripp, Aili M., Isabel Casimiro, Joy Kwesiga, and Alice Mungwa. 2009. *African Women's Movements: Changing Political Landscapes*. New York: Cambridge University Press.

Tsikata, Dzodzi. 2009. "Women's Organizing in Ghana since the 1990s: From Individual Organizations to Three Coalitions." *Development*, 52: 185–192. DOI: 10.1057/dev.2009.8.

Women's and Feminist Activism in Western Europe

ROSEMARIE BUIKEMA
Utrecht University, The Netherlands

Different generations of Western European feminists struggled to realize full access to citizenship and the creation of a participatory democracy that ensured social solidarity for all citizens. As a direct result of the struggles of twentieth-century activists, twenty-first-century women in Western Europe have the right to vote, retain control over property and capital, combine motherhood and work, receive equal wages for equal work, pay taxes, and access higher education, and to enjoy reproductive rights and gender-specific care. However, it is important to realize that the majority of these rights, accessible now for three or four generations of Western European women, still prove elusive in some contexts.

In some countries, specific so-called *first-wave* goals were generally implemented only a few decades ago. Most Western European countries passed laws to give the full right to vote for women between 1913 (Norway) and 1944 (France). Remarkably, women in Switzerland accessed suffrage as late as 1971 owing to a persistent ideology linking women to the realms of children, church, and kitchen. These private-sphere realms could presumably be dealt with through municipalities and cantons that included women's votes. The belief was that parliament should occupy itself with issues that lay beyond the "legitimate" sphere of women's influence such as questions of war and peace, the maintenance of the army and the navy, and the administration of the nation. Surprisingly, it was not only men, but also certain groups of conservative women, collectively gathered into the Federation of Swiss Women Against the Right to Vote, who embraced this separation of the private and the public spheres. So, while second-wave feminism started to challenge the patriarchal foundations of post-World War II Western Europe's welfare states, some countries were still in the process of implementing essentially first-wave goals. The Swiss example is just one of many illustrating the tenacious force of gendered, social, and cultural structures.

First- and second-wave (or pre- and postwar) feminist activists therefore stressed the fact that next to attaining legal rights, women also had symbolical hurdles to jump, such as contesting dominant images of womanhood. Virginia Woolf's famous reference in 1931 to the "Angel in the House," borrowed from Coventry Patmore's poem celebrating domestic bliss, is a case in point (Woolf 1993). This image of a selfless sacrificial woman of the nineteenth century, whose sole purpose in life was to soothe, flatter, and comfort men, resonates in the contemporary moment, capturing ongoing struggles of feminist activism. In order to be able to participate effectively in the public sphere, women and minority groups must engage with an inner struggle with these "Angels in the House" – these icons of invisibility and submission. Such consciousness-raising initiatives are usually seen as specific to second-wave feminism. However, as Woolf's essays show, they were also relevant to the first wave.

Building on the first wave, second-wave feminists made this issue one of their explicit goals, raising awareness about the feminist mantra that the personal is political. Feminists of the time argued that it was not by nature that women in mid-twentieth-century Western Europe were locked in the private sphere or took care of the reproduction of male citizens without fully sharing in their civil rights. Personal experiences of marginalization and unequal power balances, second-wave feminists argue, are nearly always the result of interacting political and societal structures. Second-wave feminism revealed that Western European women's personal experiences of marginalization and submission were shared by women in comparable geopolitical situations and positions. They challenged the idea that women in general enjoyed being voiceless or rendered a mere visual spectacle in the public sphere. Rather, second-wave feminism posited that this division of gendered positions between the private and the public was the result of a history of societal conventions and geopolitics funded by patriarchal systems – the law, the church, the class system, and so on.

Institutionalized gender roles were assigned to the female body and, as Simone de Beauvoir in 1949 famously claimed, "One is not born but rather becomes a woman" (de Beauvoir 1989, 301). Feminists contended that the structure of the private sphere was entangled with and embedded in the organization of the public sphere and equally governed by sexual politics. Therefore, Western European feminist activists continuously demonstrated how the personal and the political, the private and the public, were not neatly separated but inevitably intersecting.

Following this line of thought, second-wave feminists argued that the house as the patriarchal metaphor of seclusion, intimacy, and nourishment was not necessarily a safe space for women and did not protect them from gendered power differences, violence, and rape. Additionally, women of color pointed out that although power and the possibility of rape and violence are always present in the private sphere, the house simultaneously can function as a shelter from racism. Black feminism was thereby claiming an explicitly race-specific manifestation of feminist activism *within* feminist activism, by focusing on the complex intersection of sexual and racial politics (Carby 1982).

While politicizing and complicating the fixed connotations of the private sphere, second-wave feminists also directed their actions toward the gendered politics of the public sphere. One of the activist groups gaining international attention in this respect was the Dutch Mad Mina ("Dolle Mina" in Dutch, named after the famous first-wave suffragette Wilhelmina Drucker (1847–1925)). One of Mad Mina's early actions consisted of the public burning of bras in front of the statue of Drucker in Amsterdam, paying homage to the burning of corsets by first-generation feminists. Such feminist protests against patriarchal conventions and gender divisions were radical and political but always characterized by humor and, therefore, easily garnered international media attention (Buikema and van der Tuin 2014). Mad Mina would pinch men's bottoms in public, close down Amsterdam public toilets for men only, and occupy newsrooms and the remaining male-only educational institutions.

Other famous second-wave feminist actions involved pro-abortion politics. The United Kingdom legalized abortion in 1967 whereas the Dutch only did so in 1981. For example, Dutch feminist activists interrupted a conference of gynecologists in 1970 by showing their naked bellies painted with the slogan "boss in own belly." Thus, in the 1970s and 1980s, the streets and other public spaces were claimed as sites to demonstrate the presence and the agency of women. These kinds of actions determined, to a certain extent, the public image of second-wave feminists as bra-burning men haters and, some might suggest, may have added to the alleged generation gap between second- and third-wave activism in the West today.

In spite of this polarizing stereotypification, second-wave feminist activism playfully performed and embodied the dethronement of Virginia Woolf's "Angel in the House." One aspect continually exposed by feminist activism is that attaining any semblance of first-class citizenship is obstructed by many more factors than legislation alone. Further work is needed to investigate the ways in which womanhood and the female body are imaged and also how female bodies and other systems of stratification such as class, race, religion, and sexuality are entangled. Completing women's access to full citizenship, becoming an integral part of the democratic system of representation, is a complex and longitudinal process involving simultaneous change on many different levels. As first- and second-wave feminist activism illustrates, the intersection of the personal and the political can only ever be successfully realized if it includes the cultural analysis of the intersection of the empirical and the symbolic. As Gayatri Spivak also explained in her agenda-setting article "Can the Subaltern Speak?" (Spivak 1988), this is where global feminism and Western European feminist activism meet, be it by means of rebellious humor, political radicalism, theoretical analysis, or the struggle for other emancipatory measures.

Contemporary discussions about the effects of the two feminist waves in Western Europe invariably involve key indicators and focus on questions such as: (1) what is the proportion of women in full-time employment?; (2) what are their career opportunities for leading positions?; (3) what is the glass ceiling in Western European society?; (4) what childcare facilities are available?; (5) what is the male participation rate in care and domestic work?; and (6) what are the pay differences between men and women?. The tension between equality and difference, the ties – as well as tensions – between the law and feminist ethics, the inseparability of the private and the public, the personal and the political, the empirical and the symbolical, are all still feminist concerns.

That notwithstanding, a major concern of twenty-first-century feminist activism in Western Europe is that the achievements of the movement for women's liberation threaten to become disconnected from their initial manifestations of equality for all, understood as transnational solidarity. Instead, the outcome of the two feminist waves seems mainly to serve neoliberal capitalism and the concomitant individualization of the process of emancipation and social participation (Scott 2011). As Nancy Fraser's timely summary in *The Guardian* (Fraser 2013) suggests, this risk of female empowerment becoming the handmaiden of global neoliberal capitalism might have been implicated in the movement from the start. Western European second-wave feminist goals and strategies in the end seem to have been ambivalent and thus susceptible for two different elaborations. The initial deeply political commitment to participatory democracy and social justice included goals which, with hindsight, simultaneously served the neoliberal vocabulary of autonomy, choice, and meritocratic advancement. Contrary to the feminist postcolonial and postsocialist project which situates the female subject as subjected to patriarchal, racist, and capitalist structures – the very same structures that produced the image of women as the "Angels in the House" – neoliberal feminisms seem to promote participation in capitalism and patriarchy.

The feminist struggle for paid labor for women, economic independence, and female empowerment, for example, now threatens to serve an increasingly fluid and flexible labor market. Movements such Facebook's CEO Sheryl Sandberg's *Lean In* encourage women to develop themselves in the vocabulary of the free market (Sandberg 2013). Proceed and be bold is the mantra. Female autonomy is a brand. Neoliberal feminism is therefore at risk of serving the status quo and, in that process, reducing subjects to economic actors, to servants of capital, encouraged to invest in their own individual liberation and autonomy instead of striving for social justice for all. To paraphrase Wendy Brown (2013), neoliberal feminism seriously risks the gradual replacement of the homo politicus for the homo economicus. Additionally, the rightful second-wave feminist emphasis on differences within possible manifestations of feminine identities (black, white, colored, queer, trans, hetero, etc.) threatens to replace analysis of political economic developments and circumstances and instead takes the patriarchal capitalist vocabulary of the free market for granted. Third-wave feminism became so concerned with stressing the differences within the category of woman as such that the feminist enterprise of analysis on the level of the productivity of societal structures and transnational solidarity became undertheorized.

The challenge for twenty-first-century third-wave feminists is to develop and practice an activism that continues truly to connect the local and the global, the private and the public, the personal and the political, the empirical and the symbolical. Third-wave feminism should therefore embark on a return to the history of feminism and a relocation of the definitions of emancipation, liberation, and solidarity (Buikema and van der Tuin 2014). Inspirational texts of first- and second-wave feminism, most notably Simone de Beauvoir's 1949 book *The Second Sex* (de Beauvoir 1989), for example, already theorized liberation as a concept that not only referred to the individual but also to the simultaneous desire for a freedom for the other(s). This ethical–political second-wave nuance – one geared toward justice for all rather than merely towards equality and emancipation – needs to be reactivated in the context of twenty-first-century feminist activism; a return to the envisioned futures of the past. This implies, for example, that actions to question the glass ceiling for women in business, culture, and politics are accompanied by critical reflections concerning the ideologies of paid and unpaid work both locally and globally. Actions against the trafficking of women need to be accompanied by critical reflections on the gendered intersections of private and public, personal and political. Western feminist criticisms concerning the alleged Islamophobia of Ukraine feminist activists such as the FEMEN group need to be paired to an analysis of the sexualization of the postsocialist female subject in Eastern European discourses, and so on.

SEE ALSO: Democracy and Democratization; Gender, Politics, and the State in Western Europe

REFERENCES

Beauvoir, Simone de. 1989. *The Second Sex*. New York: Vintage Books. First published 1949.

Brown, Wendy. 2013. "Reclaiming Democracy: An Interview with Wendy Brown on Occupy, Sovereignty, and Secularism." Critical Legal Thinking, an Interview by Robin Celikates and Yolanda Jansen. Accessed January 7, 2015, at http://criticallegalthinking.com/2013/01/30/reclaiming-democracy-an-interview-with-wendy-brown-on-occupy-sovereignty-and-secularism/.

Buikema, Rosemarie, and Iris van der Tuin. 2014. "Three Feminist Waves." In *Discovering the Dutch*, edited by Emmeline Besamusca and Jaap Verheul, 211–221. Amsterdam: Amsterdam University Press.

Carby, Hazel. 1982. "White Woman Listen! Black Feminism and the Boundaries of Sisterhood." In *The Empire Strikes Back: Race and Racism in Seventies Britain*, edited by the Centre for Contemporary Cultural Studies, 212–235. London: Hutchinson.

Fraser, Nancy. 2013. "How Feminism Became Capitalism's Handmaiden." In *The Guardian* online, October 14, 2013. Accessed January 7, 2015, at http://www.theguardian.com/commentisfree/2013/oct/14/feminism-capitalist-handmaiden-neoliberal.

Sandberg, Sheryl. 2013 *Lean In: Women, Work and the Will to Lead*. New York: Alfred A. Knopf.

Scott, Joan W. 2011. *The Fantasy of Feminist History*. Durham, NC: Duke University Press.

Spivak, Gayatri Chakravorty. 1988. "Can the Subaltern Speak?" In *Marxism and the Interpretation of Culture*, edited by Cary Nelson and Lawrence Grossberg, 271–313. Urbana: University of Illinois Press.

Woolf, Virginia. 1993. "Professions for Women." In *A Room of One's Own and Three Guineas*, edited by Michèle Barrett, 356–361. London: Penguin. First published 1931.

FURTHER READING

Woolf, Virginia. 1978. "The Death of the Moth." In *The Pargiters*, edited by Mitchell A. Leaska. London: Hogarth Press.

Women's and Feminist Organizations in South Asia

KANCHANA N. RUWANPURA
University of Edinburgh, UK

NGOs are the fashionable architects of the development world, with multilateral and bilateral aid agencies electing to work via non-governmental organizations (NGOs) rather than state authorities at the national, regional, and local level. This shift to NGO-led development coincides with the neoliberal turn in the global economy, where reducing state intervention is an aspiration. Ironically these liberal ambitions toward governance of the global economy through a conservative prism also came together with feminist activists' calls for social engagement and state accountability. The upshot was that unlikely bedfellows became evangelical about NGOs.

Early feminist scholarship tended to portray NGOs as beacons of an alternative architecture of social governance and where progressive space for social, political, and economic activities could be crafted (Kabeer 1994; Molyneux 1998). However, there is increasing acknowledgment that NGOs take multiple guises and consequently the past few decades have made it apparent that some NGOs may be prone to the problems that have been conventionally leveled against the state (Hickey and Mohan 2005). Or more specifically, where NGOs have failed to appreciate and account for the local spatial politics, their status as a surrogate development arm unravels. Here we briefly outline the various strands necessary to understand the evolution of feminist research on NGO activity – how it became the modus operandi in the development sphere, why feminists were enthusiastic about its early potential, and what the more recent critical evaluations reveal about the promises and pitfalls of NGOs for feminist politics.

The initial impetus for NGOs to take an increasingly prominent role stems from a desire for civil society, the space between the state and citizen, to engage and make the state accountable for its profligacy and challenge human rights violations. NGOs were to be an instrument of strengthening civil society and social movements, which were gaining momentum in reaction to mounting market fundamentalism and disenfranchising of human rights. Consequently, the World Trade Organization (WTO) talks held in Seattle, Genoa, and Gleneagles, for instance, witnessed the culmination of numerous political strands of social movements from both the Global North and South opposing the increasing encroachment of free market policies in various sphere of life. Vandana Shiva is a notable grassroots and environmental activist for the NGO Navdanya in India, objecting to the biopiracy of native seeds found in South Asia. Similarly, feminists such as Shireen Huq and Khushi Kabir from Bangladesh have led key NGOs and social movements in the arena of advocating the rights of women and the landless, respectively. Such moments suggested that NGOs could be a potential force for progressive social transformation – where radical social politics find ground and alternative social practices find safe space for creative expression. Reinvigorating civil society, then, was a means through which the state was to be held responsible.

By making incursions into the prevailing status quo, the expectation was that such NGOs had the capacity to undermine neoliberal governance and strengthen the fabric of democratic and human rights – within individual countries as well as in the global arena. Despite these promising embryonic phases, the incremental evidence suggested that there is a need to pay attention to the complexities in the world of NGO activity and civil society activism. While this healthy skepticism toward NGOs as the panacea for civil society mobilization and development is warranted, it is necessary to appreciate how NGOs came to be the mainstream. The sections below trace the evolution of that path.

NGO formation and their latent promise as a medium through which progressive, radical, or alternative social agendas could be promoted began in the early 1990s, where Escobar's (1995) intervention was an important catalyst in social science thinking. Marshaling grassroot action was cast by critical scholars as vital in contesting the dominant development paradigm[1] and generating momentum toward a space where voices of marginal and deprived communities could be heard. In South Asia this impetus was to have particular resonance according to specificities within local contexts – whether it was war, recurrent natural disasters, or sectarian violence. The need to strengthen human security in war-torn Sri Lanka where ethnic strife was rampant, for instance, meant a proliferation of NGOs that operated around human rights issues (Wickramasinghe 2001). In contrast, given its association with its widespread poverty and numerous cyclone-related disasters, Bangladesh witnessed an explosion of service-delivery NGOs, and one of its NGOs gave birth to the globally heralded microcredit schemes (Rankin 2002). In their burgeoning days there was optimism and enthusiasm that NGOs were not simply reaching out to the most vulnerable communities within South Asia, but were particularly beneficial for women. Moreover, NGO activities and their outcomes were also portrayed as an effective instrument for feeding the concerns of these social groups into the realm of regional, national, and global policymakers. Yet this buoyancy was to be short-lived; as researchers became ever more interested in the promise of grassroots and civil society mobilization via NGOs, investigations began to reveal that there were multiple contradictions within NGOs' efforts.

A paramount concern pointed out by a number of critical social science scholars is that local communities are not devoid of unbalanced power structures and inequitable distributive practices. Hence where NGOs neglect local hierarchies and spatial politics, their activities can end up reinforcing gender, class, race, and ethnic dynamics. These scholars began to point out that without directly confronting structures that create and perpetuate corrosive social politics and practices, there is less likely to be social transformation (Hickey and Mohan 2005). More worryingly, Indian feminist scholars began to highlight how NGO activity has led to discord and violence between communities, with grassroots women's groups in Uttar Pradesh (UP) joining in sectarian violence during and after the Babri Masjid riots in 1992 (Butalia 2002). In other words, grassroots organizations and NGOS have been implicated in perpetrating the violence of development (Kapadia 2002), drifting from their incipient potential as an antidote to the worst excesses of conventional development policies.

Another strand of scholarship started to underline how the agenda of NGOs came to be hijacked by the neoliberal schema. NGOs did not become the vehicle for challenging the contours of neoliberal policies as initially envisioned; rather, these non-state institutions started to be increasingly deployed to do the bidding of neoliberal governance. Undeniably since advocates of neoliberalism were interested in reducing the presence of the state in development delivery, the rhetoric of grassroots and civil society activists on the culpability and negligence of the state conveniently fed into the neoliberal agenda as well.

Instead of making the state accountable to its civil constituency, activism by grassroots and civil society groups resulted in NGOs being treated as a credible alternative. For example, as Feldman (1997) points out, through social and economic reorganization in rural and remote communities, NGO activities, especially microcredit initiatives, reshape the everyday and become a mechanism through which the neoliberal development agenda is promoted. Similarly, where NGOs become the preferred partner in service delivery of public goods, such as primary or secondary education, as sometimes is the case in Bangladesh, the upshot is a displacement of the state, with the possible consequence of privatizing public goods – i.e., education or healthcare delivery. NGOs thus emerge as a credible armory for multilateral institutions, such as the World Bank and International Monetary Fund (IMF), and bilateral development agencies, for example the US Agency for International Development (USAID), the UK's Department for International Development (DFID), or the Australian Agency for International Development (AusAID), to work in partnership with and evade state institutions in carrying out development projects.

Feminist interventions have revealed the evolution of NGOs, from the promise of creating spaces for sweeping changes to social life and practice to social politics as usual. How NGO activity can exacerbate prevailing political and social tensions in everyday life – whether in Nepal, Sri Lanka, or Bangladesh – has been the focus of these feminist contributions (Kabeer 2001; Rankin 2002; Ruwanpura 2007). Their central tenet is that action toward social transformation and reconstituting democratic spaces and politics requires NGO institutions not simply to work in areas that have previously been inaccessible, but also to be committed to a politics of place. This implies acknowledging the social structures and constraints within which NGOs operate, and facilitates a commitment to place for the long haul. Challenging and confronting interlocking social structures that impede vulnerable communities – including women – are factors that thwart locals from achieving explicit recognition of their capabilities. Emancipation and creating the momentum and space for transformative feminist politics to take shape is possible only when social structures of caste, class, religion, ethnicity, gender, and patriarchy are confronted. As feminists point out, this hindering creates barriers for social democracy to be created and sustained – with consequential socioeconomic and sociopolitical inequities.

Kabeer (2001) illustrates how microcredit initiatives in Bangladesh are necessarily limited in what they can achieve in terms of transforming gender relations as the microcredit model assumes that access to finance alone can disentangle and dissipate the complex web of social relations in which rural Bangladeshi women find themselves. She shows how this is an impossibility because of domestic violence, for instance, which has been linked with women's access to credit. In contrast, she shows that where NGO action focuses on consciousness-raising and rights awareness – of land rights for example – marginal communities are more likely to feel empowered and realize their potential for emancipation because of the sense of entitlement encouraged by a politics of consciousness-raising.

Similarly, Rankin (2002) notes how NGOs in Nepal, working on microfinance, do not confront the ideological and material structures and consequently end up exacerbating prevailing social hierarchies. She notes how, without the collective consciousness of women's subordination, microcredit programs cannot become the catalysts for social change that they purport to be. Adding another dimension to these debates, Halim Chowdhury (2011), through an ethnographic study of acid attacks on women in Bangladesh, explores the ways in which transnational feminist activism may be necessarily inflected given the contradictions inherent in seeking gender justice via NGO organizing and transnational activism. Her focus is on Nariphokko, the well-established and long-standing local feminist body, and its actions around working together with/on acid-attacked women. She finds its initial agenda hijacked and its activists estranged from its constituency because of the way global feminist interventions consolidate along neoliberal registers, which vary from their prism for intervention (Halim Chowdhury 2011, 8). She signals, then, how it is necessary to be attentive to the broader backdrop against which diverse forms of organizing and feminist activism take place within Bangladesh in particular, and in South Asia more broadly.

Ethnic conflict and war in Sri Lanka offer another context for registering similar concerns. With regards to NGOs working on humanitarian issues, Hyndman and de Alwis (2003) suggest that the neglect of overdetermined gender identity formations results in ignoring women's fraught and multiple locations in the context of war. They remark that when the dynamics between gendered politics and practices of militarized nationalism are overlooked, the ways in which gender is conceived and disseminated by humanitarian agencies is necessarily restrictive of feminist concerns around women's security. Similarly, Ruwanpura (2007) shows for conflict-ridden Sri Lanka that NGOs which explicitly confront structures perpetuating gender, ethnic, class, religious, and caste hierarchies that women must negotiate in their everyday lives hold the greatest potential as sites of protest. These NGOs explicitly deal with the rich and complex tapestry of women's multiple roles and positions and challenge divisions that bar women from building alliances. They have the greatest implications for feminist consciousness-raising and gender rights and create the possibility for feminist-inspired transformation.

The underlying emphasis of these feminist interventions is how discourses of gender rights, which underpin NGO activity, are unlikely to have credible purchase unless facets of politics, power, and ideology are brought into discussions around civil society mobilization. They argue that incorporating political strategy and power dimensions into the analysis of NGOs is crucial for appreciating the extent to which their activities enable a space within which prevailing inequitable social relations are subverted in servicing progressive social reform. Any lapses in this direction would discount how NGOs are implicated within the prevailing neoliberal political economy. By default, how NGO activity undermines feminist politics and thwarts shifts in the ideological dimensions of social change calls for continuous scrutiny.

SEE ALSO: Empowerment; Gender Analysis; Microcredit and Microlending; NGOs and Grassroots Organizing

NOTE

[1] The Euro- and male-centric vision of economic progress historically associated with the development paradigm was progressively under critique for its lack of critical engagement with the political economy particularities of the postcolonial world (Zein-Elabdin and Charusheela 2004).

REFERENCES

Butalia, Urvashi. 2002. "Confrontation and Negotiation: The Women's Movement's Responses to Violence against Women." In *The Violence of Development: The Politics of Identity, Gender* and *Social Inequalities in India*, edited by Karin Kapadia, 207–234. London: Zed Books.

Escobar, Arturo. 1995. *Encountering Development: The Making and Unmaking of the Third World*. Princeton: Princeton University Press.

Feldman, Shelley. 1997. "NGOs and Civil Society: (Un)stated Contradictions." *American Association of Political and Social Science*, 554: 46–65.

Halim Chowdhury, Elora. 2011. *Transnationalism Reversed: Women Organizing against Gendered Violence of Bangladesh*. Albany: SUNY Press.

Hickey, Sam, and Giles Mohan. 2005. "Relocating Participation within a Radical Politics of Development." *Development and Change*, 36(2): 237–262.

Hyndman, Jennifer, and Malathi de Alwis. 2003. "Beyond Gender: Towards a Feminist Analysis of Humanitarianism and Development in Sri Lanka." *Women's Studies Quarterly*, 31(3/4): 212–226.

Kabeer, Naila. 1994. *Reversed Realities: Gender Hierarchies in Development Thought*. London: Verso.

Kabeer, Naila. 2001. "Conflicts over Credit: Re-evaluating the Empowerment Potential of Loans to Women in Rural Bangladesh." *World Development*, 29(1): 63–84.

Kapadia, Karin, ed. 2002. *Violence of Development: The Politics of Identity, Gender and Social Inequality in India*. London: Zed Books.

Molyneux, Maxine. 1998. "Analysing Women's Movements." In *Feminist Visions of Development: Gender Analysis and Policy*, edited by Cecile Jackson and Ruth Pearson, 65–85. London: Routledge.

Rankin, Katharine. 2002. "Social Capital, Microfinance and the Politics of Development." *Feminist Economics*, 8(1): 1–24.

Ruwanpura, Kanchana N. 2007. "Awareness and Action: The Ethno-Gender Dynamics of Sri Lankan NGOs." *Gender, Place and Culture*, 14(3): 317–333.

Wickramasinghe, Nira. 2001. *Civil Society in Sri Lanka: New Circles of Power*. New Delhi: Sage.

Zein-Elabdin, Eiman, and S. Charusheela, eds. 2004. *Postcolonialism meets Economics*. New York: Routledge.

Women's Banking

JANETTE RUTTERFORD
Open University Business School, UK

JOSEPHINE MALTBY
Sheffield University Management School, UK

Women's involvement with banking has taken a variety of forms worldwide, reflecting diverse and changing views of gender roles with tensions between tradition and developing practice. Anglo-American historians have emphasized a "separate spheres" model, in which women were excluded from financial activities (e.g., Hamlett and Wiggins 2009). But there is evidence that from early modern times British women invested in financial assets (Carlos, Maguire, and Neal 2009). Some companies – for example, Barclays Bank – even aimed securities at female investors (Maltby and Rutterford 2006). Working-class women made substantial use of savings bank accounts from their foundation (see, e.g., Maltby 2011), with contemporary sources describing women as "the great representatives of the virtue of providence amongst the working classes" despite legal and social restrictions on married women's property rights. Similarly, some US banks offered women's departments, with female staff providing advice (Robertson 2008).

Contemporary discussion of women's investment behavior has replaced claims of the "separate spheres" with allegations of innate female risk aversion, with a preference for "conservative investing and low turnover" (Basch and Zehner 2009, 7–8). In the banking industry, there are claims that this makes women a suitable complement to men but limits their ability to generate high profit. UK 2009 figures showed that women represented 50 percent of banking sector employees but less than 2 percent of executive directors. This is argued to reflect the male-dominated nature of the industry rather than women's career choices (House of Commons Treasury Committee 2010).

Worldwide female inclusion in the use of banks lags that of men. In developing economies, while 46 percent of men have a formal account, only 37 percent of women do (Demirguc-Kunt and Klapper 2012). The gap varies in size across regions – at its widest in South Asia, where 41 percent of men had access to an account against 25 percent of women – and impacts on all uses of financial services, including current account, savings, and borrowing (Demirguc-Kunt and Klapper 2012).

There is continuing debate about appropriate mechanisms for ensuring that women have access to banks and to finance. Women-only bank branches that were a feature of the early twentieth century in the United States and United Kingdom have been created more recently in Iran and Saudi Arabia (Malik 2011), with India opening a women-only bank in 2012, aimed at users "from the self-help groups to the small business women and from the working woman to the high net worth individual" (Bhalla 2013). The availability of microcredit has been welcomed as a means to "advance women's empowerment" (Hirut, Folmer, and Bock 2012) by enabling them to generate income and manage assets on their own, without male control. Concerns have, however, been raised about the actual benefits derived by women from microcredit. There is evidence that credit may lead to an increase in workload and to the accumulation of a burden of debt without creating a permanent improvement in well-being (e.g., Desmedt 2010 on microcredit in Europe).

It is argued that women are likely to derive more benefit from financial services provided by cooperative organizations, such as schemes developed in Ecuador by DGRV, the German Cooperative movement, or the Indian women's cooperative Sewa Bank (Biswas 2013), and from schemes that give them financial education and local control to prevent exploitation.

SEE ALSO: Microcredit and Microlending; Poverty in Global Perspective; Sustainable Livelihoods

REFERENCES

Basch, Linda, and Jacki Zehner. 2009. "Women in Fund Management: A Road Map for Achieving Critical Mass – and Why it Matters." Working paper, National Council for Research on Women.

Bhalla, N. 2013. "India Launches First Bank Exclusively for Women." Accessed July 24, 2014, at http://www.in.reuters.com/article/2013/11/19/india-women-bank-bmb-idINDEE9AI0C020131119.

Biswas, Soutik. 2013. "Does India Need a Bank for Women?" Accessed July 24, 2014, at http://www.bbc.co.uk/news/21611787.

Carlos, Ann M., Karen Maguire, and Larry Neal. 2009. "Women in the City: Financial Acumen During the South Sea Bubble." In *Women and their Money 1700–1950: Essays on Women and Finance*, edited by Anne Laurence, Josephine Maltby, and Janette Rutterford, 33–45. London: Routledge.

Demirguc-Kunt, Asli, and Leora Klapper. 2012. "Measuring Financial Inclusion: The Global Findex Database." World Bank Development Research Group Finance and Private Sector Development Team Policy Research Working Paper 6025

Desmedt, Emmanuelle. 2010. "Trapped in Ideology: The Limitations of Micro-Finance in Helping Women Creating Viable Micro-Businesses." PhD dissertation, University of York.

Hamlett, Jane, and Sarah Wiggins. 2009. "Victorian Women in Britain and the United States: New Perspectives." *Women's History Review*, 18(5): 705–717.

Hirut, Bekele Haile, Henk Folmer, and Bettina Barbara Bock. 2012. "Microfinance and Female Empowerment: Do Institutions Matter?" *Women's Studies International Forum*, 35: 256–265.

House of Commons Treasury Committee. 2010. *Women in the City: Tenth Report of Session 2009–10*. HC 482. London: HMSO.

Malik, Nesrine. 2011. "Do Women Need a Bank of their Own?" Accessed July 24, 2014, at http://www.theguardian.com/commentisfree/2011/dec/14/women-only-banks-middle-east.

Maltby, Josephine. 2011. "'The Wife's Administration of the Earnings?' Working-Class Women and Savings in the Mid-19th Century." *Continuity and Change*, 26: 1–31.

Maltby, Josephine, and Janette Rutterford. 2006. "'She Possessed Her Own Fortune': Women Investors from the Late Nineteenth Century to the Early Twentieth Century." *Business History*, 48(2): 220–253.

Robertson, Nancy. 2008. "'The Principles of Sound Banking and Financial Noblesse Oblige': Women's Departments in US Banks at the Turn of the Twentieth Century." In *Women and their Money 1700–1950: Essays on Women and Finance*, edited by Anne Laurence, Josephine Maltby, and Janette Rutterford. London: Routledge.

FURTHER READING

Rutterford, Janette, and Josephine Maltby. 2006. "'The Widow, the Clergyman and the Reckless': Women Investors in England and Wales, 1830–1914." *Feminist Economics*, 12(1–2): 111–138.

Women's Centers

CAROLYN CUNNINGHAM
Gonzaga University, USA

The term "women's center" can take on multiple meanings. In general, women's centers address a variety of women's issues including health, education, job skills training, and economic development. A common characteristic among women's centers is that they strive to empower women through offering access to material resources while creating a support system.

The history of women's centers can be linked to trends in the global women's movement. In 1946, the United Nations formed the Commission on the Status of Women (UNCSW). One of the ongoing projects of the UNCSW is the coordination of world conferences to discuss the status of women globally. These conferences, like the Fourth World Conference on Women held in Beijing in 1995, have drawn attention to specific issues affecting women and have led to platforms and policies for focused efforts and resources. Additionally, one of the strategies of the global feminist movement has been the creation of transnational advocacy networks that have been important for providing resources to various locales (Sperling, Ferree, and Risman 2001). Thus, many women's centers are connected to larger social networks in which local feminist activists contribute to larger international forums, which has been important for the funding and support of women's centers.

The structure and mission of women's centers are varied. While some women's centers are housed in physical locations, others are part of a larger network of resources. For example, in Hong Kong, the first women's center opened in 1985, providing a link to community resources, networks to other women's groups, and offering a physical place for women to organize. The Cultural Development Center for Rural Women is a non-government organization (NGO) in Beijing that offers support for migrant women. Founded in 1994, the Asia-Japan Women's Resource Center is an NGO that advocates gender equality, an end to violence against women, and sustainable development.

Other women's centers address the specific cultural needs of migrant and refugee women. For example, the Asian Women's Resource Centre is located in the UK and offers support services for Asian women and children. The Asian Women's Resource Centre supports women's professional and personal development through services that include workshops, training, domestic violence support, and sexual health information. The South Asian Women's Centre is located in Canada and is run by women from South Asia. They empower women to develop their social and cultural potential. The South Asian Women's Centre offers settlement programs and services, health groups, and student placement programs.

Examples of women's centers that are part of larger networks include the East Africa Center and Heal Africa. The East Africa Center (EAC) partners with the local communities to help empower women and children while ensuring access to education and health programs. Heal Africa works with communities in the Democratic Republic of Congo, helping to transform the status of women and bring balance back to life in villages. Heal Africa helps women get the tools they need to ensure that women have physical, psychological, and financial well-being.

While some women's centers may be funded by NGOs, others rely on charitable donations or other economic models. The Global Fund for Women advances the rights of women and girls worldwide through investing in women-led organizations and women's leadership efforts. The Global Fund for Women uses technology, education, and leadership training to provide women worldwide access to resources and knowledge. Founded in 1982, the Women's International Center (WIC) is a non-profit foundation that works with international, national and local organizations to provide economic assistance to refugees and displaced women.

A recent trend in women's centers is to link local efforts to more global issues. For example, the Center for the Rights of Ethiopian Women (CREW) promotes the "social, economic and legal rights of Ethiopian women in Ethiopia and worldwide" (CREW 2014).

In the United States, the development of women's centers is closely linked to University campuses. These arose out of feminist consciousness-raising during the 1960s and 1970s that recognized the need to provide resources for female college students. Campus-based women's centers tend to have a mission of raising awareness about gender inequality and social change. However, some argue that the relationship between advocacy and activism can be problematic because tensions can arise over the balance of offering services and enacting advocacy (Bengiveno 2000).

Women's centers can also refer to organizations that conduct research on women's issues. For example, The International Center for Research on Women (ICRW) works with women in developing countries and identifies the contributions of women in the economy and the obstacles that prevent full participation in society. ICRW's research areas include adolescence, agriculture, economy, HIV and other health programs, violence against women, and technology.

Much of the research on women's centers includes case studies that document the history of a specific center or look at the impact of women's centers on achieving outcomes, such as increased health and wellness. For example, Wilson and Jenkins (2001) evaluated the impact of 12 women's wellness centers in Kazakhstan that provided clinical and education services. They found that the centers had a number of positive outcomes for women's health, including increased acceptance and demand for family-centered birthing services and early screening for breast and cervical cancers. Future research on women's centers may identify patterns and trends among different models to better understand the economic, cultural, and political roles that women's centers play in improving women's lives.

SEE ALSO: Gender Equality; Global Restructuring; Health Disparities; NGOs and Grassroots Organizing; Women in Development

REFERENCES

Bengiveno, Teri Ann. 2013. "Feminist Consciousness and the Potential for Change in Campus Based Student Staffed Women's Centers." *Journal of International Women's Studies*, 1(1): 1–9.

Center for the Rights of Ethiopian Women (CREW). 2014. "Home." Accessed February 14, 2014, at http://centerforethiopianwomen.org/.

Sperling, Valerie, Myra M. Ferree, and Barbara Risman. 2001. "Constructing Global Feminism: Transnational Advocacy Networks and Russian Women's Activism." *Signs*, 26: 1155–1186.

Wilson, Teresa A., and Emily L. Jenkins. 2001. "Development of a Women's Wellness Center in Almaty, Kazakhstan." *Journal of Obstetric, Gynecologic, and Neonatal Nursing*, 30: 231–239.

FURTHER READING

Cheung, Fanny M. 1989. "A Community Approach to Feminism in Hong Kong." *American Journal of Community Psychology*, 17: 99–107.

Ferree, Myra M., and Aili M. Tripp, eds. 2006. *Global Feminism: Transnational Women's Activism, Organizing, and Human Rights*. New York: NYU Press.

Global Fund for Women. 2014. "Global Fund for Women." Accessed February 14, 2014, at www.globalfundforwomen.org.

Naples, Nancy A., and Manisha Desai, eds. 2002. *Women's Activism and Globalization: Linking Local Struggles and Transnational Politics*. New York: Routledge.

Women's Dirges

SELVY THIRUCHANDRAN
Women's Education and Research Centre, Sri Lanka

Dirges are associated with death and have a ritual status in some countries, and therefore they are amenable to analytical, sociological, and anthropological research. In South India and Sri Lanka the Tamils call them *oppari*, which can be translated as ritual lament songs. Etymologically, *oppari* means to make noise together (*oppu*, together; *ari*, to make noise). Usually crying or lamenting is a prerogative of women, though occasionally men take part. Apart from the ritual status there are dramatic elements involved. When a death occurs, the women in the house get together and weep loudly. Indirectly this act initially intimates to the neighbors that someone has died. The women in the neighborhood immediately assemble. They sit in a circle around the body with their hands around each other's necks and cry. Beating on the chest is also a common sight. The lamentations flow poetically with rhymes and alliterations in a tune that is symptomatic of grief. This spontaneous and instantaneous verbal outburst usually entails praising the dead person, calling attention to their virtues, personality, demeanor, deportment, and worldly achievements throughout their life history.

This genre has a cross-cultural presence across China, Finland, Ireland, Greece, and India (Alexiou 1974; Caraveli-Chaves 1980; Jordan and de Caro 1986). However, in India, Sri Lanka, China, and Finland there are other types of lament songs more closely associated with women's suffering. At a wedding, it was customary in Finland for the bride and her mother to sing lament songs as part of the ceremonies. In China the ritual can last for weeks.

We could identify one important signification that has social reality and that is the collective spirit of the communities in coming together to participate and share their grief. That this is done through an overt expressive communicative skill is yet another factor to be noted. An extension of this reality is the patriarchal norm that sees women as the emotional expressive other who binds the societies.

In Sri Lanka we have come across different kinds of lament songs particular to women's experience. They fall under particular traditional titles and could be classified as lament songs. Not all of them have ritual status like dirges, nor are they communicative events of a collective nature. There are two types of such lament songs, one called *Inamil Ilampen Olam* (which can be literally translated as the lament in a loud voice of women who have no kin group members), sung by young and orphaned widows, and the other sung by unmarried women who lament their unmarried status. These are composed and sung by individual women. The young widows choose a funeral and sit by the corner near the entrance perhaps, unseen by others, and wail.

Usually a senior woman, who in the kinship category is closely related to the dead person's family, starts the *oppari*. Groups are formed, with three or more women in each one, and the *oppari* goes from group to group. The women usually sit around the body and the ritual is performed for the public view of those who have assembled for the funeral.

In the public discourse following a funeral, one of the topics is who cried the most. Wailing becomes the social indicator of one's personal involvement and attachment to the family. Another interesting feature of this *oppari* genre is what are called the professional mourners, *Koolikku Maratital*, which literally means "beating on the chest for a payment." The *oppari* is often accompanied by wailing and the physical act of beating on the chest. The status of a person is communicated, measured, and made publicly known by the number of professional mourners who wail at the funeral. The duration and period of wailing and the depth of the voices of the wailing crowd are also equally important. It was customary then to hire mourners to come and sing funeral laments. These were usually women of the "low" caste, who by caste rules had duties and obligations to perform when their masters or their masters' wives or children died. This was done as part of the funeral rituals.

The emotions expressed through the songs vary according to the age, gender, and caste/class status of the person who has died, and also depend very much on the relationship of the deceased to the mourners. The following is typical of a mother who is the chief mourner, on the untimely death of her son.

You did not lie down on the mat,
Even for ten days (as sick)
With fever, you did not suffer,
For many days.
Why did the letter of death
Come so soon
Why did you not hide under the leaves?
Why did you hide behind people?

In addition to the soliloquy forms of *oppari* mentioned earlier, when young widows and unmarried women take part, there are other forms of soliloquy. On the third-day ritual after the death the closest kin, either the mother, wife, sisters, or first cousins, remember the dead by singing the *oppari* by which they also pay homage to the deceased and remember them with affection. This is done individually and not necessarily in groups.

There is also a belief that singing *oppari* has an otherworldly motive. It is asserted that the dead person's soul will be appeased by the *oppari*, that *oppari* helps achieve a peaceful ascent to the other world, and that the deceased really belong to the "dead island" (Shanmugasundaram 1974, 72).

Most importantly, commonsense wisdom comprehends the *oppari* from a social-psychological perspective. *Oppari* is seen as catharsis of the self. *Oppari* is explained as a process or as a technique adopted by grieving people to relieve anxiety and pent-up tensions through an outlet for their repressed feelings.

SEE ALSO: Woman-Centeredness

REFERENCES

Alexiou, Margaret. 1974. *The Ritual Lament in Greek Tradition*. Cambridge: Cambridge University Press.

Caraveli-Chaves, Anna. 1980. "Bridge Between Worlds: The Greek Women's Lament as Communicative Event." *Journal of American Folklore*, 93(368): 129–157.

Jordan, Rosan A., and F. A. de Caro. 1986: "Women and the Study of Folklore." *Signs*, 11(3): 500–518.

Shanmugasundaram, S. 1974. "Oppari." In *Nattupura Illakiya Parvaikal* (Literary Views of Folklore). Chennai: Pari Nilayam.

Women's Health Movement in the United States

BREANNE FAHS
Arizona State University, USA

At the start of the women's movement in the United States, women's health advocates in the late 1960s and early 1970s started to recognize a pattern: women's health needs were being ignored or thought to be entirely aligned with men's needs, reproductive justice floundered, and choices that affected women only (menstrual products, childbirthing options, breast cancer treatment) received little public health attention. Feminist activists at the time had developed a slogan: *The personal is political*. Taking seriously these aims, women's health advocates began a campaign to change how doctors, the government, the media, and the medical field treated women and their bodies.

The women's health movement began as an effort to help women get more in touch with their bodies, but grew to encompass a variety of goals that united the personal and political spheres. In 1971, Carol Downer used a speculum, a mirror, and a flashlight to look at her own cervix and then formed a woman's group that worked to legalize abortion. Having felt empowered by this new knowledge of her own body, Downer felt that other women would feel differently about abortion rights if they knew their own bodies in a more familiar way. Feminists all over the country began hosting groups where women would bring their own speculums, talk about reproductive health, teach women how to look at their cervices, and learn from other women's health experiences.

Shortly thereafter, Lorraine Rothman, a women's health advocate, developed a device that would allow women to extract their own menstrual fluids, a technique she termed "menstrual extraction." This functioned to allow women both to take menstruation into their own hands by shortening their periods and to self-induce an abortion. Downer and Rothman traveled throughout the country by bus carrying these devices in a box marked "TOYS" to disguise the contents, hoping to catalyze their work into the start of the women's self-help movement. They believed women needed to control their own reproductive destiny, decide about when to have children, and serve as informed decision-makers about their own healthcare needs.

Around this same time, as the women's movement gained traction around the country, 12 feminist activists met at a women's liberation conference and attended a workshop on "women and their bodies." They recognized that the medical profession did not provide information about women's bodies with enough accuracy, specificity, and care. In particular, the group felt angry at the condescending and paternalistic messages they received from doctors. Having been active in the women's movement, the civil rights movement, and the anti-war movement, they saw the chance to better disseminate information about women's health as an *activist* issue as well as a social and public health cause.

Shortly thereafter, these 12 women formed "The Doctor's Group," a forerunner to what would eventually become the Boston Women's Health Book Collective, a group that emphasized research about women, bodies, and health. Each woman in the original group chose a topic that was personally meaningful to her, with the goal of collectively assembling these topics into a book that would challenge the medical establishment and improve women's healthcare.

In 1973, the Boston Women's Health Collective published their groundbreaking book, *Our Bodies, Ourselves*, a book that would go on to sell over 3 million copies worldwide and that would catalyze the women's health movement to recognize its activist potential. Showcasing information about women's health and sexuality, the book included a range of topics that affected women's lives: body image, healthy and unhealthy eating behaviors, drugs and alcohol, exercise, emotional well-being, environmental and occupational health, violence and abuse, gender identity, relationships, sexual health, STI (sexually transmitted infections) information, contraception, parenting, abortion, pregnancy, childbirth, infertility, menopause, and political issues related to women's health. Written at home, in libraries, and around kitchen tables, *Our Bodies, Ourselves* was one of the first of its kind to address issues related to women's health by combining the latest research in scientific fields with women's experiences of their bodies, health, and medical care. Currently in its 13th edition and published in over 20 languages throughout the world, it has been called a "feminist classic." Numerous health education, advocacy, and activist projects have used the book to lobby for women's healthcare, access to abortion, safe and accessible contraception, and more widely available STD (sexually transmitted disease) and HIV testing.

During this time period, women of color raised other concerns that were not readily addressed by predominantly white women's organizations. Chicano women activists worked on behalf of women farm workers for environmental health and reproductive justice for women farm workers. Native American women organized against forced sterilization abuse, reproductive justice, and the negative health consequences of radiation poisoning and other environmental contaminants, some of which were evident in the breast milk of women in different Native American communities. African American women established a number of important organizations through which they also fought against sterilization abuse and for equal access to contraception, abortion, maternal and child health, and healthcare.

As one outgrowth of the women's health movement, the Atlanta-based Black Women's Health Initiative (BWHI) started in 1983 as a way to address health disparities between white women and women of color. Issues such as reproductive rights and reproductive justice, spiritual healing, fitness, domestic violence, and connections to women across the African diaspora (including the West Indies) became prominent issues that the BWHI sought to address.

Radical feminist groups in the United States debated with each other about the best possible way to achieve access to abortion, with some arguing that the "right to privacy" constituted the best approach, while others argued for a more radical and sweeping claim that women had a fundamental right to their own bodies. Ultimately, the infamous 1973 case, *Roe v. Wade*, decided that women had the right to abortion because of their "right to privacy." Since then, women's health activists have fought hard to stave off the continued erosions of women's right to abortion, including dictates that require minors to stay within state lines, secure parental consent, or get the father's permission for an abortion, as well as "late-term" abortion bans and even bans on abortion after 20 weeks. Recognizing the significance of abortion at the helm of women's rights advocacy, women's health activists organized the 2003 March for Women's Lives, a march in Washington, DC that drew over a million participants. This march showed solidarity around the need for abortion and reproductive justice for women and brought together women and men, as well as those from a range of class, race, and educational backgrounds.

The need for safe, effective, and accessible birth control has also formed a central component of the women's health movement, as activists, scholars, public health officials, and grassroots groups have demonstrated that women need to make decisions about their own bodies and that medical insurance should cover these methods and should make them widely available to women. Disagreements over the availability of birth control created many controversies for President Obama when he wrote into law that insurance carriers must cover birth control options like the birth control pill. Activists today argue that intrauterine devices (IUDs) should also be covered by insurance companies, as they provide long-term, highly effective, cost-efficient, and (in some versions) non-hormonal options for women to control reproduction. Women's health advocates have also been the voice around issues of racism and classism in reproductive justice, bringing attention to the differential treatment of white women and women of color, middle- and upper-class women versus working-class and poor women. As many welfare policies have built in discrimination against women of color who receive public assistance, women's health activists have argued that *all* women have the right to decide when to have children and whether to use birth control.

Along these lines, women's health activists have also prioritized women's needs to control their own childbirth. Activists have critiqued the overly medical treatment of childbirth, targeting unnecessary tests and fetal monitors, the doctors' language of "delivering" the baby (while the mother is constructed as passive and not participating), the overuse of cesarean sections, the lack of doulas and midwives in medical facilities, differential insurance coverage for different types of women, and the general assumption that pregnancy and childbirth are "illnesses."

Women's health advocates have also demanded better research and treatment for breast cancer and, in recent years, ovarian and cervical cancer. Activists have fought for a multitude of goals on this front, including more funding for research, better treatment options, better treatment facilities, a critical analysis of the corporate interest in breast cancer research, a reframing of those who "survive" and those who die, a recognition that men also get breast cancer, more analyses and understanding of reconstruction options (including not getting any reconstruction), better understandings of how toxic environments create more cancer, critical examinations of breasts and their role in producing femininity and self-worth, and more options for preventing breast cancer for women both in the United States and globally.

Targeting the health of younger women, women's health activists were also responsible for pushing through the funding, development, and dissemination of the cervical cancer vaccine Gardasil, first to girls and recently also to boys. This vaccine, designed to prevent a variety of strains of cervical cancer, is given to adolescents prior to when they become sexually active in order to prevent the growth of the human papilloma virus (HPV), which can cause cervical cancer. Debates and controversies continue to surround this drug, as some conservatives have argued that it creates "promiscuity" and serves as a parental signal for permission to have sex. As no studies have supported these claims, most public health advocates have stated that these drugs are a necessary and vital part of sexual health for young people today.

As a combination of do-it-yourself culture, anarchy, punk, and anti-consumerism, menstrual activism (also called "menstrual anarchy") has also played a part in the women's health movement. These activists have particularly targeted the corporate control over "menstrual management," arguing instead that women should avoid disposable products due to their environmental consequences and their toxicity for women's bodies. Menstrual activists have noted that commercial tampons contain chemicals like dioxin that result in the peeling of the vaginal lining and the introduction of harmful substances into women's bodies. Commercial pads result in a massive amount of waste that goes into landfills each year, adding up to a staggering number of pounds of waste during women's lifetimes. Citing the financial, environmental, social, and political benefits of reusable and make-it-yourself products, menstrual activists have made a convincing case for why reusable pads, reusable menstrual cups, and reusable sea sponges serve as good alternatives to commercial products.

Additionally, menstrual activists have also fought against the treatment of menstruation as a medical problem, as "premenstrual syndrome" (PMS) and "premenstrual dysphoric disorder" (PMDD) have recently gained more traction in recent years. Menstrual activists note that PMS has no specific criteria consistent across women and that PMDD turns women's normal bodily processes into a mental illness. Some menstrual activists have also tried to "de-pathologize" actions like menstrual sex and stating aloud that one is menstruating. Menstrual activists also have fought against the television and media portrayals of menstruation, the shame-based teachings promoted in grade school to both girls and boys, and the assumption that menstruation is dirty, shameful, and should be hidden from view. Instead, they argue, men and women need to understand women's menstrual cycles and menstrual needs and they need to fight back against a culture that silences and shames women about their bodies' natural processes.

In all, women's health advocates still face a plethora of challenges when working to secure justice for women and their bodies. Faced with continued assaults by conservatives and those who see men as "normal" and women as "deviant," women's health activists have taken a multipronged approach to fighting back, calling upon women of all ages and backgrounds to combat the negative, patriarchal, and condescending treatment of women and their bodies. The women's health movement also symbolizes the ideal union between second-wave and third-wave activism, as new generations of women carry on the struggles that continue to limit, control, and silence women's health decisions and advocacy.

SEE ALSO: Abortion, Legal Status in Global Perspective on; Activist Mothering; Birth Control, History and Politics of; Community and Grassroots Activism; Feminist Activism; Menstrual Activism; Premenstrual Syndrome (PMS); Self-Help Movements

FURTHER READING

Bobel, Chris. 2010. *New Blood: Third Wave Feminism and the Politics of Menstruation*. New

Brunswick: Rutgers University Press.
Boston Women's Health Book Collective. 2011. *Our Bodies, Ourselves*, revised and updated. New York: Touchstone Books. First published 1973.
Dubriwny, Tasha N. 2012. *The Vulnerable Empowered Woman: Feminism, Postfeminism, and Women's Health*. New Brunswick: Rutgers University Press.
Galarneau, Charlene. "Farm Labor, Reproductive Justice: Migrant Women Farmworkers in the US." *Health and Human Rights* 15: 144–160.
Roth, Benita. 2004. *Separate Roads to Feminism: Black, Chicana, and White Feminist Movements in the America's Second Wave*. New York: Cambridge University Press.
Seaman, Barbara, and Laura Eldridge. 2012. *Voice of the Women's Health Movement*, 2 vols. New York: Seven Stories Press.

Women's Movements: Early International Movements

NATALIE SPAGNUOLO
York University, Canada

Historians commonly refer to the international networks that encompassed the social and political reform efforts of women during the late nineteenth century and leading up to World War I as the early international women's movement. Whereas the early nineteenth century is often characterized by the formation of women's networks at the national level in many countries, and during the 1910s by the winning of the franchise as the result of women's political mobilization in some of these countries, the period in between was marked by the formation of international links between various national groups. These interest groups were predominantly non-governmental, free associations of women who were concerned with a range of issues, including temperance, birth control, enfranchisement, pacifism, and the unpaid labor of women in the home. Women's organizations reflected a plurality of values, ranging from radical to conservative, from feminist to anti-feminist.

International women's networks were often based on alliances formed between various voluntary, national women's associations. Many international women's conferences were the result of national initiatives, such as the World Women's Christian Temperance Union (WWCTU), which emerged in 1883 out of the US national temperance movement. Often thought to be the first international organization of women, the WWCTU was founded within the larger context of a society accustomed to a race-based "slave economy." The missionary agenda which the WWCTU combined with an interest in suffrage reflected the same racist, paternalistic ideology that led the national Women's Christian Temperance Union in the United States to segregate black and racialized women into separate temperance unions.

The American suffrage movement was also involved in the creation of the International Council of Women (ICW), which was first held in Washington in 1888 and famously associated with the leadership of American suffragist Susan B. Anthony. While the ICW hosted later meetings outside the United States, the association's international reach was limited to Western, European countries (with the exception of Argentina). The national contexts of these Western countries informed the exclusionary practices that shaped the membership and leadership of participating women's groups. In Australia, Canada, the United States, and many European countries, for instance, leadership often resided in a group of elite, white, and Christian, middle-class women.

National contexts meant that women's groups often adopted different strategies in pursuit of the same goals. The international suffrage movement known as the International Women's Suffrage Alliance (IWSA) helps to illustrate the diversity of orientations that existed among women's organizations. Formed in 1902 as the result of ICW congresses, the IWSA connected diverse women's associations across national boundaries. Women's groups in Asia, however, differed from their European and North American counterparts in their tendency to prioritize education over suffrage, seeing this as a more direct route to emancipation (Edwards and Roces 2004, 7). Hence even though women's groups outside the United States, Canada, and Western Europe were part of the broader suffrage movement represented by the IWSA, their approach to gaining political rights was shaped by their immediate, national circumstances rather than by any IWSA formula. When Chinese women created a Suffrage Alliance in 1912, they did so within the context of the Xinhai Revolution and the establishment of a new Republic. The tactics that many Chinese women practiced were more militant than the American feminist and first president of the IWSA, Carrie Chapman Catt, was comfortable condoning (Sasaki-Gayle 2009). The priorities of black American women involved in national temperance organizations such as the WWCTU also differed in important ways from those espoused by the white-dominated unions in the United States. The temperance unions led by black women tended to emphasize issues of racism and its connections to temperance and political emancipation (Terborg-Penn 1998, 85–86). By contrast, in colonial settler societies such as New Zealand, Canada, Australia, and the United States, white women commonly adopted the racist rhetoric of "civilizing" indigenous and foreign-born women.

The broad range of interests held by different women's associations at the national and international levels makes it useful to discuss multiple, international women's movements rather than a single, unified movement. Nevertheless, the shared material circumstances of women in different countries resulted in similar membership bases and thematically similar agendas among many groups. For example, many of the women's associations that began in Canada, the United Kingdom, the United States, and Australia, who were affiliated with the IWSA, were the initiatives of educated, white female elites who already enjoyed certain advantages in their respective societies. In other countries, such as Japan, China, Iran, and India, suffrage leadership was also elite and reform efforts tended to exclude women who were are already marginalized in those societies (Edwards and Roces 2004). Among black women in the United States, leadership was also concentrated among the educated, middle classes (Terborg-Penn 1998, 2). These women were non-voting at the time of their mobilization efforts and they were mainly interested in extending the franchise to a limited number of women with a similar social standing to themselves.

Alliances of non-elite women have also been documented by historians. Many working-class women formed national groups that held international connections, such as the national Association for the Representation of the Interests of Working-Class Women in Germany, which formed in 1896 as the result of trade union activity. Ideological differences and diversity in women's conditions resulted in tensions within and between different regional and national associations. Often these disagreements occurred between elite-led women's groups and those with more working-class memberships. For example, when the Second International took up enfranchisement and women's rights around 1907, they created an international network of national women's organizations that was sensitive to the elite-domination of national and international suffrage movements. The women's branch of the Second International, led by prominent German and Marxist theorist Clara Zetkin, encouraged women to abandon the American-based IWSA.

The Second International allowed women to pursue suffrage through a more class-sensitive platform than the IWSA, which was commonly viewed as a middle-class, "mainstream" women's group that focused on enfranchisement (Bluhe 1981, 222). Largely upon Zetkin's initiative, International Women's Day was created in 1910 as a way of fostering a sense of solidarity among women around the globe; this day also reflects important links between feminism and socialism, and the international orientation of both. Indeed, the Second International successfully engaged women's groups in Eastern and Southern Asia. These socialist groups in Asia, however, tended to be more radical in orientation compared with their European and North American counterparts (Moghadam 2013, 18).

The reality of a diversified population of women who experienced oppression differently formed an important part of the reform context of the late nineteenth and early twentieth centuries. The effects of elite-led political reform efforts were not evenly applied to all women, with the majority of women either being intentionally excluded from reform efforts or constituting the target of efforts initiated by middle-class reformers. In China, racialized discourses were employed by the elite-led suffrage movement that was part of the IWSA. These discourses participated in the formation of new Republican identity that alienated certain ethnic groups within China (Edwards 2004, 62). Within the context of white, settler nationalisms that were developing in countries such as Canada, women's groups with connections to international groups such as the WWCTU played an important role in defining early citizenship ideals that attempted to exclude racialized women, women with disabilities, and poor women.

Indeed, motherhood and nationalism formed complementary themes that many women's groups enacted through a moral reform agenda that focused on upholding standards of behavior purely defined by their class-based and cultural interests. These reform efforts, which largely took place during the early twentieth century, allowed women to engage in moral and sexual regulatory work that was directed at working-class and racialized women, and also women with disabilities and foreign-born women. The general goal of these maternal feminists was to ensure "healthy" children and future citizens by focusing on the role of women as "mothers of the race." Women's groups would apply arbitrary tests to the subjects of their reform efforts in an attempt to measure their capacity for rational and moral behavior and determine their suitability to serve as mothers. From the 1890s through to the 1930s and long afterwards, public interest arguments based on improving national populations were frequently used to bolster the role of women as mothers of the nation. At the same time, an emphasis on rationalism and moral constraint as necessary attributes of a healthy citizenry was used to justify elite-led demands for women's suffrage. Often women's groups who practiced this approach to nationalism espoused a pro-natalism and an interest in child welfare, claiming that they were combating the perceived threat of depopulation or degeneration that was thought to be caused by disability and immigration.

During the early twentieth century, many women's groups articulated an explicitly eugenic rationale in relation to motherhood and anti-immigrationism. Positive eugenics, or the encouragement of reproduction among a select group of women, was difficult to separate from negative eugenic practices that sought to punish and exclude women who were perceived as being unfit for citizenship and motherhood. Maternal feminist movements in Canada, for example, discouraged the use of contraceptives among elite women while supporting their use among so-called defective women. Women's associations in Canada also conducted "house visits" to poor women as part of their attempt to enforce standards of behavior through the provision of relief. These women could and often did enact punitive policies toward their female subjects. Some women actively sought out female deviant behavior, facilitating the confinement and sterilization of women who they viewed as being defective or unemployable. Women who were thought to be intellectually inferior or "mentally deficient," based on preconceived ideas about class, race, gender, and sexuality, were often the most popular targets of these eugenic practices. The fact that such socially stratifying activities were sometimes spearheaded by women's organizations demonstrates the extent to which categories such as "motherhood" failed to unite women across class and other divides. Through their voluntary involvement in eugenic discourse and practice, many women and maternal feminists gained a professional status in the managerial state that was beginning to develop in Canada, the United States, and elsewhere during World War I.

As eugenic thinking came to the forefront of public discourse in the late nineteenth and early twentieth centuries, women's groups also gained an international voice by participating in transatlantic eugenic leagues. Women's groups engaged with various brands of eugenics which reflected both feminist and anti-feminist ideologies and attracted women from the left and right of the political spectrum. In Central Europe, the League for the Protection of Mothers (BfM), founded in 1905, symbolized the compatibility between different strains of feminism and eugenics (McLaren 1990). BfM was one of the largest German feminist organizations, having been born out of a concern for single mothers, unmarried mothers, and children. This women's group was concerned with sexuality, abortion rights, paid maternity leave, and many eugenic and progressive issues. In the context of the broader eugenic movement, national women's organizations such as BfM formed international connections with sexologists and social reformers. Notably, BfM leaders collaborated with Havelock Ellis, the prominent British eugenicist and head of the Galton Institute. Ellis was influential in the work of Helene Stöcker, the feminist founder of BfM.

Most women's groups promoted heteronormative relations between men and women. Even leagues such as the BfM that defended single women were reluctant to support homosexuality among women. There was often tension within women's movements in Central Europe when lesbian women, such as feminist activist Anna Rüling, questioned normative assumptions about sexuality (Dollard 2009). European women in Central Europe seemed especially interested in discussing early theories of sexuality, and debates that ranged over issues of female emancipation often incorporated theories from psychoanalysis and sexology. The range of feminisms that emerged from these influences led some women to emphasize similarities between men and women, and others to endorse theories of female uniqueness or superiority. Such claims, however, were mitigated through practices that excluded "degenerate" women, a broad category that encompassed women who were perceived as being defective.

More recently, historians of women's movements have been challenged by the colonial nature of the many international connections that were formed between national women's groups. Efforts to balance colonial and imperial realities with recognition of the agency of historical actors in colonized contexts has raised questions as to whether and to what extent Western forms of feminism have been imported to these areas. The relationship between Japanese and American women's movements in the mid-nineteenth century helps to illustrate the complexity of power dynamics within these international exchanges. In Japan during this period, women's groups coalesced around demands for suffrage and education for women. These movements arose within the context of Japan's industrialization and what is commonly thought to be the "Westernization" of this country. The American-founded WWCTU was adopted by Japanese women following a visit to Japan by American women's leader Mary Leavitt. The creation of Tokyo Kyofukai, the Japanese branch of the WWCTU, in 1886 with Yajma Kaj as its first President has been linked to the missionary work of the American WCTU and also to earlier Japanese women's movements that had been active in attempting to abolish prostitution and gain enfranchisement since the 1870s (Matsukawa and Tachi 1994, 172–174). The difficulty in acknowledging the potentially imperialistic connections associated with international organizations such as the WWCTU, without reducing the role played by other women's groups, has led scholars to rethink the influence of Western feminisms within international networks.

An over-crediting of Western influences took place in early histories of women's movements, inspiring more contemporary scholars to consciously work against these trends. Despite these efforts, Western timelines continue to dominate many discussions of internationalism in early women's movements. The overall periodization of women's movements has been criticized for having the effect of privileging the actions of white, middle-class women of European descent, and forming chronologies which occlude the political involvement of indigenous, racialized, or working-class women in these areas. In the histories of white settler colonies such as Canada, Australia, and the United States, scholars have demonstrated that networks of resistance to colonization were shaped by women's actions. These forms of women's organizations have been included in discussions of women's activism only relatively recently.

The Eurocentric focus of women's histories is partly due to the role attributed to American and Western European women leaders in high-profile, international networks of women. Historical narratives emphasizing the role of these organizations have tended to align women's activism with Western emancipation timelines, characterizing movements as "second-generation suffrage" or "first-wave feminist." Periodization has tended to bookend these early movements with the winning of political rights in the 1910s and 1920s and the formation of national organizations during the early nineteenth century. In doing so, these timelines misleadingly suggest that women's gains in particular national contexts were universal. More and more scholars have come to rethink previously accepted timelines, and to recognize the role of indigenous or precolonial women's movements. The more recent critiques of feminist wave-theory, the move away from state-based models of political action, and criticism of the rights-based focus in studies of women's movements have led historians to consider organizations previously overlooked or viewed as being less legitimate or significant. Socialist and anti-racist feminist researchers, for example, have documented women and feminist activists who were previously ignored.

Although much attention has been paid to grassroots efforts and institutional histories, narratives often center on the role of individual leaders. Biographical approaches that focus on the writings or activities or single players in women's movements represent a dominant approach in the history of women's movements. However, many historians are now reluctant to heroize key female reformers, and instead have explored the effects of these women's activities on the lives of other women, such as women with disabilities, racialized women, and poor and working-class women. The reification of racial differences has also been questioned by scholars who are critical of strict divisionary categories. Instead, greater consideration of intersecting identities and axes of oppression has complicated earlier understandings of membership and motives within women's groups. Although the perpetuation of gender essentialism and the erasure of sexual diversity continue to characterize a large body of scholarship on women's movements, attention to the occlusion of lesbian women's histories and the histories of women with disabilities has attracted the attention of some researchers and generated fruitful links between topics such as feminisms and eugenics.

Finally, the extent to which any women's movements were truly international in scope remains unclear. Historians have pointed out that many of the documented international women's networks simply represented alliances between Western European and North American national movements, and therefore are less representative of global diversity or broad international cooperation. Other critiques draw attention to the overwhelmingly national features of the many organizations involved in international movements as evidence that certain claims to internationalism were less important in practice. At the same time, comparative studies between national women's movements remain popular, in addition to studies of cross-cultural feminisms. Approaches that emphasize cosmopolitanism, such as the multiple connections between German-speaking, elite, educated women in Central Europe, have provided an alternative to more international frameworks.

SEE ALSO: Eugenics, Historical and Ethical Aspects of; Feminism, Nineteenth-Century United States; Feminist Disability Studies; History of Women's Rights in International and Comparative Perspective; International Women's Day; Nationalism and Gender; Nationalism and Sexuality; Women's Movements: Modern International Movements

REFERENCES

Bluhe, Mari Jo. 1981. *Women and American Socialism, 1870–1920*. Urbana: University of Illinois Press.

Dollard, Catherine L. 2009. *The Surplus Woman: Unmarried in Imperial Germany, 1871–1918*. New York: Berghahn Books.

Edwards, Louise. 2004. "Chinese Women's Campaigns for Suffrage: Nationalism, Confucianism and Political Agency." In *Women's Suffrage in Asia: Gender, Nationalism and Democracy*, edited by Louise Edwards and Mina Roces, 59–78. London: RoutledgeCurzon.

Edwards, Louise, and Mina Roces. 2004. "Introduction: Orienting the Global Women's Suffrage Movement." In *Women's Suffrage in Asia: Gender, Nationalism and Democracy*, edited by Louise Edwards and Mina Roces, 1–23. London: RoutledgeCurzon.

Matsukawa, Yukiko, and Kaoru Tachi. 1994. "Women's Suffrage and Gender Politics in Japan." In *Suffrage and Beyond: International Feminist Perspectives*, edited by Caroline Daley and Melanie Nolan, 171–183. New York: NYU Press.

McLaren, Angus. 1990. *Our Own Master Race: Eugenics in Canada, 1885–1945*. Toronto: McClelland and Stewart.

Moghadam, Valentine M. 2013. *Globalization and Social Movements: Islamism, Feminism, and the Global Justice Movement*, 2nd ed. Lanham: Rowman & Littlefield.

Sasaki-Gayle, Motoe. 2009. *Entangled with Empire: American Women and the Creation of the 'New Woman' in China, 1898–1937*. PhD dissertation, Johns Hopkins University.

Terborg-Penn, Rosalyn. 1998. *African American Women in the Struggle for the Vote, 1850–1920*. Bloomington: Indiana University Press.

FURTHER READING

Janz, Oliver, and Daniel Schönpflug, eds. 2014. *Gender History in a Transnational Perspective: Networks, Biographies, Gender Orders*. New York: Berghahn Books.

Women's Movements: Modern International Movements

BRONWYN WINTER
The University of Sydney, Australia

This entry follows on from the preceding entry on the early international movement and takes as its starting point the creation, in 1915, of the Women's International League for Peace and Freedom, discussed below. It considers the themes around which international women's activism has developed since World War I and looks at various framings that have been suggested as alternatives to the "international," such as global, transnational, and decolonial feminisms.

EARLY TWENTIETH-CENTURY ORGANIZATIONS

The International Women's Congress for Peace and Freedom, held in The Hague from April 28 to 30, 1915, during the first year of the "Great War," has been characterized as "probably the most celebrated (and was at the time also the most reviled) expression of women's internationalism" (Rupp 1997, 3).

The Women's International League for Peace and Freedom (WILPF) was formed at the Congress (although the present name of the organization was not adopted until the second Congress in 1919). Although not the first international feminist initiative in the twentieth century – in fact WILPF was largely a breakaway group from the International Alliance of Women (IAW), founded in Berlin in 1904 – The Hague initiative has remained one of the most inspiring, not least because of its founding president, Jane Addams. In the 1920s, Addams was famously dubbed "the most dangerous woman in America" by J. Edgar Hoover, founding director of the Federal Bureau of Investigation, because of both her peace activism and her work for poor women and immigrants in Chicago. In 1931, she became the world's second woman to be awarded the Nobel Peace Prize, the first being the Austrian baroness Bertha Von Suttner, another peace activist and author of the influential 1889 novel *Die Waffen Nieder! (Lay Down Your Arms!)*.

WILPF and its two predecessors, the International Council of Women (ICW) (founded as an international suffrage association in 1888 in Washington) and the IAW, which like WILPF, still exists and has broadened its focus to women's human rights, development, and gender equality, foregrounded themes that have remained dominant in international feminist organizing: anti-militarism, civil and political rights, and – especially for those women aligned with socialism, communism, or trade unionism – economic equality. The issue of violence against women, and particularly sexual violence, was, although not absent, mostly raised within the context of anti-militarism and although on one level a unifying theme across cultures and classes, it was also often discussed within nationalist and racist tropes, by women who were predominantly members of Western elites (Rupp 1997). The interwar years also saw the beginnings of feminist endeavors to gain access to a platform within international organizations, particularly through the efforts of the ICW in relation to the League of Nations (LoN) (Rupp 1997; Lake 2001; Offen 2001). Then, as now, feminists internationally were divided over the usefulness of interacting with international institutions, and many in WILPF in particular – overall the most radical of the three international women's organizations mentioned here – criticized the male-dominated character of the LoN and its dismal performance on women's rights. Another point of contention within international feminist organizing in the interwar years was the relationship or otherwise of the international movement to international socialism and trade unionism, and rifts developed between bourgeois and socialist women which at times posed the risk of undermining the movements. Approaches to specific issues also created divisions. For example, with the rise of European fascism and the threat of a new war, the question arose: how unconditional is feminist pacifism? Are feminists opposed to all armed conflict, at all times, no matter the circumstances?

All of these problems continue to dog feminist organizing and theorizing beyond national borders, notwithstanding the otherwise pioneering impacts and often radical stances taken. Admittedly, such problems are not unique to feminist organizing: questions of inclusiveness or otherwise, pluralism or otherwise, which strategies to adopt or issues to prioritize, and how to frame them, and internal divisions and power struggles sometimes related to other allegiances, plague all social movements and especially international ones. They have, however, often appeared particularly acute within the international feminist movement, because of the feminist commitment not only to a radically different *vision* of global governance, but also to a fundamentally different *mode* of operating: collective, pluralist, inclusive, non-hierarchical, and indeed non-nationalist.

THEMES AND MODES OF ORGANIZING

If any two themes can be said to have drawn women most closely together across the borders of nation, race, class, language, and a host of other differences during the last century, they are surely armed conflict and violence against women. There has, unfortunately, been no lack of either to fuel international feminist activism, and some of the most successful and enduring international networks have focused on one or both of these issues (for example, the Coalition Against Trafficking in Women, founded in the United States in 1983, and Women in Black, founded in Israel in 1987).

A third issue that has emerged since roughly the 1980s to bring women together internationally is that of global capitalism. Although, as noted above, parts of the early feminist international movements also embraced socialist ideas, it is capitalist globalization of the late twentieth century that sparked a new phase of international feminist activism around economic exploitation and feminized poverty, and helped bring about closer dialogue between women of the so-called Global North and those of the so-called Global South. A number of international or regional organizations focusing on women, economic equality, and sustainable development emerged in the 1980s and early 1990s, with varying positions concerning autonomy, North–South relationships, and relationships with national and international institutions and corporate actors. For example, DAWN (Development Alternatives with Women for a New Era, founded 1984) is "a network of feminist scholars, researchers and activists from the economic South working for economic and gender justice and sustainable and democratic development" (www.dawnnet.org). It is one of the oldest and probably remains one of the most autonomous of such organizations. AWID (Association for Women's Rights in Development, founded 1982), is a feminist organization whose membership represents a broad cross-section of stakeholders involved in "gender equality, sustainable development and women's human rights" (www.awid.org); these stakeholders include business and government representatives and funding agencies. WEDO (Women's Environment and Development Organization, founded 1991), which "promotes and protects human rights, gender equality and the integrity of the environment" (www.wedo.org), was founded in the United States, largely at the initiative of former congresswoman Bella Abzug, although its founding committee included Wangari Maathai (Kenya), Thais Corral (Brazil), and Vandana Shiva (India). These networks and organizations foregrounded the connections between women's rights, economic justice, and sustainable development, and many of them were centrally involved in both anti- and alter-globalization movements, in addition to lobbying the UN to have these connections made core to development initiatives (Moghadam 2005).

The centrality of these three foci does not mean that other issues have not been addressed by feminists working across national borders. The international network Women Living Under Muslim Laws, set up in 1984 in Pakistan and France, is a case in point (the European headquarters subsequently moved to the United Kingdom). But militarism, violence, and global capitalism have arguably been the most consistent unifying factors for the international women's movement, with international feminist networks and scholarship often pointing out the connections between them (e.g., Cockburn 2007; Enloe 2007; Farr et al. 2009).

Women's international anti-war activism, moreover, not only has brought women together internationally, but has also fed the development of national movements. In Japan, for example, peace activism during the interwar years contributed substantially to the development of an autonomous Japanese women's movement (Shibahara 2014). The converse has also been true: national-level mobilization around the Israeli state's occupation of Palestine gave rise to an international network – Women in Black (WIB). WIB has also exemplified a new kind of international feminist organizing during the "second wave," along the lines of a network rather than a formally constituted organization. The first WIB vigil was a response by Ashkenazi citizens and residents of Israel to the first Palestinian intifada in December 1987, and just seven people (of whom two were men) attended (Cockburn 2007). WIB has since become a transnational network, and although the primary focus remains a call for an end to the Israeli occupation of Palestine, WIB groups in different parts of the world have focused on local or regional issues of state violence, armed violence, and violence against women. Thus, WIB India has included a focus on violence against women in India, WIB Serbia has included a focus on the Serbian state's violence and its brutal repression of gay rights activism, WIB Australia has included foci on refugee rights and Indigenous rights, and so on. Global issues thus intersect and interact with local issues in quite diverse ways within the broad WIB network, but its raison d'être remains the Israeli occupation, and it is therefore on one level a single-issue network.

Another advantage of the network model, such as that used by WIB and Women Living Under Muslim Laws, is that they accommodate, within and across the focus on the core purpose of the network's existence, a large range of views. Members of the national and international WIB network, for example, are not in agreement about a one-state versus two-state solution or about the desirability of advocating boycotts, divestment, and sanctions, but they *are* in agreement about their core issue: ending the violence, and ending the occupation. Similarly, in Women Living Under Muslim Laws there is a huge cultural diversity as well as a diversity of views concerning the degree of engagement with religion. What unites the network is resistance to the use of shari'a law (at whatever level) to discriminate against women or justify any sort of violence against them.

The network model corresponds no doubt the most closely to new ways of thinking about feminist internationalism, which Kaplan and Grewal (Kaplan and Grewal 1994, 1999; Grewal and Kaplan 2000) have theorized as transnational feminism. Transnational feminism does not posit a global sisterhood as natural and inevitable, nor does it posit divides among the world's women as insurmountable, or deny that women have common cause within a global patriarchy. It suggests, rather, that the unevenness and often instability of power relationships among the world's women need to be acknowledged and transnational feminist practices be based on the understanding that women face both contradictions and connections and these relationships will change according to the demands of historically and geopolitically specific conditions. Not unlike many of the women who came together in The Hague in 1915, Grewal and Kaplan insist on the importance of destabilizing rather than maintaining "boundaries of nation, race and gender" (Grewal and Kaplan 2000) and of refusing to choose among "economic, cultural and political concerns", but rather considering them as interlocking (Grewal and Kaplan 2000; see also Winter 2012). However, the development of this sort of analysis did not come out of nowhere: it coincided also with challenges by feminist activists and theorists from the Global South to dominant conceptualizations of feminist internationalism.

INTERNATIONAL OR WESTERN?

At the time WILPF was founded, "international" feminism remained very much a trans-Atlantic affair, notwithstanding some international connections that extended farther. The only non-European or non-Western member of the IAW at the time of WILPF's creation was China, and both organizations remained dominated by the West until the 1920s, when a number of non-Western and non-European national women's organizations began to join (Rupp 1997). The IAW's new members in 1923 included Brazil, India, Jamaica, Palestine, Japan, and Egypt, considered the birthplace of both Arab modernism and the modern Arab feminist movement. It was in 1923 that the Egyptian Feminist Union was founded, under the leadership of Huda Sha'arawi, who represented Egypt at the IAW Congress that year in Rome. Five years later, Egypt became also, somewhat ironically, the birthplace of modern political Islamism, as the Muslim Brotherhood was founded in Cairo in 1928. Egypt thus modeled quite early in the twentieth century both modernist and reactionary trends within the Arabo-Muslim world.

Notwithstanding these expanded memberships of international women's organizations, international feminist activism remained, in the interwar years, mainly the province of educated elites and dominated by Western Europe and the United States. Even if the women involved were passionately committed to working on behalf of poorer women, often through links with socialist or trade union organizations, they were not themselves poor, a statement that is no doubt self-evident as the ability to travel, especially transcontinentally, meant that one had the financial means to do so. This dominance of elites who have the most access to resources remains, unsurprisingly, largely intact today, even if those elites are more dispersed geographically and more diverse culturally and to some extent linguistically (although the dominance of English as a global lingua franca has significantly undermined linguistic diversity). Not even the Internet, often hailed as a democratizing tool that enhances women's ability to organize internationally at grassroots level, has enabled the international feminist movement to move beyond the problem of elites. Internet use is most concentrated in the West and other industrialized countries such as Japan, and the least concentrated in the poorest nations in sub-Saharan Africa, the Middle East, and Southeast Asia. Access to resources (to reliable sources of electricity for a start), to language in which to articulate claims and analyses, and to the means of travel to meetings is still a central concern for women seeking to build a grassroots international movement.

Similarly, "the world" prior to the end of World War II and the period of massive decolonization that followed was still largely conceptualized in terms of the dominant powers: Western Europe, the United States (and occasionally their Anglo-World allies Canada, Australia, and New Zealand, along with Japan, the Soviet Union and, to a lesser extent, China). Just as the Euro-American axis dominated international relations, it continued to dominate international feminism. And just as the Western-centeredness of the "international" came under increased criticism after World War II, the Western dominance in international feminism also started to be called into question, most especially with the advent of the so-called "second wave" from the late 1960s. Even then, however, those who were able to theorize and organize beyond national borders were inevitably members of elites, and the West remained dominant.

The second wave was nonetheless the moment at which thinking about international feminist organizing began to shift. The idea of the "international" started to be replaced by that of the "global," based on the idea of a commonality of women's experience of oppression that transcended barriers of nation, race, culture, and class, and here the issue of violence against women came very much to the forefront. A groundbreaking moment in thinking feminist globalism came with the publication in 1984 of *Sisterhood is Global* (edited by Robin Morgan), which included contributions from women in some 70 countries (Morgan 1984). The idea of a "global sisterhood" and a corresponding international feminist movement was, however, very strongly contested by feminists who claimed that "global sisterhood" was based on a Western idea that one model of women's liberation would fit all women, and was most famously contested in academic forums by Mohanty (1984). So that, while some feminists prioritized global commonalities among women, others argued that the differences continued to outweigh the commonalities, and privileged organizing along lines of regional and ethno-cultural commonalities.

Regional initiatives such as the Encuentros Feministas Latinoamericanos y del Caribe, the first of which took place in 1981 (the thirteenth took place in 2014), have provided a space of counter-hegemonic feminist organizing that was both international in scope and yet focused on broad cultural commonalities and regional concerns, the latter of which included the fact that feminist movements in many of the countries concerned emerged during political struggles of resistance to dictatorships. Such regional initiatives, however, can also mask internal diversity and divisions. "Latin America and the Caribbean" covers a range of cultural, racial, linguistic, and economic contexts and often very different political and social histories. Regional initiatives, although important in the construction of a feminist internationalism, have thus at some levels tended to reproduce the very homogenizing models they initially set out to counteract.

INSTITUTIONAL INTEGRATION VERSUS AUTONOMY

One problem that emerged within the Encuentros, notably since the fourth UN World conference on women (Beijing 1995), as it had emerged within WILPF some 70 years earlier, and as it has done more broadly within the international women's movement, was the debate over the degree to which international feminist activism should work with and even within institutions. The most obvious interlocutor for such engagement is the UN, but many feminists also work, for example, with development agencies of government, corporate, and financial sectors, and richer non-governmental organizations (NGOs), access to funding for various projects being an ongoing and vexed question. Since the first UN international conference on women in Mexico in 1975 (with subsequent meetings in Copenhagen 1980, Nairobi 1985, and Beijing 1995) and the signing of the Convention on the Elimination of all forms of Discrimination Against Women in 1979, the international women's movement has been confronted with the same process of "NGO-ization" that has affected other transnational social movements. Debates and divisions have re-emerged over the wisdom or otherwise of putting one's energy into working with institutions, whether the risks of co-optation and dilution of one's political agenda outweigh the benefits. Moreover, those networks not politically and legally constructed as NGOs (the case of Women in Black, for example) do not have direct access to the UN (but may have indirect access through network members' participation in other groups). The question of autonomy or otherwise thus impacts not only on political content and strategies but also on the very form of transnational organizing that women choose to adopt.

The UN is also "a broad church" – and this metaphor is not chosen randomly. Several thousand registered NGOs vie for the UN's attention, and among those who are the most ferociously opposed to women's rights – notably albeit not only in the areas of reproductive and sexual rights – are a significant number of religious groups. At post-Beijing UN meetings in New York in 2000 and 2005, for example, conservative Christian groups harassed members of reproductive choice NGOs, and many of the parallel NGO meetings, notably lesbian ones, took place semi-underground in that their time and place were circulated by word of mouth only, not published in any daily information sheet, for fear of disruption by conservative groups. Feminist interaction with the UN is thus far from a straightforward process, for many reasons.

At the same time, the UN has had clear material and symbolic importance for the international women's movement, as it is one of the few international bodies whose moral and sometimes legal authority can be used to put pressure on states. "Human rights talk" has thus became a significant part of international feminist organizing since the 1980s. Activist intellectuals such as Charlotte Bunch, Gita Sen, Eileen Pittaway, and innumerable others became outspoken advocates, in both activist and scholarly forums, for women's (including lesbians') rights as integral to the human rights project and for the participation of, and impact on, women to be considered in all international deliberations on civil and political rights protections, peace and security, health, and development. A significant body of human rights feminist scholarship has emerged, tracing these developments (e.g., Peters and Wolper 1995; Ferree and Tripp 2006; Reilly 2013). Notably, since 9/11, scholarship has further focused on the impact and application (or otherwise) of specific UN Resolutions on women in relation to conflict situations [such as Porter (2007) on UN Security Council Resolution 1325 (2000) on Women, Peace, and Security].

SEE ALSO: Feminisms, First, Second, and Third Wave; Feminist Activism; Feminist Movements in Historical and Comparative Perspective; Feminist Organizations, Definition of; Feminist Theories of Organization; Women's Centers; Women's Movements: Early International Movements; UN Decade for Women

REFERENCES

Cockburn, Cynthia. 2007. *From Where We Stand.* London: Zed Books.

Enloe, Cynthia. 2007. *Globalization and Militarism: Feminists Make the Link.* Lanham: Rowman & Littlefield.

Farr, Vanessa, Henri Myrttinen, and Albrecht Schnabel. 2009. *Sexed Pistols: The Gendered Impacts of Small Arms and Light Weapons.* Tokyo: United Nations University Press.

Ferree, Myra Marx, and Aili Mari Tripp, eds. 2006. *Global Feminism: Transnational Women's Activism, Organizing, and Human Rights.* New York: New York University Press.

Grewal, Inderpal, and Caren Kaplan. 2000. "Postcolonial Studies and Transnational Feminist Practices." *Jouvert: A Journal of Postcolonial Studies*, 5(1): 1. Accessed June 16, 2015, at http://english.chass.ncsu.edu/jouvert/v5i1/grewal.htm.

Kaplan, Caren, and Inderpal Grewal. 1994. "Transnational Feminist Cultural Studies: Beyond the Marxism/Poststructuralism/Feminism Divide." *Positions*, 2(2): 430–445.

Kaplan, Caren, and Inderpal Grewal. 1999. "Transnational Feminist Cultural Studies: Beyond the Marxism/Poststructuralism/Feminism Divides." In *Between Woman and Nation*, edited by Caren Kaplan, Norma Alarcón, and Minoo Moallem, 349–363. Durham, NC: Duke University Press.

Lake, Marilyn, 2001. "From Self-Determination (via Protection) to Equality (via Non-Discrimination): Defining Women's Rights at the League of Nations and the United Nations." In *Women's Rights and Human Rights: International Historical Perspectives*, edited by Patricia Grimshaw, Katie Holmes, and Marilyn Lake, 254–271. Basingstoke: Palgrave Macmillan.

Moghadam, Valentine M. 2005. *Globalizing Women: Transnational Feminist Networks.* Baltimore: Johns Hopkins University Press.

Mohanty, Chandra Talpade. 1984. "Under Western Eyes: Feminist Scholarship and Colonial Discourses." *Boundary 2*, 12(3)–13(1): 333–358.

Morgan, Robin, ed. 1984. *Sisterhood is Global.* New York: Doubleday/Anchor.

Offen, Karen. 2001. "Women's Rights or Human Rights? International Feminism Between the Wars." In *Women's Rights and Human Rights: International Historical Perspectives*, edited by Patricia Grimshaw, Katie Holmes, and Marilyn Lake, 243–253. Basingstoke: Palgrave Macmillan.

Peters, Julia, and Andrea Wolper, eds. 1995. *Women's Rights, Human Rights: International Feminist Perspectives.* New York: Routledge.

Porter, Elisabeth. 2007. *Peacebuilding: Women in International Perspective.* London: Routledge.

Reilly, Niamh. 2013. *Women's Human Rights: Seeking Gender Justice in a Globalising Age.* Cambridge: Polity.

Rupp, Leila. 1997. *Worlds of Women: The Making of an International Women's Movement.* Princeton: Princeton University Press.

Shibahara, Taeko. 2014. *Japanese Women and the Transnational Feminist Movement Before World War II.* Philadelphia: Temple University Press.

Winter, Bronwyn. 2012. "International vs Transnational? The Politics of Prefixes in Feminist International Relations." In *Conflict-Related Sexual Violence: International Law, Local Responses*, edited by Tonia St Germain and Susan Dewey, 15–32. West Hartford: Kumarian Press.

Women's Political Representation

DRUDE DAHLERUP
Stockholm University, Sweden

Seen in relation to their share of the population, women have been and are still systematically underrepresented in most elected political assemblies of the world. Also other groups such as national minorities and new immigrants are marginalized in political decision-making. Equal or proportional representation of women and men, today often named *parity*, can – like the representation of minorities – be seen as a goal in itself, a human right, or as a means to change political decisions taken by male-dominated political assemblies. Contemporary discourses challenge the idea that the *how* of representation, for example the decision-making structures, is much more important than the *who* of representation. Who the representatives are is seen as significant, be it in the ancient city-state of Athens or in modern deliberative governance structures. After introducing the new contemporary discourse of exclusion, this entry addresses the issue of women's political representation from three interlinked perspectives: descriptive representation (numerical), substantive representation (policies), and symbolic representation (the meaning attached to women's representation).

Often political "participation" and political "representation" are used synonymously. However, while political *participation* may in theory be open to all citizens who want to participate in, for instance, a Facebook group, a demonstration or an organization, political *representation*, in contrast, emerges from elections and is embedded in the power structures and gatekeeping mechanisms of the political system. To become a representative, one has to be nominated as a candidate for election, and in most political systems the political parties are the gatekeepers to elected positions. When the voters enter the polling station, the nomination and rank order of candidates for election have already been decided on by the political parties.

Historically, representation predates democracy, as in the representation of noblemen, priests, and the bourgeoisie in the old estates during the Middle Ages and later. The present discussion of equal representation of all citizens in relation to their share of the population is, however, linked to modern democracy. Yet, increasingly, even less democratic countries or countries in transition to democracy like Algeria, Rwanda, and Afghanistan select their political assemblies through direct public elections, which has made the question of who the representatives are a global issue.

The Platform for Action adopted by the United Nations (UN) World Conference on Women in Beijing, 1995, represented a new global discourse on women's underrepresentation, calling for "equitable distribution of power and decision-making at all levels" and supporting the use of affirmative action (Art. 181). With its focus on "discriminatory attitudes and practices," the Platform for Action provided a powerful international discourse of exclusion. Under this discourse, women's historical underrepresentation is not primarily explained by women's alleged lack of qualifications or interest in politics, which earlier had been the usual justification. Instead the rules and praxis of those who control the selection and nomination processes, usually the political parties, are the subject of scrutiny. This new focus on the lack of inclusiveness of political institutions and political parties themselves is also applicable to the underrepresentation of other marginalized groups, such as ethnic minorities and disabled persons (Dahlerup 2011).

Recent research on women in political life distinguishes between *descriptive, substantive,* and *symbolic representation,* inspired by, although not completely identical to, the classic concepts of Hanna Pitkin (1967).

DESCRIPTIVE REPRESENTATION

The claim that elected assemblies should mirror the social composition of the population has gained saliency in recent years. The classic liberal notion of representation of different political ideas needs to be supplemented by social representation, a "politics of presence," as Anne Phillips (1995) argues, either as a right in itself or as a means to change politics for the benefit of those hitherto marginalized in political life.

Even if the Beijing Platform for Action did not explicitly mention the controversial word "quota" among its affirmative action strategies, the discourse of exclusion has legitimized the global diffusion of electoral gender quotas in the past decades. If the main problem is that political parties are not sufficiently inclusive, then quotas can force parties to search more seriously for potential female candidates instead of continuing to recruit candidates from within a narrow "old boy's network."

As of 2015 more than 80 countries in the world – democratic and semi-democratic as well as non-democratic – have adopted as a matter of law electoral gender quotas, requiring, for example, that neither sex comprise less than 30 or 40 percent of the candidates (candidate quotas) or that a certain number of seats be reserved in advance for women (reserved seat quotas). In many other countries individual political parties make use of gender quotas for their own electoral lists (voluntary party quotas). Research has shown that, if designed in a way that is compatible with the electoral system in the country and if the provisions include sanctions for non-compliance and rank order rules, quotas can lead to unprecedented gains in women's political representation (Dahlerup 2006; *Atlas of Electoral Gender Quotas* 2013; Quota Project n.d.).

With this fast-track trajectory through the use of quotas, some countries – such as Rwanda, Senegal, South Africa, Algeria, and Bolivia – leaped to over 30 percent women in parliament in one or a few elections, in sharp contrast to the slow, step-wise incremental track model of the old democracies. For instance, in Sweden, it took more than 30 years after women's suffrage to pass the 10 percent threshold in women's parliamentary representation, in Germany almost 70 years, and in the United Kingdom 80 years. The 25 percent threshold was passed in the 1970s, and 1980s, respectively, in Sweden and Germany, and finally reached in the United Kingdom in the election of 2015. As the only country among these three, Sweden obtained 40 percent in 1994 (Dahlerup and Leyenaar 2013). Today, Rwanda ranks number one in the world, with 64 percent female parliamentarians, and Bolivia number two with 53.1 percent.

The world average rose from 12–13 percent in the late 1990s to 22 percent in 2015, a modest increase. Women's representation tends to be higher in countries that make use of a proportional representation (PR) electoral system than in plurality/majority systems like the United States, the United Kingdom, and India, where every party nominates only one candidate per electoral district (Kittilson and Schwindt-Bayer 2012; Inter-Parliamentary Union n.d.). Governments are still a predominantly male arena, though the number of women ministers is increasing and their portfolios are expanding. However, the number of women presidents and prime ministers in the world is still extremely low (Skard 2014).

Viewing political representation through an intersectional lens reveals the underrepresentation of minorities or marginalized social groups in general, and the lack of diversity among both male and female parliamentarians and local councilors. When racial and ethnic minority or immigrant women (with a few exceptions, e.g., Norway and Sweden) have lower representation than immigrant men – both of whom are underrepresented in general – this may be conceptualized as a result of the multiple oppressions on account of gender, ethnicity, and nationality operating simultaneously.

A decrease in women's political representation has indeed occurred, most notably in Central and Eastern Europe and in most former Soviet republics after the collapse of the Soviet Union. The recent entrance into parliament of xenophobic parties, usually with a low percentage of women, underlines the fact that it is wrong merely to assume that there will be continuous improvement in women's political representation until parity has been reached.

SUBSTANTIVE REPRESENTATION

Even if gender balance in politics may be seen as a goal in itself, most campaigns for equal representation rest on the presumption that women in politics will make a difference. Substantive representation implies "representing as acting for," "in the interest of" (Pitkin 1967, 111–113, 209).

Substantive representation is a contested concept, first because of controversies over the character of voter-representative relations, and second because it seems to require some agreement as to what constitutes "women's interests" (Mansbridge 2003; Childs and Lovenduski 2013; Escobar-Lemmon and Taylor-Robinson 2014). Critics warn against "essentialism." Poststructuralist Judith Butler has criticized feminist theory for assuming "that there is some existing identity, understood through the category of women, who not only initiates feminist interests and goals within discourse, but constitutes the subject for whom political representation is sought" (Butler 1999/1990, 3). According to Iris Marion Young, however, such arguments derive from a misunderstanding of the nature of representation more generally. Representation is not about identification or substitution but a dynamic and differentiated relationship among political actors (Young 2000, 123).

When we move from these theoretical discussions onto empirical studies of women's representation, the question becomes when and on which issues broad coalitions among women's organizations and groups have been established. Empirical studies of women's common interests through a focus on actual patterns of conflict and cooperation display examples from all over the world of cooperation between women's organizations and women politicians across party lines (often joined by supportive male politicians) on issues such as women's suffrage, women's equal representation, girls' education, childcare, maternity health, and measures to prevent violence against women.

Yet, women politicians throughout the world are being criticized by feminist activists for not being "feminist" enough. Linking descriptive and substantive representation of women, women politicians themselves have argued that it takes a critical mass, e.g., 30 percent, of women in the political institutions to be able to make a difference. Research on gender and politics has pointed to other factors that may be even more important than women's share of the legislature for the likelihood of having gender equality reforms passed, such as the ideological persuasion of the government, the strength of public gender equality agencies, strong pressure by women's movements, and the public debate on the role of women politicians. Nevertheless, in spite of scholarly reservations, this story of the critical mass theory lives on in the public debate as a powerful argument, most recently in relation to quota advocacy.

Perhaps Rosabeth Moss Kanter's seminal argument about the importance of the size of the minority (Kanter 1977), which inspired the critical mass discussion in politics (see *Politics & Gender* 2006), is mostly relevant when the issue is politics seen as a workplace, for example the conditions women meet as politicians in institutions where historically "inequality is embedded in the walls." Here the size of the minority becomes highly important. Thus, the social composition of political assemblies (the descriptive representation) seems important in itself for the possibility of women politicians or minority politicians to be effective in performing their representative tasks in the way they wish, whether they see themselves as representatives of a social group (substantive representation) or not.

SYMBOLIC REPRESENTATION

The symbolic aspect of representation is an expanding, yet somewhat diffuse field of research, related to the meaning that representatives have for those being represented, for instance the importance of female role models for the general perceptions of women in politics (Alexander 2012). Symbolic representation is also linked to the legitimacy of the political regime at large. While 50 years ago a male-dominated assembly or government was considered natural, today it would be met by protests, and the democratic legitimacy of the institution or assembly questioned (Dahlerup and Leyenaar 2013). The increased symbolic value of having a fair representation of women in politics for a country's image as modern and democratic may help to explain why also authoritarian or semi-democratic regimes today adopt gender quotas in order to increase women's representation considerably.

CONCLUSION

Just 50 or 60 years ago an all-male political assembly or government was in general considered to be the natural order of things. Since then a process of engendering politics has taken place, with considerable variations, however, in speed and results from country to country and between regions. Today, male-dominated political assemblies or governments are often met with local and international protests. Through pressure from women's movements and advocates working within the political parties, women's representation has increased, sometimes gradually, sometimes in historical leaps by the use of fast-track policies, not least by the adoption of electoral gender quotas. However, women's numerical representation in the world's parliaments (lower and upper houses) is only 22 percent as of 2015, implying that the representation of men amounts to 78 percent.

At the end of the 1990s, only five countries had passed the 30 percent threshold: Denmark, Finland, the Netherlands, Norway, and Sweden. As of 2015, as many as 44 countries have more than 30 percent women in their parliament (lower or single houses), among them many countries from the Global South. Whether women politicians make a difference in politics has been a recurring issue, ever since women obtained the right to vote and stand for election. It is, however, women's minority status in politics that makes this such a burning question, while few have engaged in the discussion about what difference men actually make in politics, even if the pressure for increasing women's political representation in parliaments and local councils derives from a critique of men's descriptive overrepresentation. Adding the perspectives of substantive and symbolic representation to the discussion of descriptive representation on the basis of gender, minority status, class, age, and ethnicity can broaden our understanding of the complex processes of exclusion and inclusion in political life.

SEE ALSO: Democracy and Democratization; Gender Equality; Governance and Gender; Intersectionality; Political Participation in Western Democracies; Politics of Representation

REFERENCES

Alexander, Amy C. 2012. "Change in Women's Descriptive Representation and the Belief in Women's Ability to Govern: A Virtuous Circle." *Politics & Gender*, 8(4): 437–464.

Atlas of Electoral Gender Quotas. 2013. Stockholm: International IDEA, Inter-Parliamentary Union, and Stockholm University.

Butler, Judith. 1999. *Gender Trouble: Feminism and the Subversion of Identity*. New York: Routledge. First published 1990.

Childs, Sarah, and Joni Lovenduski. 2013. "Political Representation." In *The Oxford Handbook of Gender and Politics*, edited by Georgina Waylen, Karen Celis, Johanna Kantola, and S. Laurel Weldon, 489–513. Oxford: Oxford University Press.

Dahlerup, Drude, ed. 2006. *Women, Quotas and Politics*. New York: Routledge.

Dahlerup, Drude. 2011. "Engendering Representative Democracy." In *The Future of Representative Democracy*, edited by Sonia Alonso, John Keane, and Wolfgang Merkel, 144–168. Cambridge: Cambridge University Press.

Dahlerup, Drude, and Monique Leyenaar, eds. 2013. *Breaking Male Dominance in Old Democracies*. Oxford: Oxford University Press.

Escobar-Lemmon, Maria C., and Michelle M. Taylor-Robinson, eds. 2014. *Representation: The Case of Women*. Oxford: Oxford University Press.

Inter-Parliamentary Union. n.d. http://www.ipu.org/english/home.htm.

Kanter, Rosabeth Moss. 1977. *Men and Women of the Corporation*. New York: Basic Books.

Kittilson, Miki Caul, and Leslie Schwindt-Bayer. 2012. *The Gendered Effects of Electoral Institutions*. Oxford: Oxford University Press.

Mansbridge, Jane. 2003. "Rethinking Representation." *American Political Science Review*, 97(4): 515–528.

Phillips, Anne. 1995. *The Politics of Presence*. Oxford: Clarendon Press.

Pitkin, Hanna. 1967. *The Concept of Representation*. Los Angeles: University of California Press.

Politics & Gender. 2006. "Do Women Represent Women? Rethinking the 'Critical Mass' Debate." Special issue, 2(4). Contributions by Sandra Grey, Manon Tremblay, Drude Dahlerup, Sarah Childs and Mona Lena Krook.

Quota Project. n.d. http://www.quotaproject.org/.

Skard, Torild. 2014. *Women of Power: Half a Century of Female Presidents and Prime Ministers Worldwide*. Bristol: Policy Press.

Young, Iris Marion. 2000. *Inclusion and Democracy*. Oxford: Oxford University Press.

Women's Ways of Knowing

SHARON A. BONG
Monash University, Malaysia

The evolution and consolidation of women's ways of knowing – premised on at least 100 years of feminist thought (e.g., liberal, radical/lesbian, existentialist, Marxist, postcolonial, postmodernist feminisms) – are feminist standpoint epistemologies (Harding 1986, 1991, 1993; Collins 1990; Haraway 1991; Hartsock 1998). They are evolutionary (as a successor epistemology) and revolutionary (as an oppositional epistemology). First, they as successor epistemologies of "malestream" theories that privilege male-centered discursive processes or "phallologocentrism": privileging of the phallus as a male signifier and logos, the written word or discourses (Beasley 1999). And in doing so, "malestream" theories often exclude ways of knowing of those on the margins, in particular, women, ethnic, cultural, religious minorities, the dispossessed such as migrant workers, refugees, and so on.

Second and more importantly, feminist standpoint epistemologies are subjugated knowledges as they debunk positivistic Truth claims of universality, hegemony, objectivity, and abstraction in the production of knowledge. The plural form of "knowledges" is not accidental as it embodies the proliferation and plurality even contestation of truth claims. Feminist standpoint epistemologies subvert "malestream" theories by asserting that "real" knowledge, premised on standpoints, is not apolitical but rather, is often and ideally, politically invested (i.e., committed to realizing gender equality and gender equity). A standpoint is defined as a "morally and scientifically preferable grounding for our interpretations and explanations of nature and social life" (Harding 1986, 26). It is therefore not disembodied from the material, temporal and spatial conditions of both feminist social researcher and subjects of knowledge (i.e., those studied) who inhabit the social order. Feminist standpoint epistemologies thus engender an "oppositional consciousness" (Haraway quoted in Harding 1986, 192) in validating knowledge that is contextualized and situated; in insisting upon the agency of social actors or those studied; and in engendering a transformative and emancipatory methodology (e.g., action-oriented research designed to influence policy or law). The three criteria of these successor and subjugated knowledges question underlying assumptions and grounds of knowledge production: whose knowledge counts (and by inference, who is counting), who knows, how women know and have it both ways – universalized *and* particularized truth claims (Harding 1993).

The first criterion of whose knowledge shows how a standpoint epistemology is embodied and embedded in the lived realities of women as subjects of local and situated knowledge. It is knowledge that manifests a moral and political imperative to make visible the prevalence of VAW (violence against women) or GBV (gender-based violence), to deploy a gendered analytical lens to show how women experience local and global phenomena differently and disproportionately from men and to foreground women-specific experiences, particularly with regard to reproductive health and sexuality rights in the twenty-first century (e.g., wombs for hire, mail-order brides, pan-sexualities). In these ways, feminists are now doing the counting of whose knowledge matters and in doing so, have considerably redressed the invisibility of women's voices.

The second criterion of who knows affirms that women know. It shows how women have accorded epistemic privilege to women as those who inhabit the margins as they are active subjects of socially situated knowledge. The margins are reclaimed as a liminal space from which feminist knowledges are produced and reproduced (i.e., the sustainability, integrity, and rigor of feminist thought lies in the internal critique levelled at feminists by other feminists). Women, as such, are not only socially marginalized but also socially marginal (Bar-On 1993): the latter position is potentially empowering where the former position is disempowering. Occupying the margins becomes a vantage point as feminists work from within and without the center margin for change. These knowers are not only feminist thinkers but also feminist activists who embody the nexus of theory and practice in showing how the value of theorizing is contingent on its political mileage – the extent to which knowledge becomes a tool to dismantle the "master's house" in engendering gender equality and gender equity.

The third criterion shows how possessing "real knowledge that is socially situated" is, as Sandra Harding postulates, "to have it both ways" (1993, 50). Socially situated knowledge is deemed a contradiction in terms because it subverts the construction of knowledge as ideally universal, abstracted from the problematic particularities of time and space and as value neutral or apolitical. Proponents of feminist standpoint epistemologies contend that such heralded but disembodied knowledge amounts merely to weak objectivity. As such, those who aspire towards "strong objectivity" (Harding 1993, 69) seek to dispel the "conquering gaze from nowhere," which "mythically inscribes all the marked bodies, that makes the unmarked category claim the power to see and not be seen, to represent while escaping representation" (Haraway 1991, 188). In drawing from feminist standpoint epistemologies, such totalizing discourses are to be contested and held accountable for reinforcing false dualisms between mind/body, spirit/matter, abstract/concrete, objective/subjective, theory/praxis, universal/particular, observer/observed, and male/female that inevitably distort knowledge claims. As such, "real knowledge that is socially situated" is embodied and embedded in women's lived realities.

SEE ALSO: Women's and Feminist Activism in Southeast Asia

REFERENCES

Bar On, Bat-Ami. 1993. "Marginality and Epistemic Privilege." In *Feminist Epistemologies*, edited by Linda Alcoff and Elizabeth Potter, 83–100. New York: Routledge.

Beasley, Chris. 1999. *What is Feminism, Anyway?* Sydney: Allen & Unwin.

Collins, Patricia Hill. 1990. *Black Feminist Thought: Knowledge, Consciousness, and the Politics of Empowerment*. Cambridge, MA: Unwin Hyman.

Haraway, Donna J. 1991. "Situated Knowledges: The Science Question in Feminism and the Privilege of Partial Perspective," In *Simians, Cyborgs and Women: The Reinvention of Nature*, 183–201. London: Free Association Books.

Harding, Sandra. 1986. *The Science Question in Feminism*. Milton Keynes: Open University Press.

Harding, Sandra. 1991. *Whose Science? Whose Knowledge? Thinking from Women's Lives*. Milton Keynes: Open University Press.

Harding, Sandra. 1993. "Rethinking Standpoint Epistemology: What Is "Strong Objectivity"?" In *Feminist Epistemologies*, edited by Linda Alcoff and Elizabeth Potter, 49–92. New York: Routledge.

Hartsock, Nancy. 1998. *The Feminist Standpoint Revisited and Other Essays*. Boulder: Westview Press.

FURTHER READING

Taman, Lucy. 2001. *Knowledge That Matters: A Feminist Theological Paradigm and Epistemology*. Cleveland: Pilgrim Press.

Women's Worlds Conference

DOROTA GOLAŃSKA
University of Łódź, Poland

Women's Worlds Conference (WWC), officially called Women's Worlds, International Interdisciplinary Congress on Women (IICW), also referred to as Women's Worlds Congress (WWC), is one of the most important feminist events worldwide that takes place every three years in different locations across the globe; it is hosted by local academic institutions and financially supported from local sources (e.g., governments, local authorities, academic institutions, nongovernmental organizations, foundations, inter- and transnational organizations, etc.). It gathers together people involved in academic research on gender issues, feminist activists, representatives of social movements and NGOs, women's interest groups, feminist artists as well as public officials and politicians. Typically, interdisciplinary feminist research provides a fundamental conceptual basis for WWCs, yet their logic is also to attract and actively engage grassroots activists as well as policymakers and public officials with an aim to translate the discussed research results into practical actions and initiatives. The main orientation of WWC is to continuously struggle against any kind of exclusion, discrimination, injustice, and violence targeted at different minority groups or those with a limited or no access to power. Gender and women's issues constitute a conceptual framework and a leading theme of each WWC; however, they are understood inclusively and also refer to other categories of difference, such as race, sexuality, class, age, ethnicity, religion, etc., that are often at the origin of diverse practices of oppression. The general theme of each congress reflects current topics and the most up-to-date debates undertaken by feminist scholars and activists. Although every WWC addresses a number of areas approached from the critical women's or gender perspective (such as patriarchy, language, representations, feminists philosophies, methodologies and epistemologies, exclusion, health, climate change, globalization, agriculture, sexualities, identities, wars and conflicts, power and leadership, welfare state, citizenship, literary and artistic production, family, reproductive and fertility rights, ICT, science and technology, violence, migration, girl child, etc.), usually the conferences also bear an imprint of the host countries and explore local contexts of feminist struggles. WWCs gather up to 3,000 participants from all over the world and offer a forum for exchange of ideas, discussions on scholarship, multilateral international and transdisciplinary networking, and for forging productive links between feminist activism and academia. The program of each conference is appended with a number of cultural and artistic events, as well as book launches, roundtables, and workshops. Usually, the site of the next congress is approved during the current one. Typically, a potential organizer should put forward a conference proposal and assure financial support for the event.

The inspiration for WWC came partly from the UN initiative of World Conferences on Women, especially after the proclamation of the UN Decade for Women; however, WWC has an academic orientation. The first WWC took place in 1981 in Israel and it was hosted by Haifa University. It centered on the topic of "The New Scholarship" and aimed at discussing research pertaining to women's issues. It gathered together approximately 600 participants from 36 countries and received wide media coverage both nationally and internationally, including *The New York Times* front-page article. Three years later, in 1984 the meeting was held at Groningen University, the Netherlands and explored the issue of "Strategies for Empowerment," mostly addressing the problem of women's access, or lack thereof, to power and leadership. In 1987 the WWC moved to Ireland, to Trinity College, Dublin and focused on "Visions and Revisions," aiming at (r)evaluating and critically assessing feminist scholarship, also from the point of view of the so-called third-wave feminists. Paramount, yet controversial, was the presence of men as chairs of the panels and presenters at the Dublin Conference, set up under the rubric "Men's Response to the Feminist Challenge" (see Schreier Rupprecht 1988). This was also widely commented in the local media. In 1990 the Conference traveled across the Atlantic to Hunter College, New York, tackling the issue of "Realities and Choice" and discussing the main barriers for women's emancipation. In 1993 the WWC moved to Costa Rica, the University of San José, to debate the theme "Search, Participation, Change," whereas the sixth WWC, held in 1996 at the University of Adelaide in

Australia, was organized around the topic "Think Global – Act Local" and focused on different contexts of common feminist struggle. In 1999 the Conference was back in Europe, hosted by Tromsø University in Norway, and explored the topic of "GenDerations," focusing on the issue of generations in feminist movements as well as addressing the need for intergenerational communication. For the first time this conference included a number of panels organized by and for profeminist men-academics involved in critical research on gender. Significant was also a paradigmatic shift from women's to gender issues, heavily critiqued by more radical feminist environments. Since then, however, the presence of panels dedicated to research on men and by profeminist male scholars has become an integral part of all subsequent WWCs. "Gendered Worlds: Gains and Challenges" was a topic of the eighth WWC hosted in 2002 by Makerere University in Kampala, Uganda. This time the conference aimed at assessing the progress made over the past decades regarding equality and emancipation. Importantly, it attracted a great number of participants from non-Western cultures. The 2005 Congress, jointly organized by the Korean Association of Women's Studies and Ewha Womans University, took place in Seoul, South Korea and debated the theme "Embracing the Earth: East–West, North–South" focusing on the deepening gaps between the living conditions of women from the North and South, and situating these considerations in the context of differing values of the West and East. In 2008 the tenth WWC was hosted by Computense University in Madrid, Spain with a motto "Equality: No Utopia" and under the conference theme "New Frontiers: Dares and Advancements." Violence and migration were the principal topics at this meeting. Three years later the WWC was jointly hosted by Carleton University and the University of Ottawa in Canada and addressed the topic of "Inclusions, Exclusions, Seclusions: Living in a Globalized World." The main focus of the eleventh Congress was on globalizations and the risks, opportunities, and challenges it posed. In Ottawa the University of Hyderabad in India proposed to host the 2014 WWC under a leading title "Gender in a Changing World" addressing the dynamic transformations of contemporary globalized and digitalized world from the critical interdisciplinary gender-informed perspective. In 2017 the WWC will eventually move to South America.

Since its inauguration in 1981, the WWC has traveled globally and thus far has reached over 40,000 people from all parts of the world and from different academic backgrounds. This makes it the largest feminist global event.

SEE ALSO: Empowerment; Feminisms, First, Second, and Third Wave; Feminist Activism; Gender Justice; NGOs and Grassroots Organizing; UN Decade for Women

REFERENCES

Schreier Rupprecht, Carol. 1988. "Third International Interdisciplinary Congress on Women." *Signs: Journal of Women in Culture and Society*, 14(1): 235–242.

FURTHER READING

Allwood, Gill. 2003. "Conference Report. The 8th Interdisciplinary Congress on Women, Women's Worlds Congress 2002, 21–6 July, Makerere University, Kampala, Uganda." *Journal of Contemporary European Studies*, 11(1): 119–121.

Geraldine, Mary R., and Amancio Sarausad. 2005. "Women's World 2005: 9th International Interdisciplinary Congress on Women." *Gender, Technology and Development*, 9: 441–443.

Pollard, Miranda. 1988. "Women's Worlds: The Third International Interdisciplinary Congress on Women." *International Labor and Working-Class History*, 34: 100–102.

Women's Writing

LIEDEKE PLATE
Radboud University Nijmegen, The Netherlands

Women and writing is a subject central to art and literature. Taking gender as its principle of categorization, the topic covers women's writings, the distinctiveness of literature by women, and its relationship to male canons of writing; female authorship and its conditions of possibility; access to means of production and distribution; and the reception, assessment, and evaluation of women's writings.

The conjunction of women and writing as a topic is premised on the condition of basic literacy. Literacy is gendered: in 2008, of the 796 million adults worldwide who reported not being able to read and write, two thirds were women. For centuries, women were refused access to literacy and education, and denied the rights to speak, to personhood, and to self-representation. This condition still obtains in many parts of the world, affecting women's relationship to the act of writing, to publishing and public speaking, and to literary and exegetical traditions.

The topic of women and writing brings the issue of gender to the fore; specifically, how social expectations of women, of their roles and tasks within the family, community, and society, clash and interfere with writing as a public activity and a profession. For instance, focusing on the so-called "Angel in the House" – the Victorian feminine ideal of a wife and mother selflessly devoted to her children and submissive to her husband – Virginia Woolf discusses the effect gender has upon the mind of the writer and maintains: "Killing the Angel in the House was part of the occupation of a woman writer" (Woolf 1979, 60). Other writers have looked at factors deterring women from writing and shaping the writings they do produce.

For women, as for men, writing is a relatively cheap and therefore accessible means of expression (compared to painting or sculpture, for instance), requiring only a pen or pencil and paper. Writing requires leisure time, which is unevenly distributed across the world and across gender. Access to means of publication and distribution also differs, not just between men and women but also among women. In addition, there are significant social, historical, and geographical differences in the constraints families, communities, and society in general place on women. These constraints determining women's writing can be identified in terms of censorship, of which there are many types, from political and religious bans on writing, to publishers' refusals to publish the writing, to forms of self-censorship, whereby women censor themselves before any other person or instance can do so.

A related concept is that of silence, for censorship silences. Tillie Olsen's *Silences* (1978) is a landmark study exploring the social and economic conditions that make creativity possible, as well as the effects of poverty, motherhood, and rigid literary norms on writing. In *How to Suppress Women's Writing* (1983), Joanna Russ builds on Olsen's work to reveal the many ways in which existing women's writing is belittled, disparaged, and ignored – and thus effectively silenced. To circumvent such forms of censorship, women have published anonymously. They have also used male pseudonyms (for instance, Charlotte Brontë published her novel *Jane Eyre* under the pen name Currer Bell). Even today, there are still women writers who hide their gender behind initials or a male name (e.g., the author of *Harry Potter*, J. K. Rowling, published her first adult novel, *The Cuckoo's Calling*, as Robert Galbraith; and the author of the sexually explicit *Fifty Shades of Grey* similarly hid her gender behind initials), although there are also men publishing under female pen names (e.g., Nicci French, the pseudonym of English husband-and-wife team Nicci Gerrard and Sean French).

Because of the constraints that determine women's relationship to writing, it has been argued that women's writing differs from men's. Such arguments served both to extoll and to denigrate it. In *A Room of One's Own* (1929), Virginia Woolf writes of a "woman's sentence" and suggests it is shaped by anger; other women writers have identified fear, despair, or, on the contrary, courage as determining women's writing. In contrast, some men have spoken of feminine sensitivity and a narrow view as the hallmarks of literature by women. In the 1970s, so-called French feminists theorized women's relationship to language and to writing, arguing it is shaped by their position within culture as a material and a symbolic system. A key concept that emerged from the search for the specificity of women's writing is that of *écriture féminine* (feminine writing) – a term coined by the Algerian-French writer Hélène Cixous to identify a writing that differs from masculine/mainstream writing and that inscribes woman's body and differences. On the other side of the Atlantic, and writing about English and American literature, Elaine Showalter identified different phases of women's writing: feminine (1840–1880), feminist (1880–1920), female (1920–1980s), and free (1980s–). Theories about the distinctiveness of women's writing did not go uncontested. Often criticized for their presumed essentialism and for focusing on themes long associated with women – i.e., the body, maternity, sexuality, and irrationality – they were also challenged for emphasizing difference.

Theories of women's writing build on theories of women's relationship to language. They divide into two main categories: psychoanalytical and material approaches. Psychoanalytical theories of women's writing focus on psychodynamics and the effects and consequences of women's position in the Symbolic Order – i.e., language, ideologies, law, and the entire social culture ruling human knowledge, communication, and relations – for their literary production. According to the psychoanalytical theory of Jacques Lacan, which is based on the work of Sigmund Freud, the child's entry into language marks its entry into the Symbolic. Because it is aligned with the Oedipus complex and requires recognition of the Name-of-the-Father, the Symbolic is identified as patriarchal and phallocentric. In consequence, it has been argued that women's truth cannot be expressed in it (Hélène Cixous, Luce Irigaray), and that feminine language arises from the Semiotic, pre-Oedipal stage of psychic development that is governed by the symbiotic relationship of mother and child (Julia Kristeva).

In contrast, material approaches focus on language as social practice, looking at the inscription of a gendered, sexist viewpoint in language, and discussing the relationship between women and writing from a historical perspective on linguistic practice. Such approaches are based on sociolinguistic insights on the effects of society on language, including gender socialization, norms, expectations, and context, and the differences between men's and women's use and styles of language as they intersect with other sources of language variation, such as class, occupation, age, and ethnicity. The relationship between social identity and language use is articulated in exemplary fashion in the writings of Gloria Anzaldúa, notably *Borderlands/La Frontera: The New Mestiza* (1987), which uses multilingualism and code-switching to capture her sense of (dis)location on the frontier between languages and cultures.

In the field of rhetoric, as in the field of literature, feminist scholars have pointed out the gendered nature of the rhetorical tradition and the absence of women from its canon. Cheryl Glenn's *Rhetoric Retold: Regendering the Tradition from Antiquity Through the Renaissance* (1997) is a groundbreaking work that "regenders" and expands the canon of persuasive writing by locating women's contributions to and participation in it from antiquity through the Renaissance, for example, Sappho, Aspasia, Diotima, Hortensia, Fulvia, Julian of Norwich, Margery Kempe, and Elizabeth I. Other scholars suggest the inclusion of women requires rhetoric be reconceived. Women's acts of invention often begin with the need to claim the right to speak and to be visible. They have used different means of persuasion, based in different contexts (e.g., the kitchen, the nursery, the garden, and the body). New topoi open up new possibilities for inventing argument, mounting evidence, and persuading audiences. Redefining and subverting traditional methods of argument, invention, arrangement, style, and ends, women's persuasive or informative writings often arise from their embodiment, physicality, and location.

The idea of gendered language use and styles can lead to stereotyping. Speaking of women writers in a 2011 interview, V. S. Naipaul claimed that he could identify whether a piece of writing was written by a man or a woman because of the latter's sentimentality and narrow perspective. Naipaul's controversial remark stands in a long tradition of stereotyping women's writing, for instance Nathaniel Hawthorne's comment on the "damned mob of scribbling women" that dominated the literary marketplace in his days, a comment that was repeated throughout the nineteenth and twentieth centuries to belittle women writers and disparage women's writing. Online text-analysis programs such as Gender Genie, which predicts the gender of the writer by analyzing and categorizing keywords, reinforce the idea of a stereotypical women's writing.

Because women were authorized to speak in public only on special occasions and in specific roles, for instance at religious festivals, weddings, and funerals, historically, the genres of women's writing differed from men's. Thus Ancient Greek women poets composed primarily in genres that belong to the private sphere and to religion, for example elegy, epithalamium, and hymn, and which reflect their lower social status, as they are not represented in the more important literary genres, notably the epic. Having access or being restricted to different places inevitably shaped women's writings in terms of themes, perspectives, and subject matter. At the same time, there is discussion whether the distinctiveness of women's writing, its genres, and themes, is simply the result of woman's position in society. Just as powerful are acts of reception, which select, categorize, anthologize, transmit, keep, and destroy writings.

The idea of women's writing as forming a distinct category can be dated back to at least the third century BCE and has been shaping the reception of women writers ever since. An early and influential example is the poet Antipater of Thessalonica (flor. 11 BCE-12 CE), who wrote a catalogue of the most respected and famous women poets, grouping the names of nine women who were writing up to 300 years apart, in different regions, and in different genres, calling them the nine earthly muses. Making a selection out of the many more women poets known at the time, praising women for qualities traditionally associated with femininity, poems such as Antipater's epigram have influenced the reception of literature by women, serving as guides for which texts to include in anthologies and thus to transmit and keep for posterity.

Women writers also have long shown a keen interest in tracing female traditions in writing. By referring to Sappho and to each other, women poets of Ancient Greece and Rome have contributed to the idea of a female tradition. In English literature, Mary Scott's poem *The Female Advocate* (1774) is identified as the first distinctively feminist response to male praise of female accomplishments, sketching a female literary tradition that runs from the sixteenth century to her own day. Since the 1970s, many feminist literary scholars have drawn such female literary lineages, for instance Elaine Showalter's study *A Literature of Their Own: British Women Novelists from Brontë to Lessing* (1978) or the *Norton Anthology of Literature by Women* (2007/2007), edited by Sandra Gilbert and Susan Gubar. Informed by identity politics, the study of women's writing pluralized to account for the distinctiveness of writings by women of color and lesbian and queer literature. The feminist reevaluation of women's contributions to society, history, and culture has also led to women's rewriting of myths, fairy tales, and other culturally dominant identity narratives, for example the Bible.

In the last decades of the twentieth century, women's writing developed as an academic field, with courses on women's writing being taught at universities and the development of feminist literary theories and criticism. Developing alongside interest in postcolonial literatures and sexuality studies, gynocriticism, the study of women's writings, brought hitherto neglected writers and genres within the purview of "literature," for instance, children's literature, journals, and letters. Efforts to get women's writings in print led to the establishment of dedicated presses and lists within academic and trade publishing houses. Today, a number of literary periodicals, academic journals, and organizations are dedicated to (areas) of women's writing. Also, several literary prizes are awarded exclusively to literature written by women, for instance the Stella Prize in Australia, the Baileys Women's Prize for Fiction (formerly Orange Prize for Fiction) in the United Kingdom, and the Opzij Literatuurprijs in the Netherlands. Aiming to celebrate women's writing, such prizes reinforce the idea of women's writing as a discrete area of literary practice.

It is important to note that many women writers have resisted categorization on the basis of gender, claiming they are writers, not women writers, and that awards singling out women writers are sexist. In 2013, controversy over gender categorization in Wikipedia erupted when it appeared that novelists of the female gender were being systematically removed from the general category to a subcategory, and were reassigned from "American novelists" to "American women novelists." The concern over (sub)categorization is legitimate, as gender continues to this day to play a role in the reception of writing by women. Literature by women is still being read differently, with preconceptions (and prejudices) about women and femininity informing critical and cultural perceptions of the writings they produce. This condition carries over to reviewing books written by women. Recent research on both sides of the Atlantic has shown that literature authored by women receives significantly less critical attention than literature authored by men, balanced around 30 percent at best.

With the advent of the Internet, born-digital writings by women have emerged. Shelley Jackson's hypertext *Patchwork Girl* (1995) is a frequently cited work of electronic literature, and Jennifer Egan's *Black Box* (2012), which was released as a series of tweets on *The New Yorker*'s Twitter account, has been lauded as an exemplary work of post-postmodernist literature. Research consistently reports women dominate social networking sites. Fan fiction, a non-commercial genre in which fans rewrite the plots and characters of their favorite television series, is largely a female affair that has taken flight as it migrated from fanzines to the Internet. Crossing the border between non-commercial and commercial publishing, the record-setting bestseller *Fifty Shades of Grey* (2011) by E. L. James began as *Twilight* fan fiction on the Internet.

SEE ALSO: Essentialism; Feminist Art; Feminist Literary Criticism; Feminist Publishing; Gynocriticism; Language and Gender

REFERENCES

Anzaldúa, Gloria. 1987. *Borderlands/La Frontera: The New Mestiza*. San Francisco: Aunt Lute Books.

Gilbert, Sandra, and Susan Gubar, eds. 2007. *The Norton Anthology of Literature by Women: The Traditions in English*, 3rd ed. New York: Norton. First published 1985.

Glenn, Cheryl. 1997. *Rhetoric Retold: Regendering the Tradition from Antiquity Through the Renaissance*. Carbondale: Southern Illinois University Press.

Olsen, Tillie. 1978. *Silences*. New York: Delacorte Press/Seymour Lawrence.

Russ, Joanna. 1983. *How to Suppress Women's Writing*. Austin: University of Texas Press.

Showalter, Elaine. 1978. *A Literature of Their Own: British Women Novelists from Brontë to Lessing*. London: Virago.

Woolf, Virginia. 1929. *A Room of One's Own*. London: Hogarth.

Woolf, Virginia. 1979. *Women and Writing*, edited by Michèle Barrett. London: Women's Press.

FURTHER READING

Burrett, Jocelyn, ed. 2004. *Word: On Being a [Woman] Writer*. New York: Feminist Press.

Cameron, Deborah, ed. 1998. *The Feminist Critique of Language: A Reader*, 2nd ed. London: Routledge.

Plate, Liedeke. 2011. *Transforming Memories in Contemporary Women's Rewriting*. Basingstoke: Palgrave Macmillan.

Ritchie, Joy, and Kate Ronald, eds. 2001. *Available Means: An Anthology of Women's Rhetoric(s)*. Pittsburgh: University of Pittsburgh Press.

UNESCO Institute for Statistics. 2010. "Adult and Youth Literacy: Global Trends in Gender Parity." UNESCO Fact Sheet 3. Accessed June 23, 2015, at http://www.unesco.org/education/ild2010/FactSheet2010_Lit_EN.pdf.

Work–Family Balance

ANDRZEJ KLIMCZUK
Warsaw School of Economics, Poland

MAGDALENA KLIMCZUK-KOCHAŃSKA
University of Warsaw, Poland

The concept of work–family balance is usually defined as the act of balancing of inter-role pressures between the work and family domains that leads to role conflict. The conflict is driven by the organizations' views of the "ideal worker" as well as gender disparities and stereotypes that ignore or discount the time spent in the unpaid work of family and community. Balancing actions are mainly aimed at the change of the women's employment by more gender equity in fields of paid employment (including career and responsibilities) and family care work to achieve equal satisfaction, engagement, and good functioning of individuals in both spheres.

A broader version of this concept is a work–life balance, which includes not only family, but also "everything else," the individual lifestyle (for example, leisure, health, spiritual practices, hobbies, community involvement). The main components are time, psychological involvement, and satisfaction balances between gendered work and family roles (Greenhaus, Collins, and Shaw 2003).

Work–family balance was coined in the 1970s in the United Kingdom based on a work–leisure dichotomy, which was invented in the mid-1800s. Early writers such as Karl

Marx underlined that industrialization leads to the separation of work and non-work into relatively independent spheres. Balancing solutions were popularized in the last decades of the twentieth century in European Union countries and the United States by legislation (for example, wage gap, gender discrimination, occupational rights), flexible workplace arrangements, and the market care services (Jain and Nair 2013). Among factors supporting this process was the economic recession of the 1970s, which accelerated women entering the labor market and changed the dominant family model with a single income of the male breadwinner into the dual-earner family. Also single-parent family and population aging continues to emerge in developed countries, which increase demand for family friendly work policies. In the 1990s, further workplace shifts were supported by technological solutions (for example, computers, Internet, cell phones) that enable more flexible work, which may be done outside the office.

Work–family balance varies in both developed and developing countries due to sociocultural, organizational, and personal conditions. Usually balance is important in wealth communities that allow more leisure time, organizations that may support gender equity with specific benefits based on market forces and individual performance, and in adulthood that implies care responsibilities of children or aging parents. Also gender is important in work–family balance due to the fact that "equal pay" required by laws usually is not a reality and women are paid less than men in similar positions, and the labor market is characterized by dualism – men and women tend to choose different career paths and, for example, women jobs in education, culture, and care are paid less than men in industry and science.

Early studies on the work–family interaction have been focused on the role stress theory or the role scarcity hypothesis that underlines negative consequences of work demands. Such pressures may lead to role overload, role conflict, increased staff turnover and absenteeism, lower performance, increased costs of contracting for personal services, and mental and physical health breakdowns (for example, cardiovascular disease, sexual health problems, smoking, and alcohol consumption) (EU-OSHA 2007). Role imbalance that heavily favors family over the other domains was also examined. More investigation recently concerns the positive role balance, which refers to the tendency of engagement in every role with equivalent and high amount of time, involvement, and satisfaction, which leads to gains such as facilitation and positive spillover. A later developed concept of enrichment further shows that work experiences may enhance the quality of family life and vice versa (Jain and Nair 2013). Supporting of positive balance and enrichment aims to a condition in which both male and female employees are good workers and caregivers.

Balance in work–family interaction is becoming important not only as a part of employment and family policies, but also as part of human resources management and corporate social responsibility due to the assumption that employees are stakeholders that create a positive image of the organization. Some employers realized that a positive balance helps with recruitment and retention of employees, build commitment and loyalty to the organization, and increase productivity. However, because the "family friendly" solutions may be criticized by employees without children, broader "life-friendly" benefits are also promoted, such as flexible working hours and telecommuting.

There are many types of benefits that were recognized as fostering a positive work–life balance (European Commission

2005; UNDESA 2012). Depending on their purpose four groups may be distinguished.

- Working time innovations, flexible forms of employment and work organization: flextime, compressed work weeks, telecommuting/working at home, part time employment, job-sharing, term-time work, saving hours.
- Leave: paid and unpaid leave – maternity, paternity, parental, for family reasons (elder-care), adoption; career break scheme.
- Dependent care: childcare arrangements – workplace nursery, contracted childcare places, child-minding, childcare resource and referral, financial assistance, early childhood education, youth care, holiday play schemes/summer camps, informal care and grandparents, care for elderly, people with disabilities.
- Supportive arrangements: employees' counseling/assistance, work–family management training, work–family coordinators, research on employees' needs, financial contributions; partnerships between employers, trade unions, and employees.

Such instruments may be combined with different methods and procedures in programs of specific organizations that adapt to their gender diversity and employees' needs. These include not only combining paid and unpaid workloads of men and women, but also the issue of leisure and care.

However, the concept of work–family balance is still in development and there is no consensus in terms of defining, measuring, researching, and theorizing balance with its components and factors (Rantanen et al. 2011). Techniques for evaluation of the benefits that are aimed at reducing the problematic life role imbalances are also not yet fully described and determined.

SEE ALSO: Division of Labor, Domestic; Gender, Politics, and the State in Central and Eastern Europe; Gender, Politics, and the State in the United States and Canada; Parental Leave in Comparative Perspective

REFERENCES

EU-OSHA (European Agency for Safety and Health at Work). 2007. Family Issues and Work–Life Balance. Accessed July 10, 2015 at https://osha.europa.eu/en/tools-and-publications/publications/e-facts/e-fact-57-family-issues-work-life-balance/view.

European Commission. 2005. *Reconciliation of Work and Private Life: A Comparative Review of Thirty European Countries*. Luxembourg: Office for Official Publications of the European Communities.

Greenhaus, Jeffrey H., Karen M. Collins, and Jason D. Shaw. 2003. "The Relation Between Work–Family Balance and Quality of Life." *Journal of Vocational Behavior*, 63(3): 510–531.

Jain, Sarika, and Shreekumar K. Nair. 2013. "Research on Work–Family Balance: A Review." *Business Perspectives & Research*, 2(1): 43–58.

Rantanen, Johanna, Ulla Kinnunen, Saija Mauno, and Kati Tillemann. 2011. "Introducing Theoretical Approaches to Work–Life Balance and Testing a New Typology Among Professionals." In *Creating Balance?*, edited by Stephan Kaiser, Max J. Ringlstetter, Doris R. Eikhof, and Miguel Pina e Cunha, 27–46. Berlin: Springer.

UNDESA (United Nations Department of Economic and Social Affairs). 2012. *Family Oriented Policies for Poverty Reduction, Work–Family Balance and Intergenerational Solidarity*. New York: United Nations.

FURTHER READING

Crane, D. Russell, and E. Jeffrey Hill, eds. 2009. *Handbook of Families and Work: Interdisciplinary Perspectives*. Lanham: University Press of America.

Lewis, Jane. 2009. *Work–Family Balance, Gender and Policy*. Northampton, MA: Edward Elgar.

X

Xenophobia and Gender

SUSANNE RIPPL
Technische Universität Chemnitz, Germany

KLAUS BOEHNKE
Jacobs University Bremen, Germany

Dictionary definitions commonly describe xenophobia as an irrational fear of "the other," that is, of out-groups categorized as foreign or strange, coupled with negative attitudes toward these groups and/or their members. An inspection of media coverage of xenophobia leads to the impression that the phenomenon is distinctly "male." However, whether there are indeed gender differences in xenophobia cannot be answered easily. While there seem to be significant differences in levels of aggressive behavior toward "the other," differences in attitudes tend to be marginal and dependent on context.

Recent research on xenophobia has mostly used gender as a control variable; the reasons for gender having an impact on xenophobia are rarely discussed conceptually. Hughes and Tuch (2003), however, offer more theoretical depth, distinguishing two broad conceptual perspectives on gender differences: socialization theories and social structure theories.

The first approach sees gender role stereotypes and gender-specific value socialization as the main cause of gender differences in xenophobia. According to the socialization approach, close ties between prosocial value orientations and the female gender stereotype reduce tendencies to favor xenophobic attitudes and behavior. The argument can be traced back to Gilligan's work on female morality, which emphasizes care and empathy, ruling out stereotypic derogation of "the other." However, these prosocial orientations are strongly shaped by culture at a given historic time. Nunner-Winkler (2005) assumes that it is less female morality and much more a socialized role model closely linked to the changing division of labor between men and women. With the increase of more androgynous gender roles in contemporary society, the gender gap in xenophobia should decrease. Gender role stereotypes also play a role in sociological accounts of gender differences in xenophobia: so-called modernization theory assumes that the increasing dissolution of traditional role assignments in the course of individualization and modernization processes generates insecurities. Among men who do not participate in these processes successfully, this is assumed to lead to an amplified return to traditional role stereotypes, linked then to increased xenophobia.

Hughes and Tuch (2003) refer to a second class of theoretical approaches as social structural theories. Here group membership

The Wiley Blackwell Encyclopedia of Gender and Sexuality Studies, First Edition. Edited by Nancy A. Naples.
© 2016 John Wiley & Sons, Ltd. Published 2016 by John Wiley & Sons, Ltd.

and status are focal theoretical concepts. Competition for power and resources is the main reason for xenophobia. According to Hughes and Tuch (2003, 386), the "same racial position" of men and women suggests that there are no differences in their tendencies to derogate others. Differences in levels of xenophobia should rather depend on the degree to which "others" are immediate competitors for power and status. From a feminist perspective, the "racial positions" of men and women do differ, because women suffer from patriarchal domination by men within any racial group. This would suggest that, as an oppressed group, women should express *more* xenophobia than men because they will see the other more as a competitor for their reduced status and power.

A combination of personality-focused and group-related arguments is found in McDonald, Navarrete, and Sidanius's (2011) theory of gendered prejudice. Based on the assumption that humans strive for social dominance and pointing to evolutionary roots, the authors assume that parental investment differs between men and women, offering men an incentive structure that favors competitive and risky behavior in the service of enhancing mating probabilities. For this reason men are primary agents (and targets) of intergroup aggression because they compete for mating partners. In contrast to this, female prejudice is more likely to originate from fearing such men. Consequently, gender differences can be expected especially in competitive areas of life and for aggressive, dominance-related forms of xenophobia. In contrast, no or only small differences should be expected in areas of xenophobia where social distance or an overrating of the ingroup is relevant. Women should express a higher level of xenophobia than men in life domains associated with care of offspring.

When confronting theoretical considerations with empirical findings, no clear-cut results emerge. Looking at morality, women show more prosocial attitudes such as caring, altruism, and empathy (e.g., Cross and Madson 1997). To what extent these findings can be transformed linearly into a statement that women are in general less xenophobic than men remains unclear. Analyses of political attitudes also reveal an inconsistent picture. In many studies on xenophobia, no or only small gender differences are found. If disparities do occur, men usually turn out to be more xenophobic. Men are more xenophobic particularly when items contain high levels of aggression toward the other and are worded explicitly (Ekehammar, Akrami, and Araya 2003). In contrast, women express more negative attitudes than men in the context of personal relationships. Also, multiple studies show that in close interethnic relationships women react with more rejection and a higher social distance than do men (Hughes and Tuch 2003). Overt violence toward the other is, on the contrary, predominantly a male form of xenophobia (Wahl 2002).

In summary, the topic of xenophobia and gender continues to need considerable research attention. There is seemingly no gender main effect in xenophobia, but the size of gender differences is moderated by the behavioral domain, suggesting greater gender differences as xenophobia becomes more aggressive. An obvious blind spot in research is that of gender-aware xenophobia victimology: who becomes a victim of xenophobia and under which circumstances?

SEE ALSO: Gender Difference Research; Gender Role Ideology; Gender Stereotypes

REFERENCES

Cross, Susan E., and Laura Madson. 1997. "Models of the Self: Self-Construct and Gender." *Psychological Bulletin*, 122: 5–37.

Ekehammar, Bo, Nazar Akrami, and Tadesse Araya. 2003. "Gender Differences in Implicit

Prejudice." *Personality and Individual Differences*, 34(8): 1509–1523.

Hughes, Michael, and Steven A. Tuch. 2003. "Gender Differences in Whites' Racial Attitudes: Are Women's Attitudes Really More Favorable?" *Social Psychology Quarterly*, 66(4): 384–401.

McDonald, Melissa M., Carlos D. Navarrete, and Jim Sidanius. 2011. "Developing a Theory of Gendered Prejudice: An Evolutionary and Social Dominance Perspective." In *Social Cognition, Social Identity, and Intergroup Relations: A Festschrift in Honor of Marilynn B. Brewer*, edited by Roderick M. Kramer, Geoffrey J. Leonardelli, and Robert W. Livingston, 189–220. New York: Psychology Press.

Nunner-Winkler, Gertrud. 2005. "Changes in Moral Understanding – an Intergenerational Comparison." In *Morality in Context*, edited by Wolfgang Edelstein and Gertrud Nunner-Winkler, 273–291. Amsterdam: Elsevier.

Wahl, Klaus. 2002. "Development of Xenophobia and Aggression." *International Journal of Comparative and Applied Criminal Justice*, 26: 247–256.

Yin-Yang

WONG KIN-YUEN
Hong Kong Shue Yan University, People's Republic of China

The two characters *yin* 陰 and *yang* 陽 first appear in *Shijing* 詩經 (*Book of Poetry*), meaning simply "shade" and "sunshine." *Yin* and *yang* are then adopted as *kun* 坤 and *qian* 乾, respectively, as the first two primary *qua*(s) 卦 in *Yijing* 易經 (*Book of Change*). As the first *qua* in *Zhouyi* 周易, *qian* etymologically is made up of a sun giving life to the plantation world, hence symbolizing *tien* 天 (sky), while *kun* figures a procreative line across the land or earth, giving rise to all life forms. Diagrammatically, *qian* is represented by two trigrams forming a hexagram of six solid lines ☰, designating the *yang* principle with qualities such as initiative, masculinity, firmness, action, and the spreading of heavenly *qi* 氣 (energy). *Kun* on the other hand and in contrast with *qian*, "responds" to *qian*'s all pervasive *qi* by opening up itself, configured by the hexagram of six broken lines ☷, and is attributed with characteristics such as passivity, submissiveness, absorption of life energies, and as obliging as the flow of water but possessing an extensive life-producing capacity. Hence, *yin-yang* embodies a correlation of the Chinese cosmology of at once coexisting and succession, modulating the vital *qi* as a dynamic processuality. All the 64 hexagrams become "combinations of continuous and discontinuous features deriving from one another according to the level of a spiral that figures the set of moments through which the transcendent descends" (Deleuze and Guattari 1994, 89). One should note that the all-male six solid lines resemble the male sex organ, whereas the all-female six broken lines represent the female sex organ both pictorially and symbolically. In science, Leibniz (1994, 73) acknowledges that such *yin-yang* "analogy to creation" would contain his "binary arithmetic" that he "rediscovered after so many years where all numbers are written by only two notations: 0 and 1." Needless to say, Leibniz's 0 and 1 easily reminds us of our being "digital" in the twenty-first century.

Although Confucius proclaims that "one *yin* and one *yang* make up *Dao*" 道 (way-making) itself, it is also under Confucianism that *yin-yang* is transformed into two hierarchical male and female principles, inscribing *yin-yang* within a set of natural laws. Originally, as beautifully configured in the famous *Tai-ji* 太極 emblem, *yin* and *yang* curve into each other, proliferating into an infinite sum of multiple, non-linear, and relational assemblages between structure and change, embracing a nuanced and overlapping difference without a concrete model, coextensive with the eventful and emergent process of fluid and rotational connectivities. Unfortunately, a part of Confucianism is responsible for having allocated *yin* and *yang* with various and contrastive values in relation to epistemology, ontology, aesthetics, and social order. Henceforth, Confucianism is described as a *yang* school of thinking and practice, whereas Daoism has kept its major tenet as a philosophy valorizing *yin* characteristics. To highlight this point we need to go to a recent translation of the famous passage in Laozi's 老子 *Daodejing* 道德經 which directly unpacks the secret of the Daoist *yin-yang* nature-thought:

> Way-making (*dao*) gives rise to continuity, continuity gives rise to difference, difference gives rise to plurality. And plurality gives rise to the manifold of everything that is happening (*wanwu*). Everything carries *yin* on its shoulders and *yang* in its arms and blend these vital energies (*qi*) together to make them harmonious (*he*). (Ames and Hall, 2003, 142–143)

This new rendition succeeds in capturing the Daoist emphasis on the graduational, at once contracting and synthesizing as an ongoing continuum of a single emanation of *yin-yang* forces. Here *yin-yang* is bodied forth in a kind of "nomad" thinking which is meant to crack open any binary structure, equating the "one" with "continuity," which entails the necessity of "two" to become creative difference. Difference as embodiment of *yin-yang* would have to be followed by "three" as "plurality" which delves into the realm of virtuality and intensity. This emanative nature of *dao*, therefore, buttresses the argument that Chinese classical thought is neither transcendental nor empirical, but rather, as Deleuze and Guattari (1994, 74) point out, aspires towards a "relative transcendence" and an "absolutization of immanence" all at once. If two is taken as becoming-difference, it reverberates with the Deleuzian difference-in-itself which disavows any dualisms rooted in patriarchal societies. Here the grid network of intersecting *yin-yang* forces borne out of the processuality of *dao* is firmly grafted not onto a platform of One and the Many, but one *with* the many. This is why Deleuze and Guattari (1994, 916) affirm that *yin-yang* functions as "a sort of to-ing and fro-ing," which "inscribes the diagrammatic movement of a Nature-thought on the plane, *yin* and *yang*." We now understand the original logic of *yin-yang* as non-hierarchical ordinals leading to coordinates of things, making up a pulverizing machine into which distributed elements are fed and out of which patterns of things emerge. It certainly runs counter to the long-time privileging and veneration of *yang* over *yin* by the hegemonic and deep-seated dualistic sexism, sedimented over centuries in popular religions and cultural practices. *Yang* has been assigned to the rational, the living, and the sublime, while *yin* degraded into chaos, death, and abjection. This means that women in China have been victimized to become despicable as being filthy, monstrous, waste or dung, as "defilement and pollution," and "exclusion or taboo" (Kristeva 1982, 17). As we know, dualisms of this kind have proliferated throughout the world, and the variegated structures of such have prompted feminists such as Donna Haraway (1991, 177) to declare that "One is too few, but two are too many"; and we contend that this might have been the reason for Ames and Hall's choice of turning the Chinese *er* 二 (two) into difference rather than the cardinal number itself.

It can then be argued that Laozi's *yin-yang* would be an essential point of reference to feminists today, especially to those who promugate difference feminism beyond egalitarianism. We know that Laozi repeatedly highlights the superiority of stillness or non-action, and the natural tendency of flowing water as the ultimate female power, giving rise to a system of coordinates of active material agents embracing astrology, mathematics, and biological elements. It also initiates the *yin-yang* cult of sex practice with religious and medical implications, emphasizing the mutual transformative of *yin* and *yang* through specific training programs of the sex act. Such a practice has become famous or notorious; and even Deleuze and Guattari (1988, 157) refer to it as the Daoist "formation of a circuit of intensities between female and male energy" in *A Thousand Plateaus*, although their understanding of "restraining from ejaculation on the part of man" as a way of making oneself a body without organs might have been questionable. At any rate, we can still reaffirm *yin-yang* as a life-producing machinery, or what Deleuze calls a "desiring machine;" and on this score we can turn to Luce Irigaray for further support. Despite the hegemonic dualisms Haraway warns us against, Irigaray turns around and revalorizes the "two" as the primordial ontological base of sexual difference. As a difference feminist, Irigaray is adamant about the creative forces she finds in the sexual coupling of a man and a woman. Echoing Darwin's natural selection, she construes sexual difference as the most fundamental source of life, since "The natural, aside from the diversity of its incarnations or ways of appearing, is at least two: male and female" (Irigaray 1996, 37). Here Irigaray is virtually agreeing with *Zhuangzi* 莊子 when he says the Dragon "riding on the clouds and feeding itself on the Vital energy of *yin* and *yang*" (*Zhuangzi* 1999, 239) and "A male insect buzzes in the distance while the female insect echoes against the wind and pregnancy (*feng-hua* 風化, wind-transformation) takes place" (1999, 243). Without mentioning the concept, Irigaray (1995, 191) is practically relying on the *yin-yang* principle when she argues that sexual difference "allows us to promote the recognition of all forms of others without hierarchy, privilege or authority over them: whether it be differences in race, age, culture, religion."

Feminists should be curious as to why in the expression *yin-yang*, *yin* categorically comes before *yang*, whereas the Chinese always say, father-mother, man-woman, sky-earth, light-darkness, life-death and *qian-kun*, and so on. This may have been attributed to our discovery of the earlier but lost *Yi*, entitled *Guicang* 歸藏, which, through fragments that have been preserved, has *kun* as the very first *qua* instead of *qian*, apparently due to its matriarchal influences during the Yin 殷 dynasty. Such a primacy granted to the *yin* principle should be taken seriously for our purpose of revitalizing the hidden collective unconscious concerning *yin-yang* itself. Armed with such a qualitative shift, we can move away from the "prudery" bias imposed on *yin-yang*, and welcome back the mythological and distributive "prurience" dynamics of *yin* power (Wawrytko 2000). This is to reinvent the kind of *yin-yang* dualism – if we still wish to keep this word – which, with its concomitantly projecting and reciprocating vicissitudes, defines what it cuts into as a dynamic continuity and difference. After all, Haraway has alerted us that there is "a need for a theory of 'difference' whose geometries, paradigms and logics break out of binaries, dialectics and nature/culture models of any kind. Otherwise, threes will always reduce to twos, which quickly became lonely ones in the vanguard. And no one learns to count to four. These things matter politically" (Haraway 1991, 129).

SEE ALSO: Cyborg Manifesto; Daoism; Feminism, Chinese

REFERENCES

Ames, Roger T., and David L. Hall. 2003. *A Philosophical Translation: Dao De Jing*. New York: Ballantine Books.

Deleuze, Gilles, and Felix Guattari. 1988. *A Thousand Plateaus: Capitalism and Schizophrenia*,

trans. Brian Massumi. London: The Athlone Press.
Deleuze, Gilles, and Felix Guattari. 1994. *What is Philosophy?* trans. Hugh Tomlinson and Graham Burchell. New York: Columbia University Press.
Haraway, Donna J. 1991. *Simians, Cyborgs, and Women: The Reinvention of Nature*. New York: Routledge.
Irigaray, Luce. 1995. "The Question of the Other." *Yale French Studies*, 87: 7–19.
Irigaray, Luce. 1996. *I Love to You: Sketch of a Possible Felicity in History*, trans. Alison Martin. London: Routledge.
Kristeva, Julia. 1982. *Powers of Horror: An Essay on Abjection*, trans. Leons Roudiez. New York: Columbia University Press.
Laozi. 1999. Trans. Arthur Waley, revised and annotated by Fu Heisheng. Hunan: Hunan People's Publishing House.
Leibniz, Gottfried Wilhelm. 1994. *Writings On China*, trans. Daniel J. Cook and Henry Rosemont Jr. Chicago: Open Court.
Wawrytko, Sandra A. 2000. "Prudery and Prurience: Historical Roots of the Confucian Conundrum Concerning Women, Sexuality, and Power." In *The Sage and the Second Sex: Confucianism, Ethics, and Gender*, edited by Chenyang Li, 163–197. Chicago: Open Court.
Zhuangzi. 1999. Trans. Wang Rongpei. Hunan: Hunan People's Publishing House.

FURTHER READING

The Complete I Ching. 1998. Trans. Alfred Huang. Rochester: Inner Traditions.

Yogyakarta Principles

RYAN RICHARD THORESON
New York, USA

The Yogyakarta Principles are a soft-law instrument that affirms that human rights protections must fully extend to those marginalized on the basis of sexual orientation and gender identity (SOGI). They are not independently binding upon states, but instead draw their force from widely accepted obligations states must follow under international law.

The Principles followed early efforts to gain formal recognition for SOGI in the international arena. At the Fourth World Conference on Women in Beijing in 1995, sexual rights activists fought unsuccessfully to ensure that a reference to "sexual orientation" would survive into the final Platform for Action (Girard 2007). In 2003, when Brazil introduced a resolution on human rights and sexual orientation for consideration by the UN Commission on Human Rights, activists again met with strong opposition. Under significant pressure from the Holy See and the Organization of the Islamic Conference, the resolution was postponed, and Brazil ultimately opted not to reintroduce it (Girard 2007). In late 2006, 54 states issued a joint statement before the UN Human Rights Council expressing "deep concern" over human rights violations on the basis of SOGI. Although these efforts made headway in building support, explicit recognition of SOGI in binding international law remained elusive.

In November 2006, a group of experts gathered at Gadjah Mada University in Yogyakarta, Indonesia, for a meeting on SOGI and human rights chaired by Sonia Onufer Corrêa and Vitit Muntarbhorn. The Yogyakarta Principles were born of this meeting, endorsed by 29 human rights experts who became its signatories, and launched in March 2007. The signatories included UN Special Rapporteurs, members of treaty monitoring bodies, and former UN High Commissioner for Human Rights Mary Robinson, in addition to activists, academics, and domestic judges and policymakers (O'Flaherty and Fisher 2008).

The Principles articulate 29 precepts of international law and affirm they must be enjoyed by all people regardless of SOGI.

The Preamble articulates the understanding of SOGI on which the Principles are based. It defines sexual orientation as referring "to each person's capacity for profound emotional, affectional and sexual attraction to, and intimate and sexual relations with, individuals of a different gender or the same gender or more than one gender," and gender identity as referring "to each person's deeply felt internal and individual experience of gender, which may or may not correspond with the sex assigned at birth, including the personal sense of the body (which may involve, if freely chosen, modification of bodily appearance or function by medical, surgical or other means) and other expressions of gender, including dress, speech and mannerisms" (Yogyakarta Principles 2007). Under this definition, gender identity is understood to encompass gender expression.

In order, the Principles affirm rights to: universal enjoyment of human rights; equality and non-discrimination; recognition before the law; life; security of the person; privacy; freedom from arbitrary deprivation of liberty; fair trial; treatment with humanity while in detention; freedom from torture and cruel, inhuman, or degrading treatment or punishment; protection from all forms of exploitation, sale, and trafficking of human beings; work; social security and other social protection measures; an adequate standard of living; adequate housing; education; the highest attainable standard of health; protection from medical abuses; freedom of opinion and expression; freedom of peaceful assembly and association; freedom of thought, conscience, and religion; freedom of movement; seek asylum; found a family; participate in public life; participate in cultural life; promote human rights; effective remedies and redress; and accountability.

The Principles canvass the rights laid out in a number of canonical international human rights instruments, particularly those enshrined in widely ratified treaties such as the International Covenant on Civil and Political Rights (ICCPR), International Covenant on Economic, Social, and Cultural Rights (ICESCR), Convention on the Elimination of All Forms of Discrimination Against Women (CEDAW), and Convention on the Rights of the Child (CRC). The Principles do not assert rights, such as same-sex marriage, that may be recognized in some jurisdictions but are not yet codified in international law. To give full force to the rights that they specify, each Principle is accompanied by recommendations detailing how states might fully comply with their obligations.

Shortly after their adoption, activists began using the Principles in pursuit of advocacy goals (Thoreson 2009). Activists have used the Principles to press for legal change, promote policy reform, bolster government responsiveness, engage in public education, and build movements, and these efforts are actively tracked and catalogued (Yogyakarta Principles 2014). They have experienced both tangible and intangible success. Perhaps most notably, the Principles were cited by the Delhi High Court in the *Naz Foundation* ruling, which decriminalized same-sex activity in India from 2009 to 2013.

The Principles have not been free from controversy. States at the UN that generally oppose recognition of SOGI, or sexual rights broadly, object that SOGI is not a recognized concept at the UN, and stress that the Principles themselves are not binding in international law. The objections have been voiced in side events before the General Assembly, efforts to pass non-binding statements and resolutions, and non-governmental organization (NGO) efforts to receive special consultative status before the UN Economic and Social Council (ECOSOC). LGBT (lesbian, gay, bisexual, and transgender) activists and supportive states have been careful to recognize that the Principles are not binding law in themselves, but do provide expert guidance on the binding human rights obligations that states parties have assumed.

SEE ALSO: Human Rights, International Laws and Policies on; Sexual Orientation and the Law

REFERENCES

Girard, Françoise. 2007. "Negotiating Sexual Rights and Sexual Orientation at the UN." *Sex-Politics: Reports from the Frontlines*, 311–358. Rio de Janeiro: Sexuality Policy Watch.

O'Flaherty, Michael, and John Fisher. 2008. "Sexual Orientation, Gender Identity and International Human Rights Law: Contextualising the Yogyakarta Principles." *Human Rights Law Review*, 8(2): 207–248.

Thoreson, Ryan Richard. 2009. "Queering Human Rights: the Yogyakarta Principles and the Norm that Dare Not Speak Its Name." *Journal of Human Rights*, 8(4): 323–339.

Yogyakarta Principles. 2007. *The Yogyakarta Principles. Principles on the Application of International Human Rights Law in Relation to Sexual Orientation and Gender Identity*. Accessed June 11, 2015, at http://www.yogyakartaprinciples.org/principles_en.pdf.

Yogyakarta Principles. 2014. *Yogyakarta Principles in Action*. Accessed June 4, 2014, at http://www.ypinaction.org.

Yoruba Culture, Religion, and Gender

MENOUKHA CASE
SUNY Empire State College, USA

The traditional religion of the Yoruba is *Ifa/Orisha* worship. Yoruba language, everyday life, and religious tenets are inextricably linked. Since the Yoruba language is largely gender neutral and traditional Yoruba culture is gender balanced, this religious family offers insights into non-Western ways of thinking about gender that are shared among many indigenous groups. Western gendering expects behavior and abilities to accord with genitalia; of particular interest are clear distinctions between anatomical sex, sexuality, personal characteristics, and social function. These distinctions remain evident in contemporary religious practices despite a history of severe patriarchal constraints through colonialism in Africa and slavery in the Americas. This entry draws on Menoukha Case, *Ori and the Ethical Subject: Pro Indigenous Readings of African Diaspora Literature in Yoruba* (Case 2007), to outline the key dimensions of gender in Yoruba culture and religion.

Indigenous to West Africa, forms of *Ifa/Orisha* worship became global through both voluntary and involuntary Diaspora and are part of religions such as Vodun (Benin), Candomble (Brazil), Santeria (Cuba, United States, Mexico), and Voodoo (United States) and also many relatives and branches. One of the earliest migrations from the stated birth place of Ile Ife, Nigeria, was to Benin, where aspects of the religion combined with local practices to become Vodun, and where the divination system is known as Fa. The latter days of the slave trade were synchronous with West African battles, which the Yoruba lost, so they comprised a large proportion of the last wave of enslaved Africans to be brought to the Americas, including the Caribbean. There the Yoruba religion flourished in many forms, sometimes combining with the religions of other ethnic groups according to the make-up of enslaved populations. Aspects of Indigenous American religions also came to be part of prayers and practices as a way of honoring the host land. Imposed aspects of Christianity also made inroads. Among each member of this family of religions there are various sects that include or sequester these facets differently, and among many, the Yoruba thread remains strong. In addition, post-slavery voluntary migrations have brought Yoruba culture and religion to all regions of the globe and revitalized theology and practices. The presence of a Yoruba thread in a religion may be indicated by specific ways in which gender matters or fails to matter in religious roles and practices.

While local variations are intrinsic to the principles of *Ifa* and *Orisha*, other changes have been wrought by patriarchal colonialism. Still, we will see how traditional gendering, carefully cordoned from biology and social function, remain vital in religious concepts and practices. Since secular and religious spheres are integrally related and mirror each other, we will begin with a foundation in the elements of everyday life, such as language, family structure, male and female social roles, and governance.

One of the most important aspects of any culture is language, the structure of which may open or close the mind and heart to specific perceptions. For the subject of this encyclopedia, gender in language is a prominent example, and one with which we need to take special care when "translating" from one culture to another. In studying Yoruba culture and religion, that translation issue is literal. For example, Yoruba pronouns are not gendered, but gender must be chosen in translation, and mistranslation can lead to misinterpretation. Such misinterpretations can prevent us from perceiving how religious practices reflect social organization based on a different way of "doing" gender that is possible when a language is largely gender neutral.

Western writers have long struggled with the way inescapably gendered pronouns permeate English, for example, replacing the "he" that stands in for all people with "s/he" or "her" and "his" with the grammatically inaccurate "their." Such adaptations may point to, rather than resolve, the problems of gender rigidity and inequity. However, the problem of circumventing or violating grammar to free imagination never existed in Yoruba. Table 1 demonstrates key words referring to persons.

Table 2 demonstrates key words referring to family roles. When shifting from persons to families, it becomes impossible to utilize English as the originating category – that only results in mistranslations and misinterpretations. The roles are so innately different that we must go the other way around. For example, while the phrase "primary family unit" brings "Mom, Dad, children" to the Western mind, in Yoruba it is a maternal line-child unit called *omoya*.

Since one's maternal uncle is greeted as "my mother," and paternal aunt as "my father," clearly lineage is privileged, not anatomical, sex. Thus what appears as gender in mistranslation instead reflects lines of responsibility. For example, a woman marrying into a compound calls her sister-in-law *oko*, and their joint responsibility for the children is determined accordingly; as an *Iya* heading an *omoya*, she also has responsibility towards her siblings' children.

Collectively, these linguistic indications of family structure demonstrate a system of communal co-mothering that does not rely on biological motherhood. Birth and infancy aside, anyone can mother, father, or take on any social role. However, motherhood in the sense of gestating, birthing, and nursing a child is clearly tied to anatomical sex (Oyeronke Oyewumi, personal communication, August 2005). Thus, while mothering is done by many and the social term for mother, *Iya*, can refer to a man in the mother's lineage, the anatomical word for motherhood, *ikunle abiyamo*, denotes a woman kneeling in the labor position; only women own motherhood. Such potential is considered god-like: "*e wo le fobinrin, orisa l'obinrin* – give women due respect, women are like gods" (Olajubu 2003). Women are co-creators of human beings, along with the androgynous deity *Orisha Obatala*, the creative artist who shapes the child within the mother's womb.

Table 1 Persons

English	Yoruba	Explanation
He, she, or it	o	There is no indication of anatomical sex
Hers, his, or its	re	Non-human beings are not set aside as objects
Human and mankind	eniyan	The word for human beings does not rely on the word for adult males
Child	omo	This is the usual terminology for both sons and daughters
Daughter	omo ti a bi li obinrin	There are relatively rare and particular situational reasons to signify a child's gender
Son	omo ti a bi li okunrin	This longer phrase can be used if there is such a reason and the sex of the child is relevant to a discussion
Anatomical adult male	okunrin	This refers to an anatomical male of reproductive age
Anatomical adult female	obinrin	This refers to an anatomical female of reproductive age

Table 2 Family roles

Yoruba	Explanation	English mistranslation
Omoya (elision of omo iya, children of one mother)	A mother, her children, and her nieces and nephews in the maternal line. Note how a woman and her siblings are "one"	Western family = parents/child, so this is misperceived as a subset of male-dominant polygamy
Iyawo	The word members born to a compound, male and female, used to refer to women marrying in	Translated as Wife, the word is used by many people other than the husband
Oko	The word women marrying into a compound used to refer to all their husband's blood relatives, male and female	Translated as Husband, the word refers to many people other than the husband
Iya	The mother and all her siblings, male and female	Translated as Mother, the word refers to all the mother's *omoya*
Baba	The father and all his siblings, male and female	Translated as Father, the word refers to all the father's *omoya*
Egbon	Older sibling	This replaces sister or brother as in "child" in Table 1
Aburo	Younger sibling	Similarly, a longer phrase can indicate the sex of the sibling

Motherhood, however, does not impede on women's social roles: "in Africa the idea of a full-time housewife is alien'" (Johnson-Phipps 2002). Yoruba culture is cosmopolitan, with many families owning both country homes (for farming, primarily attended by men) and city homes for trading (primarily women) and governance (both). Although, on the whole, traditional Yoruba culture was more economically equitable than Western European cultures, within this model there is variance in economic status, and that status differential may exist within the family itself. Since women are economically independent, they may acquire greater status than their husbands, and their reputations rely on professional accomplishments rather than marriage. However, kinship networks include multi-directional lines of redistribution of the fruits of success; this traditional model has been eroded by colonialism, which valorizes both the patriarchal nuclear family, and having more than one's neighbor.

To this day, Yoruba women in West Africa are often self-employed traders; older women care for children so they can pursue their work. A successful woman may purchase land and build her own dwelling. Since there is no stigma associated with divorce, some women retire to such homes after their children have been raised. She may also build a home at her birth compound, to reunite with siblings and/or care for elderly parents. Since the age of those born to a compound is a primary determinant of seniority regardless of sex, women who return to their *omoya* are called *Baba* by younger members of the household. Mothers and elderly women use phrases such as "*o kare, baba mi*" – "well done, my father" to praise or persuade children of both sexes (Kehinde 2002). Although there are various interpretations of this cultural practice, the point is that the child is referred to as *Baba* whether male or female, and that the *Baba* proffered as a role model may be a male or female, and may be an older woman.

Many proper names do not reveal the sex of a person, and in marriage wives do not take husbands' names. The man is as likely to be referred to as "that person's husband" as the woman is "that person's wife." Similarly, the distinction between princess and prince does not exist in Yoruba: both are called *Omo Oba* based on the gender-neutral words for "child" and "ruler." These kinds of linguistic features bypass the way in which English encodes sexism, as in the examples above, and including words that demean women. It especially forecloses demeaning language tied to reproductive usefulness, such as "old maid, spinster, hag" for a woman who is no longer valuable and therefore outside patriarchal protection. Elderly women are revered and powerful in traditional Yoruba culture, as evident in family structure and governance.

Yoruba scholars confirm that gendered social roles exist, but society follows the more powerful adage to "concede to each person his or her own character." Trading is women's realm, and other professional roles are also gendered – men carve, women make clay pots – but since the Yoruba primarily perceive a spectrum of individuals, these roles are not fixed. Thus a "woman artist … [who] carves twin figures" is "only one among many [who] … contravened normal practice; she had the power to 'act otherwise'" (Drewal and Drewal 1990). Neither men nor women, then, are excluded from any aspect of society. Because of this, elder women were traditionally found in every level of governance. One of the most important decision-making groups still extant in some Yoruba villages is the *Ogboni* council. It is composed of elder men and women whose emblem is *onile*, paired brass sculptures linked by a chain, identical except for genitalia. These represent spiritual aspects of the grandfathers and grandmothers of the council. Council deliberations may be presented to the *Oba* (ruler), who sets aside her or his personhood and allows spirit to speak. Traditional Yoruba decision-making, then, is gender-balanced consensus mediated by spirit (Fatunmbi 2005).

The women of this council are called *Iyaami Osoronga*, our powerful mothers. *Iyaami* long retained – and in some locales still retain – an intrinsic role in what became known as king-making when the gender-neutral term *Oba* became king through British decree. The *Oba*'s regalia, the crown and staff, are topped by birds, emblem of the *Iyaami*. Without the continuing ritual endorsement of these powerful mothers, no-one can be *Oba*. Andrew Apter witnessed the annual ceremony in which a mother recharged authority by holding a calabash crowned with red parrot feathers on the *Oba*'s head. Power surged through the *Oba*, expressed as a tremor of the arms. If the ruler had proved deficient, the same calabash would be delivered with the feathers inside, a signal that required abdication (Apter 1992). In another dethroning ceremony, women may convict the ruler of wrongdoing by appearing semi-nude, reminding the *Oba* of the source of life and power.

Olajubu notes that "women have been active contributors to the Yoruba polity throughout history;" that is, both men and women have had authority (Olajubu 2003). Historically, male *Iyawo* of the *Oba* of Oyo have been delegated crucial aspects of governance; women have been *Oba* in Oyo, and they too had male *Iyawo*. Authority has nothing to do with either the sexed body or virility; while the literal, generative aspect of secular motherhood, *ikunle abiyamo*, is necessarily sexed, we have seen that mothering responsibilities are not necessarily sexed, either. We can see via language, family structure, social roles, and governance that a complementary system of checks and balances between male and female is intrinsic to Yoruba philosophy, and that anatomy did not traditionally limit roles.

While no one contests the presence of sexism in contemporary life, it is not inherently Yoruba. It did, however, arrive with colonialism in West Africa, and was relentlessly present for enslaved Yoruba in the Americas. Oyeronke Olajubu (2003), Oyeronke Oyewumi (1997; personal communication, August 2005), Chandra Mohanty et al. (1991), Jacqui Alexander (2005), Andy Smith (1997), and others foreground colonization as the most severe oppression for indigenous cultures, such as the Yoruba, that do not posit male superiority over nature or women, and therefore did not have sexism to begin with (Smith 1997). Colonialism and patriarchy displaced women from traditional roles; only men were permitted to hold authoritative positions, and women were expected to become their subordinates. Among the Yoruba in Nigeria, the British appointed male puppets to governance positions, and actively persecuted entire female categories of authority. For example, the British outlawed the *Iyaami* Society to prevent them from removing the puppet kings from office. To put bite in their policy, they systematically destroyed *Iyaami* shrines. Before leaving Nigeria in the 1950s, British Christian ministers went through the country burning down the *iroko* trees where *Iyaami* meet, "based on the belief that speaking with your ancestors is the work of the devil"(Fatunmbi 2005). In Ode Remo, Nigeria, a Christian church was built on the sacred site used by the women to initiate into *Iyaami*. "When the church was completed, the women of *Iyaami* burned it to the ground and continue to use the site for the rituals" (Fatunmbi 2005).

If colonial oppression of women was severe in Africa, it was worse in the Americas, where slaves had little recourse. Still, Yoruba cultural principles, beleaguered yet intact, appear in many aspects of Diaspora religions. When two or more religions are mixed to form a third, it is called syncretism, and debates on whether this applies to *Santeria* are extensive and complex. Wande Abimbola, a Nigerian Yoruba, visited with Cubans who carried Yoruba religion through slavery as *Santeria*. He noted that "When a [priest] tells [traditional Yoruba] stories ... in Cuba, he doesn't mix it with stories from the Bible. What is called syncretism has mainly to do with ... icons ... and this is sometimes just a way of saluting the divinity of a neighbor ... if it were truly syncretic, then not just the outward and visual levels [would] be affected ... you don't find mixture in the liturgy and thought system" (Abimbola and Miller 1997). One mode of sustaining *Orisha* was to hide them in plain sight – for example, Shango worship was disguised as devotion to Saint Barbara. The saintly "masks" chosen to hide an Orisha were selected due to commonalities: Shango's colors are red and white, as are Saint Barbara's robes. More importantly, her father, who cut off her head when she refused to marry, was struck dead by Shango's lightning. That Shango can be worshipped under the guise of a female saint demonstrates how Yoruba gender norms were secretly and not-so-secretly maintained in religious praxis.

To understand how this religion survived every attempt at eradication, we need to understand how language and everyday principles made this possible. In short, being the possessor of values that obviate Western values empowered enslaved Africans to retain, secretly express, and intergenerationally transmit the inner core of Yoruba religion. This begins with the very concept of God. Returning to Table 1, note that there is one pronoun for all beings. Non-humans are not considered objects, but agents with consciousness, intelligence, and, in many cases, more wisdom than humans. This is not unusual in indigenous cultures and is often termed animism. Likewise, fluid, collective forces of nature are also considered intelligent agents, which is often perceived as polytheism. This means that the displaced or enslaved person, acting in a world brimming with active power, had resources unimagined by those who believe God to be in a separate realm.

However, just as the family in mistranslation offers no real sense of Yoruba polity and culture, words such as animism and polytheism offer no real sense of *Ifa/Orisha* religions. The selected key terms in Table 3 broach their complexity and also illustrate how gender changed in Diaspora, in this case due to Spanish patriarchy in Cuba. However, a table cannot convey the nuances of these terms in relationship to each other. We will examine how they work together step-by-step.

Olodumare, even when personified for the purposes of stories, is absolutely neither he nor she. This is easy to convey in Yoruba, but English writers refer to *Olodumare* as He. *Olodumare* is not separate from or above "his" creation as in Biblical religions. Rather, *Olodumare* is genderless, divine energy that is immanent in everything. Therefore, monotheism and immanence are not mutually exclusive. Rather, immanent monotheism, while firmly centered in a unified transpersonal Source, includes us in that Source and that Source in us, much like a matrix imprints DNA. Therefore, the Yoruba concept of God transcends and includes us: "divinity abides in humanity and vice versa" (Lawal 2001).

The divine energy permeating all creation is called *ashe*. "Olodumare, the supreme being, is a transcendent world force or 'current' known as ashe. This sacred energy becomes the power, grace, blood and life force of all reality ... Ashe is absolute illimitable, pure power, nondefinite and nondefinable" (de la Torre 2001). *Ashe* is present in "rocks, hills, streams, mountains, leaves, animals, sculpture, ancestors, and gods – prayers, songs, curses, and even everyday speech." (Drewal and Drewal 1990). While always indefinite and changeable, it simultaneously has temporary definition when it particularizes as, say, a rock.

Particularized *ashe* provides a locus in which a unique manifestation of consciousness resides. The unique consciousness identified with a given form is called *Ori*. To use the Yoruba description, *Ori* is the self that dances on the mat, the interwoven unity of Creation (Fatunmbi 2005). *Ori* is mental, emotional, physical, and transcendent:

Table 3 The sacred

Yoruba	Shorthand explanation	Santeria	Shorthand explanation	English mistranslation
Olodumare	One of many names for the Primal Source of divine universal energy	Same	Same	God
Ase, Ashe pronounced ah-shay	Divine energy enlivening and inherent in all entities	Same	Same	No equivalent
Ori – literally, head, but a complex of multiple aspects	Individual divine consciousness	Same	Same	Soul
Iponri	Collective divine consciousness	Same	Same	No equivalent
Orisha – literally, selected head	Forces of nature and/or crossroads of *ashe*	Same	Same	Gods
Egun	Ancestral collective based on family, Table 2, actively involved in daily life and energetically accessible "from the ground up"	Same	Same	Individual blood-line ancestors may be thought of as "looking down from heaven"

Ori-ode means "outer head," *Ori-inu* means "inner head" and also includes *enikeji*, a spirit with whom one makes a covenant before being born. Life consists of remembering and aligning with that covenant (Drewal and Drewal 1990). To be born physically, one selects from "a collection of … heads molded by Ajala, the heavenly potter. … these … look similar, though each is intrinsically different. … The one selected … constitut[es] the inner core … and determin[es] a person's lot on earth" (Lawal 2001). The Yoruba concept of self is thus based on the premise that one is a subject, an agent, who becomes a finite being by active choice. Importantly, since the heads are neither male nor female, the primary indicator of Yoruba identity is gender free.

There are 20 linked aspects of *Ori*: "*tikara-eni*, the Yoruba word for self … is an elision of *ti ika ara eni*, meaning one who surrounds the physical body … described as a calabash holding the head and the heart"

(Fatunmbi 2005). So, while *Ori* is associated with the head, we cannot mistake it for rational thought. The 20 aspects include intuition, feelings, and so on. *Ori* is elevated above all but *Olodumare*: "It is my *Ori* to whom I will give praise/My *Ori* it is you/All the good things I have on earth/It is *Ori* I will praise/My *Ori* it is you" (Lawal 2001). *Ori* worship consists of "specific techniques to facilitate the integration of new information and new experiences" (Fatunmbi 2005).

In addition, multiple consciousnesses interconnect as a spiritual identity called *iponri*, also associated with *egungun*, ancestral collectives. Each being, seen and unseen, past and present, contributes to a matrix of accountability. In this way, *Ori*, with its complex of concepts involving head, heart, self, others, past, and future, is the locus of the ethical subject. This critical and central concept of what it means to exist and how to exist is utterly gender free and is the foundation of all Yoruba philosophy and practices.

If we each carry internal divinity (*Ori*), then natural forces are hyper-powerful external deities. An *Orisha* is "selected" consciousness that acts with intensity beyond comprehension. The Wind, Ocean, a particular River, and so on, is understood as an enormous nexus of divine energy that dwarfs humans. *Ashe* continually permeates everything, never placing human over nature, never favoring white over black, male over female, rich over poor, distributed as the unique *Ori* in each entity – and thus there is a multiplicity of *Orisha*. *Orisha*, then, are 401 (with one standing for "more than you can imagine") proto-manifestations of *ashe*, situated at the juncture of nature and ethics, science, and art. All earthly existence and every *Ori* choice circulate in and out of these Divine Natural Forces (breathing > speaking; eating/drinking > acting); therefore, *Orisha* receive devotion as an accessible midrange between the abstract cosmological *Olodumare* and lived earthly experience.

It is in such deities that fluid, complementary gender is best preserved. Applying Western gender constructs to Yoruba deities is not strictly possible. The English word "gender" is signified with five Yoruba words: *imo ako tabi abo yato*, literally "knowledge male or female (of beasts) different." If gender does not apply to human behavior, the divine *Orisha* are often ambiguously or multiply sexed, and are always ambiguous and variable in terms of Western gendered behavior norms. A few examples illuminate this.

Orisha Shango, the virile, masculine thunder deity, wields gender balance with his two-headed butterfly/axe: "In Nigeria ... men dance for *Sango* ... either in women's clothes or with a woman's hairdo. This ... is a symbolic manifestation of the deep mystery of balance" (Fatunmbi 2005).

Orisha Yemoja is called "the great mother," but at times wears warrior's clothing, bears a machete, and fights alongside her son, *Shango*. According to Lydia Cabrera, she is "*androgino, de sexo anfibio. Asi se dice El mar. Y hembra, La Mar, lo es en otros aspetos.*" This translates as "androgynous, of amphibious sex. Thus we say The Sea [with masculine pronoun]. And The Sea, [with feminine pronoun], in other aspects" (Cabrera 1980). Cabrera had to break Spanish pronoun rules to make her point, yet *Yemoja* does not change sex when she changes clothing or behavior. Women can be warriors as well as mothers. Machete in hand, *Yemoja* remains a female and *Shango*'s mother, demonstrating a clear distinction between anatomical sex and gender norms.

Orisha Oshun, an alluringly veiled female form in some stories, bears the title *Baale*, father of the house. Referred to in popularized parlance as an "African Venus" that evokes the burden of the Hottentot Venus, stereotypical renditions of her go beyond feminine sensuality and call her a prostitute. However, to devotees, *Oshun* is known as the one who cures with cool, sweet water. She is acclaimed as a mysterious spirit who owns rivers, as the one who flew past the Sun as a peacock to ask God for cooling rain during drought and returned with the burnt bald head and singed tail feathers of a vulture. Yet *Oshun* can also be hot – "*gbona*, to be warm, to have a fever." As a protector, she is the "hot woman who blocks the road (by flooding it)/And causes men to run ... /The powerful and huge woman/Who cannot be captured" (Olajubu 2003).

Like *Yemoja* and *Shango*, *Oshun* demonstrates that "within the Yoruba philosophy of life, there is nothing intrinsically male or female. An anatomical male can be both gentle and ruthless and so can an anatomical female" (Okome 2001). Neither *obinrin* nor *okunrin* mandates "masculinity or femininity, that is, gender performance, because those categories do not exist in Yoruba life or thought" (Oyewumi 1997). The greatly venerated *Oshun*, *Oya*, and *Iyanla* (grandmother or great mother) have beards from time to time; *Obatala* and *Eshu* are sometimes hermaphroditic; *Nana Buruku* conceives children without intercourse; and no-one thinks less of them for it. On the contrary, these aspects are celebrated in their praise songs. They are not human but they do model a crucial schema that applies to humans: taking on metaphorical secondary, or even primary, sex characteristics is in absolutely no conflict with gender characteristics, because, quite simply, while human bodies are sexed, character is not gendered.

The ways of "doing" gender in language, families, governance, and the sacred are also evident in the structure of religious groups and practices, as evidenced in Table 4.

Ifa is central to Yoruba religion. It is a sacred literary corpus consisting of 256 chapters called *Odu* (literally, womb), each comprised of innumerable verses that carry Yoruba history, wisdom, and knowledge, including *Orisha* stories and lore. The reference to womb indicates that given verses transmit how particular knowledge came into existence. The reason why the verses are innumerable is that each locale may add to the core liturgy to reflect its own history and ecology. This wisdom is accessed through divination, and the *Orisha* of divination is *Orunmila*, "witness of creation." The title of *Ifa* diviners is *Awo*; in some communities those who have memorized 1000 verses are called *Babalawo*, "father of secrets," whereas in other communities that title is reserved for *Orunmila*. As described in governance, men and women share authority to assure gender balance, traditionally expressed through the relationship between *Awo* and the *Iyaami* Society. The *Iyaami* are necessary to birth an *Awo*, and must consecrate divining tools each year to renew their *ashe*. If an *Awo* has not behaved with good character, the *Iyaami* Society imposes a "time out" by refusing to consecrate the tools.

While there have always been more male than female *Awo*, again, role follows character rather than anatomy. A contemporary *Babalawo* recently told Oyewumi that his village in Oyo, Nigeria has an organization of 26 *Ifa* priests that includes eight women. The women's titles, too, are *Babalawo*, regardless of their sex (Oyeronke Oyewumi, personal communication, August 2005). Olajubu cites a verse from the first *Odu Ifa*, *Ejiogbe*: "So long as Orunmila's firstborn child/Who is female studied *Ifa*/From then on women Have studied *Ifa*/They prescribe sacrifice/And they are initiated into the *Ifa* corpus" (Olajubu 2003). Fatunmbi says that women are not *Awo* in the Ode Remo lineage, they are intrinsic to and equal in *Ifa* ritual. On the other hand, priests in Abimbola's lineage initiate female *Ifa* priests as *Awo*. Thus, while titles such as *Babalawo* may seem gendered, their application is not based on sex.

Olorisha, *Iyalorisha*, and *Babalorisha* are titles of those initiated to a given *Orisha*. The *Orisha* chooses the person, not the other way round, and does so according to character, not gender or anatomy; a male can be initiated to a female *Orisha*, and vice versa. For example, *Orisha Obatala* tends towards patience and *Orisha Ogun* tends towards quick actions. The *Iya*, *Baba*, and *Olorisha* often serve the community as conduits for the *Orisha* to whom they are initiated. In ritual context, through drum language, the *Orisha* is "called" and acts and speaks through the *Olorisha*. To outsiders, an *Orisha* ceremony can appear as a dizzying nexus of rapidly changing gender displays. Suppose *Yemoja* is called. Her *Babalorisha* spins among a rhythmically shifting wave of dancers who call *Yemoja*'s name. He makes his way to the altar, where he disappears to the floor and rises hidden by several *Olorisha*, and is accompanied inside a small white-curtained enclosure. The next

Table 4 Religious practices and practitioners

Yoruba title or practice	Shorthand explanation	Santeria	Shorthand explanation	English mistranslation
Ifa/Orunmila	Orisha called Witness of Creation who is the keeper of oral liturgy	Same	Same	Westerners may liken Orunmila to Jesus and Ifa to the Bible
Iyaami Osoronga	Spiritual Collective of powerful elder women	Same	Same, but spiritual, not human, since slavery eliminated the Iyaami Society	Witches
Awo	Diviner who interprets oral liturgy	Babalawo	Same, but exclusively male	Wizard
Olorisha – literally, owner of Orisha	Male or female Orisha initiate	Same	Same	Priest or priestess
Iyalorisha – literally, mother of Orisha	Female Orisha initiate who "births" spiritual godchildren	Madrina or Padrino	Person who "births" the new initiate	Priestess
Babalorisha – literally, father of Orisha	Male Orisha initiate who "births" spiritual godchildren	Jubona	Person who supports the person who births	Priest
Iyawo	Initiate with less seniority than the speaker	Same	Initiate in first year	Novitiate
Bi awon Orisha – literally, birth Orisha	Ceremony to make an Olorisha	Kariocha, referred to in English as "making" Ocha (Orisha)	Same; both the person who births and the supporter may be male or female	Initiation
Ebo – literally, doing	Offering	Same	Can consist of objects or actions	Sacrifice

time we see him, he *is* the mother, *he* is *she*, is *Yemoja*, and around *her* waist she wears a blue and white flowing wrap.

That the possessed body is male is irrelevant to us as we salute our mother *Yemoja*. An outsider observes a man speaking in a light voice, wearing something reminiscent of a formal skirt, and dancing the swaying "feminine" dance of the ocean in peaceful mode. If the possessed *Olorisha* happens to be a gay man – and in many houses of worship he is as likely to be as not – the outsider may also infer cross-gender performance. But to devotees, when *Yemoja*, the owner of salt waters, appears among us, she *is* herself, not a man performing *Yemoja*. We are in the presence of an *Orisha* in human clothing, a living metaphor that reveals the meaning of the invisible by clothing it. The possessed young man will not have any memory of the healing, gifts, and advice *Yemoja* bestowed on us through the medium of his body, and when she leaves *he* will dance with us again.

A ceremony like this is a form of *ebo*, the "doing" of worship, sometimes called an offering. *Ebo* can range from physical offerings (feed a deity, feed the poor, feed wild animals) to spiritual offerings (in the divination verse *Ejiogbe* good character is the *ebo*). The purpose of *ebo* is to regain harmony; *ebo* is ethics in action. The Yoruba understanding of ethics goes far in explaining gender neutral culture. *Orisha Eshu*, who is androgynous, sits at every crossroads to remind us of the ramifications of decisions. *Eshu* always receives the first share of any *ebo* because we can never know all the ramifications of any of our choices yet must live with the mystery of continually shifting results. Decisions invoke binaries – right or left? up or down? yes or no? – and Yoruba philosophy posits that consciousness continually constructs our understanding of the world via such binaries. An important distinction from Western use of evaluative binaries, though, is the recognition that they are neutral in the abstract, and that differential value accords with particular situations. We can understand, for example, how hot/cold can be positive or negative depending on the situation: we do not get any use from a hot refrigerator or a cold stove. It is harder for Westerners to imagine binaries such as male/female or dark/light as neutral, weighted as they are with the history of sexism and racism.

The absence of the relentless Western notion of good/evil that is woven tight with most binaries does not, however, point to an absence of ethics. In Yoruba terms, ethics consists of accountability to oneself, family, and the whole, a community that includes what the West calls nature. From this perspective, the crucial task of "choosing your head" is a lifelong continuous process; we continue to affect *Ori* throughout our lives, therefore we must "feed" our heads. The *ebo* – the doing – of the hard work is necessary since we are responsible for attaining the desired results: "if I am created, I will re-create myself … /Having been created, I shall now re-create myself" (Lawal 2001).

It is easy to see how such a complex, nuanced, integrated religion could be misunderstood by colonizers, especially since they had a vested interest in deeming themselves superior to those they invaded. The British refused to deal with *Babalorisha* and *Iyalorisha*, whom they termed idolaters, but they accorded a semblance of respect to *Ifa* priests. As with *Oba*, the British refused to acknowledge female *Ifa* priests and today many people believe that they do not and have never existed; today, Yoruba priests in the Cuban lineage generally will not fully initiate women to *Ifa*. Since gay men are perceived as feminine, they are prohibited from Cuban lineage *Ifa* priesthood as well – though not from *Orisha* priesthood. The appellation *Baba*, simply translated as father, along with the absence of a visible Yoruba "gay lifestyle" due to traditional conventions of sexual privacy, are considered as proof of the correctness of these exclusions. But Fatunmbi writes: "The *Awoni* are … the only people in Nigeria who have the *ase* to change *Odu*. … I asked them if gay men could be *Awo*. They said the only requirement to initiation was willingness to follow the guidance of *Ifa* and the guidance of their elders; otherwise there were no taboos or restrictions to initiation" (Fatunmbi 2005). Gay *Ifa* priests, then, were likely invisible and retained a masculine image in British eyes.

Perhaps *Ifa* also retained a higher reputation than *Orisha* because, while *Ifa* possession is two-headed – the priest remains cognizant and present – *Orisha* possession is one-headed – the priest's head is displaced by the *Orisha*. Such possession, as described above in the *Babalorisha* possessed by *Yemoja*, is highly visible, misunderstood, deemed demonic or immoral, while the apparent self-collection of an *Ifa* priest expounding upon a sacred text has some positive familiarity for Christians. This ironically ignores the fact that the *Orisha* who possess the *Olorisha* are the very same ones who speak through the *Ifa* priest. But *Ifa* priests do not dance their divination or change their clothing or behavior when the *Orisha* speak; rather, their possession is marked by a change in the eyes and hands, akin to what was witnessed by Apter.

Still, the figure of the *Babalawo* did not escape demonization by Nigerian Christians among whom one- versus two-headedness is understood. They are depicted in some videos with "horns sticking out of [their] head[s,] [with] … animal blood splattered all around and usually his house is dressed in red" (Osofisan 2003). Colonialism, patriarchy, slavery with its language loss, and the separation of the secular from the spiritual have left their marks, and some individual devotees have internalized more patriarchal values than others; when such a person has authority due to ritual knowledge or other finely developed characteristics, house members may undergo sexist, racist, or heterosexist experiences. Still, liturgy and language are alive to counter this, and gender balance has been retained in many contemporary religious practices. For a fairly universal example of how fluid role assignment has been retained in the modern-day *Orisha* house of worship, consider the fact that in religious terms, motherhood itself is not sexed; the mother who "births" a new initiate can be male or female, and the co-parent may likewise be either male or female. A new initiate is still called *Iyawo*, whether male or female. Yoruba religion, both traditionally and in Diaspora, continues to offer possibilities for gender neutral, welcoming spaces for empowering worship.

SEE ALSO: Black Feminist Thought; Capitalist Patriarchy; Child Labor in Comparative Perspective; Colonialism and Gender; Cross-Cultural Gender Roles; Gender, Politics, and the State: Overview; Intersectionality; Sexism in Language; Women's and Feminist Activism in West Africa

REFERENCES

Abimbola, Wande, and Ivor Miller. 1997. *Ifa Will Mend Our Broken World: Thoughts on Yoruba Religion and Culture in Africa and the Diaspora*. Boston, MA: Aim Books.

Alexander, Jacqui M. 2005. *Pedagogies of Crossing: Meditations on Feminism, Sexual Politics, Memory, and the Sacred*. Durham, NC: Duke University Press.

Apter, Andrew. 1992. *Black Critics and Kings: The Hermeneutics of Power in Yoruba Society*. Chicago: University of Chicago Press.

Cabrera, Lydia. 1980. *Yemaya y Ochun:Kariocha, Iyalorichas y Olorichas (Coleccion del Chichereku en el Exilio)*. Miami: Ediciones Universal.

Case, Menoukha. 2007. *Ori and the Ethical Subject: Pro Indigenous Readings of African Diaspora Literature in Yoruba*. PhD dissertation, SUNY University at Albany.

Drewal, Henry John, and Margaret Thompson Drewal. 1990. *Gelede: Art and Female Power Among the Yoruba*. Bloomington: Indiana University Press.

Fatunmbi, Awo Falookun. 2005. *Inner Peace: The Yoruba Concept of Ori*. New York: Athelia Henrietta Press.

Johnson-Phipps, Candace. 2002. "Review of Nigerian Videos: Born Again and Submission." *Ijele: Art Ejournal of the African World*, Issue 5. Accessed July 2006 at www.africaresource.com/ijele/issue5/johnson.pdf.

Kehinde, Yisa. 2002. "Sexism, English and Yoruba." *Linguistik OnLine, Language and Gender*. Accessed November 2002 at www.linguistik-online.de/11_02/yusuf_a.html.

Lawal, Babatunde. 2001. "Aworan: Representing the Self and Its Metaphysical Other in Yoruba Art." *The Art Bulletin*, 83(3): 498–526.

Mohanty, Chandra Talpade, Lourdes M. Torres, and Ann Russo, eds. 1991. *Third World Women and the Politics of Feminism*. Bloomington: Indiana University Press.

Okome, Mojubaolu Olufunke. 2001. "African Women and Power: Reflections on the Perils of Unwarranted Cosmopolitanism." *Jenda: A Journal of Culture and African Women Studies*, 1(1) (online).

Olajubu, Oyeronke. 2003. *Women in the Yoruba Religious Sphere*. Albany: State University of New York Press.

Osofisan, Sola. 2003. "Yoruba Culture Is Scientific" – The Tunde Kelani Interview. Accessed September 12, 2015, at http://www.naijarules.com/index.php?threads/%E2%80%9Cyoruba-culture-is-scientific%E2%80%9D-the-tunde-kelani-interview.317/.

Oyewumi, Oyeronke. 1997. *The Invention of Women: Making an African Sense of Western Gender Discourses*. Minneapolis: University of Minnesota Press.

Smith, Andy. 1997. "Ecofeminism Through an Anticolonial Framework." In *Ecofeminism: Women, Culture, Nature*, edited by Karen J. Warren and Nisvan Erkal, 21–37. Bloomington: Indiana University Press.

Torre, Miguel A. de la. 2001. "Ochun: (N)either the (M)other of All Cubans (N)or the Bleached Virgin." *Journal of the American Academy of Religion*, 69(4): 837–862.

Index of Names

A

Abdel Fattah, Esraa, 343
Abdel-Malke, Anouar, 1815
Abraham, Karl, 720
Abu-Lughod, Lila, 799, 800, 1315, 1459
Acconci, Vito, 1845
Adams, Carol J., 76
Adams, Margie, 1530
Addams, Jane, 637, 1646, 1828
Agassiz, Louis, 1359
Agustin, Laura, 2108
Ahmed, Leila, 1121
Ahmed, Sara, 296
Aidoo, Ama Ata, 857
Akhter, Farida, 862
al-Khawaja, Zainab and Maryam, 344
Al-Shykh, Hanan, 1815
Albee, Edward, 936
Alexander, M. Jacqui, 703, 1860, 2222
Allan, Maud, 1815
Allen, Michael Patrick, 2459
Allen, Paula Gunn, 802, 863, 1406, 2515
Allfrey, Phyllis Shand, 73
Allison, Dorothy, 858, 1515
Alloula, Malek, 309, 312
Alloway, Lawrence, 763
Almeida, Rhea, 806
Almond, Gabriel, 418
Althusser, Louis, 509, 1262–1263, 2287
Alvarez, Sonia, 419
Amin, Samir, 574–575
Anastasi, Anne, 1947
Anderson, Benedict, 705
Anderson, Elizabeth, 795
Anderson, Kim, 2513
Ang, Ien, 1858
Ansara, Y. Gavriel, 272
Anthony, Susan B., 687, 746, 1293, 1827, 2371, 2567
Antrobus, Peggy, 2484
Anzaldúa, Gloria, 161, 164, 165–166, 187–188, 661–662, 667, 703, 764, 787, 818, 863, 885, 1439, 1515, 1693–1695, 1968, 2590
Apple, Rima, 2060
Arat, Yesim, 419
Arkoun, Mohamed, 1815
Armstrong, Jeanette, 2515
Arnold, June, 857
Aronson, Lisa, 766
Asante, Molefi Kete, 575
Asch, Adrienne, 783, 785
Ashbery, John, 936
Astell, Mary, 643–644, 775, 1291
Athey, Ron, 1845
Atkinson, Ti-Grace, 856
Atwood, Margaret, 902
Auden, W. H., 936
Ausserer, Caroline, 1348
Awekotuku, Ngahuia Te, 1569
Awiakta, Marilou, 1408

B

B. Franko, 1845
Baartman, Saartjie, 306
Baartman, Sara, 1381–1382
Bachofen, Johan Jakob, 55, 1650
Bahadur, Gauitra, 657
Bahri, Deepika, 704
Bail, Kathy, 1894
Bailey, Amy, 2481
Bailey, Hannah, 1827
Baker, Ella, 98
Baker-Fletcher, Karen, 2440
Bakunin, Mikhail, 60, 61
Baldez, Lisa, 419
Baldwin, James, 936, 1968
Banaszak, Lee Ann, 911
Bandler, Faith, 619

The Wiley Blackwell Encyclopedia of Gender and Sexuality Studies, First Edition. Edited by Nancy A. Naples.
© 2016 John Wiley & Sons, Ltd. Published 2016 by John Wiley & Sons, Ltd.

Bandura, Albert, 980
Barad, Karen, 672–674, 677–678, 748, 795, 875
Bard, Christine, 652
Barlow, Maud, 505
Barlow, Tani, 633
Barnett, Ida Wells, 2422
Barnfield, Richard, 937
Barrett, Michelle, 753
Barriteau, Eudine, 2484
Barthes, Roland, 2407
Bartkowski, Frances, 901
Bashir, Danya, 344
Baudrillard, Jean, 46
Baumgardner, Jennifer, 1923
Bay, Brenda, 100
Beach, Frank A., 2016
Beale, Frances, 747
Bechdel, Alison, 858
Beckwith, Francis, 1926
Behn, Aphra, 775
Bell, Diane, 504, 620, 622, 801
Bell, Leonard, 1376
Bell, Richard, 1815
Bem, Sandra Lipsitz, 66, 1162, 1941, 1947
Bender, Rita Schwerner, 99
Benhabib, Seyla, 709
Benjamin, Harry, 2095, 2360
Benjamin, Jessica, 717, 723–725, 976
Benjamin, Walter, 2401
Bennet, Ramona, 2514
Bennett, Mary, 619
Bennholdt-Thomsen, Veronika, 213, 214, 504
Berg, Laurie, 126
Berger, John, 763, 2460
Berlant, Lauren, 1967
Bernal, Doleres Delgado, 341
Bernstein, Eduard, 509
Berque, Jacques, 1815
Bersani, Leo, 1967
Bertell, Rosalie, 505
Besant, Annie, 176
Bhabha, Homi, 1888
Bigler, Rebecca, 981
Binet, Alfred, 2161
Birkett, Dea, 311
Blachère, Régis, 1815
Blainville, Henry, 306
Blatch, Harriot Stanton, 1295, 1297
Blaugdone, Barbara, 1821
Blay, Yaba, 2248
Blee, Kathleen, 2000
Blunt, Alison, 311

Boccaccio, Giovanni, 774
Bogaert, Anthony, 118
Bograd, Michele, 806
Bollas, Christopher, 974
Bolotin, Susan, 1892
Bonaparte, Marie, 2052
Boothby, Frances, 775
Bordo, Susan, 37
Boring, Edwin G., 1946
Bornstein, Kate, 1168, 2341
Boscawen, Frances, 644
Boserup, Ester, 540
Boupacha, Djamilia, 1020
Bourdieu, Pierre, 591, 1314
Bouatta, Cherifa, 2523
Bradley, Karen, 1048
Braidotti, Rosi, 1773–1774, 1775–1776
Brassel, Daphne, 857
Bregula, Karolina, 1011
Bremer, Fredrika, 1826, 1827
Bridenthal, Renate, 772
Brockovich, Erin, 543
Brodber, Erna, 73
Brontë, Charlotte, 309
Brontë, Emily, 309
Brookes, Les, 1961
Brooks, Ann, 1892
Broude, Norma, 764
Brown Crawford, A. Elaine, 2440
Brown, Rita Mae, 667, 747, 857
Brownmiller, Susan, 2209
Bryant, E. Gay, 1214
Buckley, Thomas, 1687
Buela, Juane Rouco, 62
Bullough, Vern L., 2214
Bunch, Charlotte, 1261, 1326
Burbank, Victoria, 620
Burden, Chris, 1845
Burgmann, Meredith, 621
Burke, Edmund, 2385
Burney, Linda, 1075
Burns, Lucy, 1297
Burroughs, William S., 936
Burton, Antoinette, 312
Bushnell, Horace, 1295
Buss, David, 977
Butalia, Urvashi, 862
Butler, Josephine, 1294
Butler, Judith, 183, 260–261, 442, 447, 648, 714–715, 753, 757–758, 764, 879, 976, 1032, 1071–1072, 1807, 1966, 1970, 1975, 1980, 1981, 2116
Butler, Octavia, 902

C

Cabezas, Amalia, 2106
Cadet, Jean-Robert, 239
Cady Stanton, Elizabeth, 414–416, 686, 687, 746, 856, 1292, 1293, 1827, 2371
Cai Chang, 330
Caird, Mona, 76
Caldicott, Helen, 502, 1831
Caldwell, Paulette M., 181
Califia, Pat, 2052
Calkins, Mary Whiton, 1947
Campbell, Kim, 1505–1506
Campbell, Maria, 2515
Canaday, Margo, 2223
Capote, Truman, 936
Caron, Simone, 1926–1927
Carpenter, Mary, 307
Carr, Deborah, 36
Carson, Rachel, 416, 502, 541, 543
Carter, Elizabeth, 644
Cassatt, Mary, 764
Catt, Carrie Chapman, 736, 741, 1297, 2568
Cavafy, Constantine P., 936
Cavendish, Margaret, 775
Çetin, Fethiye, 864
Chant, Sylvia, 908
Chaperon, Sylvie, 652
Chapone, Hester, 644
Charest, Danielle, 1984
Charles, Maria, 1048
Charnas, Suzy McKee, 901
Chase, Cheryl, 1443
Chatterjee, Partha, 313
Chattopadhyay, Raghabendra, 1504
Chaudhuri, Nupur, 312
Cheng Yen, 1789
Chesler, Phyllis, 852, 1314
Chetcuti, Natacha, 653, 1984
Chicago, Judy, 763–764
Child, Lydia Maria, 1293
Chodorow, Nancy, 879, 974–975
Chopin, Kate, 2461
Christian, Barbara, 818
Christian, Meg, 1530
Chuh, Candice, 885
Cixous, Hélène, 447, 448, 648, 651, 717, 722, 756, 817–818, 879, 975, 2286–2287, 2590
Claramunt, Teresa, 62
Clark, Edward H., 1028
Clark, Helen, 1078
Clark, Septima, 98
Clarke, Cheryl, 1515
Cleaver, Eldridge, 100
Cleaver, Kathleen, 100

Cleland, John, 1878
Cliff, Michelle, 74, 885
Cobbe, Frances Power, 76, 1294
Cocteau, Jean, 936
Code, Lorraine, 794
Coleman, Monica, 2440
Collier, Mary, 645
Collins, Patricia Hill, 38, 161, 164–165, 181–182, 342, 345, 681, 867, 882, 884, 885, 1439, 1634, 1660, 1669, 1816, 2461
Comstock, Anthony, 1877
Condé, Maryse, 73
Connell, Catherine, 2001
Conradi, Peter, 1672
Cook, Judith A., 822
Cooper, Afua, 74
Cooper, Anna Julia, 165, 2421, 2422
Copeland, Shawn, 2440
Corber, Robert, 339
Cornell, Drusilla, 901
Corral, Thais, 2575
Corse, Sarah, 2461
Cotterrell, Roger, 813
Cowlishaw, Gillian, 620
Cox, Christopher, 936
Craven, Elizabeth, 307
Creed, Barbara, 1727
Crenshaw, Kimberlé, 181, 389, 764, 854, 885, 1439
Crow, Liz, 785
Cuillaumin, Colette, 1984
Culleton-Mosionier, Beatrice, 2515
Cunningham, Michael, 936
Curiel, Enriqueta Valdez, 189
Cuvier, Georges, 306

D

Dahl, Ronald, 418
d'Alembert, Jean-Baptiste le Rond, 1145
Daly, Mary, 504, 639, 1231–1232
Damasio, Antonio, 295
Dangarembga, Tsitsi, 313, 705
Darwin, Charles, 305, 565, 585, 1202, 2061
Das, Mahadai, 657
Das, Veena, 313
Davenport, Charles Benedict, 567
Davies, Emily, 1294
Davies, Jill, 153
Davis, Angela, 100, 181, 704, 747
Davis, Paulina Wright, 1294
Davy, Zowie, 273
Day, Dorothy, 1829
de Balzac, Honoré, 937

de Beauvoir, Simone, 294, 647, 649–654, 717, 720–721, 748, 753, 795, 879, 1026, 1859, 1983, 2116, 2278–2279
de Cleyre, Voltairine, 62, 624, 625
de Cristo, Antonia, 1290
de Gouges, Olympe, 413, 1144, 1145, 1291, 2293
de Gournay, Marie, 774
dé Ishtar, Zohl, 504
de la Barre, Poulain, 774–775
de la Cruz, Sor Juana Inés, 1975
de Lauretis, Teresa, 45, 1861, 1966, 1980, 2288, 2405
de Pisan, Christine, 748, 773–774, 901, 1290
Dean, Tim, 1964
d'Eaubonne, Françoise, 502
Debord, Guy, 46
Decker, Julie, 118
Defoe, Daniel, 775
Defosse, Dana Leland, 267
Degheidi, Inas, 1120
Deleuze, Gilles, 109, 1773, 1776
Delgado-Gaitan, Concha, 188
Delphy, Christine, 676
D'Emilio, John, 2177
Denfeld, Rene, 1893, 1894
Deng Yingchao, 330, 333
Deroin, Jeanne, 1292
Derrida, Jacques, 44, 76, 714, 755, 1966
Descartes, René, 1717–1718
Deshmukh, Lakshmibai, 29
Deshpande, Shashi, 705
Deutsch, Helene, 720, 2052
Devall, Bill, 417
Di Marco, Graciela, 419
Diamond, Elin, 1976
Diamond, Larry, 418
Diamond, Milton, 1444
Didrikson, Mildred "Babe", 139
Dietrich, Marlene, 953
Djebar, Assia, 1815, 2446, 2523
Dlugacz, Judy, 1530
Dobzhansky, Theodosius, 1202
Dodson, Betty, 1639
Doisy, Edward, 1319
Dolan-Del Vecchio, Kenneth, 806
Dominga, Sentime, 1975
Donovan, Josephine, 76
Dorn, Harold, 14
Douglas, Kelly Brown, 2440
Douglas, Mary, 1687, 1958
Douglass, Frederick, 1293, 2421
Dow, Bonnie, 1896
Downer, Carol, 2563
Drake, Barbara, 2351

Dreger, Alice D., 1444
Du Bois, W. E. B., 161–162, 568, 847, 2422
du Bosc, Jacques, 775
Dubow, Sara, 1927
Duby, Georges, 772
Dudgeon, Pat, 2471
Duff Gordon, Lucie, 307
Duflo, Esther, 1504
Duncan, Robert, 936
Duren, Jane, 2471–2472
Durkheim, Emile, 2259
Dux, Monica, 1894
Dworkin, Andrea, 1879, 1894
Dworkin, Ronals, 2027–2028
Dyer, Richard, 810, 1861
Dykewomon, Elana, 857

E
Eagly, Alice, 1952
Edelman, Lee, 1968
Ehrenreich, Barbara, 1920
Eisenstein, Hester, 910
Eissenstein, Zillah, 213, 216
Ekman, Paul, 296
El Saadawi, Nawal, 746, 1121
El-Solh, Camilla Fawzi, 1739
Ellis, Havelock, 1639, 2133
Elwood, Catherine, 307
Elyot, Thomas, 774
Emerson, Ralph Waldo, 1293
Engels, Friedrich, 750, 1652
Enke, A. Finn, 268
Enloe, Cynthia, 311–312, 703, 1710, 2222, 2315
Enslin, Elisabeth, 799
Ephron, Nora, 228
Erdrich, Louise, 2515, 2516
Erevelles, Nirmala, 788
Erlandson, Eddie, 41
Espinet, Ramabai, 657
Esterberg, Kristin, 1999
Etaugh, Claire, 1951
Eugenides, Jeffrey, 1964
EXPORT, VALIE, 1845

F
Faderman, Lilian, 2048, 2177
Fallon, Kathleen, 419
Falquet, Jules, 653
Faludi, Susan, 149
Fanon, Frantz, 703, 704
Fausto-Sterling, Anne, 167, 174, 306, 880, 2116
Fawcett, Millicent, 746, 1147, 1294
Feinberg, Leslie, 1964, 2338, 2343, 2344
Fénélon, Abbé, 775

Ferro, Robert, 936
Feuerbach, Ludwig, 868
Feydeau, Ernest, 314
Fiduccia, Barbara Waxman, 784
Finch, Anne, 645
Fine, Michelle, 783
Finger, Anne, 786
Finkbine, Sherry, 1920
Finley, Karen, 1845
Firestone, Shulamith, 727, 856, 879, 1847
Fiske, John, 1858
Flanagan, Bob, 1845
Flax, Jane, 756
Fletcher, Alice, 798
Flores, Yvette, 189
Fonow, Mary Margaret, 822
Ford, Clellan S., 2016
Forrest, Katherine V., 858, 901
Foucault, Michel, 109–110, 183, 260, 537, 714, 754, 801, 891, 936, 1224, 1776, 1783–1785, 1961, 1966, 1970, 1977, 1980, 2052, 2287
Fourest, Caroline, 653
Fox, George, 1821
Fox, Warwick, 417
Frankel, David, 228
Franklin, Sarah, 1745
Fraser, Nancy, 709, 1060
Freedman, Estelle, 379–380
Freeman, Elizabeth, 748
Freidus, Andrea, 2108
Freire, Paolo, 534, 561
Freud, Sigmund, 612, 713, 716–726, 973, 1639, 1806, 2133, 2259
Fricker, Miranda, 795
Friedan, Betty, 161, 162–163, 666, 798, 1302, 1665, 1847, 1859, 2371
Friedman, Ann, 1504
Fromm, Erich, 1652
Frye, Marilyn, 667
Fuh, Divine, 2247
Fuller, Loïe, 1815
Fuller, Margaret, 817, 1293
Fusae, Ichikawa, 695
Fusco, Coco, 764
Fuss, Diana, 447

G

Galland, Antoine, 1814
Galton, Francis, 565, 566
Gamble, Clarence, 568
Gamson, William, 1781
Gandhi, Mahatma Karamchand, 96
Gandhi, Mohandas, 1781
Garber, Marjori, 77
Garcia, Lorena, 663
Gardiner, Grace, 310
Gardner, Gerald, 2428
Garland-Thomson, Rosemarie, 784, 882–883
Garrard, Mary, 764
Garrison, Ednie Kaeh, 1893
Garrison, William Lloyd, 1826
Garrow, David, 1926
Garvey, Amy Ashwood, 2480
Gatens, Moira, 675
Gearhart, Sally, 901
Geary, David, 977
Genet, Jean, 936
Gentileschi, Artemisia, 764
George, Robert P., 1926
George, Rosemary Marangoly, 704
Gerster, Caroline, 1929
Ghandhi, Leela, 703
Ghose, Indira, 311
Gibbs, Lois, 543, 549
Gibbs, Pearl, 619, 1074–1075, 2472
Gide, André, 936
Gilbert, Sandra, 309, 311
Gilkes, Cheryl Townsend, 2440
Gillard, Julia, 1078
Gilligan, Carol, 558, 559, 562, 1941
Gilman, Charlotte Perkins, 66, 637, 857
Gilman, Sander, 306
Gilmore, Georgia, 99
Gilroy, Beryl, 73
Ginsberg, Allen, 936
Glaser, Michael, 265
Glendon, Mary Ann, 1927
Glenn, Cheryl, 2591
Godbole, Ramona, 2104
Godwin, William, 59
Goethe, Johann Wolfgang von, 937, 2051
Goffman, Erving, 1027, 1368, 2272
Goldman, Emma, 62, 176, 624, 1508
Gomez, Jewel, 858, 901
González-López, Gloria, 189, 2001
Goodison, Lorna, 73
Goodwin, Elizabeth, 1929
Gordon, Linda, 1927
Graham, Judy, 856
Graham-Brown, Sarah, 312
Grahn, Judy, 858
Gramsci, Antonio, 47, 449, 509, 1255, 1858, 2291
Grant, Jacqueline, 2439
Grealy, Lucy, 786
Green, Jamison, 1964
Greenberg, Steven, 1478
Greer, Germaine, 746, 856
Gregerson, Edgar, 2212

Gregory, John, 2385
Grewal, Inderpal, 183, 703
Griffen, Susan, 504
Grimes, Michael, 681
Grimke, Angelina and Sarah, 1826
Grisez, Germain, 1926
Griswold, Wendy, 2458
Gross, Larry, 1861
Grosz, Elizabeth, 674–675, 713, 757, 879
Grumley, Michael, 936
Guattari, Felix, 1773
Gubar, Susan, 309, 311
Guerroudj, Jacqueline, 1020
Guilamo-Ramos, Vincent, 2104
Guillaume, Jacquette, 775
Guillaumin, Colette, 677
Gunn, Paula, 505
Gunnarsson, Asa, 1060
Gustavo, Soledad, 61, 62
Guy-Sheftall, Beverly, 181

H
Hacker, Frederick, 2208
Hahnemann, Samuel, 50
Haignere, Lois, 825
Haines, Roger, 130
Halberstam, Judith, 1861, 1967
Hall, G. Stanley, 1028, 1946, 2259
Hall, Kim Q., 784, 787
Halperin, David, 1967
Halverson, Charles, 981
Hamer, Fannie Lou, 181
Hamilton, Annette, 620
Hanisch, Carol, 851, 1847
Hansen, Thomas Blom, 2222
Haraway, Donna, 76, 183, 407–409, 436, 541, 672, 710, 753, 794, 1669, 1745, 2465
Harding, Sandra, 639–640, 672, 683, 709, 794, 821–822, 823, 867, 869, 884, 1669, 2464
Hare-Mustin, Rachel, 1944
Hargitai, Eszter, 2460
Harjo, Joy, 2515
Harlow, Margaret Kuenne, 1948
Harper, Frances E.W., 1840
Harrex, Wendy, 857
Harrison, Cynthia Ellen, 819–820
Hartle, Alice, 1929
Hartmann, Heidi, 750, 825
Hartsock, Nancy, 683, 867, 868, 884, 1816
Hassan, Riffat, 1461
Hassan, Zoya, 1738
Hausman, Bernice L., 2332
Hawkesworth, Mary E., 794
Hawthorne, Susan, 857

Haywood, Eliza, 645
He Zhen, 62
Hearne, Vicki, 76
Hegarty, Peter, 272
Hegel, G. W. F., 509, 868
Heidegger, Martin, 520
Heim, Scott, 1962
Helfgot, Nathaniel, 1477
Hélie, Anissa, 2316
Henderson, Mae G., 882, 1968
Henson, Maria Rosa, 317–318
Hernandez, Pilar, 806
Herndl, Diane Price, 786
Herrnstein, Richard, 569
Hesen, Cai, 1299
Hideko, Fukuda, 695
Highsmith, Patricia, 937
Hintikka, Merrill B., 794
Hirdman, Yvonne, 1061
Hirschfeld, Magnus, 176, 2362
Hite, Shere, 1639
Hiu-Wan, 1789
Ho, Mae-Wan, 504
Hochschild, Arly Russell, 1216
Hocine, Baya, 1020
Hodge, Merle, 73
Hoefinger, Heidi, 2107
Holland, Allison, 619
Holleran, Andrew, 936, 1963
Hollinghurst, Alan, 936
Hollingsworth, Leta Stetter, 984
Hollister, John, 267
Holofcener, Nicole, 228
Hooker, Evelyn, 1523
hooks, bell, 164–165, 181, 215, 346, 357, 681, 704, 810, 818, 1411
Horney, Karen, 717, 720, 721, 974, 1947, 2052
Hoskins, Janet, 1687–1688
Hossain, Rokheya, 503, 504, 856
Hossain, Sara, 1314
Hourani, Albert, 1815
Hu Binxia, 699
Hubbard, Ruth, 1745
Hudson-Weems, Clenora, 2436
Hufton, Olwen, 772
Huggins, Erika, 100
Huggins, Jackie, 621, 622
Hughes, Melanie, 419
Hulme, Keri, 857
Hume, David, 561
Humphreys, Laud, 2307
Hunt, Mary E., 2468
Hurley, Michael, 1961
Hurston, Zora Neale, 165, 801–802, 857

Husserl, Edmund, 520
Hyam, Ronald, 312
Hymowitz, Carol, 1214

I
Ighilahriz, Louisette, 1020
Inge, William, 936
Inglehart, Ronald, 418, 421
Ingraham, Chris, 1262–1263
Irigaray, Luce, 447, 448, 648, 651, 713, 718, 722, 755–756, 817, 879, 975, 1807, 2286–2287, 2590
Isherwood, Christopher, 936
Isla, Ana, 506

J
Jackson, Shelley, 2592
Jacobs, Aletta, 176, 746
Jacobs, Harriet, 1840
Jaggar, Alison, 1669
Jameson, Anna, 1293
Jameson, Fredric, 47
Jaquette, Jane, 419
Jay, David, 118
Jefferson, Mildred, 1929
Jeffreys, Sheila, 244, 747
John, Mary, 802–803
Johnson, Allan, 682
Johnson, E. Patrick, 882, 1968
Johnson, Virginia, 1639, 2133, 2212
Johnston, Jill, 746, 856
Jones, Ernest, 720
Joseph, Gloria, 215
Jung, Carl, 111, 1652

K
Kabbani, Rana, 311
Kafer, Alison, 785
Kagitcibasi, Cigdem, 1411
Kahlo, Frida, 764, 787, 1975
Kamenetskaya, Nataliya, 765
Kang Keqing, 330
Kang Youwei, 699
Kanitkar, Kashibai, 29
Kant, Immanuel, 1202
Kanter, Rosabeth Moss, 2317
Kaplan, Caren, 183, 703
Kaplan, Cora, 2385
Karides, Marina, 343
Karl, Terry, 418
Karlsen, Carol, 2428
Karman, Tawakkul, 108
Kartini, Raden Ajeng, 735–736
Katz, Jonathan, 2049

Kautsky, Karl, 509
Kayberry, Phyllis, 798
Kaye/Kantrowitz, Melani, 99
Keller, Evelyn Fox, 872, 1745
Keller, Helen, 787
Kelley, Robin D.G., 346
Kelly, Petra, 1830–1831
Keneko, Fumiko, 62
Kessler, Suzanne J., 1444, 2332
Kheel, Mart, 505
Kibria, Nazli, 1394
Kilbourne, Jean, 1369
Kim, Eunjung, 117
Kim, Hak-sun, 318
King, Billie Jean, 139
King, Martin Luther Jr., 96
King, Michael Patrick, 228
King, Ynestra, 503
Kingsley, Mary, 307
Kinsey, Alfred, 178, 338–339, 1487–1489, 1639, 2133, 2176
Kipling, Rudyard, 1888
Kirby, Vicki, 748, 795
Kirchner, Albert, 1878
Kirk-Duggan, Cheryl, 2440
Kirsch, Max, 1981
Kissling, Frances, 2197
Kita, Kusunose, 694
Kittay, Eva, 787
Klein, Gloria, 1929
Klein, Melanie, 179, 974
Klein, Renate, 857
Knight, Anne, 1826
Knoll, Kristina, 786
Ko, Dorothy, 922
Koechlin, Floriane, 504
Kohlberg, Lawrence, 558, 562, 981, 1941
Kollentai, Alexandra, 328
Kolodny, Annette, 818
Kovács, Ágnes, 1670
Krafft-Ebing, Richard von, 2051, 2133, 2161
Kramer, Larry, 936
Kristeva, Julia, 447, 448, 648, 651, 713, 717, 722, 756, 817, 818, 879, 975, 1728, 2286–2287
Kushner, Tony, 936

L
Lacan, Jacques, 713, 722, 940, 976, 1386–1388, 1502–1503, 1717, 1807, 1849, 2402
Laclau, Ernesto, 510
Ladd, William, 1826
Ladd-Franklin, Christine, 1947, 1948
LaDuke, Winona, 503, 549

LaFleur, William, 14
Lahiri, Jhumpa, 313
Lake, Marilyn, 618, 619
Lakoff, Robyn, 1498, 2131
Lamarcke, Jean-Baptiste, 565–566
Lamas, Marta, 1372
Lang, Sabine, 2323
Lathrop, Julia, 1646
Laurent, Bo, 1443
Lauzen, Martha, 2459
Lawson, Louisa, 856
Layton, Lynne, 975
Laz, Cheryl, 35
Le Doeuff, Michelle, 651
Le Guin, Ursula, 901, 902, 952
Leapor, Mary, 645
Lederer, Laura, 2197
LeDoux, Joseph, 295
Lee, Ann, 2232
Lee, Vernon, 56
Leight, Carol, 2120
Leo-Rhynie, Elsa, 2484
Lepetit, Laura, 862
Lerner, Gerda, 771
LeRoy, J. T., 1964
Lessing, Doris, 902
LeVay, Simon, 2212
Lévi-Strauss, Claude, 713, 2287
Levy, Ariel, 1894
Lewin, Karl, 561
Lewis, Bernard, 1815
Lewis, Reina, 311
Lewis, Tareka "Mataliba", 100
Liben, Lynn, 981
Lieb, Kristin, 2460
Lincoln, Anne E., 2459
Linnaeus, Carl, 304
Linton, Simi, 786
Lipset, Seymour Martin, 418
Lister, Anne, 2277
Locke, John, 669
Longino, Helen, 284, 672, 795, 1670, 2465
Loomba, Ania, 305, 705
Lorber, Judith, 1024, 1052, 1053–1054
Lorde, Audre, 99, 165, 181, 667, 704, 747, 787, 818, 858, 861, 863, 1515, 2215
Loshak, Marina, 765
Loti, Pierre, 1815
Lotz, Amanda, 1893
Lowe, Lisa, 311
Luderman, Kate, 41
Luker, Kristen, 1920, 1926
Lurting, Thomas, 1822
Lyon, Eleanor, 153

Lyons, Andrew and Harriet, 2215
Lyotard, Jean-François, 754

M

Maathai, Wangari, 549, 2575
Mabro, Judy, 1739
Macaulay, Catherine, 644
Maccoby, Eleanor, 979
Machon, Louis, 775
MacKinnon, Catharine, 66, 557, 559, 813, 1879, 1894
Macmillan, Chrystal, 1828
Mahmood, Saba, 1460
Maine, Henry Sumner, 1652
Mairs, Nancy, 786
Malani, Nalini, 766
Malinowski, Bronislaw, 2259
Malthus, Thomas, 359, 565, 585, 1873
Mammucini, Maria Grazia, 504
Manalansan, Martin, 1388
Mani, Lata, 312
Mann, Sarah, 681
Mann, Thomas, 936
Maracek, Jeanne, 1944
Maracle, Lee, 2515
Marciano (Lovelace), Linda, 1879
Marlowe, Christopher, 937
Marshall, Gary, 228
Marshall, Paule, 73
Marson, Una, 73, 2481
Marston, William Moulton, 56
Marten, John, 1638
Martin, Carol, 981, 2473
Martin, Clarice, 2440
Martin, Clyde, 1487–1489, 2176
Martin, Darnise, 2440
Martin, Emily, 880
Martin, Patricia Yancey, 1052, 1053–1054
Martin, Robert K., 2049
Martinez, Josefa, 62
Marx, Karl, 60, 509, 750, 868, 1827
Massad, Joseph, 2011
Massiah, Joycelin, 73, 2484
Masson, Denise, 1815
Masters, William, 1639, 2133, 2212
Mathieu, Nicole-Claude, 1984
May, Reuben Buford, 2000
Mayer, Mónica, 764
Mazur, Amy G., 910
McBride, Dorothy, 910
McCarthy, Paul, 1845
McClaurin, Irma, 799
McClintock, Anne, 703
McCloud, Janet, 2514

McDowell, Teresa, 806
McElroy, Wendy, 1880
McGoldrick, Monica, 806
McGreevy, John, 1927
McHugh, John, 2343
McHugh, Paul, 2335–2336
McIntosh, Peggy, 847
McKeegan, Michele, 1927
McKenna, Wendy, 2332
McKlintock, Anne, 305
McLellan, Betty, 861
McLuhan, Marshall, 2401
McNab, Claire, 858
McRobbie, Angela, 1891
McRuer, Robert, 786
Mead, Margaret, 233, 798, 2259
Mecklenburg, Marjorie, 1929
Mellor, Mary, 503
Melman, Billie, 311
Mendieta, Ana, 763, 1845
Menon, Ritu, 862
Merchant, Carolyn, 505, 871
Merleau-Ponty, Maurice, 520, 521–522
Mernissi, Fatima, 1121, 1460, 2510, 2511
Merrill, James, 936
Merry, Sally Engle, 1328
Messerschmidt, James, 1635
Meyer, Ilan, 2177
Meyer, Jon, 2335
Meyer, Moe, 1968
Meyers, Nancy, 227, 228
Michel, Louise, 62, 624, 1508
Mies, Maria, 213, 214, 504, 506, 542, 703
Mill, Harriet Taylor, 670, 1147, 1294
Mill, John Stuart, 670, 1147, 1294
Millbank, Jenni, 126, 130
Miller, Arthur, 2428
Miller, Errol, 73
Miller, Jean Baker, 1941
Millet, Kate, 727, 746, 856
Millington, June, 1530
Mills, Sara, 311
Minatchy-Bogat, Arlette, 657
Minh-ha, Trinh T., 764, 803, 1774
Mitchell, Juliet, 717, 723
Mitchell, W. J. T., 2399, 2407
Mithun, Marianne, 1407
Mitter, Swasti, 703
Mohai, Paul, 551
Mohammed, Patricia, 2484
Mohanty, Chandra Talpade, 183, 311, 702, 703, 706, 802, 885, 1860, 2315
Moi, Toril, 648, 651

Mollow, Anna, 786
Monette, Paul, 936
Money, John, 167, 1030–1031, 1444
Montagu, Elizabeth, 644
Montgomery, Heather, 2107
Montseny, Federica, 61, 62
Moore, Barrington, 422
Moore, Hannah, 1826
Mooto, Shani, 657
Moraga, Cherrie, 662, 703, 747, 764, 885, 1439, 1515
More, Hannah, 644
Moreton-Robinson, Aileen, 622
Morgan, Lewis Henry, 1652
Morgan, Paula, 74
Morgan, Robin, 505
Morley, David, 1858
Morris, Jenny, 786
Morris-Knibb, Mary, 2481
Morrison, Toni, 902
Morrow, Phyllis, 1688
Mosely, LaReine-Marie, 2440
Mott, James, 1293
Mott, Lucretia, 686, 1292
Mouffe, Chantal, 510
Moutoussamy, Laure, 657
Moya, Paula M. L., 711
Moynihan, Daniel Patrick, 346
Moynihan, Patrick, 72
Mullen, Ann, 1049
Mulvey, Laura, 45, 763, 809, 1664, 1859, 2402, 2405
Mumeo, Oku, 695
Muñoz, José Estaban, 1968
Muñoz, Laurena, 1970
Murray, Anne Firth, 2197
Murray, Pauli, 181

N
Naess, Arne, 416–417
Namaste, Viviane, 2349
Nandy, Ashis, 703
Nannup, Alice, 2472
Naples, Nancy, 17–19
Negra, Diane, 1893
Nelson, Lynn Hankinson, 795
Neu, Diann L., 2468
Newton, Esther, 209
Newton, Helmut, 952–953
Newton, Huey P., 100
Nicholls, Doug, 619
Nicholson, Linda, 709
Nietzsche, Friedrich, 1652

Nightingale, Florence, 307
Nkrumah, Kwame, 1886
Nochlin, Linda, 764, 765
Norton, Mary Beth, 2428
Nott, Josiah Clark, 1359
Nussbaum, Martha, 211
Nyamnjoh, Francis, 2247

O
Oakley, Ann, 2117
O'Brien, Edna, 705
O'Donoghue, Lowitja, 1075
O'Hara, Frank, 936
O'Hara, Sabine, 504
O'Keeffe, Georgia, 764, 768
Okju, Mun, 318
Ong, Aihwa, 803, 1860
Ono, Yoko, 763
Ordover, Nancy, 568
O'Shane, Pat, 621

P
Padilla, Mark B., 2104
Paisley, Fiona, 618
Palac, Lisa, 406
Pan, Elysia, 2247–2248
Pane, Gina, 1845
Pankhurst, Christabel, 1147, 1297
Pankhurst, Emmeline, 746, 1147, 1296, 1297
Pankhurst, Sylvia, 1147
Parameswaran, Radhika, 799
Parekh, Pushpa, 786
Park Chung-hee, 698
Park, You-me, 703
Parker, Lynne, 806
Parks, Fanny, 307
Parks, Rosa, 96
Parlee, Mary Brown, 1941
Parreñas, Rhacel Salazar, 1216
Parsons, Elsi Clews, 798
Parsons, Lucy Eldine Gonzalez, 62, 1508
Pateman, Carol, 1741
Paul, Alice, 1297
Paxton, Nancy, 313, 419
Paxton, Pamela, 418
Payne, Charles, 97
Pearce, Diana, 907
Pease, Elizabeth, 1292
Pechey-Phipson, Edith, 307
Pelletier, Madeleine, 62
Penman, Mary, 1824
Peris, Nova, 2473–2474
Peristiany, J.G., 1314
Perrot, Michelle, 652, 772

Persaud, Lakshmi, 657
Peterson, Spike, 511
Phelp, Jamie, 2440
Philip, Marlene NourbeSe, 73
Philips, Katherine, 645
Picano, Felice, 936
Piccinini, Patricia, 1729
Piercy, Marge, 901
Pindell, Howardina, 763
Pinderhughes, Elaine, 806
Piper, Adrian, 763
Pirou, Eugène, 1878
Pitt-Rivers, Julian, 1314
Pitt-Taylor, Victoria, 880
Plummer, Ken, 1979, 2215
Plumwood, Val, 505
Polwhele, Elizabeth, 775
Pomeroy, Wardell, 1487–1489, 2176
Poovey, Mary, 2385
Poston, Carol, 2385
Potter, Elizabeth, 795, 1670
Pratt, Mary Louise, 304
Pratt, Minnie Bruce, 847
Preves, Sharon, 1444
Price, Janet, 785
Prince, Virginia, 2361
Probyn, Elspeth, 1896
Prosser, Jay, 1168, 2332
Proulx, Annie, 937
Proust, Marcel, 936, 2051
Przeworski, Adam, 418
Puri, Iyoti, 2224
Pyne, Jake, 273

Q
Qiu Jin, 699

R
Radcliffe-Brown, Alfred, 1650
Radjkoemar, Asha "Cádani", 657
Radway, Janice, 799, 1858
Rahimi, Sadaf, 139
Raichō, Hiratsuka, 695
Rainey, Gertrude "Ma", 165, 1529
Ramabai, Pandita, 29
Ramgoonai, Drupatie, 2480
Ramjattan, Christina, 2481
Rapoport, David C., 1508–1509, 1510
Rasing, Thera, 1689
Ray, Sangeeta, 313
Raymond, Janice, 861
Reagan, Leslie, 1927
Reagon, Bernice Johnson, 787
Reddock, Rhoda, 74, 2484

Reeve, Clara, 644
Reich, Wilhelm, 1652, 2259
Reid, Althaus, 265
Reilly, Maura, 765
Rest, James, 562–563
Reter, Donna, 2336
Reve, Gerard, 936
Reynolds, Burt, 42
Rhys, Jean, 72, 73
Rice, Anne, 937
Rice, Charles E., 1926
Rich, Adrienne, 354–355, 667, 747, 787, 861, 1261, 1725, 1984
Richards, Ellen Swallow, 543
Riggs, Marcia, 2440
Rimbaud, Arthur, 936
Ringgold, Faith, 763
Ringrose, Jessica, 1898
Risen, James, 1927
Ritvo, Harriet, 76
Rivera, Sylvia, 2339
Roberts, Emma, 307
Robin, Marie-Monique, 504, 505, 863–864
Robinson, Jo Ann, 97
Roda, Maria, 62
Rodinson, Maxime, 1815
Rogers, Carol Ann, 234
Roiphe, Katie, 1894
Romero-Daza, Nancy, 2108
Rose, Hilary, 1745
Rose, Jacqueline, 1640
Rosler, Martha, 763
Rossiter, Margaret, 872
Rothman, Barbara Katz, 1699
Rothman, Lorraine, 2563
Rousseau, Jean-Jacques, 1145, 2385
Rowbotham, Sheila, 703
Rowe, Elizabeth Singer, 645
Rowntree, Tessa, 1824
Rubin, Gayle, 283, 510, 798, 1489–1490, 1515, 1632, 1880, 1966, 2124
Ruddick, Sarah, 558
Ruether, Rosemary Radford, 2468
Rushdie, Salman, 705
Rutgers, Johannes, 176

S
Sacks, Karen, 341
Said, Edward, 310–311, 702, 704, 799, 1459, 1887
Saihi, Horria, 2523
Salleh, Ariel, 506
Sam, Michael, 142
Sandberg, Sheryl, 2077, 2373
Sanger, Margaret, 62, 176, 568, 587, 1919
Saornil, Lucia Sánchez, 63
Sarachild, Kathie, 1847
Sargent, Lydia, 215
Sargisson, Lucy, 901
Sarkar, Tanika, 28
Sarkeesian, Anita, 438
Sartre, Jean-Paul, 647
Saxton, Marsha, 784, 785
Schapiro, Miriam, 763
Scharff, Christina, 1898
Scharlieb, Mary, 307
Schellhardt, Timothy, 1214
Schlesinger, Arthur, 337–338
Schmitter, Philippe, 418
Schneemann, Carolee, 763, 1845
Schneider, David, 1489
Schor, Naomi, 447
Schuyler, James, 936
Schwarzer, Alice, 746
Schwerner, Michael, 99
Schwimmer, Rosika, 1828
Scott, Henry, 1877
Scott, Joan, 311, 771, 884
Scott, Mary, 2592
Scott, Sarah, 644
Scranton, Mary, 697
Sebbar, Leila, 1815
Sedgwick, Eve Kosofsky, 554–556, 937, 1961, 1967, 1970, 1980, 2222
Seidman, Steven, 2215
Sen, Amartya, 211, 2102
Serano, Julia, 267
Sessions, George, 417
Seward, Anna, 644
Shah, Ryhaan, 657
Shahrkhani, Wojdan Ali Seraj Abdulrahim, 139
Sharpe, Jenny, 703
Sheffield, Carole, 2208
Sherman, Cindy, 1728
Sherman, Lawrence, 154
Shewcharan, Narmala, 657
Shipley, Jenny, 1078
Shiva, Vandana, 504, 505, 506, 540, 864, 2575
Shock, Suzy, 1975
Showalter, Elaine, 818, 2590
Sidhwa, Bapsi, 313
Sigmundson, Keith, 1444
Sigusch, Volkmar, 267
Silko, Leslie Marmon, 2515
Silkwood, Karen, 503
Silvers, Anita, 787

INDEX OF NAMES

Simic, Zora, 1894
Sinha, Mrinalini, 312
Sirleaf, Ellen Johnson, 1504
Sivori, Horace, 2315
Smith, Andrea, 1408
Smith, Barbara, 99
Smith, Bessie, 165, 1529
Smith, Bonnie, 772
Smith, Dorothy, 161, 163–164, 683, 823, 884, 1669
Smith, George, 2015
Smith-Rosenberg, Carroll, 2048
Sodano, Valeria, 513
Sontag, Susan, 210, 902, 2407
Spalter-Roth, Roberta, 825
Spedding, Carole, 860
Spencer, Herbert, 565, 585
Spender, Dale, 861
Spillers, Hortense, 72
Spivak, Gayatri Chakravorty, 183, 309, 311, 702, 757, 802, 879, 885, 1887, 1889, 2279, 2291, 2292, 2314
Spretnak, Charlene, 505
Sprinkle, Annie, 1881
St. Denis, Ruth, 1815
St. Hilaire, Étienne Geoffroy, 306
Stacey, Judith, 799, 800, 801, 1893
Stack, Carol, 1490
Standing, Guy, 511
Stanhope, Hester, 307
Starhawk, 505
Staton, Mary, 901
Steel, Flora Annie, 307, 310
Stein, Arlene, 1979
Steinberg, Ronnie, 825
Steinem, Gloria, 37, 45
Stephens, Elizabeth, 1849
Steputtat, Finn, 2222
Steward, Milton and Lyman, 2021
Stewart, Maria, 165, 1292
Stoler, Ann, 310
Stoller, Robert, 2117
Stone, Sandy, 2348
Stopes, Marie, 176, 567, 1220
Strobel, Margaret, 312
Stryker, Susan, 882, 2338–2339, 2341
Suleri, Sara, 313
Sunder Rajan, Rajeswari, 703
Surridge, Lisa, 76
Suttner, Bertha von, 1827
Swinnerton, Kenneth A., 234
Sykes, Bobbi, 621

T
Tabet, Paola, 2120
Talbot, Catherine, 644
Tannen, Deborah, 639
Taraud, Christelle, 652
Tasker, Yvonne, 1893
Tatchell, Peter, 1547
Taylor, Dorceta, 549
Tekakwitha, Catherine, 1290
Terrell, Mary Church, 2422
Thomas, Carol, 785
Thomas, Judy L., 1927
Thompson, Clara, 1947
Thompson, Denise, 727
Thompson, E. P., 509
Thoreau, David, 1781
Thornton, Big Mama, 1529
Thrale, Hester, 644
Tibi, Bassam, 2020
Tollefson, Christopher, 1926
Toshiko, Kishida, 694
Toumi, Khalida, 2518, 2522
Townes, Emilie, 2440
Tremain, Shelly, 785, 787
Trilling, Lionel, 338–339
Tronto, Joan, 559
Truth, Sojourner, 165, 747, 1027–1028, 1439, 2026, 2421
Tuana, Nancy, 672
Tuchman, Gaye, 1664
Tucker, Margaret, 1075
Turcotte, Louise, 1984
Turkle, Sherry, 436
Tuttle, Carolyn, 512

U
Ulrichs, Karl Heinrich, 2360
Urry, Megan, 1670
Ussher, Jane M., 1729
Utrata, Jennifer, 36

V
Vail, Tobi, 2046
Valerio, Anita, 885
van Schurman, Anna Maria, 774
Venner, Fiametta, 653
Verlaine, Paul, 936
Vesey, Elizabeth, 644
Vicinus, Martha, 2048
Vidal, Gore, 936
Vidal, Mirta, 631
Villard, Frances Garrison, 1827
Visweswaran, Kamala, 799, 801
Viterna, Jocelyn, 419

W

Wade, Lisa, 290
Walejko, Gina, 2460
Walker, Alice, 99, 181, 319, 680–681, 818, 863, 2434–2437, 2439
Walker, Denis, 2473
Walker, Kath, 619
Walker, Lenore, 153
Walkerdine, Valerie, 1898
Wallace, Michelle, 747
Waring, Marilyn, 504
Warner, Michael, 1261, 1967
Warren, Karen, 417
Washburn, Margaret Floy, 1947
Washington, Mary Helen, 165
Watkins, Frances Ellen Harper, 1294
Watson, Lilla, 503
Waylen, Georgina, 419
Webb, Beatrice and Sidney, 2351
Weber, Lynd, 682
Weber, Max, 1223–1224
Weems, Renita J., 2439
Weinberg, George, 1259
Weismann, August, 565
Weisstein, Naomi, 852, 1939, 1950
Welchman, Lynne, 1314
Wells, Ida B., 2421
Wells-Barnett, Ida B., 165
Welzel, Christian, 418, 421
Wendell, Susan, 785, 787
Werlhof, Claudia von, 213, 214–215, 216–217
West, Candace, 35
West, Rebecca, 817
Westermarck, Edvard, 1652
Westervelt, Saundra Davis, 2461
White, Edmund, 936
White, Patrick, 1963
Whitman, Walt, 937
Whitmore, George, 936
Wieringa, Saskia, 2315
Wiesner-Hanks, Merry, 772
Wilberforce, William, 1826
Wilde, Oscar, 936
Wilken, George Alexander, 1650
Wilkerson, Abby, 786
Willard, Frances, 1827

Williams, Bernard, 1879
Williams, Bridget, 857
Williams, Dolores, 2440
Williams, Patricia, 181
Williams, Tennessee, 936
Williamson, Judith, 1859
Williamson, Laila, 1412
Willis, Ellen, 1880
Winick, Gary, 227, 228
Winterson, Jeanette, 902, 952
Wittig, Monique, 648, 667, 727, 818, 879, 901, 1261, 1262, 1983–1985
Wolchik, Sharon, 419
Wolf, Naomi, 1894, 1923
Wolfe, Cary, 76
Wollstonecraft, Mary, 645, 670, 748, 829, 855–856, 879, 1146, 1291, 1859, 2384–2386
Wood, Francis, 2440
Woodhull, Victoria, 2163
Woods, Gregory, 935
Woolf, Virginia, 703, 748, 817, 856, 937, 952, 2590
Woolley, Helen Thompson, 984
Worell, Judith, 1951
Wortley Montagu, Mary, 307, 309, 646
Wright, Doris, 680
Wright, Judith, 502
Wu Rongrong, 634
Wylie, Alison, 795
Wynter, Sylvia, 72, 73

X

X. Malcolm, 101
Xiang Jingu, 1299

Y

Yearsley, Ann, 645
Yingyi Mar, 1049
Yongsu, Yi, 318
Young, Iris Marion, 1060
Young, Rebecca, 2177

Z

Zetkin, Clara, 2569
Zimmerman, Don, 35
Ziv, Nitzan, 1689–1690
Zwick, Joel, 228

Index of Subjects

A
A Vindication of the Rights of Woman, 2384–2386
Aboriginal Australia and Torres Strait Islands
   feminisms, 618–623
   gender, politics and the state, 1073–1077
   women's and feminist activism, 2470–2475
abortion, 175
   adolescent pregnancy, 19–21
   family planning, 584–589
   fetal rights, 916–918
   fundamentalism and public policy, 925–929
   genetics testing and screening, 1206–1208
   global gag rule, 1218–1221
   Mormonism, 1729–1731
   and religion, 13–17
   reproductive health, 2030–2035
   sexual rights, 2196–2200
   United States
      pro-choice movement, 1918–1925
      pro-life movement, 1925–1933
      reproductive justice/rights, 2035–2040
      women's health movement, 2563–2567
   see also birth control
abortion laws/policies, 1–13
   barriers to abortion services, 9–13
   categories of, 3–5, 6–8
   liberalization, 8–9
Abrahamic religions *see* Christianity, gender and sexuality; Islam; Judaism
acknowledgment
   customary laws, 399–401
activism
   activist mothering, 17–19
   anarchism and gender, 59–64
   anti-globalization movements, 82–87
   anti-poverty, 92–95
   Arab Spring movements, 107–108
   asexual, 114–116
   Chicana feminism, 630–632

Chinese feminism, 632–637
community and grassroots activism, 341–345
community other mothers, 345–348
consciousness-raising, 356–358
drag, 484–490
ecofeminism, 502–509
empowerment, 534–537
environmental justice, 548–550
environmental politics and women's activism, 550–554
feminist, 759–762
feminist art practice, 767–769
feminist organizations, definition of, 842–844
feminist publishing, 855–864
first, second and third wave feminism, 745–749
French feminism, 649–654
gender and economic globalization, 511–515
Greenham Common, 1229–1230
identity politics, 1365–1367
intersex movement, 1443–1448
Kothi, 1491–1493
LGBT
   Eastern and Central Europe, 1557–1563
   Latin America, 1563–1569
   Native North America, 1578–1583
   Northern Africa, 1588–1590
   North America, 1583–1587
   South Asia, 1590–1595
   Southeast Asia, 1595–1600
   Western Europe, 1605–1612
maternal activism, 1640–1645
matrix of domination, 1660–1662
menstrual activism, 1682–1686
Northern Africa
   gender, politics and the state, 1116–1122
   LGBT, 1588–1590
Occupy movements, 1801–1805
pornography, feminist legal and political debates on, 1877–1882

The Wiley Blackwell Encyclopedia of Gender and Sexuality Studies, First Edition. Edited by Nancy A. Naples.
© 2016 John Wiley & Sons, Ltd. Published 2016 by John Wiley & Sons, Ltd.

sexual minorities, 2176–2179
sexual rights, 2196–2200
suffrage, 2293–2296
transgender politics, 2346–2351
transnational labor movements, 2351–2357
United States
 transgender movements, 2341–2345
 women's health movement, 2563–2567
United States women's movements in historical perspective, 2369–2374
women in non-traditional work fields, 2451–2458
Yogyakarta Principles, 2604–2606
activist mothering, 17–19
 community and grassroots activism, 341–345
 maternal activism, 1640–1645
 women's and feminist activism, United States and Canada, 2539–2545
 women's health movement in the United States, 2563–2567
acupressure, 49
acupuncture, 49
addiction
 drug and alcohol abuse, 490–493
 fetal alcohol syndrome, 914–916
adolescent pregnancy, 19–21
 child sex offenders, 246–249
 sexology and psychological sex research, 2133–2142
 socialization and sexuality, 2257–2262
 virginity, 2397–2399
adolescents
 Latina feminism, 661–666
adultery
 chastity, 225–227
 cultural views of, 21–24
advertising, images of gender/sexuality, 1367–1371
 beauty industry, 157–159
 eating disorders, 499–502
 men's magazines, 1676–1678
 metrosexual, 1695–1696
advocacy
 breast cancer, 194–199
aesthetic labor, 525–527
affirmative action, 24–25
 critical race theory, 384–389
 glass ceiling/glass elevator, 1214–1216
 health careers, 1243–1246
 sexism, 2129–2131
Afghanistan
 abortion laws, 3
African religions
 womanist theology & preaching, 2439–2440

Yoruba culture, religion, and gender, 2606–2618
African womanism
 AIDS-related stigma, 38–40
 womanism, 2434–2437
African Americans
 bifurcated consciousness, 161–166
Africana womanism
 womanism, 2434–2437
age of consent
 child marriage in India, 26–30
 criminal justice system and sexuality, 371–384
 historical and international perspective, 30–34
 rape law, 1989–1993
 sexual citizenship in East Asia, 2151–2157
aging and ageism, 34–38
 elder abuse
  domestic violence in United States, 467–470
  and gender, 518–520
 life expectancy, 1612–1616
 medicine and medicalization, 1671–1676
 menopause, 1680–1682
 senior women and sexuality in United States, 2078–2080
AIDS
 breastfeeding, 200–201
 sexual citizenship in the Caribbean, 2146–2151
AIDS-related stigma, 38–40
 LGBT, Latin America, 1563–1569
 sexually transmitted infections, 2225–2227
 women's and feminist activism, Southern Africa, 2534–2538
Albania
 abortion laws, 3
alchemy
 capitalist patriarchy, 213–217
Alexander technique, 50–51
Algeria
 abortion laws, 3
 LGBT, 1574–1575
 women's and feminist activism, 2522–2523
alpha male, 41–43
altered states of consciousness
 shaman priestesses, 2236–2237
alternative media, 43–47
 Riot grrrl, 2046–2047
alternative medicine see complementary and alternative medicine
Amazons, 53–57
 Dahomey, 57–59
 leftist armed struggle, women in, 1507–1512
 women in combat, 2441–2445
anarchism
 anarchist feminisms, 623–626
 and gender, 59–64

leftist armed struggle, women in, 1507–1512
women anarchists, 62–64
ancient indigenous cultures
    cohabitation and *Ekageikama* in the Kandyan Kingdom (Sri Lanka), 301–303
    traditional and indigenous knowledge, 2322–2326
    two-spirit, 2364–2365
ancient nation-states
    age of consent, 30–34
Andorra
    abortion laws, 3
androcentrism, 65–66
    environment and gender, 539–544
    existential feminism, 647–649
    feminist economics, 788–793
    gender bias in research, 955–959
    gender mainstreaming, 1062–1064
    language and gender, 1497–1502
    menstrual rituals, 1686–1691
    non-sexist language use, 1779–1781
    sexism in language, 2131–2133
androgen insensitivity syndrome, 66–68
    intersex movement, 1443–1448
androgyny, 68–71
    gender schema theory, 1162–1164
    Hijra/Hejira, 1281–1282
    trans identities, psychological perspectives, 2328–2331
anglophone Caribbean feminism, 71–75
    women's and feminist activism, 2480–2485
Angola
    abortion laws, 3
    LGBT, 1602–1603
animality
    psychology of objectification, 1956–1957
    sexism in language, 2131–2133
    taboo, 2303–2305
    and women, 76–78
anthropology
    matriarchy, 1649–1655
    sexual perspectives, 78–82
anti-abortion campaigns, 176–177
anti-civil rights movements, 96–102
anti-globalization movements, 82–87
    community and grassroots activism, 341–345
    environmental justice, 548–550
    free trade zones, 922–925
    NGOs and grassroots organizing, 1765–1769
anti-miscegenation laws, 87–91
anti-poverty activism, 92–95
    community and grassroots activism, 341–345
    household livelihood strategies, 1322–1326
    Occupy movements, 1801–1805

anti-racist and civil rights movements, 96–102
    community and grassroots activism, 341–345
    environmental justice, 548–550
    history of women's rights in international and comparative perspective, 1289–1306
    lesbian and gay movements, 1516–1522
    suffrage, 2293–2296
    women's and feminist activism, Aboriginal Australia and Torres Strait Islands, 2470–2475
Antigua & Barbuda
    abortion laws, 3
appearance psychology, 102–107
    eating disorders, 499–502
    lookism, 1616–1618
Arab, LGBT
    Middle East, 1573–1578
    Northern Africa, 1588–1590
Arab Spring movements, 107–108
    community and grassroots activism, 341–345
    gender, politics and the state, Northern Africa, 1116–1122
    history of women's rights in international and comparative perspective, 1289–1306
    Islam and gender, 1458–1463
    North African feminism, 688–694
    Occupy movements, 1801–1805
archaeology, 109–110
archaeology and genealogy
    tattooing and piercing, 2305–2307
archetype, 110–112
Argentina
    abortion laws, 3
    women's movements, 63–64
argumentation, feminist, 743–745
armed conflict
    "Don't ask, don't tell" policy, 470–473
    leftist armed struggle, women in, 1507–1512
    militarism and gender-based violence, 1701–1710
    women in combat, 2441–2445
Armenia
    abortion laws, 3
arranged marriages
    India, 26–30
    mail-order brides, 1619–1621
    South Asia, 112–114
art
    feminist, 762–767
    feminist art practice, 767–769
    monstrous-feminine, 1727–1729
    performance art, 1844–1846
    queer performance, 1974–1977

art (*Continued*)
   visual culture and gender, 2403–2408
   women as producers of culture, 2458–2462
asexual activism, 114–116
Asexual Visibility and Education Network (AVEN), 115, 116, 117
asexuality, 116–119
   celibacy, 221–222
   sexuopharmaceuticals, 2227–2232
assisted reproduction, 119–123
   eugenics movements, 570–574
   family planning, 584–589
   reproductive choice, 2027–2030
   reproductive justice/rights in the United States, 2035–2040
   sex selection, 2102–2104
   stratified reproduction, 2280–2281
   surrogacy, 2296–2298
asylum
   challenges faced by sexual minorities, 123–128
   and gender, 128–133
   and sexual orientation, 133–137
   see also immigration
athletics
   eating disorders, 499–502
   and homosexuality, 142–147
   metrosexual, 1695–1696
athletics and gender, 137–142
   eating disorders, 499–502
   gender equality/inequality in education, 993–998, 1046–1050
   steroids, 2270–2272
audiences
   Bollywood, 185–187
Australia
   abortion laws, 3
   gender, politics and the state, 1073–1082
   homelessness and gender, 1308–1311
   LGBT, 1541–1546
   poverty, 1906
   women's and feminist activism
      Aboriginal Australia and Torres Strait Islands, 2470–2475
      Australia and New Zealand, 2475–2479
Austria
   abortion laws, 3
autoeroticism
   masturbation, 1638–1640
   see also sex toys
autonomous organizing
   radical feminism, 726–729
Ayurveda, 49
Azarbaijan
   abortion laws, 3

B
backlash
   against feminism, 149–150
   feminist activism, 759–762
   postfeminism, 1891–1900
   representation, 2025–2027
Bahamas
   abortion laws, 3
Bahrain
   abortion laws, 3
Baklâ, 486
Bangladesh
   abortion laws, 3
Barbados
   abortion laws, 3
bathhouses, 150–152
battered woman syndrome, 152–155
   post-traumatic stress disorder, 1884–1886
battered women, 152–155
   intimate partner abuse, 1456–1458
   rape law, 1989–1993
   violence against women in global perspective, 2386–2392
   women's and feminist activism, Southern Africa, 2534–2538
bear culture, 155–157
beauty
   lookism, 1616–1618
beauty industry, 157–159
   cosmetic surgery, 365–367
   health careers, 1243–1246
   misogyny, 1718–1720
   sexual objectification, 2179–2181
Belarus
   abortion laws, 3
Belgium
   abortion laws, 3
Belize
   abortion laws, 3
Bem Sex-Role Inventory (BSRI), 69, 1162
Benin
   abortion laws, 3
berdache, 159–161
   gender identification, 1023–1026
   gender identity theory, 1030–1035
   Hijra/Hejira, 1281–1282
   LGBT, Native North America, 1578–1583
   traditional and indigenous knowledge, 2322–2326
   two-spirit, 2364–2365
Bhutan
   abortion laws, 3
bias
   clinical trials, bias against women, 283–288

feminist objectivity, 838–841
see also gender bias
bifurcated consciousness, 161–166
biochemistry/physiology, 166–173
    androgen insensitivity syndrome, 66–68
    gender identity theory, 1030–1035
    nature–nurture debate, 1744–1750
    occupational health and safety, 1797–1799
    sex-related difference research, 2125–2129
biological determinism, 173–174
    athletics and gender, 137–142
    essentialism, 556–558
    ethics of care, 558–560
    eugenics, history and ethics, 565–570
    existential feminism, 647–649
    feminist studies of science, 870–876
    gender, definition of, 966–968
    gender development, theories of, 977–982
    hybridity and miscegenation, 1359–1361
    nature–nurture debate, 1744–1750
    neuroscience, brain research, and gender, 1754–1759
    social constructionist theory, 2249–2251
biomedicalization
    sexuopharmaceuticals, 2227–2232
birth control, 61
    abortion and religion, 13–17
    adolescent pregnancy, 19–21
    contraception/contraceptives, 358–362
    family planning, 584–589
    fertility rates, 911–914
    global gag rule, 1218–1221
    heterosexual marriage trends in the West, 1265–1270
    history and politics, 175–177
    Mormonism, 1729–1731
    reproductive choice, 2027–2030
    reproductive health, 2030–2035
    sterilization, 2268–2270
    United States
        pro-choice movement, 1918–1925
        reproductive justice/rights, 2035–2040
        women's health movement, 2563–2567
    see also abortion
birthing practices
    midwifery, 1699–1701
    reproductive health, 2030–2035
    surrogacy, 122, 2296–2298
    wet nursing, 2419–2421
    woman-centeredness, 2431–2434
bisexuality, 177–180
    appearance psychology, 102–107
    asylum and sexual orientation, 133–137
    drug and alcohol abuse, 490–493

    health and healthcare in sexual minorities, 1250–1255
    Kinsey Scale, 1487–1489
    lesbian feminism, 666–669
    lesbian stereotypes in the United States, 1531–1536
    same-sex families, 2053–2055
    sexual identity and orientation, 2171–2174
    sexual minorities, 2176–2179
    sexualities, 2212–2217
    trans identities, psychological perspectives, 2328–2331
black
    feminisms, 626–630
    nationalism, 97
black feminist thought, 180–182
    bifurcated consciousness, 164–166
    critical race theory, 384–389
    feminist methodology, 821–827
    images of gender and sexuality in advertising, 1367–1371
    intersectionality, 1439–1443
    multiracial feminism, 678–682
    outsider within, 1816–1819
    postcolonial feminism, 702–706
    postcolonialism, theory and criticism, 1886–1891
    South Africa
        feminism, 729–735
        LGBT, 1600–1605
    white supremacy and gender, 2421–2425
    Yoruba culture, religion, and gender, 2606–2618
black lesbians
    butch/femme, 207–208
body
    material feminism, 671–676
body labor, 525–527
body politics, 182–185
    appearance psychology, 102–107
    beauty industry, 157–159
    birth control, 175–177
    boys' peer cultures, 192–194
    cisgenderism, 271–274
    Communism in Eastern Europe, 323–328
    dieting, 430–433
    eating disorders, 499–502
    embodiment and phenomenological tradition, 520–525
    fashion, 591–595
    female genital cutting, 288–293, 609–612
    feminist theories
        of body, 878–883
        of experience, 883–887
    infanticide, 1412–1415

body politics (*Continued*)
  male circumcision, 1621–1623
  menarche, 1678–1680
  menopause, 1680–1682
  menstrual activism, 1682–1686
  Nazi persecution of homosexuals, 1750–1754
  performance art, 1844–1846
  pornography, feminist legal and political debates on, 1877–1882
  sex toys, 2109–2111
  tattooing and piercing, 2305–2307
  technosexuality, 2309–2311
  women in combat, 2441–2445
body practices
  cosmetic surgery, 365–367
  female genital cutting, 288–293, 609–612
  feminist theories of body, 878–883
  footbinding, 920–922
  metrosexual, 1695–1696
  monasticism, 1720–1722
  sexual objectification, 2179–2181
  Shaker religion, 2232–2234
  steroids, 2270–2272
Bolivia
  abortion laws, 3
Bollywood, 185–187
books
  feminist publishing, 855–864
  feminist utopian writing, 901–903
  gay male literature, 935–938
borderlands, 187–191
Bosnia and Herzegovina
  abortion laws, 3
Botswana
  abortion laws, 3
bottom-up
  customary laws, 399–401
bourgeois vs socialism
  Northeast Asian feminism, 694–701
boys' peer cultures, 192–194
  bullying, 204–206
brain
  cognitive critical and cultural theory, 293–298
  female orgasm, 612–614
  incest, social practices and legal policies on, 1399–1405
  neuroscience and brain research
    gender, 1754–1759
    sexuality, 1759–1765
Brazil
  abortion laws, 3
breast cancer, 194–199
  hormone replacement therapy, 1318–1320
  women's health movement in the United States, 2563–2567
breastfeeding
  historical and comparative perspective, 199–201
  scientific motherhood, 2060–2061
  wet nursing, 2419–2421
Britain
  abortion laws, 3
  eighteenth-century feminism, 642–647
  sex education in UK and United States, 2092–2095
British colonies
  anti-miscegenation laws, 89–91
Brown, William Wells, 1840
Brunei
  abortion laws, 3
Buddhism, 201–204
  abortion, 14–15
  Daoism, 411–413
  monasticism, 1720–1722
  nuns, including Taiwan Buddhist, 1786–1791
  Shinto, 2239–2241
  virginity, 2397–2399
Bulgaria
  abortion laws, 3
bullying, 204–206
Burkina Faso
  abortion laws, 3
Burundi
  abortion laws, 3
butch/femme, 207–208
  drag, 484–490
  lesbian performance, 1527–1529
  lesbian stereotypes in the United States, 1531–1536
  social identity, 2251–2254
  stone butch, 2274–2276

C

CAM *see* complementary and alternative medicine
Cambodia
  abortion laws, 3
  feminism, 739
Cameroon
  abortion laws, 3
camp, 209–211
Canada
  abortion laws, 3
  anti-globalization movements, 85
  anti-poverty activism, 92–95
  gender, politics and the state, 1138–1144
  LGBT, 1583–1587
  obscenity laws, 1793–1797

poverty, 1906–1907
women's and feminist activism
  Native United States and Canada, 2513–2518
  United States and Canada, 2539–2545
see also North America
cancer
  breast cancer, 194–199
Canela people, 80
capabilities approach, 211–213
Cape Verde
  abortion laws, 3
capitalism
  anarchist feminisms, 623–626
  Communism and gender in China, 329–337
capitalist patriarchy, 213–217
  economic determinism, 509–510
  gender bias, 953–955
  gender as institution, 1052–1056
  governance and gender, 1223–1229
  Occupy movements, 1801–1805
  Yoruba culture, religion, and gender, 2606–2618
cardiac disease and gender, 218–220
  life expectancy, 1612–1616
career
  mentoring, 1691–1693
  see also employment
Caribbean
  anglophone Caribbean feminism, 71–75
  LGBT, 1546–1550
  poverty, 1907–1908
  religion and homophobia, 2016–2020
  sexual citizenship, 2146–2151
  women's and feminist activism, 2480–2485
  see also Latin America
Catholic
  women-church, 2468–2470
CEDAW, 25, 359, 362–365, 842–843
  customary laws, 399–401
  gender and development, 968–973
  gender indices, 1036–1046
  gender justice, 1056–1062
  gender mainstreaming, 1062–1064
  gender, politics and the state, Western Europe, 1144–1152
  history of women's rights in international and comparative perspective, 1289–1306
  honor killing, 1314–1318
  human rights, international laws and policies, 1330–1345
  leadership and gender, 1504–1506
  LGBT, Southern Africa, 1600–1605
  North African feminism, 688–694
  sexual rights, 2196–2200
  universal human rights, 2375–2377

women's and feminist activism
  East Asia, 2485–2489
  Southern Africa, 2534–2538
celibacy, 221–222
  Buddhism, 203
  chastity, 225–227
  feminist utopian writing, 901–903
  virginity, 2397–2399
censorship
  obscenity laws in United States, Canada and Europe, 1793–1797
Central African Republic
  abortion laws, 3
Central America
  maquiladora, 1623–1625
Central Europe
  Nazi persecution of homosexuals, 1750–1754
Chad
  abortion laws, 3
charivaris, 223–225
chastity, 225–227
  celibacy, 221–222
  feminist utopian writing, 901–903
  honor killing, 1314–1318
  rape law, 1989–1993
  virginity, 2397–2399
Chicanas
  bifurcated consciousness, 164–166
  borderlands, 187–191
  feminism, 630–632
  Latina feminism, 661–666
  Mestiza consciousness, 1693–1695
  multiracial feminism, 678–682
chick flicks, 227–229
  visual culture and gender, 2403–2408
  see also film
child care
  breastfeeding, 199–201
  fatherhood movements, 595–599
  scientific motherhood, 2060–2061
  stratified reproduction, 2280–2281
  wet nursing, 2419–2421
child custody and father right principle, 229–234
  fatherhood movements, 595–599
  masculinism, 1625–1627
child development
  age of consent in historical and international perspective, 30–34
  boys' peer cultures, 192–194
  bullying, 204–206
  child prostitution, 241–246
  children's literature and sexuality, 256–259
  cisgenderism, 271–274

child development (*Continued*)
  gender variance, 1169–1171
  menarche, 1678–1680
child labor in comparative perspective, 234–241
  household livelihood strategies, 1322–1326
  Yoruba culture, religion, and gender, 2606–2618
child marriage
  adolescent pregnancy, 19–21
  age of consent and child marriage in India, 26–30
child prostitution, 241–246
  child labor in comparative perspective, 234–241
  sexual slavery, 2202–2205
child sex offenders, 246–249
child sexual abuse/trauma, 249–252
  domestic violence in United States, 467–470
  fathers and parenting interventions, 600–601
  incest, social practices and legal policies on, 1399–1405
  misogyny, 1718–1720
  rape and re-victimization, treatment of, 1993–1997
  recovered memories, 1997–1999
children's literature
  and gender, 252–256
  media and gender socialization, 1662–1667
  and sexuality, 256–259
Chile
  abortion laws, 3
China
  abortion laws, 3
  Communism and gender, 329–337
  feminism, 698–701
  footbinding, 920–922
  gender/history of revolutions, 1000–1001
  Yin-Yang, 2601–2604
Chinese feminism, 632–637
Chinese religions
  abortion, 16
  nuns, including Taiwan Buddhist, 1786–1791
Chinese traditional medicine, 49
chiropractic, 50
Christianity
  monasticism, 1720–1722
  Mormonism, 1729–1731
  mysticism, 1733–1735
  pacifism, Quakers, and gender, 1821–1825
  religion and homophobia, 2016–2020
  religious fundamentalism, 2020–2025
  virginity, 2397–2399
  witches, 2427–2429
Christianity, gender and sexuality, 259–262
  abortion, 15–16
  celibacy, 221–222

chastity, 225–227
feminist Christology, 769–771
gyn/ecology, 1231–1232
homosexuality, 263–267
same-sex marriage, 259–262
Christology, feminist, 769–771
chromotherapy, 51
cisgender/cissexual, 267–271
  gender identity theory, 1030–1035
  gender violence, 1172–1175
  privilege, 1916–1918
  sex selection, 2102–2104
cisgenderism, 271–274
  lesbian, gay, bisexual, and transgender psychologies, 1522–1527
  transphobia, 2357–2360
citizen journalism, 108
civil rights law and gender
  customary laws, 399–401
  LGBT
    North America, 1583–1587
    Western Europe, 1605–1612
  sodomy law in comparative perspective, 2262–2266
  United States, 274–275
class, caste, and gender, 275–280
  anti-racist/anti-civil rights movements, 96–102
  cohabitation and *Ekageikama* in the Kandyan Kingdom (Sri Lanka), 301–303
  courtly love, 367–369
  Declaration of the Rights of Women, 413–414
  fashion, 591–595
  feminist standpoint theory, 867–870
  gender inequality and gender stratification, 1050–1052
  identity politics, 1365–1367
  India, 275–280
  queer methods and methodologies, 1969–1974
  self-esteem, 2071–2074
  suffrage, 2293–2296
cleanliness
  cult of domesticity, 394–396
  see also purity versus pollution
clerical
  celibacy, 221–222
climate change and gender, 280–283
  environment and gender, 539–544
  environmental disasters and gender, 544–548
  Mother Nature, 1731–1733
clinical trials, bias against women, 283–288
  medical and scientific experimentation and gender, 1667–1671

clitoridectomy, 288–293
  gender, politics and the state, Northern Africa, 1116–1122
  gyn/ecology, 1231–1232
  taboo, 2303–2305
coaching
  mentoring, 1691–1693
cognitive critical and cultural theory, 293–298
  feminist utopian writing, 901–903
  individualism and collectivism, critical feminist perspectives on, 1410–1412
cognitive methodologies
  cognitive critical and cultural theory, 293–298
  emotional abuse, 530
cognitive sex differences
  debates on, 298–300
  feminist studies of science, 870–876
  gender equality/inequality in education, 993–998, 1046–1050
  nature–nurture debate, 1744–1750
  neuroscience, brain research, and gender, 1754–1759
cohabitation
  heterosexual marriage trends in the West, 1265–1270
cohabitation and *Ekageikama* in the Kandyan Kingdom (Sri Lanka), 301–303
  polyamory, 1862–1866
  polygamy, polygyny and polyandry, 1866–1868
collective action
  gender and economic globalization, 511–515
  violence against women, movements against, 2392–2397
  see also community and grassroots activism
Colombia
  abortion laws, 3
colonialism
  anti-miscegenation laws, 89–91
  capitalist patriarchy, 213–217
  comfort women, 317–319
  criminal justice system and sexuality, 371–384
  cult of domesticity, 394–396
  eurocentrism, 574–576
  feminist ethnography, 796–804
  and gender, 303–314
  gender, politics and the state
    Aboriginal Australia and Torres Strait Islands, 1073–1077
    Latin America, 1104–1112
    South Asia, 1127–1133
  images of gender and sexuality
    Latin America, 1371–1376
    Southern Africa, 1380–1385

  immigration, colonialism, and globalization, 1388–1393
  indigenous knowledges and gender, 1405–1409
  non-violence, 1781–1783
  oral tradition, 1810–1813
  postcolonial feminism, 702–706
  postcolonialism, theory and criticism, 1886–1891
  religion and homophobia, 2016–2020
  Southeast Asian feminism, 735–743
  suttee (Sati), 2300–2302
  transgender politics, 2346–2351
  women's and feminist activism, Native United States and Canada, 2513–2518
  Yoruba culture, religion, and gender, 2606–2618
colonialism and gender
  gender/history of revolutions
    East Asia, 998–1005
    Northern Africa, 1015–1023
  history of women's rights in international and comparative perspective, 1289–1306
  Islam and gender, 1458–1463
  LGBT, Caribbean, 1546–1550
  nationalism and sexuality, 1741–1744
  oral tradition, 1810–1813
  orientalism, 1813–1816
  sodomy law in comparative perspective, 2262–2266
  traditional and indigenous knowledge, 2322–2326
  two-spirit, 2364–2365
  women's and feminist activism
    Aboriginal Australia and Torres Strait Islands, 2470–2475
    Eastern Africa, 2489–2494
    Native United States and Canada, 2513–2518
    West Africa, 2545–2548
  Yoruba culture, religion, and gender, 2606–2618
colonialism and sexuality, 314–317
  LGBT, Eastern Africa, 1551–1557
  regulation of queer sexualities, 2009–2014
  sodomy law in comparative perspective, 2262–2266
  traditional and indigenous knowledge, 2322–2326
  two-spirit, 2364–2365
comfort women, 317–319
  geisha, 942–943
  militarism and sex industries, 1710–1714
  sexual slavery, 2202–2205
  sexual terrorism, 2208–2210
  war, international violence, and gender, 2411–2419

coming out, 319–321
    lesbian and gay movements, 1516–1522
    passing, 1839–1841
commitment ceremonies, 321–323
common law
    sodomy law in comparative perspective, 2262–2266
communal ideology
    kibbutz/kibbutzim, 1485–1486
communication
    alternative media, 43–47
    gender discourse, 441–445
    Internet and gender, 1433–1437
    oral tradition, 1810–1813
Communism/socialism
    anarchism and gender, 59–64
    China, 329–337
    Eastern and Central Europe
        gender/history of revolutions, 1005–1015
        women's and feminist activism, 2494–2499
    Eastern Europe, 323–328
    leftist armed struggle, women in, 1507–1512
    Russia, 328–329
    United States, 337–341
community
    charivaris, 223–225
    empowerment, 534–537
    kibbutz/kibbutzim, 1485–1486
    kinship, 1489–1491
    nuns, including Taiwan Buddhist, 1786–1791
community and grassroots activism, 341–345
    Chicana feminism, 631
    intersex movement, 1443–1448
    NGOs and grassroots organizing, 1765–1769
    Occupy movements, 1801–1805
    subaltern, 2291–2293
    transnational labor movements, 2351–2357
    women's centers, 2559–2561
    women's and feminist activism
        Eastern Africa, 2489–2494
        Middle East, 2508–2513
        West Africa, 2545–2548
    women's and feminist organizations in South Asia, 2553–2557
    women's health movement in the United States, 2563–2567
    Women's Worlds Conference, 2586–2588
community other mothers, 345–348
    fictive kin, 918–920
Comoros
    abortion laws, 3
comparable worth/work of equal value, 348–351
    gender division of labor, 456–461
    governance and gender, 1223–1229

complementary and alternative medicine, 47–53, 351–354
    traditional healing, 2326–2328
compulsory heterosexuality, 354–358
    gender as institution, 1052–1056
    gender oppression, 1067–1069
    heteronormativity and homonormativity, 1257–1259
    lesbian continuum, 1512–1513
    lesbian stereotypes in the United States, 1531–1536
    monogamy, sociological perspectives on, 1724–1727
    nationalism and sexuality, 1741–1744
    Nazi persecution of homosexuals, 1750–1754
    Oedipal conflict, 716–726, 1805–1808
computing, feminist design, 776–783
conception
    assisted reproduction, 119–123
Confucianism
    abortion, 16
    gender, politics and the state, East Asia, 1093–1099
Congo
    abortion laws, 3
consciousness-raising, 356–358
    empowerment, 534–537
    feminist methodology, 821–827
    feminist organizations, definition of, 842–844
    feminist psychotherapy, 851–855
    lesbian and gay movements, 1516–1522
    maternal activism, 1640–1645
    personal is political, 1846–1848
    Riot grrrl, 2046–2047
    self-help movements, 2074–2078
contraception/contraceptives, 358–362
    family planning, 584–589
    fertility rates, 911–914
    history of women's rights in international and comparative perspective, 1289–1306
    see also abortion; birth control
Convention on the Elimination of All Forms of Discrimination against Women see CEDAW
cosmetic surgery, 365–367
    feminist theories of body, 878–883
    sexual objectification, 2179–2181
    skin lightening/bleaching, 2247–2249
Costa Rica
    abortion laws, 3
Cóte d'Ivoire
    abortion laws, 3
courtly love, 367–369

creation stories, 369–371
　feminist Christology, 769–771
　Judaism and gender, 1471–1475
crime
　comfort women, 317–319
　criminal justice system and sexuality in the United States, 371–384
　gender and death penalty, 964–966
　victimization, 2381–2384
criminal justice
　female criminality, 601–605
　gender and death penalty, 964–966
　prostitution/sex work, 1933–1938
criminal justice system and sexuality
　parenting in prison, 1836–1839
　United States, 371–384
critical race theory, 384–389
　feminist perspectives on whiteness, 846–851
　genetics and racial minorities in United States, 1199–1206
　hip-hop/rap, 1287–1289
　hybridity and miscegenation, 1359–1361
　intersectionality, 1439–1443
　Mestiza consciousness, 1693–1695
　outsider within, 1816–1819
　white supremacy and gender, 2421–2425
　womanist, 2437–2438
　womanist theology & preaching, 2439–2440
critical theory
　archaeology and genealogy, 109–110
　cisgenderism, 271–274
　cognitive critical and cultural theory, 293–298
　colonialism and gender, 303–314
　consciousness-raising, 356–358
　individualism and collectivism, critical feminist perspectives on, 1410–1412
　Yin-Yang, 2601–2604
Croatia
　abortion laws, 3
cross-cultural
　breastfeeding, 199–201
　gender roles, 389–392
　initiation rites, 1424–1428
　midwifery, 1699–1701
　Northeast Asian feminism, 694–701
　polygamy, polygyny and polyandry, 1866–1868
　self-esteem, 2071–2074
　tattooing and piercing, 2305–2307
　traditional healing, 2326–2328
　volunteerism and charitable giving, 2408–2409
cross-cultural gender roles
　geisha, 942–943
　gender identification, 1023–1026
　Hijra/Hejira, 1281–1282

　immigration and gender, 1394–1399
　internet and gender, 1433–1437
　LGBT, Eastern Africa, 1551–1557
　regulation of queer sexualities, 2009–2014
　sex-related difference research, 2125–2129
　tattooing and piercing, 2305–2307
　two-spirit, 2364–2365
　Yoruba culture, religion, and gender, 2606–2618
cross-dressing, 392–394
　drag, 484–490
　fairy tales, 579–582
　shaman priestesses, 2236–2237
　third gender, 2311–2314
　trans identities, psychological perspectives, 2328–2331
Cuba
　abortion laws, 3
　LGBT, 1548–1549
cult of domesticity, 394–396
　eighteenth-century feminism, 642–647
　scientific motherhood, 2060–2061
cults *see* sects and cults
cultural context
　feminist psychotherapy, 851–855
　self-esteem, 2071–2074
cultural criticism
　fairy tales, 579–582
　lesbian cultural criticism, 1514–1516
　popular culture and gender, 1868–1871
　queer literary criticism, 1965–1969
cultural feminism, 637–642
　feminism and argumentation, 743–745
　feminist jurisprudence, 812–816
　Marxist/Socialist feminism, 749–753
　radical feminism, 726–729
cultural practices
　adultery, 21–24
　anthropological perspectives of sex, 78–82
　arranged marriages, 112–114
　breastfeeding, 199–201
　charivaris, 223–225
　child labor in comparative perspective, 234–241
　compulsory heterosexuality, 354–358
　dowry and bride-price, 476–480
　eurocentrism, 574–576
　female genital cutting, 288–293, 609–612
　geisha, 942–943
　gender bender, 951–953
　gender, politics and the state, Māori, 1112–1116
　gender as practice, 1153–1154
　images of gender and sexuality in Latin America, 1371–1376
　indigenous knowledges and gender, 1405–1409
　Islamic feminism, 658–661

cultural practices (*Continued*)
  kinship, 1489–1491
  menstrual rituals, 1686–1691
  purity versus pollution, 1957–1959
  queer performance, 1974–1977
  suttee (Sati), 2300–2302
  traditional and indigenous knowledge, 2322–2326
  wicca, 2425–2427
  women's dirges, 2561–2563
cultural theory
  embodiment and phenomenological tradition, 520–525
  gender as institution, 1052–1056
  individualism and collectivism, critical feminist perspectives on, 1410–1412
  politics of representation, 1857–1862
culture
  body politics, 182–185
  children's literature and gender, 252–256
  cohabitation and *Ekageikama* in the Kandyan Kingdom (Sri Lanka), 301–303
  colonialism and gender, 303–314
  dowry and bride-price, 476–480
  fairy tales, 579–582
  fashion, 591–595
  feminist publishing, 855–864
  feminist utopian writing, 901–903
  oral tradition, 1810–1813
  Riot grrrl, 2046–2047
  structuralism, feminist approaches to, 2286–2291
  women as cultural markers/bearers, 2445–2449
  Yin-Yang, 2601–2604
curriculum transformation, 396–399
  sex education in UK and United States, 2092–2095
customary laws, 399–401
  civil rights law and gender, 274–275
  gender, politics and the state, Northern Africa, 1116–1122
  leadership and gender, 1504–1506
  menstrual rituals, 1686–1691
  women's and feminist activism, Southern Africa, 2534–2538
cyber intimacies, 401–405
  digital media and gender, 435–438
cyberbullying, 205
  curriculum transformation, 396–398
cybersex, 405–407
  cyber intimacies, 401–405
  digital media and gender, 435–438
  plastic sexuality, 1853–1855
  sexual addiction, 2142–2144
  technosexuality, 2309–2311
cyberspace
  alternative media, 46
  cyber intimacies, 401–405
  cybersex, 405–407
  Internet and gender, 1433–1437
  Internet sex, 1437–1439
  mail-order brides, 1619–1621
Cyborg Manifesto, 407–409
  Marxist/Socialist feminism, 749–753
  Yin-Yang, 2601–2604
Cyprus
  abortion laws, 3
Czech Republic
  abortion laws, 3

D

Dahomey Amazons, 57–59
  women in combat, 2441–2445
Daoism, 411–413
  Yin-Yang, 2601–2604
Darussalam
  abortion laws, 3
Declaration of the Rights of Women, 413–414
  history of women's rights in international and comparative perspective, 1289–1306
Declaration of Sentiments, 414–416
  history of women's rights in international and comparative perspective, 1289–1306
deep ecology, 416–418
  ecofeminism, 502–509
  Mother Nature, 1731–1733
demisexual, 117
democracy
  representation, 2025–2027
  Shaker religion, 2232–2234
democracy and democratization, 418–423
  gender equality, 990–993
  gender, politics and the state
    Eastern and Central Europe, 1082–1093
    Latin America, 1104–1112
    Western Europe, 1144–1152
  Islam and gender, 1458–1463
  LGBT, Latin America, 1563–1569
  South African feminism, 729–735
  suffrage, 2293–2296
  volunteerism and charitable giving, 2408–2409
  women's and feminist activism
    Eastern and Central Europe, 2494–2499
    Russia, Ukraine, and Eurasia, 2524–2529
    Western Europe, 2548–2552
  women's political representation, 2580–2584

Democratic People's Republic of Korea
  abortion laws, 4
Democratic Republic of Congo
  abortion laws, 3
demography
  feminization of migration, 905–907
  heterosexual marriage trends in the West, 1265–1270
  life expectancy, 1612–1616
  population control and population policy, 1872–1876
Denmark
  abortion laws, 4
denomination
  sects and cults, 2066–2069
depression, 423–426
  misogyny, 1718–1720
  occupational health and safety, 1797–1799
descent
  matrilineal/matrilocal systems, 1655–1660
desexualization, 426–428
design
  feminist design in computing, 776–783
Diagnostic and Statistical Manual of Mental Disorders (DSM), 428–430
  gender dysphoria, 987–990
  post-traumatic stress disorder, 1884–1886
  premenstrual syndrome (PMS), 1910–1912
  psychological theory, research, methodology, and feminist critiques, 1939–1944
  transgender movements in United States, 2341–2345
dieting, 430–433
  eating disorders, 499–502
difference feminism, 651
digital divide, 433–435
  Internet and gender, 1433–1437
digital media and gender, 435–438
  media and gender socialization, 1662–1667
disability
  fetal alcohol syndrome, 914–916
  disability rights movement, 439–441
  community and grassroots activism, 341–345
  sex selection, 2102–2104
  sexual rights, 2196–2200
  universal human rights, 2375–2377
disability studies
  asexuality, 116–119
  eugenics movements, 570–574
  feminist, 783–788
discourse and gender, 441–445
  A Vindication of the Rights of Woman, 2384–2386
  documentary film, 461–465

gender audit, 946–949
genderlect, 1193–1196
hegemonic masculinity, 1255–1257
language and gender, 1497–1502
non-sexist language use, 1779–1781
postcolonialism, theory and criticism, 1886–1891
sexism in language, 2131–2133
discrimination
  CEDAW, 25, 359, 362–365
  civil rights law and gender, United States, 274–275
  "Don't ask, don't tell" policy, 470–473
  employment *see* employment discrimination
  femicide, 614–616
  feminization of poverty, 788–793, 907–909
  gender and educational testing, 515–518
  gender justice, 1056–1062
  gender redistributive policies, 1155–1159
  gender wage gap, 1175–1177
  genetics testing and screening, 1206–1208
  heterosexism and homophobia, 1259–1261
  hostile work environment, United States, 1320–1322
  Islamic feminism, 658–661
  lookism, 1616–1618
  matrix of domination, 1660–1662
  sex *see* sex discrimination
  sexual orientation and law, 2181–2192
  sodomy law in comparative perspective, 2262–2266
  transphobia, 2357–2360
  universal human rights, 2375–2377
  women in non-traditional work fields, 2451–2458
discursive theories of gender, 445–450
  feminist ethnography, 796–804
  feminist literary criticism, 816–819
  feminist theories of organization, 887–892
  gender as institution, 1052–1056
  genderlect, 1193–1196
  phallocentrism/phallogocentrism, 1848–1850
  poststructural feminism, 712–716
disease symptoms, gender differences in, 450–454
disordered eating *see* eating disorders
division of labor
  domestic, 454–456
  economic determinism, 509–510
  eighteenth-century feminism, 642–647
  fatherhood movements, 595–599
  female farming systems, 605–609
  feminist standpoint theory, 867–870
  gender identity theory, 1030–1035
  gender role ideology, 1159–1162

division of labor (*Continued*)
   gendered *see* gender division of labor
   health careers, 1243–1246
   household livelihood strategies, 1322–1326
   immigration and gender, 1394–1399
   Latina feminism, 661–666
   Marxist/Socialist feminism, 749–753
   occupational segregation, 1799–1801
   parental leave in comparative perspective, 1832–1836
   patriarchy, 1841–1844
   social role theory of sex differences, 2254–2257
   volunteerism and charitable giving, 2408–2409
   work–family balance, 2593–2595
Djibouti
   abortion laws, 3
documentary film and gender, 461–465
domestic
   child labor in comparative perspective, 234–241
   cross-cultural gender roles, 389–392
   cult of domesticity, 394–396
   eighteenth-century feminism, 642–647
   fatherhood movements, 595–599
   gendered space, 1189–1191
domestic appliances
   cult of domesticity, 394–396
domestic technology, 465–467
domestic violence, 152–155
   environmental disasters and gender, 544–548
   fatherhood movements, 595–599
   gender-based violence, 1177–1181
   homelessness and gender, 1308–1311
   rape law, 1989–1993
   refugees and refugee camps, 2004–2009
   sexual coercion, 2157–2159
   United States, 467–470, 544–548
   women's and feminist activism, Native United States and Canada, 2513–2518
   see also violence against women
domesticity
   cult of, 394–396
   nineteenth-century feminism, 683–688
Dominica
   abortion laws, 4
Dominican Republic
   abortion laws, 4
"Don't ask, don't tell" policy, 470–473
   military masculinity, 1714–1716
   sexual orientation and law, 2181–2192
double standard, 473–476
   genderlect, 1193–1196
   health disparities, 1246–1250
   taboo, 2303–2305

dowry and bride-price, 476–480
   rape law, 1989–1993
dowry deaths, 480–482
   violence against women in global perspective, 2386–2392
Dowry Prohibition Act, 482–484
drag, 484–490
   camp, 209–211
   gender performance, 1071–1072
   third gender, 2311–2314
   trans identities, psychological perspectives, 2328–2331
   transvestitism, 2362–2364
drug and alcohol abuse, 490–493
   female criminality, 601–605
   fetal alcohol syndrome, 914–916
   intimate partner abuse, 1456–1458
   rape and re-victimization, treatment of, 1993–1997
   steroids, 2270–2272
DSM *see* Diagnostic and Statistical Manual of Mental Disorders
dual labor market, 493–495

E

earner-carer model, 497–499
   head of household and supplementary earner, 1241–1242
   parental leave in comparative perspective, 1832–1836
   patriarchy, 1841–1844
East Asia
   Chinese feminism, 632–637
   geisha, 942–943
   gender, politics and the state, 1093–1099
   gender/history of revolutions, 998–1005
   Northeast Asian feminism, 694–701
   poverty, 1907
   sexual citizenship, 2151–2157
   women's and feminist activism, 2485–2489
Eastern Africa
   LGBT, 1551–1557
   women's and feminist activism, 2489–2494
Eastern and Central Europe
   Communism, 323–328
   gender/history of revolutions, 1005–1015
   LGBT, 1557–1563
   women's and feminist activism, 2494–2499
Eastern Europe
   Communism, 323–328
   women's and feminist activism, Russia, Ukraine, and Eurasia, 2524–2529

eating disorders, 499–502
  dieting, 430–433
  feminist theories of body, 878–883
  misogyny, 1718–1720
  rape and re-victimization, treatment of, 1993–1997
  sexual objectification, 2179–2181
ecofeminism, 502–509
  community and grassroots activism, 341–345
  deep ecology, 416–418
  environment and gender, 539–544
  environmental justice, 548–550
  environmental politics and women's activism, 550–554
  feminist studies of science, 870–876
  feminist utopian writing, 901–903
  human–animal studies, 1350–1354
  Mother Nature, 1731–1733
  nomadic theory, 1775–1777
ecology
  deep, 416–418
  ecofeminism, 502–509
  environmental justice, 548–550
economic determinism, 509–510
  Marxist/Socialist feminism, 749–753
economic globalization
  capabilities approach, 211–213
  capitalist patriarchy, 213–217
  ecofeminism, 502–509
  free trade zones, 922–925
  and gender, 511–515
  gender and development, 968–973
  global care chain, 1216–1218
  global restructuring, 1221–1223
  household livelihood strategies, 1322–1326
  leadership and gender, 1504–1506
  NGOs and grassroots organizing, 1765–1769
  structural adjustment, 2284–2285
  women in development, 2449–2451
economics
  capabilities approach, 211–213
  child labor in comparative perspective, 234–241
  employment discrimination, 531–533
  feminist, 788–793
    gender budget, 961–964
    gender and economic globalization, 511–515
    gender indices, 1036–1046
    Occupy movements, 1801–1805
    structural adjustment, 2284–2285
  free trade zones, 922–925
  gender inequality and gender stratification, 1050–1052
  gender wage gap, 1175–1177
  informal economy *see* informal economy

  occupational segregation, 1799–1801
  structural adjustment, 2284–2285
  women's banking, 2557–2559
ecotheology
  Mother Nature, 1731–1733
Ecuador
  abortion laws, 3
education
  A Vindication of the Rights of Woman, 2384–2386
  climate change and gender, 280–283
  consciousness-raising, 356–358
  curriculum transformation, 396–399
  eighteenth-century feminism, 642–647
  feminist pedagogy, 844–846
  gender equality/inequality, 993–998, 1046–1050
  gender inequality and gender stratification, 1050–1052
  girls' peer cultures, 1212–1214
  higher education and gender in the United States, 1270–1281
  non-sexist education, 1777–1779
  sex difference research and cognitive abilities, 2085–2089
  sex segregation and education in United States, 2097–2102
  single-sex education and coeducation, 2243–2245
educational testing and gender, 515–518
Egypt
  abortion laws, 4
  LGBT, 1577
eighteenth century
  A Vindication of the Rights of Woman, 2384–2386
  Declaration of the Rights of Women, 413–414
  feminism, 642–647, 669–671
  pacifism, Quakers, and gender, 1821–1825
El Salvador
  abortion laws, 4
elder abuse
  domestic violence in United States, 467–470
  and gender, 518–520
embodied labor, 525–527
embodiment
  aging and ageism, 34–38
  cognitive critical and cultural theory, 293–298
  menopause, 1680–1682
  mind/body split, 1716–1718
  nomadic subject, 1773–1775
  queer performance, 1974–1977
  steroids, 2270–2272
  transsexuality, 2360–2362

embodiment and phenomenological tradition, 520–525
  skin lightening/bleaching, 2247–2249
emotion work, 525–527
  cognitive critical and cultural theory, 293–298
  ethics of care, 558–560
emotional abuse of women, 527–531
  elder abuse and gender, 518–520
  gender difference, 529
  sexual coercion, 2157–2159
employment
  dual labor market, 493–495
  emotion work, 525–527
  gender inequality and gender stratification, 1050–1052
  health careers, 1243–1246
  hostile work environment, United States, 1320–1322
  Latina feminism, 661–666
  occupational segregation, 1799–1801
  sexual harassment law, 2166–2171
  women in science, 2462–2466
  women's banking, 2557–2559
  work–family balance, 2593–2595
employment discrimination, 531–533
  glass ceiling/glass elevator, 1214–1216
  higher education and gender in the United States, 1270–1281
  informal economy, 1415–1419
  leadership and gender, 1504–1506
  occupational segregation, 1799–1801
  universal human rights, 2375–2377
  women's and feminist activism, East Asia, 2485–2489
empowerment, 534–537
  anarchism and gender, 59–64
  CAM, 351–354
  consciousness-raising, 356–358
  Declaration of Sentiments, 414–416
  environmental disasters and gender, 544–548
  feminist ethnography, 796–804
  feminist pedagogy, 844–846
  girls' peer cultures, 1212–1214
  matrix of domination, 1660–1662
  microcredit and microlending, 1697–1699
  Riot grrrl, 2046–2047
  sex-radical feminists, 2123–2125
  suffrage, 2293–2296
  violence against women, movements against, 2392–2397
  women's and feminist activism
    Australia and New Zealand, 2475–2479
    Northern Africa, 2518–2524

    women's and feminist organizations in South Asia, 2553–2557
    Women's Worlds Conference, 2586–2588
enigmatic
  sexual subjectivity, 2205–2208
entrepreneurship, 537–539
environment
  climate change and gender, 280–283
  deep ecology, 416–418
  and gender, 539–544
  hunger and famine, 1354–1359
  queer space, 1977–1978
environment and gender
  feminist studies of science, 870–876
  health disparities, 1246–1250
  Mother Nature, 1731–1733
  sustainable livelihoods, 2298–2300
environmental disasters and gender, 544–548
environmental justice, 548–550
  Mother Nature, 1731–1733
environmental politics and women's activism, 550–554
epistemology
  androcentrism, 65–66
  archaeology and genealogy, 109–110
  cisgenderism, 271–274
  feminist, 794–796
    feminism and argumentation, 743–745
    feminist objectivity, 838–841
    feminist studies of science, 870–876
    psychological theory, research, methodology, and feminist critiques, 1939–1944
    queer space, 1977–1978
    strong objectivity, 2282–2284
  indigenous knowledges and gender, 1405–1409
  matrix of domination, 1660–1662
  reflexivity, 1999–2001
  strong objectivity, 2282–2284
epistemology of the closet, 554–556
  feminist standpoint theory, 867–870
  gay male literature, 935–938
Equatorial Guinea
  abortion laws, 3
Eritrea
  abortion laws, 4
erotic
  masturbation, 1638–1640
  sex toys, 2109–2111
  sexual subjectivity, 2205–2208
essentialism, 556–558
  biological determinism, 173–174
  cisgenderism, 271–274
  cognitive critical and cultural theory, 293–298
  discursive theories of gender, 445–448

entrepreneurship, 537–539
ethics of care, 558–560
feminism and argumentation, 743–745
feminist art, 762–767
feminist studies of science, 870–876
gender, definition of, 966–968
gender development, theories of, 977–982
gender as practice, 1153–1154
genderlect, 1193–1196
gynocriticism, 1233–1234
hybridity and miscegenation, 1359–1361
individualism and collectivism, critical feminist perspectives on, 1410–1412
information technology, 1419–1424
Judaism and gender, 1471–1475
language and gender, 1497–1502
nomadic subject, 1773–1775
postmodern feminist psychology, 1900–1905
representation, 2025–2027
sex-related difference research, 2125–2129
sexual identity and orientation, 2171–2174
sisterhood, 2245–2247
social constructionist theory, 2249–2251
strategic essentialism, 2278–2280
subaltern, 2291–2293
women's writing, 2589–2593
Estimate of Risk of Adolescent Sexual Offense Recidivism (ERASOR), 248
Estonia
  abortion laws, 4
ethics
  eugenics movements, 570–574
  nature–nurture debate, 1744–1750
  positionality, 1882–1884
  reproductive choice, 2027–2030
  tearoom trade, 2307–2309
ethics of care, 558–560
  human–animal studies, 1350–1354
  maternal activism, 1640–1645
  Mother Nature, 1731–1733
  volunteerism and charitable giving, 2408–2409
ethics, moral development, and gender, 560–565
Ethiopia
  abortion laws, 4
ethnicity
  anti-racist/anti-civil rights movements, 96–102
  class, caste and gender, 275–280
  gangs and gender, 931–933
  images of gender and sexuality in Latin America, 1371–1376
  immigration and gender, 1394–1399
  strategic essentialism, 2278–2280

traditional healing, 2326–2328
womanist, 2437–2438
ethnography
  feminist, 796–804
    Aboriginal Australia and Torres Strait Islands, 618–623
  reflexivity, 1999–2001
  relations of ruling, 2014–2016
  tearoom trade, 2307–2309
eugenics
  age of consent in historical and international perspective, 30–34
  anti-miscegenation laws, 87–91
  contraception/contraceptives, 358–362
  criminal justice system and sexuality, 371–384
  disability rights movement, 439–441
  family planning, 584–589
  history and ethics, 565–570
  movements, 570–574
  negative, 571–572
  pro-choice movement in United States, 1918–1925
  sterilization, 2268–2270
  women's movements, early international movement, 2567–2573
Eurasia
  women's and feminist activism, 2524–2529
eurocentrism, 574–576
  feminist perspectives on whiteness, 846–851
  universal human rights, 2375–2377
Europe
  obscenity laws, 1793–1797
  poverty, 1907
European Union
  women's and feminist activism, Eastern and Central Europe, 2494–2499
evolutionary genetics
  nature–nurture debate, 1744–1750
existential feminism, 647–649
existentialism
  embodiment and phenomenological tradition, 520–525
experience
  bifurcated consciousness, 161–166
  black feminist thought, 180–182
  comfort women, 317–319
  feminist theories of, 883–887
exploitation
  child labor in comparative perspective, 234–241
extended families, 576–578
  fictive kin, 918–920
  kinship, 1489–1491

F

fairy tales, 579–582
   media and gender socialization, 1662–1667
false memories *see* recovered memories
families of choice, 582–584
   fictive kin, 918–920
   lesbians as community other mothers, 1538–1540
   monogamy, sociological perspectives on, 1724–1727
   single-parent households, 2241–2243
family law
   child custody and father right principle, 229–234
   fatherhood movements, 595–599
   fetal rights, 916–918
   incest, social practices and legal policies on, 1399–1405
   kinship, 1489–1491
   women's and feminist activism, Northern Africa, 2518–2524
family planning, 584–589
   abortion and religion, 13–17
   contraception/contraceptives, 358–362
   eugenics movements, 570–574
   fertility rates, 911–914
   heterosexual marriage trends in the West, 1265–1270
   reproductive choice, 2027–2030
   sterilization, 2268–2270
   see also birth control
family policy
   fathers and parenting interventions, 600–601
   parental leave in comparative perspective, 1832–1836
   work–family balance, 2593–2595
family roles and patterns
   masculinities, 1627–1632
   Yoruba culture, religion, and gender, 2606–2618
family violence
   honor killing, 1314–1318
   see also domestic violence; violence against women
family wage, 589–591
   feminist economics, 788–793
   household livelihood strategies, 1322–1326
   masculinities, 1627–1632
   pro-choice movement in United States, 1918–1925
family/household
   child labor in comparative perspective, 234–241
   community other mothers, 345–348
   Declaration of Sentiments, 414–416
   domestic technology, 465–467
   extended families, 576–578
   family wage, 589–591
   feminist family therapy, 804–807
   fictive kin, 918–920
   gender belief systems/ideology, 949–951
   gender division of labor, 454–456
   gender, politics and the state, East Asia, 1093–1099
   head of household and supplementary earner, 1241–1242
   heterosexual marriage trends in the West, 1265–1270
   household livelihood strategies, 1322–1326
   Judaism and gender, 1471–1475
   Judaism and sexuality, 1475–1482
   maternal activism, 1640–1645
   matrilineal/matrilocal systems, 1655–1660
   monogamy, biological perspectives on, 1722–1724
   Mormonism, 1729–1731
   pacifism, Quakers, and gender, 1821–1825
   parenting in prison, 1836–1839
   polyamory, 1862–1866
   polygamy, polygyny and polyandry, 1866–1868
   private/public spheres, 1912–1914
   religious fundamentalism, 2020–2025
   scientific motherhood, 2060–2061
   single-parent households, 2241–2243
farming systems
   female farming systems, 605–609
Fascism and Nazism
   eugenics, history and ethics, 560–565
   eugenics movements, 570–574
   pink triangle, 1850–1853
   right-wing women's movements, 2040–2046
   see also Nazi Germany; Nazi persecution of homosexuals
fashion, 591–595
   footbinding, 920–922
fatherhood
   anthropological perspectives of sex, 78–82
   child custody and father right principle, 229–234
   monogamy, biological perspectives on, 1722–1724
   parental leave in comparative perspective, 1832–1836
fatherhood movements, 595–599
   masculinism, 1625–1627
fathers and parenting interventions, 600–601
Feldenkrais method, 51
female criminality, 601–605
   gender and death penalty, 964–966
female farming systems, 605–609

female genital cutting, 288–293, 609–612
  gender, politics and the state, Northern Africa, 1116–1122
  gyn/ecology, 1231–1232
  initiation rites, 1424–1428
  North African feminism, 688–694
  sexuality and human rights, 2217–2220
  taboo, 2303–2305
female orgasm, 612–614
  masturbation, 1638–1640
  sex toys, 2109–2111
  sexology and psychological sex research, 2133–2142
femicide, 614–616
  honor killing, 1314–1318
  maternal activism, 1640–1645
  sex selection, 2102–2104
  violence against women in global perspective, 2386–2392
feminine and masculine elements, 616–618
  feminist Christology, 769–771
feminine principle, 505
femininities
  androcentrism, 65–66
  androgyny, 68–71
  appearance psychology, 102–107
  bifurcated consciousness, 162–164
  breast cancer, 194–199
  children's literature and sexuality, 256–259
  courtly love, 367–369
  feminine and masculine elements, 616–618
  gender bias, 953–955
  gender schema theory, 1162–1164
  gendered space, 1189–1191
  girls' peer cultures, 1212–1214
  initiation rites, 1424–1428
  masculinity and femininity, theories of, 1632–1638
  militarism and gender-based violence, 1701–1710
  sexuopharmaceuticals, 2227–2232
feminism
  A Vindication of the Rights of Woman, 2384–2386
  Aboriginal Australia and Torres Strait Islands, 618–623
  activist mothering, 17–19
  aging and ageism, 34–38
  Amazons, 53–59
  anarchism and gender, 59–64
  anarchist, 623–626
  anglophone Caribbean, 71–75
  and argumentation, 743–745
  backlash, 149–150
  beauty industry, 157–159
  bifurcated consciousness, 161–166
  birth control, history and politics, 175–177
  black, 626–630
  black feminist thought, 180–182
  body politics, 182–185
  borderlands, 187–191
  Buddhist, 201–204
  Chicana, 630–632
  chick flicks, 227–229
  Chinese, 632–637
  cisgender/cissexual, 267–271
  clinical trials, bias against women, 283–288
  colonialism and gender, 303–314
  Communism and gender in China, 329–337
  Communism in Russia, 328–329
  compulsory heterosexuality, 354–358
  cultural, 637–642
  Cyborg Manifesto, 407–409
  democracy and democratization, 418–423
  discourse and gender, 441–445
  discursive theories of gender, 445–448
  ecofeminism, 502–509
  economic determinism, 509–510
  eighteenth-century Britain, 642–647
  empowerment, 534–537
  entrepreneurship, 537–539
  essentialism, 556–558
  ethics of care, 558–560
  existential, 647–649
  fairy tales, 579–582
  family wage, 589–591
  feminist consciousness, historical perspective, 771–776
  feminist economics, 788–793
  first, second and third wave *see* first-wave feminism; second-wave feminism; third-wave feminism
  French, 649–654, 716–726
  gender and development, 968–973
  gender discourse, 441–445
  gender equality, 990–993
  gender justice, 1056–1062
  gender oppression, 1067–1069
  gender as practice, 1153–1154
  girls' peer cultures, 1212–1214
  gyn/ecology, 1231–1232
  history of women's rights in international and comparative perspective, 1289–1306
  homelessness and gender, 1308–1311
  human trafficking, feminist perspectives on, 1345–1350
  identity politics, 1365–1367
  indigenous knowledges and gender, 1405–1409

feminism (*Continued*)
  individualism and collectivism, critical feminist perspectives on, 1410–1412
  Indo-Caribbean, 654–658
  intersectionality, 1439–1443
  Islamic, 658–661
  Latina, 661–666
  leftist armed struggle, women in, 1507–1512
  LGBT, North America, 1583–1587
  liberal, 669–671
  masculinism, 1625–1627
  material, 671–676
  materialist, 676–678
  matriarchy, 1649–1655
  mentoring, 1691–1693
  Mestiza consciousness, 1693–1695
  monstrous-feminine, 1727–1729
  multiracial, 678–682
  nomadic subject, 1773–1775
  non-sexist language use, 1779–1781
  North Africa, 688–694
  Northeast Asia, 694–701
  Oedipal conflict, 716–726, 1805–1808
  orientalism, 1813–1816
  outsider within, 1816–1819
  patriarchy, 1841–1844
  performance art, 1844–1846
  political participation in Western democracies, 1855–1857
  positionality, 1882–1884
  postcolonial, 702–706
  postfeminism, 1891–1900
  postmodern, 753–759
  postmodern feminist psychology, 1900–1905
  poststructural, 712–716
  and psychoanalysis, 716–726
  psychology of gender, history and development of field, 1944–1955
  queer methods and methodologies, 1969–1974
  queer theory, 1978–1982
  radical *see* radical feminism
  refugees and refugee camps, 2004–2009
  right-wing women's movements, 2040–2046
  romantic friendship, 2048–2050
  scientific sexism and racism, 2061–2066
  self-help movements, 2074–2078
  sex work and sex workers' unionization, 2118–2123
  sexism in language, 2131–2133
  sisterhood, 2245–2247
  South Africa, 729–735
  Southeast Asia, 735–743
  strategic essentialism, 2278–2280
  structuralism, feminist approaches to, 2286–2291
  subaltern, 2291–2293
  suffrage, 2293–2296
  Third World women, 2314–2317
  woman-centeredness, 2431–2434
  womanist, 2437–2438
    theology & preaching, 2439–2440
  women-church, 2468–2470
  Women's Worlds Conference, 2586–2588
  Yin-Yang, 2601–2604
feminism, lesbian, 666–669
  lesbian continuum, 1512–1513
  lesbian cultural criticism, 1514–1516
  lesbian popular music, 1529–1531
  lesbian and womyn's separatism, 1536–1538
  Lesbos, 1540–1541
  radical lesbianism, 1983–1985
feminism, Marxist/Socialist, 749–753
  women in development, 2449–2451
feminism and postmodernism, 707–712
  popular culture and gender, 1868–1871
  queer methods and methodologies, 1969–1974
  visual culture, 2399–2403
feminist activism, 759–762
  documentary film and gender, 461–465
  feminist design in computing, 776–783
  gender, politics and the state, 1122–1127
    Aboriginal Australia and Torres Strait Islands, 1073–1077
    Australia and New Zealand, 1073–1082
    Eastern and Central Europe, 1082–1093
    indigenous women, 1099–1104
    Southern Africa, 1133–1138
    United States and Canada, 1138–1144
    Western Europe, 1144–1152
  gender/history of revolutions
    Eastern and Central Europe, 1005–1015
    Northern Africa, 1015–1023
  Greenham Common, 1229–1230
  menstrual activism, 1682–1686
  multiracial feminism, 678–682
  non-violence, 1781–1783
  Occupy movements, 1801–1805
  pro-choice movement in United States, 1918–1925
  radical feminism, 726–729
  sex-radical feminists, 2123–2125

United States women's movements in historical perspective, 2369–2374
violence against women, movements against, 2392–2397
women's and feminist activism
    Australia and New Zealand, 2475–2479
    Caribbean, 2480–2485
    East Asia, 2485–2489
    Eastern and Central Europe, 2494–2499
    Latin America, 2499–2504
    Māori, 2504–2508
    Native United States and Canada, 2513–2518
    Northern Africa, 2518–2524
    Russia, Ukraine, and Eurasia, 2524–2529
    Southeast Asia, 2529–2533
    Southern Africa, 2534–2538
    United States and Canada, 2539–2545
    West Africa, 2545–2548
    Western Europe, 2548–2552
women's movements, modern international movement, 2573–2579
Women's Worlds Conference, 2586–2588
feminist art, 762–767
    gynocriticism, 1233–1234
    women's writing, 2589–2593
feminist art practice, 767–769
    Riot grrrl, 2046–2047
    visual culture and gender, 2403–2408
    women as producers of culture, 2458–2462
feminist Christology, 769–771
    feminist theology, 876–878
    women-church, 2468–2470
feminist consciousness, historical perspective, 771–776
feminist critiques
    DSM, 428–430
    of Marxism
        economic determinism, 509–510
    psychological theory, research, methodology, and feminist critiques, 1939–1944
feminist design in computing, 776–783
    information technology, 1419–1424
feminist disability studies, 783–788
    feminist theories of body, 878–883
    women's movements, early international movement, 2567–2573
feminist economics, 788–793
    gender budget, 961–964
    gender and economic globalization, 511–515
    gender indices, 1036–1046
    Occupy movements, 1801–1805
    structural adjustment, 2284–2285
    see also economics

feminist epistemology, 794–796
    feminism and argumentation, 743–745
    feminist objectivity, 838–841
    feminist studies of science, 870–876
    psychological theory, research, methodology, and feminist critiques, 1939–1944
    queer space, 1977–1978
    strong objectivity, 2282–2284
    see also epistemology
feminist ethics
    ethics, moral development, and gender, 560–565
feminist ethnography, 796–804
    reflexivity, 1999–2001
feminist family therapy, 804–807
feminist film theory, 807–812
    gaze, 940–941
    lesbian cultural criticism, 1514–1516
    monstrous-feminine, 1727–1729
    visual culture and gender, 2403–2408
feminist jurisprudence, 812–816
    women's and feminist activism, Southern Africa, 2534–2538
feminist legal and political debates
    pornography, 1877–1882
    postfeminism, 1891–1900
    sex-radical feminists, 2123–2125
    sexual addiction, 2142–2144
feminist literary criticism, 816–819
    feminist publishing, 855–864
    gynocriticism, 1233–1234
    women's writing, 2589–2593
feminist magazines, 819–821
    visual culture and gender, 2403–2408
feminist methodology, 821–827
    strong objectivity, 2282–2284
feminist movements
    gender/history of revolutions in Eastern and Central Europe, 1005–1015
    historical and comparative perspective, 827–838
    pro-choice movement in United States, 1918–1925
    United Nations Decade for Women, 2367–2369
    women's movements, modern international movement, 2573–2579
feminist objectivity, 838–841
    feminist studies of science, 870–876
    nature–nurture debate, 1744–1750
    strong objectivity, 2282–2284
feminist organizations *see* women's and feminist organizations
feminist pedagogy, 844–846
feminist perspectives on whiteness, 846–851

feminist print media, 45
　radical feminism, 726–729
feminist psychotherapy, 851–855
　phallocentrism/phallogocentrism, 1848–1850
feminist publishing, 855–864
　gynocriticism, 1233–1234
　women's writing, 2589–2593
feminist sex wars, 865–867
　human trafficking, feminist perspectives on, 1345–1350
　nature–nurture debate, 1744–1750
　postfeminism, 1891–1900
　romantic friendship, 2048–2050
　sex-radical feminists, 2123–2125
　sexual freedom, feminist debates in United States, 2163–2165
　sexual slavery, 2202–2205
feminist standpoint theory, 867–870, 2464
　feminist studies of science, 870–876
　matrix of domination, 1660–1662
　outsider within, 1816–1819
　personal is political, 1846–1848
　strong objectivity, 2282–2284
feminist studies of science, 870–876
　intersex movement, 1443–1448
　medical and scientific experimentation and gender, 1667–1671
　nature–nurture debate, 1744–1750
　neuroscience, brain research, and sexuality, 1759–1765
　scientific sexism and racism, 2061–2066
　women in science, 2462–2466
feminist theology, 876–878
　gyn/ecology, 1231–1232
　Islam and gender, 1458–1463
　nuns, including Taiwan Buddhist, 1786–1791
　women-church, 2468–2470
feminist theories of body, 878–883
　nomadic subject, 1773–1775
　sexual objectification, 2179–2181
　witches, 2427–2429
feminist theories of experience, 883–887
　mind/body split, 1716–1718
feminist theories of organization, 887–892
　governance and gender, 1223–1229
　women's movements, modern international movement, 2573–2579
feminist theories of welfare state, 892–901
　governance and gender, 1223–1229
feminist utopian writing, 901–903
　matriarchy, 1649–1655
feminization of labor, 903–905
　female farming systems, 605–609
　poverty in global perspective, 1905–1910
　see also labor
feminization of migration, 905–907
　immigration and gender, 1394–1399
　see also immigration; migration
feminization of poverty, 788–793, 907–909
　homelessness and gender, 1308–1311
　household livelihood strategies, 1322–1326
　hunger and famine, 1354–1359
　microcredit and microlending, 1697–1699
　see also poverty
femocrat, 909–911
　gender, politics and the state, Southern Africa, 1133–1138
　political participation in Western democracies, 1855–1857
fertility
　anthropological perspectives of sex, 78–82
　assisted reproduction, 119–123
　contraception/contraceptives, 358–362
　control of, 61
　monogamy, biological perspectives on, 1722–1724
　population control and population policy, 1872–1876
　surrogacy, 2296–2298
fertility rates, 911–914
　heterosexual marriage trends in the West, 1265–1270
　reproductive choice, 2027–2030
　reproductive health, 2030–2035
fetal alcohol syndrome, 914–916
fetal rights, 916–918
　genetics testing and screening, 1206–1208
　pro-life movement in the United States, 1925–1933
　universal human rights, 2375–2377
fictive kin, 918–920
　kinship, 1489–1491
fidelity
　chastity, 225–227
Fiji
　abortion laws, 3
film
　alternative media, 45
　Bollywood, 185–187
　chick flicks, 227–229
　documentary film and gender, 461–465
　feminist film theory, 807–812
　gaze, 940–941
　monstrous-feminine, 1727–1729
　visual culture and gender, 2403–2408
　see also media

fiqh
    Shari'a, 2237–2239
first-wave feminism, 745–749
    cultural feminism, 637–642
    lesbian popular music, 1529–1531
    matriarchy, 1649–1655
    multiracial feminism, 678–682
    nineteenth-century feminism, 683–688
    postfeminism, 1891–1900
    radical feminism, 726–729
    sisterhood, 2245–2247
    United States women's movements in historical perspective, 2369–2374
    women's movements, modern international movement, 2573–2579
    Women's Worlds Conference, 2586–2588
    see also feminism
food and health
    climate change and gender, 280–283
    hunger and famine, 1354–1359
footbinding, 920–922
    women's and feminist activism, East Asia, 2485–2489
Former Yugoslavian Republic of Macedonia
    abortion laws, 4
France
    abortion laws, 4
    anti-miscegenation laws, 91
    materialist feminism, 676–678
    radical lesbianism, 1983–1985
free trade zones, 922–925
    maquiladora, 1623–1625
French feminism, 649–654
    existential feminism, 647–649
    feminism and psychoanalysis, 716–726
    feminist literary criticism, 816–819
    Marxist/Socialist feminism, 749–753
    postmodern feminism, 753–759
    radical feminism, 726–729
Freudian psychoanalysis
    feminist film theory, 807–812
    masturbation, 1638–1640
    monstrous-feminine, 1727–1729
    transvestitism, 2362–2364
fundamentalism and public policy, 925–929
    regulation of queer sexualities, 2009–2014
    religious fundamentalism, 2020–2025

G
Gabon
    abortion laws, 4
Gambia
    abortion laws, 4
gangs and gender, 931–933

gay
    appearance psychology, 102–107
    asylum, challenges faced by sexual minorities, 123–128
    coming out, 319–321
    criminal justice system and sexuality, 371–384
    neuroscience, brain research, and sexuality, 1759–1765
gay identity
    anti-racist/anti-civil rights movements, 98–99
Gay and Lesbian Pride Day, 933–935
    lesbian and gay movements, 1516–1522
    LGBT
        Eastern Africa, 1551–1557
        Eastern and Central Europe, 1557–1563
gay male
    bathhouses, 150–152
    bear culture, 155–157
    camp, 209–211
    epistemology of the closet, 554–556
    health and healthcare in sexual minorities, 1250–1255
    lesbian and gay movements, 1516–1522
    LGBT, Northern Africa, 1588–1590
    pink triangle, 1850–1853
    pornography, 938–940
    tearoom trade, 2307–2309
gay male couples
    commitment ceremonies, 321–323
gay male literature, 935–938
    queer anglophone literature, 1961–1965
gaze, 940–941
    feminist art, 762–767
    feminist film theory, 807–812
    images of gender and sexuality in Southern Africa, 1380–1385
    media and gender socialization, 1662–1667
    visual culture, 2399–2403
        and gender, 2403–2408
geisha, 942–943
gender, 61–62
    alternative media, 43–47
    anarchist feminisms, 623–626
    androgyny, 68–71
    anglophone Caribbean feminism, 71–75
    anti-miscegenation laws, 87–91
    anti-racist/anti-civil rights movements, 96–102
    asylum seeking, 128–133
    backlash, 149–150
    biochemistry/physiology, 166–173
    birth control, history and politics, 175–177
    bullying, 204–206
    camp, 209–211
    cardiac disease and, 218–220

gender (*Continued*)
    children's literature, 252–256
    Christianity, gender and sexuality, 259–262
    cisgender/cissexual, 267–271
    civil rights law and gender, United States, 274–275
    class, caste and gender, 275–280
    clinical trials, bias against women, 283–288
    colonialism and gender, 303–314
    colonialism and sexuality, 314–317
    Communism and gender
        China, 329–337
        United States, 337–341
    cross-dressing, 392–394
    curriculum transformation, 396–399
    cyber intimacies, 401–405
    definitions of, 966–968
    drug and alcohol abuse, 490–493
    and educational testing, 515–518
    and elder abuse, 518–520
    employment discrimination, 531–533
    environmental disasters, 544–548
    environmental justice, 548–550
    essentialism, 556–558
    family wage, 589–591
    fathers and parenting interventions, 600–601
    female criminality, 601–605
    femicide, 614–616
    feminist art practice, 767–769
    feminist Christology, 769–771
    feminist consciousness, historical perspective, 771–776
    feminist design in computing, 776–783
    feminist disability studies, 783–788
    feminist economics, 788–793
    feminist jurisprudence, 812–816
    feminization of migration, 905–907
    footbinding, 920–922
    free trade zones, 922–925
    gangs and gender, 931–933
    higher education and gender in the United States, 1270–1281
    human rights, 1326–1330
        international laws and policies, 1330–1345
    human–animal studies, 1350–1354
    and immigration, 1394–1399
    indigenous knowledges and, 1405–1409
    individualism and collectivism, critical feminist perspectives on, 1410–1412
    Internet and gender, 1433–1437
    intimate partner abuse, 1456–1458
    Islamic feminism, 658–661
    Kothi, 1491–1493
    and language, 1497–1502
    and leadership, 1504–1506
    media and gender socialization, 1662–1667
    menopause, 1680–1682
    monogamy, biological perspectives on, 1722–1724
    mysticism, 1733–1735
    and nationalism, 1737–1741
    neuroscience, brain research, and gender, 1754–1759
    non-sexist education, 1777–1779
    non-sexist language use, 1779–1781
    occupational health and safety, 1797–1799
    Oedipal conflict, 716–726, 1805–1808
    pacifism
        peace activism, and gender, 1826–1832
        Quakers, and gender, 1821–1825
    political participation in Western democracies, 1855–1857
    postmodern feminist psychology, 1900–1905
    poverty in global perspective, 1905–1910
    as practice, 1153–1154
    premenstrual syndrome (PMS), 1910–1912
    psychology of gender, history and development of field, 1944–1955
    queer space, 1977–1978
    queer theory, 1978–1982
    relations of ruling, 2014–2016
    religion and homophobia, 2016–2020
    religious fundamentalism, 2020–2025
    self-esteem, 2071–2074
    sex and culture, 2080–2085
    sex discrimination, 2089–2091
    sex education in UK and United States, 2092–2095
    sex segregation and education in United States, 2097–2102
    sex tourism, 2104–2109
    sex versus gender categorization, 2116–2118
    sexism, 2129–2131
        in language, 2131–2133
    sexuality and human rights, 2217–2220
    single-sex education and coeducation, 2243–2245
    social role theory of sex differences, 2254–2257
    sterilization, 2268–2270
    strategic essentialism, 2278–2280
    tattooing and piercing, 2305–2307
    women travelers, 2466–2468
    women's dirges, 2561–2563
    women's ways of knowing, 2584–2586
    Women's Worlds Conference, 2586–2588
    women's writing, 2589–2593
    xenophobia and gender, 2597–2599

gender analysis, 943–945
  bifurcated consciousness, 161–166
  borderlands, 187–191
  feminist family therapy, 804–807
  femocrat, 909–911
  gender audit, 946–949
  gender blind, 959–961
  gender budget, 961–964
  gender and economic globalization, 511–515
  gender as institution, 1052–1056
  gender neutral, 1065–1067
  gender as practice, 1153–1154
  gender transgression, 1167–1169
  gendered innovations in science, health, and technology, 1181–1188
  gendered time, 1191–1193
  genderlect, 1193–1196
  gyn/ecology, 1231–1232
  hegemonic masculinity, 1255–1257
  higher education and gender in the United States, 1270–1281
  homelessness and gender, 1308–1311
  hypermasculinity, 1361–1363
  medical and scientific experimentation and gender, 1667–1671
  misogyny, 1718–1720
  sadomasochism, domination, and submission, 2051–2053
  sisterhood, 2245–2247
  social role theory of sex differences, 2254–2257
  status of women reports, 2266–2268
  strategic essentialism, 2278–2280
  tomboys and sissies, 2319–2322
  women's and feminist organizations in South Asia, 2553–2557
  women's ways of knowing, 2584–2586
gender assault/gender violence, 1172–1175
  bullying, 204–206
  cisgenderism, 271–274
  comfort women, 317–319
  domestic violence in United States, 467–470
  elder abuse, 518–520
  gangs and gender, 931–933
  gender/history of revolutions in Northern Africa, 1015–1023
  genocide, 1208–1212
  LGBT, Caribbean, 1546–1550
  rape culture, 1985–1989
  refugee women and violence against women, 2001–2004
  sexual slavery, 2202–2205
  sexual terrorism, 2208–2210
  transphobia, 2357–2360
  victimization, 2381–2384

  violence against women in global perspective, 2386–2392
  see also sexual violence; violence against men; violence against women
gender audit, 946–949
gender belief systems/ideology, 949–951
  gender, definition of, 966–968
  glass ceiling/glass elevator, 1214–1216
  LGBT
    Australia and New Zealand, 1541–1546
    Native North America, 1578–1583
  popular culture and gender, 1868–1871
  sexism, 2129–2131
  social role theory of sex differences, 2254–2257
gender bender, 951–953
  genderqueer, 1196–1198
gender bias, 953–955
  clinical trials, bias against women, 283–288
  disease symptoms, gender differences in, 450–454
  DSM, 428–430
  feminist literary criticism, 816–819
  feminist objectivity, 838–841
  feminist studies of science, 870–876
  gender analysis, 943–945
  gender and educational testing, 515–518
  gender equality/inequality in education, 993–998, 1046–1050
  gender mainstreaming, 1062–1064
  information technology, 1419–1424
  media and gender socialization, 1662–1667
  sex discrimination, 2089–2091
  sexism, 2129–2131
  tomboys and sissies, 2319–2322
gender bias in research, 955–959
  medical and scientific experimentation and gender, 1667–1671
  neuroscience, brain research, and gender, 1754–1759
  oral tradition, 1810–1813
  psychological theory, research, methodology, and feminist critiques, 1939–1944
  sex-related difference research, 2125–2129
  women in science, 2462–2466
gender blind, 959–961
  refugees and refugee camps, 2004–2009
gender and Buddhism, 201–204
gender budget, 961–964
gender and death penalty, 964–966
  sodomy law in comparative perspective, 2262–2266
gender development
  biochemistry/physiology, 166–173
  biological determinism, 173–174

gender development (*Continued*)
  cultural feminism, 637–642
  female farming systems, 605–609
  feminist psychoanalytic perspective, 973–977
  gender identification, 1023–1026
  gender identity theory, 1030–1035
  gender mainstreaming, 1062–1064
  law of the father, 1502–1503
  Oedipal conflict, 1805–1808
  population control and population policy, 1872–1876
  theories of, 977–982
  women in non-traditional work fields, 2451–2458
  women's centers, 2559–2561
gender and development, 968–973
  capabilities approach, 211–213
  environment and gender, 539–544
  environmental disasters and gender, 544–548
  female farming systems, 605–609
  gender analysis, 943–945
  gender role ideology, 1159–1162
  global restructuring, 1221–1223
  hunger and famine, 1354–1359
  informal economy, 1415–1419
  leadership and gender, 1504–1506
  maquiladora, 1623–1625
  microcredit and microlending, 1697–1699
  refugees and refugee camps, 2004–2009
  structural adjustment, 2284–2285
  sustainable livelihoods, 2298–2300
  Third World women, 2314–2317
  United Nations Decade for Women, 2367–2369
  women in development, 2449–2451
  women's movements, modern international movement, 2573–2579
gender difference
  adultery, 21–24
  bifurcated consciousness, 161–166
  biological determinism, 173–174
  CAM, 351–354
  climate change and gender, 280–283
  drug and alcohol abuse, 490–493
  ethics of care, 558–560
  ethics, moral development, and gender, 560–565
  femicide, 614–616
  gender analysis, 943–945
  gender and language, 1497–1502
  gender outlaw, 1069–1071
  gender role ideology, 1159–1162
  gender schema theory, 1162–1164
  genderlect, 1193–1196

  genderqueer, 1196–1198
  Hijra/Hejira, 1281–1282
  infanticide, 1412–1415
  Judaism and gender, 1471–1475
  Judaism and sexuality, 1475–1482
  life expectancy, 1612–1616
  monasticism, 1720–1722
  mysticism, 1733–1735
  nomadic subject, 1773–1775
  non-violence, 1781–1783
  normalization, 1783–1786
  occupational segregation, 1799–1801
  purity versus pollution, 1957–1959
  queer methods and methodologies, 1969–1974
  sex difference research and cognitive abilities, 2085–2089
  sexual instinct/desire, 2174–2176
  Shakti Shanthi, 2234–2235
  social role theory of sex differences, 2254–2257
  women travelers, 2466–2468
  women's banking, 2557–2559
gender difference research, 983–987
  masculinity and femininity, theories of, 1632–1638
  neuroscience and brain research
    gender, 1754–1759
    sexuality, 1759–1765
  sex-related, 2125–2129
  xenophobia and gender, 2597–2599
gender discourse, 441–445
  bifurcated consciousness, 161–166
  charivaris, 223–225
  Communism
    Eastern Europe, 323–328
    Russia, 328–329
  Communism and gender
    China, 329–337
    United States, 337–341
  discursive theories of gender, 445–450
  feminist utopian writing, 901–903
  gender analysis, 943–945
  gender audit, 946–949
  gender, definition of, 966–968
  gender identities and socialization, 1026–1030
  gender as institution, 1052–1056
  gender neutral, 1065–1067
  gender transgression, 1167–1169
  genderlect, 1193–1196
  hypermasculinity, 1361–1363
  images of gender and sexuality in Latin America, 1371–1376
  popular culture and gender, 1868–1871

poststructural feminism, 712–716
Third World women, 2314–2317
women's ways of knowing, 2584–2586
gender division of labor, 456–461
  domestic, 454–456
  domestic technology, 465–467
  dual labor market, 493–495
  emotion work, 525–527
  employment discrimination, 531–533
  entrepreneurship, 537–539
  ethics of care, 558–560
  family wage, 589–591
  female farming systems, 605–609
  gender redistributive policies, 1155–1159
  gender role ideology, 1159–1162
  gendered time, 1191–1193
  glass ceiling/glass elevator, 1214–1216
  head of household and supplementary earner, 1241–1242
  health careers, 1243–1246
  maquiladora, 1623–1625
  private/public spheres, 1912–1914
  social role theory of sex differences, 2254–2257
  wet nursing, 2419–2421
  women in development, 2449–2451
  women in non-traditional work fields, 2451–2458
  women in science, 2462–2466
gender dysphoria, 987–990
  gender identity theory, 1030–1035
  gender outlaw, 1069–1071
  genderqueer, 1196–1198
  sex reassignment surgery, 2095–2097
  sexology and psychological sex research, 2133–2142
  third gender, 2311–2314
  trans identities, psychological perspectives, 2328–2331
gender equality, 990–993
  age of consent and child marriage in India, 26–30
  Chinese feminism, 632–637
  comparable worth/work of equal value, 348–351
  creation stories, 369–371
  Declaration of the Rights of Women, 413–414
  Declaration of Sentiments, 414–416
  division of labor, 454–461
  environmental disasters and gender, 544–548
  feminist movements in historical and comparative perspective, 827–838
  feminist theories of organization, 887–892
  fertility rates, 911–914
  gender analysis, 943–945
  gender audit, 946–949

gender bias, 953–955
gender budget, 961–964
gender discourse, 441–445
gender identities and socialization, 1026–1030
gender justice, 1056–1062
gender oppression, 1067–1069
gender, politics and the state, 1122–1127
  Australia and New Zealand, 1077–1082
  Northern Africa, 1116–1122
  United States and Canada, 1138–1144
and gender stratification, 1050–1052
gender-based violence, 1177–1181
gender/history of revolutions
  Eastern and Central Europe, 1005–1015
  Northern Africa, 1015–1023
gendered time, 1191–1193
glass ceiling/glass elevator, 1214–1216
hegemonic masculinity, 1255–1257
heterosexual marriage trends in the West, 1265–1270
higher education and gender in the United States, 1270–1281
Hijra/Hejira, 1281–1282
Hite Report on Female Sexuality, 1306–1308
homelessness and gender, 1308–1311
hostile work environment, United States, 1320–1322
human rights, international laws and policies, 1330–1345
infanticide, 1412–1415
International Women's Day, 1431–1433
Internet and gender, 1433–1437
Judaism and gender, 1471–1475
Judaism and sexuality, 1475–1482
kibbutz/kibbutzim, 1485–1486
masculinism, 1625–1627
Mormonism, 1729–1731
non-sexist education, 1777–1779
parental leave in comparative perspective, 1832–1836
patriarchy, 1841–1844
sexual harassment law, 2166–2171
sexually transmitted infections, 2225–2227
Shaker religion, 2232–2234
Shinto, 2239–2241
single-sex education and coeducation, 2243–2245
social role theory of sex differences, 2254–2257
South African feminism, 729–735
status of women reports, 2266–2268
structural adjustment, 2284–2285
suffrage, 2293–2296
transnational labor movements, 2351–2357
transphobia, 2357–2360

gender equality (*Continued*)
  United States women's movements in historical perspective, 2369–2374
  women's centers, 2559–2561
  women's and feminist activism
    Australia and New Zealand, 2475–2479
    East Asia, 2485–2489
    Southeast Asia, 2529–2533
  women's political representation, 2580–2584
gender equality in education, 993–998, 1046–1050
  sex segregation and education in United States, 2097–2102
  single-sex education and coeducation, 2243–2245
gender equality policies
  gender mainstreaming, 1062–1064
gender identification, 1023–1026
  LGBT
    Eastern and Central Europe, 1557–1563
    Southeast Asia, 1595–1600
  sexology and psychological sex research, 2133–2142
  stone butch, 2274–2276
  tattooing and piercing, 2305–2307
  see also gender identities
gender identities
  age of consent and child marriage in India, 26–30
  butch/femme, 207–208
  coming out, 319–321
  drag, 484–490
  gender belief systems/ideology, 949–951
  gender blind, 959–961
  gender discourse, 441–445
  gender dysphoria, 987–990
  gender identification, 1023–1026
  gender as institution, 1052–1056
  gender outlaw, 1069–1071
  gender, politics and the state, Māori, 1112–1116
  genderqueer, 1196–1198
  hegemonic masculinity, 1255–1257
  Hijra/Hejira, 1281–1282
  hypermasculinity, 1361–1363
  intersexuality, 1448–1451
  lesbian stereotypes in the United States, 1531–1536
  lesbians as community other mothers, 1538–1540
  LGBT
    Eastern and Central Europe, 1557–1563
    North America, 1583–1587
    Southern Africa, 1600–1605
  politics of representation, 1857–1862
  postmodern feminist psychology, 1900–1905

  Shakti Shanthi, 2234–2235
  stone butch, 2274–2276
  traditional and indigenous knowledge, 2322–2326
  transgender movements
    international perspective, 2337–2341
    United States, 2341–2345
  transgender politics, 2346–2351
  two-spirit, 2364–2365
  women as cultural markers/bearers, 2445–2449
  women travelers, 2466–2468
  women's banking, 2557–2559
  women's dirges, 2561–2563
gender identity and socialization, 1026–1030
  media and gender socialization, 1662–1667
  sex and culture, 2080–2085
  sex segregation and education in United States, 2097–2102
  socialization and sexuality, 2257–2262
  taboo, 2303–2305
gender identity theory, 1030–1035
  sexual minorities, 2176–2179
gender images
  age of consent and child marriage in India, 26–30
  androgyny, 68–71
  children's literature and gender, 252–256
  fairy tales, 579–582
  feminine and masculine elements, 616–618
  feminist art practice, 767–769
  feminist film theory, 807–812
  gaze, 940–941
  images of gender and sexuality
    advertising, 1367–1371
    Latin America, 1371–1376
    Māori, 1376–1380
    Southern Africa, 1380–1385
  men's magazines, 1676–1678
  metrosexual, 1695–1696
  visual culture, 2399–2403
gender indices, 1036–1046
  immigration, colonialism, and globalization, 1388–1393
gender inequality in education
  A Vindication of the Rights of Woman, 2384–2386
gender inequality and gender stratification, 1050–1052
  structural adjustment, 2284–2285
  tomboys and sissies, 2319–2322
  volunteerism and charitable giving, 2408–2409
gender as institution, 1052–1056
gender and Islam, 1458–1463
  Shari'a, 2237–2239

gender justice, 1056–1062
  Women's Worlds Conference, 2586–2588
gender and language
  genderlect, 1193–1196
gender mainstreaming, 1062–1064
  femocrat, 909–911
  gender and development, 968–973
  gender justice, 1056–1062
  gender redistributive policies,
      1155–1159
  LGBT, Southern Africa, 1600–1605
  war, international violence, and gender,
      2411–2419
  women's and feminist activism
    Eastern and Central Europe, 2494–2499
    Southern Africa, 2534–2538
gender neutral, 1065–1067
  genderqueer, 1196–1198
gender oppression, 1067–1069
  outsider within, 1816–1819
  tomboys and sissies, 2319–2322
  transphobia, 2357–2360
gender outlaw, 1069–1071
gender performance, 1071–1072
  Hijra/Hejira, 1281–1282
  lesbian performance, 1527–1529
  maternal activism, 1640–1645
  stone butch, 2274–2276
  tomboys and sissies, 2319–2322
gender politics
  affirmative action, 24–25
  AIDS-related stigma, 38–40
  Amazons, 53–59
  animality, 76–78
  bear culture, 155–157
  courtly love, 367–369
  Cyborg Manifesto, 407–409
  Dahomey Amazons, 57–59
  female genital cutting, 288–293, 609–612
  feminism, Aboriginal Australia and Torres Strait
      Islands, 618–623
  feminist consciousness, historical perspective,
      771–776
  feminist movements in historical and
      comparative perspective, 827–838
  feminist utopian writing, 901–903
  gender budget, 961–964
  gender identities and socialization,
      1026–1030
  gender mainstreaming, 1062–1064
  gender, politics and the state, indigenous
      women, 1099–1104
  gender redistributive policies, 1155–1159
  gender transgression, 1167–1169

gender/history of revolutions
  East Asia, 998–1005
  Eastern and Central Europe, 1005–1015
  Hite Report on Female Sexuality,
      1306–1308
  identity politics, 1365–1367
  images of gender and sexuality in Southern
      Africa, 1380–1385
  lesbian cultural criticism, 1514–1516
  lesbian feminism, 666–669
  LGBT
    Eastern and Central Europe, 1557–1563
    Latin America, 1563–1569
    Māori, 1569–1573
    Middle East, 1573–1578
    Native North America, 1578–1583
  maquiladora, 1623–1625
  maternal activism, 1640–1645
  monstrous-feminine, 1727–1729
  North African feminism, 688–694
  Northeast Asian feminism, 694–701
  Occupy movements, 1801–1805
  prostitution/sex work, 1933–1938
  right-wing women's movements, 2040–2046
  Shakti Shanthi, 2234–2235
  strategic essentialism, 2278–2280
  transgender movements in international
      perspective, 2337–2341
  United States women's movements in historical
      perspective, 2369–2374
  women in combat, 2441–2445
  women's and feminist activism
    Latin America, 2499–2504
    Russia, Ukraine, and Eurasia, 2524–2529
  Yin-Yang, 2601–2604
gender, politics and the state, 1122–1127
  A Vindication of the Rights of Woman,
      2384–2386
  Aboriginal Australia and Torres Strait Islands,
      1073–1077
  Australia and New Zealand, 1077–1082
  East Asia, 1093–1099
  Eastern and Central Europe, 1082–1093
  indigenous women, 1099–1104
  Latin America, 1104–1112
  leadership and gender, 1504–1506
  Māori, 1112–1116
  Northern Africa, 1116–1122
  political participation in Western democracies,
      1855–1857
  South Asia, 1127–1133
  Southern Africa, 1133–1138
  suffrage, 2293–2296

gender, politics and the state (*Continued*)
  traditional and indigenous knowledge, 2322–2326
  United States and Canada, 1138–1144
  Western Europe, 1144–1152
  women's and feminist activism
    Aboriginal Australia and Torres Strait Islands, 2470–2475
    East Asia, 2485–2489
    Eastern and Central Europe, 2494–2499
    Middle East, 2508–2513
    Native United States and Canada, 2513–2518
    West Africa, 2545–2548
    Western Europe, 2548–2552
  work–family balance, 2593–2595
  Yoruba culture, religion, and gender, 2606–2618
gender as practice
  stigma, 2272–2274
  women as cultural markers/bearers, 2445–2449
gender practices
  entrepreneurship, 537–539
gender redistributive policies, 1155–1159
  population control and population policy, 1872–1876
gender relations
  Communism in Eastern Europe, 323–328
  Communism and gender in China, 329–337
  matriarchy, 1649–1655
  militarism and gender-based violence, 1701–1710
gender role ideology, 1159–1162
  health disparities, 1246–1250
  hypermasculinity, 1361–1363
  women in combat, 2441–2445
  xenophobia and gender, 2597–2599
gender roles
  charivaris, 223–225
  children's literature and gender, 252–256
  Communism in Russia, 328–329
  courtly love, 367–369
  cross-cultural, 389–392
  discursive theories of gender, 445–448
  fatherhood movements, 595–599
  female criminality, 601–605
  gender as practice, 1153–1154
  Judaism and gender, 1471–1475
gender schema theory, 1162–1164
gender socialization
  boys' peer cultures, 192–194
  children's literature and gender, 252–256
  civil rights law and gender, United States, 274–275
  cross-cultural gender roles, 389–392
  double standard, 473–476

gender belief systems/ideology, 949–951
gender development, theories of, 977–982
  and gender identities, 1026–1030
gender as institution, 1052–1056
gender neutral, 1065–1067
gender outlaw, 1069–1071
gender role ideology, 1159–1162
gender schema theory, 1162–1164
gender transgression, 1167–1169
Internet and gender, 1433–1437
menstrual activism, 1682–1686
obscenity laws in United States, Canada and Europe, 1793–1797
psychology of objectification, 1956–1957
self-esteem, 2071–2074
sex and culture, 2080–2085
sex segregation and education in United States, 2097–2102
sex-related difference research, 2125–2129
tomboys and sissies, 2319–2322
gender stereotypes, 1164–1167
  children's literature
    gender, 252–256
    sexuality, 256–259
  Communism and gender in United States, 337–341
  comparable worth/work of equal value, 348–351
  disease symptoms, gender differences in, 450–454
  eating disorders, 499–502
  fathers and parenting interventions, 600–601
  feminist film theory, 807–812
  gender identities and socialization, 1026–1030
  gender role ideology, 1159–1162
  gender schema theory, 1162–1164
  glass ceiling/glass elevator, 1214–1216
  health disparities, 1246–1250
  homelessness and gender, 1308–1311
  hypermasculinity, 1361–1363
  images of gender and sexuality
    advertising, 1367–1371
    Latin America, 1371–1376
  Internet and gender, 1433–1437
  masculinities, 1627–1632
  nationalism and gender, 1737–1741
  nuns, including Taiwan Buddhist, 1786–1791
  passing, 1839–1841
  popular culture and gender, 1868–1871
  post-traumatic stress disorder, 1884–1886
  sex discrimination, 2089–2091
  sex selection, 2102–2104
  sexism, 2129–2131
  sexual orientation and law, 2181–2192
  social role theory of sex differences, 2254–2257

tomboys and sissies, 2319–2322
victimization, 2381–2384
women in non-traditional work fields, 2451–2458
xenophobia and gender, 2597–2599
gender transgression, 1167–1169
genderqueer, 1196–1198
LGBT, Southern Africa, 1600–1605
shaman priestesses, 2236–2237
gender variance, 1169–1171
berdache, 159–161
children's literature and sexuality, 256–259
genderqueer, 1196–1198
LGBT
Australia and New Zealand, 1541–1546
Native North America, 1578–1583
third gender, 2311–2314
gender wage gap, 1175–1177
family wage, 589–591
feminization of labor, 903–905
head of household and supplementary earner, 1241–1242
hunger and famine, 1354–1359
informal economy, 1415–1419
Internet and gender, 1433–1437
occupational segregation, 1799–1801
patriarchy, 1841–1844
poverty in global perspective, 1905–1910
sex discrimination, 2089–2091
gender-based terrorism
sexual terrorism, 2208–2210
gender-based violence, 1177–1181
asylum and sexual orientation, 133–137
child prostitution, 241–246
dowry deaths, 480–482
Dowry Prohibition Act, 482–484
emotional abuse of women, 527–531
female genital cutting, 288–293, 609–612
femicide, 614–616
gender and death penalty, 964–966
gender oppression, 1067–1069
genocide, 1208–1212
homelessness and gender, 1308–1311
human rights, international laws and policies, 1330–1345
hypermasculinity, 1361–1363
International Women's Day, 1431–1433
intimate partner abuse, 1456–1458
maternal activism, 1640–1645
militarism and gender-based violence, 1701–1710
military masculinity, 1714–1716
misogyny, 1718–1720

pacifism, peace activism, and gender, 1826–1832
pornography, feminist legal and political debates on, 1877–1882
rape culture, 1985–1989
refugees
refugee women and violence against women, 2001–2004
refugees and refugee camps, 2004–2009
sex trafficking, 2111–2116
sexuality and human rights, 2217–2220
sexually transmitted infections, 2225–2227
transgender politics, 2346–2351
transphobia, 2357–2360
war, international violence, and gender, 2411–2419
women's and feminist activism, Southern Africa, 2534–2538
gender/history of revolutions
East Asia, 998–1005
Eastern and Central Europe, 1005–1015
Northern Africa, 1015–1023
gendered innovations
digital media and gender, 435–438
feminist design in computing, 776–783
in science, health, and technology, 1181–1188
gendered relationships, 61–62
gendered space, 1189–1191
private/public spheres, 1912–1914
queer space, 1977–1978
gendered time, 1191–1193
glass ceiling/glass elevator, 1214–1216
genderlect, 1193–1196
language and gender, 1497–1502
genderqueer, 1196–1198
cisgender/cissexual, 267–271
gender identity theory, 1030–1035
gender variance, 1169–1171
gender violence, 1172–1175
Hijra/Hejira, 1281–1282
neuroscience, brain research, and sexuality, 1759–1765
politics of representation, 1857–1862
sex selection, 2102–2104
third gender, 2311–2314
trans identities, psychological perspectives, 2328–2331
genealogy, 109–110
genetics
androgen insensitivity syndrome, 66–68
biological determinism, 173–174
eugenics

genetics (*Continued*)
    history and ethics, 565–570
    movements, 570–574
genetics and racial minorities in United States, 1199–1206
    hybridity and miscegenation, 1359–1361
    scientific sexism and racism, 2061–2066
genetics testing and screening, 1206–1208
    genetics and racial minorities in United States, 1199–1206
genital mutilation
    clitoridectomy and female genital cutting, 288–293, 609–612
    taboo, 2303–2305
genocide, 1208–1212
    sexual terrorism, 2208–2210
    see also violence; war and international violence
Georgia
    abortion laws, 4
Germany
    abortion laws, 4
    anti-miscegenation laws, 91
Ghana
    abortion laws, 4
girls
    female genital cutting, 288–293, 609–612
    feminist psychotherapy, 851–855
girls' peer cultures, 1212–1214
    bullying, 204–206
    gangs and gender, 931–933
glass ceiling/glass elevator, 1214–1216
    employment discrimination, 531–533
    gender division of labor, 456–461
    gender equality, 990–993
    leadership and gender, 1504–1506
    patriarchy, 1841–1844
global care chain, 1216–1218
    immigration and gender, 1394–1399
    informal economy, 1415–1419
    stratified reproduction, 2280–2281
Global Fund for Women, 2197–2198
global gag rule, 1218–1221
global restructuring, 1221–1223
    women's centers, 2559–2561
globalization
    abortion laws/policies, 1–13
    anti-globalization movements, 82–87
    asylum and sexual orientation, 133–137
    capabilities approach, 211–213
    capitalist patriarchy, 213–217
    deep ecology, 416–418
    female farming systems, 605–609

feminist movements in historical and comparative perspective, 827–838
feminization of labor, 903–905
feminization of migration, 905–907
free trade zones, 922–925
Gay and Lesbian Pride Day, 933–935
global care chain, 1216–1218
global restructuring, 1221–1223
human trafficking, feminist perspectives on, 1345–1350
immigration, colonialism, and globalization, 1388–1393
informal economy, 1415–1419
international laws and policies
LGBT, Latin America, 1563–1569
poverty in global perspective, 1905–1910
women's and feminist activism, Western Europe, 2548–2552
governance
    Declaration of Sentiments, 414–416
    feminization of poverty, 907–909
    global restructuring, 1221–1223
    relations of ruling, 2014–2016
    status of women reports, 2266–2268
governance and gender, 1223–1229
    A Vindication of the Rights of Woman, 2384–2386
    gender, politics and the state, Eastern and Central Europe, 1082–1093
    leadership and gender, 1504–1506
    political participation in Western democracies, 1855–1857
    sexual regulation and social control, 2192–2196
    women's political representation, 2580–2584
grassroots activism *see* community and grassroots activism
gray-A, 117
Great Britain *see* Britain
Greece
    abortion laws, 4
Greenham Common, 1229–1230
    war, international violence, and gender, 2411–2419
    see also activism; community and grassroots activism; women's movements
Grenada
    abortion laws, 4
Guatemala
    abortion laws, 4
Guinea
    abortion laws, 4
Guinea-Bissau
    abortion laws, 4

Guyana
    abortion laws, 4
gyn/ecology, 1231–1232
    Mother Nature, 1731–1733
gynocentric science, 51–52
gynocriticism, 1233–1234
    feminist literary criticism, 816–819
    feminist publishing, 855–864
    women's writing, 2589–2593

H
Haiti
    abortion laws, 4
    LGBT, 1547–1548
hate crimes/hate crime law, 1235–1240
head of household and supplementary earner, 1241–1242
health careers, 1243–1246
health disparities, 1246–1250
    occupational health and safety, 1797–1799
    transgender health and healthcare, 2333–2337
    women's centers, 2559–2561
health and healthcare, 1–13
    AIDS-related stigma, 38–40
    androgen insensitivity syndrome, 66–68
    athletics and gender, 137–142
    CAM, 47–53, 351–354
    cardiac disease and gender, 218–220
    climate change and gender, 280–283
    depression, 423–426
    disease symptoms, gender differences in, 450–454
    drug and alcohol abuse, 490–493
    female genital cutting, 288–293, 609–612
    life expectancy, 1612–1616
    midwifery, 1699–1701
    occupational health and safety, 1797–1799
    premenstrual syndrome (PMS), 1910–1912
    reproductive health, 2030–2035
    reproductive justice/rights in the United States, 2035–2040
    scientific motherhood, 2060–2061
    self-help movements, 2074–2078
    sexual assault/sexual violence, 2144–2146
    sexual minorities, 1250–1255
    sexually transmitted infections, 2225–2227
    steroids, 2270–2272
    transgender health and healthcare, 2333–2337
    women's centers, 2559–2561
    women's health movement in the United States, 2563–2567
health impact
    breast cancer, 194–199
    skin lightening/bleaching, 2247–2249

hegemonic masculinity, 1255–1257
    capitalist patriarchy, 213–217
    entrepreneurship, 537–539
    gender violence, 1172–1175
    homosexual reparative therapy, 1312–1314
    hypermasculinity, 1361–1363
    images of gender and sexuality in advertising, 1367–1371
    masculinities, 1627–1632
    masculinity and femininity, theories of, 1632–1638
    military masculinity, 1714–1716
    phallocentrism/phallogocentrism, 1848–1850
    rape culture, 1985–1989
    see also masculinities
heteronormativity and homonormativity, 1257–1259
heterosexism
    lesbian, gay, bisexual, and transgender psychologies, 1522–1527
    lesbian stereotypes in the United States, 1531–1536
    lesbians as community other mothers, 1538–1540
    privilege, 1916–1918
    sexualities, 2212–2217
    tomboys and sissies, 2319–2322
heterosexism and homophobia, 1259–1261
    alpha male, 41–43
    Christianity and homosexuality, 263–267
    drug and alcohol abuse, 490–493
    hegemonic masculinity, 1255–1257
    heteronormativity and homonormativity, 1257–1259
    homosexual reparative therapy, 1312–1314
    immigration, colonialism, and globalization, 1388–1393
    information technology, 1419–1424
    lesbian, gay, bisexual, and transgender psychologies, 1522–1527
    Nazi persecution of homosexuals, 1750–1754
    neuroscience, brain research, and sexuality, 1759–1765
    oral tradition, 1810–1813
    privilege, 1916–1918
    queer methods and methodologies, 1969–1974
    regulation of queer sexualities, 2009–2014
    religion and homophobia, 2016–2020
    sex and culture, 2080–2085
    sexual minorities, 2176–2179
    sexualities, 2212–2217
    tomboys and sissies, 2319–2322
    transphobia, 2357–2360

heterosexual imaginary, 1261–1265
  popular culture and gender, 1868–1871
heterosexual marriage trends in the West, 1265–1270
  same-sex marriage, 2055–2057
heterosexual matrix, 104
heterosexuality
  charivaris, 223–225
  compulsory, 354–358
  desexualization, 426–428
  double standard, 473–476
  kinship, 1489–1491
  private/public spheres, 1912–1914
  radical lesbianism, 1983–1985
  sex and culture, 2080–2085
hierarchy
  sexual subjectivity, 2205–2208
higher education and gender in the United States, 1270–1281
Hijra/Hejira, 1281–1282
  gender identity theory, 1030–1035
  gender, politics and the state, South Asia, 1127–1133
  gender variance, 1169–1171
  Kothi, 1491–1493
  LGBT, South Asia, 1590–1595
  politics of representation, 1857–1862
  third gender, 2311–2314
  trans identities, psychological perspectives, 2328–2331
Hinduism, 1282–1287
  abortion, 15
  Bollywood, 185–187
  celibacy, 221–222
  monasticism, 1720–1722
  Mother Nature, 1731–1733
  religious fundamentalism, 2020–2025
  Shakti Shanthi, 2234–2235
  Shinto, 2239–2241
  suttee (Sati), 2300–2302
  virginity, 2397–2399
hip-hop/rap, 1287–1289
historical materialism
  materialist feminism, 676–678
history
  Amazons, 53–59
  birth control, 175–177
  child custody and father right principle, 229–234
  colonialism and gender, 303–314
  Dahomey Amazons, 57–59
  Daoism, 411–413
  feminist consciousness, historical perspective, 771–776

  feminist movements in historical and comparative perspective, 827–838
  lesbian continuum, 1512–1513
  orientalism, 1813–1816
  pacifism, peace activism, and gender, 1826–1832
  rape law, 1989–1993
  romantic friendship, 2048–2050
  single-sex education and coeducation, 2243–2245
  transnational labor movements, 2351–2357
  United States women's movements in historical perspective, 2369–2374
  women's and feminist activism
    Aboriginal Australia and Torres Strait Islands, 2470–2475
    United States and Canada, 2539–2545
  women's rights in international and comparative perspective, 1289–1306
Hite Report on Female Sexuality, 1306–1308
  Kinsey Scale, 1486–1489
  masturbation, 1638–1640
HIV *see* AIDS
home
  cult of domesticity, 394–396
  see also domestic
homelessness and gender, 1308–1311
homeopathy, 50
homonormativity *see* heteronormativity and homonormativity
homophobia
  Christianity and homosexuality, 263–267
  Communism in Eastern Europe, 323–328
  Communism and gender in United States, 337–341
  desexualization, 426–428
  drug and alcohol abuse, 490–493
  heteronormativity and homonormativity, 1257–1259
  homosexual reparative therapy, 1312–1314
  Islam and homosexuality, 1463–1469
  Judaism and gender, 1471–1475
  Judaism and sexuality, 1475–1482
  lesbian feminism, 666–669
  lesbians as community other mothers, 1538–1540
  LGBT
    North Africa, 1588–1590
    South Asia, 1590–1595
  masculinity and femininity, theories of, 1632–1638
  Mormonism, 1729–1731
  open and reaffirming religious organizations, 1808–1810

pink triangle, 1850–1853
religion and homophobia, 2016–2020
sex and culture, 2080–2085
homosexual reparative therapy, 1312–1314
homosexuality
    asylum and sexual orientation, 133–137
    and athletics, 142–147
    Buddhism, 203
    butch/femme, 207–208
    Christianity and, 263–267
    coming out, 319–321
    Communism
        Eastern Europe, 323–328
        Russia, 328–329
    Communism and gender
        China, 329–337
        United States, 337–341
    "Don't ask, don't tell" policy, 470–473
    Gay and Lesbian Pride Day, 933–935
    gay male literature, 935–938
    genocide, 2008–2012
    and Islam, 1463–1469
    Kinsey Scale, 1487–1489
    LGBT
        Middle East, 1573–1578
        Northern Africa, 1588–1590
        North America, 1583–1587
        Southern Africa, 1600–1605
    Nazi persecution of homosexuals, 1750–1754
    pink triangle, 1850–1853
    private/public spheres, 1912–1914
    same-sex families, 2053–2055
    same-sex marriage, 2055–2057
    same-sex sexuality in India, 2057–2059
    sexual identity and orientation, 2171–2174
    sexual minorities, 2176–2179
    sexual orientation and law, 2181–2192
    sodomy law in comparative perspective, 2262–2266
Hong Kong
    abortion laws, 3
honor killing, 1314–1318
    violence against women in global perspective, 2386–2392
hormone replacement therapy, 1318–1320
hostile work environment, United States, 1320–1322
    occupational health and safety, 1797–1799
household livelihood strategies, 1322–1326
    hunger and famine, 1354–1359
    lesbians as community other mothers, 1538–1540

housewifization
    capitalist patriarchy, 213–217
    cult of domesticity, 394–396
housework
    cult of domesticity, 394–396
human rights *see* universal human rights; women's rights
human trafficking
    child labor in comparative perspective, 234–241
    child prostitution, 241–246
    feminist perspectives on, 1345–1350
    feminist sex wars, 865–867
    mail-order brides, 1619–1621
    sex trafficking *see* sex trafficking
    women's and feminist activism, Russia, Ukraine, and Eurasia, 2524–2529
human–animal studies, 1350–1354
    nature–nurture debate, 1744–1750
Hungary
    abortion laws, 4
hunger and famine, 1354–1359
hybridity and miscegenation, 1359–1361
hypermasculinity, 1361–1363
    hip-hop/rap, 1287–1289
    masculinities, 1627–1632
    military masculinity, 1714–1716
    steroids, 2270–2272
hypersexuality, 42, 116
hypoactive sexual desire disorder, 116
hysteria
    feminism and psychoanalysis, 716–726

I

Iceland
    abortion laws, 3
identity politics, 1365–1367
    anti-racist/anti-civil rights movements, 96–102
    bear culture, 155–157
    class, caste and gender, 275–280
    coming out, 319–321
    disability rights movement, 439–441
    gender outlaw, 1069–1071
    gender performance, 1071–1072
    gender, politics and the state, Māori, 1112–1116
    individualism and collectivism, critical feminist perspectives on, 1410–1412
    intersectionality, 1439–1443
    intersex movement, 1443–1448
    intersexuality, 1448–1451
    LGBT
        North America, 1583–1587
        Southern Africa, 1600–1605
        Western Europe, 1605–1612
    nomadic theory, 1775–1777

identity politics (*Continued*)
  personal is political, 1846–1848
  queer anglophone literature, 1961–1965
  queer theory, 1978–1982
  Riot grrrl, 2046–2047
  self-esteem, 2071–2074
  sisterhood, 2245–2247
  subaltern, 2291–2293
  transgender movements in international perspective, 2337–2341
ideology
  Bollywood, 185–187
  kibbutz/kibbutzim, 1485–1486
ijtihad
  Shari'a, 2237–2239
images of gender and sexuality
  alternative media, 43–47
  beauty industry, 157–159
  dieting, 430–433
  eating disorders, 499–502
  entrepreneurship, 537–539
  fashion, 591–595
  gender bender, 951–953
  infanticide, 1412–1415
  Latin America, 1371–1376
  LGBT
    Latin America, 1563–1569
    Māori, 1569–1573
  Māori, 1376–1380
  media and gender socialization, 1662–1667
  men's magazines, 1676–1678
  misogyny, 1718–1720
  politics of representation, 1857–1862
  popular culture and gender, 1868–1871
  sexual objectification, 2179–2181
  Southern Africa, 1380–1385
  visual culture and gender, 2403–2408
images of gender and sexuality in advertising, 1367–1371
  visual culture, 2399–2403
  and gender, 2403–2408
  women as producers of culture, 2458–2462
imaginary, 1386–1388
  heterosexual, 1261–1265
immigration
  arranged marriages, 112–114
  asylum
    challenges faced by sexual minorities, 123–128
    and gender, 128–133
    and sexual orientation, 133–137
  borderlands, 187–191
  colonialism, and globalization, 1388–1393
  feminist theories of welfare state, 892–901

  and gender, 1394–1399
  human trafficking, feminist perspectives on, 1345–1350
  informal economy, 1415–1419
  LGBTI, 123–128
  mail-order brides, 1619–1621
  oral tradition, 1810–1813
incest
  extended families, 576–578
  social practices and legal policies on, 1399–1405
India
  abortion laws, 3
  age of consent and child marriage, 26–30
  Bollywood, 185–187
  class, caste and gender, 275–280
  Dowry Prohibition Act, 482–484
  feminism, 654–658
  LGBT, South Asia, 1590–1595
  same-sex sexuality, 2057–2059
  suttee (Sati), 2300–2302
indigenous knowledges and gender, 1405–1409
  subaltern, 2291–2293
  two-spirit, 2364–2365
  women's and feminist activism, Aboriginal Australia and Torres Strait Islands, 2470–2475
indigenous women
  gender, politics and the state, 1099–1104
  images of gender and sexuality of Māori, 1376–1380
  traditional and indigenous knowledge, 2322–2326
  women's and feminist activism
    Aboriginal Australia and Torres Strait Islands, 2470–2475
    Māori, 2504–2508
    Native United States and Canada, 2513–2518
individualism and collectivism
  critical feminist perspectives on, 1410–1412
  postfeminism, 1891–1900
Indo-Caribbean
  feminism, 654–658
  Latina feminism, 661–666
  women's and feminist activism, Caribbean, 2480–2485
Indonesia
  abortion laws, 4
  feminism, 735–737
industrialization
  maquiladora, 1623–1625
inequality/inequalities
  aging and ageism, 34–38
  animality, 76–78
  climate change and gender, 280–283

community and grassroots activism, 341–345
comparable worth/work of equal value, 348–351
critical race theory, 384–389
Dahomey Amazons, 57–59
depression, 423–426
digital divide, 433–435
gender bias in research, 955–959
gender equality/inequality in education, 993–998, 1046–1050
gender inequality and gender stratification, 1050–1052
gender justice, 1056–1062
heterosexism and homophobia, 1259–1261
Internet and gender, 1433–1437
privilege, 1916–1918
sexual harassment law, 2166–2171
tomboys and sissies, 2319–2322
infanticide, 1412–1415
infidelity *see* adultery
informal economy, 1415–1419
    microcredit and microlending, 1697–1699
    privatization, 1914–1916
    sex work and sex workers' unionization, 2118–2123
information technology, 1419–1424
    cultural views of adultery, 21–24
    cyber intimacies, 401–405
    digital divide, 433–435
    feminist design in computing, 776–783
    Internet and gender, 1433–1437
informed consent, 32
inheritance
    matrilineal/matrilocal systems, 1655–1660
initiation rites, 1424–1428
    menstrual rituals, 1686–1691
    tattooing and piercing, 2305–2307
institutional micropolitics, 1428–1431
international laws and policies
    abortion, 1–13
    affirmative action, 24–25
    CEDAW, 25, 359, 362–365
    child labor in comparative perspective, 234–241
    child prostitution, 241–246
    civil rights law and gender, 274–275
    female genital cutting, 288–293, 609–612
    fundamentalism and public policy, 925–929
    and gender, 1326–1330
    gender equality, 990–993
    gender identification, 1023–1026
    hate crimes/hate crime law, 1235–1240
    LGBT
        Eastern Africa, 1551–1557
        Eastern and Central Europe, 1557–1563
        Western Europe, 1605–1612
    sex trafficking, 2111–2116
    sexual slavery, 2202–2205
    sexual terrorism, 2208–2210
    status of women reports, 2266–2268
    transgender movements in international perspective, 2337–2341
    universal human rights, 1330–1345, 2375–2377
    war, international violence, and gender, 2411–2419
    Yogyakarta Principles, 2604–2606
International Women's Day, 1431–1433
    women's and feminist activism, East Asia, 2485–2489
    women's movements, early international movement, 2567–2573
Internet and gender, 1433–1437
    digital divide, 433–435
    information technology, 1419–1424
Internet sex, 1437–1439
    gay male pornography, 938–940
    masturbation, 1638–1640
    prostitution/sex work, 1933–1938
    see also cybersex
intersectionality, 1439–1443
    aging and ageism, 34–38
    black feminisms, 626–630
    borderlands, 187–191
    cisgender/cissexual, 267–271
    cross-cultural gender roles, 389–392
    feminist art, 762–767
    feminist disability studies, 783–788
    feminist family therapy, 804–807
    Gay and Lesbian Pride Day, 933–935
    gender identity theory, 1030–1035
    gender, politics and the state, 1122–1127
        indigenous women, 1099–1104
    gender violence, 1172–1175
    gendered innovations in science, health, and technology, 1181–1188
    homelessness and gender, 1308–1311
    identity politics, 1365–1367
    images of gender and sexuality in advertising, 1367–1371
    information technology, 1419–1424
    lesbian feminism, 666–669
    matrix of domination, 1660–1662
    outsider within, 1816–1819
    privilege, 1916–1918
    psychology of gender, history and development of field, 1944–1955
    representation, 2025–2027

intersectionality (*Continued*)
  stratified reproduction, 2280–2281
  women's political representation, 2580–2584
  Yoruba culture, religion, and gender, 2606–2618
intersex movement, 1443–1448
  LGBT, Southern Africa, 1600–1605
  sex selection, 2102–2104
intersexuality, 1448–1451
  androgen insensitivity syndrome, 66–68
  androgyny, 68–71
  asylum, challenges faced by sexual minorities, 123–128
  biochemistry/physiology, 166–173
  cisgenderism, 271–274
  gender identification, 1023–1026
  gender outlaw, 1069–1071
  gender violence, 1172–1175
  intersex movement, 1443–1448
  LGBT, Southern Africa, 1600–1605
  neuroscience, brain research, and sexuality, 1759–1765
  sex versus gender categorization, 2116–2118
  sexualities, 2212–2217
  trans identities, psychological perspectives, 2328–2331
  transsexuality, 2360–2362
intimacy and sexual relationships, 1451–1453
  plastic sexuality, 1853–1855
  sexology and psychological sex research, 2133–2142
  sexual subjectivity, 2204–2208
intimate citizenship, 1453–1456
intimate labor, 525–527
intimate partner abuse, 1456–1458
  domestic violence in United States, 467–470
  elder abuse and gender, 518–520
  emotional abuse of women, 527–531
  female criminality, 601–605
  gender violence, 1172–1175
  gender-based violence, 1177–1181
  rape law, 1989–1993
  sexual assault/sexual violence, 2144–2146
  violence against women in global perspective, 2386–2392
Iran
  abortion laws, 4
Iraq
  abortion laws, 4
  LGBT, 1575
Ireland
  abortion laws, 4
Islam
  abortion, 15–16
  celibacy, 221–222
  and gender, 1458–1463
  gender, politics and the state, Northern Africa, 1116–1122
  male circumcision, 1621–1623
  religious fundamentalism, 2020–2025
  Shari'a, 2237–2239
  virginity, 2397–2399
  women's and feminist activism, Middle East, 2508–2513
Islam and homosexuality, 1463–1469, 1573–1578
  Shari'a, 2237–2239
Islamic feminism, 658–661
  Shari'a, 2237–2239
Israel
  abortion laws, 4
  LGBT, 1575
istanbe, 486
Italy
  abortion laws, 4

J

Jamaica
  abortion laws, 4
  LGBT, 1547
Japan
  abortion laws, 3
  feminism, 694–696
  Shinto, 2239–2241
Jewish *see* Judaism
jockocracy, 142–147
Jordan
  abortion laws, 4
Judaism
  abortion, 15–16
  celibacy, 221–222
  and gender, 1471–1475
  male circumcision, 1621–1623
  niddah, 1769–1773
  religious fundamentalism, 2020–2025
Judaism and sexuality, 1475–1482
  virginity, 2397–2399
Julian of Norwich
  feminist Christology, 769–771
jurisprudence
  asylum
    and gender, 128–133
    and sexual orientation, 133–137
  Declaration of the Rights of Women, 413–414
  feminist, 812–816
justice
  gender justice, 1056–1062
  reproductive *see* reproductive justice/rights
  see also law

Juvenile Sex Offender Assessment Protocol-II (J-SOAP-II), 248
Juvenile Sexual Offense Recidivism Risk Assessment Tool-II (JSORRATII), 248

K

Kama Sutra
   Hinduism, 1282–1287
Kathoey, 1483–1485
   gender identification, 1023–1026
   gender identity theory, 1030–1035
   gender variance, 1169–1171
   ladyboys, 1495–1497
   LGBT, South Asia, 1590–1595
   third gender, 2311–2314
   trans identities, psychological perspectives, 2328–2331
Kazakhstan
   abortion laws, 4
Kenya
   abortion laws, 4
kibbutz/kibbutzim, 1485–1486
   incest, social practices and legal policies on, 1399–1405
killing
   taboo, 2303–2305
   see also violence
Kinsey Scale, 1487–1489
   neuroscience, brain research, and sexuality, 1759–1765
kinship, 1489–1491
   assisted reproduction, 119–123
   community other mothers, 345–348
   Dahomey Amazons, 57–59
   dowry and bride-price, 476–480
   extended families, 576–578
   fictive kin, 918–920
   immigration, colonialism, and globalization, 1388–1393
   incest, social practices and legal policies on, 1399–1405
   matrilineal/matrilocal systems, 1655–1660
   polyamory, 1862–1866
   polygamy, polygyny and polyandry, 1866–1868
   same-sex families, 2053–2055
Kiribati
   abortion laws, 4
Klein Grid, 179
knowledge
   indigenous *see* indigenous knowledges and gender; traditional and indigenous knowledge
   material feminism, 671–676

Korea
   feminism, 696–698
   gender/history of revolutions, 1003–1005
Kosovo
   abortion laws, 3
Kothi, 1491–1493
   gender variance, 1169–1171
Kuwait
   abortion laws, 4
Kyrgyzstan
   abortion laws, 3
kyriarchy
   women-church, 2468–2470

L

labor
   capitalist patriarchy, 213–217
   child labor in comparative perspective, 234–241
   domestic division, 454–456
   dual labor market, 493–495
   embodied, 525–527
   feminization of, 903–905
      female farming systems, 605–609
      poverty in global perspective, 1905–1910
   gender division, 456–461
   gender wage gap, 1175–1177
   health careers, 1243–1246
   hostile work environment, United States, 1320–1322
   household livelihood strategies, 1322–1326
   informal economy, 1415–1419
   militarism and sex industries, 1710–1714
   transnational labor movements, 2351–2357
   women in non-traditional work fields, 2451–2458
labor market
   comparable worth/work of equal value, 348–351
   emotion work, 525–527
   glass ceiling/glass elevator, 1214–1216
   head of household and supplementary earner, 1241–1242
   work–family balance, 2593–2595
ladyboys, 1495–1497
   gender variance, 1169–1171
   Kathoey *see* Kathoey
   third gender, 2311–2314
language
   discourse and gender, 441–445
   documentary film and gender, 461–465
   feminism and postmodernism, 707–712
   feminist publishing, 855–864
   gender, definition of, 966–968
   genderlect, 1193–1196
   gynocriticism, 1233–1234

language (*Continued*)
  male bias, 44
  non-sexist language use, 1779–1781
  postmodern feminism, 753–759
  sexism in, 2131–2133
  women's writing, 2589–2593
  Yoruba culture, religion, and gender, 2606–2618
language and gender, 1497–1502
  popular culture and gender, 1868–1871
  tomboys and sissies, 2319–2322
  women's writing, 2589–2593
Laos
  abortion laws, 5
Latin America
  gender, politics and the state, 1104–1112
  images of sex and gender, 1371–1376
  LGBT, 1563–1569
  maquiladora, 1623–1625
  Mestiza consciousness, 1693–1695
  poverty, 1907–1908
  women's and feminist activism, 2499–2504
  see also Caribbean; Chicanas; Latina feminism
Latina feminism, 631, 661–666
  see also Chicanas
Latvia
  abortion laws, 3
law
  affirmative action, 24–25
  asylum and sexual orientation, 133–137
  battered women, 153–155
  civil rights law and gender, United States, 274–275
  criminal justice system and sexuality in the United States, 371–384
  customary laws, 399–401
  Declaration of Sentiments, 414–416
  "Don't ask, don't tell" policy, 470–473
  female genital cutting, 288–293, 609–612
  feminist jurisprudence, 812–816
  gender, politics and the state, Northern Africa, 1116–1122
  rape law, 1989–1993
  reproductive justice/rights in the United States, 2035–2040
  sexual harassment law, 2166–2171
  sexual orientation and law, 2181–2192
  sexual violence and the military, 2210–2212
  sodomy law in comparative perspective, 2262–2266
law of the father, 1502–1503
leadership
  and gender, 1504–1506
  glass ceiling/glass elevator, 1214–1216
  mentoring, 1691–1693
Lebanon
  abortion laws, 5
  LGBT, 1575–1576
leftist armed struggle
  militarism and gender-based violence, 1701–1710
  women in, 1507–1512
legal and political debates
  affirmative action, 24–25
  age of consent in historical and international perspective, 30–34
  feminist sex wars, 865–867
  obscenity laws in United States, Canada, and Europe, 1793–1797
  pornography, feminist legal and political debates on, 1877–1882
  self-defense and violence against women in United States, 2069–2071
  sexual slavery, 2202–2205
  women in combat, 2441–2445
legal status in global perspective
  women's health movement in the United States, 2563–2567
legal systems
  parenting in prison, 1836–1839
lesbian
  aging and ageism, 37
  appearance psychology, 102–107
  asylum, challenges faced by sexual minorities, 123–128
  athletics and gender, 137–142
  butch/femme, 207–208
  clinical trials, bias against women, 283–288
  coming out, 319–321
  compulsory heterosexuality, 354–358
  criminal justice system and sexuality, 371–384
  feminist film theory, 807–812
  feminist publishing, 855–864
  feminist utopian writing, 901–903
  Gay and Lesbian Pride Day, 933–935
  genocide, 2008–2012
  Greenham Common, 1229–1230
  health and healthcare in sexual minorities, 1250–1255
  Kinsey Scale, 1486–1489
  Lesbos, 1540–1541
  neuroscience, brain research, and sexuality, 1759–1765
  radical lesbianism *see* radical lesbianism
  romantic friendship, 2048–2050
  same-sex families, 2053–2055
  same-sex sexuality in India, 2057–2059
  stone butch, 2274–2276

lesbian continuum, 1512–1513
  lesbian stereotypes in the United States, 1531–1536
lesbian couples
  commitment ceremonies, 321–323
lesbian cultural criticism, 1514–1516
lesbian feminism, 638, 666–669
  abortion laws, 3
  radical feminism, 726–729
lesbian, gay, bisexual, and transgender psychologies, 1522–1527
lesbian and gay movements, 1516–1522
  feminist activism, 759–762
  intersex movement, 1443–1448
  intimate citizenship, 1453–1456
  Judaism and sexuality, 1475–1482
  LGBT
    Eastern Africa, 1551–1557
    Eastern and Central Europe, 1557–1563
    Latin America, 1563–1569
    North America, 1583–1587
    Southeast Asia, 1595–1600
    Southern Africa, 1600–1605
    Western Europe, 1605–1612
  neuroscience, brain research, and sexuality, 1759–1765
  same-sex marriage, 2055–2057
  sexual minorities, 2176–2179
lesbian performance, 1527–1529
lesbian popular music, 1529–1531
lesbian stereotypes
  postfeminism, 1891–1900
  in the United States, 1531–1536
lesbian and womyn's separatism, 1536–1538
  Lesbos, 1540–1541
  LGBT, North America, 1583–1587
  radical lesbianism, 1983–1985
lesbians as community other mothers, 1538–1540
Lesbos, 1540–1541
Lesotho
  abortion laws, 4
LGB
  families of choice, 582–584
  Latina feminism, 661–666
  same-sex sexuality in India, 2057–2059
LGBT
  Australia and New Zealand, 1541–1546
  bullying, 205
  Caribbean, 1546–1550
    sexual citizenship, 2146–2151
  East Asia, sexual citizenship, 2151–2157
  Eastern Africa, 1551–1557
  Eastern and Central Europe, 1557–1563
  gender, politics and the state, Northern Africa, 1116–1122
  Islam and homosexuality, 1463–1469
  Judaism and sexuality, 1475–1482
  Latin America, 1563–1569
  Māori, 1569–1573
  Middle East, 1573–1578
  Native North America, 1578–1583
  Northern Africa, 1588–1590
    activism, 1588–1590
  North America, 1583–1587
  passing, 1839–1841
  postmodern feminist psychology, 1900–1905
  print media, 45
  South Asia, 1590–1595
  Southeast Asia, 1595–1600
  Southern Africa, 1600–1605
  traditional and indigenous knowledge, 2322–2326
  Western Europe, 1605–1612
  women's and feminist activism, Southeast Asia, 2529–2533
LGBTI
  asylum, challenges faced by sexual minorities, 123–128
LGBTIQ
  LGBT, Middle East, 1573–1578
LGBTQ
  asexuality, 116–119
  asylum and sexual orientation, 133–137
  children's literature and gender, 252–256
  Chinese feminism, 632–637
  cisgender/cissexual, 267–271
  coming out, 319–321
  criminal justice system and sexuality in the United States, 371–384
  curriculum transformation, 396–399
  "Don't ask, don't tell" policy, 470–473
  drag, 484–490
  Gay and Lesbian Pride Day, 933–935
  genderqueer, 1196–1198
  health and healthcare in sexual minorities, 1250–1255
  heteronormativity and homonormativity, 1257–1259
  hostile work environment, United States, 1320–1322
  information technology, 1419–1424
  lesbian, gay, bisexual, and transgender psychologies, 1522–1527
  lesbian and gay movements, 1516–1522
  open and reaffirming religious organizations, 1808–1810
  queer performance, 1974–1977

LGBTQ (*Continued*)
   queer space, 1977–1978
   romantic friendship, 2048–2050
   same-sex families, 2053–2055
   same-sex marriage, 2055–2057
   sex tourism, 2104–2109
   sexual minorities, 2176–2179
   sexual orientation and law, 2181–2192
   stone butch, 2274–2276
   transgender movements in United States, 2341–2345
   transnational labor movements, 2351–2357
   transsexuality, 2360–2362
   transvestitism, 2362–2364
   two-spirit, 2364–2365
   Yogyakarta Principles, 2604–2606
liberal feminism, 669–671, 888
   A Vindication of the Rights of Woman, 2384–2386
   Marxist/Socialist feminism, 749–753
   pro-choice movement in United States, 1918–1925
Liberation Tigers of Tamil Eelam (LTTE), 2429–2431
Liberia
   abortion laws, 4
Libya
   abortion laws, 5
Liechtenstein
   abortion laws, 4
life expectancy, 1612–1616
   population control and population policy, 1872–1876
literary criticism
   gay male literature, 935–938
   gynocriticism, 1233–1234
   queer anglophone literature, 1961–1965
   queer literary criticism, 1965–1969
   sadomasochism, domination, and submission, 2051–2053
   subaltern, 2291–2293
   women's writing, 2589–2593
literature
   children's literature and gender, 252–256
   gay male literature, 935–938
   gynocriticism, 1233–1234
   queer anglophone literature, 1961–1965
   women's writing, 2589–2593
Lithuania
   abortion laws, 3
lookism, 1616–1618
Luxembourg
   abortion laws, 3

M
Madagascar
   abortion laws, 5
mail-order brides, 1619–1621
   human trafficking, feminist perspectives on, 1345–1350
Malawi
   abortion laws, 5
Malaysia
   abortion laws, 4
   feminism, 739
Maldives
   abortion laws, 4
male circumcision, 1621–1623
   intersex movement, 1443–1448
   medicine and medicalization, 1671–1676
Mali
   abortion laws, 5
Malta
   abortion laws, 3
Māori
   gender, politics and the state, 1112–1116
   images of gender and sexuality, 1376–1380
   LGBT, 1569–1573
   traditional and indigenous knowledge, 2322–2326
   women's and feminist activism, 2504–2508
maquiladora, 1623–1625
marriage
   anti-miscegenation laws, 87–91
   charivaris, 223–225
   child custody and father right principle, 229–234
   dowry and bride-price, 476–480
   Dowry Prohibition Act, 482–484
   fundamentalism and public policy, 925–929
   heterosexual marriage trends in the West, 1265–1270
   incest, social practices and legal policies on, 1399–1405
   mail-order brides, 1619–1621
   matrilineal/matrilocal systems, 1655–1660
   monogamy, sociological perspectives on, 1724–1727
   polyamory, 1862–1866
   polygamy, polygyny and polyandry, 1866–1868
   same-sex marriage, 2055–2057
   sex education in UK and United States, 2092–2095
   see also arranged marriages; child marriage; same-sex marriage
marriage equality
   commitment ceremonies, 321–323

Marshall Islands
  abortion laws, 3
Marxism
  economic determinism, 509–510
  see also Communism/socialism
Marxist/Socialist feminism, 749–753
  leftist armed struggle, women in, 1507–1512
  sex work and sex workers' unionization, 2118–2123
masculinism, 1625–1627
  feminine and masculine elements, 616–618
  hypermasculinity, 1361–1363
  men's magazines, 1676–1678
masculinities, 1627–1632
  alpha male, 41–43
  androcentrism, 65–66
  androgyny, 68–71
  appearance psychology, 102–107
  athletics
    and gender, 137–142
    and homosexuality, 142–147
  bear culture, 155–157
  boys' peer cultures, 192–194
  children's literature and sexuality, 256–259
  colonialism and sexuality, 314–317
  Communism and gender in China, 329–337
  courtly love, 367–369
  feminine and masculine elements, 616–618
  gender bias, 953–955
  gender, definition of, 966–968
  gender, politics and the state, 1122–1127
  gender schema theory, 1162–1164
  gendered space, 1189–1191
  hegemonic masculinity, 1255–1257
  hip-hop/rap, 1287–1289
  homosexual reparative therapy, 1312–1314
  hypermasculinity, 1361–1363
  information technology, 1419–1424
  initiation rites, 1424–1428
  Islam and homosexuality, 1463–1469
  male circumcision, 1621–1623
  metrosexual, 1695–1696
  militarism and gender-based violence, 1701–1710
  military masculinity, 1714–1716
  mysticism, 1733–1735
  nationalism and gender, 1737–1741
  Nazi persecution of homosexuals, 1750–1754
  pacifism, Quakers, and gender, 1821–1825
  phallocentrism/phallogocentrism, 1848–1850
  postmodern feminist psychology, 1900–1905
  sexuopharmaceuticals, 2227–2232
  steroids, 2270–2272
  stone butch, 2274–2276
  tattooing and piercing, 2305–2307
  tomboys and sissies, 2319–2322
masculinity and femininity, theories of, 1632–1638
  psychological theory, research, methodology, and feminist critiques, 1939–1944
masturbation, 1638–1640
  Internet sex, 1437–1439
  sex toys, 2109–2111
material feminism, 671–676
materialism
  Marxist/Socialist feminism, 749–753
  nomadic theory, 1775–1777
materialist conception of history
  economic determinism, 509–510
materialist feminism, 676–678
  sex work and sex workers' unionization, 2118–2123
maternal activism, 1640–1645
maternalism, 1645–1649
mathematics
  cognitive sex differences, debates on, 298–300
matriarchy, 1649–1655
  Amazons, 53–59
  capitalist patriarchy, 213–217
  community other mothers, 345–348
  cult of domesticity, 394–396
matrilineal/matrilocal systems, 1655–1660
matrix of domination, 1660–1662
Mauritania
  abortion laws, 3
Mauritius
  abortion laws, 5
media
  alternative, 43–47
  backlash, 149–150
  chick flicks, 227–229
  children's literature
    gender, 252–256
    sexuality, 256–259
  documentary film and gender, 461–465
  feminist magazines, 819–821
  images of gender and sexuality in advertising, 1367–1371
  mainstream, 43–44
  men's magazines, 1676–1678
  obscenity laws in United States, Canada, and Europe, 1793–1797
  popular culture and gender, 1868–1871
  Riot grrrl, 2046–2047
  visual culture, 2399–2403
    and gender, 2403–2408
  see also film

media and gender socialization, 1662–1667
  visual culture, 2399–2403
    and gender, 2403–2408
medical practices
  breast cancer, 194–199
  clinical trials, bias against women, 283–288
  depression, 423–426
  female genital cutting, 288–293, 609–612
  intersexuality, 1448–1451
  male circumcision, 1621–1623
  midwifery, 1699–1701
  wet nursing, 2419–2421
medical and scientific experimentation and gender, 1667–1671
  neuroscience, brain research, and sexuality, 1759–1765
medicine and medicalization, 1671–1676
  assisted reproduction, 119–123
  breastfeeding, 199–201
  CAM, 47–53, 351–354
  disability rights movement, 439–441
  disease symptoms, gender differences in, 450–454
  DSM, 428–430
  gender bias in research, 955–959
  gendered innovations in science, health, and technology, 1181–1188
  intersex movement, 1443–1448
  medical and scientific experimentation and gender, 1667–1671
  premenstrual syndrome (PMS), 1910–1912
  self-help movements, 2074–2078
  sex-related difference research, 2125–2129
  sexually transmitted infections, 2225–2227
  sexuopharmaceuticals, 2227–2232
  traditional healing, 2326–2328
  transgender health and healthcare, 2333–2337
Megan's Law, 33
memory repression
  recovered memories, 1997–1999
men
  alpha male, 41–43
  appearance psychology, 102–107
  athletics and gender, 137–142
  athletics and homosexuality, 142–147
  cardiac disease and gender, 218–220
  men's magazines, 1676–1678
  violence against, 54
  see also masculinism; masculinities; patriarchy
MENA
  orientalism, 1813–1816
  poverty, 1908

menarche, 1678–1680
  menstrual rituals, 1686–1691
  niddah, 1769–1780
menopause, 1680–1682
  hormone replacement therapy, 1318–1320
  senior women and sexuality in United States, 2078–2080
menstrual activism, 1682–1686
  menarche, 1678–1680
  niddah, 1769–1780
  premenstrual syndrome (PMS), 1910–1912
  purity versus pollution, 1957–1959
  women's health movement in the United States, 2563–2567
menstrual rituals, 1686–1691
  Judaism and gender, 1471–1475
  niddah, 1769–1773
  purity versus pollution, 1957–1959
menstruation
  anthropological perspectives of sex, 78–82
  Judaism and gender, 1471–1475
  menarche, 1678–1680
  menopause, 1680–1682
  menstrual activism, 1682–1686
  menstrual rituals, 1686–1691
  misogyny, 1718–1720
  premenstrual syndrome (PMS), 1910–1912
  purity versus pollution, 1957–1959
mentoring, 1691–1693
methodology
  archaeology and genealogy, 109–110
  gender bias in research, 955–959
  queer methods and methodologies, 1969–1974
  reflexivity, 1999–2001
  sexology and psychological sex research, 2133–2142
metrosexual, 1695–1696
Mexico
  abortion laws, 3
  anti-globalization movements, 84–85
microcredit and microlending, 1697–1699
  gender and development, 968–973
  household livelihood strategies, 1322–1326
  self-help movements, 2074–2078
  women in development, 2449–2451
  women's banking, 2557–2559
  women's and feminist organizations in South Asia, 2553–2557
Micronesia
  abortion laws, 3
Middle East
  gender, politics and the state, Northern Africa, 1116–1122

LGBT, 1573–1578
poverty, 1908
women's and feminist activism, 2508–2513
Middle East and North Africa *see* MENA
midwifery, 1699–1701
    scientific motherhood, 2060–2061
    wet nursing, 2419–2421
    see also breastfeeding
migration
    feminization of, 905–907
    global care chain, 1216–1218
    human trafficking, feminist perspectives on, 1345–1350
    immigration, colonialism, and globalization, 1388–1393
    see also immigration
militarism
    comfort women, 317–319
    leftist armed struggle, women in, 1507–1512
    masculinities, 1627–1632
    Nazi persecution of homosexuals, 1750–1754
    pacifism, peace activism, and gender, 1826–1832
militarism and gender-based violence, 1701–1710
    sexual violence and the military, 2210–2212
    violence against women in global perspective, 2386–2392
    war, international violence, and gender, 2411–2419
militarism and sex industries, 1710–1714
    pornography, feminist legal and political debates on, 1877–1882
    sexual violence and the military, 2210–2212
military
    "Don't ask, don't tell" policy, 470–473
    genocide, 2008–2012
    women in combat, 2441–2445
military masculinity, 1714–1716
    war, international violence, and gender, 2411–2419
mind reading
    cognitive critical and cultural theory, 293–298
mind-body therapies
    CAM, 47–53, 351–354
    cognitive critical and cultural theory, 293–298
mind/body split, 1716–1718
misogyny, 1718–1720
    hip-hop/rap, 1287–1289
    rape culture, 1985–1989
Mestiza consciousness, 1693–1695
modernization
    religious fundamentalism, 2020–2025
moffies, 486

Moldova
    abortion laws, 3
Monaco
    abortion laws, 3
monasticism, 1720–1722
Mongolia
    abortion laws, 3
monogamy
    biological perspectives on, 1722–1724
    plastic sexuality, 1853–1855
    sociological perspectives on, 1724–1727
monstrous-feminine, 1727–1729
Montenegro
    abortion laws, 3
moral development
    ethics, moral development, and gender, 560–565
    nature–nurture debate, 1744–1750
    reproductive choice, 2027–2030
    volunteerism and charitable giving, 2408–2409
Mormonism, 1729–1731
Morocco
    abortion laws, 3
    LGBT, 1576
    women's and feminist activism, 2521–2522
mosaic masculinities, 103
Mother Earth
    Mother Nature, 1731–1733
Mother Goddess
    Hinduism, 1282–1287
Mother Nature, 1731–1733
    lesbian and womyn's separatism, 1536–1538
motherhood
    activist mothering, 17–19
    breastfeeding, 199–201
    child custody and father right principle, 229–234
    feminist standpoint theory, 867–870
    maternal activism, 1640–1645
    maternalism, 1645–1649
    parental leave in comparative perspective, 1832–1836
    parenting in prison, 1836–1839
    right-wing women's movements, 2040–2046
    scientific motherhood, 2060–2061
    status-of-the-mother laws, 88
    surrogacy, 2296–2298
    women's movements, early international movement, 2567–2573
    Yoruba culture, religion, and gender, 2606–2618
mothering/mother work
    activist mothering, 17–19
    community other mothers, 345–348
    gender division of labor, 456–461

mothering/mother work (*Continued*)
   maternalism, 1645–1649
   scientific motherhood, 2060–2061
   stratified reproduction, 2280–2281
   wet nursing, 2419–2421
   women as cultural markers/bearers, 2445–2449
movements
   activist mothering, 17–19
   anarchism and gender, 59–64
   anarchist feminisms, 623–626
   anti-globalization *see* anti-globalization movements
   Arab Spring, 107–108
   asexual activism, 114–116
   community and grassroots activism, 341–345
   democracy and democratization, 418–423
   disability rights movement, 439–441
   eugenics movements, 570–574
   fatherhood movements, 595–599
   feminist activism, 759–762
   Gay and Lesbian Pride Day, 933–935
   identity politics, 1365–1367
   intersex *see* intersex movement
   masculinism, 1625–1627
   maternalism, 1645–1649
   Occupy movements, 1801–1805
   pacifism, peace activism, and gender, 1826–1832
   pro-choice *see* pro-choice movement
   pro-life *see* pro-life movement
   reproductive justice/rights in the United States, 2035–2040
   right-wing women's movements, 2040–2046
   self-help movements, 2074–2078
   transnational labor movements, 2351–2357
   wicca, 2425–2427
   women's *see* women's movements
moxibustion, 49
Mozambique
   abortion laws, 3
   LGBT, 1603
Mujeres Libres, 62–64
multicultural
   dowry and bride-price, 476–480
   feminist family therapy, 804–807
   feminist jurisprudence, 812–816
   feminist movements in historical and comparative perspective, 827–838
   social constructionist theory, 2249–2251
   traditional healing, 2326–2328
multiracial
   feminism, 678–682
   hybridity and miscegenation, 1359–1361
Muñoz, José Estaban, 1975

music
   lesbian popular music, 1529–1531
   Riot grrrl, 2046–2047
Muslims in the West
   Shari'a, 2237–2239
   see also Islam
mysticism, 1733–1735
   feminine and masculine elements, 616–618
   feminist Christology, 769–771
   Judaism and gender, 1471–1475
   Mother Nature, 1731–1733
   sects and cults, 2066–2069
   wicca, 2425–2427
   witches, 2427–2429

N

Namibia
   abortion laws, 3
natalism
   religiously encouraged, 16
nationalism
   gender, politics and the state, Southern Africa, 1133–1138
   gender/history of revolutions
      East Asia, 998–1005
      Northern Africa, 1015–1023
   genocide, 2008–2012
   intimate citizenship, 1453–1456
   Islam and gender, 1458–1463
   Mestiza consciousness, 1693–1695
   North African feminism, 688–694
   Northeast Asian feminism, 694–701
   postcolonial feminism, 702–706
   South African feminism, 729–735
   Southeast Asian feminism, 735–743
nationalism and gender, 1737–1741
   women as cultural markers/bearers, 2445–2449
   women suicide bombers, 2429–2431
   women's and feminist activism, East Asia, 2485–2489
   women's movements, early international movement, 2567–2573
nationalism and sexuality, 1741–1744
   women's movements, early international movement, 2567–2573
Native North America
   berdache, 159–161
   indigenous knowledges and gender, 1405–1409
   LGBT, 1578–1583
   traditional and indigenous knowledge, 2322–2326
   two-spirit, 2364–2365

Native United States and Canada
women's and feminist activism, 2513–2518
natural medicine, 49–50
nature–nurture debate, 1744–1750
feminist studies of science, 870–876
genetics and racial minorities in United States, 1199–1206
incest, social practices and legal policies on, 1399–1405
social constructionist theory, 2249–2251
Nauru
abortion laws, 3
Nazi Germany
eugenics, history and ethics, 560–565
eugenics movements, 570–574
genocide, 2008–2012
nationalism and sexuality, 1741–1744
see also Fascism and Nazism
Nazi persecution of homosexuals, 1750–1754
pink triangle, 1850–1853
neoliberalism
gender and economic globalization, 511–515
postfeminism, 1891–1900
privatization, 1914–1916
Nepal
abortion laws, 3
Netherlands
abortion laws, 3
neuroscience
biological determinism, 173–174
cognitive critical and cultural theory, 293–298
female orgasm, 612–614
incest, social practices and legal policies on, 1399–1405
nature–nurture debate, 1744–1750
neuroscience, brain research, and gender, 1754–1759
psychological theory, research, methodology, and feminist critiques, 1939–1944
neuroscience, brain research, and sexuality, 1759–1765
new religious movements
sects and cults, 2066–2069
new sexisms, 444
New Zealand
abortion laws, 3
gender, politics and the state, 1077–1082
LGBT, 1541–1546
women's and feminist activism, 2475–2479
Māori, 2504–2508
NGOs
and grassroots organizing, 1765–1769
LGBT
South Asia, 1590–1595
Western Europe, 1605–1612
subaltern, 2291–2293
transnational labor movements, 2351–2357
volunteerism and charitable giving, 2408–2409
women in development, 2449–2451
women's centers, 2559–2561
women's and feminist activism
Middle East, 2508–2513
West Africa, 2545–2548
women's and feminist organizations in South Asia, 2553–2557
women's movements, modern international movement, 2573–2579
Women's Worlds Conference, 2586–2588
Yogyakarta Principles, 2604–2606
see also community and grassroots activism
Nicaragua
abortion laws, 3
niddah, 1769–1773
menarche, 1678–1680
menstrual activism, 1682–1686
menstrual rituals, 1686–1691
purity versus pollution, 1957–1959
Niger
abortion laws, 3
Nigeria
abortion laws, 3
nineteenth-century feminism, 683–688
history of women's rights in international and comparative perspective, 1289–1306
women's movements, early international movement, 2567–2573
nomadic subject, 1773–1775
nomadic theory, 1775–1777
non-governmental organizations see NGOs
non-sexist education, 1777–1779
non-sexist language use, 1779–1781
discourse and gender, 441–445
gender neutral, 1065–1067
language and gender, 1497–1502
sexism in language, 2131–2133
non-violence, 1781–1783
normalization, 1783–1786
disability rights movement, 439–441
sexual regulation and social control, 2192–2196
stigma, 2272–2274
North Africa
activism
gender, politics and the state, 1116–1122
LGBT, 1588–1590
feminism, 688–694
gender/history of revolutions, 1015–1023

North Africa (*Continued*)
  poverty, 1908
  women's and feminist activism, 2518–2524
North America
  LGBT, 1583–1587
  women's and feminist activism, 2539–2545
  see also Canada; United States
Northeast Asia
  feminism, 694–701
Northern Ireland
  abortion laws, 3
Norway
  abortion laws, 3
nuns, including Taiwan Buddhist, 1786–1791

O

object relations theory
  feminism and psychoanalysis, 716–726
objectification *see* sexual objectification
objectivity
  feminist, 838–841
  feminist economics, 788–793
  reflexivity, 1999–2001
  strong objectivity, 2282–2284
obscenity laws
  gay male pornography, 938–940
  United States, Canada, and Europe, 1793–1797
obstetrics
  midwifery, 1699–1701
  reproductive health, 2030–2035
occupational health and safety, 1797–1799
occupational segregation, 1799–1801
  poverty in global perspective, 1905–1910
  women in non-traditional work fields, 2451–2458
Occupy movements, 1801–1805
  self-help movements, 2074–2078
Oedipal conflict, 716–726, 1805–1808
  feminist psychotherapy, 851–855
  incest, social practices and legal policies on, 1399–1405
  law of the father, 1502–1503
Oman
  abortion laws, 3
online dating, 401–405
open and reaffirming religious organizations, 1808–1810
  religion and homophobia, 2016–2020
  sects and cults, 2066–2069
  women-church, 2468–2470
oral tradition, 1810–1813
Organization for Refuge, Asylum and Migration (ORAM), 127

organized hate groups
  hate crimes/hate crime law, 1235–1240
orientalism, 1813–1816
  immigration, colonialism, and globalization, 1388–1393
  Islam and gender, 1458–1463
  mail-order brides, 1619–1621
  nationalism and sexuality, 1741–1744
  postcolonialism, theory and criticism, 1886–1891
  sex selection, 2102–2104
osteopathy, 50
othermothering, 345–348
  kinship, 1489–1491
outsider within, 1816–1819
  intersectionality, 1439–1443

P

pacifism
  ecofeminism, 502–509
  LGBT, Latin America, 1563–1569
  non-violence, 1781–1783
  North African feminism, 688–694
  peace activism and gender, 1826–1832
  Quakers and gender, 1821–1825
  Shaker religion, 2232–2234
  war, international violence, and gender, 2411–2419
Pakistan
  abortion laws, 3
Palau
  abortion laws, 3
Palermo Protocol
  human trafficking, feminist perspectives on, 1345–1350
Panama
  abortion laws, 3
Papua New Guinea
  abortion laws, 3
Paraguay
  abortion laws, 3
parental leave in comparative perspective, 1832–1836
  work–family balance, 2593–2595
parenting in prison, 1836–1839
  fathers and parenting interventions, 600–601
partial androgen insensitivity syndrome (PAIS), 67
passing, 1839–1841
paternity, 79–80
patriarchy, 1841–1844
  alpha male, 41–43
  Amazons, 53–59
  arranged marriages, 112–114

capitalist, 213–217
child custody and father right principle, 229–234
Communism and gender in China, 329–337
creation stories, 369–371
Dahomey Amazons, 57–59
discursive theories of gender, 445–448
dowry deaths, 480–482
economic determinism, 509–510
empowerment, 534–537
eurocentrism, 574–576
extended families, 576–578
feminism and argumentation, 743–745
feminist psychotherapy, 851–855
feminization of poverty, 788–793, 907–909
footbinding, 920–922
gender bias, 953–955
gender and economic globalization, 511–515
gender, politics and the state, Southern Africa, 1133–1138
Greenham Common, 1229–1230
health careers, 1243–1246
heterosexual imaginary, 1261–1265
honor killing, 1314–1318
Indo-Caribbean feminism, 654–658
Islamic feminism, 658–661
lesbian continuum, 1512–1513
lesbian feminism, 666–669
lesbian and womyn's separatism, 1536–1538
liberal feminism, 669–671
masculinism, 1625–1627
masculinities, 1627–1632
menstrual activism, 1682–1686
mind/body split, 1716–1718
misogyny, 1718–1720
monasticism, 1720–1722
Mother Nature, 1731–1733
nationalism and sexuality, 1741–1744
phallocentrism/phallogocentrism, 1848–1850
privilege, 1916–1918
queer theory, 1978–1982
radical feminism, 726–729
sexism, 2129–2131
sexual coercion, 2157–2159
woman-centeredness, 2431–2434
women in non-traditional work fields, 2451–2458
peace activism
  non-violence, 1781–1783
  pacifism, Quakers, and gender, 1821–1825
  war, international violence, and gender, 2411–2419
pedagogy
  consciousness-raising, 356–358

peer cultures
  boys' peer cultures, 192–194
  bullying, 204–206
  fictive kin, 918–920
  girls' peer cultures, 1212–1214
  sex education in UK and United States, 2092–2095
peer pressure
  boys' peer cultures, 192–194
perceived partner responsiveness
  intimacy and sexual relationships, 1451–1453
performance
  camp, 209–211
  drag, 484–490
  geisha, 942–943
  gender bender, 951–953
  gender, definition of, 966–968
  gender performance, 1071–1072
  lesbian performance, 1527–1529
  queer performance, 1974–1977
  sadomasochism, domination, and submission, 2051–2053
performance art, 1844–1846
performativity
  discursive theories of gender, 445–450
  feminism and postmodernism, 707–712
  gender identity theory, 1030–1035
  gender performance, 1071–1072
  gender as practice, 1153–1154
  lesbian performance, 1527–1529
  nomadic subject, 1773–1775
  postmodern feminism, 753–759
  poststructural feminism, 712–716
  queer performance, 1974–1977
  trans theorizing, 2331–2333
Personal Attributes Questionnaire (PAQ), 70
personal is political, 1846–1848
  lesbian and womyn's separatism, 1536–1538
  private/public spheres, 1912–1914
  radical feminism, 726–729
  women's health movement in the United States, 2563–2567
Peru
  abortion laws, 3
phallocentrism/phallogocentrism, 1848–1850
  feminist literary criticism, 816–819
  nomadic subject, 1773–1775
phenomenology
  embodiment and, 520–525
  mind/body split, 1716–1718
Philippines
  abortion laws, 3
  feminism, 740–742
  ladyboys, 1495–1497

philosophy/ethics
   animality, 76–78
   archaeology and genealogy, 109–110
   eighteenth-century feminism, 642–647
   existential feminism, 647–649
   feminist studies of science, 870–876
   mind/body split, 1716–1718
   nomadic theory, 1775–1777
   see also ethics
physical appearance
   lookism, 1616–1618
   see also beauty industry
physiology *see* biochemistry/physiology
physiotherapy, 50
Pilates, 51
pink triangle, 1850–1853
plastic sexuality, 1853–1855
pluralism
   alternative media, 44
   feminist studies of science, 870–876
poetry
   Daoism, 411–413
   gay male literature, 935–938
Poland
   abortion laws, 3
policymaking
   gender equality, 990–993
   gender mainstreaming, 1062–1064
political behavior/political participation
   militarism and gender-based violence, 1701–1710
   political participation in Western democracies, 1855–1857
   see also women's political representation
political economy
   global restructuring, 1221–1223
   hunger and famine, 1354–1359
political ideologies
   A Vindication of the Rights of Woman, 2384–2386
   homosexual reparative therapy, 1312–1314
   institutional micropolitics, 1428–1431
political participation in Western democracies, 1855–1857
   women's political representation, 2580–2584
political representation
   gender, politics and the state, Aboriginal Australia and Torres Strait Islands, 1073–1077
   institutional micropolitics, 1428–1431
   lesbian cultural criticism, 1514–1516
   representation, 2025–2027
   women's political representation, 2580–2584

politics
   Communism in Eastern Europe, 323–328
   Communism and gender in China, 329–337
   Communism and gender in United States, 337–341
   Communism in Russia, 328–329
   Declaration of the Rights of Women, 413–414
   environmental politics and women's activism, 550–554
   gender equality, 990–993
   gender, politics and the state, 1122–1127
      Australia and New Zealand, 1077–1082
      East Asia, 1093–1099
      Eastern and Central Europe, 1082–1093
      Latin America, 1104–1112
      South Asia, 1127–1133
      Southern Africa, 1133–1138
      United States and Canada, 1138–1144
      Western Europe, 1144–1152
   identity politics, 1365–1367
   institutional micropolitics, 1428–1431
   leftist armed struggle, women in, 1507–1512
   lesbian and womyn's separatism, 1536–1538
   pacifism, peace activism, and gender, 1826–1832
   pro-life movement in the United States, 1928–1932
   transgender politics, 2346–2351
   women's and feminist activism, Australia and New Zealand, 2475–2479
politics of representation, 1857–1862
   political participation in Western democracies, 1855–1857
   representation, 2025–2027
   suffrage, 2293–2296
pollution
   niddah, 1769–1773
   Shinto, 2239–2241
   see also purity versus pollution
polyamory, 1862–1866
   monogamy, sociological perspectives on, 1724–1727
   plastic sexuality, 1853–1855
polygamy, polygyny and polyandry, 1866–1868
   cohabitation and *Ekageikama* in the Kandyan Kingdom (Sri Lanka), 301–303
   Hinduism, 1282–1287
   monogamy
      biological perspectives on, 1722–1724
      sociological perspectives on, 1724–1727
   Mormonism, 1729–1731
   plastic sexuality, 1853–1855
   women's and feminist activism, Southern Africa, 2534–2538

poor *see* poverty
popular culture
    charivaris, 223–225
    chick flicks, 227–229
    feminist film theory, 807–812
    hip-hop/rap, 1287–1289
    images of gender and sexuality in Latin America, 1371–1376
    lesbian popular music, 1529–1531
    men's magazines, 1676–1678
    oral tradition, 1810–1813
    women as producers of culture, 2458–2462
popular culture and gender, 1868–1871
    women as cultural markers/bearers, 2445–2449
popular legislation
    customary laws, 399–401
population control
    contraception/contraceptives, 358–362
    eugenics, history and ethics, 565–570
    family planning, 584–589
    fertility rates, 911–914
    and population policy, 1872–1876
    see also abortion
pornography
    cybersex, 405–407
    feminist legal and political debates on, 1877–1882
    feminist sex wars, 865–867
    gay male, 938–940
    obscenity laws in United States, Canada, and Europe, 1793–1797
    postfeminism, 1891–1900
    sex-radical feminists, 2123–2125
    sexual addiction, 2142–2144
Portugal
    abortion laws, 3
positionality, 1882–1884
post-Marxism
    economic determinism, 509–510
post-structuralism
    phallocentrism/phallogocentrism, 1848–1850
post-traumatic stress disorder, 1884–1886
    battered woman syndrome, 152–155
    feminist psychotherapy, 851–855
    intimate partner abuse, 1456–1458
    rape and re-victimization, treatment of, 1993–1997
    recovered memories, 1997–1999
    sexual violence and the military, 2210–2212
postcolonial/postcolonialism
    colonialism and gender, 303–314
    feminism, 702–706
    feminist ethnography, 796–804

feminist methodology, 821–827
gender, politics and the state
    indigenous women, 1099–1104
    Latin America, 1104–1112
    South Asia, 1127–1133
    Southern Africa, 1133–1138
images of gender and sexuality of Māori, 1376–1380
Mestiza consciousness, 1693–1695
nomadic subject, 1773–1775
refugees and refugee camps, 2004–2009
sex tourism, 2104–2109
strategic essentialism, 2278–2280
subaltern, 2291–2293
theory and criticism, 1886–1891
Third World women, 2314–2317
women's and feminist activism, Eastern Africa, 2489–2494
postfeminism, 1891–1900
    chick flicks, 227–229
    monstrous-feminine, 1727–1729
    representation, 2025–2027
    womanist, 2437–2438
    women's and feminist activism, Australia and New Zealand, 2475–2479
postmodern feminism, 753–759
    cultural feminism, 637–642
    existential feminism, 647–649
    feminism and postmodernism, 707–712
    imaginary, 1386–1388
    material feminism, 671–676
    positionality, 1882–1884
postmodern feminist psychology, 1900–1905
    psychological theory, research, methodology, and feminist critiques, 1939–1944
postmodern/postmodernism
    empowerment, 534–537
    gender blind, 959–961
    institutional micropolitics, 1428–1431
    mentoring, 1691–1693
    nomadic subject, 1773–1775
    positionality, 1882–1884
    queer theory, 1978–1982
    social constructionist theory, 2249–2251
    visual culture, 2399–2403
poststructural/poststructuralism
    discursive theories of gender, 445–450
    feminism and postmodernism, 707–712
    feminist ethnography, 796–804
    feminist theories of organization, 887–892
    gender as practice, 1153–1154
    institutional micropolitics, 1428–1431
    normalization, 1783–1786
    poststructural feminism, 712–716

poststructural/poststructuralism (*Continued*)
   queer theory, 1978–1982
   romantic friendship, 2048–2050
   sisterhood, 2245–2247
   structuralism, feminist approaches to, 2286–2291

poverty
   anti-poverty activism, 92–95
   child prostitution, 241–246
   feminization of, 788–793, 907–909
   gender and development, 968–973
   gender difference, 36–37
   gender and economic globalization, 511–515
   household livelihood strategies, 1322–1326
   hunger and famine, 1354–1359
   microcredit and microlending, 1697–1699

poverty in global perspective, 1905–1910
   privatization, 1914–1916
   women in development, 2449–2451
   women's banking, 2557–2559

power
   discursive theories of gender, 445–448
   gendered space, 1189–1191
   sexual subjectivity, 2205–2208
   see also empowerment

pregnancy, 81
   assisted reproduction, 119–123
   midwifery, 1699–1701

premenstrual syndrome (PMS), 1910–1912
   medicine and medicalization, 1671–1676
   menstrual activism, 1682–1686
   women's health movement in the United States, 2563–2567

Principe
   abortion laws, 4

private prisons, 1914–1916

private/public spheres, 1912–1914
   feminist theories of welfare state, 892–901
   gender equality, 990–993
   intimate citizenship, 1453–1456
   oral tradition, 1810–1813
   personal is political, 1846–1848
   queer space, 1977–1978
   right-wing women's movements, 2040–2046
   scientific motherhood, 2060–2061

privatization, 1914–1916
   private/public spheres, 1912–1914

privilege, 1916–1918
   gender bias in research, 955–959
   heterosexism and homophobia, 1259–1261
   nationalism and sexuality, 1741–1744
   queer methods and methodologies, 1969–1974

pro-choice movement
   family planning, 584–589

   fetal rights, 916–918
   right-wing women's movements, 2040–2046
   United States, 1918–1925
      women's and feminist activism, United States and Canada, 2539–2545

pro-environmental behavior, 552

pro-life movement
   family planning, 584–589
   fetal rights, 916–918
   United States, 1925–1933

professional ethics
   ethics, moral development, and gender, 560–565

proscribed behavior
   taboo, 2303–2305

prostitution, 31, 1933–1938
   child prostitution, 241–246
   comfort women, 317–319
   criminal justice system and sexuality, 371–384
   feminist sex wars, 865–867
   human trafficking, feminist perspectives on, 1345–1350
   militarism and sex industries, 1710–1714
   sex tourism, 2104–2109
   sex work and sex workers' unionization, 2118–2123
   sex-radical feminists, 2123–2125
   sexual citizenship in East Asia, 2151–2157
   sexual slavery, 2202–2205

pseudoscience
   alternative medicine, 47–53

psychiatry
   DSM, 428–430

psychoanalysis
   DSM, 428–430
   feminism and, 716–726
   gender development, feminist psychoanalytic perspective, 973–977
   imaginary, 1386–1388
   incest, social practices and legal policies on, 1399–1405
   Oedipal conflict, 716–726, 1805–1808
   phallocentrism/phallogocentrism, 1848–1850
   poststructural feminism, 712–716
   transvestitism, 2362–2364

psychological aggression
   emotional abuse of women, 527–531

psychological sex research
   senior women and sexuality in United States, 2078–2080

psychological theory, research, methodology, and feminist critiques, 1939–1944

psychology
    of appearance, 102–107
    cosmetic surgery, 365–367
    depression, 423–426
    DSM, 428–430
    feminist psychotherapy, 851–855
    gender difference research, 983–987
    gender dysphoria, 987–990
    gender identity theory, 1030–1035
    gender variance, 1169–1171
    heterosexual imaginary, 1261–1265
    homosexual reparative therapy,
        1312–1314
    imaginary, 1386–1388
    individualism and collectivism, critical feminist
        perspectives on, 1410–1412
    internet sex, 1437–1439
    lesbian, gay, bisexual, and transgender
        psychologies, 1522–1527
    neuroscience, brain research, and gender,
        1754–1759
    postmodern feminist psychology,
        1900–1905
    sex difference research and cognitive abilities,
        2085–2089
    sex-related difference research, 2125–2129
    sexology and psychological sex research,
        2133–2142
    sexual fetishism, 2161–2163
    sexual instinct/desire, 2174–2176
    sexual objectification, 2179–2181
    traditional healing, 2326–2328
    transphobia, 2357–2360
psychology of gender, history and development of
        field, 1944–1955
    sexual assault/sexual violence,
        2144–2146
psychology of objectification, 1956–1957
psychotherapy
    archetype, 110–112
    feminist, 851–855
    feminist family therapy, 804–807
    social constructionist theory, 2249–2251
Psyképo, 650–651
public policy
    bathhouses, 150–152
    fatherhood movements, 595–599
    gender and development, 968–973
    gender, politics and the state, Latin America,
        1104–1112
    gender redistributive policies, 1155–1159
    status of women reports, 2266–2268
public sex venues
    bathhouses, 150–152

publishing
    feminist magazines, 819–821
    feminist publishing, 855–864
    women as producers of culture, 2458–2462
Puerto Rico
    abortion laws, 3
pulchronomics
    lookism, 1616–1618
purity
    chastity, 225–227
purity versus pollution, 1957–1959
    sexually transmitted infections, 2225–2227
    taboo, 2303–2305

Q
Qatar
    abortion laws, 3
qi gong, 51
Quakers
    non-violence, 1781–1783
    pacifism, Quakers, and gender, 1821–1825
queer
    lesbian popular music, 1529–1531
    masculinity and femininity, theories of,
        1632–1638
    regulation of queer sexualities, 2009–2014
queer anglophone literature, 1961–1965
    gay male literature, 935–938
queer literary criticism, 1965–1969
    politics of representation, 1857–1862
    queer performance, 1974–1977
queer literature and arts
    performance art, 1844–1846
    queer anglophone literature, 1961–1965
    queer literary criticism, 1965–1969
    queer methods and methodologies, 1969–1974
    queer space, 1977–1978
    queer theory, 1978–1982
queer performance, 1974–1977
    gender performance, 1071–1072
    lesbian performance, 1527–1529
    performance art, 1844–1846
queer space, 1977–1978
    Gay and Lesbian Pride Day, 933–935
queer theory, 1978–1982
    coming out, 319–321
    epistemology of the closet, 554–556
    feminist disability studies, 783–788
    gender blind, 959–961
    gender oppression, 1067–1069
    genderqueer, 1196–1198
    heteronormativity and homonormativity,
        1257–1259

queer theory (*Continued*)
  identity politics, 1365–1367
  monogamy, sociological perspectives on, 1724–1727
  normalization, 1783–1786
  Oedipal conflict, 716–726, 1805–1808
  queer anglophone literature, 1961–1965
  queer literary criticism, 1965–1969
  queer methods and methodologies, 1969–1974
  queer space, 1977–1978
  romantic friendship, 2048–2050
  sexual orientation and law, 2181–2192
  sexual regulation and social control, 2192–2196
  sexualities, 2212–2217
  sisterhood, 2245–2247
  traditional and indigenous knowledge, 2322–2326
  transvestitism, 2362–2364

R
race
  black feminisms, 626–630
  multiracial feminism, 678–682
race and racism
  affirmative action, 24–25
  anti-miscegenation laws, 87–91
  anti-racist/anti-civil rights movements, 96–102
  black feminist thought, 180–182
  class, caste and gender, 275–280
  colonialism and sexuality, 314–317
  community other mothers, 345–348
  critical race theory, 384–389
  eugenics, history and ethics, 565–570
  feminist perspectives on whiteness, 846–851
  genetics and racial minorities in United States, 1199–1206
  hip-hop/rap, 1287–1289
  hybridity and miscegenation, 1359–1361
  intersectionality, 1439–1443
  outsider within, 1816–1819
  reproductive justice/rights in the United States, 2035–2040
  scientific sexism and racism, 2061–2066
  South African feminism, 729–735
  women's and feminist activism
    Aboriginal Australia and Torres Strait Islands, 2470–2475
    Latin America, 2499–2504
    Māori, 2504–2508
radical feminism, 638, 726–729, 888–889
  feminist jurisprudence, 812–816
  feminist sex wars, 865–867

French feminism, 649–654
liberal feminism, 669–671
materialist feminism, 676–678
radical lesbianism, 1983–1985
woman-centeredness, 2431–2434
radical lesbianism, 1983–1985
  French feminism, 649–654
  materialist feminism, 676–678
  radical feminism, 726–729
radicalism
  aging and ageism, 37
rape
  child sex offenders, 246–249
  comfort women, 317–319
  definition, 30
  double standard, 473–475
  gender, politics and the state, Northern Africa, 1116–1122
  militarism and gender-based violence, 1701–1710
  sexual terrorism, 2208–2210
rape culture, 1985–1989
  domestic violence in United States, 467–470
  gender-based violence, 1177–1181
  sexual coercion, 2157–2159
  victim blaming, 2379–2381
  violence against women in global perspective, 2386–2392
  white supremacy and gender, 2421–2425
rape law, 1989–1993
  sexual assault/sexual violence, 2144–2146
rape and re-victimization
  intimate partner abuse, 1456–1458
  sexual coercion, 2157–2159
  treatment of, 1993–1997
recovered memories, 1997–1999
  rape and re-victimization, treatment of, 1993–1997
reflexivity, 1999–2001
  positionality, 1882–1884
  psychological theory, research, methodology, and feminist critiques, 1939–1944
  strong objectivity, 2282–2284
refugee women and violence against women, 2001–2004
  war, international violence, and gender, 2411–2419
refugees and refugee camps, 2004–2009
  asylum
    challenges of sexual minorities, 123–128
    and gender, 128–133
    and sexual orientation, 133–137

immigration, colonialism, and globalization, 1388–1393
war, international violence, and gender, 2411–2419
regulation of queer sexualities, 2009–2014
reiki, 51
relations of ruling, 2014–2016
relationship forms
  cyber intimacies, 401–405
  fictive kin, 918–920
  intimate citizenship, 1453–1456
  monogamy, sociological perspectives on, 1724–1727
  polyamory, 1862–1866
  see also intimacy and sexual relationships
religion
  abortion and religion, 13–17
  celibacy, 221–222
  creation stories, 369–371
  eighteenth-century feminism, 642–647
  feminine and masculine elements, 616–618
  feminist Christology, 769–771
  feminist theology, 876–878
  fundamentalism and public policy, 925–929
  gender, politics and the state, Northern Africa, 1116–1122
  global gag rule, 1218–1221
  and homophobia, 2016–2020
  homosexual reparative therapy, 1312–1314
  initiation rites, 1424–1428
  male circumcision, 1621–1623
  monasticism, 1720–1722
  mysticism, 1733–1735
  nuns, including Taiwan Buddhist, 1786–1791
  open and reaffirming religious organizations, 1808–1810
  purity versus pollution, 1957–1959
  suttee (Sati), 2300–2302
  volunteerism and charitable giving, 2408–2409
  wicca, 2425–2427
  womanist theology & preaching, 2439–2440
  women as cultural markers/bearers, 2445–2449
  women's and feminist activism, Southeast Asia, 2529–2533
  Yoruba culture, religion, and gender, 2606–2618
  see also Buddhism; Christianity, gender and sexuality; Hinduism; Islam; Judaism
religious fundamentalism, 2020–2025
  Islam and gender, 1458–1463
  open and reaffirming religious organizations, 1808–1810
  polygamy, polygyny and polyandry, 1866–1868
  sects and cults, 2066–2069
  sexual citizenship in East Asia, 2151–2157

representation, 2025–2027
  archetype, 110–112
  Bollywood, 185–187
  feminist magazines, 819–821
  gender, politics and the state
    East Asia, 1093–1099
    United States and Canada, 1138–1144
    Western Europe, 1144–1152
  images of gender and sexuality in advertising, 1367–1371
  men's magazines, 1676–1678
  menstrual activism, 1682–1686
  queer anglophone literature, 1961–1965
  queer literary criticism, 1965–1969
  visual culture, 2399–2403
  women as producers of culture, 2458–2462
  women's and feminist activism
    Eastern Africa, 2489–2494
    Russia, Ukraine, and Eurasia, 2524–2529
reproduction
  assisted, 119–123
  contraception/contraceptives, 358–362
  female orgasm, 612–614
  fertility rates, 911–914
  global care chain, 1216–1218
  global gag rule, 1218–1221
  Latina feminism, 661–666
  menarche, 1678–1680
  menopause, 1680–1682
  midwifery, 1699–1701
  mind/body split, 1716–1718
  Shinto, 2239–2241
  sterilization, 2268–2270
  stratified reproduction, 2280–2281
  surrogacy, 2296–2298
reproduction genetics
  nature–nurture debate, 1744–1750
reproductive choice, 2027–2030
  genetics testing and screening, 1206–1208
  pro-choice movement in United States, 1918–1925
reproductive health, 2030–2035
  hormone replacement therapy, 1318–1320
  medicine and medicalization, 1671–1676
  menarche, 1678–1680
  menopause, 1680–1682
  taboo, 2303–2305
  war, international violence, and gender, 2411–2419
  woman-centeredness, 2431–2434
  women's and feminist activism, Southern Africa, 2534–2538

reproductive justice/rights
  intimate citizenship, 1453–1456
  sexual citizenship in the Caribbean, 2146–2151
  sexuality and human rights, 2217–2220
  United States, 2035–2040
    pro-choice movement, 1918–1925
    sterilization, 2268–2270
    women's and feminist activism, United States and Canada, 2539–2545
  white supremacy and gender, 2421–2425
Republic of Korea
  abortion laws, 3
research
  gender bias in, 955–959
  gender difference, 983–987
  imaginary, 1386–1388
  sex *see* sex research
revictimization
  rape and re-victimization, treatment of, 1993–1997
revolutions
  community and grassroots activism, 341–345
  gender/history of revolutions
    East Asia, 998–1005
    Eastern and Central Europe, 1005–1015
    Northern Africa, 1015–1023
  leftist armed struggle, women in, 1507–1512
  subaltern, 2291–2293
right-wing women's movements, 2040–2046
  white supremacy and gender, 2421–2425
Riot grrrl, 2046–2047
  lesbian popular music, 1529–1531
rites of passage
  boys' peer cultures, 192–194
  initiation rites, 1424–1428
  menstrual rituals, 1686–1691
Romania
  abortion laws, 3
romantic relationships
  intimacy and sexual relationships, 1451–1453
  romantic friendship, 2048–2050
Russian Federation
  abortion laws, 3
  Communism, 328–329
  women's and feminist activism, 2524–2529
Rwanda
  abortion laws, 3

S

sadomasochism, domination, and submission, 2051–2053
Saint Kitts & Nevis
  abortion laws, 3
Saint Lucia
  abortion laws, 3
Saint Vincent & Grenadines
  abortion laws, 3
same-sex families, 2053–2055
  extended families, 576–578
  fictive kin, 918–920
  health and healthcare in sexual minorities, 1250–1255
  kinship, 1489–1491
  reproductive choice, 2027–2030
  sexual orientation and law, 2181–2192
  single-parent households, 2241–2243
same-sex marriage, 2055–2057
  Christianity, gender and sexuality, 259–262
  commitment ceremonies, 321–323
  gender equality, 990–993
  health and healthcare in sexual minorities, 1250–1255
  heterosexual imaginary, 1261–1265
  identity politics, 1365–1367
  intimate citizenship, 1453–1456
  Judaism and sexuality, 1475–1482
  LGBT
    Northern Africa, 1588–1590
    Western Europe, 1605–1612
  religion and homophobia, 2016–2020
  sexual citizenship in East Asia, 2151–2157
  sexual orientation and law, 2181–2192
same-sex sexuality
  Christianity, gender and sexuality, 259–262
  health and healthcare in sexual minorities, 1250–1255
  India, 2057–2059
  Judaism and sexuality, 1475–1482
  Kothi, 1491–1493
  sexual orientation and law, 2181–2192
Samoa
  abortion laws, 4
San Marino
  abortion laws, 3
sapphism, 1540
Saudi Arabia
  abortion laws, 4
  anti-miscegenation laws, 91
saunas *see* bathhouses
science
  biochemistry/physiology, 166–173
  clinical trials, bias against women, 283–288
  Cyborg Manifesto, 407–409
  feminist objectivity, 838–841
  feminist studies, 870–876
  feminist theories of body, 878–883

gendered innovations in science, health, and
    technology, 1181–1188
  material feminism, 671–676
  nature–nurture debate, 1744–1750
  neuroscience, brain research, and gender,
    1754–1759
  sex selection, 2102–2104
  strong objectivity, 2282–2284
  women in science, 2462–2466
scientific experiments
  gender bias in research, 955–959
  medical and scientific experimentation and
    gender, 1667–1671
scientific motherhood, 2060–2061
scientific sexism and racism, 2061–2066
second sight *see* bifurcated consciousness
second-wave feminism, 745–749
  cultural feminism, 637–642
  feminist art, 762–767
  feminist sex wars, 865–867
  French feminism, 649–654
  Greenham Common, 1229–1230
  gynocriticism, 1233–1234
  lesbian popular music, 1529–1531
  materialist feminism, 676–678
  matriarchy, 1649–1655
  multiracial feminism, 678–682
  nineteenth-century feminism, 683–688
  postfeminism, 1891–1900
  psychology of gender, history and development
    of field, 1944–1955
  radical feminism, 726–729
  sisterhood, 2245–2247
  social constructionist theory,
    2249–2251
  United States women's movements in historical
    perspective, 2369–2374
  woman-centeredness, 2431–2434
  women's and feminist activism, Australia and
    New Zealand, 2475–2479
  women's health movement in the United States,
    2563–2567
  women's movements, modern international
    movement, 2573–2579
  Women's Worlds Conference, 2586–2588
  see also feminism
secondary victimization
  victim blaming, 2379–2381
sects and cults, 2066–2069
  cult of domesticity, 394–396
self-concept
  social identity, 2251–2254
self-defense and violence against women in United
  States, 2069–2071

self-dysregulation
  rape and re-victimization, treatment of,
    1993–1997
self-esteem, 2071–2074
  cosmetic surgery, 365–367
  eating disorders, 499–502
  emotional work, 525–527
  rape and re-victimization, treatment of,
    1993–1997
  self-help movements, 2074–2078
  sexual objectification, 2179–2181
  skin lightening/bleaching, 2247–2249
  women travelers, 2466–2468
self-help movements, 2074–2078
  women's health movement in the United States,
    2563–2567
semisexual, 117
Senegal
  abortion laws, 4
senior women
  menopause, 1680–1682
  and sexuality in the United States, 2078–2080
separatism
  radical lesbianism, 1983–1985
Serbia
  abortion laws, 3
settler states
  gender, politics and the state, Aboriginal
    Australia and Torres Strait Islands,
    1073–1077
sex
  anthropological perspectives, 78–82
  clinical trials, bias against women, 283–288
  transsexuality, 2360–2362
sex beliefs and customs
  anthropological perspectives of sex, 78–82
  child sexual abuse/trauma, 249–252
  cultural views of adultery, 21–24
  Hite Report on Female Sexuality, 1306–1308
  intimate citizenship, 1453–1456
  purity versus pollution, 1957–1959
  sex education in UK and United States,
    2092–2095
  sexual addiction, 2142–2144
  sexual instinct/desire, 2174–2176
  sexual regulation and social control,
    2192–2196
  sexual scripts, 2200–2202
  Shaker religion, 2232–2234
sex and culture, 2080–2085
  taboo, 2303–2305
sex difference research and cognitive abilities,
  2085–2089
  sex and culture, 2080–2085

sex differences
    cognitive critical and cultural theory, 293–298
    cognitive, debates on, 298–300
sex discrimination, 2089–2091
    sexual harassment law, 2166–2171
    universal human rights, 2375–2377
    see also discrimination
sex education in UK and United States, 2092–2095
    socialization and sexuality, 2257–2262
sex industries
    child prostitution, 241–246
    feminist sex wars, 865–867
    human trafficking, feminist perspectives on, 1345–1350
    militarism and sex industries, 1710–1714
    pornography, feminist legal and political debates on, 1877–1882
    prostitution/sex work, 1933–1938
    sex tourism, 2104–2109
    sex toys, 2109–2111
    sex work and sex workers' unionization, 2118–2123
    sex-radical feminists, 2123–2125
    sexual slavery, 2202–2205
    strap-on sex, 2276–2278
sex reassignment surgery, 2095–2097
    intersexuality, 1448–1451
    Judaism and sexuality, 1475–1482
    passing, 1839–1841
    sexology and psychological sex research, 2133–2142
    trans identities, psychological perspectives, 2328–2331
    transsexuality, 2360–2362
sex research
    biochemistry/physiology, 166–173
    female orgasm, 612–614
    feminist studies of science, 870–876
    gender dysphoria, 987–990
    gendered innovations in science, health, and technology, 1181–1188
    Internet sex, 1437–1439
    Kinsey Scale, 1487–1489
    masturbation, 1638–1640
    prostitution/sex work, 1933–1938
    sex and culture, 2080–2085
    sexology and psychological sex research, 2133–2142
    sexual coercion, 2157–2159
    sexual fetishism, 2161–2163
    sexual instinct/desire, 2174–2176
    sexual scripts, 2200–2202
    tearoom trade, 2307–2309
sex segregation and education in United States, 2097–2102
    single-sex education and coeducation, 2243–2245
sex selection, 2102–2104
    genetics testing and screening, 1206–1208
    infanticide, 1412–1415
    intersexuality, 1448–1451
sex tourism, 2104–2109
    Caribbean, 1550
    child prostitution, 241–246
    human trafficking, feminist perspectives on, 1345–1350
    ladyboys, 1495–1497
    militarism and sex industries, 1710–1714
    post-traumatic stress disorder, 1884–1886
    prostitution/sex work, 1933–1938
    sex work and sex workers' unionization, 2118–2123
sex toys, 2109–2111
    masturbation, 1638–1640
    strap-on sex, 2276–2278
    technosexuality, 2309–2311
sex trafficking, 2111–2116
    child labor in comparative perspective, 234–241
    child prostitution, 241–246
    misogyny, 1718–1720
    prostitution/sex work, 1933–1938
    sex tourism, 2104–2109
    sex work and sex workers' unionization, 2118–2123
    sexual slavery, 2202–2205
    sexual terrorism, 2208–2210
sex versus gender categorization, 2116–2118
    sex-related difference research, 2125–2129
sex work, 1933–1938
    comfort women, 317–319
    militarism and sex industries, 1710–1714
    sex tourism, 2104–2109
    sexual citizenship in East Asia, 2151–2157
    sexual slavery, 2202–2205
    see also prostitution
sex work and sex workers' unionization, 2118–2123
    prostitution/sex work, 1933–1938
    sexual rights, 2196–2200
    technosexuality, 2309–2311
sex workers' rights movement
    prostitution/sex work, 1933–1938
    sex work and sex workers' unionization, 2118–2123
sex workers' unions *see* sex work and sex workers' unionization
sex-radical feminists, 2123–2125

sex-related difference research, 2125–2129
　gender difference research, 983–987
sex/gender
　neuroscience, brain research, and sexuality,
　　1759–1765
sexism, 2129–2131
　discourse and gender, 441–445
　fairy tales, 579–582
　gender bias, 953–955
　gender, definition of, 966–968
　gender equality/inequality in education,
　　993–998, 1046–1050
　images of gender and sexuality in Southern
　　Africa, 1380–1385
　information technology, 1419–1424
　mentoring, 1691–1693
　mind/body split, 1716–1718
　privilege, 1916–1918
　scientific sexism and racism, 2061–2066
　sex selection, 2102–2104
　sexual harassment law, 2166–2171
　tokenism, 2317–2319
　women in science, 2462–2466
　women's and feminist activism, East Asia,
　　2485–2489
　women's health movement in the United States,
　　2563–2567
sexism in language, 2131–2133
　language and gender, 1497–1502
　non-sexist language use, 1779–1781
　Yoruba culture, religion, and gender, 2606–2618
sexology
　and psychological sex research, 2133–2142
　　sexual fetishism, 2161–2163
　　sexually transmitted infections,
　　　2225–2227
　senior women and sexuality in United States,
　　2078–2080
sexual addiction, 2142–2144
　cybersex, 405–407
　drug and alcohol abuse, 490–493
　Internet sex, 1437–1439
sexual assault *see* sexual violence
sexual behaviors
　alpha male, 41–43
　bathhouses, 150–152
　bisexuality *see* bisexuality
　child sex offenders, 246–249
　child sexual abuse/trauma, 249–252
　cultural views of adultery, 21–24
　female orgasm, 612–614
　Hite Report on Female Sexuality, 1306–1308
　Internet sex, 1437–1439
　masturbation, 1638–1640

　plastic sexuality, 1853–1855
　sex tourism, 2104–2109
　sex toys, 2109–2111
　sexology and psychological sex research,
　　2133–2142
　sexual addiction, 2142–2144
　sexual contract, 2159–2161
　sexual fetishism, 2161–2163
　sexual identity and orientation, 2171–2174
　sexual scripts, 2200–2202
　sexually transmitted infections, 2225–2227
sexual citizenship
　age of consent in historical and international
　　perspective, 30–34
　asexual activism, 114–116
　Caribbean, 2146–2151
　East Asia, 2151–2157
　immigration, colonialism, and globalization,
　　1388–1393
　LGBT, Caribbean, 1546–1550
　monogamy, sociological perspectives on,
　　1724–1727
　sex selection, 2102–2104
　sexual minorities, 2176–2179
　women's and feminist activism, Middle East,
　　2508–2513
sexual coercion, 2157–2159
　child sexual abuse/trauma, 249–252
　emotional abuse of women, 527–531
　radical lesbianism, 1983–1985
　sexual slavery, 2202–2205
　sexual subjectivity, 2204–2208
sexual contract, 2159–2161
sexual cultures
　bisexuality, 177–180
　cybersex, 405–407
　double standard, 473–476
　drag, 484–490
　plastic sexuality, 1853–1855
　polyamory, 1862–1866
　sexual contract, 2159–2161
　sexual fetishism, 2161–2163
　strap-on sex, 2276–2278
sexual desire *see* sexual instinct/desire
sexual development
　androgen insensitivity syndrome, 66–68
　gender dysphoria, 987–990
　sexual contract, 2159–2161
　sexual identity and orientation, 2171–2174
sexual dysfunction
　alternative medicine, 52
　asexuality, 116–119
　sexology and psychological sex research,
　　2133–2142

sexual dysfunction (*Continued*)
   sexual addiction, 2142–2144
   sexuopharmaceuticals, 2227–2232
sexual fetishism, 2161–2163
   footbinding, 920–922
   Internet sex, 1437–1439
sexual freedom, feminist debates in United States, 2163–2165
sexual harassment law, 2166–2171
   sexual violence and the military, 2210–2212
   women in non-traditional work fields, 2451–2458
   women's and feminist activism, East Asia, 2485–2489
sexual identity and orientation, 2171–2174
   coming out, 319–321
   criminal justice system and sexuality, 371–384
   Daoism, 411–413
   "Don't ask, don't tell" policy, 470–473
   identity politics, 1365–1367
   Islam and homosexuality, 1463–1469
   Judaism and sexuality, 1475–1482
   Kinsey Scale, 1486–1489
   lesbian continuum, 1512–1513
   lesbian, gay, bisexual, and transgender psychologies, 1522–1527
   monogamy, sociological perspectives on, 1724–1727
   open and reaffirming religious organizations, 1808–1810
   sexology and psychological sex research, 2133–2142
   sexual freedom, feminist debates in United States, 2163–2165
   stone butch, 2274–2276
sexual instinct/desire, 2174–2176
   sex toys, 2109–2111
   sexual subjectivity, 2204–2208
sexual intimacy
   intimacy and sexual relationships, 1451–1453
sexual minorities, 2176–2179
   asexual activism, 114–116
   asexuality, 116–119
   asylum, challenges faced by, 123–128
   bisexuality, 177–180
   Communism in Russia, 328–329
   cross-dressing, 392–394
   desexualization, 426–428
   employment discrimination, 531–533
   epistemology of the closet, 554–556
   families of choice, 582–584
   gender dysphoria, 987–990
   heteronormativity and homonormativity, 1257–1259
   heterosexism and homophobia, 1259–1261
   intersexuality, 1448–1451
   Kathoey, 1483–1485
   LGBT
      Australia and New Zealand, 1541–1546
      Eastern and Central Europe, 1557–1563
   nomadic theory, 1775–1777
   open and reaffirming religious organizations, 1808–1810
   private/public spheres, 1912–1914
   sadomasochism, domination, and submission, 2051–2053
   sexual identity and orientation, 2171–2174
   sexual orientation and law, 2181–2192
   sexual rights, 2196–2200
   trans identities, psychological perspectives, 2328–2331
   transvestitism, 2362–2364
   victimization, 2381–2384
sexual objectification, 2179–2181
   beauty industry, 157–159
   cosmetic surgery, 365–367
   eating disorders, 499–502
   mail-order brides, 1619–1621
   men's magazines, 1676–1678
   misogyny, 1718–1720
   psychology of, 1956–1957
sexual orientation and law, 2181–2192
   asylum seeking, 133–137
   bathhouses, 150–152
   criminal justice system and sexuality, 371–384
   "Don't ask, don't tell" policy, 470–473
   hate crimes/hate crime law, 1235–1240
   heterosexism and homophobia, 1259–1261
   intimate citizenship, 1453–1456
   LGBT
      Australia and New Zealand, 1541–1546
      Eastern and Central Europe, 1557–1563
      North America, 1583–1587
      Southeast Asia, 1595–1600
      Western Europe, 1605–1612
   Nazi persecution of homosexuals, 1750–1754
   same-sex sexuality in India, 2057–2059
   sexual citizenship in East Asia, 2151–2157
   sexual identity and orientation, 2171–2174
   Yogyakarta Principles, 2604–2606
sexual pleasure
   female orgasm, 612–614
   geisha, 942–943
   intimacy and sexual relationships, 1451–1453
   masturbation, 1638–1640
   sex toys, 2109–2111
   sex-radical feminists, 2123–2125
   sexual regulation and social control, 2192–2196

stone butch, 2274–2276
strap-on sex, 2276–2278
sexual politics
   asexual activism, 114–116
   coming out, 319–321
   compulsory heterosexuality, 354–358
   courtly love, 367–369
   epistemology of the closet, 554–556
   feminist sex wars, 865–867
   lesbian continuum, 1512–1513
   lesbian cultural criticism, 1514–1516
   open and reaffirming religious organizations, 1808–1810
   sadomasochism, domination, and submission, 2051–2053
   sex-radical feminists, 2123–2125
   sexual citizenship in the Caribbean, 2146–2151
   sexual regulation and social control, 2192–2196
   sisterhood, 2245–2247
sexual regulation and social control, 2192–2196
   medicine and medicalization, 1671–1676
   regulation of queer sexualities, 2009–2014
   sexual freedom, feminist debates in United States, 2163–2165
sexual rights, 2196–2200
   lesbian popular music, 1529–1531
   LGBT, Southern Africa, 1600–1605
   sexual citizenship
      in the Caribbean, 2146–2151
      in East Asia, 2151–2157
   sexual contract, 2159–2161
   universal human rights, 2375–2377
sexual scripts, 2200–2202
   sexual subjectivity, 2204–2208
sexual slavery, 2202–2205
   child labor in comparative perspective, 234–241
   comfort women, 317–319
   Dahomey Amazons, 57–59
   human trafficking, feminist perspectives on, 1345–1350
   sexual contract, 2159–2161
   sexual subjectivity, 2204–2208
   sexual terrorism, 2208–2210
sexual subjectivity, 2205–2208
   child sex offenders, 246–249
   feminism and psychoanalysis, 716–726
sexual terrorism, 2208–2210
sexual violence, 2144–2146
   battered women, 152–155
   child sex offenders, 246–249
   child sexual abuse/trauma, 249–252
   comfort women, 317–319
   desexualization, 426–428
   domestic violence in United States, 467–470
   emotional abuse of women, 527–531
   fairy tales, 579–582
   genocide, 1208–1212
   higher education and gender in the United States, 1270–1281
   incest, social practices and legal policies on, 1399–1405
   intimate partner abuse, 1456–1458
   militarism and gender-based violence, 1701–1710
   militarism and sex industries, 1710–1714
   misogyny, 1718–1720
   pornography, feminist legal and political debates on, 1877–1882
   rape culture, 1985–1989
   rape law, 1989–1993
   rape and re-victimization, treatment of, 1993–1997
   refugees and refugee camps, 2004–2009
   sex trafficking, 2111–2116
   sexual coercion, 2157–2159
   sexual harassment law, 2166–2171
   sexual slavery, 2202–2205
   sexual terrorism, 2208–2210
   sexual violence and the military, 2210–2212
   victimization, 2381–2384
   violence against women in global perspective, 2386–2392
   women's and feminist activism, Native United States and Canada, 2513–2518
   see also gender assault/gender violence; violence
sexual violence and the military, 2210–2212
   war, international violence, and gender, 2411–2419
sexuality, 2212–2217
   bathhouses, 150–152
   bisexuality, 177–180
   camp, 209–211
   Christianity, gender and sexuality, 259–262
   compulsory heterosexuality, 354–358
   creation stories, 369–371
   cross-dressing, 392–394
   curriculum transformation, 396–399
   cyber intimacies, 401–405
   Cyborg Manifesto, 407–409
   desexualization, 426–428
   double standard, 473–476
   drag, 484–490
   drug and alcohol abuse, 490–493
   empowerment, 534–537
   female orgasm, 612–614
   gender, politics and the state

sexuality (*Continued*)
    Northern Africa, 1116–1122
    South Asia, 1127–1133
  Hinduism, 1282–1287
  Hite Report on Female Sexuality, 1306–1308
  and human rights, 2217–2220
  human rights, international laws and policies, 1330–1345
  images of *see* images of sexuality
  information technology, 1419–1424
  Judaism and sexuality, 1475–1482
  Kinsey Scale, 1487–1489
  Kothi, 1491–1493
  Latina feminism, 661–666
  lesbian feminism, 666–669
  lesbian stereotypes in the United States, 1531–1536
  Lesbos, 1540–1541
  LGBT
    Australia and New Zealand, 1541–1546
    Native North America, 1578–1583
  monasticism, 1720–1722
  monogamy, biological perspectives on, 1722–1724
  monogamy, sociological perspectives on, 1724–1727
  nationalism
    and gender, 1737–1741
    and sexuality, 1741–1744
  neuroscience, brain research, and sexuality, 1759–1765
  normalization, 1783–1786
  Oedipal conflict, 716–726, 1805–1808
  plastic sexuality, 1853–1855
  polyamory, 1862–1866
  prostitution/sex work, 1933–1938
  regulation of queer sexualities, 2009–2014
  same-sex families, 2053–2055
  same-sex sexuality in India, 2057–2059
  sects and cults, 2066–2069
  sex toys, 2109–2111
  sexology and psychological sex research, 2133–2142
  sexual addiction, 2142–2144
  sexual fetishism, 2161–2163
  sexual instinct/desire, 2174–2176
  sexual orientation and law, 2181–2192
  sexual regulation and social control, 2192–2196
  sexual rights, 2196–2200
  sexual scripts, 2200–2202
  sexual subjectivity, 2205–2208
  sexually transmitted infections, 2225–2227
  sexuopharmaceuticals, 2227–2232
  stone butch, 2274–2276
  strap-on sex, 2276–2278
  tearoom trade, 2307–2309
  Third World women, 2314–2317
  trans identities, psychological perspectives, 2328–2331
  virginity, 2397–2399
sexualization
  postfeminism, 1891–1900
  sexualizing the state, 2220–2225
sexualizing the state, 2220–2225
sexually transmitted infections, 2225–2227
  AIDS-related stigma, 38–40
  sexology and psychological sex research, 2133–2142
sexuopharmaceuticals, 2227–2232
Seychelles
  abortion laws, 4
Shaker religion, 2232–2234
  feminist Christology, 769–771
  sects and cults, 2066–2069
Shakti Shanthi, 2234–2235
  Hinduism, 1282–1287
shaman priestesses, 2236–2237
  Shinto, 2239–2241
Shari'a, 2237–2239
Shinto, 2239–2241
  geisha, 942–943
Sierra Leone
  abortion laws, 4
simultaneity
  black feminisms, 626–630
Singapore
  abortion laws, 4
single-parent households, 2241–2243
single-sex education and coeducation, 2243–2245
  sex segregation and education in United States, 2097–2102
siskana, 486
sisterhood, 2245–2247
skin lightening/bleaching, 2247–2249
  cosmetic surgery, 365–367
  fashion, 591–595
  passing, 1839–1841
  sexual objectification, 2179–2181
Slovak Republic
  abortion laws, 4
Slovenia
  abortion laws, 4
social constructionist theory, 2249–2251
  gender development, theories of, 977–982
  gender inequality and gender stratification, 1050–1052
  gender as institution, 1052–1056

gender neutral, 1065–1067
gender as practice, 1153–1154
masculinities, 1627–1632
sexual identity and orientation, 2171–2174
social identity, 2251–2254
A Vindication of the Rights of Woman, 2384–2386
disability rights movement, 439–441
popular culture and gender, 1868–1871
trans theorizing, 2331–2333
social justice
  feminist movements in historical and comparative perspective, 827–838
  women-church, 2468–2470
social location
  social identity, 2251–2254
social media, 46
  Arab Spring movements, 107–108
  skin lightening/bleaching, 2247–2249
  technosexuality, 2309–2311
social networks
  families of choice, 582–584
social policy
  gender and development, 968–973
  gender redistributive policies, 1155–1159
  global care chain, 1216–1218
  parental leave in comparative perspective, 1832–1836
  women in non-traditional work fields, 2451–2458
  work–family balance, 2593–2595
social regulation
  regulation of queer sexualities, 2009–2014
social role theory
  gender development, theories of, 977–982
  of sex differences, 2254–2257
  trans theorizing, 2331–2333
social structure
  xenophobia and gender, 2597–2599
social support
  families of choice, 582–584
socialism
  feminist theories of organization, 887–892
  gender, politics and the state, Eastern and Central Europe, 1082–1093
  Marxist/Socialist feminism, 749–753
  see also Communism/socialism
socialization
  androcentrism, 65–66
  child labor in comparative perspective, 234–241
  child sex offenders, 246–249
  children's literature and gender, 252–256
  gender role ideology, 1159–1162
  heterosexism and homophobia, 1259–1261

higher education and gender in the United States, 1270–1281
media and gender socialization, 1662–1667
normalization, 1783–1786
self-esteem, 2071–2074
sexual instinct/desire, 2174–2176
sexual subjectivity, 2204–2208
and sexuality, 2257–2262
xenophobia and gender, 2597–2599
sodomy
  Communism in Russia, 328–329
  LGBT, Southeast Asia, 1595–1600
  sexual orientation and law, 2181–2192
  sexuality and human rights, 2217–2220
sodomy law in comparative perspective, 2262–2266
Soloman Islands
  abortion laws, 4
Somalia
  abortion laws, 4
South Africa
  abortion laws, 4
  feminism, 729–735
  see also Southern Africa
South Asia
  arranged marriages, 112–114
  Buddhism, 201–204
  cohabitation and *Ekageikama* in the Kandyan Kingdom (Sri Lanka), 301–303
  dowry deaths, 480–482
  Dowry Prohibition Act, 482–484
  gender, politics and the state, 1127–1133
  Hijra/Hejira, 1281–1282
  Kothi, 1491–1493
  LGBT, 1590–1595
  poverty, 1908–1909
  sex trafficking, 2111–2116
  subaltern, 2291–2293
  suttee (Sati), 2300–2302
  women's and feminist organizations, 2553–2557
  see also individual countries
South Sudan
  abortion laws, 4
Southeast Asia
  feminism, 735–743
  LGBT, 1595–1600
  women's and feminist activism, 2529–2533
Southern Africa
  gender, politics and the state, 1133–1138
  images of gender and sexuality, 1380–1385
  LGBT, 1600–1605
  women's and feminist activism, 2534–2538
  see also South Africa
space *see* cyberspace; gendered space; queer space

Spain
  abortion laws, 4
spatial ability
  cognitive sex differences, debates on, 298–300
spirituality
  Buddhism, 201–204
  CAM, 351–354
  deep ecology, 416–418
  ecofeminism, 502–509
  feminine and masculine elements, 616–618
  Mestiza consciousness, 1693–1695
  Shaker religion, 2232–2234
  shaman priestesses, 2236–2237
  two-spirit, 2364–2365
  womanist theology & preaching, 2439–2440
sports
  athletics *see* athletics; athletics and gender
  metrosexual, 1695–1696
Sri Lanka
  abortion laws, 4
  cohabitation and *Ekageikama* in the Kandyan Kingdom, 301–303
  women suicide bombers, 2429–2431
standpoint theory
  feminist objectivity, 838–841
state
  sexualizing of, 2220–2225
  see also gender, politics, and the state
state feminism
  femocrat, 909–911
status degradation ceremonies, 528
status position
  social identity, 2251–2254
status of women reports, 2266–2268
status-of-the-mother laws, 88
STEM
  cognitive sex differences, debates on, 298–300
stereotypes
  athletics and gender, 137–142
  lesbian stereotypes in the United States, 1531–1536
sterilization, 2268–2270
  family planning, 584–589
  reproductive justice/rights in the United States, 2035–2040
steroids, 2270–2272
stigma, 2272–2274
  AIDS-related, 38–40
  fetal alcohol syndrome, 914–916
  sex work and sex workers' unionization, 2118–2123
  sexual rights, 2196–2200

sexually transmitted infections, 2225–2227
tokenism, 2317–2319
stone butch, 2274–2276
  lesbian stereotypes in the United States, 1531–1536
strap-on sex, 2276–2278
  sex toys, 2109–2111
strategic essentialism, 2278–2280
  subaltern, 2291–2293
  transphobia, 2357–2360
stratification
  family wage, 589–591
  gender inequality and gender stratification, 1050–1052
  heteronormativity and homonormativity, 1257–1259
stratified reproduction, 2280–2281
  surrogacy, 2296–2298
strong objectivity, 2282–2284
structural adjustment, 2284–2285
  feminist economics, 788–793
  privatization, 1914–1916
structuralism
  feminist approaches to, 2286–2291
  feminist literary criticism, 816–819
  heterosexual imaginary, 1261–1265
  imaginary, 1386–1388
  masculinity and femininity, theories of, 1632–1638
  social constructionist theory, 2249–2251
Sub-Saharan Africa
  poverty, 1909
subaltern, 2291–2293
subcultures
  bear culture, 155–157
  fictive kin, 918–920
  outsider within, 1816–1819
  polyamory, 1862–1866
subject position
  social identity, 2251–2254
subjective transnationalism, 187–191
substance use
  drug and alcohol abuse, 490–493
Sudan
  abortion laws, 4
  LGBT, 1577
suffrage, 2293–2296
  gender, politics and the state, United States and Canada, 1138–1144
  history of women's rights in international and comparative perspective, 1289–1306
  Mormonism, 1729–1731
  non-violence, 1781–1783

right-wing women's movements, 2040–2046
women's and feminist activism
   East Asia, 2485–2489
   United States and Canada, 2539–2545
women's movements, early international
   movement, 2567–2573
see also women's movements
Suffragettes
   family planning, 584–589
   gender, politics and the state, Western Europe, 1144–1152
   history of women's rights in international and comparative perspective, 1289–1306
Suriname
   abortion laws, 4
surrogacy, 122, 2296–2298
sustainable livelihoods, 2298–2300
   women's banking, 2557–2559
suttee (Sati), 2300–2302
   subaltern, 2291–2293
swardspeak, 486
Swaziland
   abortion laws, 4
Sweden
   abortion laws, 4
Switzerland
   abortion laws, 4
Syria
   abortion laws, 4

T
taboo, 2303–2305
   incest, social practices and legal policies on, 1399–1405
   masturbation, 1638–1640
   menstrual activism, 1682–1686
   menstrual rituals, 1686–1691
   monstrous-feminine, 1727–1729
   post-traumatic stress disorder, 1884–1886
   purity versus pollution, 1957–1959
   sadomasochism, domination, and submission, 2051–2053
   sexual fetishism, 2161–2163
   strap-on sex, 2276–2278
Taiwan
   abortion laws, 3
   nuns, including Taiwan Buddhist, 1786–1791
Tajikistan
   abortion laws, 4
tantrism
   Hinduism, 1282–1287
Tanzania
   abortion laws, 4
   LGBT, 1603
Taoism
   abortion, 16
tattooing and piercing, 2305–2307
tearoom trade, 2307–2309
   queer space, 1977–1978
technology
   clinical trials, bias against women, 283–288
   Cyborg Manifesto, 407–409
   digital divide, 433–435
   domestic, 465–467
   gendered innovations in science, health, and technology, 1181–1188
   information technology, 1419–1424
   Internet and gender, 1433–1437
   intimate citizenship, 1453–1456
   surrogacy, 2296–2298
technosexuality, 2309–2311
   digital media and gender, 435–438
   nomadic theory, 1775–1777
teledildonics
   cybersex, 405–407
terms for women
   Amazons, 53–59
   cohabitation and *Ekageikama* in the Kandyan Kingdom (Sri Lanka), 301–303
   geisha, 942–943
   womanist, 2437–2438
Thailand
   abortion laws, 4
   feminism, 740
   Kathoey, 1483–1485
   ladyboys, 1495–1497
Thatcherism
   privatization, 1914–1916
theology
   creation stories, 369–371
   feminine and masculine elements, 616–618
   feminist, 876–878
   wicca, 2425–2427
   womanist theology & preaching, 2434–2437
   see also religion
theory
   A Vindication of the Rights of Woman, 2384–2386
   archaeology and genealogy, 109–110
   archetype, 110–112
   compulsory heterosexuality, 354–358
   critical race theory, 384–389
   discursive theories of gender, 445–450
   feminist theories of body, 878–883
   French feminism, 649–654
   gender development, theories of, 977–982
   gender identity theory, 1030–1035
   gender as institution, 1052–1056

theory (*Continued*)
  heterosexual imaginary, 1261–1265
  imaginary, 1386–1388
  materialist feminism, 676–678
  nature–nurture debate, 1744–1750
  trans theorizing, 2331–2333
theory and criticism
  postcolonialism, 1886–1891
  Third World women, 2314–2317
therapies
  CAM, 47–53, 351–354
third genders, 2311–2314
  fairy tales, 579–582
  gender identity theory, 1030–1035
  gender variance, 1169–1171
  genderqueer, 1196–1198
  Kathoey, 1483–1485
  regulation of queer sexualities, 2009–2014
  trans identities, psychological perspectives, 2328–2331
third sex
  berdache, 159–161
  Kathoey, 1483–1485
third wave
  democracy and democratization, 418–423
  intersectionality, 1439–1443
third-wave feminism, 745–749
  cultural feminism, 637–642
  gender, politics and the state, United States and Canada, 1138–1144
  lesbian popular music, 1529–1531
  matriarchy, 1649–1655
  multiracial feminism, 678–682
  nineteenth-century feminism, 683–688
  postfeminism, 1891–1900
  radical feminism, 726–729
  Riot grrrl, 2046–2047
  sisterhood, 2245–2247
  structuralism, feminist approaches to, 2286–2291
  United States women's movements in historical perspective, 2369–2374
  women's and feminist activism
    Australia and New Zealand, 2475–2479
    Western Europe, 2548–2552
  women's movements, modern international movement, 2573–2579
  Women's Worlds Conference, 2586–2588
  see also feminism
Third World, 2314–2317
  anti-globalization movements, 82–87
  feminist ethnography, 796–804
  feminist methodology, 821–827

  global gag rule, 1218–1221
  Indo-Caribbean feminism, 654–658
  Islam and gender, 1458–1463
  maquiladora, 1623–1625
  multiracial feminism, 678–682
  NGOs and grassroots organizing, 1765–1769
  postcolonial feminism, 702–706
  women in development, 2449–2451
  women suicide bombers, 2429–2431
  women's and feminist activism, Eastern Africa, 2489–2494
Timor-Leste
  abortion laws, 4
Title IX, 140–141
Togo
  abortion laws, 4
tokenism, 2317–2319
tomboys and sissies, 2319–2322
  gender variance, 1169–1171
  third gender, 2311–2314
Tonga
  abortion laws, 4
traditional Chinese medicine, 49
traditional healing, 2326–2328
  two-spirit, 2364–2365
traditional and indigenous knowledge, 48, 49, 2322–2326
  medical and scientific experimentation and gender, 1667–1671
  shaman priestesses, 2236–2237
trans identities
  Kathoey, 1483–1485
  neuroscience, brain research, and sexuality, 1759–1765
  psychological perspectives, 2328–2331
  sexual minorities, 2176–2179
  sexualities, 2212–2217
  stone butch, 2274–2276
  transgender health and healthcare, 2333–2337
  transgender movements in international perspective, 2337–2341
  transgender politics, 2346–2351
  transphobia, 2357–2360
trans theorizing, 2331–2333
  trans identities, psychological perspectives, 2328–2331
  transgender movements in international perspective, 2337–2341
  transgender politics, 2346–2351
transgender
  asylum, challenges faced by sexual minorities, 123–128
  asylum and sexual orientation, 133–137
  cisgender/cissexual, 267–271

cross-dressing, 392–394
drag, 484–490
fairy tales, 579–582
gender dysphoria, 987–990
gender equality, 990–993
gender identification, 1023–1026
gender identity theory, 1030–1035
gender oppression, 1067–1069
gender outlaw, 1069–1071
gender violence, 1172–1175
genderqueer, 1196–1198
Kathoey, 1483–1485
ladyboys, 1495–1497
lesbian feminism, 666–669
queer anglophone literature, 1961–1965
sex versus gender categorization, 2116–2118
trans identities, psychological perspectives, 2328–2331
trans theorizing, 2331–2333
transgender politics, 2346–2351
transsexuality, 2360–2362
transvestitism, 2362–2364
transgender health and healthcare, 2333–2337
transgender movements
in international perspective, 2337–2341
LGBT
North America, 1583–1587
South Asia, 1590–1595
Western Europe, 1605–1612
masculinity and femininity, theories of, 1632–1638
Occupy movements, 1801–1805
sexual citizenship in East Asia, 2151–2157
transgender politics, 2346–2351
transsexuality, 2360–2362
transvestitism, 2362–2364
United States, 2341–2345
transgender politics, 2346–2351
sexual minorities, 2176–2179
trans identities, psychological perspectives, 2328–2331
transgender health and healthcare, 2333–2337
transgender movements
international perspective, 2337–2341
United States, 2341–2345
transsexuality, 2360–2362
translation
French feminism, 649–654
transnational labor movements, 2351–2357
transnationalism
feminist movements in historical and comparative perspective, 827–838
Northeast Asian feminism, 694–701

transphobia, 2357–2360
cisgenderism, 271–274
gender dysphoria, 987–990
lesbian feminism, 666–669
lesbian, gay, bisexual, and transgender psychologies, 1522–1527
sexuality and human rights, 2217–2220
transgender movements in international perspective, 2337–2341
transgender politics, 2346–2351
transsexuality, 2360–2362
asylum and sexual orientation, 133–137
cisgender/cissexual, 267–271
cross-dressing, 392–394
drag, 484–490
gender dysphoria, 987–990
gender outlaw, 1069–1071
Hijra/Hejira, 1281–1282
Kathoey, 1483–1485
passing, 1839–1841
sex reassignment surgery, 2095–2097
sexual minorities, 2176–2179
sexualities, 2212–2217
trans theorizing, 2331–2333
transgender health and healthcare, 2333–2337
transgender movements in international perspective, 2337–2341
transgender politics, 2346–2351
transvestitism, 2362–2364
transvestitism, 2362–2364
cross-dressing, 392–394
Nazi persecution of homosexuals, 1750–1754
trans theorizing, 2331–2333
trauma
post-traumatic stress disorder, 1884–1886
see also gender assault/violence; sexual violence; violence
treatment
rape and re-victimization, treatment of, 1993–1997
Trinidad & Tobago
abortion laws, 4
Trobriand people, 78–79
Tunisia
abortion laws, 4
LGBT, 1576–1577
women's and feminist activism, 2519–2521
tunten, 488
Turkey
abortion laws, 4
Turkmenistan
abortion laws, 4
Tuvalu
abortion laws, 4

two-spirit, 2364–2365
   berdache, 159–161
   gender identification, 1023–1026
   gender identity theory, 1030–1035
   gender variance, 1169–1171
   indigenous knowledges and gender, 1405–1409
   LGBT, Native North America, 1578–1583
   politics of representation, 1857–1862
   third gender, 2311–2314
   traditional and indigenous knowledge, 2322–2326
   trans identities, psychological perspectives, 2328–2331
   transgender politics, 2346–2351

U

Uganda
   abortion laws, 4
Ukraine
   abortion laws, 4
   women's and feminist activism, 2524–2529
uncleanliness
   taboo, 2303–2305
   see also purity versus pollution
United Arab Emirates
   abortion laws, 4
United Kingdom *see* Britain
United Nations
   anti-globalization movements, 85–86
   CEDAW, 25, 359, 362–365
   gender equality, 990–993
   International Women's Day, 1431–1433
United Nations Decade for Women, 2367–2369
   sexuality and human rights, 2217–2220
   women's and feminist activism, East Asia, 2485–2489
   women's movements, modern international movement, 2573–2579
   Women's Worlds Conference, 2586–2588
United States
   abortion
      pro-choice movement, 1918–1925
      pro-life movement, 1925–1933
      reproductive justice/rights, 2035–2040
      women's health movement, 2563–2567
   abortion laws, 4
   activism
      transgender movements, 2341–2345
      women's health movement, 2563–2567
   anti-globalization movements, 84
   anti-miscegenation laws, 87–89
   anti-poverty activism, 92–95
   birth control
      reproductive justice/rights, 2035–2040
      women's health movement, 2563–2567
   civil rights law and gender, 274–275
   Communism and gender, 337–341
   cosmetic surgery, 365–367
   criminal justice system and sexuality, 371–384
   domestic violence, 467–470
   "Don't ask, don't tell" policy, 470–473
   feminist family therapy, 804–807
   gender equity in education, 993–998
   gender, politics and the state, 1138–1144
   genetics and racial minorities, 1199–1206
   hate crimes/hate crime law, 1235–1240
   higher education and gender, 1270–1281
   hostile work environment, 1320–1322, 1797–1799
   Jim Crow laws, 422
   lesbian stereotypes, 1531–1536
   LGBT, 1583–1587
   materialist feminism, 676–678
   nineteenth-century feminism, 683–688
   non-sexist education, 1777–1779
   obscenity laws, 1793–1797
   poverty, 1909
   reproductive justice/rights, 2035–2040
      pro-choice movement, 1918–1925
      sterilization, 2268–2270
      women's and feminist activism, United States and Canada, 2539–2545
   self-defense and violence against women, 2069–2071
   senior women and sexuality, 2078–2080
   sex education, 2092–2095
   sex segregation and education, 2097–2102
   sexual freedom, feminist debates, 2163–2165
   suffrage, 1781–1783
   Title IX, 140–141
   Violence Against Women Act (1994), 154
   volunteerism and charitable giving, 2408–2409
   women's and feminist activism
      Native United States and Canada, 2513–2518
      United States and Canada, 2539–2545
   women's movements
      early international movement, 2567–2573
      in historical perspective, 2369–2374
      women's health movement, 2563–2567
      see also North America
universal human rights, 2375–2377
   abortion, 1–13
   asylum
      challenges faced by sexual minorities, 123–128
      and sexual orientation, 133–137
   capabilities approach, 211–213

CEDAW, 25, 359, 362–365
child labor in comparative perspective, 234–241
child prostitution, 241–246
civil rights law and gender, 274–275
customary laws, 399–401
disability rights movement, 439–441
eugenics movements, 570–574
female genital cutting, 288–293, 609–612
feminist jurisprudence, 812–816
feminization of poverty, 907–909
fetal rights, 916–918
fundamentalism and public policy, 925–929
and gender, 1326–1330
gender and development, 968–973
gender and economic globalization, 511–515
gender identification, 1023–1026
gender indices, 1036–1046
genetics testing and screening, 1206–1208
hate crimes/hate crime law, 1235–1240
human trafficking, feminist perspectives on, 1345–1350
international laws and policies, 1330–1345
LGBT
  Eastern Africa, 1551–1557
  Eastern and Central Europe, 1557–1563
  Latin America, 1563–1569
  Middle East, 1573–1578
  Southern Africa, 1600–1605
  Western Europe, 1605–1612
male circumcision, 1621–1623
maternal activism, 1640–1645
nationalism and gender, 1737–1741
Nazi persecution of homosexuals, 1750–1754
NGOs and grassroots organizing, 1765–1769
non-violence, 1781–1783
sex trafficking, 2111–2116
sexual citizenship
  Caribbean, 2146–2151
  East Asia, 2151–2157
sexual rights, 2196–2200
sexual slavery, 2202–2205
sexuality and human rights, 2217–2220
sodomy law in comparative perspective, 2262–2266
suffrage, 2293–2296
taboo, 2303–2305
transgender movements in international perspective, 2337–2341
transgender politics, 2346–2351
war, international violence, and gender, 2411–2419
Yogyakarta Principles, 2604–2606
see also women's rights

universalism
  disability rights movement, 439–441
  essentialism, 556–558
  eurocentrism, 574–576
unmarried status
  celibacy, 221–222
Uruguay
  abortion laws, 4
Uzbekistan
  abortion laws, 4

V
Vanuatu
  abortion laws, 4
Venezuela
  abortion laws, 5
verbal ability
  cognitive sex differences, debates on, 298–300
victim blaming, 2379–2381
victimization, 2381–2384
  bullying, 204–206
  child labor in comparative perspective, 234–241
  Indo-Caribbean feminism, 654–658
  rape culture, 1985–1989
Vietnam
  feminism, 737–739
  gender/history of revolutions, 1002–1003
violence
  bullying, 204–206
  child sex offenders, 246–249
  domestic violence in United States, 467–470
  elder abuse and gender, 518–520
  female criminality, 601–605
  gangs and gender, 931–933
  genocide, 2008–2012
  intimate partner abuse, 1456–1458
  pacifism, Quakers, and gender, 1821–1825
  pink triangle, 1850–1853
  post-traumatic stress disorder, 1884–1886
  rape culture, 1985–1989
  victimization, 2381–2384
violence against children
  child labor in comparative perspective, 234–241
  child prostitution, 241–246
  child sexual abuse/trauma, 249–252
  infanticide, 1412–1415
violence against men, 54
violence against women
  adolescent pregnancy, 19–21
  age of consent and child marriage in India, 26–30
  battered women, 152–155
  domestic violence in United States, 467–470

violence against women (*Continued*)
  dowry deaths, 480–482
  elder abuse and gender, 518–520
  emotional abuse of women, 527–531
  environmental disasters and gender, 544–548
  femicide, 614–616
  gangs and gender, 931–933
  gender-based violence, 1177–1181
  global perspective, 2386–2392
  higher education and gender in the United States, 1270–1281
  honor killing, 1314–1318
  intimate partner abuse, 1456–1458
  militarism and gender-based violence, 1701–1710
  movements against, 2392–2397
  radical feminism, 726–729
  rape and re-victimization, treatment of, 1993–1997
  refugee women and violence against women, 2001–2004
  self-defense and violence against women in United States, 2069–2071
  sex trafficking, 2111–2116
  sexual *see* sexual violence
  sexual coercion, 2157–2159
  victimization, 2381–2384
  women's and feminist activism, Southern Africa, 2534–2538
Violence Against Women Act (1994), 154
virginity, 2397–2399
  chastity, 225–227
  purity versus pollution, 1957–1959
visual culture, 2399–2403
  documentary film and gender, 461–465
  feminist film theory, 807–812
  gaze, 940–941
  and gender, 2403–2408
  lookism, 1616–1618
  mail-order brides, 1619–1621
  men's magazines, 1676–1678
  performance art, 1844–1846
  popular culture and gender, 1868–1871
  queer performance, 1974–1977
  women as producers of culture, 2458–2462
volunteerism and charitable giving, 2408–2409
voyeurism
  gaze, 940–941

W

war and international violence
  comfort women, 317–319
  genocide, 2008–2012
  military masculinity, 1714–1716
  non-violence, 1781–1783
  sexual slavery, 2202–2205
  women's movements, modern international movement, 2573–2579
war, international violence, and gender, 2411–2419
  women in combat, 2441–2445
  women suicide bombers, 2429–2431
welfare state
  feminist theories of, 892–901
  gender, politics and the state, Western Europe, 1144–1152
  gender redistributive policies, 1155–1159
welfare state policy
  earner-carer model, 497–499
West Africa
  women's and feminist activism, 2545–2548
West Bank & Gaza strip
  abortion laws, 5
Western Europe
  gender, politics and the state, 1144–1152
  leftist armed struggle, women in, 1507–1512
  LGBT, 1605–1612
  women's and feminist activism, 2548–2552
westernization
  arranged marriages, 112–114
  subaltern, 2291–2293
wet nursing, 2419–2421
  surrogacy, 2296–2298
white supremacy
  critical race theory, 384–389
  feminist perspectives on whiteness, 846–851
  and gender, 2421–2425
    women's and feminist activism, Aboriginal Australia and Torres Strait Islands, 2470–2475
  genetics and racial minorities in United States, 1199–1206
  hybridity and miscegenation, 1359–1361
  skin lightening/bleaching, 2247–2249
  subaltern, 2291–2293
whiteness
  anti-miscegenation laws, 87–91
  critical race theory, 384–389
  feminist perspectives on, 846–851
wicca, 2425–2427
  lesbian and womyn's separatism, 1536–1538
  matriarchy, 1649–1655
  witches, 2427–2429
witches, 2427–2429
  fairy tales, 579–582
  misogyny, 1718–1720

shaman priestesses, 2236–2237
wicca, 2425–2427
woman-centeredness, 2431–2434
womanism, 2434–2437
  black feminisms, 626–630
womanist, 2437–2438
  theology & preaching, 2434–2437, 2439–2440
women
  AIDS-related stigma, 38–40
  and animality, 76–78
  anti-racist/anti-civil rights movements, 96–102
  appearance psychology, 102–107
  athletics and gender, 137–142
  CAM, 351–354
  cardiac disease and gender, 218–220
  chick flicks, 227–229
  colonialism and gender, 303–314
  emancipation, 61
  feminist psychotherapy, 851–855
  gender and death penalty, 964–966
  violence against *see* violence against women
  virginity, 2397–2399
Women Against Violence Against Women (WAVAW), 2393
women anarchists, 62–64
women in combat, 2441–2445
  Amazons, 53–59
  comfort women, 317–319
women in computing, 776–783
women as cultural markers/bearers, 2445–2449
  oral tradition, 1810–1813
women in development, 2449–2451
  capabilities approach, 211–213
  democracy and democratization, 418–423
  environment and gender, 539–544
  environmental disasters and gender, 544–548
  female farming systems, 605–609
  gender analysis, 943–945
  gender and development, 968–973
  gender role ideology, 1159–1162
  global restructuring, 1221–1223
  hunger and famine, 1354–1359
  informal economy, 1415–1419
  leadership and gender, 1504–1506
  maquiladora, 1623–1625
  refugees and refugee camps, 2004–2009
  structural adjustment, 2284–2285
  Third World women, 2314–2317
  United Nations Decade for Women, 2367–2369
  women's centers, 2559–2561
  women's movements, modern international movement, 2573–2579

women in law
  feminist jurisprudence, 812–816
women in non-traditional work fields, 2451–2458
women as producers of culture, 2458–2462
  oral tradition, 1810–1813
women in science, 2462–2466
  clinical trials, bias against women, 283–288
  cognitive sex differences, debates on, 298–300
  environment and gender, 539–544
  feminist design in computing, 776–783
  feminist epistemology, 794–796
  feminist studies of science, 870–876
  gender equality/inequality in education, 993–998, 1046–1050
  gendered innovations in science, health, and technology, 1181–1188
  information technology, 1419–1424
  medical and scientific experimentation and gender, 1667–1671
  nature–nurture debate, 1744–1750
  single-sex education and coeducation, 2243–2245
women suicide bombers, 2429–2431
  leftist armed struggle, women in, 1507–1512
women travelers, 2466–2468
women-centeredness
  feminist theology, 876–878
  women-church, 2468–2470
  women's dirges, 2561–2563
women-church, 2468–2470
  feminine and masculine elements, 616–618
  feminist theology, 876–878
women's banking, 2557–2559
women's centers, 2559–2561
  women's movements, modern international movement, 2573–2579
Women's Christian Temperance Union (WCTU), 31
women's conferences
  Women's Worlds Conference, 2586–2588
women's dirges, 2561–2563
women's and feminist activism
  Aboriginal Australia and Torres Strait Islands, 2470–2475
  Australia and New Zealand, 2475–2479
  Caribbean, 2480–2485
  East Asia, 2485–2489
  Eastern Africa, 2489–2494
  Eastern and Central Europe, 2494–2499
  Latin America, 2499–2504
  Māori, 2504–2508
  Middle East, 2508–2513
  Native United States and Canada, 2513–2518
  Northern Africa, 2518–2524

women's and feminist activism (*Continued*)
  Russia, Ukraine, and Eurasia, 2524–2529
  Southeast Asia, 2529–2533
  Southern Africa, 2534–2538
  United States and Canada, 2539–2545
  West Africa, 2545–2548
  Western Europe, 2548–2552
  women's ways of knowing, 2584–2586
  Yoruba culture, religion, and gender, 2606–2618
women's and feminist organizations
  animality, 76–78
  anti-globalization movements, 82–87
  definition of, 842–844
  feminist organizations, definition of, 842–844
  history of women's rights in international and comparative perspective, 1289–1306
  Marxist/Socialist feminism, 749–753
  occupy movements, 1801–1805
  pro-choice movement in United States, 1918–1925
  South Asia, 2553–2557
  Southeast Asian feminism, 735–743
  transnational labor movements, 2351–2357
  United Nations Decade for Women, 2367–2369
  women's and feminist activism
    East Asia, 2485–2489
    Eastern and Central Europe, 2494–2499
    Latin America, 2499–2504
    Russia, Ukraine, and Eurasia, 2524–2529
    Southeast Asia, 2529–2533
    United States and Canada, 2539–2545
    West Africa, 2545–2548
  women's and feminist organizations in South Asia, 2553–2557
  women's health movement in the United States, 2563–2567
  women's movements,
    early international movement, 2567–2573
    modern international movement, 2573–2579
  women's political representation, 2580–2584
  Women's Worlds Conference, 2586–2588
women's health
  clinical trials, bias against women, 283–288
  hormone replacement therapy, 1318–1320
  intersex movement, 1443–1448
  menstrual activism, 1682–1686
  woman-centeredness, 2431–2434
women's health movement in the United States, 2563–2567
women's liberation
  radical feminism, 726–729

women's movements
  A Vindication of the Rights of Woman, 2384–2386
  anarchist, 62–64
  black feminist thought, 180–182
  Buddhism, 201–204
  CEDAW, 25, 359, 362–365
  early international movement, 2567–2573
  empowerment, 534–537
  environment and gender, 539–544
  environmental justice, 548–550
  environmental politics and women's activism, 550–554
  feminist activism, 759–762
  feminist movements in historical and comparative perspective, 827–838
  feminist organizations, definition of, 842–844
  feminist theology, 876–878
  gender, politics and the state,
    Australia and New Zealand, 1077–1082
    Eastern and Central Europe, 1082–1093
    United States and Canada, 1138–1144
  gender/history of revolutions in Eastern and Central Europe, 1005–1015
  higher education and gender in the United States, 1270–1281
  history of women's rights in international and comparative perspective, 1289–1306
  International Women's Day, 1431–1433
  lesbian and gay movements, 1516–1522
  modern international movement, 2573–2579
  nineteenth-century feminism, 683–688
  non-sexist education, 1777–1779
  non-violence, 1781–1783
  Northeast Asian feminism, 694–701
  sex-radical feminists, 2123–2125
  sisterhood, 2245–2247
  South African feminism, 729–735
  suffrage, 2293–2296
  transnational labor movements, 2351–2357
  United Nations Decade for Women, 2367–2369
  United States women's movements in historical perspective, 2369–2374
  violence against women, movements against, 2392–2397
  woman-centeredness, 2431–2434
  womanism, 2434–2437
  women's and feminist activism
    Australia and New Zealand, 2475–2479
    East Asia, 2485–2489
    Māori, 2504–2508
    Russia, Ukraine, and Eurasia, 2524–2529
    Southeast Asia, 2529–2533
    Southern Africa, 2534–2538

United States and Canada, 2539–2545
  West Africa, 2545–2548
  Western Europe, 2548–2552
women's and feminist organizations in South Asia, 2553–2557
women's health movement in the United States, 2563–2567
women's policy agencies
  femocrat, 909–911
women's political representation, 2580–2584
  political participation in Western democracies, 1855–1857
  suffrage, 2293–2296
  women's and feminist activism
    Eastern Africa, 2489–2494
    Northern Africa, 2518–2524
women's rights
  abortion, 1–13
  CEDAW, 25, 359, 362–365
  child labor in comparative perspective, 234–241
  class, caste and gender, 275–280
  Communism in Eastern Europe, 323–328
  Communism and gender in China, 329–337
  Communism in Russia, 328–329
  Declaration of the Rights of Women, 413–414
  feminist activism, 759–762
  feminist consciousness, historical perspective, 771–776
  feminist movements in historical and comparative perspective, 827–838
  feminist organizations, definition of, 842–844
  feminist theology, 876–878
  feminization of poverty, 788–793, 907–909
  fetal rights, 916–918
  gender and asylum seeking, 128–133
  gender, politics and the state, Western Europe, 1144–1152
  gender/history of revolutions in Northern Africa, 1015–1023
  higher education and gender in the United States, 1270–1281
  history in international and comparative perspective, 1289–1306
  human rights and gender, 1326–1330
  human rights, international laws and policies, 1330–1345
  Islamic feminism, 658–661
  nineteenth-century feminism, 683–688
  Northeast Asian feminism, 694–701
  nuns, including Taiwan Buddhist, 1786–1791
  reproductive justice/rights in the United States, 2035–2040
  self-defense and violence against women in United States, 2069–2071
  sexual rights, 2196–2200
  sexuality and human rights, 2217–2220
  suttee (Sati), 2300–2302
  United Nations Decade for Women, 2367–2369
  women's and feminist activism,
    East Asia, 2485–2489
    West Africa, 2545–2548
  women's movements
    early international movement, 2567–2573
    modern international movement, 2573–2579
  women's political representation, 2580–2584
  see also universal human rights
women's ways of knowing, 2584–2586
women's ways of managing
  feminist theories of organization, 887–892
Women's Worlds Conference, 2586–2588
women's writing, 2589–2593
  feminist literary criticism, 816–819
  feminist publishing, 855–864
  feminist utopian writing, 901–903
  gynocriticism, 1233–1234
  women's and feminist activism, Northern Africa, 2518–2524
womyn
  lesbian and womyn's separatism, 1536–1538
work
  comparable worth/work of equal value, 348–351
  domestic technology, 465–467
  dual labor market, 493–495
  emotion work, 525–527
  feminization of poverty, 788–793, 907–909
  gender budget, 961–964
  gender division of labor, 456–461
  glass ceiling/glass elevator, 1214–1216
  global care chain, 1216–1218
  health careers, 1243–1246
  higher education and gender in the United States, 1270–1281
  hostile work environment, United States, 1320–1322
  informal economy, 1415–1419
  maquiladora, 1623–1625
  occupational health and safety, 1797–1799
work/family arrangements
  cult of domesticity, 394–396
  dual labor market, 493–495
  earner-carer model, 497–499
  feminist theories of welfare state, 892–901
  gender redistributive policies, 1155–1159

work/family arrangements (*Continued*)
  gender wage gap, 1175–1177
  higher education and gender in the United States, 1270–1281
  parental leave in comparative perspective, 1832–1836
work–family balance, 2593–2595
world religions *see* religions
World Social Forum, 86

X
xenophobia
  and gender, 2597–2599
  right-wing women's movements, 2040–2046
  see also race and racism

Y
Yemen
  abortion laws, 5
Yin-Yang, 2601–2604
  Daoism, 411–413
  feminine and masculine elements, 616–618
yoga, 51
Yogyakarta Principles, 2604–2606
  human rights, international laws and policies, 1330–1345
  sexuality and human rights, 2217–2220
  universal human rights, 2375–2377
Yoruba culture, religion, and gender, 2606–2618

Z
Zambia
  abortion laws, 3
  LGBT, 1603
zero balancing therapy, 51
Zimbabwe
  abortion laws, 4